Fodor's 95 Caribbean

Fodor's Travel Publications, Inc.
New York • Toronto • London • Sydney • Auckland

Contents

Maps and Plans

Contents

Foreword

We would like to thank the Caribbean Tourism Association, all the island tourist boards, and the people at American Airlines, British West Indies Airlines, and Leeward Island Air Transport for their help and support.

While every care has been taken to assure the accuracy of the information in this guide, the passage of time will always bring change, and consequently, the publisher cannot accept responsibility for errors that may occur.

All prices and opening times quoted here are based on information supplied to us at press time. Hours and admission fees may change, however, and the prudent traveler will avoid inconvenience by calling ahead.

Fodor's wants to hear about your travel experiences, both pleasant and unpleasant. When a hotel or restaurant fails to live up to its billing, let us know and we will investigate the complaint and revise our entries where the facts warrant it.

Send your letters to the editors of Fodor's Travel Publications, 201 E. 50th Street, New York, NY 10022.

Highlights'95 and Fodor's Choice

Highlights '95

A decade ago some Caribbean islands put more emphasis on tourism than others. St. Maarten and the Virgin Islands actively sought tourists, while St. Lucia relied on its banana crop and Guadeloupe on sugarcane for revenue. Now, however, the scramble for tourists and the dollars that they bring is fast becoming the primary focus of all the Caribbean islands.

While the competition for tourists hasn't led to lower prices—in fact some governments have been increasing tourist taxes to pay for advertising costs—it has created more options for the traveler. New hotels open all the time, old hotels are renovated, and transportation options to and from the islands are multiplying.

Interisland air transportation, as well as service to and from the Caribbean is expanding. **American Airlines** now covers most of the islands with either direct flights from the mainland or with connecting flights through San Juan on its subsidiary, American Eagle. **ALM,** the Antillean airline, is also becoming a major carrier to many of the islands, with departures from Atlanta and Miami as well as interisland flights. **Turks & Caicos Islands Airways** began non-stop service from Miami to both Provo and Grand Turk in late 1993. Improvements are under way on the departure areas of the **Barbados Airport** and Trinidad's **Piarco Airport,** and the customs area of the **Las Américas International Airport** in the Dominican Republic has undergone changes aimed at keeping baggage problems and taxi hustlers at bay.

Those who cruise to the Caribbean will appreciate the new **cruise-ship terminal** in Guadeloupe's Pointe-à-Pitre, with its complex of 80 shops, three restaurants, and a hotel. Martinique also has a new **berthing facility** within a 10-minute walk to downtown Fort-de-France. In Montserrat, the first phase of a $30 million **seaport** has been completed, including a new jetty able to berth cruise ships up to 600 feet long. Phase two will include a duty-free shopping complex.

Hotel and resort development continues throughout the Caribbean, with an emphasis on **all-inclusive properties.** Not only are new all-inclusives opening, but some hotels that formerly had various meal plans are changing to the all-inclusive format. It definitely has its advantages: No fighting over where to go for dinner, no worries about how many activities you can afford, and perhaps the biggest plus, no need to carry a wallet for the entire trip. The drawbacks are that you'll probably end up seeing less of the island and sticking more to your particular resort. New all-inclusive resorts include **LaSource** in Grenada and **Jalousie Plantation** in St. Lucia. **Sandals** has masterfully renovated the Cunard Paradise Village & Beach Club in Barbados and the Halcyon Beach Club in St. Lucia to create two new couples-only all-inclusive resorts. Also in St. Lucia, the Hotel Pullman has been converted into the all-inclusive **Wyndham Morgan Bay Resort.**

Aggressive hotel expansion is taking place in the **Dominican Republic,** with Juan Dolio, Punta Cana, and Playa Grande leading the charge. In Juan Dolio, a 276-room Sheraton and 240-room Costa Carib Beach Resort are slated to open in 1995, and the 283-room Capella Beach Renaissance Resort was close to completion at press time. **Puerto Rico** is another development hot spot. The **El Conquistador Resort and Country Club,** the first new resort on the island since 1970, opened its doors in early 1994. Thirty-one miles from San Juan, in Las Croabas, the 926-room resort is perched on a cliff between the Atlantic Ocean and the Caribbean Sea. Among other facilities, the complex has myriad restaurants and lounges, the Caribbean's largest convention center, a 13,000-square-foot casino, and an 18-hole golf course. The **San Juan Marriott Hotel and Casino** (a renovation of the old Dupont Plaza) and the 237-room **Wyndham Hotel and Casino** are both slated to open in late 1994.

Golfers will be pleased to hear that **The Links at Safehaven,** the Cayman Islands' first 18-hole championship golf course, was near completion at press time. The Roy Case–designed, par 71, 6,519-yard course caters to golfers of all skill levels by offering five placements at each tee. In Aruba, construction is under way on an 18-hole course at the **Tierra del Sol** recreation complex.

Fodor's Choice

No two people will agree on what makes a perfect vacation, but it's fun and helpful to know what others think. We hope you'll have the chance to experience some of Fodor's Choices yourself while visiting the Caribbean. For detailed information about each entry, refer to the appropriate chapter in this guidebook.

Scenic Views

Dows Hill Interpretation Centre, Antigua

Trafalgar Falls, Dominica

Appleton Estate Express train ride out of Montego Bay into the Jamaica mountains

Grand Etang National Park, Grenada

El Yunque Rain Forest, Puerto Rico

Brimstone Hill, St. Kitts

The Pitons (Petit and Gros), St. Lucia

Drake's Seat, St. Thomas

Beaches

Shoal Bay, Anguilla

Palm Beach, Aruba

Seven Mile Beach, Grand Cayman

Negril, Jamaica

Macaroni Beach, Mustique

Anse du Gouverneur, St. Barthélemy

Magens Bay, St. Thomas, U.S. Virgin Islands

Trunk Bay, St. John, U.S. Virgin Islands

Diving/Snorkeling

Reefs around Bonaire

Wreck of the Rhone, British Virgin Islands

Cayman Islands (especially Sting Ray City)

Southern coast of Curaçao

Scotts Head, Dominica

Bequia, Grenadines

Saba's pinnacles

Reefs around Speyside, Tobago

Turks and Caicos Islands' reefs

Buck Island Reef, St. Croix, U.S. Virgin Islands

Golf

Britannia Golf Course, Grand Cayman (played with a Jack Nicklaus–designed ball that goes half the normal distance)

Tryall Golf, Tennis and Beach Club, Jamaica

Four Seasons, Nevis (Robert Trent Jones II's latest masterpiece in green)

Hyatt Dorado Beach, Puerto Rico

Mount Irvine, Tobago

Mahogany Run, St. Thomas, U.S. Virgin Islands

Fishing

The waters around

Caicos Island

Little Cayman

Port Antonio, Jamaica

Puerto Rico

U.S. Virgin Islands

Parks and Gardens

Andromeda Gardens, Barbados

Washington/Slagbaai National Park, Bonaire

Christoffel Park, Curaçao

Morne Trois Pitons National Park, Dominica

Parc Naturel, Basse-Terre, Guadeloupe

Las Cabezas de San Juan Nature Reserve, Puerto Rico

Pigeon Island, St. Lucia

Asa Wright Nature Center, Trinidad

National Parks Service–protected land, St. John, U.S. Virgin Islands

Shopping

Oranjestad, Aruba

Willemstad, Curaçao

George Town, Grand Cayman

St. George's, Grenada (if just for those incredible spices)

Old San Juan, Puerto Rico

Philipsburg, St. Maarten, and Marigot, St. Martin

Charlotte Amalie, St. Thomas, U.S. Virgin Islands

Casinos

The Royal Cabana, Aruba

Sonesta Beach Hotel and Casino, Curaçao

Hyatt Regency/Cerromar Beach, Puerto Rico

Nightlife and Bars

Coco Lobo, Martinique

Condado Beach Hotel, Puerto Rico

Le Club disco, St. Maarten

Mas Camp Pub, Trinidad

Piccola Marina Cafe, St. Thomas, U.S. Virgin Islands

Hotels

Cap Juluca, Anguilla (*Very Expensive*)

Curtain Bluff, Antigua (*Very Expensive*)

Gran Bahía, Dominican Republic (*Very Expensive*)

Grand Palazzo, St. Thomas,
U.S. Virgin Islands (*Very Expensive*)

Habitation Lagrange, Martinique (*Very Expensive*)

Half Moon Club, Jamaica (*Very Expensive*)

Le Toiny, St. Barthélemy (*Very Expensive*)

Palm Island, Grenadines (*Very Expensive*)

Sandy Lane Hotel and Golf Club, Barbados (*Very Expensive*)

Secret Harbour, Grenada (*Very Expensive*)

Ladera, St. Lucia (*Expensive–Very Expensive*)

Arnos Vale, Tobago (*Expensive*)

Crane Beach Hotel, Barbados (*Expensive*)

La Belle Creole, St. Martin (*Expensive*)

Restaurants

Dasheene, St. Lucia (*Very Expensive*)

Malliouhana, Anguilla (*Very Expensive*)

Ramiro's, Puerto Rico (*Very Expensive*)

Bistro Le Clochard, Curaçao (*Expensive*)

Château de Feuilles, Guadeloupe (*Expensive*)

Chef Tell's, Grand Cayman (*Expensive*)

Chez Mathilde, Aruba (*Expensive*)

Columbo's, Antigua (*Expensive*)

Lafayette, Martinique (*Expensive*)

La Perouche, Antigua (*Expensive*)

Sandy Bay, Barbados (*Expensive*)

Wall House, St. Barthélemy (*Moderate–Expensive*)

Canboulay, Grenada (*Moderate*)

Ile de France, Barbados (*Moderate*)

Richard's Waterfront Dining, Bonaire (*Moderate*)

Getaways

Anse Chastanet Hotel, St. Lucia

Jumby Bay, Long Island, off Antigua

Peter Island Resort and Yacht Harbour,
British Virgin Islands

Mustique, The Grenadines (where you can rent Princess
Margaret's house)

PSV Resort, Petit St. Vincent

The Golden Lemon, Dieppe Bay, St. Kitts

Rawlins Plantation, St. Kitts

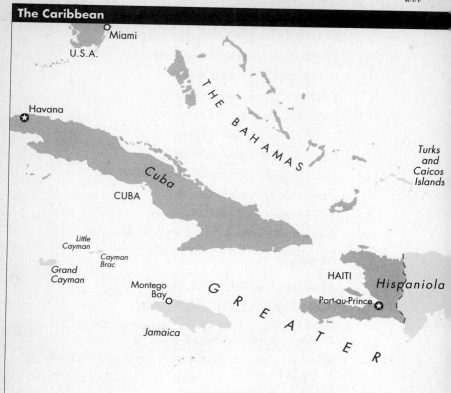

The Caribbean

Miami

U.S.A.

THE BAHAMAS

Havana

Cuba

CUBA

Turks
and
Caicos
Islands

Little
Cayman

Cayman
Brac

Grand
Cayman

Montego
Bay

G R E A T E R

HAITI

Hispaniola

Port-au-Prince

Jamaica

Caribbean

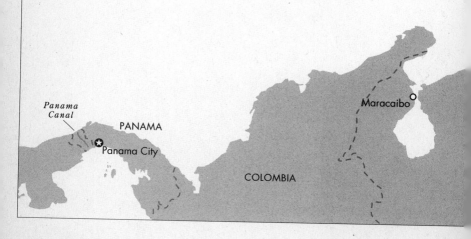

Panama
Canal

PANAMA

Maracaibo

Panama City

COLOMBIA

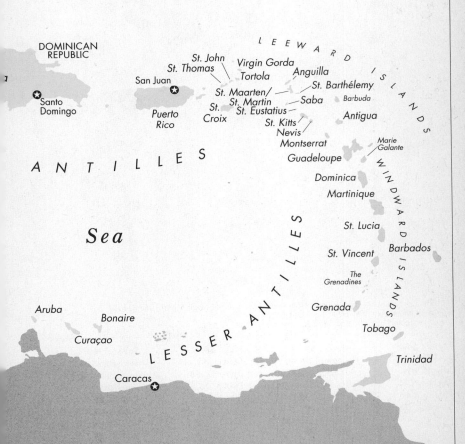

0 | 200 miles
0 | 300 km

N

ATLANTIC · OCEAN

LEEWARD ISLANDS

DOMINICAN
REPUBLIC

Santo
Domingo

San Juan

Puerto
Rico

St. John
St. Thomas
Virgin Gorda
Tortola
Anguilla
St. Barthélemy
St. Maarten/
St. Martin
Saba
Barbuda
St.
Croix
St. Eustatius
St. Kitts
Nevis
Antigua
Montserrat
Guadeloupe
Marie
Galante

Dominica

Martinique

St. Lucia

Barbados

St. Vincent

The
Grenadines

Grenada

Tobago

Trinidad

A N T I L L E S

Sea

WINDWARD ISLANDS

Aruba

Bonaire

Curaçao

L E S S E R   A N T I L L E S

Caracas

VENEZUELA

World Time Zones

Numbers below vertical bands relate each zone to Greenwich Mean Time (0 hrs.).
Local times frequently differ from these general indications,
as indicated by light-face numbers on map.

Algiers, **29**

Anchorage, **3**

Athens, **41**

Auckland, **1**

Baghdad, **46**

Bangkok, **50**

Beijing, **54**

Berlin, **34**

Bogotá, **19**

Budapest, **37**

Buenos Aires, **24**

Caracas, **22**

Chicago, **9**

Copenhagen, **33**

Dallas, **10**

Delhi, **48**

Denver, **8**

Djakarta, **53**

Dublin, **26**

Edmonton, **7**

Hong Kong, **56**

Honolulu, **2**

Istanbul, **40**

Jerusalem, **42**

Johannesburg, **44**

Lima, **20**

Lisbon, **28**

London (Greenwich), **27**

Los Angeles, **6**

Madrid, **38**

Manila, **57**

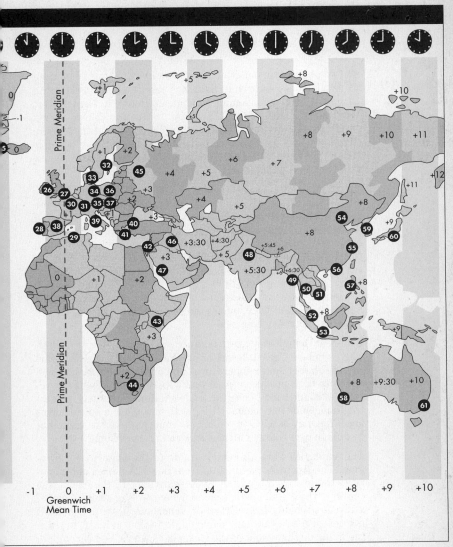

Introduction

If you have seen one island you have by no means seen them all. Tiny 5-square-mile Saba has less in common with the vast 19,000-square-mile Dominican Republic than Butte, Montana, has with Biloxi, Mississippi. Butte and Biloxi, however different in terrain and traits, sit in the same country and the citizenry speak more or less the same language. Saba, which is Dutch, and the Dominican Republic, whose roots are in Spain, simply sit in the same sea.

The Caribbean has towering volcanic islands, such as Saba; islands with forests, such as Dominica and Guadeloupe; and some islands, notably Puerto Rico, that boast both rain forests and deserts. Glittering discos, casinos, and dazzling nightlife can be found on such islands as Aruba and the Dominican Republic, and throughout the region there are isolated cays with only sand, sea, sun, lizards, and mosquitoes. Some islands, St. Kitts among them, have ancient forts to view, while Puerto Rico and the Caicos Islands have caverns and caves to explore. There are also places like Grand Turk, where the only notable sights to see are beneath the translucent sea.

Different though they are in many ways, the islands are stylistically similar. The style-setter is the tropical climate. Year-round summertime temperatures and a plethora of beaches on which to bask produce a pace that's known throughout the region as "island time." Only the trade winds move swiftly. Operating on island time means, "I'll get to it when the spirit moves me." You may hate it, or you may become addicted to it and not be able to peel yourself off the beach and return home.

The similarities are also attributable to the history of the region. The Arawaks paddled up from South America and populated the islands more than 1,000 years ago. In the early 14th century, the cannibalistic Caribs, who gave the area its name, arrived, probably from Brazil or Venezuela, then polished off the peaceful Arawaks and managed, for a time at least, to scare the living daylights out of the Europeans who sailed through in search of gold. (The original name of the Caribs was Galibi, a word the Spanish corrupted to *Canibal*—the origin of the word "cannibal.") Christopher Columbus made four voyages through the region between 1492 and 1504, christening the islands while dodging the Carib arrows. He landed on or sailed past all of the Greater Antilles and virtually all of the eastern Caribbean islands.

From the 16th century until the early 19th century, the Dutch, Danes, Swedes, English, French, Irish, and Spanish fought bitterly for control of the islands. Some islands have almost as many battle sites as sand flies. Having gained control of the islands and annihilated the Caribs, the Europeans established vast sugar plantations and brought in Africans to work the fields. With the abolition of slavery in the mid-19th century, Asians were imported as indentured laborers. Today, the Caribbean population is a rich gumbo of numerous nationalities, including Americans and Canadians who have retired to and invested in the islands.

It must be remembered that the Caribbean, like the European continent, is made up of individual countries, replete with customs, immigration officials, and, in some instances, political difficulties. Most of the islands/nations have opted for independence; others retain their ties to the mother country. They are developing nations, and many have severe economic and unemployment problems.

Virtually all of the islands depend upon tourism, which is an industry that moves on island time. Human nature being what it is, many islanders are resentful of their dependency on tourist dollars. Like as not, the person who serves you has stood in a long line, vying with other anxious applicants for the few available jobs. After serving your meals and cleaning your luxurious room, he or she returns to a tiny shack knowing full well that in less than a week you will have shelled out more than an islander makes in a month. If you encounter fewer smiling faces than you anticipated, consider chalking it up to your perceived great wealth and life of leisure.

Mother Nature has endowed most of these islands with the proverbial sun-kissed beaches, swaying palms, and year-round summer. These pleasures notwithstanding, there are some who deem it overrated. They object to encountering resentment when all they seek is a pleasant vacation for which they have paid dearly. Some feel rather keenly that they'd always like hot water—or at least *some* water— when they turn on the shower; in even the most luxurious resorts there are times when things simply don't work, and that's a fact of Caribbean life. And other visitors simply have no patience with island time.

On the other hand, there are those who travel to the Caribbean year after year. Some return to the same familiar hotel on the same familiar beach on the same familiar island, while the more adventurous try to sample as much as this smorgasbord has to offer.

Defining the Caribbean

The Caribbean Sea, an area of more than a million square miles, stretches south of Florida down to the coast of Venezuela. In the northern Caribbean are the **Greater Antilles**— the islands closest to the United States—composed of Cuba, Jamaica, Haiti, the Dominican Republic, and Puerto Rico. (Due to the political unrest in Haiti and Cuba, they are not included in this book.) The Cayman Islands lie south of Cuba. The Lesser Antilles— greater in number but smaller in size than the Greater Antilles—are divided into three groups: the Leewards and the Windwards in the eastern Caribbean, and the islands in the southern Caribbean. The eastern Caribbean islands, from the

Virgin Islands in the north all the way south to Grenada, form an arc between the Atlantic Ocean and the Caribbean Sea. Islands in the Leeward chain in order of appearance are the U.S. and British Virgin Islands, Anguilla, St. Martin/St. Maarten, St. Barthélemy, Saba, St. Eustatius, St. Kitts, Nevis, Antigua, Barbuda, Montserrat, Guadeloupe, and Dominica; the Windwards are composed of Martinique, St. Lucia, St. Vincent and the Grenadines, and Grenada. Barbados is just east of this group. In the southern Caribbean, off the coast of Venezuela, Trinidad and Tobago are anchored in the east, while Aruba, Bonaire, and Curaçao (known as the ABC Islands) bathe in the western waters. The Turks and Caicos Islands, which lie in the Atlantic Ocean between Florida and the north coast of Hispaniola (Haiti and the Dominican Republic), are part of the Bahamas but are included in this book because of their proximity to and affinity with the Caribbean islands.

When to Go?

"The Season" in the Caribbean traditionally coincides with winter in North America—that is, roughly, from mid-December till mid-April. But, contrary to common North American belief, the islands are not completely deserted during the summer. That's the time when the islanders themselves and many Europeans travel in the region. While the climate varies less than 10° between summer and winter, many hotels slash prices 30% or more in the summer. And Mother Nature is at her glamorous best then, with brilliant flamboyant trees as well as other spectacular tropical plants that bloom from summer till fall.

You will find it easier to rent a car and to make hotel and restaurant reservations in summer; easier, that is, if the facilities are open. Many hotels and restaurants close during August and September or have limited facilities; some are also closed in October. They close to renovate, to rest . . . and to wait out the season for hurricanes and tropical depressions, which are most likely to occur between June and October. Storms, such as Hurricane Gilbert in 1988 and the even nastier Hugo in 1989, can wreak great havoc.

Finding Your Own Place in the Sun

The glory of the Caribbean, aside from the guaranteed qualities of warm sun and warm sea, is that no one island is exactly like another, so that they cater to a variety of tastes. Below is a list of the Caribbean islands broken down by their specialties. Consult the Island-Finder chart on the following pages to help you choose your destination.

Luxury Resorts A wealth of posh resorts awaits those who seek comfort in the lap of luxury. **Anguilla,** rapidly becoming one of the Caribbean's most popular destinations, has the dazzling Malliouhana and the Moroccan-style Cap Juluca. **Antigua's** elegant Curtain Bluff has a long list of well-heeled repeat guests. The Four Seasons resort on **Nevis** combines European elegance, state-of-the-art sports facilities, and Caribbean casualness. On **Jamaica** there's the well-established Half Moon Club, Montego Bay. **Puerto Rico's** new El Conquistador Resort and Country Club, with five individual hotels, is a luxurious world unto itself. On French **St. Martin,** La Samanna is a favorite hideaway of the rich and not-so-famous, and La Belle Creole is a re-creation of a Mediterranean village, replete with a village square and opulent villas. For the ultimate in luxurious privacy, the **British Virgin Islands** has the Peter Island Resort and Yacht Club on its own 1,300-acre private island. Sapore di Mare and Le Toiny on **St. Barts** draw worldly personalities to its intimate setting. And Caneel Bay resort on **St. John, U.S. Virgin Islands,** has seven beaches and takes up 170 acres adjacent to the Virgin Islands National Park.

Casinos and Nightlife You can flirt with Lady Luck until the wee small hours in the dazzling casinos of Santo Domingo, **Dominican Republic;** San Juan, **Puerto Rico; St. Maarten;** and **Curaçao. Aruba** is loaded with lively night places, and San Juan's glittering floor shows are legendary. The merengue, born in the **Dominican Republic,** is exuberantly danced everywhere on the island. Both **Guadeloupe** and **Martinique** claim to have begun the beguine, and on both islands it is danced with great gusto, although the *zouk* (all-night revelry) is now the rage.

Getting Away from It All If you're looking to back out of the fast lane, you can park at one of the secluded, spartan mountain lodges on **Dominica,** which is one of the friendliest islands in the Caribbean. Or opt for the quiet grandeur of a renovated sugar plantation on **Nevis,** where you can feast in an elegant dining room or enjoy a barbecue on the beach. Tranquil **Anguilla,** with soft white beaches nudged by incredibly clear water, offers posh resorts as well as small, inexpensive, locally owned lodgings. From the low-key **Turks and Caicos Islands,** which lie in stunning blue-green waters, you can boat to more than a score of isolated cays to which even the term "low-key" would imply too fast a pace. **St. Kitts** is another peaceful green oasis, with lovely beaches and upscale, "great house" accommodations in the bargain. **St. Lucia** offers a plethora of places, from the simple to the simply elegant, for "liming"

Island-Finder

	Cost of Island	Number of rooms	Nonstop flights	Cruise ship port	U.S. dollars accepted	Historic sites	Natural beauty	Lush	Arid	Mountainous	Rain forest	Beautiful beaches	Good roads
Anguilla	$$$	662			•				•			•	
Antigua	$$$$	1878	•	•	•	•	•		•			•	
Aruba	$$	5582	•	•	•				•			•	•
Barbados	$$	3690	•	•	•	•						•	
Bonaire	$$	609	•		•							•	
British Virgin Islands	$$$	892		•	•	•	•	•	•	•		•	
Cayman Islands	$$$$	2259	•	•	•				•			•	•
Curaçao	$$	1790	•	•	•	•						•	
Dominica	$	180					•	•		•	•		
Dominican Republic	$	13455	•				•	•				•	
The Grenadines	$	400					•	•		•	•	•	
Grenada	$$$	1070		•	•		•	•		•	•	•	
Guadeloupe	$$	4320	•				•	•		•	•	•	
Jamaica	$$$	10622	•	•			•	•		•		•	•
Martinique	$$$	3945	•				•	•		•	•	•	
Montserrat	$$	86		•			•	•		•	•	•	
Nevis	$$$	363		•	•	•				•		•	
Puerto Rico	$	6520	•	•	•	•	•	•		•	•	•	•
Saba	$	100		•						•	•		
St. Barthélemy	$$$$	715	•			•				•		•	
St. Eustatius	$	102		•	•						•		
St. Kitts	$$	705		•			•	•		•	•	•	
St. Lucia	$$	2135	•	•			•	•		•	•	•	
St. Martin/St. Maarten	$$$	5264		•	•			•		•		•	•
St. Vincent	$$	339		•	•	•	•	•		•	•	•	
Trinidad	$	1257	•								•		
Tobago	$$	1057								•		•	
Turks and Caicos	$$$	1115	•		•				•			•	
U.S. Virgin Islands:													
St. Croix	$$	1026		•	•	•		•		•			
St. John	$$	1271		•	•		•	•				•	
St. Thomas	$$	3105	•	•	•					•		•	•

Public transportation	Fine dining	Local cuisine	Shopping	Music	Casinos	Nightlife	Diving and Snorkeling	Sailing	Golfing	Hiking	Ecotourism	Villa rentals	All-inclusives	Campgrounds	Luxury resorts	Secluded getaway	Good for families	Romantic hideaway
	•	•	•	•			•								•	•		•
	•	•	•		•	•	•	•	•				•		•		•	
•	•	•	•	•	•	•		•					•		•		•	
•	•			•			•		•				•		•		•	
							•	•		•	•							
•	•	•	•	•		•	•	•		•	•	•	•	•	•	•	•	•
	•	•					•	•	•			•	•	•			•	
•	•	•	•			•	•			•							•	
•							•			•	•					•		
		•			•	•			•				•				•	
•							•	•		•	•				•	•	•	•
		•	•				•	•	•			•	•		•		•	•
	•	•	•		•	•				•	•			•			•	
•	•	•		•	•	•	•		•			•	•	•	•	•	•	•
		•			•	•		•						•				
•	•	•					•	•	•	•	•	•				•	•	
	•	•		•			•	•	•	•					•	•		•
	•	•	•				•	•	•	•	•		•		•	•		•
							•			•	•					•		
	•	•					•					•			•			
							•				•					•		
	•	•	•	•	•	•	•	•	•	•			•		•	•	•	•
•			•					•		•			•		•		•	•
	•	•	•		•	•	•	•		•		•	•		•		•	•
•	•	•					•	•		•	•				•		•	•
•				•			•										•	
							•	•	•	•	•	•	•		•	•		•
		•	•			•	•		•	•					•			
•							•		•	•	•	•		•	•		•	•
•	•	•	•			•	•	•					•	•	•			

(we call it "hanging out"), the favorite local pastime. On tiny **Saba** there is little to do but tuck into a small guest house, admire the lush beauty of the island, and chat with the friendly Sabans. Nearby **St. Eustatius** is another friendly, laid-back island, as is **Montserrat. The Grenadines** offers three tiny, private-island luxury resorts: Young Island, Palm Island, and Petit St. Vincent.

Foreign **Trinidad** moves with the rhythm of calypso and is the stomping
Culture ground of a flat-out, freewheeling Carnival that rivals the pre-
African Lenten celebrations in Rio and New Orleans. The Trinidadians, whose African heritage has been augmented by many Asian races, have built up one of the most prosperous commercial centers in the Caribbean. Politically volatile Haiti is not included in this book, but exotic and unique Haitian artwork is prominently displayed throughout the Caribbean.

British **St. Kitts** is known as the Mother Colony of the West Indies; it was from here that British colonists were dispatched in the 17th century to settle Antigua, Barbuda, Tortola, and Montserrat. If you're a history buff, you won't want to miss Nelson's Dockyard at **Antigua's** English Harbour or the hunkering fortress of Brimstone Hill on St. Kitts. Sports fans who understand the intricacies of cricket can watch matches between **Nevis** and St. Kitts teams. And the waters around Antigua and the **British Virgin Islands** are a mecca for serious sailors. **Barbados,** with its lovely tradewinds, has cricket, horseracing at Garrison Savannah, and rugby. A British colony from 1627, the island gained independence in 1966.

Dutch **Saba, St. Eustatius, St. Maarten, Bonaire,** and **Curaçao** all fly the Dutch flag, but there the similarity ends. Saba is a tiny volcanic island known for its beauty, its friendly inhabitants, and its gingerbread-trimmed houses. Curaçao's colorful waterfront shops and restaurants are reminiscent of Amsterdam. Quiet St. Eustatius—affectionately called Statia—has well-preserved historical sites and is famed for being the first foreign nation to salute the new American flag in 1776. The main streets of Philipsburg, the capital of St. Maarten, are lined with colorful Dutch colonial buildings replete with fretwork and verandas. Bonaire is best known for its excellent scuba diving.

French **Martinique, Guadeloupe, St. Martin,** and **St. Barthélemy** (often called St. Barts or St. Barths) compose the French West Indies. The language, the currency, the cuisine (the most imaginative in the Caribbean), the culture, and the style are très French. St. Barts is the quietest, Martinique the liveliest, St. Martin the friendliest, and Guadeloupe the lushest. And as an extra added attraction, you can wing over from Guadeloupe to see what life is like on the nearby islands of Les Saintes, Marie Galante, and Désirade.

Spanish In the **Dominican Republic,** which occupies the eastern two-thirds of the island of Hispaniola, the language and culture are decidedly Spanish. The Colonial Zone of Santo Domingo is site of the oldest city in the Western Hemisphere, and its restored buildings reflect the 15th-century Columbus period. One also gets a sense of the past in **Puerto Rico's** Old San Juan, with its narrow cobblestone streets and filigreed iron balconies.

The Beauties of Nature   **Dominica,** laced with rivers and streams, is a ruggedly beautiful island with arguably the lushest, most untamed vegetation in the Caribbean. **Puerto Rico's** luxuriant 28,000-acre El Yunque is the only rain forest in the U.S. forestry system. Little **Saba** is awash with giant vegetation, and the island's Mt. Scenery is justly named. **Guadeloupe's** 74,000-square-acre Natural Park boasts dramatic waterfalls, cool pools, and miles of hiking trails. Majestic Mt. Pelée, a not entirely dormant volcano, towers over **Martinique's** rain forest; on **St. Eustatius,** adventurers can crawl down into a jungle cradled within a volcanic crater; and on **St. Lucia** you can drive right through a volcano.

The Lure of History   **Antigua's** well-preserved Nelson's Dockyard is a must for history aficionados. The ancient colonial zones of both Santo Domingo, **Dominican Republic,** and Old San Juan, **Puerto Rico,** should also be high on your "history" list. The Historical Society in **St. Eustatius** (Statia) publishes an excellent walking tour of sites to be seen. Brimstone Hill on **St. Kitts** is a well-maintained fortress with several museums full of military memorabilia. **Nevis** has many sugar mills restored as comfortable hotels. Port Royal, outside Kingston, **Jamaica,** was a pirates' stronghold until an earthquake shook things up in 1692.

Cuisine   The cuisine on **Martinique** and **Guadeloupe** is a marvelous marriage of Creole cooking and classic French dishes; you'll find much of the same on the other French islands of **St. Martin** and **St. Barts.** You'll also find a fine selection of French wines in the French West Indies. **Grenada,** the spice island, has an abundance of seafood available and an incredible variety of vegetables.

Music   Calypso was born in **Trinidad; Jamaica** is the home of reggae; the **Dominican Republic** gave the world the merengue; and both **Martinique** and **Guadeloupe** claim to be the cradle of the beguine. The music of **Barbados** ranges from that heard during the Crop-Over Festival (mid-July–early August) to the hottest jazz. Steel drums, limbo dancers, and jump-ups are ubiquitous in the Caribbean. Jump-up? Simple. You hear the music, jump up, and begin to dance.

Diving   Jacques Cousteau named Pigeon Island, off the west coast of **Guadeloupe,** one of the 10 best dive sites in the world. The Wall off Grand Turk in the **Turks and Caicos Islands** is a sheer drop of 7,000 feet and has long been known by scuba divers. The eruption of **Martinique's** Mt. Pelée at 8 AM on May 8, 1902, resulted in the sinking of several ships. **St. Eustatius** boasts an undersea "supermarket" of ships, as well as entire 18th-century warehouses, somewhat the worse for wear, below the surface of Oranjestad Bay. The waters surrounding all three of the **Cayman Islands** are acclaimed by experts, who also make pilgrimages to **Bonaire's** 86 spectacular sites.

Boating   **Guadeloupe's** Port de Plaisance and the marinas on Tortola in the **British Virgin Islands, St. Vincent and the Grenadines,** and St. Thomas in the **U.S. Virgin Islands** are the starting points for some of the Caribbean's finest sailing. Yachtsmen also favor the waters around **Antigua** and put in regularly at Nelson's Dockyard, which hosts a colorful regatta in late April or early May.

Golfing   According to those who have played it, the course at Casa de Campo in the **Dominican Republic** is one of the best in the Caribbean. The newest contender is the challenging (and breathtaking) course at the Four Seasons Resort on **Nevis.** Golfers on St. Thomas, **U.S. Virgin Islands,** play the spectacular Mahogany Run. There are superb courses in **Puerto Rico,** including four shared by the Hyatt Dorado Beach and the Hyatt Regency Cerromar Beach. **Jamaica** has nine courses, with Tryall west of Montego Bay rated among the top. And the **Cayman Islands'** first 18-hole championship golf course, The Links at Safehaven, was near completion at press time.

Day Trips   There are many day trips from St. Martin/St. Maarten. **Saba** is just 28 miles away; **St. Eustatius** is another 17 miles south; and **Anguilla,** the new "in" place in the Caribbean, is less than an hour's boat ride away from St. Martin/St. Maarten. **Nevis** is a mere 2 miles south of **St. Kitts,** while **Dominica** sits about halfway between **Martinique** and **Guadeloupe. Barbuda,** 30 miles from **Antigua,** is noted for hunting and diving. **Les Saintes, Désirade,** and **Marie Galante** are easily accessible from Guadeloupe. Islands like these are small enough to explore in a day and so seductive that you'll probably insist upon returning.

Water Sports

Sunbathing

Before abandoning yourself to the pleasures of the tropics, you would be well advised to take precautions against the ravages of its equatorial sun. Be sure to use a sunscreen with a high sun-protection factor, or SPF (an SPF of under 15 offers little protection); if you're engaging in water sports, be sure the sunscreen is waterproof. At this latitude, the safest hours for sunbathing are 4–6 PM, but even during these hours it is wise to limit exposure during your first few days to short intervals of 15–20 minutes. Keep your system plied with fruit juices and water; avoid coffee, tea, and alcohol, which have a dehydrating effect.

Touring the island in an open Jeep or dangling an arm out of a car window can also expose you to sunburn, so be sure to use sunscreen. If you have permed or color-treated hair, you may wish to use a sun-protective gel to keep it from becoming brittle; if you have a bald head, apply sunscreen. While snorkeling, *always* wear a T-shirt and apply sunscreen to protect the top and backs of your thighs from "duck burn."

Swimming

Any resort you visit is likely to offer a variety of swimming experiences, depending on which side of the island you choose.

The calm, leeward, Caribbean side of most islands has the safest and most popular beaches for swimming. There are no big waves, there is little undertow, and the saltwater— which buoys the swimmer or snorkeler—makes staying afloat almost effortless.

The windward, or Atlantic, side of the islands, however, is a different story: Even strong, experienced swimmers should exercise caution here. The ocean waves are tremendously powerful and can be rough to the point of being dangerous; unseen currents, strong undertows, and uneven, rocky bottoms may scuttle the novice. Some beaches post signs or flags daily to alert swimmers to the water conditions. Pay attention to them! Where there are no flags, limit your water sports to wading and sunbathing.

Swimmers on these islands must also be aware of underwater rocks, reefs, shells, and sea urchins—small, spike-covered creatures whose spines, while not fatal, can cause very painful punctures if you step on them, even through snorkel fins. Moray eels, which are harmless unless provoked, almost never leave the crevices they live in. But don't *ever* poke at one, or even point closely at them—they're lightning fast and may mistake your finger for a predator. It's possible to receive a minor cut while swimming and not feel it until you're out of the water, so make a habit of checking yourself over after leaving the beach. If you do get a small cut from a broken glass or shell, clean it immediately with soap and water.

Nike, Inc., manufactures an athletic shoe for wear in water sports. The Aqua Sock, a lightweight slip-on shoe with a waffle rubber outsole and Spandex mesh upper, offers protection from rocky beaches and underwater hazards such as coral and broken shells, and cushions the foot against the impact of windsurfing. It floats, is unaffected by salt and chlorine, and dries quickly.

How much truth is there to the old saw that you should wait an hour after eating before going for a swim? According to Mark Pitman, MD, director of Sports Medicine at the Hospital for Joint Diseases in New York City, blood travels from the muscles to the intestines after a meal to absorb the digesting food. This leaves the muscles "cold" and more likely to cramp. It is safe to float or dog-paddle after a light lunch, but save the Olympic lap-swimming for later.

Never dive, particularly from a boat or cliff, without checking the depth of the water and the bottom conditions. And even when the Caribbean is mirror-calm, never run blindly into the water, even if the beach is familiar. Changes in the tide can turn what was a sandy bottom yesterday into a collection of broken shells today.

Few beaches or pools in the Caribbean—even those at the best hotels—are protected by lifeguards, so you and your children swim at your own risk.

Sharks Nearly two decades after the release of the film *Jaws*, shark phobia endures. Sharks *are* among the fish that populate Caribbean waters; they can swim in water as shallow as three feet and are attracted by the splashing of swimmers. But there are only about a dozen shark attacks reported each year worldwide, and most of these take place off the coasts of California and Florida. You are unlikely to see a shark while swimming or diving in the Caribbean, especially if you spot dolphins nearby. The dolphin is a natural enemy of the shark and will attack its most vulnerable points—the gills and the tip of the nose—so sharks steer clear of them.

Snorkeling

Snorkeling requires no special skills, and most hotels that rent equipment have a staff member or, at the very least, a booklet offering instruction in snorkeling basics.

As with any water sport, it's never a good idea to snorkel alone, especially if you're out of shape. You don't have to be a great swimmer to snorkel, but occasionally currents come up that require stamina. The four dimensions as we know them seem altered underwater. Time seems to slow and stand still, so wear a water-resistant watch and let someone on land know when to expect you back. Your sense of direction may also fail you when you're submerged. Many a vacationer has ended up half a mile or more from shore—which isn't a disaster unless you're already tired, chilly, and it's starting to get dark.

Remember that taking souvenirs—shells, pieces of coral, interesting rocks—is forbidden. Many reefs are legally protected marine parks, where removal of living shells is prohibited because it upsets the ecology. Because it is impossible to tell a living shell from a dead one, the wisest course is simply not to remove any. Needless to say, underwater is also not the place to discard your cigarette packs, gum wrappers, or any other litter.

Good snorkel equipment isn't cheap, and you may not like the sport once you've tried it, so get some experience with rented equipment, which is always inexpensive, before investing in quality mask, fins, and snorkel. The best prices for gear, as you might imagine, are not to be found at seaside resorts.

Scuba Diving

Diving is America's fastest-growing sport. While scuba (which stands for *s*elf-contained *u*nderwater *b*reathing *a*pparatus) looks and is surprisingly simple, *phone your physician before your vacation and make sure that you have no condition that should prevent you from diving!* Possibilities include common colds and other nasal infections, which can be worsened by diving, and ear infections, which can be worsened and cause underwater vertigo as well. Asthmatics can usually dive safely but must have their doctor's okay. A full checkup is an excellent idea, especially if you're over 30. Since it can be dangerous to travel on a plane after diving, you should schedule both your diving courses and travel plans accordingly.

At depths of below 30 feet, all sorts of physiological and chemical changes take place in the body in response to an increase in water pressure, so learning to dive with a reputable instructor is a must. Nitrogen, for example, which ordinarily escapes from the body through respiration, forms bubbles in the diver's bloodstream. If the diver resurfaces at a rate of more than one foot per second, these nitrogen bubbles may accumulate; the severe joint pains caused by this process are known as "the bends." If the nitrogen bubbles travel to your heart or brain, the result can be fatal.

In addition to training you how to resurface slowly enough, a qualified instructor can teach you to read "dive tables," the charts that calculate how long you can safely stay at certain depths.

The ideal way to learn this sport is to take a resort course once you've arrived at your Caribbean destination. The course will usually consist of two to three hours of instruction on land, with time spent in a swimming pool or waist-deep water to get used to the mouthpiece and hose (known as the regulator) and the mask. A shallow 20-foot dive from a boat or beach, supervised by the instructor, follows.

Successful completion of this introductory course may prompt you to earn a certification card—often called a C-card—from one of the major accredited diving organizations: NAUI (National Association of Underwater Instructors), CMAS (Confederation Mondiale des Activités Subaquatiques, which translates into World Underwater Federation), NASE (National Association of Scuba Educators), or PADI (Professional Association of Diving Instructors). PADI offers a free list of training facilities; write PADI for information (1251 E. Dyer Rd., #100, Santa Ana, CA 92705).

A certification course will keep you very busy and pleasantly tired for most of your vacation. If your travel plans include a great deal of sightseeing as well, you'll have little time left to relax. You may wish to complete the classroom instruction and basic skills training at your hometown YMCA, for example, then do your five required open-water dives on vacation.

Unfortunately, there are a few disreputable individuals who may try to assure you that they can teach you everything you need to know about diving even though they aren't certified instructors. DON'T BELIEVE IT! Reputable diving shops proudly display their association with the organizations mentioned above. If you have any doubt, ask to see evidence of accreditation. Legitimate instructors will happily show you their credentials and will insist on seeing *your* C-card before a dive.

Keep in mind that your presence can easily damage the delicate underwater ecology. By standing on the bottom you can break fragile coral that took centuries to grow. Many reefs are legally protected marine parks; spearfishing or taking living shells and coral is rude and destructive, and often strictly prohibited. When in doubt, remember the diver's caveat: "Take only pictures, leave only bubbles."

Snuba

Not quite ready for scuba diving? Not to worry. For those kept from diving by poor health or claustrophobia, there is snuba, a combination of snorkeling and scuba diving. The snuba system consists of an inflatable raft that supports a tank of compressed air and a 20-foot air hose for one or two persons. The raft not only warns boats of your presence, but also provides a convenient resting place when you're tired. (There is even a clear window in the raft so you can still have an underwater view while taking a break.) The rental cost is approximately $45 an hour, and it takes only about an hour to become a certified snuba user.

Caribbean snuba outlets include **Pineapple Beach Club Resort,** Antigua (tel. 809/463–2006), and **SNUBA of St. John,** U.S. Virgin Islands (tel. 809/776–6922). At press time several additional Caribbean islands were slated to get snuba equipment. Check with your travel agent or the tourism board of the island you plan to visit for availability and information.

Waterskiing

Some large hotels have their own waterskiing concessions, with special boats, equipment, and instructors. Many beaches (especially those in Barbados), however, are patrolled by private individuals who own boats and several sizes of skis; they will offer their services through a hotel or directly to vacationers or can be hailed like taxis. Ask your hotel staff or other guests about their experiences with these entrepreneurs. Be *sure* they provide life vests and at least two people in the boat: one to drive and one to watch the skier at all times.

Windsurfing

Windsurfing is as strenuous as it is exciting, so it may not be the sport to try on your first day out, unless you're already in excellent shape. As with most water sports, it is essential to windsurf with someone else around who can watch you and go for help if necessary.

Always wear a life vest and preferably a diveskin to protect your own skin from the sun. Avoid suntan oil, which can make your feet slippery and interfere with your ability to stand on the board. Nike, Inc., makes athletic shoes specifically for water sports (*see* Swimming, *above*).

Sailing

Whether you charter a yacht with crew or captain a boat yourself, the waters of the Caribbean—especially those around the Virgin Islands and the Grenadines—are excellent for sailing, and the many secluded bays and inlets provide ideal spots to drop anchor and picnic or explore. Like hotel rates, charter prices are lower during the off-season.

St. Thomas, U.S. Virgin Islands, and Tortola and Virgin Gorda in the British Virgin Islands do most of the charter and marina business. In St. Thomas, contact the **Virgin Island Charter Yacht League** (tel. 809/774–3944); in Tortola, **The Moorings** (tel. 809/494–2332) and **North South Yacht Vacations** (tel. 809/494–0096). The cost of chartering a yacht varies widely, depending on the number of passengers, the season, and the length of the cruise. Contact the charter companies for exact rates.

Sailing out of St. Vincent to Grenada is also recommended, and many charters are available. From Guadeloupe, you can sail to Dominica and Antigua and anchor at the isles of Marie Galante and Les Saintes.

1 Essential Information

Before You Go

Government Tourist Offices

Each island has a U.S.–based tourist board, listed with its name and address under Important Addresses in the individual island chapters that follow; they can be good sources of general information, up-to-date calendars of events, and listings of hotels, restaurants, sights, and shops. The **Caribbean Tourism Organization** (20 E. 46th St., New York, NY 10017–2452, tel. 212/682–0435) is another resource, especially for information on the islands that have very limited tourist offices in the United States.

The U.S. Department of State's **Overseas Citizens Emergency Center** (Room 4811, Washington, DC 20520; enclose S.A.S.E.) issues Consular Information Sheets, which cover crime, security, political climate, and health risks as well as embassy locations, entry requirements, currency regulations, and other routine matters. For the latest information, stop in at any U.S. passport office, consulate, or embassy; call the interactive hot line (tel. 202/647–5225, fax 202/647–3000); or, with your PC's modem, tap into the Bureau of Consular Affairs' computer bulletin board (tel. 202/647–9225).

Tours and Packages

Should you buy your travel arrangements to the Caribbean packaged or do it yourself? There are advantages either way. Buying packaged arrangements saves you money, particularly if you can find a program that includes exactly the features you want. You also get a pretty good idea of what your trip will cost from the outset. For most destinations, you have two options: fully escorted tours and independent packages. Since most travelers to the Caribbean visit one island and stay at one resort, there is little need for escorted tours. (Cruises fill the gap here; *see* Cruises, *below*.) There is a wide variety of independent packages for every budget and taste, whether you want golf, tennis, water sports, activities for kids, hiking, or culture, as well as a number of special-interest programs. Travel agents are your best source of recommendations. They will have the largest selection, and the cost to you is the same as buying direct. Whatever program you ultimately choose, be sure to find out exactly what is included: taxes, tips, transfers, meals, baggage handling, ground transportation, entertainment, excursions, sports or recreation (and rental equipment for any sport you plan to pursue). Ask about the type of hotel (budget, deluxe, etc.), its location, the size of its rooms, the kind of beds, and its amenities, such as pool, room service, or programs for children, if they're important to you. One other important point: If the beach is the centerpiece of your vacation, ask exactly where your hotel is located with respect to the nearest one—the words "beach nearby" can have a disturbing number of meanings.

Find out the operator's cancellation penalties. Nearly everyone charges them, and the only way to avoid them is to buy trip-cancellation insurance (*see* Insurance, *below*). Also ask about the single supplement, a surcharge assessed to solo travelers. Some operators do not make you pay it if you agree to be matched up with a roommate of the same sex, even if one is not found by departure time. Remember that a program that has features you won't use, whether for rental sporting equipment or discounted museum admissions, may not be the most cost-wise choice for you. Note that when pricing different packages, it sometimes pays to purchase the same arrangements separately, as when a rock-bottom promotional airfare is being offered. Base your choice on what's available at your budget for the destinations you want to visit.

Independent Packages Independent packages are offered by airlines, tour operators who may also do escorted programs, and any number of other companies from large, established firms to small, new entrepreneurs.

One excellent source is **Tour-Scan, Inc.** (1051 Boston Post Rd., Darien, CT 06820, tel. 203/655–8091 or 800/962–2080), a one-stop travel shop that sells, direct to the public, more than 15,000 Caribbean packages, from the least to the most expensive, for all kinds of interests, most containing hotel and airfare along with transfers and various activities. Attesting that his staff checks out each resort personally, President Arthur Mehmel promises savings of "up to several hundred dollars" and says it makes the Caribbean affordable, even islands with a reputation for being pricey. The $4 you pay for the catalogue listing all the offerings is refundable if you book, which entails no fee.

Airline packages almost always include round-trip airfare, accommodations, and transfers. Contact **American Airlines Fly AAway Vacations** (tel. 800/321–2121), **Cayman Airtours** (tel. 800/247–2966), **Continental Airlines' Grand Destinations** (tel. 800/634–5555), **Delta Dream Vacations** (tel. 800/872–7786), **TWA Getaway Vacations** (tel. 800/438–2929), and **United Airlines Vacations** (tel. 800/328–6877). Independent packages are also available from **Certified Vacations** (Box 1535, Ft. Lauderdale, FL 33023, tel. 800/446–6234); **Horizon Tours** (1010 Vermont Ave. NW, Suite 202, Washington, DC 20005, tel. 202/393–8390 or 800/395–0025), with over 50 different programs; and **GWV International** (300 First Ave., Needham, MA 02194, tel. 617/449–5460 or 800/225–5498). **Domenico Tours** (750 Broadway, Bayonne, NJ 07002, tel. 800/554–8687) and **Sunbrella Vacations** (2655 Lejeune Rd., Suite 400, Coral Gables, FL 33134, tel. 800/874–0027) offer a variety of packages in the area. **Club Med** (tel. 800/258–2633) has numerous all-inclusive resorts throughout the region.

Such programs come in a wide range of prices based on levels of luxury and options—in addition to hotel and airfare, sightseeing, car rental, transfers, admission to local attractions, and other extras.

Special-Interest Travel Golf, tennis, scuba diving, and sailing vacations are available throughout the Caribbean. In addition, many more specialized programs are available. Some require a certain amount of expertise, but most are for the average traveler with an interest and are usually hosted by experts in the subject matter. When the program is escorted, it enjoys the advantages and disadvantages of all escorted programs; because your fellow travelers are apt to be passionate or knowledgeable about the subject, they can prove as enjoyable a part of your travel experience as the destination itself. The price range is wide, but the cost is usually higher—sometimes a lot higher—than for ordinary escorted tours and packages, because of the expert guiding and special activities.

Adventure **American Wilderness Experience** (Box 1486, Boulder, CO 80306, tel. 303/444–2622 or 800/444–0099) offers island adventure cruises on a luxury catamaran—scuba, kayak, fish, and swim with wild dolphins.

Clothing Optional **Caribbean Travel Naturally** (Box 897, Lutz, FL 33549, tel. 813/948–1303 or 800/462–6833) offers a range of clothing-optional resorts and cruises throughout the Caribbean.

Diving **Oceanic Society Expeditions** (Fort Mason Center, Building E, San Francisco, CA 94123 tel. 415/441–1106 or 800/326–7491) has scuba-diving packages to a number of Caribbean islands. They also offer whale-watching trips and various research-oriented trips. **Tropical Adventures** (111 Second Ave. North, Seattle, WA 98109, tel. 206/441–3483 or 800/247–3483) has packages for both divers and nondivers, including the awesome, massive underwater pinnacles of Saba.

Environmental and Natural History Programs **Earthwatch** (680 Mount Auburn St., Watertown, MA 02272, tel. 617/926–8000) recruits volunteers to serve in its EarthCorps as short-term assistants to scientists on research expeditions; explore your interest in ecotourism, marine biology, electronics, or mammalogy while collecting data on sea turtles and mongooses. **Lindblad's Special Expeditions** (720 5th Ave., New York, NY 10019, tel. 212/765–7740 or 800/762–0003) hosts journeys by boat combining swimming, hiking through a rain forest, and exploring some of the lesser-known islands of the Windward Chain: St. Lucia, Dominica,and the Grenadines. The **National Audubon Society** (700 Broadway, New York, NY 10003, tel. 212/979–3000, fax 212/979–3188) offers cruises to the Grenadines and Windward and Leeward islands with guest speakers focusing on the cultural diversity and natural beauty of the islands. **Questers Worldwide Nature Tours** (257 Park Ave. S, New York, NY 10010, tel. 212/673–3120) focuses in the Caribbean on Trinidad and Tobago, exploring rain forests, beaches, and swamps in the company of an experienced environmentalist. The **Smithsonian National Associate Program** (1100 Jefferson Dr. SW, Room 3045, Washington, DC 20560, tel. 202/357–4700) offers natural-history programs and cruises in the Caribbean. Smithsonian membership ($22 annually) is required.

Golf **ITC Golf Tours** (4134 Atlantic Ave., Suite 205, Long Beach, CA 90807, tel. 310/595–6905 or 800/257–4981) has packages to Jamaica, Barbados, Bermuda, Tobago, Nassau, and St. Martin.

Horseback Riding **FITS Equestrian** (685 Lateen Rd., Solvang, CA 93463, tel. 805/688–9494 or 800/600–3487) offers a "tan & ride" package to the Chukka Cove resort on Jamaica island with as much or as little as you wish of locally arranged dressage, stadium and cross country jumping, and polo.

Singles **Gramercy's SingleWorld** (401 Theodore Fremd Ave., Rye, NY 10580, tel. 914/967–3334 or 800/223–6490) offers separate singles-only cruise programs for those 20–30 and for those of any age.

Tips for British Travelers

Tourist Information There is no overall tourist organization for the Caribbean, but check the phone book for individual island tourist offices.

Passports and Visas See the Before You Go section in each island chapter for specific passport and visa requirements. Some islands require passports; others do not but may require a British Visitor's Passport.

How to Apply Applications for new and renewal passports are available from main post offices as well as at the six passport offices, located in Belfast, Glasgow, Liverpool, London, Newport, and Peterborough. You may apply in person at all passport offices or by mail to all except the London office; Londoners should mail applications to the Glasgow office (3 Northgate, 96 Milton St., Cowcaddens, Glasgow G4 0BT, tel. 041/332–0271). For your first passport, you must submit the completed form plus the original of your birth or adoption certificate; two recent, identical photographs measuring 35 millimeters by 45 millimeters; and, if you're a married or divorced woman, the original of your marriage certificate or divorce documents. The form and one of the photographs must be countersigned by an eligible witness. For a renewal passport, you may submit the renewal application along with your old passport and new photos. The fee is £18 for a 32-page passport, £27 for a 48-page document. Children under 16 may travel on a parent's passport when accompanying them. All passports are valid for 10 years. Allow a month for processing.

A British Visitor's Passport can include both partners of a married couple. You must apply in person at a main post office and present your uncanceled British passport or valid ID. In addition, you need two recent, identical photographs 35 millimeters by 45 millimeters and the fee (£12, or £18 if your spouse is included on the document). A British Visitor's Passport is valid for one year and will be issued on the same day that you apply.

Customs Exact customs regulations vary slightly from island to island, but in general, from countries outside the EC, you may bring home duty-free 200 cigarettes, 100 cigarillos, 50 cigars or 250 grams of tobacco; 1 liter of spirits or 2 liters of fortified or sparkling wine; 2 liters of still table wine; 60 milliliters of perfume; 250 milliliters of toilet water; plus £36 worth of other goods, including gifts and souvenirs.

For further information or a copy of "A Guide for Travellers," which details standard customs procedures as well as what you may bring into the United Kingdom from abroad, contact HM Customs and Excise (New King's Beam House, 22 Upper Ground, London SE1 9PJ, tel. 071/620–1313).

Insurance Most tour operators, travel agents, and insurance agents sell specialized policies covering accident, medical expenses, personal liability, trip cancellation, and loss or theft of personal property. Some policies include coverage for delayed departure and legal expenses, winter sports, accidents, or motoring abroad. You can also purchase an annual travel-insurance policy valid for every trip you make during the year in which it's purchased (usually only trips of less than 90 days). Before you leave, make sure you will be covered if you have a preexisting medical condition or are pregnant; your insurers may not pay for routine or continuing treatment or may require a note from your doctor certifying your fitness to travel.

For advice by phone or a free booklet, "Holiday Insurance," that sets out what to expect from a holiday-insurance policy and gives price guidelines, contact the Association of British Insurers (51 Gresham St., London EC2V 7HQ, tel. 071/600–3333; 30 Gordon St., Glasgow G1 3PU, tel. 041/226–3905; Scottish Provincial Bldg., Donegall Sq. W, Belfast BT1 6JE, tel. 0232/249176; call for other locations).

Tour Operators Packages to the Caribbean are available from **Caribbean Connection** (93 Newman St., London W1P 4BJ, tel. 071/344–0101), which publishes a 100-page catalogue devoted to Caribbean holidays; **Caribtours** (161 Fulham Rd., London SW3 6SN, tel. 071/581–3517), another Caribbean specialist; **Kuoni Travel** (Kuoni House, Dorking, Surrey RH5 4AZ, tel. 0306/742222); and **Tradewinds Faraway Holidays** (Station House, 81/83 Fulham High St., London SW6 3JP, tel. 071/731–8000).

Airlines and **British Airways, British West Indian Airways,** and **Caledonian** are the
Airfares only airlines with direct flights from London to the Caribbean. It is
always worth checking the small ads in *Time Out* magazine or the
Sunday papers for cheaper charter flights.

Travelers with Main information sources include the **Royal Association for Disabili-**
Disabilities **ty and Rehabilitation** (RADAR, 25 Mortimer St., London W1N
8AB, tel. 071/637–5400), which publishes travel information for
people with disabilities in Britain, and **Mobility International** (228
Borough High St., London SE1 1JX, tel. 071/403–5688), the headquarters of an international membership organization that serves as
a clearinghouse of travel information for people with disabilities.

Festivals and Seasonal Events

Regardless of when Carnival season starts on each island, it always
means days and nights of continuous partying. There's a celebration
going on from January through August, it's just a matter of being on
the right island!

The first Carnival of the season is also the longest. **Martinique's** Carnival begins in early January and lasts through the first day of Lent,
in mid-February. **Guadeloupe's** Carnival starts a day later and also
continues until Lent, finishing with a parade of floats and costumes
on "Mardi Gras" and a huge bash on Ash Wednesday. **Curaçao's** Carnival season lasts from late January to early February. All of these
Carnivals feature music, dance, and a costumed parade.

February brings a flood of Carnival events, including those on **Bon-**
aire, Puerto Rico, St. Lucia, St. Martin (the French side of the island), **St. Barthélemy,** and **Trinidad and Tobago,** all of which combine
feasting, dancing, music, and parades. During Carnival on **Trinidad**
and Tobago, adults and children alike are swept up in the excitement
of Playing Mas'—the state of surrendering completely to the rap-
ture of fantastic spectacle, parades, music, and dancing. For those
who feel the urge, places in a genuine "mas' band" can be purchased
(long in advance) for fees that vary according to the prestige of the
group and the intricacy of the costumes.

Spring brings the **St. Thomas (U.S. Virgin Islands)** and the **Sint**
Maarten (Dutch side of the island) Carnivals in April and the **Cay-**
man Islands' Carnival, which begins on Grand Cayman in May. In
July, the season reaches **Saba** and the **Dominican Republic,** whose
popular 10-day Merengue Festival features entertainment from
outdoor bands and orchestras and the best cuisine from local hotel
chefs. **Anguilla** and the **British Virgin Islands** start Carnival in early
August with street dancing, calypso competitions, the Carnival
Queen Coronation, and sumptuous beach barbecues. The **Turks and**
Caicos islands finish the string of festivals during the last days of the
month.

There are many other festivals each year around the islands that celebrate their rich local cultures. Barbados's **Holetown Festival** commemorates the first settlement of Barbados on February 17, 1627,
with a week of fairs, street markets, and revelry. During the **Tobago**
Heritage Festival in July, each village on Trinidad and Tobago
mounts a different show or festivity. Beginning in July and continuing through August, Barbados celebrates the **Crop-Over Festival,** a
monthlong cheer for the end of the sugarcane harvest. Calypsonians
battle for the coveted Calypso Monarch award, and Bajan cooking
abounds at the massive "Bridgetown Market" street fair. On a Sunday in early August, Guadaloupe holds a **Fête des Cuisinières** and cel-

ebrates the masters of Creole cuisine with a five-hour banquet that is open to the public. The **Hatillo Festival of the Masks,** held in December in Puerto Rico, is a carnival featuring folk music and dancing, as well as parades in which islanders don brightly colored masks and costumes.

Swimming, splashing, and snorkeling aren't the only things going on in these gorgeous green and blue waters. Sports enthusiasts, tourists, and islanders travel throughout the Caribbean to watch the many regattas. Grenada's **New Year Fiesta Yacht Race** in late January is highlighted by the "Around Grenada" sailing contest. Antigua's **Sailing Week** in April brings together more than 300 yachts from around the world. The British Virgin Islands' **Spring Regatta,** the **Curaçao Regatta,** the **Grenada Easter Regatta,** and the U.S. Virgin Islands' **International Rolex Cup Regatta** take place in April. Boat racing is the national sport in Anguilla, and the most important competitions take place on **Anguilla Day,** May 30. Just about every type of competition that can be held on or in water constitutes the weeklong **"Aqua Action" Festival** held in St. Lucia at the end of June. Canoe racing, Sunfish sailing, windsurfing, sportfishing, waterskiing, and a nonmariners race are some of the main attractions. The U.S. and British Virgin Islands share the **Hook In & Hold On Boardsailing Regatta** in June and July. Grenada's annual **Carriacou Regatta,** which takes place on this island some 16 miles to the north, brings a week of racing and partying at the end of July. Martinique hosts the **Tour des Yoles Rondes** point-to-point yawl race in early August, and the annual **Sailing Regatta** in Bonaire takes place in October. The **Route du Rosé,** a transatlantic regatta of tall ships that set sail from St-Tropez in early November, is welcomed to St. Barts in December with a round of festivities.

Music lovers should also take note of several annual events. In January, St. Barthélemy is host to an international collection of soloists and musicians as part of the **Annual St. Barts Music Festival.** The **Barbados Caribbean Jazz Festival** in Bridgetown features performances of original compositions and traditional jazz for three days at the end of May. At the end of June, the **Aruba Jazz and Latin Music Festival** is held in Oranjestad, offering well-known entertainers performing Latin, pop, jazz, and salsa music at Mansur stadium. And the **August Reggae Sunsplash International Music Festival** is getting hotter every year, as the best, brightest, and newest of the reggae stars gather to perform in open-air concerts in MoBay on Jamaica.

When to Go

The Caribbean "season" has traditionally been a winter one, usually extending from December 15 to April 14. This "season" exists because northern weather is at its worst, not because the Caribbean weather is at it's best. In fact, winter is when the Caribbean is at its windiest. However, the winter months are the most fashionable, the most expensive, and the most popular, and most hotels are heavily booked. You have to make your reservations at least two or three months in advance for the very best places (and sometimes a year in advance for the most exclusive spots). Hotel prices are at their highest in winter; the 20%–50% drop in rates for "summer" (after April 15) is one of the chief advantages of off-season travel. Cruise prices also rise and fall with the seasons. Saving money isn't the only reason to visit the Caribbean during the off-season. Temperatures in summer are only a few degrees warmer than in winter. It used to be that there were also fewer fellow travelers, but the summer is growing ever busier, and more and more hotels and restaurants are staying open year-round. September, October, and November are the least crowded months, but hotel facilities can be limited and some restaurants will be closed. Singles in search of partners should visit during the high season or in summer, or choose a resort with a high year-round occupancy rate.

The flamboyant flowering trees are at their height in summer, and so are most of the flowers and shrubs of the West Indies. The water is clearer for snorkeling, and smoother for sailing in the Virgin Islands and the Grenadines, in May, June, and July .

Climate   The Caribbean climate is fairly constant. Average year-round temperature for the region is 78°F–85°F. The extremes of temperature are 65°F low, 95°F high, but as everyone knows, it's the humidity, not the heat, that makes you suffer, especially when the two go hand in hand. You can count on downtown shopping areas being hot at midday any time of the year, but air-conditioning provides some respite. Stay near beaches, where water and trade winds can keep you cool, and shop early or late in the day.

High places can be cool, particularly when the Christmas winds hit Caribbean peaks (they come in late November and last through January). Since most Caribbean islands are mountainous (notable exceptions being the Caymans, Aruba, Bonaire, and Curaçao), the altitude always offers an escape from the latitude. Kingston (Jamaica), Port-of-Spain (Trinidad), and Fort-de-France (Martinique) swelter in summer; climb 1,000 feet or so and everything is fine.

Hurricanes occasionally sweep through the Caribbean in the fall, and officials on many islands are not well equipped to warn locals, much less tourists. Check the news daily and keep abreast of brewing tropical storms by reading stateside papers if you can get them. The rainy season, usually in fall, consists mostly of brief showers interspersed with sunshine. You can watch the clouds come over, feel the rain, and remain on your lounge chair for the sun to dry you off. A spell of overcast days is "unusual," as everyone will tell you.

Generally speaking, there's more planned entertainment in winter. The peak of local excitement on many islands, most notably Trinidad, St. Vincent, and the French West Indies, is Carnival (*see* Festivals and Seasonal Events, *above*).

For More Information   For current weather conditions for cities in the United States and abroad, plus the local time and helpful travel tips, call the **Weather Channel Connection** (tel. 900/932–8437; 95¢ per minute) from a Touch-Tone phone.

What to Pack

Pack light because baggage carts are scarce at airports and luggage restrictions are tight.

Clothing   Dress on the islands is light and casual. Bring loose-fitting clothes made of natural fabrics to see you through days of heat and high humidity. Take a cover-up for the beaches, not only to protect you from the sun, but also to wear to and from your hotel room. Bathing suits and immodest attire are frowned upon off the beach on many islands. A sun hat is advisable, but you don't have to pack one, since inexpensive straw hats are available everywhere. For shopping and sightseeing, bring walking shorts, jeans, T-shirts, long-sleeve cotton shirts, slacks, and sundresses. You'll need a sweater in the many glacially air-conditioned hotels and restaurants, for protection from the trade winds, and at higher altitudes. Evenings are casual, but "casual" can range from really informal to casually elegant, depending on the establishment. A tie is rarely required but jackets are sometimes required in the fancier restaurants and casinos.

Adapters, Converters, Transformers The general rule in the Caribbean is 110 and 120 volts AC, and the outlets take the same two-prong plugs found in the United States, but there are a number of exceptions , particularly on the French islands and on some islands with a British heritage. To be sure, check with your hotel when making reservations.

You may need an adapter plug, plus a converter, which reduces the voltage entering the appliance from 220 to 110 volts. There are converters for high-wattage appliances (such as hair dryers), low-wattage items (such as electric toothbrushes and razors), and combination models. Hotels sometimes have outlets marked "For Shavers Only" near the sink; these are 110-volt outlets for low-wattage appliances; don't use them for a high-wattage appliance. If you're traveling with an older laptop computer, carry a transformer. Newer laptop computers are auto-sensing, operating equally well on 110 and 220 volts, so you need only the appropriate adapter plug. For a copy of the free brochure "Foreign Electricity is No Deep Dark Secret," send a self-addressed, stamped envelope to adapter-converter manufacturer Franzus (Customer Service, Dept. B-50, Murtha Industrial Park, Box 142, Beacon Falls, CT 06403, tel. 203/723–6664).

Miscellaneous Bring a spare pair of eyeglasses, sunglasses, or contact lenses, and if you have a health problem that may require you to purchase a prescription drug, have your doctor write a prescription using its generic name, since nomenclature varies from island to island. Better still, take enough to last the duration of the trip: Although you can probably find what you need in the pharmacies, you may need a local doctor's prescription. You'll want an umbrella during the rainy season; leave the plastic or nylon raincoats at home, since they're extremely uncomfortable in hot, humid weather. Bring suntan lotion and film from home; they're much more expensive on the islands. You'll need insect repellent, too, especially if you plan to walk through rain forests or visit during the rainy season. Don't forget to pack a list of the addresses of offices that supply refunds for lost or stolen traveler's checks.

Luggage *Regulations* Free airline baggage allowances depend on the airline, the route, and the class of your ticket; ask in advance. In general, on domestic flights and on international flights between the United States and foreign destinations, you are entitled to check two bags—neither exceeding 62 inches, or 158 centimeters (length + width + height), or weighing more than 70 pounds (32 kilograms). A third piece may be brought aboard as a carry-on; its total dimensions are generally limited to less than 45 inches (114 centimeters) so it will fit easily under the seat in front of you or in the overhead compartment. In the United States, the Federal Aviation Administration (FAA) gives airlines broad latitude to limit carry-on allowances and tailor them to different aircraft and operational conditions. Charges for excess, oversize, or overweight pieces vary.

If you are flying between two foreign destinations, note that baggage allowances may be determined not by piece but by weight, which generally allows 88 pounds (40 kilograms) of luggage in first class, 66 pounds (30 kilograms) in business class, and 44 pounds (20 kilograms) in economy. If your flight between two cities abroad *connects* with your transatlantic or transpacific flight, the piece method still applies.

Safeguarding
Your Luggage Before leaving home, itemize the contents of your bags and their worth in case they go astray. To minimize that risk, tag them inside and out with your name, address, and phone number. (If you use your home address, cover it so that potential thieves can't see it.) Put a copy of your itinerary inside each bag, so that you can easily be tracked. At check-in, make sure that the tag attached by baggage handlers bears the correct three-letter code for your destination. If your bags do not arrive with you, or if you detect damage, file a written report with the airline immediately—before you leave the airport.

Taking Money Abroad

Traveler's checks and all major U.S. credit cards are accepted in the Caribbean. Although large hotels, restaurants, and department stores accept credit cards readily, some smaller restaurants and shops operate on a cash-only basis. U.S. dollars are also accepted on most islands; paying in dollars may even allow you to bargain for a lower price.

Traveler's Traveler's checks are preferable in metropolitan centers, although
Checks you'll need cash in rural areas and small towns. The most widely recognized checks are **American Express, Citicorp, Diners Club, Thomas Cook,** and **Visa,** which are sold by major commercial banks. Both American Express and Thomas Cook issue checks that can be countersigned and used by you or your traveling companion. Typically the issuing company or the bank at which you make your purchase charges 1% to 3% of the checks' face value as a fee. Some foreign banks charge as much as 20% of the face value as the fee for cashing traveler's checks in a foreign currency. Buy a few checks in small denominations to cash toward the end of your trip so you won't be left with excess foreign currency. Record the numbers of checks as you spend them, and keep this list separate from the checks.

You can also buy traveler's checks in the currency of some of the islands, a good idea if the dollar is dropping in relation to the local currency. The value of some currencies changes with great frequency and very radically; some are subject to inflation, others to devaluation, while still others float with the U.S. dollar.

Currency Banks offer the most favorable exchange rates. If you use currency
Exchange exchange booths at airports, rail and bus stations, hotels, stores, and privately run exchange firms, you'll typically get less favorable rates, but you may find the hours more convenient.

You can get good rates and avoid long lines at airport currency-exchange booths by getting a small amount of currency at **Thomas Cook Currency Services** (630 5th Ave., New York, NY 10111, tel. 212/757–6915 or 800/223–7373 for locations in major metropolitan areas throughout the U.S.) or **Ruesch International** (tel. 800/424–2923 for locations) before you depart. Check with your travel agent to be sure that the currency of the country you will be visiting can be imported.

Getting Money from Home

Cash Many automated-teller machines (ATMs) are tied to international
Machines networks such as **Cirrus** and **Plus,** both of which have expanded their service in the Caribbean. You can use your bank card at ATMs away from home to withdraw money from an account and get cash advances on a credit-card account if your card has been programmed with a personal identification number, or PIN. Check in advance on

limits on withdrawals and cash advances within specified periods. Ask whether your bank-card or credit-card PIN number will need to be reprogrammed for use in the area you'll be visiting. Four digits are commonly used overseas. Note that Discover is accepted only in the United States. On cash advances you are charged interest from the day you receive the money from ATMs as well as from tellers. Although transaction fees for ATM withdrawals abroad may be higher than fees for withdrawals at home, Cirrus and Plus exchange rates tend to be good. Be sure to plan ahead: Obtain ATM locations and the names of affiliated cash-machine networks before departure. For specific foreign Cirrus locations, call 800/424–7787; for foreign Plus locations, consult the Plus directory at your local bank.

Wiring Money You don't have to be a cardholder to send or receive a **MoneyGram from American Express** for up to $10,000. Go to a MoneyGram agent in retail and convenience stores and American Express travel offices, pay up to $1,000 with a credit card and anything over that in cash. You are allowed a free long-distance call to give the transaction code to your intended recipient, who needs only present identification and the reference number to the nearest MoneyGram agent to pick up the cash. MoneyGram agents are in more than 70 countries (call 800/926–9400 for locations). Fees range from 3% to 10%, depending on the amount and how you pay.

You can also use **Western Union.** To wire money, take either cash or a check to the nearest office or call and use your MasterCard or Visa. Money sent from the United States or Canada will be available for pickup at agent locations in the Caribbean within minutes. Once the money is in the system it can be picked up at *any* one of 22,000 locations (call 800/325–6000 for the one nearest you).

Long-Distance Calling

AT&T, MCI, and Sprint have several services that make calling home or the office more affordable and convenient when you're on the road. Use one of them to avoid pricey hotel surcharges. **AT&T** Calling Card (tel. 800/225–5288) and the AT&T Universal Card (tel. 800/662–7759) give you access to the service. With AT&T's USADirect (tel. 800/874–4000 for codes in the countries you'll be visiting) you can reach an AT&T operator with a local or toll-free call. **MCI**'s Call USA (MCI Customer Service, tel. 800/444–4444) allows that service from 85 countries or from country to country via MCI WorldReach. **Sprint** Express (tel. 800/793–1153) has a toll-free number travelers abroad can dial to reach a Sprint operator in the U.S.

Passports and Visas

If your passport is lost or stolen abroad, report it immediately to the nearest embassy or consulate and to the local police. If you can provide the consular officer with the information contained in the passport, he or she will usually be able to issue you a new passport promptly. For this reason, keep a photocopy of the data page of your passport separate from your money and traveler's checks. Also leave a photocopy with a relative or friend at home.

See individual island chapters for entrance requirements to specific islands.

U.S. Citizens You can pick up new and renewal application forms at any of the 13 U.S. Passport Agency offices and at quite a number of post offices and courthouses. Although passports are usually mailed within two weeks of your application's receipt, it's best to allow three weeks for delivery in low season, five weeks or more from April through summer. Call the Department of State Office of Passport Services' information line (tel. 202/647–0518) for fees, documentation requirements, and other details.

Canadian Citizens Application forms are available at 23 regional passport offices as well as at post offices and travel agencies. Whether applying for a first or subsequent passport, you must apply in person. Children under 16 may be included on a parent's passport but must have their own passport to travel alone. Passports are valid for five years and are usually mailed within two weeks of an application's receipt. For fees, documentation requirements, and other information in English or French, call the passport office (tel. 514/283–2152 or 800/567–6868).

Customs and Duties

U.S. Customs If you've been out of the country for at least 48 hours and haven't already used the exemption, or any part of it, in the past 30 days, you may bring $600 worth of goods home duty-free from *most* Caribbean countries. This amount—more generous than the $400 duty-free exemption allowed on return from almost everywhere else—applies to two dozen Caribbean Basin Initiative beneficiary countries. If you're returning from the U.S. Virgin Islands, the duty-free allowance is even higher—$1,200. A flat 10% duty (5% from the U.S. Virgin Islands) applies to the next $1,000 of goods; above that, the rate varies with the merchandise. These exemptions may be pooled among family members, regardless of age, so that one may bring in more if another brings in less. If the 48-hour or 30-day limits apply, your duty-free allowance drops to $25, which may *not* be pooled.

Some wrinkles to the above: If you are visiting more than one island, say the U.S. Virgins and the Dominican Republic (a beneficiary country), you may bring in a total of $1,200 duty-free, of which no more than $600 may be from the Dominican Republic. If you visit a beneficiary country and an excluded one, such as Martinique, you may bring in a total of $600 goods duty-free, of which no more than $400 may be from Martinique.

In addition, the Generalized System of Preferences, aimed at helping developing countries improve their economies through trade, exempts certain items from the same beneficiary countries from duty entirely, meaning that they do not count toward the duty-free total at all. At press time, however, the future of GSP beyond its July 4, 1994, expiration date was unknown.

Travelers 21 or older may bring back 2 liters of alcohol duty-free from most Caribbean countries, provided the beverage laws of the state through which they reenter the U.S. allow it. In the case of the U.S. Virgin Islands, 5 liters are allowed. If you are visiting a beneficiary country and an excluded one, no more than 1 of the 2 liters allowed may be from the excluded country; if you are visiting the U.S. Virgin Islands and a beneficiary country, no more than 2 liters of the 5 allowed may be from the beneficiary country.

Regardless of age, you may bring 100 non-Cuban cigars and 200 cigarettes back to the U.S. From the U.S. Virgin Islands, 1,000 cigarettes are allowed, but only 200 of them may have been acquired elsewhere.

Gifts valued at less than $50 ($100 from the U.S. Virgin Islands) may be mailed to the United States duty-free, with a limit of one package per day per addressee (do not send alcohol or tobacco products, or perfume valued at more than $5). These gifts do not count as part of your exemption, although if you bring them home with you, they do. Mark the package "Unsolicited Gift" and include the nature of the gift and its retail value.

The free brochure "Know Before You Go" lists all Caribbean Basin Initiative beneficiary countries and details what you may and may not bring back to this country, rates of duty, and other pointers; to obtain it, contact the U.S. Customs Service (Box 7407, Washington, DC 20044, tel. 202/927–6724). A copy of "GSP and the Traveler" is available from the same source.

Canadian Customs Once per calendar year, when you've been out of Canada for at least seven days, you may bring in $300 worth of goods duty-free. If you've been away less than seven days but more than 48 hours, the duty-free exemption drops to $100 but can be claimed any number of times (as can a $20 duty-free exemption for absences of 24 hours or more). You cannot combine the yearly and 48-hour exemptions, use the $300 exemption only partially (to save the balance for a later trip), or pool exemptions with family members. Goods claimed under the $300 exemption may follow you by mail; those claimed under the lesser exemptions must accompany you.

Alcohol and tobacco products may be included in the yearly and 48-hour exemptions but not in the 24-hour exemption. If you meet the age requirements of the province through which you reenter Canada, you may bring in, duty-free, 1.14 liters (40 imperial ounces) of wine or liquor *or* two dozen 12-ounce cans or bottles of beer or ale. If you are 16 or older, you may bring in, duty-free, 200 cigarettes, 50 cigars or cigarillos, and 400 tobacco sticks or 400 grams of manufactured tobacco. Alcohol and tobacco must accompany you on your return.

An unlimited number of gifts valued up to C$60 each may be mailed to Canada duty-free. These do not count as part of your exemption. Label the package "Unsolicited Gift—Value under $60." Alcohol and tobacco are excluded.

For more information, including details of duties on items that exceed your duty-free limit, ask the Revenue Canada Customs and Excise Department (Connaught Bldg., MacKenzie Ave., Ottawa, Ontario, K1A OL5, tel. 613/957–0275) for a copy of the free brochure "I Declare/Je Déclare."

Traveling with Cameras, Camcorders, and Laptops

Film and Cameras If your camera is new or if you haven't used it for a while, shoot and develop a few rolls of film before leaving home. Store film in a cool, dry place—never in the car's glove compartment or on the shelf under the rear window.

Airport security X-rays generally aren't harmful to film with ISO below 400. To protect your film, carry it with you in a clear plastic bag and ask for a hand inspection. Such requests are honored at U.S. airports, up to the inspector abroad. Don't depend on a lead-lined bag to protect film in checked luggage—the airline may increase the radiation to see what's inside. Call the Kodak Information Center (tel. 800/242–2424) for details.

Camcorders Before your trip, put camcorders through their paces, invest in a skylight filter to protect the lens, and check all the batteries. Most newer camcorders are equipped with a universal or worldwide AC adapter charger (or multivoltage converter) usable whether the voltage is 110 or 220. All that's needed is the appropriate plug.

Videotape Videotape is not damaged by X-rays, but it may be harmed by the magnetic field of a walk-through metal detector, so ask for a hand-check. Airport security personnel may want you to turn on the camcorder to prove that it's what it appears to be, so make sure the battery is charged. Note that while most Caribbean islands operate on the National Television System Committee video standard (NTSC), used by the United States and Canada, Guadeloupe and Martinique use a different technology, known as Secam. For that reason, you will not be able to view your tapes through the local TV set or view movies bought there in your home VCR. (Blank tapes bought in the Caribbean can be used for NTSC camcorder taping, but they are pricey.)

Laptops Security X-rays do not harm hard-disk or floppy-disk storage, but you may request a hand-check, at which point you may be asked to turn on the computer to prove that it is what it appears to be. (Check your battery before departure.) Most airlines allow you to use your laptop aloft except during takeoff and landing (so as not to interfere with navigation equipment). For international travel, register your foreign-made laptop with U.S. Customs as you leave the country. If your laptop is U.S.-made, call the consulate of the country you'll be visiting to find out whether it should be registered with customs upon arrival. Before departure, find out about repair facilities at your destination, and don't forget any transformer or adapter plug you may need (*see* Electricity, *above*).

Staying Healthy

Few real hazards threaten the health of a visitor to the Caribbean. The small lizards that seem to have overrun the islands are harmless, and poisonous snakes are hard to find, although you should exercise caution while bird-watching in Trinidad. The worst problem may well be a tiny sand fly known as the "no-see-um," which tends to appear after a rain, near wet or swampy ground, and around sunset. If you feel particularly vulnerable to insect bites, bring along a good repellent.

Sunburn or sunstroke can also be serious problems. Even people who are not normally bothered by strong sun should head into this area with a long-sleeve shirt, a hat, and long pants or a beach wrap. These are essential for a day on a boat but are also advisable for midday at the beach and whenever you go out sightseeing. Also carry some sunblock lotion for nose, ears, and other sensitive areas such as eyelids, ankles, etc. Limit your sun time for the first few days until you become used to the heat. And be sure to drink enough liquids.

Since health standards vary from island to island, inquire on local conditions before you go. No special shots are required for most destinations; where they are, we have made note of it.

Scuba divers take note: PADI (the Professional Association of Diving Instructors) recommends that you not scuba dive and fly within a 24-hour period.

Finding a The **International Association for Medical Assistance to Travellers**
Doctor (IAMAT, 417 Center St., Lewiston, NY 14092, tel. 716/754–4883; 40 Regal Rd., Guelph, Ontario N1K 1B5; 57 Voirets, 1212 Grand-

Lancy, Geneva, Switzerland) publishes a worldwide directory of English-speaking physicians whose qualifications meet IAMAT standards and who have agreed to treat members for a set fee. Membership is free.

Assistance Companies Pretrip medical referrals, emergency evacuation or repatriation, 24-hour telephone hot lines for medical consultation, dispatch of medical personnel, relay of medical records, up-front cash for emergencies, and other personal and legal assistance are among the services provided by several membership organizations specializing in medical assistance to travelers. Among them are **International SOS Assistance** (Box 11568, Philadelphia, PA 19116, tel. 215/244–1500 or 800/523–8930; Box 466, Pl. Bonaventure, Montréal, Québec, H5A 1C1, tel. 514/874–7674 or 800/363–0263), **Medex Assistance Corporation** (Box 10623, Baltimore, MD 21285, tel. 410/296–2530 or 800/874–9125), **Near Services** (450 Prairie Ave., Suite 101, Calumet City, IL 60409, tel. 708/868–6700 or 800/654–6700), and **Travel Assistance International** (1133 15th St. NW, Suite 400, Washington, DC 20005, tel. 202/331–1609 or 800/821–2828). Because these companies will also sell you death-and-dismemberment, trip-cancellation, and other insurance coverage, there is some overlap with the travel-insurance policies discussed under Insurance, *below.*

Publications *The Safe Travel Book* by Peter Savage ($12.95; Lexington Books, 866 Third Ave., New York, NY 10022, tel. 212/702–4771 or 800/257–5755, fax 800/562–1272) is packed with handy lists and phone numbers to make your trip smooth. *Traveler's Medical Resource* by William W. Forgey ($19.95; ICS Books, Inc., 1 Tower Plaza, 107 E. 89th Ave., Merrillville, IN 45410, tel. 800/541–7323) is also a good, authoritative guide to care overseas.

Insurance

Most tour operators, travel agents, and insurance agents sell specialized health-and-accident, flight, trip-cancellation, and luggage insurance as well as comprehensive policies with some or all of these features. But before you make any purchase, review your existing health and home-owner policies to find out whether they cover expenses incurred while traveling.

Health-and-Accident Insurance Specific policy provisions of supplemental health-and-accident insurance for travelers include reimbursement for from $1,000 to $150,000 worth of medical and/or dental expenses caused by an accident or illness during a trip. The personal-accident or death-and-dismemberment provision pays a lump sum to your beneficiaries if you die or to you if you lose a limb or your eyesight; the lump sum awarded can range from $15,000 to $500,000. The medical-assistance provision may reimburse you for the cost of referrals, evacuation, or repatriation and other services, or it may automatically enroll you as a member of a particular medical-assistance company (*see* Assistance Companies, *above*).

Flight Insurance Often bought as a last-minute impulse at the airport, flight insurance pays a lump sum when a plane crashes either to a beneficiary if the insured dies or sometimes to a surviving passenger who loses eyesight or a limb. Like most impulse buys, flight insurance is expensive and basically unnecessary. It supplements the airlines' coverage described in the limits-of-liability paragraphs on your ticket. Charging an airline ticket to a major credit card often automatically entitles you to coverage and may also embrace travel by bus, train, and ship.

Baggage Insurance In the event of loss, damage, or theft on international flights, airlines' liability is $20 per kilogram for checked baggage (roughly about $640 per 70-pound bag) and $400 per passenger for unchecked baggage. On domestic flights, the ceiling is $1,250 per passenger. Excess-valuation insurance can be bought directly from the airline at check-in for about $10 per $1,000 worth of coverage. However, you cannot buy it at any price for the rather extensive list of excluded items shown on your airline ticket.

Trip Insurance **Trip-cancellation-and-interruption insurance** protects you in the event you are unable to undertake or finish your trip, especially if your airline ticket, cruise, or package tour does not allow changes or cancellations. The amount of coverage you purchase should equal the cost of your trip should you, a traveling companion, or a family member fall ill, forcing you to stay home, plus the nondiscounted one-way airline ticket you would need to buy if you had to return home early. Read the fine print carefully, especially sections defining "family member" and "preexisting medical conditions." **Default or bankruptcy insurance** protects you against a supplier's failure to deliver. Such policies often do not cover default by a travel agency, tour operator, airline, or cruise line if you bought your tour and the coverage directly from the firm in question. Tours packaged by one of the 33 members of the United States Tour Operators Association (USTOA, 211 E. 51 St., Suite 12B, New York, NY 10022, tel. 212/750–7371), which requires members to maintain $1 million each in an account to reimburse clients in case of default, are likely to present the fewest difficulties. Even better, pay for travel arrangements with a major credit card, so that you can refuse to pay the bill if services have not been rendered—and let the card company fight your battles.

Comprehensive Policies Companies supplying comprehensive policies with some or all of the above features include **Access America, Inc.** (Box 90315, Richmond, VA 23230, tel. 800/284–8300); **Carefree Travel Insurance** (Box 310, 120 Mineola Blvd., Mineola, NY 11501, tel. 516/294–0220 or 800/323–3149); **Tele-Trip** (Mutual of Omaha Plaza, Box 31762, Omaha, NE 68131, tel. 800/228–9792); **The Travelers Companies** (1 Tower Sq., Hartford, CT 06183, tel. 203/277–0111 or 800/243–3174); **Travel Guard International** (1145 Clark St., Stevens Point, WI 54481, tel. 715/345–0505 or 800/782–5151); and **Wallach and Company, Inc.** (107 W. Federal St., Box 480, Middleburg, VA 22117, tel. 703/687–3166 or 800/237–6615).

Student and Youth Travel

The Caribbean is not as far out of a student's budget as you might expect. All but the toniest islands such as St. Barthélemy have fine camping facilities, inexpensive guest houses, or small no-frills hotels. You're most likely to meet students from other countries in the French and Dutch West Indies, where many go on holiday or sabbatical. Puerto Rico, Jamaica, Grenada, and Dominica, among others, have large resident international student populations at their universities.

Travel Agencies **Council Travel Services (CTS),** a subsidiary of the nonprofit Council on International Educational Exchange, specializes in low-cost travel arrangements abroad for students and is the exclusive U.S. agent for several discount cards. Also newly available from CTS are domestic air passes for bargain travel within the United States. CIEE's twice-yearly *Student Travels* magazine is available at the CTS office at CIEE headquarters (205 E. 42nd Street, 16th Floor,

New York, NY 10017, tel. 212/661–1450) and in Boston (tel. 617/266–1926), Miami (tel. 305/670–9261), Los Angeles (tel. 310/208–3551), and at 43 branches in college towns nationwide (free in person, $1 by mail). **Campus Connections** (1100 East Marlton Pike, Cherry Hill, NJ 08034, tel. 800/428–3235) specializes in discounted accommodations and airfares for students. The **Educational Travel Center** (438 N. Frances St., Madison, WI 53703, tel. 608/256–5551) offers low-cost domestic and international airline tickets, mostly for flights departing from Chicago, and rail passes. Other travel agencies catering to students include **TMI Student Travel** (1146 Pleasant St., Watertown, MA 02172, tel. 617/661–8187 or 800/245–3672) and **Travel Cuts** (187 College St., Toronto, Ontario M5T 1P7, tel. 416/979–2406).

Discount Cards For discounts on transportation and on museum and attractions admissions, buy the **International Student Identity Card** (ISIC) if you're a bona fide student or the **International Youth Card** (IYC) if you're under 26. In the United States, the ISIC and IYC cards cost $15 each and include basic travel accident and sickness coverage. Apply to **CIEE** (*see* address *above*, tel. 212/661–1414; the application is in *Student Travels*). In Canada, the cards are available for $15 each from **Travel Cuts** (*see above*). In the United Kingdom, they cost £5 and £4, respectively, at student unions and student travel companies, including Council Travel's London office (28A Poland St., London W1V 3DB, tel. 071/437–7767).

Traveling with Children

The Caribbean islands and their resorts are increasingly sensitive to the needs of families. Children's programs are part of a growing number of major new developments. Baby food is easy to find, but outside major hotels you may not find such items as high chairs and cribs. Another thing to consider is whether or not English is spoken widely; the language barrier can be frustrating for children.

Tour Operators **Grandtravel** (6900 Wisconsin Ave., Suite 706, Chevy Chase, MD 20815, tel. 301/986–0790 or 800/247–7651) offers international and domestic tours for people traveling with their grandchildren. The catalogue, as charmingly written and illustrated as a children's book, positively invites armchair traveling with lap-sitters aboard. **Rascals in Paradise** (650 5th St., Suite 505, San Francisco, CA 94107, tel. 415/978–9800 or 800/872–7225) specializes in programs for families.

Publications
Newsletter *Family Travel Times,* published 10 times a year by **Travel With Your Children** (TWYCH, 45 W. 18th St., 7th Floor Tower, New York, NY 10011, tel. 212/206–0688; annual subscription $55), covers destinations, types of vacations, and modes of travel. TWYCH also publishes *Cruising with Children.*

Books *Great Vacations with Your Kids,* by Dorothy Jordon and Marjorie Cohen ($13; Penguin USA, 120 Woodbine St., Bergenfield, NJ 07621, tel. 800/253–6476), and *Traveling with Children—And Enjoying It,* by Arlene K. Butler ($11.95 plus $3 shipping; Globe Pequot Press, Box 833, 6 Business Park Rd., Old Saybrook, CT 06475, tel. 800/243–0495; in CT, 800/962–0973) help you plan your trip with children, from toddlers to teens. From the same publisher are *Recommended Family Resorts in the United States, Canada, and the Caribbean,* by Jane Wilford with Janet Tice ($12.95), and *Recommended Family Inns of America* ($12.95).

Getting On international flights, the fare for infants under age 2 not occupy-
There ing a seat is generally either free or 10% of the accompanying adult's
Airfares fare; children ages 2 to 11 usually pay half to two-thirds of the adult
fare. On domestic flights, children under 2 not occupying a seat travel free, and older children currently travel on the "lowest applica-
ble" adult fare. Some routes in the Caribbean are considered neither
international nor domestic and have still other rules; check with
your airline.

Baggage In general, infants paying 10% of the adult fare are allowed one carry-on bag, not to exceed 70 pounds or 45 inches (length + width +
height) and a collapsible stroller; check with the airline before departure, because you may be allowed less if the flight is full. The
adult baggage allowance applies to children paying half or more of
the adult fare.

Safety Seats The FAA recommends the use of safety seats aloft and details approved models in the free leaflet **"Child/Infant Safety Seats Recommended for Use in Aircraft"** (available from the Federal Aviation
Administration, APA–200, 800 Independence Ave. SW, Washington, DC 20591, tel. 202/267–3479; Inormation Hotline, tel. 800/322–
7873). Airline policy varies. U.S. carriers allow FAA-approved models bearing a sticker declaring their FAA approval. Because these
seats are strapped into regular passenger seats, airlines may require that a ticket be bought for an infant who would otherwise ride
free. Foreign carriers may not allow infant seats, may charge the
child's rather than the infant's fare for their use, or may require you
to hold your baby during takeoff and landing, thus defeating the
seat's purpose.

Facilities Aloft Some airlines provide other services for children, such as children's
meals and freestanding bassinets (only to those with seats at the
bulkhead, where there's enough legroom). Make your request when
reserving. The annual February/March issue of *Family Travel
Times* details children's services on dozens of airlines ($10; *see
above*). "Kids and Teens in Flight" (free from the U.S. Department
of Transportation's Office of Consumer Affairs (R-25, Washington,
D.C. 20590, tel. 202/366–2220) offers tips for children flying alone.

Lodging Children are welcome except in the most exclusive resorts; many ho-
Hotels tels allow children under 12 or 16 to stay free in their parents' room
(be sure to ask the cutoff age when booking). In addition, several hotel chains have developed children's programs that free parents to
explore or relax, and many hotels and resorts arrange for baby-sitting. The following brief list is representative of the kinds of services and activities offered by some of the major chains and resorts.

In **Aruba,** the **Aruba Sonesta Hotel, Beach Club & Casino** (tel. 800/
766–3782) operates a complimentary "Just Us Kids" program for
children ages 5–12. The daily, year-round program features field
trips to local Aruban attractions, sports and games, arts-and-crafts
classes, and special bonfire nights. Baby-sitting services are also offered.

In **Puerto Rico,** the **Hyatt Regency Cerromar Beach** and the **Hyatt
Dorado Beach** operate a camp (tel. 800/233–1234) for children ages
5–12 all summer, at Christmastime, and at Easter. One of the
camp's main attractions is a meandering, free-form freshwater pool
with waterfalls, bridges, and a 187-foot water slide. The camp's
staff includes bilingual college-age counselors. The cost at both hotels is $25 per child per day. The **El San Juan** (tel. 800/468–2818) in
Puerto Rico has a program for children in the same age group that

features swimnastics, treasure hunts, beach walks, exercise classes, tennis, and an always-open games room.

SuperClubs Boscobel Beach (tel. 800/858–8009) in **Jamaica** is an all-inclusive resort that specializes in families. Seven-night packages are in the $1,000-per-person range, and two children under 14 are allowed to stay free if they occupy the same room as their parents. A small army of SuperNannies is on hand to take charge. The activities are scheduled in half-hour periods so children can drop in and out. For younger children there are morning "Mousercises," a petting zoo, shell hunts, and crafts classes; for teens, "Coke-tail" parties at a disco and "No-Talent" shows.

Casa de Campo (tel. 800/223–6620) in the **Dominican Republic** has a summer and holiday camp that children can attend on a day-by-day basis. The program includes lessons in sailing, tennis, golf, painting, and pottery as well as donkey polo and softball and soccer games. "Campers" are divided into two groups: ages 7–10 and 11–13.

On **St. Thomas** in the U.S. Virgin Islands the **Stouffer Grand Beach Resort** (tel. 800/233–4935) has half-day and full-day programs for children ages 3–12. In addition to supervising volleyball matches, arts-and-crafts classes, water games, and iguana hunts, the staff arranges outings to the Coral World Marine Life Park and Observatory.

Club Med (tel. 800/CLUB–MED) has Mini Club programs for children as well as a regular roster of activities at resorts in the **Dominican Republic** and **St. Lucia.** Designed for children ages 2–11 and scheduled from 9 AM to 9 PM, the fully supervised Mini Club activities include tennis, waterskiing, sailing, scuba experience in a pool, costume parties, painting and pottery classes, and circus workshops.

Four Seasons (tel. 800/332–3442) on **Nevis** has a complete program for children age 2 and above, with story-telling, crafts, and supervised beach sports.

Villa Rentals   Villa rentals are abundant, often economical, and great for families; island tourist boards can usually refer you to the appropriate realtors. When you book these, be sure to ask about the availability of baby-sitters, housekeepers, and medical facilities. (*See* Staying in the Caribbean, *below.*)

Hints for Travelers with Disabilities

The Caribbean has not progressed as far as other areas of the world in terms of accommodating travelers with disabilities, and very few attractions and sights are equipped with ramps, elevators, or wheelchair-accessible rest rooms. However, major new properties are beginning to do their planning with the needs of travelers with mobility problems and hearing and visual impairments in mind. Wherever possible in our lodging listings, we indicate if special facilities are available.

Lodging   A number of cruise ships, such as the *QE II* and the Norwegian Cruise Line's *Seaward*, have recently adapted some of their cabins to meet the needs of passengers with disabilities. To make sure that a given establishment provides adequate access, ask about specific facilities when making a reservation or consider booking through a travel agent who specializes in travel for people with disabilities (*see below*).

Divi Hotels (tel. 800/367–3484), which has six properties in the Caribbean, runs one of the best dive programs for people with disabilities at its resort in **Bonaire**. The facility is equipped with ramps; guest rooms and bathrooms can accommodate guests using wheelchairs; and the staff is specially trained to assist divers with disabilities.

Organizations Several organizations provide travel information for people with disabilities, usually for a membership fee, and some publish newsletters and bulletins. Among them are the **Information Center for Individuals with Disabilities** (Fort Point Pl., 27–43 Wormwood St., Boston, MA 02210; in MA, tel. 617/727–5540 between 11 and 4 or leave message; outside MA, tel. 800/462–5015; TDD 617/345–9743); **Mobility International USA** (Box 10767, Eugene, OR 97440, tel. and TDD 503/343–1284, fax 503/343–6812), the U.S. branch of an international organization based in Britain (*see below*) that has affiliates in 30 countries; **MossRehab Hospital Travel Information Service** (tel. 215/456–9603, TDD 215/456–9602); the **Travel Industry and Disabled Exchange** (TIDE, 5435 Donna Ave., Tarzana, CA 91356, tel. 818/344–3640, fax 818/344–0078); and **Travelin' Talk** (Box 3534, Clarksville, TN 37043, tel. 615/552–6670, fax 615/552–1182).

Travel Agencies and Tour Operators **Tomorrow's Level of Care** (TLC, Box 470299, Brooklyn, NY 11247, tel. 718/756–0794 or 800/932–2012) was started by two Barbadian nurses who develop unique vacation programs tailored to travelers with mobility problems and their families. They can arrange everything from accommodations to entire packages. **Accessible Journeys** (35 West Sellers Ave., Ridley Park, PA 19078, tel. 610/521–0339 or 800/846–4537, fax 610-521-6959) arranges escorted trips for travelers with disabilities and provides licensed caregivers to accompany those who require aid. **Flying Wheels Travel** (143 W. Bridge St., Box 382, Owatonna, MN 55060, tel. 507/451–5005 or 800/535–6790) is a travel agency specializing in domestic and worldwide cruises, tours, and independent travel itineraries for people with mobility impairments.

Publications Two free publications are available from the U.S. Consumer Information Center (Pueblo, CO 81009): "New Horizons for the Air Traveler with a Disability" (include Dept. 608Y in the address), a U.S. Department of Transportation booklet describing changes resulting from the 1986 Air Carrier Access Act and from the 1990 Americans with Disabilities Act, and the Airport Operators Council's *Access Travel: Airports* (Dept. 5804), which describes facilities and services for people with disabilities at more than 500 airports worldwide.

Travelin' Talk Directory (*see* Organizations, *above*) was published in 1993. This 500-page resource book ($35) is packed with information for travelers with disabilities. Twin Peaks Press (Box 129, Vancouver, WA 98666, tel. 206/694–2462 or 800/637–2256) publishes the *Directory of Travel Agencies for the Disabled* ($19.95), listing more than 370 agencies worldwide, and *Wheelchair Vagabond* ($14.95), a collection of personal travel tips. Add $2 per book for shipping.

Hints for Older Travelers

Special facilities, rates, and package deals for older travelers are rare. When planning your trip, be sure to inquire about everything from senior-citizen discounts to available medical facilities. Focus on your vacation needs: Are you interested in sightseeing, activities, golf, ecotourism, the beach? Accessibility is an important consideration. When booking, inquire whether you can easily get to the things that you enjoy. The more remote islands have fewer options and amenities.

Organizations The **American Association of Retired Persons** (AARP, 601 E St. NW, Washington, DC 20049, tel. 202/434–2277) provides independent travelers who are members of the AARP (open to those age 50 or older; $8 per person or couple annually) with the Purchase Privilege Program, which offers discounts on hotels, car rentals, and sightseeing. AARP also arranges group tours, cruises, and apartment living through AARP Travel Experience from American Express (400 Pinnacle Way, Suite 450, Norcross, GA 30071, tel. 800/927–0111 or 800/745–4567).

Two other organizations offer discounts on lodgings, car rentals, and other travel products, along with such nontravel perks as magazines and newsletters: The **National Council of Senior Citizens** (1331 F St. NW, Washington, DC 20004, tel. 202/347–8800; membership $12 annually) and **Mature Outlook** (6001 N. Clark St., Chicago, IL 60660, tel. 800/336–6330; $9.95 annually).

Note: Mention your senior-citizen identification card when booking hotel reservations for reduced rates, not when checking out. At restaurants, show your card before you're seated; discounts may be limited to certain menus, days, or hours. If you are renting a car, ask about promotional rates that might improve on your senior-citizen discount.

Educational Travel **Elderhostel** (75 Federal St., 3rd floor, Boston, MA 02110, tel. 617/426–7788) has offered inexpensive study programs for people 60 and older since 1975. Held at more than 1,800 educational institutions, courses cover everything from marine science to Greek myths and cowboy poetry. Participants usually attend lectures in the morning and spend the afternoon sightseeing or on field trips; they live in dorms on the host campuses. Fees for two- to three-week international trips—including room, board, and transportation from the United States—range from $1,800 to $4,500.

Tour Operators If you want to take your grandchildren, look into **Grandtravel** (*see* Traveling with Children, *above*); **Saga International Holidays** (222 Berkeley St., Boston, MA 02116, tel. 800/343–0273), caters to those over age 60 who like to travel in groups. **SeniorTours** (508 Irvington Rd., Drexel Hill, PA 19026, tel. 215/626–1977 or 800/227–1100) arranges motorcoach tours throughout the United States and Nova Scotia, as well as Caribbean cruises.

Publications *The 50+ Traveler's Guidebook: Where to Go, Where to Stay, What to Do,* by Anita Williams and Merrimac Dillon ($12.95; St. Martin's Press, 175 Fifth Ave., New York, NY 10010) is available in bookstores and offers many useful tips. "The Mature Traveler" (Box 50820, Reno, NV 89513, tel. 702/786–7419; $29.95), a monthly newsletter, contains many travel deals for older travelers.

Hints for Gay and Lesbian Travelers

Organizations The **International Gay Travel Association** (Box 4974, Key West, FL 33041, tel. 305/292–0217, 800/999–7925, or 800/448–8550), which has 700 members, will provide you with names of travel agents and tour operators who specialize in gay travel. The **Gay & Lesbian Visitors Center of New York, Inc.** (135 West 20th St., 3rd Floor, New York, NY 10011, tel. 212/463–9030 or 800/395–2315; $100 annually) mails a monthly newsletter, valuable coupons, and more to its members.

Travel Agencies and Tour Operators The dominant travel agency in the market is **Above and Beyond** (3568 Sacramento St., San Francisco, CA 94118, tel. 415/922–2683 or 800/397–2681). Tour operator **Olympus Vacations** (8424 Santa Monica Blvd., Suite 721, West Hollywood, CA 90069, tel. 310/657–2220 or 800/965–9678) offers all-gay-and-lesbian resort holidays. **Skylink Women's Travel** (746 Ashland Ave., Santa Monica, CA 90405, tel. 310/452–0506 or 800/225–5759) handles individual travel for lesbians all over the world and conducts two international and five domestic group trips annually.

Publications The premier international travel magazine for gays and lesbians is *Our World* (1104 North Nova Rd., Suite 251, Daytona Beach, FL 32117, tel. 904/441–5367; $35 for 10 issues). **"Out & About"** (tel. 203/789–8518 or 800/929–2268; $49 for 10 issues) is a 16-page monthly newsletter with extensive information on resorts, hotels, and airlines that are gay-friendly.

Further Reading

Caribbean Style (Crown Publishers) is a coffee-table book with magnificent photographs of the interiors and exteriors of homes and buildings in the Caribbean. The collection runs the gamut from splendid plantations to ramshackle shanties.

Don't Stop the Carnival, by Herman Wouk, is a hilarious novel about a New York press agent who left his old life behind and bought a resort hotel in the Caribbean. The novel is slightly dated, but the vicissitudes of the hero are acknowledged by everyone who has ever tried to run a hotel in the islands. It is a marvelous romp through the region.

Short stories—some dark, some full of laughs—about life in the southern Caribbean made *Easy in the Islands* by Bob Schacochis a National Book Award winner. Schacochis's ear for local patois and eye for the absurd make this book required reading.

If you want to familiarize yourself with the sights, smells, and sounds of the West Indies, pick up Jamaica Kincaid's *Annie John*, a richly textured, coming-of-age novel about a girl growing up on the island of Antigua. *At the Bottom of the River*, also by Kincaid, is a collection of short stories that depicts the mysteries and manners of a world replete with merengue music, bay rum, and blooming red hibiscus in the dreams and reminiscences of a young adult.

Omeros is Nobel Prize–winning Trinidadian poet Derek Walcott's imaginative Caribbean retelling of the *Odyssey*.

Michelle Cliff is the author of *The Land of Look Behind* and, most recently, *No Telephone to Heaven*, a structurally daring, often violent novel set in Jamaica—a landscape of wild bamboo and jasmine populated by refugees moving through the outskirts of Kingston.

Anthony C. Winkler's novels, *The Great Yacht Race*, *The Lunatic*, and *The Painted Canoe*, provide scathingly witty glimpses into Jamaica's class structure.

Another notable chronicle of Caribbean life and customs is the provocative *Wide Sargasso Sea*, by Jean Rhys. Published in 1968, the novel has an imaginative construction that still entices the reader into a world of exotic, haunting beauty that Rhys herself encountered growing up on the Windward Islands of the West Indies.

James Michener's islands saga, titled *Caribbean*, was published in 1989. Michener headquartered himself in Coral Gables, Florida, to facilitate his 10 extensive research expeditions through the Caribbean region, and he has publicly expressed both the dramatic assets and liabilities inherent in a culture so rich in diversity.

If you're interested in probing this very issue more deeply, head for V. S. Naipaul. *Guerrillas*, *The Loss of El Dorado*, and *The Enigma of Arrival* all examine the multicultural origins of Caribbean society and the complexities of colonization, enslavement, and economic dispossession. Two other excellent books on the subject are *From Columbus to Castro* by Eric Williams and *Conquest of Eden* by Michael Paiewonsky.

Staying in the Caribbean

Dining

For the longest time, cuisine in the Caribbean was thought to be the weakest part of many an island vacation. In recent years, however, island visitors have come to realize that most of what they had been eating and complaining about was not Caribbean at all—just poorly prepared Continental fare garnished with a papaya slice or banana leaf.

The cuisine of the islands is difficult to pin down because of the region's history as a colonial battleground and ethnic melting pot. The gracefully sauced French presentations of Martinique, for example, are far removed from the hearty Spanish casseroles of Puerto Rico, and even further removed from the pungent curries of Trinidad.

The one quality that best defines Caribbean-style cooking has to be its essential spiciness. While reminiscent of Tex-Mex and Cajun, Caribbean cuisine is more varied and more subtle than its love of peppers implies. There is also the seafood that is unique to and abundant in the region. Caribbean lobster, closer in comparison to crawfish than to Maine lobster, have no claws and tend to be much tougher than the New England variety.

Another local favorite is conch, biologically quite close to land-loving escargots. Conch chowder, conch fritters, conch salad, conch cocktail—no island menu would be complete without at least a half-dozen conch dishes.

For many vacationers, much of the Caribbean experience has to do with the consumption of frothy blended fruit drinks, whose main and potent ingredient is Caribbean rum. Whether you are staying in a superdeluxe resort or a small, locally operated guest house, you will find that rum flows as freely as water.

After each restaurant review, we have indicated only when reservations are necessary or suggested. Since dining is usually casual throughout the region, we have mentioned attire only when formal attire is needed.

Lodging

Plan ahead and reserve a room well before you travel to the Caribbean. If you have reservations but expect to arrive later than 5 or 6 PM, advise the hotel, inn, or guest house in advance. Unless so advised, some places will not hold your reservations after 6 PM. Also, be sure to find out what the rate quoted includes—use of sports facilities and equipment, airport transfers, and the like—and whether it operates on the European Plan (EP, with no meals), Continental Plan (CP, with Continental breakfast), Breakfast Plan (BP, with full breakfast), Modified American Plan (MAP, with two meals), or Full American Plan (FAP, with three meals), or is All-inclusive (with three meals, all facilities, and drinks unless otherwise noted). At the end of each review, we have listed the meal plans that the hotel offers. Not all plans are offered all-year round. Be sure to bring your deposit receipt with you in case any questions arise when you arrive at your hotel.

A Full American Plan may be ideal for travelers on a budget who don't want to worry about additional expenses, but travelers who enjoy a different dining experience each night will prefer to book rooms on a European Plan. Since some hotels insist on a Modified American Plan, particularly during the high season, you might want to find out whether you can exchange dinner for lunch or for meals at neighboring hotels.

Decide whether you want a hotel on the leeward side of the island (with calm water, good for snorkeling) or the windward (with waves, good for surfing). Decide, too, whether you want to pay the extra price for a room overlooking the ocean or pool. Also find out how close the property is to a beach; at some hotels you can walk barefoot from your room onto the sand; others are across a road or a 10-minute drive away.

Nighttime entertainment is alfresco in the Caribbean, so if you go to sleep early or are a light sleeper, ask for a room that doesn't overlook the dance floor.

Air-conditioning is not a necessity on all islands, most of which are cooled by trade winds; but an air conditioner can be a plus if you enjoy an afternoon snooze. Breezes are stronger in second-floor rooms, particularly corner rooms, which enjoy cross ventilation. If you like to sleep without air-conditioning, make sure that windows can be opened and are equipped with screens.

Given the vast differences in standards and accommodations in the various islands covered in this book, it would be impossible (and misleading) to establish uniform categories such as deluxe, first class, and so forth. Instead, we have used categories to indicate price rather than quality. Prices are intended as a guideline only. The larger resort hotels with the greater number of facilities will, naturally, be more expensive, but the Caribbean is full of smaller places that make up in charm, individuality, and price for what they lack in activities—and the activity is generally available on a pay-per-use basis everywhere.

Apartment and Villa Rentals If you want a home base that's roomy enough for a family and comes with cooking facilities, a furnished rental may be the solution. It's generally cost-wise, too, although not always—some rentals are luxury properties (economical only when your party is large). Home-exchange directories do list rentals—often second homes owned by prospective house swappers—and there are services that can not only look for a house or apartment for you (even a castle if that's your fancy) but also handle the paperwork. Some send an illustrated catalogue and others send photographs of specific properties, sometimes at a charge; up-front registration fees may apply.

Among the companies with properties in the Caribbean are **At Home Abroad** (405 E. 56th St., Suite 6H, New York, NY 10022, tel. 212/421–9165); **Europa-Let** (92 North Main St., Ashland, OR 97520, tel. 503/482–5806 or 800/462–4486); **Overseas Connection** (31 N. Harbor Dr., Sag Harbor, NY 11963, tel. 516/725–9308); **Rent a Home International** (7200 34th Ave. NW, Seattle, WA 98117, tel. 206/789–9377 or 800/488–7368); **Vacation Home Rentals Worldwide** (235 Kensington Ave., Norwood, NJ 07648, tel. 201/767–9393 or 800/633–3284); **Villa Leisure** (Box 209, Westport, CT 06881, tel. 407/624–9000 or 800/526–4244), which specializes in the Caribbean; **Villas and Apartments Abroad** (420 Madison Ave., Suite 1105, New York, NY 10017, tel. 212/759–1025 or 800/433–3020); and **Villas International** (605 Market St., Suite 510, San Francisco, CA 94105, tel. 415/281–0910 or 800/221–2260). **Hideaways International** (15 Goldsmith St., Box 1270, Littleton, MA 01460, tel. 508/486–8955 or 800/843–4433), with properties in the Caribbean, functions as a travel club. Membership ($99 yearly per person or family at the same address) includes two annual guides plus quarterly newsletters; rentals are arranged directly between members, not by the club staff.

Home Exchange You can find a house, apartment, or other vacation property to exchange for your own by becoming a member of a home-exchange organization, which then sends you its annual directories listing available exchanges and includes your own listing in at least one of them. Arrangements for the actual exchange are made by the two parties to it, not by the organization. For more information contact the **International Home Exchange Association** (IHEA, 41 Sutter St., Suite 1090, San Francisco, CA 94104, tel. 415/673–0347 or 800/788–2489). Principal clearinghouses include **HomeLink International** (Box 650, Key West, FL 33041, tel. 800/638–3841), with thousands of foreign and domestic listings, which publishes four annual directories plus updates (the $50 membership includes your listing in one book), and **Loan-a-Home** (2 Park La., Apt. 6E, Mount Vernon, NY 10552, tel. 914/664–7640), which specializes in long-term exchanges; there is no charge to list your home, but the directories cost $35 or $45 depending on the number you receive. **Villa Leisure** (Box 209, Westport, CT 06881, tel. 407/624–9000 or 800/526–4244) facilitates swaps.

Credit Cards

The following credit card abbreviations have been used: AE, American Express; D, Discover Card; DC, Diners Club; MC, MasterCard; V, Visa. It's a good idea to call ahead to check current credit card policies.

Cruises

Cruising the Caribbean is perhaps the most relaxed and convenient way to tour this beautiful part of the world: You get all of the amenities of a stateside hotel and enough activities to guarantee fun, even on rainy days. Cruising through the islands is an entirely different experience from staying on an island.

Cruise ships usually call at several Caribbean ports on a single voyage but are at each port for only one night. Thus, although a cruise passenger may be exposed to a variety of sightseeing opportunities, and view the geographic and topographic characteristics of several islands, the visits are too quick to get a true feel for each island. A cruise passenger does have the opportunity to select favorite islands for in-depth discovery on a later visit.

As a vacation, a cruise offers total peace of mind. All important decisions are made long before boarding the ship. The itinerary is set in advance, and the costs are known ahead of time and are all-inclusive, with no additional charge for meals, accommodations, entertainment, or recreational activities. (Only tips, shore excursions, and shopping are extra.) A cruise ship is a floating Caribbean resort. For details beyond the basics, given below, see *Fodor's Cruises and Ports of Call 1995*.

When to Go

Cruise ships sail the Caribbean year-round—the waters are almost always calm, and the prevailing breezes keep temperatures fairly steady. Tropical storms are most likely September through November, but modern navigational equipment warns ships well in advance of impending foul weather, and, when necessary, cruise lines vary their itineraries to avoid storms.

Cruises are in high demand—and therefore also higher priced—during the standard vacation times, in winter and around Easter. Some very good bargains are usually available during the immediate postvacation periods such as fall to mid-December, early spring, and the first few weeks after the Christmas and New Year's holidays. Christmas sailings are usually quite full and are priced at a premium.

Choosing a Cabin

Write to the cruise line or ask your travel agent for a ship's plan. This elaborate layout, with cabins numbered, will show you all facilities available on all decks (usually, the higher the deck, the higher the prices). Outside cabins have dramatic portholes or picture-windows that contribute to the romance of cruising, and, though usually sealed shut, most provide expansive sea views. Some windows overlook a public promenade, probably less desirable. Inside cabins are less expensive, but check the plan—you don't want to be over the galley, near the engine room, or next to the elevators. Then check on the facilities offered. Those prone to motion sickness would do best in a cabin at midship, on one of the middle decks. The higher you go, the more motion you'll experience.

Tipping

Although some ships have no-tipping policies, tipping is a major expense on most Caribbean ships. The ship's service personnel depend on tips for their livelihood, and you may feel pressure to help them out. It is customary to tip the cabin steward, the dining-room waiter, the maître d', the wine steward, and the bartender; most cruise lines distribute guidelines with suggested amounts the night before the voyage ends—which is when gratuities are normally given. Figure on tipping about $60 per passenger per week.

Shore Excursions

Tour options, which typically cost $20–$140 per port, are heavily promoted during shore-excursion talks a day or two prior to reaching your post. Better deals are often had by choosing a tour offered by one of the local vendors or renting a car yourself. However, it's always riskier to explore on your own than to leave your one day at port in the hands of the cruise line (*see* Guided Tours and Getting Around sections of the individual island chapters).

Cruise Lines

To find out which ships are sailing where and when they depart, contact the **Caribbean Tourism Organization** (20 E. 46th St., 4th floor, New York, NY 10017, tel. 212/682–0435). The CTO carries up-to-date information about cruise lines that sail to its member nations. Full-service and cruise-only travel agencies are also a good source; they stock brochures and catalogues issued by most of the major lines and have the latest information about prices, departure dates, and itineraries. The **Cruise Lines International Association** (CLIA) publishes a useful pamphlet entitled "Cruising Answers to Your Questions"; to order a copy send a self-addressed business-size envelope with 52¢ postage to CLIA (500 5th Ave., Suite 1407, New York, NY 10110).

The following chart gives the names and ports of call of a sampling of cruise ships that sail in the Caribbean. A complete list of cruise lines that operate in the Caribbean appears below.

American Canadian Caribbean Line (Box 368, Warren, RI 02885, tel. 401/247–0955 or 800/556–7450).
American Family Cruises (World Trade Center, 80 S.W. 8th St., Miami, FL 33130, tel. 800/232–0567).
Carnival Cruise Lines/FiestaMarina Cruises (Carnival Pl., 3655 N.W. 87th Ave., Miami, FL 33178, tel. 305/599–2600).
Celebrity Cruises (5200 Blue Lagoon Dr., Miami, FL 33126, tel. 800/437–3111).
Clipper Cruise Line (7711 Bonhomme Ave., St. Louis, MO 63105, tel. 800/325–0010).
Club Med (40 W. 57th St., New York, NY 10019, tel. 800/CLUB-MED).
Commodore Cruise Line (800 Douglas Rd., Coral Gables, FL 33134, tel. 305/529–3000).
Costa Cruise Lines (World Trade Center, 80 S.W. 8th St., Miami, FL 33130, tel. 800/462–6782).
Crystal Cruises (2121 Ave. of the Stars, Los Angeles, CA 90067, tel. 800/446–6645).
Cunard Line (555 5th Ave., New York, NY 10017, tel. 800/221–4770).
Diamond Cruise Inc. (600 Corporate Dr., Suite 410, Fort Lauderdale, FL 33334, tel. 800/333–3333).
Dolphin/Majesty Cruise Lines (901 South American Way, Miami, FL 33132, tel. 800/532–7788).
Fantasy Cruise (5200 Blue Lagoon Dr., Miami, FL 33126, tel. 800/437–3111).
Holland America Line (300 Elliott Ave. W, Seattle, WA 98119, tel. 800/426–0327).
Norwegian Cruise Line (95 Merrick Way, Coral Gables, FL 33134, tel. 800/327–7030).
Premier Cruise Line (Box 517, Cape Canaveral, FL 32920, tel. 800/473–3262).
Princess Cruises (10100 Santa Monica Blvd., Los Angeles, CA 90067, tel. 310/553–1770).

Caribbean Cruises

Class/Ship	Number of passengers	Length (days)	Alternate lengths (segments) available	Departs from	Anguilla	Antigua	Aruba	Barbados	Bonaire	BVI	Cayman Islands
CARNIVAL CRUISE LINES											
Celebration	1486	7		Miami							
Festivale	1146	7		San Juan				●			
Sensation	1486	7		Miami							●
CELEBRITY CRUISES											
Horizon and Zenith	1374	7		NY, San Juan, Ft. Lauderdale		●		●			●
Meridian	1006	7	10, 11	NY, San Juan			●	●			
COSTA CRUISES											
CostaAllegra	800	7		Miami							●
CostaClassica-Romantica	1300	7		Miami, San Juan				●			●
CUNARD LINE											
Countess	791	7	14	San Juan		●		●	●		
Cunard Crown Jewel	800	7	7	Fort Lauderdale							●
Queen Elizabeth II	1800	10		New York		●		●			
Sagafjord	618	13	14, 16	Ft. Lauderdale		●	●	●			●
Sea Goddess I	116	7		St. Thomas						●	
Vistafjord	749	11	15	Ft. Lauderdale		●		●		●	●
DIAMOND CRUISE INC.											
Radisson Diamond	354	7		San Juan		●		●		●	●
HOLLAND AMERICA LINE											
Nieuw Amsterdam	1214	7		Tampa							●
Noordam	1214	10		Ft. Lauderdale							●
Ryndham	1266	11	10	Ft. Lauderdale			●	●			●
Statendam	1266	10		Ft. Lauderdale				●			
Westerdam	1500	7		Ft. Lauderdale							
NORWEGIAN CRUISE LINE											
Norway	2044	7		Miami							
Starward	758	7		San Juan							
Windward	800	7		San Juan			●	●	●		
PRINCESS CRUISES											
Crown Princess	1562	7		Ft. Lauderdale							●
Star Princess	1470	7		San Juan				●			
REGENCY CRUISES											
Regent Sun	836	7		San Juan		●		●			
ROYAL CARIBBEAN CRUISE LINE											
Maj.-Sov. of the Seas	2278	7		Miami							●
Monarch of the Seas	2354	7		San Juan		●		●			
Song of America	1402	7		San Juan							
Sun Viking	714	7		San Juan							
SEAWIND CRUISE LINE											
Seawind Crown	624	7		Aruba			●				

Curaçao	Dominica	Dominican Rep.	Grenada	Guadeloupe	Jamaica	Martinique	Montserrat	Nevis	Puerto Rico	Saba	St. Barthélemy	St. Eustatius	St. Kitts	St. Lucia	St. Maarten	St. Vincent & the Grenadines	Trinidad/Tobago	Turks & Caicos	USVI	Bahamas	Bermuda	Mexico
									●						●				●			
	●					●									●				●			
				●					●										●	●		●
					●	●			●					●					●	●	●	●
●			●		●	●			●					●	●				●		●	
		●			●				●										●	●		
		●			●	●			●						●				●	●		●
			●	●		●							●	●	●				●			
		●			●				●						●				●	●		●
															●				●		●	
●			●	●		●	●					●		●	●				●			●
								●				●			●				●			
						●						●		●	●	●			●			●
			●			●			●					●	●	●			●			●
					●																	●
					●				●										●	●		
	●																●		●			
●	●		●			●								●	●				●	●		
●															●				●	●		●
									●						●				●	●		
			●								●		●	●	●			●	●			
●						●									●				●			
					●										●				●	●		●
						●									●	●			●	●		●
			●			●						●	●	●	●				●			
					●				●										●	●		●
						●							●		●		●		●			
				●									●		●				●		●	
				●								●			●				●			
●			●												●							

Regency Cruises (260 Madison Ave., New York, NY 10016, tel. 212/972-4499).

Renaissance Cruises (1800 Eller Dr., Suite 300, Box 350307, Fort Lauderdale, FL 33335, tel. 800/525-2450).

Royal Caribbean Cruise Line (1050 Caribbean Way, Miami, FL 33132, tel. 800/327-6700).

Royal Cruise Line (1 Maritime Plaza, San Francisco, CA 94111, tel. 415/956-7200).

Royal Viking Line (Kloster Cruise Limited, 95 Merrick Way, Coral Gables, FL 33134, tel. 800/422-8000).

Seabourn Cruise Line (55 Francisco St., San Francisco, CA 94133, tel. 800/351-9595).

Seawind Cruise Line (1750 Coral Way, Miami, FL 33145, tel. 800/258-8006).

Silversea Cruises (110 E. Broward Blvd., Fort Lauderdale, FL 33301, tel. 305/522-4477 or 800/722-6655).

Special Expeditions (720 5th Ave., New York, NY 10019, tel. 800/762-0003).

Star Clippers (4101 Salzedo Ave., Coral Gables, FL 33146, tel. 800/442-0551).

Sun Line Cruises (1 Rockefeller Plaza, Suite 315, New York, NY 10020, tel. 800/872-6400).

Windstar Cruises (300 Elliott Ave. W, Seattle, WA 98119, tel. 800/258-7245).

2 Anguilla

*Updated by
Pamela
Acheson*

Beach lovers become giddy when they first see Anguilla (rhymes with vanilla) from the air and spot the blindingly white beaches and neon blue and aquamarine waters that rim this scrubby piece of land. The highest point on the dry, limestone isle is 213 feet above sea level, and there are neither streams nor rivers, only saline ponds used for salt production. If you don't like beaches, you won't find a lot to do here. There are no glittering casinos and nightclubs, no duty-free shops stuffed with irresistible buys (although you're only about 30 watery minutes away from the bustle of St. Martin/St. Maarten's resorts and casinos).

Anguilla's beauty lies in its stunning beaches, its exceptionally clear waters, and its coral reefs. Peace, quiet, and pampering account for the island's growing popularity among travelers searching for a Caribbean getaway. You can swim, do some diving, practice your backhand, catch up on your reading, compare the relative merits of the beaches, or just find one that suits you and sink down on it to worship the sun. Times are slowly changing, however, and there are now six traffic lights on the island instead of the solitary signal of years past.

This is the most northerly of the Leeward Islands, lying between the Caribbean Sea and the Atlantic Ocean. Stretching from northeast to southwest, it's about 16 miles long and only 3 miles across at its widest point. Christopher Columbus seems not to have spotted this island. *Anguilla* means "eel" in Italian, but the Spanish *anguila* or French *anguille* (both of which also mean "eel") may have been the original name. New archaeological evidence shows that the island was inhabited as many as 2,000 years ago by Indians who named the island Malliouhana, a more mellifluous title that's been adopted by some of the island's shops and resorts.

In 1631, the Dutch built a fort here, but no one has been able to locate its site. English settlers from St. Kitts colonized the island in 1650, and, despite a brief period of independence with St. Kitts–Nevis in the 1960s, Anguilla has remained a British colony ever since.

There were the obligatory Caribbean battles between the English and the French, and in 1688 the island was attacked by a party of "wild Irishmen," some of whom settled on the island. But Anguilla's primary discontent was over its status vis-à-vis the other British colonies, particularly St. Kitts. In the 18th century, Anguilla, as part of the Leeward Islands, was administered by British officials in Antigua. In 1816, Britain split the islands into two groups, one of them composed of Anguilla, St. Kitts, Nevis, and the British Virgin Islands and administered by a magistrate in St. Kitts. For more than 150 years thereafter various island units and federations were formed and disbanded, with Anguilla all the while simmering over its subordinate status and enforced union with St. Kitts. Anguillans twice petitioned for direct rule from Britain, and twice were ignored. In 1967, when St. Kitts, Nevis, and Anguilla became an associated state, the mouse roared, kicked St. Kitts policemen off the island, held a self-rule referendum, and for two years conducted its own affairs. In 1968, a senior British official arrived and remained for a year working with the Anguilla Council. A second referendum in 1969 confirmed the desire of the Anguillans to remain apart from St. Kitts-Nevis, and the following month a British "peacekeeping force" parachuted down to the island, where it was greeted with flowers, fluttering Union Jacks, and friendly smiles. When the paratroopers were not working on their tans, they helped a team of royal engineers improve the port and build roads and schools. Today Anguilla elects a House of Assembly and its own leader to handle internal affairs, while a British governor is responsible for public service, the police, and judiciary and external affairs.

The territory of Anguilla includes a few islets or cays, such as Scrub Island to the east, Dog Island, Prickly Pear Cays, Sandy Island, and Sombrero Island. The island's population numbers about 8,000, predominantly of African descent but also including descendants of Europeans, especially Irish. Historically, because the limestone land was hardly fit for agriculture, attempts at slavery and colonization never lasted long; thus Anguilla doesn't bear the scars of slavery found on so many Caribbean islands. Because the island couldn't be farmed, Anguillans became experts at making a living from the sea and are known for their boatbuilding and fishing skills. Tourism is the growth industry of the island's stable economy, but the government is determined to keep this expansion at a slow and cautious pace to protect the island's natural resources and beauty. New hotels, scattered throughout the islands, are being kept small, select, and casino-free, and promotion of the island emphasizes its high-quality service, serene surroundings, and friendly people.

Before You Go

Tourist Information Contact the very helpful **Anguilla Tourist Information and Reservation Office** (c/o Medhurst & Associates, 775 Park Ave., Huntington NY 11743, tel. 516/425–0900 or 800/553–4939, fax 516/425–0903). In the United Kingdom, contact the **Anguilla Tourist Office** (3 Epirus Rd., London SW6 7UJ, tel. 071/937–7725).

Arriving and Departing By Plane **American Airlines** (tel. 800/433–7300) is the major airline with non-stop flights from the United States to its hub in San Juan, from which the airline's **American Eagle** flies twice daily to Anguilla, the first flight connecting with East Coast and Canadian flights, the second with those from the Midwest and West. **Windward Islands Airways** (Winair) (tel. 809/775–0183) wings in five times a day from St. Maarten's Juliana Airport. **LIAT** (tel. 809/465–2286) comes in from Antigua, Nevis, St. Kitts, St. Maarten, and St. Thomas. **Air Anguilla** (tel. 809/497–2643) provides air-taxi service on request from neighboring islands, as does **Tyden Air** (tel. 809/497–2719).

From the Airport At **Wallblake Airport** you'll find taxis lined up to meet the planes. A trip from the airport to Sandy Ground will cost about $8, to west-end resorts between $14 and $20. Fares, which are government regulated, should be listed in brochures the drivers carry. If you are traveling in a group, the fares apply to the first two people; each additional passenger adds $3 to the total. Tipping is welcome.

By Boat Ferryboats run frequently between Anguilla and St. Martin. They leave from Blowing Point on Anguilla every half hour from 7:30 to 5 and from Marigot on St. Martin every half hour from 8 to 5:40. There are also Friday night ferries. You pay the $9 one-way fare on board and a $2 departure tax before boarding. Don't buy a round-trip ticket, because it restricts you to the boat on which it is purchased. On very windy days the 20-minute trip can be bouncy, and if you suffer from motion sickness, you may want medication. An information booth outside the customs shed in Blowing Point, Anguilla, is usually open daily from 8:30 to 5, but sometimes the attendant wanders off.

From the Docks Taxis are always waiting to pick passengers up at the Blowing Point landing. It costs $12 to get to the Malliouhana Hotel, $15 to the Cap Juluca Hotel, and $17 to Island Harbour. Rates are fixed by the government; the taxi driver should have a list of these fares.

Passports and Visas U.S. and Canadian citizens need proof of identity. A passport is preferred (even one that has expired within the last five years). A photo ID, such as a driver's license, *along with* a birth certificate (with raised seal), voter's registration card, or naturalization papers is also acceptable. Visitor's passes are valid for stays of up to three months. British citizens must have a passport. All visitors must also have a return or ongoing ticket.

Language English, with a strong West Indian lilt, is spoken on Anguilla.

Precautions The manchineel tree, which resembles an apple tree, shades many beaches. The tree bears poisonous fruit, and the sap from the tree causes painful blisters. Avoid sitting beneath the tree, because even dew or raindrops falling from the leaves can blister your skin.

Be *sure* to take along a can of insect repellent—mosquitoes can be pesky in the late afternoon.

Anguilla is a quiet, relatively safe island, but there's no point in tempting fate by leaving your valuables unattended in your hotel room, on the beach, or in your car.

Staying in Anguilla

Important Addresses **Tourist Information:** The **Anguilla Tourist Office** (The Social Security Building, The Valley, tel. 809/497–2759) is open weekdays 8–noon and 1–4.

Emergencies **Police** and **Fire:** 809/497–2333. **Hospital:** There is a 24-hour emergency room at the **Cottage Hospital** (The Valley, tel. 809/497–2551); by 1995, the new Princess Alexandra Hospital in Stoney Ground, under construction at press time, may have supplanted it. **Ambulance:** 809/497–2551. **Pharmacies:** The **Government Pharmacy** (The Valley, tel. 809/497–2551) is located in the Cottage Hospital; the **Paramount Pharmacy** (Waterswamp, tel. 809/497–2366) is open Monday–Saturday 8:30–8:30 and has a 24-hour emergency service.

Currency Legal tender here is the Eastern Caribbean dollar (E.C.), but U.S. dollars are widely accepted. (You'll often get change in E.C. dollars.) The E.C. dollar is fairly stable relative to the U.S. dollar, hovering between E.C.$2.60 and $2.70 to U.S.$1. Credit cards are not always accepted, and it's hard to predict where you'll need cash. Some resorts will only settle in cash; a few will also accept personal checks. Be sure to carry lots of small bills; change for a $20 bill is often difficult to obtain.

Taxes and Service Charges The government imposes an 8% tax on accommodations. The departure tax is $7 at the airport, $2 if you leave by boat. A 10% service charge is added to all hotel bills and most restaurant bills. If you're not certain about the restaurant service charge, ask. If you are particularly pleased with the service, you can certainly leave a little extra. Tip taxi drivers 10% of the fare.

Guided Tours A round-the-island tour by taxi will take about 2½ hours and will cost $40 for one or two people, $5 for each additional passenger. **Bennie's Tours** (Blowing Point, tel. 809/497–2788) and **Malliouhana Travel and Tours** (The Valley, tel. 809/497–2431) put together personalized package tours on and around the island.

Getting Around
Taxis Taxi rates are regulated by the government, and there are fixed fares from point to point. Posted rates are for one to two people; each additional person pays $3.

Rental Cars This is your best bet for maximum mobility if you're comfortable driving on the left and don't mind some jostling. Anguilla's roads are

generally paved (in a manner of speaking), but those that are not can be incredibly rutted, even those leading to a fancy hotel. Observe the 30 miles per hour speed limit and watch out for the four-legged critters—goats, sheep, and cows—that amble across the road. To rent a car you'll need a valid driver's license and a local license, which can be obtained for $6 at any of the car rental agencies. Among the agencies are **Avis** (tel. 809/497–6221 or 800/331–2112), **Budget** (tel. 809/497–2217 or 800/527–0700), **Connors (National)** (tel. 809/ 497–6433 or 800/328–4567), and **Island Car Rental** (tel. 809/497– 2723). Count on $35 to $45 per day's rental, plus insurance. Motorcycles and scooters are available for about $30 per day from **R & M Cycle** (tel. 809/497–2430).

Telephones and Mail To call Anguilla from the United States, dial area code 809 + 497 + the local four-digit number. International direct dial is available on the island. **Cable & Wireless** (Wallblake Rd., tel. 809/497–3100) is open weekdays 8–6, Saturday 9–1, Sunday and holidays 10–2 and sells Caribbean Phone Cards ($5, $10, $20 denominations) for use in specially marked phone booths. The card can be used for local calls, calls to other islands, and to call the United States and charge the call to MasterCard or Visa. To make a local call on the island, just dial the four-digit number. Inside the departure lounge at the Blowing Point Ferry and at the airport, there is an AT&T USADIRECT access telephone for collect or credit card calls to the United States.

Airmail letters to the United States cost E.C.60¢; postcards, E.C.25¢.

Opening and Closing Times Banks are open Monday–Thursday 8–3 and Friday 8–5. Shopping hours are variable. No two shops seem to have the same hours, but many are certainly open between 10 and 4. Call, or ask at the tourist office for opening and closing times, or adopt the island way of doing things; if they're not open when you stop by, stop by again.

Exploring Anguilla

Numbers in the margin correspond to points of interest on the Anguilla map.

Exploring on Anguilla is mostly about checking out the spectacular beaches and classy resorts. There are only a few roads on the island, but none of them are marked, so it's still pretty easy to get lost your first time out. Having a map, and checking it frequently against passing landmarks, is essential. If you didn't get a map at the airport or the ferry dock or your hotel, then head to the Tourist Office in The Valley, where administrative offices, banks, markets, and a few boutiques, guest houses, and eateries are located.

While you're in town you might want to visit the island's historic **❶ Wallblake House,** a plantation house that was built around 1787 by Will Blake (Wallblake is probably a corruption of his name). Legends of murders, invasions by the French in 1796, and high living surround the house. Now owned and actively used by the Catholic church, the estate has spacious rooms, some with tray ceilings edged with handsome carving. On the grounds is an ancient vaulted stone cistern and an outbuilding called the Bakery (which wasn't used for breadmaking but for baking turkeys and hams). The oven measures 12 feet across and rises 3 feet up through a stepped chimney. *Cross Roads, The Valley. Call Father John, tel. 809/497–2405, to make an appointment to tour the plantation.*

Anguilla

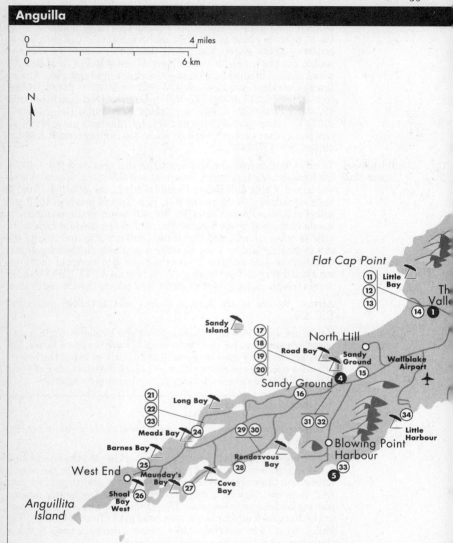

0 ———— 4 miles
0 ———— 6 km

N

Flat Cap Point

Little Bay — 11 12 13

The Valle — 14 1

Sandy Island — 17 18 19 20

North Hill

Road Bay

Sandy Ground — 4 15

Wallblake Airport

Sandy Ground — 16

21 22 23 — Long Bay

Meads Bay — 24

29 30

31 32 — 34

Little Harbour

Barnes Bay — 25

West End — 26 Maunday's Bay

Shoal Bay West

27 — Cove Bay

28 — Rendezvous Bay

Blowing Point Harbour — 33 5

Anguillita Island

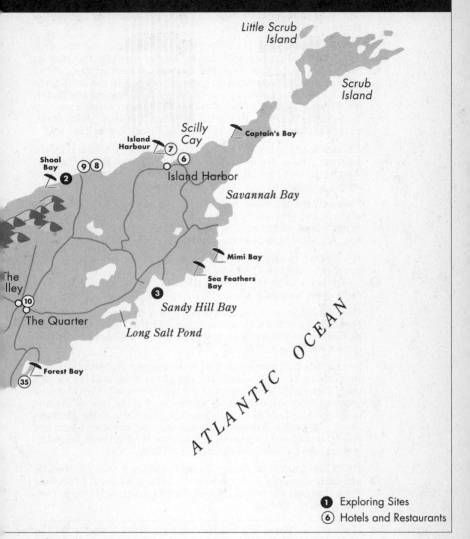

Little Scrub
Island

Scrub
Island

*Scilly
Cay*

Captain's Bay

Island
Harbour

7

6

Shoal
Bay

9 8

2

Island Harbor

Savannah Bay

Mimi Bay

Sea Feathers
Bay

The
lley

3

10

Sandy Hill Bay

The Quarter

Long Salt Pond

ATLANTIC OCEAN

Forest Bay

35

1 Exploring Sites
6 Hotels and Restaurants

Lodging	Fountain Beach, **9**	Rendezvous Bay Hotel, **30**
Arawak Beach Resort, **7**	Frangipani Beach Club, **24**	Shoal Bay Villas, **8**
Cap Juluca, **27**	Inter-Island Hotel, **13**	Syd–an's, **20**
Casablanca Resort, **28**	La Sirena, **22**	
Cinnamon Reef Beach Club, **34**	Malliouhana, **23**	
Coccoloba Plantation, **25**	The Mariners, **19**	
The Ferryboat Inn, **33**	Pineapple Beach Club, **29**	

From the **Wallblake House** follow the sign to the Cottage Hospital, and you'll come to a dirt road that leads to **Crocus Bay** and several strips of white-sand beaches.

Head northeast out of The Valley, following the occasional marker to Shoal Bay and its beautiful beach. As you approach the coast at
② **Shoal Bay,** you'll pass near **The Fountain,** where Arawak petroglyphs have been discovered. Presently closed to the public, the area is being researched by the Anguilla Archaeological and Historical Society. The AAHS (tel. 809/497–2767) plans to open a museum in the former Customs House in The Valley. The next stretch of this road is a bumpy mess. Hang in there. The beach is worth the trip.

Backtrack on the road from Shoal Bay and take your first real left. In about 2 miles you'll reach the fishing village of **Island Harbour,** where you'll see colorful, handcrafted fishing boats pulled up on the shore.

Follow rutted dirt roads from Island Harbour to the easternmost tip of the island. On the way to the aptly named **Scrub Island** and **Little Scrub Island** off the eastern tip of Anguilla, you'll pass Captain's Bay, with its isolated, windswept beach, on the north coast.

If you want to skip the easternmost end of the island, follow the paved road south (not the road you came in on) from Island Harbour.
③ It continues to **Sandy Hill Bay.** If you're an aficionado of ruined forts, there's one here you may want to explore.

Four miles farther down the coast, beyond the Long Salt Pond, is **Forest Bay,** a fit place for scuba diving. South of Forest Bay lies **Little Harbour,** with a lovely horseshoe-shape bay and the splendid **Cinnamon Reef Beach Club.**

From Little Harbour, follow the paved road past Wallblake Airport, just outside The Valley, and turn left on the main road. In about a mile, bear right, following signs for Sandy Ground, then continue
④ for another two miles to **Sandy Ground,** one of the most active and most developed of the island's beaches. It is home to **the Mariners** resort, **Tamariain Watersports,** a dive shop, a commercial pier, and several small guest houses and restaurants. A ferry leaves frequently from here for Sandy Island, 2 miles offshore.

If you backtrack from Sandy Ground to the main road you were on
⑤ and continue south, you'll pass (at the light) the turnoff to **Blowing Point Harbour,** where you'll have docked if you arrived by ferry from Marigot in St. Martin.

Time Out   If you plan to picnic (on the beach or in your room), try the **Fat Cat** (George Hill, tel. 809/497–2307) for escargots to go, as well as takeout quiche, soups, chili, chicken, and conch dishes. **Amy's Bakery** (Blowing Point, tel. 809/497–6775) turns out homemade pies, cakes, tarts, cookies, and breads.

The main paved road continues more or less down the center of the island. Teeth-jarring dirt roads lead to the coasts, the beaches, and some of the best resorts on the island.

On the south coast, just west of Blowing Point, is the crescent-shape home of **Rendezvous Bay,** the island's first hotel, built in 1959.

Farther south, you'll pass a number of fancy resorts. Left-hand turnoffs will take you to the **Casablanca Resort** and to **Cap Juluca,** which is on beautiful **Maunday's Bay.** Right-hand turnoffs head to **Meads Bay,** where you'll find the **Malliouhana** and the **Frangipani**

Beach Club, and to **Barnes Bay** and Coccoloba Plantation. At the very end of the road you'll come to beautiful **Shoal Bay West** and the striking architecture of **Cove Castles.**

Beaches

The island's big attractions are its dozens and dozens of dazzling, white-sand beaches. Each one is different. You'll find wild Atlantic waves, supercalm bays, dunes, long beaches that are great for walking, deserted beaches, and beaches lined with bars and restaurants. It's your choice. Good snorkeling is almost everywhere, but nude bathing is a no-no.

Unfortunately it's no longer a secret that **Shoal Bay** is one of the prettiest beaches in the Caribbean. But this 2-mile L-shape beach of talcum-powder-soft white sand is definitely still worth a visit. There are beach chairs, umbrellas, a backdrop of sea-grape and coconut trees, and for seafood and tropical drinks there's Trader Vic's, Uncle Ernie, and the Round Rock. Souvenir shops for T-shirts, suntan lotion, and the like abound. Head to Shoal Bay for good snorkeling in the offshore coral reefs, and visit the water-sports center to arrange diving, sailing, and fishing trips.

Island Harbour is a long, slender beach that forms a gentle harbor. For centuries Anguillans have put out from these sands in their colorful, handmade fishing boats to seek the day's catch. There are several beach bars and restaurants, and you can depart from here for the three-minute boat ride to **Scilly Cay.** You can get snorkeling equipment on the ferrying motorboat, but at times the waters are too rough to see much. On Scilly Cay there is a beach bar that serves drinks and grilled lobster and seafood.

The reward for traveling along an inhospitable dirt road via four-wheel drive is complete isolation at **Captain's Bay** on the northeastern end of the island. The surf slaps the sands with a vengeance, and the undertow is quite strong here. Wading is the safest water sport.

Mimi Bay is a difficult-to-reach, isolated, half-mile beach east of Sea Feathers. But the trip is worth it. When the surf is not too rough, the barrier reef makes for great snorkeling.

Also not far from Sea Feathers is **Sandy Hill,** a base for fishermen. Here you can buy fresh fish and lobster right off the boats and snorkel in the warm waters. Don't plan to sunbathe—the beach is quite narrow here.

Rendezvous Bay is 1½ miles of pearl-white sand. Here the water is calm, and there's a great view of St. Martin. The Pineapple Beach Club's open-air beach bar is handy for snacks and frosty island drinks.

The good news and the bad news about **Cove Bay** is the same—it's virtually deserted. There are no restaurants or bars, just calm waters, coconut trees, and soft sand that stretches down to Maunday's Bay.

One of the most popular beaches, wide, mile-long **Maunday's Bay** is known for good swimming and snorkeling. Rent water-sports gear at Tropical Watersports. Try Pimms at Cap Juluca for fine food and drink (*see* Dining, *below*).

Adjacent to Maunday's Bay, **Shoal Bay West** is a dazzling beach with several striking villa complexes, including the sculpturelike, futuristic Cove Castles. Stop for lunch at the Paradise Cafe (*see* Dining, *below*) and ask someone there to point out the best snorkeling spot. Comb this beach for lovely conch shells as well.

Barnes Bay is a superb spot for windsurfing and snorkeling. The elegant Coccoloba Plantation perches above and offers a poolside bar. In high season this beach can get a bit crowded with day-trippers from St. Martin.

The clear blue waters of **Road Bay** beach, also referred to as Sandy Ground, are usually dotted with yachts. The Mariners resort, several restaurants (*see* Lodging, *below*), a water-sports center, and lots of windsurfing and waterskiing activity make this an active commercial area. It's a typical Caribbean scene daily, as fishermen set out in their boats and goats ramble the littoral at will. The snorkeling is not very good here, but do visit this bay for its glorious sunsets.

Sandy Island, nestled in coral reefs about 2 miles offshore from Road Bay, is a tiny speck of sand and sea and a few spindly palm trees. From the distance it has the look of a classic "deserted island," but it's got the modern-day comforts of a beach boutique, beach bar, and restaurant and free use of snorkeling gear and underwater cameras. There is a ferry that heads there every hour from Sandy Ground.

At **Little Bay** sheer cliffs embroidered with agave and creeping vines plummet to a small gray-sand beach, usually accessible only by water (it's a favored spot for snorkeling and night dives). But virtually assured of total privacy, the hale and hearty can clamber down a rope to explore the caves and surrounding reef.

Sports and the Outdoors

Bicycling There are plenty of flat stretches, making wheeling pretty easy. Bikes can be rented at **Boothes** (tel. 809/497–2075).

Boating Sunfish and Hobie Cats are available at **Tropical Watersports** (tel. 809/497–6666 or 809/497–6779). *Sundancer,* a 30-foot powerboat, is available for charters at **Tamariain Watersports** (tel. 809/497–2020). Sailboats and speedboats can be rented at **Sandy Island Enterprises** (tel. 809/497–6395).

Deep-Sea Fishing Albacore, dolphin, and kingfish are among the sea creatures angled after off Anguilla's shores. Trips can be arranged through Elbert or Trevor Richardson in Long Bay (tel. 809/497–6397); or you can head to Sandy Ground and see which of the many locals who provide trips is available. Fishing tackle, diving gear, and other sports equipment are available at the **Tackle Box Sports Center** (tel. 809/497–2896).

Fitness Lest you go flabby lolling around on the beach, you'll find exercise equipment, aerobics, and martial arts instruction at **Highway Gym** (George Hill Rd., tel. 809/497–2363).

Jogging There are miles and miles of broad, flat beaches. Just pick one out and jog away.

Sea Excursions Picnic, swimming, and diving excursions to Prickly Pear, Sandy Island, and Scilly Cay are available through **Sandy Island Enterprises** (tel. 809/497–6395), **Enchanted Island Cruises** (tel. 809/497–3111), **Suntastic Cruises** (tel. 809/497–3400), and **Tropical Watersports** (tel. 809/497–6666 or 809/497–6779).

Tennis For professional instruction, contact the Peter Burwash International pro at **Coccoloba Plantation** (tel. 809/497–6871), where there are two lighted courts. There are two courts at the **Carimar Beach Club** (tel. 809/497–6881); four Laykold (hard) courts at **Malliouhana**

(tel. 809/497–6111); two Deco Turf tournament courts at **Cinnamon Reef** (tel. 809/497–2727); two courts at the **Fountain Beach and Tennis Club** (tel. 809/497–6395) and **Rendezvous Bay** (tel. 809/497–6549); and one court each at **the Mariners** (tel. 809/497–2671), **Masara** (tel. 809/497–3400), **Pelicans** (tel. 809/497–6593), **Sea Grapes** (tel. 809/ 497–6433), and **Spindrift Apartments** (tel. 809/497–4164).

Water Sports The major resorts offer complimentary Windsurfers, paddleboats, and water skis to their guests. If your hotel has no water-sports facilities, you can get in gear at **Tropical Watersports** (tel. 809/497–6666 or 809/497–6779) or **Tamariain Watersports** (tel. 809/497–2020). Tamariain Watersports also has PADI (Professional Association of Diving Instructors) instructors, short resort courses, and more than a dozen dive sites.

Shopping

Shopping tips are readily available in the informative free publications *Anguilla Life* and *What We Do in Anguilla*, but you have to be a really dedicated shopper to peel yourself off the beach and poke around in Anguilla's few shops. If you really want to shop, catch the ferry to Marigot on St. Martin for the day and spend your time in chic boutiques showcasing the latest in Italian and French fashion.

Clothing Head for **La Romana** (Meads Bay, tel. 809/497–6181), cloned from the St. Martin and St. Barts boutiques; **Boutique at Malliouhana** (Meads Bay, tel. 809/497–6111); **Whispers** (Cap Juluca, tel. 809/497–6666); and **Sunshine Shop** (South Hill, tel. 809/497–6964) for island cotton *pareos* (Polynesian-style wraps), silk-screened items, cotton resort wear, and hand-painted wood items from Haiti. **La Sirena Boutique** (Meads Bay, tel. 809/467–6827) offers a colorful range of dresses, slacks, belts, and other accessories. **Beach Stuff** (Back St., South Hill, tel. 809/497–6814) has just what you'd expect, bathing suits and cover-ups, sunglasses, T-shirts, and other sportswear for all ages. **The Valley Gap** (Shoal Bay Beach, tel. 809/497–2754) has local crafts, T-shirts, and swimwear. **Vanhelle Boutique** (Sandy Ground, tel. 809/497–2965) carries gift items, as well as Brazilian swimsuits for men and women. **Java Wraps** (George Hill Rd., tel. 809/497–5497) carries superb batikwear. **Caribbean Style** (Rendezvous Bay, tel. 809/497–6717) has an eclectic collection of everything from sandals to jewelry to furniture.

Native Crafts The **Anguilla Arts and Crafts Center** (The Valley, tel. 809/497–2200) has a wide selection of island crafts. **Alicea's Place** (The Quarter, tel. 809/497–3540) has some locally made ceramics and pottery. The **New World Gallery** (The Valley, tel. 809/407–5950) holds frequent exhibits and sells artwork, jewelry, textiles, and antiquities. The **Scruples Gift Shop** (Social Security Bldg., tel. 809/497–2800) has shells, handmade baskets, wood dolls, hand-crocheted mats, lace tablecloths, and bedspreads. **Devonish Art Gallery** (The Valley, tel. 809/ 497–2949) displays the ceramics and sculpture of Courtney Devonish, as well as works by other prominent local artists. **Cheddie's Carving Shop** (The Cove, tel. 809/497–6027), just down the road from Coccoloba Plantation, showcases Cheddie's own work, wonderfully textured, fanciful creatures fashioned from driftwood. Even the whimsically carved desk and balustrade in his studio testify to his vivid imagination. Many artists hold open studios; the tourism board can provide brochures.

Dining

Anguilla's eateries range from the truly elegant to down-home seaside shacks. Casual chic prevails; a jacket (no tie) is usually required
in high season at the top resorts. Call ahead—in the winter to make
a reservation and in the summer to see if the place you've chosen is
open. Most restaurants not affiliated with a hotel tack on an additional 5% to the service charge if you pay by credit card.

Highly recommended restaurants are indicated by a star ★.

Category	Cost*
Very Expensive	over $45
Expensive	$35–$45
Moderate	$25–$35
Inexpensive	under $25

per person, excluding drinks, service, and sales tax (8%)

★ **Malliouhana.** Sparkling crystal and fine china, exquisite service,
and a spectacularly romantic, candlelit, open-air setting are the perfect match for this restaurant's exceptional Haute French cuisine.
Michel Rostang, renowned for his Paris boîte, created the menu and
is still the consulting chef. Try the goat cheese wrapped in fresh
salmon or warm stewed lobster with pumpkin and French corn salad, then segue into lobster medallions with seasoned polenta or
Bresse chicken breasts stuffed with asparagus. Don't pass up desserts, especially the roast pear in Sauternes with walnut brioche
and cinnamon ice cream. The wine cellar contains about 25,000 bottles. *Meads Bay, tel. 809/497–6111. Reservations required. AE,
MC, V. Closed Sept. and Oct. Very Expensive.*
Pimms. You expect Rudolph Valentino to sweep in beneath the
domes, arches, and billowing canvas of this Arabian Nights setting
on the edge of a half-moon bay. Water laps almost unnervingly close
to the outer tables, but from them you can see brightly colored tropical fish swim up for a spare bit of your roll. French chefs prepare
picture-perfect plates of mostly Continental-style items with a
touch of Creole or West Indian flavor. Entrées include grilled Black
Angus sirloin and fresh local lobster or grouper in a spicy tomato
sauce. *Cap Juluca, Maunday's Bay, tel. 809/497–6666. Reservations required. AE, MC, V. Very Expensive.*
Capers. This appealing newcomer faces the beach at Meads Bay. The
simple, open-air design lets fresh breezes reach all of the diners.
Bright Caribbean paintings line the inside walls, but the most romantic tables are those on the beachside veranda, with nothing
overhead but a canopy of stars. This is a good place to come for
grilled lobster with melted herb butter and for steaks cut from imported Black Angus beef. *Meads Bay, tel. 809/497–6369. Reservations advised in season. MC, V. Closed Sept. and Oct. Expensive.*
Coccoloba Plantation. Dining here is either indoors or on a lovely
terrace overlooking the sea. Your choices might include red pepper
and orange soup perfumed with cardamom; the nightly lobster special, such as lobster cassoulet in vermouth saffron cream or duck
magret in plum and Beaumes des Venise sauce. Lunch is a poolside
buffet of salads, burgers, fish, and homemade desserts. Monday's
remarkable buffet features local specialties and international dishes—goat-cheese salad, carrot soup, baby lamb chops, veal in West
Indian white sauce, bananas in coconut sauce—prepared by the

skilled and well-traveled chef. *Barnes Bay, tel. 809/497–6871. Reservations required in season. AE, D, MC, V. Expensive.*

Hibernia. Hibernia, set in unspoiled Island Harbour in an absolutely delightful seaside cottage with wood beams, bamboo furniture, raspberry latticework, and East Indian paintings, boasts one of the island's most creative menus. Unorthodox yet delectable pairings include fricassee of lobster in mustard cinnamon sauce and breast of chicken cooked with honey and mild chiles. There is also an unusual Thai-inspired bouillabaisse of assorted local seafood. For dessert, don't miss their famous pruneaux in Armagnac chocolate sauce with homemade chestnut ice cream. *Island Harbour, tel. 809/497–4290. Reservations suggested. AE, D, MC, V. Closed Mon. Expensive.*

La Fontana. Set back from the beach, this small restaurant has an ambitious northern Italian menu, deftly seasoned with island touches by the Rastafarian chef. You can select from a range of pastas including *fettucine al limone* (with a sauce of black olives, lemon, parmesan, and butter), pasta with lobster and fresh herbs, and the daily rasta pasta special. There is also a delicious lobster dish cooked with black olives, capers, and tomatoes plus grilled duck, steak, fish, and chicken. *Fountain Beach hotel, Shoal Bay, tel. 809/497–3492. Reservations accepted. AE, MC, V. Closed May to Nov. Expensive.*

★ **The Palm Court.** This stylish eatery in the Cinnamon Reef Beach Club has a long palm-lined corridor with red terra-cotta tile floors, Haitian furniture, local murals, and huge arched picture windows fronting the Caribbean. Frenchman Didier Rochat and Anguillan Vernon Hughes collaborate on an exciting nouvelle Caribbean cuisine, their strengths complementing each other beautifully. Signature dishes you might select include char-grilled tuna with cinnamon tomato raisin sauce, queenfish roasted in phyllo and served with saffron capellini, and swordfish steak in passion fruit salsa. The mango puffs in caramel sauce are justly famous. *Cinammon Beach Club, Little Harbour, tel. 809/497–2727. Reservations advised in season. AE, MC, V. Closed mid-Sept.–mid-Oct. Expensive.*

Paradise Cafe. The twinkling music of wind chimes and seductive aromas from the kitchen waft through this informal, breezy, beachfront restaurant. Selections of local seafood (snapper, conch, lobster), chicken, and beef are prepared with an interesting blend of French and Oriental influences. Among the standouts are West Indian bouillabaisse; rack of lamb chinois in a black bean sauce; and rockfish filet flash-fried in peanut oil with sake, hoisin, and tamarind sauce. Lunches feature hamburgers, salads and soups, and individual pizzas. *Shoal Bay West, tel. 809/497–6010. Reservations suggested in season. AE, MC, V. Closed Mon. Expensive.*

★ **The Ferryboat Inn.** Just a short walk from the Ferry Dock at Blowing Point is this charming waterside restaurant with tables open to the breezes and to the romantic nighttime views of the twinkling lights of St. Martin in the distance. Come here for the delicious French onion or black bean soup, grilled local lobster, lobster thermidor (the house specialty), and *entrecôte du vin au poivre* (a house version of steak au poivre with a red wine sauce). There are also veal and chicken dishes, hamburgers, and omelets. *Cul de Sac Road, Blowing Point, tel. 809/497–6613. Reservations advised in season. AE, MC, V. Closed Sun. lunch. Moderate.*

★ **Koal Keel.** When you want a break from the island's many beachfront restaurants, head to this beautifully restored 18th-century great house that was part of a cotton and sugar plantation. Here you will dine in comfort amid handwrought stone walls and richly upholstered period furniture. Light island breezes come in through the open, window-size spaces that are a unique part of the house's island architecture. A replica of the house's original large rock oven is used to bake fresh breads and to roast chickens and racks of lamb. The chefs have created what they call "EuroCaribe" cuisine, and the menu has such offerings as Anguilla Pea Soup, lobster crêpes, smoked grouper on a bed of leeks, and grilled breast of duck. *The Valley, tel. 809/497-2930. Reservations required in season. Closed Sept.-mid-Oct. AE, MC, Visa. Moderate.*

Lucy's Harbour View Restaurant. Passing through a swinging wood gate, you'll step up to a terrace restaurant with a splendid sea view. The specialty is "Lucy's delicious whole red snapper," but there is a wide selection here, including several curried and Creole dishes, such as conch and goat. Be sure to try Lucy's sautéed potatoes (and be very sparing with the tableside hot sauce!). Live music Wednesday and Friday. *South Hill, tel. 809/497-6253. Reservations accepted. No credit cards. Closed Sun. Moderate.*

★ **The Old House.** Set on a hill near the airport, this lovely house is the place to come for a relaxing breakfast and for West Indian specialties at lunch and dinner. White and green tablecloths grace tables set with fresh flowers, even at breakfast, when those in the know head here for the island fruit pancakes. Lunch and dinner specialties include conch simmered in lime juice and wine, curried local lamb with pigeon peas and rice, and Anguillan pot fish cooked in a sauce of limes, garlic, and tomatoes. *George Hill, tel. 809/497-2228. Reservations advised. AE, D, MC, V. Moderate.*

Riviera Bar & Restaurant. This is a small and informal beachside bistro serving French and Creole specialties with an Oriental accent. A three-course lobster meal is featured, and the fish soup à la Provençale is highly recommended. French cheese and homemade pâté, sushi, sashimi, and oysters sautéed in soy sauce and sake are also among the eclectic offerings. There's a very happy Happy Hour from 6 to 7 daily. Live entertainment is featured frequently in season. *Sandy Ground, tel. 809/497-2833. Reservations advised in season. AE, V. Moderate.*

Smuggler's Grill. Somewhat out of the way on Forest Bay, this romantic, nautically decorated restaurant offers fresh Anguillan lobster prepared 10 ways. Recipes are based on cuisines from around the world, including French, Southeast Asian, Indian, and Tunisian. The menu includes escargot, onion soup, and other French bistro fare, and a good selection of steaks and chops. There is also an ample salad bar. *Forest Bay, tel. 809/497-3728. MC, V. Dinner only. Closed Sun. and Aug.-Sept. Moderate.*

★ **Arlo's.** Perched on a hill, this popular Italian restaurant offers indoor and terrace seating and the best pizza on the island. If you don't want pizza as a main course, share one as an appetizer then choose from a list of entrées that includes spaghetti Bolognese, lasagna, tortellini du jour, various preparations of fettucine, and veal or chicken parmigiana. There's always a nightly appetizer and entrée special. *South Hill, tel. 809/497-6810. MC, V. Dinner only. Closed Sun. and Sept.-Oct. Inexpensive.*

Aquarium. An upstairs terrace, the Aquarium is all gussied up with gingerbread trim, bright blue walls, and red tablecloths. The lunch menu lists sandwiches and burgers. Stewed lobster, curried chicken, barbecued chicken, and mutton stew are offered at night. This is a popular spot with locals. *South Hill, tel. 809/497-2720. Reservations accepted. No credit cards. Closed Sun. Inexpensive.*

Cross Roads. Millie Philip's roadside bar features hearty breakfasts and, at lunch, seafood salads, fish, and chicken. Hearty fare at low prices. *Wallblake, The Valley, tel. 809/497-2581. Reservations accepted. No credit cards. Inexpensive.*

Johnno's. This is *the* place to be on Sunday afternoons for barbecue and music by the island band Dumpa and the AnvVibes, but grilled or barbecued lobster, kingfish, snapper (all of which Johnno catches himself), and chicken are good anytime. This is a classic Caribbean beach bar, attracting a funky eclectic mix, from locals to movie stars. *Sandy Ground, tel. 809/497–2728. No credit cards. Inexpensive.*

Pepper Pot. Cora Richardson's small eatery in the center of town offers *roti* aficionados some of the best rotis on the island. These Trinidadian specialties are made of boneless chicken, *tania* (a local vegetable), celery, pepper, onion, garlic, and peas, all wrapped in dough and baked. Dumpling dinners, lobster, whelk, and conch are also good choices. *The Valley, tel. 809/497–2328. Reservations accepted. No credit cards. Inexpensive.*

Roy's. The dainty pink-and-white-covered deck belies the rowdy reputation of Roy and Mandy Bosson's pub, an Anguillan mainstay. One of the island's best buys, it features Roy's fish-and-chips, cold English beer, pork fricassee, and a wonderful chocolate rum cake. Sunday lunch special is roast beef and Yorkshire pudding. A faithful clientele gathers in the lively bar. *Crocus Bay, tel. 809/497–2470. Reservations accepted. MC, V. Closed Mon. and Sat. lunch. Inexpensive.*

Lodging

Anguilla has a wide range of accommodations. There are grand and glorious resorts; apartments and villas from the deluxe to the simple; and small, very simple, locally owned guest houses. Because Anguilla has so many beautiful and uncrowded beaches, it is not necessary (the way it is on some other islands) for beach lovers to choose a property because of its beach. When you call to reserve a room in a resort, be sure to inquire about special packages. Meal plans are available, but the particulars vary from resort to resort.

Highly recommended lodgings are indicated by a star ★.

Category	Cost*
Very Expensive	over $400
Expensive	$275–$400
Moderate	$150–$275
Inexpensive	under $150

*All prices are for a standard double room for two, excluding 8% tax and a service charge, which is typically 10%.

Hotels
★ **Cap Juluca.** This spectacular 179-acre resort wraps around the edge of Maunday's Bay and almost 2 miles of sugary white-sand beach. Its sparkling white, Moorish-style two-story villas with domes, arches, and turrets are some of the most luxurious and oversize accommodations in the Caribbean. Rooms are minimally but elegantly decorated, with built-in, plumply cushioned seating areas, Moroccan fabrics, and Brazilian hardwood, and are air-conditioned and have ceiling fans, safes, and minibars. Giant, luxurious bathrooms vary, but many include private sunporches or gardens and two-person soaking tubs. Breakfast can be served on your private spacious terrace, and breakfast or a light lunch can be served poolside. At the end of the bay is Chatterton's, the hotel's casual Mediterranean-style grill, which overlooks the water and is open for lunch and din-

ner. Elegant dinners are served at the adjoining waterside restaurant, Pimms. *Box 240, Maunday's Bay, tel. 809/497–6666/6779 or 800/235–3505, fax 809/497–6617. 98 units, 7 private villas. Facilities: 3 restaurants, bar, boutique, room service, laundry service, library, VCRs and cassettes for rent, pool, 3 tennis courts, watersports and fitness centers. AE, V. CP, MAP. Very Expensive.*

★ **Malliouhana.** This ultrasophisticated resort, Anguilla's classiest, sits on 25 lush tropical acres on a promontory that juts out between two exquisite beaches. The lobby entrance, boutique, restaurants, and bar are in a grand, multitiered, open-air building. Accommodations are sleekly decorated, with white walls and tile floors, high-quality rattan furniture, Haitian prints, minibars, oversize tubs in marble baths, and ceiling fans (as well as air-conditioning). The restaurant is the most elegant on the island. Peter Burwash International manages the tennis program here. *Box 173, Meads Bay, tel. 809/497–6111 or 800/372–1323, fax 809/497–6011. 20 doubles, 15 junior suites, 15 1-bedroom suites, 4 2-bedroom suites. Facilities: restaurant, bar, boutique, beauty salon, concierge, 3 pools, 4 lighted tennis courts, Nautilus-equipped exercise room, massage room, water-sports center, drugstore. No credit cards. EP, MAP. Very Expensive.*

Casablanca Resort. This pink and green Moorish beachside fantasia is the largest, and by far the gaudiest-looking, resort on Anguilla. The entranceway to reception, restaurants, bars, and the 1,200-square-foot pool is through a long, domed, open-air hallway of authentic Moroccan mosaics past a long reflecting pool. The rooms are done up in pastel green and pink prints, pale green rattan furniture, and Moroccan throw rugs. TV, VCR, radio, safe, minibar, air-conditioning, and ceiling fan are standard throughout. The feel here, despite the unusual architecture, is closer to a stateside hotel than a Caribbean resort and is sure to be popular with affluent tour groups. On another, more developed, island, Casablanca might not seem so garish. *Box 444, Rendezvous Bay West, tel. 809/496–6999 or 800/231–1945, fax 809/496–6899. 76 rooms and suites. Facilities: 3 restaurants, bar, pool, 2 lit tennis courts, boutique, library, jewelry store, sundry shop, piano bar, health club, water-sports center. AE, D, MC, V. EP. Expensive.*

★ **Cinnamon Reef Beach Club.** Low-key luxury sets the tone at this small, appealing resort. Most of the whitewashed, split-level villas line the narrow beach, while five are tucked on a bluff. Each casually decorated, white-stucco villa has a living room, raised bedroom, dressing room, sunken shower, and patio, along with little extras such as a hammock, built-in hair dryer, and minibar. This is a friendly place with a gracious staff and lots of repeat guests. The restaurant chefs have won the last several Anguilla Chefs of the Year Awards, and the Friday-night barbecue is an island favorite. Meal plans and packages are available. *Box 141, Little Harbour, tel. 809/ 497–2727 or 800/223–1108; in Canada, 416/485–8724; fax 809/497–3727. 14 studios, 8 1-bedroom suites. Facilities: restaurant, lounge, pool, 2 tennis courts, room service, all water sports. AE, MC, V. EP, MAP. Expensive.*

Coccoloba Plantation. Casual chic is the style of this resort set above a stunning beach. Guests stay in individual, gingerbread-trimmed villas that overlook the ocean and are done in bright Caribbean colors, with raised bedroom areas, marble bathrooms, and comfortable exposed patios. All rooms and one-bedroom suites are air-conditioned, with ceiling fans, and have a small library of books, safe-deposit box, hair dryer, amenity package, and complimentary fully stocked refrigerator and minibar. Most bathrooms have showers only. Peter Burwash International directs the tennis program, and tennis and other special packages are available. *Box 332, Barnes Bay, tel. 809/497-6871 or 800/351-5656; in Canada, 800/468-0023; fax 809/497-6332. 44 rooms. Facilities: restaurant, 2 bars, library, concierge, boutique, 2 tennis courts, 2 pools, Jacuzzi, TV/reading room, sauna, massage, exercise rooms, water sports. AE, DC, MC, V. EP, MAP. Expensive.*

Frangipani Beach Club. This splashy newcomer on stunning Meads Bay beach consists of pink, multilevel, Spanish Mediterranean-style buildings with archways, stone balustrades, wrought-iron railings, and roofs of red clay tiles. Grounds are lushly landscaped with colorful tropical flowers and greenery. Each one-, two-, or three-bedroom suite is tastefully decorated with white rattan furniture and fabrics in colorful prints and bold stripes. All units have marble bathrooms, oversize terraces or balconies, and air-conditioning as well as ceiling fans. Many units have full kitchens. *Box 328, Meads Bay, tel. 809/497-6442 or 800/892-4564. 24 units. Facilities: pool, restaurant, 2 bars, tennis court, all water sports. AE. EP. Expensive.*

Arawak Beach Resort. Set on the actual site of an ancient Arawak village, this new waterfront resort is perhaps the first in the Caribbean to showcase the Amerindian heritage of the region. Hexagonal, breezy, two-story villas are furnished with hand-carved replicas of Amerindian furniture. The restaurant serves Caribbean and Amerindian food, and the courtyard is planted with cassava, cotton, papaya, and other traditional island crops. A small museum displays artifacts uncovered during construction. Canoes are available in addition to the usual water sports. Although the hotel beach is not one of Anguilla's best, Scilly Cay and its beautiful beaches are just a minute away by launch. This is a no-smoking property; alcoholic beverages are not served, but you may bring your own. *Box 98, Island Harbour, tel. 809/497-4888, fax 809/497-4898. 10 rooms, 3 junior suites, 1 luxury suite. Facilities: restaurant, pool, museum, boutique, all water sports. AE. EP. Moderate-Expensive.*

★ **Fountain Beach.** The family who owns this tiny, delightful property along beautiful Shoal Bay is of Italian descent, and their heritage is evident in the resort's Mediterranean style. Each unit comes with a fully equipped kitchen, a large bathroom with an open sunken shower (the studio also has a deep tub), and a view of the sea. Furnishings are in rattan and colorfully painted wicker, with Haitian art decorating the walls. Despite the long and bumpy road to the hotel, guests from all over the island head to La Fontana, the hotel's Italian restaurant, for dinner (*see* Dining, *above*). Additional units, some with plunge pool, are planned over the next few years. *Shoal Bay, tel. and fax 809/497-3491. 8 1-bedroom suites, 2 junior suites. Facilities: restaurant, 2 pools, 2 tennis courts. AE, MC, V. EP, MAP. Closed Sept. Moderate-Expensive.*

The Mariners. This popular and casual resort is located at the far end of one of Anguilla's busiest beaches and is a short stroll from a number of beach bars and restaurants. It has offered all-inclusive rates for several years, although EP is just as popular with the honeymooners and businesspeople on retreat who make up much of the clientele. Accommodations vary considerably, ranging from deluxe two-bedroom, two-bath cottages with full kitchens to small rooms with twin beds, minibars, and shower baths. Charter the resort's Boston whaler for picnics, snorkeling, and fishing trips. The Thursday-night barbecue and Saturday West Indian night in the beachfront restaurant are popular island events. The Mariners is very West Indian in style and ambience, which means 19th-century gingerbread cottages, standard muted pastel decor, and service that, while friendly, seems laid-back verging on lackadaisical.

Box 139, Sandy Ground, tel. 809/497–2815, 809/497–2671, or 800/223–0079; fax 809/497–2901. 25 1–bedroom suites, 25 studios. Facilities: 2 restaurants, 2 bars, Jacuzzi, laundry service, boutique, pool, lighted tennis court, water-sports center. AE, MC, V. EP, MAP, FAP, all-inclusive (drinks not included). Moderate–Expensive.

Pineapple Beach Club. This is the new name for the small property formerly known as the Anguilla Great House. The exterior looks the same, but the one-bedroom suites have been turned into individual bedrooms, and the rates are now all-inclusive, meaning everything from room to water sports to alcoholic beverages is included in one price. Set along Rendezvous Bay, one of Anguilla's longest beaches, these one-story, white, West Indian–style bungalows feature chaise longues on verandas with vine-covered trellises and gingerbread trim. The rooms (five in each bungalow) feature mahogany furnishings, hand-embroidered linens, huge tile showers, and ceiling fans (no air-conditioning). *Box 157, Rendezvous Bay, tel. 809/497–6061 or 800/223–0079, fax 809/497–6019. 27 rooms. Facilities: restaurant, pool, gallery/boutique, gym. AE, MC, V. All-inclusive. Moderate–Expensive.*

Shoal Bay Villas. On two splendid miles of sand, this small condominium/hotel is surrounded by palm trees. Units are brightly decorated in Caribbean pinks and blues. Furniture is painted rattan. All units except the poolside doubles come with fully equipped kitchens. None are air-conditioned, but all have ceiling fans. The adjoining Reefside Beach Bar and open-air restaurant is an informal, pleasant spot for breakfast, lunch, and dinner. All water sports can be arranged, and meal and room packages can be tailored to fit your needs. Children are not allowed during the winter. *Box 81, Shoal Bay, tel. 809/497–2051 or 800/722–7045; in NY, 212/535–9530; in Canada, 416/283–2621; fax 809/497–3631. 2 studios, 2 2-bedroom units, 7 1-bedroom units, 2 poolside doubles. Facilities: restaurant, bar, pool. AE, MC, V. EP, BP, MAP. Moderate–Expensive.*

★ **La Sirena.** Overlooking Meads Bay—its beach is just a two-minute walk by a path—La Sirena is a personable, well-run hotel that is one of Anguilla's best values. The second-floor restaurant, open to the sea breezes, serves West Indian and international cuisine. Rooms sport the typical Caribbean decor of rattan furniture and pastel-printed fabrics and are cooled with ceiling fans. La Sirena does not have the chic elegance of Malliouhana, but it's just down the beach and you can stay here for three weeks for the price of one at Malliouhana. *Box 200, Meads Bay, tel. 809/497–6827 or 800/331–9358; in NY, 212/545–843; fax 809/497–6829. 20 rooms, 3 villas. Facilities: 2 pools, restaurant, bar, car rental, picnic and snorkeling equipment. AE, MC, V. EP, MAP. Moderate.*

Rendezvous Bay Hotel. Anguilla's first resort, which opened over 20 years ago, sits amid 60 acres of coconut groves on the fine white sand of Rendezvous Bay just a mile from the ferry dock. The main building is simple and rather undecorated, but it has a breezy, broad front patio and a lounge that showcases owner Jeremiah Gumb's elaborate electric train set, complete with tunnels and multiple tracks. The original rooms, which are about 100 yards from the beach, are quite simple, with one double and one single bed, a private shower bath, Haitian art, and ceiling fans (no air-conditioning). New two-story villas contain spacious, one-bedroom suites decorated in natural wicker and pastel prints, with refrigerators or kitchenettes and air-conditioning. These new units can be joined to form larger suites and are built either along the wide beach or on more rocky stretches of the coast that offer excellent snorkeling.

Box 31, Rendezvous Bay, tel. 809/497–6549; in the United States, 908/738–0246 or 800/274–4893; in Canada, 800/468–0023; fax 809/497–6026. 20 rooms, 24 1-bedroom villa suites. Facilities: restaurant, lounge, game and TV room, 2 tennis courts, water-sports center. No credit cards. EP, MAP. Inexpensive–Moderate.

Ferryboat Inn. This small family-run complex is an enjoyable bargain. It's just a short walk from the ferry dock and on a small beach. Simply furnished but spacious units are decorated with white or pastel fabrics; all have full kitchens, dining areas, cable TV, and ceiling fans, and the two-bedroom beach house is air-conditioned. Marjorie McClean, the owner and manager, is eager to please. All rooms and the open-air restaurant look out across the water to views of hilly St. Martin, which is stunning at night, when it's covered with sparkling lights. *Box 189, Blowing Point, tel. 809/497–6613, fax 809/497–3309. 6 1- and 2-bedroom apartments, 1 beach house (air-conditioned). Facilities: restaurant, bar. AE, MC, V. EP. Inexpensive.*

Inter-Island Hotel. This modest establishment is simply furnished with wicker and rattan. There is no air-conditioning, but some rooms in the hotel have a breezy open balcony. Most rooms have refrigerators and cramped shower baths that define the term "water closet." In addition to the hotel are two small one-bedroom apartments, each with a separate entrance on the ground floor. A homey dining room serves hearty breakfasts and fine West Indian dinners. *Box 194, The Valley, tel. 809/497–6259 or 800/223–9815; in Canada, 800/468–0023; fax 809/497–5381. 12 rooms, 2 1-bedroom apartments. Facilities: restaurant, bar, TV lounge, transportation to beach ½ mi away. AE, D, MC, V. EP. Inexpensive.*

★ **Syd-an's.** Just across the street from all the activity on Road Bay, these pleasant, clean efficiencies contain comfortable furnishings, kitchenette, and shower bath. A tremendous bargain. *Sandy Ground, tel. 809/497–3180, fax 809/497–2332. 6 studios. Facilities: gift shop. AE, MC, V. EP. Inexpensive.*

Villa and Apartment Rentals The Tourist Office has a complete listing of vacation rentals. You can also contact **Sunshine Villas** (Box 142, Blowing Point, tel. 809/497–6149, fax 809/497–6021), the **Anguilla Connection** (Island Harbour, tel. 809/497–4403, fax 809/497–4402) or **Select Villas of Anguilla** (Box 256, George Hill, tel. 809/497–5810). Housekeeping accommodations are plentiful and well organized. The following are a selection:

★ **Cove Castles Villa Resort.** These glistening white, futuristic sculptures in the sand are actually luxuriously comfortable, very private, beachfront apartments decorated with custom-made wicker furniture, raw silk cushions, and hand-embroidered sheets. Kitchens are state of the art. Some units are air-conditioned. *Shoal Bay West, Box 248, tel. 809/497–6801 or 800/348–4716; in Canada, 800/468–0023; fax 809/497–6051. 4 3-bedroom villas, 8 2-bedroom villas. Facilities: restaurant, boutique, tennis court. No credit cards. Very Expensive.*

Sea Grape Beach Club. Also on Meads Bay, these luxurious 2,000-square-foot two-bedroom condos are laid out on five levels. Each unit features acres of glass, affording spectacular views, enormous closets, three baths, king-size beds, elegant furnishings, and spacious, very private decks. *Box 65, The Valley, tel. 809/497–6433, 809/497–6541, or 800/223–9815; fax 809/497–6410. 10 condos. Facilities: restaurant, bar, 2 tennis courts, satellite TV, water-sports center. No credit cards. Very Expensive.*

Blue Waters. These glistening white, Moorish-style buildings sit at the far end of a spectacular beach. Sunny one- and two-bedroom units are decorated with pastel fabrics and white tile floors and have dining areas, full kitchens, and terraces. *Box 69, Shoal Bay West, tel. 809/497–6292, fax 809/497–3309. 9 apartments. AE, MC, V. Moderate.*

Easy Corner Villas. These one-, two-, and three-bedroom apartments are adequately furnished and include well-equipped kitchens with microwaves. Only three of the units are air-conditioned; all have only shower baths. No. 10 is a deluxe two-bedroom villa. Not located on the beach but on a bluff overlooking Road Bay, this is a good buy for families. *Box 65, South Hill, tel. 809/497–6433, 809/497–6541, or 800/223–8815; fax 809/497–6410. 17 units. AE, MC, V. Moderate.*

Rainbow Reef. These secluded units are set on three dramatic seaside acres. A gazebo with beach furniture and barbecue facilities perches right above the beach. Each self-contained villa has two bedrooms, fully equipped kitchen, spacious dining and living area, and a large gallery overlooking the sea. *Box 130, Sea Feather Bay, tel. 809/497–2817 or 708/325–2299. 14 units. No credit cards. Moderate.*

★ **Skiffles Villas.** These self-catering villas, perched on a hill overlooking Road Bay, are usually booked a year in advance. The one-, two-, and three-bedroom apartments have fully equipped kitchens, floor-to-ceiling windows, and pleasant porches. *Box 82, Lower South Hill, tel. 809/497–6619, 219/642–4855, or 219/642–4445; fax 809/495–6110. 5 units. Facilities: pool. No credit cards. Moderate.*

Nightlife

The **Mayoumba Folkloric Theater,** a group made up of the best performers in the Anguilla Choral Circle, performs complete song-and-dance skits depicting Antillean and Caribbean culture with African drums and a string band. They appear every Thursday night at **La Sirena** (Meads Bay, tel. 809/497–6827). Be on the lookout for Bankie Banx, Anguilla's own reggae superstar. He has his own group called New Generations. If you're lucky, you'll catch him playing solo at the **Malliouhana** (Meads Bay, tel. 809/497–6111) during cocktail hours. You'll appreciate his true talent—no electronics here, just a remarkable voice and great guitar playing. Other local groups include Keith Gumbs and The Mellow Tones; Spracka; Megaforce; Sleepy and the All-Stars, a string-and-scratch band; Joe and the Invaders; and Dumpa and the AnvVibes. Steel Vibrations, a pan band, often entertains at barbecues and West Indian evenings. Most of the major hotels feature some kind of live entertainment in season. A Calypso combo plays most nights at **Cinnamon Reef Beach Club** (Little Harbour, tel. 809/497–2727). **The Mariners** (Sandy Ground, tel. 809/497–2671) has regularly scheduled Thursday-night barbecues and Saturday-night West Indian parties, both with live entertainment by local groups. During high season, **Pimms** and **Chatterton's** (Cap Juluca, tel. 809/497–6666) have live music at dinner. Things are pretty loose and lively at **Johnno's** beach bar (tel. 809/497–2728) in Sandy Ground, which has live music and alfresco dancing Wednesday and Saturday nights and Sunday afternoons, when it feels as if the entire island population is in attendance. The **Red Dragon Disco** (South Hill, tel. 809/497–2687) is a hot spot on weekends after midnight. The **Coconut Paradise** restaurant (Island Harbour, tel. 809/497–4150) has nightly entertainment ranging from disco to limbo. For soft dance music after a meal, go to **Lucy's Palm Palm** (tel. 809/497–2253) at Sandy Ground. There is usually a live band on Tuesday and Friday evenings. Sunday is the big night in restaurants. In addition to the above, **Uncle Ernie's** (Shoal Bay, no tel.), **Round Rock** (Shoal Bay, tel. 809/497–2076), and **Smitty's** (Island Harbour, tel. 809/497–4300) swing all day and well into the night.

3 Antigua

Updated by
Pamela
Acheson

One could spend an entire year—and a leap year, at that—exploring Antigua's (*An-TEE-ga*) beaches; the island has 366 of them, many with snow-white sand. All the beaches are public, some absolutely deserted and others with resorts stretching right along the water's edge and offering sailing, diving, windsurfing, and snorkeling. This is an island with hotels to please travelers of all kinds, from those seeking refined elegance, to those in search of casual beachfront merriment or quiet beachside snoozing, to those charmed by beautifully restored historic inns.

Antigua, the largest of the British Leeward Islands (108 square miles), is an island with a strong sense of national identity and rich, historic inheritance. Its cricketers, like the legendary Viv Richards, arguably the greatest batsmen the game has ever seen, are famous throughout the Caribbean. Its people are known for their sharp, commercial spirit; their wit; and, unfortunately at the government level, their corruption.

In the colonial era, Antigua was the headquarters of Lord Horatio Nelson's fleet. English Harbour, in the southeast of the island, is steeped in the history of that time. At its center is Nelson's Dockyard, now a national park. It is Antigua's answer to Williamsburg, Virginia—a carefully restored gem of British Georgian architecture. Accommodations here are generally in smaller, inn-type hotels. For Anglophiles and those interested in history, English Harbour and the surrounding villages and historic sites will be immensely rewarding.

Those in search of good beaches, plenty of nightlife, and a wide choice of restaurants will want to head to the northwestern end of the island, where resorts and hotels are scattered from Five Islands Harbour, south of St. John, to Dickenson Bay and the northwest shore. If you like to walk from one beach bar and restaurant to another, then Dickenson Bay and its long sliver of white sand is the spot for you.

One of the least developed parts of the island is in the southwest, in the shadow of Antigua's highest mountain, Boggy Peak. At beaches like Fry's Bay and Darkwood Beach, visitors will find long, unspoiled beaches.

The original inhabitants of Antigua were a people called the Siboney. They lived here as early as 4,000 years ago and disappeared mysteriously, leaving the island unpopulated for about 1,000 years. When Columbus arrived in 1493, the Arawaks had set up housekeeping. The English took up residence 139 years later in 1632. After 30-odd years of bloody battles involving the Caribs, the Dutch, the French, and the English, the French ceded the island to the English in 1667. Unlike many other Caribbean islands, which spent centuries being reflagged like political ping-pong balls, Antigua remained under English control until achieving full independence, with its sister island Barbuda (26 miles to the north), on November 1, 1981.

The combined population of the two islands is about 90,000, only 1,200 of whom live on Barbuda. Tourism is the main industry here—there has been a recent building boom in tourism properties, with the construction of condominiums and the extensive renovation and expansion of the major hotels—and the government is seeking to broaden its monetary resources by reintroducing agriculture and manufacturing into the economy.

Before You Go

Tourist Information Contact the **Antigua and Barbuda Tourist Offices** in the United States (610 5th Ave., Suite 311, New York, NY 10020, tel. 212/541–4117, or 121 S.E. 1st St., Suite 1001–1004, Miami, FL 33131, tel. 305/381–6762), in Canada (60 St. Clair Ave. E, Suite 205, Toronto, Ontario M4T 1N5, tel. 416/961–3085), and in the United Kingdom (Antigua House, 15 Thayer St., London W1M 5LD, England, tel. 071/486–7073).

Arriving and Departing
By Plane **American Airlines** (tel. 800/433–7300) has daily direct service from New York and Miami, as well as several flights from San Juan that connect with flights from more than 100 U.S. cities. **BWIA** (tel. 800/ JET–BWIA) has nonstop service from New York, Miami, and Toronto; **Air Canada** (tel. 800/422–6232) from Toronto; **British Airways** (tel. 800/247–9297) from London; and **Lufthansa** (tel. 800/645–3880) from Frankfurt. **LIAT** (tel. 809/462–0701) has daily flights from Antigua to Barbuda, 15 minutes away, as well as to and from many other Caribbean islands.

V. C. Bird International Airport is, on the tiniest of scales, to the Caribbean what O'Hare is to the Midwest. It's a major hub for traffic between Caribbean islands, and it is always busy with tiny planes taking off and landing.

From the Airport Taxis meet every flight, and drivers will offer to guide you around the island. The taxis are unmetered, but rates are posted at the airport and drivers are required to carry a rate card with them. The fixed rate from the airport to St. John's is $8 in U.S. currency (although drivers have been known to *quote* Eastern Caribbean dollars) and from the airport to English Harbour, $18.75.

Passports and Visas U.S. and Canadian citizens need proof of identity. A valid passport is most desirable, but a birth certificate is acceptable provided it has a raised or embossed seal and has been issued by a county or state (not a hospital) *and* provided that you also have some type of photo identification, such as a driver's license. A driver's license by itself is *not* sufficient. British citizens need a passport. All visitors must present a return or ongoing ticket.

Language Antigua's official language is English.

Precautions Some beaches are shaded by manchineel trees, whose leaves and applelike fruit are poisonous to touch. Most of the trees are posted with warning signs and should be avoided; even raindrops falling from them can cause painful blisters. If you should come in contact with one, rinse the affected area and contact a doctor.

Throughout the Caribbean, incidents of petty theft are increasing. Leave your valuables in the hotel safe-deposit box; don't leave them unattended in your room or on the beach. Also, the streets of St. John's are fairly deserted at night, so it's not a good idea to wander out alone.

Staying in Antigua

Important Addresses **Tourist Information:** The Antigua and Barbuda Department of Tourism (Thames and Long Sts., St. John's, tel. 809/462–0480) is open Monday–Thursday 8–4:30, Friday 8–3. There is also a tourist-information desk at the airport, just beyond the immigration checkpoint. The tourist office gives limited information. You may have more success with the **Antigua Hotels Association** (Long St., St. John's, tel. 809/462–3702), which also provides assistance.

Emergencies **Police:** tel. 809/462–0125. **Fire:** tel. 809/462–0044. **Ambulance:** tel. 809/462–0251. **Hospital:** There is a 24-hour emergency room at the 210-bed **Holberton Hospital** (Hospital Rd., St. John's, tel. 809/462–0251/2/3). **Pharmacies: Joseph's Pharmacy** (Redcliffe St., St. John's, tel. 809/462–1025) and **Health Pharmacy** (Redcliffe St., St. John's, tel. 809/462–1255).

Currency Local currency is the Eastern Caribbean dollar (E.C.\$), which is tied to the U.S. dollar and fluctuates only slightly. At hotels, the rate is E.C.\$2.60 to U.S.\$1; at banks, it's about E.C.\$2.70. American dollars are readily accepted, although you will usually receive change in E.C. dollars. Be sure you understand which currency is being used, since most places quote prices in E.C. dollars. Most hotels, restaurants, and duty-free shops take major credit cards, and all accept traveler's checks. It's a good idea to inquire at the tourist office or your hotel about current credit card policy. Note: Prices quoted are in U.S. dollars unless indicated otherwise.

Taxes and Hotels collect a 7% government room tax. The departure tax is \$10.
Service Hotels add a 10% service charge to your bill. In restaurants, a 10%
Charges service charge is usually added to your bill, and it is customary to leave another 5% if you are pleased with the service. Taxi drivers expect a 10% tip.

Guided Tours Virtually all **taxi** drivers double as guides, and you can arrange an island tour with one for about \$20 an hour. The most reliable and informed driver-guides are at **Capital Car Rental and Tours** (High St., St. John's, tel. 809/462–0863). A four-hour island tour costs about \$70. These prices are sometimes negotiable, particularly off-season.

Bryson's Travel (St. John's, tel. 809/462–0223) offers personalized tours of the island, as well as cruises and deep-sea-fishing trips. **Alexander, Parrish Ltd.** (St. John's, tel. 809/462–0387) specializes in island tours and can also arrange overnight stays. **Antours** (St. John's, tel. 809/462–4788) gives half- and full-day tours of the island. Antours is also the **American Express** representative on the island.

Until **Tropikelly** (tel. 809/461–0383) came along, it was hard to get into the bush in Antigua. There are few marked trails, and roads are poor. For \$55 per person you will get an insider's guide to Antigua—deserted plantation houses, rainforest trails, and ruined sugar mills and forts—as well as drinks and a picnic lunch. One highlight is the luxuriant tropical forest around the island's highest point, Boggy Peak.

Getting You'll see two bus stations in St. John's, near the Botanical Gardens
Around and near Central Market, but don't expect to see many buses. Bus
Buses schedules here epitomize what is called "island time," which is to say they roll when the spirit (infrequently) moves them.

Taxis If you're uncomfortable about driving on the left or prone to getting lost, a taxi is your best bet, although you'll find fares will mount up quickly. Taxis are unmetered, but rates are fixed from here to there and drivers are required to carry a rate card at all times. They'll even take you from the St. John's area to English Harbour and wait for a "reasonable" amount of time (about a half hour) while you look around for about \$35.

Rental Cars To rent a car, you'll need a valid driver's license and a temporary permit (\$12), which is available through the rental agent. Rentals average about \$50, in season, per day, with unlimited mileage. Generally, as in the United States, you'll get a better daily rate if you rent for several days. Most agencies rent automatic, stick-shift, and right- and left-hand-drive vehicles, as well as Jeeps. Although these four-wheel-drive vehicles will get you more places and are refreshingly open, beware that the roads are full of potholes, and a day in a Jeep can leave you feeling as if you've been through a paint-mixing machine! Remember to drive on the left (pay particular attention getting in and out of rotaries and making turns) and know that virtually all roads are unmarked. Fortunately, you will not have to deal with the incredibly steep curves that are on so many Caribbean islands.

Among the agencies are **Budget** (St. John's, tel. 809/462–3009 or 800/648–4985), **National** (St. John's, tel. 809/462–2113 or 800/468–0008), **Carib Car Rentals** (St. John's, tel. 809/462–2062), and **Avis** (at the airport or the St. James's Club, tel. 809/462–2840).

Telephones and Mail To call Antigua from the United States, dial 1, then area code 809, then the local seven-digit number. Few hotels have direct-dial telephones, but connections are easily made through the switchboard. The Caribbean Phone Card, available in $5, $10, and $20 amounts, can be used for local and long distance calls and for access to AT&T USA Direct lines. There are now quite a few phones that accept the phone cards, and they work much better than the regular pay phones. You can purchase the card from most hotels or from a post office.

To place a call to the United States, dial 1, the appropriate area code, and the seven-digit number, or use the phone card or one of the AT&T USA DIRECT phones, which are available at several locations including the airport departure lounge, the cruise terminal at St. John's, and the English Harbour Marina. To place an interisland call, dial the local seven-digit number.

In an emergency, you can make calls from Cable & Wireless (WI) Ltd. (42–44 St. Mary's St., St. John's, tel. 809/462–9840, and Nelson's Dockyard, English Harbour, tel. 809/463–1517).

Airmail letters to North America cost E.C.60¢; postcards, E.C.40¢. The post office is at the foot of High Street in St. John's.

Opening and Closing Times Although some stores still follow the tradition of closing for lunch, most shops, especially in season, are open Monday–Friday 8:30–4 and Saturday 8–noon or 8–3. Hours vary from bank to bank, but generally they are open Monday–Thursday 8–2 and Friday 8–4.

Exploring Antigua

Numbers in the margin correspond to points of interest on the Antigua (and Barbuda) map.

St. John's The capital city of **St. John's,** home to some 40,000 people (nearly half ❶ the island's population), lies at sea level at the inland end of a sheltered bay on the northwest coast of the island. The city has seen better days, but it is in the midst of a face-lift, and there are some notable historic sights, pleasant shopping areas, and good restaurants. Although much of the city looks shabby, it is definitely worth a visit. Most of the gift stores and restaurants are located near the waterfront. Up the hill is Antigua's downtown, with stores carrying major appliances, plumbing supplies, and other goods unlikely to be of interest to tourists.

All major hotels provide free maps and island brochures, or, if you happen to be in St. John's, stop in at the Tourist Bureau, at the corner of Long and Thames streets.

Cross Long Street and walk one block to Church Street. The **Museum of Antigua and Barbuda** is a "hands-on history" opportunity. Signs say Please Touch, with the hope of welcoming both citizens and visitors into Antigua's past. Try your hand at the educational video games. Exhibits interpret the history of the nation from its geological birth to political independence in 1981. There are fossil and coral remains from some 34 million years ago, a life-size Arawak house, models of a sugar plantation and a wattle-and-daub house, and a minishop with handicrafts, books, historical prints, and paintings. The colonial building that houses the museum is the former courthouse, which dates from 1750. *Church and Market Sts., tel. 809/463–1060 or 809/462–3946. Admission free. Open weekdays 8:30–4, Sat. 10–1.*

Walk two blocks east on Church Street to the **Anglican Cathedral of St. John the Divine.** At the south gate, there are figures of St. John the Baptist and St. John the Divine said to have been taken from one of Napoléon's ships and brought to Antigua. The original church was built in 1681, replaced by a stone building in 1745, and destroyed by an earthquake in 1843. The present building dates from 1845. With an eye to future earthquakes, the parishioners had the interior completely encased in pitch pine, hoping to forestall heavy damage. The church was elevated to the status of cathedral in 1848. *Between Long and Newcastle Sts., tel. 809/461–0082. Admission free.*

Recross Long Street, walk one block, and turn left on High Street. At the end of High Street, you'll see the **Cenotaph,** which honors Antiguans who lost their lives in World Wars I and II. Trek 7 blocks to the **Westerby Memorial,** which was erected in 1888 in memory of the Moravian bishop George Westerby.

One block south of the memorial is **Heritage Quay,** a new multimillion-dollar shopping complex that keeps expanding. Two-story buildings showcase stores specializing in duty-free goods, sportswear, T-shirts, imports from down-island (paintings, T-shirts, straw baskets), and local crafts, plus several restaurants and a casino. Cruise ship passengers disembark here from the 500-foot-long pier.

Redcliffe Quay, set at the water's edge just south of Heritage Quay, is the most appealing part of St. John's. Landscaped walks crisscross courtyards and lead between attractively restored buildings housing shops, restaurants, and boutiques. This is the shopping area favored by both residents and return guests. There are no duty-free shops here, but there are many other interesting shopping choices. There are also cafés where you can sit and ponder the scene of two centuries ago. On this site, slaves were held captive prior to being sold.

Time Out At **Hemingway's** (Jardine Court, tel. 809/462–2763), a historic clapboard house in the center of St. John's, you can sit on the upstairs veranda and drink local juices like papaya and mango or have breakfast and watch the bustling life of the streets below.

At the far south end of town, where Market Street forks into Valley Road and All Saints Road, a whole lot of haggling goes on every Friday and Saturday during the day, when locals jam the public **marketplace** to buy and sell fruits, vegetables, fish, and spices. Be sure to ask before you aim a camera; expect the subject of your shot to ask for a tip.

Antigua (and Barbuda)

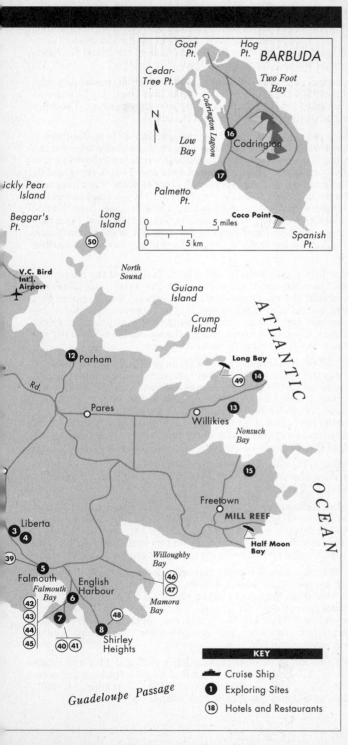

BARBUDA

Goat Pt.

Hog Pt.

Cedar-Tree Pt.

Two Foot Bay

N

Codrington Lagoon

Low Bay

16

Codrington

17

Palmetto Pt.

0 — 5 miles

0 — 5 km

Coco Point

Spanish Pt.

ickly Pear Island

Beggar's Pt.

Long Island

50

V.C. Bird Int'l. Airport

North Sound

Guiana Island

Crump Island

ATLANTIC

12 Parham

Rd.

Long Bay

49 14

Pares

Willikies

13

Nonsuch Bay

15

OCEAN

Freetown

MILL REEF

Liberta

3
4

Half Moon Bay

39

5

Falmouth

Falmouth Bay

English Harbour

Willoughby Bay

46

47

Mamora Bay

42

43

44

45

6

7

40 41

48

8

Shirley Heights

Guadeloupe Passage

KEY

🚢 Cruise Ship

❶ Exploring Sites

⑱ Hotels and Restaurants

Elsewhere on the Island After touring Fort James, divide the island into two more tours. First, you can take in English Harbour and Nelson's Dockyard on the south coast, returning to St. John's along the Caribbean (western) coast. Then travel to the eastern side of the island for sights ranging from historical churches to Devil's Bridge.

It's a good idea to wear a swimsuit under your clothes while you're sightseeing—one of the sights to strike your fancy may be an enticing secluded beach. Be sure to bring your camera along. There are some picture-perfect spots around the island.

Before you start, study your map for a minute or two. Road names are not posted, so you will need to have a sense of where you are heading if you hope to find it. The easiest way to get to anything is to see if a popular restaurant is near it, since easy-to-spot signs leading the way to restaurants are posted all over the island. (You'll see tons of them nailed to a post at every crossroad.) If you start to feel lost along the way, don't hesitate to ask anyone you see. Bear in mind that locals generally give directions in terms of landmarks that may not seem much like landmarks to you (turn left at the yellow house, or right at the big tree), so you will have to keep a close lookout for them.

Fort James Follow Fort Road northwest out of town, turn left at the Barrymore Hotel, turn left again when you reach the water, and follow the ❷ beach until the road ends (a total of 2 miles). You'll come to **Fort James,** named after King James II. The fort was constructed between 1704 and 1739 as a lookout point for the city and St. John's Harbour. The ramparts overlooking the small islands in the bay are in ruins, but 10 cannons still point out to sea.

English Harbour Take All Saints Road south out of St. John's (handmade signs point the way to English Harbour hotels and restaurants). Eight miles out ❸ of town—almost to the south coast—is **Liberta,** one of the first settlements founded by freed slaves. East of the village, on Monk's ❹ Hill, is the site of **Fort George,** built from 1689 to 1720. The fort wouldn't be of much help to anybody these days, but among the ruins you can make out the sites for its 32 cannons, its water cisterns, the base of the old flagstaff, and some of the original buildings.

❺ **Falmouth,** 1½ miles farther south, sits on a lovely bay backed by former sugar plantations and sugar mills. **St. Paul's Church** was rebuilt on the site of a church once used by troops during the Nelson period.

❻ **English Harbour** lies on the coast, just south of Falmouth. This is the most famous of Antigua's attractions. In 1671, the governor of the Leeward Islands wrote to the Council for Foreign Plantations in London pointing out the advantages of this land-locked harbor, and by 1704 English Harbour was in regular use as a garrisoned station.

In 1784, 26-year-old Horatio Nelson sailed in on HMS *Boreas* to serve as captain and second in command of the Leeward Island Station. Under his command was the captain of HMS *Pegasus*, Prince William Henry, duke of Clarence, who was to ascend the throne of England as William IV. The prince was Nelson's close friend and acted as best man when Nelson married the young widow Fannie Nisbet on Nevis in 1787.

The Royal Navy abandoned the station in 1889, and it fell into a state of decay. The Society of the Friends of English Harbour began restoring it in 1951, and on Dockyard Day, November 14, 1961, ❼ **Nelson's Dockyard** was opened with much fanfare.

Nelson's Dockyard is reminiscent, albeit on a much smaller scale, of Williamsburg, Virginia. Within the compound there are crafts shops, hotels, and restaurants. It is a hub for oceangoing yachts and serves as headquarters for the annual Sailing Week Regatta. A lively community of mariners keeps the area active in season. Beach lovers tend to stay elsewhere on the island, but visitors who enjoy history and who are part of (or like being around) the nautical scene often choose one of the hotels in the area of English Harbour.

The **Admiral's House Museum** has several rooms displaying ship models, a model of English Harbour, silver trophies, maps, prints, and Nelson's very own telescope and tea caddy. *English Harbour, tel. 809/463–1053 or 809/463–1379. Admission: $1.60. Open daily 8–6.*

On a ridge overlooking the dockyard is **Clarence House** (tel. 809/463–1026), built in 1787 and once the home of the duke of Clarence. Princess Margaret and Lord Snowdon spent part of their honeymoon here in 1960, and Queen Elizabeth and Prince Philip have dined here. It is now used by the governor-general as a country home; visits are possible when he is not in residence. The place is decorated pretty much as it was in the 18th century and is definitely worth a visit.

As you leave the dockyard, turn right at the crossroads and drive to **⑧** **Shirley Heights** for a spectacular view of English Harbour. The heights are named for Sir Thomas Shirley, the governor who fortified the harbor in 1787.

Not far from Shirley Heights is the **Dows Hill Interpretation Centre.** Observation platforms afford excellent views of the whole English Harbour area, but the highlight of the center is the multimedia presentation. Visitors sit in a darkened room and watch as different displays incorporating lifelike figures and colorful tableaux are illuminated. A commentary, synchronized TV displays, and music combine to give a cheery, if rather bland, portrait of the island's history and culture from Amerindian times to the present. *Admission: E.C.$15. Open daily 9–5.*

Time Out   Cool off with the yachting crowd on the terrace of the **Admiral's Inn** (English Harbour, tel. 809/463–1027), where the deeply tanned crews can keep an eye on their multimillion-dollar babies offshore—and on each other. The people-watching is first-rate, and so are the banana daiquiris (with or without Antiguan rum).

Drive back up to Liberta. Four and a half miles north of town, oppo-**⑨** site the Catholic church, turn left and head southwest on **Fig Tree Drive.** (Forget about plucking figs; *fig* is the Antiguan word for banana.) This drive takes you through the rain forest, which is rich in mangoes, pineapples, and banana trees. This is also the hilliest part of the island—**Boggy Peak,** to the west, is the highest point, rising to 1,319 feet. Fig Tree Drive runs into Old Road, which leads down **⑩** to **Curtain Bluff,** an unforgettable sight. On this peninsula, between Carlisle Bay and Morris Bay, the Atlantic Ocean meets the Caribbean Sea, resulting in wonderful color contrasts in the water.

From here, the main road sweeps along the southwest coast, where there are lovely beaches and spectacular views. The road then veers away from the water and goes through the villages of Bolans and Jennings.

⑪ From Jennings, a road turns right to the **Megaliths of Greencastle Hill,** an arduous climb away (you'll have to walk the last 500 yards).

Some say the megaliths were set up by humans for the worship of the sun and moon; others believe they are nothing more than unusual geological formations.

The East End St. John's is 6 miles northeast of Jennings. To explore the other half of the island, take Parham Road east out of St. John's. Drive 5½ miles and turn left on the side road that leads 1¼ miles to the settlement of **Parham. St. Peter's Church,** built in 1840 by Thomas Weekes, an English architect, is an octagonal Italianate building whose facade was once richly decorated with stucco, though it suffered considerable damage during the earthquake of 1843.

⑫

Backtrack and continue east on Parham Road for about ¾ mile, to a fork in the road. One branch veers to the right in a southeasterly direction toward Half Moon Bay, and the other continues toward the northeast coast. The latter route runs through the villages of Pares and Willikies to **Indian Town,** a national park, where archaeological digs have revealed evidence of Carib occupation.

⑬

⑭ Less than a mile farther along the coast is **Devil's Bridge,** a natural formation sculpted by the crashing breakers of the Atlantic at Indian Creek. This is now a national park. Amazing blowholes have been carved by the waves. They may seem hard to spot at first, but just wait until a wave bursts through!

Backtrack again to Parham Road and take the fork that runs southeast. You'll travel 9 miles to Half Moon Bay. Just before the coast are the village of **Freetown** and the **Mill Reef area,** where many pre-Columbian discoveries have been made.

⑮ **Harmony Hall,** northeast of Freetown, is an interesting art gallery. A sister to the Jamaican gallery near Ocho Rios, Harmony Hall is built on the foundation of a 17th-century sugar-plantation great house. Artist Graham Davis and Peter and Annabella Proudlock, who founded the Jamaican gallery, teamed up with local entrepreneur Geoffrey Pidduck to create an Antiguan art gallery specializing in high-quality West Indian art. A large gallery is used for one-man shows, and another exhibition hall displays watercolors. A small bar and an outside restaurant under the trees are open in season. *Brown's Mill Bay, tel. 809/463–2057. Open daily 10–6.*

Barbuda Twenty-six miles north of Antigua is Barbuda—a flat, 62-square-mile coral atoll with 17 miles of stunning pinkish white sand beaches. Almost all the island's 1,200 people live in **Codrington.** Barbuda's 8-mile **Coco Point Beach** lures beachcombers, and the island is ringed by wrecks and reef, which makes it a great draw for divers and snorkelers. Ornithologists and bird lovers come here, too. The Bird Sanctuary, a wide mangrove-filled lagoon, is home to an estimated 170 species of birds, including frigate birds with 8-foot wingspans.

⑯

⑰ The sole historic ruin here is **Martello Tower,** which is believed to have been a lighthouse built by the Spaniards before the English occupied the island. LIAT (*see* Before You Go, *above*) has regularly scheduled daily flights from Antigua to Barbuda (with departure times just right for day-trippers); air and boat charters are also available (contact the Department of Tourism). Those wishing to overnight here can choose from two superluxury resorts and several guest houses.

Beaches

All of Antigua's beaches are public, and many are dotted with resorts that provide water-sports-equipment rentals and a place to grab a cool drink. Sunbathing topless or in the buff is strictly illegal except on one of the small beaches at Hawksbill Beach Club, where allover tans are possible. Beware that on the one or two days a week that cruise ships dock in St. John's (check with your hotel for specific dates), buses drop off loads of cruise ship passengers on virtually all the west coast beaches. Choose this day to tour the island by car, visit one of the more remote east end beaches, or take a day trip to Barbuda, unless you are amused by watching hundreds of tourists laden with overstuffed beach bags and blaring radios frantically finding a sandy spot for a few hours of sun.

Antigua **Dickenson Bay** has a lengthy stretch of powder-soft white sand and exceptionally calm water. Here you'll find both small and large hotels, supercasual beach bars, beachfront restaurants, and several of the finest restaurants (Clouds, Coconut Grove) on Antigua. Watersports equipment can be rented at Halcyon Cove Beach Hotel.

The white sand of **Runaway Beach** is home to the Barrymore Beach Hotel and the Runaway Beach Hotel, so things can get crowded. Refresh yourself with hot dogs and beer at the Barrymore's Satay Hut.

Five Islands has four secluded beaches of fine tan sand and coral reefs for snorkeling, including a nudist beach. The Hawksbill Hotel is here.

Pigeon Point, which is very near English Harbour, is a fine whitesand beach with very calm water; there are several restaurants and bars nearby.

Johnson's Point is a deliciously deserted beach of bleached white sand on the southwest coast.

A large coconut grove adds to the tropical beauty of **Carlisle Bay** and the two long snow-white beaches over which the estimable Curtain Bluff resort sits. Standing on the bluff of this peninsula, you can see the almost-blinding blue waters of the Atlantic Ocean drifting into the Caribbean Sea.

Half Moon Bay is a ¾-mile crescent of sand, a prime area for snorkeling and windsurfing. It is on the Atlantic side of the island and can be quite rough at times.

Long Bay, on the far eastern coast, has coral reefs in water so shallow that you can actually walk out to them. Here is a lovely beach, as well as the Long Bay Hotel and the rambling Pineapple Beach Club.

Barbuda **Coco Point,** on Barbuda, is an uncrowded 8-mile stretch of white sand. Barbuda is great for scuba diving, with dozens of shipwrecks off reefs that encircle the island.

Sports and the Outdoors

Almost all the resort hotels can come up with fins and masks, Windsurfers, Sunfish, glass-bottom boats, catamarans, and other water-related gear (*see* Lodging, *below*).

Bicycling Try **Sun Cycles** (tel. 809/461–0324) for short- or long-term leases.

Boating **Halcyon Cove Watersports** (tel. 809/462–0256), at Dickenson Bay, offers waterskiing and other water rides and rents small boats. **Shorty's** (tel. 809/462–6066), also at Dickenson Bay, has some of the best water sports on the island, accompanied by a somewhat hectic pace. They also have several glass-bottom-boat cruises daily. **Nicholson Yacht Charters** (tel. 800/662–6066) are the real professionals. A long-established island family, they can charter you anything from a 20-foot ketch to a giant schooner for $10,000 per week.

Fitness Center The **Benair Fitness Club** (Country Club Rd., Hodges Bay, tel. 809/462–1540) has fitness equipment, Jacuzzi, aerobic classes, and a juice bar. The **Lotus Health Centre** (Dickenson Bay, tel. 809/462–2231) offers spa treatments, including Swedish massage, foot reflexology, and various kinds of facials.

Golf There is an 18-hole course at **Cedar Valley Golf Club** (tel. 809/462–0161) and a 9-hole course at **Half Moon Bay Hotel** (tel. 809/460–4300).

Horseback Riding First-rate Texas quarter horses and former racehorses are found at the **St. James Stables,** attached to the St. James's Club (tel. 809/463–1430).

Sailing The **Antigua School of Sailing** (tel. 809/462–2026) offers short resort courses.

Scuba Diving With all the wrecks and reefs, there are lots of undersea sights to see. Contact **Dive Antigua** (tel. 809/462–0256) or **Aquanaut Dive Center** (Halcyon Cove Hotel, tel. 809/462–3483), which offers certification courses and day and night dives from three separate locations: the St. James's Club (tel. 809/460–5000), Galleon Beach Club (tel. 809/460–1024), and the Royal Antiguan (tel. 809/462–3733). Dive packages are offered by the **Runaway Beach Club** (tel. 809/462–2626). If you are in the English Harbour area, Captain A. G. Fincham, a British ex-merchant seaman and proprietor of **Dockyard Divers** (tel. 809/464–8591, fax 809/460–1179), one of the oldest established outfits on the island, offers diving and snorkeling trips, PADI (Professional Association of Diving Instructors) courses, and dive packages with accommodations.

Sea Excursions Join in the fun on a real pirate ship when you choose one of the *Jolly Roger* (tel. 809/462–2064) cruises, complete with "pirate" crew, limbo dancing, plank walking, and other pranks. *Paradise I* (tel. 809/462–4158) is a 45-foot Beneteau yacht that offers lunches or sunset cruises. The *Black Swan* (tel. 809/462–7245) is a 47-foot racing yacht that offers several different cruises including one to deserted beaches, one to English Harbour, and one to gaze at the sunset. *Titi 1* (tel. 809/460–1452) is a 34-foot motorboat powered with twin 300 Evinrudes that will take you to nearby islets, remote beaches, or out for specially tailored snorkeling trips. They're based in Falmouth Harbour, but they'll pick you up almost anywhere.

Tennis The **Temo Sports Complex** (Falmouth Bay, tel. 809/463–1781) has two floodlit tennis courts, three glass-backed squash courts, showers, a sports shop, and snack bars. There are also seven courts at the **St. James's Club** (tel. 809/460–5000); five are lighted for night play.

Waterskiing **Halcyon Cove Watersports** (tel. 809/462–0256), at Dickenson Bay, will take you waterskiing.

Windsurfing The **High Wind Centre** at the Lord Nelson Hotel is the spot for serious board sailors, run by expert Patrick Scales (tel. 809/462–3094). Rentals and instruction are also available at **Halcyon Cove Watersports** (tel. 809/462–0256), and most major hotels offer boardsailing equipment.

Spectator Sports For information about sports events, contact **Antigua Sports and Games** (tel. 809/462–1925).

Cricket Practically the only thing most Americans know about this game is that there's something called a sticky wicket. Here, as in Britain and all the West Indies, the game is a national passion. Youngsters play on makeshift pitches, which apparently are comparable to sandlots, and international matches are fought out in the stadium on Independence Avenue, St. John's.

Shopping

Antigua's duty-free shops are at Heritage Quay; they're the reason so many cruise ships call here. Bargains can be found in perfumes, liqueurs and liquor (including, of course, Antiguan rum), jewelry, china, and crystal. As for local items, look for straw hats, baskets, batik, pottery, and hand-printed cotton clothing.

Shopping **Redcliffe Quay,** on the waterfront at the south edge of St. John's, is
Areas by far the most appealing shopping area. Here several restaurants and over 30 boutiques, many with interesting one-of-a-kind items, are set around landscaped courtyards shaded by colorful trees. **Heritage Quay** (also in St. John's) has some 35 shops—including many that are duty-free—that cater primarily to the cruise ship crowd that docks almost at its doorstep. The main tourist shops in St. John's are along **St. Mary's, High,** and **Long streets.**

Good Buys It looks like, and is, a flower shop, but the **Flower Basket** (Nevis
Books and Street—on the left, keep going, it's really there; tel. 809/462–0411)
Magazines also has the latest U.S. magazines, newspapers, and best-selling paperback books. A "must" buy at the **Map Shop** (St. Mary's St., tel. 809/462–3993) for those interested in Antiguan life is the paperback *To Shoot Hard Labour* (The Life and Times of Samuel Smith, an Antiguan Workingman); it costs $12, but you won't regret spending. Also check out any of the books of Jamaica Kincaid, whose works on her native Antigua have won international, albeit controversial, acclaim.

China and **Specialty Shoppe** (St. Mary's St., tel. 809/462–1198), **The Scent Shop**
Crystal (High St., tel. 809/462–0303), and **Norma's Duty-Free Shop** (Heritage Quay Shopping Center and Halcyon Cove Hotel, tel. 809/462–0172) have wares that make impressive presents. **Little Switzerland** (Heritage Quay, tel. 809/462–3108) houses pricey buys in a luxurious, and air-conditioned, setting.

Clothing and **Base,** in Redcliffe Quay (tel. 809/462–0920), is the brainchild of En-
Fabrics glish designer Steven Giles, whose stripey cotton-and-Lycra beachwear is now all the rage on the island. Janie Easton designs many of the original finds in her two **Galley Boutiques** (the main shop in a historic building in English Harbour, tel. 809/462–1525; another at the upscale St. James's Club, tel. 809/463–1333) with pizzazz and reasonable prices. The **CoCo Shop** (St. Mary's St., tel. 809/462–1128) is a favorite source for Sea Island cotton designs, Daks clothing, and Liberty of London fabrics, along with the shop's own designs for the country-club set. **Karibbean Kids of Antigua** (Redcliffe Quay, tel. 809/462–4566) has great gifts and clothing for youngsters. **A Thousand Flowers** (Redcliffe Quay, tel. 809/462–4264) sells resortwear made of comfortable silks, linens, and batiks from all over the world and has many unusual items.

Jewelry Hans Smit is **The Goldsmitty** (Redcliffe Quay, tel. 809/462–4601), a European-trained expert goldsmith who turns gold, black coral, and precious and semiprecious stones into one-of-a-kind works of art that adorn the wrists and necks of the rich and famous. (Be aware that environmental groups discourage tourists from purchasing corals that are designated as endangered species because the reefs are often harvested carelessly.) **Colombian Emeralds** (Heritage Quay, tel. 809/462–2086) is the largest retailer of Colombian emeralds in the world. Jewelry bargains are also at **Norma's Duty-Free Shop** (Heritage Quay Shopping Center and the Halcyon Cove Hotel, tel. 809/462–0172).

Liquor and Liqueurs **The Warehouse** (St. Mary's St., tel. 809/462–0495) and **Manuel Diaz Liquor Store** (Long and Market Sts., tel. 809/462–0440) should whet your appetite. Cuban cigars are found at **The Cigar Shop** (Heritage Quay, tel. 890/462–2677) but can't be brought legally back to the United States.

Local Art and Crafts Trinidadian Natalie White sells her sculptured cushions and wall hangings, all hand-painted on silk and signed, from her home-studio (tel. 809/463–2519) and from her **Craft Originals Studio** on the Coast Road. Artist-filmmaker Nick Maley and his wife, Gloria, have turned the **Island Arts Galleries** (three locations: their home-studio, Alton Place, on Sandy Lane, behind the Hodges Bay Club, tel. 809/461–3332; Heritage Quay, tel. 809/462–2787; and the St. James's Club, tel. 809/460–5000). into a melting pot for Caribbean artists, with prices ranging from $10 to $15,000. **Harmony Hall** (at Brown's Bay Mill, near Freetown, tel. 809/460–4120) is the Antiguan sister to the original Jamaica location. In addition to "Annabella Boxes," books, and cards, there are pottery and ceramic pieces, carved wooden fantasy birds, and an ever-changing roster of exhibits.

Perfume Try the **CoCo Shop** (St. Mary's St., tel. 809/462–1128) and **The Scent Shop** (High St., tel. 809/462–0303) in downtown St. John's. In Heritage Quay, two shops, **La Parfumerie** (tel. 809/462–2601) and **Little Switzerland** (tel. 809/462–3108), have extensive selections of European scents for men and women.

Dining

Antigua has a wide variety of restaurants, and you can find excellent food whether you feel like dressing up or dressing down. There are elegant Continental and French restaurants, casual waterfront bistros, and barefoot beach bars. It's impossible not to find fresh seafood on the menu, and virtually every chef incorporates local ingredients and elements of West Indian and Creole cuisine. Because of the island's British heritage, Antiguans tend to dress more formally for dinner than is the custom on many of the other Caribbean islands. A few places, which will be noted, require a jacket.

Most prices on menus are listed in E.C. dollars; some are listed in both E.C. and U.S. dollars. Be sure to ask if credit cards are accepted and in which currency the prices are quoted. Prices below are in U.S. dollars. Dinner reservations are needed during high season.

Highly recommended restaurants are indicated by a star ★.

Category	Cost*
Very Expensive	over $45
Expensive	$25–$45
Moderate	$15–$25
Inexpensive	under $15

*per person, excluding drinks, service, and 7% sales tax

Jumby Bay. This exclusive, 300-acre, private island resort, just a 10-minute launch ride from Antigua's shores, accepts a limited number of outside guests for lunch or dinner when advance reservations are made. For a set price of $55 (plus 10% government service tax), guests board the noon boat for a nonstop buffet at the resort. The management will also give an informal tour of their special island on request. A dinner reservation means catching the 6 or 7 PM launch and, for $85, a choice of five entrées. Although the menu changes nightly, a few of the favored dishes are sautéed breast of chicken filled with wild mushrooms, Mediterranean seafood terrine sprinkled with saffron, and soufflé of scallops with basil puree. *Long Island, tel. 809/ 462–6000. No outside dinner reservations Wed. or Sun. nights. AE, MC, V. Very Expensive.*

Alberto's. Set above Willoughby Bay on Antigua's southeast side, this Italian restaurant is a bit out of the way but popular nevertheless. Specialties here include local seafood prepared with an Italian accent. Try fresh island lobster, cockles Alberto, the chef's creation of the evening, or more traditional dishes such as eggplant parmigiana, veal pizzaiola, or linguini with clams. Tables line a balcony open to the breezes and hung with bougainvillea. *Willoughby Bay, tel. 809/460–3007 or via VHF 68. Reservations required. AE, MC, V. Closed Mon. and July–Nov. Dinner only. Expensive.*

Cacubi Room. This restaurant used to be known as "the" place to go on Antigua, but unfortunately it has not kept up with its reputation. It still has a romantic candlelight setting and the menu describes a mouthwatering array of choices, but the food is disappointingly ordinary and the service uneven at best. *Blue Waters Hotel, Boon Pt., tel. 809/462–0290. AE, MC, V. Expensive.*

★ **Coconut Grove.** There are few more pleasant places to eat in Antigua than this open-air restaurant with coconut palms growing up through the roof and waves lapping the white coral sand a few feet away. For a stunningly romantic evening, head here when there's a full moon and reserve table #1, closest to the water and under the stars. The menu always includes freshly grilled local lobster, choices of other fresh fish, plus lamb, steak, a vegetarian dish, and an excellent marinated and grilled chicken breast. For starters, the chilled gazpacho is a house specialty. *Siboney Beach Club, Dickenson Bay, tel. 809/462–1538, fax 809/461–4555. Reservations suggested in peak season. MC, V. Expensive.*

★ **Colombo's.** This is the best Italian restaurant in Antigua and one of the best in the Caribbean. A blackboard lists the remarkable assortment of items available each day: a large variety of pasta, fresh local seafood, veal, chicken, and beef. Come here for exquisitely thin carpaccio, spaghetti Bolognese, freshly grilled lobster or lobster Mornay, or veal scallopine. At lunchtime there are also light salads, hamburgers, and sandwiches. The Sardinians who run this restaurant make every effort to please. This open-air restaurant is on a small bay in English Harbour, with views of palm trees, historic cannons, and the water. On Wednesday nights a reggae band entertains. *Galleon Beach Club, English Harbour, tel. 809/460–1452. Reservations suggested. AE, MC, V. Expensive.*

La Perouche. The chef here trained at the Culinary Institute of America and did a stint at L'Esperance in France before turning La Perouche into one of the best restaurants on the island. Among the feats of culinary magic he performs nightly is the *escalar,* a rare deep-sea fish from Ecuador with a mild, slightly lemony taste, served in a polenta and lobster bordelaise sauce. An avocado mousse with sweet potato wafers arranged like petals around the wooden serving bowl is typical of the restaurant's determination to please the eye as well as the taste buds. The fruit plate—rock-fig bananas, black pineapple, fresh kidney mango, and passion fruit arranged around a hub of Antiguan golden apple—is a work of art. The plant-filled patio itself is a pleasure, with pretty green-and-white trim, crystal glasses, and a profusion of painted wooden parrots that hang everywhere—hence, the restaurant's name. *English Harbour, tel. 809/460–3040. Dinner only. AE, MC, V. Closed Sun. and Sept. Expensive.*

★ **Redcliffe Tavern.** Located on the second floor of a beautifully restored colonial warehouse set amid the courtyards of Redcliffe Quay, this appealing restaurant has a dinner menu that is part Northern Italian, part Continental, and all fresh. Come here for delicious pastas, marinated grilled chicken, and fresh local lobster. The lunch menu also includes salads, sandwiches, and hamburgers, and one can choose to eat inside or on the treetop-level terrace. The brick and stone walls are decorated with antique water-pumping equipment still bearing the original maker's crests from England. Salvaged from all over the island, these beautiful old machines, with their flywheels and pistons, have been imaginatively integrated into the restaurant's structure (one supports the buffet bar, for instance). *Redcliffe Quay, St. John's, tel. 809/461–4557. AE, MC, V. Moderate–Expensive.*

The Wardroom Restaurant. On the ground floor of the beautifully restored Copper and Lumber Store, around a charming central courtyard hung with bougainvillea, this restaurant, with its massive brick walls, stained beams, and views of the floodlit battlements of English Harbour, breathes the atmosphere of Olde England in the Caribbean. The menu is international, mixing dishes like West African peanut soup with lobster in puff pastry, a good selection of local fish dishes, and even lamb cutlets. *Nelson's Dockyard, tel. 809/460–1058. Reservations advised. Closed Wed. Moderate–Expensive.*

Wari Pier. Perched on stilts above the sea, this restaurant is reached by a walkway extending from the beach at Dickenson Bay. The lunch menu is served from noon to 6:00, and dinner is served from 6:00 until midnight. The selection of appetizers for both meals includes Caesar salad, lobster bisque, shrimp cocktail, and a tropical fruit platter. For lunch, choose from the selection of hamburgers and sandwiches, or have the popular Ocean Pasta—linguine topped with a seafood medley in white wine sauce. For dinner, try the rack of lamb with rosemary, grilled Antiguan lobster, or Chateaubriand for two. The most irresistible desserts are the Tradewinds Treat, a banana baked in rum sauce with vanilla ice cream, and the American Dream, homemade key lime pie with strawberry coulis. While you're on the walkway, be sure to look into the water—it's filled with schools of colorful fish. *Halcyon Cove Beach Resort, tel. 809/462–0256. AE, MC, V. Moderate–Expensive.*

Admiral's Inn. Known as the Ad to yachtsmen around the world, this historic inn, in the heart of English Harbour, is a must for Anglophiles and mariners. At the bar inside, you can sit and soak up the centuries under dark, timbered wood (the bar top even has the names of sailors from Nelson's fleet carved into it), but most guests tend to sit on the terrace under shady Australian pines to enjoy the splendid views of the harbor complex and Clarence House opposite. Specialties include curried conch, fresh snapper with equally fresh limes, and lobster thermidor. The pumpkin soup is not to be missed. *Nelson's Dockyard, tel. 809/460–1027. Reservations required. AE, MC, V. Moderate.*

Lemon Tree. This air-conditioned, art-deco restaurant, on the second floor of a historic building in the old part of St. John's, is a smart, upbeat eating place, popular with cruise ship guests. Live music is offered every night, varying from soft classical piano to funky reggae. The menu is eclectic, mixing minipizzas and ribs with beef Wellington, Cornish hen, lobster, vegetarian crepes, very spicy Cajun garlic shrimp, and pasta dishes. For those who like Mexican food, the Lemon Tree offers unbeatable burritos, as well as chili, nachos, and fajitas. *Long and Church Sts., St. John's, tel. 809/462–1969. AE, DC, MC, V. Open 10 AM–11 PM. Moderate.*

Lobster Pot. This beachfront restaurant has a fishing boat in the center of its large flagstone dining room and is open to the sea breeze (the best seats are in the gallery right on the water). The long (seven pages!) and diverse menu is a mix of fresh seafood, pasta, and Creole- and Caribbean-style dishes. Starters include lobster and pineapple in a spicy West Indian sauce and grilled baby eggplant stuffed with cheese and herbs. Entrées include coconut-milk curry; baked breast of chicken stuffed with goat cheese, broccoli, and sun-dried tomatoes; and good local seafood (lobster, mahimahi, and red snapper). *Runaway Bay, tel. 809/462–2856. Reservations advised. D, MC, V. Moderate.*

Shirley Heights Lookout. This restaurant is set in an 18th-century fortification high on a bluff, with a breathtaking view of English Harbour below. The first-floor pub opens onto the lookout point. Upstairs, there's a cozy, windowed room with hardwood floors and beamed ceilings. Pub offerings include burgers, sandwiches, and barbecue, while the upstairs room serves the likes of pumpkin soup and lobster in lime sauce. If you like to be at the center of things, come here on Sunday around 3 PM, when locals, yachters, and visitors troop up the hill for the barbecue. Livened by steel-band and reggae music, it lasts well into the evening. *Shirley Heights, tel. 809/463–1785. Reservations required in season in the dining room. AE, MC, V. Moderate.*

Calypso. This cheerful outdoor spot is a favorite with the St. John's professional set. At lunchtime it is packed with smartly dressed lawyers and government functionaries smoking cigars and chatting over traditional Caribbean food. Tables are arranged under green umbrellas on a sunny patio dominated by the remains of a brick kiln. Specials change every day but generally include stewed lamb, grilled lobster, and baked chicken served with *fungi,* a pastelike vegetable dish made of cornmeal and okra, rice, and dumplings. *Redcliffe St., St. John's, tel. 809/462–1965. No credit cards. Inexpensive–Moderate.*

★ **Big Banana-Pizzas on the Quay.** This tiny, often crowded spot is tucked into one side of a beautifully restored warehouse with broad plank floors and stonework archways. Here you'll find some of the best pizza on the island, topped with traditional and not-so-traditional items. It's a busy lunch and dinner spot, and there is live entertainment some evenings. *Redcliffe Quay, St. John's, tel. 809/462–2621. AE, MC, V. Inexpensive.*

Brother B's. It's impossible to miss this funky restaurant in the appropriately named Soul Alley, with its yellow-painted wooden fence and hand-painted boards advertising its fare. If you want to try such local specialties as pepper pot and *fungi; pelleau,* a seasoned rice dish with chicken, meat, and peas; saltfish and *ducana;* or bull's foot soup, a Caribbean variant of a 19th-century dish from Manchester, England, this is the place to do it. *Soul Alley, St. John's, tel. 809/462–0616. Also open for breakfast. No credit cards. Inexpensive.*

Lodging

Scattered along Antigua's fine sandy beaches and tropical hillsides are resorts of all kinds, from exclusive, elegant hideaways and romantic restored inns to casual go-barefoot-everywhere places and all-inclusive hot spots for couples. Pick a spot near St. John's—anywhere between Dickenson Bay and Five Islands Harbour—if you want to be close to restaurants and shopping or want lots of action. If you stay right on Dickenson Bay you can easily walk to quite a few restaurants, beach bars, and resorts. English Harbour, though far from St. John's, has the best collection of inns, several excellent restaurants, and is the hangout for the yachting crowd. The resorts scattered elsewhere on the island tend to cater more to guests who want to stay put or are seeking seclusion. The price categories below reflect the room cost during high season.

Highly recommended lodgings are indicated by a star ★.

Category	Cost*
Very Expensive	over $350
Expensive	$250–$350
Moderate	$150–$250
Inexpensive	under $150

All prices are for a standard double room for two, excluding 7% tax and 10% service charge.

★ **Curtain Bluff.** Curtain Bluff is in a league of its own and deserves all the praise it has received through the years. The hotel could be called Howard Hulford's Dream, after the man who built it over 30 years ago on a spectacular bluff bordered on one side by the wild Atlantic Ocean and on the other by the calm Caribbean. Most rooms are in the two-story beachfront buildings and have terraces or balconies. The suites zigzag their way up the bluff on the Atlantic side and are arguably the finest accommodations on Antigua—huge split-level apartments with two large balconies offering spectacular views, a large, tastefully decorated living room, and, up a flight of steps, a spacious and inviting bedroom. Meals, served in an open-air restaurant surrounded by greenery, are prepared by a Swiss chef and served by an army of waiters who are ready to please. Jacket and tie are required for dinner, except on Wednesday and Sunday. For those who want exceptional service and comfort, Curtain Bluff is worth every penny. *Box 288, St. John's, tel. 809/462–8400; in NY, 212/289–8888; fax 809/462–8409. 61 rooms and suites. Facilities: 2 restaurants, lounge, 4 tennis courts, squash court, fitness center, pro shop, croquet, putting green, water-sports center. AE. Closed mid-May–mid-Oct. All-inclusive. Very Expensive.*

★ **Jumby Bay.** Just five minutes by taxi and another 10 minutes by launch from Antigua is this exclusive, 300-acre, private island retreat. Spanish-style white stucco buildings with orange tile roofs line the beach. Rooms are in the two-story Pond Bay House and in individual rondavels (circular bungalows) and cottages spread around the property. All are spacious, and even those not labeled suites have separate sitting areas. Some bathrooms open out to small areas filled tropical greenery. For an extra $600 per day, you can rent an expansive and well-furnished two-bedroom villa with a kitchen/dining room and a small swimming pool that's shared with several other villas. Lunch is an alfresco buffet, while the more elegant and formal dinner is in the old manor house's dining room, which is open to the ocean breezes. There are lots of walking trails. Everything is spread out, so if you hate to walk or bicycle, you might want to stay elsewhere. No children under age eight are permitted during high season. There is occasional jet noise from the nearby airport, a small price to price for such a delightful retreat. *Box 243, St. John's, tel. 809/462–6000 or 800/421–9016, fax 809/462–6020. 38 suites, 18 villas. Facilities: 2 restaurants, 3 bars, tennis, bicycles, sailboats, croquet, water-sports center. AE, MC, V. All-inclusive (including liquor and wine). Very Expensive.*

St. James's Club. This out-of-the-way hotel is on the 100-acre spit of land that helps form Mamora Bay. Rooms and one-bedroom suites are in the main buildings at the water's edge on the tip of the peninsula. Units are beautifully furnished and painted in pastel colors, a refreshing change from the typical white Caribbean hotel room. Some have romantic canopy beds. You enter past the "villa village," a group of tightly clustered two-bedroom villas that rest on the top of the hills that spill down toward the main hotel. Although nicely decorated, they include views of your neighbor's roof. You can dine at the three restaurants in the main building: the Rainbow Garden, an elegant spot for dinner; the Docksider Cafe, with an elegant menu but casual al fresco setting; or the Poolside Reef Deck, a breakfast and lunch spot. Also part of the Club is the Italian Piccolo Mondo, but the food there could be better. Overall, the St. James tends to live off its *renommé* (it is affiliated with other like-named resorts in London, Paris, and Los Angeles), rather than what it delivers. That said, the beaches and sports facilities—snorkeling on the nearby Mamora Reef, a good tennis program (Martina Navratilova is their roving tennis pro, but don't expect to see her), stable of horses, fitness center, and children's playground—plus such amenities as a hotel helicopter that can be chartered for sightseeing, make this a fine, full-service resort. *Box 63, St. John's, tel. 809/460–5000 or 800/274–0008, fax 809/460–3015. 178 total accommodations. Facilities: 3 restaurants, 5 bars, 24-hour room service; 3 swimming pools, Jacuzzi, minigym, 4 boutiques, beauty salon and masseuse, nightclub, casino, 7 tennis courts (5 hard, 2 omniturf; 5 lighted), water sports and scuba diving, lawn croquet, children's playground, golf privileges at the 18-hole Cedar Valley Golf Club, horseback riding. AE, MC, V. EP, MAP. Very Expensive.*

Galley Bay. Set between what is virtually a private curving beach of white sand and a blue lagoon, this established hotel is an all-inclusive quiet retreat. Beachfront villas have king-size beds, ceiling fans, showers, tiled floors, and tropical-print coverlets and drapes. Ten designated "executive rooms" are on the quietest section of the beach and offer slightly more space and a private patio with a hammock to swing in. Units in Gauguin Village consist of two round thatch-roof Tahitian-style rooms linked by a patio. One room is for sleeping, the other is the bathroom with a shower for two and a dressing table. These cottages are cutesy romantic to some and confining huts to others. *Box 305, St. John's, tel. 809/462–0302 or 800/223–6510, fax 809/462–4551. 30 rooms. Facilities: restaurant, bar, tennis court, water-sports center. AE, MC, V. All-inclusive. Expensive–Very Expensive.*

Pineapple Beach Club (formerly the New Horizons). A broad stone walk leads directly from the reception area to the beach of this bustling, beachside, all-inclusive resort. There are no phones or TVs in rooms, but fax and phone service is available at the front desk. The most comfortable rooms are the larger air-conditioned ones on the beach and on a hill overlooking it. All rooms are on or very near the beach, some with partial ocean or garden views. This is an activity-oriented place with a full array of water sports, nightly entertainment, and an electronic casino, but it does quiet down soon after midnight. Be sure to bring the letter confirming your reservation; sometimes the hotel overbooks and reservation information is lost. *Box 54, St. John's, tel. 809/463–2006 or 800/345–0356; in Canada, 800/468–0023; fax 809/465–2452. 125 rooms. Facilities: restaurant, bar, pool, 4 tennis courts, kayaking, volleyball, horseshoes, croquet. AE, MC, V. All-inclusive. Expensive–Very Expensive.*

Blue Waters Beach Hotel. Although Blue Waters has drawn rave reviews in the past, both the charm and level of service of the resort have unfortunately faded with time. Its setting on Antigua's northwest tip is stunning, with views across beautifully manicured tropical gardens to the sea, but the buildings are ordinary, the beach is small and not particularly good for swimming, and the service is mediocre at best. Accommodations are in several long, two-story buildings strung out above the beach (stairways at several locations lead to the beach below). Rooms are air-conditioned, decorated with rattan and pastel prints, have sliding doors that open onto a small patio or balcony (within easy earshot of your neighbors right and left), and nice ocean views. There are also several two- and three-bedroom villas. Breakfast is a haphazard affair, but lunch on the terrace is delightful, and there is nightly dancing under the stars. The hotel has a variety of meal plans, and it is important that you fully understand them and agree to one when you check in. You might prefer EP, as there are excellent restaurants a short cab ride away. *Box 256, St. John's (Boon Pt.), tel. 809/462–0290 or 800/372–1323; in the United Kingdom, 081/367–5175; fax 809/462–0293. 67 rooms. Facilities: 2 restaurants, 2 bars, pool, 1 lighted tennis court, gift shop, water-sports center. AE, MC, V. EP, MAP. Expensive.*

Dickenson Bay Cottages. This small, pleasant development on Marble Hill, just above Dickenson Bay, opened in 1992. The rooms, in two-story, villa-style buildings surrounded by gardens, are elegantly furnished with high-quality painted rattan and soft pastel fabrics. Downstairs is a large living-room area and well-equipped kitchen. The bedroom and bathroom are up a flight of stairs in a galleried area. Larger units have two bedrooms upstairs and a large veranda overlooking the ocean. One annoying feature is the lack of a cross breeze, which pretty much obliges you to keep the air conditioner on. There are beach privileges at the excellent but busy beach at Halcyon Cove Beach Resort, just a five-minute walk away, and the resort has an arrangement for the use of the tennis and water-sports facilities there at a 20% discount. Several other resorts nearby give you a selection of lively entertainment and eating as well as secluded hillside tranquillity. *Box 1379, St. John's, tel. 809/462–4940, fax 809/462–4941. 13 rooms. Facilities: pool, cable TV, room service, telephone with direct U.S. dial. AE, MC, V. EP. Expensive.*

Hawksbill Beach Hotel. Named after the spectacular rock that juts out of the bay south of St. John's, this beachfront resort sprawls over 37 acres of the bucolic Five Islands peninsula. It boasts four beaches of fine tan sand—one of which permits sunbathing in the buff. The main building, reception area, and dining room are on a small bluff that commands a sweeping view of the sea and Montserrat beyond, set off by the restored ruins of a sugar mill in the foreground. The classiest accommodations aren't the cottage guest rooms but the three-bedroom West Indian Great House, an old, colonial-style building with king-size beds, tile floors, wicker furniture, and kitchenette. Deluxe rooms are in gingerbread-trimmed, West Indian–style cottages surrounded by grass lawns and facing the sea. The less expensive rooms are in cottages with garden views. Bedrooms, even in the deluxe category, are quite small, but guests here spend most of their time outside. Gentlemen are requested not to wear short sleeves into the dining room after 7 PM. And though children are more welcome than they used to be ("screamers" not included), Hawksbill is more a place for young couples and singles. Breakfast and the use of most water-sports facilities are complimentary. *Box 108, St. John's, tel. 809/462–0301 or 800/223–6510; in Canada, 416/622–8813; fax 809/462–1515. 90 rooms. Facilities: 2 restaurants, 2 bars, pool, tennis court, boutique, water-sports center. AE, DC, MC, V. BP. Expensive.*

Halcyon Cove Beach Resort. Set on beautiful Dickenson Bay, this busy large hotel attracts a great number of discount tour groups from Europe and the United States—so it's typically crowded and your neighbor may be paying a third of what you are. Adequately furnished accommodations, all with air-conditioning and private balcony or patio, are in two- and three-story, flat-roofed buildings scattered around the courtyard pool or along the beach. A water-sports center offers excursions on a glass-bottom boat and waterskiing in addition to the other usual water sports at the very busy beach. There are three restaurants, including the Wari Pier, set on stilts over the ocean and serving excellent fare all day long. *Box 251, St. John's, tel. 809/462–0256, fax 809/462–0271. 129 rooms, 16 1-bedroom suites. Facilities: 4 restaurants, 3 bars, room service, pool, 4 lighted tennis courts, boutiques, water-sports center. AE, DC, MC, V. EP, MAP. Expensive.*

Hodges Bay Club. Close to the airport, and about 10 minutes by cab from St. John's, this newly renovated condominium property is on a great snorkeling beach on the prestigious north shore facing Prickley Pear Island. Connected one- and two-bedroom villas line the beach or overlook the pool. All are spacious, comfortably decorated, and have fully equipped kitchens, king-size beds, balconies, and daily maid service. All are air-conditioned and have ceiling fans, and each bedroom has a private bath. A golf course is five minutes away. The on-site restaurant, The Pelican Club, is considered one of the best on the island. *Box 1237, St. John's, tel. 809/462–2300 or 800/432–4229; in NY, 212/535–9530; fax 809/462–1962. 4 1-bedroom villas, 22 2-bedroom villas. Facilities: restaurant, pool, 2 tennis courts, water-sports center. AE, DC, MC, V. EP. Expensive.*

The Inn at English Harbour. The reception area, bar and dining room, and six of the guest rooms of this inn sit atop a hill with stunning views of English Harbour. The bar, with its green leather chairs, wooden floors, and maritime prints, is one of the most pleasant on the island. Off to the side of the main house are the hilltop rooms, housed in individual, cottage-style units. Just down the steep hill, right on the beach, are 22 additional rooms in two-story wooden buildings surrounded by hibiscus and bougainvillea. The superior rooms are slightly larger, but all rooms have phones, wall safes, refrigerators, and hair dryers and are attractively furnished with wicker furniture and pastel fabrics. Also on the beach is a second bar-restaurant that stays open until 6 PM. A shuttle bus runs guests up and down the hill. The beach, like all those in English Harbour, is not the best. During high season only MAP bookings are accepted. *Box 187, St. John's, tel. 809/460–1014, fax 809/460–1603. 28 rooms. Facilities: 2 restaurants, 2 bars, water sports. AE, MC, V. EP, MAP. Moderate–Expensive.*

Ramada Renaissance Royal Antiguan Resort. This nine-story, high-rise hotel, possibly the island's ugliest, is set on the waterside a few miles south of St. John's. The hotel caters to groups and conventions and is by far the most "stateside-like" hotel on Antigua. Rooms and suites are air-conditioned, with minibars and TVs, and there are numerous facilities: three restaurants, three bars, a huge ballroom used for meetings and cocktail parties, and a 5,500-square-foot casino with blackjack, roulette, craps, baccarat, and 130 slot machines, all played by Atlantic City rules. *Deep Bay, St. John's, tel. 809/462–3733 or 800/228–9898, fax 809/462–3732. 300 rooms. Facilities: 3 restaurants, 4 bars, casino, swimming pool with swim-up bar, full water sports (snorkeling, Sunfish sailing, windsurfing, waterskiing, fishing), a certified dive master, 5 tennis courts, golf arranged at nearby 18-hole Cedar Valley course, a minicrafts market on site. AE, D, MC, V. EP. Moderate–Expensive.*

★ **Sandals.** This all-inclusive, couples-only resort is hopping day and night. Pool olympics and beach volleyball, aerobics sessions, and evening social events, including all kinds of group games, are organized by a social hostess who will veritably scowl if you don't join in the fun; but you can still enjoy the place if you just want to read and relax (assuming, of course, that you can read and relax in the midst of cacophony). Everything, from the tennis coaching to the pedal boats, the scuba diving to the swim-up pool-bars, discos, and meals, is included in the price. For a little extra, you can even get married in front of a miniature waterfall. Rooms, facing the beach or the garden, and rondavels facing the beach are spacious. Food is served in three restaurants offering Continental, West Indian, and Oriental fare. All it lacks is true island atmosphere. *Box 147, St. John's, tel. 809/462–0267, fax 809/462–4135; U.S. reservations, tel. 800/SANDALS. Facilities: 3 restaurants, 4 bars, 4 pools, 4 Jacuzzis, health spa, 4 tennis courts, and water sports. AE. All-inclusive. Moderate–Expensive.*

★ **Siboney Beach Club.** When Tony Johnson arrived in Antigua in the late '50s, he planned to stay just a few weeks. Instead, he ended up building or refurbishing some of the island's finest resorts, and eventually opened his own small gem set in an exquisite tropical garden on Dickenson Bay. Each suite has a small bedroom, a cleverly designed Pullman kitchen, a modestly furnished living room, and a plant-filled patio or balcony that looks out to tropical greenery. Some units are air-conditioned. Those that are not have louvers that do not fully close and, although the hotel supplies mosquito coils, you might want to bring along bug repellent. A few yards away is an excellent, although often busy, calm-water beach and one of the best restaurants on the island, The Coconut Grove (*see* Dining, *above*). Here, guests can enjoy great breakfasts and lunches as well as candlelight dinners at the water's edge. The staff is exceptionally friendly. *Box 222, St. John's, tel. 809/462–0806 or 800/533–0234, fax 809/462–0806. 12 suites. Facilities: restaurant, bar, pool. AE, MC, V. EP, MAP. Moderate–Expensive.*

Trade Winds Hotel. This German-run resort, on the crest of Marble Hill, has spectacular views of Dickenson Bay and the ocean beyond, including views of Montserrat. The beach is close to a mile away, but there are Jeeps to take you back and forth. Apartments are in attractive Spanish-style villas, built along the edge of the hillside. Every unit has a full kitchen, living area, and private terrace overlooking the ocean. Studios have foldaway beds, and suites have separate bedrooms. Furniture is lacquered bamboo, and there are art posters on the wall. On site is a fine French restaurant and a piano bar. *Box 1390, St. John's, tel. 809/462–1223, fax 809/462–5007. 30 rooms. Facilities: restaurant, bar, pool, cable TV, room service. AE, MC, V. EP. Moderate–Expensive.*

★ **Copper and Lumber Store Hotel.** Overlooking the marina at English Harbour, this former supply store for Nelson's Caribbean fleet and

fine example of Georgian British architecture has been beautifully
transformed into a gracious inn. The warm brick, hardwood floors,
timbered ceilings, and burgundy leather, button armchairs and
sofas give it an Old World charm unique in the West Indies. Each of
the 14 suites is meticulously decorated with authentic Georgian period furnishings, including antique washstands, secretaries, and
four-poster canopy beds. All suites have showers, and although they
lack air-conditioning, ceiling fans capture nice breezes. A ferry
service shuttles guests to a beach on the other side of English Harbour. Be warned that the hotel sits inside a national park and visitors stream through the area during the day. *Box 184, St. John's,
tel. 809/460–1058, fax 809/460–1529. 14 suites. Facilities: 2 restaurants, pub. AE, MC, V. EP, MAP. Moderate.*

Yepton Beach Resort. This Swiss-designed, full-service, all-suites
resort is set on Hog John Bay on the Five Islands peninsula, not far
from St. John's. The Mediterranean-style white-stucco buildings
are situated so that accommodations have views on one side of the
resort's own attractive beach and on the other side of a lagoon dotted
with pelicans and egrets. Some of the rooms are two-room suites,
with a bedroom and large living-room-cum-kitchenette. Others are
studios, with a folding Murphy bed and kitchenette. By putting together a double bedroom and a studio, one can also make an apartment that sleeps four. All rooms are air-conditioned. Live reggae,
calypso, and jazz groups appear three nights a week. Many different
packages are available. *Box 1427, St. John's, tel. 809/462–2520 or
800/361–4621. Facilities: restaurant, 2 tennis courts, pool, Sunfish
sailing, and snorkeling. AE, MC, V. EP, MAP. Moderate.*

★ **Admiral's Inn.** This lovingly restored 18th-century Georgian inn is
the centerpiece of the magnificent Nelson's Dockyard complex.
Once the engineers' office and warehouse (the bricks were originally
used as ballast for British ships), the Admiral's Inn reverberates
with history. The best rooms, upstairs in the main building, have
the original timbered ceilings, complete with iron braces, and massive whitewashed brick walls. Straw floor mats from Dominica and
views through wispy Australian pines to the sunny harbor beyond
complete the effect. The rooms in the garden annex are smaller and a
bit airless. The Loft, which used to be the dockyard's joinery, has
two big bedrooms, an enormous kitchen, and a magnificent view
from the timbered living room onto the busy harbor. Be aware that
this inn sits smack in the middle of a bustling daytime tourist attraction. *Box 713, St. John's, tel. 809/460–1027 or 800/223–5695; in NY,
914/833–3303; in Canada, 416/447–2335; fax 809/460–1534. 14
rooms. Facilities: restaurant, pub. AE, MC, V. EP. Inexpensive.*

Falmouth Beach Apartments. This is the sister hotel of the Admiral's Inn at English Harbour. The best accommodations are in an attractive colonial-style house at the water's edge on the hotel's own
small palm-lined beach. These units are basically one large room—a
bedroom-living-room-kitchenette combination—and a bathroom
with a shower. All open onto the house's timbered wraparound veranda with a view of the water and the hilly peninsula opposite.
Since the beach is very sheltered, it is perfect for toddlers and small
children who are learning to swim. There is no air-conditioning and
no telephones or TVs. Other rooms are located in four modern buildings perched on the hillside and have a separate kitchen, a bedroom
with twin beds, and a bathroom with shower. All apartments have
daily maid service. Quiet and simple—a good value. *Box 713, Falmouth Harbour, tel. 809/460–1094 or 800/223–5695, fax 809/460–
1534. 28 rooms. Facilities: sailing. AE, MC, V. EP. Inexpensive.*

★ **Lord Nelson Beach Hotel.** This small, family-owned, casual beachfront resort is a perfect place for children to scamper about and explore. If you don't mind a bit of chipped paint and organized chaos, you'll love it, too (as did Eugene Fodor when he once stayed here). An extensive collection of windsurfing boards, easy access to the water, and a dedicated pro have also made it a mecca for windsurfers. The best rooms are in a two-story, apricot-colored building looking directly onto the property's own horseshoe-shape beach. Each room is slightly different (one has beautiful tiled floors and an ornately carved bed from Dominica that is so high you almost need to be a pole-vaulter to get into it). The timbered dining room, dominated by a full-size replica of the boat in which Captain Bligh was cast off from the *Bounty*, serves hearty dishes like stuffed pork chops, wahoo, and snapper. Because the resort is fairly isolated (5 miles from St. John's), the price of a meal anywhere else will automatically have E.C.$20 added to it for the taxi fare there and back. *Box 155, St. John's, tel. 809/462–3094, fax 809/462–0751. Facilities: restaurant, bar, maid service, dive shop, windsurfing. AE, MC, V. EP, MAP, FAP. Inexpensive.*

Murphy's Place. Mrs. Murphy, a hard-working, talkative woman, first started taking guests into her home, a modern bungalow on the outskirts of St. John's, to pay for her children's education. The rooms, in a simple wooden annex, hung with yellow bella flowers, are either single, with a double bed, shower, and fan, or larger, with two bedrooms, a large living-room area, and a well-equipped kitchen. The furnishing is simple enough, but Mrs. Murphy sews many of the curtains and bedspreads herself and takes a lot of trouble seeing that everything is shipshape and clean. On a patio festooned with plants she serves afternoon tea for those who want it and a pancake breakfast on Saturday. As a result, the guest book is full of signatures of (mostly young) people from all over the world. At the Dolphin Restaurant, a few yards away, her son serves good Caribbean food at reasonable prices. Excellent value. *Box 491, St. John's, tel. 809/461–1183. 4 rooms. Facilities: patio. No credit cards. EP. Inexpensive.*

Nightlife

Most of Antigua's evening entertainment centers on the resort hotels, which feature calypso singers, steel bands, limbo dancers, and folkloric groups on a regular basis. Check with the Department of Tourism for up-to-date information.

Shirley Heights Lookout (Shirley Heights, tel. 809/463–1785) does Sunday-afternoon barbecues that continue into the night with music and dancing. It's *the* place to be Sunday afternoons, when local residents, visitors, and the yachting crowd gather for boisterous fun and to exchange the latest gossip. The crowd at **Millers by the Sea** (Dickenson Bay, tel. 809/462–2393) spills over onto the beach for its ever-popular happy hour and live nightly entertainment. This is the place to come and dance on the beach way into the night. The *Jolly Roger* (from Dickenson Bay, tel. 809/462–2064) gets a boisterous group for its Saturday night cruises. Head out on this replica of a pirate ship for a four-hour sail under the stars with a barbecue, open bar, and dancing to live island music.

Casinos   There are four casinos on Antigua. Hours vary depending on the season and whether or not cruise ships are in, so it's best to inquire upon your arrival to the island. The "world's largest slot machine" as well as gaming tables are at the **King's Casino** (tel. 809/462–1727), at Heritage Quay. The **St. James's Club** (Mamora Bay, tel. 809/463–

1113) has a rather elegant casino with a European ambience. Ramada has turned the casino at the **Ramada Renaissance Royal Antiguan Resort** (tel. 809/462–3733) into a model of those in Atlantic City, New Jersey.

Discos **The Lime** (Redcliffe Quay, St. John's, no tel.) is a new spot at Redcliffe Quay. It opens at 10:30 PM on Friday and Saturday and draws a frenetic mix of locals and visitors. On Wednesday nights, **Columbo's** (Galleon Beach Club, English Harbour, tel. 809/463–1452) is the place to be for live reggae, and the **Lemon Tree Restaurant** (Long and Church Sts., St. John's, tel. 809/461–1969) swings every night in season until at least 11 PM.

4 Aruba

Updated by
Jordan
Simon

Imagine Aruba as one big Love Boat cruise. Most of its 25 hotels sit side by side down one major strip along the southwestern shore, with restaurants, exotic boutiques, fiery floor shows, and glitzy casinos right on their premises. Nearly every night there are organized theme parties, treasure hunts, beachside barbecues, and fish fries with steel bands and limbo dancers.

The "A" in the ABC Islands, Aruba is small—only 19.6 miles long and 6 miles across at its widest point, approximately 70 square miles. Once a member of the Netherlands Antilles, Aruba became an independent entity within the Netherlands in 1986, with its own royally appointed governor, a democratic government, and a 21-member elected Parliament. With education, housing, and health care financed by an economy based on tourism, the island's population of 70,000 recognizes visitors as valued guests. The national anthem proclaims, "The greatness of our people is their great cordiality," and this is no exaggeration. Waiters serve you with smiles and solid eye contact, English is spoken everywhere, and hotel hospitality directors appear delighted to serve your special needs. Good direct air service from the United States makes Aruba an excellent choice for even a short vacation.

Time-sharing units bring back the committed year after year, and the huge high-rise hotel complexes fill their rooms with special package rates. Overbuilding has caused the government to place a five-year moratorium on new hotel construction while unfinished hotel construction waits for refinancing.

The island's distinctive beauty lies in its countryside—an almost extraterrestrial landscape full of rocky deserts, cactus jungles, secluded coves, and aquamarine vistas with crashing waves. With its low humidity and average temperature of 82°F, Aruba has the climate of a paradise; rain comes mostly during November. Sun, cooling trade winds, friendly and courteous service, modern and efficient amenities, and 10 modern casinos are Aruba's strong suit to fill the 7,156 hotel rooms.

Before You Go

Tourist
Information

Contact the **Aruba Tourism Authority,** 1000 Harbor Blvd. (ground level), Weehawken, NJ 07087, tel. 201/330–0800 or 800/TO–ARUBA, fax 201/330–8757; in Miami, 2344 Salzedo St., Miami, FL 33134, tel. 305/567–2720, fax 305/567–2721; in Canada, 86 Bloor St. W, Suite 204, Toronto, Ontario, M5S 1M5, tel. 416/975–1950.

Arriving and
Departing
By Plane

Flights leave daily to Aruba from New York area airports and Miami International Airport with easy connections from most American cities. **Air Aruba** (tel. 800/882–7822), the island's official airline, flies nonstop to Aruba daily from Miami and five days a week from Newark. **American Airlines** (tel. 800/433–7300) offers daily nonstop service from both Miami International and New York's JFK airport. **ALM** (tel. 800/327–7230), the major airline of the Dutch Caribbean islands, flies five days a week nonstop from Miami to Aruba; two nonstop and two direct flights a week leave out of Atlanta with connecting services (throughfares) to most major U.S. gateways tied in with Delta. Air Aruba and ALM also have connecting flights to Caracas, Bonaire, Curaçao, and St. Maarten as well as other Caribbean islands. ALM also offers a "Visit Caribbean Pass" for interisland travel. From Toronto and Montreal, you can fly to Aruba on American Airlines via San Juan. American also has connecting flights from several U.S. cities via San Juan. **VIASA** (tel. 800/327–5454) has Monday and Thursday nonstop flights out of Houston. **AeroPostal** (tel.

800/468–9419) offers nonstop flights from Atlanta three times a
week and from Orlando three times a week.

Passports U.S. and Canadian residents need show proof only of identity—a
and Visas valid passport, birth certificate, naturalization certificate, green
card, valid nonquota immigration visa, or a valid voter registration
card. All other nationalities must submit a valid passport.

Precautions Aruba is a party island, but only up to a point. A police dog sniffs for
drugs at the airport.

The strong trade winds are a relief in the subtropical climate, but
don't hang your bathing suit on a balcony—it will probably blow
away. Help Arubans conserve water and energy: Turn off air-conditioning when you leave your room and keep your faucets turned off.

Staying in Aruba

Important **Tourist Information:** The **Aruba Tourism Authority** (L. G. Smith
Addresses Blvd. 172, Box 1019, tel. 297/8–23777) has free brochures and guides
who are ready to answer any questions.

Emergencies **Police:** tel. 100. **Hospital:** Horaceo Oduber, tel. 24300. **Pharmacy:**
Botica del Pueblo, tel. 21254. **Ambulance** and **fire:** tel. 115. All hotels
have house doctors on call 24 hours a day. Call the front desk.

Currency Arubans happily accept U.S. dollars virtually everywhere, so
there's no real need to exchange money, except for necessary pocket
change (cigarettes, soda machines, or pay phones). The currency
used, however, is the Aruban florin (AFl), which at press time exchanged to the U.S. dollar at AFl1.78 for cash, AFl1.80 for traveler's checks, and to the Canadian dollar at AFl1.30. The Dutch
Antillean florin (used in Bonaire and Curaçao) is not accepted in
Aruba. Major credit cards and traveler's checks are widely accepted, but you will probably be asked to show identification when
cashing a traveler's check. Prices quoted here are in U.S. dollars unless otherwise noted.

Taxes and Hotels collect a 5% government tax and usually add an 11% service
Service charge to room bills. Restaurants usually add a 15% service charge
Charges to your bill. The departure tax is $10. There is no sales tax.

Guided Tours Aruba's highlights can be seen in a day. While most highways are in
Orientation excellent condition, signs and directions are haphazard, making a
guided tour your best option for exploring if you have only a short
time. **De Palm Tours** (L. G. Smith Blvd. 142, tel. 297/8–24400 or 297/
8–24545, telex 5049 DPALM NA, fax 297/8–23012) has a near mo-
nopoly on the Aruban sightseeing business; reservations may be
made through its general office or at hotel tour-desk branches. The
basic 3½-hour tour hits the high spots of the island, including popular spots that are difficult to find on your own, such as the Ayo and
Casibari rock formations. Wear tennis or hiking shoes (there'll be
optional climbing) and note that the air-conditioned bus can get cold.
The tour, which begins at 9:30 AM, picks you up in your lobby and
costs $17.50 per person. De Palm also offers full-day tours of Caracas,
Venezuela ($225, passport required), and Curaçao ($185). Prices include round-trip airfare, transfers, sightseeing, and lunch; there is also
free time for shopping.

General Travel Bureau (Elleboogstraat 23, tel. 297/8–26609 or 297/
8–34717) also offers trips to Caracas on Thursday, Friday, and Monday. The full-day tour ($225) includes round-trip airfare, transfers,
a historical sightseeing tour, shopping, and lunch.

Friendly Tours (tel. 297/8–23230) offers guided 3½-hour sightseeing tours to the island's main sights twice a day ($20).

Special Interest **Corvalou Tours** (tel. 297/8–21149) offers unusual excursions for specialized interests. The Archaeological/Geological Tour involves a four- to six-hour field trip through Aruba's past, including the huge monoliths and rugged, desolate north coast. Also available are architectural, bird-watching, and botanical tours. The fee for all tours is $40 per person and $70 per couple, with special prices for parties of five or more.

A new way of exploring Aruba is by Jeep caravan. **De Palm Tours** (tel. 297/8–24400) offers full-day, on-and-off-the-road tours every Wednesday and Thursday. The $49.50 per person price (four people per Jeep) includes a tour guide, lunch, and snorkeling equipment. Bring a bathing suit, lots of sunblock, and a camera.

For a three-in-one tour of prehistoric Indian cultures, volcanic formations, and natural wildlife, contact archaeologist Eppie Boerstra of **Marlin Booster Tracking, Inc.**, at Charlie's Bar (tel. 297/8–45086 or 297/8–41513). The fee for a six-hour tour is $35 per person, including a cold picnic lunch and beverages. Tours can be given in English, Dutch, German, French, and Spanish.

Hikers will enjoy a guided three-hour trip to remote sites of unusual natural beauty accessible only on foot. The fee is $25 per person, including refreshments and transportation; a minimum of four people is required. Contact **De Palm Tours** (tel. 297/8–24545).

Private Safaris Educational Tours (tel. 297/8–34869) offers adventure safaris by land cruiser into Aruba's interior. The half-day ($30) and full-day ($40) tours explore the island's history, geology, and wildlife.

Landlubbers can now explore an underwater reef teeming with marine life without getting wet. **Atlantis Submarines** (Seaport Village Marina, tel. 297/8–36090) operates a 65-foot, modern, air-conditioned sub that takes 46 passengers 50–90 feet below the surface along Aruba's Barcadera Reef. The 50-minute plunge costs $68 for adults, half price for children. If you are not a scuba diver, the hour in the submarine is the next best thing to being down among the fish and coral.

Boat Cruises If you try a cruise around the island, know that trimarans are much smoother than monohull boats. People with queasy stomachs will be helped by lemon or lime candy, and everyone should avoid going on an empty stomach. The most popular and reputable sailing cruises are offered by **De Palm Tours** (tel. 297/8–24400 or 297/8–24545), **Mi Dushi** (tel. 297/8–26034), **Red Sail Sports** (tel. 297/8–24500), **Pelican Watersports** (tel. 297/8–24739), **Wave Dancer** (tel. 297/8–25520), and **Topaz** (tel. 297/8–24401).

Moonlight cruises, though stunning, are appreciated most by honeymooners. Prices run about $25 per person. Contact **Red Sail Sports** (tel. 297/8–24500), **Pelican Watersports** (tel. 297/8–24739) or **De Palm Tours** (tel. 297/8–24400). De Palm Tours' three-hour trimaran cruise with an hour's stop for swimming and snorkeling runs daily except Sunday; the cost is $22.50 per person. Four-hour snorkel, sail, and lunch cruises aboard a 53-foot catamaran plus sunset sails and a romantic dinner cruise are among the on-the-water delights offered at prices that range from $27.50 to $49.50 per person. Contact Red Sail Sports.

If you've ever wanted to walk the plank, take a swing from the yard-arm, or be a swashbuckler defending his lady, then take a pirate cruise aboard the *Topaz*, the original tall ship used in Walt Disney's production *Return to Treasure Island*. The $39.50 cost includes unlimited drinks, a barbecue dinner, and a sunset swim. Runs daily. Call De Palm Tours.

Getting Around
Remember the island's winding roads are poorly marked, if at all. The major tourist attractions are fairly easy to find; others you'll happen upon only by sheer luck (or with an Aruban friend).

Taxis
A dispatch office is located at Alhambra Bazaar and Casino (tel. 297/8–21604 or 297/8–22116); you can also flag down taxis on the street. Since taxis do not have meters, rates are fixed and should be confirmed before your ride begins. All Aruba's taxi drivers have participated in the government's Tourism Awareness Programs and have received their Tourism Guide Certificate. An hour's tour of the island by taxi will run you about $30, for a maximum of four people per car. A taxi from the airport to most hotels will run $8–$10.

Rental Cars
You'll need a valid U.S. or Canadian driver's license to rent a car, and you must be able to meet the minimum age requirements of each rental service, implemented for insurance reasons. **Budget** (tel. 800/527–0700) requires drivers to be between 25 and 65, **Avis** (tel. 800/331–2112) requires drivers to be between 23 and 70, and **Hertz** (tel. 800/654–3131) requires drivers to be older than 21. Insurance is available starting at $10 per day, and all companies offer unlimited mileage. Local car rental companies generally have lower rates.

Local addresses and phone numbers for the rental agencies are **Avis** (Kolibristraat 14, tel. 297/8–28787; airport, tel. 297/8–25496), **Budget Rent-A-Car** (Kolibristraat 1, tel. 297/8–28600; airport, tel. 297/8–25423; at Divi resorts, tel. 297/8–35000), **Hertz, De Palm Car Rental** (L. G. Smith Blvd. 142, Box 656, tel. 297/8–24545; airport, tel. 297/8–24886), **Dollar Rent-a-Car** (Grendeaweg 15, tel. 297/8–22783; airport, tel. 297/8–25651; Manchebo, tel. 297/8–26696), **National** (Tank Leendert 170, tel. 297/8–21967; airport, tel. 297/8–25451; Holiday Inn tel. 297/8–23600), **Thrifty** (airport, tel. 297/8–35335), and **Hedwina Car Rental** (airport, tel. 297/8–37393; Fortheuvelstraat 32, tel. 297/8–26442).

Motorcycle Rentals
Rates vary according to the make of the vehicle. For Suzuki scooters ($24 day, $132 week), contact **George Cycle Center** (L. G. Smith Blvd. 136, tel. 297/8–25975). Other moped, scooter, and motorcycle rental companies are **Ron's Motorcycle Rental** (Bakval 17A, tel. 297/8–32090), **Nelson Motorcycle Rental** (Gasparito 10A, tel. 297/8–26801), and **Semver Cycle Rental** (Noord 22, tel. 297/8–26851).

Buses
For inexpensive trips between the beach hotels and Oranjestad, buses run hourly. Round-trip fare is $1.50, and exact change is preferred. Buses also run down the coast from Oranjestad to San Nicolas for the same fare. Contact the Aruba Tourism Authority (tel. 297/8–27089) for a bus schedule, or inquire at the front desk of your hotel.

Telephones and Mail
To dial direct to Aruba from the United States, dial 011–297–8, followed by the number in Aruba. Local and international calls in Aruba can be made via hotel operators or from the Government Long Distance Telephone, Telegraph, and Radio Office, SETAR, which is in the post office in Oranjestad. When dialing locally in Aruba, simply dial the five-digit number. To reach the United States, dial 001, then the area code and number.

Telegrams and telexes can be sent through SETAR, at the Post Office Building in Oranjestad or via your hotel. There is also a SETAR office in front of the Hyatt Regency hotel, adjacent to the hotel's parking lot (tel. 297/8–37138).

You can send an airmail letter from Aruba to anywhere in the world for AFl1.00, a postcard for AFl.70.

Opening and Closing Times Shops are generally open between 8 AM and 6 PM, Monday through Saturday. Most stores stay open through the lunch hour, noon–2 PM. Many stores open when cruise ships are in port on Sundays and holidays. Nighttime shopping at the Alhambra Bazaar runs 5 PM–midnight. Bank hours are weekdays from 8 to noon and 1:30 to 4. The Aruba Bank at the airport is open on Saturday from 9 to 4 and on Sunday from 9 to 1.

Exploring Aruba

Numbers in the margin correspond to points of interest on the Aruba map.

Oranjestad Aruba's charming Dutch capital, **Oranjestad,** is best explored on ❶ foot. Take a taxi or bus from your hotel to the **Port of Call Marketplace,** a new shopping mall. After exploring the boutiques and shops, head up L. G. Smith Boulevard to the colorful **Fruit Market,** located along the docks on your right.

Continue walking along the harbor until you come to **Harbourtown Market,** a festive shopping, dining, and entertainment mall. Next door (one block southwest) is **Wilhelmina Park,** a small grove of palm trees and flowers overlooking the sea.

Cross L. G. Smith Boulevard to Oranjestraat and walk one block to **Fort Zoutman,** one of the island's oldest buildings. It was built in 1796 and used as a major fortress in the skirmishes between British and Curaçao troops. The Willem III Tower, named for the Dutch monarch of that time, was added in 1868. The fort's Historical Museum displays centuries' worth of Aruban relics and artifacts in an 18th-century Aruban house. *Oranjestraat, tel. 297/8–26099. Admission: $1. Open weekdays 9–noon and 1–4.*

Turn left onto Zoutmanstraat and walk two blocks to the **Archeology Museum,** where there are two rooms of Indian artifacts, farm and domestic utensils, and skeletons. *Zoutmanstraat 1, tel. 297/8–28979. Admission free. Open weekdays 8–noon and 1:30–4:30.*

Across the street you'll see the handsome Protestant Church. Turn right on Kazernestraat. On your left side are the Sonesta Hotel and Seaport Village Mall; on your right are the **Strada Complex I** and **Strada Complex II.** Both are shopping malls, and both are excellent examples of Dutch Colonial architecture. Behind Strada Complex II is the **Holland Aruba Mall,** a new shopping complex built to resemble a Dutch Colonial village. Upstairs is an international food court.

Time Out The motto at **Le Petit Café** (at Mainstreet, corner of Schlepstraat, tel. 297/8–33716) is "Romancing the Stone"—referring to tasty cuisine cooked on hot stones. The low ceiling and hanging plants make this an intimate lunch spot for shoppers. Jumbo shrimps, sandwiches, ice cream, and fresh fruit dishes are light delights. *Open lunch and dinner, Mon.–Sat. Closed Sun.*

At the intersection of Kazernestraat and Caya G. F. Betico Croes, turn right. This is Oranjestad's main street. When you come to

Aruba

California Pt.

California Sand Dunes

⑨

Malmok Beach

Altovista

Fisherman's Hut

Bushiribana ○

⑧

Palm Beach

⑩ – ⑭

⑮ – ㉒

Noord

㉓
㉔

Paradera ○

Eagle Beach

㉕
㉖
㉗

㉘
㉙
㉚

②

Manchebo Beach

Santa Cruz ○

Divi Beach

㉛

Druif Bay

①

Reina Beatrix International Airport

Oranjestad

㉜ – ㊱

Balashi ○

N

0   4 miles
0   6 km

Exploring
Balashi Gold Mine, **4**
California Lighthouse, **9**
Frenchman's Pass, **3**
Guadirikiri/Fontein caves, **7**

Hooiberg (Haystack Hill), **2**
Natural Bridge, **8**
Oranjestad, **1**
San Nicolas, **6**
Spanish Lagoon, **5**

Dining
Bon Appetit, **15**
Boonoonoonoos, **35**
Brisas del Mar, **37**
Buccaneer Restaurant, **10**
Chez Mathilde, **33**
La Paloma, **11**

Mi Cushina, **38**
The Old Cunucu House, **16**
The Old Mill, **24**
Papiamento, **12**
Talk of the Town Restaurant, **34**
Valentino's, **13**

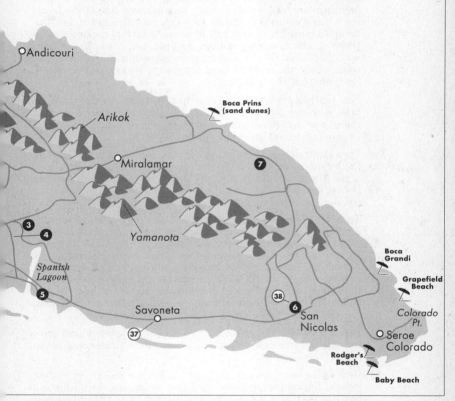

Caribbean Sea

O Exploring Sites

10 Hotels and Restaurants

Andicouri

Boca Prins
(sand dunes)

Arikok

Miralamar

7

3
4

Yamanota

Boca
Grandi

Spanish
Lagoon

Grapefield
Beach

5

38

Savoneta

6 San
Nicolas

Colorado
Pt.

37

Seroe
Colorado

Rodger's
Beach

Baby Beach

Lodging

Americana Aruba
Beach Resort &
Casino, **17**

Amsterdam Manor, **25**

Aruba Beach Club, **28**

Aruba Hilton Hotel
and Casino, **19**

Aruba Palm Beach
Hotel & Casino, **18**

Bucuti Beach
Resort, **29**

Bushiri Beach
Resort, **32**

Caribbean Palm
Village, **14**

Casa del Mar Beach
Resort, **30**

Divi Aruba Beach
Resort, **31**

Hyatt Regency Aruba
Resort & Casino, **20**

La Cabana All Suite
Beach Resort &
Casino, **26**

La Quinta Beach
Resort, **27**

The Mill Resort, **23**

Playa Linda Beach
Resort, **21**

Radisson Aruba
Caribbean Resort &
Casino, **22**

Sonesta Hotel, Beach
Club & Casino, **36**

Hendrikstraat, turn left and continue walking until you come to the **St. Francis Roman Catholic Church.** Next to the church is the **Numismatic Museum,** displaying coins and paper money from more than 400 countries. *Iraussquilnplein 2-A, tel. 297/8–28831. Admission free. Open weekdays 8:30–noon and 1–4:30 PM.*

Diagonally across from the church is the **post office,** where you can buy colorful Aruban stamps. Next door is SETAR, where you can place overseas phone calls.

The Countryside The "real Aruba"—what's left of a wild, untamed beauty—can be found only in the countryside. Either rent a car, take a sightseeing tour, or hire a cab for $30 an hour (for up to four people). The main highways are well paved, but on the windward side of the island some roads are still a mixture of compacted dirt and stones. Although a car is fine, a Jeep will allow you to explore the unpaved interior. Traffic is sparse, and you can't get lost. If you do lose your way, just follow the divi-divi trees (because of the direction of the trade winds, the trees are bent toward the leeward side of the island, where all the hotels are).

Few beaches outside the hotel strip have refreshment stands, so take your own food and drink. And one more caution: Note that there are *no* public bathrooms—anywhere—once you leave Oranjestad, except in the infrequent restaurant.

East to San Nicolas For a shimmering vista of blue-green sea, drive east on L. G. Smith Boulevard toward San Nicolas, on what is known as the Sunrise side of the island. Past the airport, you'll soon see the towering 541-foot

❷ peak of **Hooiberg** (Haystack Hill). If you have the energy, climb the 562 steps up to the top for an impressive view of the city.

Turn left where you see the drive-in theater (a popular hangout for Arubans). Drive to the first intersection, turn right, and follow the

❸ curve to the right to **Frenchman's Pass,** a dark, luscious stretch of highway arbored by overhanging trees. Local legend claims that the French and native Indians warred here during the 17th century for

❹ control of the island. Nearby are the cement ruins of the **Balashi Gold Mine** (take the dirt road veering to the right)—a lovely place to picnic, listen to the parakeets, and contemplate the towering cacti. A magnificent gnarled divi-divi tree guards the entrance.

Backtrack all the way to the main road, past the drive-in, and drive

❺ through the area called **Spanish Lagoon,** where pirates once hid to repair their ships.

❻ Back on the main highway, pay a visit to **San Nicolas,** Aruba's oldest village. During the heyday of the Exxon refineries, the town was a bustling port; now it's dedicated to tourism, with the main-street promenade full of interesting kiosks. The **China Clipper Bar** on Main Street used to be a famous "whore" bar frequented by sailors docked in port.

Time Out Now an institution, **Charlie's Bar** has been a San Nicolas hangout for more than 50 years. During the oil-refinery days, it was a hopping bar for all kinds of rough-and-scruffs. Now it is owned by the second-generation Charlie, who is eager to promote San Nicolas as a historic town. Tourists flock here, if only to gawk at the unusual decor: license plates, hard hats, baseball pennants, and old credit cards cover and crowd every inch of the walls and ceiling. The specialty is "shrimps—jumbo and dumbo." Ask Charlie for his special "honeymoon sauce." The bus to San Nicolas stops right at the door.

Zeppenfeldstraat 56, San Nicolas, tel. 297/8–45086. Open Mon.– Sat. noon–10 PM.

Anyone looking for geological exotica should head for the northern coast, driving northwest from San Nicolas. Stop at the two old Indian caves **Guadirikiri** and **Fontein.** Both were used by the native Indians centuries ago, but you'll have to decide for yourself whether the "ancient Indian inscriptions" are genuine—rumor has it they were added by a European film company that made a movie here years ago. You may enter the caves, but there are no guides available, and bats are known to make appearances. Wear sneakers and take a flashlight or rent one from the soda vendor who has set up shop here. Just before the Fontein and Guadirikiri caves lies the **Tunnel of Love,** a heart-shape tunnel containing naturally sculpted rocks that look just like the Madonna, Abe Lincoln, even a jaguar. The climb through the tunnel is strenuous and should not be attempted by anyone not in good physical condition. It's definitely not recommended for elderly people or young children. Remember, admission is free to all three caves—don't be deterred by the occasionally pushy vendors.

A few miles up the coast is the **Natural Bridge,** sculpted out of coral rock by centuries of raging wind and sea. To get to it, you'll have to follow the main road inland and then the signs that lead the way. Nearby is a café overlooking the water and a souvenir shop stuffed with trinkets, T-shirts, and postcards for reasonable prices. The dirt road continues west a half mile to the massive ruins of the Bushiribana Gold Smelter, which resembles a crumbling fortress.

West of Palm Beach Drive or take a taxi west from the hotel strip to Malmok, where Aruba's wealthiest families reside. Open to the public, **Malmok Beach** is considered one of the finest spots for shelling, snorkeling, and windsurfing (*see* Beaches, *below*). Right off the coast here is the wreck of the German ship *Antilla,* which was scuttled in 1940—a favorite haunt for divers. At the very end of the island stands the **California Lighthouse,** now closed, which is surrounded by huge boulders that look like extraterrestrial monsters; in this stark landscape, you'll feel as though you've just landed on the moon.

From here a rugged dirt road curls around the northwest corner of the island to the lonely Alto Vista Chapel. The wind whistles through the simple mustard-colored walls, eerie boulders, and looming cacti. Along the side of the road back to civilization are miniature coffins painted with depictions of the Stations of the Cross, and hand-lettered signs exhorting "pray for us, sinner," and the like—a primitive yet powerful evocation of faith.

Off the Beaten Track

Aruba has another natural bridge on its desolate, magnificent east coast. To reach it, keep bearing east out of San Nicolas, and continue uphill past the oil refinery and residential development of Seroe Colorado. While the cathedrallike formation is not as spectacular as its celebrated sister, the raw elemental power of the sea that created it certainly is. The hike down to the best vantage point is fairly arduous, but you won't find a more pristine, isolated spot on Aruba for a picnic.

Beaches

Beaches in Aruba are legendary in the Caribbean: white sand, turquoise waters, and virtually no garbage, for everyone takes the "no littering" sign—"No Tira Sushi"—very seriously, especially with an AFl500 fine. The influx of tourists in the past decade, however, has crowded the major beaches, which back up to the hotels along the southwestern strip. These beaches are public, and you can make the two-hour hike from the Holiday Inn to the Bushiri Beach Hotel free of charge and without ever leaving sand. If you go strolling during the day, make sure you are well protected from the sun—it scorches fast. Luckily, there's at least one covered bar (and often an ice-cream stand) at virtually every hotel you pass. If you take the stroll at night, you can hotel-hop for dinner, dancing, gambling, and late-night entertainment. On the northern side of the island, heavy trade winds make the waters too choppy for swimming, but the vistas are great and the terrain is wonderfully suited to sunbathing and geological explorations. Among the finer beaches are:

Rodger's Beach. Next to Baby Beach on the eastern tip of the island, this is a beautiful curving stretch of sand only slightly marred by the view of the oil refinery at the far side of the bay.

Baby Beach. On the island's eastern tip, this semicircular beach borders a bay that is as placid as a wading pool and only four to five feet deep—perfect for tots and terrible swimmers. Thatched shaded areas are good for cooling off.

Grapefield Beach. On the north of San Nicolas, this gorgeous beach is perfect for professional windsurfing.

Boca Grandi. Just west of Bachelor's Beach, on the northwest coast (near the Seagrape Grove and the Aruba Golf Club), Boca Grandi is excellent for wave jumping and windsurfing.

Boca Prins. Near the Fontein Cave and Blue Lagoon, this beach is about as large as a Brazilian bikini, but with two rocky cliffs and tumultuously crashing waves, it's as romantic as you get in Aruba. This is not a swimming beach, however. Boca Prins is famous for its backdrop of enormous vanilla sand dunes. Most folks bring a picnic lunch, a beach blanket, and sturdy sneakers.

Malmok Beach. On the southwestern shore, this lackluster beach borders shallow waters that stretch out 300 yards from shore, making it perfect for beginners learning to windsurf.

Fisherman's Hut. Next to the Holiday Inn, this beach is a windsurfer's haven. Take a picnic lunch (tables are available) and watch the elegant purple, aqua, and orange Windsurfer sails struggle in the wind.

Palm Beach. Once called one of the 10 best beaches in the world by the *Miami Herald*, this is the stretch behind the Americana Aruba, Aruba Hilton Hotel and Casino, Aruba Palm Beach, and Holiday Inn hotels. It's the center of Aruban tourism, offering the best in swimming, sailing, and fishing. During high season, however, it's a sardine can.

Eagle Beach. Across the highway from what is quickly becoming known as Time-Share Lane is Eagle Beach on the southern coast. Not long ago, it was a nearly deserted stretch of pristine sands dotted with the occasional thatched picnic hut. Now that the new time-share resorts are completed, this beach is one of the more hopping on the island.

Manchebo Beach (formerly Punta Brabo Beach). In front of the Manchebo Beach Resort, this impressively wide stretch of white powder is where officials turn a blind eye to those who wish to sunbathe topless. Elsewhere on the island, topless sunbathing is not permitted (though officials rarely enforce the ban).

Sports and the Outdoors

Bowling Opened in 1991, the **Eagle Bowling Palace** (Pos Abou, tel. 297/8–35038) has 12 lanes, a cocktail lounge, and snack bar. The cost is $8.25 a game from 10 AM to 3 PM, $10.25 a game from 3 PM to 2 AM, and $1.20 for shoe rentals. Open 10 AM–2 AM.

Deep-Sea Fishing With catches ranging from barracuda to kingfish, bonito, and black and yellow tuna, deep-sea fishing is great sport on Aruba, and many charter boats are available. Sail for a half day or a full day. **De Palm Tours** (L. G. Smith Blvd. 142, Box 656, tel. 297/8–24400) can arrange parties for up to six people, in boats that range from 24 to 27 feet. Half-day tours, including all equipment, can be arranged for $220–$250 for up to six people. Private yachts, manned by independent sea captains, can also be arranged. Check with the Aruba Tourism Authority or your hotel. Half-day tours run about $200, full-day about $425. **Pelican Tours** (tel. 297/8–31228 or 297/8–24739) and **Red Sail Sports** (tel. 297/8–24500) also arrange deep-sea fishing charters.

Golf The **Aruba Golf Club** (Golfweg 82, near San Nicolas, tel. 297/8–42006) features a nine-hole course with 25 sand traps, roaming goats, and lots of cacti. There are 11 AstroTurf greens, making 18-hole tournaments a possibility. The clubhouse contains a bar, storage rooms, workshop, and separate men's and women's locker rooms. The course's official U.S. Golf Association rating is 67; greens fees are $7.50 for 9 holes, $10 for 18 holes. There are no caddies, but golf carts are available. Golfers should also check with the tourism authority on the status of the par 72 Robert Trent Jones Jr. 18-hole golf course, which, at press time, was planned for the area known as Arashi.

Horseback Riding One-hour jaunts ($15) arranged through **Rancho El Paso** (Washington 44, tel. 297/8–23310) or **De Palm Tours** (tel. 297/8–24400) will take you through countryside flanked by cacti, divi-divi trees, and aloe vera plants; two-hour trips ($30) also go to the beach. Remember to wear a hat and take lots of suntan lotion.

Land Sailing Carts with a Windsurfer-type sail are rented at **Aruba SailCart** (Bushire 23, tel. 297/8–35133) at $15 (single seater) and $20 (double seater) for 30 minutes of speeding back and forth across a dirt field. The sport is new to Aruba and thrilling for landbound sailors. Anyone can learn the rudiments of driving the cart in just a few minutes. Open 10 AM–7 PM. Food and drinks are served until 10 PM.

Miniature Golf Two elevated 18-hole minigolf courses surrounded by a moat are available at **Joe Mendez Adventure Golf** (Eagle Beach. 297/8–36625). There are also paddleboats and bumper boats, a bar, and a snack stand. Fees are $6 for a round of minigolf, $5 for 30 minutes of paddleboating, and $5 for 10 minutes of bumper boating.

Parasailing Motorboats from Eagle and Palm beaches tow people up and over the water for about 15 minutes ($40).

Snorkeling and Scuba Diving With visibility up to 90 feet, Aruban waters are excellent for snorkeling in shallow waters, and scuba divers will discover exotic marine life and coral. Certified divers can go wall diving, reef diving, or explore wrecks sunk during World War II. The *Antilla* ship-wreck—a German freighter sunk off the northwest coast of Aruba near Palm Beach—is a favorite spot with divers and snorkelers.

De Palm Tours (tel. 297/8–24545 or 297/8–24400, fax 297/8–23012) offers daily snorkeling and scuba-diving trips. However, its rates are the most expensive on the island.

Pelican Watersports (J. G. Emanstraat 1, Oranjestad, tel. 297/8–31228 or 297/8–23600, ext. 329) also offers snorkeling and scuba diving.

Red Sail Sports (tel. 297/8–24500, ext. 109, or 800/255–6425) offers scuba packages, resort courses, PADI-certification courses, night diving, and underwater camera rental.

Aruba Pro Dive (Ponton 88, tel. 297/8–25520) offers resort courses, daily one-tank dives, two-tank dives, and night dives. Other reputable dive operators offering daily one- and two-tank dives are **Charlie's Buddies S.E.A. Scuba** (San Nicolas, tel. 297/8–41640 or 800/252–0557), **Mermaid Sports Divers** (Manchebo Beach Resort, tel. 297/8–35546 or 800/223–1108), and **Hallo Aruba Dive Shop** (Talk of the Town Hotel, L. G. Smith Blvd. 2, tel. 297/8–38270).

Windsurfing **Pelican Watersports** (J. G. Emanstraat 1, tel. 297/8–23600) rents equipment and offers instruction with a certified Mistral instructor. Stock boards and custom boards rent for $30 per two hours, $55 per day.

Red Sail Sports (tel. 297/8–24500 or 800/255–6425) offers two-hour beginner lessons for $44 and advanced lessons for $33 per hour. It also offers Fanatic board and regular windsurfing board rentals by the hour, day, and week.

Windsurfing instruction and board rental are also available through **Carib Asurf** (Manchebo Beach Resort, tel. 297/8–23444), **Sailboard Vacation** (L. G. Smith Blvd. 462, tel. 297/8–21072), **Roger's Windsurf Place** (L. G. Smith Blvd. 472, tel. 297/8–21918), **Windsurfing Aruba** (Boliviastraat 14, Box 256, tel. 297/8–33472), and **De Palm Tours** (L. G. Smith Blvd. 142, Box 656, tel. 297/8–24545).

Shopping

Caya G. F. Betico Croes—Aruba's chief shopping street—makes for a pleasant diversion from the beach and casino life. *Duty-free* is a magic word here. Major credit cards are welcome virtually everywhere, U.S. dollars are accepted almost as often as local currency, and traveler's checks can be cashed with proof of identity. Shopping malls have arrived in Aruba, so when you finish walking the main street, stop in at a mall to browse through the chic new boutiques.

Aruba's souvenir and crafts stores are full of Dutch porcelains and figurines, as befits the island's Netherlands heritage. Dutch cheese is a good buy (you are allowed to bring up to one pound of hard cheese through U.S. customs), as are hand-embroidered linens and any products made from the native plant aloe vera—sunburn cream, face masks, and skin refresheners. Since there is no sales tax, the price you see on the tag is the price you pay. But one word of warning: Don't pull any bargaining tricks. Arubans consider it rude to haggle.

Specialty Crafts can be found at several stores. At **Artesania Arubiano** (L. G.
Shops Smith Blvd. 142, next to the Aruba Tourism Authority, tel. 297/8–37494) you'll find charming Aruban home-crafted pottery, silk-

screened T-shirts and wall hangings, and folklore objects. The **Artistic Boutique** (Caya G. F. Betico Croes 25, tel. 297/8–23142, with branches at the Aruba Hilton, tel. 297/8–24466, ext. 3508; La Cabana, tel. 297/8–20675; Seaport Village Mall, tel. 297/8–32567; and the Holiday Inn, tel. 297/8–33383) sells Aruban hand-embroidered linens, gold and silver jewelry, Persian carpets and dhurries, porcelain and pottery from Spain, and lots of antiques. **Mopa Mopa** (L. G. Smith Blvd. 47, tel. 297/8–33581) sells intriguing items that look hand-painted but aren't: a special process extracts color from a mineral that is used to treat the wood. **Creative Hands** (Scotorolaan 5, Oranjestad, tel. 297/8–35665) sells porcelain and ceramic *cunucu* houses and divi-divi trees, but the store's real draw is its exquisite Japanese dolls.

For duty-free perfumes and cosmetics, stop in at **Aruba Trading Company** (Caya G. F. Betico Croes 14, tel. 297/8–22600), whose name is synonymous with old-fashioned reliability. ATC offers internationally known brand names at discounts, but you have to hunt for them. Perfumes and cosmetics are on the first floor, jewelry on the second. Both men's and women's clothes are sold.

Clothing is also sold at **Wulfsen's** (Caya G. F. Betico Croes 52, tel. 297/8–23823). For 18 years one of the highest-rated stores in the Netherlands Antilles, Wulfsen's offers Italian, French, German, and Dutch fashions for both sexes. The Dutch-line Mexx is a favorite of hip teens; Betty Buckley and Mondo are popular for women.

J. L. Penha & Son's (Caya G. F. Betico Croes 11, tel. 297/8–24161), another venerated name in Aruban merchandising, also sells clothes and cosmetics and features Boucheron, Lanvin, Dior, and Cartier for women and Givenchy and Pierre Cardin for men.

For jewelry and watches, stop in at **Gandelman's Jewelers** (Caya G. F. Betico Croes 5-A, tel. 297/8–32121 or 297/8–34433) for Gucci and Swatch watches at reasonable prices, gold bracelets, pink and red coral, and a full line of Gucci accessories, from key chains to handbags. More watches can be found at **Little Switzerland** (Caya G. F. Betico Croes 14, tel. 297/8–21192). The Curaçao-based giant in china, crystal, and fine tableware offers good buys on Omega and Rado watches, Swarovski silver, Baccarat crystal, and Lladro figurines. If you don't see what you want, ask and they'll ship it to you.

Shopping Malls

Seaport Village Mall (located on L. G. Smith Blvd., tel. 297/8–23754) is landmarked by the Crystal Casino Tower. This covered mall is located only five minutes away from the cruise terminal. It has more than 85 stores, boutiques, and perfumeries, featuring merchandise to meet every taste and budget. The arcade is lined with tropical plants and caged parrots, and the casino is located just at the top of the escalator.

There are several other shopping malls in Oranjestad, all of which are worth visiting. The **Holland Aruba Mall** (Havenstraat 6, right downtown) houses a collection of smart shops and eateries. Nearby are the **Strada I** and **Strada II,** two small complexes of shops in tall Dutch buildings painted in pastels.

In **Harbourtown** (Swain Wharf), a blue-and-white postmodern version of a seaside village, look for handmade china by Venezuelan artists, discounted perfumes, and embroidered linens from China.

Port of Call Marketplace (L. G. Smith Blvd. 17) features fine jewelry, perfumes, duty-free liquors, batiks, crystal, leather goods, and fashionable clothing.

Dining

Aruba's restaurants serve a cosmopolitan variety of cuisines, although most menus are specifically designed to please American palates—you can get fresh surf and New York turf almost anywhere. Make the effort to try Aruban specialties—*pan bati* is a delicious beaten bread that resembles a pancake, and plantains are similar to cooked bananas.

Dress ranges from casual to elegant, but even the finest restaurants require at the most only a jacket for men and a sundress for women. The air-conditioning does get cold, so don't go bare-armed. And anytime you plan to eat in the open air, remember to douse yourself first with insect repellent—the mosquitoes can get unruly, especially in July and August, when the winds drop.

On Sunday, it may be difficult to find a restaurant outside of the hotels that's open for lunch. One of the best bets is the extensive buffet at the Holiday Inn.

For good or for bad, fast food has arrived in Aruba. For those who are homesick, there's McDonald's, Kentucky Fried Chicken, Burger King, and Wendy's. For breakfast and lunch, the restaurants in the hotels tend to be more expensive than the ones in town. Most hotels offer several food plans, which you can purchase either in advance or upon arrival. But before you purchase a Full American Plan (FAP), which includes breakfast, lunch, and dinner, remember that Aruba has numerous excellent and reasonably priced restaurants from which to choose, and that eating at different places can be part of the fun of a vacation. Nonetheless, most resorts here do offer better-than-average hotel dining; for more information consult the lodging listings.

Highly recommended restaurants are indicated by a star ★.

Category	Cost*
Expensive	over $30
Moderate	$20–$30
Inexpensive	under $20

Prices are for a main course only and are per person, excluding drinks, service, and 15% sales tax.

★ **Chez Mathilde.** This elegant restaurant is in a renovated private home, one of the last surviving 19th-century dwellings in Aruba. Though the previous chef and maître d' left to open another restaurant, the new Dutch chef maintains his predecessor's high culinary standards. The French-style menu is constantly being re-created. To the tune of Strauss waltzes, dine on artfully presented smoked leg of lamb in papaya-ginger-thyme dressing, crepes filled with roast duck and spring onions in blueberry sauce, or veal chops topped with foie gras and madeira sauce. The wine list is one of the best on the island. Ask to sit in the swooningly romantic Pavilion Room, which has an eclectic mix of turn-of-the-century Italian and French decor. *Havenstraat 23, Oranjestad, tel. 297/8–34968. Reservations required. AE, MC, V. Closed for lunch Sun. Expensive.*

Valentino's. The airy, two-level dining room here is inviting, with its rose and sparkling-white color scheme. The tables are placed comfortably far apart, and the service is attentive without being overbearing. The menu is Italian, and the *gamberoni di teresa* (shrimps sautéed in garlic and fresh tomatoes) and fettucine in smoked salmon cream sauce are knockouts. The atmosphere is festive, since the restaurant is popular with celebrating Arubans. You'll find their gaiety infectious. *Caribbean Palm Village, Noord, tel. 297/8–69455. Reservations requested. AE, DC, MC, V. Expensive.*

Bon Appetit. With its white tablecloths, clay-potted plants, low lighting, and warm-looking wood beams, this restaurant glows like a beautiful tan—but it's the savory smells that hook you. The international cuisine wins acclaim—*Gourmet* magazine once requested the recipe for *keshi yena,* baked cheese stuffed with meat and condiments. Generous portions of seafood and beef (especially the gargantuan prime rib) adorn the plates of this midpriced restaurant. The kitchen won a Dutch award for being the cleanest in Aruba. Leave room for the flaming Max dessert, named after owner and charming host Max Croes. *Palm Beach 29, tel. 297/8–25241. Reservations advised. AE, D, DC, MC, V. Moderate.*

Buccaneer Restaurant. Imagine you're in a sunken ship—fishnets and turtle shells hang from the ceiling, and through the portholes you see live sharks, barracudas, and groupers swimming by. That's the Buccaneer, a virtual underwater grotto snug in an old stone building flanked by heavy black chains and boasting a fantastic 5,000-gallon saltwater aquarium, plus 12 more porthole-size tanks. The surf-and-turf cuisine is prepared by the chef-owners with European élan, and the tables are always full. Order the fresh catch of the day or more exotic fare, such as shrimps with Pernod; smoked pork cutlets with sausage, sauerkraut, and potatoes; or the turtle steak with a light cream sauce. Go early (around 5:45 PM) to get a booth next to the aquariums. *Gasparito 11-C., Noord, tel. 297/8–26172. AE, MC, V. Closed Sun. Moderate.*

The Old Mill (Die Olde Molen). A gift from the queen of Holland, this real Dutch mill was shipped brick by brick to Aruba in 1920 and reassembled here. For starters, try the seafood crepe Neptune, nestled in a delicate cheese bed. Also excellent is the shrimp with spinach and cream sauce, or the Dutch fries—crunchy little nuggets of potato. Order the ice cream with chocolate liqueur and take the bottle home as a souvenir of Aruba's oldest restaurant. *L. G. Smith Blvd. 330, Palm Beach, tel. 297/8–22060. Reservations required. AE, MC, V. 2 dinner seatings: 6:30 and 9 PM. Moderate.*

★ **Papiamento.** Longtime restaurateurs Lenie and Eduardo Ellis decided Aruba needed a bistro that was cozy yet elegant, intimate, and always romantic. So they converted their 130-year-old home into just such a dining spot. Guests can feast sumptuously indoors surrounded by antiques, or outdoors in a patio garden decorated with enormous ceramics (designed by Lenie) and filled with ficus and palm trees adorned with lights. The service is impeccable at this family-run establishment. The chef utilizes flavors from both Continental and Caribbean cuisines to produce favorites that include seafood and meat dishes. Try the Dover sole, the Caribbean lobster, shrimps and red snapper cooked tableside on a hot marble stone, or the "claypot" for two—a medley of seafoods prepared in a sealed clay pot. *Washington 61, Noord, tel. 297/8–64544. Reservations advised. AE, MC, V. Dinner only. Moderate.*

Talk of the Town Restaurant. Here you'll find candlelight dining and some of the best steaks in town—the owner comes from a family of Dutch butchers. Located in the Best Western Talk of the Town Resort, between the airport and Oranjestad, this fine restaurant is now a member of the elite honorary restaurant society, Chaine de Rotisseurs. Saturday night is prime-rib-as-much-as-you-can-eat night ($18.95), but seafood specialties are popular, too—such as the crabmeat crepes and the *escargots à la bourguignonne.* For late-night suppers, the poolside grill stays open until 2 AM. The adjoining motel is a good bargain bet for those on a budget. *L. G. Smith Blvd. 2, Oranjestad, tel. 297/8–23380. AE, DC, MC, V. Moderate.*

Boonoonoonoos. The name—say it just as it looks!—means extraordinary, which is a bit of hyperbole for this Austrian-owned Caribbean bistro in the heart of town, but in the fiercely competitive Aruban restaurant business, you gotta have a gimmick. The specialty here is Pan-Caribbean cuisine. The decor is simple in bright and pastel colors, but the tasty food, served with hearty portions of peas and rice and plantains, makes up for the lack of tablecloths, china, and crystal. It should be avoided when crowded, since the service and the quality of the food deteriorate. The roast chicken Barbados is sweet and tangy, marinated in pineapple and cinnamon and simmered in fruit juices. The Jamaican jerk ribs (a 300-year-old recipe) are tiny but spicy, and the satin-smooth hot pumpkin soup drizzled with cheese and served in a pumpkin shell may as well be dessert. *Wilhelminastrat 18A, Oranjestad, tel. 297/8–31888. Reservations advised. AE, V. Dinner only. Closed Sun. Inexpensive–Moderate.*

★ **Brisas del Mar.** This friendly 10-table place overlooking the sea makes you feel as if you're dining in an Aruban home. The menu features old family recipes and utilizes traditional indigenous ingredients like the aromatic *yerbiholé* leaf and the sizzling Mme. Jeanette pepper. Try the smashing steamy fish soup (which would do a Marseillaise proud), *keri keri* (shredded fish kissed with annatto seed), or some of the best pan bati on the island. The brightly hued fishing boats bobbing in the harbor attest to the freshness of the food. It's so good, it justifies a taxi ride to reach it—10 miles east of Oranjestad in the town of Savoneta. *Savoneta 22A, tel. 297/8–47718. Reservations suggested. AE, D, MC, V. Closed Mon. Inexpensive–Moderate.*

The Old Cunucu House. Situated on a small estate in a residential neighborhood three minutes from the high-rise hotels, this 72-year-old white stucco home with slanting roofs, wood beams, and a terracotta courtyard crawling with bougainvillea has been converted to a seafood-and-international restaurant of casual élan. Dine on local recipes for red snapper, almond-fried shrimp with lobster sauce, Cornish hen, and New York sirloin, or beef fondue à deux. An Aruban trio sings and plays background music every Friday, and on Saturday evenings a mariachi band serenades the patrons. Happy hour 5–6 PM. *Palm Beach 150, tel. 297/8–61666. Reservations suggested. AE, DC, MC. Closed Mon. Inexpensive–Moderate.*

La Paloma. "The Dove" is a no-frills, low-key neighborhood joint enlivened by hanging plants and chianti bottles, and it's usually packed. The cuisine is international and Italian, but there's conch stew with pan bati and fried plantains for exotic tastes. The Caesar salad and minestrone soup are house specialties. This is not the place for a romantic interlude; come for the family atmosphere, American-style Italian food, and reasonable prices. *Noord 39, tel. 297/8–62770. AE, MC, V. Closed Tues. Inexpensive–Moderate.*

Mi Cushina. The name means "My Kitchen," and the menu lists such Aruban specialties as *sopi di mariscos* (seafood soup) and *kreeft stoba* (lobster stew). The walls are hung with antique farm tools, coffee bags, and old family photos, and there's a small museum devoted to the aloe vera plant. You'll need a car to get here, about a mile from San Nicolas. *Cura Cabai 24, San Nicolas, tel. 297/8–48335. Reservations advised. AE, MC, V. Closed Thurs. Inexpensive.*

Lodging

Most of the hotels in Aruba are located west of Oranjestad along L. G. Smith Boulevard, and at press time a couple of new properties were scheduled to open by the end of the 1994 winter season. You may want to check with the Aruba Tourism Authority (tel. 201/330–0800 or 800/TO–ARUBA) about the status of these new ones. Most hotels include a host of facilities—drugstores, boutiques, health spas, beauty parlors, casinos, restaurants, pool bars, and gourmet delis. Do not arrive in Aruba without a reservation; many hotels are booked months in advance, especially in the winter season. All hotels offer packages, and these are considerably less expensive than the one-night rate. Hotel restaurants and clubs are open to all guests on the island, so you can visit other properties no matter where you're staying. Most hotels, unless specified, do not include meals in their room rates. The meal plans offered are optional and incur an additional per-day expense. Off-season rates are discounted approximately 40%.

Look for Charlie, the island's coconut expert, who makes the rounds of the hotels demonstrating his special talent: slicing a coconut samurai-style in three seconds without losing a drop of the precious milk.

Highly recommended lodgings are indicated by a star ★.

Category	Cost*
Very Expensive	over $250
Expensive	$200–$250
Moderate	$125–$200
Inexpensive	under $125

All prices are for a standard double room for two, excluding 5% tax and 10% service charge.

Americana Aruba Beach Resort & Casino. This established high-rise hotel on Palm Beach underwent a $20 million renovation that was completed in early 1992, yet it already seems to need sprucing up. The new clover-leaf-shape pool area has a waterfall and two Jacuzzis in its center. The hotel teems with activity, from beer-drinking contests to bikini shows around the pool, and a social director cajoles your participation in events. Children are treated to a daily activities program, which is free, as well as a video arcade. White bamboo and bleached-wood furniture are complemented by tropical blue, green, and peach fabrics in the rooms. Cable TV with remote control and hair dryers are added niceties. Rooms on the top floors tend to be nicer than those on the lower floors. Americans and Canadians, mostly in tour groups, make up 80% of the clientele. The staff can be a tad lackadaisical. *L. G. Smith Blvd. 83, Palm Beach, tel. 297/8–24500 or 800/447–7462, fax 297/8–23191; in NY, 212/661–4540. 419 rooms. Facilities: 2 restaurants, swimming pool with swim-up bar, TV, 2 lighted tennis courts, tour desk, water-sports concession, children's activities program, weight room/gym, casino, laundry/valet, 2 car rentals, company desks, telex/fax/typewriters, boutiques, beauty parlor/barbershop. AE, DC, MC, V. EP, MAP, All-inclusive. Very Expensive.*

Bushiri Beach Resort. Two long, low buildings—built around a lush Jacuzzi garden and situated on a wide expanse of beach—make up this all-inclusive resort, Aruba's first. These buildings are old and nondescript, and although the rooms were renovated in 1992, they remain ordinary. But the Bushiri is a hotel-training school, a factor that shows in the enthusiastic staff. The best rooms are in the West Wing; "deluxe" rooms, the largest, have minifridges, safe-deposit boxes, and balconies that face the oceans. Where this resort shines is in its full daily activities program for adults. Snorkeling (with instruction and equipment), tennis, sailing, windsurfing, pool volleyball, and casino gambling classes are among the offerings. Kids are kept busy with their own day-long supervised program. Three sightseeing tours around the island, three meals daily, a poolside barbecue, and a midnight buffet, as well as all soft drinks and alcoholic beverages, are included in the single tab—and it still just reaches the very expensive category. In other words, this is quite a bargain. *L. G. Smith Blvd. 35, Oranjestad, tel. 297/8–25216, 800/ GO–BOUNTY, or 800/462–6868; fax 297/8–26789. 150 rooms. Facilities: 2 restaurants, pool bar, cocktail lounge, piano bar, pool, satellite TV, 2 tennis courts, nightly entertainment, beach, watersports center, drugstore, health club, 3 Jacuzzis, free nightly shuttle to the Holiday Inn casino. AE, DC, MC, V. All-inclusive. Very Expensive.*

★ **Hyatt Regency Aruba Resort & Casino.** The center of this $57 million resort—resembling a Spanish grandee's palace with art deco flourishes—is spectacular, with a multilevel pool, two-story waterslide, waterfalls, and a lagoon stocked with tropical fish and black swans. Beyond is a white-sand beach dotted with palms. All the spacious rooms here are the same size, so the view determines their price. The decor is southwestern, with rattan and bleached-wood furniture and luxury appointments. All the air-conditioned rooms have a digital safe, stocked minibar, remote-control color TV, clock radio, ceiling fan, oversized bathroom, and a tiny balcony that's more for show than use. There's a no-smoking floor. The top floor houses the hedonistic Regency Club rooms, each with two huge his-and-her marble bathrooms loaded with every amenity, plus a private-floor lounge where free breakfast, afternoon tea, and happy hour drinks are served. Camp Hyatt keeps children ages 3–15 busy day and night, so parents can enjoy time alone. Four excellent restaurants are on the premises, among them Olé and Ruinas del Mar. Their design is exquisite: stone and marble "ruins" surrounded by moats, waterfalls, and splashing fountains. The food is equally luscious. Lighted tennis courts; a comprehensive water-sports center offering scuba diving, sailing cruises, windsurfing, waterskiing, and jet skiing; a sleek health-and-fitness center; and a shopping arcade, plus a host of well-managed services and a fine staff have turned this property into the top luxury resort on the island. *L. G. Smith Blvd. 85, tel. 297/8–31234 or 800/233–1234; fax 297/8–35478. 325 rooms and 25 suites. Facilities: free-form pool with swim-up bar, 4 restaurants, 2 bars, snack bar, casino, fitness center, 2 lighted tennis courts, water-sports center, tour desk, baby-sitting, shops. AE, DC, MC, V. EP, MAP. Very Expensive.*

Aruba Hilton Hotel and Casino. Hilton Hotels took over this rundown 18-story high rise and gutted it completely. The new slogan promises "In Aruba, some of the hotels have changed their names. At the Aruba Hilton, we are changing the hotel." At press time $20 million had been poured into the rooms, the lobby, and the casino. The vast grand public areas are dazzling in ocher, apricot, and aqua. The rooms are done in dusty rose, peach, and sea-foam green; all feature ocean-view balconies, safe, and satellite TV, with superior and deluxe rooms adding a minibar and hair dryer. Fountains splash playfully into the free-form pool, and the casino is draped like a sultan's tent. Still, the hotel lacks warmth—probably the result of its newness. *Irausquin Blvd. 77, Palm Beach, tel. 297/ 8–64466 or 800/HILTONS; fax 297/8–68217. 483 rooms. Facilities: 5 restaurants, 3 cocktail lounges, nightclub, casino, pool, children's wading pool, 2 lighted tennis courts, fitness center, games room, car rental, tour desk, water-sports desk, beach bar, ballroom with meeting and banquet rooms, shops, beauty parlor, deli, children's corner. AE, DC, MC, V. EP, CP, MAP, FAP. Expensive–Very Expensive.*

Divi Aruba Beach Resort. The motto at this popular Mediterranean-style low rise, taken over by Doral Resorts in 1993, remains "barefoot elegance," which means you can streak through the lobby in your bikini. The main section has 90 standard guest rooms, 20 beachfront lanai rooms, and 40 casitas (garden bungalows) that look out onto individual courtyards amid astonishingly verdant grounds. A newer section, Divi Dos, contains 49 luxury rooms and a bridal suite, all with minirefrigerators and Jacuzzi bathtubs. The rooms were redecorated in 1992 in yellow, green, and creamy white, and they have balconies, cable TV, safe-deposit boxes, and air-conditioning. The Divi Dos section is known as a honeymoon haven: Special packages include champagne breakfast, "just married" signs, photo albums, colorful beach towels, and fruit baskets. Divi Dos's free-form pool includes a small island at the center, accessible by a bridge. Special theme nights include Tuesday's Carnival and Saturday's Beach BBQ Fiesta, with folkloric show and steel band. *L. G. Smith Blvd. 93, Divi Beach, tel. 297/8–23300 or 800/22–DORAL; fax 297/8–34002. 203 rooms. Facilities: 2 restaurants, 2 bars, 2 pools, Jacuzzi, tennis court, shuffleboard, shops, tour desk, water-sports concession, adult activities program, baby-sitting. AE, D, DC, MC, V. EP, MAP, FAP. Expensive–Very Expensive.*

Casa del Mar Beach Resort. This beachfront, low-rise time-share hotel has combined its facilities with its time-share neighbor, the Aruba Beach Club. As time-shares go, Casa del Mar's completely furnished suites are among the most expensive on the island. Each has a dining table seating six, and the kitchen comes fully stocked. Baby-sitters are on call, and a social hostess provides children's programs. *L. G. Smith Blvd. 53, Punta Brabo Beach, tel. 297/8–27000 or 800/346–7084; in NJ, 201/617–8877; fax 297/8–26557. 107 2-bedroom, 2-bath suites. Facilities: restaurant (2 restaurants and pool bar at sister property), lobby bar, TVs with in-room movie satellite, fitness center, sauna and massage, pool, 2 Jacuzzis, 4 lighted tennis courts, children's playground, games room, 2 pools, 2 kiddie pools, baby-sitting, shops. AE, DC, MC, V. EP. Expensive.*

Playa Linda Beach Resort. Designed in a ziggurat of receding balconies, this time-share complex, sheathed in a facade of terra-cotta and cream, sits on one of the most beautiful and enticing sections of Palm Beach. Accommodations are comfortable and stylishly appointed in peach and taupe with an abundance of mirrors; each is outfitted with cable TV, smallish bathroom, full kitchen, ocean-view veranda, and air-conditioning. Units (all of which are suites) sleep four to six. All three hearty meals are served poolside, overlooking the ocean, at the open-air Linda Vista Restaurant. Water sports and tennis can be arranged. *L. G. Smith Blvd. 87, Palm Beach, tel. 297/8–31000 or 800/346–7084; in NJ, 201/617–8877; fax 297/8–25210. 194 1- and 2-bedroom suites and studio apartments. Facilities: 2 restaurants, 2 bars, activities center, adults' and children's pools, 3 lighted tennis courts, minimarket/gift shop. AE, MC, V. EP, MAP, FAP. Expensive.*

Radisson Aruba Caribbean Resort & Casino. Called La Grande Dame of the Caribbean, this resort was the first high rise on the island. Liz Taylor used to stay here when she was married to Eddie Fisher, and the queen of Holland still stays in the Royal Suite (available on request), so the staff is used to filling special needs. The turquoise-and-white tiled lobby gives the feeling of an art deco tropical palazzo. The sunny air-conditioned rooms, all with either an ocean or a garden view, are scattered among four buildings. When Radisson took over, it provided a much-needed infusion of funds for renovations, but even the newly refurbished rooms—best described as dainty and floral—seem old-fashioned. All feature cable TV, safety-deposit box, and balcony. The fitness center near the tennis courts offers a Universal weight system and aerobics classes. Bands play every Saturday night in the blue-and-gold Fandango Nightclub. *L. G. Smith Blvd. 81, Palm Beach, tel. 297/8–33555 or 800/777–1700; fax 297/8–23260. 378 rooms and suites. Facilities: 4 restaurants, 4 bars, nightclub, meeting and banquet rooms, casino, pool, 4 lighted tennis courts, fitness center, tour desk, car rental, baby-sitting, water sports, video-game room, shops, beauty parlor, deli. AE, MC, V. EP, MAP, All-inclusive. Expensive.*

★ **Sonesta Hotel, Beach Club & Casino.** If falling out of bed and onto a beach isn't important to you, then Sonesta's in-town location is ideal—especially if you like to shop, eat, and gamble. This new (1992) hotel stands out amid the Dutch architecture of Oranjestad: In the lobby, sleek low couches wrap around pink stucco pillars while glass elevators rise above the circular deep-water grotto; brilliantly hued toucans and parrots squawk at you from their baroque cages; and motor skiffs board guests headed for the hotel's 40-acre private island. The 300 tropical green-and-pink guest rooms and suites are spacious and modern, with tiny balconies, cable TV, hair dryers, safe-deposit boxes, and stocked minibars. The free daily "Just Us Kids" program offers children ages 5 to 12 supervised activities, including kite flying, bowling, movies, storytelling, and field trips. For adults there are free casino classes, volleyball, and beach bingo. The gourmet restaurant, L'Escale, is one of Aruba's most creative—and expensive. The neighboring Crystal Casino houses the Caribbean's largest $1 slot machine. Dancers should head for the Desires Lounge, which features live entertainment every night except Sunday. By 1995, the Sonesta will have completed renovations of the Harbourside Hotel and Complex, adding its facilities to what is already the most complete resort on the island. *L. G. Smith Blvd. 82, tel. 297/8–36000, 800/SONESTA, or 800/343–7170; fax 297/8–34389. 274 rooms and 25 suites. Facilities: 3 restaurants, bar, minispa and fitness center, pool, 40-acre private island with watersports center, casino, nightclub, 85 shops, children's program, tour desk, beauty salon. AE, DC, MC, V. EP. Expensive.*

Aruba Beach Club. This attractive low-rise resort on Druif Beach also doubles as a time-share. The open-air lobby leads to a patio, gardens, and pool, with the beach only a few steps beyond. Action settles around the pool bar, with a clientele that's mostly American, mostly young-to-middle-aged couples with children. The pastel rooms are more basic than luxurious, even though they're refurbished every two years. Each features a kitchenette, cable TV, room safe, and balcony. Guests may use all the facilities at the Casa del Mar resort next door. *L. G. Smith Blvd. 53, Punta Brabo Beach, tel. 297/8–23000 or 800/346–7084; fax 297/8–26557. 131 studio and 1-bedroom suites. Facilities: 2 restaurants, cocktail lounge, pool bar, ice-cream parlor, adults' and children's pools, 4 lighted tennis courts, playground, baby-sitting. AE, MC, V. EP. Moderate.*

Aruba Palm Beach Hotel & Casino. Formerly a Sheraton, this pink, eight-story Moorish palazzo even has pink-swaddled palm trees dotting its drive. The lobby, with its impressive grand piano, is a haze of pink and purple, underlaid with cool marble. The large backyard sunning grounds are a well-manicured tropical garden, with a fleet of pesky parrots guarding the entrance. The oversize guest rooms are roomy and cheerful, decorated in either burgundy and mauve or emerald and pink. Each has a walk-in closet, color cable TV, and a tiny balcony. All overlook either the ocean, the pool, or the gardens. For a peaceful meal, eat alfresco in the rock-garden setting of the Seawatch Restaurant. For live music, try the Players Club lounge, open nightly until 3 AM. *L. G. Smith Blvd. 79, Palm Beach, tel. 297/ 8–23900 or 800/428–9933; in FL, 305/539–9933; fax 297/8–21941. 202 rooms. Facilities: 2 restaurants, pizza parlor, deli, 2 bars, car rental desk, pool, coffee shop, disco, TV, shops, casino, 2 lighted tennis courts, water sports, tour desk, beauty salon. AE, DC, MC, V. EP, MAP. Moderate.*

★ **Bucuti Beach Resort.** This is not your typical Best Western. The small, European-style Bucuti Beach is a refreshing antidote to the impersonal feel at some larger resorts. These hacienda-style buildings house enormous rooms with bright floral decor and sparkling tile floors. All boast cable TV, air-conditioning, minibar, microwave, coffeemaker, room safe, and terrace or balcony with ocean view. The resort has an enviable location on a gleaming stretch of sand, just across from all the action at the Alhambra Casino and Shopping Center. The breezy Pirate's Nest restaurant is well-known islandwide for its excellent theme dinners. *Box 1299, Aruba, tel. 297/8–36141 or 800/528–1234; fax 297/8–25272. 63 rooms. Facilities: restaurant, bar, pool. AE, DC, MC, V. EP, CP, MAP. Moderate.*

Caribbean Palm Village. In the giant strip mall that is Noord, this is an unexpected oasis. The two-story Mediterranean-style buildings sport porticoed balconies perfumed by frangipani and cooled by fountains. All units feature a full kitchen (including dishwasher and microwave), cable TV, safe, and air-conditioning; a standard room can be closed off from the suite. But what sets these suites apart from the standard sterile Caribbean room is the work of the original developer, who animated the spacious suites with throw rugs, local artworks, potted plants, and cleverly placed divans. Add to that a staff unusually courteous and helpful by Aruban standards. If it weren't so far from the beach, or at least offered a shuttle, it would qualify as Aruba's greatest bargain. *Palm Beach Rd., Noord 43E, tel. 297/8–62700, fax 297/8–62380. 114 units. Facilities: 2 restaurants, bar, 2 pools, lighted tennis court, exercise room. AE, DC, MC, V. EP, MAP. Moderate.*

La Cabana All Suite Beach Resort & Casino. At the top end of Eagle Beach and across the road from the sand is Aruba's largest timesharing condominium/hotel complex. The large four-story building forms a horseshoe around a huge free-form pool complex with a water slide, poolside bar, outdoor cafe, and water-sports center. The entire complex faces the pristine white sands of Eagle Beach just across the street. One-third of the rooms have a full sea view; two-thirds have a partial view. All the oddly configured, but comfortable, rooms—studios or one-bedroom suites—come with a fully equipped kitchenette, a small balcony, and a Jacuzzi, and all have air-conditioning and ceiling fans. The tropically decorated suites have interconnecting doors so that three of them may be linked together to form two- and three-bedroom units. The ground-floor living rooms do not offer as much privacy as do the higher floors because they look out onto the pool area. This complete resort has much to offer: a modern fitness and health center, an ice cream and espresso shop, a budget restaurant, a small grocery store, several shops, and an activities center in the main complex. Shuttle buses run guests over to the upscale casino, the island's largest, where the hotel has another three restaurants and the *rouge et noir* Tropicana nightclub that features top shows. In addition, comedians perform every weekend. At press time, another 400 deluxe suites were scheduled to come on-line by early 1994, yet the unfailingly gracious staff makes it seem like a resort one-third its size. *L. G. Smith Blvd. 250, tel. 297/8–39000 or 800/835–7193; in NY, 212/251–1710; fax 297/8–37208. 440 rooms. Facilities: 5 restaurants, including poolside bar; shops; casino; racquetball, squash, and tennis courts; health and fitness center. AE, DC, MC, V. EP, MAP. Moderate.*

The Mill Resort. Two-story red-roof buildings flank the open-air common areas of this small condominium hotel, which opened in September 1990 and continues to expand. Unlike time-share resorts, this hotel sells each unit to an individual, who then leases the unit back to the resort for use as a hotel room. The decor is soft country French, with a delicate rose-and-white color scheme, white wicker furniture, and wall-to-wall silver carpeting. The junior suites feature a king-size bed, sitting area, and kitchenette. The studios have a full kitchen, but only a queen-size convertible sofa bed and a tiny bathroom. There's no kitchen in the hedonistic Royal Den, but there's a marble Jacuzzi tub big enough for two. This resort is popular with couples seeking a quiet getaway and with families vacationing with small children. There is no restaurant on the premises, but The Old Mill is next door (*see* Dining, *above*). There are also no bars, no tour desk, and no organized evening activities. The theme here is one of peaceful bliss. Action can be found at the nearby large resorts, and the beach is only a five-minute walk away. *L. G. Smith Blvd. 330, Palm Beach, tel. 297/8–37700, fax 297/8–37271. 204 studio, junior, and Royal Den suites. One- and 2-bedroom suites are available by combining two of the above units. Facilities: pool, kiddie pool, mini food market, baby-sitting, car rental, 2 lighted tennis courts, fitness center, pool snack bar. AE, DC, MC, V. EP. Moderate.*

Amsterdam Manor. This attractive gabled russet- and mustard-colored hotel looks like part of a Dutch colonial village. You feel as if you're stepping back three centuries the moment you walk through the gate. Rooms are furnished either in Dutch modern or quaint provincial style, ranging from smallish studios with a balcony, cable TV, and kitchenette to deluxe two-bedroom suites with a Jacuzzi and full kitchen. Alas, even this cozy enclave (and a lovely pool with waterfall) can't quite shut out the noise of traffic from Palm Beach Road. At least that glorious beach is just across the street. *L. G. Smith Blvd. 252, tel. 297/8–31492, fax 297/8–31463. 73 units. Facilities: restaurant, bar, pool, minimart. MC, V. EP. Inexpensive–Moderate.*

La Quinta Beach Resort. Across the road from Eagle Beach is this moderately priced time-share complex with a friendly staff. The efficiency and one-bedroom units were completed in 1993 and are small but well designed and stylish, with full cooking facilities, TVs, and hair dryers in the tiled bathrooms. One-, two-, and three-bedroom units also have sleep sofas and VCRs; some even boast a Jacuzzi. *Eagle Beach, tel. 297/8–35010 or 800/223–9815, fax 297/8–26263. 54 units. Facilities: bar, 2 pools, cable TV, tennis courts. AE, DC, MC, V. EP. Inexpensive–Moderate.*

Nightlife

Casinos   Casinos are all the rage in Aruba. At last count there were 10. The crowds seem to flock to the newest of the new: The Crystal Casino enjoyed the business until the Hyatt Regency's ultramodern gaming room stole the show (the marquee above the bar at this casino opens to reveal a live band). Then it was the wildly popular new **Royal Cabana Casino** (L. G. Smith Blvd. 250, tel. 297/8–39000) with its sleek interior, multitheme three-in-one restaurant, and showcase Tropicana nightclub. Smart money's on the just-opened Hilton Casablanca Casino, quietly elegant with a Moorish theme (Irausquin Blvd. 77, tel. 297/8–64466). One place where you'll always find some action is the **Alhambra Casino** (L. G. Smith Blvd. 93, Oranjestad, tel. 297/8–35000), where a "Moorish slave" gives every gambler a hearty handshake upon entering.

There's also action along the Oranjestad "strip" in the casinos at the **Aruba Hilton Hotel and Casino** (L. G. Smith Blvd. 77, tel. 297/8–24466) and the **Golden Tulip Caribbean** (L. G. Smith Blvd. 81, tel. 297/8–33555). The **Holiday Inn**'s casino (L. G. Smith Blvd. 230, tel. 297/8–23419) is open 19 hours a day, with an adjacent New York–style deli open until 5 AM. The **Americana Aruba Beach Resort & Casino** (L. G. Smith Blvd. 83, tel. 297/8–24500) opens daily at 1 PM for slots, 5 PM for all games. The **Aruba Palm Beach Hotel Casino** (L. G. Smith Blvd. 79, tel. 297/8–23900) opens at 10 AM for slots, 6 PM for all games. You can also woo Lady Luck at the Sonesta Hotel's **Crystal Casino** (L. G. Smith Blvd. 82, tel. 297/8–36000), where the action is nonstop from 10 AM to 4 AM for slots; 1 PM to 4 AM for the gaming tables. And there's the new **Hyatt Regency Aruba Resort Casino** (L. G. Smith Blvd. 85, tel. 297/8–31234), a 10,000-square-foot complex with a Carnival-in-Rio theme and live entertainment. Low-key gambling can be found at the new waterside **Harbourtown Casino** (L. G. Smith Blvd. 9, tel. 297/8–35600 or 297/8–32165).

Disco and Dancing Arubans usually start partying late, and action doesn't start till around midnight, mostly on the weekends. The newest "in" place is **Papas & Beer** (L. G. Smith Blvd. 184, tel. 297/8–60300), whose purple-and-pink neon signs can be seen lighting up the night from as far away as hotel row. Live bands perform nightly, waiters in funky costumes do dance routines under flickering strobe lights, video screens flash, and food and drinks are served almost round-the-clock. Another popular nightclub is **Blue Wave** (Shellstraat, tel. 297/8–38856) with live bands on Saturday nights and a "Ladies Night" drawing in the crowds on Thursday. For a young adult–style "amusement park," stop in at **La Visage** (L. G. Smith Blvd. 152A, tel. 297/8–22397), the disco for the young set, both Arubans and tourists. Jazz lovers will prefer the quiet piano bar atmosphere of **La Nota** (Emmastraat 7, tel. 297/8–32739), which gets lively around 10 PM until close at 2 AM.

One truly different evening out is **Chiva Parranda** (tel. 297/8–37643), which means "bus out on the town." Every Tuesday and Thursday at 6:30 PM, this nightlife tour boards up to 40 people on a hand-painted 1947 Ford bus and whisks them off to the five hot local nightspots. The $49.50-per-person price includes a drink at each rum shop and dinner. You're picked up (and poured off) at your hotel. As your affable host remarks, "I finally learned how to cash in on being a party animal."

Theater **Aladdin Theater** (L. G. Smith Blvd. 93, tel. 297/8–35000). This cabaret theater tucked into the Alhambra Bazaar features a variety of shows, including Broadway musicals.

Tropicana (L. G. Smith Blvd. 250, tel 297/8–39000). Aruba's newest cabaret theater and nightclub, part of the La Cabana All Suite Beach Resort complex, features first-class Las Vegas–style reviews and modern shows, plus a special revolving comedy series every weekend.

Twinklebones's House of Roast Beef (Noord 24, tel. 297/8–26780) does serve succulent prime rib and the like. But it's best known for the fun cabaret put on by the staff twice nightly. Customers eat it up.

Specialty Theme Nights One of the unique things about Aruba's nightlife is the number of specialty theme nights offered by the hotels: At last count there were more than 30. Each "party" features dinner and entertainment, followed by dancing. For a complete list, contact the Aruba Tourism Authority (tel. 297/8–23777).

An Aruban must is the **Bon Bini Festival,** held every Tuesday evening from 6:30 to 8:30 PM in the outdoor courtyard of the Fort Zoutman Museum. *Bon Bini* is Papiamento for "welcome," and this tourist event is the Aruba Institute of Culture and Education's way of introducing visitors to all things Aruban. Stroll by the stands of Aruban foods, drinks, and crafts, or watch Aruban entertainers perform Antillean music and folkloric dancing. A master of ceremonies explains the history of the dances, instruments, and music. It's a fun event, and a good way to meet other tourists. Look for the clock tower. *Oranjestraat, tel. 297/8–22185. Admission: Afl2 adults, Afl1 children.*

Weekend evenings are lively all over town, so the theme-night pickings are fewer. The best ones are Divi Aruba Beach Resort's **Beach BBQ Fiesta** (L. G. Smith Blvd. 93, tel. 297/8–23300) on Saturday nights and the Mexican fiesta **Fajitas and 'ritas** (L. G. Smith Blvd. 85, tel. 297/8–31234) held Friday nights at the beachside Palms Restaurant in the Hyatt Regency.

5 Barbados

Updated by
Susan Ryan

Barbados has a life of its own that goes on after the tourists have packed their sun oils and returned home. Since the government is stable and unemployment is relatively low, the difference between haves and have-nots is less marked—or at least less visible—than on other islands, and visitors are neither fawned upon nor resented for their assumed wealth. Genuinely proud of their country, the quarter million Bajans (Barbadians) welcome visitors as privileged guests. Barbados is fine for people who want nothing more than to offer their bodies to the sun; yet the island, unlike many in the Caribbean, is also ideal for travelers who want to discover another life and culture.

Because the beaches of Barbados are open to the public, they lack the privacy that some visitors seek, but the beaches themselves are lovely, and many along the tranquil west coast—in the lee of the northwest trade winds—are backed by first-class resorts. Most of the hotels are situated along the beaches on the southern and southwestern coasts. The British and Canadians often favor the hotels of St. James Parish; Americans (couples more often than singles) tend to prefer the large south-coast resorts.

To the northeast are rolling hills and valleys covered by acres of impenetrable sugarcane. The Atlantic surf pounds the gigantic boulders along the rugged east coast, where the Bajans themselves have their vacation homes. Elsewhere on the island, linked by almost 900 miles of good roads, are historic plantation houses, stalactite-studded caves, a wildlife preserve, and the Andromeda Gardens, one of the most attractive small tropical gardens in the world.

No one is sure whether the name Los Barbados ("the bearded ones") refers to the beardlike root that hangs from the island's fig trees or to the bearded natives who greeted the Portuguese "discoverer" of the island in 1536. The name Los Barbados was still current almost a century later when the British landed—by accident—in what is now Holetown in St. James Parish. They colonized the island in 1627 and remained until it achieved independence in 1966.

Barbadians retain a British accent. Afternoon tea is a ritual at numerous hotels. Cricket is still the national sport, and Barbados produces some of the world's top players. Polo is played in winter. The British tradition of dressing for dinner is firmly entrenched; a few luxury hotels require tie and jacket at dinner, and in good restaurants most women will consider themselves inappropriately dressed in anything less formal than a sundress. (A daytime stroll in a swimsuit is as inappropriate in Bridgetown as it would be on New York's 5th Avenue.) Yet the island's atmosphere is hardly stuffy. When the boat you ordered for noon doesn't arrive until 12:30, you can expect a cheerful response, "He okay, mon, he just on Caribbean time."

Before You Go

Tourist Information

Contact the **Barbados Board of Tourism**, 800 2nd Ave., New York, NY 10017, tel. 212/986–6516, or 3440 Wilshire Blvd., Suite 1215, Los Angeles, CA 90010, tel. 213/380–2198. **In Canada:** 5160 Yonge St., Suite 1800, N. York, Ontario M2N–6L9, tel. 416/512–6569; 615 Dorchester, Montreal, Suite 960, Montreal, Québec H3B 1P5, tel. 514/861–0085. **In the United Kingdom:** 263 Tottenham Court Rd., London W1P 9AA, tel. 441/636–9448.

Arriving and Departing
By Plane

Grantley Adams Airport in Barbados is a Caribbean hub. There are daily flights from New York via San Juan, and **American Airlines** (tel. 800/433–7300) and **BWIA** (tel. 800/538–2942) both have nonstop flights from New York. There are direct flights from Miami on BWIA. From Canada, **Air Canada** (tel. 800/776–3000) connects from Montreal through New York or Miami and flies nonstop from Toronto. From London, **British Airways** (tel. 800/247–9297) has nonstop service and BWIA connects through Trinidad.

Flights to St. Vincent, St. Lucia, Trinidad, and other islands are scheduled on LIAT (tel. 809/495–1187) and BWIA; Air St. Vincent/Air Mustique links Barbados with St. Vincent and the Grenadines.

From the Airport   Airport taxis are not metered. A large sign at the airport announces the fixed rate to each hotel or area, stated in both Barbados and U.S. dollars (about $20 to the west coast hotels, $13 to the south coast ones). The new highway around Bridgetown saves time and trouble in getting up the western coast.

By Boat   A popular cruise port, Barbados has room for eight ships (which is some indication of how crowded the Bridgetown shops can be). Bridgetown Harbour is located on the northwest side of Carlisle Bay, and most cruise ships organize transportation to and from the **Carlisle Bay Centre,** a "hotel without rooms" for passengers on shore excursions. The CBC provides changing facilities, a restaurant, gift shops, and water-sports facilities—including floats, snorkel equipment, Sunfish sailboats, water skis, Windsurfers—for a nominal fee.

Passports and Visas   U.S. and Canadian citizens need proof of citizenship plus a return or ongoing ticket to enter the country. Acceptable proof of citizenship is a valid passport or an original birth certificate and a photo ID; a voter registration card is not acceptable. British citizens need a valid passport.

Language   English is spoken everywhere, sometimes accented with the phrases and lilt of a Bajan dialect.

Precautions   Beach vendors of coral jewelry and beachwear will not hesitate to offer you their wares. The degree of persistence varies, and some of their jewelry offerings are good; sharp bargaining is expected on both sides. One hotel's brochure gives sound advice: "Please realize that encouraging the beach musicians means you may find yourself listening to the same three tunes over and over for the duration of your stay."

Water   The water on the island, both in hotels and in restaurants, has been treated and is safe to drink.

Insects   Insects aren't much of a problem on Barbados, but if you plan to hike or spend time on secluded beaches, it's wise to use insect repellent.

Toxic Tree   The little green apples that fall from the large branches of the manchineel tree may look tempting, but they are poisonous to eat and toxic to the touch. Even taking shelter under the tree when it rains can give you blisters. Most manchineels are identified with signs; if you do come in contact with one, go to the nearest hotel and have someone there phone for a physician.

Crime   Don't invite trouble by leaving valuables unattended on the beach or in plain sight in your room, and don't pick up hitchhikers.

Staying in Barbados

Important Addresses   **Tourist Information:** The **Barbados Board of Tourism** is on Harbour Road in Bridgetown (tel. 809/427–2623). Hours are 8:30–4:30 Monday–Friday. There are also information booths, staffed by board

Exploring

Dining

Lodging

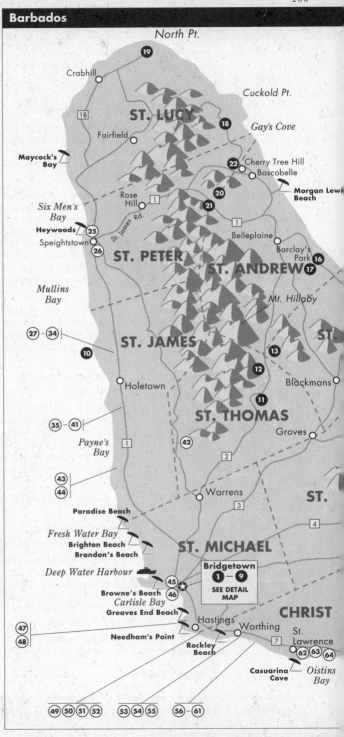

Barbados

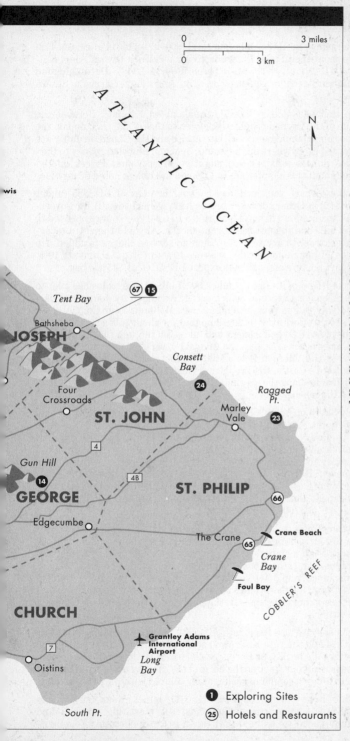

representatives at Grantley Adams International Airport and at Bridgetown's Deep Water Harbour.

Emergencies   **Emergency:** tel. 119. **Ambulance:** tel. 809/426–1113. **Police:** tel. 112. **Fire department:** tel. 113. **Scuba diving accidents:** Divers' Alert Network (DAN; tel. 809/684–8111 or 919/684–2948). **Decompression chamber:** Barbados Defense Force, St. Ann's Fort, Garrison, St. Michael Parish, tel. 809/436–6185.

Currency   One Barbados dollar (BDS$1) equals about U.S.50¢. Because the value of the Barbados dollar is pegged to that of the U.S. dollar, the ratio remains constant. Both currencies and the Canadian dollar are accepted everywhere on the island, but changing your money to Barbados dollars will get you slightly better value. Prices quoted throughout this chapter are in U.S. dollars unless noted otherwise.

Taxes and   At the airport you must pay a departure tax of BDS$25 (about
Service   U.S.$12) in either currency before leaving Barbados. A 5% govern-
Charges   ment tax is added to hotel bills, and a 10% service charge is added to hotel bills and to most restaurant checks. Any additional tip recognizes extraordinary service. When no service charge is added, tip maids $1 per room per day, waiters 10% to 15%, taxi drivers 10%. Airport porters and bellboys expect BDS$2 (U.S.$1) per bag.

Guided Tours   For an island of its size (14 miles by 21 miles), Barbados has a lot to see. A bus or taxi tour, which can be arranged by your hotel, is a good way to get your bearings. **L. E. Williams Tour Co.** (tel. 809/427–1043) offers an 80-mile island tour for about $50; a bus picks you up between 8:30 and 9:30 AM and takes you through Bridgetown, the St. James beach area, past the Animal Flower Cave, Farley Hill, Cherry Tree Hill, Morgan Lewis Mill, the east coast, St. John's Church, Sam Lord's Castle, Oistin's fishing village, and to St. Michael Parish, with drinks along the way and a West Indian lunch at the Atlantis Hotel in Bathsheba.

Sally Shern operates **VIP Tours** (Hillcrest Villa, Upton, St. Michael Parish, tel. 809/429–4617), custom-tailored to each client, whom she picks up in an air-conditioned Mercedes-Benz. Bajan-born Ms. Shern knows her island well and provides the unusual and unique: a champagne lunch at Sunbury Plantation House, a swim at her favorite beach. **Bajan Helicopters** offers an eagle's-eye view of Barbados (the Wharf, Bridgetown, tel. 809/431–0069). Depending upon the time spent aloft, prices per person range from U.S.$65 for 20 minutes to U.S.$100 for 30 minutes.

Custom Tours (tel. 809/425–0099) arranges personalized tours for one to four persons at a cost of U.S. $25 per hour (minimum four hours). Staff members determine your particular interests (such as gardens, plantation houses, swimming at secluded beaches), pack a picnic lunch, and drive you in their own cars. They offer a familiarization tour for first-time visitors and often can take you to places that aren't normally open to the public. Ask for Margaret Leacock, the owner.

Getting   Taxis operate at a fixed rate (BDS$30 for the first hour, less after
Around   that); settle the rate before you start off, and be sure you agree on
Taxis   whether it's in U.S. or Barbados dollars. Most drivers will cheerfully narrate a tour, though the noise of the car may make it difficult for you to follow a rambling commentary colored with Bajan inflections.

Buses   Public buses along Highway 1, St. James Road, are cheap (BDS$1.50, exact change appreciated), plentiful, reliable, and usually packed. The buses provide a great opportunity to experience local color, and your fellow passengers will be eager to share their knowledge.

Rental Cars It's a pleasure to explore Barbados by car, provided you take the time to study a good map and don't mind asking directions frequently. The more remote roads are in good repair, yet few are well lighted at night, and night falls quickly—at about 6 PM. Even in full daylight, the tall sugarcane fields lining a road can create near-zero visibility. Yet local residents are used to pointing travelers in the right direction, and some confused but intelligent drivers have been known to flag a passing taxi and pay to follow it back to a city area. Use caution: Pedestrians are everywhere. And remember, traffic keeps to the left throughout the island.

To rent a car you must have an international driver's license, obtainable at the airport and major car-rental firms for $5 if you have a valid driver's license. More than 40 offices rent minimokes (open-air vehicles) for upward of $45 a day plus insurance (about $215 a week), usually with a three-day or four-day minimum; cars with automatic shift are $45–$55 a day, or approximately $285 a week. Gas costs just over BDS$1 a liter (about $2 a gallon) and is extra. The speed limit, in keeping with the pace of life, is 37 miles per hour (60 kilometers per hour) in the country, 21 miles per hour in town. Operating a motorbike also requires an international driver's license—and some skill and daring.

The principal car-rental firms are **National** (tel. 809/426–0603), **Dear's Garage** on the south coast (tel. 809/429–9277 or 809/427–7853), **Sunny Isle** in Worthing (tel. 809/428–8009 or 809/428–2965), and **Sunset Crest Rentals** in St. James (tel. 809/432–1482). **P&S Car Rentals** (Spring Garden Hwy., tel. 809/424–2052) offers air-conditioned cars and Jeeps with free customer delivery; it also arranges visitor driving permits.

Telephones The area code for Barbados is 809. Except for emergency numbers,
and Mail all phone numbers have seven digits and begin with 42 or 43.

An airmail letter from Barbados to the United States or Canada costs BDS95¢ per half ounce; an airmail postcard costs BDS65¢. Letters to the United Kingdom are BDS$1.10; postcards are BDS70¢.

Opening and Stores are open weekdays 8–4, Saturday 8–1. Some supermarkets
Closing Times are open daily 8–6. Banks are open Monday to Thursday 9–3, Friday 9–1 and 3–5.

Exploring Barbados

Numbers in the margin correspond to points of interest on the Bridgetown map.

The island's most popular sights and attractions can be seen comfortably in four or five excursions, each lasting one day or less. The five tours described here begin with Bridgetown and then cover central Barbados, the eastern shore, north-central Barbados, and the south shore. Before you set out in a car, minimoke, or taxi, ask at your hotel or the Board of Tourism for a free copy of the detailed Barbados Holiday Map and check performance or opening times.

Bridgetown **Bridgetown** is a bustling city, complete with rush hours and traffic congestion; you'll avoid hassle by taking the bus or a taxi. Sightseeing will take only an hour or so, and the shopping areas are within walking distance.

In the center of town, overlooking the picturesque harbor known as
1 the Careenage, is **Trafalgar Square,** with its impressive monument

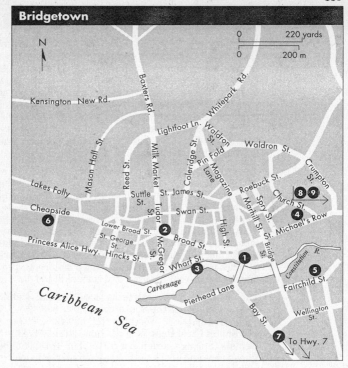

Bridgetown

to Horatio, Lord Nelson. It predates the Nelson's Column in London's Trafalgar Square by about two decades (and for more than a century Bajans have petitioned to replace it with a statue of a Bajan). Here are also a war memorial and a three-dolphin fountain commemorating the advent of running water in Barbados in 1865.

② Bridgetown is a major Caribbean free port. The principal shopping area is **Broad Street,** which leads west from Trafalgar Square past the House of Assembly and Parliament buildings. These Victorian Gothic structures, like so many smaller buildings in Bridgetown, stand beside a growing number of modern office buildings and shops. Small colonial buildings, their balconies trimmed with wrought iron, reward the visitor who has patience and an appreciative eye.

③ The water that bounds Trafalgar Square is called the **Careenage,** a finger of sea that made early Bridgetown a natural harbor and a gathering place. Here working schooners were careened (turned on their sides) to be scraped of barnacles and repainted. Today the Careenage serves mainly as a berth for fiberglass pleasure yachts.

④ Although no one has proved it conclusively, George Washington, on his only visit outside the United States, is said to have worshiped at **St. Michael's Cathedral** east of Trafalgar Square. The structure was nearly a century old when he visited in 1751, and it has since been destroyed by hurricanes and rebuilt twice, in 1780 and 1831.

⑤
⑥ The two bridges over the Careenage are the Chamberlain Bridge and the Charles O'Neal Bridge, both of which lead to Highway 7 and south to the **Fairchild Market.** On Saturdays the activity there and at the **Cheapside Market** (on the north end of Lower Broad Street,

across from St. Mary's Church Square) recall the lively days before the coming of the supermarket and the mall, when the outdoor markets of Barbados were the daily heart and soul of shopping and socializing.

❼ About a mile south of Bridgetown on Highway 7, the unusually interesting **Barbados Museum** has artifacts and mementos of military history and everyday life in the 19th century. Here you'll see cane-harvesting implements, lace wedding dresses, ancient (and frightening) dentistry instruments, and slave sale accounts kept in a spidery copperplate handwriting. Wildlife and natural history exhibits, a well-stocked gift shop, and a good café are also here, in what used to be the military prison. *Hwy. 7, Garrison Savannah, tel. 809/427-0201. Admission: BDS$10 adults, BDS$5 children under 12. Open Mon.–Sat. 9–5, Sun. 2–6.*

❽ East of St. Michael's Cathedral, **Queen's Park,** now being restored to its original splendor, is home to one of the largest trees in Barbados:
❾ an immense baobab more than 10 centuries old. The historic **Queen's Park House,** former home of the commander of the British troops, has been converted into a theater—with an exhibition room on the lower floor—and a restaurant. Queen's Park is a long walk from Trafalgar Square or the museum; you may want to take a taxi. *Open daily 9–5.*

Central *Numbers in the margin correspond to points of interest on the Bar-*
Barbados *bados map.*

❿ The **Folkstone Underwater Park,** north of Holetown, has a land museum of marine life and an underwater snorkeling trail around Dottin's Reef (glass-bottom boats are available for nonswimmers). A dredge barge sunk in shallow water is the home to myriad fish, and it and the reef are popular with scuba divers. Huge sea fans, soft coral, and the occasional giant turtle are sights to see.

⓫ Highway 2 will take you to **Harrison's Cave.** These pale-gold limestone caverns, complete with subterranean streams and waterfalls, are entirely organic and said to be unique in the Caribbean. Open since 1981, the caves are so extensive that tours are made by electric tram (hard hats are provided, but all that may fall on you is a little dripping water). *Tel. 809/438-6640. Admission: BDS$15 adults, BDS$7.50 children. Reservations recommended. Open daily 9–4.*

⓬ The nearby **Welchman Hall Gully,** a part of the National Trust in St. Thomas, gives you another chance to commune with nature. Here are acres of labeled flowers and trees, the occasional green monkey, and great peace and quiet. *Tel. 809/438-6671. Admission: BDS$10 adults, BDS$5 children. Open daily 9–5.*

⓭ Continue along Highway 2 to reach the **Flower Forest,** 8 acres of fragrant flowering bushes, canna and ginger lilies, and puffball trees. Another hundred species of flora combine with the tranquil views of Mt. Hillaby to induce in visitors what may be a relaxing and very pleasant light-headedness. *Tel. 809/433-8152. Admission: BDS$10. Open daily 9–5.*

⓮ Go back toward Bridgetown and take Highway 4 and smaller roads to **Gun Hill** for a view so pretty it seems almost unreal: Shades of green and gold cover the fields all the way to the horizon, the picturesque gun tower is surrounded by brilliant flowers, and the white limestone lion behind the garrison is a famous landmark. Military invalids were once sent here to convalesce. *No tel. Admission: BDS$5 adults, BDS$2.50 children.*

The Eastern Shore Take Highway 3 across the island to Bathsheba and the phenomenal view from the **Atlantis,** one of the oldest hotels in Barbados, where you may need help getting up from the table after sampling the lunch buffet.

⑮ In the nearby **Andromeda Gardens** (tel. 809/433–9261), a fascinating small garden set into the cliffs overlooking the sea, are unusual and beautiful plant specimens from around the world, collected by the late horticulturist Iris Bannochie and now administered by the Barbados National Trust. *Tel. 809/426–2421. Admission: BDS$10 adults, BDS$5 children. Open daily 9–5.*

⑯ North of Bathsheba, **Barclay's Park** offers a similar view and picnic
⑰ facilities in a wooded seafront area. At the nearby **Chalky Mount Potteries,** you'll find craftspersons making and selling their wares.

A drive north to the isolated Morgan Lewis Beach (*see* Beaches, *below*) or to Gay's Cove, which every Bajan calls Cove Bay, will put you
⑱ in reach of the town of **Pie Corner.** Pie Corner is known not for baked goods but for artifacts left by the Cariband Arawak tribes who once lived here.

⑲ The **Animal Flower Cave** at North Point, reached by Highway 1B, displays small sea anemones, or sea worms, that resemble jewel-like flowers as they open their tiny tentacles. For a small fee you can explore inside the cavern and see the waves breaking just outside it. *Tel. 809/439–8797. Admission: BDS$3 adults, BDS$1.50 children under 12. Open daily 9–4.*

North-Central Barbados The attractions of north-central Barbados may well be combined with the tour of the eastern shore.

⑳ The **Barbados Wildlife Reserve** can be reached on Highway 1 from Speightstown on the west coast. Here are herons, land turtles, a kangaroo, screeching peacocks, innumerable green monkeys and their babies doing all manner of things, geese, brilliantly colored parrots, and a friendly otter. The fauna are not in cages, so step carefully and keep your hands to yourself. The preserve has been much improved in recent years with the addition of a giant walk-in aviary and natural-history exhibits. Terrific photo opportunities are everywhere. *Tel. 809/422–8826. Admission: BDS$15 adults, BDS$10 children under 12 with adult. Open daily 10–5.*

㉑ Just to the south is **Farley Hill,** a national park in northern St. Peter Parish; the rugged landscape explains why they call this the Scotland area. The imposing ruins of a once-magnificent plantation great house are surrounded by gardens, lawns, an avenue of towering royal palms, and gigantic mahogany, whitewood, and casuarina trees. Partially rebuilt for the filming of *Island in the Sun,* the structure was later destroyed by fire. *Admission: BDS$2 per car; walkers free. Open daily 8:30–6.*

㉒ **St. Nicholas Abbey** near Cherry Tree Hill, was named for a former owner and is the oldest (ca. 1650) great house in Barbados. It's well worth visiting for its stone and wood architecture in the Jacobean style. Fascinating home movies, made by the present owner's father, record scenes of Bajan town and plantation life in the 1920s and 1930s. There are no set showing times; you need only ask to see them. *Tel. 809/422–8725. Admission: $2.50. Open weekdays 10–3:30.*

The South Shore Driving east on Highways 4 and 4B, you'll note the many **chattel houses** along the route; the property of tenant farmers, these ever-expandable houses were built to be dismantled and moved when

㉓ necessary. On the coast, the appropriately named **Ragged Point Lighthouse** is where the sun first shines on Barbados and its dramatic Atlantic seascape. About 4 miles to the northwest, in the eastern corner of St. John Parish, the coral-stone buildings and serenely **㉔** beautiful grounds of **Codrington Theological College,** founded in 1748, stand on a cliff overlooking Consett Bay.

Take the smaller roads southeast to reach **Marriott's Sam Lord's Castle** (*see* Lodging, *below*), the Regency house built by the buccaneer. Most of the rooms are furnished with the fine antiques he is said to have acquired from passing ships (note the mahogany four-poster), but he had to hire Italian artisans to create the elaborate plaster ceilings. The tour is free to guests; others pay a small fee.

Beaches

Barbados is blessed with some of the Caribbean's most beautiful beaches, all of them open to the public. (Access to hotel beaches may not always be public, but you can walk onto almost any beach from another one.)

West Coast Beaches The west coast has the stunning coves and white-sand beaches that are dear to postcard publishers—plus calm, clear water for snorkeling, scuba diving, and swimming. The afternoon clouds and sunsets may seem to be right out of a Turner painting; because there is nothing but ocean between Barbados and Africa, the sunsets are rendered even more spectacular by the fine red sand that sometimes blows in from the Sahara.

While beaches here are seldom crowded, the west coast is not the place to find isolation. Owners of private boats stroll by, offering waterskiing, parasailing, and snorkel cruises. There are no concession stands per se, but hotels welcome nonguests for terrace lunches (wear a cover-up). Picnic items and necessities can be bought at the Sunset Crest shopping center in Holetown.

Beaches begin in the north at **Heywoods** (about a mile of sand) and continue almost unbroken to Bridgetown at **Brighton Beach,** a popular spot with locals. There is public access through the Barbados Beach Club and the Barbados Pizza House (both good for casual lunches), south of the Discovery Bay Hotel.

Good spots for swimming include **Paradise Beach; Brandon's Beach,** a 10-minute walk south; **Browne's Beach,** in Bridgetown; and **Greaves End Beach,** south of Bridgetown at Aquatic Gap, between the Grand Barbados Beach Resort and the Barbados Hilton International in St. Michael Parish.

The west coast is the area for scuba diving, sailing, and lunch-and-rum cruises on the red-sailed *Jolly Roger* "pirate" party ship (Fun Cruises, tel. 809/436–6424 or 809/429–4545). Somewhat more sedate sea experiences can be had on the *Wind Warrior* (tel. 809/427–7245) and the *Secret Love* (tel. 809/427–7245).

You can go to depths of 150 feet off wrecks and reefs in the *Atlantis* (tel. 809/436–8929 or 809/436–8932), a Canadian-built 50-foot submarine that seats 28 passengers at a time, each at his or her own porthole. Classical music plays while an oceanography specialist informs. *Cost: $69.50 adults, $39.75 children 4–12.*

South Coast Beaches The heavily traveled south coast of Christ Church Parish is much more built up than the St. James Parish coast in the west; here you'll find condos, high-rise hotels, many places to eat and shop, and the traffic (including public transportation) that serves them. These busier beaches generally draw a younger, more active crowd. The quality of the beach itself is consistently good, the reef-protected waters safe for swimming and snorkeling.

Needham's Point, with its lighthouse, is one of Barbados's best beaches, crowded with locals on weekends and holidays. Two others are in the St. Lawrence Gap area, near **Casuarina Cove.** The **Benston Windsurfing Club Hotel** in Maxwell caters specifically to windsurfing aficionados, and most hotels and resorts provide boards or rent them for a nominal fee.

Crane Beach has for years been a popular swimming beach. As you move toward the Atlantic side of the island, the waves roll in bigger and faster; the waves at the nearby Crane Hotel are a favorite with bodysurfers. (But remember that this is the ocean, not the Caribbean, and exercise caution.)

Nearby **Foul Bay** lives up to its name only for sailboats; for swimmers and alfresco lunches, it's lovely.

North Coast Beaches Those who love wild natural beauty will want to head north up the east-coast highway. With secluded beaches and crashing ocean waves on one side, rocky cliffs and verdant landscape on the other, the windward side of Barbados won't disappoint anyone who seeks dramatic views. But be cautioned: Swimming here is treacherous and *not* recommended. The waves are high, the bottom tends to be rocky, and the currents are unpredictable. Limit yourself to enjoying the view and watching the surfers—who have been at it since they were kids.

A worthwhile little-visited beach for the adventurous who don't mind trekking about a mile off the beaten track is **Morgan Lewis Beach,** on the coast east of Morgan Lewis Mill, the oldest intact windmill on the island. Turn east on the small road that goes to the town of Boscobelle (between Cherry Tree Hill and Morgan Lewis Mill), but instead of going to the town, take the even less traveled road (unmarked on most maps; you will have to ask for directions) that goes down the cliff to the beach. What awaits is more than 2 miles of unspoiled, uninhabited white sand and sweeping views of the Atlantic coastline. You may see a few Barbadians swimming, sunning, or fishing, but for the most part you'll have privacy.

Return to your car, cross the island's north point on the secondary roads until you reach the west coast. About a mile west from the end of Highway 1B is **Maycock's Bay,** an isolated area in St. Lucy Parish about 2 miles north of Heywoods, the west coast's northernmost resort complex.

Sports and the Outdoors

Golfing The Royal Westmoreland Golf and Country Club is still in its planning stages and until it is completed, golfers favor the 18 holes at the **Sandy Lane Club** (tel. 809/432–1145), whose dramatic 7th hole is famous both for its elevated tee and its incredible view. There is also a 9-hole course at the **Rockley Resort** (tel. 809/435–7873) and another 9 holes at **Heywoods** (tel. 809/422–4900). All are open (for various fees) to nonguests.

Hiking/Jogging Hilly but not mountainous, the interior of Barbados is ideal for hiking. The **Barbados National Trust** (Belleville, St. Michael, tel. 809/426–2421) sponsors free walks year-round on Sunday, from 6:30 AM to about 9:30 AM and from 3:30 PM to 5:30 PM, as well as special moonlight hikes when the heavens permit. Newspapers announce the time and meeting place (or you can call the trust).

Horseback Riding The **Caribbean International Riding Center** (Christ Church, tel. 809/433–1453) offers one-hour to half-day rides that range in price from BDS$55 to BDS$175. On the west coast, **Brighton Stables** (tel. 809/425–9381) offers one-hour rides along beaches and palm groves for BDS$55. Prices for both operators include transportation to and from your hotel.

Parasailing Parasailing, during which you wear a parachute harness and take off from a raft as you're towed by a speedboat, is available, wind conditions permitting, on the beaches of St. James and Christ Church. Just ask at any hotel, then flag down a speedboat (though it may have found you first).

Sailing and Fishing **Blue Jay Charters** (tel. 809/422–2098) has a 45-foot, fully equipped fishing boat, with a crew that knows the waters where blue marlin, sailfish, barracuda, and kingfish play. You can also try **Sailing Charter Tiami Cruises** (tel. 809/427–7245) for chartered sails or fishing trips.

Scuba Diving Barbados, with a rich and varied underwater world, is one of the few islands in the Caribbean that offers activity for both divers and nondivers. Many dive shops provide instruction (the three-hour beginner's "resort courses" and the week-long certification courses) followed by a shallow dive, usually on Dottin's Reef. Trained divers can explore reefs, wrecks, and the walls of "blue holes," the huge circular depressions in the ocean floor. Not to be missed by certified, guided divers is the *Stavronikita*, a 368-foot Greek freighter that was deliberately sunk at about 125 feet; hundreds of butterfly fish hang out around its mast, and the thin rays of sunlight that filter down through the water make exploring the huge ship a wonderfully eerie experience.

Dive Barbados (Watersports, Sunset Crest Beach, near Holetown, St. James Parish, tel. 809/432–7090) provides beginner's instruction (resort course) and reef and wreck dives with a friendly, knowledgeable staff. At the **Dive Shop, Ltd.** (Grand Barbados Beach Resort, tel. 809/426–9947), experienced divers can participate in deep dives to old wrecks to look for bottles and other artifacts (and you can usually keep what you find). **Willie's Watersports** (Heywoods Barbados hotel, tel. 809/422–4900, ext. 2831) offers instruction and a range of diving excursions. **Exploresub Barbados** (Divi Southwinds Beach Resort, tel. 809/367–3484, ext. 349) operates a full range of daily dives. **Dive Boat Safari** (Barbados Hilton, tel. 809/427–4350) offers full diving and instruction services.

Snorkeling Snorkeling gear can be rented for a small charge from nearly every hotel.

Squash Squash courts can be reserved at the **Rockley Resort** (tel. 809/435–7880) and **Barbados Squash Club** (Marine House, Christ Church, tel. 809/427–7913).

Submarining Submarines are enormously popular with families and those who enjoy watching fish without getting wet, and the 28-passenger *Atlantis* turns the Caribbean into a giant aquarium. The 45-minute trip takes you as much as 150 feet below the surface for a look at what even sport divers rarely see. The nighttime dives, using high-power searchlights, are spectacular. *Tel. 809/436–8929 or 809/436–8932. Cost: $69.50 adults, $39.75 children 4–12.*

Surfing The best surfing is available on the east coast, and most wave riders congregate at the Soup Bowl, near Bathsheba. An annual international surfing competition is held on Barbados every November.

Tennis Most hotels have tennis courts that can be reserved day and night. Be sure to bring your whites; appropriate dress is expected on the court.

Waterskiing Waterskiing is widely available, often provided along St. James and Christ Church by the private speedboat owners. Inquire at your hotel, which can direct you to the nearest Sunfish sailing and Hobie Cat rentals as well.

Windsurfing Windsurfing boards and equipment are often guest amenities at the larger hotels and can be rented by nonguests. The best place to learn and to practice is on the south coast at the **Benston Windsurfing Club Hotel** (Maxwell, Christ Church Parish, tel. 809/428–9095).

Spectator Sports
Cricket The island is mad for cricket, and you can sample a match at almost any time of year. While the season is June through late December, test matches are played in the first half of the year. The newspapers give the details of time and place.

Horse Racing Horse racing takes place on alternate Saturdays, from January to May and from July to November, at the **Garrison Savannah** in Christ Church, about 3 miles south of Bridgetown. Appropriate dress might be described as "casual elegant." *Tel. 809/426–3980. Admission: BDS$10 adults, BDS$5 children under 12. Opens race days at 2:30.*

Polo Polo, the sport of kings, is played seriously in Barbados. Matches are held at the **Polo Club** in St. James on Wednesday and Saturday from September to March. Hang around the club room after the match. That's where the lies, the legends, and the invitations happen. *Admission: about $2.50.*

Rugby The rough-and-tumble game of rugby is played at the Garrison Savannah; schedules are available from the **Barbados Rugby Club.** Contact Victor Roach (tel. 809/435–6543).

Soccer The "football," or soccer, season runs from January through June. For game schedules write to the **Barbados Football Association,** Box 1362, Bridgetown, Barbados.

Shopping

Traditionally, Broad Street and its side streets in Bridgetown have been the center for shopping action. Hours are generally weekdays 8–4, Saturday 8–1. Many stores have an in-bound (duty-free) department where you must show your travel tickets or a passport in order to buy duty-free goods.

Recently, several new areas opened their freshly painted doors. The mall-like **Sheraton Centre** (at Sargeant's Village in Christ Church) has toys for tots, togs for teens, and temptations for all. The **Quayside Shopping Center** (at Rockley in Christ Church) is smaller and more select.

Best 'N The Bunch is both a wildly colored chattel house at the Chattel House Village (at St. Lawrence Gap) and its own best advertisement. Here the expert jewelry of Bajan David Trottman sells for that rarity—reasonable prices. **Perfections** also has good finds—all from Bajan artists—for men, women, and children, and **Beach Bum** offers teens "barely" bikinis.

Luxury Goods Bridgetown stores have values on fine bone china, crystal, cameras, stereo and video equipment, jewelry, perfumes, and clothing. **Cave Shepherd** and **Harrison's** department stores offer wide selections of goods at many locations and at the airport. **De Lima's** and **Da Costa's Ltd.** stock high-quality imports. Among the specialty stores are **Louis I. Bayley** (gold watches), **J. Baldini** (Brazilian jewelry and Danish silver), and **Correia's** (diamonds, pearls, semiprecious stones). The 20 small shops of **Mall 34** in Bridgetown's central district sell everything from luxury goods to crafts.

Handicrafts Island handicrafts are everywhere: woven mats and place mats, dresses, dolls, handbags, shell jewelry. The **Best of Barbados** shops, at the Sandpiper Inn, Mall 34, in Bridgetown (tel. 809/436–1416) and three other locations, offer the highest-quality artwork and crafts, both "native style" and modern designs. A resident artist, Jill Walker, sells her watercolors and prints here and at **Walker's World** shops near the south shore hotels in St. Lawrence Gap.

At the **Pelican Village Handicrafts Center** on the Princess Alice Highway near the Cheapside Market in Bridgetown, in a cluster of conical shops, you can watch goods and crafts being made before you purchase them. Rugs and mats made from pandanus grass and khuskhus are good buys.

For native Caribbean arts and crafts, including items from Barbados and Haiti, try the Guardhouse Gallery near the Grand Barbados Hotel in St. Michael. A selection of wooden, straw, and ceramic items is available.

Antiques Antiques and fine memorabilia are the stock of **Greenwich House Antiques** (tel. 809/432–1169) in Greenwich Village, Trents Hill, St. James Parish, and at **Antiquaria** (tel. 809/426–0635) on St. Michael's Row next to the Anglican cathedral in Bridgetown.

Chic Shops Hidden in separate corners of Barbados are some very upscale, little-known shops that can hold their own in New York or London. Carol Cadogan's **Cotton Days Designs** at Rose Cottage (Lower Bay St., tel. 809/427–7191) and on the Wharf in Bridgetown sets the international pace with all-cotton, collage creations that have been declared "wearable art." These are fantasy designs, with prices that begin at U.S.$250. Fortunately, she takes credit cards.

Another shop worth a visit on the Wharf is **Origins** (tel. 809/436–8522), where original hand-painted and dyed clothing, imported cottons, linens and silks for day and evening, and handmade jewelry and accessories are the order of the day. The hand-painted T-shirts are especially good here.

In St. Michael, stop in at **Petal's** in the Barbados Hilton shopping arcade for fashionable shoes and handbags: Friendly service and good-quality items make this shop special.

Dining

The better hotels and restaurants of Barbados have employed chefs trained in New York and Europe to attract and keep their sophisticated clientele. Gourmet dining here usually means fresh seafood, beef, or veal with finely blended sauces.

The native West Indian cuisine offers an entirely different dining experience. The island's West African heritage brought rice, peas, beans, and okra to its table, the staples that make a perfect base for slowly cooked meat and fish dishes. Many side dishes are cooked in oil (the pumpkin fritters can be addictive). And be cautious at first with the West Indian seasonings; like the sun, they are hotter than you think.

Every menu features dolphin (the fish, not the mammal), kingfish, snapper, and flying fish prepared every way imaginable. Shellfish abound; so does steak. Everywhere for breakfast and dessert you'll find mangoes, soursop, papaya (called pawpaw), and, in season, "mammy apples," a basketball-size, thick-skinned fruit with giant seeds.

Cou-cou is a mix of cornmeal and okra with a spicy Creole sauce made from tomatoes, onions, and sweet peppers; steamed flying fish is often served over it. A version served by the Brown Sugar restaurant, called "red herring," is smoked herring and breadfruit in Creole sauce.

Pepper-pot stew, a hearty mix of oxtail, beef chunks, and "any other meat you may have," simmered overnight, is flavored with *cassareep*, an ancient preservative and seasoning that gives the stew its dark, rich color.

Christophines and **eddoes** are tasty, potatolike vegetables that are often served with curried shrimp, chicken, or goat.

Buljol is a cold salad of codfish, tomatoes, onions, sweet peppers, and celery, marinated and served raw.

Callaloo is a soup made from okra, crabmeat, the spinachlike vegetable that gives the dish its name, and seasonings.

Among the liquid refreshments of Barbados, in addition to the omnipresent Banks Beer and Mount Gay rum, there are **falernum,** a liqueur concocted of rum, sugar, lime juice, and almond essence, and **mauby,** a refreshing nonalcoholic beerlike drink made by boiling bitter bark and spices, straining the mixture, and sweetening it.

Barbados's British heritage and large resident population keep the island's dress code modest. While this does not always mean a tie and jacket, jeans, shorts, and beach shirts are frowned upon at dinnertime.

Highly recommended restaurants are indicated by a star ★.

Category	Cost*
Expensive	over $40
Moderate	$25–$40
Inexpensive	under $25

per person, excluding drinks and 10% service charge

Expensive **Bagatelle Great House.** Occupying a converted plantation house in a hilly area, Bagatelle Great House gives diners an impression of colonial life. The terrace allows intimate dining at tables for two, while inside the castlelike walls there are much larger round tables. The superb ambience is somewhat more memorable than the expensive Continental dishes. *St. Thomas Parish, tel. 809/421–6767. Reservations necessary. Dress: smart casual. AE, MC, V.*

★ **Carambola.** This romantic al fresco restaurant is set on a cliff overlooking the Caribbean in St. James Parish. Here, by candlelight, you can enjoy what is considered some of the best food in Barbados, created by British chef Paul Owens. The menu is a mix of Thai and Continental dishes, all prepared with a Caribbean touch. Start with a spicy, Caribbean-style crab tart, served with hollandaise sauce on a bed of sweet pepper coulis. Entrées include Thai fillet of kingfish broiled with ginger, coriander, and spring onions, and sliced duck breast with a wild mushroom fumet served with stuffed tomatoes and *gratin dauphinoise* (potatoes au gratin). When you think you can't eat another bite, the *citron gâteau* (lime mousse on a bed of lemon coulis) makes a light but superb finish. *Derricks, St. James Parish, tel. 809/432-0832. Reservations required. AE, MC, V. No lunch.*

La Cage aux Folles. Acclaimed as one of the island's finest restaurants, La Cage aux Folles has moved to a new location, in the restored Summerland Great House amid 2 acres of tropical gardens, and is lovelier than ever. The exotic five-course menu features international cuisine. Items include fresh fish with orange and Cointreau, sweet-and-sour shrimp, Malaysian satay, and sesame prawn pâté. *Prospect, St. James Parish, tel. 809/424-2424. Reservations necessary. Jacket and tie required. AE, D, DC, MC, V. No lunch. Closed Tues.*

The Palm Terrace. The Palm's young British chef, who came here from London's Le Gavroche, applies his talents to combine Barbadian produce with top-quality imports. The result is modern European creations, such as *mille feuille* of home-smoked chicken with tomato, chives, and carrots in a light mustard cream sauce for an appetizer. Home-grown mint accents New Zealand rack of lamb, and panfried crab becomes a stuffing for the breast of chicken entrée. Widely spaced tables, comfortable chairs, and indoor palms swaying under floor-to-ceiling arches create an ambience that is formal yet relaxed as you dine facing the Caribbean Sea. *Royal Pavilion, Porters, St. James Parish, tel. 809/422-5555. Reservations advised. AE, D, DC, MC, V. No lunch.*

★ **Raffles.** Young, international owners have made this one of Barbados's top restaurants. Forty guests can be seated at beautifully decorated tables featuring a tropical safari theme. Main dishes may be shrimp saki, blackened fish, steak served in a wine-and-lime sauce, basil-curry chicken, and sweet-and-sour pork. The desserts are both delicious and decadent. *1st St., Holetown, St. James Parish, tel. 809/432-6557 or 809/432-1280. Reservations necessary. AE, D, DC, MC, V. No lunch.*

Sandy Bay Restaurant. Located at the renowned Sandy Lane Hotel, this is the perfect place for an elegant meal overlooking one of the best beaches on the island. The hotel's general manager brought British chef Mel Rumbles to the restaurant to create a menu that is both tasty and healthful. Grilled dolphin; lobster; and grilled lamb with honey, thyme, and wild rosemary are among the entrées. The vegetables, including local christophines and the delicate puréed pumpkin soup, are tasty. To ensure that the best produce is used, a van is sent out every morning to scour the island for the freshest vegetables and fish. The chef has also begun cultivating a spice and vegetable garden specifically to meet the hotel's needs. The desserts, created by a French pastry chef, are not to be missed, especially the dark chocolate truffle and the pecan pie with almond sauce. *Sandy Lane Hotel and Golf Club, St. James Parish, tel. 809/432-1311. AE, MC, V.*

Moderate **Brown Sugar.** A special-occasion atmosphere prevails at Brown Sugar, which is set in a restored West Indian wooden house across the road from the Grand Barbados Beach Resort outside Bridgetown. Dozens of ferns and hanging plants decorate the breezy multilevel restaurant. An extensive and authentic West Indian lunch buffet—everything from cou-cou to pepper-pot stew—served between 12:00 and 2:30, is popular with local businessmen. The dinner menu adds entrées such as Creole orange chicken and homemade desserts, including angel food chocolate mousse cake, passion fruit and nutmeg ice cream, and lime cheesecake with guava sauce. *Aquatic Gap, St. Michael Parish, tel. 809/426–7684. Reservations recommended. AE, DC, MC, V. No lunch Sat.*

★ **Fathoms.** The newest property of veteran restaurateurs Stephen and Sandra Toppin is open seven days a week for lunch and dinner, with 22 well-dressed tables scattered from the inside dining rooms to the patio's ocean edge. Dinner may bring a grilled lobster, island rabbit, jumbo baked shrimp, or cashew-crusted kingfish. This place is casual by day, candlelit by night. *Payne's Bay, St. James Parish, tel. 809/432–2568. Reservations advised for dinner. AE, MC, V.*

★ **Ile de France.** French owners Martine (from Lyon) and Michel (from Toulouse) Gramaglia have adapted the pool and garden areas of the Windsor Arms Hotel and turned them into an island "in" spot. White latticework opens to the night sounds; soft taped French music plays; and a single, perfect hibiscus dresses each table. Their specialties include foie gras, tournedos Rossini, lobster-and-crepe flambé, and filet Mignon with a choice of pepper, béarnaise, or champignon sauce. *Windsor Arms Hotel, Hastings, Christ Church Parish, tel. 809/435–6869. Reservations required. No credit cards. No lunch. Closed Mon.*

Josef's. Swede Nils Ryman created a menu from the unusual combination of Caribbean cooking—blackened fish in which the fish is fried, rolled in Cajun spices, and seared in oil before being slightly baked in the oven—and Scandinavian fare—toast Skagen made from diced shrimp blended with mayonnaise and fresh dill. Stroll around the garden before moving to the alfresco dining room downstairs or to the simply decorated room upstairs for a table that looks out over the sea. *Waverly House, St. Lawrence Gap, tel. 809/435–6541. Reservations advised. AE, DC, MC, V.*

La Maison. The elegant, colonial-style Balmore House reopened in October 1990 under the ownership of Geoffrey Farmer. The atmosphere is created by English country furnishings and a paneled bar opening onto a seaside terrace for dining. A French chef from the Loire Valley creates seafood specials, including a flying-fish parfait appetizer. Passion-fruit ice cream is the dessert special. *Holetown, St. James Parish, tel. 809/432–1156. Reservations recommended. AE, D, MC, V. Closed Mon.*

★ **Ocean View Hotel.** This elegant pink grande dame hotel is dressed in fresh fabrics, with great bunches of equally fresh flowers and sparkling crystal chandeliers. Bajan dishes are featured for lunch and dinner, and the Sunday-only Planter's Luncheon Buffet in the downstairs Club Xanadu (which fronts the beach) offers course after course of traditional dishes. *Hastings, Christ Church Parish, tel. 809/427–7821. Reservations recommended. AE, MC, V.*

Pisces. For Caribbean seafood at the water's edge, this restaurant in lively St. Lawrence Gap specializes in seasonal dishes. Fish is the way to go here—flying fish, dolphin, crab, kingfish, shrimp, prawns, and lobster—prepared any way from charbroiled to sautéed. There are also some chicken and beef dishes. Other items include conch fritters, tropical gazpacho, and seafood terrine with a mango sauce. Enjoy a meal in a contemporary setting filled with hanging tropical plants. *St. Lawrence Gap, Christ Church Parish, tel. 809/435–6564. Reservations recommended. AE, MC, V. No lunch.*

Plantation. Wednesday's Bajan buffet and entertainment on Wednesday, Friday, and Saturday, are big attractions here. The Plantation is set in a renovated Barbadian residence surrounded by spacious grounds above the Southwinds Resort; its cuisine combines

French and Barbadian influences, and you can eat indoors or on the terrace. *St. Lawrence, Christ Church Parish, tel. 809/428–5048. Reservations suggested. AE, MC, V. No lunch.*

Rose and Crown. The casual Rose and Crown serves a variety of fresh seafood, but it's the local lobster that's high on diners' lists. Indoors is a paneled bar, outdoors are tables on a wraparound porch. *Prospect, St. James Parish, tel. 809/425–1074. Reservations suggested. AE, MC, V. No lunch. Closed Sat.*

The Virginian. The locally popular Virginian offers intimate surroundings and some of the island's best dining values. The lunch and dinner specialties are seafood, shrimp, and steaks. *Sea View Hotel, Hastings, Christ Church Parish, tel. 809/427–7963, ext. 121. Reservations suggested. AE, MC, V.*

Witch Doctor. The interior of the Witch Doctor is decorated with pseudo-African art that gives a lighthearted, carefree atmosphere to this casual hangout across the street from the sea; the menu features traditional Barbadian dishes, American fare, and local seafood. *St. Lawrence Gap, Christ Church Parish, tel. 809/435–6581. Reservations recommended. MC, V. No lunch.*

Inexpensive **Atlantis Hotel.** While the surroundings may be simple and the rest room could use a coat of paint, the nonstop food and the magnificent ocean view at the Atlantis Hotel in Bathsheba make it a real find. Owner-chef Enid Maxwell serves up an enormous Bajan buffet daily, where you're likely to find pickled souse (marinated pig parts and vegetables), pumpkin fritters, spinach balls, pickled breadfruit, fried "fline" (flying) fish, roast chicken, pepper-pot stew, and West Indian–style okra and eggplant. Among the homemade pies are an apple and a dense coconut. *Bathsheba, St. Joseph Parish, tel. 809/ 433–9445. Reservations suggested. AE.*

★ **David's Place.** Here you'll be served first-rate dishes in a first-rate location—a black-and-white Bajan cottage overlooking St. Lawrence Bay. Specialties include Baxters Road chicken, local flying fish, pepper-pot (salt pork, beef, and chicken boiled and bubbling in a spicy cassareep stock), and curried shrimp. Homemade cheesebread is served with all dishes. Desserts might be banana pudding, coconut-cream pie, carrot cake with rum sauce, or cassava pone. *St. Lawrence Main Rd., Worthing, Christ Church Parish, tel. 809/435–6550. Reservations preferred. AE, MC, V. No lunch Sat.– Mon.*

Nico's. This small bistro, overlooking Second Street from its second-story location, is a cheery, intimate gathering spot for ex-patriates and visitors. An oval bar, surrounded by stools, stands in the middle of the room, with the tables on the perimeter and a few more on the terrace above the street. Come to Nico's for drinks and to socialize, as well as order off the blackboard menu something small like deep-fried Camembert or more substantial, such as seafood thermidor. *Second St., Holetown, tel. 809/432–6386. AE, MC, V. Closed Sun.*

The Waterfront Cafe. Located on the Careenage, a sliver of sea in Bridgetown, this is the perfect place to enjoy a drink, snack, or meal. Locals and tourists gather here for sandwiches, salads, fish, steak-and-kidney pie, and casseroles. The panfried flying-fish sandwich is especially tasty. From the brick and mirrored interior you can gaze through the arched windows, enjoy the cool trade winds and let time pass. *Bridgetown, St. Michael Parish, tel. 809/427– 0093. MC, V. Dress: casual. Live jazz Mon.–Sat. Food served 10– 10, open until midnight.*

Lodging

The southern and western shores of Barbados are lined with hotels and resorts of every size and price, offering a variety of accommodations ranging from private villas to modest but comfortable rooms in simple inns. At the same time, apartment and home rentals and time-share condominiums have become widely available and are growing increasingly popular among visitors to the island. A few of Barbados's hotels have recently become all-inclusive, though most still offer either EP or MAP meal plans.

Choosing the location of your hotel is important. Hotels to the north of Bridgetown, in the parishes of St. Peter, St. James, and St. Michael, tend to be self-contained resorts with stretches of empty road between them that discourage strolling to a neighborhood bar or restaurant. Southwest of Bridgetown, in Christ Church Parish, many of the hotels cluster near or along the busy strip known as St. Lawrence Gap, where small restaurants, bars, and nightclubs are close by.

Hotels listed are grouped here by parish, beginning with St. James in the west and St. Peter to the north, then St. Michael, Christ Church, St. Philip, and St. Joseph.

Highly recommended lodgings are indicated by a star ★.

Category	Cost*
Very Expensive	over $350
Expensive	$250–$350
Moderate	$150–$250
Inexpensive	under $150

All prices are for a standard double room, excluding 5% government tax and 10% service charge.

Hotels St. James Parish

Coral Reef Club. Days here are spent relaxing on the white-sand beach or around the pool, with time taken out for the hotel's superb afternoon tea. The public areas ramble along the beach and face the Caribbean Sea, with small coral-stone cottages scattered over the surrounding 12 flower-filled acres. (The cottages farthest from the beach are a bit of a hike to the main house.) The accommodations are spacious, each with air-conditioning and ceiling fans, a small patio terrace, and fresh flowers. The restaurant, under the direction of Bajan chef Graham Licorish, is noted for its inventive cuisine that combines local cooking with European flair. Most guests are on a MAP plan that includes a complimentary buffet lunch. Another convenience is the free shuttle into Bridgetown. *Porters, St. James Parish, tel. 809/422-2372, fax 809/422-1776. 68 rooms. Facilities: pool, entertainment. AE, MC, V. EP. Very Expensive.*

★ **Glitter Bay.** In the 1930s, Sir Edward Cunard, of the English shipping family, bought this estate, built the main Great House and a beach house similar to his palazzo in Venice, and began hosting famous parties in honor of visiting aristocrats and celebrities, making Glitter Bay synonymous with grandeur. Today, new buildings, angled back from the beach, house 81 one- to three-bedroom suites with full kitchens, and the beach house has been transformed into five garden suites. Manicured landscaped gardens separate the reception area and large, comfortable tea lounge from the pool; the alfresco dining room where evening entertainment is held; and the

half mile of crunchy beach. Glitter Bay is more casual and family oriented than its next-door sister property, the Royal Pavilion, but
they share facilities, including complimentary water sports, and
guests at either have dining privileges at both. *Porters, St. James
Parish, tel. 809/422–4111, fax 809/422–3940. 74 rooms. Facilities:
restaurant, pool, water sports, 2 lighted tennis courts, golf course
nearby. AE, DC, MC, V. EP, MAP. Very Expensive.*

★ **The Royal Pavilion.** Of the 75 rooms here, 72 are oceanfront suites;
the remaining three are nestled in a garden villa. The ground-floor
ocean-front rooms allow guests simply to step through sliding doors,
cross their private patio, and walk onto the sands. Second- and
third-floor rooms, however, have the advantage of an elevated view
of the sea. Breakfast and lunch are served alfresco along the edge of
the beach. Afternoon tea and dinner are in the Palm Terrace (*see*
Dining, *above*). The Royal Pavilion attracts sophisticated guests
who want serenity (bringing children under the age of 12 is discouraged during the winter months), but they are welcome to share the
facilities of its adjoining sister hotel, the more informal Glitter Bay.
*Porters, St. James Parish, tel. 809/422–5555, fax 809/422–3940. 75
rooms. Facilities: 2 restaurants, 2 bars, 2 lighted, artificial-grass
tennis courts, supper-club entertainment, water-sports center, golf
course nearby. AE, D, DC, MC, V. EP. Very Expensive.*

★ **Sandy Lane Hotel.** The complete renovation of this prestigious hotel
has given it good reason to remain the island's most expensive property. If you like low-key luxury set on one of the best beaches in Barbados, Sandy Lane is the place. One choice room is 310, with a large
private balcony for eating breakfast and watching magnificent sunsets in the evening. It has a huge king-size bed and a vast bathroom,
complete with double washbasin, a deep oval tub, and bidet. Afternoon tea, fine dining, and personalized service all add to the charm.
The white coral structure, finished with Zandobbio marble throughout and a staircase leading to the beach shaded with mahogany
trees, is reminiscent of the *Great Gatsby. Hwy. 1, St. James Parish,
tel. 809/432–1311, fax 809/432–2954. 90 doubles, 30 suites. Facilities: two oceanfront restaurants, poolside snack bar, 5 bars, live entertainment nightly, fitness facility, free water sports, 18-hole golf
course and club, pool, 5 tennis courts (4 floodlit). AE, DC, MC, V.
EP, MAP. Very Expensive.*

Settlers' Beach. The accommodations at Settlers' Beach are two-story, two-bedroom homes with full kitchen and dining room (or one-
story villas with atrium), arranged asymmetrically around a large
courtyard filled with towering palms and a pool. The property is
small, squeezed between newer resorts, and attracts those seeking a
quiet vacation. *Hwy. 1, St. James Parish, tel. 809/422–3052, fax
809/422–1937. 22 villas. Facilities: restaurant, pool. AE, MC, V.
EP. Very Expensive.*

Coconut Creek Club. A luxury cottage colony, the Coconut Creek
Club is set on handsomely landscaped grounds with a small but adequate private beach and a bar pavilion for entertainment and dancing. The atmosphere here is more casual than that of its sister hotel,
the Colony Club. *Reservations: Box 249, Bridgetown; Hwy. 1, St.
James Parish, tel. 809/432–0803, fax 809/422–1726. 53 rooms. Facilities: dining room, pub, pool. AE, DC, MC, V. EP, MAP. Expensive.*

Discovery Bay Hotel. The rooms of the quiet, white-columned Discovery Bay Hotel open onto a central lawn and a pool. Some rooms
have ocean views. *Hwy. 1, Holetown, St. James Parish, tel. 809/
432–1301, fax 809/422–1726. 87 rooms. Facilities: terrace restaurant, pool, table tennis, boutique. AE, D, DC, MC, V. EP. Expensive.*

Treasure Beach. Most of the small one-bedroom suites of this compact resort overlook the small garden; a few have sea views. The ground-floor rooms offer little privacy from other guests unless the shutters are closed, so you may wish to be on the second or third floor. The atmosphere is casual, and the staff is equally so. *Payne's Bay, St. James Parish, tel. 809/432–1346, fax 809/432–1740. 24 one-bedroom, air-conditioned suites; 1 two-bedroom penthouse suite. Facilities: restaurant, pool, water sports. AE, DC, MC, V. EP, MAP. Expensive.*

Almond Beach Club. In this hotel, everything is included in the price of the room—all you want to eat and drink (that includes wine and liquor); water sports; boat trips; tennis; tours of the island; shopping excursions to Bridgetown; accommodations, mostly in one-bedroom suites with balconies; departure transportation to the airport; and service and taxes. The food is excellent, from the breakfast buffet and a four-course lunch to the afternoon tea and pastries and the extensive dinner menu. The menus offer plenty of choice, but if your stay is seven days or more and you want something different, the Almond Beach Club offers a dine-around program—dinner or lunch at a number of area restaurants with round-trip transportation included. The Almond Beach Club doesn't have the enforced-activity, "whistle-blowing" atmosphere of some all-inclusives. *Vauxhall, St. James, tel. 809/432–7840 or 800/966–4737, fax 407/994–6344. 151 rooms. Facilities: 2 restaurants, 3 pools, snorkeling, fishing, windsurfing, waterskiing, tennis, squash, sauna, fitness center. AE, MC, V. All-inclusive. Moderate–Expensive.*

Barbados Beach Village. Vacationers choose from twin-bedded rooms, studios, apartments, and duplexes at the Barbados Beach Village. The beach has a terrace bar, and the restaurant is seaside. *Hwy. 1, St. James Parish, tel. 809/432–8280, fax 809/424–0996. 89 rooms. Facilities: restaurant, disco nightclub, pool. AE, D, DC, MC, V. EP. Moderate.*

St. Peter Parish **Cobblers Cove Hotel.** This all-suite hotel, renovated in 1992 and lo-
★ cated 12 miles up the west coast from Bridgetown, combines comfort and informal elegance. Each luxury suite has a balcony or patio and wet bar. The pink-and-white buildings contrasting with tropical gardens overlooking the sea create a fine retreat that is now part of the Relais et Château marketing group. The atmosphere is casual and smart, with a clublike lounge-library and a bar that becomes the evening gathering spot. *Hwy. 1, St. Peter Parish, tel. 809/422–2291, fax 809/422–1460. 38 suites plus the Camelot Suite, with king-size, four-poster bed; whirlpool bath; private pool; and lounge. Facilities: pool, floodlit tennis court, water sports, child care available, but no children under 12 allowed late Jan.–late March. Closed Sept. AE, MC, V. CP, MAP. Very Expensive.*

Heywoods Barbados. Everything is on a grand scale here: The seven buildings of the Heywoods Barbados, each with its own theme and decor, house a total of nearly 300 rooms. The mile-long beach has space for all water sports. Now a Wyndham resort, the property is well laid out to accommodate large groups. *Hwy. 1, St. Peter Parish, tel. 809/422–4900, fax 809/422–1581. 288 rooms. Facilities: 4 restaurants, bars, 3 pools, 5 lighted tennis courts, squash courts, 9-hole golf course, boutiques, entertainment. AE, DC, MC, V. All-inclusive. Moderate.*

St. Michael **Grand Barbados Beach Resort.** A mile from Bridgetown on Carlisle
Parish Bay, this convenient hotel has pleasant rooms and suites. The white-sand beach is lapped by a surprisingly clear sea, despite the oil refinery close by. The Aquatic Club executive floor has rooms that include a Continental breakfast and secretarial services suitable for

business travelers. A 260-foot-long pier for romantic walks, live music, and a dance floor, add to the enjoyment of a stay here. *Box 639, Bridgetown, St. Michael Parish, tel. 809/436–9823 or 800/223–9815, fax 809/424–0096. 133 rooms. Facilities: 2 restaurants, beach, pool, exercise room, whirlpool, sauna, shopping arcade, beauty salon/ barber shop. AE, DC, MC, V. EP. Expensive.*

Barbados Hilton International. This large resort, just five minutes from Bridgetown, is for those who like activity and having plenty of people around. Expect to rub shoulders with seminar attendees and conventioneers, and don't be surprised by the strong odor from the nearby oil refinery. Attractions here include an atrium lobby, a 1,000-foot-wide man-made beach with full water sports, and lots of shops. All rooms and suites have balconies. *Needham's Point, St. Michael Parish, tel. 809/426–0200, fax 809/436–8646. 184 rooms. Facilities: restaurant, lounge, pool, 4 lighted tennis courts, health club. AE, D, DC, MC, V. EP. Moderate–Expensive.*

Christ Church **Divi Southwinds Beach Resort.** In this resort, situated on 20 lush
Parish acres, the toss-up is whether to take one of the one-bedroom suites, with a balcony and kitchenette overlooking the gardens and pool, or one of the smaller and older-looking rooms, just steps from the white sandy beach. Though all the rooms are pleasant, the buildings themselves have a barracks ambience. Dining facilities next to the pool have the tour-package feel, with the emphasis on self-service. Guests come here for a rollicking good time that includes making full use of the scuba and water-sports facilities. *St. Lawrence, Christ Church Parish, tel. 800/367–3484, fax 809/428–4674. 166 rooms. Facilities: 2 restaurants, 3 pools, 2 lighted tennis courts, putting green, shopping arcade. AE, MC, V. EP, MAP. Expensive.*

Southern Palms. A plantation-style hotel on a 1,000-foot stretch of pink sand near the Dover Convention Center, Southern Palms is a convenient businessperson's hotel. You may choose from standard bedrooms, deluxe oceanfront suites with kitchenettes, and a four-bedroom penthouse. Each wing of the hotel has its own small pool. *St. Lawrence, Christ Church Parish, tel. 809/428–7171, fax 809/ 428–7175. 93 rooms. Facilities: dining room, 2 pools, duty-free shop, small conference center, miniature-golf course, tennis court, water sports. AE, D, DC, MC, V. EP. Expensive.*

Casuarina Beach Club. This luxury apartment hotel on 900 feet of pink sand takes its name from the casuarina pines that surround it, and the quiet setting provides a dramatic contrast to that of the platinum-coast resorts. The bar and restaurant are on the beach. A new reception area includes small lounges where guests can get a dose of TV—there aren't any in the bedrooms. Scuba diving, golf, and other activities can be arranged. The Casuarina Beach is popular with those who prefer self-catering holidays in a secluded setting, convenient to nightlife and shopping. *St. Lawrence Gap, Christ Church Parish, tel. 809/428–3600, fax 809/428–1970. 134 rooms. Facilities: restaurant, bar, pool, tennis courts, squash courts, minimarket, duty-free shop. AE, D, DC, MC, V. EP. Moderate.*

Club Rockley Barbados. At press time, some of these time-share condominiums were being transformed into an all-inclusive resort with air-conditioned one- and two-bedroom accommodations with balcony or patio. The extensive list of amenities includes a massage center, seven swimming pools, five tennis courts (three lighted), a 9-hole golf course, two air-conditioned squash courts, a shuttle bus to the beach (five minutes), a disco for late-night revelry, a children's program, and two dining rooms, one offering buffet dinners and another with an à la carte menu. *Christ Church Parish, tel. 809/435–*

7880, fax 809/435–8015. 288 rooms. AE, D, DC, MC, V. All-inclusive. Moderate.

Sandy Beach Hotel. On a wide, sparkling white beach, this comfortable hotel has a popular poolside bar and the Beachfront Restaurant, which serves a West Indian buffet Tuesday and Saturday nights. All rooms have kitchenettes. Water sports, at extra cost, include scuba-diving certification, deep-sea fishing, harbor cruises, catamaran sailing, and windsurfing. Guests can walk to St. Lawrence Gap for other restaurants and entertainment. *Worthing, Christ Church Parish, tel. 809/435–8000, fax 809/435–8053. 89 units. Facilities: restaurant, bar, entertainment, pool. AE, D, DC, MC, V. EP. Moderate.*

Benston Windsurfing Club Hotel. A small hotel that began as a gathering place for windsurfing enthusiasts, the Benston Windsurfing Club is now a complete school and center for the sport. The rooms are spacious and sparsely furnished to accommodate the active and young crowd who choose this bare-bones hotel right on the beach. The bar and restaurant overlook the water. All sports can be arranged, but windsurfing (learning, practicing, and perfecting it) is king. *Maxwell Main Rd., Christ Church Parish, tel. 809/428–9095, fax 809/435–6621. 14 rooms. Facilities: restaurant, bar, entertainment. AE, D, MC, V. EP. Inexpensive.*

Little Bay Hotel. This small hotel is a find for anyone who wants to go easy on the wallet and yet sleep to the sounds of the sea. Each room has a private balcony, bedroom, small lounge, and kitchenette. Room 100 is a favorite. At press time, owner Charlene Paterson from Toronto had plans to throw away the drab carpets and replace them with a clay-tile floor. There are no TVs in the rooms, but guests can catch up on the news and watch sports in the small lounge next to the popular restaurant, Southern Accents. *St. Lawrence Gap, tel. 809/435–8574, fax 809/435–8586. 10 rooms. Facilities: restaurant, lounge, bar. AE, MC, V. EP. Inexpensive.*

★ **Ocean View.** Possibly the best-kept secret in the Caribbean, the 40 rooms and suites of this individualistic hideaway are home to celebrities on their commute to private villas in Mustique. The rooms vary considerably, and their charm depends on whether you appreciate the eclectic furnishings. Although it lacks modern amenities, bear in mind that this is an old colonial-style building and enjoy it for that. Owner John Chandler places his personal antiques throughout his three-story grande dame nestled against the sea, adds great bouquets of tropical flowers everywhere, and calls it home. In season, the downstairs Xanadu Club presents very good, off-off-Broadway reviews. *Hastings, Christ Church Parish, tel. 809/427–7821, fax 809/427–7826. 40 rooms. Facilities: restaurant and bar, supper club. AE, MC, V. CP. Inexpensive.*

Sichris Hotel. The Sichris is a "discovery," more attractive inside than seen from the road, a comfortable and convenient self-contained resort that can be ideal for businesspeople who need a quiet place in which to work. Just minutes from the city, the air-conditioned one-bedroom suites all have kitchenettes and private balconies or patios. It's a walk of two or three minutes to the beach. *Worthing, Christ Church Parish, tel. 809/ 435–7930, fax 809/435–8232. 24 rooms. Facilities: restaurant, bar, pool. AE, D, DC, MC, V. EP. Inexpensive.*

St. Philip Parish ★ **Crane Beach Hotel.** This remote hilltop property on a cliff overlooking the dramatic Atlantic coast remains one of the special places of Barbados. The Crane Beach has suites and one-bedroom apartments in the main building. Room rates vary considerably. Corner suite 1 is one of the nicest, with its two walls of windows and patio terrace. The Roman-style pool with columns separates the main house from the dining room. To reach the beach, you walk down some 200 steps onto a beautiful stretch of sand thumped by waves that are good for both body surfing and swimming. *Crane Bay, St. Philip Parish, tel. 809/423–6220, fax 809/423–5343. 18 rooms. Facilities: restaurant, bar, pool. AE, D, DC, MC, V. EP, MAP. Expensive.*

Marriott's Sam Lord's Castle. Set on the Atlantic coast about 14 miles east of Bridgetown, Sam Lord's Castle is not a castle with moat and towers but a sprawling great house surrounded by 72 acres of grounds, gardens, and beach. The seven rooms in the main house have canopied beds; downstairs, the public rooms have furniture by Sheraton, Hepplewhite, and Chippendale—unfortunately, for admiring, not for sitting. Additional guest rooms in surrounding cottages have conventional hotel furnishings. The beach is a mile long, the Wanderer Restaurant offers Continental cuisine, and there are even a few slot machines, as befits a pirate's lair. *Long Bay, St. Philip Parish, tel. 809/423–7350, fax 809/423–5918. 234 rooms. Facilities: 3 restaurants, 3 pools, 7 lighted tennis courts, entertainment. AE, D, DC, MC, V. EP, MAP. Moderate.*

St. Joseph Parish **Atlantis Hotel.** The Atlantis provides a warm, pleasant atmosphere in a pastoral location overlooking a majestically rocky Atlantic coast. The hotel is modest, yet the congeniality and the Bajan food more than make up for that. *Bathsheba, St. Joseph Parish, tel. 809/433–9445. 16 rooms. Facilities: dining room. AE. EP. Inexpensive.*

Rental Homes and Apartments Private homes are available for rent south of Bridgetown in the Hastings–Worthing area, along the coast of St. James Parish, and in St. Peter Parish. The **Barbados Board of Tourism** (tel. 809/427–2623) has a listing of rental properties and prices.

Villas and private home rentals are also available through Barbados realtors. Among them are **Alleyne, Aguilar & Altman,** Rosebank, St. James (tel. 809/432–0840); **Bajan Services,** St. Peter (tel. 809/422–2618); and **Ronald Stoute & Sons Ltd.,** St. Philip (tel. 809/423–6800).

In the United States, contact **At Home Abroad** (tel. 212/421–9165) or Jan Pizzi at **Villa Vacations** (tel. 617/593–8885 or 800/800–5576).

The Arts and Nightlife

The Arts **Barbados Art Council.** The gallery shows drawings, paintings, and other art, with a new show about every two weeks. *2 Pelican Village, Bridgetown, tel. 809/426–4385. Admission free. Open Mon.–Fri. 10–5, Sat. 9–1.*

A selection of private art galleries offers Bajan and West Indian art at collectible prices. **The Studio Art Gallery** (Fairchild St., Bridgetown, tel. 809/427–5463) exhibits local work (particularly that of Rachael Altman) and will frame purchases. The **Queen's Park Gallery** (Queen's Park, Bridgetown, tel. 809/427–2345) is run by the National Culture Foundation and is the island's largest gallery, presenting month-long exhibits.

Nightlife When the sun goes down, the musicians come out, and folks go limin' in Barbados (anything from hanging out to a chat-up or jump-up). Competitions among reggae groups, steel bands, and calypso singers are major events, and tickets can be hard to come by, but give it a try.

Most of the large resorts have weekend shows aimed at visitors, and there is a selection of dinner shows that are a Barbados-only occasion. The cultural, folklore dinner show **1627 And All That** is held at the Barbados Museum on Thursday and Sunday. There's transportation to and from your hotel, hot hors d'oeuvres, a buffet dinner (with a l-o-n-g line), an open bar, and a good show put on by the Barbados Dance Theatre that combines history and folklore with calypso, limbo, and stilt dancing. *Hwy. 7, Garrison Savannah, tel. 809/ 435–6900 or 809/429–3633 after hours and weekends. $44. Reservations recommended. AE, D, MC, V. Show and dinner, Sun. and Thurs.*

If it's Saturday, it must be the **Plantation Tropical Spectacular II** at the Plantation and Garden Theatre, with the internationally known Merrymen making the music and dance. It's a high-energy calypso show with fire-eaters, flaming limbo dancers, steel bands, and calypso, preceded by dinner and drinks, for $44 (show and drinks only, $17.50). Wednesday and Friday, the contemporary group Barbados By Night with Spice performs. *St. Lawrence Rd., Christ Church Parish, tel. 809/428–5048. Reservations recommended. AE, DC, MC, V.*

Club Xanadu is a mid-December through April cabaret, and on Thursday and Friday nights, it's the hottest ticket in town. David McCarty, who danced on Broadway and with the New York City Ballet, has joined forces with chanteuse Jean Emerson, and, along with local strutters, they put on a great show. Dinner—served in the upstairs flower-decked dining room—and show is $44; cabaret admission only, approximately $12.50. *Ocean View Hotel, Hastings, tel. 809/427–7821. Reservations required.*

Island residents have their own favorite night spots that change with the seasons. The most popular one is still **After Dark** (St. Lawrence Gap, Christ Church, tel. 809/435–6547), with the longest bar on the island and a jazz-club annex.

Harbour Lights claims to be the "home of the party animal," and most any night features live music with dancing under the stars. *On the Bay, Marine Villa, Bay St., St. Michael, tel. 809/436–7225.*

Another "in" spot, **Front Line** (Wharf St., tel. 809/429–6160) at the Wharf in Bridgetown, attracts a young crowd for its Reggae music.

Club Miliki (tel. 809/422–4900), a dusky disco, takes center stage at the Heywoods Barbados resort in St. Peter. Live music begins at 9 PM Friday and Saturday.

A late-night (after 11) excursion to **Baxter Road** is de rigueur for midnight Bajan street snacks, local rum, great gossip, and good lie-telling. **Enid & Livy's** and **Collins** are just two of the many long-standing favorites. The later, the better.

Bars and Inns   Barbados supports the rum industry in more than 1,600 "rum shops," simple bars where men congregate to discuss the world's ills, and in more sophisticated inns, where you'll find world-class rum drinks and the island's renowned Mount Gay and Cockspur rums. The following offer welcoming spirits: the **Ship Inn** (St. Lawrence Gap, Christ Church Parish, tel. 809/435–6961), the **Coach House** (Paynes Bay, St. James Parish, tel. 809/432–1163), and **Harry's Oasis** (St. Lawrence, Christ Church Parish, no tel.). **Bert's Bar** at the Abbeville Hotel (Rockley, Christ Church Parish, tel. 809/ 435–7924) serves the best daiquiris in town . . . any town. Also try the **Boat Yard** (Bay Street, Bridgetown, tel. 809/436–2622), the **Waterfront Cafe** (Bridgetown, tel. 809/427–0093), the **Warehouse** (Bridgetown, tel. 809/436–2897), and **TGI Boomers** (St. Lawrence Gap, Christ Church Parish, tel. 809/428–8439).

6 Bonaire

Updated by
Jordan
Simon

Bonaire is a stark desert island, perfect for the rugged individualist who is turned off by the overcommercialized high life of the other Antillean islands. The island boasts a spectacular array of exotic wildlife—from fish to fowl to flowers—that will keep nature watchers awestruck for days. It's the kind of place where you'll want to rent a Jeep and go dashing off madly in search of the wild flamingo, the wild iguana, or even the wild yellow-winged parrot named the Bonairian lora.

A mecca for divers, Bonaire offers one of the most unspoiled reef systems in the world. The water is so clear that you can lean over the dock and look the fish straight in the eye.

Kudos for the preservation of the 112-square-mile isle go to the people and government of Bonaire, who, in 1970, with the help of the World Wildlife Fund, developed the Bonaire Marine Park—a model of ecological conservation. The underwater park includes, roughly, the entire coastline, from the high-water tidemark to a depth of 200 feet, all of which is protected by strict laws. Because the Bonairians desperately want to keep their paradise intact, any diver with a reckless streak is firmly requested to go elsewhere.

This is not the island for connoisseurs of fine cuisine, shopping maniacs, beachcombers, or those who prefer hobnobbing with society. The island itself may be lacking in splendor, but what lies off its shores keeps divers enthralled. With only 11,000 inhabitants, the island has the feeling of a small community with a gentle pace.

Before You Go

Tourist Information
Contact the **Bonaire Government Tourist Office** (444 Madison Ave., Suite 2403, New York, NY 10022, tel. 212/832–0779 or 800/U–BONAIR, fax 212/838–3407) for advice and information on planning your trip.

Arriving and Departing
By Plane
ALM (tel. 800/327–7230) and **Air Aruba** (tel. 800/882–7822) will get you to Bonaire. ALM has eight direct flights (through Curaçao), two nonstop flights a week from Miami, and five flights a week from Atlanta through Curaçao, with connecting service (thoroughfares) to most U.S. gateways tied in with Delta and other airlines, making ALM Bonaire's major airline. ALM also flies to Caracas, Aruba, Curaçao, and St. Maarten, as well as other Caribbean islands, using Curaçao as its Caribbean hub. Air Aruba flies six days a week from Newark and daily from Miami to Aruba with connecting service to Bonaire. **American Airlines** (tel. 800/433–7300) offers daily flights from New York to Aruba, but you must connect to Bonaire through ALM or Air Aruba. ALM also offers a Visit Caribbean Pass, which allows easy interisland travel.

From the Airport
Bonaire's Flamingo Airport is tiny, but you'll appreciate its welcoming ambience. The customs check is perfunctory if you are arriving from another Dutch isle; otherwise you will have to show proof of citizenship, plus a return or ongoing ticket. Rental cars and taxis are available at the airport, but try to arrange the pickup through your hotel. A taxi will run between $8 and $12 (for up to four people) to most hotels.

Passports and Visas
U.S. and Canadian citizens need offer only proof of identity, so a passport, notarized birth certificate, or voter registration card will suffice. British subjects may carry a British Visitor's Passport, available from any post office. All other visitors must carry an official passport. In addition, any visitor who steps onto the island must

have a return or ongoing ticket and is advised to confirm that reservation 48 hours before departure.

Language The official language is Dutch, but few speak it, and even then only on official occasions. The street language is Papiamento, a mixture of Spanish, Portuguese, Dutch, English, African, and French—full of colorful Bonairian idioms that even Curaçaoans sometimes don't get. You'll light up your waiter's eyes, though, if you can remember to say *Masha danki* (thank you). English is spoken by most people working at the hotels, restaurants, and tourist shops.

Precautions Because of violent trade winds pounding against the rocks, the windward (eastern) side of Bonaire is much too rough for diving. The *Guide to the Bonaire Marine Park* (available at dive shops around the island) specifies the level of diving skill required for 44 sites, and it knows what it's talking about. No matter how beautiful a beach may look, heed all warning signs regarding the rough undertow.

From October through December the mosquitoes in Bonaire are nearly vampiric. Spray your hotel room before you go to bed. Smart, happy people douse themselves, including their arms, legs, and face, with repellent all day long.

Get an orientation on what stings underwater and what doesn't. As the island's joke goes, you won't appreciate Bonaire until you've stepped on a long-spined urchin, but by then, you won't appreciate the joke.

Bonaire used to have a reputation for being the friendliest and safest island in the Caribbean, but lately, even residents are locking their car doors. Don't leave your camera in an open car, and leave your money, credit cards, jewelry, and other valuables in your hotel's safety-deposit box.

Staying in Bonaire

Important Addresses **Tourist Information:** The **Bonaire Tourist Board** (Kaya Simon Bolivar 12, tel. 599/7–8322 or 599/7–8649, fax 599/7–8408).

Emergencies **Police:** For assistance call 7–8000; in an emergency, dial 11. **Ambulance:** tel. 14. **Hospital: St. Franciscus Hospital,** Kralendijk (tel. 599/7–8900).

Currency The great thing about Bonaire is that you don't need to convert your American dollars into the local currency, the NAf guilder. U.S. currency and traveler's checks are accepted everywhere, and the difference in exchange rates is negligible. Banks accept U.S. dollar banknotes at the official rate of NAf1.78 to the U.S. dollar, traveler's checks at NAf1.80. The rate of exchange at shops and hotels ranges from NAf1.75 to NAf1.80. The guilder is divided into 100 cents. Note: Prices quoted here are in U.S. dollars unless indicated otherwise.

Taxes and Service Charges Hotels charge a room tax of $4.10 per person, per night, and many hotels (not all) add a 10% maid service charge to your bill. Most restaurants add a 10% service charge to your bill. There's no sales tax on purchases in Bonaire. Departure tax when going to Curaçao is $5.75. For all other destinations it's $10.

Guided Tours If you don't like to drive, **Bonaire Sightseeing Tours** (tel. 599/7–8778 or 599/7–8300, ext. 212) will chauffeur you around the island on various tours, among them a two-hour Northern Island Tour ($13) that visits the 1,000 steps, Goto Lake, and Rincon, the oldest settlement on the island, and a two-hour Southern Island Tour ($13) that covers Akzo Salt Antilles N.V., a modern salt-manufacturing facility where flamingos gather, Lac Bay, and the oldest lighthouse on the island. A half-day tour ($19) visits sites in both the north and south. For $30, you can take a half-day tour of Bonaire's Washington/ Slagbaai National Park (entrance fee included), 13,500 acres of majestic scenery, wildlife, unspoiled beaches, and tropical flora. A full-day tour of the park costs $50. Day trips to Curaçao are offered for $125 per person and include round-trip airfare and transfers, an island tour of Curaçao, and lunch. **Ayubi's Tours** (tel. 599/7–5338) also offers several half- and full-day island tours.

Getting Around You can zip about the island in a car or a Suzuki Jeep. Scooters and bicycles, which are also available, are less practical but can be fun, too. Just remember that there are at least 20 miles of unpaved road; the roller-coaster hills at the national park require a strong stomach; and during the rainy season, mud—called Bonairian snow—is unpleasant. All traffic stays to the right and, delightfully, there is yet to be a single traffic light. Signs or green arrows are usually posted to leading attractions; if you stick to the paved roads and marked turnoffs, you won't get lost.

Rental Cars **Budget** has cars and Jeeps available from its six locations, but reservations can be made only at the head office (tel. 599/7–8300, ext. 225). Pickups are at the airport (tel. 599/7–8315) and at several hotels. It's always a good idea to make advance reservations (fax 599/ 7–8865 or 599/7–8118; cable BUDGET BONAIRE; in the U.S., tel. 800/472–3325). Prices range from $31 a day for a Volkswagen to $60 a day for an automatic, air-conditioned four-door sedan. Other agencies are **Avis** (tel. 599/7–5795, fax 599/7–5791, telex 1900 ROCAR), **Dollar Rent-A-Car** (tel. 599/7–8888; at the airport, tel. 599/7–5588; fax 599/7–7788), **Sunray** (tel. 599/7–5230, fax 599/7–4888), and **AB Car Rental** (tel. 599/7–8980 or 599/7–5410, fax 599/7–5034). There is also a new government tax of $2 per day per car rental.

Scooters Two-seater scooters are available from **Bonaire Bicycle & Motorbike Rental** (tel. 599/7–8226) and **S. F. Wave Touch** (tel. 599/7–4246) for about $26 a day and $165 a week.

Bicycles **Bonaire Bicycle & Motorbike Rental** (tel. 599/7–8226) rents bicycles for $15 a day. **Captain Don's Habitat** (tel. 599/7–8290 or 599/7–8913) rents mountain bicycles for $6 per day plus a $250 deposit. **Harbour Village Beach Resort** (tel. 599/7–7500) rents Hybrid bikes for $11 a day to nonhotel guests, but hotel guests get first dibs.

Taxis Taxis are unmetered; they have fixed rates controlled by the government. A trip from the airport to your hotel will cost between $8 and $12 for up to four passengers. A taxi from most hotels into town costs between $5 and $8. Fares increase from 7 PM to midnight by 25% and from midnight to 6 AM by 50%. Taxi drivers are usually knowledgeable enough about the island to conduct half-day tours; they charge about $60 for a northern-route tour and $40 for a southern-route tour. Call **Taxi Central Dispatch** (tel. 599/7–8100 or dial 10), or inquire at your hotel.

Telephones and Mail It's difficult for visitors to Bonaire to get involved in dramatic, heart-wrenching phone conversations or *any* phone discussions requiring a degree of privacy: Only about one-third of the major hotels have phones in their rooms, so calls must be made from hotel front desks or from the central telephone company office in Kralendijk. Telephone connections have improved, but static is still common. To call Bonaire from the United States, dial 011–599–7 + the local four-digit number. When making interisland calls, dial the local four-digit number. Local phone calls cost NAf25¢.

Airmail postage rates to the United States and Canada are NAf1.75 for letters and NAf.90 for postcards; to Britain, NAf2.50 for letters and NAf1.25 for postcards.

Opening and Closing Times Stores in the Kralendijk area are generally open Monday through Saturday 8–noon and 2–6 PM. On Sundays and holidays, when cruise ships arrive, most shops open for a few extra hours. Most restaurants are open for lunch and dinner, but few not affiliated with hotels are open for breakfast. Banks stay open from 8:30–4 Monday through Friday.

Exploring Bonaire

Numbers in the margin correspond to points of interest on the Bonaire map.

Kralendijk
❶
Bonaire's capital city of **Kralendijk** (population: 2,500) is five minutes from the airport and a short walk from Bruce Bowker's Carib Inn and the Divi Flamingo Beach Resort. There's really not much to explore here, but there are a few sights worth noting in this small, very tidy city.

Kralendijk has one main drag, J. A. Abraham Boulevard, which turns into **Kaya Grandi** in the center of town. Along it are most of the island's major stores, boutiques, restaurants, duty-free shops, and jewelry stores (*see* Shopping, *below*).

Across Kaya Grandi, opposite the Spritzer & Fuhrmann jewelry store, is Kaya L. D. Gerharts, with several small supermarkets, the ALM office, a handful of snack shops, and some of the better restaurants, including Bistro des Amis and The Rendez-Vous (*see* Dining, *below*). Walk down the narrow waterfront avenue called Kaya C.E.B. Hellmund, which leads straight to the **North** and **South piers.** In the center of town, stop in at the new Harbourside Mall, which has 13 chic boutiques. Along this route you will see **Fort Oranje,** with cannons pointing to the sea. From December through April, cruise ships, including the *Seabourn Pride* and the *Regent Suns*, dock in the harbor every few days. The *Ocean Breeze* stops at Bonaire year-round. The elegant white structure that looks like a tiny Greek temple is the **Fish Market,** where local fishermen sell their early-morning haul, along with vegetables and fruits.

Elsewhere on the Island Two tours, north and south, are possible of the 24-mile-long island; both will take from a few hours to a full day, depending upon whether you stop to snorkel, swim, dive, or lounge.

South Bonaire The trail south from Kralendijk is chock-full of icons—both natural and man-made—that tell the minisaga of Bonaire. Rent a Jeep (a car will do, but during the rainy months the roads can become muddy, making traction difficult) and head south along the Southern Scenic Route.

❷
The first icon you'll come to is the unexpected symbol of modernism—the towering 500-foot antennas of **Trans-World Radio,** one of the most powerful stations in Christian broadcasting. From here, evangelical programs and gospel music are transmitted daily in five languages to all of North, South, and Central America, as well as the entire Caribbean.

❸
Keep on cruising past the salt pans until you come to the **salt flats,** voluptuous white drifts that look something like huge mounds of va-

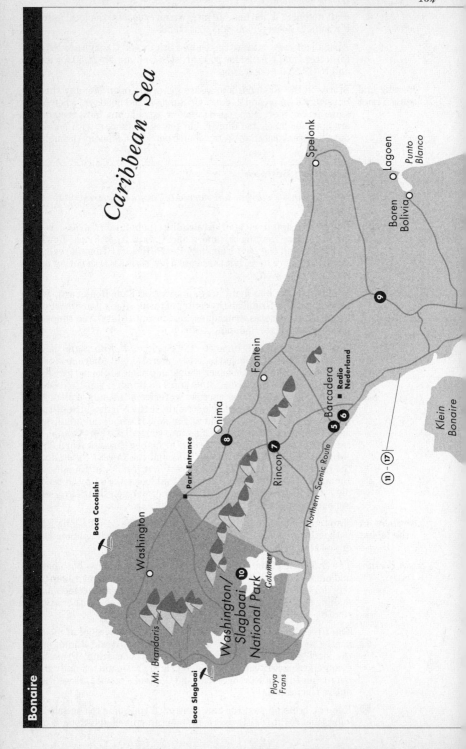

Bonaire

Caribbean Sea

Boca Cocolishi

Washington

Mt. Brandaris

Boca Slagbaai

Playa Frans

Washington/
Slagbaai
National Park

Gotomeer

Park Entrance

Onima

Rincon

Fontein

Barcadera

Radio Nederland

Northern Scenic Route

Spelonk

Lagoen

Punto Blanco

Boren Bolivia

Klein Bonaire

10

8

7

5

6

9

11 – 17

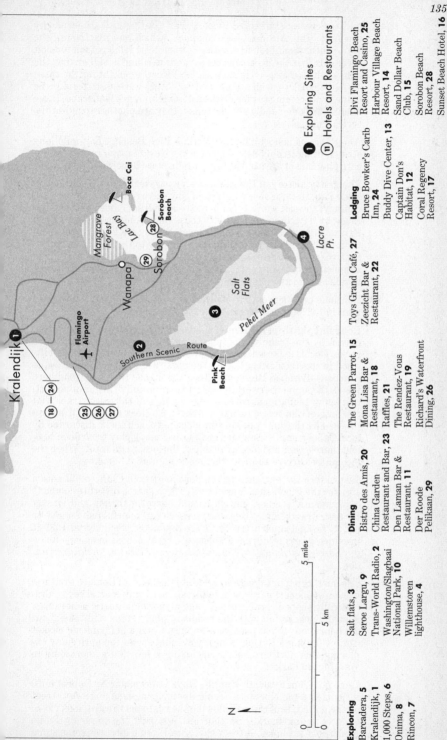

135

Exploring Sites ①

Hotels and Restaurants ⑪

Exploring
Barcadera, **5**
Kralendijk, **1**
1,000 Steps, **6**
Onima, **8**
Rincon, **7**
Salt flats, **3**
Seroe Largu, **9**
Trans-World Radio, **2**
Washington/Slagbaai
National Park, **10**
Willemstoren
lighthouse, **4**

Dining
Bistro des Amis, **20**
China Garden
Restaurant and Bar, **23**
Den Laman Bar &
Restaurant, **11**
Der Roode
Pelikaan, **29**
The Green Parrot, **15**
Mona Lisa Bar &
Restaurant, **18**
Raffles, **21**
The Rendez-Vous
Restaurant, **19**
Richard's Waterfront
Dining, **26**
Toys Grand Café, **27**
Zeezicht Bar &
Restaurant, **22**

Lodging
Bruce Bowker's Carib
Inn, **24**
Buddy Dive Center, **13**
Captain Don's
Habitat, **12**
Coral Regency
Resort, **17**
Divi Flamingo Beach
Resort and Casino, **25**
Harbour Village Beach
Resort, **14**
Sand Dollar Beach
Club, **15**
Sorobon Beach
Resort, **28**
Sunset Beach Hotel, **16**

nilla ice cream. Harvested twice a year, the "ponds" are owned by the Akzo Salt Antilles N.V. company, which has reactivated the 19th-century salt industry with great success. (One reason for that success is that the ocean on this part of the island is higher than the land—which makes irrigation a snap.) Keep a lookout for the three 30-foot obelisks—white, blue, and red—that were used to guide the trade boats coming to pick up the salt. On this stark landscape, these obelisks look decidedly phallic; today, they are photographed as historical curiosities.

Along the sea just a bit farther south is **Pink Beach,** a half-mile-long stretch of incredibly soft sand that derives its name from the delicate pink hue of the sand at the shoreline (*see* Beaches, *below*).

The gritty history of the salt industry is revealed down the road in **Rode Pan,** the site of two groups of tiny slave huts. During the 19th century, the salt workers, imported slaves from Africa, worked the fields by day, then crawled into these huts at night to sleep. Each Friday afternoon, they walked seven hours to Rincon to weekend with their families, returning each Sunday to the salt pans. In recent years, the government has restored the huts to their original simplicity. Only very small people will be able to go inside, but take a walk around and put your head in for a look.

❹ Continue heading south to **Willemstoren,** Bonaire's first lighthouse, built in 1837 and still in use, but closed to visitors.

Rounding the tip of the island, head north and notice how the waves, driven by the trade winds, play a crashing symphony against the rocks. Locals make a habit of stopping here to collect pieces of driftwood in spectacular shapes. To the north are two more picturesque beaches—**Sorobon Beach** and **Boca Cai** at Lac Bay. The road here winds through otherworldly desert terrain, full of organ-pipe cacti and spiny-trunk mangroves—huge stumps of saltwater trees that rise out of the marshes like witches. At Boca Cai, you'll be impressed by the huge piles of sun-bleached conch shells discarded by local fishermen. On Sundays at Cai, live bands play from noon to 8, and there's beer and food available at the local restaurant. When the mosquitoes arrive at dusk, it's time to hightail it home.

Just before the entrance to the Sorobon Beach Club, you'll note a sign for the Fundashon Marcultura. The research institute conducts experimental studies, cultivates and harvests shrimp and lobster for restaurants, and raises several species of colorful fish for sale to pet stores and aquariums. Tours are conducted weekdays at 1:30. It provides a fascinating and informative crash course in marine biology. *Sorobon, tel. 599/7-7799. Admission: $2 adults, $1 children under 12.*

North Bonaire The northern tour takes you right into the heart of Bonaire's natural wonders—desert gardens of towering cacti, tiny coastal coves, dramatically shaped coral grottoes, and plenty of fantastic panoramas. A snappy excursion with the requisite photo stops will take about 2½ hours, but if you pack your swimsuit and a hefty picnic basket (forget finding a Burger King), you could spend the entire day exploring this northern sector, including a few hours snorkeling in Washington Park.

Head out from Kralendijk on the Kaya Gobernador N. Debrot until it turns into the Northern Scenic Route, a one-lane, one-way street on the outskirts of town. Following the route northward, look closely for a yellow marker on your left just past the towering Radio Nederland antennas. A few yards ahead, you'll discover some stone steps that lead down into a cave full of stalactites and vegetation. Once used to trap goats, this cave, called **Barcadera,** is one of the oldest in Bonaire; there's even a tunnel that looks intriguingly spooky.

Note that once you pass the antennas of Radio Nederland, you cannot turn back to Kralendijk. The road becomes one-way, and you will have to follow the cross-island road to Rincon and return via the main road through the center of the island.

The road weaves through spectacular eroded pink-and-black limestone walls and eerie rock formations with fanciful names like the Devil's Mouth and Iguana Head. Opposite the turnoff to the Bonaire Caribbean Club is a site called **1,000 Steps,** a limestone staircase carved right out of the cliff on the left side of the road. If you take the trek down them, you'll discover a great place to snorkel and scuba dive. Actually, you'll only climb 67 steps, but it feels like 1,000 when you walk up them carrying scuba gear.

If you continue toward the northern curve of the island, the green storage tanks of the Bonaire Petroleum Corporation become visible. Follow the sign to **Goto Meer,** a saltwater lagoon that is a popular flamingo hangout. Bonaire is one of the few places in the world where pink flamingos nest. The spiny-legged creatures—affectionately called "pink clouds"—at first look like swizzle sticks. But they're magnificent birds to observe—and there are about 15,000 of them in Bonaire. The best time to catch them at home is January–June, when they tend to their gray-plumed young. For the best view of these shy birds, take the dirt access road to the left, which slices through a virtual jungle of cacti. Back on the paved surface, the road will loop around and pass through **Rincon,** a well-kept cluster of pastel cottages and century-old buildings that constitute Bonaire's oldest village. Watch your driving—both goats and dogs often sit right in the middle of the main drag.

Rincon was the original Spanish settlement on the island: It became home to the slaves brought from Africa to work on the plantations and salt fields. Superstition and voodoo lore still have a powerful impact here, more so than in Kralendijk, where they work hard at suppressing the old ways. Rincon has a couple of local eateries, but the real temptation is **Prisca's Ice Cream** (tel. 599/7–6334), to be found at her house on Kaya Komkomber.

Pass through Rincon on the road that heads back to Kralendijk, but take the left-hand turn before Fontein to **Onima.** Small signposts direct the way to the **Indian inscriptions** found on a 3-foot limestone ledge that juts out like a partially formed cave entrance. Look up to see the red-stained designs and symbols inscribed on the limestone, said to have been the handiwork of the Arawak Indians when they inhabited the island centuries ago.

Backtrack to the main road and continue on to Fontein and then to **Seroe Largu,** the highest point on the southern part of the island. During the day, a winding path leads to a magnificent view of Kralendijk's rooftops and the island of Klein Bonaire; at night, the twinkling city lights below make this a romantic stop.

Washington/ Slagbaai National Park Once a plantation producing divi-divi trees (whose pods were used for tanning animal skins), aloe (used for medicinal lotions), charcoal, and goats, **Washington/Slagbaai National Park** is now a model of conservation, designed to maintain fauna, flora, and geological treasures in their natural state. Visitors may easily tour the 13,500-acre tropical desert terrain along the dirt roads. As befits a wilderness sanctuary, the well-marked, rugged roads force you to drive slowly enough to appreciate the animal life and the terrain. A four-wheel-drive is a must. (Think twice about coming here if it rained the day before—the mud you may encounter will be more than inconvenient.) If you are planning to hike, bring a picnic lunch, camera, sunscreen, and plenty of water. There are two different routes: The long one, 22 miles (about 2½ hours), is marked by yellow arrows; the short one, 15 miles (about 1½ hours), is marked by green arrows. Goats and donkeys may dart across the road, and if you keep your eyes peeled, you may catch sight of large, camouflaged iguanas in the shrubbery. Some folks even look out for shooting cacti.

Bird-watchers are really in their element here. Right inside the park's gate, flamingos roost on the salt pad known as **Salina Mathijs,** and exotic parakeets dot the foot of **Mt. Brandaris,** Bonaire's highest peak at 784 feet. Some 130 species of colorful birds fly in and out of the shrubbery in the park. Keep your eyes open and your binoculars at hand. (For choice beach sites in the park, *see* Beaches, *below*.) Swimming, snorkeling, and scuba diving are permitted, but visitors are requested not to frighten the animals or remove anything from the grounds. There is absolutely no hunting, fishing, or camping allowed. A useful guidebook to the park is available at the entrance for about $6. *Admission: $5 adults, $1 children under 15. The park is open daily 8–5, but you must enter before 3:30.*

What to See and Do with Children

Captain Don's Habitat offers all-inclusive **Family Weeks** in August, with packages that provide a variety of activities, in and out of the water, for both children and adults (*see* Lodging, *below*).

The Sand Dollar Beach Club resort has the daily, year-round **Sand Penny Club** for the children (ages 3–15) of guests. The kids can learn to snorkel and will have a chance to participate in a number of activities and games (*see* Lodging, *below*).

The **Sunset Beach Hotel** and the **Divi Flamingo Beach Resort** also offer family packages and programs for children (*see* Lodging, *below*).

Beaches

Beaches in Bonaire are not the island's strong point. Don't come expecting Aruba-length stretches of glorious white sand. Bonaire's beaches are smaller, and though the water is indeed blue (several shades of it, in fact), the sand is not always white. You can have your pick of beach in Bonaire according to color: pink, black, or white. The best hotel beaches are found at Harbour Village, Sunset Beach, and Sorobon (*see* Lodging, *below*).

Hermit crabs can be found along the shore at **Boca Cocolishi,** a black-sand beach in Washington/Slagbaai National Park on the northeast coast. The dark hues of tiny bits of dried coral and shells form the basin and beach, giving the sand an unusual look. This beach gives new meaning to the term windswept: cooling breezes whip the water into a frenzy as the color of the sea changes from midnight blue to aquamarine. Located on the windward side of the island, the water is too rough for anything more than wading; however, the spot is perfect for an intimate picnic *à deux*. To get there, take the Northern Scenic Route to the park, then ask for directions at the gate.

Also inside Washington Park is **Boca Slagbaai,** a beach of coral fossils and rocks with interesting coral gardens that are good for snorkeling just offshore. Bring scuba boots or canvas sandals to walk into the water because the "beach" is rough on bare feet. The gentle surf makes it an ideal place for picnicking or swimming, especially for children.

The exquisite ocher-and-russet building here was constructed by the first plantation owner and included a customs office and slaughterhouse. Today it houses a restaurant serving fine lunches Thursday–Sunday.

Playa Funchi, another Washington Park beach, is notable for the lagoon on one side where flamingos nest, and the superb snorkeling on the other, where iridescent green parrotfish swim right up to shore.

As the name suggests, the sand at **Pink Beach** boasts a pinkish tint that takes on a magical shimmer in the late-afternoon sun. The water is suitable for swimming, snorkeling, and scuba diving. Take the Southern Scenic Route on the western side of the island, past the Trans-World Radio station, close to the slave huts. A favorite hangout for Bonairians on the weekend, it is virtually deserted during the week.

For uninhibited sun worshipers who'd rather enjoy the rays in the altogether, the private, "clothes-optional" beach, at the **Sorobon Beach Resort,** offers calm water, soft clean sand, and delightfully strong tropical breezes. Nonguests are welcome and can purchase a $15 day pass at the entrance gate.

Boca Cai is across Lac Bay, which is an ideal spot for windsurfing.

If you enjoy water sports, find out which beaches are best for a specific sport (*see* Sports and the Outdoors, *below*).

Sports and the Outdoors

Scuba Diving   Bonaire has some of the best reef diving this side of Australia's Great Barrier Reef. The island is unique primarily for its incredible dive sites; it takes only 5–25 minutes to reach your site, the current is usually mild, and while some reefs have very sudden, steep drops, most begin just offshore and slope gently downward at a 45° angle. General visibility runs 60 to 100 feet, except during surges in October and November. An enormous range of coral can be seen, from knobby brain and giant brain coral to elkhorn, staghorn, mountainous star, gorgonian, and black coral. You're also likely to encounter schools of parrotfish, surgeonfish, angelfish, eels, snappers, and groupers. Beach diving is excellent just about everywhere on the leeward side of the island.

The well-policed Bonaire Marine Park, which encompasses the entire coastline around Bonaire and Klein Bonaire, remains an underwater wonder because visitors take the rules here seriously. Do not even think about (1) spearfishing, (2) dropping anchor, or (3) touching, stepping on, or collecting coral. Divers must pay an admission charge of $10, for which they receive a colored plastic tag (to be attached to an item of scuba gear) entitling them to one calendar year of unlimited diving in the Marine Park. The fees are used to maintain the underwater park. Tags are available at all scuba facilities and from the marine park headquarters in the Old Fort in Kralendijk (tel. 599/7–8444). To help preserve the reef, all dive operations on Bonaire now offer free buoyancy-control, advanced buoyancy-control, and photographic buoyancy-control classes. Check with any dive shop for the schedule.

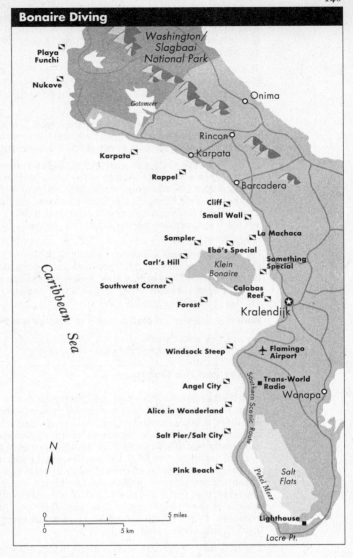

Bonaire Diving

Washington/
Slagbaai
National Park

Playa
Funchi

Nukove

Gotomeer

Onima

Rincon

Karpata

Karpata

Rappel

Barcadera

Cliff

Small Wall

Sampler

La Machaca

Ebo's Special

Carl's Hill

Klein
Bonaire

Something
Special

Southwest Corner

Calabas
Reef

Forest

Kralendijk

Caribbean Sea

Windsock Steep

Flamingo
Airport

Angel City

Trans-World
Radio

Wanapa

Alice in Wonderland

Salt Pier/Salt City

N

Southern Scenic Route

Pink Beach

Pekel Meer

Salt
Flats

0   5 miles

0   5 km

Lighthouse

Lacre Pt.

There is a hyperbaric decompression chamber located next to the hospital in Kralendijk (tel. 599/7–8187 or 599/7–8900 for emergencies).

*Dive
Operations* Organized tours are not necessary on Bonaire, as many dive sites are easily accessible from shore and clearly marked by yellow stones on the roadside. Most of the hotels listed in this guide have dive centers. The competition for quality and variety is fierce. Before making a room reservation, inquire about specific dive/room packages that are available. Many of the dive shops also have boutiques where you can purchase T-shirts, color slides showing underwater views, postcards, and tropical jewelry. **Peter Hughes Dive Bonaire** (Divi Flamingo Beach Resort, tel. 599/7–8285 or 800/367–3484), **Sand Dollar Dive and Photo** (Sand Dollar Beach Club, Kaya Gobrenador

Debrot 79, tel. 599/7–5252), and **Habitat Dive Center** (Captain Don's Habitat, Kaya Gobrenador Debrot 103, tel. 599/7–8290 or 800/327–6709) are all PADI (Professional Association of Diving Instructors) five-star dive facilities qualified to offer both PADI and NAUI (National Association of Underwater Instructors) certification courses. Sand Dollar Dive and Photo is also qualified to certify dive instructors. Other centers include **Bonaire Scuba Center** (Black Durgon Inn; in the U.S., write Box 775, Morgan, NJ 08879, or call 908/566–8866 or 800/526–2370), **Buddy Dive Resort** (Kaya Gobrenador N., Debrot 85, tel. 599/7–8647), **Dive Inn** (Kaya C.E.B. Hellmund 27, tel. 599/7–8761 and at the Sunset Beach Hotel, tel. 599/7–8448), **Neal Watson's Bonaire Undersea Adventures** (Coral Regency Resort, Kaya Gobrenador Debrot 90, tel. 599/7–5580 or 800/327–8150), **Great Adventures Bonaire** (Harbour Village Beach Resort, tel. 599/7–7500 or 800/424–0004), and **Bruce Bowker's Carib Inn Dive Center** (Bruce Bowker's Carib Inn, tel. 599/7–8819; fax 599/7–5295).

Americans Jerry Schnabel and Suzi Swygert of **Photo Tours N.V.** (Kaya Grandi 68, tel. 599/7–8060) specialize in teaching and guiding novice-through-professional underwater photographers. They also offer land-excursion tours of Bonaire's birds, wildlife, and vegetation. **Dee Scarr's Touch the Sea** (Box 369, tel. 599/7–8529) is a personalized (two people at a time) diving program that provides interaction with marine life; it is available to certified divers.

Dive Sites The *Guide to the Bonaire Marine Park* lists 44 sites that have been identified and marked by moorings. In the past few years, however, an additional 42 designated mooring and shore diving sites have been added through a conservation program called Sea Tether. Guides associated with the various dive centers can give you more complete directions. The following are a few popular sites to whet your appetite; these and selected other sites are pinpointed on our Bonaire Diving map.

Take the track down to the shore just behind the Trans-World Radio station; dive in and swim south to **Angel City,** one of the shallowest and most popular sites in a two-reef complex that includes **Alice in Wonderland.** The boulder-size green-and-tan coral heads are home to black margates, Spanish hogfish, gray snappers, and the large purple tube sponges.

Calabas Reef, located off the Divi Flamingo Beach Resort, is the island's most popular dive site. All divers using the hotel's facilities take their warm-up dive here where they can inspect the wreck sunk by Don Stewart for just this purpose. The site is replete with Christmas-tree sponges and fire coral adhering to the ship's hull. Fish life is frenzied, with the occasional octopus putting in an appearance.

You'll need to catch a boat to reach **Forest,** a dive site off the coast of Klein Bonaire, so named for the abundant black-coral forest found there. Responsible for occasional currents, this site gets a lot of fish action, including what's been described as a "friendly" spotted eel that lives in a cave.

Small Wall is one of Bonaire's only complete vertical wall dives. Located off the Black Durgon Inn, it is one of the island's most popular night-diving spots. Access is made by boat (Black Durgon guests can access it from shore). The 60-foot wall is frequented by seahorses, squid, turtles, tarpon, and barracudas and has dense hard and soft coral formations; it also allows for excellent snorkeling.

Rappel is one of the most spectacular dives, near the Karpata Ecological Center. The shore is a sheer cliff, and the lush coral growth is home to an unusual variety of marine life, including orange seahorses, squid, spiny lobsters, and a spotted trunkfish named Sir Timothy that will befriend you for a banana or a piece of cheese.

Something Special, just south of the entrance of the marina, is famous for its garden eels, which slither around the relatively shallow sand terrace.

Windsock Steep, situated in front of the small beach opposite the airport runway, is an excellent first-dive spot and a popular place for snorkeling close to town.

Snorkeling Don't consider snorkeling the cowardly diver's sport; in Bonaire the experience is anything but elementary. For only $6–$11 per day, you can rent a mask, fins, and snorkel at any hotel with a watersports center (*see* Lodging, *below*). The better spots for snorkeling are on the leeward side of the island, where you have access to the reefs.

Swimming Beaches good for swimming can be found anywhere along the western coast of the island. Excellent sites are **Pink Beach, Sorobon,** and **Boca Cai.** The best resort beaches are found at **Harbour Village Beach Resort, Sunset Beach Hotel,** and **Divi Flamingo Beach Resort and Casino.** Or take a water taxi ($12 round-trip) to **Klein Bonaire,** an islet where you can spend the day playing king of the dune. Except for a few forgotten sneakers, there is absolutely *nothing* on Klein Bonaire, so remember to take some food along. And don't miss the boat back home.

Tennis Tennis is available for free to the guests at the **Sunset Beach Hotel, Divi Flamingo Beach Resort and Casino,** and the **Sand Dollar Beach Club.** Nonguests can play for free during the day at the **Divi Flamingo Beach Resort and Casino** and even take the free tennis clinics on Tuesday and Wednesday mornings (8:30–10). At night, there's a $10-an-hour charge. At press time, the Sunset Beach Hotel was considering charging nonguests $10 an hour to use its two courts.

Windsurfing Lac Bay, a protected cove on the east coast, is ideal for windsurfing. Novices will find it especially comforting since there's no way to be blown out to sea. **Windsurfing Bonaire,** known locally as "Jibe City" (fax 599/7–5363; U.S. representative, 800/748–8733), offers courses for beginning to advanced board sailors. Lessons cost $20; board rentals start at $20 an hour, $40 for a half day. There are regular pickups at all the hotels at 9 AM and 1 PM.

Deep-Sea Fishing **Captain Rich** (tel. 599/7–5421) will take you on his 30-foot twin diesel sportfishing boat, the *Slamdunk*, to fish for wahoo, marlin, tuna, and sailfish. Rates are $275 for a half day, $375 for a full day (maximum six people). **Piscatur Charters** (tel. 599/7–8774) offers the light-tackle angler reef fishing for jacks, barracudas, and snappers from a 15-foot skiff. Rates are $125 for a half day, $225 for a full day. The 30-foot sportfisherman *Piscatur* is available for charter at $275 for a half day, $375 for a full day.

Sailing Cruises The *Samur* (tel. 599/7–5433), the *Oscarina* (tel. 599/7–8290 or 599/7–8819), and the *Woodwind* (tel. 599/7–8285) offer a variety of cruises for snorkeling, picnicking, and watching the sunset. A private day's cruise on the sailboat *Oscarina* (tel. 599/7–8290) is $350 for a party of four. Glass-bottom-boat trips are offered on the *Bonaire Dream.* The 1½-hour trip costs $15 for adults, $7.50 for children, and leaves daily, except Sunday, from the Harbour Village Marina.

Shopping

You can get to know all the shops in Bonaire in a matter of a few hours, but sometimes there's no better way to enjoy some time out of the sun and sea than to go shopping, particularly if your companion is a dive fanatic and you're not. Almost all the shops are situated on the Kaya Grandi or in adjacent streets and tiny malls. There are several snazzy boutiques worth a browse. One word of caution: Buy as many flamingo T-shirts as you want, but don't take home items made of goatskin or tortoiseshell; they are not allowed into the United States.

Clothing   **Benetton** (19 Kaya Grandi, tel. 599/7–5107) has added Bonaire to its list of franchises in the Caribbean and makes the claim that prices here are 20% less than in New York. At **Caro's Boutique** (34 Kaya Grandi, tel. 599/7–8308) men can find designs by LaCoste and Guy LaRoche.

One shop that's sure to inspire a purchase is the **Ki Bo Ke Pakus,** or **What Do You Want?** (Divi Flamingo Beach Resort, tel. 599/7–8239), with an exquisite line of batiks, material for dashikis, island-made jewelry, and chic designer swimsuits and beach coverups.

Perfume and   **D'Orsy's** (Harborside Mall, tel. 599/7–5288) sells name-brand, duty-
Cosmetics   free perfumes and makeup from Lancôme, Clinique, Estee Lauder, Chanel, Nina Ricci, and Ralph Lauren, to name a few.

Souvenirs and   The hippest boutique in Bonaire is **Birds of Paradise** (Bonaire Shop-
Crafts   ping Gallery, 36 Kaya Grandi, tel. 599/7–8998), with merchandise ranging from wooden fish earrings and other desert-chic jewelry to Esprit sportswear and stylish swimsuits. **Dalila Shop** (Bonaire Shopping Gallery, 36-A Kaya Grandi, tel. 599/7–8460) specializes in decorations for the home, including locally made *chibichibi* (sugar birds), tile paintings, Dutch souvenirs, and unusual stuffed fish and cloth parrots. **Littman Gifts** (35 Kaya Grandi, tel. 599/7–8091) is the place for gourmet foods—mouth-watering Dutch cheeses, rye breads, Dutch and American chocolates, and fine wines. Batik cloth by the yard, European costume jewelry, T-shirts, framed underwater pictures, wooden divers, and glass flamingos are also sold. **Caribbean Arts and Crafts** (38-A Kaya Grandi, tel. 599/7–5051) offers unique Mexican onyx, papier-mâché clowns, woven wall tapestries, painted wooden fish and parrots, straw carrying bags, and hand-blown glass vases. **Things Bonaire** (Sunset Beach Hotel, Kaya Grandi 38C, DL Two problems with address. DL tel. 599/7–8423) offers T-shirts, shorts, colorful earrings, batik dresses, souvenirs, and guidebooks. A government-funded crafts center, **Fundashon Arte Industri Bonairiano** (J. A. Abraham Blvd., Kralendijk, next to the post office, no phone), offers locally made necklaces of coral in a variety of colors, hand-painted shirts and dresses, and the "fresh craft of the day."

Dining

Gourmets have not been sneaking off to Bonaire for five-star cuisine, but with a healthy variety of dining experiences, visitors should not go home hungry. Dress on the island is casual but conservative.

Highly recommended restaurants are indicated by a star ★.

Category	Cost*
Expensive	over $25
Moderate	$15–$25
Inexpensive	under $15

Per person, excluding drinks and service. There is no sales tax.

Bistro des Amis. The Bistro's creative French menu and its simple yet elegant setting are both designed by owner Lucille Martyn. Try to get this engaging Dutch woman to talk about her specialties, then savor the Dutch chef's unforgettable red-pepper soup, duck with orange sauce, smoked salmon in honey-lemon sauce, and grouper sautéed in dill and white wine. Or just have a drink around the mahogany bar. *1 Kaya L. D. Gerharts, tel. 599/7–8003. Reservations required. AE, MC, V. Dinner only. Closed Sun. Expensive.*

★ **Der Roode Pelikaan.** The Red Pelican is by far the most soigné eatery on Bonaire: a harmonious blend of white tile floors, heavy wood beams, comfortable rattan furnishings, coral pink napery, and the owner's splendid collection of medieval Dutch crafts, from chamber pots to ale steins, all imaginatively incorporated into the decor. Add to that constantly changing art exhibits and tinkling ivories, and you have the stuff of a most civilized evening out. The Dutch chefs weave culinary magic with their light versions of such traditional Dutch fare as marinated fish salad, *stoofpot* (a thick sultry seafood stew), and chicken in walnut sauce. Connected to the new Lac Bay development, this is a quietly glamorous enclave. *Kaminda Sorobon 64, Lac Bay, tel. 599/7–8198. Reservations recommended. AE, MC, V. Expensive.*

Raffles. In one of the oldest two-story houses on Bonaire, this air-conditioned oasis of green and white is a find for seekers of a romantic tête-à-tête. Inside, soft jazz plays in the background, tables are intimate and candlelit, and the service is unobtrusive. More casual, café-style dining can be found outside on the terrace, where you can watch the strolling passersby. There's an à la carte menu, imaginatively blending Caribbean influences with Continental standards, and three fixed-priced complete dinners. Excellent beginners include the seven-seafood soup and fish pâté. Order the Seafood Platter Caribe (lobstertail, shrimp, scallops, and a fillet of grouper) or the salmon cascade. Save room for a mango parfait, dark and white chocolate mousse, or homemade fruit sherbets. Look for the landmark red British phone box that sits outside the door. *Kaya C.E.B. Hellmund 5, tel. 599/7–8617. Reservations suggested. AE, MC, V. Dinner only. Closed Mon. Expensive.*

Mona Lisa Bar & Restaurant. This restaurant offers Continental fare, along with a few authentic Dutch and Indonesian dishes. Lunch prices are considerably more reasonable than those on the dinner menu. Its most famous plate is the pork tenderloin *sate* drizzled with a special peanut-butter sauce. Somehow, Mona Lisa has become renowned for fresh vegetables, though who knows where they come from, since nearly everything in Bonaire has to be imported. This is a late-night hangout for local schmoozing and light snacks, which are served until about 2 AM in a colorful bar adorned with various team and business baseball-style caps. The intimate dining room features brick-and-iron grillwork, lace curtains, and whirring ceiling fans. *15 Kaya Grandi, tel. 599/7–8718. Closed Sun. MC, V. Moderate–Expensive.*

Den Laman Bar & Restaurant. A 6,000-square-foot aquarium provides the backdrop to this casual, nautically decorated, sea-breeze-cooled restaurant. Eat indoors next to the glass-enclosed "ocean show" (request a table in advance) or outdoors on the noisier patio overlooking the sea. Pick a fresh Caribbean lobster from the lobster tank, or choose red snapper Creole, which is a hands-down winner. *77 Gobrenador Debrot, next to the Sunset Beach Hotel, tel. 599/7–8599. Reservations advised. AE, MC, V. Dinner only. Closed Tues. Moderate.*

The Rendez-Vous Restaurant. The terrace of this bistrolike café, draped with a canopy of electric stars, is the perfect place to watch the world of Bonaire go by as you fill up on warm bread, hearty soups, seafood, steaks, and vegetarian specialties. Or munch on light pastries accompanied by steamy espresso. Those in the know swear the Rendez-Vous is the place to go to recover from disco-burn-out. *3 Kaya L. D. Gerharts, tel. 599/7–8454. AE. Dinner only. Closed Tues. Moderate.*

★ **Richard's Waterfront Dining.** Animated and congenial owner Richard Beady's alfresco eatery on the water is casually romantic and has become the most recommended restaurant on the island—a reputation that's well deserved. Richard, originally from Boston, sets the tone by personally checking on every table. Although the menu is limited, the food is consistently excellent, catering to American palates with flavorful, not spicy, preparations. Among the best dishes are conch *alajillo* (fillet of conch with garlic and butter), shrimp primavera, and grilled wahoo. Start with the fish soup, a tasty broth with chunks of the catch of the day. A new pier lets you arrive by boat. The Sunset Happy Hour is popular with locals. *60 J. A. Abraham Blvd., a few houses away from Bruce Bowker's Carib Inn, tel. 599/7–5263. Reservations advised. AE, MC, V. Dinner only. Closed Mon. Moderate.*

★ **Toys Grand Café.** Restaurants don't come much more playful than this hip Dutch paean to high camp. Murals of everyone from Elvis to Chaplin to Mickey Mouse enliven the walls. Toy trains and crazy puppets jut out from the walls, and jack-in-the-boxes seem poised for assault at any minute. Potted plants engulf the wicker chairs. The food, with a strong Indonesian influence, is first-rate: try the snails in blue cheese, the *nasi goreng* (fried rice), or the pork medallions in peach sauce. During happy hour you can get the daily special for five bucks! *J. A. Abraham Blvd., Kralendijk, tel. 599/7–6666. No credit cards. Moderate.*

The Green Parrot. This family-run restaurant, on the dock of the Sand Dollar Beach Club, features the biggest hamburgers and the best strawberry margaritas on the island. Try the onion string appetizer, which consists of onion rings shaped into a small bread loaf. Bagels with cream cheese, char-grilled steaks, Creole fish, and barbecued chicken and ribs are also served. This is where you'll find both the American expatriates and visiting tourists hanging out. It's also a good place for viewing the setting sun. *Sand Dollar Beach Club, tel. 599/7–5454. Reservations suggested in high season. AE, MC, V. Inexpensive–Moderate.*

Zeezicht Bar & Restaurant. Zeezicht (pronounced *zay-zeekt* and meaning sea view) is one of the better restaurants in town that is open for three meals a day. At breakfast and lunch you'll get basic American fare with an Antillean touch, such as a fish omelet. Dinner is either on the terrace overlooking the harbor or in the homey, rough-hewn main room. Locals are dedicated to this hangout, especially for the ceviche, conch sandwiches, local snails in hot sauce, and the Zeezicht special soup with conch, fish, shrimps, and oysters. After dessert, stop in the garden to see the monkey and parrots. *10 Kaya Corsow, across from Karel's Beach Bar, tel. 599/7–8434. AE, MC, V. Inexpensive–Moderate.*

China Garden Restaurant and Bar. Despite its name, this place has

an everything-you-could-ever-want menu, from American sandwiches to shark's-fin soup, steaks, lobster, even omelets. But Cantonese dishes are still the specialty. Try the goat Chinese-style,
anything in black-bean sauce, or one of the sweet-and-sour dishes.
Lots of locals turn up between 5 and 7 PM to have a drink and watch
the latest in sports on the bar's cable TV. The formerly sleazy decor
has been brightened with Chinese lanterns and scarlet tablecloths. *47
Kaya Grandi, tel. 599/7–8480. Reservations suggested in season.
AE, DC, MC, V. Closed Tues. Inexpensive.*

Lodging

Hotels on Bonaire, with the exception of Harbour Village, cater primarily to avid divers who spend their days underwater and come up
for air only for evening festivities. Hence, hotel facilities tend to be
modest with small swimming pools and limited service. Groomed
sandy beaches are not a requisite for a hotel, but an efficient dive
shop is. Many resort accommodations have fully equipped kitchens.
Although the larger hotels offer a variety of meal plans, most are on
the European Plan. As a general rule, hotel restaurants can be significantly more expensive than restaurants in town.

Highly recommended lodgings are indicated by a star ★.

Category	Cost*
Very Expensive	over $225
Expensive	$150–$225
Moderate	$100–$150
Inexpensive	under $100

**All prices are for a standard double room for two in high season,
excluding a $4.10 per person, per night, government room tax and a
10% service charge.*

Hotels
★

Harbour Village Beach Resort. This is the resort for divers who want
the best of both an upscale resort and a dive vacation. Wide walkways bordered by lush foliage and blooming tropical flowers separate eight low-rise, southwestern-style buildings, with Moorish
arches, red barrel-tile roofs, and a pastel color scheme. The palm
tree–lined beach is wide and inviting. While not as impressive as the
grounds or building exteriors, the pleasant rooms and suites are
done in dusty rose and aqua and have French doors leading to a terrace or patio (except for second-story courtyard rooms), white tile
floors, and pale wood and wicker furniture. Rooms are similar in decor, with price categories determined by the view—garden courtyard, marina, or ocean. Each room has a hair dryer, cable TV,
amenity package, and direct-dial telephone. There is a full-service
dive shop and a water-sports concession that offers sailing,
windsurfing, deep-sea fishing, kayaking, and powerboat rentals at
the resort's marina. A new fitness center offers an air-conditioned
state-of-the-art workout. This exclusive enclave appeals to those
who like the quiet life. The Kasa Coral restaurant, which overlooks
the'pool, serves full American buffet breakfasts, international *à la
carte* lunches, and gourmet, fixed-price, multicourse dinners. *Box
312, tel. 599/7–7500 or 800/424–0004, fax 599/7–7507. 60 rooms, 8
oceanfront suites, 30 condominium units. Facilities: 2 restaurants,
2 bars/lounges, dive center, dive lockers at beach, fitness center,
meeting room, water-sports center, pool, bicycles, baby-sitting,*

marina, gift shop. AE, DC, MC, V. EP, MAP, FAP. Very Expensive.

Captain Don's Habitat. With its recent (1992) expansion and massive renovation, the Habitat, once a sort of extended home of Captain Don Stewart, the island's wildest sharpshooting personality, can no longer pass itself off as a mere guest house for divers. Stewart's Curaçaon partners have poured money into this resort, adding a set of upscale rooms (Junior suites) and then a long row of private villas (the Hamlet section) that rank among the island's best: all are spacious, with ocean-view verandas, full kitchens, and stylish appointments. The rooms in the original 11 cottages are also spacious but in need of refurbishing. The atmosphere at the Habitat is laid-back and easygoing, with the emphasis on the staff's personal warmth rather than on spick-and-span efficiency. It's also one of few dive resorts that welcomes families. The beachfront property units—with glorious views of Klein Bonaire—are spaced widely apart, and the grounds have been landscaped with rocks and cacti. Be sure to meet Captain Don, who shows up twice a week just to say hello, shoot the breeze, and tell his incredible tales, most of which are actually true. A full dive center with seven boats, complete with a resident photo pro, rounds out the picture. *Kaya Gobrenador Debrot 103, Box 88, tel. 599/7–8290. U.S. representative: Habitat North American, tel. 800/327–6709, fax 599/7–8240. 11 cottages, 11 villas, 16 rooms. Facilities: 2 bars, restaurant, gift shop, pool, cruises, baby-sitting, laundry facilities, bicycles, dive center, photo labs. AE, DC, MC, V. EP, MAP, FAP. Expensive.*

Coral Regency Resort. This time-share resort's 32 studios and one- and two-bedroom suites are in 10 coral-pink, two-story buildings set around a quadrangle containing a small pool and sunbathing area—there's no beach for lounging. As a result, for privacy, the rooms on the second floor are more desirable than those on the first. The studio apartments have a small but complete kitchen, while the suites have a spacious living room with overhead fan, a large balcony looking out to sea (wonderful for morning breakfasts), and a fully equipped kitchen—including microwave and blender. All feature cable TV, direct-dial phone, and air-conditioning. The plain but clean bedrooms are compact, with little space left over after the huge king-size bed or two twins, but the marble-tiled bathrooms are large. Paul's Oceanfront Bar & Restaurant and the dive shop, a Neal Watson Undersea Adventures affiliate, add to the offerings. More villa units are planned, but these will be in a separate area several hundred yards from the waterfront. *Kaya Gob, Debrot 90, Box 380, tel. 599/7–5580; in the U.S., tel. 800/327–8150; fax 599/7–5680. 32 units. Facilities: bar, restaurant, pool, dive center. AE, DC, MC, V. CP, MAP, FAP. Expensive.*

★ **Sand Dollar Beach Club.** These elegant, spacious time-share apartments combine a European design with a tropical rattan decor, though this varies according to the individual owner's taste. Each has cable TV, air-conditioning, a full kitchen, a large bathroom, a couch that turns into a queen-size bed, and a private patio or terrace that looks out to the sea (though the views from the ground-floor units are obstructed by foliage). Some units also have telephones. This American enclave is for serious divers and their families. There's daily maid service, and the maids will even do your laundry for $4 a load. There's an on-premise PADI five-star dive center, a limited activities club for children and two lighted tennis courts. There is a beach, but it's minuscule and disappears at high tide. The resort's waterfront Green Parrot restaurant serves breakfast, lunch, and dinner, and there's a grocery store for those who like to cook. *Kaya Grandi, tel. 599/7–8738; in the U.S., tel. 800/766–6016*

or 617/821–1012; fax 599/7–8760. 77 studio, 1-, 2-, and 3-bedroom
units and 8 2-bedroom town houses. Facilities: restaurant, bar, dive
center, photo lab, pool, 2 lighted tennis courts, outdoor showers,
strip shopping center, grocery/convenience store. AE, DC, MC, V.
EP, MAP, FAP. Expensive.

Sorobon Beach Resort. Here's the perfect place for acting out all
your *Swept Away* fantasies. The Sorobon is a secluded cluster of cottages on a lovely private sandy beach at Lac Bay, on the southeast
shore. This delightfully unpretentious small resort is for "natural-
ists" who take its clothing-optional motto literally. Guests are a fair
mix of Europeans and Americans. New Agers will like the natural
look of the Scandinavian pine furniture. The chalets are arranged in
a "V" shape so as to give the resort more openness and access to the
beach. Each chalet consists of two small one-bedroom units, each
with simple furnishings, an older-style kitchen, and a shower-only
bath. In keeping with the get-away-from-it-all concept, there's no
air-conditioning, TV, or telephone. A daily shuttle will take you to
town. Relax sitting around full-moon bonfires, playing ping-pong,
or enjoying a shiatsu massage, all right on the beach. The heady
windsurfing in Lac Bay, a result of the unbeatable combo of shallow
bay and strong trade winds, draws raves. Restaurant, bar, volleyball, nature-oriented book and video library, even a telescope to
view the stunning night skies are all for the asking. But act blasé
when the manager arrives wrapped in a towel. *Box 14, tel. 599/7–
8080, fax 599/7–5363. 25 cottages. Facilities: kitchenettes, restaurant, bar, library . AE, MC, V. EP. Expensive.*

Divi Flamingo Beach Resort and Casino. The Divi Flamingo is the
closest thing you'll find to a small village on Bonaire—a plantation-
style resort that will serve your every need. No matter which hotel
you're staying at, reserve a table at the Chibi Chibi Restaurant,
where you can hear ocean waves pounding beneath the floorboards.
The resort consists of the hotel and the Club Flamingo studio apartments, which have the newest and nicest rooms. This is the oldest
hotel on the island—a former internment camp for German POWs
during World War II, and even those rooms that have been "renovated" still cry out for new furnishings and another coat of fresh
paint. Though the resort is definitely showing signs of age, because
of its dive facility and upbeat activities programs it still receives a
fair share of repeat guests. Dive Bonaire was founded by world-class
expert Peter Hughes and features some of the best photo labs in the
Caribbean. Several rooms are accessible to travelers using wheelchairs, and the dive operation even has specially trained masters
who teach scuba diving to individuals with disabilities and dive with
them. The on-premise tennis pro offers free clinics every Tuesday
and Wednesday morning, there's a daily activities program, live
bands perform several nights a week, and the island's only casino—
billed as the world's only barefoot gaming center—is here as well.
The all-inclusive package offers great value for the price. *J. A.
Abraham Blvd., tel. 599/7–8285. U.S. representative: Divi Hotels,
tel. 800/367–3484, fax 599/7–8238. 105 rooms, 40 time-share units.
Facilities: 2 restaurants, 3 bars, casino, 2 pools, 2 dive shops, photo
shop, jewelry store, lighted tennis court, 2 car-rental desks, tour
desk, Jacuzzi, boutique. AE, D, MC, V. EP, MAP, All-inclusive.
Moderate–Expensive.*

Sunset Beach Hotel. In 1990 a group of businessmen purchased this
hotel (then called the Bonaire Beach Hotel) and began renovations.
New beds and drapes were brought in, walls painted, and wood
floors polished. Each sizable room got a digital safety vault, direct-
dial telephone, remote-control color TV, minirefrigerator, and coffeemaker. Age, however, has its drawbacks, and here the drawback

is the location of the original buildings: They are all set back from the shore, giving even the best rooms only garden views. And in spite of the new amenities, the old-looking rooms and bathrooms lack brightness and appeal. Still, the 12 acres encompass one of the island's better hotel beaches (in contrast to the swimming pool, which is tiny), a miniature golf course, a water-sports concession that offers more than any other on the island, and a romantic thatch-roof restaurant overlooking the sea. Unfortunately, the food is not the island's best, and although the service is superfriendly, it is not always efficient. Divers come for the complete on-premise scuba center, Dive Inn, which has three dive boats. Nondivers can rent Sunfish, Windsurfers, and snorkeling gear, or go parasailing or boogie boarding. The Bonairian Theme night, with native buffet, folkloric dance show, steel band, and dancing waitresses, costs $20 per person. *Kaya Gobrenador Debrot 75, Box 333, tel. 599/7–8448, fax 599/7–8118. U.S./Canada representative: tel. 800/333–1212, 800/ 344–4439, or 800/223–9815. 142 rooms, 3 1-bedroom suites. Facilities: restaurant, bar/lounge, pool, 3 hot tubs, dive center, watersports center, water taxi to Klein Bonaire, miniature golf, shuffleboard, 2 lighted tennis courts, game room, tour desk, gift shop, car rental. AE, D, DC, MC, V. EP, MAP. Moderate.*

★ **Bruce Bowker's Carib Inn.** Sixteen years ago, American diver Bruce Bowker started his small diving lodge out of a private home, continually adding onto and refurbishing the air-conditioned inn. New rattan furnishings, cable TVs, completely renovated kitchens, and a family-style atmosphere have turned his homey hostelry into one of the island's best bets, albeit one that gets booked far in advance by repeat guests. Bowker knows everybody by name and loves to fill special requests. The two units with no kitchen have a refrigerator and electric kettle, but for more involved dining, you'll have to leave the premises—there's no restaurant. (Richard's Waterfront Restaurant is right next door.) Those who prefer to cook can shop for supplies at the grocery store just across the street. Nervous virgin divers will enjoy Bowker's small scuba classes (one or two people); PADI certification is available. You'll have to drive to the nearest beach. *Box 68, tel. 599/7–8819, fax 599/7–5295. U.S. representative: ITR, tel. 800/223–9815 or 212/545–8649. 9 units. Facilities: pool, scuba classes, dive center, retail dive store. AE, MC, V. EP. Inexpensive.*

Buddy Dive Center. Europeans who tend to eschew luxury, requiring only basic amenities with matching rates, enjoy this growing complex situated on the beach. In keeping with its no-frills style, the five units on the ground level have no air-conditioning and no TV; the five second-floor units have air-conditioning. All these original 10 "apartments" are tiny but clean, with a kitchenette, tile floors, twin beds, a sleep sofa, and a shower-only bathroom. In January 1993, the first of two new buildings housing more upscale, spacious, and air-conditioned two- and three-bedroom apartments opened. A dive operation and pool is also on the premises. *Kaya Gobrenador Debrot, Box 231, tel 599/7–8065 or 800/ 359–0747; fax 599/7–2647. 10 apartments and 15 2- and 3-bedroom condominium units. Facilities: pool with bar, dive shop. AE, MC, V. EP. Inexpensive.*

Home and Apartment Rentals The **Bonaire Government Tourist Office** (tel. 800/U–BONAIR) can help you locate suitable guest houses and smaller rental apartments in Bonaire. Rental apartments are also available through **Bonaire Sunset Villas** (tel. 800/223–9815, fax 599/7–8118), **Sunset Oceanfront Apartments** (tel. 800/223–9815, fax 599/7–8865), **Club Laman Caribe**

(fax 599/7–7741), or **Black Durgon Inn Properties** (tel. 800/526–2370).

The Arts and Nightlife

The Arts Slide shows of underwater scenes keep both divers and nondivers fascinated in the evenings. Dee Scarr, a dive guide, presents the fascinating "Touch the Sea" show Monday night at 8:45, from the beginning of November to the end of June, at **Captain Don's Habitat** (tel. 599/7–8290). Check with the Habitat for other shows throughout the week. **Sunset Beach Hotel** (tel. 599/7–8448) offers a free one-hour slide show every Wednesday evening at 7. **Divi Flamingo Beach Resort** (tel. 599/7–8285) offers a free underwater video, "Discover the Caribbean," on Sunday night at 7 PM.

The best singer on the island is guitarist **Cai-Cai Cecelia,** who performs with his duo Monday night at the **Divi Flamingo Beach Resort,** Wednesday night at **Sunset Beach Hotel,** and Thursday night at **Captain Don's Habitat.** He sings his own compositions, as well as Harry Belafonte classics. A local duo also sings and plays music every Thursday night at the **Divi Flamingo Beach Resort.** The Kunuku Band plays every Friday and Sunday for happy hour at **Captain Don's Habitat.** The M & M Duo also entertains three nights a week at the Chibi Chibi Restaurant at the **Divi Flamingo Beach Resort.**

Nightlife Most divers are exhausted after they finish their third, fourth, or fifth dive of the day, which probably explains why there's only one disco in Bonaire. Nevertheless, **E Wowo** (Kralendijk, at the corner of Kaya Grandi and Kaya L. D. Gerharts, no phone) is usually packed in high season, so get there early. The name E Wowo means "eye" in Papiamento and is illustrated with two flashing op-art eyes on the wall. Recorded music is loud, and the large circular bar seats a lot of action. The entrance fee varies according to the season.

The popular bar **Karel's** (tel. 599/7–8434), on the waterfront across from the Zeezicht Restaurant, sits on stilts above the sea and is *the* place for mingling with islanders, dive pros, and tourists, especially Friday and Saturday nights, when there's live music.

Mi Ramada (Rincon, tel. 599/7–6338) is a hopping joint, splashed with neon colors and adorned with everything from license plates to creatively carved driftwood, that serves fine local Creole food to the accompaniment of top bands from all three ABC islands. Friday and Saturday nights are party time, when Bonairians gather along the main street of Kralendijk to dance to informal bands that set up on the sidewalk.

The island has only one casino, the **Divi Flamingo Beach Casino,** which opens at 8 PM and is closed on Sunday.

7 The British Virgin Islands

Tortola, Virgin Gorda, and Outlying Islands

*Updated by
Pamela
Acheson*

At several points, the British Virgin Islands are less than a mile from the U.S. Virgin Islands, yet the B.V.I. have remained happily free of the runaway development that has detracted from the charm of so many West Indian islands. Here you will find about 50 islands, islets, and cays that are serene, seductive, and spectacularly beautiful. The pleasures to be found here are of the understated sort— sailing around the multitude of tiny, nearby islands; diving to the wreck of the RMS *Rhone*, sunk off Salt Island by a nasty hurricane in 1867; snorkeling in one of hundreds of wonderful spots; walking empty beaches; seeing some spectacular views from the island's peaks; and settling down on some breeze-swept terrace to admire the sunset.

One reason the B.V.I. have retained this sense of blissful simplicity is their strict building codes. No building can rise higher than the surrounding palms—two stories is the limit. The lack of direct air flights from the mainland United States also helps the British islands retain the endearing qualities of yesteryear's Caribbean. One first has to get to Puerto Rico, 60 miles to the west, or to nearby St. Thomas in the United States Virgin Islands and catch a small plane to the little airports on Beef Island/Tortola and Virgin Gorda. Many of the travelers who return year after year prefer arriving by water, either aboard their own ketches and yawls or on one of the convenient ferryboats that cross the turquoise waters between St. Thomas and Tortola.

Tortola, about 10 square miles, is the largest of the islands, and Virgin Gorda, with 8 square miles, ranks second. The islands scattered around them include Jost Van Dyke, Great Camanoe, Norman, Peter, Salt, Cooper, Ginger, Dead Chest, and Anegada, among others.

Sailing has always been a popular activity in the B.V.I. The first arrivals here were a romantic seafaring tribe, the Siboney Indians. Christopher Columbus was the first European to visit, during his second voyage to the New World, in 1493. The redoubtable "Admiral of the Ocean Seas," impressed by the number of islands dotting the horizon, named them *Las Once Mil Virgines* (The 11,000 Virgins) in honor of the 11,000 virgin-companions of Saint Ursula, martyred in the fourth century.

In the ensuing years, the Spaniards passed through these waters seeking gold, and, finding none, they quickly moved on to the richer pastures of Mexico. The next seafarers to arrive were a number of pirates who found the islands' hidden coves and treacherous reefs an ideal base from which to prey on passing galleons crammed with Mexican and Peruvian gold, silver, and spices. Among the most notorious of these predatory men were Blackbeard Teach; Bluebeard; Captain Kidd; and Sir Francis Drake, who lent his name to the channel that sweeps through the two main clusters of the B.V.I.

In the 17th century, these colorful cutthroats were replaced by the Dutch. The Dutch, in turn, were soon sent packing by the British, who retained control of the islands for nearly three centuries. The British established a plantation economy, and for the next 150 years they developed the sugar industry. African slaves were brought in to work the cane fields while the plantation owners and their families reaped the benefits. When slavery was abolished in 1838, the plantation economy quickly faltered, and the majority of the white population returned to Europe.

The islands dozed, a forgotten corner of the British empire, until the early 1960s. In 1966, a new constitution, granting greater autonomy to the islands, was approved. While the governor is still appointed by the queen of England, his limited powers concentrate on external affairs and local security. Other matters are administered by the legislative council, consisting of representatives from nine island districts. General elections are held every four years. The arrangement seems to suit the British Virgin Islanders just fine: The mood is serene, with none of the occasional political turmoil found on other islands. Having had tacit control over their destinies for more than a century and a half, local residents now have no reason to feel that visitors are more than welcome guests.

The 1960s also saw the arrival of a few profit-seeking souls, notably Laurance Rockefeller and American-expatriate Charlie Cary, who became convinced that the islands' balmy weather, powder-soft beaches, and splendid sailing would make them an ideal holiday destination. Attempts at building a small tourist industry began in 1965, when Rockefeller set about creating the Little Dix resort on Virgin Gorda. A few years later, Cary and his wife, Ginny, established the Moorings marina complex on Tortola, and sailing in the area burgeoned. Today the majority of jobs on the islands are tourism-related. British Virgin Islanders love their unspoiled tropical home and are determined to maintain its easygoing charms, for both themselves and the travelers who are their guests.

Before You Go

Tourist Information Information about the B.V.I. is available through the **British Virgin Islands Tourist Board** (370 Lexington Ave., Suite 416, New York, NY 10017, tel. 212/696–0400 or 800/835–8530) or at the **British Virgin Islands Information Office** in San Francisco (1686 Union St., Suite 305, San Francisco, CA 94123, tel. 415/775–0344 or 800/232–7770). British travelers can write or visit the **BVI Information Office** (110 St. Martin's Lane, London WC2N 4DY, tel. 071/2404259).

Arriving and Departing
By Plane No nonstop service is available from the United States to the B.V.I.; connections are usually made through San Juan, Puerto Rico, or St. Thomas, U.S.V.I. Airlines serving both San Juan and St. Thomas include **American** (tel. 800/433–7300), **Continental** (tel. 800/231–0856), and **Delta** (tel. 800/323–2323). **Sunaire Express** (809/495–2480) flies from San Juan and St. Thomas to both Beef Island/Tortola and Virgin Gorda and between St. Croix and Beef Island/Tortola. **American Eagle** (tel. 800/433–7300) flies from San Juan to Tortola. Regularly scheduled service between the B.V.I. and most other Caribbean islands is provided by **Leeward Islands Air Transport (LIAT)** (tel. 809/495–1187). Many Caribbean islands can also be reached via **Gorda Aero Service** (Tortola, tel. 809/495–2271), a charter service.

By Boat Various ferries connect St. Thomas, U.S.V.I., with Tortola and Virgin Gorda. **Native Son, Inc.** (tel. 809/495–4617), operates three ferries—(*Native Son, Oriole,* and *Voyager Eagle*)—and offers service between St. Thomas and Tortola (West End and Road Town) daily and between St. Thomas and Spanish Town, Virgin Gorda, on Wednesday and Sunday. **Smiths Ferry Services** (tel. 809/494–4430 or 809/494–2355) carries passengers between downtown St. Thomas and Road Town and West End on Monday through Saturday, offers daily service between Red Hook on St. Thomas and Tortola's West End, and travels between St. Thomas and Spanish Town on Sunday. **Inter-Island Boat Services'** *Sundance II* (tel. 809/776–6597) connects St. John and West End on Tortola daily.

Passports and Visas Upon entering the B.V.I., U.S. and Canadian citizens are required to present some proof of citizenship—if not a passport, then a birth

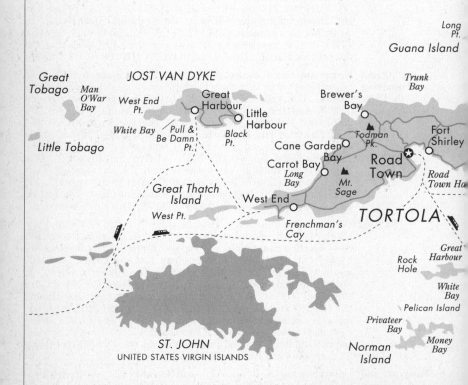

ATLANTIC

Long
Pt.

Guana Island

Great
Tobago

Man
O'War
Bay

JOST VAN DYKE

West End
Pt.

Great
Harbour

Brewer's
Bay

Trunk
Bay

Little Tobago

White Bay

Pull &
Be Damn
Pt.

Little
Harbour

Black
Pt.

Cane Garden
Bay

Todman
Pk.

Fort
Shirley

Carrot Bay

Long
Bay

Road
Town

Great Thatch
Island

West Pt.

West End

Mt.
Sage

Road
Town Ha

Frenchman's
Cay

TORTOLA

Great
Harbour

Rock
Hole

White
Bay

Pelican Island

Privateer
Bay

Money
Bay

ST. JOHN
UNITED STATES VIRGIN ISLANDS

Norman
Island

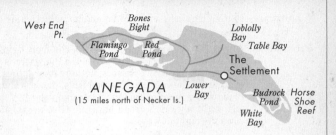

West End
Pt.

Bones
Bight

Flamingo
Pond

Red
Pond

Loblolly
Bay

Table Bay

The
Settlement

ANEGADA
(15 miles north of Necker Is.)

Lower
Bay

Budrock
Pond

Horse
Shoe
Reef

White
Bay

O C E A N

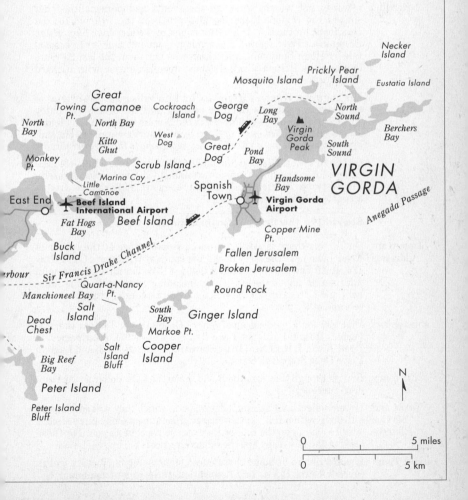

Necker
Island

Prickly Pear
Island

Eustatia Island

Mosquito Island

Great
Camanoe

Towing
Pt.

Cockroach
Island

George
Dog

Long
Bay

North
Sound

North Bay

North
Bay

West
Dog

Virgin
Gorda
Peak

South
Sound

Berchers
Bay

Kitto
Ghut

Great
Dog

Pond
Bay

VIRGIN
GORDA

Monkey
Pt.

Scrub Island

Marina Cay

Handsome
Bay

Anegada Passage

Little
Camanoe

Spanish
Town

East End

Beef Island
International Airport

Virgin Gorda
Airport

Fat Hogs
Bay

Beef Island

Copper Mine
Pt.

Buck
Island

Fallen Jerusalem

Sir Francis Drake Channel

Broken Jerusalem

rbour

Quart-a-Nancy
Pt.

Round Rock

Manchioneel Bay

Salt
Island

South
Bay

Ginger Island

Dead
Chest

Markoe Pt.

Salt
Island
Bluff

Cooper
Island

Big Reef
Bay

Peter Island

N

Peter Island
Bluff

0   5 miles

0   5 km

certificate or voter-registration card with a driver's license or photo ID.

Language British English, with a West Indian inflection, is the language spoken.

Precautions Although there are generally no perils from drinking the water in these islands it is a good idea to ask if the water is potable when you check into your hotel. Insects, notably mosquitoes, are not usually a problem in these breeze-blessed isles, but it is always a good idea to bring some repellent along. Animals in the B.V.I. are not dangerous, but they can be road hazards. Give goats, sheep, horses, and cows the right of way.

Beware of the little varmints called "no-see-ums." They're for real and are especially pesky at twilight near the water. So if you're going for an evening stroll on the beach, apply some type of repellent liberally. No-see-um bites itch worse than mosquito bites and take a lot longer to go away. Prevention is the best cure, but witch hazel (or a dab of gin or vodka) offers *some* relief if they get you.

Further Reading Vernon Pickering's *Concise History of the British Virgin Islands* is a wordy but worthy guide to the events and personalities that shaped the region. Pickering also produces the *Official Tourist Handbook* for the B.V.I. Look for copies of *A Place Like This: Hugh Benjamin's Peter Island*, a charming, eloquent, and very personal tale by Hugh Benjamin, a Kittitian who has spent the last 20 years living in the British Virgin Islands, in collaboration with Richard Myers, a New York writer.

For linguists, *What a Pistarckle!* by Lito Valls gives the origins of the many expressions you'll be hearing, and historians will enjoy *Eyewitness Accounts of Slavery in the Danish West Indies* by Isidor Paiewonsky and *Conquest of Eden* by Michael Paiewonsky. For sailors, Simon Scott has written a *Cruising Guide to the Virgin Islands*.

On the B.V.I., the *Island Sun* and the *BVI Beacon* are the best local papers for everything from entertainment listings to local gossip. The *Welcome Tourist Guide* is comprehensive and available free at airports and larger hotels.

Staying in the British Virgin Islands

Important Addresses On Tortola there is a **B.V.I. Tourist Board Office** at the center of Road Town near the ferry dock, just south of Wickham's Cay I (Box 134, Road Town, Tortola, tel. 809/494–3134). For all kinds of useful information about these islands, including rates and phone numbers, get a free copy of the *Welcome Tourist Guide*, available at hotels and other places.

Emergencies Dial 999 for a medical emergency. **Hospital:** On Tortola there is **Peebles Hospital** in Road Town (tel. 809/494–3497). **Pharmacies:** in Road Town, **J. R. O'Neal Drug Store** (tel. 809/494–2292) and **Lagoon Plaza Drug Store** (tel. 809/494–2498).

Currency British though they are, the B.V.I. have the U.S. dollar as the standard currency.

Taxes and Service Charges Hotels collect a 7% accommodations tax, which they will add to your bill along with a 10% service charge. Restaurants may put a similar service charge on the bill, or they may leave it up to you. For those leaving the B.V.I. by air, the departure tax is $5; by sea it is $4.

Guided Tours If you'd like to do some chauffeured sightseeing on Tortola, get in touch with the **B.V.I. Taxi Association** (three-person minimum, tel.

809/494–2875, 809/494–2322, or 809/495–2378), **Style's Taxi Service** (tel. 809/494–2260 during the day or 809/494–3341 at night), or **Travel Plan Tours** (tel. 809/494–2872). **Scato's Bus Service** (tel. 809/494–2365), in Road Town, provides public transportation, special tours with group rates, and beach outings. Guided tours on Virgin Gorda can be arranged through **Andy's Taxi and Jeep Rental** (tel. 809/495–5252) or **Mahogany Rentals and Island Tours** (tel. 809/495–5469).

Getting Around Boats
Speedy's Fantasy (tel. 809/495–5240) makes the run between Road Town, Tortola, Spanish Town and Virgin Gorda daily. Running daily between Virgin Gorda's North Sound (Bitter End Yacht Club) and Beef Island, Tortola are **North Sound Express** (tel. 809/494–2746) boats. There are also daily boats between Peter Island's private dock on Tortola just east of Road Town and Peter Island. **Jost Van Dyke Ferry Service** (tel. 809/495–2997) makes the Jost Van Dyke–Tortola run several times a day via the *When* ferry.

Cars
Driving on Tortola and Virgin Gorda is not for the timid. Rollercoaster roads with breathtaking ascents and descents and tight turns that give new meaning to the term "hairpin curves" are the norm. It's a challenge well worth trying, however; the ever-changing views of land, sea, and neighboring islands are among the most spectacular in the Caribbean. Most people will strongly recommend renting a four-wheel drive vehicle. Driving is *à l'Anglais*, on the left side of the road. It's easy to become accustomed to it if you drive slowly, think before you make a turn, and pay attention when driving in and out of the occasional traffic circle, locally called a "roundabout." Speed limits are 30–40 mph outside town and 10–15 mph in residential areas. A valid B.V.I. driver's license is required and can be obtained for $10 at car-rental agencies. You must be at least 25 and have a valid driver's license from another country to get one.

On Tortola, car rentals are available from **Avis** (tel. 809/494–3322), **Budget** (tel. 809/494–2639), **Hertz** (tel. 809/495–4405), and **National** (tel. 809/494–3197). On Virgin Gorda, try **Mahogany Rentals** (tel. 809/495–5469) or **Andy's Taxi and Jeep Rental** (tel. 809/495–5252).

Taxis
Your hotel staff will be happy to summon a taxi for you. On Tortola, there is a B.V.I. Taxi Association stand in Road Town near the ferry dock (tel. 809/494–2875) and Wickham's Cay I (tel. 809/494–2322) and one on Beef Island, at the airport (tel. 809/495–2378). You can also usually find a taxi at the Sopers Hole ferry dock, West End, where ferries from St. Thomas arrive. On Virgin Gorda, Mahogany or Andy's (*see above*) also provide taxi service.

Buses
For information about rates and schedules on Tortola, call **Scato's Bus Service** (tel. 809/494–2365).

Mopeds and Bicycles
Scooters and bicycles can be rented on Tortola from **Hero's Bicycle Rental** (tel. 809/494–3536). On Virgin Gorda, **Honda Scooter Rental** (tel. 809/495–5212) rents mopeds.

Telephones and Mail
The area code for the B.V.I. is 809. To call anywhere in the B.V.I. once you've arrived, dial only the last five digits: Instead of dialing 494–1234, just dial 4–1234. A local call from a public pay phone costs 25¢. Coin-operated pay phones are frequently on the blink, but phones that use the **Caribbean Phone Card**, available in $5, $10, and $20 denominations, are a handy alternative. The cards are sold at most major hotels and many stores and can be used all over the Caribbean (except the French islands) in special Phone Card telephones. You can call anywhere in the world with them (although rates to the U.S. are cheaper if you use AT&T, *see below*). For credit-card or collect long-distance calls to the United States, look for

special U.S.A. Direct phones that are linked to an AT&T operator, or dial 111 from a pay phone and charge the call to your MasterCard or Visa. U.S.A. Direct and pay phones can be found at most hotels and in towns.

There are post offices in Road Town on Tortola and in Spanish Town on Virgin Gorda. Postage for a first-class letter to the United States is 35¢ and for a postcard 20¢. (It might be noted that postal efficiency is not first class in the B.V.I.) For a small fee, **Rush It** in Road Town (tel. 809/494–4421) or Spanish Town (tel. 809/495–5821) offers most U.S. mail and UPS services via St. Thomas the next day.

Opening and Closing Times   Stores are generally open from 9 to 5 Monday through Saturday. Bank hours are Monday through Thursday 9–2:30 and Friday 9–2:30 and 4:30–6.

Exploring Tortola

Numbers in the margin correspond to points of interest on the Tortola map.

The drives on Tortola are dramatic, with dizzying roller-coaster dips and climbs and glorious views. Leave plenty of time to negotiate the hilly roads and drink in the irresistible vistas at nearly every hairpin turn. Distractions are the real danger here, from the glittering mosaic of azure sea, white skies, and emerald islets to the ambling cattle and grazing goats roadside.

Before setting out on your tour of Tortola, you may want to devote an hour or so to strolling down Main Street and along the waterfront ❶ in **Road Town,** the laid-back island capital. A good place to start is at the General Post Office facing **Sir Olva Georges Square,** across from the ferry dock and customs office. (Locals don't use street names much because they *know* where everything is, so if you ask directions, ask how to get to such-and-such restaurant or store, rather than how to find the street.) The hands of the clock atop this building permanently point to 10 minutes to 5, rather appropriate in this drowsy town, where time does seem to be standing still.

The eastern side of Sir Olva Georges Square is open to the harbor, and a handful of elderly Tortolans can generally be found sitting under the square's shade trees enjoying the breeze that sweeps in from the water here. The General Post Office is at the opposite side of the square. From the front of the post office follow Main Street to the right past a number of small shops housed in traditional pastel-painted West Indian buildings with high-pitched, corrugated tin roofs, bright shutters, and delicate fretwork trim.

On the left, about half a block from the post office, you'll encounter the **British Virgin Islands Folk Museum.** Founded in 1983, the museum has a large collection of artifacts from the Arawak Indians, some of the early settlers of the islands. Of particular interest are the triangular stones called *zemis*, which depict the Arawak gods Julihu and Yuccahu. The museum also has a display of a number of bottles, bowls, and plates salvaged from the wreck of the RMS *Rhone*, a British mail ship sunk off Salt Island in a hurricane in 1867. *Main St., no tel. Admission free. Open Mon., Tues., Thurs., Fri. 10–4; Sat. 10–1, though hours may vary.*

From Main Street, turn right onto Challwell Street, cross Waterfront Drive, and proceed a few hundred yards to **Wickham's Cay** to admire the boats moored at **Village Cay Marina.** Enjoy a broad view of the wide harbor, home of countless sailing vessels and yachts and a base of the well-known yacht-chartering enterprise the Moorings. You'll find a **B.V.I. Tourist Board** office to serve you right here as well as banks, a post office, and more stores and boutiques.

When you've finished wandering about Wickham's Cay, take Fishlock Road up to the courthouse, and make a right to get back on Main Street. At the police station, turn left onto Station Avenue and follow it to the **J. R. O'Neal Botanic Gardens.** These 2.8 acres of lush gardens include hothouses for ferns and orchids, gardens of medicinal herbs and plants and plants that bloom around Christmas, and plants and trees indigenous to the seashore. A number of flower shows and special events are held here during the year. *Station Ave., tel. 809/494–4557. Admission free. Open Mon.–Sat. 8–4, Sun. noon–5.*

Retrace your steps to Sir Olva Georges Square to pick up your car. From Road Town, head southwest along Waterfront Drive. Follow the coastline for 5 miles or so of the easiest driving in the B.V.I.: no hills; little traffic; lots of curves to keep things interesting; and the lovely, island-studded channel on your left. At Sea Cows Bay the road bends inland just a bit to pass through a small residential area, but it soon rejoins the water's edge. Sir Francis Drake Channel provides a kaleidoscope of turquoise, jade green, and morning glory blue on your left, and further entertainment is provided by pelicans diving for their supper.

The next development you come to is **Nanny Cay.** Jutting out into the channel, this villagelike complex, with brightly painted buildings trimmed with lacy wood gingerbread, also contains a marina that can accommodate more than 200 yachts.

From Nanny Cay the route continues westward as St. John, the smallest of the three main U.S.V.I., comes into view across the channel. The road curves into **West End** past the ruins of the 17th-century Dutch **Fort Recovery,** a historic fort 30 feet in diameter, on the grounds of Fort Recovery Villas. There are no guided tours, but the public is welcome to stop by. The road ends at **Sopers Hole.** The waterfront here is dominated by the boat terminal and customs office that service the St. Thomas/St. John/Tortola ferries. Turn around and head back, taking your very first right over a bridge; follow signs to **Frenchman's Cay** and bear right on the other side of the bridge. There's a marina and a captivating complex of pastel-hued West Indian–style buildings with shady second-floor balconies, colonnaded arcades, shuttered windows, and gingerbread trim that showcase art galleries, boutiques, and restaurants. **Pusser's Landing** is a lively place where you can stop for a cold drink and a sandwich and watch the boats come and go from the harbor.

Retrace your route out of West End, turn left, and head across the island on Zion Hill Road, a steep byway that rises and then drops precipitously to the other side of the island. Follow the road to the end and then turn left, drive up a steep hill, and be prepared for a dazzling view of **Long Bay,** a mile-long stretch of white sand secured on the west end by **Belmont Point,** a sugar-loaf promontory that has been described as "a giant, green gumdrop." On this stretch of beach is the Long Bay Hotel, one of Tortola's more appealing resorts, which is home to one of the island's two pitch-and-putt golf courses (Prospect Reef has the other). The large island visible in the distance is Jost Van Dyke.

Time Out   After you've had a swim or a walk on the beach, turn your car around and head back past Long Bay Hotel, over the hill to **Sebastian's On**

Tortola

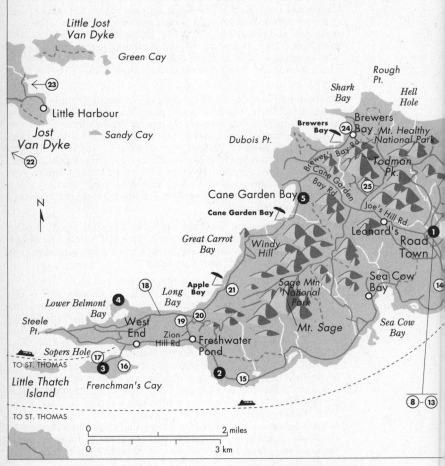

ATLANTIC OCEAN

Little Jost
Van Dyke

Green Cay

23

Little Harbour

Jost
Van Dyke

22

Sandy Cay

Dubois Pt.

Shark
Bay

Rough
Pt.

Hell
Hole

**Brewers
Bay** 24 Brewers Bay Mt. Healthy
National Park

Todman
Pk.

Brewer's Bay Rd.

Cane Garden
Bay Rd.

Cane Garden Bay 5

25

Joe's Hill Rd.

Cane Garden Bay

Leonard's

1

Road
Town

N

Great Carrot
Bay

Windy
Hill

Sage Mtn.
National
Park

Sea Cow
Bay

14

18

**Apple
Bay** 21

Sea Cow
Bay

Lower Belmont
Bay

4

Long
Bay

Steele
Pt.

West
End

19 20

Freshwater
Pond

Mt. Sage

Zion
Hill Rd

Sopers Hole

17

3 16

2

15

TO ST. THOMAS

Little Thatch
Island

Frenchman's Cay

8 13

TO ST. THOMAS

0   2 miles

0   3 km

Exploring
Beef Island, **6**
Belmont Point, **4**
Cane Garden Bay, **5**
Fort Recovery, **2**
Frenchman's Cay, **3**
Queen Elizabeth II
Bridge, **7**
Road Town, **1**

Dining
The Apple, **20**
Brandywine Bay, **28**
Capriccio di Mare, **8**
The Fishtrap, **9**
Pusser's Landing, **17**
Skyworld, **25**
Spaghetti Junction, **10**

Sugar Mill, **21**
Tradewinds, **29**
The Upstairs, **14**
Virgin Queen, **13**

Lodging
Anegada Reef
Hotel, **27**
Brewer's Bay
Campground, **24**
Fort Recovery, **15**
Frenchman's Cay, **16**

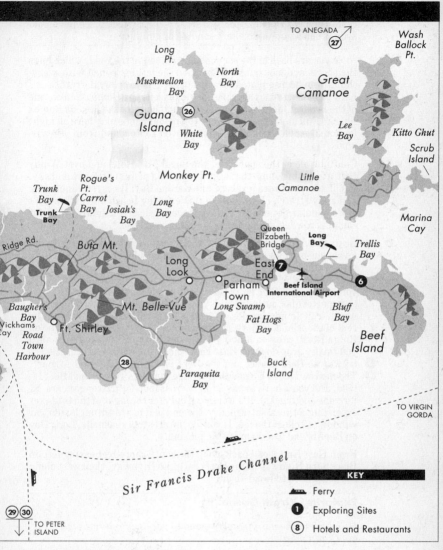

the Beach Hotel (tel. 809/495–4212), where you'll find an excellent restaurant overlooking the water. It's the perfect place for a cold soda, a snack, or an excellent sandwich.

Once you are back in the car continue following the road, which hugs the shore, and look out for a shack on the left festooned with everything from license plates to crepe paper leis to colorful graffiti. It's hard to believe that this ramshackle place is the *Bomba Shack*, one of the liveliest night spots on Tortola and home of the famous Bomba Shack "Full Moon" party. Every full moon, bands play here all night long and people flock here from all over Tortola and from other islands.

Continue along the shore past the **Sugar Mill Hotel** and over **Windy Hill,** a gripping climb that affords splendid vistas of the sea and sky.

⑤ You'll descend to sea level at **Cane Garden Bay:** Its crystalline water and silky stretch of sand make this enticing beach one of Tortola's most popular getaways. Its existence is no secret, however, and it can get crowded, though never uncomfortably so.

Go up Cane Garden Bay Road, up, up, and up. When the road finally levels out high up on the ridge, you can decide what to do next. To return to Road Town, take Joe's Hill Road, the first right after the sign to Skyworld. Follow this right and bear left (and down) when you come to the "Y." The road's steep grade may make you gasp, but the spectacular, nearly aerial view of Road Town and the harbor is worth a little nervousness. If you'd rather continue exploring the rest of the island, follow that first sign to Skyworld, and you'll be on Ridge Road. Stay on it and you'll twist and turn through hills until you finally drop down at East End, the sleepy village that is the en-

⑥ tryway to **Beef Island,** and the Beef Island International Airport.

⑦ The narrow **Queen Elizabeth II Bridge** connects Tortola and Beef Island, and you'll have to pay a toll to cross (50¢ for passenger cars, $1 for vans and trucks). It's worth it if only for the sight of the tolltaker extending a tin can attached to the end of a board through your car window to collect the fee. If you like interesting seashells, **Long Bay** on Beef Island has them for the picking.

From East End, head back along the south shore by bearing left on Blackburn Highway to Sir Francis Drake Highway, then west along the coast back to Road Town.

Exploring Virgin Gorda

Numbers in the margin correspond to points of interest on the Virgin Gorda map.

Virgin Gorda's main settlement, located on the island's southern

❶ wing, is **Spanish Town,** a peaceful village so tiny that it barely qualifies as a town at all. Also known as The Valley, Spanish Town is home to a marina, a small cluster of shops, and a couple of car-rental agencies. Just north of town is the ferry slip. At the **Virgin Gorda Yacht Harbour** you can enjoy a stroll along the dockfront or do a little browsing in the shops there.

Having rented a vehicle (you'll find a four-wheel drive the most satisfactory for negotiating some of the rougher terrain; remember that many of the roads are unmarked, so be prepared to stop and ask for directions), turn right from the marina parking lot onto Lee Road and head through the more populated, flat countryside of the south for about 15 minutes. You'll pass the Fischer's Cove Beach Hotel on your right. Keep driving until the road ends in a round park-

② ing area. From here it's a 35-yard walk to **the Baths,** Virgin Gorda's most celebrated site. Giant boulders, brought to the surface eons ago by a vast volcanic eruption, are scattered about the beach and in the water. They are the size of small houses and form remarkable grottoes. Climb between these rocks to swim in the many pools. Early morning and late afternoon are the best times to visit, since the Baths and the beach here are usually crowded with day-trippers visiting from Tortola.

Time Out   There is a small bar called **Mad Dog's** (tel. 809/495–5830) just before the parking area where you may want to pause for a cool drink and a BLT or hot dog after making the climb back from the Baths. Piña coladas are its specialty.

If it's privacy you crave, follow the shore north for a few hundred yards to reach several other quieter bays—Spring, The Crawl, Little Trunk, and Valley Trunk—or head south to Devil's Bay. These beaches have the same giant boulders as those found at the Baths.

Back in the car, retrace your route along Lee Road until you reach the southern edge of Spanish Town. After you pass a school and sports field on your right, take the next right and proceed to a T-intersection, then make another right and follow Copper Mine Road,
③ part of it unpaved, to **Copper Mine Point.** Here you will discover a tall, stone shaft silhouetted against the sky and a small stone structure overlooking the sea. These are the ruins of a copper mine established here 400 years ago and worked first by the Spanish, then by English miners until the early 20th century. This is one of the few places in the B.V.I. where you won't see islands along the horizon.

Pass through town and continue north to **Savannah Bay** and **Pond Bay,** two pristine stretches of sand that mark the thin neck of land connecting Virgin Gorda's southern extension to the larger north-
④ ern half. The view from this scenic elbow, called **Black Rock,** is of the Sir Francis Drake Channel to the northeast and the Caribbean Sea to the southwest. The road forks as it goes uphill. The unpaved left prong winds past the Mango Bay Club resort (and not much else) to Long Bay and not quite to Mountain Point. To continue exploring, take the road on the right, which winds uphill and looks down on beautiful South Sound. You'll notice nary a dwelling nor sign of mundane civilization up here, only a green mountain slope on your left and a spectacular view down to South Sound on the right. From here, too, you can also look back and get a wonderful, living sense of Virgin Gorda's stringy, crooked shape: Back there, looking flat and almost like a separate island, is the Valley, which you've just left. Because of this shape, Virgin Gorda is one of those places where you can get a bird's-eye (or map's-eye) view of things from right inside your car.

You should see a small sign on the left for the trail up to the 265-acre
⑤ **Virgin Gorda Peak National Park** and the island's summit at 1,359 feet. (Sometimes the sign is missing, so keep your eyes open for a set of stairs that disappears into the trees.) It's about a 15-minute hike up to a small clearing, where you can climb a ladder to the platform of a wood observation tower. If you're keen for some woodsy exercise or just want to stretch your legs, go for it. Unfortunately, the view at the top is somewhat tree-obstructed. A bit farther on, the road forks again. The right fork leads to **Gun Creek,** where launches pick up passengers for the Bitter End and Biras Creek, two of Virgin Gorda's most appealing hostelries.

Virgin Gorda

Mountain Pt.

George Dog

Cockroach Island

Great Dog

West Dog

Long Bay

Sir Francis Drake Channel

Pond Bay

Little Dix Bay

Savannah Bay

④

Colison Pt.

⑫

⑬

Handsome Bay

TO TORTOLA

St. Thomas Bay

Virgin Gorda Airport

Spanish Town

⑨

Fort Pt.

① ⑩ ⑪

Valley Trunk Bay

Little Trunk Bay

Copper Mine Bay

The Crawl

Spring Bay

⑧

②

③

Copper Mine Pt.

Crook's Bay

Stoney Bay

Fallen Jerusalem

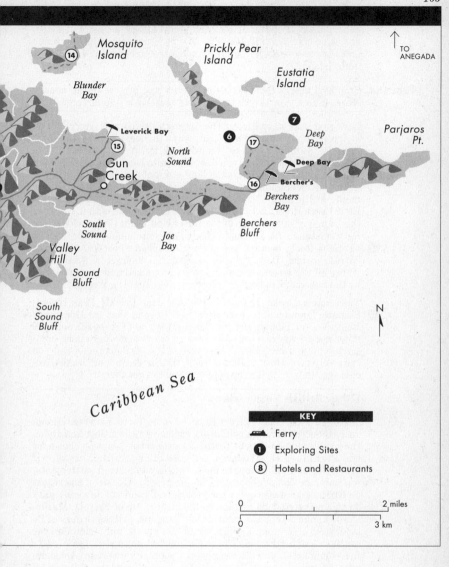

Mosquito Island

Prickly Pear Island

Eustatia Island

TO ANEGADA

Blunder Bay

Parjaros Pt.

Deep Bay

Leverick Bay

North Sound

Gun Creek

Deep Bay

Bercher's

Berchers Bay

South Sound

Joe Bay

Berchers Bluff

Valley Hill

Sound Bluff

South Sound Bluff

Caribbean Sea

N

KEY

Ferry

Exploring Sites

Hotels and Restaurants

0   2 miles

0   3 km

The left fork will bring you to **Leverick Bay. Leverick Bay Resort** is here, plus a cozy beach and marina, a restaurant, a cluster of shops, and some luxurious hillside villas to rent. This is also where a launch picks up passengers for Drake's Anchorage, a resort on nearby Mosquito Island.

Time Out Stop by **Pusser's Beach Bar** for a snack and browse in the nearby stores before your return trip to your vacation headquarters.

Low-gear your way up one of the narrow hillside roads (you're not on a driveway, it only seems that way) to one of those top-most Leverick dwellings, where you can park for a moment. Out to the left, across Blunder Bay, you'll see **Mosquito Island,** home of Drake's Anchorage Resort; the hunk of land straight ahead is **Prickly Pear,** which has been named a national park to protect it from development. At the neck of land to your right, across from Gun Creek, is **Biras Creek Hotel,** and around the bend to the north of that you'll see the Danish-roof buildings of the **Bitter End Yacht Club and Marina.** Between the Bitter End and Prickly Pear you should be able to make
❻ out **Saba Rock,** home of one of the Caribbean's best-known diving entrepreneurs, Bert Kilbride—a colorful character who knows where all the wrecks are and who is recognized and commissioned by the queen of England as Honorary Keeper of the Wrecks.

That magical color change in the sea near Prickly Pear reveals
❼ **Eustatia Sound** and its extensive reef. Beyond that are Horseshoe Reef, Necker Island, and the flat coral island of Anegada some 20 miles north, where most of those wrecks *are* and where bare-boaters are not permitted to sail because of the perilous reefs. But you can easily take a boat to Biras Creek, the Bitter End, or Drake's Anchorage. In fact, that's the only way you can get there.

Other British Virgin Islands

Just across the channel from Road Town on Tortola is **Peter Island,** an 1,800-acre island known for its exclusive resort. **Jost Van Dyke,** the sizable island north of Tortola's western tip, is a good choice for travelers in search of isolation and good hiking trails; it has several hostelries and two campgrounds, but only two small settlements, few cars, and small generators for electricity. Guests of the resort on **Guana Island** also enjoy the nature trails and wildlife sanctuary on this private island just above the eastern tip of Tortola. **Marina Cay** is a snug 6-acre islet near Great Camanoe, just north of Beef Island, east of Tortola. **Cooper Island** is a green, hilly island on the south side of Sir Francis Drake Channel. It has a restaurant and a four-room hotel, and has long been a popular anchorage. **Anegada,** about 20 miles north of Virgin Gorda's North Sound, is a flat mass of coral 11 miles long and 3 miles wide with a population of only about 250. Visitors are chiefly scuba divers, snorkelers, lovers of deserted beaches, and fishermen, some of whom come for the bonefishing here. (For more information on these islands, *see* Lodging, *below*.)

Off the Beaten Track

Sage Mountain National Park. At 1,716 feet, Sage Mountain is the highest peak in the B.V.I. The best unobstructed views up here are from the parking area, from which a trail will lead you in a loop not only to the peak itself but also to the island's rain forest, sometimes shrouded in mist. Most of the island's forest was cut down over the centuries to clear land for sugarcane, cotton, and other crops, as well as pastureland and timber. But in 1964 this park was established to preserve the remaining rain forest. Up here you can see mahogany trees, white cedars, mountain guavas, elephant-ear vines, mamey trees, and giant bulletwoods, to say nothing of such birds as mountain doves and thrushes. Take a taxi from Road Town or drive up Joe's Hill Road and make a left onto Ridge Road toward Chalwell and Doty villages. The road dead-ends at the park. *Ridge Rd., no tel. (contact the tourist office for information). Admission free.*

Beaches

Beaches here are less developed than, say, on St. Thomas or St. Croix. You'll also find fewer people. Try to get out on a boat at least one day during your stay in these islands, whether a dive-snorkeling boat or a day-trip sailing vessel. It's sometimes the best way to get to the most virgin Virgin beaches (some have no road access).

Tortola Tortola's north side has a number of postcard-perfect, palm-fringed white-sand beaches that curl luxuriantly around turquoise bays and coves. Nearly all are accessible by car (preferably with four-wheel drive), albeit down bumpy roads that corkscrew precipitously. Facilities range from none to several beach bars with rest rooms.

If you want to surf, **Apple Bay** (Capoon's Bay) is the spot, although the beach itself is pretty narrow. Sebastian's, the very casual hotel here, caters especially to those in search of the perfect wave. Good waves are never a sure thing, but January and February are usually high times here. **Josiah's Bay** is another favored place to hang-10. The beach is wide, very often deserted, and a nice place to come for a quiet picnic.

The water at **Brewers Bay** is good for snorkeling. There's a campground here, but in the summer you'll find almost nobody around. The beach and its old sugar mill and rum-distillery ruins are just north of Cane Garden Bay (up and over a steep hill), just past Luck Hill.

Cane Garden Bay rivals St. Thomas's Magens Bay in beauty, but is Tortola's most popular beach (it's the closest beach to Road Town—one steep up- and down-hill drive) and one of the B.V.I.'s best-known anchorages. It's a grand beach for jogging if you can resist staying out of that translucent water. You can rent sailboards and such, and for noshing or sipping you have a choice of going to Stanley's Welcome Bar; Rhymer's The Wedding; or Quito's Gazebo, where local recording star Quito Rhymer sings island ballads four nights a week. For true romance, nothing beats an evening of stargazing from the bow of a boat, listening to Quito's love songs drift across the bay.

Long Bay (East) is a stunning mile-long stretch of white sand, and the road that leads to it offers panoramic views of the bay (bring your camera). Long Bay Hotel sits along part of it, but the whole beach is open to the public. The water is not as calm as that at Cane Garden or Brewer's Bay, but it is still very swimmable.

Long Bay (West) on Beef Island offers scenery that draws superlatives and is visited only by a knowledgeable few. The view of Little Camanoe and Great Camanoe islands is appealing, and if you walk around the bend to the right, you can see little Marina Cay and Scrub Island. Take the Queen Elizabeth II Bridge to Beef Island and watch for a small dirt turnoff on the left before the airport. Drive across that dried-up marsh flat—there really is a beach (with interesting seashells) on the other side.

After bouncing your way to beautiful **Smuggler's Cove** (Lower Belmont Bay), you'll really feel as if you've found a hidden paradise (although don't expect to be alone on weekends). Have a beer or a toasted cheese sandwich, the only items on the menu, at the *extremely casual* snack bar. There is a fine view of the island of Jost Van Dyke, and the snorkeling is good.

About the only thing you'll find moving at **Trunk Bay** is the surf. It's directly north of Road Town, midway between Cane Garden Bay and Beef Island, and you'll have to hike down a *ghut* (gully) from the high Ridge Road.

Virgin Gorda   The best beaches are most easily reached by water, although they are accessible on foot, usually after a moderately strenuous hike of 10 to 15 minutes. But your persistence is amply rewarded.

Anybody going to Virgin Gorda must experience swimming or snorkeling among its unique boulder formations. But why go to **the Baths**, which is usually crowded, when you can catch some rays just north at **Spring Bay** beach, which is a gem, and, a little farther north, at **the Crawl**? Both are easily reached from the Baths on foot or by swimming.

Leverick Bay is a small, busy beach-cum-marina that fronts a resort restaurant and pool. Don't come here to be alone or to jog. But if you want a lively little place and a break from the island's noble quiet, take the road north and turn left before Gun Creek. The view of Prickly Pear Island is an added plus, and there's a dive facility right here to motor you out to beautiful Eustatia Reef just across North Sound.

It's worth going out to **Long Bay** (near Virgin Gorda's northern tip, past the Diamond Beach Club) for the snorkeling (Little Dix Bay resort has outings here). Going north from Spanish Town, go left at the fork near Pond Bay. Part of the route there is dirt road.

The North Shore has many nice beaches. From Biras Creek or Bitter End you can walk to **Bercher's** and **Deep Bay** beach. Two of the prettiest beaches in North Sound are accessible only by boat: Mosquito Island's **Hay Point Beach** and Prickly Pear's **Vixen Point Beach.**

Savannah Bay is a lovely long stretch of white sand, and though it may not always be deserted, it seems wonderfully private for a beach just north of Spanish Town (on the north side of where the island narrows, at Black Rock). From town it's about 30 minutes on foot.

Other Islands   Beaches on other islands, reachable only by boat, include Jost Van Dyke's **Great Harbour** and **White Bay; Marina Cay;** Peter Island's **Big Reef Bay, White Bay,** and **Dead Man's Bay;** Mosquito Island's **Limetree Beach, Long Beach,** and **Honeymoon Beach;** and Cooper Island's **Manchioneel Bay.** Farther off, and reachable by plane as well as by boat, is beach-ringed, reef-laced **Anegada.**

Sports and the Outdoors

Horseback Riding   On Tortola, equestrians should get in touch with **Shadow Stables** (tel. 809/494–2262).

Sailboarding   One of the best spots for sailboarding is at Trellis Bay on Beef Island. **Boardsailing B.V.I.** (Trellis Bay, Beef Island, tel. 809/495–2447) has rentals, private lessons, and group rates. On Virgin Gorda, the **Nick Trotter Sailing School** (Bitter End Yacht Club,

North Sound, tel. 800/872–2392) has beginner and advanced courses.

Sailing/ Boating   The B.V.I. offer some of the finest sailing waters in the world, with hundreds of boats available for charter—with or without crew—as well as numerous opportunities for day-sails. For help in chartering a boat and crew for an extended trip, contact **Virgin Island Sailing** (Box 146, Road Town, Tortola, B.V.I., tel. 800/233–7936), a top brokerage house. For sailors interested in renting a bare boat, contact **the Moorings** (1305 U.S. 19 S, Suite 402, Clearwater, FL 34624, tel. 800/535–7289). Based in Road Town, it is the largest operator in the Caribbean and offers sailboats in a wide range of sizes, with or without crew.

Scuba Diving and Snorkeling   The famed wreck of the RMS *Rhone*, off Salt Island, is reason enough to dive during your B.V.I. stay. For snorkelers, perhaps the most popular spot is at the famed Baths on Virgin Gorda. Dive and snorkel sites also abound near the smaller islands of Norman, Peter, Cooper, Ginger, the Dogs, and Jost Van Dyke; the North Sound area of Virgin Gorda; Brewer's Bay and Frenchman's Cay on Tortola; and the wreck-strewn waters off Anegada. In addition to renting equipment, many of the dive operators here also offer instruction, hotel/ dive packages, and snorkeling excursions. On Tortola, contact **Baskin-in-the-Sun** (Box 108, Road Harbour, tel. 809/494–2858 or 800/ 233–7938) or **Underwater Safaris Ltd.** (Box 139, Road Town, tel. 809/ 494–3235 or 800/537–7032). **Dive BVI** (VG Yacht Harbour, tel. 809/ 495–5513 or 800/848–7078) has locations on Virgin Gorda and Peter Island.

Sportfishing   A number of companies can transport and outfit you for fishing. On Tortola try **Charter Fishing Virgin Islands** (Prospect Reef, tel. 809/ 494–3311). On Virgin Gorda contact **Captain Dale** (809/495–5225), who operates the 38-foot Bertram *Classic* out of Biras Creek.

Tennis   Several resorts on Tortola have tennis courts for guests' use. For a fee, nonguests may use courts at **Prospect Reef** (Road Town, tel. 809/ 494–3311) and at Peter Island Resort and Yacht Harbour (a 20-minute ferry ride from Road Town). On Virgin Gorda, nonguests can use the courts at **Biras Creek** (tel. 809/494–3555) for a fee.

Shopping

The British Virgins are not known as a shopping haven, but there are interesting finds, particularly artwork. Don't be put off by an informal shop entrance. Some of the best finds in the B.V.I. lie behind a shopworn door.

Shopping Districts   Most of the shops and boutiques on Tortola are clustered on and off Road Town's **Main Street** and at **Wickham's Cay** shopping area adjacent to the Marina. There is also an ever-growing group of art, jewelry, clothing, and souvenir stores at **Sopers Hole** on Tortola's West End. On Tortola's resort-crested sister isles, boutiques are located within the individual hotel complexes. One of the best is the one in **Little Dix Bay** on Virgin Gorda. Other properties on the same island—**Biras Creek and Bitter End**—have small but equally select boutiques. There is a small collection of shops at Leverick Bay and there's a more-than-respectable and diverse scattering of stores in the minimall adjacent to the bustling yacht harbor in Spanish Town.

Specialty Stores
Art and Antiques   **Antiquities and Presents Unlimited** (Waterfront Dr., Road Town, tel. 809/495–2439) has a small but excellent collection of 18th- and 19th-century furniture, wall hangings, rugs, and pottery from Africa, Asia, and South America, as well as some B.V.I. pottery. **Collector's**

Corner (Columbus Centre, Wickham's Cay, tel. 809/494–3550) carries antique maps; watercolors by local artists; gold and silver jewelry; coral; and larimar, a pale blue Caribbean gemstone. **The Courtyard Gallery** (Main St., Road Town, no tel.) shows its exclusive Carinia Collection, delicate crushed-coral sculptures created on the premises and depicting darting hummingbirds, angelfish, nesting pelicans, and flowers. The place to find watercolors, paintings, pottery, sculpture, model ships, coffee-table books on the Caribbean, and prints of Caribbean maps and scenes is **Islands Treasures** (Sopers Hole Marina, tel. 809/495–4787). **Caribbean Fine Arts Ltd.** (Main St., Road Town, tel. 809/494–4240) has a wide range of Caribbean art, including original watercolors, oils, and acrylics, as well as signed prints, limited-edition serigraphs, and turn-of-the-century sepia photographs. **Sunny Caribbee Art Gallery** (Main Street, Road Town, tel. 809/494–2178) has one of the largest displays of paintings in the Caribbean.

Clothing **Bonker's Gallery** (Main St., Road Town, tel. 809/494–2535) carries trendy resort wear for women, including cotton and washable-silk tops and bottoms and cover-ups. There is also a small collection of pants and shirts for men. **Next Wave** (Virgin Gorda Yacht Harbour, tel. 809/495–5623) sells bathing suits, T-shirts, and canvas tote bags. **Pelican's Pouch Boutique** (Virgin Gorda Yacht Harbour, tel. 809/495–5599). At the Pelican's Pouch you'll find a large selection of swimsuits plus cover-ups, beach hats, T-shirts, and accessories. **Sea Urchin** (Columbus Centre, Road Town, tel. 809/494–2044; Soper's Hole Marina, tel. 809/495–4850) has a good selection of island-living designs: print shirts and shorts, slinky swimsuits, sandals, and T-shirts. **Violet's** (Wickham's Cay I, tel. 809/494–6398) has a beautiful collection of silk lingerie and a small line of designer dresses.

Food and Drink The **Ample Hamper** (Village Cay Marina, Wickham's Cay, tel. 809/494–2494; Soper's Hole Marina, tel. 809/495–4684), and the **Gourmet Galley** (Wickham's Cay II, Road Town, tel. 809/494–6999) offer fine selections of wines, cheeses, fresh fruits and vegetables, and canned goods from the United Kingdom and the United States and provide full provisioning for yachtspeople and villa renters. At the Bitter End resort, **Bitter End's Emporium** (North Sound, tel. 809/494–2745) is the place to look for such edible treats as local fruits, bakery goods, and cheeses. **Virgin Island Bakery** (Virgin Island Yacht Harbour, no tel.) sells freshly baked loaves of bread, rolls, muffins, and cookies and has sandwiches and sodas to go.

Gifts **J. R. O'Neal, Ltd.** (Main St., Road Town, tel. 809/494–2292) carries fine crystal, Royal Worcester china, a wonderful selection of hand-painted Italian dishes, hand-blown Mexican glassware, ceramic housewares from Spain, and woven rugs and tablecloths from India. A remarkable array of gift items, from wearable artwork and hand-painted jewelry to watercolors and batik fabric can be found at **Pink Pineapple** (Prospect Reef Hotel, tel. 809/494–3311). **The Pusser's Company Store** (Main St. and Waterfront Rd., Road Town, tel. 809/494–2467; Soper's Hole Marina, tel. 809/495–4603; Leverick Bay, tel. 809/495–7369) features nautical memorabilia, ship models, marine paintings, an entire line of clothes and gift items bearing the Pusser's logo, and handsome decorator bottles of Pusser's rum. **The Sunny Caribbee Herb and Spice Company** (Main St., Road Town, tel. 809/494–2178), located in a brightly painted West Indian house, packages its own herbs, teas, coffees, herb vinegars, hot sauces, natural soaps, skin and suntan lotions, Caribbean art, and hand-painted decorative accessories. A small branch of this store is located at the Skyworld Restaurant (*see above*). **Turtle Dove Boutique**

(Flemming St., Road Town, tel. 809/494–3611) is among the best in the B.V.I. for French perfume, international swimwear, and silk dresses, as well as gifts and accessories for the home.

Jewelry **Felix Gold and Silver Ltd.** (Main St., tel. 809/494–2406) handcrafts exceptionally fine jewelry in their on-site workshop. Choose from island or nautical themes or have something custom made (in most cases, they'll make it for you within 24 hours!). **Flaxcraft Jewellers** (Main St., Road Town, tel. 809/494–2892) carries fine gold and silver jewelry; many of the pieces are one-of-a-kind creations incorporating shells and fragments of coral. **Samarkand** (Main St., Road Town, tel. 809/494–6415) features handmade gold and silver pendants, earrings, bracelets, and pins.

Local Crafts **Caribbean Handprints** (Main St., Road Town, tel. 809/494–3717) creates silkscreened fabric and sells it by the yard and fashioned into dresses, shirts, pants, bathrobes, beach cover-ups, and beach bags. **Virgin Gorda Craft Shop** (Virgin Gorda Yacht Harbour, no tel.) features the work of island artisans and carries West Indian jewelry and crafts styled in straw, shells, and other local materials. It also stocks clothing and paintings by Caribbean artists.

Textiles **Zenaida** (Cutlass House, Wickham's Cay, Road Town, tel. 809/494–2113) displays the fabric finds of Argentinean Vivian Jenik Helm, who travels through South America, Africa, and India in search of batiks, hand-painted and hand-blocked fabrics, and interesting weaves that can be made into pareos or wall hangings. The shop also offers a selection of unusual bags, belts, sarongs, scarves, and ethnic jewelry.

Dining

The most popular choices in B.V.I. restaurants are seafood dishes. You'll find a greater range of eateries on Tortola than on more remote Virgin Gorda and the other islands, where most hotels offer a meal plan. On both islands, except where noted, the way to dress is casual but neat.

Highly recommended restaurants are indicated by a star ★.

Category	Cost*
Very Expensive	over $35
Expensive	$25–$35
Moderate	$15–$25
Inexpensive	under $15

per person for three courses, excluding drinks and service; there is no sales tax in the B.V.I.

Tortola **Tradewinds.** Catch the Peter Island ferry for a 25-minute ride to this
★ elegant restaurant on Peter Island and dine and dance under the stars. The excellent à la carte menu offers Continental selections prepared with Caribbean flair. Appetizers such as grilled assorted vegetables or medallions of cold lobster are followed by entrées that may include grilled local grouper, baby lamb chops, pasta with slices of grilled chicken in a tomato-basil sauce, or a veal chop with shiitake mushrooms. For a truly decadent finish, choose one of the sinfully rich desserts (maybe Strawberry Romanoff) *and* have a tasty Sprat Bay Coffee. *Peter Island, tel. 809/494–2561. Reserva-*

tions essential. Dress: casual elegant (no shorts or jeans; collared shirts for men). AE, MC, V. Closed Mon. Very Expensive.

★ **Brandywine Bay.** For the best in romantic dining, don't miss this hillside gem, where candlelit alfresco tables have a sweeping view of neighboring islands. Italian owner/chef Davide Pugliese prepares food the Tuscan way—grilled with lots of fresh herbs. The remarkable menu, which hostess Cele Pugliese describes tableside, can include homemade mozzarella, grilled portobello mushrooms, grilled local wahoo, and grilled veal chops with ricotta and sun-dried tomatoes. Roast duck, a house specialty, is always served with an exotic sauce such as berry, mango, orange-and-ginger, or passion fruit. The lemon tart and the tiramisu are irresistible. There's also an excellent wine list. *Sir Francis Drake Hwy., east of Road Town, tel. 809/495–2301. Reservations advised. AE, MC, V. Closed lunch and Sun. Expensive.*

Skyworld. You'll want to arrive early for dinner at this mountaintop aerie; the sunset views are breathtaking. Watch the western horizon become ablaze with color, then settle back in the casually elegant dining room to feast on chef George Petcoff's delectable offerings. Try the veal in lemon caper sauce, the local swordfish with sun dried–tomato pesto, or the passion-fruit sorbet. This is also a special place for lunch. Not only are the sandwiches on home-baked bread delicious, but both the restaurant and the observation tower above offer the B.V.I.'s highest (and absolutely spectacular) 360-degree view of numerous islands and cays. Even St. Croix and Anegada (both 20 miles away) can be seen on a clear day. *Ridge Rd., tel. 809/494–3567. Reservations advised. AE, MC, V. Expensive.*

Sugar Mill Restaurant. The candles gleam and the background music is pleasingly mellow in this well-known restaurant. Well-prepared selections on the very limited menu may include smoked duck breast with honey-lemon glaze, herbed prawns with drawn butter, or His Majesty's West Indian Regimental beef curry. *Apple Bay, tel. 809/495–4355. Reservations advised. AE, MC, V. Expensive.*

★ **The Upstairs.** Ask for a window table here and you'll be bathed in gentle tropical breezes as you gaze out at the stars. Excellent service and food are hallmarks of this elegant and romantic restaurant overlooking a small marina. For a truly exceptional meal, try the superbly cooked filet mignon that comes with peaches and an outstanding port wine sauce. Other specialties include a delicious lobster au gratin appetizer, grilled local fish, roast duck, and key lime pie. A 10% service charge is included in the bill. *On Prospect Reef Hotel grounds (turn left just after the entrance), Road Town, tel. 809/494–2228. Reservations accepted. AE, MC, V. Expensive.*

Pusser's Landing. Yachters flock to the two-story home of this popular waterfront restaurant. Downstairs, belly up to the large, comfortable mahogany bar or choose a waterside table for drinks, sandwiches, or a light dinner. Head upstairs for quieter alfresco dining and a delightfully eclectic menu that includes homemade black bean soup, freshly grilled local fish, pasta, and such pub favorites as "bubble and squeak" (mashed potatoes with sautéed onions). The air-conditioned Dinner Theater, with its 15-foot screen, features fixed-price, three-course meals and shows movie combos and sports events. *Sopers Hole, tel. 809/495–4554. AE, MC, V. Moderate–Expensive.*

The Apple. This small, inviting restaurant is located in a small West Indian house. Soft candlelight provides a relaxed atmosphere for diners as they sample fish steamed in lime butter, conch or whelks in garlic sauce, and other local seafood dishes. There is a traditional West Indian barbecue and buffet every Sunday evening from 7 to 9. The excellent new lunch menu includes a variety of sandwiches, meat and vegetarian lasagna, lobster quiche, seafood crepes, and croissants with ham and Swiss or spinach and feta. *Little Apple Bay, tel. 809/495-4437. Reservations accepted. AE, MC, V. Moderate.*

The Fishtrap. Dine alfresco at this restaurant, which serves grilled local fish, steaks, and chicken. Friday and Saturday there's a barbecue with a terrific salad bar; Sunday prime rib is featured. *Columbus Centre, Wickham's Cay, Road Town, tel. 809/494-2636. AE, MC, V. Closed for Sun. lunch. Moderate.*

Spaghetti Junction. This funky spot is popular with the boating crowd. Nightly specials complement the tasty and traditional Italian menu (veal or chicken parmigiana, pastas, etc.), and sun-dried tomato in the Caesar salad is a nice twist. Check out the gorilla in the rest room. *Waterfront Dr., Road Town, tel. 809/494-4880. No credit cards. Closed lunch, holidays, and Sept. Moderate.*

★ **Virgin Queen.** The sailing and rugby crowd and locals gather here to play darts, drink beer, and eat Queen's Pizza (some say it's the best pizza in the Caribbean) or some of the excellent West Indian and English fare. A delicious menu includes saltfish, barbecued ribs with beans and rice, bangers and mash, shepherd's pie, and chili. *Fleming St., Road Town, tel. 809/494-2310. No reservations. No credit cards. Closed Sun. Moderate.*

★ **Capriccio di Mare.** The owners of well-known Brandywine Bay restaurant (*see above*) have now opened an authentic Italian café. People stop by for cappuccino and espresso, a fresh pastry or a tiramisu, delicious toast Italiano (grilled ham and Swiss cheese sandwiches), bowls of perfectly cooked linguini or penne with a variety of sauces, and crispy crust tomato-and-mozzarella pizzas topped with hot Italian sausage or fresh grilled eggplant. Drink specialties include the Mango Bellini, a mango and Italian sparkling wine mixture that's a variation on the famous Bellini Cocktail served by Harry's Bar in Venice. *Waterfront Dr., Road Town, tel. 809/494-5369. No reservations. Dress: casual. No credit cards. Closes at 5 PM Sat. Closed Sun. Inexpensive–Moderate.*

Virgin Gorda **Biras Creek.** You come by boat (provided free) to this serene and elegant restaurant. Candlelit tables are set on a turretlike stonework terrace with the wild Caribbean on one side and calm North Sound on the other. The menu for the four-course fixed-price dinner changes nightly and always includes a choice of four entrées. *North Sound, tel. 809/494-3555 or 809/495-4356. Reservations advised. Dress: neat but casual (no shorts at dinner). AE, MC, V. Very Expensive.*

Olde Yard Inn. Civilized and charming, the dining room here is suffused with gentle classical melodies and the scent of herbs. A cedar roof covers the breezy, open-air room decorated with old-style Caribbean charm. The French-accented cuisine includes lamb chops with mango chutney, chicken breast in a rum cream sauce, and grilled local fish and steaks. *The Valley, north of the marina, tel. 809/495-5544. Reservations advised. AE, MC, V. Expensive.*

★ **The Bath and Turtle.** This informal patio tavern with its friendly staff is a popular spot to sit back and relax. Burgers, well-stuffed sandwiches, pizzas, pasta dishes, and daily specials round out the casual menu. Live entertainment is presented on Wednesday and Sunday nights. *Virgin Gorda Yacht Harbour, tel. 809/495-5239. Reservations accepted. MC, V. Moderate.*

The Crab Hole. This homey hangout serves West Indian specialties such as callaloo soup, saltfish, stewed goat, rice and peas, green bananas, and curried chicken roti. *The Valley, tel. 809/495-5307. Reservations accepted. No credit cards. Inexpensive–Moderate.*

Lodging

The number of rooms available in the B.V.I. is small compared with other destinations in the Caribbean; what is available is also often in great demand, and the prices are not low. The top-of-the-line resorts here are among the most expensive in the Caribbean and are sometimes difficult to book even off-season. Even the more moderately priced hotels command top dollar during the season; off-season, however, they are legitimate bargains at about half the price. In addition, many of the hotels offer rates that include all three meals.

Highly recommended lodgings are indicated by a star ★.

Category	Cost*
Very Expensive	over $300
Expensive	$200–$300
Moderate	$100–$200
Inexpensive	under $100

All prices are for a standard double room in high season, excluding 7% hotel tax and 10% service charge.

Tortola   **Frenchman's Cay.** This resort consists of one- and two-bedroom villas that overlook Sir Francis Drake Channel. Each unit includes a full kitchen, dining area, and sitting room—ideal for families or couples. Rooms are done in neutral colors, with cream-color curtains and bedspreads and tile floors. Ceiling fans and pleasant breezes keep the rooms cool. There is a pool and a small man-made beach that is sandy to the water's edge but rocky offshore. It's not good for wading without shoes but does offer good snorkeling. The alfresco bar and dining room are breeze-swept and inviting. *Box 1054, West End, tel. 809/495–4844, fax 809/495–5046. 9 units. Facilities: restaurant, bar, tennis court, beach, pool, water sports. AE, D, MC, V. EP. Expensive.*

Long Bay Hotel. Set on a mile-long arc of white sand, this hotel offers a wide variety of accommodations, including 32 deluxe beachfront rooms, with two queen beds or one king-size four-poster bed, marble-top wet bars, and showers with Italian tiles. There are also smaller beach cabanas, 10 rustic, tropical hideaways set on stilts at the water's edge. Hillside choices include small but adequate rooms, studios with a comfortable seating area, and roomy one- and two-bedroom villas; all have balconies with lovely views. The Beach restaurant offers all-day dining, and the Garden restaurant serves fixed-price three-course dinners in a romantic, candlelit setting. Unfortunately, the staff here is disappointingly sullen and unresponsive. *Box 433, Road Town, tel. 809/495–4252 or 800/729–9599, fax 809/495–4677. 62 rooms. Facilities: 2 restaurants, 2 bars, beach, pool, pitch-and-putt golf, small tennis court, commissary. AE, MC, V. EP, MAP. Expensive.*

Sugar Mill Hotel. The owners of this small, out-of-the-way hotel are Jeff and Jinx Morgan, who opened it two decades ago after becoming well-established travel and food writers. The reception area, bar, and restaurant are located in the ruins of a centuries-old sugar mill and are decorated with bright Haitian artwork. Rather plain guest houses are scattered on the hillside; the rooms are furnished in soft pastels and rattan and have ceiling fans but no air conditioners. (Light sleepers may be disturbed by the roosters, who start crowing long before dawn.) There's a circular swimming pool set into the hillside and a tiny beach where lunch is served on a shady terrace. The Sugar Mill Restaurant is well known on the island. (*see* Dining, *above*). *Box 425, Road Town, tel. 809/495–4355, fax 809/495–4696. 20 rooms. Facilities: restaurant, 2 bars, beach, pool, water sports. AE, MC, V. EP, MAP. Expensive.*

Prospect Reef Resort. A much-needed face-lift of this sprawling resort overlooking Sir Francis Drake Channel included a fresh coat of paint in bright pinks, purples, blues, and yellows and new fabrics in light tropical prints to brighten the rooms. There are 11 types of units, including variously sized rooms with kitchenettes and two-story, two-bedroom units with private interior courtyards. All have a balcony, patio, or both and may face either the water or the hotel's gardens. There are 7 acres of neatly manicured grounds with creative rock paths and a network of lagoons. In addition to the hotel's Junior Olympic–size swimming pool and diving pool, Prospect Reef features a saltwater pool sectioned off from the sea with large rocks and a narrow, artificial beach. The resort also boasts its own harbor with sailboats available for day trips or longer excursions. *Box 104, Road Town, tel. 809/494–3311, fax 809/494–5595. 131 rooms. Facilities: 2 restaurants, beach, beachside snack bar, 2 bars, 3 pools (2 freshwater: 1 Junior Olympic–size, 1 for diving), children's splash pool, 6 tennis courts, pitch-and-putt golf, water sports, unisex hair salon, gift shop, beachwear shop, commissary, conference center. AE, MC, V. EP. Moderate–Expensive.*

★ **Fort Recovery.** Built around the remnants of a Dutch fort, this appealing group of one- to four-bedroom bungalows stretches along a small beach facing Sir Francis Drake Channel. The grounds are bright with tropical flowers. All units have patios, kitchens, and equally excellent views. A new kitchen provides gourmet room-service meals; and yoga classes, exercise classes, massages, and special fitness packages are available. *Box 239, Road Town, tel. 809/ 495–4467, fax 809/495–4036. 10 units. Facilities: beach, commissary selling basic food supplies and frozen homemade entrées. AE, MC, V. EP. Moderate.*

Moorings-Mariner Inn. Headquarters for the Moorings Charter operation and popular with yachting folk who find its full-service facilities convenient and the companionship of fellow "boaties" congenial, this is also a good choice for those who want to be within easy walking distance of town. The atmosphere is a combination of laid-back and lively and the rooms, including four full-size suites, are large and comfortable. The rooms' pale peach decor is picked up in the peach tiles on the floors, and bright, tropical print bedspreads and curtains add color. All rooms have a small kitchenette (with sink, refrigerator, and two-burner stove) and a balcony. Most rooms face the water except for eight, which overlook the pool or the tennis court. *Box 139, Road Town, tel. 809/494–2331, fax 809/494–2226. 40 rooms. Facilities: restaurant, bar, pool, tennis court, volleyball court, dive shop, gourmet shop. AE, MC, V. EP. Moderate.*

★ **Sebastian's on the Beach.** The eight beachfront rooms here are the best beach rooms on Tortola's north shore. Airy white rooms, simply decorated with floral print curtains and bedspreads, open out to either terraces or balconies and great ocean breezes and views. Bathrooms only have stall showers, and there is no air-conditioning; but ceiling fans and louvered windows keep the rooms cool, and you are lulled sleep to the sound of the ocean. The 18 non-beach front rooms are very simple, lack views, and can be noisy; but they are a comfortable size and quite a bit cheaper than the beach rooms. The restaurant here is excellent. *Box 441, Road Town, tel. 809/495–4212, fax 809/495–4466. 26 rooms. Facilities: restaurant, bar, beach, water sports, commissary. AE, EP. Moderate.*

Treasure Isle Hotel. Owned by the Moorings, this hillside hotel, painted in bright shades of lemon, violet, and mango pink, is one of the prettiest properties on the island. The air-conditioned rooms are spacious and accented with fabrics printed with Matisse-like patterns. Set on a hillside overlooking the harbor, Treasure Isle makes a handy base for in-town shopping and visits to nearby marinas. Open to the breezes and the heady aroma of tropical flowers, the Spy Glass Bar with its comfortable lounge is the perfect place to relax and look out at a stunning view of the harbor and islands in the distance. There is daily transportation to Cane Garden Bay and Brewer's Bay. *Box 68, Road Town, tel. 809/494–2501, fax 809/494–2507. 40 rooms. Facilities: restaurant, 2 bars, pool, water sports. AE, MC, V. EP. Moderate.*

Campgrounds **Brewer's Bay Campground.** Both prepared and bare sites are located on Brewer's Bay, one of Tortola's prime snorkeling spots. Check out the ruins of the distillery that gave the bay its name. *Box 185, Road Town, tel. 809/494–3463. Facilities: beach, bar, restaurant, commissary, water sports, baby-sitters available.*

Virgin Gorda **Biras Creek Hotel.** This enchanting 150-acre hideaway is so secluded that the only way to reach it is by launch. The hilltop open-air bar and restaurant area is made perfectly of stonework and offers stunning views of North Sound. Each guest cottage is a suite, with bedroom, bath, and living room. Perhaps its loveliest feature is the sensuous open-air walled shower in each bathroom. Guests can explore the grounds on foot or on bicycles provided by the hotel. There's a pool set right at the edge of the sea; and there's a beach for swimming, although it's a bit grassy. Sailing, boardsailing, and snorkeling equipment is available for guest use, and there are 2 lighted tennis courts. Guests are pampered here, and the atmosphere is one of casual elegance. *Box 54, North Sound, tel. 809/494– 3555, fax 809/494–3557. 34 rooms. Facilities: restaurant, bar, 2 beaches, 2 lighted tennis courts, marina, pool, water sports, hiking and biking trails. AE, MC, V. FAP. Very Expensive.*

★ **Bitter End Yacht Club and Marina.** Stretching along the coastline of North Sound, the BEYC enjoys panoramic views of the Sound, Leverick Bay, and nearby islands. Accommodations range from hillside or beachfront villas and chalets to live-aboard yachts, all of which include the basics, but are refreshingly no-frills. What's most inviting about this property, however, is the friendly, unpretentious welcome the staff extends to all its guests. The resort organizes daily snorkeling and diving trips to nearby reefs, windsurfing lessons, and excursions to local attractions, but the BEYC is most touted for its Nick Trotter Sailing School. Judged by many to offer the best sailing instruction in the Caribbean, the school helps both seasoned salts and beginners sharpen their nautical skills. When the sun goes down, the festivities continue at either the elegant Carvery, where themed buffets are served on special occasions, or at the Clubhouse, an open-air restaurant overlooking the Sound. The hotel's character is one of the liveliest and most convivial in the B.V.I. (but is considered a bit too frenetic by some). *Box 46, North Sound, tel. 809/494–2746, fax 809/494–3557. 100 rooms. Facilities: 2 restaurants, bar, beach, marina, pool. AE, MC, V. FAP. Very Expensive.*

★ **Little Dix Bay.** The luxury resort that first set the standards for understated elegance in the B.V.I. was taken over by Rosewood Resorts and closed for the fall of 1993 for refurbishing. Telephones, new fabrics, and new furniture have been added to all rooms. At press time, air-conditioning had been installed in half of the rooms, with the remaining installation to be completed by the end of 1995.

The duplex cottages used to be open to noise as well as breezes, and the air-conditioning has transformed them into peaceful retreats. There's a new Italian restaurant in the Sugar Mill; and dining in the open, peak-roofed Pavilion restaurant is a memorable experience. There are beautifully manicured lawns, the reef-protected beach is long and silken, and tennis, sailing, snorkeling, waterskiing, and bicycling are included in the rate. Popular with honeymooners and older couples who have apparently been coming back for years, Little Dix may leave the single traveler feeling slightly left out occasionally. Nonetheless, the accommodations are superb, the service is thoughtful and attentive, and the setting is unforgettable. *Box 70, tel. 809/495-5555, fax 809/495-5561. 102 rooms. Facilities: 3 restaurants, 2 bars, beach, water sports, marina, 7 tennis courts, boutique. AE, MC, V. EP, MAP, FAP. Very Expensive.*

Guavaberry Spring Bay Vacation Homes. These unusual hexagonal cottages are perched on stilts, and you'll feel as if you are in a tree house, with chirping birds and branches swaying in the breezes. These one- and two-bedroom units are situated on a hill, a short walk down to a tamarind-shaded beach and not far from the mammoth boulders and cool basins of the famed Baths. *Box 20, Virgin Gorda, tel. 809/495-5227, fax 809/495-7367. 16 units. Facilities: commissary, beach. No credit cards. EP. Moderate.*

Leverick Bay Resort. This small hotel offers 16 hillside rooms, decorated in pastels and with original artwork. All rooms have refrigerators, balconies, and lovely views of North Sound. Four two-bedroom condos are also available. A Spanish Colonial–style main building houses a restaurant operated by Pusser's of Tortola. A dive operation, a crafts shop, commissary, coin-operated laundry, and beauty salon are also on-site. *Box 63, tel. 809/495-7421, fax 809/495-7367. 20 rooms. Facilities: restaurant, bar, beach, marina, pool, shopping arcade, water sports. AE, D, MC, V. EP. Moderate.*

Olde Yard Inn. Owners Charlie Williams and Carol Kaufman have cultivated a refreshingly unique atmosphere at this quiet retreat just outside Spanish Town. Classical music plays in the small bar; a large and varied collection of books lines the walls of the octagonal library cottage. The restaurant's French-accented menu is lovingly prepared and served with style in the high-ceilinged dining rooms. The guest rooms are cozy and simply furnished. Though the hotel is not on the beach (Savannah Bay and Pond Bay are only a 20-minute walk away) and has no pool, it does have a loyal group of repeat guests. You may want to request one of the air-conditioned rooms; the hotel's location in the Valley means trade winds are less noticeable here. *Box 26, Spanish Town, tel. 809/495-5544, fax 809/495-5986. 14 rooms. Facilities: restaurant, bar, library, horseback riding. AE, MC, V. EP, MAP. Moderate.*

The Wheelhouse. This hotel is easy on the pocketbook for those seeking a no-frills vacation headquarters. The cinder-block building has rooms that are air-conditioned and have recently been redecorated with pastel print bedspreads and curtains. However, the rooms are still small, and the restaurant and bar can get noisy. It is conveniently close to the Virgin Gorda marina and shopping center. *Box 66, tel. 809/495-5230. 12 rooms. Facilities: restaurant, bar. AE, MC, V. CP. Inexpensive.*

Anegada **Anegada Reef Hotel.** This hotel is away from it all in every sense of the phrase: It's the only hotel on Anegada, and the island itself is off the beaten path. Rooms are motel-like and rustic, but people come here for peace rather than luxury. Snorkeling and diving are as good here as anywhere else in the islands. Bonefishing in the flats is a favorite activity, and deep-sea fishing trips can be arranged. If you favor true laid-back living and absolutely no schedules, this is the spot for you. *Anegada, tel. 809/495–8002, fax 809/495–9362. 16 rooms. Facilities: restaurant, bar, beach, gift shop, water sports. FAP. Expensive.*

Guana Island **Guana Island Club.** Fifteen guest rooms are spread among seven houses scattered along one of the many hillsides of this totally private island. The houses are simply decorated in Caribbean style, with rattan furniture and ceiling fans, and each has its own porch. The island's many trails make it a favorite spot for hikers, and it's a bird-watching paradise. *Box 32, Road Town, Tortola, tel. 809/494–2354, fax 914/967–8048. 15 rooms. Facilities: restaurant, wildlife sanctuary, tennis, croquet, hiking trails, water sports. FAP. Very Expensive.*

Jost Van Dyke **Sandcastle.** This tiny, four-cottage hideaway (with a staff of five) is set on a half-mile of white beach on remote White Bay. There's "nothing" to do here, except maybe snooze in a hammock, read, gaze, walk, swim, rest, and enjoy sophisticated cuisine and dining by candlelight. Arrangements can be made for diving, sailing, and sportfishing trips. *White Bay, tel. 809/775–5262, fax 809/775–5262. Facilities: restaurant, bar, beach. No credit cards. Moderate.*
Sandy Ground Estates. Tucked into the foliage along the edge of one of Jost Van Dyke's East End beaches is this collection of eight privately owned one- and two-bedroom houses. Each one is architecturally different, and interiors range from spartan to stylish. Kitchens are fully equipped and can be pre-stocked (you'll want to do this, since supplies are limited on the island), and there are four very casual restaurants within walking distance. *Sandy Ground, East End of Jost Van Dyke, tel. 809/495–3391. Facilities: beach. No credit cards. Moderate.*

Mosquito Island ★ **Drake's Anchorage.** Manager Albert Wheatley ensures that this small, secluded getaway offers true privacy and the pampering of the more elegant resorts without the formality. Changing for dinner here means switching from a bathing suit to comfortable cottons. The three West Indian–style, waterfront bungalows contain 10 comfortably furnished rooms, including two suites. There are also two fully equipped villas for rent. There are hiking trails, water-sports facilities, four delightful beaches with hammocks here and there, and a highly regarded restaurant—a truly peaceful, rejuvenating experience. *Box 2510, North Sound, Virgin Gorda, tel. 809/494–2254 or 800/624–6651, fax 809/494–2254. Facilities: restaurant, bar, 4 beaches, water sports, hiking trails, gift shop. AE, MC, V. FAP. Very Expensive.*

Peter Island ★ **Peter Island Resort and Yacht Harbour.** This resort is close to the last word in luxury in all the Caribbean. General Manager Jamie Holmes has made sure that every imaginable living, dining, and recreational amenity is available, including a gourmet restaurant, stunning freshwater pool, and tennis courts complete with a resident pro. There are also small sailboats, Sunfish, kayaks, mountain bicycles, Windsurfers, Hobie Cats, a 20-station fitness trail, an exercise room, 10 miles of walking trails, a dive shop, and a masseuse. The 50 guest rooms are in quadraplex cottages that are tucked among beds of radiant tropical flowers either at the edge of the beach or near the pool. *Box 211, Road Town, Tortola, tel. 809/494–2561 or 800/346–4451, fax 809/494–2313. 50 rooms, 2 villas. Facilities: 2 restaurants, 2 bars, 5 beaches, pool, 4 lighted tennis courts, tennis pro, 2 gift shops, fitness trail, five-star PADI dive facility, marina (limited services), helicopter pad. AE, MC, V. EP, MAP, FAP. Very Expensive.*

8 Cayman Islands

Nightlife

On Tortola, live bands play at **Pusser's Landing** (Sophers Hole, tel.
809/494–4554) Thursday through Sunday, the **Jolly Rodger** (West
End, tel. 809/495–4559) Tuesday, Wednesday, Friday and Saturday, **Sebastian's** (Apple Bay, tel. 809/495–4214) Saturday and Sunday, and **Bomba's Shack** (Apple Bay, tel. 809/495–4148) on Sunday,
Wednesday, and every full moon. At **Quito's Gazebo** (Cane Garden
Bay, tel. 809/495–4837), B.V.I. recording star Quito Rhymer sings
his own island ballads Sunday, Tuesday, Thursday, and Friday
nights, starting at 8:30. **Stanley's Welcome Bar** (Cane Garden Bay,
tel. 809/495–4520) gets rowdy when crews stop by to party. On Virgin Gorda, **Andy's Chateau de Pirate** (Fischer's Cove Beach Hotel,
The Valley, tel. 809/495–5252) has live music and dancing on the
weekends, and **The Bath and Turtle** has local bands Wednesday and
Sunday evenings. One of the busiest nocturnal spots in the B.V.I. is
little Jost Van Dyke. Check out **Rudy's Mariner Rendezvous** (tel. 809/
495–9282), **Foxy's Tamarind** (tel. 809/495–9258), and **Sydney's Peace
and Love** (tel. 809/495–9271).

Updated by
Laurie S.
Senz

The venerable old *Saturday Evening Post* dubbed them "the islands that time forgot." But the past decade has changed all that: The Cayman Islands, a British Crown colony that includes Grand Cayman, Cayman Brac, and Little Cayman, are now one of the Caribbean's hottest destinations.

Why do metropolis-weary visitors trek 480 miles south of Miami, filling the hotels and condominiums that line famed Seven Mile Beach, even during the traditionally slow summer season? Their dollars certainly go farther in other Caribbean destinations, for in Grand Cayman—which positively reeks of suburban prosperity, bulging as it does with some 544 offshore banks located in George Town, the capital—the U.S. dollar is worth 80 Cayman cents, and the cost of living is 20% higher than in the United States.

Effective advertising accounts for some visitors, but the secret is word-of-mouth testimonials. The Cayman Islanders—the population is 25,000, almost all of it residents of Grand Cayman—are renowned for the courteous and civil manners befitting their British heritage. Visitors will find no hasslers or panhandlers and no need to look apprehensively over their shoulder on dark evenings, for the colony is virtually crime-free. Add to that permanent political and economic stability, and you have a fairly rosy picture.

The Caymans fully deserve their reputation as a paradise for divers: Translucent waters and a colorful variety of marine life are protected by the government, which has created a marine parks system in all three islands.

Columbus is said to have sighted the islands in 1503, but he didn't stop off to explore. He did note that the surrounding sea was alive with turtles, so the islands were named Las Tortugas. The name was later changed to Cayman.

The islands stayed largely uninhabited until the late 1600s, when Britain took over the Cayman Islands and Jamaica from Spain under the Treaty of Madrid. Cayman attracted a mixed bag of settlers, pirates, refugees from the Spanish Inquisition, shipwrecked sailors, and deserters from Oliver Cromwell's army in Jamaica. Today's Caymanians are the descendants of those nationalities.

The caves and coves of the islands—still fascinating to explore—were a perfect hideout for pirates like Blackbeard and Sir Henry Morgan, who plundered Spanish galleons hauling riches from the New World of South America to Spain. Many a ship also fell afoul of the reefs surrounding the islands, often with the help of the Caymanians, who lured the vessels to shore with beacon fires. Some of the old pioneer homes on the islands were made from the remains of those galleons.

The legend of the Wreck of the Ten Sails was to have a lasting effect on the Caymanians. In 1788, a convoy of 10 Jamaican ships bound for England foundered on the reefs, but the islanders managed to rescue everyone. Royalty was purportedly aboard, and a grateful George III decreed that Caymanians should forever be exempt from conscription and never have to pay taxes.

The Cayman Islands are still a British colony. A governor appoints three official members to the Legislative Assembly and has to accept the advice of the Executive Council in all matters except foreign affairs, defense, internal security, and civil service appointments.

Before You Go

Tourist Information
For the latest information on activities and lodging, write or call any of the following offices of the **Cayman Islands Department of Tourism:** 6100 Waterford Bldg., 6100 Blue Lagoon Dr., Suite 150, Miami, FL 33126–2085, tel. 305/266–2300; 2 Memorial City Plaza, 820 Gessner, Suite 170, Houston, TX 77024, tel. 713/461–1317; 420 Lexington Ave., Suite 2733, New York, NY 10170, tel. 212/682–5582; 9525 West Bryn Mawr Ave., Suite 160, Rosemont, IL 60018, tel. 708/678–6446; 3440 Wilshire Blvd., Suite 1202, Los Angeles, CA 90010, tel. 213/738–1968; 234 Eglinton Ave. E, Suite 306, Toronto, Ont. M4P 1K5, tel. 416/485–1550; Trevor House, 100 Brompton Rd., Knightsbridge, London SW3 1EX, tel. 071/581–9960.

Arriving and Departing
By Plane
Cayman Airways (tel. 800/422–9626) flies nonstop to Grand Cayman from Miami daily, from Tampa and Atlanta four times a week, and from Houston three times a week. **American Airlines** (tel. 800/433–7300) has daily nonstop flights from both Miami and Raleigh/Durham, North Carolina. **United** (tel. 800/538–2929) and **Northwest** (tel. 800/447–4747) both have regularly scheduled nonstop flights from Miami. **U.S. Air** (tel. 800/428–4322) flies nonstop four times a week from Tampa and three times a week from Charlotte, North Carolina. **Cayman Airtours** (tel. 800/247–2966) offers package deals. Air service from Grand Cayman to Cayman Brac and Little Cayman is offered via Cayman Airways and **Island Air** (809/949–0241 or 809/949–6027). Flights land at Owen Roberts Airport, Gerrard-Smith Airport, or Edward Bodden Airfield. **Airport Information:** For flight information, call 809/949–7733.

Upon arrival, some hotels offer free pickup at the airport. Taxi service and car rentals are also available.

Passports and Visas
American and Canadian citizens do not have to carry passports, but they must show some proof of citizenship, such as a birth certificate or voter registration card, plus a return ticket. British and Commonwealth subjects do not need a visa, but must carry a passport. Visitors to the islands cannot be employed without a work permit.

Language
English is spoken everywhere; all local publications are in English as well.

Precautions
Locals make a constant effort to conserve fresh water, so don't waste a precious commodity.

Penalties for drug importation and possession of controlled substances include large fines and prison terms.

Theft is uncommon, but be smart: Lock up your room and car and secure valuables as you would at home. Outdoors, marauding blackbirds called "ching chings" have been known to carry off jewelry if it is left out in the open.

There are several poisonous plants on the island—the Maiden Plum, the Lady Hair, and the manchineel tree. If in doubt, don't touch, and don't seek shelter under a manchineel tree in the rain.

Staying in the Cayman Islands

Important Addresses
Tourist Information: The main office of the **Department of Tourism** is located in the Harbour Center (N. Church St., tel. 809/949–0623). Information booths are at the airport (tel. 809/949–2635); in the George Town Craft Market, on Cardinal Avenue, open when cruise ships are in port (tel. 809/949–8342); and in the kiosk at the cruise

ship dock in George Town (no tel.). There is also an islandwide tourist hotline (tel. 809/949-8989).

Emergencies **Police and Hospitals:** 911. **Ambulance:** 555. **Pharmacy:** The most central pharmacy is **Cayman Drug** (tel. 809/949-2597), in downtown George Town on Panton Street. **Divers' Recompression Chamber:** Call 809/949-4234.

Currency Although the American dollar is accepted everywhere, you'll save money if you go to the bank and exchange U.S. dollars for Cayman Island (C.I.) dollars, which are worth about $1.25 each. The Cayman dollar is divided into a hundred cents with coins of 1¢, 5¢, 10¢, and 25¢ and notes of $1, $5, $10, $25, $50, and $100. There is no $20 bill.

Prices are often quoted in Cayman dollars, so it's best to ask. All prices quoted here are in U.S. dollars unless otherwise noted.

Taxes and Service Charges Hotels collect a 6% government tax. The departure tax is C.I. $7.50 (U.S. $9). Hotels add a 10% service charge to your bill. Many restaurants add a 10%–15% service charge.

Guided Tours The most impressive sights are underwater. Snorkeling, diving, glass-bottom-boat and submarine rides can be arranged at any of the major aquatic shops: **Bob Soto's Diving Ltd.** (tel. 809/947-4631), **Red Sail Sports** (tel. 809/949-8745), **Don Foster's Dive Grand Cayman** (tel. 809/949-5679), **Aqua Delights** (tel. 809/947-4786), **Ocean Safari** (tel. 809/949-8613), and **Atlantis Submarine** (tel. 809/949-7700).

To see the island, rent a car or take a tour with a taxi driver (call **Taxi Services,** tel. 809/949-5702) or with a local tour service. **Evco Tours** (tel. 809/949-2118) offers six-hour, round-island tours from the Tortuga Club at the East End to the Turtle Farm and village of Hell in West Bay. All-day tours also can be arranged with **Tropicana Tours** (tel. 809/949-0944), **Rudy's** (tel. 809/949-3208), **Reids** (tel. 809/949-6531), and **GreyLine** (tel. 809/949-2791). Half-day tours average $45 a person; full-day tours average $65 and include lunch.

Getting Around If your accommodations are along Seven Mile Beach, you can walk to the shopping centers, restaurants, and entertainment spots along West Bay Road.

Taxis Taxis offer islandwide service. Fares are determined by an elaborate rate structure set by the government, and although it may seem pricey for a short ride (fare from Seven Mile Beach for four people to the airport ranges from $10 to $12), cabbies rarely try to rip off tourists. Ask to see the chart if you want to double-check the quoted fare. **Cayman Cab Team** offers 24-hour service (tel. 809/947-1173), as does **Holiday Inn Taxi Stand** (tel. 809/947-4491).

Rental Cars To rent a car, bring your current driver's license, and the car-rental firm will issue you a temporary permit ($5). Most firms have a range of models available, from compacts to Jeeps to minibuses. Rates range from $35–$55 a day. The major agencies have offices in a plaza across from the airport terminal, where you can pick up and drop off vehicles. Just remember, driving is on the left.

Car-rental companies are **Ace Hertz** (tel. 809/949-2280 or 800/654-3131), **Budget** (tel. 809/949-5605 or 800/527-0700), **CICO-Avis** (tel. 809/949-2468 or 800/331-1212), **Coconut** (tel. 809/949-4037 or 800/262-6687), **Dollar** (tel. 809/949-2981), and **National** (tel. 809/949-4790 or 800/227-7368).

Grand Cayman is flat as a pancake, making it perfect for zipping around on a motor scooter or bicycle. Just don't forget the sunblock and that driving is on the left. Bicycles ($12.50 a day), scooters ($24–

$30 a day), and motorcycles ($30–$33 a day), can be rented from **Caribbean Motors** (tel. 809/949–4051 or 809/947–8878), **Cayman Cycle** (tel. 809/947–4020), **Honda** (tel. 809/947–4466), and **Soto Scooters** (tel. 809/947–4652).

Telephones and Mail
For international dialing to Cayman, the area code is 809. To call outside, dial 0 + 1 + area code and number. You can call anywhere, anytime, through the cable and wireless system and local operators. To make local calls, dial the seven-digit number.

Beautiful stamps and first day covers are available at the main post office in downtown George Town weekdays from 8:30 to 4 and from the philatelic office in West Shore Plaza weekdays from 8:30 to 3:30. Sending a postcard to the United States, Canada, the Caribbean, or Central America costs C.I.10¢. An airmail letter is C.I.25¢ per half ounce. To Europe and South America, the rates are C.I.15¢ for a postcard and C.I.50¢ per half ounce for airmail letters.

Opening and Closing Times
Banking hours are generally Monday–Thursday 9–2:30 and Friday 9–1 and 2:30–4:30. Shops are open Monday–Friday 9–5, and on Saturday in George Town from 10 to 2; in outer shopping plazas, from 10 to 5. Shops are usually closed on Sunday except in hotels.

Exploring the Cayman Islands

Numbers in the margin correspond to points of interest on the Grand Cayman map.

George Town
①
Begin exploring **George Town** at the **Cayman Islands National Museum** on Harbour Drive, slightly south of the Cruise Ship Dock Gazebo. Built in 1833, this building was used as a courthouse, a jail, and a dance hall before being reopened in 1990 as a museum. It is small but fascinating, with excellent displays and videos illustrating the history of Cayman plant, animal, human, and geological life. *Harbour Drive, tel. 809/949–8368. Admission: $5. Open Mon.–Fri. 9–5, Sat. 10–4.*

Just one block over on South Church Street is the headquarters of the **Atlantis Submarine** (*see* What to See and Do with Children). From the museum, turn right onto Harbour Drive for a leisurely stroll along the waterfront. The circular gazebo is where visitors from the cruise ships disembark. Diagonally across the street is the **Elmslie Memorial United Church,** named after Scotsman James Elmslie, the first Presbyterian missionary to serve in the Caymans. The church was the first concrete block building built in the Cayman Islands. Its vaulted ceiling, with wood arches and sedate nave, reflect the quietly religious nature of island residents.

Continue north on Harbour Drive past the **War Memorial** erected in memory of the Caymanian Royal Navy volunteers who died in defense of Great Britain during World Wars I and II. Next you come to **Fort George Park,** established to preserve the stone wall remnants of the circa-1790 fort, reputedly one of the smallest ever built in the Caribbean.

Turn right onto **Fort Street,** a main shopping street where you'll find the People's Boutique and a whole row of jewelry shops featuring black coral products—Bernard Passman, Finiterre, Smith's, and the Jewellery Factory.

At the end of the block is the heart of downtown George Town. At the corner of Fort Street and **Edward Street,** notice the small clock tower dedicated to Britain's King George V and the huge fig tree

Grand Cayman

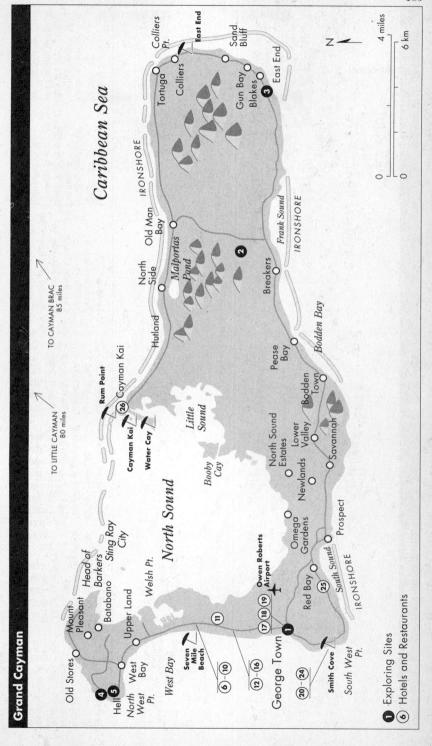

Caribbean Sea

TO CAYMAN BRAC
85 miles

TO LITTLE CAYMAN
80 miles

Colliers Pt.

East End

Sand
Bluff

Colliers

Colliers

Tortuga

Gun Bay

Blakes

❸ East End

*Old Man
Bay*

North
Side

*Malportas
Pond*

❷

Breakers

IRONSHORE

Frank Sound

IRONSHORE

Hutland

Rum Point

Cayman Kai

❷⑥ Cayman Kai

Cayman Kai

Water Cay

*Little
Sound*

Pease
Bay

Bodden Bay

*Booby
Cay*

North Sound
Estates

Lower
Valley

Bodden
Town

Savannah

North Sound

Newlands

Mount
Pleasant

*Head of
Barkers*

Old Stores

*Sting Ray
City*

Batabano

Upper Land

Welsh Pt.

West Bay

Omega
Gardens

Red Bay

Prospect

South Sound

IRONSHORE

Hell

❹ ❺

North
West Pt.

West
Bay

⑪

**Seven
Mile Beach**

⑥–**⑩**

⑫–**⑯**

⑰ ⑱ ⑲

**Owen Roberts
Airport**

❶ George Town

⑳–**㉔**

Smith Cove

South West
Pt.

㉕

❶ Exploring Sites

⑥ Hotels and Restaurants

N

4 miles

6 km

0

0

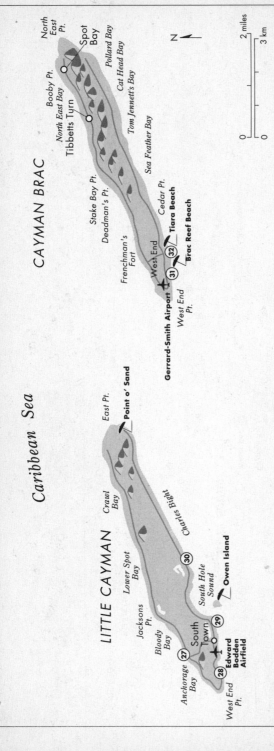

Cayman Brac and Little Cayman

Exploring
Botanic Park, **2**
East End, **3**
George Town, **1**
Hell, **5**
Turtle Farm, **4**

Dining
The Almond Tree, **19**
Chef Tell's Grand Old
House, **20**
Corita's Copper
Kettle, **18**

The Cracked Conch, **11**
Crow's Nest, **25**
Garden Loggia Cafe, **9**
Golden Pagoda, **10**
Hemingway's, **12**
Hog Sty Bay Cafe, **21**

Lantana's, **7**
Lobster Pot, **17**
Ottmar's, **24**
The Wharf, **13**
White Hall Bay, **14**

Lodging
Brac Reef Beach
Resort, **31**
Caribbean Club, **7**
Cayman Islander, **16**
Cayman Kai Resort, **26**
Coconut Harbour, **22**

Divi Tiara Beach
Resort, **32**
Holiday Inn Grand
Cayman, **8**
Hyatt Regency Grand
Cayman, **9**
Indies Suites, **6**
Little Cayman Beach
Resort, **30**

Pirates Point
Resort, **28**
Radisson Resort
Grand Cayman, **15**
Sam McCoy's Diving
and Fishing Lodge, **27**
Southern Cross
Club, **29**
Sunset House, **23**

manicured into an umbrella shape. The Cayman Islands **Legislative Assembly Building** is next door to the 1919 **Peace Memorial Building.**

Turning right on Edward Street, you'll find the charming **library,** built in 1939; it has English novels, current newspapers from the United States, and a small reference section. It's worth a visit just for the Old World atmosphere and a look at the shields depicting Britain's prominent institutions of learning that decorate the ceiling. Across the street is the **courthouse.** Down the next block is the "financial district," where banks from all over the world have offices.

Straight ahead is the **General Post Office,** also built in 1939, with its strands of decorative colored lights and some 2,000 private mailboxes on the outside. (Mail is not delivered on the island.) Behind the post office is **Elizabethan Square,** a new shopping and office complex on **Shedden Road** that houses various food, clothing, and souvenir establishments. The courtyard has a pleasant garden and fountain as well as outdoor tables at La Fontaine, a German restaurant.

Exiting Elizabethan Square onto Shedden Road and walking past Anderson Square and Caymania Freeport, turn right back onto Edward Street, then left at the Royal Bank of Canada onto **Cardinal Avenue.** This is the main shopping area. On the right is the chic Kirk Freeport Plaza, known for its fine jewelry, plus duty-free bargains in china, crystal, Gucci items, perfumes, and fine cosmetics.

Turn left on **Harbour Drive** and make your way back to Shedden Road, passing the English Shoppe, a souvenir outlet that looks more as if it belongs on Shaftesbury Avenue in London than in the West Indies, and the Cayside Galleries, with its maritime antiques and cameras.

The **Treasure Museum,** a quick taxi ride away on West Bay Road, in front of the Hyatt Regency, is a real find. Dioramas show how Caymanians became seafarers, boat builders, and turtle breeders. An animated figure of Blackbeard the Pirate spins salty tales about the pirates and buccaneers who "worked" the Caribbean. Since the museum is owned by a professional treasure-salvaging firm, it's not surprising that there are a lot of artifacts from shipwrecks. There is even a gold bar that visitors can lift to appreciate its weight. *West Bay Rd., tel. 809/947–5033. Admission: $5 adults, $2.50 children 6– 12. Open Mon.–Sat. 9–5.*

The Outer Districts To see the rest of the island, rent a car or scooter, or take a guided tour. The flat road that circles the island is in good condition, with clear signs; you'd have to work to get lost here. Reserve a half day for a visit to the West End attractions and another half to full day to visit the East End. Venturing away from the Seven Mile Beach strip, travelers will encounter the more down-home character of the islands. Heading out on South Church Street, you can see some of the old houses, which feature elaborate Victorian gingerbread on modest frame homes. Heading east in a district called **Pantonville,** after the Pantons who live there, there are three pretty cottages with lacy woodwork. Then at **South Sound** you see larger residences, some with fine detail and gracious verandas.

In the Savannah district, **Pedro's Castle,** built in 1780, lays claim to being the oldest structure on the island. Legends linked to this structure abound, but what is known is that the building was struck by lightning in 1877 and left in ruins until bought by a restaurateur in the 1960s. Gutted once again by fire in 1970, the building was purchased by the government in 1991 for restoration as a historic landmark. At **Bodden Town**—the island's original capital—you'll find an old cemetery on the shore side of the road. Graves with A-frame structures are said to contain the remains of pirates, but, in fact, they may be those of early settlers. A curio shop serves as the entrance to what's called the **Pirate's Caves,** and you'll pass a minizoo en route to these partially underground caves. The natural formations are interesting, but the place is more hokey than spooky.

Time Out The large and airy **Lighthouse at Breakers Restaurant** (Breakers, tel. 809/947–2047) has booth seating around spectacular waterfront windows and offers seafood and Italian cuisine.

At Frank Sound Road, turn left (north) to get to the Cayman Islands

2 National Trust **Botanic Park,** a 60-acre preserve of wooded land recently established as the site for future botanical gardens. About a mile of walking trail has been completed; small yellow and green

3 signs identify the island's flora. The village of **East End** is the first recorded settlement on the island. Its major claim to fame these days is that it's where a renowned local musician called the "Violin Man," aka Radley Gourzong, lives and occasionally performs his distinctive form of music (more akin to Louisiana's backwater zydeco than reggae) with his band, the Happy Boys. It's also the site of a number of shipwrecks and **Morritt's Tortuga Club** (55 time-share units), whose guests include avid divers and windsurfers.

At the other end of the island is the **West Bay** community, whose

4 main attraction is the **Turtle Farm.** The farm, which was started about 25 years ago, is the most popular attraction on the island today, with some 70,000 visitors a year. There are turtles of all ages, from ping-pong-ball-size eggs to day-old hatchlings to huge 600-pounders that can live to be 100 years old. The Turtle Farm was set up both as a conservation and a commercial enterprise; it releases about 5% of its stock back out to sea every year, harvests turtles for local restaurants, and exports the by-products. (Note: U.S. citizens cannot take home any turtle products because of a U.S. regulation banning their import.) In the adjoining café, you can sample turtle soup or turtle sandwiches while looking over an exhibit about turtles. *West Bay Rd., tel. 809/949–3893. Admission: $5 adults, $2.50 children 6–12. Open daily 8:30–5.*

The other area of West Bay that is of brief interest is the tiny village

5 of **Hell,** which is little more than a patch of incredibly jagged rock formations called ironshore. The big attraction here is a small post office, which does a land-office business selling stamps and postmarking cards from Hell, and lots of T-shirt and souvenir shops. Almost unbelievably, a nearby nightclub, called the Club Inferno, is run by the McDoom family.

Cayman Brac

Brac, the Gaelic word for "bluff," aptly identifies this island's most distinctive feature, a rugged limestone cliff that runs down the center of the island's 12-mile length. At the eastern end, the bluff soars to 140 feet—rather dramatic for the Caribbean. Cayman Brac lies 89 miles east of Grand Cayman via Cayman Airways. It's a spelunker's paradise: you can explore the island's half-dozen large caves, some of which are still used for hurricane protection. You can get to the caves via moped or taxi. Wear sneakers for exploring, not flip-flops; some of the paths to the caves are steep and rocky. Only 1,700 people live on this island, in communities such as Watering Place and Halfway Ground. The variety of flora includes unusual orchids, mangoes, and papaya, and the endangered Caymanian parrot lives among the Brac's bird population. Parts of the island are unpopulated, so visitors can explore truly isolated areas both inland and along the shore.

Two hotels catering to divers, the Divi Tiara Beach and the Brac Reef Beach Resort, are located on sandy beaches in a lagoon on the southwest coast. Swimming is possible, but the bottom is much rockier than on Seven Mile Beach.

Little Cayman

Only 7 miles away from Cayman Brac is Little Cayman Island, which boasts a population of about three dozen on its 12 square miles. This tiny place really is paradise for those intent on getting away from crowds—it has only two small shops and a Jeep-rental office in the "plaza" by the airstrip, with a few private phones and one pay phone on the entire island. It does have ample accommodations for visitors, however, in five small lodges—the Southern Cross Club, Sam McCoy's Diving and Fishing Lodge, the Village Inn, the Little Cayman Beach Resort, and Pirates Point. In addition to privacy, the real attractions of Little Cayman are diving in spectacular Bloody Bay, off the north coast, and fishing, which includes angling for tarpon and bonefish.

And if Little Cayman ever gets too busy, there is one final retreat—**Owen Island,** which is just 200 yards offshore. Accessible by rowboat, it has a blue lagoon and a sandy beach. Take your own picnic if you plan to spend the day.

What to See and Do with Children

Don't miss the one-hour **Atlantis Submarine** (tel. 809/949–7700) ride, which takes 48 passengers, a driver, and a guide down along the Cayman Wall to depths of up to 90 feet. This $2.8 million submarine has entertained hundreds of thousands of passengers, has all sorts of safety features, including a constantly circling surface monitor boat, and is air-conditioned. Through its large windows, you can see huge barrel sponges, corals of extraterrestrial-like configurations, strange eels, and schools of beautiful and beastly fish. Night dives are quite dramatic, because the artificial lights of the ship make the colors more vivid than they are in daytime excursions.

Turtle Farm (*see* Exploring the Cayman Islands, *above*).

Older children can also enjoy many of the water sports and beach games available. Only the Hyatt Regency has a (seasonal) children's program. Other hotels politely say that they do not organize children's activities; be prepared to do so yourself.

Off the Beaten Track

Two architectural curiosities are worth a look if you are driving around. One is the little pink-and-white house on West Bay Road just past the cemetery. This 100-year-old cottage is made of mahogany and ironwood. Another odd residence is the conch house, near the power plant. This house was covered with conch shells years ago, but a recent renovation has added modern skylights and a garish satellite dish in the front yard.

Carey Cayman Coral (no tel.) is a workshop out on South Sound Road, east of the Crow's Nest Restaurant, run by Carey Hurlstone.

Carey, a gentle bear of a man with tattoos covering his skin, professes he was a biker with the Hell's Angels before coming home to Cayman to work as a craftsman. He also carves glass. Carey's workmanship is superb, and his prices are quite reasonable for the quality.

Beaches

Grand
Cayman

You may read or hear about the "dozens of beaches" of these islands, but that's more exaggeration than reality. Grand Cayman's west coast, the most developed area of the entire colony, is where you'll find its famous **Seven Mile Beach** (actually 5½ miles long) and its expanses of powdery white sand. The beach is litter-free and sans peddlers, so you can relax in an unspoiled, hassle-free (if somewhat crowded) atmosphere. This is also Grand Cayman's busiest vacation center, and most of the island's accommodations, restaurants, and shopping centers are on this strip. The seaside bar and pool at the Holiday Inn are "party central" to repeat visitors on the island. You'll find headquarters for the island's aquatic activities here are scattered along the strip (*see* Sports and the Outdoors, *below*).

Grand Cayman has several smaller beaches that may better be called coves, including **Smith Cove,** off South Church Street, south of the Grand Old House—a popular bathing spot with residents on weekends.

The best snorkeling locations are off **the ironshore** (coral ledge area) south of **George Town** on Grand Cayman's west coast and in the reef-protected shallows of the island's north and south coasts, where coral and fish life are much more varied and abundant.

The best windsurfing is just off the beaches in **East End,** at Colliers, by Morritt's Tortuga Club. The beach can be lovely if it's kept clean of seaweed tossed ashore by trade winds, but the windsurfing is the real draw here. Seldom discovered by visitors unless they're staying there are the beautiful beach areas of **Cayman Kai, Rum Point,** and, even more isolated and unspoiled, **Water Cay.** These are favored hideaways for residents and popular Sunday picnic spots.

Cayman Brac

Both **Divi Tiara Beach** and **Brac Reef Beach** resorts have fine small beaches, better for sunning than for snorkeling. Excellent snorkeling can be found immediately offshore of the now-defunct **Buccaneer's Inn** on the north coast.

Little Cayman

The beaches **Point o' Sand,** on the eastern tip, and **Owen Island,** off the south coast, are exquisite isolated patches of powder that are great for sunbathing and worth every effort to reach by car, bike, or boat.

Sports and the Outdoors

Deep-Sea
Fishing

If you enjoy action fishing, Cayman waters have plenty to offer—blue and white marlin, yellowfin tuna, sailfish, dolphin, and wahoo. Bonefish and tarpon are also plentiful off Little Cayman. Some 25 boats are available for charter, offering fishing options that include deep-sea, reef, bone, tarpon, light-tackle, and fly fishing. Charter operators to contact are **Charter Boat Headquarters** (tel. 809/947–4340), **Crosby Ebanks** (tel. 809/947–4049), **Island Girl** (tel. 809/947–3029), and **Capt. Eugene's Watersports** (tel. 809/949–3099 or 800/453–8984). Since 1984 a Million Dollar Month fishing tournament has been held in June, and registered anglers can win cash and vacation prizes by landing record-breaking catches. Each of the five tournaments has its own rules, records, and entrance fees. For information and applications, write Million Dollar Month Committee (Box 878 GT, Grand Cayman, Cayman Islands, B.W.I.).

Diving To say that the Cayman Islands are a scuba diver's paradise is not overstating the case. Jacques Cousteau called Bloody Bay (off Little Cayman) one of the world's top dives. Pristine water (often exceeding 100-foot visibility), breathtaking coral formations, and plentiful and exotic marine life await divers. A host of top-notch dive operations offer a variety of services, instruction and equipment. Unfortunately, most of Grand Cayman's dive boats tend to be full all year; however, the sister islands are far less crowded. A Grand Cayman must-see for adventurous souls is **Sting Ray City,** which has been called the best 12-foot dive (or snorkel) in the world. Here are dozens of unsually tame sting rays who, accustomed to being fed first by fishermen and now by divers, suction squid off divers' outstretched palms and gracefully swim and twist around the divers in the shallow waters.

Divers are required to be certified and possess a "C" card or take a short resort or full certification course. A certification course, including classroom, pool, and boat sessions as well as checkout dives, takes five or six days and costs $300–$400. A short resort course usually lasts a day and costs about $75–$90. It introduces the novice to the sport and teaches the rudimentary skills needed to make a shallow, instructor-monitored dive.

All dive operations on Cayman are more than competent; among them are **Bob Soto's** (tel. 809/947–4631 or 800/262–7686), **Don Foster's** (tel. 809/949–5679 or 800/83–DIVER), **Red Sail Sports** (tel. 809/949–8745 or 800/255–6425), **Quabbin Dives** (tel. 809/949–5597), and **Sunset Divers** (tel. 809/949–7111 or 800/854–4767). Request full information on all operators from the Department of Tourism (*see* Before You Go, *above*). A single-tank dive averages $35–$40; a two-tank dive about $55. Snorkel equipment rents run from $8–$12.50 a day, so consider purchasing your own before you come.

On Cayman Brac, **Brac Aquatics** (tel. 809/858–7429 or 809/858–7323) and **Divi Tiara** (tel. 809/948–7553) offer scuba and snorkeling. On Little Cayman, contact the **Southern Cross Club** (tel. 809/948–3255). Each hotel also has its own instructors.

Most operations can rent all diving gear, including equipment for underwater photography; Bob Soto's, Don Foster's, Fisheye Photographic, and Sunset U/W Photo have facilities for film processing and underwater photo courses.

One week live-aboard dive cruises are available aboard a 110-foot ship that's part of the **Aggressor Fleet** (tel. 800/DIV–BOAT).

Fitness A **Nautilus Fitness Center** (tel. 809/949–5132), with machines, weights, sauna, and whirlpool, is in operation on Grand Cayman on Crewe Road, in the Crighton Building just across from the airport. Daily membership is $10; weekly, $25. **Fitness Connection** (tel. 809/949–8485) offers aerobics classes, private instruction, and fitness counseling at three locations in George Town.

Golf The **Grand Cayman–Britannia** golf course (tel. 809/949–8020), next to the Hyatt Regency, was designed by Jack Nicklaus. The course is really three in one—a 9-hole regulation course, an 18-hole executive course, and a Cayman course, played with a Cayman ball that goes about half the distance of a regulation ball. Greens fees range from $25 to $50.

The Cayman's first 18-hole championship golf course, **The Links at Safehaven** (tel. 809/947–4155), was just opening at press time (Sept. 1994). The Roy Case–designed par 71, 6,519-yard course caters to golfers of all skill levels, with five placements available at each tee. Facilities will include a two-story clubhouse, locker rooms, a pro shop, and a bar and restaurant.

Tennis Most hotels and condo complexes have tennis courts for guests.

Water Sports Water skis, Windsurfers, Hobie Cats, and jet skis are available at many of the aquatic shops along Seven Mile Beach (*see* Diving, *above*). **Sailboards Caribbean** (tel. 809/949–1068) offers windsurfing lessons for beginners and a full gamut of courses through high-wind advanced levels. **Cayman Windsurf** (tel. 809/947–7492) offers windsurfing lessons and rentals at the East End of the island at Morritt's Tortuga Club.

Shopping

If your motto is "Born to Shop," then Grand Cayman has two money-saving attributes—duty-free merchandise and the absence of a sales tax. Prices on imported merchandise—English china, Swiss watches, French perfumes, and Japanese cameras and electronic goods—are often less expensive than elsewhere, but not always. To ensure you are getting a bargain, come prepared with a price list of items you are thinking of buying and comparison shop. Unusual jewelry can also be found, ranging from authentic sunken treasure and ancient coins made into necklaces and pins to relatively inexpensive rings and earrings made from semiprecious stones, coral, and seashells. For an unusual and relatively inexpensive souvenir, try the island perfume, Cayman Caress, found at a number of boutiques, or the **Tortuga Rum Company's** (tel. 809/949–7701) scrumptious rum cake.

Good Buys Debbie van der Bol runs an arts and crafts shop called **Pure Art** (tel. 809/949–9133) on South Church Street and at the Hyatt Regency (tel. 809/347–5633). She features watercolors, wood carvings, and lacework by local artists, as well as her own sketches and cards.

Arts and Crafts

The **Heritage Crafts Shop** (tel. 809/949–7093), near the harbor in George Town, sells local crafts and gifts. The new **West Shore Shopping Center,** on Seven Mile Beach near the Radisson, offers good-quality island art, beachwear, ice cream, and more. Original prints, paintings, and sculpture with a tropical theme are found at **Cayman Fine Art** (tel. 809/949–8007). The **Oasis Boutique** (tel. 809/947–4444) at the Holiday Inn has a superior selection of contemporary, unique art pieces: jewelry, gifts, carvings, and clothing. T-shirt shops abound all over town.

Black Coral Black coral products are a popular and exquisite choice; however, environmental groups discourage tourists from purchasing any coral that is designated as endangered species because the reefs are not always harvested carefully. If you feel differently, there are a number of local craftsmen who create original designs and finish their own work. Among those who have retail outlets in downtown George Town are **Coral Art Collections by Mitzi** (tel. 809/949–5086), in the Old Fort building on North Church Street; **Bernard Passman** (tel. 809/949–0123), whose creations won the approval of the English royal family, on Fort Street; and **Black Coral Jewelry and Other Fine Gems** (tel. 809/949–7156), whose creators, Richard and Rafaela Barile, have attracted lots of celebrities to their shop on Harbour Drive.

Dining

Grand Cayman's restaurants satisfy every palate and pocketbook. Gourmet Continental cuisine is available to the high rollers; ethnic food can be had at moderate prices. West Indian fare in dining spots serving locals is the best in taste and value.

Seafood, not surprisingly, appears on most restaurant menus. Fish—including grouper, snapper, dolphin, tuna, wahoo, and marlin—is served either simply or Cayman style, with peppers, onions, and tomatoes. Conch, the meat of a large pink mollusk, is ubiquitous in stews and chowders and as fritters or panfried ("cracked"). Caribbean lobster is available but is often quite expensive, and other shellfish are in short supply in local waters. The only traditional culinary treat of the islands is turtle soup, stew, or steak, but only a few restaurants carry it these days.

Dining out on Grand Cayman can be expensive, so replenish your billfold, because some places do not accept plastic.

All the restaurants reviewed below are located on Grand Cayman. Highly recommended restaurants are indicated by a star ★.

Category	Cost*
Expensive	over $30
Moderate	$20–$30
Inexpensive	under $20

per person, excluding drinks and service charge

★ **Chef Tell's Grand Old House.** TV celebrity chef Tell Erhardt has been running this popular establishment since 1986. His menu features Continental entrées and a few local specialties. Among the spicier appetizer choices is grouper Beignete, marinated and deep-fried grouper served with curry sauce and minted yogurt. On the nonspicy side is Lobster Chef Fred's Way, dipped in egg batter and sautéed with shallots, mushrooms, and white wine. The back-porch dining room, with its Victorian trim and ceiling fans, is the liveliest and best spot for dining. The excellent service adds to this gracious dining experience. *S. Church St., tel. 809/949–9333. Reservations necessary for dinner, suggested for lunch. AE, MC, V. Closed for lunch weekends. Expensive.*

Garden Loggia Cafe. The Hyatt's indoor-outdoor café opens onto the most beautifully landscaped garden courtyard on the island. The Caribbean decor includes pastel colors, ceiling fans, and marble-top tables. The menu combines European and Caribbean tastes. The Friday-night seafood buffet and sumptuous Sunday champagne brunch feature everything from roast suckling pig, king crab, and lobster to waffles and custom-made omelets. Live music is featured at breakfast and dinner every day except Sunday. *Hyatt Regency Grand Cayman, West Bay Rd., tel. 809/949–1234. Reservations necessary. AE, MC, V. Expensive.*

★ **Hemingway's.** Located right on Seven Mile Beach, this classy restaurant features open-air dining with a sea view and breezes. Nouvelle Caribbean and seafood dishes include conch and turtle steak prepared in coconut milk and green bananas or beer-batter coconut shrimp. For a tropical drink, try the Seven Mile Meltdown, with dark rum, peach schnapps, pineapple juice, and fresh coconut. There is superb service and Caribbean decor. Buffet dinner is served on the *Spirit of Ppalu*, a glass-bottom catamaran. *Hyatt/Bri-*

tannia Beach Club, West Bay Rd., tel. 809/949–1234. Reservations accepted. AE, MC, V. Expensive.

★ **Lantana's.** Alfred Schrock, longtime chef at the top-rated Wharf Restaurant, now serves his own excellent southwestern cuisine at lunch and dinner. The decor is as tasteful and imaginatively authentic as the food: Enjoy blackened Canadian salmon with banana fritters, sweet-and-sour salsa, and cilantro pasta, or Cayman conch fritters with chile mayonnaise and cilantro pesto. *Caribbean Club, West Bay Rd., tel. 809/947–5595. Reservations necessary. AE, MC, V. Expensive.*

Ottmar's. This quietly elegant restaurant is styled after a West Indian great house. Jade carpeting, peach walls, linen, and glass chandeliers create an attractive setting for the excellent service. The mesquite-grilled entrées, seafood, and French cuisine are no less exciting. Start the meal with drinks on a garden terrace. *In the Transnational Conference Center, West Bay Rd., tel. 809/941–5879 and 809/947–5882. Reservations required. Dinner only; closed Sun. AE, MC, V. Expensive.*

The Wharf. Stylishly decorated in blue and white, The Wharf looks onto a veranda and the nearby sea. On the menu are such Caribbean specialties as turtle steak, conch chowder, and sea scallops Provençal. Daily specials include seafood paella and soft-shell and stone crabs. Live music entertains diners. The Ports of Call bar is a perfect spot from which to watch the sun set. *West Bay Rd., tel. 809/949–2231. MC, V. Closed lunch weekends. Expensive.*

Lobster Pot. The second-floor terrace of this cozy restaurant overlooks the bay downtown, so the sunsets are an extra attraction. Its menu features both Continental dishes and such Caribbean specialties as conch chowder, turtle soup, steak, seafood curry, and, of course, lobster. This place is popular, so the constant turnover makes the atmosphere feel rushed. If you can't make dinner, drop by the pub and have a frozen banana daiquiri. *N. Church St., tel. 809/949–2736. Reservations recommended. MC, V. Moderate–Expensive.*

★ **Crow's Nest.** With the ocean right in its backyard, this secluded small restaurant is a great spot for snorkeling as well as lunching. One drawback: Insect repellent is required for patio dining in the evening. The gourmet shrimp and conch dishes are excellent, as is the dessert of raisins and rum cake. *South Sound, tel. 809/949–9366. Reservations required. MC, V. Closed Sun. Moderate.*

White Hall Bay. Formerly the Cook Rum, the White Hall Bay has moved across the street to a restored waterfront Caymanian house, but it hasn't lost any of its casual ambience and charm. The hearty West Indian menu includes turtle stew, salt beef and beans, and pepper-pot stew. Follow up with dessert specials, such as yam cake and coconut cream pie. *N. Church St., tel. 809/949–8670. AE, D, MC, V. Moderate.*

The Cracked Conch. This popular seafood restaurant has the ambience of a crowded fish house. Specialties include conch fritters, conch chowder, spicy Cayman-style snapper, and three types of turtle steak. The key lime pie is divine. Take-out service is available. The bar has live entertainment and is a local hangout. *Selkirk's Plaza, West Bay Rd., tel. 809/947–5217. Reservations suggested in winter. AE, MC, V. Inexpensive–Moderate.*

The Almond Tree. Looking for authentic island atmosphere in modern Grand Cayman? This eatery combines architecture from the South Seas isle of Yap with bones, skulls, and bric-a-brac from Africa, South America, and the Pacific. Sample good-value seafood entrées, including environmentally correct turtle steak, with "All-U-Can-Eat" entrées for C.I.$11 on Wednesday and Friday. *N. Church*

St., tel. 809/459–2893. Dinner reservations recommended. AE, MC, V. Closed Tues. Inexpensive.

Corita's Copper Kettle I & II. Here is a tidy downtown diner featuring Jamaican breakfasts and such native specialties as conch and lobster burgers. The fare is simple and tasty. *I: Edward St., tel. 809/ 949–2696. II: Dolphin Center on Eastern Ave., tel. 809/949–7078. No reservations. No credit cards. Open breakfast and lunch only. Inexpensive.*

Golden Pagoda. The well-known Chinese restaurant in the Caymans features Hakka-style cooking. Among its specialties are Mahlah chicken, butterfly shrimp, and chicken in black-bean sauce. Takeout is available. *West Bay Rd., tel. 809/949–5475. Reservations accepted. Dress: no shorts at dinner. AE, MC, V. No lunch weekends. Inexpensive.*

Hog Sty Bay Cafe. Lots of socializing goes on in the casual atmosphere of this English-style café on the harbor in George Town. A simple menu of sandwiches, hamburgers, and Caribbean dishes will satisfy you for lunch and dinner. Come and watch the sun set from the seaside patio or for the weekday happy hour. *N. Church St., tel. 809/949–6163. AE, MC, V. Closed lunch Sat. Inexpensive.*

Lodging

The success of the Cayman Islands as a resort destination means visitors should book ahead for holidays, especially at Christmastime. During the summer season, it's possible to find suitable lodging even on short notice. If you choose to stay in a condominium, you can book on a daily basis and stay any length of time. While about a third of the visitors come for the diving, a growing number are young honeymooners. There are few accommodations in the economy range, so guests must be prepared for resort prices. Money-saving packages (everything from honeymoon trips to air/hotel deals) are offered through hotels and through **TourScan, Inc.** (tel. 800/962– 2080 or 203/655–8091) and **Cayman Airtours** (tel. 800/247–2966). Most of the larger hotels along Seven Mile Beach don't offer meal plans. The smaller properties that are more remote from the restaurants usually offer MAP or FAP. The rates for most hotels on Cayman Brac and Little Cayman include meals, and in some cases drinks and diving as well, making them a better value than their prices reveal at first glance. Cayman Islands Hotel Reservations: 800/327–8777.

Highly recommended lodgings are indicated by a star ★.

Category	Cost*
Very Expensive	over $260
Expensive	$200–$260
Moderate	$145–$200
Inexpensive	under $145

All prices are for a standard double room for two in winter, excluding 6% tax and 10% service charge. To estimate rates for hotels offering MAP/FAP, add about $40 per person per day to the average price ranges above.

Hotels
Grand Cayman

Caribbean Club. Eighteen one- and two-bedroom villas (six located on the beach) make up this quiet island condominium getaway. All units were renovated in 1990. They are air-conditioned, individually decorated, and have full kitchens, living and dining rooms, TVs, patios, and a bathroom for every bedroom. While secluded, these units are not quite on a par with the truly deluxe properties on the island. Children under age 11 are not allowed in the winter season. *Box 504, Grand Cayman, tel. 809/947–4099 or 800/327–8777, fax 809/947–4443. 18 villas. Facilities: restaurant (open for lunch and dinner), bar, tennis court, maid service. AE, MC, V. EP. Very Expensive.*

★ **Hyatt Regency Grand Cayman.** Painted sky-blue and white and set amid gorgeous grounds, the Hyatt is adjacent to the only golf course on Grand Cayman. The rooms are exquisite, each with a marble entrance, oversize bathtub, bar, French doors, and a veranda. Across the street, the Hyatt's beach club offers every water sport imaginable. Regency Club accommodations include complimentary Continental breakfast, early-evening hors d'oeuvres, and 24-hour concierge service. Camp Hyatt offers a supervised activities program for children 3–15 at a cost of $35 a child per day. *Box 1698, Grand Cayman, tel. 809/949–1234 or 800/553–1300. 236 rooms; 43 rooms in Regency Club; 1-, 2-, and 3-bedroom Britannia villas. Facilities: 3 restaurants, 4 bars, 3 pools (one with a swim-up bar), dive shop, golf course, 2 lighted tennis courts, full-service water-sports center, conference rooms. AE, D, MC, V. EP, BP, MAP. Very Expensive.*

Holiday Inn Grand Cayman. This hotel, home of the Coconuts Comedy Club, was the pioneer resort establishment on the beach, and it's still loose and fun. The property is cheerful yet unpretentious, a sprawling modern hotel with bright tropical colors in the spacious public rooms and one of the widest and nicest beaches on the strip. The guest rooms are standard Holiday Inn: large and comfortable, if not luxurious, with pool or ocean views, air-conditioning, TV, phone, radio, and either two doubles or one king-size bed. The huge breakfast buffet is a good value, and don't miss the "Barefoot Man," who performs four nights a week outside on the patio. *Box 904, Grand Cayman, tel. 809/947–4444 or 800/421–9999. 215 rooms. Facilities: 3 restaurants, 3 bars, ice cream parlor, water-sports center, dive shop, pool, car rental, conference facilities, wheelchair-accessible rooms. AE, D, MC, V. EP, BP, MAP. Expensive.*

★ **Indies Suites.** Cayman's first and only all-suite hotel is attractive, comfortable, and across the road from the beach. One- or two-bedroom suites are done in cream and burnt orange, with contemporary wood furniture. Each has a fully equipped modern kitchen with a microwave oven, a living-dining room with a sleeper sofa), a terrace, and a storeroom for dive gear. All suites are air-conditioned and have two phones and a TV. Free Continental buffet breakfast daily and a live band that entertains in the lushly landscaped courtyard twice a week are nice extras. *Box 2070 GT, Seven Mile Beach, Grand Cayman, tel. 809/947–5025 or 800/654–3130, fax 809/947–5024. 40 suites. Facilities: water-sports shop, pool, poolside bar, snack shop, small convenience store, Jacuzzi, maid service, dive shop, snorkeling, conference facilities, laundry facilities. AE, MC, V. CP. Expensive.*

★ **Radisson Resort Grand Cayman.** This is a five-story luxury property on Seven Mile Beach, just 1 mile from George Town. Designed in colonial style with arched doorways, the hotel's airy pale yellow and marble lobby opens onto a plant-filled courtyard. Families like the adjoining large, air-conditioned rooms, done in bright tropical colors; all have color TVs and balconies facing either the ocean or a garden court. There's an inviting beach bar near the pool, a dive shop offering every possible water sport, and a lively comedy club with performers Wednesday through Sunday nights. There is a good snorkeling reef just 50 feet offshore, and the hotel offers a dine-around meal plan with reciprocity at several restaurants in town. *Box 30371, Grand Cayman, tel. 809/949–0088 or 800/333–3333, fax 809/949–0288. 315 rooms, 4 suites. Facilities: restaurant, snack bar, bar, pool, nightclub, Jacuzzi, water sports through Don Foster's, baby-sitting, car rental, room service. AE, DC, MC, V. EP, MAP. Expensive.*

Coconut Harbour. There's only one drawback to this serious diver's retreat: It's located near a field of oil storage tanks. This delightful resort has a dive shop, waterfront thatch-roof bar, and an informal restaurant. There's excellent diving offshore at Waldo's Reef, which is known for its population of tame marine life. The air-conditioned studios are carpeted and have a kitchenette, ceiling fan, and phone, but no TV. Continental breakfast is included in the rate. *Box 2086, Grand Cayman, tel. 809/949–7468 or 800/552–6281, fax 809/949–7117. 35 studios, all with kitchenette. Facilities: bar/restaurant, dive shop, pool, Jacuzzi. AE, MC, V. CP. Moderate.*

Cayman Islander. New management has done a lot for this simple, casual hotel across the road from Seven Mile Beach. The small but pleasant pool area was refurbished in 1992, as were the 67 rooms. Although the rooms aren't fancy, they're comfortable and more than adequate with new air-conditioning, carpeting, phones, satellite TVs, and a brighter decor. The three efficiency apartments have microwaves and refrigerators. A complete dive shop is on the premises. This motel-like hotel is a good value. *Box 30081, Seven Mile Beach, Grand Cayman, tel. 809/949–0990 or 800/327–8777; fax 809/949–7896. 67 rooms and 3 efficiencies. Facilities: small restaurant, bar/lounge, dive shop, pool. AE, MC, V. EP. Inexpensive.*

Cayman Kai Resort. Nestled next to a coconut grove, each sea lodge features a full kitchen, dining and living areas, and two screened-in porches overlooking the ocean. The hotel is on a beach at the north-central tip of the island—quite remote. You need a car to get anywhere, but many guests are content to stay put and dive. Not all of the rooms have air-conditioning, so be sure to request it if it's important to you. *Box 1112, North Side, tel. 809/947–9055 or for reservations, 800/223–5427. 26 sea lodges, 1 beach villa. Facilities: restaurant, 2 bars, tennis court, diving, fishing and water-sports shop. AE, MC, V. EP. Inexpensive.*

★ **Sunset House.** Low-key and laid-back describe this resort on the ironshore south of George Town. A well-run dive operation, congenial staff, popular bar, and excellent seafood restaurant, Seaharvest, make this resort a favorite with divers. The relaxed atmosphere on the deck in the evening makes it a great place for meeting people. All rooms are air-conditioned and have a phone and radio. Some also have ceiling fans, and minirefrigerators are available upon request for $5 a day. Full dive services include free waterside lockers, two- and three-tank dives to the eastern end of the island, and a U/W photo center. *Box 479, S. Church St., tel. 809/949–7111 or 800/854–4767, fax 809/949–7101. 57 rooms, 2 suites. Facilities: restaurant, bar, dive shop, U/W photo center, dive packages, pool, whirlpool, gift shop. AE, D, DC, MC, V. EP, BP, MAP. Inexpensive.*

Cayman Brac **Brac Reef Beach Resort.** Designed, built, and owned by Bracker Linton Tibbets, the resort lures divers and vacationers who come to savor the special ambience of this tiny island. The recently (1990) renovated rooms, air-conditioning, pool, beach, snorkeling, guest bicycles, and waterside two-story covered deck are additional reasons to stay here. The modest all-inclusive package rates here include three buffet meals daily, all drinks, airport transfers, and taxes and service charges. There's even an all-inclusive dive package. *Box 56, Cayman Brac, tel. 809/948–7323 or 800/327–3835, fax 809/948–7207. 40 rooms. Facilities: restaurant, 2 bars, pool, Jacuzzi, beach, dive shop, lighted tennis court, bicycles. AE, MC, V. EP, MAP, FAP, All-inclusive. Inexpensive–Moderate.*

Divi Tiara Beach Resort. This resort is dedicated to divers and has an excellent new diving facility. At press time, refurbishment of the guest rooms was still under way, with all 28 rooms in the west wing completed and cable TVs installed in most rooms. We recommend asking for a renovated room (these have new bedspreads, curtains, and paint), although all of the rooms feature tile floors, louvered windows, and balconies. A number of rooms also have an ocean view. The 12 Club Divi time-share apartments are also scheduled for renovations. *Box 238, Cayman Brac, tel. 809/948–7553; in the U.S., 800/FOR–DIVI; fax 809/948–7316. 70 rooms. Facilities: restaurant, bar, pool, Jacuzzi, tennis, dive operation, water-sports center, fishing. AE, MC, V. EP. Inexpensive–Moderate.*

Little Cayman **Pirates Point Resort.** A 1993 renovation of this comfortably informal
★ beach resort included the addition of four large air-conditioned rooms and two duplex cabins to the six octagonal units—all located a few minutes from the airstrip. Rooms feature tiled floors, white wicker furnishings, ceiling fans, louvered windows, and tropical colors. Owner Gladys Howard, a native Texan, leads nature walks and is a cordon bleu chef. "Relaxing" rates include only the mouthwatering meals and wine; all-inclusive rates include meals, wine, dives, fishing, and picnics on uninhabited Owen Island. Sunset wine-and-cheese parties are held weekly on the beachside dock. *Little Cayman, tel. 809/948–4210 or 800/654–7537, fax 809/948–4610. 10 rooms, 2 cabins. Facilities: restaurant, dive operation, fishing. No credit cards. FAP, All–inclusive. Very Expensive.*

Southern Cross Club. Three family-style meals a day are included in the rates at this relaxing retreat that caters to fishers and divers. The rooms, which are not air-conditioned, have a simple white-on-white decor with wicker furniture and ceiling fans. The draw here is the excellent diving and fishing, with deep-sea fishing, fly fishing, light-tackle fishing, bottom fishing, and bone-fishing offered. You're on a pretty beach here, with good views. A motorboat makes trips to uninhabited Owen Island nearby. *Little Cayman, tel. 809/948–3255; in the U.S., 317/636–9501; fax 317/636–9503. 10 rooms. Facilities: dining on premises, diving, fishing, bird-watching in sanctuary. No credit cards. FAP. Very Expensive.*

Sam McCoy's Diving and Fishing Lodge. Be prepared for an ultracasual experience: This is really a large, ordinary family house with very simple bedrooms and baths. There's no bar or restaurant per se; guests just eat at a few tables outdoors or with Sam and his family. Fans like it for its owner's infectious good nature, the superb diving and snorkeling right offshore, and the family atmosphere. "Relaxing" rates include three meals a day and airport transfers; all-inclusive rates also include beach and boat diving. *Little Cayman, tel. 809/948–4526 or 800/626–0496, fax 809/949–6821. 6 rooms. No credit cards. FAP, All–inclusive. Expensive–Very Expensive.*

★ **Little Cayman Beach Resort.** This two-story property, on the south side of the island, opened in early 1993. Considerably less rustic than those of other Little Cayman resorts, the 32 air-conditioned, water-view rooms here have modern furnishings in pastel tropical colors, tile floors, and satellite TVs. The formal dining room overlooking the pool and bar area seats 50 for family-style buffet meals. Double hammocks are slung on the two-story pier. The resort offers diving and fishing packages and also caters to bird-watchers and soft adventure ecotourists. Paddleboats, Windsurfers, a complete dive operation, tennis, and free bicycles provided for exploring the island keep guests busy. All-inclusive packages are available for both divers and nondivers and include three meals daily, all alcoholic and soft drinks, airport transfers, taxes, and gratuities. *Blossom Village, Little Cayman, tel. 809/948–4533 or 800/327–3835, fax 809/ 948–4507. 32 rooms. Facilities: bar/restaurant, dive shop, pool, Jacuzzi, tennis court, gift shop, deep-sea fishing charters, bicycles, dive packages available. AE, MC, V. EP, MAP, FAP, All-inclusive. Inexpensive.*

Condominiums and Villas The **Cayman Islands Department of Tourism** provides a complete list of condominiums and small rental apartments in the Inexpensive to Moderate range. Rates are higher during the winter season, so check before you book. **Hospitality World Ltd.** (tel. 800/232–1034 or 809/949–8098) has daily and weekly condominium rentals for one to six people starting from $150 a day in summer and $265 a day in winter. **Cayman Villas** (Box 681, Grand Cayman, tel. 809/947–4144) can help you locate a rental house or cottage. **Reef House Ltd. Property Management** (Box 1540, Grand Cayman, tel. 809/949–7093) also rents villas, houses, and apartments on all three islands.

Nightlife

Each of the island hot spots attracts a different clientele. The **Holiday Inn** (tel. 809/947–4444) offers something for everyone: **Coconuts** (tel. 809/947–5757), the hotel's original comedy club, features young American stand-up comedians who entertain year-round every Wednesday through Sunday. Crowds also gather poolside, where the island-famous "Barefoot Man" sings and plays four nights a week. Dancing is spontaneous and welcome, and it's a great spot to people-watch. Free karaoke sing-alongs are held Wednesday through Friday nights in the hotel's **Ten Sails Lounge.**

Silver's Nightclub (tel. 809/949–7777), at the Ramada Treasure Island Resort, is a spacious, tiered club that is usually filled to capacity on Monday nights when *CMX-5*, one of the island's top bands, plays there. Other acts perform from Tuesday through Saturday. The **BWI Comedy Zone** (tel. 809/949–0088), at the Radisson Resort Grand Cayman, features stand-up comedians from the United States every Wednesday through Sunday. **Island Rock Nightclub** (Falls Shopping Center, tel. 809/947–5366), a popular disco and bar, features live bands some nights.

For current entertainment, look at the freebie magazine *What's Hot*, which gives listings of music, movies, theater, and other entertainment possibilities.

9 Curaçao

Updated by
Jordan
Simon

Thirty-five miles north of Venezuela and 42 miles east of Aruba is Curaçao, the largest of the islands in the Netherlands Antilles. The sun smiles down on Curaçao, but it never gets stiflingly hot: The gentle trade winds refresh. Water sports attract enthusiasts from all over the world, and some of the best reef diving is here. Though the island claims 38 beaches, Curaçao does not have long stretches of sand or enchanting scenery. The island is dominated by an arid countryside, rocky coves, and a sprawling capital situated around a natural harbor. Until recently, the island's economy was based not on tourism but on oil refining and catering to offshore corporations seeking tax hedges. Although tourism has become a major economic force in the past five years, with millions of dollars invested in restoring old colonial landmarks and modernizing hotels, the atmosphere on the island remains comparatively low-key—offering an appealing alternative to the commercialism found on many other Caribbean islands.

As seen from the Otrabanda of Willemstad by the first-time visitor, Curaçao's "face" will be a surprise—spiffy rows of pastel-colored town houses that look as though they were transplanted from Holland. Although the gabled roofs and red tiles show a Dutch influence, the absurdly gay colors of the facades, as novelist Christopher Isherwood once described them, are peculiar to Curaçao. It is said that the first governor of Curaçao developed a terrible allergy to the color white (it gave him migraines), so all the houses were painted in colors. The dollhouse look of the *landhuizen* (plantation houses) makes a cheerful contrast to the stark cacti and the austere shrubbery dotting the countryside.

The history books still cannot agree on who discovered Curaçao—one school of thought believes it was Alonzo de Ojeda, another says it was Amerigo Vespucci—but they seem to agree that it was around 1499. The first Spanish settlers arrived in 1527. In 1634, the Dutch came via the Netherlands West India Company. They promptly shipped off the Spaniards and the few remaining Indians—survivors of the battles for ownership of the island, famine, and disease—to Venezuela. Eight years later, Peter Stuyvesant began his rule as governor, which lasted until he left for New York around 1645. Twelve Jewish families arrived from Amsterdam in 1651 and built a synagogue; today, it is the oldest synagogue still in use in the Western Hemisphere. Over the years, the city built massive fortresses to defend itself against French and British invasions—many of those ramparts now house unusual restaurants and hotels. The Dutch claim to Curaçao was finally recognized in 1815 by the Treaty of Paris. In 1954, Curaçao became an autonomous part of the Kingdom of the Netherlands, with an elected parliament and island council. It is ruled by a governor appointed by the queen.

Today Curaçao's population is derived from more than 50 nationalities blending together in an exuberant mix of Latin, European, and African roots and a Babel of tongues, resulting in a legacy of superb restaurants and an active cultural scene. The island is known for its religious tolerance, and tourists are warmly welcomed.

Before You Go

Tourist
Information
Contact the **Curaçao Tourist Office** (400 Madison Ave., New York, NY 10017, tel. 212/751–8266 or 800/332–8266, and at 330 Biscayne Blvd., Suite 330, Miami, FL 33132, tel. 305/374–5811) for information.

Arriving and Departing
By Plane

ALM (tel. 800/327–7230) has 4 nonstop and 10 direct flights a week from Miami and 4 direct flights a week from Atlanta. For Atlanta departures, ALM has connecting services (throughfares) to most U.S. gateways with Delta. This arrangement makes ALM Curaçao's major carrier. ALM uses Curaçao as its hub to fly to Aruba, Bonaire, Caracas, Trinidad, Puerto Rico, and St. Maarten. ALM also offers a Visit Caribbean Pass, allowing easy interisland travel. **Air Aruba** (tel. 800/882–7822) has direct flights to Curaçao (flights make brief stops in Aruba) from both Miami and Newark airports. Air Aruba also has regularly scheduled service from Curaçao to Aruba and Bonaire. Every Saturday, **Key Air** (tel. 800/786–2386) offers connecting flights from Chicago, Baltimore/Washington, DC, Newark, Philadelphia, and Boston into its hub in Savannah, Georgia, for a nonstop flight into Curaçao.

Passports and Visas

U.S. and Canadian citizens traveling to Curaçao need only proof of citizenship and a valid photo ID. A voter's registration card or a notarized birth certificate (not a photocopy) will suffice—a driver's license will *not*. British citizens must produce a passport. All visitors must show an ongoing or return ticket.

Language

Dutch is the official language, but the vernacular is Papiamento—a mixture of Dutch, Portuguese, Spanish, and English. Developed during the 18th century by Africans, Papiamento evolved in Curaçao as the mode of communication between landowners and their slaves. These days, however, English, as well as Spanish, and, of course, Dutch, are studied by schoolchildren. Anyone involved with tourism—shopkeepers, restaurateurs, and museum guides—speaks English.

Precautions

Mosquitoes on Curaçao do not seem as vicious and bloodthirsty as they do on Aruba and Bonaire, but that doesn't mean they don't exist. To be safe, keep perfume to the minimum, be prepared to use insect repellent before dining alfresco, and spray your hotel room at night—especially if you've opened a window.

If you plan to go into the water, beware of long-spined sea urchins, which can cause pain if you come in contact with them.

Do not eat any of the little green applelike fruits of the manchineel tree: They're poisonous. In fact, steer clear of the trees altogether; raindrops or dewdrops dripping off the leaves can blister your skin. If contact does occur, rinse the affected area with water and, in extreme cases, get medical attention. Usually, the burning sensation won't last longer than two hours.

Staying in Curaçao

Important Addresses

Tourist Information: The **Curaçao Tourism Development Foundation** has three offices on the island where multilingual guides are ready to answer questions. You can also pick up maps, brochures, and a copy of *Curaçao Holiday*. The main office is located in Willemstad at Pietermaai No. 19 (tel. 599/9–616000); other offices are in the Waterfort Arches (tel. 599/9–613397), across from the Van Der Valk Plaza Hotel, and at the airport (tel. 599/9–686789).

Emergencies

Police or **fire:** tel. 114. The **main police station** number is 599/9–611000. **Hospitals:** For medical emergencies, call **St. Elisabeth's Hospital** (tel. 599/9–624900) or an ambulance (tel. 112). **Pharmacies: Botica Popular** (Madurostraat 15, tel. 599/9–611269), or ask at your hotel for the nearest one.

Currency U.S. dollars—in cash or traveler's checks—are accepted nearly everywhere, so there's no need to worry about exchanging money. However, you may need small change for pay phones, cigarettes, or soda machines. The currency in the Netherlands Antilles is the guilder, or florin, as it is also called, indicated by an fl. or NAf. on price tags. The U.S. dollar is considered very stable; the official rate of exchange at press time was NAfl.78 to U.S. $1. Note: Prices quoted here are in U.S. dollars unless indicated otherwise.

Taxes and Service Charges Hotels collect a 7% government tax and add a 12% service charge to the bill; restaurants add 10%–15%. The airport departure tax is U.S. $10 ($5.75 for Bonaire).

Guided Tours You don't really need a guide to show you downtown Willemstad— it's an easy taxi or bus ride from most major hotels and small enough for a self-conducted walking tour (follow the one outlined in the free tourist booklet *Curaçao Holiday*). The Curaçao Museum (tel. 599/9–623777) conducts architectural and historical walking tours of the town Wednesday and Thursday afternoons starting at Brionplein for $5.75 a person (a drink at a typical bar is included). To see the rest of the island, however, a guided tour can save you time and energy, though it is easy to cover the island yourself in a rented car. Most hotels have tour desks where arrangements can be made with reputable tour operators. For very personal, amiable service, try **Casper Tours** (tel. 599/9–653010 or 599/9–616789). For $25 per person, you'll be escorted around the island in an air-conditioned van, with stops at the Juliana Bridge, the salt lakes, Knip Bay for a swim, the grotto at Boca Tabla, and lunch at Jaanchi Christiaan's, which is famous for its native cuisine. **Taber Tours** (tel. 599/9–376637) offers a 3½-hour city and country tour ($10) that includes visits to the Curaçao Liqueur Factory, the Curaçao Museum, and the Bloempot shopping center. A full-day tour includes a visit to the Seaquarium and a snorkel trip; it costs $25 per person. Taber Tours also offers a two-hour sunset cruise ($29.50 for adults and $20 for children) with a feast of French bread, cheese, and wine. A day trip to Aruba or Bonaire is also available. **Curven Tours** (tel. 599/9–379806) offers island tours and special packages to Venezuela.

Getting Around
Taxis Taxi drivers have an official tariff chart, with fares from the airport vicinity running about $10–$15 to Willemstad and the nearby beach hotels. Taxis tend to be moderately priced, but since there are no meters, you should confirm the fare with the driver before departure. There is an additional 25% surcharge after 11 PM. Taxis are readily available at hotels; in other cases, call Central Dispatch at tel. 599/9–616711.

Rental Cars You can rent a car from **Budget** (tel. 599/9–683420), **Avis** (tel. 599/9–681163), or **National Car Rental** (tel. 599/9–683489) at the airport or have it delivered free to your hotel. A typical rate is about $46 a day for a Toyota Starlet to about $73 for a four-door sedan. The least expensive car-rental companies at press time were **Love Car Rental** (tel. 599/9–690444) and **Dollar** (tel. 599/9–690262). Their prices range from $33 for a Starlet to $50 for a four-door sedan. Off-season prices are about $25 a day. If you're planning to do country driving or rough it through Christoffel Park, a Jeep is best. All you'll need is a valid U.S. or Canadian driver's license. Scooters ($20), mopeds ($15), and bikes ($12.50) can be rented from **Easy Going** (tel. 599/9–695056).

Telephones and Mail Phone service through the hotel operators in Curaçao is slow, but direct-dial service, both on-island and to the United States, is fast and clear. Hotel operators will put the call through for you, but if you make a collect call, do check immediately afterward that the hotel does not charge you as well. To call Curaçao direct, dial 011–599–9 plus the number in Curaçao. To place a local call on the island, dial the six-digit local number. An airmail letter to anywhere in the world costs NAf2.50, a postcard NAf1.25.

Opening and Closing Times Most shops are open Monday–Saturday 8–noon and 2–6. Banks are open weekdays 8:00–3:30.

Exploring Curaçao

Numbers in the margin correspond to points of interest on the Curaçao map.

Willemstad The capital city, **Willemstad,** is a favorite cruise stop for two rea-
❶ sons: The shopping is considered among the best in the Caribbean, and a quick tour of most of the downtown sights can be managed within a six-block radius. Santa Anna Bay slices the city down the middle: On one side is the Punda, and on the other is the Otrabanda (literally, the "other side"). Think of the Punda as the side for tourists, crammed with shops, restaurants, monuments, and markets. Otrabanda is less touristy, with lots of narrow winding streets full of private homes notable for their picturesque gables and Dutch-influenced designs.

There are three ways to make the crossing from one side to the other: (1) drive or take a taxi over the Juliana Bridge, (2) traverse the Queen Emma Pontoon Bridge on foot, or (3) ride the free ferry, which runs when the bridge is open for passing ships. All the major hotels outside of town offer free shuttle service to town twice daily. Shuttles coming from the Otrabanda side leave you at Rif Fort. From there it's a short walk north to the foot of the Pontoon Bridge. Shuttles coming from the Punda side leave you near the main entrance to Fort Amsterdam.

Our walking tour of Willemstad starts at the **Queen Emma Bridge,** affectionately called the Lady by the natives. During the hurricane season in 1988, the 700-foot floating bridge practically floated right out to sea; it was later taken down for major reconstruction. If you're standing on the Otrabanda side, take a few moments to scan Curaçao's multicolored "face" on the other side of Santa Anna Bay. If you wait long enough, the bridge will swing open (at least 30 times a day) to let the seagoing ships pass through. The original bridge, built in 1888, was the brainchild of the American consul Leonard Burlington Smith, who made a mint off the tolls he charged for the bridge. Initially, the charge was 2¢ per person for those wearing shoes, free to those crossing barefoot. Today it's free to everyone.

Take a breather at the peak of the bridge and look north to the 1,625-foot-long **Queen Juliana Bridge,** completed in 1974 and standing 200 feet above water. That's the bridge you drive over to cross to the other side of the city, and although the route is time-consuming (and more expensive if you're going by taxi), the view from this bridge is worth it. At every hour of the day, the sun casts a different tint over the city, creating an ever-changing panorama; the nighttime view, rivaling Rio's, is breathtaking.

When you cross the Pontoon Bridge and arrive on the Punda side, turn left and walk down the waterfront, along **Handelskade.** You'll soon pass the ferry landing. Now take a close look at the buildings you've seen only from afar; the original red tiles of the roofs came from Europe and arrived on trade ships as ballast.

Walk down to the corner and turn right at the customs building onto Sha Caprileskade. This is the bustling **floating market,** where each morning dozens of Venezuelan schooners arrive laden with tropical fruits and vegetables. Fresh mangoes, papayas, and exotic vegetables vie for space with freshly caught fish and herbs and spices. It's probably too much to ask a tourist to arrive by 6:30 AM, when the buying is best, but there's plenty of action to see throughout the afternoon. Any produce bought here, however, should be thoroughly washed before eating.

Keep walking down Sha Caprileskade. Head toward the Wilhelmina Drawbridge, which connects Punda with the once-flourishing district of **Scharloo,** where the early Jewish merchants first built stately homes. Scharloo is now a red-light district.

If you continue straight ahead, Sha Caprileskade becomes De Ruyterkade. Soon you'll come to the post office, which will be on your left. Behind it is the **Old Market** (Marche). Here you'll find local women preparing hearty Antillean lunches. For $4–$6 you can enjoy such Curaçaon specialties as *funchi* (cornbread), *kesi yena* (Gouda cheese stuffed with meat), goat stew, fried fish, peas and rice, and fried plantains. After lunch, return to the intersection of De Ruyterkade and Columbusstraat and turn left.

Walk up Columbusstraat to the **Mikveh Israel-Emmanuel Synagogue,** founded in 1651 and the oldest temple still in use in the Western Hemisphere. One of the most important sights in Curaçao, it draws 20,000 visitors a year. Enter through the gates around the corner on Hanchi Di Snoa and ask the front office to direct you to the guide on duty. A unique feature is the brilliant white sand covering the synagogue floor, a remembrance of Moses leading his people through the desert and of the Diaspora. The Hebrew letters on the four pillars signify the names of the Four Mothers of Israel: Sarah, Rebecca, Rachel, and Leah. A fascinating museum (tel. 599/9-611633, admission $2) in the back displays Jewish antiques (including a set of circumcision instruments) and artifacts from Jewish families collected from all over the world. The gift shop near the gate has excellent postcards and commemorative medallions. *Hanchi Di Snoa 29, tel. 599/9-611067. Open weekdays 9–11:45 and 2:30–4:45. English and Hebrew services conducted by an American rabbi are held Fri. at 6:30 PM and Sat. at 10 AM. Jacket and tie required.*

Continue down Columbusstraat and cross Wilhelminaplein (Wilhelmina Park). Now you will be in front of the courthouse, with its stately balustrade, and the impressive Georgian facade of the Bank of Boston. The statue keeping watch over the park is of Queen Wilhelmina, a deceased popular monarch of the Netherlands, who gave up her throne to her daughter Juliana after her Golden Jubilee in 1948. Cut back across the park and turn left at Breedestraat, Punda's main street and a window-shopper's delight. Take Breedestraat down to the Pontoon Bridge, then turn left at the waterfront. At the foot of the bridge are the mustard-colored walls of **Fort Amsterdam.** Take a few steps through the archway and enter another century. The entire structure dates from the 1700s, when it was actually the center of the city and the most important fort on the island. Now it houses the governor's residence, the Fort Church, the ministry, and several other government offices. Outside the entrance a series of majestic gnarled *wayaka* trees are fancifully carved with a dragon, giant squid, mermaid, and a portrait of the queen—the work of noted local artist Mac Alberto, who can be seen strolling the streets impeccably garbed in blinding white suits, a

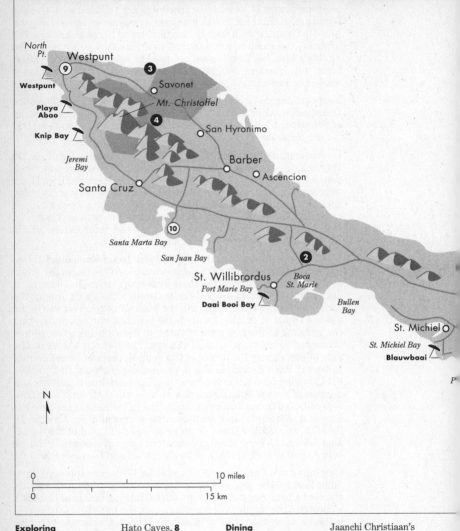

North Pt.

Westpunt

Westpunt

Playa Abao

Knip Bay

9

3

Savonet

Mt. Christoffel

4

San Hyronimo

Jeremi Bay

Barber

Ascencion

Santa Cruz

10

Santa Marta Bay

San Juan Bay

2

St. Willibrordus

Port Marie Bay

Boca St. Marie

Daai Booi Bay

Bullen Bay

St. Michiel

St. Michiel Bay

Blauwbaai

P

N

0   10 miles

0   15 km

Caribbean Sea

Curaçao
International
Airport
❽

Brievengat ❼

Santa
Catarina

St. Joris Bay

Great St. Joris

Little St. Joris

Santa Rosa

Mt. Tafelberg

Ostpunt

Julianadorp

St. Anna
Bay

Bottelier

Brakkeput

⑯

㉓ ㉔

Willemstad

㉚ ㉙

Spanish
Water

⑪

❶

Bapor
Kibra

⑫ ⑬ ⑭

❺

Piscadera
Bay

Jan
Thiel Bay

Caracas
Bay

Santa
Barbara
Beach

Nieuwpoort

❻

㉕ ㉖

⑰ — ㉒

Curaçao Underwater Marine Park

courtly boutonniere in his lapel. Next door is the **Plaza Piar,** dedicated to Manuel Piar, a native Curaçaoan who fought for the independence of Venezuela under the liberator Simon Bolívar. On the other side of the plaza is the **Waterfort,** a bastion dating from 1634. The original cannons are still positioned in the battlements. The foundation, however, now forms the walls of the Van Der Valk Plaza Hotel. Following the sidewalk around the plaza, you'll discover one of the most delightful shopping areas on the island, newly built under the **Waterfort Arches** (*see* Shopping, *below*, for details).

Western Side The road through the village of Soto that leads to the northwest tip of the island winds through landscape that Georgia O'Keefe might have painted—towering cacti, flamboyant dried shrubbery, and aluminum-roof houses. Throughout this *cunucu*, or countryside, you'll see native fishermen hauling in their nets, women pounding cornmeal, and an occasional donkey blocking traffic. Landhouses, large estate houses from centuries past, dot the countryside, though most are closed to the public. Their facades, though, can often be glimpsed from the highway. For a splendid view, and some unusual island tales of ghosts, follow Wespunt Highway to the intersection at Cunucu Abao, then veer left onto Weg Naar San Willibrordo until ❷ you come to **Landhuis Jan Kock** (tel. 599/9–648087), located across from the salt pans. Since the hours are irregular, be sure to call ahead to arrange a tour of this reputedly haunted mid-17th-century house, or stop by on Sunday mornings, when the proprietor occasionally opens the small restaurant behind her home and serves delicious Dutch pancakes. Continuing north on this road, you'll come to the village of Soto. From here the road leads to the northwest tip of the island, where it becomes Wespunt Highway again and heads ❸ south to **Boca Tabla,** where the sea has carved a magnificent grotto. Safely tucked in the back, you can watch and listen to the waves crashing ferociously against the rocks. A short distance farther is ❹ **Christoffel Park,** a fantastic 4,450-acre garden and wildlife preserve with the towering Mt. Christoffel at its center. Open to the public since 1978, the park consists of three former plantations with individual trails that take about 1 to 1½ hours each to traverse. You may drive your own car (heavy-treaded wheels) or rent a Jeep with an accompanying guide($15). Start out early (by 10 AM the park starts to feel like a sauna), and if you're going solo, first study the *Excursion Guide to Christoffel Park* that's sold at the front desk of the elegant if dilapidated Landhuis Savonet; it outlines the various routes and identifies the flora and fauna found here. No matter what route you take, you'll be treated to interesting views of hilly fields full of prickly pear cacti, divi-divi trees, bushy-haired palms, and exotic flowers that bloom unpredictably after April showers. There are also caves—the strong at heart will revel in the rustling of bat wings and the sight of scuttling scorpion spiders (scary but not poisonous)—and ancient Indian drawings.

As you drive through the park, keep a lookout for tiny deer, goats, and other small wildlife that might suddenly dart in front of your car. The whip snakes and minute silver snakes you may encounter are not poisonous. White-tail hawks may be seen on the green route, white orchids and crownlike passion flowers on the yellow route. Climbing the 1,239-foot Mt. Christoffel on foot is an exhilarating experience and a definite challenge to anyone who hasn't grown up scaling the Alps. The guidebook claims the round-trip will take you one hour, and Curaçaoan adolescent boys do make a sport of racing up and down, but the last few feet are deadly. The view from the peak, however, *is* thrilling—a panorama of the island, including

Santa Marta Bay and the tabletop mountain of St. Hironimus. On a clear day, you can even see the mountain ranges of Venezuela, Bonaire, and Aruba. *Savonet, tel. 599/9–640363. Admission: $5 adults, $3 children 6–15. Open Mon.–Sat. 8–5, Sun. 6–3.*

Eastern Side To explore the eastern side of the island, take the coastal road— Martin Luther King Blvd.—out from Willemstad about 2 miles to Bapor Kibra. There you'll find the Seaquarium and the Underwater Park.

❺ The **Curaçao Seaquarium** is *the* place to see the island's underwater treasures without getting your feet wet. In fact, it's the world's only public aquarium where sea creatures are raised and cultivated totally by natural methods. You can spend several hours here, mesmerized by the 46 freshwater tanks full of more than 400 varieties of exotic fish and vegetation found in the waters around Curaçao, including sharks, lobsters, turtles, corals, and sponges. Look out for the over 5-foot-long mascot, Herbie the lugubrious jewfish. Four sea lions from Uruguay are the most recent pride of the aquarium. If you get hungry, stop at the excellent Italian restaurant or the steak house–cum–Mexican eatery. There are also glass-bottom-boat tours, fun feeding shows, and a viewing platform overlooking the wreck of the steamship SS *Oranje Nassau*, which sank in 1906 and now sits in 10 feet of water. A nearby 495-yard man-made beach of white sand is well suited to novice swimmers and children, and bathroom and shower facilities are available. A souvenir shop sells some of the best postcards and coral jewelry on the island. *Tel. 599/9–616666. Admission: $6 adults, $3 children. Open daily 9 AM–10 PM.*

❻ **Curaçao Underwater Marine Park** (tel. 599/9–618131) consists of about 12½ miles of untouched coral reefs that have been granted the status of national park. Mooring buoys have been placed at the most interesting dive sites on the reef to provide safe anchoring and to prevent damage to the reef. The park stretches along the south shore from the Princess Beach Hotel in Willemstad to the eastern tip of the island.

❼ **Landhuis Brievengat** (tel. 599/9–378344) is a 10-minute drive northeast of Willemstad, near the Centro Deportivo sports stadium. On the last Sunday of the month (from 10 AM to 3 PM), this old estate holds an open house with crafts demonstrations and folkloric shows. You can see the original kitchen still intact, the 18-inch-thick walls, fine antiques, and the watchtowers once used for lovers' trysts. The restaurant, which is open only on Wednesday and Friday, serves a fine *rijstaffel* (Indonesian smorgasbord). Every Friday night a party is held on the wide wraparound terrace, with two bands and plenty to drink.

Head northwest toward the airport (take a right onto Gosieweg, follow the loop right onto Schottegatweg, take another right onto Jan Norduynweg, a final right onto Rooseveltweg, and follow the signs)
❽ to the island's newest attraction, **Hato Caves.** Hour-long guided tours wind down into the various chambers to the water pools, voodoo chamber, wishing well, fruit bats' sleeping quarters, and Curaçao Falls, where a stream of silver joins with a stream of gold (they're colored by lights) and is guarded by a limestone "dragon" perched nearby. Hidden lights illuminate the limestone formations and gravel walkways. One of the better Caribbean caves open to the public. *Tel. 599/9–680378. Admission: $4.25 adults, $2.75 children. Open Tues.–Sun. 10 AM–5 PM. Closed Mon.*

Curaçao for Free

Located on Salina Arriba, in the Landhouse Chobolobo, the **Senior Liqueur Factory** (tel. 599/9–613526) distills and distributes the original Curaçao liqueur. Don't expect to find a massive factory—it's just a small showroom in the open-air foyer of a beautiful 17th-century landhouse. There are no guides, but you can read the story of the distillation process on posters, and you'll be graciously offered samples in various flavors. If you're interested in buying—the orange-flavored chocolate liqueur is fantastic over ice cream—you can choose from a complete selection, which is bottled in a variety of fascinating shapes, including Dutch ceramic houses.

The **Amstel Brewery Tours** (Blvd. Rijkseenheid, Salina, tel. 599/9–612944) offer insights into the world's only beer made from distilled seawater. Free tours (followed by all-you-can-drink beer tastings) are held every Tuesday and Thursday morning at 10 AM. *Closed June 15–Aug. 6.*

What to See and Do with Children

The **Curaçao Seaquarium,** *see* Exploring, *above.*

Beaches

Curaçao has some 38 beaches, but unfortunately many are extremely rocky and litter-strewn. The best way to find "your" beach is to rent a Jeep, motor scooter, or heavy-treaded car. Ask your hotel to pack a picnic basket for you and go exploring. Getting lost and ending up in some undiscovered cove is half the fun. Curaçao doesn't have Aruba's long, powdery stretches of sand; instead, you'll discover the joy of inlets: tiny bay openings to the sea marked by craggy cliffs, exotic trees, and scads of interesting pebbles. Imagine a beach that's just big enough for your party of four—or a party of just two. Beware of thorns and keep an eye out for flying fish. They propel their tails through the water until they reach a speed of 44 mph, then spread their fins and soar.

Hotels with the best beach properties include the new **Sonesta Beach Hotel** (impressively long), the **Princess Beach** (impressively sensuous), and the **Coral Cliff Resort** (impressively deserted). No matter which hotel you're staying at, beach hopping to other hotels can be fun. Nonguests are supposed to pay the hotels a beach fee, but often there is no one to collect.

One of the largest, more spectacular, beaches on Curaçao is **Blauwbaai** (Blue Bay). There's plenty of white sand and lots of shady places, showers, and changing facilities, but since it's a private beach, you'll pay an entrance fee of about $2.50 per car. Take the road that leads past the Holiday Beach Hotel and the Curaçao Caribbean north toward Julianadorp. At the end of the stretch of straight road, a sign will instruct you to bear left for Blauwbaai and the fishing village of St. Michiel. The latter is a good place for diving.

Starting from the church of St. Willibrordus, signs will direct you to **Daai Booi Bay,** a sandy shore dotted with thatched shelters. The road to this public beach is a small paved highway flanked on either side by thick lush trees and huge organ-pipe cacti. The beach is curved, with shrubbery rooted into the side of the rocky cliffs—a great place for swimming.

Knip Bay has two parts: Big (Groot) Knip and Little (Kleine) Knip. Only Little Knip is shaded with trees, but these are manchineels, so steer clear of them. Also beware of cutting your feet on beer bottle caps. Both beaches have alluring white sand, but only Big Knip has changing facilities. Big Knip also has several tiki huts for shade and calm turquoise waters that are perfect for swimming and lounging. The protected cove, flanked by sheer cliffs, is usually a blast on Sundays, when there is live music. To get there, take the road to the Knip Landhouse, then turn right. Signs will direct you.

Playa Forti, just south of Westpunt (the island's northwest point), is a double cove of beige sand with a splendid view of Westpunt Church, colorful fishing boats bobbing in the turquoise water, and a little café in the shade where you can watch local boys dive from the cliffs on weekends.

Playa Lagun, farther southeast, is dotted with powder blue camping huts and caught between towering gunmetal gray cliffs. Cognoscenti know this is one of the best places to snorkel—you may even go nose to nose with the resident giant squid.

To reach **Santa Barbara,** a popular family beach on the eastern tip, you'll drive through one of Curaçao's toniest neighborhoods, Spanish Water, where gleaming white yachts replace humble fishing fleets. The beach has changing facilities and a snack bar but charges a small admission fee, usually around $3.35 per car. Around the bend, **Caracas Bay** is a popular dive site, with a sunken ship so close to the surface that snorkelers can balance their flippers on the helm.

Sports and the Outdoors

Golf Visitors are welcome to play golf at the **Curaçao Golf and Squash Club** (tel. 599/9–373590) in Emmastad. The nine-hole course offers a challenge because of the stiff trade winds and the sand greens. *Open 8–12:30.*

Horseback Riding **Ashari's Ranch** (tel. 599/9–686254) is the only stable to offer romps to the beach ($15 an hour).

Jogging The **Rif Recreation Area,** locally known as the *corredor*, stretches from the water plant at Mundo Nobo to the Curaçao Caribbean Hotel along the sea. It consists of more than 1.2 miles of palm-lined beachfront, a wading pond, and a jogging track with an artificial surface, as well as a big playground. There is good security and street lighting along the entire length of the beachfront.

Sailing **Sail Curaçao** (Yachtclub Asiento, Spanish Water, tel. 599/9–676003) offers day sails, sailing instruction, snorkeling trips and windsurfing.

Tennis Most hotels (including Sonesta Beach, Curaçao Caribbean, Las Palmas, Princess Beach, and Holiday Beach) offer well-paved courts, illuminated for day and night games.

Water Sports Curaçao has facilities for all kinds of water sports, thanks to the government-sponsored **Curaçao Underwater Marine Park** (tel. 599/9–618131), which includes almost a third of the island's southern diving waters. Scuba divers and snorkelers can enjoy more than 12½ miles of protected reefs and shores, with normal visibility from 60 to 80 feet (up to 150 feet on good days). With water temperatures ranging from 75° to 82°F, wet suits are generally unnecessary. No coral collecting, spearfishing, or littering is allowed. An exciting wreck to explore is the SS *Oranje Nassau*, which ran aground over 80 years ago and now hosts hundreds of exotic fish and unusually shaped coral.

Most hotels either offer their own program of water sports or will be happy to make arrangements for you. An introductory scuba resort course usually runs about $50–$65.

Underwater Curaçao (tel. 599/9–618131) offers complete vacation/dive packages in conjunction with the Lions Dive Hotel & Marina. Its fully stocked dive shop, located between the Lions Dive Hotel and the Curaçao Seaquarium, offers equipment for both sale and rental. Personal instruction and group lessons are conducted on state-of-the art dive boats personally designed by "Dutch" Schrier. One dive will run you $33; dive-only packages are available. Take a dive/snorkeling trip on the *Coral Sea*, a 40-foot twin diesel yacht-style dive boat. Landlubbers can see beneath the sea aboard *The Coral View*, a monohull flat-top glass-bottom boat that makes four excursions a day. *Seaworld Explorer* (tel. 599/9–6044892) is a semi-submarine that leaves from the Seaquarium dock.

Seascape (tel. 599/9–625000, ext. 177), at the Curaçao Caribbean Hotel, specializes in snorkeling and scuba-diving trips to reefs and underwater wrecks in every type of water vehicle—from pedal boats and water scooters to waterskis and Windsurfers. A six-dive package costs $155 and includes unlimited beach diving plus one free night dive. Snorkeling gear costs about $5 an hour or $10 a day to rent. Die-hard fishermen with companions who prefer to suntan will enjoy the day trip to Little Curaçao, the "clothes optional" island between Curaçao and Bonaire, where the fish are reputed to be lively: Plan on $25 per person. Deep-sea fishing for a maximum of six people can also be arranged; it costs $300 for a half day, $500 for a full day.

Peter Hughes Diving (tel. 599/9–367888, ext. 5047) at the Princess Beach Hotel rents equipment and conducts diving and snorkeling trips. Also available is a cabin cruiser for half-day ($200) or full-day ($500) deep-sea fishing excursions.

For windsurfing, check out the **Curaçao High Wind Center** (Princess Beach Hotel, tel. 599/9–614944). Lessons cost $20 an hour.

Coral Cliff Diving (tel. 599/9–642822) offers scuba certification courses ($320), a one-week windsurfing school ($170), a one-week basic sailing course ($255), and a full schedule of dive and snorkeling trips to Curaçao's southwest coast. It also rents pedal boats, Hobie Cats, and underwater cameras.

Spectator Sports Soccer matches and baseball games, from March through October, are held in the modern and comfortable **Centro Deportivo** stadium, located about 10 minutes from town at Bonamweg 49. *Tel. 599/9–376620. Open daily 9:30–12:30 and 3–6.*

Shopping

Curaçao has long enjoyed the reputation of having some of the best shops in the Caribbean, but don't expect posh Madison Avenue boutiques. With a few exceptions (such as Benetton, which recently moved into the Caribbean with a vengeance), the quality of women's fashions here lies along the lines of sales racks.

If you're looking for bargains on Swiss watches, cameras, crystal, perfumes, or electronic equipment, do some comparison shopping back home and come armed with a list of prices. Willemstad is no longer a free port.

Shopping Areas Most of the shops are concentrated in **Willemstad's Punda** within about a six-block area. The main shopping streets are **Heerenstraat, Breedestraat,** and **Madurostraat. Heerenstraat** and **Gomezplein** are pedestrian malls, closed to traffic, and their roadbeds have been raised to sidewalk level and covered with pink inlaid tiles.

The hippest shopping area lies under the **Waterfort Arches,** along with a variety of restaurants and bars. Our two favorite shops under the arches are **Bamali** (tel. 599/9–612258), which sells Indonesian batik clothing, leather bags, and charming handicrafts, and **Clarisa & Laura Kemper** (tel. 599/9–618313), which specializes in exquisite leather and silk creations.

Good Buys **Julius L. Penha & Sons** (Heerenstraat 1, tel. 599/9–612266), in front of the Pontoon Bridge, sells French perfumes, Hummel figurines, linen from Madeira, delftware, and handbags from Argentina, Italy, and Spain. The store also has an extensive cosmetics counter. **Boolchand's** (Heerenstraat 4B, tel. 599/9–616233) handles an interesting variety of merchandise behind a facade of red-and-white checked tiles. Stock up here on French perfumes, British cashmere sweaters, Italian silk ties, Dutch dolls, Swiss watches, and Japanese cameras.

Clothing **Benetton** (Madurostraat 4, tel. 599/9–614619) has winter stock in July and summer stock in December; both stocks are 20% off the retail price. **Crazy Look** (Madurostraat 6, tel. 599/9–611440) has French, Italian, and Dutch fashions with a hip Eurotrash look, as well as trendy sweatshirts and baggy pants. **Boutique Liska** (Schottegatweg Oost 191-A, tel. 599/9–613111) is where local residents shop for smart women's fashions. **Boutique Aquarius** (Breedestraat 9, tel. 599/9–612618) sells Fendi merchandise for 25% less than in the United States. Fendi fanatics can stock up on belts, shoes, pocketbooks, wallets, and even watches. If you've always longed for Dutch clogs, try **Clog Dance** (De Rouvilleweg 9B, tel. 599/ 9–623280).

Delicacies **Toko Zuikertuintje** (Zuikertuintjeweg, tel. 599/9–370188), a supermarket built on the original 17th-century Zuikertuintje Landhuis, is where most of the local elite shop. Enjoy the free tea and coffee while you stock up on all sorts of European and Dutch delicacies. Shopping here for a picnic is a treat in itself.

Jewelry/ Watches The leading jewelers in the Netherlands Antilles, **Spritzer & Fuhrmann** (Gomezplein 1, tel. 599/9–612600), carries gold jewelry, watches, French crystal, diamonds, emeralds, and china.

La Zahav N.V. (Curaçao International Airport, tel. 599/9–689594) is one of the best places to buy gold jewelry—with or without diamonds, rubies, and emeralds—at true discount prices. The shop is located in the airport transit hall, just at the top of the staircase.

Linens **New Amsterdam** (Gomezplein 14, tel. 599/9–613823) is the place to price hand-embroidered tablecloths, napkins, and pillowcases.

Local Crafts Native crafts and curios are on hand at **Fundason Obra di Man** (Bargestraat 57, tel. 599/9–612413). Particularly impressive are the posters of Curaçao's architecture. **Black Coral** (Princess Beach Hotel, tel. 599/9–614944) is owned by Dutch-born artisan Bert Knubben, one of Curaçao's true characters. For the past 30 years, he's been designing and sculpting the most exciting black-coral jewelry in the Caribbean—and he even dives for the coral himself, with special permission from the government. Dolphin pendants and twiglike earrings finished in 14-karat gold are excellent buys. Call before you drop by. Artisans with disabilities at **Landhuis Groot**

Santa Martha (tel. 599/9–641950) fashion handicrafts of varying types. **Arawak Clay Products** (Cruise Terminal, Otrabanda, tel. 599/9–627249) has a factory showroom of native-made crafts. You can purchase a variety of tiles, plates, pots, and tiny replicas of landhouses. **Gallery 86** (tel. 599/9–613417), in the Bloksteeg (Punda) opposite the Bank of the Netherlands Antilles, features the works of local artists and occasionally those of South Americans and Africans.

Dining

Restaurateurs in Curaçao believe in whetting appetites with a variety of cuisines and intriguing ambience: Dine under the boughs of magnificent old trees, in the romantic gloom of wine cellars in renovated landhouses, or on the ramparts of 18th-century forts. Curacaoans partake of some of the best Indonesian food in the Caribbean, and they also find it hard to resist the French, Swiss, Dutch, and Swedish delights. Dress in restaurants is almost always casual, but if you feel like putting on your finery, there will always be a place for you. Do take a wrap or a light sweater with you—for some reason, most restaurants have their air conditioners going full blast.

Highly recommended restaurants are indicated by a star ★

Category	Cost*
Very Expensive	over $40
Expensive	$30–$40
Moderate	$15–$30
Inexpensive	under $15

per person, excluding drinks and service charge

★ **De Taveerne.** From the intricate detail of its antiques and brickwork to its impressive Continental menu, this restaurant is the most elegant, romantic spot on the island. Dining is in the whitewashed wine cellar of this magnificent renovated octagonal country estate, built in the 1800s by an exiled Venezuelan revolutionary. The best appetizer is the salmon carpaccio with laurel bay dressing en brioche. The entrées are as rich and decadent as the ambience: velvety lobster bisque finished with armagnac, sautéed goose liver in plum sauce, and smoked eel with horseradish. For dessert, there's the absolutely unforgettable broiled pears, topped with vanilla ice cream and drenched with Curaçao chocolate liqueur. *Landhuis Groot Davelaar, on Silena, near the Promenade Shopping Center, tel. 599/9–370669. Reservations required. AE, DC, MC, V. Closed Sun. Very Expensive.*

Bistro Le Clochard. A romantic gem, the bistro is built into the 18th-century Rif Fort and is suffused with the cool, dark atmosphere of ages past—an oasis of arched entryways, exposed brickwork, wood beams, and lace curtains. The use of fresh ingredients in the consistently well-prepared French and Swiss dishes makes dining here a dream, though a pricey one. Try the fresh-fish platters or the tender veal in mushroom sauce. The chef is especially adroit at preparing game: Try the wild boar cutlet in honey and sesame. Savor the fondue and let yourself get carried away by the unusual setting; just save room for the chocolate mousse. Try not to go on weekends, when an inexplicably hokey duo regales diners with a violin and jarring electric piano. *On the Otrabanda Rif Fort, tel. 599/9–625666.*

Reservations required. AE, DC, MC, V. Closed Sat. for lunch and Sun. off-season. Expensive–Very Expensive.

★ **L'Alouette.** With only eight tables, this cozy space defines intimate. Tasteful touches include fanciful stemware, art deco lamps, and severe black and white tables that provide a stunning contrast to the peach walls and voluminous lushly folded drapery. Maria Eugenia Saban's cooking is equally subtle and sophisticated, wonderfully textured; everything is lovingly prepared and slow-cooked in its own juices. You might begin with two cheese flans (goat cheese–leek and gruyere-mushroom), perfectly complemented by a tomato sauce perfumed with basil or a seafood sausage in lobster velouté. Your entrée might be the sublime salmon in lime and *ciboulette* (chive) sauce. Maria is an amateur chef in the best sense of the word: she cooks because she loves it. Her exquisite presentations and creative counterpoints can't fail to seduce even the most discriminating palate. *Orionweg 12, tel. 599/9–618222. Reservations suggested. AE, DC, MC, V. Closed Sun. Expensive–Very Expensive.*

Fort Nassau Restaurant. This is *the* place from which to witness the twinkling magic of Curaçao at night. High on a hilltop overlooking Willemstad, the restaurant is built into an 18th-century fort and gives a 360-degree view of the city's rooftops. Go for a drink in the breezy, couple-filled Battery Terrace bar or dine in air-conditioned civility in front of the huge bay windows. The view is superb. The menu is diverse, from duck with a molasses sauce to lightly broiled fish (ask the waiter what's fresh—and not on the menu), but the price that you pay is more for the views and ambience. Avoid the enticing yet overly complex stabs at innovative cuisine, such as roast hare in sesame oil drizzled with star anise sauce, the simple selections are the best here. *Near Juliana Bridge, tel. 599/9–613086. Reservations required. AE, DC, MC, V. Expensive.*

La Pergola. Built into the stuccoed walls of the Waterfort, with huge picture windows fronting the rambunctious sea and a pretty pink-and-white arbor wound with bunches of grapes, La Pergola offers creative variations on Italian standards. Try the smoked salmon drizzled with olive oil and studded with cloves; grouper siciliana with capers, olives, anchovies, tomatoes, and garlic; and the tiramisu and zuppa inglese, both some of the most authentic in the Caribbean. *Waterfort Arches, Willemstad, tel. 599/9–613482. Reservations recommended. AE, DC, MC, V. Closed for lunch Sun. Expensive.*

Pirates. This new restaurant in the Curaçao Caribbean Hotel gets the nod over owner Luis Chavarria's popular El Marinero, if only because he is devoting more time and energy here. The decor is lighthearted nautical, with an anchor, a watchtower and, of course, a presiding mermaid. The dominant color scheme is olive and periwinkle. The waiters are dressed in white sailor suits. Service is both friendly and efficient, and the chef whips up one superb seafood dish after another, including such delicacies as oyster soup, ceviche, paella, and conch. The sea bass Creole-style is delicious, as is the red snapper in almond sauce. Diners with a hearty appetite are likely to accumulate a large tab. *Curaçao Caribbean Hotel, tel. 599/9–625000. Reservations suggested. AE, DC, MC, V. Moderate–Expensive.*

Fort Waarzaamreid. High on a hill overlooking Willemstad and the harbor, this fort was captured by Captain Bligh of HMS *Bounty* two centuries ago. Now it is controlled by an Irishman, Tom Farrel, who operates an open-air restaurant and bar in the evening. The atmosphere is informal, and the food is primarily barbecued seafood and steaks decorated with your own makings from a salad bar. You will be equally well greeted if you go just for cocktails and snacks—and the sunsets are magnificent. *Seru Domi, Willemstad, tel. 599/9–623633. Located off the main highway on the Otrabanda side of the suspension bridge. Dinner only. AE, V. Moderate.*

Rijstaffel Indonesia Restaurant. An antique rickshaw guarding the entrance sets the mood for this tranquil spot. No steaks or chops here, just one dish after another of exotic delicacies that make up the traditional Indonesian banquet called rijstaffel. Choose from 16 to 25 traditional dishes that are set buffet-style around you. Lesser appetites will enjoy the lighter meals, such as the fried noodles, fresh jumbo shrimp in garlic, or combination meat-and-fish platters. Desserts are nearly mystical: A "ladies only" ice cream comes with a red rose, and the coconut ice cream comes packed in a coconut shell you can take home. The walls are hung with beautiful Indonesian puppets ($25–$40) that make stunning gifts. *Mercurriusstraat 13–15, Salinja, tel. 599/9–612999. Open Mon.–Sat. for lunch and dinner, Sun. for dinner only. Reservations required. AE, DC, MC, V. Moderate.*

Seaview. Seaview is nestled snugly in the corner of the Waterfort Arches, where the surf pounds against the rocks—you expect the sea to drench you at any minute. This casual terrace eatery offers sterling fresh seafood. Try the tangy *salpicon de mariscos*, a version of ceviche that includes everything from octopus to shrimp seasoned with a saffron, bay leaf, and lime vinaigrette. Landlubbers won't be disappointed by the tender pepper fillet. The chef can surprise with such specialties as green and white asparagus en brioche kissed by a delicate fragrant herbal cream sauce. It's a marvelous place to watch the pyrotechnics of the sun at dusk. *Waterfort Arches, Willemstad, tel/ 599/9–616688. AE. Closed lunch Sun. Moderate.*

Cactus Club. A veritable grove of aloe and cacti greets you in the courtyard of this Caribbean version of Bennigan's or TGIFriday's. The inside is surprisingly subdued: faux Tiffany lamps, hanging plants, whirring ceiling fans—hardly the honky-tonk atmosphere the name leads you to expect. Food is cheap and filling, tending toward pub favorites like fettucine alfredo, fajitas, buffalo wings, and cajun snapper. And of course there are burgers, prepared to your liking. It's predictably popular with both locals and homesick Americans. *Mahaai, tel. 371600. DC, MC, V. Inexpensive.*

★ **Golden Star Restaurant.** This place looks and feels more like a friendly roadside diner than a full-fledged restaurant, but the native food here is among the best in town. Owner Marie Burke turns out such Antillean specialties as *bestia chiki* (goat stew), shrimp Creole, and delicately seasoned grilled conch, all served with generous heaps of rice, fried plantains, and avocado. Steaks and chops can be had for the asking. *Socratestraat 2, tel. 599/9–654795. AE, DC, MC, V. Inexpensive.*

Jaanchi Christiaan's Restaurant. Tour buses stop regularly at this open-air restaurant for lunch and for weird-sounding but mouth-watering native dishes. The main-course specialty is a hefty platter of fresh-caught fish, potatoes, and vegetables. Curaçaoans joke that Jaanchi's "iguana soup is so strong it could resurrect the dead"—truth is, it tastes just like chicken soup, only better. But Jaanchi, Jr., says if you want iguana, you must order in advance "because we have to go out and catch them." He's not kidding. *Westpunt 15, tel. 599/9–640126. AE, DC, MC, V. Inexpensive.*

Lodging

Hotels in Curaçao all have their pluses and minuses. If you're a business traveler, you'll appreciate the modest Van Der Valk Plaza,

Otrabanda and new Porto Paseo, with easy access to the city center, but you'll have a long trek to the beach. Guests at the sophisticated Avila Beach, Sonesta Beach, Curaçao Caribbean, Princess Beach, Las Palmas, and Holiday Beach hotels enjoy their own beaches, but they're a 10-minute drive from town. The Curaçao Caribbean and the Sonesta Beach Hotel are across the road from the International Trade Center. Most hotels offer free shuttle bus services to the downtown area. They also either include breakfast or offer a large buffet breakfast at a reasonable price. Full American Plans are not popular because of the abundance of good restaurants in all price ranges.

Highly recommended lodgings are indicated by a star ★.

Category	Cost*
Expensive	over $175
Moderate	$110–$175
Inexpensive	under $110

All prices are for a standard double room for two and include tax and service charges.

Hotels   **Curaçao Caribbean Hotel and Casino.** This five-story complex is self-contained, with one of the best organized activities program on the island, including rum-swizzle parties, volleyball, T-shirt painting contests, Papiamento lessons, walking tours, and special theme nights for dinner and dancing. The lovely champagne-colored coves can become crowded, but there is a lounging area above them that is perfect for sunbathing. Water sports include everything imaginable. Guest rooms on the first four floors are run-down and old-looking in spite of the new burgundy rugs and a minor face-lift. The top floor, dedicated to business guests, has its own reception area, breakfast area, and fax and computer capabilities. It's the only floor that was completely renovated, yet still appears ramshackle, though nice extras include hair dryers and coat presses. All the hotel rooms have small balconies, but only half face the sea. Plans are in progress to extend the hotel's beach area and build new town-house time-sharing units. *Box 2133, Piscadera Bay, Willemstad, tel. 599/ 9–625000 or 800/344–1212, fax 599/9–625846. 200 rooms. Facilities: 3 restaurants, 24-hour coffee shop, 2 bars, pool, casino, beauty salon, barbershop, lighted tennis courts, health spa, boutiques, drugstore, secretarial services, telex, fax, meeting and convention rooms. AE, D, DC, MC, V. EP, MAP. Expensive.*
Princess Beach Hotel and Casino. The beach, lined with palm trees and one of the most beautiful in Curaçao, is located right in front of the underwater park. The rooms are huge, most with breathtaking ocean or garden views. The garden-view rooms are the more spacious of the two; however, the sea-view rooms are newer and are much more tropical, modern, and upscale. All rooms include a hair dryer, air-conditioning, color cable TV, and either a balcony or a patio. The pathway to guest rooms is through lush, tropical grounds full of chirping birds. The freshwater pool has the added bonus of a staff to offer drinks to guests as they paddle about on floats. The casino is one of the more exciting ones in Curaçao. This is a high-energy place, with lively happy hours, popular theme buffet dinners, and a slew of sports activities to keep guests busy, including those offered by the Curaçao High Wind Center. New luxury one-bedroom suites are in the planning, but these are off to the side and should not interfere with the day-to-day functioning of the hotel. *Martin Lu-*

ther King Blvd. 8, tel. 599/9–614944 or 800/327–3286, fax 599/9–614131. 202 rooms. Facilities: restaurant, pool with bar, boutiques, drugstore, dive shop, tour desk, car- and scooter-rental agent, casino, beauty salon, baby-sitting services, facilities and rooms for people with disabilities. AE, DC, MC, V. EP, BP, MAP, FAP. Expensive.

★ **Sonesta Beach Hotel & Casino.** Curaçao's newest resort is a sprawling, burnished ocher low rise, built to blend in with the surrounding Dutch Colonial–style architecture. The approach through lushly landscaped grounds brimming with oleander, hibiscus, and gently swaying palms, is impressive. Striking contemporary artworks adorn the walls. The beach is one of Curaçao's finest. The air-conditioned accommodations have a muted tropical pastel color scheme, TVs, minibars, tiled showers and baths, and either a terrace or a balcony. Price is determined solely by view, though all rooms boast at least a partial ocean vista. Two children under age 12 stay free when sharing the room with their parents, and the free daily "Just Us Kids" program offers supervised activities for children ages 5 to 12. *Box 6003, Piscadera Bay, tel. 599/9–368800 or 800/SONESTA, fax 599/9–627502. 214 rooms, 34 suites. Facilities: 3 restaurants, 2 bars, casino, water-sports and dive center, free-form swimming pool with swim-up bar, children's wading pool, 2 lighted tennis courts, health club, shopping arcade, 2 whirlpools, baby-sitting service, children's program. AE, DC, MC, V. EP. Expensive.*

★ **Avila Beach Hotel.** The royal family of Holland and its ministers stay at this 200-year-old mansion for three good reasons: the privacy, the personalized service, and the austere elegance. The civilized reception area is cooled by whirring fans and graced with brass lanterns, porcelain statuary, and a baby grand, suggesting colonial plantation living at its ultimate. Americans used to luxurious resorts will find the air-conditioned rooms rather plain and old-fashioned, but the double quarter-moon-shape beach is enchanting. The original guest rooms are charming but basic-looking, with hardwood or tile floors and small baths with showers only. Most guests will prefer the newer La Belle Alliance section, on its own beach adjacent to the main property. The Mediterranean-style yellow-and-gold low-rise buildings feature Moorish arches, Dutch red-gabled roofs, and lighted walkways. Sold as condominium units and leased back to the hotel as guest accommodations, these 45 rooms and 18 one- and two-bedroom apartments all have either balconies or patios with sea views. Half the rooms are equipped with kitchenettes. While these rooms may have less charm than the old ones do, their larger size and modern amenities make them the more desirable—and more expensive. The hotel has a unique outdoor dining area shaded by the leafy intertwining boughs of an enormous tree. The Danish chefs, who specialize in a Viking pot, local dishes, and weekly smorgasbord, also smoke their own fish and bake their own bread. Classical concerts performed by the owner, a recorded artist, take place once a month on Sunday mornings. Recent additions include a new café/ jazz club with an open-air sea view, a tennis court, and a conference room. *Box 791, Penstraat 130134, Willemstad, tel. 599/9–614377 or 800/448–8355, fax 599/9–611493. 95 rooms. Facilities: restaurant, coffee shop, tennis court, bar, baby-sitting service, cable TV, conference room, shuttle bus to city center. AE, DC, MC, V. EP. Moderate.*

Holiday Beach Hotel and Casino. This ex–Holiday Inn is a four-story, 26-year-old, U-shape, aquamarine-colored building surrounding a pool area. Over the past four years, the rooms have been completely renovated and refurnished in a beige, emerald, and rose color scheme, with bleached wood and rattan furniture, TVs, showers and baths, and balconies. Half the rooms face the parking lot; most of the others face the pool area, and only a few have sea views. The air-conditioned lobby is spacious to permit the assembly of tour groups, and the island's largest casino is off to the lobby's left. The hotel's outstanding feature is its crescent beach, quite large for Curaçao and dotted with palm trees. There's also a water-sports concession and a tiki-hut beach bar. Guests are encouraged to join in the voluminous daily selection of activities. The lobby bar happy hour is one of the most popular on the island. While this hotel is an older property, the completed renovation, along with the friendly service, makes it a good choice for people seeking good value on a middle-of-the-road budget. *Box 2178, Otrabanda, Pater Euwensweg, Willemstad, tel. 599/9–625400, fax 599/9–624397. 197 rooms; 2 suites. Facilities: playground, 2 tennis courts, beauty shop, boutique, drugstore, gift shop, car-rental agent, baby-sitting service, casino. AE, DC, MC, V. EP. Moderate.*

Coral Cliff Resort and Beach Club. Seclusion and rustic simplicity are everything here. A 45-minute ride from the center of Willemstad, the grounds of the resort boast a beach so alluring that it attracts even native islanders seeking a weekend retreat. (The beach is open to the public for a $5 admission charge.) This resort exudes a European atmosphere—replete with wood beams to enhance the lavender, mint, olive, cream, and teal colors—and is very popular with Dutch tourists. Americans used to luxurious or amenity-laden resorts will find the rooms stark and in sore need of modernizing. However, all are air-conditioned, have spectacular views of the sea, and are equipped with satellite TV, direct-dial phone, and an old but functional kitchenette. The hotel recently installed a children's playground and miniature golf course, a tennis court, and slot machines in the bar. Regrettably, they plan further expansion, with another 70 rooms to be added by early 1995. All guests receive complimentary airport transfers. *Box 3782, Santa Marta Bay, tel. 599/9–641820 or 800/344–1212, fax 599/9–641781. 35 rooms. Facilities: restaurant, bar, pool, car-rental agent, marina, water-sports center, and PADI 4-star dive shop. AE, DC, MC, V. EP, BP, MAP, FAP. Inexpensive.*

Lions Dive Hotel & Marina. This recent addition to the Curaçao vacation scene is a hop, skip, and plunge away from the Seaquarium. The pink-and-green caravansary is set next to a quarter mile of private beach. The rooms are airy, modern, and light-filled, with tile floors, large bathrooms, and lots of windows. A pair of French doors leads out to a spacious balcony or terrace, and every room has a view of the sea. The Sunday-night happy hour is especially festive, with a local merengue band playing poolside. By midnight, however, the only sound to be heard is the whir of your room's air conditioner. Pluses include a young, attractive staff who are eager to please and a top-notch scuba center. Dive packages are offered with Underwater Curaçao, and most, if not all, of the guests are dive enthusiasts. *Bapor Kibra, Curaçao, tel. 599/9–618100, fax 599/9–618200. 72 air-conditioned rooms with color TV. Facilities: Antillean restaurant, terrace bar, pool, scuba-diving center with 2 dive boats, each with a 25-passenger capacity, water-sports concession, video-rental shop. AE, DC, MC, V. CP. Inexpensive.*

Otrabanda Hotel & Casino. Built in 1991, this city hotel is across the harbor from downtown Willemstad. Rooms are tiny but appealing, decorated with rattan furnishings and light pastels and paintings of country life, with smashing harbor views. All feature cable TV, air-conditioning and full bath. If you're watching your budget, this hotel offers superior value. *Breedestraat (O), Otrabanda, tel. 599/*

9–627400, fax 599/9–627299. 45 rooms. Facilities: coffee shop, restaurant, bar, casino. AE, V. CP. Inexpensive.

★ **Porto Paseo Hotel and Casino.** The tropical gardens, flagstone courtyard, rock walls, and mustard-colored red tile roof buildings of this charming new (1993) small hotel on the Otrabanda side of the harbor were designed to duplicate a typical landhouse. It's a remarkably peaceful, private place amid the city's bustle. Squawking white cockatoos preside over the entrance to an open-air bar splashed with murals depicting island life and overlooking Santa Anna Bay. The unadorned but pleasant rooms shimmer in silver, mauve, and ecru and feature satellite TV, air-conditioning, and a shower bath. *De Rouvilleweg 47, Willemstad, tel. 599/9–627878 or 800/328–7222, fax 599/9–627969. 44 rooms, 1 suite, 1 apartment. Facilities: restaurant, bar, pool, casino. AE, DC, MC, V. Inexpensive.*

Van Der Valk Plaza Hotel and Casino. "Please don't touch the passing ships" is the slogan of the Van Der Valk Plaza, the only hotel in the world with marine-collision insurance. The ships do come close to the island's first high-rise hotel, which is built right into the massive walls of a 17th-century fort at the entrance of Willemstad's harbor. At the Plaza, you give up beachfront (you have beach privileges at major hotels, however) for walking access to the city's center— consequently, it's a business traveler's oasis, complete with secretarial service, fax and telex machines, and typing and translation services. The ramparts rising from the sea offer a fantastic evening view of the twinkling lights of the city. A new, enlarged casino has been completed, the fine restaurants are a splendid place to watch the ships anchor in the harbor, and the lobby is now a vision in marble, with handsomely upholstered furniture, vaulting trees, and a winding lagoon and waterfall. Regrettably, the rooms are sorely lacking in style and decor and are awash in garish hot pink, chartreuse, and kelly green: '50s kitsch. One hundred and thirty-five of the rooms are in the tower, many with a sea view and some with balconies. All rooms have color cable TV, air-conditioning, and a minifridge. *Box 229, Plaza Piar, Willemstad, tel. 599/9–612500, fax 599/9–616543. 254 rooms. Facilities: restaurant, coffee shop, 3 bars, casino, room service, dive shop, drugstore, gift shop, car-rental agent, tour desk, pool. Baby-sitter and house physician on call. AE, DC, MC, V. CP. Inexpensive.*

Home and Apartment Rentals   There are many rentals available on the island. Your best bet is to contact the **Curaçao Tourist Board** (Box 3266, Curaçao, Netherlands Antilles) at least two months before you plan to go; it will send you a list of available properties.

The Arts and Nightlife

The Arts   **The Curaçao Museum,** housed in a century-old former plantation house, is filled with artifacts, paintings, and antique furnishings that trace the island's history. *Across from the Holiday Beach Hotel, off Pater Euwensweg, tel. 599/9–623777. Admission: $1.50. Open Tues.–Fri. 9–noon and 2–5, Sat. 10–4.*

Nightlife   Friday is the big night out, with rollicking happy hours, most with live music, at several hotels, most notably the Holiday Beach and Avila Beach (*see* Lodging, *above*). The once-a-month open house at Landhuis Brievengat (*see* Exploring, Curaçao, Eastern Side, *above*) is a great way to meet interesting locals—it usually offers a folkloric show, snacks, and local handicrafts. Every Friday night the landhouse holds a big party with two bands. Check with the tourist board for the schedule of folkloric shows at various hotels. The Sonesta Beach, Van Der Valk Plaza, Curaçao Caribbean, Holiday

Beach, Las Palmas, Otrabanda, and Princess Beach hotels all have casinos that are open 1 PM–4 AM.

Salinja is the spot for clubbing, depending on your musical tastes: You'll find everything from merengue to house. **The Pub** (Salinja 144A, tel. 599/9–612190) is a crowded, energetic dancing-and-drinking club. It's the place for the loud, the hip, the young, and the wannabes checking on the latest Curaçao fads and fancies. The dress is casual to funky, so leave your heels at home. Open Friday 8 PM–4 AM, Saturday 9 PM–4 AM, Monday–Thursday and Sunday 9 PM–3 AM.

Considered the most colorful disco in town, **Facade** (Lindbergweg 32, Salina, tel. 599/9–614640) is about as hip as Curaçao gets. It's dark and cool, with huge bamboo chairs for lounging. The men cruise and the women are dressed to kill. There are two disco floors with flashing lights and an intense aural assault. It's packed on Thursday, Friday, and Saturday nights from 10 PM to 4 AM. Closed Tuesday.

L'Aristocrat (Lindbergweg-Salina, tel. 599/9–614353) attracts the more mature crowd seeking late-night pleasures, and on Saturday night the line to get in stretches down the block. Inside, the trendy clientele gyrates to a heavy beat while silent large-screen TVs flash sensual images. The place to see and be seen. There's a $9 cover charge, and it's open Friday and Saturday 10 PM to 4 AM; closed Monday.

Rum Runner (Otrobanda Waterfront, De Rouvilleweg 9, tel. 599/9–623038) is another casual hot spot. This well-lit indoor/outdoor bar and eatery serves up tapas in an atmosphere that's reminiscent of a college fraternity hall. There's music nightly. The crowd stays until about midnight, after which the majority switch to **Facade, The Pub,** or **L'Aristocrat.**

10 Dominica

Updated by
Andrew
Collins

The national motto emblazoned on the coat of arms of the Common-wealth of Dominica reads *"Après Bondi, c'est la ter."* It is a French-Creole phrase meaning "After God, it is the land." On this unspoiled isle, the land is indeed the main attraction: It turns and twists, tow-ers to mountain crests, then tumbles to falls and valleys. It is a land that the Smithsonian Institution called a giant plant laboratory, un-changed for 10,000 years. Indeed, after a heavy rain you half expect to see things grow before your very eyes; the island is a virtual rain-bow in entirely green hues.

The grandeur of Dominica (pronounced *dom-in-EE-ka*) is not man-made. This untamed, ruggedly beautiful land, located in the eastern Caribbean between Guadeloupe to the north and Martinique to the south, is a 305-square-mile nature retreat; 29 miles long and 15 miles wide, the island is dominated by some of the highest elevations in the Caribbean and is laced with 365 rivers, "one for every day of the year." Much of the interior is covered by a luxuriant rain forest, a wild place where you almost expect Tarzan to swing howling by on a vine. Straight out of Conan Doyle's *Lost World*, everything here is larger than life, from the towering tree ferns to the enormous in-sects. This exotic spot is home to such unusual critters as the Sisserou (or Imperial) parrot and the red-necked (or Jacquot) par-rot, neither of which can be found anywhere else in the world.

Dominica is home, too, to the last remnants of the Carib Indians, whose ancestors came paddling up from South America more than a thousand years ago. The fierce Caribs kept Christopher Columbus at bay when he came to call during his second voyage to the New World. Columbus turned up at the island on Sunday, November 3, 1493. In between Carib arrows he hastily christened it Dominica (Sunday Island) and then sailed on.

For almost two centuries the British and French tried unsuccessful-ly to subdue the Caribs, and in 1748 they agreed to let the Caribs keep the island. However, French and English planters, unable to resist the lure of the fertile land, began to fight one another for squatter's rights. The Caribs had named their island *waitukubuli* ("tall is her body"), but it was *Dominica* that remained in history. In 1805, the English paid a "ransom" of £12,000 to the French, and Dominica became a British possession. In 1967, the British colony became self-governing, and on November 3, 1978, Dominica became a fully independent republic, officially called the Commonwealth of Dominica. Despite (or perhaps because of) its ferocious past, Dominica today is a quiet, peaceful place. There are about 75,000 people living on the island, and they are some of the friendliest peo-ple in all of the Caribbean.

Before You Go

Tourist Information

Contact the **Caribbean Tourism Organization,** 20 E. 46th St., New York, NY 10017, tel. 212/682–0435. In the United Kingdom, contact the **Dominica Tourist Office** (1 Collingham Gardens, London SW5 0HW, tel. 071/835–1937 or 071/370–5194).

Arriving and Departing
By Plane

No major airlines fly into Dominica, but **LIAT** (tel. 809/462–0700) connects with flights from the United States on Antigua, Barbados, Guadeloupe, Martinique, St. Lucia, St. Maarten, and San Juan. **Air Martinique** (tel. 809/448–2181) flies from Fort de France, and **Air Guadeloupe** (tel. 809/448–2181) from Pointe-à-Pitre. **Air BVI** (tel. 809/774–6500) connects from Tortola, BVI. **BWIA** (tel. 809/462–0262) connects from Antigua, and **Winair** (tel. 809/448–2181) con-nects from St. Maarten.

From the Airport	**Canefield Airport** (about 3 miles north of Roseau) handles only small aircraft and daytime flights; landing here is a hair-raising experience and not for those uneasy about flying. Cab fare is about $8 to Roseau. **Melville Hall Airport**, on the northeast coast, handles larger planes; although interesting, the 90-minute drive through the island's rain forest to Roseau is bumpy, exhausting, and costs about $50 by private taxi or $17 per person by co-op cab.
By Ferry	**The Caribbean Express** (c/o Whitchurch Shipping & Tours, tel. 809/448–5787) has scheduled service Monday, Wednesday, Friday, and Saturday from Guadeloupe in the north to Martinique in the south, with stops at Les Saintes and Dominica. **Madikera** (c/o Trois Pitons Travel, tel. 809/448–6977) began offering similar service in 1993, stopping in Roseau on Wednesday, Friday, Saturday, and Sunday.
Passports and Visas	U.S. and Canadian citizens must produce a driver's license or passport and a return or ongoing ticket. British citizens must show a passport.
Language	The official language is English, but most Dominicans also speak a French-Creole patois.
Precautions	Be sure to bring insect repellent. Bring along pills for motion sickness; the roads twist and turn dramatically, and the local drivers barrel across them at a dizzying pace. If you plan on hiking even the simplest trail, bring along extra clothing and hiking boots or athletic sneakers to change into; trails are very rugged and very muddy.

Staying in Dominica

Important Addresses	**Tourist Information:** Contact the main office of the **Division of Tourism,** National Development Corp. (Bath Estate, Box 73, Roseau, tel. 809/448–2186 or 809/448–2351). The tourist desk at the **Old Market Plaza** (Roseau, tel. 809/448–2186) is open Monday 8–5, Tuesday–Friday 8–4, Saturday 9–1. The offices at **Canefield Airport** (tel. 809/449–1242) and **Melville Hall Airport** (tel. 809/445–7051) are open weekdays 6:15–11 AM and 2–5:30 PM.
Emergencies	**Police, fire, and ambulance:** Call 999. **Hospital: Princess Margaret Hospital** (Federation Dr., Goodwill, tel. 809/448–2231 or 809/448–2233). **Pharmacy: Jolly's Pharmacy** (33 King George V St., Roseau, tel. 809/448–3388).
Currency	The official currency is the Eastern Caribbean dollar (E.C.$). Figure about E.C.$2.70 to the U.S.$1. U.S. dollars are readily accepted, but you'll usually get change in E.C. dollars. Major credit cards are widely accepted, as are traveler's checks. Prices quoted here are in U.S. dollars unless indicated otherwise.
Taxes and Service Charges	Hotels collect a 5% government tax; restaurants a 3% tax. The departure tax is $8 or E.C.$20. A security service charge tax of $2 or E.C.$5 is also imposed. Most hotels and restaurants add a 10% service charge to your bill. Taxi drivers appreciate a 10% tip.
Guided Tours	A wide variety of hiking and photo safari tours are conducted by **Dominica Tours** (tel. 809/448–2638) in sturdy four-wheel-drive vehicles. Prices range from $15 to $100 per person, depending upon the length of the trip and whether picnics and rum punches are included. There are also boat tours that include snorkeling, swimming, and rum or fruit drinks.
	Rainbow Rover Tours (tel. 809/448–8650) are conducted in air-conditioned Land Rovers. Tours take in the island for a half or full day at a per-person cost of $30–$60, which includes food and drink. **Ken's**

Hinterland Adventure Tours (tel. 809/448–4850) provides tours in vans with knowledgeable guides and can design expeditions to fit your needs. If you're uneasy about some of the more dangerous hikes, Ken's is the best choice: They use two-way radios at all times, which you'll appreciate if ever there's an emergency.

Any taxi driver will be happy to offer his services as a guide at the cost of $18 an hour, with tip extra. It's a good idea to get a recommendation from your hotel manager or the Dominica Division of Tourism (*see* Tourist Information, *above*) before selecting a guide and driver. **Mally's Tour & Taxi Service** (tel. 809/448–3114) is one of the better operators.

Getting Around
Vans
This is a cheap, though not always dependable, means of transportation. Minivans cruise the island and, like taxis, will stop when hailed. You can also catch a minivan in Roseau by the bridges crossing the Roseau River.

Rental Cars
If it doesn't bother you to drive on the left on potholed mountainous roads with hairpin curves, rent a car and strike out on your own. Daily car-rental rates begin at $35 (weekly about $190), plus collision damage insurance at $6 a day and personal accident insurance at $2 a day, and you'll have to put down a deposit and purchase a visitor's driving permit for E.C.$20. You can rent a car from **Wide Range Car Rentals** (79 Bath Rd., Roseau, tel. 809/448–2198), **Valley Rent-A-Car** (Goodwill Rd., Roseau, tel. 809/448–3233), **Anselm's Car Rental** (3 Great Marlborough, Roseau, tel. 809/448–2730), or **S.T.L. Rent-A-Car** (Goodwill Rd., Roseau, tel. 809/448–2340 or 809/448–4525); **Budget Rent-A-Car** (Canefield Industrial Estate, Canefield, tel. 809/449–2080) offers daily rates, three-day specials, and weekly and monthly rates.

Telephones, Electricity, and Mail
To call Dominica from the United States, dial area code 809 and the local access code, 44, followed by the five-digit local number. On the island, you need to dial only the five-digit number. The island has efficient and quick direct-dial international service. All pay phones are equipped for local and overseas dialing.

Electric voltage is 220/240 AC, 50 cycles. American appliances require an adaptor.

First-class (airmail) letters to the United States and Canada cost E.C.95¢; postcards cost E.C.50¢.

Opening and Closing Times
Business hours are weekdays 8–1 and 2–4, Saturday 8–1. Banks are open Monday–Thursday 8–3, Friday 8–5.

Exploring Dominica

Numbers in the margin correspond to points of interest on the Dominica map.

Despite the small size of this almond-shape island, it can take a couple of hours to get between many of the island's popular destinations; roads are in poor shape and travel is relatively slow. The amount of time you spend hiking, mountain climbing, bird-watching, or just enjoying the scenery will determine how much you can see during one round-the-island trip. It takes about four days of solid trekking to take in the whole of Dominica. The highways ringing most of the island's perimeter have been upgraded in recent years; but more remote destinations remain somewhat inaccessible, and it's wise to hire a car and driver or to take an escorted tour (*see* Guided Tours, *above*).

Roseau All the hotels and virtually all the island's population are on the lee-ward, or Caribbean, side of the island. Twenty thousand or so inhab-

① itants reside in the capital, **Roseau** (pronounced *Rose-OH*). This noisy, ragged town on the flat delta of the Roseau River reminds one of a somewhat more tattered version of New Orlean's French Quarter. A new waterfront and pier have upgraded the coastal side of town, but Roseau, which is one of the poorest capitals in the Caribbean, lacks the grand colonial architecture and the regal layout typical of the region. Walking through town you will notice the French West Indian construction of most homes and shops—small wood-and-stone or wood-and-concrete shanties, many with balustrades and French doors. One impressive sight, on Victoria Street, is the **Fort Young Hotel,** built as a fort in the 18th century. Directly across the street is the **state house;** the **public library** and the **old court house** are both nearby.

The National Park Office, fittingly located in the 40-acre Botanical Gardens in Roseau, can provide tour guides and a wealth of printed information. *Tel. 809/448–2401, ext. 417. Open Mon. 8–1 and 2–5, Tues.–Fri. 8–1 and 2–4.*

Time Out Sit in the garden of the late Jean Rhys, the Dominican-born novelist who won Britain's Royal Literary Award. The garden has now been turned into an informal garden eatery, the **World of Food** (Queen Mary St. and Field's La., tel. 809/448–6125). If you've never read Rhys, stop off at **Paperbacks** (6 Cork St., tel. 809/448–2370) and purchase her *Wide Sargasso Sea* or any of her many other books.

Elsewhere on **Morne Trois Pitons** is a blue-green hill of three peaks, the highest of
the Island which is 4,403 feet. The mountain is usually veiled in swirling mists
② and clouds, and the 16,000-acre national park over which it looms is awash with cool mountain lakes, waterfalls, and rushing rivers. Ferns grow 30 feet tall, and wild orchids sprout from trees. Sunlight leaks through green canopies, and a gentle mist rises over the jungle floor.

The road from the capital to the Morne Trois Pitons National Park runs through the **Roseau River Valley** toward Laudat. About 5 miles out of Roseau, the Wotton Waven Road branches off toward the
③ **Sulphur Springs,** where you'll see the belching, sputtering, and gur-gling release of hot springs along a river and nearby field—evidence of the area's restless volcanic activity. Double back and continue up the road to Laudat, taking the next side road to the spectacular twin
④ **Trafalgar Falls.** The road ends at **Papillote Wilderness Retreat** (*see* Dining and Lodging, *below*). Both are visible from a viewing plat-form that is an easy hike from Papillote's driveways—guides there will happily show you the way. If you're in decent shape and possess agility and balance, it's worth hiking up the riverbed to the cool pools at the bases of both falls. The taller of the two is where hot, orange-colored sulfuric and ferric waters mix with the crash of cold river water; it's an exhilarating experience.

Again, double back to the main road from Roseau and continue to
⑤ **Laudat,** a small mountaintop village about 7 miles from Roseau and a good starting point for a venture into the national park. Two miles
⑥ northeast of Laudat, at the base of **Morne Micotrin** (4,006 feet), you'll find **Freshwater Lake,** and farther on, **Boeri Lake,** which is fringed with greenery and has purple hyacinths floating on its sur-face.

Laudat is the starting point for the most talked about—and most
⑦ treacherous—hike in Dominica: the trek to **Boiling Lake** and the

Valley of Desolation. You should only go with a guide (*see* Hiking, *below*) and will have to leave at about 8 AM for this steep and slippery, all-day, 6-mile (round-trip) ramble. You will return covered with mud, nicks, and scrapes; exhausted; and satisfied that you've seen one of the world's true wonders. Guides keep small groups of hikers (usually six to eight maximum) under their eye at all times. This is for serious hikers only: Make sure you're in excellent condition, and bring your own drinking water. The lake, the world's second-largest boiling lake, is like a caldron of gurgling gray-blue water. It's 70 yards wide, and the temperature of the water ranges from 180°F to 197°F. Its depth is unknown. It is believed that the lake is not a volcanic crater but a flooded fumarole—a crack through which gases escape from the molten lava below.

On your way to the lake, you'll pass through the Valley of Desolation, a sight that definitely lives up to its name. Harsh sulfuric fumes have destroyed virtually all the vegetation in what was once a lush forested area. Stay on the trail to avoid breaking through the crust that covers the hot lava below.

8 You'll have to backtrack to Roseau and head north toward the Pont Casse rotary to reach **Emerald Pool.** At the rotary, follow signs for Castle Bruce for about 3½ miles until you come to the trail that leads to Emerald Pool. Lookout points along this short 20-minute trail provide sweeping views of the windward (Atlantic) coast and the forested interior. Emerald Pool is a swirling, fern-bedecked basin into which a 50-foot waterfall splashes. This is the most accessible of Dominica's natural wonders—and fittingly its least wondrous.

Time Out Peter Kaufmann and his friendly dogs are the proprietors of a terrific diversion a short drive from the Emerald Pool: Welcome to the **Emerald Bush Bar–Restaurant–Bush Hotel–Nature Park** (tel. 809/448–4545, answering machine). Here you can stop for a glass of fresh juice or a rum punch, wander along a couple hours' worth of unbelievably lush trails, or spend the night in an A-frame cottage that is barely a cut above camping (rooms cost as little as $18 per night). The list of non-amenities is long: No electricity, no phone, no TV, etc. Be prepared to rough it—but this is one of the most beautiful settings in Dominica. The bar and restaurant are open only until about sundown.

9 A good map and steady nerves are necessary for driving along the rugged, ragged windward coast. If you head back from the Emerald Pool toward Pont Casse and turn left at the intersection a couple miles before the rotary, the road leads to **Rosalie,** where there is a river for swimming, a black-sand beach, an old aqueduct, and a waterwheel. There is also a waterfall that dashes down a cliff into the ocean.

10 From here, head north along the coast to the little fishing village of **Castle Bruce.** On the beach here you can watch dugout canoes being made from the trunks of gommier trees using traditional Carib methods (after the tree is cut it gets stretched). About 6 miles north **11** of Castle Bruce lies the **Carib Indian Reservation,** which was established in 1903 and covers 3,700 acres. Don't expect a lot in the way of ancient culture and costume. The folks who gave the Caribbean its name live pretty much like other West Indians, as fishermen and farmers. However, they have maintained their traditional skills at wood carving, basket weaving, and canoe building. Their wares are displayed and sold in little thatch-top huts lining the road. The reservation's Roman Catholic church at Salibia has an altar that was

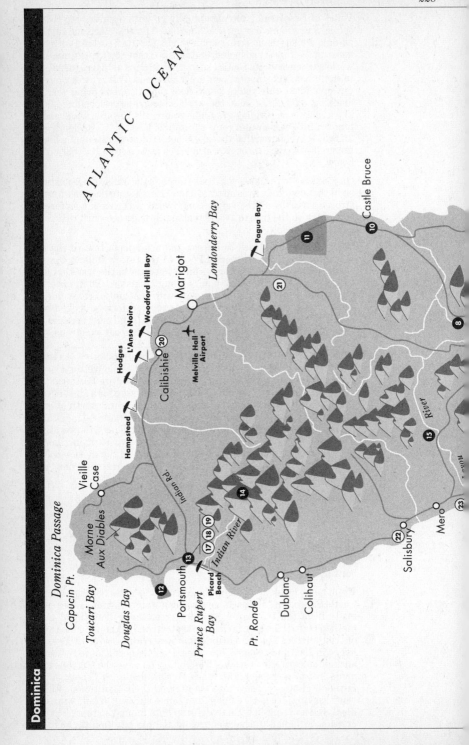

Dominica

ATLANTIC OCEAN

Dominica Passage

Capucin Pt.

Toucari Bay

Douglas Bay

Vieille
Case

Morne
Aux Diables

Prince Rupert
Bay

Portsmouth

Picard
Beach

Indian River

Pt. Ronde

Dublanc

Colihaut

Salisbury

Mero

Castle Bruce

Pagua Bay

Londonderry Bay

Marigot

Woodford Hill Bay

L'Anse Noire

Hodges

Hampstead

Calibishie

Melville Hall
Airport

River

Indian Rd.

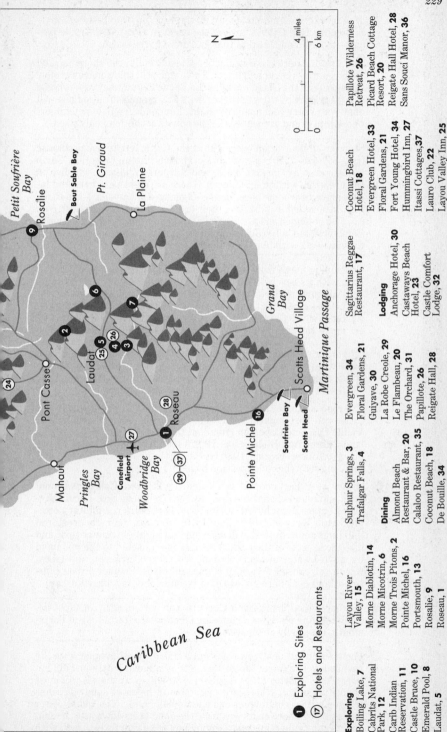

once a canoe. Another point of interest on the reservation is **L'Escalier Tête Chien** ("trail of the snake staircase" in Creole patois)—a hardened lava flow that juts down to the ocean.

The Atlantic here is particularly fierce and roily, the shore marked with countless coves and inlets. The Carib still tell wondrous colorful legends of the island's origins: La Roche Pagua, they say, is home to a fragrant white flower; bathe in its petals and your loved one will obey your every command. By night, Londonderry Islets metamorphose into grand canoes to take the spirits of the dead out to sea.

Time Out Stop for an hour or an overnight at the **Carib Territory Guesthouse** (tel. 809/445–7256), a very basic and fascinating wayside Carib house owned by Caribs Charles and Margaret Williams, who live on the premises with their children. There are eight very bare and inexpensive bedrooms here for the adventurous traveler—the three new ones added in 1994 have their own baths and are comfiest. You can also get lunch and a cold drink, not to mention a good selection of Carib crafts. Call Williams in advance and schedule a half-day or full-day walk with him through the territory.

Continuing north from the reservation, you'll go past lovely **Pagua Bay,** with its beach of dark sand. A bit farther along, near Melville Hall Airport, is **Marigot,** the largest (population: 5,000) settlement on the east coast. On the northeast coast, steep cliffs rise out of the Atlantic, which flings its frothy waters over dramatic reefs, and rivers crash through forests of mangroves and fields of coconut. The beaches at **Woodford Hill, Hampstead, Anse Noir,** and **Hodges** are excellent for snorkeling and scuba diving, though all this wind-tossed beauty can be dangerous to swimmers, since there are strong underwater currents as well as whipped-cream waves. From here you can see the French island of Marie Galante in the distance.

The road continues across the top of the island through banana plantations to Portsmouth, but a side road leads up to the village of **Vieille Case** and **Capucion Pointe,** at the northernmost tip of the island. **Morne Aux Diables** soars 2,826 feet over this area and slopes down to **Toucari Bay** and **Douglas Bay** on the west coast, where you'll find long stretches of dark-sand beach.

⑫ In northern Portsmouth, you'll find the 250-acre **Cabrits National Park,** surrounded on three sides by the Caribbean Sea. Local historian Lennox Honychurch has restored **Fort Shirley,** a military complex built between 1770 and 1815. You can tour the restored buildings and visit the small museum that highlights the natural and historic aspects of the park. The park is connected to the mainland by a freshwater swamp, verdant with ferns, grasses, and trees, where you can see a variety of migrant birds. Smaller cruise ships sometimes dock here instead of at Woodbridge Bay, near Roseau.

Time Out The bar in the **Purple Turtle Guest House** (Portsmouth, tel. 809/445–5296) is a fine place for a rum punch before or after a tour of Portsmouth, especially at sunset.

⑬ **Portsmouth** is a small town of about 5,000; it's most popular with the yachting set. **Prince Rupert Bay,** site of a naval battle in 1782 between the French and the English, is far and away the island's most beautiful harbor. There are more than 2 miles of sandy beaches fringed with coconut trees and a few small hotels. The **Indian River** flows through here on its way from the mountains down into the sea, and a canoe ride takes you through an exotic rain forest thick with mangrove trees and exotic bird life. Board a rowboat (not power) for total tranquillity, to be able to hear fish jumping and exotic birds calling. The guides here are notoriously overeager: Choose carefully or ask your hotel to recommend someone.

Just south of Indian River is **Pointe Ronde,** the starting point for an **⑭** expedition to **Morne Diablotin,** at 4,747 feet the island's highest summit. This is not an expedition you should attempt alone; the uninhabited interior is an almost impenetrable primeval forest. You'll need a good guide (*see* Hiking, *below*), sturdy shoes, a warm sweater, and firm resolve.

Heading back to Roseau, the west-coast road dips down through the little villages of **Dublanc** (with a side road off to the Syndicate Estate), **Colihaut,** and **Salisbury** before reaching the mouth of the **⑮** Layou River. The **Layou River valley** is rich with bananas, cacao, citrus fruits, and coconuts. The remains of Hillsborough Estate, once a rum-producing plantation, are here. The river is the island's longest and largest, with deep gorges, quiet pools and beaches, waterfalls and rapids—a great place for a full day's outing of swimming and shooting the rapids, or just sunning and picnicking.

The road at the bend near Dublanc that leads to the Syndicate Estate also leads to the 200-acre site of the **Project Sisserou.** This protected site has been set aside with the help of some 6,000 schoolchildren, each of whom donated 25¢ for the land where the endangered Sisserou parrot (found only in Dominica) flies free. At last estimate, there were only about 60 of these shy and beautiful birds, covered in rich green feathers with a mauve front.

Just south of Roseau the road forks, with a treacherous prong leading east to **Grand Bay,** where bay leaves are grown and distilled. If **⑯** you continue due south from Roseau you'll go through **Pointe Michel,** settled decades ago by Martinicans who fled the catastrophic eruption of Mont Pelée. The stretch all the way from Roseau to **Scotts Head** at the southernmost tip of the island has excellent beaches for scuba diving and snorkeling.

Beaches

Don't come to Dominica in search of powdery white-sand beaches. The travel-poster beaches do exist on the northeast coast, but this is still an almost totally undeveloped area. You'll see mostly dark-sand beaches, evidence of the island's volcanic origins, the best of which sit at the mouths of rivers and in protected bays. Scuba diving, snorkeling, and windsurfing are all excellent here.

Layou River has the best river swimming on the island, and in some places, you can sunbathe on its banks.

Picard Beach, on the northwest coast, is the island's best beach. Great for windsurfing and snorkeling, it's a 2-mile stretch of brown sand fringed with coconut trees. The Picard Beach Cottage Resort and Coconut Beach hotel are along this beach.

Pagua Bay, a quiet, secluded beach of dark sand, is on the Atlantic coast.

Woodford Hill Bay, Hampstead, L'Anse Noir, and **Hodges,** all on the northeast coast, are excellent beaches for snorkeling and scuba diving.

In the southeast, near La Plaine, **Bout Sable Bay** is not much good for swimming, but the surroundings are stirringly elemental: towering red cliffs challenge the rollicking Atlantic.

The beaches south of Roseau to **Scotts Head** at the southernmost tip of the island are good for scuba diving and snorkeling because of the dramatic underwater walls and sudden drops.

The scuba diving is excellent at **Soufrière Bay,** a sandy beach south of Roseau. Volcanic vents puff steam into the sea; the experience has been described as "swimming in champagne."

Sports and the Outdoors

Boating Motorboat and sailing trips can be arranged through **Dominica Tours** (tel. 809/448–2638) and the **Castaways Hotel** (tel. 809/449–6245).

Hiking Trails range from the easygoing to the arduous. For the former, all you'll need are sturdy, rubber-soled shoes and an adventurous spirit.

For the hike to Boiling Lake or the climb up Morne Diablotin you will need hiking boots, a guide, and water. Guides will charge about $30–$35 per person and can be contacted through the Dominica tourist office or the Forestry Division (tel. 809/448–2401 or 809/448–2638).

Scuba Diving *Skin Diver* magazine recently ranked Dominica among the top five Caribbean dive destinations. **Dive Dominica** (Castle Comfort, tel. 809/448–2188 or 800/544–7631, fax 809/448–6088), with three boats, is one of the oldest dive shops on the island, run by owners Derek and Ginette Perryman, NAUI-approved instructors. They offer snorkeling and resort dives for beginners and, for the advanced set, dives on drop-offs, walls, and pinnacles—by day or night. The owners of the **Dominica Dive Resorts, Waitukubuli** (there are two: one at the Anchorage Hotel, tel. 809/448–2638, the other at the Portsmouth Beach Hotel, tel. 809/445–5142), are PADI-certified and offer both resort courses and full certification. **The Castaways Hotel,** 11 miles north of Roseau, has diving at its water-sports center (tel. 809/449–6244 or 800/525–3833). The going rate at all of the above is about $65 for a two-tank dive or $90 for a resort course with two open-water dives.

Snorkeling Major island operators rent equipment: **Anchorage Hotel** (tel. 809/448–2638), **Castaways Hotel** (tel. 809/449–6244), **Coconut Beach Hotel** (tel. 809/445–5393), **Portsmouth Beach Hotel** (tel. 809/551–4255), **Sunshine Village** (tel. 809/445–5066), and **Picard Beach Cottage Resort** (tel. 809/445–5131).

Swimming River swimming is extremely popular on Dominica, and the best river to jump into is the Layou River (*see* Exploring Dominica, *above*). Also see Beaches, above, for our pick of the best beaches at which to swim, snorkel, or surf.

Windsurfing Contact either **Anchorage Hotel, Picard Beach Cottage Resort,** or **Castaways Hotel** (*see* Snorkeling, *above*).

Shopping

Gift Ideas The distinctive handicrafts of the Carib Indians include traditional baskets made of dyed *larouma* reeds and waterproofed with tightly woven *balizier* leaves. These crafts are sold on the reservation, as well as in Roseau's shops. Dominica is also noted for its spices, hot peppers, bay rum, and coconut-oil soap; its vetiver-grass mats are sold all over the world.

One of the nicest buys here (or anywhere) is a "then-and-now" book of photography and prose, *Views in the Island of Dominica, 1849*, that shows 1849 Dominica in sepia prints and again some 100 years later in color. Try the Aquarela Gallery on King George V Street.

Good gifts are stylized candles from **Starbrite Industries** (Canefield Industrial Estate, tel. 809/449–1006) that come in the shape of the Dominican parrot, cupids, and trees, as well as more traditional shapes. Open weekdays 8–4. **The Old Mill Culture Centre and Historic Site** on Canefield Road presents exhibits on the historical, cultural, and political development of Dominica. In addition, the center exhibits and sells wood carvings by a master carver, Louis Desire, and those of his students—all lovingly carved from Dominican woods. Open weekdays 9–1 and 2–4. There are excellent gift shops at both Papillote (magnificent carvings) and Floral Gardens (domestic goods and crafts). (*See* Lodging, *below*.)

Stop in at **Caribana Handcrafts** (31 Cork St., Roseau, tel. 809/448–2761) or **Tropicrafts** (41 Queen Mary St., Roseau, tel. 809/448–2747), where you'll find soaps, spices, and stacks of handmade hats, baskets, and woven straw mats.

Siblings **Arnold** and **Roberta Toulon** hand-paint T-shirts at their studio-home (54 Queen Mary St., tel. 809/448–3740) that sell so well, stock is always limited. They will, however, make up a special order within two days. Arnold's canvases of fine art are also on display.

Dining

The fertile Dominican soil produces a cornucopia of fresh vegetables, and chefs here utilize them to great advantage, most often with a Creole flair. There are sweet green bananas, *kushkush* yams, breadfruit, and dasheen (a tuber similar to the potato called taro elsewhere)—these and other staples are known as ground provisions. You'll find fresh fish on virtually every menu, and occasionally "mountain chicken"—a euphemism for a large frog called *crapaud*. Two rare delicacies for the intrepid diner are *manicou* (a small opossum) and the tender, gamey *agouti* (a large, indigenous rodent)—both are best smoked or stewed. You will not find fast-food restaurants or a variety of ethnic options, but the local cuisine is delicious.

Dominica is far from the chic fashion world. Clothes here are practical—for dinner it's shirt and trousers for men and modest dresses for women.

Highly recommended restaurants are indicated by a star ★.

Category	Cost*
Expensive	over $35
Moderate	$15–$35
Inexpensive	under $15

*per person, excluding drinks, service charge, and 3% tax

★ **La Robe Creole.** A cozy place with wood rafters, ladderback chairs, and colorful Madras cloths, this restaurant has an eclectic à la carte listing. A specialty is callaloo and crab soup, made with dasheen and coconut. You can also have crepes of lobster and conch, charcoal-grilled fish and meats, barbecued chicken, and salads. The down-stairs take-out annex, The Mouse Hole, is an inexpensive place to stock up for your picnic. *3 Victoria St., Roseau, tel. 809/448–2896. Reservations advised. AE. Closed Sun. Expensive.*

Reigate Hall. In this stylish but rustic restaurant with green linen napery and formal place settings—a rarity in Dominica—guests and perhaps a few locals mingle over some of the better hotel food on the island. While some new, health-oriented dishes have been added, favored specialties remain mountain chicken in champagne sauce and coq au vin. *Reigate Hall Hotel, Roseau, tel. 809/448–4031. Reservations recommended. AE, MC, V. Expensive.*

De Bouille. The attractive dining room at the Fort Young Hotel—with its stone walls and wood-raftered ceiling—is usually filled with the businesspeople who frequent the hotel. The upscale restaurant has an Indian chef, who adds a touch of his homeland cuisine to inter-national and Dominican specialties. The menu includes callaloo and pumpkin soup, grilled lobster, steak, curried chicken, and mountain chicken. *Fort Young Hotel, Roseau, tel. 809/448–5000. Reservations recommended. AE, MC, V. Moderate.*

★ **Evergreen.** This large, airy dining room, which opens onto a small terrace overlooking the sea, has a slightly European feel. Decorated with antiques, marble-tiled floors, and the paintings and wood carv-ings of local artist Carl Winston—and replete with classical back-ground music—it is a peaceful place in which to enjoy a meal. Dinner includes an interesting choice of soup and salad; entrées of chicken, fish, and beef are served with local fruits and vegetables, such as kushkush and plantains. Homemade desserts include fresh fruit, cake, and ice cream. *Evergreen Hotel, Roseau, tel. 809/448–3288. Reservations recommended. AE, MC, V. Moderate.*

Floral Gardens. You feel as if you're eating in a private home at this warm, welcoming restaurant. The food is delectable; it's the perfect spot to sample local specialties, such as crapaud and agouti. *Floral Gardens Hotel, Concord, tel. 809/445–7636. AE, MC, V. Moderate.*

Guiyave. Have a drink at the second-floor bar and then repair to the table-filled balcony for dining. Spareribs, lobster, rabbit, and moun-tain chicken are offered, along with homemade beef or chicken pat-ties, spicy rotis (Caribbean burritos), and a variety of light snacks and sandwiches. This restaurant is noted for its fresh tropical fruit juices (a local cherry, guava, passion fruit, and barbadine) and its homemade pies, tarts, and cakes. *15 Cork St., Roseau, tel. 809/448–2930. No credit cards. No dinner. Moderate.*

Le Flambeau. This open-air beach restaurant at the Picard Beach Cottage Resort serves an American-style breakfast of pancakes and French toast that will keep you from being homesick. Lunch and dinner entrées are not memorable, but leave room for the homemade ice cream—peanut, coconut, or mixed berry. *Picard Beach Cottage Resort, Portsmouth, tel. 809/445–5131. AE, D, MC, V. Moderate.*

The Orchard. You can dine indoors in a spacious, unadorned dining room or in a pleasant covered courtyard surrounded by latticework. Chef Joan Cools-Lartique offers Creole-style coconut shrimp, lob-ster, black pudding, mountain chicken, and callaloo soup with crabmeat, among other delicacies, on a changing menu. Sandwiches are also served. *31 King George V St., Roseau, tel. 809/448–3051. AE, D, MC, V. Moderate.*

Papillote. This open-air restaurant, with trellises of woven orchids and ferns, and popular with birds, butterflies, and tour groups, seems hacked from the undergrowth. Try the bracing callaloo soup, the knockout rum punches and, if they're on the menu, the succulent *souk* (tiny, delicate river shrimp). *Papillote Wilderness Retreat, tel. 809/448–2287. AE, D, MC, V. Moderate.*

Calaloo Restaurant. Up the stairs of a verandaed building on a busy Roseau street is this small, informal eatery decorated with local crafts. Changing lunch and dinner specials might include pepper-pot soup, curried conch, or crab callaloo. Most everything here is homemade, including juices and ice cream. *63 King George V St., Roseau, tel. 809/448–3386. No credit cards. Inexpensive–Moderate.*
Almond Beach Restaurant & Bar. If you're visiting one of the island's northeast beaches, stop here for a lunch of callaloo soup, lobster, or octopus. Select from tantalizing fruit juices, including guava, passion fruit, tangerine, soursop, and papaya, or one of the bewitching spice rums steeped for more than two months in various herbs and spices. Try the *pweve* (patois for pepper), the aniselike *nanie*, or *lapsenth*, a violet-scented pick-me-up and digestive. *Calibishi, tel. 809/445–7783. No credit cards. Inexpensive.*
Coconut Beach. This casual, low-key beachfront restaurant and bar is popular with both visiting yacht owners (moorings are available) and anyone interested in an afternoon on a stretch of white-sand beach. Fresh tropical drinks and local seafood dishes are the specialty here; sandwiches and rotis are also served. *Coconut Beach Hotel, Portsmouth, tel. 809/445–5393. AE, D, MC, V. Inexpensive.*
Sagittarius Reggae Restaurant. This funky place, plastered with astrological paraphernalia, serves johnnycakes that have Egg McMuffins beat by a country mile and sublime fresh fruit juices. Weekends it's transformed into a hopping club that blasts reggae and soca. *Portsmouth, no tel. No credit cards. Inexpensive.*

Lodging

Most hotels here are locally owned, and standards are often not up to what seasoned Caribbean travelers expect. Rooms may be dark—even creepy—bathrooms simple, and linens a bit threadbare at some properties. On the plus side, prices are low, and staffs are usually friendly and down-to-earth. It pays to compare rates and call for hotel brochures, as everything from bare-bones motels to charming hilltop retreats is comparably priced here.

The only beachfront hotels are in the Portsmouth area, the one exception being the Castaways on Mero Beach. Roseau's seaside facilities have splendid Caribbean views but are beachless. Since you're on this lush, tropical island, try to spend at least two nights at one of the wonderful nature retreats set in the rain forest—these are Dominica's greatest assets, at least where lodging is concerned.

Most hotels offer a MAP plan; considering the uniformity of Dominica's restaurants and difficulty of getting around, this option makes sense. Dominican hoteliers seldom differentiate between high and low season—though a few have caught on.

Highly recommended lodgings are indicated by a star ★.

Category	Cost*
Expensive	over $100
Moderate	$65–$100
Inexpensive	under $65

*All prices are for a standard double room for two, excluding 5% tax, 3% sales tax, and 10%–15% service charge.

Hotels **Castaways Beach Hotel.** This beachfront hotel in Mero, 11 miles north of Roseau, is popular with divers and younger guests. Daytime activity centers on its mile-long, dappled gray beach; evenings, the focus is on the restaurant and terrace, which are attractive, although the food leaves something to be desired. Rooms are spacious, have balconies overlooking the beach, and were refurbished in 1992; however, they are still dark, a bit musty, and decorated in 1970s colors and styles. Some have air-conditioning and cable TV. *Box 5, Roseau, tel. 809/449–6245 or 800/742–4276, fax 809/449–6246. 27 rooms. Facilities: restaurant, 2 bars, beach, tennis, water-sports center, scuba, dive packages offered. AE, MC, V. EP, MAP. Expensive.*

★ **Fort Young Hotel.** Roseau's top downtown hotel, it reopened in the summer of 1989 following a total renovation. Now Dominican paintings and prints from the late 1700s decorate massive stone walls of the same era, built when this was the island's main fort. Set on a cliff in Roseau, the hotel has rooms with small balconies, air-conditioning, ceiling fans, shower baths, cable TV, and modern furnishings. Ocean-view rooms cost the most but are worth it. Business travelers usually stay here, but plenty of tourists do, too. *Box 519, Roseau, tel. 809/448–5000, fax 809/448–5006. 73 rooms. Facilities: restaurant, bar, pool, entertainment, disco. AE, MC, V. EP. Expensive.*

★ **Lauro Club.** From the dining room's bright linen napery, cheerful wall mural, and fresh flowers to the cottages' bold colors and contemporary furniture, the Lauro Club has a neat European feel that, oddly enough, works well in the Caribbean. Each unit has a kitchenette on the large veranda but no TVs or air-conditioning. Six units have direct sea views, a sitting area, and daybed; four others are up the hill a bit but still have angled sea views and the same clean look found throughout the property. Below is a swimming pool, a sandy beach area, and a long wooden staircase that twists down to the ocean below. The Club is in Salisbury, between Roseau and Portsmouth and about 13 miles from each, so you'll probably need to rent a car. *Box 483, Roseau, tel. 809/449–6602, fax 809/449–6603. 10 units. Facilities: restaurant, bar, pool. AE, MC, V. EP, MAP. Expensive.*

Picard Beach Cottage Resort. Eight small wood cottages dot the grounds of this former coconut plantation, on the island's northwest coast. Units have a simple, rustic appeal, with louvered windows, locally made furniture, and small porches. Rooms have kitchens, but the restaurant here serves large breakfasts as well as lunch and dinner. The beach is right out your door, and pool privileges are next door, at the Portsmouth Beach Hotel. These are a bit overpriced but probably the best rooms in Portsmouth. *Box 34, Roseau, tel. 809/445–5131 or 800/424–5500, fax 809/445–5599. 8 cottages. Facilities: restaurant, bar, beach, pool, dive center with scuba, snorkeling, and windsurfing. AE, MC, V. EP. Expensive.*

Reigate Hall Hotel. Perched like a treehouse high on a steep wooded cliff a mile above Roseau and the ocean, this is a lovely stone-and-wood dwelling. It's the fanciest hotel in Dominica but is still quite casual. Rooms have locally made furnishings—such as embroidered bedspreads–air-conditioning, and private balconies; the higher priced rooms 17 and 18 have sea views. Some rooms have exposed brick, beam ceilings, and antiques; others have wet bars and refrigerators. Room amenities and arrangement are sort of a hodgepodge, with every room a bit different. *Reigate, tel. 809/448–4031; in the U.S., 800/223–9815; in Canada, 800/468–0023; fax 809/448–4034. 14 rooms, 2 suites, 1 apartment. Facilities: restaurant, 2 bars, pool, tennis, sauna. AE, MC, V. EP, MAP. Expensive.*

★ **Sans Souci Manor.** Three luxury apartments and one bungalow sit in a prosperous suburb high above Roseau. The bungalow and huge two-bedroom apartments have clay-tile floors, locally made wood and wicker furniture, fully equipped kitchens, large verandas with sweeping views of Roseau and the hills, and museum-quality Caribbean and Latin American art. Urbane owner John Keller hosts a sophisticated crowd of Americans and Europeans. Dinners are three-course affairs prepared by Mr. Keller, a gourmet cook, and served house-party style on his plant-filled terrace. *Box 373, St. Aromet, Roseau, tel. 809/448–2306, fax 809/448–6202. 3 apartments, 1 bungalow. Facilities: dining, honor bar, pool, airport transfers. AE, MC, V. Expensive.*

★ **Evergreen Hotel.** A recent expansion has added six bright, modern rooms with balconies and an airy bar and restaurant with terrace to this small hotel 2 miles from downtown Roseau. While the squeaky-clean new annex is somewhat lacking in authentic island charm (the older building, a stone-and-wood structure with a red roof, has more character), it's still where you want to stay. Air-conditioned rooms have bright print fabrics, rattan furnishings, cable TV, large shower baths, and lovely sea views. Other new additions include a pool, Italian ceramic tiles in the public areas, and a small garden. The new restaurant is excellent and another good reason to stay here. *Box 309, Roseau, tel. 809/448–3288, fax 809/448–6800. 16 rooms. Facilities: restaurant, bar, pool, dive shop, yacht moorings. AE, D, MC, V. EP, MAP. Moderate–Expensive.*

Anchorage Hotel. Years of wear have taken their toll on this hotel, although it still becomes an active scene during the season. Make sure you reserve one of the renovated rooms, with clay-tile floors and madras fabrics, in the two-story galleried section; don't bother with any of the other dark, lifeless units until they've seen a refurbishment—hopefully soon. *Box 34, Roseau, tel. 809/448–2638, fax 809/448–5680. 36 rooms. Facilities: restaurant, bar, pool, squash court. AE, D, MC, V. EP. Moderate.*

Coconut Beach Hotel. Rooms and baths here are bare and depressing, and amenities are nonexistent (only those staying a week get utensils to use in their kitchenettes). But the island's best beach, lovely Picard, is right outside your door. Another plus is an open-air bar and restaurant where a crowd of yachties (moorings are available here) and locals keeps things lively and friendly. The staff is friendly and laid-back, but only backpackers and budget travelers will truly feel at home here. *Box 37, Roseau, tel. 809/445–5393, fax 809/445–5693. 22 rooms. Facilities: restaurant, bar, dive shop, yacht moorings. AE, D, MC, V. EP, MAP. Inexpensive.*

Papillote Wilderness Retreat. This inn is in the rain forest, only a short hike from the 200-foot Trafalgar Falls and near river bathing. The spectacular setting includes a botanical garden, created by owner Anne Jean-Baptiste, with a mind-boggling assortment of plants and flowers. Rooms are low-ceilinged and somewhat dark, with a rustic, log-cabin feel. Bird calls and rushing water are your background music at meals, served in an open-air restaurant. *Box 67, Roseau, tel. 809/448–2287, fax 809/448–2286. 10 rooms. Facilities: restaurant, bar, gift shop. AE, DC, MC, V. EP, MAP. Inexpensive.*

Guest Houses/ Lodges

Castle Comfort Lodge. This small dive lodge, sandwiched between the Anchorage and Evergreen hotels and run by the enthusiastic
★ Derek and Ginette Perryman, wins a loyal following for its first-rate dive shop and excellent-value dive packages. Rooms are nothing special, although the five oceanfront units are more modern and cheerful than many you will find on the island. The Perrymans can also arrange various inland adventures and nature walks. *Box 63, Roseau, tel. 809/448–2188, fax 809/448–6088. 10 rooms. Facilities: restaurant, dive shop. AE, MC, V. EP. Moderate.*

★ **Hummingbird Inn.** This simple and perfect hilltop retreat is just a short drive from Roseau and Canefield Airport. The friendly and enthusiastic Finucane family built these 10 rooms, set in 2 bunga-lows with outstanding Caribbean views, in 1992. Rooms have white walls, terra-cotta-tile floors, and peaked wooden ceilings; varnished wooden hurricane windows can be left open all night to let in fresh breezes and the sounds of tree frogs and the ocean a few hundred yards down below. There's no air-conditioning, TV, or phones. Ceil-ing fans were added in 1994, and other nice touches include hand-made quilts and tables fashioned out of the trunks of local gommier trees. One large suite also has a four-poster bed and kitchen. The Hummingbird's cook is perhaps the best of any guest house on Dominica, and nonguests can arrange for dinner here if they call a day in advance—it's worth it to sample the fresh and expertly pre-pared local cuisine. *Box 20, Roseau, tel. or fax 809/449-1042. 9 rooms, 1 suite. Facilities: restaurant, bar. AE, MC, V. EP, MAP. Moderate.*

Itassi Cottages. The brochure pretty well lives up to its promise: "...for discerning travelers who are not necessarily loaded." These three self-contained cottages built within the past couple years can hold from two to six people each. They're much homier than most island lodgings, with a mix of antiques, straw mats, beautiful hand-made floral bedspreads, and wraparound porches with hammocks and sweeping views of Roseau, Scotts Head, and the Caribbean. These are ideal for long-term stays. Each has a kitchen, ceiling fans, and cable TV, and there is a shared laundry facility. Grounds are beautifully landscaped and include a tennis court. *Box 319, Roseau, tel. 809/448-4313, fax 809/448-3045. 3 cottages. Facilities: kitchens, laundry facility, tennis. No credit cards. Moderate.*

Floral Gardens. This 15-room motel looks like a Swiss Chalet—com-plete with latticed windows and flower boxes—plunked down on the edge of Dominica's rain forest reserve, on the island's windward side. Although rooms are carefully decorated with island crafts and homey fabrics, they are small and dark, with a slightly claustropho-bic feel. New, larger units closer to the beautiful Layou River were scheduled for completion in 1994. The restaurant here (*see* Dining, *above*) is a favorite among residents and tour groups, and the hotel's location is convenient for river bathing, hiking, and relaxing on northeast coast beaches. Congenial O. J. Seraphin, the former inter-im prime minister, is the owner. *Concord, tel. 809/445-7636, fax 809/445-7636. 15 rooms. Facilities: restaurant, gift shop. AE, MC, V. EP, MAP. Inexpensive.*

Layou Valley Inn. Tamara Holmes and her late husband built this tasteful house in the foothills of the national park, under the peaks of Morne Trois Pitons. She's a Russian who once translated for NASA but now devotes her talents to the kitchen. The rooms are simple and clean, and the sunken lounge and glass-fronted dining area are com-fortable, attractive places where guests mingle. Unless you plan on going nowhere (which suits some guests just fine), you'll need a car—even buses pass only infrequently. *Box 196, Roseau, tel. 809/449-6203, fax 809/448-5212. 10 rooms. Facilities: restaurant, bar, swimming in nearby rivers. AE, MC, V. EP, MAP. Inexpensive.*

Nightlife

Discos If you're not too exhausted from mountain climbing, swimming, and the like, you can join the locals on weekends at **The Warehouse** (tel. 809/449-1303), outside Roseau toward the airport, or the **Night Box** (Goodwill Road, no tel.), which attracts a rowdier clientele. Another favorite with locals is the easygoing **Good Times** (2 mi north of Roseau in Checkhall, tel. 809/449-1660), a reggae bar with an out-door patio and a sizable crowd on weekends.

Nightclubs When the moon comes up, most visitors go down to the dining room in their resident hotel for the music or chat offered there, which is always liveliest on weekends. Newly reopened Fort Young has upscale entertainment, as do many of the better hotels—the Castaways, Anchorage, and Reigate Hall in particular.

The **Shipwreck,** in the Canefield industrial area (tel. 809/449–1059), has live reggae and taped music on weekends and a Sunday bash that starts at noon and continues into the night.

The best insider's spot is definitely **Wykie's La Tropical** (51 Old St., Roseau, tel. 809/448–8015). This classic Caribbean hole-in-the-wall is a gathering spot for the island's movers and shakers, especially during Friday's happy hours from 5 to 7, when they nibble on stewed chicken or black pudding, then stay on for a local calypso band or Jing-Ping—a group playing local music on the accordion, *quage* (a kind of washboard instrument), drums, and a boom boom (a percussive instrument). Another resident favorite is **Lenville** (tel. 809/446–6598), a very basic rum shop with barbecued chicken and dancing in the village of Coulivistrie.

11 Dominican Republic

Updated by
Jordan
Simon

Sprawling over two-thirds of the island of Hispaniola, the Dominican Republic is the spot where European settlement of the Western Hemisphere really began. Santo Domingo, its capital, is the oldest continuously inhabited city in this half of the globe, and history buffs who visit have difficulty tearing themselves away from the many sites that boast of antiquity in the city's 16th-century Colonial Zone. Sun-seekers head for the beach resorts of Puerto Plata, Barahona, Samaná, and La Romana; at Punta Cana, beachcombers tan on the Caribbean's longest stretch of white-sand beach. The highest peak in the West Indies is here: Pico Duarte (10,128 feet) lures hikers to the central mountain range, and ancient sunken galleons and coral reefs divert divers and snorkelers.

Columbus happened upon this island on December 5, 1492, and on Christmas Eve his ship, the *Santa María*, was wrecked on the Atlantic shore. He named it La Isla Española ("the Spanish island"), established a small colony, and sailed back to Spain on the *Pinta*. A year later he returned, only to find that the Spanish colony had been destroyed by the Taino Indians, the island's original inhabitants. But Columbus established another colony nearby, leaving his brother Bartholomew in charge. Santo Domingo, which is located on the south coast where the Río Ozama spills into the Caribbean Sea, was founded in 1496 by Bartholomew Columbus and Nicolás de Ovando and during the first half of the 16th century became the bustling hub of Spanish commerce and culture in the New World.

Hispaniola (a derivation of *La Isla Española*) has had an unusually chaotic history, replete with bloody revolutions, military coups, yellow-fever epidemics, invasions, and bankruptcy. In the 17th century, the western third of the island was ceded to France; a slave revolt in 1804 resulted in the establishment there of the first black republic, Haiti. Dominicans and Haitians battled for control of the island on and off throughout the 19th century. The Dominicans declared themselves independent from Haiti in 1844 and from Spain in 1865. The country was, however, bankrupt by the turn of the century. The United States helped to administer the island's finances, and eventually U.S. Marines occupied the country from 1916 to 1924, until a new Dominican constitution was signed. Rafael Trujillo ruled the Dominican Republic with an iron fist from 1930 until his assassination in 1961. A short-lived democracy was overthrown soon thereafter, followed by another occupation by the U.S. Marines in 1965. The country has been relatively stable since the early 1970s, and administrations have been staunch supporters of the United States.

American influence looms large in Dominican life. If Dominicans do not actually have relatives living in the United States, they know someone who does; and many speak at least rudimentary English. Still, it is a vibrantly Latin country, and the Hispanic flavor contrasts sharply with the culture of the British, French, and Dutch islands in the Caribbean.

Dominican towns and cities are generally not quaint, neat, or particularly pretty. Poverty is everywhere, but the country is also alive and chaotic, sometimes frenzied, sometimes laid-back. Dominicans love music—there is dancing in the streets every summer at Santo Domingo's Merengue Festival—and they have a well-deserved reputation for being one of the friendliest people in the region. This is a tropical country; there is less urgency to get things done, and tempers don't flare up quickly. Blackouts, for instance, are a daily occurrence in much of the country, but this does not cause much discomfort for visitors, since most major hotels have emergency generators.

In recent years, tourism has played an increasingly important role in the government's scheme of things. Like Puerto Rico, its cousin to the east across the Mona Channel, the Dominican Republic used the 500th anniversary of its "discovery" by Christopher Columbus to give the tourist industry a much-needed boost. Its tourist zones are incredibly varied and include extravagant Casa de Campo, the manicured hotels of Playa Dorada, Santa Domingo's exquisite Colonial Zone, the neglected streets of Jarabacoa in its gorgeous mountain setting, and the world-weary beauty of the Samaná peninsula. Tourism officials hope the attractions, beaches, friendly people, and some of the Caribbean's lowest hotel rates will help recapture the lost American travel market.

Before You Go

Tourist Information

Contact the **Dominican Republic Department of Tourism,** Dominican Consulate, 1 Times Sq., 11th Floor, New York, NY 10036, tel. 212/768–2480; 2355 Salzedo Ave., Suite 305, Coral Gables, FL 33134, tel. 305/444–4592; 1464 Crescent St., Montreal, Quebec, Canada H3A 2B6, tel. 514/933–6126. The best source of information is the **Dominican Tourist Information Office** in Santo Domingo (tel. 800/752–1151), which will advise on all tourist matters. Be prepared to wait at least two weeks to get requested material sent to you.

Arriving and Departing
By Plane

The Dominican Republic has two major international airports: Las Américas International Airport, about 20 miles outside Santo Domingo, and La Unión International Airport, about 25 miles east of Puerto Plata on the north coast. **American Airlines** (tel. 800/433–7300) has the most extensive service to the Dominican Republic. It and **Dominicana** (tel. 212/765–7310) fly nonstop from New York to Santo Domingo; American, **Continental** (tel. 800/231–0856), and Dominicana fly nonstop from New York to Puerto Plata; Continental flies nonstop from Newark to Santo Domingo; **Carnival** (tel. 800/437–2110) offers daily service to Santo Domingo from New York, Miami, and Orlando; American and Dominicana fly nonstop from Miami to Santo Domingo; and American and Dominicana fly nonstop from Miami to Puerto Plata. Minneapolis-based **TransGlobal Tours** (tel. 800/338–2160) offers weekly charters from the Twin Cities to Puerto Plata. Continental has connecting service from Puerto Plata to Santo Domingo; American offers connections to both Santo Domingo and Puerto Plata from San Juan, Puerto Rico; and American Eagle has two flights a day from San Juan to La Romana and several flights weekly to Punta Cana.

Several regional carriers serve neighboring islands. **ALM** (tel. 800/327–7230) connects Santo Domingo to St. Maarten and Curaçao. There is also limited domestic service available from La Herrera Airport in Santo Domingo to smaller airfields in La Romana, Samaná, and Santiago. The new Barahona International Airport, opening in mid-1994, will handle large jet aircraft.

The remodeled and enlarged Las Américas (Santo Domingo) and La Unión (Puerto Plata) facilities are sophisticated by Latin American standards. Still, overworked customs and immigration officials are often less than courteous, and luggage theft is rife. Try to travel with carry-on luggage, and keep a sharp eye on it. Be prepared for a daunting experience as you leave customs. However, some order is being imposed—taxis now line up and, for the most part, charge the official established rates. If you have arranged for a hotel transfer, a representative should be waiting for you in the immigration hall.

From the Airport Taxis are available at the airport, and the 25-minute ride into Santo Domingo averages R.D.$250 (about U.S.$21). Taxi fares from the Puerto Plata airport average R.D.$200.

Passports and Visas U.S. and Canadian citizens must have either a valid passport or proof of citizenship, such as an original (not photocopied) birth certificate, and a tourist card. Legal residents of the United States must have an alien registration card (green card), a valid passport, and a tourist card. British citizens need only a valid passport; no entry visa is required. The requisite tourist card costs $10, and you should be sure to purchase it at the airline counter when you check in and then fill it out on the plane. You can purchase the card on arrival at the airport, but you may encounter long lines. Keep the bottom half of the card in a safe place because you'll need to present it to immigration authorities when you leave. There is also a U.S.$10 departure tax (payable only in U.S. dollars).

Language Before you travel to the Dominican Republic, you should know at least a smattering of Spanish. Guides at major tourist attractions and front-desk personnel in the major hotels speak a fascinating form of English, though they often have trouble understanding tourists. Traffic signs and restaurant menus, except at popular tourist establishments, are in Spanish. Using smiles and gestures will help, but a nodding acquaintance with the language or a phrase book is more useful.

Precautions Beware of the *buscones* at the airports. They offer to assist you, and do so by relieving you of your luggage and disappearing with it. Also avoid the black marketers, who will offer you a tempting rate of exchange for your U.S. dollars. If the police catch you changing money on the street, they'll haul you off to jail (the *calabozo*). Also, buy amber only from reputable shops. The attractively priced piece offered by the street vendor is more than likely plastic. Guard your wallet or pocketbook in Santo Domingo, especially around the Malecón (waterfront boulevard), which seems to teem with pickpockets.

Staying in the Dominican Republic

Important Addresses **Tourist Information:** The **Secretary of Tourism** is in Santo Domingo in a complex of government offices at the corner of Avenida Mexico and Avenida 30 de Marzo (Officinas Guberbamentales Building D, tel. 809/221–4660, fax 809/682–3806). Unless you are seeking special assistance, it is not worth making the trek here for the limited material offered to tourists. The **tourist office** is in Puerto Plata (Playa Long Beach, tel. 809/586–3676). Both offices are open weekdays 9–2:30, but the Puerto Plata office often opens late and closes early.

Emergencies **Police:** In Santo Domingo, call 711; in Puerto Plata, call 586–2804; in Sosúa, call 571–2233. However, do not expect too much from the police, aside from a bit of a hassle and some paperwork that they will consider the end of the matter. In general, the police and government bureaucrats take a hostile approach to visitors.

Hospitals: Santo Domingo emergency rooms that are open 24 hours are **Centro Médico Universidad Central del Este** (UCE) (Av. Máximo Gómez 68, tel. 809/682–1220), **Clínica Abreu** (Calle Beller 42, tel. 809/688–4411), and **Clínica Gómez Patino** (Av. Independencia 701, tel. 809/685–9131 or 685–9141). In Puerto Plata, you can go to **Clínica Dr. Brugal** (Calle José del Carmen Ariza 15, tel. 809/586–2519). In Sosúa, try the **Centro Médico Sosúa** (Av. Martinez, tel. 809/571–2305).

Pharmacies: Pharmacies that are open 24 hours a day are, in Santo Domingo, **San Judas Tadeo** (Av. Independencia 57, tel. 809/689–2851 or 809/685–8165); in Puerto Plata, **Farmacia Deleyte** (Av. John F. Kennedy 89, tel. 809/571–2515); in Sosúa, **San Rafael** (Carretera Cabarete Km. 1, tel. 809/571–0777).

Currency The coin of the realm is the Dominican peso, which is divided into 100 centavos. It is written R.D.$, and fluctuates relative to the U.S. dollar. At press time, U.S.$1 was equivalent to R.D.$12.30. Always make certain you know in which currency any transaction is taking place (any confusion will probably not be to your advantage). There is a growing black market for hard currency, so be wary of offers to exchange U.S. dollars at a rate more favorable than the official one.

Taxes and Hotels and restaurants add a service charge (15% in hotels, 10% in
Service restaurants) and 8% government tax. U.S. visitors must buy a $10
Charges tourist card before entering the Dominican Republic. All foreign visitors must pay a $10 departure tax. Both must be paid in U.S. dollars.

Although hotels add the 15% service charge, it is customary to leave a dollar per day for the hotel maid. At restaurants and nightclubs you may want to leave an additional 5%–10% tip for a job well done. Taxi drivers expect a 10% tip. Skycaps and hotel porters expect at least R.D.$5 per bag.

Guided Tours **Prieto Tours** (tel. 809/685–0102 or 809/688–5715) operates Gray Line of the Dominican Republic. It offers half-day bus tours of Santo Domingo, nightclub tours, beach tours, tours to Cibao Valley and the Amber Coast, and a variety of other tours.

Turinter (tel. 809/685–4020) tours include dinner and a show or casino visit, a full-day tour of Samaná, as well as specialty tours (museum, shopping, fishing).

Cafemba Tours (tel. 809/586–2177) runs various tours of the Cibao Valley and the Amber Coast, including Puerto Plata, Sosúa, and Rio San Juan.

Apolo Tours (tel. 809/586–5329) offers a full-day tour of Playa Grande and tours to Santiago (including a casino tour) and Sosúa. It will also arrange transfers between your hotel and the airport, day sightseeing tours, and custom and small-group tours along the north coast, which include stops along the way for swimming and an overnight stay at Samaná.

Ecoturista (tel. 809/221–4104) arranges ecological tours and cultural and scientific expeditions, many of them tailored to the clients' needs. **Mountain Jeep Safaris** (tel. 809/571–1924) runs Jeep tours in the mountains behind Puerto Plata and Sosúa, ending up at the new Cabarete Adventure Park, where you can swim in an underground pool and explore caves with Taino rock paintings. Buffet lunch and unlimited drinks are included in the R.D.$600 price.

Getting Taxis, which are government regulated, line up outside hotels and
Around restaurants. The taxis are unmetered, and the minimum fare within
Taxis Santo Domingo is about R.D.$50, but you can bargain for less if you order a taxi away from the major hotels. Hiring a taxi by the hour and with any number of stops is R.D.$125 per hour with a minimum of two hours. Be sure to establish the time that you start; drivers like to advance the time a little. Just be certain it is clearly understood in advance which currency is to be used in the agreed-upon fare. Taxis can also drive you to destinations outside the city. Rates are posted in hotels and at the airport. Sample fares are R.D.$930 to

La Romana and R.D.$1,830 to Puerto Plata. Round-trips are considerably less than twice the one-way fare. Call **Taxi la Paloma** (tel. 809/562-3460), **Taxi Raffi** (tel. 809/689-5468), or **Centro Taxi** (tel. 809/687-6128).

In a separate category are radio taxis, which are convenient if you'd like to schedule a pickup—and a wise choice if you don't speak Spanish. The fare is negotiated over the phone when you make the appointment. The most reliable company is **Apolo Taxi** (tel. 809/541-9595). The standard charge is R.D.$90 per hour during the day, R.D.$110 at night, no minimum, with as many stops as you like.

Avoid unmarked street taxis—there have been numerous incidents of assaults and robberies, particularly in Santo Domingo.

Buses   *Públicos* are small blue-and-white or blue-and-red cars that run regular routes, stopping to let passengers on and off. The fare is R.D.$2. Competing with the públicos are the *conchos* or *colectivos* (privately owned buses), whose drivers tool around the major thoroughfares, leaning out of the window or jumping out to try to persuade passengers to climb aboard. It's a colorful, if cramped, way to get around town. The fare is about R.D.$1. Privately owned air-conditioned buses make regular runs to Santiago, Puerto Plata, and other destinations. Avoid night travel, because the country's roads are full of potholes. You should make reservations by calling **Metro Buses** (Av. Winston Churchill, tel. in Santo Domingo, 809/566-6590, 809/566-6587, or 809/566-7126; in Puerto Plata, 809/586-6063; in Santiago, 809/583-9111; and in Nagua, 809/584-2259) or **Caribe Tours** (Av. 27 de Febrero at Leopoldo Navarro, tel. 809/687-3171). One-way bus fare from Santo Domingo to Puerto Plata is R.D.$70. *Voladoras* ("fliers") are vans that run from Puerto Plata's Central Park to Sosúa and Cabarete a couple of times each hour for R.D.$10. They don't run on a reliable schedule and are not always labeled with their destination.

Motorbike Taxis   Known as *motoconchos*, these bikes are a popular and inexpensive way to get around such tourist areas as Puerto Plata, Sosúa, and Jarabacoa. Bikes can be flagged down both on the road and in town; rates vary from R.D.$3 to R.D.$20 per person, depending upon distance.

Rental Cars   You'll need a valid driver's license from your own country and a major credit card and/or cash deposit. Cars can be rented at the airports and at many hotels. Among the known names are **Avis** (tel. 809/532-8786), **Budget** (tel. 809/567-0175), **Hertz** (tel. 809/221-5333), and **National** (tel. 809/562-1444). Rates average U.S.$70 and up per day, depending upon the make and size of the car. Driving is on the right. Many Dominicans drive recklessly, often taking their half of the road out of the middle, but they will flash their headlights to warn against highway patrols.

If for some unavoidable reason you must drive on the narrow, unlighted mountain roads at night, exercise extreme caution. Many local cars are without headlights or taillights, bicyclists do not have lights, and cows stand by the side of the road. Traffic and directional signs are less than adequate, and unseen potholes can easily break a car's axle. The 80-kph (50-mph) speed limit is strictly enforced. Finally, keep in mind that gas stations are few and far between in some of the remote regions. Police supplement their income by stopping drivers on various pretexts and expecting a "gift." Locals give R.D.$20 or R.D.$40.

Plane If you lack the time to travel overland, you can charter a small plane for trips around the island and to neighboring countries, and for surprisingly inexpensive rates. Contact Jimmy or Irene Butler at **Air Taxi** (Núñez de Cáceres 2, Santo Domingo, tel. 809/541–5333 or 809/541–7366).

Telephones and Mail To call the Dominican Republic from the United States, dial area code 809 and the local number. Connections are clear and easy to make. Fortunately, service from the Dominican Republic is much improved. There is direct-dial service to the United States; just dial 1, followed by area code and number.

Airmail postage to North America for a letter or postcard costs R.D.$2; to Europe, R.D.$4, and may take up to three weeks to reach the destination.

Opening and Closing Times Regular office and shop hours are weekdays 8–12:30 and 2:30–5, Saturday 8–noon. Government offices are open weekdays 7:30–2:30. Banking hours are weekdays 8:30–4:30.

Exploring the Dominican Republic

Numbers in the margin correspond to points of interest on the Santo Domingo map.

Santo Domingo We'll begin our tour where Spanish civilization in the New World began, in the 12-block area of **Santo Domingo** called the Colonial Zone. This historical area is now a bustling, noisy district with narrow cobbled streets, shops, restaurants, residents, and traffic jams. Ironically, all the noise and congestion make it somehow easier to imagine this old city as it was when the likes of Columbus, Cortés, Ponce de León, and pirates sailed in and out and colonists were settling themselves in the New World. Tourist brochures boast that "history comes alive here"—a surprisingly truthful statement.

A quick taxi tour of the old section takes about an hour, but if you're interested in history, you'll want to spend a day or two exploring the many old "firsts," and you'll want to do it in the most comfortable shoes you own. Be aware that wearing shorts, miniskirts, and halters in churches is considered inappropriate. (Note: Hours and admission charges are erratic; check with the tourist office in Puerto Plata for up-to-date information.)

One of the first things you'll see as you approach the Colonial Zone is a statue, only slightly smaller than the Colossus of Rhodes, staring
❶ out over the Caribbean Sea. It is **Montesina,** the Spanish priest who came to the Dominican Republic in the 16th century to appeal for human rights for Indians.

❷ **Parque Independencia** (Independence Park), on the far western border of the Colonial Zone, is a big city park dominated by the marble and concrete **Altar de la Patria.** The impressive mausoleum was built in 1976 to honor the founding fathers of the country (Duarte, Sánchez, and Mella).

❸ To your left as you leave the square, the **Concepción Fortress,** within the old city walls, was the northwest defense post of the colony. *Calle Palo Hincado at Calle Isidro Duarte, no tel. Admission free. Open Tues.–Sun. 9–6.*

From Independence Park, walk eight blocks east on Calle El Conde
❹ and you'll come to **Parque Colón.** The huge statue of Columbus dates from 1897 and is the work of French sculptor Gilbert. On the west side of the square is the **old town hall** and on the east, the **Palacio de**

Borgella, residence of the governor during the Haitian occupation of 1822–44 and presently the seat of the Permanent Dominican Commission for the **Fifth Centennial of the Discovery and Evangelization of the Americas.** Gallery spaces house architectural and archaeological exhibits pertaining to the fifth centennial.

Towering over the south side of the square is the coral limestone facade of the **Catedral Santa María la Menor, Primada de América,** the first cathedral in America. Spanish workmen began building the cathedral in 1514 but left off construction to search for gold in Mexico. The church was finally finished in 1540. Its facade is composed of architectural elements from the late Gothic to the plateresque style. Inside, the high altar is made of beaten silver, and in the treasury there is a magnificent collection of gold and silver. Some of its 14 lateral chapels serve as mausoleums for noted Dominicans, including Archbishop Meriño, who was once president of the Dominican Republic. Of interest is the Chapel of Our Lady of Antigua, which was reconsecrated by John Paul II in 1984. In the nave are four baroque columns, carved to resemble royal palms, which for more than four centuries guarded the magnificent bronze and marble sarcophagus containing (say Dominican historians) the remains of Christopher Columbus, whose last wish was to be buried in Santo Domingo. The sarcophagus has recently been moved to the Columbus Memorial Lighthouse (*see below*)—only the latest in the Great Navigator's posthumous journeys. *Calle Arzobispo Meriño, tel. 809/689–1920. Admission free. Open Mon.–Sat. 9–4; Sun. masses begin at 6 AM.*

When you leave the cathedral, turn right, walk to Columbus Square, and turn left on Calle El Conde. Walk one more block and turn right on Calle Hostos and continue for two more blocks. You'll see the ruins of the **Hospital de San Nicolás de Bari,** the first hospital in the New World, which was built in 1503 by Nicolás de Ovando. *Calle Hostos, between Calle de Las Mercedes and Calle Luperon, no tel.*

Continue along Calle Hostos, crossing Calle Emiliano Tejera, up the hill, and about midblock on your left you'll see the majestic ruins of the **San Francisco Monastery.** (If you look toward the horizon, you will see the impressive Columbus Memorial Lighthouse.) Constructed between 1512 and 1544, the monastery contained the church, chapel, and convent of the Franciscan order. Sir Francis Drake's demolition squad significantly damaged the building in 1586, and in 1673 an earthquake nearly finished the job, but when it's floodlit at night, the old monastery is indeed a dramatic sight. Plans are in the works to begin holding occasional cultural events here.

Walk east for two blocks along Calle Emiliano Tejera. Opposite the Telecom building on Calle Isabel la Católica, the **Casa del Cordón** is recognizable by the sash of the Franciscan order carved in stone over the arched entrance. This house, built in 1503, is the Western Hemisphere's oldest surviving stone house. Columbus's son Diego Colón, viceroy of the colony, and his wife lived here until the Alcázar was finished. It was in this house, too, that Sir Francis Drake was paid a ransom to prevent him from totally destroying the city. The house is now home to the Banco Popular. *Corner of Calle Emiliano Tejera and Calle Isabel la Católica, no tel. Admission free. Open weekdays 8:30–4:30.*

Walk one block east along Calle Emiliano Tejera to reach the imposing **Alcázar de Colón,** with its balustrade and double row of arches. The Renaissance structure has strong Moorish, Gothic, and Isabelline influences. The castle of Don Diego Colón, built in 1514,

Dominican Republic

Cofresí Beach
Luperón Beach
Montecristi
Guayubin
Dajabón
Puerto Plata
La Unión International Airport
Playa Dorada
Sosúa
Cabarete Beach
Santiago de los Caballeros
Moca
San Francisco de Macorís
Jarabacoa
HAITI
Bánica
San Juan
Lago Enriquillo
Neiba
Azua
Duvergé
Bahía de Ocoa
Bani
Pedernales
Barahona
HISPANIOLA
Oviedo
Isla Beata
Cabo Beata

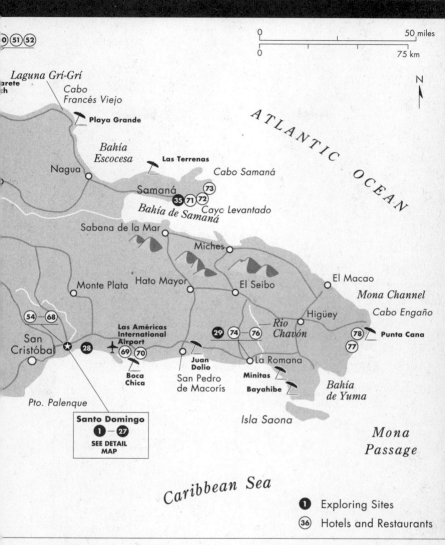

Laguna Grí-Grí

Cabo
Francés Viejo

▲ Playa Grande

Bahía
Escocesa

Las Terrenas

Cabo Samaná

Nagua

Samaná (73)

(35)(71)(72)

Cayo Levantado

Bahía de Samaná

Sabana de la Mar

Miches

El Macao

Monte Plata

Hato Mayor

El Seibo

Mona Channel
Cabo Engaño

Higüey

Río
Chavón

(54)—(68)

(29)(74)(76)

(78) Punta Cana

San
Cristóbal

(28)

Las Américas
International
Airport

(69)(70)

(77)

Boca
Chica

Juan
Dolio

La Romana

Minitas

Bahía
de Yuma

San Pedro
de Macorís

Bayahibe

Pto. Palenque

Santo Domingo
(1)—(27)
SEE DETAIL
MAP

Isla Saona

Mona
Passage

Caribbean Sea

(1) Exploring Sites

(36) Hotels and Restaurants

ATLANTIC OCEAN

N

0   50 miles
0   75 km

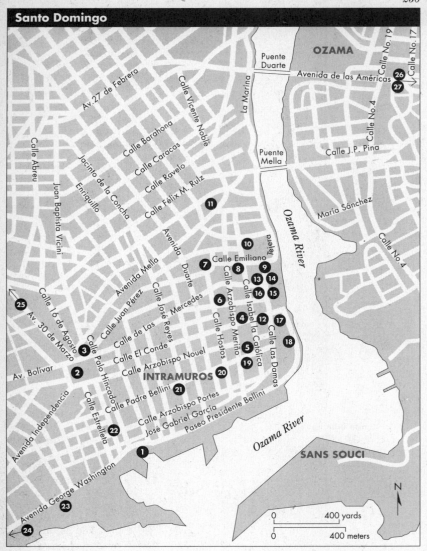

Santo Domingo

OZAMA

Puente
Duarte

Calle No. 19

Calle No. 17

Avenida de las Américas

26
27

Av. 27 de Febrero

La Marina

Calle Vicente Noble

Calle J.P. Pina

Calle No. 4

Puente
Mella

Calle Barahona

Calle Caracas

Calle Abreu

Jacinto de la Concha

Enriquillo

Juan Baptista Vicini

Calle Ravelo

Calle Félix M. Ruiz

11

María Sánchez

Calle No. 4

Ozama River

Avenida Duarte

Avenida Mella

10

Calle Emiliano

7

8

9

13   14

16   15

La Joleta

25

Av. 30 de Marzo

Calle 16 de Agosto

Calle Juan Pérez

Calle José Reyes

Calle de Las Mercedes

6

Calle Arzobispo Merino

Calle Isabel la Católica

4   12

17

Calle Hostos

Calle Las Damas

18

3

Calle Palo Hincado

Calle El Conde

Calle Arzobispo Nouel

5

19

INTRAMUROS

2

Av. Bolívar

Avenida Independencia

Calle Estrelleta

Calle Padre Bellini

20

21

Calle Arzobispo Portes

José Gabriel García

Paseo Presidente Bellini

Ozama River

22

1

SANS SOUCI

N

0   400 yards

0   400 meters

23

Avenida George Washington

24

Acuario Nacional, **26**
Alcázar de Colón, **9**
Calle Las Damas, **12**
Capilla de los
Remedios, **14**
Casa de Bastidas, **17**
Casa de Tostado, **19**
Casa del Cordón, **8**
Catedral Santa María
la Menor, **5**

Concepción
Fortress, **3**
El Faro a Colón, **27**
Hospital de San
Nicolás de Bari, **6**
Hostal Palacio Nicolás
de Ovando, **15**
Iglesia y Convento
Domínico, **20**
Jardín Botánico
Nacional Dr. Rafael
M. Moscoso, **25**

La Atarazana, **10**
La Iglesia de Regina
Angelorum, **21**
Malecón, **23**
Montesina, **1**
Museo de las Casas
Reales, **13**
National Pantheon, **16**
Parque Colón, **4**
Parque Indepen-
dencia, **2**

Plaza de la Cultura, **24**
Puerta de la
Misericordia, **22**
San Francisco
Monastery, **7**
Santa Bárbara
Church, **11**
Torre del
Homenaje, **18**

was painstakingly reconstructed and restored in 1957. Forty-inch-thick coral limestone walls were patched and shored with blocks from the original quarry. There are 22 rooms, furnished in a style to which the viceroy of the island would have been accustomed—right down to the dishes and the viceregal shaving mug. Many of the period paintings, statues, tapestries, and furnishings were donated by the University of Madrid. *Just off Calle Emiliano Tejera at the foot of Calle Las Damas, tel. 809/687–5361. Admission: R.D.$10. Open Mon. and Wed.–Fri. 9–5, Sat. 9–4, Sun. 9–1. Closed Tues.*

⑩ Across from the Alcázar, **La Atarazana** (the Royal Mooring Docks) was once the colonial commercial district, where naval supplies were stored. There are eight restored buildings, the oldest of which dates from 1507. It now houses crafts shops, restaurants, and art galleries.

Time Out If your walking tour leads you to La Atarazana by midday, join the Reserve Bank and Telecom staff at the **Café Montesinos** (Calle La Atarazana 23) for a typical Dominican noonday meal. For R.D.$50 the hearty specials may include fish or beef in a succulent Creole sauce and a tasty bean soup with plantains. If you happen to be in that area in the late afternoon, stop in for a pizza and a drink at **Drake's Pub** (Calle La Atarazana 25). There's a fine view of the Alcázar from here, and the place fills up with congenial locals and foreigners.

⑪ To reach the **Santa Bárbara Church,** go back to Calle Isabel la Católica, turn right, and walk several blocks. This combination church and fortress, the only one of its kind in Santo Domingo, was completed in 1562. *Av. Mella, between Calle Isabel la Católica and Calle Arzobispo Meriño, no tel. Admission free. Open weekdays 8–noon. Sun. masses begin at 6 AM.*

⑫ Retrace your steps to Calle Isabel la Católica, turn left on Calle de Las Mercedes, and walk one block right to **Calle Las Damas,** where you'll make a right turn to the New World's oldest street. The "Street of the Ladies" was named after the elegant ladies of the court who, in the Spanish tradition, promenaded in the evening.

On your left you'll see a sundial dating from 1753 and the **Casa de los Jesuitas,** which houses a fine research library for colonial history as well as the Institute for Hispanic Culture. *Admission free. Open weekdays 8–4:30.*

⑬ Across the street is the **Museo de las Casas Reales** (Museum of the Royal Houses). The collections in the museum are displayed in two early-16th-century palaces that have been altered many times over the years. Exhibits cover everything from antique coins to replicas of the *Niña,* the *Pinta,* and the *Santa María.* There are statue and cartography galleries, coats of armor and coats of arms, coaches and a royal court room, gilded furnishings, and Indian artifacts. The first room of the former Governor's Residence has a wall-size map marking the routes sailed by Columbus's ships on expeditions beginning in 1492. If you like museums, you may have a hard time taking leave of this one. *Calle Las Damas, corner Calle Mercedes, tel. 809/ 682–4202. Admission: R.D.$10. Open Tues.–Sat. 9–4:45, Sun. 10–1.*

⑭ Across the street is the **Capilla de los Remedios** (Chapel of Our Lady of Remedies), which was originally built in the 17th century as a private chapel for the family of Francisco de Dávila. Early colonists also worshiped here before the completion of the cathedral. Its architectural details, particularly the lateral arches, are evocative of the Castilian-Romanesque style. *Calle Las Damas, at the foot of Calle Mercedes, no tel. Admission free. Open Mon.–Sat. 9–6; Sun. masses begin at 6 AM.*

⑮ Just south of the chapel on Calle Las Damas, the **Hostal Palacio Nicolás de Ovando** (*see* Lodging, *below*), now a highly praised hotel, was once the residence of Nicolás de Ovando, one of the principal organizers of the colonial city.

⑯ Across the street from the hotel looms the massive **National Pantheon.** The building, which dates from 1714, was once a Jesuit monastery and later a theater. Trujillo had it restored in 1955 with an eye toward being buried there. (He is buried instead at Père Lachaise in Paris.) An allegorical mural of his assassination is painted on the ceiling above the altar, where an eternal flame burns. The impressive chandelier was a gift from Spain's Generalissimo Franco. *Calle Las Damas, near the corner of Calle Mercedes, no tel. Admission free. Open Mon.–Sat. 10–5.*

Continue south on Calle Las Damas and cross Calle El Conde. Look
⑰ on your left for the **Casa de Bastidas,** where there is a lovely inner courtyard with tropical plants and temporary exhibit galleries. *Calle Las Damas, just off Calle El Conde, no tel. Admission free. Open Tues.–Sun. 9–5.*

⑱ You won't have any trouble spotting the **Torre del Homenaje** (Tower of Homage) in the Fort Ozama. The fort sprawls two blocks south of the Casa de Bastidas, with a brooding crenellated tower that still guards the Ozama River. The fort and its tower were built in 1503 to protect the eastern border of the city. The sinister tower was the last home of many a condemned prisoner. *On Paseo Presidente Bellini, overlooking Río Ozama, no tel. Admission: R.D.$10. Open Tues.–Sun. 8–7.*

When you leave the fortress, turn left off Calle Las Damas onto
⑲ Calle Padre Bellini. A two-block walk will bring you to **Casa de Tostado.** The house was built in the first decade of the 16th century and was the residence of writer Don Francisco Tostado. Its twin Gothic windows are the only ones that are still in existence in the New World. It now houses the **Museo de la Familia Dominicana** (Museum of the Dominican Family), which features exhibits on the well-heeled Dominican family in the 19th century. *Calle Padre Bellini, near Calle Arzobispo Meriño, tel. 809/689–5057. Admission: R.D.$10. Open Thurs.–Tues. 9–2.*

Walk two blocks west on Calle Padre Bellini to the corner of Avenida
⑳ Duarte. The graceful building with the rose window is the **Iglesia y Convento Domínico** (Dominican Church and Convent), founded in 1510. In 1538, Pope Paul III visited here and was so impressed with the lectures on theology that he granted the church and convent the title of university, making it the oldest institution of higher learning in the New World. *Calle Padre Bellini and Av. Duarte, tel. 809/682–3780. Admission free. Open Tues.–Sun. 9–6.*

Continue west on Calle Padre Bellini for two blocks, and at the cor-
㉑ ner of Calle José Reyes you'll see another lovely church, **La Iglesia de Regina Angelorum** (Church of Regina Angelorum), which dates from 1537. The church was damaged during the Haitian regime, from 1822 to 1844, but you can still appreciate its Baroque dome, Gothic arches, and traceries. *Corner of Calle Padre Bellini and Calle José Reyes, tel. 809/682–2783. Admission free. Open Mon.–Sat. 9–6.*

㉒ Walk four blocks west on Calle Padre Bellini, turn left on Calle Palo Hincado, and keep going straight till you reach the **Puerta de la Misericordia** (Gate of Mercy), part of the old wall of Santo Domingo. It was here on the plaza, on February 27, 1844, that Ramón Mata Mella, one of the country's founding fathers, fired the shot that began the struggle for independence from Haiti.

Parque Independencia separates the old city from the new. Avenidas 30 de Marzo, Bolívar, and Independencia traverse the park and mingle with avenues named for George Washington, John F. Kennedy, and Abraham Lincoln. Modern Santo Domingo is a sprawling, noisy city with a population of close to 2 million.

Avenida George Washington, which features tall palms and Las Vegas–style tourist hotels, breezes along the Caribbean Sea. The
㉓ Parque Litoral de Sur, better known as the **Malecón,** borders the avenue from the colonial city to the Hotel Santo Domingo, a distance of about 3 miles. The seaside park, with its cafés and places to relax, is a popular spot, but beware of pickpockets.

Time Out Before leaving the seafront, check out **Baseball Blues** (Av. George Washington 503, tel. 809/686–7103). Locals come here to watch TV *béisbol* (baseball), the ocean, and one another. There's a happy hour from 5 to 8, when jazz is played.

Avenida Máximo Gómez comes down from the north. Take a right turn on it, cross Avenida Bolívar, and you'll come to the landscaped
㉔ lawns, modern sculptures, and sleek buildings of the **Plaza de la Cultura.** Among the buildings are the **National Theater** (tel. 809/687–3191), which stages performances in Spanish; the **National Library,** in which the written word is Spanish; and museums and art galleries, whose notations are also in Spanish. The following museums on the plaza are open Tuesday–Saturday from 10 to 5, and admission to each is R.D.$10: The **Museum of Dominican Man** (tel. 809/687–3622) traces the migrations of Indians from South America through the Caribbean islands. The **Museum of Natural History** (tel. 809/689–0106) examines the flora and fauna of the island. In the **Gallery of Modern Art** (tel. 809/682–8260), the works of 20th-century Dominican and foreign artists are displayed.

㉕ North of town in the Arroyo Hondo district is the **Jardín Botánico Nacional Dr. Rafael M. Moscoso** (Dr. Rafael M. Moscoso National Botanical Gardens), the largest garden in the Caribbean. Its 445 acres include a Japanese garden, a great ravine, a glen, a gorgeous display of orchids, and an enormous floral clock. You can tour the gardens by train, boat, or horse-drawn carriage. *Arroyo Hondo, no tel. Admission: R.D.$2. Open daily 10–6.*

In the 320-acre **Parque Zoológico Nacional** (National Zoological Park), not far from the botanical gardens, animals roam free in natural habitats. There is an African plain, a children's zoo, and what the zoo claims is the world's largest bird cage. *Av. Máximo Gómez at Av. de los Proceres, tel. 809/562–2080. Admission: R.D.$10. Open daily 10–6.*

㉖ Now head east and cross the Río Ozama at Puente Duarte. Take Avenida de las Américas to the **Acuario Nacional** (National Aquarium). The largest aquarium in the Caribbean, with an impressive collection of tropical fish and dolphins, its construction was a controversial public expenditure. *In the Sans Souci district on the Avenida de las Américas. Admission: R.D.$10. Open daily 10–6.*

㉗ Follow the signs to the nearby **El Faro a Colón** (Columbus Memorial Lighthouse). This striking lighthouse monument and museum complex dedicated to the Great Navigator is shaped like a pyramid cross. Completed in 1992, its inauguration was set to coincide with the 500th anniversary of Christopher Columbus's landing on the island. Along with its showpiece laser-powered lighthouse, the complex holds the tomb of Columbus (recently moved there after 400 years in the Catedral Santa María la Menor) and six museums featuring exhibits related to Columbus and early exploration of the New World. One museum focuses on the long, rocky, and often controversial history of the lighthouse memorial itself and another on the Great Navigator's posthumous peregrinations (Cuba, Spain, and the Dominican Republic have all laid claim to—and hosted—his remains, which even today are a subject of controversy). *Av. España. No tel. Admission: R.D.$5, children under 12 R.D.$1. Open Tues.–Sun. 9–4.*

The East *Numbers in the margin correspond to points of interest on the Do-*
Coast *minican Republic map.*

Continue east on Las Américas Highway toward La Romana, about a two-hour drive along the southeast coast. All along the highway are small resort-hotel complexes where you can find refreshments or stay overnight. About 1½ miles outside the capital, you'll come to
㉘ the **Parque de los Tres Ojos** (Park of the Three Eyes). The "eyes" are cool blue pools peering out of deep limestone caves, and it's actually a four-eyed park. If you've a mind to, you can look into the eyes more closely by climbing down into the caves.

About 20 minutes east of the city is **Boca Chica Beach,** popular because of its proximity to the capital. Another 45 minutes or so farther east is the city of **San Pedro de Macorís,** where the national sport and the national drink are both well represented. Some of the country's best béisbol games are played in **Tetelo Vargas Stadium,** which you can see off the highway to your left. The grander homes in the area most likely belong to Dominican baseball stars like George Bell. The **Macorís Rum distillery** is on the eastern edge of the city. Outside town is Juan Dolio, another beach popular with *capitaleños*.

The two big businesses around La Romana used to be cattle and sugarcane. That was before Gulf & Western created (and subsequently sold) the **Casa de Campo** resort (*see* Lodging, *below*), which is a very big business, indeed, and **Altos de Chavón,** a re-creation of a 16th-century village and art colony on the resort grounds.

㉙ **Altos de Chavón** sits on a bluff overlooking the Río Chavón, about 3 miles east of the main facility of Casa de Campo. You can drive there easily enough, or you can take one of the free shuttle buses from the resort. In this re-creation of a medieval Spanish village, there are cobblestone streets lined with lanterns, wrought-iron balconies, and courtyards swathed with bougainvillea. More than a museum piece, this village is a place where artists live, work, and play. There is an art school, affiliated with New York's Parsons School of Design; a disco; an archaeological museum; five restaurants; and a 5,000-seat outdoor amphitheater (used about four times a year) where Frank Sinatra and Julio Iglesias have entertained. The focal point of the village is **Iglesia St. Stanislaus,** which is named after the patron saint of Poland in tribute to the Polish Pope John Paul II, who visited the Dominican Republic in 1979 and left some of the ashes of St. Stanislaus behind.

From here the road continues east to Punta Cana and Bavaro, glorious beaches on the sunrise side of the island. On the way you'll pass through Higüey, an undistinguished collection of ramshackle buildings notable only for its controversial church, consecrated by Pope John Paul II in 1984, which resembles a pinched McDonald's arch.

The Cibao Valley The road to the north coast cuts through the lush banana plantations, rice and tobacco fields, and royal poinciana trees of the Cibao Valley. All along the road there are stands where, for a few centavos, you can buy ripe pineapples, mangoes, avocados, *chicharrones* (either fried pork rinds or chicken pieces), and fresh fruit drinks. To ❸⓪ the west is **Pico Duarte,** at 10,128 feet the highest peak in the West Indies.

In the heart of the Cibao is La Vega. Founded in 1495 by Columbus, it is the site of one of the oldest settlements in the New World. The inquisitive will find the tour of the ruins of the original settlement, ❸① **La Vega Vieja** (The Old La Vega), a rewarding experience. About 3 miles north of La Vega is **Santo Cerro** (Holy Mount), site of a miraculous apparition of the Virgin and therefore many local pilgrimages. The **Convent of La Merced** is located there, and the views of the Cibao Valley are breathtaking.

About 90 miles north of the capital, you'll come to the industrial city of **Santiago de los Caballeros,** where a massive monument honoring the restoration of the republic guards the entrance to the city. Many past presidents were born in Santiago, and it is currently a center for processing tobacco leaf. You can gain an appreciation of the art and skill of Cuban cigar–making with a tour of **La Aurora Tabacalera** (tel. 809/582–1131).

The Amber Coast The Autopista Duarte ultimately leads (in three to four hours from Santo Domingo) to the Amber Coast, so called because of its large, rich, and unique deposits of amber. The coastal area around Puerto Plata is a region of splashy resorts and megadevelopments like Costambar and Playa Dorada. The north coast boasts more than 70 miles of beaches, with condominiums and villas going up fast.

❸② **Puerto Plata,** although now quiet and almost sleepy, was a dynamic city in its heyday. Visitors can get a feeling for this past in the magnificent Victorian **Glorieta** (Gazebo) in the central **Parque Independencia.** Next to the park, the recently refurbished **Catedral de San Felipe** recalls a simpler, colonial past. On Puerto Plata's own Malecón, the **Fortaleza de San Felipe** protected the city from many a pirate attack and was later used as a political prison. The fort is most dramatic at night.

Puerto Plata is also the home of the **Museum of Dominican Amber,** a lovely galleried mansion and one of several tenants in the Tourist Bazaar. The museum displays and sells the Dominican Republic's national stone. Semiprecious, translucent amber is actually fossilized pine resin that dates back about 50 million years, give or take a few millennia. The north coast of the Dominican Republic has the largest deposits of amber in the world (the only other deposits are found in Germany and the formerU.S.S.R.), and jewelry crafted from the stone is the best-selling item on the island. *Calle Duarte 61, tel. 809/586–2848. Admission: R.D.$10. Open Mon.–Sat. 9–5.*

❸③ Southwest of Puerto Plata (follow the signs from the Autopista), you can take a cable car (when it is working) to the top of **Mt. Isabel de Torres,** which soars 2,600 feet above sea level. On the mountain there is a botanical garden, a huge statue of Christ, and a spectacular view. The cable was first laid in 1754, although rest assured that it's been replaced since then. Lines can be long, and once on top of the mountain you will wonder if it was worth the time. Don't eat at the restaurant at the top—the food is awful. *No phone. Cable car operates Tues., Thurs., Fri., Sat., and Sun. 8–6. Round-trip is R.D.$20.*

34 Take the Autopista east from Puerto Plata about 15 miles to **Sosúa,** a small community settled during World War II by 600 Austrian and German Jews. After the war, many of them returned to Europe or went to the United States, and most of those who remained married Dominicans. Only a few Jewish families reside in the community today, and there is only one small one-room synagogue. The flavor of the town is decidedly Spanish. (Note: Be warned that the roads off the Autopista are horribly punctured with potholes.)

Sosúa has become one of the most frequently visited tourist destinations in the country, favored by French Canadians and Europeans. Hotels and condos are going up at breakneck speed. It actually consists of two communities, **El Batey,** the modern hotel development, and **Los Charamicos,** the old quarter, separated by a cove and one of the island's prettiest beaches. The sand is soft and white, the water crystal clear and calm. The walkway above the beach is packed with tents filled with souvenirs, pizzas, and even clothing for sale—a jarring note in this otherwise idyllic setting.

Time Out   **The Albatros** (Calle Pedro Clisante, tel. 809/571–2325), in the center of Sosúa, is a hot spot for tacos, hamburgers, and a rum punch or two. It also serves as an impromptu library filled with an eclectic collection of paperbacks that are ideal for beach reading.

Continue east on the Autopista past **Cabarete,** a popular windsurfing haunt, and **Playa Grande.** The powdery white beach remains miraculously undisturbed and unspoiled by development.

35 The Autopista rolls along eastward and rides out onto a "thumb" of the island, where you'll find **Samaná.** Back in 1824, a sailing vessel called the *Turtle Dove,* carrying several hundred escaped American slaves from the Freeman Sisters' underground railway, was blown ashore in Samaná. The escapees settled and prospered, and today their descendants number several thousand. The churches here are Protestant; the worshipers live in villages called Bethesda, Northeast, and Philadelphia; and the language spoken is an odd 19th-century form of English.

The wealth of marine life in the surrounding waters is beginning to attract more specialty tourists. Sportfishing at Samaná is considered to be among the best in the world. In addition, about 3,000 humpback whales winter off the coast of Samaná from December to March. Major whale-watching expeditions like those out of Massachusetts, are being organized and should boost the region's economy without scaring away the world's largest mammals.

Samaná makes a fine base for exploring the area's natural splendors. Most hotels on the peninsula arrange tours to the **Los Haitises National Park,** a remote unspoiled rain forest with limestone knolls, crystal lakes, mangrove swamps teeming with aquatic birds, and caves stippled with Taino petroglyphs. **Las Terrenas,** a remote stretch of beautiful, nearly deserted beaches on the north coast of the Samaná peninsula, is barely known to North American tourists, although French Canadians and Europeans, especially Germans, have begun making the long trek to this latter-day hippie haven that also attracts surfboarders and windsurfers. There are several modest restaurants (the best is **Boca Fina,** no tel.) for fresh seafood, a dusty main street in the town of Las Terrenas, a small airfield, the

El Portillo Beach Club (tel. 809/688–5785), and several congenial hotels right on the beach at Punta Bonita. If you're seeking tranquillity and are happy just hanging out drinking beer and soaking up sun, this is the place for you. The road from Samaná, even though it is longer and not paved, is a lot less strenuous than coming over the hills from Sanchez.

Dominican Republic for Free

Concerts. The quadrangle of Santo Domingo's Plaza de la Cultura is the site of occasional classical music concerts that you can hear for a song. There are also open-air concerts along the Malecón. Check with local newspapers, your hotel, or the tourist office for dates and programs.

Colonial Zone. Many of the ancient buildings have no admission charge, notably the Catedral Santa María la Menor, the San Francisco Monastery, and the Casa del Cordón (*see* Exploring the Dominican Republic, *above*).

What to See and Do with Children

Acuario Nacional (*see* Exploring the Dominican Republic, *above*).

Columbus Memorial Lighthouse (*see* Exploring the Dominican Republic, *above*) fascinates kids, who especially love the hourly changing of the guard.

Parque Zoológico Nacional (*see* Exploring the Dominican Republic, *above*).

Parque de los Tres Ojos (*see* Exploring the Dominican Republic, *above*).

Off the Beaten Track

The Dominican Republic offers vastly different microclimates in an area that is only twice the size of Massachusetts.

Laguna Grí-Grí is a swampland smack out of the Louisiana bayou country, with the added attraction of a cool blue grotto that almost outdoes the Blue Grotto of Capri. Laguna Grí-Grí is only about 90 minutes west of Puerto Plata, in Río San Juan (ask for directions off the Autopista). Contact the tourist office for arrangements.

Nature lovers should consider a trip to **Jarabacoa,** in the mountainous region known rather wistfully as the Dominican Alps. There is little to do in the town itself but eat and rest up for excursions on foot, horseback, or by motorbike taxi to the surrounding waterfalls and forests—quite incongruous in such a tropical country. Accommodations in the area are rustic but comfortable.

Less accessible and vastly different is the largest lake in the Antilles, **Lago Enriquillo,** near the Haitian border. The salt lake is also the lowest point in the Antilles: 114 feet below sea level. The lake encircles wild, arid, and thorny islands that serve as sanctuary to such exotic birds and reptiles as the flamingo, the iguana, and the caiman—the indigenous crocodile.

Equally wild and pristine is **Barahona,** just to the south and the latest area to be developed. Here mountains carpeted with emerald rain forests and laced with silvery streams slope down into sugary white stretches of sand.

Just off the east coast of Hispaniola lies **Isla Saona,** now a national park inhabited by sea turtles, pigeons, and other wildlife. Caves on the island were once used by Indians. The beaches are beautiful, and legend has it that Columbus once strayed ashore here.

Beaches

The Dominican Republic has more than 1,000 miles of beaches, including the Caribbean's longest strip of white sand—Punta Cana. Many beaches are accessible to the public and may tempt you to stop for a swim. Be careful: Some have dangerously strong currents.

Boca Chica is the beach closest to Santo Domingo (2 miles east of Las Américas Airport, 21 miles from the capital), and it's crowded with city folks on weekends. Five years ago, this beach was virtually a four-lane highway of fine white sand. "Progress" has since cluttered it with plastic beach tables, chaise longues, pizza stands, and beach cottages for rent. But the sand is still fine, and you can walk far out into clear blue water, which is protected by natural coral reefs that help keep the big fish at bay.

About 20 minutes east of Boca Chica is another beach of fine white sand, **Juan Dolio.** The Metro Hotel and Marina, the all-inclusive Decameron, Villas del Mar Hotel, and Punta Garza Beach Club are on this beach.

Moving counterclockwise around the island, you'll come to the La Romana area, with its miniature **Minitas** beach and lagoon, and the long, white-sand, palm-lined crescent of **Bayahibe** beach, which is accessible only by boat. La Romana is the home of the 7,000-acre Casa de Campo resort (*see* Lodging, *below*), so you're not likely to find any private place in the sun here.

The gem of the Caribbean, **Punta Cana** is a 20-mile strand of pearl-white sand shaded by trees and coconut palms. Located on the easternmost coast, it is the home of several top resorts.

Las Terrenas, on the north coast of the Samaná peninsula, looks like something from *Robinson Crusoe*: Tall palms list toward the sea, away from the mountains; the beach is narrow but sandy; and best of all, there is nothing man-made in sight—just vivid blues, greens, and yellows. Two adjacent hotels are right on the beach at nearby Punta Bonita.

Playa Grande, on the north coast, is a long stretch of powdery sand that is slated for development. At present, it's undisturbed, but you'd better hurry if you want to enjoy it in solitude. Actually, the entire northeast coast seems like one unbroken golden stretch, unmaintained and littered with kelp, driftwood, and the occasional beer bottle. If you don't mind the lack of facilities and upkeep, you have your pick of deserted beaches.

The ideal wind and surf conditions of **Cabarete Beach,** also on the north coast, have made it an integral part of the international windsurfing circuit.

Farther west is the lovely beach at **Sosúa,** where calm waters gently lap at long stretches of soft white sand. Unfortunately the backdrop here is a string of tents, with hawkers pushing cheap souvenirs. You can, however, get snacks and rent water-sports equipment from the vendors.

On the north Amber Coast, still-developing **Puerto Plata** is about to outdo San Juan's famed Condado strip. The beaches are of soft ecru or white sand, with lots of reefs for snorkeling. The Atlantic waters are great for windsurfing, waterskiing, and fishing expeditions.

About an hour west of Puerto Plata lies **Luperón Beach,** a wide white-sand beach fit for snorkeling, windsurfing, and scuba diving. The Luperón Beach Resort is handy for rentals and refreshments.

Sports and the Outdoors

Although there is hardly a shortage of outdoor activities here, the resorts have virtually cornered the market on sports, including every conceivable water sport. In some cases, facilities may be available only to guests. You can check with the tourist office for more details. Listed below is a mere smattering of the island's athletic options:

Bicycling Pedaling is easy on pancake-flat beaches, but there are also steep hills in the Dominican Republic. Bikes are available at **Villas Doradas** (Playa Dorada, Puerto Plata, tel. 809/586–3000), **Dorado Naco** (Dorado Beach, tel. 809/586–2019), **Jack Tar Village** (Puerto Plata, tel. 809/586–3800), and the **Hotel Cofresi** (Puerto Plata, tel. 809/586–2898).

Boating Hobie Cats and pedal boats are available at **Heavens** (Playa Dorada, tel. 809/586–5250). Check also at **Casa de Campo** (La Romana, tel. 809/682–2111) and **Club Med** (Punta Cana, tel. 809/567–5228).

Deep-Sea Fishing Marlin and wahoo are among the fish that folks angle for here. Arrangements can be made through **Casa de Campo** (La Romana, tel. 809/682–2111) or **Actividas Acuaticás** (Playa Dorada, tel. 809/506–3988). Fishing is best between January and June.

Golf **Casa de Campo** has two 18-hole Pete Dye courses and a third for the private use of villa owners. Two new 18-hole courses are planned for the **Punta Cana Beach Resort** and the **Bávaro Beach.** The Playa Dorada hotels have their own 18-hole Robert Trent Jones–designed course; there is also a 9-hole course nearby at the **Costambar** complex. Guests in Santo Domingo hotels are usually allowed to use the 18-hole course at the **Santo Domingo Country Club** on weekdays— *after* members have teed off. There is a 9-hole course outside of town, at Lomas Lindas. A new Pete Dye course is under construction outside Santo Domingo.

Horseback Riding **Casa de Campo** (La Romana) has a dude ranch on its premises, saddled with 2,000 horses. You can even arrange for polo lessons (it's a major stop on the international circuit). In Puerto Plata, **Gran Chapparal** (tel. 809/320–4250) offers beach rides.

Sailing Sailboats are available at **Club Med** (Punta Cana) and **Casa de Campo** (La Romana).

Scuba Diving and Snorkeling Ancient sunken galleons, undersea gardens, and offshore reefs are the lures here. For equipment and trips, contact **Mundo Submarino** (Santo Domingo, tel. 809/566–0344). A new Diving Instructors World Association (DIWA) scuba-certification school has been opened at the **Demar Beach Club** in Boca Chica, outside the capital, offering three-day and one-week programs.

Tennis There must be a million nets laced around the island, and most of them can be found at the large resorts (*see* Lodging, *below*).

Windsurfing Between June and October, **Cabarete Beach** offers what many consider to be optimal windsurfing conditions: wind speeds at 20–25 knots and 3- to 15-foot waves. The Professional Boardsurfers Association has included Cabarete Beach in its international windsurfing slalom competition. But the novice is also welcome to learn and train on modified boards stabilized by flotation devices. **CaribBIC Windsurfing Center,** on Caberete Beach (tel. 800/635–1155 or 800/243–9675), offers accommodations, equipment, training, and professional coaching.

Spectator Baseball is the national pastime and passion. Major leaguers hone
Sports their skills in the Professional Winter League, which plays from late
Baseball October through January. Call **Liga de Beisbol** (tel. 809/567–6371) for details on the five teams and their schedule of play. You can also consult newspaper listings, or your hotel can reserve tickets. You may not reach an English-speaking representative at Liga de Beisbol.

Greyhound The dogs make tracks every Monday, Wednesday, Friday, and Sun-
Races day at **Canódromo El Coco.** *Av. Monumental, La Yuca—about 15 min north of the capital, tel. 809/560–6968 or 560–8342. Admission: R.D.$1–R.D.$4. Races Mon., Wed., Fri. 7:30 PM, Sun. and holidays 4 PM.*

Horse Racing There are races year-round at the **Hipódromo Perla Antillana.** *Av. San Cristóbal, Santo Domingo, tel. 809/565–2353. Admission free. Post time: Tues., Thurs., Sat. 3 PM.*

Polo The ponies pound down the field at **Sierra Prieta** (Santo Domingo) and at **Casa de Campo** (La Romana). The season runs from October through May. For information about polo games, call 809/565–6880.

Shopping

The hot ticket in the Dominican Republic is amber jewelry. This island has the world's largest deposits of amber, and the prices here for the translucent, semiprecious stones, which range in color from pale lemon to dark brown, are unmatched. The most valuable stones are those in which tiny insects or small leaves are embedded. (Don't knock it till you've seen it.)

The Dominican Republic is the homeland of designer Oscar de la Renta, and you may want to stop at some of the chic shops that carry his creations. In the crafts department, hand-carved wood rocking chairs are big sellers, and they are sold unassembled and boxed for easy transport. Look also for the delicate ceramic lime figurines that symbolize the Dominican culture.

Bargaining is both a game and a social activity in the Dominican Republic, especially with street vendors and at the stalls in El Mercado Modelo. Vendors are disappointed and perplexed if you don't haggle. They also tend to be tenacious, so unless you really have an eye on buying, don't even stop to look—you may get stuck buying a souvenir just to get rid of an annoying vendor.

Shopping **El Mercado Modelo** in Santo Domingo is a covered market in the Co-
Districts lonial Zone bordering Calle Mella. The restored buildings of **La Atarazana** (across from the Alcázar in the Colonial Zone) are filled with shops, art galleries, restaurants, and bars. The main shopping streets in the Colonial Zone are **Calle El Conde,** which has been transformed into an exclusively pedestrian thoroughfare, and **Calle Duarte.** (Some of the best shops on Calle Duarte are north of the Colonial Zone, between Calle Mella and Avenida de Las Américas.) **Plaza Criolla** (corner of Avenida 27 de Febrero and Avenida Anacaona) is filled with shops that sell everything from scents to nonsense. Duty-free shops selling liquors, cameras, and the like are at the **Centro de los Héroes** (Avenida George Washington), the **Hotel**

El Embajador, the Santo Domingo Sheraton, and at Las Américas Airport. The two major commercial malls in Santo Domingo are Unicentro (406 Avenida Abraham Lincoln) and Plaza Central (Avenidas Bolívar and 27 de Febrero).

In Puerto Plata, the seven showrooms of the Tourist Bazaar (Calle Duarte 61) are in a wonderful old galleried mansion with a patio bar. Another cluster of shops is at the Plaza Shopping Center (Calle Duarte at Avenida 30 de Marzo). A popular shopping street for jewelry and local souveniers is Calle Beller.

In Altos de Chavón, art galleries and shops are grouped around the main square.

Good Buys Ambar Tres (La Atarazana 3, Colonial Zone, Santo Domingo, tel.
Amber/Jewelry 809/688–0474) carries a wide selection of the Dominican product.

Dominican Art Galleries in Santo Domingo are Arawak Gallery (Avenida Pasteur 104, tel. 809/685–1661) and Galería de Arte Nader (La Atarazana 9, Colonial Zone, tel. 809/688–0969). Novo Atarazana (Atarazana 21, tel. 809/689–0582) has a varied assortment of artifacts made by locals.

Macaluso's (Calle Duarte 32, and in Plaza Turisol, tel. 809/586–3433) and the Collector's Corner Gallery and Gift Shop (Plaza Shopping Center, Calle Duarte at Avenida 30 de Marzo, no tel.) are the better-known galleries in Puerto Plata.

Check out the Dominican fashions at Jenny Polanco's boutiques in the Santo Domingo Sheraton (tel. 809/221–6666, ext. 2270), Plaza Central (tel. 809/541–5929), and the Paradise Beach Resort in Playa Dorada (tel. 809/586–3663, ext. 314).

Mink One does not necessarily think mink (or fox) in the tropics, but the Dominican Republic has the largest mink and fox factory in the Western Hemisphere. Mink America furnishes lavish collections not only to New York's Seventh Avenue but also to the individual buyer. Whether made to order or prêt-à-porter, the merchandise is tax- and duty-free and therefore an attractive buy at almost half the price (Puerto Plata Free Zone, showroom and factory by appointment). Tel. 809/586–4396. AE, MC, V.

Wood Crafts Visit the stalls of El Mercado Modelo in the Colonial Zone and El Conde Gift Shop (Calle El Conde 153, tel. 809/682–5909), both in Santo Domingo, for exquisite mahogany carvings.

In Puerto Plata, browse and shop at Macaluso's (Calle Duarte 32, tel. 809/586–3433) and at the Collector's Corner Gallery and Gift Shop (Plaza Shopping Center, no tel.). In Santiago, try Artesanía Lime (Autopista Duarte, Km. 2½, Santiago, tel. 809/582–3754).

Dining

Dining out is a favorite form of entertainment for Dominicans, and they tend to dress up for the occasion. Most restaurants begin serving dinner around 6 PM, but the locals don't generally turn up until 9 or 10. There are French, Italian, and Chinese restaurants, as well as those serving traditional Dominican fare. Hotel restaurants are uniformly good; consult lodging listings for additional recommendations. Some favorite local dishes you should sample are paella, sancocho (a thick stew usually made with five different meats, though sometimes as many as seven), arroz con pollo (rice with chicken), plátanos (plantains) in all their tasty varieties, and tortilla de jamón (spicy ham omelet). Country snacks include chichar-

rones (fried pork rinds or chicken pieces) and *galletas* (flat biscuit crackers). Many a meal is topped off with *majarete*, a tasty cornmeal custard. Presidente, Bohemia, and Quisqueya are the local beers, Barceló, Bermúdez, and Brugal the local rums. Wine is on the expensive side because it has to be imported.

Highly recommended restaurants are indicated by a star ★.

Category	Cost*
Expensive	over $30
Moderate	$20–$30
Inexpensive	under $20

per person, excluding drinks, 10% service charge, and 8% sales tax

Boca Chica **Neptuno's Club.** This breezy seaside eatery is little more than a shack perched above the water, seemingly held together by the barnacles of marine memorabilia. While you can order good local preparations of chicken and pork, it goes without saying that seafood reigns supreme. Try the Neptuno's fish casserole in coconut water or kingfish in bechamel sauce. *Boca Chica Beach, tel. 809/523–4703. MC, V. Closed Mon. Inexpensive–Moderate.*

La Romana **Casa del Rio.** This ultraromantic space, a cool candlelit stone cellar
★ in a 16th-century-style castle, overlooks the virtual jungle of the Rio Chavón. But even this elegant decor becomes a mere backdrop for the imaginative creations put forth by chef Philippe Mongereau. His New Caribbean cuisine is a combination of classic French methods of preparation and savory indigenous ingredients and culinary traditions. The seasonally changing menu includes such standouts as leg of lamb baked in creole marmalade, lobster tail glazed with vanilla vinaigrette, and mango napoleon on a bed of julienne shrimp and artichoke hearts. Mongereau is experimenting with Asian ingredients like lemongrass, coriander, and garam masala, and the subtle counterpoint of textures and flavors is truly heavenly. This restaurant's success is measured not only by the heavy repeat clientele, but by the capitaleños who swear it's worth the two-hour drive from Santo Domingo. *Altos de Chavón, tel. 809/523–3333, ext. 2345. Jacket and reservations required. AE, DC, MC, V. Dinner only. Expensive.*
Villa Casita. This small and intimate restaurant serves creative Dominican cooking amid candles and muted lights. Start with octopus vinaigrette, spinach crepes, or pasta with anchovies and clams before feasting on sea bass or local lobster. Meat eaters fare slightly less well with steak or—the better choice—veal rollatine. Piano music accompanies your dinner, and the polished wood bar is a relaxing place for cognac and coffee. *Francisco Richer 71, La Romana, tel. 809/556–2808. Reservations accepted. Dress: smart casual. AE, MC, V. Moderate.*

The Amber **De Armando.** Set in a pretty aqua-and-white house, this charmingly
Coast old-fashioned eatery feels like a proper old relative's dining room, with high-backed embroidered chairs, crisp white napery, and dark-wood tables. Steak, seafood, and Continental dishes are featured, all served to the tune of a guitar trio. Try the snapper in green peppercorn sauce or sea bass in champagne mushroom velouté. *Av. Mota 23, at Av. Separación, tel. 809/586–3418. Reservations required. MC, V. Moderate–Expensive.*
Another World. It defines hokey and kitschy. The brochures exhort you to "spend an unforgettable evening with Stuart and his charming mother Jeanette, from Miami, Florida, in their 120-year-old re-

stored Victorian 'haunted' farmhouse." (Stuart is a former singer/ actor known to belt his rendition of "My Way." Jeanette calls the ghosts their "friendly boarders.") And then there's the minizoo, including a 350-pound Bengal tiger, a honey bear, and a capuchin monkey appropriately named Hanky Panky. The food selection is straight from Noah's Ark as well: frogs' legs tempura, river prawns, escargots, rabbit, and quail are just a few choices from the enormous—and surprisingly well-prepared—menu. Free pickup and return to Puerto Plata hotels, as well as complimentary hors d'oeuvres and cordials make this a pitch difficult to resist. *Puerto Plata, tel. 809/543–8116. Reservations advised. MC, V. Dinner only. Moderate.*

Caribae. The most striking decoration in this warm, unassuming spot is the aquariums teeming with all manner of sea creatures. You can choose your own lobster, shrimp, and oysters for the barbecue. Costs are low, because this health-conscious restaurant raises its own shrimp at a farm and grows its own 100% organic vegetables. *Camino Libre 70, Sosúa, tel. 809/571–3138. MC, V. Moderate.*

Hemingway's. This tropical variation on an English pub (maybe they should have called it Maugham's) is a cool retreat with polished hardwood floors and tables, nautical paraphernalia, trellises, and a sizable aquarium. Food is strictly of the happy-hour variety: burgers, chicharrones (we call them chicken McNuggets—theirs are tastier), and "wings from hell." But you can't beat beers and cuba libres for R.D.$20! *Playa Dorada Plaza, no tel. AE, MC, V. Inexpensive.*

Roma II. This is just a simple wood shack with a glass wall and metal roof, but the pizzas, cooked in a wood-burning oven, are surprisingly delicious. The pizza dough and pasta are made fresh daily. Other specialties include *spaghetti con pulpo* (octopus), *filete chito* (steak with garlic), and a host of other pastas and special sauces. *Corner Calle E. Prudhomme and Calle Beller, tel. 809/586–3904. No reservations. No credit cards. Inexpensive.*

Samaná **Café de France.** This small, intimate bistro on the waterfront, with white stucco walls and red tablecloths, couldn't be simpler. But local aficionados swear the beef (try the fillet in mushroom or peppercorn sauce) is among the best in the Dominican Republic. Seafood here is also dependable: one standout is shrimp (or grouper) in garlic-coconut sauce. The even more casual annex serves knockout pizzas. *Malecon, Samaná, no tel. Reservations advised (stop by the restaurant). MC, V. Moderate.*

Santo **Vesuvio.** Capital-city denizens flock to this superb Italian restau-
Domingo rant, where everything on the lengthy menu is either freshly
★ caught, homemade, or homegrown. On most islands it's a struggle to get (and keep) things fresh, thus the crisp vegetables here are nothing short of miraculous. Vesuvio has spent 40 years as the best in its business, yet refuses to rest on its laurels. Part of the restaurant's appeal is the gay, social ambience of Dominican families relishing their meal. The chef doesn't shy away from strong, bold flavors in perfect combinations. Start with antipasti: kingfish carpaccio dancing in zesty capers, onions, and basil-infused olive oil; *calamares al vino blanco* (squid in white-wine sauce); *scaloppina al tarragon* (veal with tarragon); or, if they have it, succulent river crayfish grilled simply and memorably with butter and garlic. The *piéce de résistance* is the dessert tray—maybe it can also come by to roll you out! (**Vesuvio II** is at Av. Tiradentes 17, tel. 809/562–6090.) *Av. George Washington 521, tel. 809/689–2141. No reservations. Jacket required. DC, MC, V. Expensive.*

El Caserio. An extensive menu lists such specialties as paella valenciana, seafood zarzuela, bluefish with anchovies, and leg of lamb Segovia. For dessert, forget your diet and order chocolate cake Caserio. Adjacent to the formal dining room, reminiscent of a white-washed Andalusian cottage, is **La Taverna,** with a bistro-like atmosphere that offers an appetite-whetting range of *tapas* (appetizers). *Av. George Washington 459, tel. 809/685–3392. Jacket and reservations required. AE, DC, MC, V. Moderate–Expensive.*

★ **Lina.** Lina was the personal chef of Trujillo, and she taught her secret recipes to the chefs of this stylish contemporary restaurant, still a favorite of Santo Domingo movers and shakers. The extensive menu favors Continental and haute Dominican dishes. Paella is the best-known specialty, but other offerings include chateaubriand in béarnaise sauce and a casserole of mixed seafood flavored with Pernod. *Gran Hotel Lina, Av. Máximo Gómez at Av. 27 de Febrero, tel. 809/686–5000. Jacket and reservations required. AE, DC, MC, V. Moderate–Expensive.*

Mesón de la Cava. The capital's most unusual restaurant is more than 50 feet below ground in a natural cave complete with stalagmites and stalactites. Guests clamber down a circular staircase ducking rock protrusions to dine on Continental standards like prime fillet with Dijon flambé, and tournedos Roquefort. Seafood preparations tend to be more adventurous, such as red snapper poached in white wine and coconut sauce, but the food takes a back seat to the spectacular setting. There is live music and dancing nightly until 1 AM, although sometimes you may wish they'd stop playing Jackson Five renditions and allow a majestic silence to fall over the cathedralesque grotto. *Av. Mirador del Sur, tel. 809/533–2818. Jacket and reservations required. AE, DC, MC, V. Moderate–Expensive.*

★ **Café St. Michel.** The decor is rather odd, sort of a contemporary indoor take on a gazebo, but it is creations like the cream of pumpkin soup and steak tartare that have made this popular restaurant the winner of many gastronomical awards. You can choose from a French bistro–style menu or a list of local fare. Desserts include a prize-winning chocolate torte and spectacular soufflés. *Av. Lope de Vega 24, tel. 809/562–4141. Jacket and reservations suggested. AE, MC, V. Moderate.*

Fonda de la Atarazana. This patio restaurant, set in a 17th-century building with whitewashed stucco walls and red brick floors in the Colonial Zone, is especially romantic at night, when music and dancing are added. Try the kingfish, shrimp, or *chicharrones de pollo* (bits of fried Dominican chicken). *La Atarazana 5, tel. 809/689–2900. AE, MC, V. Moderate.*

★ **El Conuco.** Conuco means countryside—and it's hard to believe that this open-air thatched hut, alive with hanging plants, hibiscus, and frangipani and decorated with basketry, sombreros, license plates, and graffiti (you're encouraged to leave your mark) is smack in the center of Santo Domingo. This is a superb place to sample typical Dominican cuisine, from *la bandera* (white rice, *habichuelas* [kidney beans], and stewed beef duplicating the colors of the flag) to a magnificent, delicately flaky *bacalao de la comai* (cod in white cream sauce with garlic and onions). The ambience is always happy and celebratory; waiters occasionally take to makeshift drum sets to accompany the merengue tapes. *152 Casimiro de Moya, tel. 809/221–3231. MC, V. Inexpensive.*

La Bahía. This is an unpretentious spot where the catch of the day is tops. Conch appears in a variety of dishes. For starters, try the *sopa palúdica*, a thick soup made with fish, shrimp, and lobster and served with tangy garlic bread. Then move on to kingfish in coconut sauce or *espaguettis a la canona* (spaghetti heaped with seafood).

Av. George Washington 1, tel. 809/682–4022. No reservations. AE, MC, V. Inexpensive.

★ **Ludovino's** and **Joaquin's.** Shacks and stands serving cheap eats for people on the run are a Dominican tradition, as much a part of the culture and landscape as the Colonial Zone. Two such shacks have become legends in Santo Domingo; both are located in working-class districts outside the normal tourist loop. El Palacio de los Yaniqueques (everyone calls it Ludovino's after the nutty owner) is famed for its johnnycakes—fried dough stuffed with everything from chicken to seafood. Ludovino started off with these egg McMuffins of the Caribbean, then expanded his horizons to "gourmet" offerings like shrimp and clams. You pay the cashier when you order and get a free thimbleful of strong, sweet coffee while you wait for your food. Joaquin's serves up the best pork sandwich—laden with onions, tomatoes, pickles, and seasonings—in the Western World (yes, even Texas BBQ takes a back seat). The price for a filling meal? Two bucks at either. *Ludovino's: 19 Summer Wells, no tel. Open daily 7AM–8PM. Joaquin's: Av. Abraham Lincoln and Max Henríquex Ureña St., no tel. Open nightly 7PM–2AM.*

Lodging

Your options here vary from the New World's first hotel to some of the world's newest and poshest resorts. An ambitious development plan continues, especially on the north coast. The Dominican Republic has the largest hotel inventory (24,000 rooms and growing) in the Caribbean. Puerto Plata alone features 8,000 rooms and hosts 250,000 tourists a year. There are already so many adjoining resorts that when you go out for a stroll you have to flag landmarks to find your way back to the one where your luggage is. The fierce competition translates into some of the best hotel buys in the Caribbean. Be sure to inquire about special packages when you call to reserve; arranging your room as a package through a tour operator will cost considerably less. Be aware that many hotels, especially on the north coast, turn their water supply off at midnight as a conservation measure. Rooms are air-conditioned unless otherwise noted.

Hotels in Santo Domingo base their tariffs on the EP and maintain the same room rates through the year. In contrast, resorts have high winter and low summer rates, with the low rate reducing the room prices by as much as 50%. All-inclusive properties are concentrated especially along the north coast. Those that aren't all-inclusive offer EP or MAP. Our prices, in U.S. dollars, are based on a double room during the high season.

Highly recommended lodgings are indicated by a star ★.

Category	Cost*
Very Expensive	over $175
Expensive	$125–$175
Moderate	$75–$125
Inexpensive	under $75

All prices are for a standard double room for two, excluding 15% service charge and 8% tax.

Boca Chica   **Hamaca Beach Hotel.** This MAP resort is half an hour east of Santo Domingo and just a few minutes from Las Américas Airport and the exclusive Santo Domingo Yacht Club. The impressive teal, mustard, and primrose reception area has terra-cotta floors, wicker furnishings, water walls, and huge floral arrangements. Rooms are furnished in painted rattan and dark woods, with sea-foam tile floors, floral bedspreads, full bath, and cable TV. The lovely champagne-colored beach is especially popular with Germans. *Boca Chica Beach, tel. 809/523–4455 or 800/828–8895, fax 809/523–4438. 209 rooms. Facilities: 3 restaurants, 2 bars, grill, terrace, 2 tennis courts, scuba diving, archery, bicycling, horseback riding, snorkeling, sailing, windsurfing, excursions to Catalina Island, transportation to Santo Domingo casinos. AE, MC, V. MAP. Very Expensive.*

The Amber Coast

Bayside Hill Resort and Beach Club. Part of the Costambar development—a 15-hotel complex including a 9-hole golf course, residential community, and supermarket—this hotel is an adroit blend of classic and contemporary elements: modern artworks and Corinthian columns, marble floors and metal sculptures. The centerpiece is a majestic split-level pool and jacuzzi with waterfalls and cavorting mermaid statuary. The Cafemba restaurant is highly respected for its innovative Continental cuisine. The rooms, primarily in olive, chartreuse, and salmon with tile floors, cable TV, and small terrace or balcony, are pleasant but disappointing compared to the public areas. The best rooms are those with stunning panoramic vistas of Puerto Plata. A free shuttle runs guests from the hillside development to the beach. Costambar is pleasantly quiet compared to Playa Dorada. *Costambar, Puerto Plata, tel. 809/586–5260 or 800/322–2388, fax 809/586–5545. 150 rooms. Facilities: 2 restaurants, 3 bars, beach club and water-sports center, pool, golf, beauty parlor, gift shop, disco. AE, MC, V. All-inclusive. Very Expensive.*

Caribbean Village Club and Resort. Colonnaded walkways connect the 44 two-story, pastel-colored villas at this sprawling resort complex, popular with active types. Rooms in the newer Royale building are simple but fresh, predominantly in peach, all with cable TV and kitchenette. The older Tropicale is a series of small houses with connecting skywalks. Rooms are really like mini-apartments, perfect for families, all with terrace or balcony, kitchenette, small sitting area, marble floors, and light pastel decor. One free-form pool has a swim-up terrace, and there's free shuttle service to the beach, or you can make the 10-minute hike. On the beach is the hotel's La Tortuga, a snack bar, and the water-sports facilities. Nightly entertainment and dancing take place in the patio lounge and lobby bar. The staff genuinely works hard to compensate for the off-beach location. *Playa Dorada, tel. 809/586–25350 or 800/852–4523, fax 809/320–5386. 310 rooms, 26 suites. Facilities: 3 restaurants, 3 bars/lounges, grill, 2 pools, 2 lighted tennis courts, minimart, disco, child care, beach club and water-sports center, medical clinic, shopping arcade, golf. AE, MC, V. CP, MAP. Very Expensive.*

Dorado Naco and Playa Naco. These two sister hotels make up a sprawling complex. Dorado Naco, the elder of the two, is currently being renovated. The design is a cluster of villas with spacious carpeted one- and two-bedroom apartments. The living and dining area have a sofa bed, cable TV, two phones, dining table that seats four, and a counter bar. Each apartment has a large patio or terrace surrounded by tropical flowers and plants. The more expensive rooms have views of the pool, surrounded by restaurants. The new hacienda-style Playa Naco, with 346 rooms, abuts the beach, although the main lobby and standard hotel rooms, overlooking the pool and tennis courts, are a four-minute walk from the sands. The more expensive accommodations are the one- and two-bedroom units in the two-story buildings that follow the path to the beach. The pleasing decor includes tile floors and mauve, lilac, and olive tones. The bustling free-form pool spouts several waterfalls. The resort was scheduled to go all-inclusive in early 1994. *Box 162, Playa Dorada. Dorado Naco: tel. 809/586–2019, fax 809/320–3608. Playa Naco: tel. 809/ 320–6226, fax 809/320–6225. U.S. reservations for both, tel. 800/ 322–2388. 496 units. Facilities: 6 restaurants, 3 bars, coffee shop, 2 pools, shopping arcade, beauty salon, car rental, games room, minimarket, bicycle rental, horseback riding, 4 lighted tennis courts, golf, disco, pub, 3 Jacuzzis, beach club and water-sports center, convention center. AE, DC, MC, V. EP, MAP, FAP, All-inclusive. Very Expensive.*

★ **Flamenco Beach Resort, Villas Doradas,** and **Playa Dorada Beach Resort.** Guests can use the facilities at all three of these hotels that are lined up one after the other on the mile-long white-sand beach. They're all known for their lively nightlife and variety of social and sports programs, but the similarities end there. Rooms at the older Playa Dorada are pleasant enough, with light pastels, navy or maroon carpets, cable TV, and minibar; but they are dowdy and sadly in need of refurbishment. Service is efficient but unenthusiastic. The Villas Doradas units are in earth tones (a refreshing change of pace) with abstract paintings, all with cable TV, safe, and minibar. But the new Flamenco is a real jewel. The glorious public spaces include cobblestone and Andalusian brick floors, hand-painted tiles, stuccoed walls, and antique carved doors. There are four magnificent restaurants inlcuding Via Veneto, a lively trattoria, and gourmet Spanish El Cortijo. The main free-form pool (with swim-up bar) is designed to resemble a lake, complete with waterfall and lapping waves. Rooms and suites are tasteful, with hardwood furnishings, terra-cotta floors, bright floral upholstery, native crafts, minibar, cable TV, and balcony or terrace. Club Miguel Angel is a hotel within a hotel offering premium concierge service. The only thing missing at the Flamenco is an ocean view. *Flamenco: Playa Dorada, Puerto Plata, tel. 809/320–5084, fax 809/ 320–6319. 518 units. Facilities: 4 restaurants, 3 bars, pizzeria, 2 pools, water-sports center, 2 lighted tennis courts, shopping arcade. Villas Doradas: Box 1370, Puerto Plata, tel. 809/320–3000, fax 809/ 320–4790. 207 rooms. Facilities: 5 restaurants, 2 bars, pool, water-sports center, car rental, 3 tennis courts, gift shop. Playa Dorada: Box 272, Puerto Plata, tel. 809/586–3988 or 800/423–6902, fax 809/ 320–1190. 252 rooms, 1 suite. Facilities: 4 restaurants, 2 bars, pool, disco, casino, ice-cream parlor, golf, tennis courts, horseback riding, bikes, jogging trail, water-sports center. AE, DC, MC, V. EP. Very Expensive.*

★ **Paradise Beach Resort and Club.** Of the 12 hotels in the Playa Dorada complex, this hotel stands out on two counts: It is one of the few that fronts the beach and that has any individuality of design. Its cluster of low-rise buildings with white-tile roofs and latticed balconies and windows follow the winding paths through palms, birds-of-paradise, and hibiscus from the reception area down to the beach. Bold, imaginative designs contrast with a carefully chosen palette of pastel greens and blues. Standard rooms have one double or two twin beds; some of the one-bedroom apartments have kitchens. In the center of the resort is the free-form pool, with a water channel that winds its way from the pool to the beach. There guests can dine in open-air restaurants or take advantage of the water-sports facilities. *Box 337, Playa Dorada, tel. 809/586–3663 or 800/752–0836, fax 809/320–4858. 216 rooms, 186 suites. Facilities: 3 restaurants, 3 bars, boutiques, 2 lighted tennis courts, golf, horseback riding, water-sports clinic, bicycles, scooters. AE, DC, MC, V. All-inclusive. Very Expensive.*

Sand Castle. The name says it all. This resort is a fantasy of curves, balconies, and balustrades set high above coral cliffs. Royal palms rise majestically from the beachside gardens. Rooms are simple and comfortable in muted mint and primrose pastels, with stained glass fixtures on the sliding doors and cable TV. Your stay here will be made more enjoyable if you have a room with a view, especially of the small curving beach down below. Though the hotel is by itself on a peninsula, lots of organized activities and the nearby village of Sosúa keep guests busy. Service is polite but distant. *Puerto Chiquito, Sosúa, tel. 809/571–2420 or 800/445–5963, fax 809/571–2000. 240 rooms. Facilities: 3 restaurants, 5 bars, 2 pools, Jacuzzi, shopping arcade, disco, convention center, water-sports center including dive shops, horseback riding, bicycling. AE, MC, V. EP, MAP. Expensive–Very Expensive.*

Hotel Cofresi. The rooms here are rather basic and somewhat cramped, but the staff is unfailingly courteous and the setting is breathtaking. This still- expanding, all-inclusive resort is built on the reefs along the Atlantic, which spritzes its waters into the peaceful man-made lagoon and pools along the beach. Most rooms include cable TV, hair dryer, safe, and kitchenette. There are jogging and exercise trails, paddleboats for the lagoon, scuba-diving clinics, and evening entertainment, including a disco. The cost covers drinks and all. *Box 327, Costambar, tel. 809/586–2898, fax 809/586–8064. 145 rooms, 5 suites. Facilities: 2 restaurants, 2 bars, disco, 3 pools (1 saltwater), bicycling, horseback riding, paddleboats, 2 lighted tennis courts, game room, water-sports center. AE, MC, V. All-inclusive. Expensive.*

Puerto Plata Beach Resort and Casino. This is a seven-acre village with cobblestone pathways, colorful gardens, and suites in 23 porticoed two- and three-story buildings. Accommodations have terracotta floors and a primarily mint and jade decor, with cable TV, minifridge, and balcony or terrace. An activities center sets up water-sports clinics, rents bicycles, and so forth. The resort also caters to the little ones, with children's games and enclosures for them at the shallow end of the pool. Bogart's is the glitzy disco. Ylang-Ylang, named after the evening flower that blooms here, is a highly rated gourmet restaurant and catering service. The Neptune restaurant across the road on the beach is good for seafood. This resort is just outside of town and a ways from Playa Dorada, which will be an added attraction to some. *Box 600, Av. Malecón, Puerto Plata, tel. 809/586–4243 or 800/223–9815, fax 809/586–4377. 216 units. Facilities: 4 restaurants, bar, pool, outdoor Jacuzzi, horseback riding, casino, gift shop, nightclub, 4 lighted tennis courts, water-sports center. AE, MC, V. EP, MAP. Expensive.*

Hotel Montemar. Located on the Malecón, between Puerto Plata and Playa Dorada, a five-minute walk from the town's Long Beach, this is a good choice for a cost-conscious holiday. All rooms have an ocean view. Superior rooms are air-conditioned, but small standard rooms are not. There is a daily schedule of activities and transportation to the beaches at Playa Dorada. It's a fine, inexpensive alternative to Playa Dorada, with an appealingly warm atmosphere, thanks to a staff composed of hotel-school trainees. *Box 382, Puerto Plata, tel. 809/586–2800 or 800/332–4872, fax 809/586–2009. 95 rooms. Facilities: restaurant, coffee shop, bar, 2 tennis courts, beach club, golf, horseback riding. AE, MC, V. All-inclusive. Moderate–Expensive.*

Punta Goleta Beach Resort. This bare-bones resort is set on a tangle of 100 overgrown tropical acres across the road from Cabarete Beach, where windsurfing is the big deal. The apricot-and-jade buildings boast lacy Victorian-style gingerbread trim, but rooms are unexceptional in typical soft pastels. There is a lot of activity here, such as volleyball in the pool or on the beach, frog and crab racing, board games, merengue lessons, disco, and boating on the lagoon. The uninterested staff is lethargic at best, but the resort still offers fairly good value. *Box 318, Cabarete, tel. 809/571–0700, fax 809/571–0707. 126 rooms and 10 villas. Facilities: 2 restaurants, 4 bars, disco, jogging track, pool, lagoon, horseback riding, golf, tennis, water-sports center. AE, DC, MC, V. All-inclusive. Moderate–Expensive.*

Playa Chiquita. In this new (1992) Sosúa resort you register in a broad breezeway that leads past the free-form pool (with swim-up bar and shallow children's section) right to the delightful private cove. The rooms boast standard contemporary tropical decor, with pastel upholstery and rattan furnishings, terra-cotta floors, cable TVs, double or king-size beds, and wet bars; most have patios or balconies. Fortunately, plans to double the size of this intimate resort have been shelved. In the meantime, a new casino has opened. *Sosúa, tel. 809/689–6191 or 800/922–4272, fax 809/571–2460. 90 rooms. Facilities: restaurant, coffee shop, pool, gift shop, nightclub, casino, water sports. AE, MC, V. EP, MAP. Moderate.*

Club Marina. This is a wonderfully unusual budget option. Former owner Eduardo de Lora, a master stained-glass craftsman, designed this charming beige stucco and red tile hotel. Everything displays his creative touch: the pool is landscaped with rocks, giving it a natural grotto feel, spiral staircases are embedded with shards of glass (there are no exposed edges!). The rooms themselves are plain but impeccably neat, with a well-worn integrity. The blue-and-white tiles, lilac bedspreads, and closets painted jade green brighten them up. The restaurant serves wonderful home-cooking—and the prices here are sensational. All units have cable TV, private bath, and small French balcony. The beach is a five-minute walk. *Alejo Martínez Street, Sosúa, tel. 809/571–3939. Facilities: restaurant, pool. AE, MC, V. Inexpensive.*

Hostal Jimessón. One of the few hotels in downtown Puerto Plata, the Jimessón is a gingerbread, century-old clapboard house right out of New Orleans. There are rocking chairs on the front porch, and the parlor houses a veritable museum of antique grandfather clocks, Victrolas, and mahogany and wicker furniture. Other superb, homey touches include a live parrot, hanging plants, and the owners' genuine hospitality. The drawback is that the air-conditioned guest rooms are actually in the newer concrete addition at the back and have nothing more than a bed, a table, and a basic bathroom. *Calle John F. Kennedy 41, Puerto Plata, tel. 809/586–5131, fax 809/586–6313. 22 air-conditioned rooms. Facilities: bar, cable TV. AE, MC, V. EP. Inexpensive.*

La Romana
★

Casa de Campo. Casa de Campo means "house in the country," an interesting appellation for this resort that sprawls over 7,000 acres and accommodates some 3,000 guests. It includes 350 casitas, casita-suites, and one-, two-, and three-bedroom villas, and offers two public golf courses (one of them, a teeth-clencher called Teeth of the Dog, has seven holes that skirt the sea), 16 tennis courts, horseback riding, polo, archery, trap shooting, and every imaginable water sport. Minibuses provide free transportation around the resort, but you can also rent electric carts, scooters, and bicycles. Oscar de la Renta designed much of the resort, owns a villa, and has a boutique in Altos de Chavón, the recreated medieval village and art colony on the property (*see* Exploring the Dominican Republic, *above*). Some rooms and villas are decorated in Laura Ashley style, others with bolder, more abstract touches. This luxury resort is—in a word—awesome. The advantage of staying here is that American Eagle flies in twice a day from San Juan to the La Romana airstrip. The disadvantage is that there are few attractions in the vicinity of the hotel other than the hotel's own campus—not that most guests mind. *Box 140, La Romana, tel. 809/523–3333 or 800/223–6620, fax 809/523–8548. 740 rooms. Facilities: 9 restaurants, 8 bars, 13 pools, 16 tennis courts (6 lighted), fitness center, Jacuzzi, sauna, polo fields, horseback riding, shooting and archery ranges, 2 18-hole golf courses, boutiques, marina, airstrip. AE, DC, MC, V. EP, MAP. Very Expensive.*

Punta Cana **Bavaro Beach Resort.** This four-star luxury resort, actually part of a complex of five low-rise hotels, is situated on the glorious twenty-mile stretch of Punta Cana beach. Each room has a private balcony or terrace, cable TV, and refrigerator. The biggest rooms are at the Bavaro Beach Hotel, with hemp and wood furnishings and bright striped upholstery. The Bavaro Gardens is decorated in vivid primary colors. The Bavaro Casino Hotel has several duplex suites ideal for families. The Bavaro Golf Hotel is the only thoroughly self-contained property; the new Bavaro Palace is the most refined and subdued, with touches like marble vanities. A social director coordinates a wide variety of daily activities, but it is a very impersonal resort. *Higüey, tel. 809/682–2162 or 800/336–6612, fax 809/682–2169. 1,001 rooms. Facilities: 8 restaurants, 12 bars, 2 grills, 5 pools, 3 discos, casino, nightclub, shopping arcade, beauty salon, medical center, golf, archery, bicycles, horseback riding, 6 lighted tennis courts, water-sports center. AE, MC, V. EP, MAP. Very Expensive.*

Punta Cana Beach Resort. Several pretty coral-and-aquamarine buildings dot the lush grounds of this rambling resort, and expansion is planned for 1995, including a new golf course and an additional 350-room hotel. The handsome lobby sets a civilized tone with Dominican crafts, birdcages, and lots of plants. Rooms are spare but pleasant, primarily in jade, coral, and eggshell with wicker furnishings. The half-mile private beach is gorgeous, and there are nature walks into the mahogany forest, including dips in a secret freshwater pool. There are lots of activities here too, including nightly musical entertainment by the staff (perhaps taking a cue from the Club Med next door). *Box 1083, Santo Domingo (mailing address). Punta Cana Beach, tel. 809/686–0084, fax 809/689–8745. 341 units. Facilities: 5 restaurants, 2 bars, disco, boutique, gift shop, beauty parlor, minimart, medical clinic, pool, water-sports center, 4 lighted tennis courts, playground, day care and children's minicamp. AE, DC, MC, V. EP, MAP. Expensive–Very Expensive.*

Samaná **Hotel Gran Bahía.** This new luxury resort is built at the water's edge
★ in an area yet to be spoiled with overdevelopment. The grand yet welcoming reception area and three-story white colonnaded atrium surround a spectacular fountain flanked with numerous cozy nooks for cocktails or reading. The modern colonial Victorian has graceful verandas and balconies looking out over the pool and the sea beyond (you can see schools of whales frolicking offshore during the winter). The superb views make breakfast on your room's private terrace a treat. The large guest rooms are furnished with cheerful floral prints, tiled floors, and pastel watercolor paintings. Dining alfresco is pleasant, though you would be wise to stay with the fresh seafood rather than try the meat dishes. This small elegant hotel has a delightfully European ambience that appeals to a select, chic crowd. *Box 2024, Santo Domingo, tel. 809/538–3111 or 800/372–1323, fax 809/538–2764. 98 rooms. Facilities: 2 restaurants, bar, pool, 2 ten-*

nis courts, gym, archery, 9-hole golf course, beauty salon, boutique, whale-watching arranged. AE, MC, V. CP, MAP. Very Expensive.

Cayo Levantado. This tranquil new hotel is tucked into the lush greenery of the tiny island national park just off the Samaná coast. The exquisite fringe of pearly white beach is regrettably overrun weekends with day-trippers, but many enjoy the party atmosphere, with makeshift stalls hawking T-shirts, paintings, beer, and delicious grilled items. (There's another, smaller beach on the other side of the island for the romantically inclined.) The rooms, either in the main building or bungalows, are simple and appealing, with writing desks, wicker furnishings, and bright pastels. They're planning on adding cable TVs—but promise no phones. The food is good, solid Creole: A fortunate thing, since the hotel operates on a FAP (that includes four drinks per day). *Cayo Levantado, tel. 809/538–3131. 44 rooms. Facilities: restaurant, bar, pool, boutique, water sports. AE, MC, V. Expensive.*

Santo Domingo ★

Jaragua Renaissance Resort and Casino. This ultramodern complex is set on 14 acres of gardens, waterfalls, and fountains. Top-name entertainers are booked into the 800-seat nightclub, master chefs from four countries tend to the cuisine, and a staff doctor supervises the diet program in the spa. The resort was featured on "Lifestyles of the Rich and Famous" and is still the class act in town. Accommodations are in garden or tower rooms, and all have three phones, 21-channel satellite TVs, minibars, and hair dryers. Each floor sports different decor, one in peach and burgundy, another apricot and mint. Rates are based on view (garden, pool, or ocean). Twelve cabanas surround the Olympic-size free-form pool, and the casino covers 20,000 square feet. *Av. George Washington 367, Santo Domingo, tel. 809/221–2222 or 800/331–3542, fax 809/686–0528. 337 rooms, 18 suites. Facilities: 6 restaurants, 5 bars, casino, pool, 4 tennis courts (1 lighted), golf (at the Santo Domingo Country Club), and European spa with exercise/diet programs, saunas, Jacuzzis, whirlpool. AE, MC, V. EP. Very Expensive.*

Hotel V Centenario. Santo Domingo's newest five-star hotel opened in late 1992 on the Malecón. Marble floors and pillars give the hotel a crisp, fresh feel. The rooms are furnished in attractive earth tones, Dominican handicrafts, and burnished rattans and come with up-to-date features, including a minifridge, cable TV, and electronic safe. Guests can try their luck at the casino or take time out to relax in the lounge bar area with subdued lighting and enticing easy chairs. The cellar tapas bar has become a favorite after-work hangout for locals in the know. A casual coffee shop looks out over the Caribbean, and the pool shares a terrace with a bar and an alfresco seafood restaurant. *Av. George Washington 218, Santo Domingo, tel. 809/221–0000, fax 809/221–2020. 167 rooms, 33 suites. Facilities: 3 restaurants, 2 bars, pool, shops, casino. 1 tennis and 2 squash courts, sauna, gym, parking. AE, MC, V. EP. Expensive.*

Santo Domingo Sheraton Hotel and Casino. This 11-story, modern hotel is on Avenida George Washington in the center of the Malecón action. Rooms are fair-sized, in taupe and teal; many have French balconies (more like a ledge) overlooking the sea, and all include minibar and cable TV. The two restaurants are fine by any standard: one serving Continental cuisine, the other local specialties. Service is disorganized, but the staff tries to be helpful. *Box 1493, Santo Domingo, tel. 809/686–6666 or 800/325–3535, fax 809/687–8150. 260 rooms. Facilities: 2 restaurants, coffee shop, bar, casino, pool, disco, 2 lighted tennis courts, beauty salon, shops, health club, facilities for the disabled. AE, DC, MC, V. EP. Expensive.*

★ **Hotel Santo Domingo.** This complex actually consists of two different hotels: **Hotel Hispaniola** and **Hotel Santo Domingo.** Catering to a younger crowd, the Hispaniola has 165 rooms, with an active pool, a modern disco favored by capitaleños, and a recently refurbished casino. There are two restaurants here, Las Cañas and La Pizetta, as well as the Hispaniola Bar, which has a small dance area. The bar is very dark, very intimate, and very, very red. Guest rooms are spacious, furnished in the usual tropical motif, with stylish trimmings, but they're a tad worn. In dramatic juxtaposition is the Hotel Santo Domingo. This is the epitome of an haute hotel. Oscar de la Renta designed the interiors: with the black- and red-lacquered accents of hall lamps, conch-shell mirrors, bold colors, and handcrafted Dominican furniture. The rooms have balconies and cable TVs, and most have double beds. Located on 14 delicately manicured acres overlooking the Caribbean, the hotel caters to the executive. Many VIPs check into the Premier Club for the extra perks. The elegant Alcázar features excellent Continental dining in de la Renta's romantic Moorish rendition. The regular merengue combo at dimly lit Las Palmas makes it a local favorite for music and dancing. The hotels are at the Western edge of the Malecón—often more convenient for businessmen who want to be close to the new commercial section of town than for tourists who prefer being closer to the historic area. *Av. Independencia and Abraham Lincoln. Box 2112, Santo Domingo, tel. 809/535-1511 or 800/223-6620, fax 809/535-4050. 220 rooms. Facilities: 3 restaurants, 2 bars, pool, sun deck, sauna, 3 lighted tennis courts, conference rooms, and helipad. AE, MC, V. EP. Moderate (Hispaniola)-Expensive.*

Gran Hotel Lina and Casino. The whitewashed modern cinderblock structure of this hotel gives little hint of its stylish, exquisite interior, which gleams with marble floors, mirrored brass colonnades, and striking modern artworks. The rather plain rooms, mostly in dusky rose, are air-conditioned with double beds, minifridges, huge marble baths, and cable TVs, and exude a staid secure ambience. A private Jacuzzi and solarium are planned for the executive floor. The staff is friendly and helpful. *Box 1915, Santo Domingo, tel. 809/686-5000 or 800/942-2461, fax 809/686-5521. 205 rooms, 15 suites. Facilities: restaurant, piano bar, casino, nightclub, coffee shop, health club, 2 tennis courts, pool facilities for people with disabilities. AE, DC, MC, V. EP. Inexpensive-Moderate.*

Hotel El Embajador and Casino. This hotel radiates an air of faded gentility; it seems caught in a '50s time warp—Hollywood's idea of a top hotel in an exotic locale. But though the exterior needs sprucing up, the public rooms are imposing by Dominican standards. The bedrooms are spacious but spare, with tatty carpeting and bare walls; all include minibar, cable TV, and private balcony with either a mountain or an ocean view (choose the latter). An executive concierge floor is good for business travelers. The newly renovated Jardin de Jade serves marvelous Chinese food. The pool is a popular weekend gathering place for resident foreigners. *Av. Sarasota 65, Santo Domingo, tel. 809/221-2131 or 800/457-0067, fax 809/532-4494. 304 rooms, 12 suites. Facilities: 2 restaurants, 2 bars, casino, pool, free transport to beach, 4 tennis courts (1 lighted), nightclub, shopping arcade, facilities for people with disabilities. AE, DC, MC, V. EP. Inexpensive-Moderate.*

★ **Hostal Palacio Nicolás de Ovando.** The oldest hotel in the New World, and one of the few in the Colonial Zone, was home to the first governor in the early 1500s. The decor is Spanish, with carved mahogany doors, beamed ceilings, tapestries, arched colonnades, and three courtyards with splashing fountains. The spartan rooms are reminiscent of monks' cells but have views of the port, the pool, or the Colonial Zone. Dominican specialties are served in the restaurant. This is Santo Domingo's only hotel with the charm of antiquity. Its disadvantage is its location. At night, the area can be deserted and unpleasant for walking alone. *Calle Las Damas 44, Apdo. 89-2, Santo Domingo, tel. 809/687–3101, fax 809/686–5170. 55 rooms. Facilities: restaurant, bar, pool. AE, MC, V. EP. Inexpensive.*

The Arts and Nightlife

Get a copy of the magazine *Vacation Guide* and the newspaper *Touring*, both of which are available free at the tourist office and at hotels, to find out what's happening around the island. Also look in the *Santo Domingo News* and the *Puerto Plata News* for listings of events. The monthly *Dominican Fiesta!* also provides up-to-date information.

Cafés   **Café Atlantico** (J.A. Aybar at Abraham Lincoln, tel. 809/565–1841) is responsible for bringing happy hour and Tex-Mex cooking to the Dominican Republic. (Its sister restaurant of the same name is a hot spot in Washington, D.C.) It has been attracting well-to-do Dominicans and an international crowd for more than six years. Usually young, very lively, and very friendly, the late-afternoon yuppie crowd comes for the music, the food, the exotic drinks, and the energetic atmosphere.

Exquesito (Av. Tiradentes 8, tel. 809/541–0233) is in a striking setting that mixes traditional Dominican decor with deconstructivist provincial Italian. The fare includes French cheeses, Italian antipasti, and a local version of the deli. Talk, relax, and try the fondue at this top gathering spot that appeals to the young and terminally hip.

A recent annex to the Café St. Michel, the **Grand Café** (Av. Lope de Vega 26, tel. 809/562–4141) attracts a relaxed local crowd. You can escape the music by going upstairs to the Tree House. The menu is informal and generally light, but try the Creole oxtail *fradiabolo* served with crabmeat patties.

Casinos   Most of the casinos are concentrated in the larger hotels of Santo Domingo, but there are others here and there, and all offer blackjack, craps, and roulette. Casinos are open daily 3 PM–4 AM. You must be 18 to enter, and jackets are required. In Santo Domingo, the most popular casinos are in the **Dominican Fiesta** (Calle Anacaona, tel. 809/562–8222), the **Jaragua** (Av. Independencia, tel. 809/686–2222), the **Embajador** (Av. Sarasota, tel. 809/533–2131), the **Gran Hotel Lina** (Av. Máximo Gómez, tel. 809/689–5185), the **Naco Hotel** (Av. Tiradentes 22, tel. 809/562–3100), and the **San Géronimo** (Av. Independencia 1067, tel. 809/533–8181).

You'll soon discover that there is no such thing as last call in the Dominican Republic. Customers usually decide when closing time will be.

Music and   An active and frenzied young crowd dances to new wave, house, and, Dance   of course, merengue at **Alexander's** club (Av. Pasteur 23, tel. 809/685–9728). An institution, it is open till all hours.

The neon palm tree outside **Bella Blue** (Av. George Washington 165, tel. 809/689–2911) is a noticeable night beacon for a fun time. The crowd at this Malecón dance club is definitely over 21, and no jeans are allowed.

A favorite of locals for live music featuring local merengue bands, **Las Palmas** (Hotel Santo Domingo, Av. Independencia at Abraham

Lincoln, tel. 809/535–1511) has a happy hour from 6 to 8 PM. The newest sensation is **Guácara Taína** (655 Rómulo Betancourt Avenue, tel. 809/530–2666), a cultural center/disco set in a cave, hosting folkloric dances during the early evening and transforming into the city's hottest night spot later on. The world's only disco grotto, it boasts two dance floors, three bars, and lots of nooks and crannies.

An aptly named club, **Tops** (Plaza Naco Hotel, Av. Tiradentes, tel. 809/541–6226) offers excellent views of the city. Located on the 12th floor of the hotel, it features a variety of special events, from lingerie fashion shows to the latest bands.

When all the partying is over, capitaleños will guide you to **La Aurora** (Av. Hermanos Deligne, tel. 809/685–6590), a lush after-hours supper club in a rustic garden setting. Savor typical dishes, even sancocho, at four in the morning. Here you'll see not only party goers but also the musicians who entertained them. It's a spot of preference for Santo Domingo's hottest band, 4:40.

Nearly every hotel in Puerto Plata has a disco and frequent live entertainment. Among the most popular spots are **La Roca Club** (Sosúa, tel. 809/571–2179), **Crazy Moon** (Paradise Beach Club, tel. 809/320–3663), and **Andromeda** (Heavens, tel. 809/586–5250).

12 Grenada

Updated by
Kate Sekules

Grenada, a tiny island only 21 miles long and 12 miles wide, is bordered by dozens of beaches and secluded coves, crisscrossed by nature trails, and filled with spice plantations, tropical forests, and select hotels clinging to hillsides overlooking the sea.

Known as the Isle of Spice, Grenada is a major producer of nutmeg, cinnamon, mace, cocoa, and many other common household spices. The pungent aroma of spices fills the air at the outdoor markets, where they're sold from large burlap bags; in the restaurants, where chefs believe in using them liberally; and in the pubs, where cinnamon and nutmeg are sprinkled on the rum punches. If the Irish hadn't beaten them to the name, Grenadans might have called their land the Emerald Isle, for the lush pine forests and the thick brush on the hillsides give it a great, green beauty that few Caribbean islands duplicate.

Located in the Eastern Caribbean 90 miles north of Trinidad, Grenada is the most southerly of the Windward Islands. It is a nation composed of three inhabited islands and a few uninhabited islets: Grenada island is the largest, with 120 square miles and about 91,000 people; Carriacou, 16 miles north of Grenada, is 13 square miles and has a population of about 5,000; and Petit Martinique, 5 miles northeast of Carriacou, has 486 acres and a population of 700. Although Carriacou and Petit Martinique are popular for day trips and fishing and snorkeling excursions, most of the tourist action is on Grenada. Here, too, you will find the nation's capital, St. George's, and its largest harbor, St. George's Harbour.

Until 1983, when the United States/Eastern Caribbean invasion of Grenada catapulted this tiny nation into the forefront of international news, it was a relatively obscure island providing a quiet hideaway for those who love fishing, snorkeling, or simply lazing in the sun.

Today Grenada is back to normal, a safe and secure vacation spot with enough good shopping, restaurants, and pubs to make it a regular port of call for major cruise lines, and plenty of beaches and coves for those who want to scuba dive, snorkel, or just sit and stare at the waves.

Although Grenada's tourism industry is undergoing an expansion, it is a controlled expansion, counterbalanced by the island's West Indian flavor. No building can stand taller than a coconut palm, and new construction on the beaches must be at least 165 feet from the high-water mark. The hotels, resorts, and restaurants remain small and are mostly family-owned by people who get to know their guests and pride themselves on giving personalized service. They're typical of the islanders as a whole—friendly and hospitable.

Grenada was sighted by Columbus in 1498. Although he never set foot on the island, he nevertheless named it Concepción. Throughout the 17th century it was the scene of bloody battles between the indigenous Carib Indians and the French. The Caribs finally lost to the French in 1651, committing mass suicide by leaping off a cliff rather than submitting to their captors. The French, however, lost the island again in 1762 to the British, thus beginning the seesaw of power between the two nations that became a familiar tale on many of the Windward Islands.

In 1967 Grenada became part of the British Commonwealth; seven years later it was granted total independence. The New Jewel Movement (NJM) seized power in 1979, formed the People's Revolutionary Government, and named as prime minister Maurice Bishop, who established controversial ties with Cuba. Bishop's prime ministry lasted until 1983, when a coup d'état led to his execution, along with those of many of his supporters. Bernard Coard, NJM deputy prime minister, and Army Commander Hudson Austin took over the government. U.S. troops invaded the island on October 25, 1983, and evacuated the American students who were attending St. George's University Medical School. Coard and Austin were arrested, and resistance to the invasion was quickly put down. Since then, the annual number of U.S. residents alone traveling to this splendid isle has more than tripled.

Herbert A. Blaize was elected prime minister in December 1984. With $57.2 million in U.S. aid, his government began reorganizing Grenada's economy to focus on agriculture, light manufacturing, and tourism. The country started to rebuild roads, and a new telephone system, with direct dial from the United States, replaced the outdated one. Point Salines International Airport opened in 1984, enabling jets to land on the island and allowing night landings, both firsts for Grenada.

The most recent election (Nicholas Braithwaite as prime minister) took place in March 1990, bringing more peaceful progress to this island nation with a stable and U.S.-friendly government.

Before You Go

Tourist Information
Contact the **Grenada Tourist Office:** in the United States (820 2nd Ave., Suite 900D, New York, NY 10017, tel. 212/687–9554 or 800/927–9554, fax 212/573–9731); in Canada (Suite 820, 439 University Ave., Toronto, Ontario M5G 1Y8, tel. 416/595–1339, fax 416/595–8278); or in Britain (1 Collingham Gardens, Earl's Court, London SW5 0HW, tel. 071/370–5164 or 071/370–5165, fax 071/370–7040).

Arriving and Departing
By Plane
BWIA (tel. 800/JET–BWIA) flies from New York, Miami, Toronto, and London to Grenada and also connects with Aruba and Curaçao. **American Airlines** (tel. 800/334–7400) has daily flights during high season from major U.S. and Canadian cities via their San Juan hub; **Air Canada** (tel. 800/776–3000) flies from Toronto to Barbados, where **LIAT** (Leeward Islands Air Transport, tel. 809/440–2796 or 809/440–2797) connects with flights to Grenada. LIAT has scheduled service between Barbados, Grenada, and Carriacou and also serves Trinidad, St. Lucia, Martinique, Antigua, and Venezuela.

From the Airport
Taxis are readily available at the airport. Rates to St. George's and the hotels of Grand Anse and L'Anse aux Epines are $10–$12. Rides taken between 6 PM and 6 AM incur a 33.3% surcharge.

Passports and Visas
Passports are not required of U.S., Canadian, or British citizens, provided they have two proofs of citizenship (one with photo) and a return air ticket. A passport, even an expired one, is the best proof of citizenship; a driver's license with photo *and* an original birth certificate or voter registration card will also suffice.

Language
English is the official language of Grenada.

Precautions
Secure your valuables in the hotel safe. A problem with walking late at night in the Grand Anse/L'Anse aux Epines (pronounced *lance-au-peen*) hotel districts is that it's dark enough to bump into things, maybe even into one of the cows that graze silently by the roadside. Starving mosquitoes adore tourists, especially after heavy rains; bring repellent, though U.S. brands are available in supermarkets.

Staying in Grenada

Important Addresses

Tourist Information: The **Grenada Tourist Office** is located in St. George's (the Carenage, tel. 809/440–2001, fax 809/440–6637). It has maps, brochures, and information on accommodations, tours, and other services.

Emergencies

Police, fire, and **ambulance:** In St. George's, Grand Anse, and L'Anse aux Epines, call 911. For other areas, check with your hotel. **Hospital: St. George's Hospital** (tel. 809/440–2051; 809/440–2052; 809/440–2053). **Pharmacies: Gitten's** (Halifax St., St. George's, tel. 809/440–2165) is open Monday–Wednesday and Friday–Saturday 8–5 and Thursday 8–noon and 1–5. **Gitten's Drugmart** (Grand Anse, tel. 809/444–4954) is open weekdays and Saturday 9–8, Sunday and public holidays 9–noon. **Parris' Pharmacy Ltd.** (Victoria St., Grenville, tel. 809/442–7330), on the windward side of the island, is open Monday–Wednesday and Friday 9–4:30, Thursday 9–1, and Saturday 9–7.

Currency

Grenada uses the Eastern Caribbean (E.C.) dollar. At press time, the exchange rate was E.C.\$2.67 in banks to U.S.\$1. Money can be exchanged at any bank or hotel. U.S. currency and traveler's checks are widely accepted, but be sure to ask which currency is referred to when you make purchases and business transactions; prices are often quoted in E.C. dollars. Hotels are unable by law to give foreign currency in change or on departure. Most hotels and major restaurants accept credit cards. *Note:* Prices quoted here are in U.S. dollars unless indicated otherwise.

Taxes and Service Charges

Hotels add an 8% government tax; restaurants add a 10% tax. The departure tax is E.C.\$35 for adults and E.C.\$17.50 for children ages 5 to 12. Children under 5 are exempt. Hotels and some restaurants add a 10% service charge to your bill. If not, a 10%–15% gratuity should be added for a job well done.

Guided Tours

Arnold's Tours (tel. 809/440–0531 or 809/440–2213) offers several tours, from two-hour sails to Carriacou trips. "LanSea Frolic," for instance, is a five-hour island tour that takes in the Annandale Falls, Grand Etang Lake, and Gouyave and includes a coastal cruise with lunch and drinks for \$45 per person. **Edwin Frank** (tel. 809/443–5143, after 5 PM) handles public relations for the tourist board by day, making him probably the best-informed tour guide around. He will tailor a weekend tour to your requirements. Dennis Henry of **Henry's Safari Tours** (tel. 809/444–5313) offers a program of adventurous hikes and Jeep safaris and is happy to discuss alternative itineraries, with discounts for groups of six or more.

A most unusual way to see Grenada is to join a scientific research project for a day. Options offered by the **Foundation for Field Research** (Box 771, St. George's, tel. 809/440–8854, fax 809/440–2330) include an underwater excavation of a 17th-century town and recording the social behavior of mona monkeys in the wild. This is no tourist bus trip, since you donate labor as well as a portion of the project cost, which is tax-deductible. Write for more details.

Getting Around
Buses

Minivans ply the winding road between St. George's and Grand Anse Beach, where many of the hotels are located. Hail one anywhere along the way, pay E.C.\$1, and hold on to your hat. They are available from about 6 to 8 daily except Sundays and public holidays. By minivan, you can get anywhere on the island for E.C.\$1–E.C.\$6—a bargain by any standard—but be prepared for packed vehicles, unpredictable schedules, and some hair-raising maneuvers on mountainous roads and byways.

Taxis   Taxis are plentiful, and rates are posted at the hotels and at the pier on the Carenage in St. George's. The trip from the airport to Grand Anse is E.C.$25, and from the airport to St. George's, E.C.$30. A surcharge of 33.3% is added to all fares for rides taken between 6 PM and 6 AM. Cabs are plentiful at all hotels, at the pier, and near the tourist office on the Carenage.

Rental Cars   To rent a car, you will need a valid driver's license, with which you may obtain a local permit from the traffic department (next to the fire station on the Carenage) or certain car rental firms, at a cost of E.C.$30. Driving is on the left. Rental cars cost about $45 a day or $250 a week with unlimited mileage. A Jeep and automatic drive run about $50 a day and $275 a week. Gas costs about $2.25 per gallon. Your hotel can arrange a rental for you. Car-rental agencies in St. George's are numerous. **David's** (tel. 809/440–2399, 809/440–3038, or 809/444–4310) maintains four offices: Point Salines International Airport, Ramada's Grenada Renaissance Resort, Archibold Avenue in St. George's, and South Wind Cottages in Grand Anse. **Avis** at Spice Isle Rental (tel. 809/440–3936 or 809/440–2624; after hours 809/444–4563) is on Paddock and Lagoon roads in St. George's. Look for **McIntyre Bros. Ltd.** (tel. 809/440–2044 or 809/440–2901; after hours 809/440–4053) on Lagoon Road in the capital.

Telephones and Mail   Grenada can be dialed directly from the United States and Canada. The area code is 809. Long-distance calls from Grenada can now be dialed directly as well.

Airmail rates for letters to the United States and Canada are E.C.75¢ for a half-ounce letter and E.C.35¢ for a postcard.

Opening and Closing Times   Store hours are generally from 8–noon and 1–4 weekdays; 8–noon, Saturday; they are closed Sunday. Banks in St. George's are open 8–2 or 3 Monday–Thursday; 8–noon and 2:30–5 on Friday.

Exploring Grenada

Numbers in the margin correspond with points of interest on the Grenada (and Carriacou) map.

St. George's   Grenada's capital city and major port is one of the most picturesque and truly West Indian towns in the Caribbean. Pastel warehouses cling to the curving shore along the horseshoe-shape Carenage, the harborside thoroughfare; rainbow-colored houses rise above it and ❶ disappear into the green hills. A walking tour of **St. George's** can be made in about two hours.

Start on the **Carenage,** a walkway along St. George's Harbour and the town's main thoroughfare. Ocean liners dock at the pier at the eastern end, and the **Delicious Landing** restaurant (tel. 809/440–3948), with outdoor tables, is at the western end. In between are the **public library,** a number of small **shops,** the **Grenada Tourist Office,** and two more good restaurants, **Rudolf's** and **The Nutmeg** (*see* Dining, *below*), which boasts a huge open window that provides a great view of the harbor.

You can reach the **Grenada National Museum** by walking along the west end of the Carenage and taking Young Street west to Monckton Street. The museum has a small, interesting collection of ancient and colonial artifacts and recent political memorabilia. *Young and Monckton Sts., tel. 809/440–3725. Admission: $1 adults, 25¢ children under 18. Open weekdays 9–4:30, Sat. 10–1:30.*

Walk west along Young Street, turn left on Cross Street, and you'll reach the **Esplanade,** the thoroughfare that runs along the ocean

Grenada (and Carriacou)

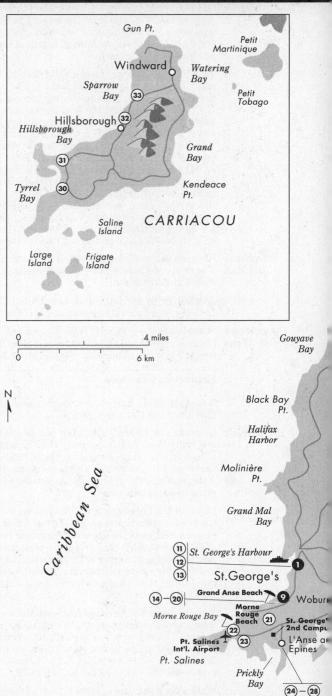

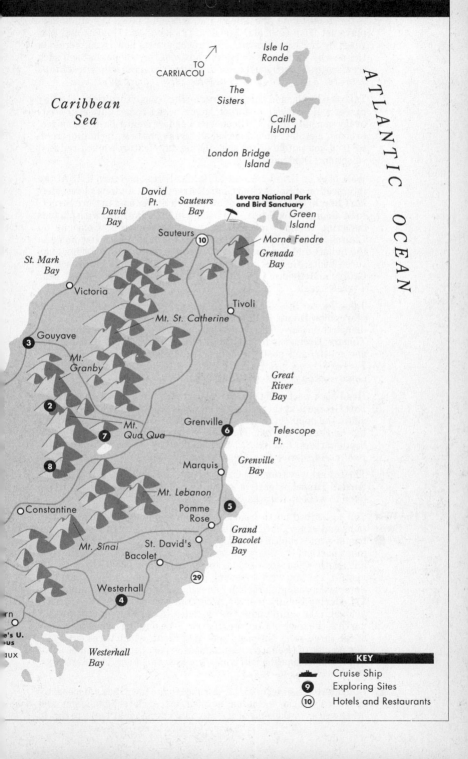

Isle la Ronde

TO CARRIACOU

The Sisters

Caille Island

Caribbean Sea

London Bridge Island

ATLANTIC OCEAN

David Pt.

David Bay

Sauteurs Bay

Levera National Park and Bird Sanctuary

Green Island

Sauteurs ⑩

Morne Fendre

Grenada Bay

St. Mark Bay

Victoria

Tivoli

Mt. St. Catherine

❸ Gouyave

Mt. Granby

Great River Bay

❷

Grenville ❻

Telescope Pt.

❼ *Mt. Qua Qua*

❽

Marquis

Grenville Bay

Mt. Lebanon

Constantine

Pomme Rose ❺

Grand Bacolet Bay

Mt. Sinai

St. David's

Bacolet

㉙

rn

e's U.
us

ux

Westerhall ❹

Westerhall Bay

KEY

Cruise Ship

❾ Exploring Sites

⑩ Hotels and Restaurants

side of town. At the intersection of Cross Street and the Esplanade is the **Yellow Poui Art Gallery** (tel. 809/440–3001). The studio displays art from Grenada, Jamaica, Trinidad, and Guyana and canvases by British, German, and French artists now living here. On the nearby Esplanade you'll find a row of tiny shops that sell such treats as guava jelly and coconut fudge. *Shopping hours: weekdays 9:15–12:15 and 1:15–3:15, Sat. 9:15–12:15; closed Sun.*

Take the Esplanade north to Granby Street and turn right. Granby Street will take you to **Market Square,** which comes alive every Saturday morning from 8 to noon with vendors selling baskets, spices, brooms, clothing, knickknacks, and fresh produce, including tropical fruit you can eat on the spot. (Other days feature a much-reduced selection.) Don't miss it!

Walk back on Granby Street to Halifax Street and turn left. At the intersection of Halifax and Church streets is **St. Andrew's Presbyterian Church,** built in 1830. Follow Church Street east to Gore Street, to **St. George's Anglican Church,** built in 1828. It's lined with plaques depicting Grenada in the 18th and 19th centuries. Continue up Church Street to the **York House,** built around 1800. Now home to the Senate and Supreme Court, it's open to the public for unstructured visits. Go back to Market Square and turn left to reach **St. George's Methodist Church,** built in 1820, on Green Street near Tyrrel Street.

Take Tyrrel Street east to the corner of Park Lane to see the **Marryshow House.** Built in 1917, it combines Victorian and West Indian architecture. The Marryshow also houses the **Marryshow Folk Theatre,** Grenada's first cultural center. Plays, West Indian dance and music, and poetry readings are presented here on occasion. *Tyrrel St., near Bain Alley, tel. 809/440–2451. Admission free. Open weekdays 8:30–4:30, Sat. 9–1.*

Head back west on Tyrrel Street and turn left onto Church Street. **Fort George** is at the southern tip of Church Street. The fort, rising above the point that separates the harbor from the ocean, was built by the French in 1705. The inner courtyard now houses the police headquarters. *Church St., no phone. Outer courtyard open to the public. Admission free. Open daily during daylight hours.*

The fastest way from the Carenage to the Esplanade is through the **Sendall Tunnel,** slightly north of Fort George. Take it if you're too tired to walk up the steep hill.

The West Coast ❷ The coast road north from St. George's winds past soaring mountains and valleys covered with banana and breadfruit trees, palms, bamboo, and tropical flowers. You can drive to **Concord Falls,** about 8 miles north of St. George's, and then hike 2 miles to the main falls, and another hour to a second, spectacular waterfall. There's a small visitors' center, with a viewing platform, the inevitable spice vendors, and a changing room for donning your bathing suit (admission $1). During the dry months, when the currents aren't too strong, you can take a dip under the cascades. About 15 minutes farther north is the town of **Gouyave,** center of the nutmeg industry. A tour of the three-story **Nutmeg Processing Plant,** which turns out 3 million pounds of Grenada's most famous export per year, makes a fragrant and fascinating half hour. *Gouyave, no phone. Admission $1. Open weekdays 10–1, 2–4.*

❸ **Dougaldston Estate,** near the entrance to the town, has a spice factory where you can see cocoa, nutmeg, mace, cloves, cinnamon, and other spices in their natural state, laid out on giant trays to dry in the sun. Pick up a bag of cinnamon bark, cloves, bay leaves, red mace, or nutmeg for $2. *Gouyave, no phone. Admission free. Open weekdays 9–4.*

Continuing along the coast road to the northernmost tip of the island brings you to Leapers' Hill, known by the French word for leapers, Sauteurs. It was off this 100-foot cliff that the Carib Indians flung themselves in 1651, preferring to die rather than submit to the French invaders.

Time Out   For lunch take the short drive to Betty Mascoll's old plantation house, **Morne Fendue** (St. Patrick's Parish, tel. 809/440–9330). The large, two-story house was built by Mrs. Mascoll's father in 1912 of hand-chiseled, colored stones mortared with lime and molasses. Outside, poinsettias grow in profusion; inside, amid Victorian antiques and dainty lace curtains, you'll meet every one of the day's tour groups, since Betty's is the only lunch you can get this far north—but what a lunch! The West Indian buffet is deservedly famous, as is the restorative rum punch. Reservations are essential.

The East   Start your tour at **Westerhall**, a residential area about 5 miles south-
Coast   east of St. George's, known for its beautiful villas, gardens, and pan-
④ ⑤   oramic views. From here, take a dirt road north to **Grand Bacolet
Bay**, a jagged peninsula on the Atlantic where the surf pounds
⑥   against deserted beaches. Some miles north is **Grenville**, the island's second-largest city, reminiscent of a French market town. From here you can watch schooners set sail for the outer islands. As in St. George's, Saturday is market day, and the town fills with local people doing their shopping for the week. Cooking enthusiasts may want to see the town's spice-processing factory, which is open to the public.

If you take the interior route back to St. George's, you'll get a full sense of the lush, mountainous nature of the island. There is only one paved road that cuts across the island. Leaving Grenville and heading for St. George's, you'll wind upward through the rain forest until you're surrounded by mist, then you'll descend onto the sunny
⑦   hillsides. In the middle of the island is **Grand Etang National Park.** Visit the informative Welcome Center, with displays on the local flora and fauna and a forest manager on hand to answer questions. The lake, in the crater of an extinct volcano, is a 13-acre glasslike expanse of cobalt blue water. The area is a bird sanctuary and forest reserve where you can go fishing and hiking. *Main interior road, halfway between Grenville and St. George's, tel. 809/442–7425. Admission $1. Open daily 8:30–4.*

⑧   Another place to visit is **Annandale Falls and Visitors' Centre,** where a mountain stream cascades 50 feet into a pool surrounded by such exotic tropical flora as liana vines and elephant ears. This is a good swimming and picnic spot. *Main interior road, 15 min east of St. George's, tel. 809/440–2452. Open daily 9–5.*

Grand Anse   Most of the island's hotels and its nightlife are in Grand Anse or the
and the   adjacent community of L'Anse aux Epines, which means Cove of
South End   Pines. Here you will find one of the two campuses of **St. George's
⑨   University Medical School,** which is due to move to its other campus at True Blue sometime this year, leaving another prime hotel site on Grand Anse.

True Blue, a residential area near L'Anse aux Epines, can be reached from the Grand Anse Road by turning left onto an unnamed road before the airport.

The **Grand Anse Shopping Centre** has a supermarket/liquor store, clothing store, shoe store, fast-food joint, and several small gift shops with good-quality souvenirs and such luxury items as English china and Swedish crystal (*see* Shopping, *below*). Prices are competitive with duty-free shops elsewhere in the Caribbean.

Grenada's Grenadines **Carriacou, Petit Martinique,** and a handful of uninhabited specks that constitute the nation of Grenada, are north of Grenada island and part of the Grenadines, a chain of 32 tiny islands and cays.

Carriacou is a little island (13 square miles) with a lot of punch. A hideaway with "over a hundred rum shops and only one gasoline station," this place moves even the fastest Manhattan metabolism down several notches and exudes the kind of ebullient spirit and goodwill that you want to find in a Caribbean retreat but usually find only in a travel brochure. Don't come here if you don't want peace, if you do want luxurious amenities, or if you would suffer coldly a parrot on your breakfast table.

Carriacou's colonial history parallels Grenada's; its tiny size has restricted its political role to a minor part in the area's history. A chain of hills cuts a wide swath through its center, from Gun Point in the north to Tyrrel Bay in the south. LIAT has seven daily flights (flying time approximately 20 minutes) to and from Grenada island, and schooners leave from St. George's Harbour twice a week. Hillsborough is the main town. In August, the Carriacou Regatta attracts yachts and sailing vessels from throughout the Caribbean.

The only museum in the eastern Caribbean that is owned by the people, not the government, is the **Carriacou Museum,** located in Hillsborough behind Gramma's Bakery. This operation, housed in an old cotton ginnery, displays unearthed Amerindian, European, and African artifacts and features a gift shop loaded with locally made wares.

Five miles northeast of Carriacou is Petit Martinique, the smallest of Grenada's inhabited islands. Like Carriacou and Grenada, Petit Martinique was settled by the French.

Grenada for Free

A good way to spend an afternoon without spending money is to watch fishing boats of all sizes and descriptions pull in and out of St. George's Harbour. On Tuesday afternoons you can watch the boats being loaded with crates and bags of fruits and vegetables bound for Trinidad. It's also fun to roam through St. George's and Grenville's Saturday markets, which are ablaze with color and humming with activity. Farm women sitting under umbrellas sell bananas, papayas, oranges, yams, plantains, exotic roots and vegetables, and fresh spices; ask the women for their permission before grabbing a photo opportunity. At the nearby fish market, just a short stroll down the Esplanade, you can see the day's catch on display. Bird- or butterfly-watchers can view a multitude of species at Levera National Park (*see* Beaches, *below*) or La Sagesse Nature Center (*see* Lodging, *below*).

Beaches

Grenada has some 80 miles of coastline, 65 bays, and 45 white-sand beaches, many with secluded little coves. All the beaches are public and within an easy cab ride of St. George's. Most are located on the Caribbean, south of St. George's in the Grand Anse and L'Anse aux

Epines areas, where most of the hotels are clustered. Virtually every hotel, apartment complex, and residential area has its own beach or tiny cove.

The loveliest and most popular beach is **Grand Anse,** about a 10-minute taxi ride from St. George's. It's a gleaming, 2-mile curve of sand and clear, gentle surf. At its southern end is a palm-covered point; to the north you can see the narrow mouth of St. George's Harbour and the pastel houses with fish-scale-tile rooftops on the hillsides above it. Constant visits from vendors selling spices, palm baskets, T-shirts, and brown coral jewelry punctuate a day on this beach. They are, for the most part, licensed, and their wares are worth a look. The sunset is particularly beautiful at Grand Anse—enjoy it over cocktails at Spice Island Inn, where tables line the beach.

Morne Rouge Beach is on the Caribbean side, about 1 mile south of Grand Anse Bay and 3 miles south of St. George's Harbour. The beach forms a half-mile-long crescent and has a gentle surf excellent for swimming. A small café serves light meals during the day. In the evening, there's a disco, Fantasia 2001 (*see* Nightlife, *below*).

Levera National Park and Bird Sanctuary is at the northern tip of the island, where the Caribbean meets the Atlantic. The first of the Grenadines is visible in the distance. The surf is rougher here than on the Caribbean beaches, but it is great for body surfing or watching the waves roll in. In 1991, this area, with its thick mangroves for food and protection, became an official sanctuary for nesting seabirds and seldom-seen tropical parrots. There are some fine Arawak ruins and petroglyphs to be seen as well.

Sports and the Outdoors

Bicycling Level ground is about as common here as are reindeer, but that doesn't stop the aerobically primed. What's more, 15-speed mountain bikes are available for a much more reasonable rate than are four-wheel-drive vehicles; you can find them at **Ride Grenada** (L'Anse aux Epines, tel. 809/444–1157). A word of caution to women cyclists: you are a novelty on Grenada and will attract an alarming amount of attention.

Fishing Deep-sea fishing around Grenada is excellent, with marlin, sailfish, tuna, yellowfin, and dolphin topping the list of good catches. The annual **Game Fishing Tournament** is held in late January. Half-day and full-day excursions are available, plus tours to Sandy Island, Carriacou, and the Grenadines. Your hotel can help you charter a fishing boat.

Golf The Grenada Golf Club in Grand Anse (tel. 809/444–4128) has a nine-hole course. Your hotel will make arrangements for you.

Sailing, Diving, and Snorkeling The Moorings (tel. 809/444–4548; in the U.S., 800/535–7289; in Canada, 800/633–7348) has taken over Secret Harbour on the southeast shore and added some of its finest charter yachts and a range of Shore 'n' Sail programs developed by America's cup racer Steve Colgate for beginning and experienced sailors. You can rent 32- to 45-foot yachts, with or without crew, from **Seabreeze Yacht Charters** at the Spice Island Marine Centre (tel. 809/444–4924; from the United States, 800/387–3998). Diving in this area is excellent, with visibility as far as 200 feet. Hundreds of varieties of fish and more than 40 species of coral await underwater explorers. The best snorkeling is found around Carriacou's offshore islands. A superb spot for scuba diving is at the site of what is sometimes dubbed "the *Titanic* of the Caribbean," the *Bianca C*, a 600-foot cruise ship that caught fire and sank in 1961. It settled in waters more than 100 feet deep and is now home to giant turtles, spotted eagle rays with 15-foot wingspans, and a 350-pound grouper that lives in the ship's smokestack.

Dive Grenada at Grand Anse Beach (Grenada Renaissance Resort, tel. 809/444–4371, ext. 638) offers a variety of scuba courses, as well as certification for novices. It also takes expert divers to the reefs and shipwrecks.

Swimming Take your pick from Grenada's 45 beaches and secluded coves, but don't miss Grand Anse Beach.

Other Water Sports The major hotels on Grand Anse Beach have water-sports centers where you can rent small sailboats, Windsurfers, and Sunfish equipment. The centers are located in front of the hotels. Your hotel can make arrangements for you, or you can call one of the major hotels for information.

Tennis Several hotels have tennis courts that are free to their guests, including **Calabash** (tel. 809/444–4234), **Secret Harbour** (tel. 809/444–4548), **Coyaba** (tel. 809/444–4129), **Spice Island Inn** (tel. 809/444–4258), **Grenada Renaissance** (tel. 809/444–4371), **Coral Cove** (tel. 809/444–4217), and **Twelve Degrees North** (tel. 809/444–4580). If there are no courts where you're staying, you can play at some private clubs on the island. Your hotel desk clerk can contact them for you.

Shopping

The best souvenirs in Grenada are little spice baskets filled with cinnamon, nutmeg, mace, bay leaf, vanilla, "saffron" (the local name for turmeric), and ginger. You can find them in practically every shop. Vendors who stroll the beach in Grand Anse also sell spice baskets as well as fabric dolls, T-shirts, hats, fans, visors woven from green palm, and brown coral jewelry. (Be aware that environmental groups discourage tourists from buying black coral.)

Good Buys **St. George's** **The Yellow Poui Art Gallery** (Cross St., tel. 809/440–3001) offers the most serious art finds, with canvases from Grenada, Jamaica, Guyana, and Trinidad and offerings by overseas artists who have settled here. Prices range from $2 to $2,000. Barbara Minors's shop, **Gifts Remembered** (Cross St., tel. 809/440–2482), and her daughter Alison's branch (at the Coyaba beach resort, tel. 809/444–4129), are both crammed with amazing and inexpensive stuff, including wonderful, brightly painted boats, houses, and trucks, laden with fruit and smiling people, from the local Tropica ceramic studio, and T-shirts that are better quality than usual. **Spice Island Perfumes** on the Carenage (tel. 809/440–2006) is a treasure trove of local perfumes, body oils, and natural extracts of spices and herbs. Best of all are the tiny wooden pots of solid fragrances, including bitter orange, jasmine, or spice for around $8. At the far end of the Carenage, **White Cane Industries** (tel. 809/444–2014) stocks bargain baskets, hats, and spectacularly colored rag rugs, all handwoven locally by blind craftspeople; they receive the proceeds from the shop. Pricier is **Tikal** (Young St., tel. 809/440–2310), a long-established boutique well known for its exquisite handicrafts and fashions, both local and imported.

Grand Anse In Grand Anse, the **Grand Anse Shopping Centre,** houses **the Gift Shop,** an outlet for imported luxury items such as watches, leather goods, fine jewelry, crystal, and china, all at competitive prices, and

Imagine, which specializes in island handicrafts, including batik fabrics.

Carriacou In L'Esterre on Carriacou, hand-painted signs announce "This way to the great artist," **Canute Calliste.** If you get lost, one of his many (more than 20) grandchildren will lead the way. Works by Calliste are also available at the Carriacou Museum, as are the creations of Frankie Francis.

Dining

Unlike most Caribbean islands, which have a scarcity of fresh produce, Grenada has everything from cabbages and tomatoes to bananas, mangoes, papaya (called pawpaw), plantains, melons, callaloo (similar to spinach), breadfruits, oranges, tangerines, limes, christophines (similar to squash), and avocados—the list is endless. In addition, fresh seafood of all kinds, including lobster and oyster, is also plentiful. Conch, known here as *lambi*, is very popular and appears on most menus in some form, but usually as a stew. Be sure to try one of the exotic ice creams made from avocado or nutmeg. Almost all the Grenadan restaurants serve local dishes, which are varied enough to be continually interesting.

Rum punches are served everywhere, but no two places make them exactly alike, except for the nutmeg always grated on top. The local beer, Carib, is also very popular.

Highly recommended restaurants are indicated by a star ★.

Category	Cost*
Expensive	over $40
Moderate	$20–$40
Inexpensive	under $20

*per person, excluding drinks, service, and 10% sales tax

Grenada **The Calabash.** The open-air restaurant at the hotel of the same name is small and pretty, surrounded by palms and tropical flowers. There is a prix fixe dinner each evening with a set menu that may include fillet of kingfish with roast potatoes, mixed vegetables, and fried plaintains or chicken with ginger and chive sauce, accompanied by a salad and cauliflower in mustard sauce. Cheese and biscuits with coffee, tea, or cocoa top off the meal. *L'Anse aux Epines, tel. 809/444–4234. Reservations suggested. AE, MC, V. Expensive.*

★ **Canboulay.** With their exciting reconfigurations of local cuisine, the Trinidadian couple Erik and Gina-Lee Johnson put Canboulay on the map as soon as it opened its shutters to the Grand Anse view and hilltop breezes. The menu changes often, but regulars include crab crepes with a purée of callaloo, breadfruit vichyssoise, grilled tuna steak with citrus-pepper sauce, African *bobotie* (spiced, raisin-studded ground beef topped with a baked custard), and five-star versions of the ubiquitous *roti* (curried meat, potatoes, and beans wrapped in a giant tortilla) and nutmeg ice cream. The frozen chocolate-mocha cheesecake has broken hearts, and anything they do with shrimp—coconut-beer-batter-it, or peanut-sauce-it—is memorable. There's now a veranda terrace with a more casual ambience. *Morne Rouge, St. George's, tel. 809/444–4401. Reservations suggested. Dress: casual to elegant. AE, D, MC, V. Open for lunch and dinner weekdays, dinner only Sat., closed Sun. Expensive.*

★ **La Belle Creole.** This restaurant is celebrated for its creative nouvelle West Indian cuisine and wraparound hilltop view of St. George's. The lunch and dinner menus are always changing, but if you're lucky, there will be an appetizer made from Grenadan caviar (roe of the white sea urchin), soursop mousse, or lobster-egg flan. Entrées may be stuffed baked rainbow runner, Creole saffron pork chops, or callaloo quiche. The Sunday barbecue features many of the delicate dishes along with live entertainment. The graciousness with which you are served at this restaurant is bound to impress even the most jaded traveler. *Blue Horizons Cottage Hotel, Morne Rouge, St. George's, tel. 809/444–4316. Reservations required for nonhotel guests. AE, MC, V. Expensive.*

Red Crab. This is a favorite meeting and eating spot (especially on Saturday nights) where guests dine in a relaxed pub or outside under trees and stars, although the food itself is not exemplary and remains overpriced. The accent is on fresh seafood, local lobster in particular, but the steak is what draws homesick Americans back. Hot garlic bread comes with all orders. *L'Anse aux Epines (near The Calabash). tel. 809/444–4424. AE, MC, V. Expensive.*

★ **Spice Island Inn.** Diners tend to dress elegantly for the five-course evening meal at this nicest of hotel dining rooms (reservations for nonhotel guests are limited) that boasts an ivy-hung terrace and is open on three sides and separated from the beach by the narrowest of paths. Roast beef or calves' liver are as likely to appear on the menu as are more local or innovative fare, of which the unlikely-sounding grapefruit consommé is a sublime example. Lobster usually plays support, taking the title role at the Saturday "Seafood Night" buffet, upstaged only by a dessert table groaning with pineapple pie, nutmeg ice cream, chocolate truffle torte, and the like. Wednesdays are *the* night, "Grenadan Night," in fact, when crab back, sea egg, roast suckling pig, and such is on the table, and there's dancing under the stars. Fridays feature an equally festive barbecue. *Grand Anse, tel. 809/444–4258 or 809/444–4423. Reservations required late Dec.–mid-Apr. AE, D, MC, V. Expensive.*

★ **Betty Mascoll's Great House.** Betty herself is now over 80 and not at all well, which is sad news indeed for the thousands who have pigged out at her lunchtime West Indian buffet in the beautiful, secluded Morne Fendue plantation house that her father built in 1912. Still, for now, her helpers provide just as fine a spread, including the legendary pepper pot—a rich and spicy Guyanese stew of pork and oxtail, rumored to have been bubbling for years, and alone worth the hour's drive north. You may find the appetizer is callaloo soup, the dessert some seasonal fruit, and the rum punches very good and very strong. *St. Patrick's Parish, near Sauteurs, tel. 809/440–9330. Reservations required. No credit cards. Moderate.*

The Boatyard. Smack in the middle of a marina, this restaurant is a lively place, filled with embassy personnel and expatriates. Lunches include burgers, fish-and-chips, and deep-fried shrimp. Dinner features club steaks, lobster, and different types of meat and seafood brochettes. In season (late December–mid-April) there's a steel band on Saturday night, jazz on Sunday, and disco music on Friday night. *L'Anse aux Epines, tel. 809/444–4662. MC, V. Closed Mon. Moderate.*

The Flamboyant. The night to come to the Flamboyant hotel's exquisite terrace with its vista of St. George's lights, its pyramid-roofed bar, and white-wicker bucket chairs, is definitely Monday. Monday is ebullient Hotel Managing Director Lawrence Lambert's crab-racing night, and you haven't lived until you've bet a few cents on the confused hermit crab racing in your country's colors. (Don't worry, Mr. Lambert collects them personally from the hills and feeds them coconut. They lead happy lives.) The Monday food—a Grenadan buffet—is the week's best, too; other nights, tropical fruit cocktail, orange-grilled tuna, beef stew, and a tendency to fry all vegetables doesn't add up to the best-value meal, though there are two other buffet-and-party nights (Wednesday's party has a steel band; Friday features calypso, limbo, and barbecue) that are definitely worth your attention. *Grand Anse, tel. 809/444–4247. AE, D, DC, MC, V. Expensive.*

The Nutmeg. Fresh seafood is the specialty of this second-floor restaurant that has a great view of the harbor. Try the grilled turtle steaks, lobsters, or shrimp with fries, or go for the chicken rôti. *The Carenage, St. George's, tel. 809/440–2539. Dress: informal. AE, D, MC, V. Moderate.*

Rudolf's. This informal, publike place offers fine West Indian fare. Skip the attempts at haute cuisine "Viennoise" or "Parisienne," and enjoy the crab back, lambi, and delectable nutmeg ice cream. This is *the* place for eavesdropping on local gossip. Even for Grenada the rum punches are lethal. *The Carenage, St. George's, tel. 809/440–2241. No credit cards. Closed Sun. Moderate.*

Cot Bam. Wedged between the Coyaba resort and the medical school on Grand Anse beach, this bar/restaurant/night spot with a tin roof and bamboo railings is a place to kick back and enjoy. Order a chicken *roti* served with coleslaw for E.C.$6, and a Carib beer, and you're set for the evening. It's within walking distance of all the Grand Anse hotels; the staff is a delight; and you can hop over in your shorts after a long day at the beach to dance or socialize with abandon. *Grand Anse, tel. 809/444–2050. Open Sun.–Thurs. 10 AM–midnight, Fri.–Sat. 10 AM–3 AM. AE. Inexpensive.*

Mamma's. This restaurant is more like a diner, West Indian style, and very charming. One of Mamma's daughters will set generous helpings of local specialties before you—probably some roast turtle, lobster salad, christophine salad, cabbage salad, or fried plantain, as well as such exotica as armadillo, opossum, and sea urchin. Menus don't list prices, but the broad buffet offerings are available at a fixed E.C.$45 per person. Request the iguana in advance. You will not leave hungry, although word is that standards have slipped a little of late. *Lagoon Rd., St. George's, tel. 809/440–1459. Reservations required. No credit cards. Inexpensive.*

Carriacou **Barba's Oyster Shell.** This place is basic, but it is the only one that offers Carriacou's rare and succulent mangrove oysters. *Tyrrel Bay, Carriacou, tel. 809/443–7454. No credit cards. Inexpensive.*

Scrapers. Good things are happening at Tyrrel Bay. Scrapers serves up lobster, conch, and an assortment of fresh catches, along with an artless spirit and decor seasoned with occasional calypsonian serenades (owner Steven Gay "Scraper" is a pro). Order a rum punch and exercise your right to do nothing. *Tyrrel Bay, Carriacou, tel. 809/443–7403. AE, D, MC, V. Inexpensive.*

Lodging

Grenada's accommodations range from simply furnished kitchenette apartments to suites of overwhelming Caribbean-style elegance. There are no pretentious hotels—Grenada is a simple place, and its hotels have been furnished in "casual tropical" decor. Most of the hotels are owned and operated by Grenadans; those that aren't are usually run by British or American expatriates who thrive on the simplicity of Grenadan life. The hotels tend to be small (10 to 20 rooms in most cases), but they exude a sense of intimacy, with friendly managers or owners.

For confirmation on reservations at any of the 24 members of the **Grenada Hotel Association,** call, in the United States or Canada, 800/ 223–9815; in New York State, 212/545–8469.

Most posted daily room rates at Grenadan hotels are quoted in U.S. currency and represent the room rate only, without meals. Visitors can often opt for CP or MAP, depending on the season. The plans specified in the individual listings below apply year-round unless otherwise noted. Prices for the summer are discounted by 20% to 40%.

Highly recommended lodgings are indicated by a star ★.

Category	Cost*
Very Expensive	over $200
Expensive	$150–$200
Moderate	$100–$150
Inexpensive	under $100

All prices are for a standard double room for two during high season, excluding 8% tax and 10% service charge.

Hotels
Grenada

The Calabash. This all-suite hotel is set on a wide green lawn in 8 acres of tropical gardens overlooking a curved beach, a yacht harbor, and charter-boat anchorage in "Prickly Bay," L'Anse aux Epines, a few minutes away from the hotel row of Grand Anse. A major renovation has just been completed, adding a casual beach bar and restaurant, and equipping an additional nine suites with whirlpool baths, making a total of 14 such suites in all; eight suites with their own private pool were added as well. All suites have air-conditioning and a veranda, where breakfast is delivered. You'll have to live with the noise generated by the nearby Point Salines International Airport: Early-morning flights can bounce you out of bed. *Box 382, St. George's, tel. 809/444–4234, fax 809/444–4804. 22 suites. Facilities: restaurant, beach bar/restaurant, pool, water-sports center, tennis. AE, MC, V. BP, MAP. Very Expensive.*

LaSource. The brand-new sister of St Lucia's LeSport, this serene spa resort promises great things. A towering, louvered wood-and-stained-glass reception hall leads into a courtyard around which treatment rooms, restaurant (consume *cuisine légère* in the mint-and-raspberry colonnaded terrace or the colonial teak and plush Great Room), piano bar, and pool are ranged. The stunning bedrooms—with Persian rugs on Italian marble floors; tall, sloping wooden ceilings; balconies; and marble bathrooms with hair dryers and illuminated make-up mirrors—are housed in separate four-story buildings on or above the main beach. Rates seem steep at first glance, but include *everything*, down to three meals, snacks, drinks at the bar, wine with dinner, tipping (it's banned), sports, plus, of course, spa treatments. Massages, facials, and saunas are scheduled for you pre-arrival and augmented by local concoctions made with lemons, limes, papayas, or whatever's in season. The array of sports facilities is impressive—the best on Grenada. *Pink Gin Beach, Box 852, St. George's, tel. 809/444–2556 or 800/544–2883, fax 809/444–2561. 100 rooms. Facilities: 2 restaurants, full spa with treatment rooms, sauna, hot tub, hair salon, etc, piano bar, 2 beaches, pool, poolside bar service, water sports, gym, aerobics, yoga, stretch, and meditation classes, par-3, 9-hole golf course, 2 lighted tennis courts, fencing, archery, volleyball, cycling, table tennis, entertainment. AE, MC, V. All-inclusive. Very Expensive.*

★ **Secret Harbour.** The Moorings (which specializes in sailing vacations) has taken over this deluxe resort, and it's an ideal match. The hotel has oversize rooms tucked into Mediterranean-style villas on a bluff overlooking Mt. Hartman Bay. Both these and the spacious lobby/bar/terrace restaurant have burnished terra-cotta floors, aged-brick arches, nooks and crannies of exposed stone with simple local art, Moorish furniture, and black-stained, carved wood; arty knickknacks are scattered about judiciously. Outside, yachts dock at the door (all with professional crew), ready for a day at sea or, if you opt for the hotel's Club Mariner plans, four nights ashore and three cruising the offshore islands. Secret Harbour may not lie on Grand Anse beach, but its tropical gardens, marina, and windward position (this side of the island receives less rainfall than does the west coast) boost its desirability quotient to the top. *Box 11, St. George's, tel. 809/444-4548 or 800/334-2435;outside continental U.S., 813/538-8760; fax 809/444-4819. 20 rooms. Facilities: restaurant, lounge, tennis, beach with bar, pool, sailboats (day sailers, bareboat to crewed). AE, DC, MC, V. EP, MAP. Very Expensive.*

★ **Spice Island Inn.** There are three types of suites here, all luxuriously oversize, shiny with the colors of sand, cloud and coral, and equipped with air-conditioning, fan, phone, hair dryer, minibar, vast mirrored closets, and patios. Some prefer the original suites, built *on* Grand Anse beach, others the later, second-floor suites with their white-ballustraded terraces overlooking garden, sea, and sunset. Beneath those are the pool suites, with a private splash-pool. What really distinguishes Spice from the pack, though, are the fabulous bathrooms. The size of a small parking garage, they're equipped with spa-Jacuzzis that could submerge a family of four, heaps of big, white towels, and skylights for watching the moon rise. In some pool suites, you forgo the Jacuzzi but you still get your courtyard cleverly shielded from prying eyes by wooden decking and curtains of hibiscus blossom. Since Grand Anse is Grenada's prime stretch of sand, the location can't be better for beach bums—with the restaurant (*see* Dining, *above*) and bar in the center of the complex, your feet need never touch concrete. *Box 6, Grand Anse, St. George's, tel. 809/444-4258 or 800/223-9815, fax 809/444-4807. 39 whirlpool suites and 17 private-pool suites. Facilities: restaurant, bar, tennis courts, water-sports center, boutique, fitness center, entertainment most nights, 18-hole golf course nearby. AE, MC, V. MAP, All-inclusive. Very Expensive.*

Grenada Renaissance Resort. Fifteen million dollars were spent on this property in 1991, when Ramada took it over. It's well located, on the beach directly across from the Grand Anse shopping center, but the place still suffers from an American motel decor. The ceilings are low, the rooms less spacious than those at competing resorts, and the interior spaces tend to be dark. Still, all rooms have king-size or extra-large beds, satellite TVs, and hair dryers, and the Ramada is also the hub of a Grand Anse night out—sooner or later everyone seems to end up here for drinks. Whether that will continue to be the case now that the Grenadian has overtaken this in both size and degree of international flavor remains to be seen. *Box 441, Grand Anse, St. George's, tel. 809/444-4371, fax 809/444-4800. 184 doubles, 2 luxury suites. Facilities: 2 restaurants, lounge, pool, tennis, barber shop/beauty salon, 2 gift shops. AE, DC, MC, V. EP, MAP. Expensive-Very Expensive.*

Coyaba. Coyaba means "heaven" in the Arawak Indian language, which doesn't *quite* describe the ambience here, but this Grand Anse beach resort next to the medical school is certainly well equipped. Leading off the lawns are tennis and volleyball courts, a sizable pool with swim-up bar, and a bamboo-walled terrace restaurant. The carpeted rooms, housed in four two-story concrete, tiled-roof blocks, have air-conditioning, cable TV, phone, hair dryer, and a balcony (or strip of grass with lounge chair), but they're mostly set back too far from the beach to overlook anything but the grounds and are still a brief amble away from the water. Plants, dark-stained wood, and Arawak-inspired folk art adorn both rooms and public areas. *Box 336, Grand Anse, St. George's, tel. 809/444–4129 or 800/ 223–9815, fax 809/444–4808. 40 rooms. Facilities: restaurant, bar, pool with swim-up bar, tennis courts, water-sports center, lounge boutique. AE, D, DC, MC, V. EP, CP, BP, MAP, FAP. Expensive.*

The Grenadian. This massive, British-owned resort near the airport has overtaken the Grenada Renaissance in size and business facilities; this means you're likely to be vacationing alongside a convention group. However, you may not notice them, since the conference suites and executive rooms are housed in a wing of their own in the central building, a faux-Palladian white palace of lofty, pink-limed oak ceilings, vast arched windows, trellised walkways, and tiled terraces. Eight two-story blocks house the other rooms, of robin's-egg blue and taupe with rattan furniture, king or large twin beds, and balconies; $25 more adds air- conditioning, tub, and hair dryer; a further $50 buys a beachfront suite with cable TV. Enthusiastic landscaping includes a lake and fountain, which many rooms overlook, and a pool terrace above one of two beaches, with restaurant and bar. All manner of activity is laid on—water sports, rainy-day programs (bingo, local dialect classes, dance lessons), evening shows, happy hours. It's the capital city of resorts. *Point Salines, Box 893, St. George's, tel. 809/444–3333 or 800/255–5859; fax 809/444–1111. 212 rooms. Facilities: 3 restaurants, café, lounge, 2 beaches, beach bar, pool with bar/restaurant, piano bar, executive lounge, conference facilities, water sports, fitness center, tennis, entertainment. AE, D, DC, MC, V. EP. Moderate–Expensive.*

★ **Blue Horizons Cottage Hotel.** This comfortable resort appointed in handsome mahogany furnishings, white walls, and cool, tiled floors is a very good value. Set among the palms around a large, sunny lawn and swimming pool on 6½ acres, the suites are air-conditioned and equipped with kitchenette, terrace, TV, phone, fan, and hair dryer. Grand Anse beach is a six-minute walk down the hill, where sister hotel Spice Island Inn sprawls along 1,600 feet of beach. Water sports are free for guests at either hotel. Guests may eat here at La Belle Creole or at Spice Island, and evening entertainment alternates between the two. *Box 41, Grand Anse, St. George's, tel. 809/ 444–4316 or 809/444–4592; in the U.S., 800/223–9815; fax 809/444– 2815. 32 suites. Facilities: restaurant, 2 bars, lounge, pool. AE, MC, V. EP, CP, MAP. Moderate.*

The Flamboyant Hotel and Cottages. Home of the famous Monday-night crab-racing spectacular, this Grenadan-owned cross between hotel and self-catering resort is a particularly friendly place, with one of the island's best views, sweeping over the entire Grand Anse bay to St George's. Enjoy this from any of the rooms, all simply furnished with air-conditioning, minibar, cable TV, phone, and balcony; some with kitchen, lounge, and extra bedrooms for an additional $25 (one-bedroom apartment) to $100 (two-bedroom cottage). Pass the freshwater pool along the path down to the beach, where the cabana bar serves snacks and holds barbecues. You get a lot for a little here. *Box 214, St. George's, tel. 809/444–4247, fax 809/444–1234. 16 rooms, 20 suites (with kitchenettes), and 2 cottages. Facilities: restaurant, bar, beach bar, pool, cable TV, free snorkeling equipment. AE, D, MC, V. EP, BP, MAP. Inexpensive–Moderate.*

La Sagesse Nature Center. Set on a bay 10 miles from Point Salines International Airport, the center has a guest house with basic high-ceilinged rooms with fans, kitchenettes, and hot-water baths. Mangroves, a salt-pond bird sanctuary, and hiking trails provide a peaceful, unspoiled setting, making this a best bet for avoiders of nightlife. Though the center is away from St. George's and Grand Anse, Mike Meranski, its American owner-manager, cheerfully runs guests into town for grocery supplies and shopping when he takes his daughter to school. Of course he's cheerful—he lives on a secluded beach in a paradisial setting. *Box 44, St. David's, tel. 809/ 444–6458, fax 809/444–6458. 4 double rooms. Facilities: restaurant, bar, beach, satellite TV. MC, V. EP. Inexpensive.*

Carriacou **Cassada Bay Resort.** This resort doesn't just offer a breathtaking panorama of the ocean, you have the use of a private island for snorkeling and windsurfing and some of the finest lemonade this side of the equator. Cabins here, on the south side of Carriacou, shimmy down the side of a hilltop overlooking the sea and offer an unadorned, but peaceful, sea-sprayed hideaway. *Carriacou, tel. 809/ 443–7494, fax 809/443–7672. 20 doubles. Facilities: restaurant, bar, water-sports center. AE, DC, MC, V. EP, CP, MAP. Moderate.*

Silver Beach Resort. This 18-room hotel is tucked away on stretches of pristine beach on Carriacou, Grenada's sister isle. All rooms have private patios and ocean views. An owner-managed hotel, it has the biggest scuba facilities in the Grenadines and, incidentally, is the best place on the island for a hearty, early-morning breakfast in its open-air restaurant by the water. *Silver Beach, Carriacou, tel. 809/ 443–7337, fax 809/443–7165. 12 doubles (2 with kitchenettes) and 6 cottages. Facilities: restaurant, snorkeling, windsurfing, spearfishing, day trip to offshore islets, boutique, gift shop, floating dock, moorings, docking facilities, showers and garbage disposal for yachts, complete scuba certification course, island bus service, car rental. AE, MC, V. EP, CP, MAP. Inexpensive–Moderate.*

Apartment These fully equipped units often represent a great Inexpensive–
Hotels Moderate alternative, especially for families. Contact the tourist office for additional listings.

Twelve Degrees North is top of the line (and most expensive), with eight one- and two-bedroom apartments, maid service (which includes cooking your breakfast and lunch and doing your laundry), private beach, pool, and tennis. A minimum stay of one week is required during high season, and children under 12 are not allowed. *Box 241, L'Anse aux Epines, St. George's, tel. 809/444–4580, fax 809/444–4580. 8 apartments. Facilities: pool, water sports, tennis. AE, V. EP. Expensive–Very Expensive.*

Wave Crest Holiday Apartments. Joyce Dabrieo runs a tight ship. She lives here with her husband (owner-managed properties make all the difference in the world) and takes great pains to keep all 20 air-conditioned, sunny rooms and apartments, some of which are self-catering, spotless and well-maintained. Wave Crest, an excellent value, is a five-minute walk to Grand Anse beach. *Box 278, St. George's, tel. 809/444–4116, fax 809/444–4847. 14 1-bedroom apartments, 2 2-bedroom apartments, 4 double rooms. AE, D, MC, V. Inexpensive.*

Villa and Several local agencies handle rentals of villas and private homes:
Private-Home The most reliable is **Grenada Property Management** (Melville St.,
Rentals St. George's, tel. 809/440–1896). In-season rates range from about $600 a week for a two-bedroom home with a pool to about $3,500 for a six-bedroom home on the beach.

Nightlife

Grenada's nightlife centers on the hotel lounges and bars. During winter, many of the hotel lounges have steel, reggae, and pop bands in the evenings. **Spice Island Inn, The Calabash, Coyaba,** and the **Grenada Renaissance** are among the most lively, but check out the new **Grenadian** too (*see* Lodging, *above*). Check with your hotel or the tourist information office to find out where various bands are performing on a given night.

Fantasia 2001 (Gem Apartments premises, Morne Beach, tel. 809/444–4224) is a popular disco on Morne Rouge Beach where soca, reggae, and cadence are played, along with international favorites. There is a small cover charge on Friday and Saturday nights. **Le Sucrier** (Grand Anse, tel. 800/444–1068) is open on Wednesday, Thursday, Friday, and Saturday from 9 PM to 3 AM, with local comedy and a disco on Thursday and "oldies" night on Wednesday. Friday night only is "the" night at the **Boatyard Restaurant and Bar** (L'Anse aux Epines beach in the Marina, tel. 809/444–4662), from 11 PM till sunup, with international discs spun by a smooth-talkin' local DJ. Check out **Cot Bam** (tel. 809/444–2050) on Grand Anse beach for a night of dancing, dining, and socializing. The place is open until 3 AM on Friday and Saturday, and it definitely hits the spot for visitors who want something simple, lively, and friendly for little money. Don't forget the **Beachside Terrace** (St. George's, tel. 809/444–4247) at the Flamboyant Hotel in Grand Anse. Crab racing on Monday nights, a live steel band on Wednesdays, and a beach barbecue with calypso music on Friday evenings draw an international set who savor a casual, unpretentious environment.

Brave the twin otter to Carriacou (you may note the solo pilot becoming deeply immersed in a Sidney Sheldon novel), then buy yourself a drink at the **Hillsborough Bar** (Carriacou, tel. 809/443–7932). The bar is a small, white, flat-topped structure on the main street of the island's seat of government—a town populated by no more than about 600 citizens—and one Edward Primus owns the place. Rum flows freely.

13 Guadeloupe

Updated by
Susan M.
Bain

It's a steamy hot Saturday in August. There may be a tropical depression brewing somewhere to the west—it's that time of year. But the mood in Pointe-à-Pitre, Guadeloupe's commercial center, is anything but depressing. Amid music and laughter, women adorned with gold jewelry and dressed in clothes made of the traditional madras and foulard parade through the streets. Balanced on their heads are huge baskets decorated with miniature kitchen utensils and filled with mangoes, papayas, breadfruits, christophines, and other island edibles. The procession wends its way to the Cathédrale de St-Pierre et St-Paul, where a high mass is celebrated. A five-hour feast with music, song, and dance will follow.

The Fête des Cuisinières (Cooks' Festival) takes place annually in honor of St. Laurent, patron saint of cooks. The parading *cuisinières* are the island's women chefs, an honored group. This festival gives you a tempting glimpse of one of Guadeloupe's stellar attractions—its cuisine. The island's more than 200 restaurants serve some of the best food in the Caribbean.

But there is more here than meets the palate. Night owls and nature enthusiasts, hikers and bikers, scuba divers, sailors, mountain climbers, beachcombers, and hammock potatoes all can indulge themselves in Guadeloupe.

Sugar, not tourism, is Guadeloupe's primary source of income. As a result, the island's attractions are less commercialized than are those of neighboring isles. However, Guadeloupe is eager to pull in a larger share of the tourist trade, and each year more field workers opt for jobs in resorts and restaurants. Currently, about 10% of the work force is employed in the tourism industry, compared with the situation in St. Martin/St. Maarten, where the whole island is sold to tourists. At harvesttime here in late January, the fields teem with workers cutting the sugarcane, and the roads are clogged with trucks taking the cane to distilleries.

French is Guadeloupe's official language. But even if your tongue twirls easily around a few French phrases, you will sometimes receive a bewildered response. The Guadeloupeans' Creole patois greatly affects their French pronunciation. However, their friendliness allows for repeated attempts at communication, so eventually you'll be understood. If not, don't despair—most hotels and many of the restaurants have some English-speaking staff.

Guadeloupe looks like a giant butterfly resting on the sea between Antigua and Dominica. Its two wings—Basse-Terre and Grande-Terre—are the two largest islands in the 659-square-mile Guadeloupe archipelago, which includes the little islands of Marie-Galante, La Désirade, and Les Saintes, as well as French St. Martin and St. Barthélemy to the north. Mountainous 312-square-mile Basse-Terre ("low land") lies on the leeward side, where the winds are "lower." Smaller, flatter Grande-Terre (218 square miles) gets the "bigger" winds on its windward side. The Rivière Salée, a 4-mile seawater channel flowing between the Caribbean and the Atlantic, forms the "spine" of the butterfly. A drawbridge over the channel connects the two islands. Driving around the islands is the best way to fully appreciate their diversity.

If you're seeking resort hotels, casinos, and white sandy beaches, your target is Grande-Terre. By contrast, Basse-Terre's National Park, laced with mountain trails and washed by waterfalls and rivers, is a 74,100-acre haven for hikers, nature lovers, and anyone yearning to peer into the steaming crater of an active volcano. If you

want to get away from it all, head for the islands of Les Saintes, La
Désirade, and Marie-Galante.

Christopher Columbus "discovered" Guadeloupe on November 4,
1493, when he landed at Ste-Marie on the southern shore of Basse-
Terre. He named the island for Santa Marie de Guadeloupe de
Estremadura. The Carib inhabitants, who had already polished off
the peaceful Arawaks, had no intention of relinquishing the land
they called Karukéra (Island of Beautiful Waters), and the Spaniards gave up on the island in 1604. In 1635, the French laid claim to
it. They ran the Caribs off and brought in African slaves to work
their sugar plantations, and in 1674 Guadeloupe was annexed by
France. The British also had designs on the island, and they controlled it from 1759 until 1763, when they relinquished it in exchange
for all French rights to Canada. During the French Revolution, battles broke out between royalists and revolutionaries on the island. In
1794, Britain responded to the call from Guadeloupe royalists to
come to their aid, and that same year France dispatched Victor
Hugues to sort things out. (In virtually every town and village you'll
run across a "Victor Hugues" street, boulevard, or park.) After his
troops banished the British, Hugues issued a decree abolishing slavery and guillotined recalcitrant planters. The ones who managed to
keep their heads fled to Louisiana or hid in the hills of Grande-Terre,
where their descendants now live. Hugues was soon relieved of his
command, slavery was reestablished by Napoléon, and the French
and English continued to battle over the island. The 1815 Treaty of
Paris restored Guadeloupe to France, and in 1848, due largely to the
efforts of Alsatian Victor Schoelcher, slavery was permanently
abolished. The island has been a full-fledged *département* of France
since 1946, and in 1974 it was elevated to a *région*, administered by a
prefect appointed from Paris by the minister of the interior.

Before You Go

Tourist
Information

For information contact the **French West Indies Tourist Board** by
calling France-on-Call at 900/990–0040 (50¢ per minute 9 AM–7 PM
EST), or write to the **French Government Tourist Office,** 610 5th
Ave., New York, NY 10020; 9454 Wilshire Blvd., Beverly Hills, CA
90212; 645 N. Michigan Ave., Chicago, IL 60611; 750 N. St. Paul,
Suite 570, Dallas, TX 75201. In Canada contact the French Govern-
ment Tourist Office, 1981 McGill College Ave., Suite 490, Montreal,
Québec H3A 2W9, tel. 514/288–4264 or 30 St. Patrick St., Suite 700,
Toronto, Ontario M5T 3A3, tel. 416/593–6427. In the United King-
dom the tourist office can be reached at 178 Piccadilly, London,
United Kingdom W1V 0AL, tel. 071/499–6911.

Arriving and
Departing
By Plane

American Airlines (tel. 800/433–7300) is usually the most convenient, with year-round daily flights from more than 100 U.S. cities
direct to San Juan and nonstop connections to Guadeloupe via American Eagle. **Air Canada** (tel. 800/422–6232) flies direct from Montreal and Toronto. **Air France** (tel. 800/237–2747) flies nonstop from
Paris and Fort-de-France and has direct service from Miami and San
Juan. **Air Guadeloupe** (tel. 590/82–47–47) flies daily from St. Martin
and St. Maarten, St. Barts, Marie-Galante, La Désirade, and Les
Saintes. **LIAT** (tel. 212/251–1717) flies from St. Croix, Antigua, and
St. Maarten in the north and is your best bet from Dominica, Martinique, St. Lucia, Grenada, Barbados, and Trinidad.

*From the
Airport*

You'll land at La Raizet International Airport, 2½ miles from
Pointe-à-Pitre. Cabs are lined up outside the airport. The metered
fare is about 35F to Pointe-à-Pitre, 60F to Gosier, and 170F to St-

François. Fares go up 40% on Sundays and holidays and from 9PM to 7AM nightly. For 5F, you can take a bus from the airport to downtown Pointe-à-Pitre.

By Boat   Major cruise lines call regularly, docking at berths in downtown Pointe-à-Pitre about a block from the shopping district. **Trans Antilles Express** (tel. 590/91–13–43) and **Transport Maritime Brudey Frères** (tel. 590/90–04–48) provide ferry service to and from Marie-Galante and Les Saintes. The *Jetcat* and *Madras* ferries depart daily from the pier at Pointe-à-Pitre for Marie-Galante starting at 8 AM (check the schedule). The trip takes one hour, and the fare is 160F round-trip. For Les Saintes, Trans Antilles Express connects daily from Pointe-à-Pitre at 8 AM and from Terre-de-Haut at 4 PM. The trip takes 45 minutes and costs 160F round-trip. The *Socimade* (tel. 590/83–32–67) runs between La Désirade and St-François, departing Monday, Wednesday, and Friday–Sunday at 8:30 AM; Tuesday at 3 PM; and Thursday at 4:30 PM. Return ferries depart Monday, Wednesday, Friday, and Saturday at 6:15 AM and 4 PM; Tuesday and Thursday at 6:15 AM; and Sunday at 4 PM. These schedules are subject to change and should be verified through your hotel or at the tourist office. The **Caribbean Express** (tel. 590/83–04–43) operates from Guadeloupe's Pointe-à-Pitre to Dominica and Martinique. The fare to Dominica is 450F, and the ride takes 2½ hours; the fare to Martinique is 450F and takes 4 hours. The ferry departs from Pointe-à-Pitre at 8 AM four days a week, but check the schedules because they frequently change.

Passports   U.S. and Canadian citizens need only proof of citizenship. A pass-
and Visas   port is best (even one that expired up to five years ago). Other ac-
ceptable documents are a notarized birth certificate with a raised seal (not a photocopy) or a voter registration card accompanied by a government-authorized photo ID. A free temporary visa, good only for your stay in Guadeloupe, will be issued to you upon your arrival at the airport. British citizens need a valid passport, but no visa. In addition, all visitors must hold an ongoing or return ticket.

Language   The official language is French. Everyone also speaks a Creole pa-
tois, which you won't be able to understand even if you're fluent in French. In the major tourist hotels, most of the staff knows some English. However, communicating may be more difficult in the smaller hotels and restaurants in the countryside. Some taxi drivers speak a little English. Arm yourself with a phrase book, a dictionary, patience, and a sense of humor.

Precautions   Put your valuables in the hotel safe. Don't leave them unattended in your room or on the beach. Keep an eye out for motorcyclists riding double, as they sometimes play the notorious game of veering close to the sidewalk and snatching shoulder bags. It isn't a good idea to walk around Pointe-à-Pitre at night because it's almost deserted after dark. If you rent a car, always lock it with luggage and valuables stashed out of sight.

The rough Atlantic waters off the northeast coast of Grande-Terre are dangerous for swimming.

Ask permission before taking a picture of an islander, and don't be surprised if the answer is a firm "No." Guadeloupeans are also deeply religious and traditional. Don't offend them by wearing short shorts or swimwear off the beach.

Staying in Guadeloupe

Important Addresses **Tourist Information:** The **Office Départemental du Tourism** has an office in Pointe-à-Pitre (5 Square de la Banque B.P. 1099, 97181 Cedex, tel. 590/82–09–30). The office is open weekdays 8–5, Saturday 8–noon. A tourist information booth is at the airport.

Emergencies **Police:** In Pointe-à-Pitre (tel. 590/82–00–17), in Basse-Terre (tel. 590/81–11–55). **Fire:** In Pointe-à-Pitre (tel. 590/83–04–76), in Basse-Terre (tel. 590/81–19–22). **SOS ambulance:** Tel. 590/82–89–33. **Hospitals:** There is a 24-hour emergency room at the main hospital, **Centre Hopitalier de Pointe-à-Pitre** (Abymes, tel. 590/82–98–80 or 590/82–88–88). There are 23 clinics and five hospitals located around the island. The tourist office or your hotel can assist you in locating an English-speaking doctor. **Pharmacies:** Pharmacies alternate in staying open around the clock. The tourist office or your hotel can help you locate the one that's on duty.

Currency Legal tender is the French franc, which is equal to 100 centimes. At press time (spring 1994), U.S.$1 bought 5.55F and 1 bought 8.10F, but currencies fluctuate daily. Check the current rate of exchange. Some places accept U.S. dollars, but it's best to change your money into the local currency. Credit cards are accepted in most major hotels, restaurants, and shops, less so in smaller places and in the countryside. Prices are quoted here in U.S. dollars unless otherwise noted.

Taxes and Service Charges The *taxe de séjour* varies from hotel to hotel but never exceeds $1.50 per person, per day. Most hotel prices include a 10%–15% service charge; if not, it will be added to your bill.

Restaurants are legally required to include 15% gratuity in the menu price, and no additional gratuity is necessary. Tip skycaps and porters about 5F. Many cab drivers own their own cabs and don't expect a tip. You won't have any trouble ascertaining if a 10% tip is expected.

Guided Tours There are set fares for taxi tours to various points on the island. The tourist office or your hotel can arrange for an English-speaking taxi driver and even organize a small group for you to share the cost of the tour.

George-Marie Gabrielle (Pointe-à-Pitre, tel. 590/82–05–38) offers half- and full-day excursions around the island. A modern bus with an English-speaking guide will pick you up at your hotel.

Organisation des Guides de Montagne de la Caraibe, O.G.M.C., (Maison Forestière, Matouba, tel. 590/94–29–11) provides guides for hiking tours in the mountains.

Getting Around Fares are regulated by the government and posted at the airport, at taxi stands, and at major hotels. During the day you'll pay about 35F from the airport to Pointe-à-Pitre, about 60F to Gosier, and about 170F to St-François. On Sundays, holidays, and between 9 PM and 7 AM, fares increase 40%. If your French is in working order, you can contact radio cabs at 590/82–15–09, 590/83–64–27, and 590/84–37–65.

Taxis

Buses Modern public buses run from 5:30 AM to 7:30 PM. They stop along the road at bus stops and shelters marked ARRET-BUS, but you can also flag one down along the route.

Vespas or Bikes If you opt to tour the island by bike, you won't be alone. Biking is a major sport here (*see* Sports and the Outdoors, *below*, for rental information).

Vespas (motorbikes) can be rented at **Vespa Sun** (many locations in Pointe-à-Pitre, tel. 590/91–30–36). A scooter generally costs 170F per day including insurance. You'll need to put down a 1000F deposit.

Rental Cars   Your valid driver's license will suffice for up to 20 days, after which you'll need an international driver's permit. Guadeloupe has 1,225 miles of excellent roads (marked as in Europe), and driving around Grande-Terre is relatively easy. On Basse-Terre it will take more effort to navigate the hairpin bends that twist through the mountains and around the eastern shore. Guadeloupeans are skillful drivers, but they do like to drive fast. Cars can be rented at **Avis** (tel. 590/82–33–47 or 800/331–1212), **Budget** (tel. 590/82–95–58 or 800/527–0700), **Hertz** (tel. 590/82–00–14 or 800/654–3131), and **Eurorent** (tel. 590/88–48–96). There are rental offices at the airport as well as at the major resort areas. Car rentals cost a bit more on Guadeloupe than on the other islands: Count on about $60 a day for a small rental car.

Telephones   To call from the United States, dial 011–590 + the local six-digit
and Mail   number. (To call person-to-person, dial 01–590.) It is not possible to place collect or credit card calls to the United States from Guadeloupe. Coin-operated phones are rare but can be found in restaurants and cafés. If you need to make many calls outside of your hotel, purchase a Telecarte at the post office or other outlets marked "Telecarte en Vente Ici." Telecartes look like credit cards and are used in special booths labeled "Telecom." Local and international calls made with the cards are cheaper than operator-assisted calls.

To call the United States from Guadeloupe, dial 19 + 1 + the area code and phone number. To dial locally in Guadeloupe, simply dial the six-digit phone number.

Postcards to the United States cost 3.50F; letters up to 20 grams, 4.40F. Stamps can be purchased at the post office, *café-tabacs*, hotel newsstands, or souvenir shops. Postcards and letters to the United Kingdom cost 3.40F.

Opening and   Banks are open weekdays 8–noon and 2–4. Credit Agricole, Banque
Closing Times   Populaire, and Société Générale de Banque aux Antilles have branches that are open Saturday. During the summer most banks are open 8–3. Banks close at noon the day before a legal holiday that falls during the week. As a rule, shops are open weekdays 8 or 8:30–noon and 2:30–6, but hours are flexible when cruise ships are in town.

Exploring Guadeloupe

Numbers in the margin correspond to points of interest on the Guadeloupe map.

Pointe-à-Pitre   **Pointe-à-Pitre** is a city of some 100,000 people in the southwest of
❶   Grande-Terre. It lies almost on the "backbone" of the butterfly, near the bridge that crosses the Salée River. In this bustling, noisy city, with narrow streets, honking horns, and traffic jams, there is a faster pulse than in many other Caribbean capitals, though at night the city streets are deserted.

Life has not been easy for Pointe-à-Pitre. The city has suffered severe damage over the years as a result of earthquakes, fires, and hurricanes. The most recent damage was done in 1979 by Hurricane Frederick, in 1980 by Hurricane David, and in 1989 by Hurricane Hugo. Standing on the rue Frébault, you can see on one side the remaining French colonial structures and on the other, the modern city. However, downtown is rejuvenating itself while maintaining its old charm. Completion of the Centre St-John Perse has meant the transformation of old warehouses into a new cruise-terminal complex that consists of a hotel (the Hotel St-John), three restaurants, space for 80 shops, and the headquarters for Guadeloupe's Port Authority.

Stop at the Office of Tourism, in Place de la Victoire across from the quays where the cruise ships dock, to pick up maps and brochures. *Bonjour, Guadeloupe*, the free visitors' guide, is very useful. Outside, the tourist-office stalls take over the sidewalk, selling everything from clothes to kitchen utensils. Across the road along the harbor, a gaggle of colorfully dressed women sells fruits and vegetables.

When you leave the office, turn left, walk one block along rue Schoelcher, and turn right on rue Achille René-Boisneuf. Two more blocks will bring you to the **Musée St-John Perse.** The restored colonial house is dedicated to the Guadeloupean poet who won the 1960 Nobel Prize in Literature. (Nearby, at No. 54 rue René-Boisneuf, a plaque marks his birthplace.) The museum contains a complete collection of his poetry, as well as some of his personal belongings. There are also works written about him and various mementos, documents, and photographs. *Corner rues Noizières and Achille René-Boisneuf, tel. 590/90–01–92. Admission: 10F. Open Mon.–Fri. 9–5, Sat. 9–12:30.*

Rues Noizières, Frébault, and Schoelcher are Pointe-à-Pitre's main shopping streets. In sharp contrast to the duty-free shops is the bustling **marketplace,** which you'll find by backtracking one block from the museum and turning right on rue Frébault. Located between rues St-John Perse, Frébault, Schoelcher, and Peynier, the market is a cacophonous and colorful place where housewives bargain for papayas, breadfruits, christophines, tomatoes, and a bright assortment of other produce.

Take a left at the corner of rues Schoelcher and Peynier. The **Musée Schoelcher** honors the memory of Victor Schoelcher, the 19th-century Alsatian abolitionist who fought against slavery in the French West Indies. The museum contains many of his personal effects, and the exhibits trace his life and work. *24 rue Peynier, tel. 590/82–08–04. Admission: 10F. Open weekdays 8:30–12:30 and 2:30–5:30 (except Wed. PM), Sat. 8:30–12:30.*

Walk back along rue Peynier past the market for three blocks. You'll come to **Place de la Victoire,** surrounded by wood buildings with balconies and shutters. Many sidewalk cafés have opened up on this revitalized square, making it a good place for lunch or light refreshments. The square was named in honor of Victor Hugues's 1794 victory over the British. The sandbox trees in the park are said to have been planted by Hugues the day after the victory. During the French Revolution, Hugues's guillotine in this square lopped off the heads of many a white aristocrat. Today the large palm-shaded park is a popular gathering place. The tourist office is at the harbor end of the square.

Rue Duplessis runs between the southern edge of the park and La Darse, the head of the harbor, where fishing boats dock and fast motorboats depart for the choppy ride to Marie-Galante and Les Saintes.

Guadeloupe

Guadeloupe Passage

Anse Laborde

Anse-Bertrand **13** **76**

Souffleur **N6**

Port–Louis **14**

Beauport

Anse du Vieux Fort

Pte. Allègre

Anse du Canal

Petit-Canal **N**

La Grande Anse **37**

36 **35** Ste-Rose

Vieux-Bourg

Grand Cul-de-Sac Marin

Jabrun du Sud

Abymes

Deshaies

N2

Lamentin

La Raizet International Airport

38 **N2**

39

Destrelan

N1

R. Salée

Pointe- Noir

Anse Caraïbe

20

NATIONAL

PARK

La Traversée

Mahaut **19**

17

18

16

Vernou

D23

Petit- Bourg **47**

Pointe-à-Pitre **1** **48**

Bas-du-fort

3

2

N1

Petit Cul-de-Sac Marin

49 **50**

Malendure

Pigeon Island

40

Bouillante **21**

BASSE-TERRE

Goyave

N2

Marigot

Vieux- Habitants **22**

Plage de Rocroy

Matouba **25**

St-Claude **24**

La Soufrière

28

Carbet

30 Ste-Marie

N1

Capesterre- Belle-Eau

29

St-Sauveur

Basse-Terre **23**

Caribbean Sea

Anse Turlet

D11

D6

26

Gourbeyre

Bananier

N1

Trois-Rivières

27

D6

Vieux-Fort

41

KEY

🚢 Cruise Ship

⛴ Ferry

1 Exploring Sites

35 Hotels and Restaurants

31 Iles des Saintes (Les Saint

Terre- de-Bas

32 Terre-de-Haut

Place Crawen

42 – **46**

Le Côte Jardin, **50**

Le Flibustier, **60**

Le Karacoli, **37**

Le Rocher de Malendure, **40**

Les Gommiers, **39**

Les Oiseaux, **64**

Relais des Iles, **43**

Relais du Moulin, **63**

Lodging

Auberge de la Distillerie, **47**

Auberge de la Vieille Tour, **51**

Auberge du Grand Large, **59**

Bois Joli, **46**

Canella Beach Residence, **57**

Cap Sud Caraibes, **56**

Club Méditerranée La Caravelle, **61**

Golf Marine Club Hotel, **71**

Grand Anse Hotel, **41**

Hamak, **70**

La Cocoteraie, **68**

La Créole Beach Hotél, **54**

La Plantation Ste Marthe, **73**

La Sucrerie du Comté, **36**

La Toubana, **62**

L'Auberge Les Petits Saints aux L'Anacardies, **45**

Le Domaine de l'Anse des Rochers, **65**

Le Méridien St. Françios, **69**

L'Orchidée, **55**

Mini-Beach, **58**

Relais du Moulin, **63**

Tropical Club Hotel, **74**

Village Créole, **44**

Rue Bebian is the western border of the square. Walk north along it (away from the harbor) and turn left on rue Alexandre Isaac. You'll see the imposing **Cathédrale de St-Pierre et St-Paul,** which dates from 1847. Mother Nature's rampages have wreaked havoc on the church, and it is now reinforced with iron ribs. Hurricane Hugo took out many of the upper windows and shutters, but the lovely stained-glass windows survived intact.

Grande-Terre This round-trip tour of **Grande-Terre** will cover about 85 miles. Drive south out of Pointe-à-Pitre on Route N4 (named the "Riviera Road" in honor of the man-made beaches and resort hotels of Bas-du-Fort). The road goes past the marina, which is always crowded with yachts and cabin cruisers. The numerous boutiques and restaurants surrounding the marina make it popular in the evening.

The road turns east and heads along the coast. In 2 miles you'll sight **②** **Fort Fleur d'Epée,** an 18th-century fortress that hunkers on a hillside behind a deep moat. This was the scene of hard-fought battles between the French and the English. You can explore the well-preserved dungeons and battlements and, on a clear day, take in a sweeping view of Iles des Saintes and Marie-Galante.

③ The **Guadeloupe Aquarium** is just past the fort off the main highway. This aquarium, the Caribbean's largest and most modern, also ranks fourth in all of France. *Place Créole (just off Rte. N4), tel. 590/ 90–92–38. Admission: 38F adults, 20F children. Open daily 9–7.*

④ **Gosier,** a major tourist center 2 miles farther east, is a busy place indeed, with big hotels and tiny inns, cafés, discos, shops, a casino, and a long stretch of sand. The Creole Beach, the Auberge de la Vieille Tour, and the Canella Beach are among the hotels here.

Breeze along the coast through the little hamlet of St-Felix and on to **⑤** **Ste-Anne,** about 8 miles east of Gosier. Only ruined sugar mills remain from the days in the early 18th century when this village was a major sugar-exporting center. Sand has replaced sugar as the town's most valuable asset. The soft white-sand beaches here are among the best in Guadeloupe. The Club Med Caravelle occupies a secluded spot on Caravelle Beach to the west of town, and there are several small Relais Creoles with their "feet in the sand." The hotel La Toubana sits on a bluff with its bungalows tumbling down to the beach, and the Relais du Moulin occupies one of the old sugar mills. On a more spiritual note, you'll pass Ste-Anne's lovely cemetery with stark-white above-ground tombs.

Don't fret about leaving the beaches of Ste-Anne behind you as you head eastward. The entire south coast of Grande-Terre is scalloped with white-sand beaches. Eight miles along, just before coming to **⑥** the blue-roof houses of **St-François,** you'll come to the Raisins-Clairs beach, another beauty.

St-François was once a simple little village primarily involved with fishing and tomatoes. The fish and tomatoes are still here, but so are some of the island's ritziest hotels. This is the home of the Hamak and Le Méridien's extension, La Cocoteraie, two very plush properties. Avenue de l'Europe runs between the well-groomed 18-hole Robert Trent Jones municipal golf course and the man-made marina. On the marina side, a string of shops, hotels, and restaurants caters to tourists. Just inland is the 120-room Plantation Ste-Marthe hotel, and just to the south is the 356-room La Domaine de l'Anse des Rochers.

⑦ To reach **Pointe des Châteaux,** take the narrow road east from St-François and drive 8 miles out onto the rugged promontory that is the easternmost point on the island. The Atlantic and the Caribbean waters join here and crash against huge rocks, carving them into castlelike shapes. The jagged, majestic cliffs are reminiscent of the headlands of Brittany. The only human contribution to this dramatic scene is a white cross high on a hill above the tumultuous waters. From this point there are spectacular views of the south and east coasts of Guadeloupe and the distant cliffs of La Désirade.

Time Out **Paillote** (no tel.) is a tiny roadside stand right on the *pointe* where you can get libations and light bites.

About 2 miles from the farthest point, a rugged dirt road crunches off to the north and leads to the nudist beach Pointe Tarare.

A mile closer to St-François is another beach, Anse de la Gourde, where at least half of a bikini is kept on. The half-mile stretch of coarse white sand and reef-protected waters makes it a choice beach, and off the parking lot is **La Langouste** (tel. 590/88–52–19), a lunch spot popular on the weekends.

8 Take Route N5 north from St-François for a drive through fragrant silvery-green seas of sugarcane. About 4 miles beyond St-François you'll see **Zévalos,** a handsome colonial mansion that was once the manor house of the island's largest sugar plantation.

9 Four miles northwest you'll come to **Le Moule,** a port city of about 17,000 people. This busy city was once the capital of Guadeloupe. It was bombarded by the British in 1794 and 1809 and by a hurricane in 1928. Canopies of flamboyants hang over narrow streets, where colorful vegetable and fish markets do a brisk business. The small buildings are of weathered wood with shutters, balconies, and bright awnings. The town hall, with graceful balustrades, and a small 19th-century neoclassical church are on the main square. Le Moule also has a beautiful crescent-shape beach. A mile to the east is an excellent beach protected by a reef, making it perfect for windsurfing; boards may be rented from the Tropical Club Hotel (tel. 590/93–97–97).

10 North of Le Moule archaeologists have uncovered the remains of Arawak and Carib settlements. The **Edgar-Clerc Archaeological Museum,** 3 miles out of Le Moule in the direction of Campêche, contains Amerindian artifacts from the personal collection of this well-known archaeologist and historian. There are several rooms with displays pertaining to the Carib and Arawak civilizations. *La Rosette, tel. 590/23–57–43. Admission free. Open Mon., Wed.–Fri., and Sun. 9:30–12:30 and 2:30–5:30, Sat. 9:30–5:30.*

From Le Moule you can turn west on Route D101 to return to Pointe-à-Pitre or continue northwest to see the rugged north coast.

To reach the coast, drive 8 miles northwest along Route D120 to Campêche, going through Gros-Cap.

Time Out **Château de Feuilles** (tel. 590/22–30–30), between Le Moule and Campêche (nearer Gros-Cap), is an absolutely superb place for a long lunch. A mini-estate, the château has style and excellent cuisine. Bring your swimming togs and use the pool while lunch is being prepared (*see* Dining, *below*).

11 Turn north on Route D122 1½ miles north of Campêche. **Porte d'Enfer** (Gate of Hell) marks a dramatic point on the coast where two jagged cliffs are stormed by the wild Atlantic waters. One legend has it that a Madame Coco strolled out across the waves carrying a parasol and vanished without a trace.

⑫ Four miles from Porte d'Enfer is **La Pointe de la Grande Vigie,** the northernmost tip of the island. Park your car and walk along the paths that lead right out to the edge. There is a splendid view of the Porte d'Enfer from here, and on a clear day you can see Antigua, 35 miles away.

⑬ **Anse-Bertrand,** the northernmost village in Guadeloupe, lies 4 miles south of La Pointe de la Grande Vigie along a gravel road. Drive carefully. En route to Anse-Bertrand you'll pass Anse Laborde, another good beach. The area around Anse-Bertrand was the last refuge of the Caribs. Most of the excitement these days takes place in the St-Jacques Hippodrome, where horse races and cockfights are held.

⑭ Route N6 will take you 5 miles south to **Port-Louis,** a fishing village of about 7,000. As you come in from the north, look for the turnoff to the Souffleur beach. It was once one of the island's prettiest, but it has become a little shabby. Still, the sand is fringed by flamboyant trees whose brilliant orange-red flowers bloom during the summer and early fall, and though the beach is crowded on weekends, it's blissfully quiet during the week. The sunsets here are something to write home about.

Time Out **Poisson d'Or** is a rustic seaside restaurant that features spicy Creole dishes. *Rue Sadi Carnot, Port-Louis, tel. 590/22–88–63. No credit cards.*

From Port-Louis the road leads 5 miles south through mangrove swamps and turns inland at Petit Canal. Three miles east of Petit Canal, turn right on the main road. Head 6 miles south to ⑮ **Morne-à-l'Eau,** an agricultural city of about 16,000 people. Morne-à-l'Eau's unusual amphitheater-shape cemetery is the scene of a moving (and photogenic) candlelight service on All Saints' Day. Take Route N5 out of town along gently undulating hills past fields of sugarcane and dairy farms.

Just south of Morne-à-l'Eau are the villages of **Jabrun du Sud** and **Jabrun du Nord,** which are inhabited by the descendants of the "Blancs Matignon," the whites who hid in the hills and valleys of the Grands Fonds after the abolition of slavery.

Continue on Route N5 to Pointe-à-Pitre.

Basse-Terre: There is high adventure on the butterfly's west wing, which swirls **The Southern** with mountain trails and lakes, waterfalls, and hot springs. Basse-**Half** Terre is the home of the Old Lady, as the Soufrière volcano is called locally, as well as of the capital, also called Basse-Terre.

Guadeloupe's de rigueur tour takes you through the 74,100-acre **Parc National de la Guadeloupe,** a sizable chunk of Basse-Terre. (The park's administrative headquarters is in Basse-Terre, tel. 590/80–24–25.) Before going, pick up a *Guide to the National Park* from the tourist office, which rates the hiking trails according to difficulty.

The Route de la Traversée (La Traversée) is a good paved road that runs east–west, cutting a 16-mile-long swath through the park to the west-coast village of Mahaut. La Traversée divides Basse-Terre into two almost equal sections. The majority of mountain trails are in the southern half. Allow a full day for the following excursion.

Wear rubber-soled shoes, and take along both swimsuit and sweater, and perhaps food for a picnic.

Begin your tour by heading west from Pointe-à-Pitre on Route N1, crossing the Rivière Salée on the Pont de la Gabare drawbridge. At the Destrelan traffic circle turn left and drive 6 miles south through sweet-scented fields of sugarcane to the Route de la Traversée (aka D23), where you'll turn west.

As soon as you cross the bridge you'll begin to see the riches produced by Basse-Terre's fertile volcanic soil and heavier rainfall. La Traversée is lined with masses of thick tree ferns, shrubs, flowers, tall trees, and green plantains that stand like soldiers in a row.

Five miles from where you turned off Route N1 you'll come to a junction. Turn left and go a little over a mile south to **Vernou**. Traipsing along a path that leads beyond the village through the lush forest you'll come to the pretty waterfall at **Saut de la Lézarde**, the first of many you'll see.

Back on La Traversée, 3 miles farther, you'll come to the next one, **Cascade aux Ecrevisses**. Park your car and walk along the marked trail that leads to a splendid waterfall dashing down into the Corossol River (a fit place for a dip). Walk carefully—the rocks along the trail can be slippery.

Two miles farther along La Traversée you'll come to the **Parc Tropical de Bras-David,** where you can park and explore various nature trails. The **Maison de la Forêt** (admission free, open daily 9–5) has a variety of displays that describe (for those who can read French) the flora, fauna, and topography of the national park. There are picnic tables where you can enjoy your lunch in tropical splendor.

Two and a half miles more will bring you to the two mountains known as **Les Mamelles**—Mamelle de Petit-Bourg at 2,350 feet and Mamelle de Pigeon at 2,500 feet. (*Mamelle* means "breast," and when you see the mountains you'll understand why they are so named.) There is a spectacular view from the pass that runs between the Mamelles to the south and a lesser mountain to the north. From this point, trails ranging from easy to arduous lace up into the surrounding mountains. There's a glorious view from the lookout point 1,969 feet up Mamelle de Pigeon. If you're a climber, you'll want to spend several hours exploring this area.

You don't have to be much of a hiker to climb the stone steps leading from the road to the **Zoological Park and Botanical Gardens.** Titi the Raccoon is the mascot of the park. There are also cockatoos, iguanas, and turtles. A snack bar is open for lunch daily except Monday. *La Traversée, tel. 590/98–83–52. Admission: 30F adults, 20F children. Open daily 9–5.*

On the winding 4-mile descent from the mountains to **Mahaut** you'll see patches of the blue Caribbean through the green trees. In the village of Mahaut turn left on Route N2 for the drive south along the coast. In less than a mile you'll come to **Malendure.** The big attraction here is offshore on **Pigeon Island.** Club Nautilus and Chez Guy, both on the Malendure Beach, conduct diving trips, and the glass-bottom *Aquarium* and *Nautilus* make daily snorkeling trips to this spectacular site.

Time Out   Though there are a couple of café/bars on Malendure Beach, the restaurant for lunch is **Le Rocher de Malendure** (tel. 590/98–70–84). Perched on a bluff overlooking Pigeon Island, the open-air restaurant is a gem, with dining on a series of terraces affording marvelous views. The owner can also arrange deep-sea fishing expeditions.

㉑ From Malendure continue through neighboring **Bouillante,** where
㉒ hot springs burst up through the earth, and **Vieux-Habitants,** one of the oldest settlements on the island. Pause to see the restored church, which dates from 1650, before driving 8 miles south to the capital city.

㉓ **Basse-Terre,** the capital and administrative center, is an active city of about 15,000 people. Founded in 1640, it has had even more difficulties than Pointe-à-Pitre. The capital has endured not only foreign attacks and hurricanes but sputtering threats from La Soufrière as well. More than once it has been evacuated when the volcano began to hiss and fume. The last major eruption was in the 16th century. But the volcano seemed active enough to warrant the evacuation of more than 70,000 people in 1975.

The centers of activity are the port and the market, both of which you'll pass along boulevard Général de Gaulle. The 17th-century **Fort St. Charles,** at the extreme south end of town, and the **Cathedral of Our Lady of Guadeloupe,** to the north across the Rivière aux Herbes, are worth a short visit. Drive along boulevard Felix Eboue to see the colonial buildings that house government offices. Follow the boulevard to the **Jardin Pichon** to see its beautiful gardens. Stop off at **Champ d'Arbaud,** an Old World square surrounded by colonial buildings. Continue along the boulevard to the **botanical gardens.** A
㉔ steep, narrow road leads 4 miles up to the suburb of **St-Claude,** on the slopes of La Soufrière. In St-Claude there are picnic tables and good views of the volcano. You can also get a closer look at the volcano by driving up to the Savane à Mulets. From there leave your car and hike (with an experienced guide) the strenuous two-hour climb to the summit at 4,813 feet, the highest point in the Lesser Antilles. Water boils out of the eastern slope of the volcano and spills into the Carbet Falls.

㉕ Drive 2 miles farther north from St-Claude to visit **Matouba,** a village settled by East Indians whose descendants still practice ancient rites including animal sacrifice. If you've an idle 10 hours or so, take off from Matouba for a 19-mile hike on a marked trail through the Monts Caraibes to the east coast.

Descend and continue east on Route N1 for 4 miles to **Gourbeyre.**
㉖ Visit **Etang As de Pique.** Reaching this lake, located 2,454 feet above the town, is another challenge for hikers, but you can also get to it in an hour by car via paved Palmetto Road. The 5-acre lake, formed by a lava flow, is shaped like an *as de pique* (ace of spades).

From Gourbeyre you have the option of continuing east along Route N1 or backtracking to the outskirts of Basse-Terre and taking the roller coaster–like Route D6 along the coast. Either route will take you through lush greenery to **Trois-Rivières.**

㉗ Not far from the ferry landing for Les Saintes is the **Parc Archéologique des Roches Gravées,** which contains a collection of pre-Columbian rock engravings. Pick up an information sheet at the park's entrance. Displays interpret the figures of folk and fauna depicted on the petroglyphs. The park is set in a lovely botanical garden that is off the beaten track for many tourists, so it remains a haven of tranquility. *Trois-Rivières, no tel. Admission: 4F. Open daily 9–5.*

Continue for 5 miles, through banana fields and the village of Bananier, to reach the village of **St-Sauveur,** gateway to the magnificent **Chutes du Carbet** (Carbet Falls). Three of the chutes, which drop from 65 feet, 360 feet, and 410 feet, can be reached by following the narrow, steep, and spiraling Habituée Road for 5 miles up past the **Grand Etang** (Great Pond). At the end of the road you'll have to proceed on foot. Well-marked but slippery trails lead to viewing points of the chutes.

Time Out You can have a hearty lunch of Creole chicken, curried goat, or crayfish at **Chez Dollin-Le Crepuscule** (Habituée Village, tel. 590/86–34–56) before or after viewing the falls. There's also a four-course menu.

Continue along Route N1 for 3 miles toward **Capesterre-Belle-Eau.** You'll cross the Carbet River and come to **Dumanoir Alley,** lined with century-old royal palms.

Three miles farther along, through fields of pineapples, bananas, and sugarcane, you'll arrive at **Ste-Marie,** where Columbus landed in 1493. In the town there is a monument to the Great Discoverer.

Seventeen miles farther north you'll return to Pointe-à-Pitre.

Iles des This eight-island archipelago, usually referred to as **Les Saintes,**
Saintes dots the waters off the south coast of Guadeloupe. The islands are Terre-de-Haut, Terre-de-Bas, Ilet à Cabrit, Grand Ilet, La Redonde, La Coche, Le Pâté, and Les Augustins. Columbus discovered the islands on November 4, 1493, and christened them Los Santos in honor of All Saints' Day.

Of the islands, only Terre-de-Haut and Terre-de-Bas are inhabited, with a combined population of 3,260. Les Saintois, as the islanders are called, are fair-haired, blue-eyed descendants of Breton and Norman sailors. Fishing is the main source of income for les Saintois, and the shores are lined with their fishing boats and *filets bleus* (blue nets dotted with burnt-orange buoys). The fishermen wear hats called *salakos,* which look like inverted saucers or coolie hats. They are patterned after a hat said to have been brought here by a seafarer from China or Indonesia.

With 5 square miles and a population of about 1,500, Terre-de-Haut is the largest island and the most developed for tourism. Its "big city" is Bourg, which boasts one street and a few bistros, cafés, and shops. Clutching the hillside are trim white houses with bright red or blue doors, balconies, and gingerbread frills.

Getting to Terre-de-Haut is an exhilarating affair, whether by land or sea. Air Guadeloupe has regularly scheduled flights, and your whole life may flash before your eyes as you soar down to the tiny airstrip. However, the flight is mercifully brief, and you may prefer it to the choppy 35-minute ferry crossing from Trois-Rivières or the 60-minute ride from Pointe-à-Pitre. Ferries leave Trois-Rivières at about 8:30 AM (7:30 AM on Sunday) and return about 3 PM. From Pointe-à-Pitre the usual departure time is 8 AM, with return at 4 PM. The round-trip fare is 160F. Check with the tourist office for up-to-date ferry schedules.

Terre-de-Haut's ragged coastline is scalloped with lovely coves and beaches, including the nudist beach at Anse Crawen. The beautiful bay, complete with sugarloaf, has been called a mini Rio. This is a quiet, peaceful getaway, but it may not remain unspoiled. At present, tourism accounts for 20%–30% of the economy. Although government plans call for a total of only 250 hotel rooms, the tourist-related industries are making a major pitch for more facilities for tourists.

There are three paved roads on the island, but don't even think about driving here. The roads are ghastly, and backing up is a minor art form choreographed on those frequent occasions when two vehicles meet on one of the steep, narrow roads. The four minibuses that transport passengers from the airstrip and the wharf and double as tour buses. However, the island is so small you can get around by walking. It's a mere five-minute stroll from the airstrip and ferry dock to downtown Bourg.

③② **Fort Napoléon** is a relic from the period when the French fortified these islands against the Caribs and the English, but nobody has ever fired a shot at or from it. The nearby museum contains a collection of 250 modern paintings. You can also visit the well-preserved barracks, prison cells, and museum and admire the surrounding botanical gardens. From the fort you can see Fort Josephine across the channel on the Ilet à Cabrit. *Bourg, no tel. Admission: 10F. Open daily 9–noon.*

For such a tiny place, Terre-de-Haut offers a variety of hotels and restaurants. For details, *see* Dining and Lodging, *below.* There is also the **Centre Nautique des Saintes** (Plage de la Coline, tel. 590/99–54–25), should you wish to scuba dive off the islands.

Marie-Galante The ferry to this flat island departs from Pointe-à-Pitre at 8 AM, 2 **③③** PM, and 5 PM with returns at 6 AM, 9 AM, and 3:45 PM. (Schedules often change, especially on the weekends, so check them at the tourist office or the harbor offices.) The round trip costs 160F. You'll put in at Grand Bourg, the major city, with a population of about 8,000. A plane will land you 2 miles from Grand Bourg. If your French or phrase book is good enough, you can negotiate a price with the taxi drivers for touring the island.

About 60 square miles, Marie-Galante is the largest of Guadeloupe's islands. It is dotted with ruined 19th-century sugar mills, and sugar is still one of its major products—the others are cotton and rum. One of the last refuges of the Caribs when they were driven from the mainland by the French, the island is now a favorite retreat of Guadeloupeans, who come on weekends to enjoy the beach at Petit-Anse.

Columbus sighted the island on November 3, 1493, the day before he landed at Ste-Marie on Basse-Terre. He named it for his flagship, the *Maria Galanda,* and sailed on.

There are several places near the ferry landing where you can get an inexpensive meal of seafood and Creole sauce. If you want to stay over, you can choose from Le Salut, in St-Louis (15 rooms, tel. 590/97–02–67), Auberge de l'Arbre à Pain (7 rooms, tel. 590/97–73–69), or Hotel Hajo (4 rooms, tel. 590/97–32–76) in Capesterre. An entertainment complex in Grand Bourg El Rancho has a 400-seat movie theater, a restaurant, terrace grill, snack bar, disco, and a few double rooms.

La Désirade According to legend, this island is the "desired land" of Columbus's **③④** second voyage. He spotted it on November 3, 1493. The 8-square-mile island, 5 miles east of St-François, was for many years a leper colony. Most of today's 1,600 inhabitants are fishermen. The main settlement is Grande-Anse, where there is a pretty church and a hotel called La Guitoune. The restaurant is not fancy, but it serves excellent seafood.

There are good beaches here, notably Souffleur and Baie Mahault, and there's little to do but loll around on them. The island is virtually unspoiled by tourism and is likely to remain so in the foreseeable future.

Three or four minibuses meet the flights and ferries, and you can negotiate with one of them to get a tour. Ferries depart from St-François Monday, Wednesday, and Friday–Sunday at 8:30, Tuesday and Thursday at 4:30. The return ferry departs (at varying hours) afternoons daily except Tuesday and Thursday. However, be sure to check schedules.

Beaches

Guadeloupe's beaches, all free and open to the public, generally have no facilities. For a small fee, hotels allow nonguests to use changing facilities, towels, and beach chairs. You'll find long stretches of white sand on Grande-Terre. On the south coast of Basse-Terre the beaches have gray volcanic sand, and on the northwest coast the color is golden-tan. There are several nudist beaches (noted below), and topless bathing is commonplace at the resort hotels. Note that the Atlantic waters on the northeast coast of Grande-Terre are too rough for swimming.

Ilet du Gosier is a little speck off the shore of Gosier where you can bathe in the buff. Make arrangements for water-sports rentals and boat trips to the island through the Creole Beach Hotel in Gosier (tel. 590/90–46–00). Take along a picnic for an all-day outing. *Beach closed weekends.*

Some of the island's best beaches of soft white sand lie on the coast of Grande-Terre from Ste-Anne to Pointe des Châteaux.

One of the longest and prettiest stretches is just outside the town of Ste-Anne at **Caravelle Beach,** though there are rather dilapidated shacks and cafés scattered about the area. Protected by reefs, the beach makes a fine place for snorkeling. Club Med, with its staggering array of activities, occupies one end of this beach.

Just outside of St-François is **Raisin-Clairs,** home of the Le Méridien (tel. 590/88–51–00), which rents Windsurfers, water skis, and sailboats.

Between St-François and Pointe des Châteaux, **Anse de la Gourde** is a beautiful stretch of sand that becomes very popular on weekends. A restaurant and snack bar are at the entrance to the beach.

Tarare is a secluded strip just before the tip of Pointe des Châteaux; many bathe naked there. There is a small bar/café located where you park, a four-minute walk from the beach.

Located just outside of Deshaies on the northwest coast of Basse-Terre, **La Grande Anse** is a secluded beach of soft beige sand sheltered by palms. There's a large parking area but no facilities other than the Karacoli restaurant, which sits with its "feet in the water," ready to serve you rum punch and Creole dishes.

All along the western shore of Basse-Terre you'll see signposts to small beaches. The sand starts turning gray as you reach Pigeon Island; it becomes volcanic black as you work your way farther south.

From **Malendure** beach, on the west coast of Basse-Terre, Pigeon Island lies just offshore. Jacques Cousteau called it one of the 10 best diving places in the world. C.I.P., the International Diving Center (tel. 590/98–81–72) at Malendure is the island's top scuba operation.

There are also glass-bottom-boat trips for those who prefer keeping their heads above water.

Souffleur, on the west coast of Grande-Terre north of Port-Louis, has brilliant flamboyant trees that bloom in the summer. There are no facilities on the beach, but you can buy the makings of a picnic from nearby shops. Be sure to stick around long enough for a super sunset.

Place Crawen, Les Saintes' quiet, secluded beach for skinny-dipping, is a half mile of white sand on Terre-de-Haut. Facilities are within a five-minute walk at Bois Joli hotel (tel. 590/99–50–38).

Petit-Anse, on Marie-Galante, is a long gold-sand beach crowded with locals on weekends. During the week it's quiet, and there are no facilities other than the little seafood restaurant, La Touloulou.

Sports and the Outdoors

Bicycling The relatively flat terrain of Grande-Terre makes for easy wheeling. You can rent bikes in Pointe-à-Pitre or in St. François at Easy Rent (tel. 590/88–76–27).

Boating If you plan to sail these waters, you should be aware that the winds and currents of Guadeloupe tend to be strong. There are excellent, well-equipped marinas in Pointe-à-Pitre, Bas-du-Fort, Deshaies, St-François, and Gourbeyre. Bare-boat or crewed yachts can be rented in Bas-du-Fort at **Locaraibes** (tel. 590/90–82–80), **Vacances Yachting Antilles** (tel. 590/90–82–95), and **Soleil et Voile** (tel. 590/90–81–81). Most beachfront hotels rent Hobie Cats, Sunfish, pedal boats, motorboats, and water skis.

Deep-Sea Fishing Half- and full-day trips in search of bonito, dolphin, captainfish, barracuda, kingfish, and tuna can be arranged through **Le Rocher de Malendure** (Pigeon, Bouillante, tel. 590/98–70–84) and **Caraibe Peche** (Marina, Bas-du-Fort, tel. 590/90–97–51). Count on about 3,500F for a half-day's boat charter and 4,500F for a full day.

Fitness The **PLM-Azur Marissol** (Bas-du-Fort, tel. 590/90–84–44) offers gym facilities for calisthenics, stretching, water exercises in pool or sea, yoga, and beauty care. **Viva Forme** (Bas-du-Fort, tel. 590/90–98–74) has equipment for muscle toning as well as two squash courts. **Lydia Deshauteurs** (Pointe-à-Pitre, tel. 590/83–49–77) offers fitness and dance.

Flying Popular with the Europeans are ULMs (Ultra Léger Motorisé). These extremely lightweight seaplanes soar along the coast at approximately 100 feet. Try one at **Holywind** (Canella Beach Residence, Pointe de la Verdure, Gosier, tel. 590/90–44–00). The cost is 170F for 10 minutes.

Golf **Golf Municipal Saint-François** (St-François, tel. 590/88–41–87) has an 18-hole Robert Trent Jones course, an English-speaking pro, a clubhouse, a pro shop, and electric carts for rental. Expect to pay 250F for a day's greens fees.

Hiking Basse-Terre's national park is laced with fascinating trails, many of which should be attempted only with an experienced guide. Trips for up to 12 people are arranged by **Organisation des Guides de Montagne de la Caraibe** (Maison Forestière, Matouba, tel. 590/94–29–11).

Horseback Riding Beach rides, picnics, and lessons are available through **Le Criolo** (St-Felix, Gosier, tel. 590/84–38–90).

Scuba Diving The main diving area is the Cousteau Underwater Park off Pigeon Island (west coast of Basse-Terre). Guides and instructors here are certified under the French CMAS rather than PADI or NAUI. To explore the wrecks and reefs, contact **Chez Guy et Christian** (Bouillante, tel. 590/98–82–43). This outfit also arranges dives elsewhere around Guadeloupe and weekly packages that include accommodations in bungalows. On the Isle des Saintes, the new **Centre Nautique des Saintes** (Plage de la Coline, Terre-de-Haut, tel. 590/99–54–25) will arrange dives.

Sea Excursions and Snorkeling Most hotels rent snorkeling gear and post information about excursions. The *King Papyrus* (Marina Bas-du-Fort, tel. 590/90–92–98) is a catamaran you can snorkel from that offers full-day outings replete with rum, dances, and games, as well as moonlight sails.

Tennis Courts are located at many hotels, including **Auberge de la Vieille Tour** (2 courts), **Caravelle/Club Med** (6 courts), **La Créole Beach** (2 courts), **Golf Marine Club** (2 courts), **Hamak** (1 court), **Le Méridien** (2 courts), **Relais du Moulin** (1 court), and **Toubana** (1 court). You can also play at the **Marina Club** in Pointe-à-Pitre (tel. 590/90–84–08) and at the Tennis League of Guadeloupe at the Centre Lamby-Lambert Stadium in Glosier (tel. 590/90–90–97).

Windsurfing Windsurfing is immensely popular here. Rentals and lessons are available at all beachfront hotels. Windsurfing buffs congregate at the **UCPA Hotel Club** (tel. 590/88–64–80) in St-François. You can also rent a *planche-à-voile* (Windsurfer)—try the **Callinago** (Gosier, tel. 590/84–25–25).

Shopping

If shopping is your goal and you want to do it on a French island, head for Martinique—selection is better and you are more likely to be understood. But shopping can be fun in Pointe-à-Pitre at the street stalls around the harbor quay, in front of the tourist office, and at the market. Moreover, numerous small boutiques selling unique designs have opened in town. The more touristy shops are down at the St-John Perse cruise terminal, where an attractive mall is home to two dozen shops. Get an early start, because it gets very hot and sticky around midday.

Many stores offer a 20% discount on luxury items purchased with traveler's checks or, in some cases, major credit cards. You can find good buys on anything French—perfumes, crystal, china, cosmetics, fashions, scarves. As for local handcrafted items, you'll see a lot of junk, but you can also find woodcarvings, madras table linens, island dolls dressed in madras, finely woven straw baskets and hats, and salako hats made of split bamboo. And, of course, the favorite Guadeloupean souvenir—rum.

Shopping Areas In Pointe-à-Pitre the main shopping streets are **rue Schoelcher, rue de Noizières,** and **rue Frébault.** Bas-du-Fort's two shopping districts are the **Mammouth Shopping Center** and the **Marina,** where there are 20 or so boutiques and several restaurants. In **St-François** there are also several shops surrounding the marina. Many of the resorts have fashion boutiques. There are also a number of duty-free shops at Raizet Airport.

Good Buys
China, Crystal, and Silver For Baccarat, Lalique, Porcelaine de Paris, Limoges, and other upscale tableware, check **Selection** (rue Schoelcher, Pointe-à-Pitre, no tel.) and **Rosebleu** (5 rue Frébault, Pointe-à-Pitre, tel. 590/82–93–44).

Cosmetics Guadeloupe's exclusive purveyor of Stendhal and Germaine Monteil
and Lingerie is **Vendome** (8–10 rue Frébault, Pointe-à-Pitre, tel. 590/83–42–84).
Tickle someone's fancy with the delicate, fanciful, and very French
lingerie found at **Soph't** (41, Immeuble Lesseps, Centre St-John
Perse, Pointe-à-Pitre, tel. 590/83–07–73).

Native Crafts **Tim Tim** (15 rue Henri IV, tel. 590/83–48–71) is a nostalgia shop
with elegant (and expensive) antiques ranging from Creole furni-
ture to maps. For dolls, straw hats, baskets, and madras table
linens, try **Au Caraibe** (4 rue Frébault, Pointeà-Pitre, no tel.). Anthuriums and other plants that pass muster at U.S. customs are
packaged at **Floral Antilles** (80 rue Schoelcher, tel. 590/82–18–63).
For imaginative art, visit the **Centre d'Art Haitien** (Rue Delgres,
Pointe-à-Pitre, tel. 590/82–54–46, and 65 Montauban, Gosier, tel.
590/84–04–84).

Perfumes Sweet buys can be found at **Phoenicia** (Bas-du-Fort, Gosier, tel. 590/
90–85–56; 8 rue Frébault, Pointe-à-Pitre, tel. 590/83–50–36; and
121 bis rue Frébault, Pointe-à-Pitre, tel. 590/82–25–75), **Au Bon-
heur des Dames** (49 rue Frébault, Pointe-à-Pitre, tel. 590/82–00–
30), and **L'Artisan Parfumeur** (rue Schoelcher, Pointe-à-Pitre, no
tel.).

Rum and **Delice Shop** (45 rue Achille René-Boisneuf, Pointe-à-Pitre, tel. 590/
Tobacco 82–98–24), **Ets Azincourt** (13 rue Henry IV, Pointe-à-Pitre, no tel.),
and **Comptoir sous Douane** (Raizet Airport, tel. 590/82–22–76) have
good choices of island rum as well as tobacco.

Dining

The food here is superb. Many of Guadeloupe's restaurants feature
seafood (shellfish is a great favorite), often flavored with rich herbs
and spices à la Creole. Favorite appetizers are *accras* (codfish fritters), *boudin* (highly seasoned pork sausage), and *crabes farcis*
(stuffed land crabs). Christophines, a type of vegetable pear, are
prepared in a variety of ways. Plantains, served as a side dish, are
considered a vegetable banana. *Blaff* is a spicy fish stew. Lobster,
turtle steak, and *lambi* (conch) are often among the main dishes, and
homemade coconut ice cream is a typical dessert. The island boasts
more than 200 restaurants, including those serving classic French,
Italian, African, Indian, Vietnamese, and South American fare.
The local libation of choice is the *petit punch* ("'ti poonch," as it is
pronounced)—a heady concoction of rum, lime juice, and sugarcane
syrup. The innocent-sounding little punch packs a powerful wallop.

Highly recommended restaurants are indicated by a star ★.

Category	Cost*
Expensive	over $35
Moderate	$25–$35
Inexpensive	under $25

per person, excluding drinks

Grande-Terre **Auberge de la Vieille Tour.** Lionel Péan superb cuisine is artistically
★ presented in a stylish, air-conditioned room with intimate lighting.
The large windows afford a splendid view of Ilet du Gosier; be sure
to request a window table when you make your reservations. The
highlights of the menu include fresh duck foie gras, sliced pork fillet
in saffron sauce, and salmon and dorado with banana butter. The

menu dégustation is the best opportunity to test Péan's skills. There is an extensive (and expensive) wine list. A band plays cool jazz Wednesday–Saturday evenings. *Gosier, tel. 590/84–23–23. Reservations advised. AE, DC, MC, V. No lunch. Expensive.*

★ **Auberge de St-François.** Claude Simon's country home is set in an orchard, and his tables are set with Royal Doulton china and fine crystal. Dining is indoors or on one of the flower-filled patios, with a superb view of Marie-Galante and Pointe des Châteaux. The house specialty is crayfish prepared in several different ways. Also try brochette of smoked shark with a pepper sauce or conch. A *menu touriste* (for 180F) of three courses, each with a choice of three dishes, makes an affordable alternative to the à la carte offerings. Monsieur Simon has also developed a superior wine cellar to complement his cuisine. *St-François, tel. 590/88–51–71. Reservations advised. MC, V. No lunch. Closed Sun. Expensive.*

★ **Château de Feuilles.** This restaurant is worth a special trip. You will savor no finer luncheon than in this relaxed, stylish country setting, hosted by Martine and Jean-Pierre Dubost. Take a dip in the pool or stroll around the 2-acre farm of this country home while waiting for your lunch. For an aperitif, about 20 different punch concoctions are made with different juices and flavors—sample all if you dare. The changing menu may include goose *rillettes* (pâté), breaded conch, tuna carpaccio (with olive and lemon), swordfish with sorrel, or the deep-sea fish *capitan* grilled with lime and green pepper. For dessert, try the pineapple flan. The estate is 9 miles from Le Moule on the Campêche road, between Gros-Cap and Campêche. *Campêche, tel. 590/22–30–30. Reservations advised. V. No dinner. Closed Mon. Expensive.*

La Canne à Sucre. A favorite over the years for its innovative Creole cuisine, La Canne à Sucre has the reputation for being the best restaurant in Pointe-à-Pitre. Once in a gingerbread house, the restaurant has moved to the complex adjacent to the cruise-ship terminal, with a commanding position at the corner of the quay. There are two dining rooms with separate menus; the views from the upstairs dining room are wide-ranging—as are the prices. Fare at the main-floor Brasserie ranges from crayfish salad with smoked ham to a puff pastry of skate with saffron sauce. Dining upstairs is more elaborate and twice as expensive, with *foie gras frais de canard au vieux rhum* (fresh duck liver in old rum) or *papillotte de perroquet* (red parrot baked in a paper bag and served with basil sauce). Gerard Virginius masterminds the creative recipes coming from the kitchen. *Quai No. 1, Port Autonome, Pointe-à-Pitre, tel. 590/82–10–19. Reservations suggested. Jacket required upstairs. Closed Sun. AE, V. Expensive.*

★ **La Louisiane.** The owner, chef Daniel Hogon, who hails from the Carlton in Cannes, prepares such traditional favorites as duck-liver confit with raspberry vinaigrette or smoked fish as starters; then crayfish with cassis or roast rack of lamb; and, *miroir aux framboises*, a raspberry treat, for dessert. The dozen tables of this small restaurant are on a terrace decorated with paintings and flower-filled hanging pots. Since the restaurant is on the road to Ste-Marthe, about 2 miles from St-François, Monsieur Hogon will send a car for you on request. *St-François, tel. 590/88–44–34. Reservations suggested. MC, V. Closed Mon. Expensive.*

★ **Le Balata.** This commanding restaurant sits high on a bluff above the main Gosier Bas-du-Fort highway (the entrance road is off the highway at the Elf gas station traveling from Gosier in the direction of Fort-de-France). Madame Guynamant presents classic French cuisine and a selection of good French wines at reasonable prices. A fixed menu is available at 155F, including wine. Choose a table by the window (reserve early) and enjoy the magnificent view of Fort Fleur d'Epée. *Route de Labrousse, Gosier, tel. 590/90–88–25. AE, MC, V. Closed Sat. lunch, Sun. Expensive.*

Le Côte Jardin. The marina between Bas-du-Fort and Pointe-à-Pitre is a lively evening venue with a dozen restaurants, bar lounges, and shops around the quay. Diners may take their pick from pizzas to hamburgers. Try something more formal with a view of the harbor at La Plantation (tel. 590/90–84–83) or creative cuisine at Le Côte Jardin. This plant-filled, intimate restaurant offers haute French Creole dishes that range from the safe—lamb Provençal and baked red snapper—to the more exotic, such as escargots de la mer with garlic butter. *La Marina, tel. 590/90–91–28. Reservations advised. AE, MC, V. Expensive.*

Le Flibustier. This rustic hilltop farmhouse is a favorite with staffers from neighboring Club Med. It's a lively, fun place that warms up after 8 PM. You can order a complete dinner—mixed salad, grilled lobster, coconut ice cream, petit punch, and half a pitcher of wine—or à la carte off the blackboard menu. *La Colline, Fonds Thézan (between Ste-Anne and St-Felix), tel. 590/88–23–36. No credit cards. Closed Mon., no lunch Sun. Moderate–Expensive.*

Les Oiseaux. Claudette and Arthur Rolle's menu includes *filet en croûte* with red-wine sauce as well as such unusual dishes as *marmite de Robinson*, a fish fondue with dorado, kingfish, tuna, shrimp, and local vegetables. Shellfish aficionados should try *cassolette de fruits de mer*, a seafood casserole. The stone house of Les Oiseaux, on the coast road south of St-François, has a small pool good for a refreshing dip. *Anse des Rochers, tel. 590/88–56–92. Reservations essential. MC, V. No lunch Mon.–Wed. Moderate–Expensive.*

★ **Relais du Moulin.** The restaurant of this inn overlooks a restored windmill. Inside, sunlight floods through large windows during the day; by night, candles flicker on crisp white cloths. The nouvelle cuisine served here includes the house specialty: grouper and lobster served with Creole sauce or stuffed with fresh homemade pâté. Crème caramel in coconut sauce is among the sumptuous desserts. A *menu dégustation* for 220F offers seven courses so you can sample Creole cooking. *Châteaubrun (between Ste-Anne and St-François), tel. 590/88–13–78. Reservations advised. AE, DC, MC, V. Moderate–Expensive.*

La Grande Pizzeria. Open late and very popular, this seaside spot serves pizza, pasta, salads, and some Milanese, Bolognese, and other Italian seafood specialties. *Bas-du-Fort, tel. 590/90–82–64. Moderate.*

La Mouette. Tables in a gazebo and in the front yard set the tone for barefoot and bathing-suit lunching here. Grilled lobster, curried goat, ragouts, accras, and stuffed or roasted trunkfish are on the menu. *Pointe des Châteaux, tel. 590/88–43–53. No credit cards. Closed Wed. and Sun. dinner. Moderate.*

★ **Chez Violetta-La Creole.** As head of Guadeloupe's association of cuisinières (female chefs), the late Violetta Chaville established an à la carte menu of traditional Creole dishes here. Her brother now continues the tradition. You'll be served by waitresses in madras and foulard garb. The restaurant is popular with American visitors. *Eastern outskirts of Gosier Village, tel. 590/84–10–34. AE, MC, V. Inexpensive–Moderate.*

Folie Plage. This lovely spot, north of Anse-Bertrand, is especially popular with families on weekends. Prudence Marcelin prepares reliable Creole food—superb court bouillon and imaginative curried dishes are among the specialties. There is a children's wading pool here. *Anse Laborde, tel. 590/22–11–17. Reservations suggested. No credit cards. Inexpensive.*

Basse-Terre **Le Rocher de Malendure.** The setting on a bluff above Malendure
★ Bay overlooking Pigeon Island makes this restaurant worth a trip. The tiered terrace is decked with flowers, and the best choices of the menu are the fresh fish, but there are also such meat selections as veal in raspberry vinaigrette and tournedos in three sauces. The owners, Monsieur and Madame Nouy, also have five bungalows for rent at very reasonable prices and can arrange deep-sea fishing trips. Even if you do not want a large lunch, stop here for a drink and, perhaps, a plate of accras. *Malendure Beach, Bouillante, tel. 590/98–70–84. Reservations suggested on weekends. DC, MC, V. Closed Sun. dinner. Moderate.*

★ **Chez Clara.** Clara Laseur, who gave up a jazz-dancing career in Paris to run her family's seaside restaurant with her mother, dishes out delicious Creole meals. Clara takes the orders (her English is excellent), and the place is often so crowded (even in the off-season) with her friends and fans that you may have to wait at the bar before being seated. The food is worth the wait, however—check the daily specials listed on the blackboard. *Ste-Rose, tel. 590/28–72–99. Reservations advised. MC, V. Closed Wed., Sun. dinner, Oct. Inexpensive–Moderate.*

Le Karacoli. Lucienne Salcede's rustic seaside restaurant is well established and well regarded. The restaurant has its feet firmly planted in the sands of Grande-Anse, a great place for a swim. Creole boudin is a hot item here, as are accras. Other offerings include coquilles Karacoli, court bouillon fried chicken, and turtle ragout. For dessert, try the banana flambé. *Grande-Anse, north of Deshaies, tel. 590/28–41–17. MC, V. No dinner Sat.–Tues. Inexpensive–Moderate.*

Chez Jacky. Jacqueline Cabrion serves Creole and African dishes in her cheerful seaside restaurant. Creole boudin is featured, as are lobster (grilled, vinaigrette, or fricassee), fried crayfish, and ragout of lamb. There's also a wide selection of omelets, sandwiches, and salads. For dessert, try peach melba or banana flambé. *Anse Guyonneau, Pte. Noire, tel. 590/98–06–98. DC, MC, V. Closed Sun. dinner. Inexpensive.*

Les Gommiers. Lovely peacock chairs grace the bar of this stylish restaurant. The changing menu may list beef tongue in mango sauce, lobster in sauce piquante, fillet beef Roquefort, escallops of veal, and grilled entrecôte. Banana splits and profiteroles are on the dessert list. Light lunches include salade Niçoise. *Rue Baudot, Pte. Noire, tel. 590/98–01–79. MC, V. No dinner Sun. and Mon. Inexpensive.*

Iles des **La Saladerie.** This delightful seaside terrace restaurant serves a so-
Saintes, phisticated mélange of grilled fish, meats, and salads. The wine list
Terre-de-Haut is also pleasantly varied. This is the place for a light meal with a fab-
★ ulous view. *Anse Mirre, tel. 590/99–50–92. MC, V. Inexpensive–Moderate.*

★ **Relais des Iles.** Select your lobster from the *vivier* (tank) and enjoy the splendid view from this hilltop eatery while your meal is expertly prepared by Bernard Mathieu and then served by his wife Nanette. Imaginative things are done with local vegetables. For dessert, try the melt-in-your-mouth white chocolate mousse. Choose your libations from an excellent wine list. *Rte. de Pompierre, tel. 590/99–53–04. Reservations suggested in high season. MC, V. Closed Tues. Inexpensive–Moderate.*

Lodging

Guadeloupe doesn't have the selection of elegant, tasteful hotels found on other islands, but you can opt for a splashy hotel with a full complement of resort activities or head for a small inn called a Relais Creole. If French is not your forte, you'll fare better in the large hotels. Gosier and Bas-du-Fort have been the main venues for resort hotels, but the areas around Ste-Anne and St-François especially also have their fair share of resorts. Le Méridien's deluxe extension, La Cocoteraie, is one of the newer wonders along St-François's marina. To the south at Anse des Rochers is a relatively new 360-room hotel. The Domaine de Petit Anse has incorporated the Hotel Lagrange at Bouillante and now offers 40 bungalows and 112 rooms total, making it one of the larger hotels on Basse Terre. Additionally, some small hotels exist: La Sucrerie du Comté (tel. 590/28–60–17), with 26 rooms; Les Villas de Petit Anse (tel. 590/98–80–28), with 10 bungalows; and Domaine de Malendure in Bouillante (tel. 590/28–60–17), geared to divers, with 44 rooms. There are also small hotels on Iles des Saintes and Marie-Galante. Most hotels include buffet breakfast in their rates. Prices decline 25% to 40% in the off-season.

Highly recommended lodgings are indicated by a star ★.

Category	Cost*
Very Expensive	over $300
Expensive	$225–$300
Moderate	$150–$225
Inexpensive	under $150

*All prices are for a standard double room for two, excluding a taxe de séjour, which varies from hotel to hotel, and a 10%–15% service charge.

La Cocoteraie. This annex to Le Méridien serves as an enclave for guests who are willing to pay almost $600 for the privilege of privacy while having access to all of its parent facilities (see below). La Cocoteraie consists of 52 suites, each with a view of either the marina or the pool, a private balcony, a round tub and separate shower in the bathroom. It has a restaurant exclusively for its clientele, tennis courts, and a very small beach area at the entrance to a marina. The management caters to the French bourgeois—the booking office is in Paris—and expresses little interest in attracting English-speaking guests. Avenue de l'Europe, St-François 97118, tel. 590/88–79–81 or 800/543–4300, fax 590/88–78–33. 52 suites. Facilities: restaurant, pool, 2 tennis courts, access to Méridien's facilities. AE, DC, MC, V. CP. Very Expensive.

Hamak. Five landscaped acres, a private white-sand beach, and attentive service make this one of the smartest places on Guadeloupe. Golfers will be delighted that Guadeloupe's municipal golf course is across the street, and gardeners appreciate the hotel's array of flowers and shrubs. One-bedroom suites are in bungalows; each unit has a living room, a small bedroom, a kitchenette, a private rear patio with outdoor freshwater shower, and a front terrace with a hammock. All are air-conditioned, with twin beds, hair dryers, and international direct-dial phones. TVs and videos are available. You pay a high price for the bungalows, which have small rooms, bathrooms no bigger than closets, and a tiny and crowded beach. Thirty-six were recently refurbished. St-François 97118, tel. 590/88–59–99 *or 800/633–7411, fax 590/88–41–92. 56 units. Facilities: restaurant, 2 bars, lighted tennis court, water-sports center. AE, MC, V. BP. Very Expensive.*

★ **Auberge de la Vieille Tour.** Since being acquired by the PLM hotel group, the hotel has added an arc-shape row of town-house units, thereby doubling its room capacity. It's really no longer an auberge but a large chain hotel—the personal flavor and individual service have gone; nevertheless, the hotel still has a desirable location three blocks from the Gosier center. The main building occupies the hilltop on a four-acre estate. Steep steps go down to the pool and beach. The older rooms are in the main building, with another series of rooms in a long building facing Ilet du Gosier. These older rooms tend to be rather small and dully furnished, though this may be forgiven if your room has a sea view. The new rooms, in the town houses on the other side of the pool, are larger and have cheerful contemporary furnishings. In high season, breakfast, lunch, and barbecues are served in the terrace restaurant at the pool level, and Robert Zarkis's orchestra plays nightly in the formal dining room. Watersports equipment is available for guests at the sister hotel, Callinago-PLM Azur. *Montauban Gosier 97190, tel. 590/84–23–23 or 800/223–9862, fax 590/84–33–43. 160 rooms. Facilities: 2 restaurants, bar, boutiques, 2 lighted tennis courts, pool. AE, DC, MC, V. BP. Expensive.*

La Creole Beach Hotel. Set in 10 acres of tropical greenery, this three-star hotel boasts two beaches and spacious rooms. All rooms have individually controlled air conditioners, TVs, radios, international direct-dial phones, and sliding glass doors that open onto a balcony. Water activities include boat excursions to Ilet du Gosier. La Creole Beach was extensively refurbished and added a 63-room extension in 1992. Mazelike corridors and pathways can be somewhat confusing here. *Box 19, Gosier 97190, tel. 590/90–46–46 or 800/755–9313, fax 590/90–46–96. 321 rooms. Facilities: 2 restaurants, bar, pool, 2 lighted tennis courts, car-rental desk, boat excursions, water-sports center. AE, DC, MC, V. CP. Expensive.*

Club Méditerranée La Caravelle. This version of the well-known club has air-conditioned twin-bed rooms, some with balconies, and 50 secluded acres at the western end of a magnificent white-sand beach. Facilities include a French-English language lab and spaces for volleyball, calisthenics, and water sports. The property has never been the finest of Club Med's villages, but it draws a fun-loving, younger crowd, most of whom are from France, and serves as the home port for Club Med's sailing cruises. *Ste-Anne 97180, tel. 590/88–21–00 or 800/258–2633, fax 590/88–06–06. 275 rooms. Facilities: restaurant, pub, boutique, 6 lighted tennis courts (with pro), water-sports center. AE, MC, V. All-inclusive (drinks extra). Moderate–Expensive.*

La Plantation Ste-Marthe. This hotel, on 15 acres, is a few miles inland from the coast, but the ocean can be seen from some guest rooms. In four three-story Creole-style buildings, the guest rooms, most of which are standard doubles, open onto terraces that overlook the large pool. In addition, 34 duplex suites have loft-style bedrooms looking down upon the salon. Bathrooms, with separate toilets, are cheerfully patterned with red-and-blue tiles. The furniture throughout the hotel combines a modern rendering of period French with cane-pattern work. The main reception house is large and grand enough to process incentive groups, accommodate several conference rooms, and serve those in need of a refreshing drink at the bar. A separate building, with its own kitchens, has a grand dining hall for as many as 500 guests. Next to the large free-form pool is the main restaurant, with indoor and terrace dining. The chef is from Paris, where his most recent position was at the renowned Taillevant. *St-François 97110, tel. 590/88–43–58 or 800/333–1970, fax 590/88–72–47. 96 rooms and 24 duplexes. Facilities: restaurant, bar, conference rooms. MC, V. EP. Moderate–Expensive.*

La Toubana. Red-roof bungalows are sprinkled on a hilltop overlooking the Caravelle Peninsula, arguably the best beach on the island. The bungalows are air-conditioned, and all rooms have private bath, phone, kitchenette, private terraced garden, and ocean view. Despite renovations made after Hurricane Hugo, La Toubana requires more work and maintenance. There's a French-Creole restaurant with evening entertainment and a small pool here. Pets are welcome. *Box 63, Ste-Anne 97180, tel. 590/88–25–78, fax 590/88–38–90. 33 bungalows. Facilities: restaurant, bar, pool, tennis court, watersports center. AE, DC, MC, V. CP. Moderate–Expensive.*

Le Méridien St. François. This hotel is recommended for those who want to pack as much activity as possible into a vacation. The 150-acre resort puts out its own *A to Z Leisure Guide* and broadcasts from Télé Méridien to let you know about resort activities. The activities director organizes everything from bocci to book lending. The hotel's beach hut is a busy place even off-season (partly because the Air France crews use the hotel). The spacious, breezy lobby is filled with Haitian artwork and fresh flowers. Standard rooms are rather modest, and wear and tear has taken its toll, but all are air-conditioned with double or twin beds, radios, direct-dial phones, and balconies, about half of which face the sea. *St-François 97118, tel. 590/88–51–00 or 800/543–4300, fax 590/88–40–71. 265 rooms, 10 suites. Facilities: 3 restaurants, 2 bars, disco, boutiques, pool, 2 lighted tennis courts, car-rental desk, water-sports center. AE, DC, MC, V. CP. Moderate–Expensive.*

Canella Beach Residence. One of the latest additions to the Gosier hotels is this 150-room resort built to resemble a Creole village. Guests have a choice of single-level and duplex studios and junior and duplex suites. Each has its own terrace or balcony with a small kitchenette. Guests are assigned their own direct telephone line, making the hotel desirable for business travelers. Water sports are free, and there is a beach bar for refreshments. Set back from the beach is the swimming pool and tennis courts. The staff, with inspiration from Jean-Pierre Reuff, the general manager, is enthusiastic and enjoys speaking English. Anotherplus is the Verandah restaurant, which offers dining indoors with air-conditioning or outdoors cooled by the sea breezes. The menu offers Creole and French dishes; the salad with warm goat cheese makes an excellent light meal or an appetizer. *Pointe de la Verdure, Gosier 97190, tel. 590/90–44–00 or 800/223–9815, fax 590/90–44–44; in NY, 212/251–1800. 146 rooms. Facilities: restaurant, pool, 4 tennis courts, water sports, excursions arranged to nearby islands. AE, DC, MC, V. EP. Moderate.*

Cap Sud Caraibes. This is a tiny Relais Creole on a country road between Gosier and Ste-Anne, just a five-minute walk from a quiet beach. The staff does its best to make you feel at home. Individually decorated rooms are air-conditioned, and each has a balcony and either a shower or an enormous bath. *Gosier 97190, tel. 590/85–96–02, fax 590/85–80–39. 12 rooms. Facilities: transfer from airport to hotel, bar, dry-cleaning, laundry, snorkeling equipment. AE, MC, V. CP. Moderate.*

Golf Marine Club Hotel. Near the town's newer shops and restaurants, this small hotel offers a more moderately priced alternative to Hamak and Le Méridien. But the hotel's name overpromises: It is not a club, the municipal golf course is across the street, and it has neither marina nor beach. Guests must walk two blocks to the nearest public beach. The rooms, however, are clean, pristine, and softly furnished in light blues. Each has a balcony, but those facing the street tend to be noisy—reserve one looking onto the gardens. A third of the rooms are called mezzanine suites. These have loft bedrooms and a roll-out couch in the lounge. The space is pleasant for two people, and a small family can squeeze in. The patio terrace facing the small pool is a relaxed, informal restaurant where meals are served. *Avenue de l'Europe, B.P. 204, St-François 97118, tel. 590/ 88–60–60, fax 590/88–68–98. 38 rooms, 32 suites. Facilities: restaurant, pool, 2 tennis courts. AE, MC, V. CP. Moderate.*

Le Domaine de l'Anse des Rochers. This 27-acre complex is on the coast a few miles from St.-François. Guests can choose rooms in Creole-style buildings or the 34 villas that climb the rise behind the hotel. All rooms have red-tile floors, rich russet-patterned bedspreads, and functional bathrooms. A formal restaurant offers à la carte dining, and the terrace bar serves casual drinks. On most evenings, guests eat in a different building, at the "theme-buffet dinner" at the Blanc Mangé restaurant, where performers entertain on the large piazza in front. Across the piazza is an open-sided disco, good for late-night revelry. The complex is so large that the trek to the man-made beach at one end can prompt you to use the car. And though Anse des Rochers may not have the best beach on the island, it does boast the largest swimming pool. Dramatically set, the pool creates the effect of water cascading into the sea. Your travel agent should be able to obtain discounted rates for you, which can make this hotel very reasonable. *Anse des Rochers, St-François 97118, tel. 590/93–90–00, fax 590/93–91–00. 356 rooms. Facilities: 2 restaurants, beach snack bar, pool, 2 lighted tennis courts, archery, conference rooms. MC, V. EP. Moderate.*

L'Orchidée. Right in the center of Gosier, this hotel is perfect for the businessperson who does not need resort facilities or a beach. Its studios have a small kitchenette, a balcony, a direct-dial telephone, and air-conditioning. On the ground floor a small eatery makes morning coffee and The owner-manager, Madame Karine Chenaf, speaks English and can help you arrange your day. *32, blvd. Général de Gaulle, Gosier 97130, tel. 590/84–54–20, fax 590/84–54–90. 20 rooms. MC, V. EP. Moderate.*

★ **Relais du Moulin.** A restored windmill serves as the reception room for this Relais Creole tucked in Châteaubrun, near Ste-Anne. A spiral staircase leads up to a TV/reading room from which there is a splendid view. Accommodations are in air-conditioned bungalows; the rooms are immaculate but tiny, with twin beds, small terraces, and kitchenettes. The hotel is on a small hill, and there is usually a pleasant, cooling breeze. The beach is a 10-minute hike away. Guests are advised to have their own rental car. Bikes are available. The owner-manager speaks English. *Châteaubrun, Ste-Anne 97180, tel. 590/88–23–96 or 800/223–9815, fax 590/88–03–92. 40 rooms. Facilities: restaurant, bar, pool, tennis court, archery. AE, DC, MC, V. CP. Moderate.*

Tropical Club Hotel. At this hotel, on the northeastern coast of Grand-Terre, you'll get the best of both worlds: Constant cooling trade winds from the Atlantic make for great windsurfing, and a reef about 100 yards offshore creates gentle waves that wash up on a dark, golden beach, making it perfect for swimming. Set back from the beach is an almond-shaped pool, adjacent to an open-sided dining room that serves French and Creole fare. The guest rooms are in three buildings on a rise at the back of the main hotel building. Each room has a double bed, two bunk beds, TV, air-conditioning, telephone, and fan. The bunk beds are in an entrance annex—ideal for children. The bathroom has a shower only, and the toilet is in a separate area. Every room has a private balcony with a small kitchenette, table and chairs, and a view of the sea; better views are from the rooms on the top (third) floor. *Le Moule, 97160, tel. 590/93–97–97, fax 590/93–97–00. 72 rooms. Facilities: restaurant, bar, pool, windsurfing, pétanque area, gym, boutique, and 3 lighted tennis courts nearby. AE, MC, V. CP. Moderate.*

★ **Auberge de la Distillerie.** This is an excellent choice for those who want to be close to the national park and its hiking trails. The small country inn has air-conditioned studios with phone, minibar, and TV. There's also a rustic wood chalet that sleeps two to four people. Boat trips on the Lezarde River can be arranged, and you can also swim in the river. *Vernou 97170, D23, Petit-Bourg, tel. 590/94–25–91 or 800/223–9815, fax 590/94–11–91. 14 rooms. Facilities: restaurant, bar, piano bar. AE, MC, V. CP. Inexpensive.*

Auberge du Grand Large. This casual family-style inn on the grand Ste-Anne beach has bungalows on the beach or tucked in a garden. All are air-conditioned with private baths. The restaurant serves Creole specialties. Pets are welcome, as long as they're not too big. *Ste-Anne 97180, tel. 590/88–20–06, fax 590/88–16–69. 10 rooms. Facilities: restaurant, bar. AE, MC, V. EP. Inexpensive.*

Grand Anse Hotel. Less than a mile from a black-sand beach, and offering spectacular mountain views, this Relais Creole is a good choice for nature-lovers. It's also near the ferry landing from which you leave for Les Saintes. You'll stay in air-conditioned bungalows with shower bath, phone, and small balcony. Water sports can be arranged. *Trois-Rivières 97114, tel. 590/92–92–21 fax 590/92–93–69. 16 bungalows. Facilities: restaurant, pool, bar. MC, V. CP. Inexpensive.*

La Sucrerie du Comté. Pristine white bungalows dot this former sugar plantation and offer clean, simple, air-conditioned accommodations at reasonable prices. Though the rooms are small, the pool in the center court, the alfresco restaurant, and the bar-lounge are large, pleasant gathering spots. The enthusiastic French owner, Monsieur Girard Jean-Luc, will have you speaking French in no time as you try the home-made fruit punches lined up in great jars on the bar in the evening. Although the hotel is a mile inland from the sea, there are numerous small beaches close by. To find the hotel, look for a left turn off the main road just after Ste-Rose. Once at its gates, you'll recognize the hotel by the ancient remains of a sugar factory and a rusted, twisted steam train that looks like a modern-art sculpture. *Comté de Lohéac, Ste-Rose 97115, tel. 590/28–60–17, fax 590/28–65–63. 26 rooms. Facilities: restaurant, bar, pool, 1 tennis court. AE, DC, MC, V. CP. Inexpensive.*

Mini-Beach. This small hotel at the northern end of Ste-Anne's beach has a comfortable open-front lounge and dining area with wicker chairs, hanging plants, and an open-hearth kitchen, all contributing to a relaxed atmosphere. There are piano concerts every Tuesday evening. Six simply furnished rooms with private bath can be found in the main house. Three bungalows are scattered around: one at the water's edge, another on the beach, and the third in the gardens. Like the rooms in the main house, these bungalows are very simply furnished but are more than adequate for a beachcombing life. *B.P. 77, Ste-Anne 97180, tel. 590/88–21–13, fax 590/88–19–29. 6 rooms, 3 bungalows. Facilities: restaurant, pool table. MC, V. CP. Inexpensive.*

Iles des Saintes **Village Créole.** Baths by Courreges, dishwashers, freezers, satellite TV, videos, and international direct-dial phones are among the amenities in this apartment hotel. Ghyslain Laps, the English-speaking owner, will help you whip up meals in the kitchen. If you'd prefer not to cook, he can provide you with a cook and housekeeper for an extra charge. A sailboat is available for excursions to Marie-Galante and Dominica. *Pte. Coquelet 97137, Terre-de-Haut, tel. 590/ 99–53–83, fax 590/99–55–55. 22 duplexes. Facilities: airport shuttle service, daily maid service, safe deposit, business center, scooter and boat rentals, water-sports center. MC, V. EP. Moderate–Inexpensive.*

★ **L'Auberge les Petits Saints aux L'Anacardies.** Trimmed with trellises, topped by dormers, and formerly owned by the mayor, this inn offers air-conditioned, twin-bed rooms with phones and baths. Casement windows open to a splendid view of the gardens, the hills, and the bay. Furnishings are an odd assortment of antiques. This hostelry has the island's only swimming pool, and the owners, Jean-Paul Coles and Didier Spindler, have installed a sauna alongside. There's a bungalow next to the main house. Steak au poivre, grilled lobster, and fish are among the restaurant's offerings. The hotel's private boat will take guests on excursions around the islands. *La Savane 97137, Terre-de-Haut, tel. 590/99–50–99, fax 590/99–54–51. 10 rooms. Facilities: restaurant, boutique, bar, pool. AE, MC, V. CP. Inexpensive.*

★ **Bois Joli.** In high season, you'll need to reserve a room here three months in advance. Facing the "Sugarloaf" on the island's beautiful bay, the hotel consists of modern rooms in bungalows, 14 of which are air-conditioned. Eight rooms and eight bungalows have private baths. The more modern and fresher rooms are in the recently added, fully equipped bungalows. The hotel restaurant serves wonderful clams in Creole sauce on a terrace that overlooks the sea. Water sports can be arranged, and the Anse Crawen nudist beach is a 10-minute walk away. Pets are allowed. *Terre-de-Haut 97137, tel. 590/99–52–53 or 800/223–9815, fax 590/99–55–05. 29 rooms. Facilities: restaurant, bar, pool, airport transfers. MC, V. CP. Inexpensive.*

Home and Apartment Rental For information about villas, apartments, and private rooms in modest houses, contact **Gîtes de France** (tel. 590/91–64–33). For additional information about apartment-style accommodations, contact the **ANTRE Association** (tel. 590/88–53–09).

The Arts and Nightlife

Cole Porter notwithstanding, Guadeloupeans maintain that the beguine began here (the Martinicans make the same claim for their island). Discos come, discos go, and the current music craze is "zouk," but the beat of the beguine remains steady. Many of the resort hotels feature dinner dancing, as well as entertainment by steel bands and folkloric groups.

Bars and Nightclubs There's nightly entertainment at the **Lele Bar** (Le Méridien, St-François, tel. 590/88–51–00). **Le Jardin Brésilien** (Marina, Bas-du-Fort, tel. 590/90–99–31) has light music in a relaxed setting on the waterfront.

Casinos There are two casinos on the island. Neither has one-armed bandits, but both have American-style roulette, blackjack, and chemin de fer. The legal age is 21. Admission is $10, and you'll need a photo ID. Tie and jacket are not required, but "proper attire" means no shorts. The **Casino de Gosier les Bains** (Gosier, tel. 590/84–18–33) has a bar and restaurant and is open Monday–Saturday 9 PM–dawn. Slot machines open at 10 AM. The **Casino de St-François** (Marina, St-François, tel. 590/84–41–40) has a snack bar and nightclub and is open Tuesday–Sunday 9 PM–3 AM.

Discos A mixed crowd of locals and tourists frequents the discos. Night owls should note that carousing is not cheap. Most discos charge an admission of at least $8, which includes one drink (drinks cost about $5 each). Some of the enduring hot spots are **Le Foufou** (Hotel Frankel, Bas-du-Fort, tel. 590/84–35–59), the very Parisian **Elysée Matignon** (Rte. des Hôtels, Bas-du-Fort, tel. 590/90–89–05), **Le Caraibe** (Salako, Gosier, tel. 590/84–22–22), and **New Land** (Rte. Riviera, Gosier, tel. 590/84–37–91).

14 Jamaica

Updated by
Laurie S.
Senz

The third-largest island in the Caribbean (after Cuba and Puerto Rico), the English-speaking nation of Jamaica enjoys a considerable self-sufficiency based on tourism, agriculture, and mining. Its physical attractions include jungle mountaintops, clear waterfalls, and unforgettable beaches, yet the country's greatest resource may be the Jamaicans themselves. Although 95% of the population trace their bloodlines to Africa, their national origins lie in Great Britain, the Middle East, India, China, Germany, Portugal, South America, and many of the other islands in the Caribbean. Their cultural life is a wealthy one; the music, art, and cuisine of Jamaica are vibrant, with a spirit easy to sense but as hard to describe as the rhythms of reggae or a flourish of the streetwise patois.

Jamaica is unusual in that in addition to such pleasure capitals of the north coast as Montego Bay and Ocho Rios, it has a real capital in Kingston. For all its congestion and for all the disparity between city life and the bikinis and parasails to the north, Kingston is the true heart and head of the island. This is the place where politics, literature, music, and art wrestle for acceptance in the largest English-speaking city south of Miami, its actual population of nearly 1 million bolstered by the emotional membership of virtually all Jamaicans.

The first people known to have reached Jamaica were the Arawaks, Indians who paddled their canoes from the Orinoco region of South America about a thousand years after the death of Christ. Then, in 1494, Christopher Columbus stepped ashore at what is now called Discovery Bay. Having spent four centuries on the island, the Arawaks had little notion that his feet on their sand would mean their extinction within 50 years.

What is now St. Ann's Bay was established as New Seville in 1509 and served as the Spanish capital until the local government crossed the island to Santiago de la Vega (now Spanish Town). The Spaniards were never impressed with Jamaica; their searches found no precious metals, and they let the island fester in poverty for 161 years. When 5,000 British soldiers and sailors appeared in Kingston Harbor in 1655, the Spaniards did not put up a fight.

The arrival of the English, and the three centuries of rule that followed, provided Jamaica with the surprisingly genteel underpinnings of its present life—and the rousing pirate tradition fueled by rum that enlivened a long period of Caribbean history. The British buccaneer Henry Morgan counted Jamaica's governor as one of his closest friends and enjoyed the protection of His Majesty's government no matter what he chose to plunder. Port Royal, once said to be the "wickedest city of Christendom," grew up on a spit of land across from present-day Kingston precisely because it served so many interests. Morgan and his brigands were delighted to have such a haven, and the people of Jamaica profited by being able to buy pirate booty there at terrific bargains.

Morgan enjoyed a prosperous life; he was knighted and made lieutenant governor of Jamaica before the age of 30, and, like every good bureaucrat, he died in bed and was given a state funeral. Port Royal fared less well. On June 7, 1692, an earthquake tilted two-thirds of the city into the sea, the tidal wave that followed the last tremors washed away millions in pirate treasure, and Port Royal simply disappeared. In recent years divers have turned up some of the treasure, but most of it still lies in the depths, adding an exotic quality to the water sports pursued along Kingston's reefs.

The very British 18th century was a time of prosperity in Jamaica. This was the age of the sugar baron, who ruled his plantation great house and made the island the largest sugar-producing colony in the world. Because sugar fortunes were built on slave labor, however, production became less profitable when the Jamaican slave trade was abolished in 1807 and slavery was ended in 1838.

As was often the case in colonies, a national identity came to supplant allegiance to the British in the hearts and minds of Jamaicans. This new identity was given official recognition on August 6, 1962, when Jamaica became an independent nation with loose ties to the Commonwealth. The island today has a democratic form of government led by a prime minister and a cabinet of fellow ministers.

Before You Go

Tourist Information Contact the **Jamaica Tourist Board,** 801 2nd Ave., 20th Floor, New York, NY 10017, tel. 212/856–9727, 800/233–4JTB; fax 212/856–9730; 500 North Michigan Ave., Suite 1030, Chicago, IL 60611, tel. 312/527–1296, fax 312/527–1472; 1320 S. Dixie Hwy., Coral Gables, FL 33146, tel. 305/665–0557, fax 305/666–7239; 8214 Westchester, Suite 500, Dallas, TX 75225, tel. 214/361–8778, fax 214/361–7049; 3440 Wilshire Blvd., Suite 1207, Los Angeles, CA 90010, tel. 213/384–1123, fax 213/384–1123. **In Canada:** 1 Eglinton Ave. E, Suite 616, Toronto, Ontario M4P 3A1, tel. 416/482–7850, fax 416/482–1730. **In the United Kingdom:** 1–2 Prince Consort Rd., London, SW7 2BZ, tel. 071/224–0505, fax 071/224–0551.

Arriving and Departing
By Plane **Donald Sangster International Airport** in Montego Bay (tel. 809/952–3009) is the most efficient point of entry for visitors destined for Montego Bay, Ocho Rios, Runaway Bay, and Negril. **Norman Manley Airport** in Kingston (tel. 809/924–8024) is better for visitors to the capital or Port Antonio. **Trans Jamaica Airlines** (tel. 809/952–5401) provides shuttle services on the island. Be sure to reconfirm your departing flight a full 72 hours in advance.

Air Jamaica (tel. 800/523–5585) and **American Airlines** (tel. 212/619–6991 or 800/433–7300) fly nonstop daily from New York and Miami; Air Jamaica provides the most frequent service from U.S. cities, also flying in from Atlanta, Philadelphia, Baltimore, and Orlando. American also flies in from San Juan. **Continental** (tel. 800/231–0856) flies in four times a week from Newark, **Northwest Airlines** (tel. 212/563–7200 or 800/447–4747) has daily direct service to Montego Bay from Minneapolis and Tampa, and **Aeroflot** (tel. 809/929–2251) flies in from Havana. **Air Canada** (tel. 800/776–3000) offers daily service from Toronto and Montreal in conjunction with Air Jamaica, and both **British Airways** (tel. 800/247–9297) and Air Jamaica connect the island with London.

Passports and Visas Passports are not required of visitors from the United States or Canada, but every visitor must have proof of citizenship, such as a birth certificate or a voter registration card (a driver's license is *not* enough). British visitors need passports but not visas. Each visitor must possess a return or ongoing ticket. Declaration forms are distributed in flight to keep customs formalities to a minimum.

Language The official language of Jamaica is English. Islanders usually speak a patois among themselves, and they may use it when they don't want you to understand something.

Precautions Do not let the beauty of Jamaica cause you to relax the caution and good sense you would use in your own hometown. Never leave money or other valuables in your hotel room; use the safe-deposit boxes that most establishments make available. Carry your funds in traveler's checks, not cash, and keep a record of the check numbers in a secure place. Never leave a rental car unlocked, and never leave valuables, even in a locked car. Finally, resist the call of the wild when it presents itself as a scruffy-looking native offering to show you the "real" Jamaica. Jamaica *on* the beaten path is wonderful enough; don't take chances by wandering far from it. And ignore efforts, however persistent, to sell you a ganja joint.

Staying in Jamaica

Important Addresses
Tourist Information: The main office of the **Jamaica Tourist Board** is in Kingston (2 St. Lucia Ave., New Kingston, Box 360, Kingston 5, tel. 809/929–9200). There are also JTB desks at both Montego Bay and Kingston airports and JTB offices in all resort areas.

Emergencies
Police, fire, and ambulance: Police and air-rescue is 119; fire department and ambulance is 110. **Hospitals: University Hospital** at Mona in Kingston (tel. 809/927–1620), **Cornwall Regional Hospital** (Mt. Salem, in Montego Bay, tel. 809/952–5100), **Port Antonio General Hospital** (Naylor's Hill in Port Antonio, tel. 809/993–2646), and **St. Ann's Bay Hospital** (near Ocho Rios, tel. 809/972–2272). **Pharmacies: Pegasus Hotel** in Kingston (tel. 809/926–3690), **McKenzie's Drug Store** (16 Strand St. in Montego Bay, tel. 809/952–2467), and **Great House Pharmacy** (Brown's Plaza in Ocho Rios, tel. 809/974–2352).

Currency
The Jamaican government abolished the fixed rate of exchange for the Jamaican dollar, allowing it to be traded publicly and subject to market fluctuations. At press time the Jamaican dollar was worth about J$30 to U.S.$1. Currency can be exchanged at airport bank counters, exchange bureaus, or commercial banks. Prices quoted below are in U.S. dollars unless otherwise noted.

Taxes and Service Charges
Hotels collect a 12% government consumption tax on room occupancy. The departure tax is J$200, or approximately $7. Most hotels and restaurants add a 10% service charge to your bill. Otherwise, tips may average 15%–20%.

Guided Tours
Half-day tours are offered by a variety of operators in the important areas of Jamaica. The best great-houses tours include Rose Hall, Greenwood, and Devon House. Plantations to tour are Prospect and Sun Valley. The Appleton Estate Express Tour uses a diesel railcar to visit villages, plantations, and a rum distillery. The increasingly popular waterside folklore feasts are offered on the Dunn's, Great, and White rivers. The significant city tours are those in Kingston, Montego Bay, and Ocho Rios. Quality tour operators include **Martin's Tours** (tel. 809/922–5245), **Tropical Tours** (tel. 809/952–1110), **Greenlight Tours** (tel. 809/952–2650), **SunHoliday Tours** (tel. 809/952–5629), and **Jamaica Tours** (tel. 809/952–8074). The highlight of the **Hilton High Day Tour** (tel. 809/952–3343), which has been dubbed "Up, Up, and Buffet," is a meet the people, experience Jamaican food, and learn some of its history day, all on a private estate ($55, including transportation). **Helitours Jamaica Ltd.** offers a way to see Jamaica from the air, with helicopter tours ranging from 10 minutes to an hour aloft at prices that vary accordingly ($50–$250). Contact the Ocho Rios office (tel. 809/974–2265). **South Coast Safaris Ltd.** has guided boat excursions up the Black River for some 10 miles (round-trip), into the mangroves and marshlands, aboard the 25-passenger *Safari Queen* and 25-passenger *Safari Princess* (tel. 809/965–2513 or, after 7 PM, 809/962–0220).

Getting Around
Taxis
Some but not all of Jamaica's taxis are metered. If you accept a driver's offer of his services as a tour guide, be sure to agree on a price *before* the vehicle is put into gear. All licensed taxis display red Pub-

lic Passenger Vehicle (PPV) plates, as well as regular license plates. Cabs can be summoned by telephone or flagged down on the street. Taxi rates are per car, not per passenger, and 25% is added to the metered rate between midnight and 5 AM. Licensed minivans are also available and bear the red PPV plates.

Rental Cars Jamaica has dozens of car-rental companies throughout the island. Because rentals can be difficult to arrange once you've arrived, you *must* make reservations and send a deposit before your trip. (Cars are scarce, and without either a confirmation number or a receipt you may have to walk.) Best bets are **Avis** (tel. 800/331–1212), **Dollar** (tel. 800/800–4000), **Hertz** (tel. 800/654–3131), and **National** (tel. 800/227–3876). In Jamaica, try the branch offices in your resort area or try **United Car Rentals** (tel. 809/952–3077) or **Jamaica Car Rental** (tel. 809/952–5586). You must be at least 21 years old to rent a car (at least 25 years old at several agencies), have a valid driver's license (from any country), and have a valid credit card. Rates average $90 a day.

Traffic keeps to the left in Jamaica, and those who are unfamiliar with driving on the left will find that it takes some getting used to. Be cautious until you are comfortable with it.

Trains The diesel train run by the Jamaica Railway Corporation (tel. 809/ 922–6620) between Kingston and Montego Bay reveals virtually every type of scenery Jamaica has to offer in a trip of nearly five hours. At press time operation was temporarily suspended.

Buses Buses are the mode of transportation Jamaicans use most, and consequently buses are very crowded and slow. They're also not air-conditioned, and rather uncomfortable. Yet the service is fairly frequent between Kingston and Montego Bay and between other significant destinations. Schedule or route information is available at bus stops or from the bus driver.

Cycles The front desks of most major hotels can arrange the rental of bicycles, mopeds, and motorcycles. Daily rates run from about $45 for a moped to $70 for a Honda 550. Deposits of $100–$300 or more are required. However, we highly recommend that you NOT rent a moped or motorcycle. The strangeness of driving on the left, the less-than-cautious driving style that prevails on the island, the abundance of potholes, and the prevalence of vendors who will approach you at every traffic light are just a few reasons to skip cycles. If you want to adventure out on your own, rent a car.

Telephones and Mail The area code for all Jamaica is 809. Direct telephone, telegraph, telefax, and telex services are available.

At press time, airmail postage from Jamaica to the United States or Canada was J$1.10 for letters, J90/ for postcards.

Opening and Closing Times Normal business hours for stores are weekdays 9–5, Saturday 9–6. Banking hours are generally Monday–Thursday 9–2, Friday 9–noon, 2:30–5.

Exploring Jamaica

Numbers in the margin correspond to points of interest on the Jamaica map.

Montego Bay ❶ The number and variety of its attractions make **Montego Bay,** on the island's north coast, the logical place to begin an exploration of Jamaica. Confronting the string of high-rise developments that crowd the water's edge, you may find it hard to believe that little of what is

Jamaica

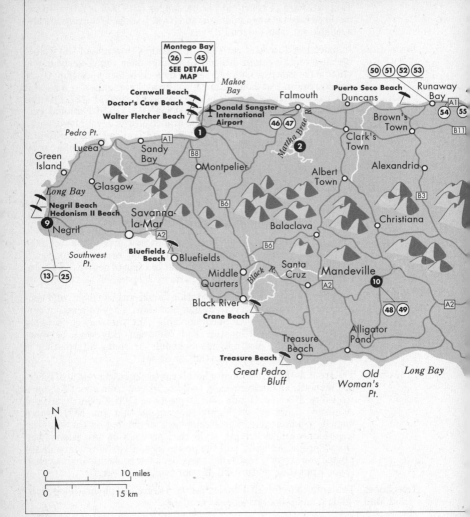

Montego Bay
(26) — (45)
SEE DETAIL
MAP

Mahoe Bay

Cornwall Beach
Doctor's Cave Beach
Walter Fletcher Beach

Falmouth

Puerto Seco Beach Duncans
Runaway Bay

(50)(51)(52)(53)

(54) A1

(55)

Pedro Pt.

Lucea

Sandy Bay

A1

Donald Sangster International Airport
(1)

(46)(47)

Martha Brae R.

(2)

Brown's Town

Clark's Town

B11

Green Island

Glasgow

Montpelier

B8

Albert Town

Alexandria

B3

Long Bay

Negril Beach
Hedonism II Beach

Savanna-la-Mar

A2

(9)
Negril

Southwest Pt.

(13) — (25)

Bluefields Beach

Bluefields

Middle Quarters

Black River

Crane Beach

B6

Balaclava

Christiana

B6

Black R.

Santa Cruz

Mandeville

A2

(10)

(48)(49)

A2

Treasure Beach

Treasure Beach

Great Pedro Bluff

Alligator Pond

Old Woman's Pt.

Long Bay

N

0   10 miles
0   15 km

Exploring	Dining		Lodging
Firefly, **5**	Almond Tree, **60**	The Palm Court, **77**	Astra Hotel, **48**
Golden Eye, **4**	Blue Mountain Inn, **73**	Paradise Yard, **22**	Bonnie View Plantation Hotel, **82**
Kingston, **11**	Cafe au Lait, **13**	Peppers, **79**	Boscobel Beach, **70**
Mandeville, **10**	Cosmo's Seafood Restaurant and Bar, **21**	Rick's Cafe, **14**	Boscobel Beach, **70**
Martha Brae River, **2**		The Ruins, **59**	Boscobel Beach, **70**
Montego Bay, **1**	Evita's, **66**	Tan-ya's, **24**	Charela Inn, **20**
Negril, **9**	The Hot Pot, **76**	Temple Hall, **72**	Chukka Cove, **54**
Ocho Rios, **3**	Hotel Four Seasons, **75**		Ciboney, Ocho Rios, **67**
Port Antonio, **6**	Ivor Guest House, **78**		Club Caribbean, **52**
Port Royal, **12**	Le Pavillon, **74**		Couples, **69**
Rio Grande River, **7**			DeMontevin Lodge, **85**
Somerset Falls, **8**			

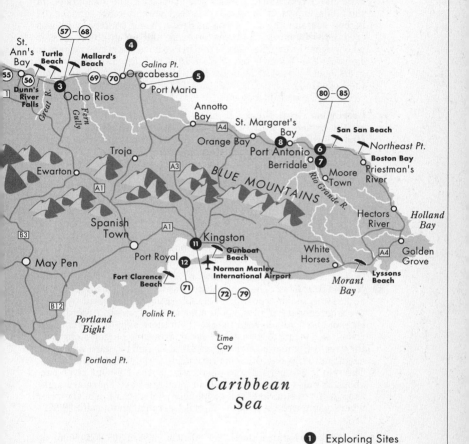

St. Ann's Bay

Turtle Beach

Mallard's Beach

Galina Pt.

57 – 68

4

35

56

Dunn's River Falls

3

69 70 Oracabessa

5

Ocho Rios

Port Maria

1

Great R.

Fern Gully

Annotto Bay

A4

St. Margaret's Bay

80 – 85

Orange Bay

8

Port Antonio

San San Beach

6

Berridale

7

Northeast Pt.

Boston Bay

Moore Town

Priestman's River

Troja

BLUE MOUNTAINS

Rio Grande R.

Ewarton

Hectors River

Holland Bay

A3

A1

Spanish Town

B3

A1

Kingston

11

Gunboat Beach

White Horses

A4

Golden Grove

May Pen

Port Royal

12

Norman Manley International Airport

Fort Clarence Beach

71

Morant Bay

Lyssons Beach

B12

72 – 79

Portland Bight

Polink Pt.

Lime Cay

Portland Pt.

Caribbean Sea

● 1   Exploring Sites

⑬   Hotels and Restaurants

The Enchanted Garden, **57**
FDR, Franklyn D. Resort, **53**
Fern Hill Club, **84**
Fisherman's Inn Dive Resort, **46**
Goblin Hill, **81**
Grand Lido, **15**
H.E.A.R.T. Country Club, **51**

Hedonism II, **16**
Hibiscus Lodge, **68**
Jamaica Grande, **64**
Jamaica Inn, **62**
Jamaica, Jamaica, **50**
Jamaica Palace, **83**
Jamaica Pegasus, **74**
Jamel Continental, **55**
Mandeville Hotel, **49**

Morgan's Harbour Hotel, Beach Club, and Yacht Marina, **71**
Negril Cabins, **25**
Negril Gardens, **19**
Negril Inn, **17**
Plantation Inn, **63**
Sandals Dunn's River, **56**
Sandals Negril, **18**
Sandals Ocho Rios, **61**

Sans Souci Lido, **58**
Shaw Park Beach Hotel, **65**
Swept Away, **23**
Trelawny Beach Hotel, **47**
Trident Villas and Hotel, **80**
Wyndham New Kingston, **77**

now Montego Bay (the locals call it MoBay) existed before the turn of the century. Today many explorations of Montego Bay are conducted from a reclining chair on Doctor's Cave Beach, with a table nearby to hold frothy drinks.

Rose Hall Great House, perhaps the greatest in the West Indies in the 1700s, enjoys its popularity less for its architecture than for the legend surrounding its second mistress, Annie Palmer, who was credited with murdering three husbands and a plantation overseer who was her lover. The story is told in two novels sold everywhere in Jamaica: *The White Witch of Rose Hall* and *Jamaica White*. The great house is east of Montego Bay, just across the highway from the Rose Hall resorts. *Tel. 809/953–2323. Admission: $10 adults, $6 children. Open daily 9:30–6.*

Greenwood Great House, 15 miles east of Montego Bay, has no spooky legend to titillate visitors, but it's much better than Rose Hall at evoking the atmosphere of life on a sugar plantation. The Barrett family, from which the English poet Elizabeth Barrett Browning was descended, once owned all the land from Rose Hall to Falmouth, and the family built several great houses on it. The poet's father, Edward Moulton Barrett ("the Tyrant of Wimpole Street"), was born at Cinnamon Hill, currently the private estate of country singer Johnny Cash. Highlights of Greenwood include oil paintings of the Barretts, china made especially for the family by Wedgwood, a library filled with rare books printed as early as 1697, fine antique furniture, and a collection of exotic musical instruments. *Tel. 809/ 953–1077. Admission: $7. Open daily 9–6.*

One of the most popular excursions in Jamaica is rafting on the **❷ Martha Brae River.** The gentle waterway takes its name from that of an Arawak Indian who killed herself because she refused to reveal the whereabouts of a local gold mine to the Spanish. According to legend, she finally agreed to take them there and, on reaching the river, used magic to change its course, drowning herself along with the greedy Spaniards. Her *duppy* (ghost) is said to guard the mine's entrance to this day. Bookings are made through hotel tour desks. The trip is $40 per raft (two per raft) for the 1½-hour river run, about 28 miles from most hotels in Montego Bay. There are a gift shop, a bar-restaurant, and swimming pool at the top of the river where you purchase tickets. To make arrangements call 809/952–0889.

The **Appleton Estate Express** (tel. 809/952–3692 or 809/952–6606), an air-conditioned diesel railcar, takes you through the lush hills and countryside around Montego Bay. You'll get a look at Jamaican villages, plantations growing banana and coconut, coffee groves, and the facility that turns out Appleton Rum. The full-day excursion leaves from the Appleton Estate station every Monday, Thursday, and Friday at 8:50 AM and returns at 4:45 PM. The $70 fare includes transfers to and from your hotel, Continental breakfast prior to departure from the station, buffet lunch, and open bar.

There is also **Mountain Valley Rafting** on the river Lethe, approximately 12 miles (about 50 minutes) southwest of Montego Bay. The trip is $40 per raft (two per raft), lasting an hour or so, through unspoiled hillside country. Bookings are made through hotel tour desks or by calling 809/952–0527.

An Evening on the Great River is a must for tour groups, yet fun nonetheless. The adventure includes a boat ride up the torchlit river, a full Jamaican dinner, a native folklore show, and dancing to a reggae band. *Tel. 809/952–5047 or 809/952–5097. $55 per person* with hotel pickup and return; $50 if you arrive via your own transport. Sun., Tues., and Thurs.

Ocho Rios Perhaps more than anywhere else in Jamaica, **Ocho Rios**—67 miles
❸ east of Montego Bay—presents a striking contrast of natural beauty
and recreational development. The Jamaicans can fill the place by
themselves, especially on a busy market day, when cars and buses
from the countryside clog the heavily traveled coastal road that
links Port Antonio with Montego Bay. Add a tour bus or three and
the entire passenger list from a cruise ship, and you may find yourself
mired in a considerable traffic jam.

Time Out **Double V Jerk Centre** (109 Main St., tel. 809/974–2084) is a good
place to park yourself for frosty Red Stripe beer and fiery jerk pork
or chicken. It's lively at lunch, when you can tour the adjacent
minizoo, with fish and tropical birds.

Yet a visit to Ocho Rios is worthwhile, if only to enjoy its two chief
attractions—Dunn's River Falls and Prospect Plantation. A few
steps away from the main road in Ocho Rios are waiting some of the
most charming inns and oceanfront restaurants in the Caribbean.
Lying on the sand of what will seem to be your private cove or
swinging gently in a hammock with a tropical drink in your hand,
you'll soon forget the traffic that's only a brief stroll away.

The dispute continues as to the origin of the name Ocho Rios. Some
claim it's Spanish for "eight rivers"; others maintain that the name is
a corruption of *chorreras*, which describes a seemingly endless series
of cascades that sparkle from the limestone rocks along this
stretch of coast. For as long as anyone can remember, Jamaicans
have favored Ocho Rios as their own escape from the heat and the
crowds of Kingston.

Dunn's River Falls (tel. 809/974–2857) is an eye-catching sight: 600
feet of cold, clear mountain water splashing over a series of stone
steps to the warm Caribbean. The best way to enjoy the falls is to
climb the slippery steps. Don a swimsuit, take the hand of the person
ahead of you, and trust that the chain of hands and bodies leads
to an experienced guide. Those who lead the climbs are personable
fellows who reel off bits of local lore while telling you where to stop.
Admission: $3 adults, $1 children.

Prospect Plantation Tour (tel. 809/974–2058) is the best of several offerings
that delve into the island's former agricultural lifestyle. It's
not just for specialists; virtually everyone enjoys the beautiful views
over the White River Gorge and the tour by jitney (a canopied open-
air cart pulled by a tractor) through a plantation with exotic fruits
and tropical trees planted over the years by such celebrities as
Winston Churchill and Charlie Chaplin. Horseback riding over
1,000 acres is available. *Admission: $10.*

The only major historic site in Ocho Rios is **the Old Fort,** built in 1777
as a defense against invaders from the sea. The original "defenders"
spent much of their time sacking and plundering as far afield as St.
Augustine, Florida, and sharing their bounty with the local plantation
owners who financed their missions. Fifteen miles west is Discovery
Bay, site of Columbus's landing, with a small museum of
artifacts and Jamaican memorabilia.

Other excursions of note are the one to Runaway Bay's Green Grotto
Caves (and a boat ride on an underground lake), a ramble through
the Shaw Park Botanical Gardens, a visit to Sun Valley, a working
plantation with banana, coconut, and citrus trees, and a drive

through Fern Gully, a natural canopy of vegetation filtered by sunlight (Jamaica has the world's largest number of fern species, over 350). Ocho Rios's newest attraction is **Coyaba River Garden and Museum,** featuring exhibits from Jamaica's many cultural influences (the national motto is "Out of Many One People"). The museum covers the island's history from the time of the Arawak Indians up to the modern day. The complex includes an art gallery, crafts shop, and snack bar.

4 Two area residences are of more than passing interest. **Golden Eye,** just east of Ocho Rios on the main coast road, was used in wintertime by Ian Fleming, the creator of James Bond, from 1946 until his death in 1964. Later Golden Eye served as home to reggae legend Bob Marley and to the founder of Island Records, Chris Blackwell. Today it can be seen only by those who can afford to rent it from the record company. It's an airy complex of deep-blue buildings, walls and bookcases bursting with Bond memorabilia, and a private cove reached by stone steps that would have delighted 007.

5 **Firefly,** about 20 miles east of Ocho Rios in Port Maria, was once Sir Noël Coward's vacation residence and is now preserved in all its hilltop wonder by the Jamaican National Heritage Trust. Coward used to entertain jet-setters and royalty in the surprisingly Spartan digs in an Eden-like setting. The Jamaicans who give impromptu tours of Firefly for a cost of $2 used to work for Sir Noël, and they show a moving reverence for his simple grave on the grounds. At press time, plans called for a small theater to be built on the grounds, where Coward's plays will be performed.

Further information on Ocho Rios is available from the Ocho Rios JTB office (tel. 809/974–2570).

Port Antonio

6 Every visitor's presence in **Port Antonio** pays homage to the beginnings of Jamaican tourism. Early in the century the first tourists arrived here on the island's northeast coast, 133 miles east of Montego Bay, drawn by the exoticism of the island's banana trade and seeking a respite from the New York winters. The original posters of the shipping lines make Port Antonio appear as foreign as the moon, yet in time it became the tropical darling of a fast-moving crowd and counted Clara Bow, Bette Davis, Ginger Rogers, Rudyard Kipling, J. P. Morgan, and William Randolph Hearst among its admirers. Its most passionate devotee was the actor Errol Flynn, whose spirit still seems to haunt the docks, devouring raw dolphin and swigging gin at 10 AM. Flynn's widow, Patrice Wymore Flynn, owns a boutique in the Palace Hotel and operates a working cattle farm.

Although the action has moved elsewhere, the area can still weave a spell. Robin Moore wrote *The French Connection* here, and Broadway's tall and talented Tommy Tune found inspiration for the musical *Nine* while being pampered at Trident.

Recent renovations make a stroll through the town suggest a step into the past. **Queen Street,** in the residential Titchfield area, a couple of miles north of downtown Port Antonio, has several fine examples of Georgian architecture. **DeMontevin Lodge** (21 Fort George St., on Titchfield Hill, tel. 809/993–2604), owned by the Mullings family (the late Gladys Mullings was Errol Flynn's cook), and the nearby **Musgrave Street** (the Craft Market is here) are in the traditional sea-captain style that one finds along coasts as far away as New England.

The town's best-known landmark is **Folly,** on the way to Trident, a Roman-style villa in ruins on the eastern edge of East Harbor. The creation of a Connecticut millionaire in 1905, the manse was made almost entirely of concrete. Unfortunately, the cement was mixed with seawater, and it began to crumble as it dried. According to local lore, the millionaire's bride took one look at her shattered dream, burst into tears, and fled forever. Little more than the marble floor remains today.

Time Out **Navy Island Resort and Marina** is the 64-acre island made famous by Errol Flynn when he bought it. The present operator welcomes visitors, who catch the private launch to his restaurant for lunch (or dinner, by prior reservation: tel. 809/993–2667). Lunch can be as simple as a thick pepper pot soup and grilled fish with lime; dinner can be a five-course spectacular.

7 Rafting on the **Rio Grande River** (yes, Jamaica has a Rio Grande, too) is a must. This is the granddaddy of the river-rafting attractions, an 8-mile-long swift green waterway from Berrydale to Rafter's Rest. Here the river flows into the Caribbean at St. Margaret's Bay. The trip of about three hours is made on bamboo rafts pushed along by a raftsman who is likely to be a character. You can pack a picnic lunch and eat it on the raft or along the riverbank; wherever you lunch, a vendor of Red Stripe beer will appear at your elbow. A restaurant, bar, and souvenir shops are at Rafter's Rest (tel. 809/993–2778). About $40 per two-person raft.

8 Another interesting excursion takes you to **Somerset Falls,** a special sun-dappled spot crawling with flowering vines where you can climb the 400 feet with some assistance from a concrete staircase. A brief raft ride takes you part of the way. **Athenry Gardens** (tel. 809/993–3740), a 3-acre tropical wonderland, and **Nonsuch Cave** are some 6 miles northeast of Port Antonio in the village of Nonsuch. The cave's underground beauty has been made accessible by concrete walkways, railed stairways, and careful lighting.

A short drive east from Port Antonio deposits you at **Boston Bay,** which is popular with swimmers and has been enshrined by lovers of jerk pork. The spicy barbecue was originated by the Arawaks and perfected by runaway slaves called the Maroons. Eating almost nothing but wild hog preserved over smoking coals enabled the Maroons to survive years of fierce guerrilla warfare with the English.

For as long as anyone can remember, Port Antonio has been a center for some of the finest deep-sea fishing in the Caribbean. Dolphins (the delectable fish, not the lovable mammal) are the likely catch here, along with tuna, kingfish, and wahoo. In October the week-long Blue Marlin Tournament attracts anglers from around the world. By the time enough beer has been consumed, it's a bit like the running of the bulls at Pamplona, except that fish stories carry the day.

Further information on Port Antonio is available from the Port Antonio JTB office (tel. 809/993–3051).

Crystal Springs (tel. 809/993–2609), about 18 miles west of Port Antonio, has more than 15,000 orchids, and hummingbirds dart among the blossoms, landing on visitors' outstretched hands. Hiking and camping are available here. *Admission: 50¢. Open daily.*

Negril Situated 52 miles southwest of Montego Bay on the winding coast
9 road, **Negril** is no longer Jamaica's best-kept secret. In fact, it has begun to shed some of its bohemian, ramshackle atmosphere for the attractions and activities traditionally associated with Montego Bay. Applauding the sunset from Rick's Cafe may still be the high-

light of a day in Negril, yet increasingly the hours before and after
have come to be filled with conventional recreation.

One thing that has not changed around this west coast center (whose
only true claim to fame is a 7-mile beach) is the casual approach to
life. As you wander from lunch in the sun to shopping in the sun to
sports in the sun, you'll find that swimsuits are common attire. Want
to dress for a special meal? Slip a caftan over your bathing suit.

Negril's newest attraction is the **Anancy Family Fun & Nature Park**
(tel. 800/468–6728 or 809/957–4100), just across the street from the
family-oriented Poinciana Beach Resort. Named after the mischie-
vous spider character in Jamaican folktales, the 3-acre site features
an 18-hole miniature golf course, go-cart rides, a fishing pond, and a
nature trail, with more attractions planned. Another new attraction
is the **Negril Hills Golf Club.** The 18-hole championship course, designed by Roy Case and Robert Simons, is slated to open by mid-
1995.

Even though you may be staying at one of the charming smaller inns
in Negril, you may enjoy spending a day at **Hedonism II** (*see* Lodging, *below*), a kind of love poem to health, Mother Nature, and good
(mostly clean) fun. The owners love to publicize the occasional nude
volleyball game in the pool at 3 AM, but most of the pampered campers
are in clothes and in bed well before that hour. And what if Hedonism
II is not the den of iniquity it likes to appear to be? What it is, and what
your day pass ($50) gets you, is a taste of the spirit as well as the food
and drink—and participation in water sports, tennis, squash, and daily activities.

Next to Hedonism II is a sister resort, the **Grand Lido** (*see* Lodging,
below), that offers a "night pass" for nonguests that includes dinner
at the Cafe Lido, live entertainment, and dusk-to-dawn dancing.
The price is a hefty $75, and reservations are a must.

Further information on Negril is available from the Negril JTB office (tel. 809/957–4243).

After sunset, activity centers on **West End Road,** Negril's main (and
only) thoroughfare, which comes to life in the evening with bustling
bistros and earsplitting discos. West End Road may still be unpaved, yet it leads to the town's only building of historical significance, the **Lighthouse.** All anyone can tell you about it, however, is
that it's been there for a while. Even historians find it hard to keep
track of the days in Negril.

Negril today stretches along the coast south from the horse-shoe-
shaped **Bloody Bay** (named during the period when it was a whale-
processing center) along the calm waters of **Long Bay** to the Lighthouse section and the landmark **Rick's Cafe** (tel. 809/957–4335).
Sunset at Rick's is a Negril tradition. Divers spiral downward off 50-
foot-high cliffs into the deep green depths as the sun turns into a ball
of fire and sets the clouds ablaze with color.

In the 18th century Negril was where the English ships assembled
in convoys for the dangerous ocean crossing. Not only were there pirates in the neighborhood, but the infamous Calico Jack and his crew
were captured right here, while they guzzled the local rum. All but
two of them were hanged on the spot; Mary Read and Anne Bonney
were pregnant at the time, and their execution was delayed.

Mandeville More than a quarter of a century after Jamaica achieved its indepen-
❿ dence from Great Britain, **Mandeville** seems like a hilly tribute to all
that is genteel and admirable in the British character. At 2,000 feet

above sea level, 70 miles southeast of Montego Bay, Mandeville is considerably cooler than the coastal area 25 miles to the south. Its vegetation is more lush, thanks to the mists that drift through the mountains. The people of Mandeville live their lives around a village green, a Georgian courthouse, tidy cottages and gardens, even a parish church. The entire scene could be set down in Devonshire, were it not for the occasional poinciana blossom or citrus grove.

Mandeville is omitted from most tourist itineraries even though its residents are increasingly interested in showing visitors around. It is still much less expensive than any of the coastal resorts, and its diversions include horseback riding, cycling, croquet, hiking, tennis, golf, and people-meeting.

The town itself is characterized by its orderliness. You may stay here several days, or a glimpse of the lifestyle may satisfy you and you'll scurry back to the steamy coast. **Manchester Club** features tennis, nine holes of golf, and well-manicured greens; **Mrs. Stephenson** conducts photographic tours of her **Gardens** (tel. 809/962–2328), an arboretum filled with lovely orchids and fruit trees; and the natural **Bird Sanctuary** at **Marshall's Penn Great House** (tel. 809/962–2260) is visited by more than 25 species indigenous to Jamaica. Tours of this bird sanctuary are by appointment only and are led by owner Robert Sutton, one of Jamaica's leading ornithologists. Other sites worth visiting are **Lover's Leap,** where legend has it that two slave lovers leapt off the 1,700-foot-high cliff rather than be recaptured by their plantation owner, and the **High Mountain Coffee Plantation** (tel. 809/962–1072 or 809/962–3265) in nearby Williamsfield, where free tours (by appointment only) show how coffee beans are turned into one of American's favorite morning drinks.

Further information on Mandeville is available from the Mandeville office of the JTB (tel. 809/962–1072).

Kingston   The reaction of most visitors to the capital city, situated on the southeast coast of Jamaica, is anything but love at first sight. In fact, ⑪ only a small percentage of visitors to Jamaica see it at all. **Kingston,** for the tourist, may seem as remote from the resorts of Montego Bay as the loneliest peak in the Blue Mountains. Yet the islanders themselves can't seem to let it go. Everybody talks about Kingston, about their homes or relatives there, about their childhood memories. More than the sunny havens of the north coast, Kingston is a distillation of the true Jamaica. Parts of it may be dirty, crowded, often raucous, yet it is the ethnic cauldron that produces the cultural mix that is the nation's greatest natural resource. Kingston is a cultural and commercial crossroads of international and local movers and shakers, art-show openings, theater (from Shakespeare to pantomime), and superb shopping. Here, too, the University of the West Indies explores Caribbean art and literature, as well as science. As one Jamaican put it, "You don't really know Jamaica until you know Kingston."

The first-time business or pleasure traveler may prefer to begin with New Kingston, which glistens with hotels, office towers, apartments, and boutiques. Newcomers may feel more comfortable settling in here and venturing forth from comfort they know will await their return.

Kingston's colonial past is very much alive away from the high rises of the new city. **Devon House** (tel. 809/929–7029), our first stop, is reached through the iron gates at 26 Hope Road. Built in 1881 and bought and restored by the government in the 1960s, the mansion has period furnishings. Shoppers will appreciate Devon House, for the firm Things Jamaican has converted portions of the space into some of the best crafts shops on the island. On the grounds you'll find one of the few mahogany trees to survive Kingston's ambitious but not always careful development. *Devon House, open Tues.–Sat. 10–5. Admission: $1.50. Shops open Mon.–Sat. 10–6.*

Further information on Kingston is available at the Kingston JTB office (tel. 809/929–9200).

Time Out Bob Marley's former cook has opened her own restaurant, on two floors of a simple wooden rondavel. **Minnie's Ethiopian Herbal-Health Food** (176 Old Hope Rd., tel. 809/927–9207) sells food and fresh juices (at last count, there were more than 15 fresh fruit juices), prepared Rasta health-food style. From early in the AM, this is the place for a true Jamaican breakfast of *ackee* with "festival" (cornmeal bread) or callaloo with "food" (ground tubers), then on to a lunch of vegetable run-down (vegetables cooked with coconut milk and spices) or gungo-pea stew. On Friday nights musicians drop by to jam and juice.

Among nearby residences, **King's House,** farther along Hope Road, is the home of Jamaica's governor-general, and **Vale Royal** on Montrose Road is home to the prime minister. The latter structure, originally built as a plantation house in the 1700s, is one of the few still standing in the capital that has a lookout tower for keeping an eye on ships in the harbor. *Tel. 809/927–6424. King's House is only open Mon.–Sat. 10–5.*

Once you have accepted the fact that Kingston doesn't look like a travel poster—too much life goes on here for that—you may see your trip here for precisely what it is, the single best introduction to the people of Jamaica. Near the waterfront, the **Institute of Jamaica** (tel. 809/922–0620) is a museum and library that traces the island's history from the Arawaks to current events. The charts and almanacs here make fascinating browsing; one example, famed as the Shark Papers, is made up of damaging evidence tossed overboard by a guilty sea captain and later recovered from the belly of a shark.

From the institute, push onward to the **University of the West Indies** (tel. 809/927–1660) in the city's Mona section. A cooperative venture begun after World War II by several West Indian governments, the university is set in an eye-catching cradle of often misty mountains. In addition to a bar and a disco where you can meet the students (they pay dues, while tourists enter free), the place seems a monument to the conviction that education and commitment lead to a better life for the entire Caribbean.

Jamaica's rich cultural life is evoked at the **National Gallery** (12 Ocean Blvd., tel. 809/922–1561), which was once at Devon House and can now be found at Kingston Mall near the reborn waterfront section. The artists represented here may not be household words in other nations, yet the paintings of such intuitive masters as John Dunkley, David Miller, Sr., and David Miller, Jr., reveal a sensitivity to the life around them that transcends academic training. Among other highlights from the 1920s through the 1980s are works by Edna Manley and Mallica Reynolds, better known as Kapo. Reggae fans touring the National Gallery will want to look for Christopher Gonzalez's controversial statue of Bob Marley.

Reggae fans will also want to see **Tuff Gong International** (56 Hope Rd.). Painted in Rastafarian red, yellow, and green, this recording studio was built by Marley at the height of his career. The house has since become the **Bob Marley Museum** (tel. 809/927–9152), with impromptu tours given by just about anyone who may be around. Certainly there is much here to help the outsider understand Marley, reggae, and Jamaica itself. The Ethiopian flag is a reminder that Rastas consider the late Ethiopian emperor Haile Selassie to be the Messiah, a descendant of King Solomon and the Queen of Sheba. A striking mural by Everald Brown, *The Journey of Superstar Bob Marley*, depicts the hero's life from its beginnings in a womb shaped like a coconut to enshrinement in the hearts of the Jamaican people.

While no longer lovingly cared for, the **Royal Botanical Gardens at Hope** (tel. 809/927–1257) is a nice place to while away an afternoon. Donated to Jamaica by the Hope family following the abolition of slavery, the garden consists of 50 acres filled with tropical trees, plants, and flowers, most clearly labeled for those taking a self-guided tour. Free concerts are given here on the first Sunday of each month.

12 Unless your visit must be very brief, you shouldn't leave Kingston without a glimpse of "the wickedest city in the world." **Port Royal** has hardly been that since an earthquake tumbled it into the sea in 1692, yet the spirits of Henry Morgan and other buccaneers add a great deal of energy to what remains. The proudest possession of **St. Peter's Church,** rebuilt in 1725 to replace Christ's Church, is a silver communion plate said to have been donated by Morgan himself.

You can no longer down rum in Port Royal's legendary 40 taverns, but you can take in a draft of the past at the **Archaeological and Historical Museum** (tel. 809/924–8706), located within the Police Training School building, and explore the impressive remains of Fort Charles, once the area's major garrison. On the grounds are a small **maritime museum** and **Giddy House,** an old artillery storehouse that gained its name after being permanently tilted by the earthquake of 1907. Nearby is a graveyard in which rests a man who died twice. According to the tombstone, Lewis Galdy was swallowed up in the great earthquake of 1692, spewed into the sea, rescued, and lived another four decades in "Great Reputation." Port Royal attractions are open daily 9–5.

Jamaica for Free

Sixteen years ago Jamaica introduced the "Meet the People" concept that has become so popular in the Caribbean. One of the best free attractions anywhere, it allows visitors to get together with islanders who have compatible interests and expertise. The nearly 600 Jamaican families who participate in Meet the People on a voluntary basis offer their guests a spectrum of activities from time at a business or home to musical or theatrical performances. The program's theme is Forget Me Not, the name of a tiny blue flower that grows on Jamaican hillsides. Once you've met these people, you're not likely to forget them. It's helpful to arrange your occasion through the Jamaica Tourist Board in advance of your trip.

Off the Beaten Track

The Cockpit Country, 15 miles inland from Montego Bay and one of the most primitive areas in the West Indies, is a terrain of pitfalls and potholes carved by nature in limestone. For nearly a century after 1655 it was known as the Land of Look Behind because British soldiers rode their horses back-to-back in pairs, looking out for the savage freedom fighters known as Maroons. Fugitive slaves who refused to surrender to the invading English, the Maroons eventually won a treaty of independence and continue to live apart from the rest of Jamaica in the Cockpit Country. The government leaves them alone, untaxed and ungoverned by outside authorities. Minibus tours from Montego Bay to Maroon headquarters at Accompong are offered through the **Maroon Tourist Attraction Co.** (tel. 809/952–4546).

The **Blue Mountains** are lush, with deep valleys and soaring peaks that climb into the clouds. Admirers of Jamaica's wonderful coffee may wish to take a tour to **Pine Grove** or to the Jablum coffee plant at **Mavis Bank.** Unless you are traveling with a local, do not rent a car and go on your own, as the mountain roads wind and dip, hand-lettered signs blow away, and a tourist can easily get lost—not just for hours, but for days. Pine Grove, a working coffee farm that doubles as an inn, has a restaurant that serves owner Marcia Thwaites's Jamaican cuisine. Mavis Bank is delightfully primitive—considering the retail price of the beans it processes. There is no official tour; ask someone to show you around.

If your calf muscles are in good shape, another way to see the **Blue Mountains** is by the downhill bicycle tour offered by Paul and Becky Lemoine (tel. 809/974–0635). The day-long adventure costs $80 and includes lunch. Or visit Gloria Palomino's café restaurant **the Gap** (tel. 809/923–5617; open for lunch Tues.–Sun.), 4,200 feet above sea level, adjacent to several well-defined nature walking trails. Her gift shop sells the coveted Blue Mountain coffee. On your way up (or back) stop in World's End for a free tour of **Dr. Sangster's Rum Factory** (call ahead, tel. 809/926–8888). The small factory produces wonderful liqueurs flavored with local coffee beans, oranges, coconuts, and other Jamaican produce; samples are part of the tour.

Spanish Town, 12 miles west of Kingston on A1, was the island's capital under Spanish rule. The town boasts the tiered Georgian **Antique Square,** the **Jamaican People's Museum of Crafts and Technology** (in the Old King's House stables), and the oldest cathedral (**St. James**) in the Western Hemisphere. Spanish Town's original name was Santiago de la Vega, which the English corrupted to St. Jago de la Vega, both meaning St. James of the Plains.

Beaches

Jamaica has some 200 miles of beaches, some of them still uncrowded. The beaches listed below are public places (there is usually a small admission charge), and they are among the best Jamaica has to offer. In addition, nearly every resort has its own private beach, complete with towels and water sports. Some of the larger resorts sell day passes to nonguests. Generally, the farther west you travel, the lighter and finer the sand.

Doctor's Cave Beach at Montego Bay shows a tendency toward population explosion, attracting Jamaicans and tourists alike; at times it may resemble Fort Lauderdale at spring break. The 5-mile stretch of sugary sand has been spotlighted in so many travel articles and brochures over the years that it's no secret to anyone. On the bright side, Doctor's Cave is well fitted for all its admirers with changing rooms, colorful if overly insistent vendors, and a large selection of snacks.

Two other popular beaches in the Montego Bay area are **Cornwall Beach,** farther up the coast, which is smaller, also lively, with lots of food and drink available and a water-sports concession, and **Walter**

Fletcher Beach, on the bay near the center of town. Fletcher offers protection from the surf on a windy day and therefore unusually fine swimming; the calm waters make it a good bet for children, too.

Ocho Rios appears to be just about as busy as MoBay these days, and the busiest beach is usually **Mallards.** The **Jamaica Grande** hotel, formerly the Mallards Beach and Americana hotels, is here, spilling out its large convention groups at all hours of the day. Next door is **Turtle Beach,** which islanders consider *the* place for swimming in Ocho Rios.

In Port Antonio, head for **San San Beach** or **Boston Bay.** Any of the shacks spewing scented smoke along the beach at Boston Bay will sell you the famous peppery delicacy, jerk pork.

Puerto Seco Beach at Discovery Bay is a sunny, sandy beach.

There are no good beaches in Kingston. Beach goers can travel outside of the city, but the beaches there, as a rule, are not as beautiful as those in the resort areas. The most popular stretch of sand is **Hellshire Beach** in Bridgeport, about a 20–30 minute drive from Kingston. **Fort Clarence,** a beach in the Hellshire Hills area southwest of the city, has changing facilities and entertainment. Sometimes Kingstonians are willing to drive 32 miles east to the lovely golden **Lyssons Beach** in Morant Bay or, for a small negotiable fee, to hire a boat at the Morgan's Harbor Marina at Port Royal to ferry them to **Lime Cay.** This island, just beyond Kingston Harbor, is perfect for picnicking, sunning, and swimming.

Not too long ago, the 7 miles of white sand at **Negril Beach** offered a beachcomber's vision of Eden. Today much of it is fronted by modern resorts, although the 2 miles of beach fronting Bloody Bay remain relatively untouched. The nude beach areas are found mostly along sections of the beach where no hotel or resort has been built, such as the area adjacent to Cosmo's (*see* Dining, *below*). A few resorts have built accommodations overlooking their nude beaches, thereby adding a new dimension to the traditional notion of "ocean view."

Those who seek beaches off the main tourist routes will want to explore Jamaica's unexploited south coast. Nearest to "civilization" is **Bluefields Beach** near Savanna-La-Mar, south of Negril along the coast. **Crane Beach** at Black River is another great discovery. And the best of the south shore has to be **Treasure Beach,** 20 miles farther along the coast beyond Crane.

Sports and the Outdoors

The tourist board licenses all operators of recreational activities, which should ensure you of fair business practices as long as you deal with companies that display the decals.

Fishing Deep-sea fishing can be great around the island. Port Antonio gets the headlines with its annual Blue Marlin Tournament, and Montego Bay and Ocho Rios have devotees who talk of the sailfish, yellowfin tuna, wahoo, dolphin, and bonito. Licenses are not required. Boat charters can be arranged at your hotel.

Golf The best courses are found around Montego Bay at **Tryall** (tel. 809/952–5110), **Half Moon** (tel. 809/953–2560), **Rose Hall,** (tel. 809/953–2650), and **Ironshore** (tel. 809/953–2800). Good courses are also found at **Caymanas** (tel. 809/926–8144) and **Constant Spring** (tel. 809/924–1610) in Kingston and at **SuperClubs Runaway Bay** (tel. 809/973–2561) and **Sandals Golf and Country Club** (tel. 809/974–2528), formerly Upton, in Ocho Rios. A 9-hole course in the hills of Mandeville is called **Manchester Club** (tel. 809/962–2403). Great golf and spectacular scenery also go hand in hand at the new **Negril Hills Golf Club** in Negril, which is scheduled to open by early-to-mid 1995. **Prospect Plantation** (tel. 809/974–2058) in Ocho Rios has an 18-hole minigolf course.

Horseback Riding Jamaica is fortunate to have the best equestrian facility in the Caribbean, **Chukka Cove** (write Box 160, Ocho Rios, St. Ann, tel. 809/972–2506), near Ocho Rios. The resort, complete with stylishly outfitted villas, offers full instruction in riding, polo, and jumping, as well as hour-long trail rides, three-hour beach rides, and rides to a great house. Weekends, in-season, this is the place for hot polo action and equally hot social action. **Rocky Point Stables** (tel. 809/953–2286), just east of the Half Moon Club in Montego Bay, **Rhodes Hall Plantation Ltd.**, between Green Island and Negril (tel. 809/957–4258), and **Prospect Plantation** (tel. 809/974–2058) also offer rides.

Tennis Many hotels have tennis facilities that are free to their guests, but some will allow nonguests to play for a fee. The sport is a highlight at **Tryall** (tel. 809/952–5110), **Round Hill Hotel and Villas** (tel. 809/952–5150), **Sandals Montego Bay** (tel. 809/952–5510), and **Half Moon Club** (tel. 809/953–2211) in Montego Bay; **Swept Away** (tel. 809/957–4061) in Negril; and **Sandals Dunn's River** (tel. 809/972–1610), **Sans Souci Lido** (tel. 809/974–2353), and **Ciboney** (tel. 809/974–5503) in Ocho Rios.

Water Sports The major areas for swimming, windsurfing, snorkeling, and scuba diving are Negril in the west and Port Antonio in the east. All the large resorts rent equipment for a deposit and/or a fee. Diving is perhaps the only option that requires training, because you need to show a C-card in order to participate. However, some dive operators on the island are qualified to certify you. **Blue Whale Divers** (Negril, tel. 809/957–4438), **Sun Divers** (Poinciana Beach Hotel, Negril, tel. 809/957–4069, and Ambiance Hotel, Runaway Bay, tel. 809/973–2346), **Garfield Dive Station** (Ocho Rios, tel. 809/974–5749), **Sea World Resorts Ltd.** (Montego Bay, tel. 809/953–2180, fax 809/952–5018), and **Sandals Beach Resort Watersports** (Montego Bay, tel. 809/979–0104) offer certification courses and dive trips. Most all-inclusive resorts offer free scuba diving to their guests. Some tour operators offer day trips that include an offshore excursion, snorkeling equipment, lunch, and cocktails. **Aqua Action at San San Beach** (tel. 809/993–3318) and **Lady Godiva** (Dragon Bay, tel. 809/993–3281) in Port Antonio both offer scuba diving and snorkeling.

Shopping

Shopping in Jamaica goes two ways: things Jamaican and things imported. The former are made with style and skill; the latter are duty-free luxury finds. Jamaican crafts take the form of resortwear, hand-loomed fabrics, silk screens, wood carvings, paintings, and other fine arts.

Jamaican rum is a great take-home gift. So is Tia Maria, Jamaica's world-famous coffee liqueur. The same goes for the island's prized Blue Mountain and High Mountain coffees and its jams, jellies, and marmalades.

Some bargains, if you shop around, include Swiss watches, Irish crystal, jewelry, cameras, and china. The top-selling French perfumes are also available alongside Jamaica's own fragrances.

Shopping A shopping tour of the Kingston area should begin at **Constant**
Areas **Spring Road** or **King Street.** No matter where you begin, keep in
Kingston mind that the trend these days is shopping malls, and in Jamaica
they caught on with a fever and an ever-growing roster: **Twin Gates**
Plaza, New Lane Plaza, the **New Kingston Shopping Centre, Tropical**
Plaza, Manor Park Plaza, the **Village,** the **Springs,** and the newest
(and some say nicest), **Sovereign Shopping Centre** (tel. 809/927–
5955).

A day at **Devon House** (26 Hope Rd., Kingston, tel. 809/929–6602)
should be high on your shopping list. This is the place to find old and
new Jamaica. The great house is now a museum with antiques and
furniture reproductions and the Lady Nugent's Coffee Terrace outside. There are boutiques in what were once the house's stables: a
branch of Things Jamaican, Tanning and Turning for leather finds,
first-rate furnishings and antique reproductions at Jacaranda, silver and pewter re-creations (many from centuries-old patterns) at
the Olde Port Royal, and some of the best tropical-fruit ice cream
(mango, guava, pineapple, and passion fruit) at I-Scream.

Montego Bay While you should not rule out a visit to the "crafts market" on Mar-
and ket Street in MoBay, you should consider first how much you like
Ocho Rios pandemonium and haggling over prices and quality. The crafts markets in Ocho Rios are less hectic unless a cruise ship is in port, and
the crafts markets in Port Antonio and Negril are good fun. You'll
find a plethora of T-shirts; straw hats, baskets, and place mats;
carved wood statues; colorful Rasta berets; and cheap jewelry.

If you're looking to spend money, head for **City Centre Plaza,**
Overton Plaza, Miranda Ridge Plaza, St. James's Place, and **Westgate**
Plaza in Montego Bay; in Ocho Rios, the shopping plazas are **Pine-**
apple Place, Ocean Village, the **Taj Mahal, Coconut Grove,** and **Island**
Plaza. It's also a good idea to chat with salespeople, who can enlight-
en you about the newer boutiques and their whereabouts.

Specialty Silk batiks, by the yard or made into chic designs, are at **Caribatik**
Shops (tel. 809/954–3314), the studio of the late Muriel Chandler, 2 miles
Arts and east of Falmouth. Drawing on patterns in nature, Chandler trans-
Crafts lated the birds, seascapes, flora, and fauna into works of art.

The **Gallery of West Indian Art** (1 Orange La., MoBay, tel. 809/952–
4547 and at Round Hill, tel. 809/952–5150) is the place to find Jamaican and Haitian paintings. A corner of the gallery is devoted to
hand-turned pottery (some painted) and beautifully carved and
painted birds and jungle animals.

Harmony Hall (an 8-minute drive east on A1 from Ocho Rios; tel.
809/975–4222), a restored great house, is where Annabella
Proudlock sells her unique wood Annabella Boxes. The covers feature reproductions of Jamaican paintings. Larger reproductions of
paintings, lithographs, and signed prints of Jamaican scenes are
also for sale, along with hand-carved wood combs—all magnificent-
ly displayed. Harmony Hall is also well known for its year-round art
shows by local artists.

Belts, bangles, and beads are the name of the game at the factory of
Ital-Craft (Shop 8, Upper Manor Park Shopping Plaza, 184C Spring
Rd., Kingston, tel. 809/931–0477). Belts are the focus of this savvy
operation, but it also produces some intriguing jewelry and purses
(many made from reptile skins). While Ital-Craft's handmade treasures are sold in boutiques throughout Jamaica, we recommend a
visit to the factory for the largest selection of these belts, made of

spectacular shells, combined with leather, feathers, or fur. (The most ornate belts sell for about $75.)

Go to **Patoo** (Upper Manor Park Plaza, Kingston, tel. 809/924–1552) for fine art, folk art, crafts, and collectibles.

Sprigs and Things (Miranda Ridge Plaza, Gloucester Ave., MoBay, tel. 809/952–4735) is where artist Janie Soren sells T-shirts featuring her hand-painted designs of birds and animals. She also paints canvas bags and tennis dresses.

Things Jamaican (Devon House, 26 Hope Rd., Kingston, tel. 809/ 929–6602, and 44 Fort St., MoBay, tel. 809/952–5605) has two outlets and two airport stalls that display and sell some of the best native crafts made in Jamaica, with items that range from carved wood bowls and trays to reproductions of silver and brass period pieces.

Bikinis **Vaz Enterprises, LTD.** Teeny-weeny bikinis, which more than rival Rio's, are designed by **Sonia Vaz** and sold at her manufacturing outlet (77 East St., Kingston, tel. 809/922–9200), at Sandals, and other resorts (*see* Lodging, *below*).

Jewelry **L. A. Henriques** (Shop 11, Upper Manor Park Plaza, tel. 809/931– 0613) sells high-quality jewelry made to order.

Records Reggae tapes by world-famous Jamaican artists, such as Bob Marley, Ziggy Marley, Peter Tosh, and Third World, can be found easily in U.S. or European record stores, but a pilgrimage to **Randy's Record Mart** (17 N. Parade, Kingston, tel. 809/922–4859) should be high on the reggae lover's list. Also worth checking are the **Record Plaza** (Tropical Plaza, Kingston, tel. 809/926–7645), **Record City** (14 King St., Port Antonio, tel. 809/993–2836), and **Top Ranking Records** (Westgate Plaza, Montego Bay, tel. 809/952–1216). While Kingston is the undisputed place to make purchases, the determined somehow (usually with the help of a local) will find **Jimmy Cliff's Records** (Oneness Sq., MoBay, no tel.), owned by reggae star Cliff.

Sandals Cheap sandals are good buys in shopping centers throughout Jamaica. While workmanship and leathers don't rival the craftsmanship of those found in Italy or Spain, neither do the prices (about $20 a pair). In Kingston there's **Lee's** (New Kingston Shopping Centre, tel. 809/929–8614). In Ocho Rios, the **Pretty Feet Shoe Shop** (Ocean Village Shopping Centre, tel. 809/974–5040) is a good bet. In Montego Bay, try **Overton Plaza** or **Westgate Plaza.**

Gift Ideas Fine Macanudo handmade cigars make sensational gifts. They can be bought on departure at Montego Bay airport (call 809/925–1082 for outlet information). Blue Mountain coffee can be found at **John R. Wong's Supermarket** (1 Tobago Ave., Kingston, tel. 809/926–4811) and the **Sovereign Supermarket** (Hope Rd., tel. 809/927–5955). If they're out of stock, you'll have to settle for High Mountain coffee, the natives' second-preferred brand. If you're set on Blue Mountain, you may try **Magic Kitchen Ltd.** (Village Plaza, Kingston, tel. 809/ 926–8894).

Jamaican-brewed rums and Tia Maria can be bought at either the Kingston or MoBay airports before your departure. As a general rule, only rum factories, such as Sangster's, are less expensive than the airport stores, and if you buy at the airport there's no toting of heavy, breakable bottles from your hotel.

Dining

Sampling the island's cuisine introduces you to virtually everything the Caribbean represents. Every ethnic group that has made significant contributions on another island has made them on Jamaica, too, adding to a Jamaican stockpot that is as rich as its melting pot. So many Americans have discovered the Caribbean through restaurants owned by Jamaicans that the very names of the island's dishes have come to represent the region as a whole.

Jamaican food represents a true cuisine, organized, interesting, and ultimately rewarding. It would be a terrible shame for anyone to travel to the heart of this complex culture without tasting several typically Jamaican dishes. Here are a few:

Rice and Peas. A traditional dish, known also as Coat of Arms and similar to the *moros y christianos* of Spanish-speaking islands: white rice cooked with red beans, coconut milk, scallions, and seasoning.

Pepper Pot. The island's most famous soup—a peppery combination of salt pork, salt beef, okra, and the island green known as callaloo—it is green, but at its best it tastes as though it ought to be red.

Curry Goat. Young goat is cooked with spices and is more tender and has a gentler flavor than the lamb for which it was substituted by immigrants from India.

Ackee and Saltfish. Salted fish was once the best islanders could do between catches, so they invented this incredibly popular dish that joins saltfish (in Portuguese, *bacalao*) with ackee, a vegetable (introduced to the island by Captain Bligh of *Bounty* fame) that reminds most people of scrambled eggs.

Jerk Pork. Created by the Arawaks and perfected by the Maroons, jerk pork is the ultimate island barbecue. The pork (the purist cooks the whole pig) is covered with a paste of hot peppers, pimento berries (also known as allspice), and other herbs and cooked slowly over a coal fire. Many think that the "best of the best" jerk comes from Boston Beach in Port Antonio.

Patties are spicy meat pies that elevate street food to new heights. Although they in fact originated in Haiti, Jamaicans can give patty lessons to anybody.

Where restaurants are concerned, Kingston has the widest selection; its ethnic restaurants offer Italian, French, Rasta natural foods, Cantonese, German, Thai, Indian, Korean, and Continental fare. There are fine restaurants as well in all the resort areas, and the list includes many that are in large hotels.

Dress is casual chic (just plain casual at the local hangouts), except at the top resorts, some of which require semiformal wear in the evening during high season.

Highly recommended restaurants are indicated by a star ★.

Category	Cost*
Very Expensive	over $40
Expensive	$30–$40

Moderate	$20–$30
Inexpensive	under $20

per person, excluding drinks and service charge (or tip)

Kingston **Blue Mountain Inn.** The elegant Blue Mountain Inn is a 30-minute
★ taxi ride from downtown and worth every penny of the fare. On a
former coffee plantation, the antique-laden inn complements its English Colonial atmosphere with Continental cuisine. All the classics
of the beef and seafood repertoires are here, including steak Diane
and lobster thermidor. *Gordon Town, tel. 809/927–1700. Reservations required. AE, MC, V. Expensive–Very Expensive.*
Le Pavillon. Situated just off the Jamaica Pegasus lobby and noted
for its afternoon teas, this is *the* place to go for lunch and dinner. The
setting is sophisticated, the menu international with a Jamaican
flair, and the service top-notch. The wine list is excellent and costly.
A value-packed seafood buffet lunch is served on Friday. *Jamaica
Pegasus Hotel, tel. 809/926–3690. Reservations required. AE, DC,
MC, V. Expensive.*
The Palm Court. Nestled on the mezzanine floor of the Wyndham
Kingston, the elegant Palm Court is open for lunch and dinner
(lunch is noon to 3 PM; dinner from 7 PM). The menu is Continental,
with a heavy Italian accent: tagliatelle Alfredo, with ham and fresh
mushrooms; tricolor pasta with shrimp, fish, and lobster; and a seafood
kebab. *Wyndham New Kingston, tel. 809/926–5430. Reservations
recommended. AE, DC, MC, V. Moderate–Expensive.*
Temple Hall. Located in the hills, 30 minutes from New Kingston,
this restaurant has the ambience of a 17th-century plantation house.
The menu features home-grown vegetables, meats, and poultry ef-
fectively combining Caribbean nouvelle with Jamaican cuisine.
*Stony Hill, tel. 809/942–2340. Reservations required. AE, MC, V.
Moderate–Expensive.*
Hotel Four Seasons. The Four Seasons has been pleasing local resi-
dents for more than 25 years with its cuisine from the German and
Swiss schools as well as local seafood. The setting tries to emulate
Old World Europe without losing its casual island character. *18
Ruthven Rd., tel. 809/926–8805. Reservations recommended. AE,
DC, MC, V. Moderate.*
Ivor Guest House. Serving international and Jamaican cuisines, this
elegant yet cozy restaurant has an incredible view of Kingston from
2,000 feet above sea level. Go for dinner, when the view is dramatically caught between the stars and the glittering brooch of
Kingston's lights. Owner Hellen Aitken is an animated and cordial
hostess. *Jack's Hill, tel. 809/977–0033. Reservations required. AE,
MC, V. Moderate.*
★ **The Hot Pot.** Jamaicans love the Hot Pot for breakfast, lunch, and
dinner. Fricassee chicken is the specialty, along with other local
dishes, such as mackerel run-down (salted mackerel cooked down
with coconut milk and spices) and ackee and salted cod. The restaurant's fresh juices "in season" are the best—tamarind, sorrel, coconut water, soursop, and cucumber. *2 Altamont Terr., tel. 809/929–
3906. V. Inexpensive.*
Peppers. This casual outdoor bar is the "in" spot in Kingston, particularly on weekends. Sample the jerk pork and chicken with the local
Red Stripe beer. *31 Upper Waterloo Rd., tel. 809/925–2219. MC, V.
Inexpensive.*

Montego Bay **Georgian House.** A landmark restaurant in the heart of town, the
Georgian House occupies a restored 18th-century building set in a
shady garden courtyard. An extensive wine cellar complements the

Continental and Jamaican cuisines, the best of which are the steaks and the dishes made with the local spiny lobster. Free pickup from Montego Bay hotels. *Union and Orange Sts., tel. 809/952–0632. Reservations required. AE, DC, MC, V. Expensive–Very Expensive.*

Julia's. Couples flock to this romantic Italian restaurant set up in the hills overlooking the twinkling lights of MoBay. Diners choose from an à la carte or four-course fixed-price menu ($34 per person) that includes homemade soups and pastas; entrées of fish, chicken, and veal; and scrumptious desserts. *Bogue Hill, tel. 809/952–1772. Reservations required. AE, MC, V. Expensive.*

★ **Sugar Mill.** Seafood is served with flair at this terrace restaurant. Caribbean specialties, steak, and lobster are usually offered in a pungent sauce that blends Dijon mustard with Jamaica's own Pickapeppa. Other wise choices are the daily à la carte specials and anything flamed. *At Half Moon Golf Course, tel. 809/953–2228. Reservations required for dinner, recommended for lunch. AE, DC, MC, V. Expensive.*

Norma at the Wharf House. This sister property to creative chef and entrepreneur Norma's successful Kingston restaurant has gathered rave reviews as a supper club. Set in a converted 300-year-old stone sugar warehouse on the water, this savvy eatery with blue and white decor offers innovative Jamaican cuisine ranging from Caribbean lobster steamed in Red Stripe beer to jerk chicken with mangoes flambé. Nightly jazz bands enliven the bar and sometimes play out on the wharf. Free pickup service from MoBay-area hotels. Open daily from 9 AM–2 AM. *10 minutes west of MoBay in Reading, tel. 809/979–2745. Reservations necessary for dinner. MC, V. Moderate–Expensive.*

Pier 1. Despite the fact that it shares a name with the American imports store, Pier 1 writes the book daily on waterfront dining. After tropical drinks at the deck bar, you'll be ready to dig into the international variations on fresh seafood, the best of which are the grilled lobster and any preparation of island snapper. *Just off Howard Cooke Blvd., tel. 809/952–2452. Reservations recommended. AE, MC, V. Moderate–Expensive.*

Town House. Most of the rich and famous who have visited Jamaica over the decades have eaten at the Town House. You will find specials of the day and good versions of standard ideas (red snapper papillot is the specialty, with lobster, cheese, and wine sauce) in an 18th-century Georgian house complete with shuttered windows. The restaurant offers free pickup service from your hotel. *16 Church St., tel. 809/952–2660. Reservations recommended. AE, DC, MC, V. Moderate.*

Hemingway's Pub. Opened in 1990, this eatery has been a great success with the local business community, which enjoys the pub lunches and dinners. It's an air-conditioned casual bar-restaurant with satellite TV and the added bonus of a terrace for watching the sun go down. *At Miranda Ridge Plaza, Gloucester Ave., tel 809/952–8606. No credit cards. Inexpensive.*

★ **Le Chalet.** Don't let the French name fool you. This Denny's look-alike, set in a nondescript shopping mall, serves heaping helpings of some of the best Chinese and Jamaican food in MoBay. Its staff will even pick you up from your hotel. *32 Gloucester Ave., tel. 809/952–5240. AE, MC, V. Inexpensive.*

★ **Pork Pit.** This open-air hangout three minutes from the airport must introduce more travelers to Jamaica's fiery jerk pork than any other place on the island. The Pork Pit is a local phenomenon down to the Red Stripe beer, yet it's accessible in both location and style. Plan to arrive around noon, when the jerk begins to be lifted from its bed of coals and pimento wood. *Adjacent to Fantasy Resort, tel. 809/952–1046. No reservations. No credit cards. Inexpensive.*

Negril **Cafe au Lait.** The proprietors of Cafe au Lait are French and Jamaican, and so is the cuisine. Local seafood and produce are prepared with delicate touches and presented in a setting overlooking the sea. *Mirage Resort on Lighthouse Rd., tel. 809/957–4471. Reservations recommended. MC, V. Moderate.*

Tan-ya's. This alfresco restaurant is on the edge of the beach of its hotel, Seasplash. It features Jamaican delicacies with an international flavor for breakfast, lunch, and dinner. *Seasplash Hotel, Norman Manley Blvd., tel. 809/957–4041. AE, DC, MC, V. Moderate.*

Rick's Cafe. Here it is, the local landmark complete with cliffs, cliff divers, and powerful sunsets, all perfectly choreographed. It's a great place for a sunny brunch of omelets or eggs Benedict. In the sunset ritual, the crowd toasts Mother Nature with rum drinks, shouts and laughter, and ever-shifting meeting and greeting. When the sun slips below the horizon, there are more shouts, more cheers, and more rounds of rum. *Lighthouse Rd., tel. 809/957–4335. MC, V. Inexpensive–Moderate.*

Cosmo's Seafood Restaurant and Bar. Owner Cosmo Brown has made this seaside open-air bistro a pleasant place to spend a lunch, an afternoon, and maybe stay on for dinner. (He's also open for breakfast. In fact, he only closes from 5 PM to 6:30 PM for a scrub-down.) The fresh fish is the main attraction, and the conch soup that's the house specialty is a meal in itself. There's also lobster (grilled or curried), fish-and-chips, and a catch-of-the-morning. Customers often drop cover-ups to take a beach dip before coffee and dessert and return later to lounge in chairs scattered under almond and sea-grape trees. (There's an entrance fee for the beach alone, but it's less than $1.) *Norman Manley Blvd., tel. 809/957–4330. MC, V. Inexpensive.*

Paradise Yard. Locals enjoy this alfresco restaurant on the Savanna-La-Mar side of the roundabout in Negril. Sit back and relax in the casual atmosphere while eating Jamaican dishes or the house special Rasta Pasta. Open for breakfast, lunch, and dinner. *Tel. 809/957–4006. V. Inexpensive.*

Ocho Rios **Almond Tree.** One of the most popular restaurants in Ocho Rios, the
★ Almond Tree offers Jamaican dishes enlivened by a European culinary tradition. The swinging rope chairs of the terrace bar and the tables perched above a lovely Caribbean cove are great fun. You'll also find pumpkin and pepper-pot soups and fresh fish served in many wonderful ways. *83 Main St., Ocho Rios, tel. 809/974–2813. Reservations required. AE, DC, MC, V. Moderate–Expensive.*

The Ruins. A 40-foot waterfall dominates the open-air Ruins restaurant, and in a sense it dominates the food as well. Surrender to local preference and order the Lotus Lily Lobster, a stir-fry of the freshest local shellfish, then settle back and enjoy the tree-shaded deck and the graceful footbridges that connect the dining patios. *DaCosta Dr., tel. 809/974–2442. Reservations recommended. AE, DC, MC, V. Moderate.*

★ **Evita's.** The setting here is a sensational, nearly 100-year-old gingerbread house high on a hill overlooking Ocho Rios Bay (but also convenient from MoBay). More than 18 kinds of pasta are served here, ranging from lasagna Rastafari (vegetarian) to *rotelle alla Eva* (crabmeat with white sauce and noodles). There are also excellent fish dishes—sautéed fillet of red snapper with orange butter, red snapper stuffed with crabmeat—and several meat dishes, among them grilled sirloin with mushroom sauce and barbecued ribs glazed with honey-and-ginger sauce. *Mantalent Inn, Ocho*

Rios, tel. 809/974–2333. Reservations required. AE, MC, V. Inex-pensive–Moderate.

Lodging

The island has a variety of destinations to choose from, each of which offers its own unique expression of the Jamaican experience. **Monte-go Bay** has miles of hotels, villas, apartments, and duty-free shops. Although lacking much in the way of cultural stimuli, MoBay pre-sents a comfortable island backdrop for the many conventions and conferences it hosts.

Ocho Rios, on the northeast coast halfway between Port Antonio and Montego Bay, is hilly and lush, with rivers, riotous gardens, and a growing number of upscale resorts, many of which are all-inclu-sive. Ocho Rios's hotels and villas are all situated within short driv-ing distance of shops and one of Jamaica's most scenic attractions, Dunn's River Falls.

Port Antonio, described by poet Ella Wheeler Wilcox as "the most exquisite port on earth," is a seaside town nestled at the foot of ver-dant hills toward the east end of the north coast. The two best exper-iences to be had here are rafting the Rio Grande and a stop at the Trident, arguably the island's classiest resort. Today, Port Antonio enjoys the reputation of being Jamaica's most favored out-of-the-way resort.

Negril, some 50 miles west of Montego Bay, was long a sleepy Bohe-mian retreat. In the last decade the town has bloomed considerably and added a number of classy all-inclusive resorts (Sandals Negril, Grand Lido, and Swept Away), with a few more on the drawing board. Negril itself is only a small village, so there isn't much of his-torical significance to seek out. Then again, that's not what brings the sybaritic singles and couples here. The crowd is young, hip, laid-back, and here for the sun, the sand, and the sea.

Mandeville, 2,000 feet above the sea, is noted for its cool climate and proximity to secluded south coast beaches.

The smallest of the resort areas, **Runaway Bay** has a handful of mod-ern hotels and an 18-hole golf course.

Kingston is the most culturally active place on Jamaica. Some of the island's finest business hotels are here, and those high towers are filled with rooftop restaurants, English pubs, serious theater and pantomime, dance presentations, art museums and galleries, jazz clubs, upscale supper clubs, and disco dives.

Jamaica was the birthplace of the Caribbean all-inclusive, the vaca-tion concept that took the Club Med idea and gave it a lusty, excess-in-the-tropics spin. The all-inclusive resort has become the most popular vacation option on Jamaica, offering incredible values with rates from $175–$350 per person per night. Rates include airport transfers; hotel accommodations; three meals a day plus snacks; all bar drinks, often including premium liquors; wine, beer, and soft drinks; a plethora of land and water sports, including instruction and equipment; and all gratuities and taxes. The only surcharges are usually for such luxuries as massages, souvenirs, and sightsee-ing tours. At times they may feel a bit like Pleasure Island, as all of your needs and most of your wants are taken care of. The all-inclu-sives have branched out, some of them courting families, others go-ing after an upper crust that would not even have picked up a brochure a few years ago.

If you're the exploring type who likes to get out and about, you may prefer an EP property. Many offer MAP or FAP packages that include extras like airport transfers and sightseeing tours. Even if you don't want to be tied down to a meal plan, it pays to inquire because the savings can be considerable.

Please note that the price categories listed below are based on winter rates. As a general rule, rates are reduced anywhere from 10%–30% from April 30–Dec. 15.

Highly recommended lodgings are indicated by a star ★.

Category	Cost EP*	Cost MAP**	Cost AI***
Very Expensive	over $245	over $345	over $500
Expensive	$175–$245	$265–$345	$400–$500
Moderate	$105–$175	$130–$265	$335–$400
Inexpensive	under $105	under $130	under $335

EP prices are for a standard double room for two in winter, excluding 12% tax and any service charge.
**MAP prices include breakfast and dinner for two daily in winter. Often MAP packages come with use of nonmotorized water sports and other benefits.*
***All-inclusive (AI) winter prices include tax, service, all meals, drinks, facilities, lessons, airport transfers.*

Falmouth **Trelawny Beach Hotel.** The dependable Trelawny Beach resort offers seven stories of rooms overlooking 4 miles of beach. Off the beaten path, it's run as a semi-inclusive resort (lunch and liquor are excluded) with an emphasis on families. During the off-season, one child under 15 gets free room and board when sharing accommodations with his or her parents. There's a daily activities program for children, a free shopping shuttle into MoBay, and a designated area of beach for nude sunbathing. *Box 54, Falmouth, tel. 809/954–2450 or 800/223–0888, fax 809/954–2173. 350 rooms. Facilities: 2 dining rooms, 4 lighted tennis courts, pool, complimentary use of water-sports equipment, shopping arcade, beauty salon, disco, nightly entertainment. AE, DC, MC, V. MAP, FAP. Expensive.*

★ **Fisherman's Inn Dive Resort.** A charming red-tile-and-stucco building fronts a phosphorescent lagoon at this welcoming hotel run by divers for divers. At night the hotel restaurant offers a free boat ride to diners; dip your hand in the water, and the bioluminescent microorganisms glow. It's really a treat. The bright breezy rooms all face the water, with air-conditioning, satellite TV, patio, and full bath. A great bargain, whether you dive (excellent packages are available) or not. Rates include three dives daily and MAP meal plan; nondiving spouses or mates do get a slight discount. *Falmouth P.O., tel. and fax 809/954–3427. 12 rooms. Facilities: restaurant, bar, pool, water sports (include PADI dive shop). AE, MC, V. MAP. Moderate.*

Kingston **Jamaica Pegasus.** The Jamaica Pegasus is one of two fine business
★ hotels in the New Kingston area. The 17-story complex near downtown boasts an efficient and accommodating staff, meeting rooms, a top-notch restaurant and a hearty café, handsome Old World decor, a pampering ambience, and an international crowd in the lobby. The

Polo Bar Lounge in the hotel lobby is a comfortable place to sit and have a drink. Advantages here include an excellent business center, duty-free shops, and 24-hour room service. *Box 333, Kingston, tel. 809/926–3690 or 800/225–5843, fax 809/929–4062. 397 rooms, 16 suites. Facilities: restaurants, cocktail lounge, meeting rooms for 1,000, audiovisual services, shops, Olympic-size pool, jogging track, health club, 2 lighted tennis courts. AE, DC, MC, V. EP, MAP. Expensive.*

Morgan's Harbour Hotel, Beach Club, and Yacht Marina. A favorite of the sail-into-Jamaica set, this small property boasts 22 acres of beachfront at the very entrance to the old pirate's town. Rooms are decorated in either a provincial or 18th-century nautical style that the pirate Captain Morgan would have appreciated. *Port Royal, Kingston, tel. 809/924–8464 or 800/JAMAICA, fax 809/924–8562. 66 rooms. Facilities: restaurant, pier bar, full-service marina, disco, access to Lime Cay and other cays. AE, MC, V. EP. Moderate.*

Wyndham New Kingston. The main competition to the Jamaica Pegasus on the Kingston business beat, the high-rise Wyndham New Kingston also has 17 stories but adds seven cabana buildings. A renovation in 1993 upgraded the facilities; the pleasant modern rooms all include air-conditioning, satellite TV, direct-dial phone, and hair dryer. *Box 112, Kingston, tel. 809/926–5430 or 800/JAMAICA; fax 809/929–7439. 300 rooms, 14 1-bedroom suites. Facilities: 2 restaurants, bars, Olympic-size pool, gardens, conference space for 800, meeting rooms, business center, 2 lighted tennis courts, health club, disco. AE, DC, MC, V. EP, MAP. Moderate.*

Mandeville **Astra Hotel.** A hotel with guest-house charm, the Astra is situated ★ 2,000 feet up in the hills, providing an ideal getaway for nature lovers and outdoors enthusiasts. *Ward Ave., Box 60, Mandeville, tel. 809/962–3265 or 800/JAMAICA, fax 809/962–1461. 22 rooms. Facilities: restaurant and bar, swimming pool, golf course and 1 tennis court nearby, horseback riding, bird-watching, sauna, satellite TV. AE, V. EP. Inexpensive.*

Mandeville Hotel. The Victorian Mandeville Hotel, set in tropical gardens, has redecorated for the 1990s. Rooms are simple and breeze-cooled; breakfast and lunch are served in a new flower-filled garden terrace. *Box 78, Mandeville, tel. 809/962–2460, fax 809/962–0700. 62 rooms. Facilities: restaurant, cocktail lounge, golf privileges at nearby Manchester Club. AE, MC, V. EP. Inexpensive.*

Montego Bay **Half Moon Club.** For four decades the 400-acre Half Moon Club resort has been a destination unto itself with a reputation for doing the little things right. Although it has mushroomed from 30 to over 200 units, it has maintained its intimate, luxurious feel. The rooms, suites, and villas, whether in modern or Queen Anne style, are decorated in exquisite taste, with marvelous touches like Oriental throw rugs and antique radios. *Box 80, east of Montego Bay (7 mi), tel. 809/953–2211 or 800/227–3237, fax 809/953–2731. 53 rooms, 159 suites and villas. Facilities: 3 restaurants, 3 bars, golf course, 4 squash courts, 13 tennis courts (7 lighted), horseback riding, health spa, water-sports center, 19 pools, children's pool. AE, DC, MC, V. EP, MAP, FAP, All-inclusive. Very Expensive.*

★ **Round Hill.** Eight miles west of town on a hilly peninsula, this peaceful resort is popular with the Hollywood set. Twenty-seven villas housing 74 suites are scattered over 98 acres, and each villa has a maid who cooks breakfast. There are also 36 hotel rooms in a two-story building overlooking the sea. The refined rooms all feature mahogany furnishings and terra-cotta floors. The privately owned villas vary in decor, but jungle motifs are a favorite. *Box 64, Montego*

Montego Bay Dining and Lodging

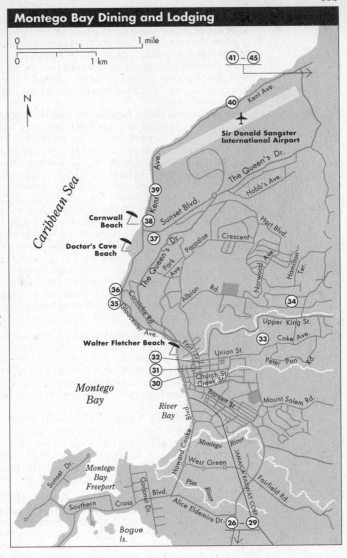

Bay, tel. 809/952–5150 or 800/237–3237, fax 809/952–2505. 36 rooms, 74 villa suites. Facilities: restaurant, pool, 5 lighted tennis courts, spa and fitness center, nearby horseback riding, water-sports center. AE, DC, MC, V. EP, MAP, FAP, All-inclusive. Very Expensive.

Tryall Golf, Tennis, and Beach Club. Part of a posh residential development 12 miles west of Montego Bay, Tryall clings to a hilltop overlooking the golf course and the Caribbean. Here you choose between accommodations in the former great house of a 3,000-acre island plantation and one of the private villas dotting the landscape, each with its own pool. Box 1206, Sandy Bay, Hanover, Montego Bay, tel. 809/952–5110 or 800/237–3237, fax 809/952–0401. 52 rooms, 41 villas. Facilities: 2 restaurants, golf course, 9 tennis courts (5

*lighted), pool with swim-up bar, water sports. AE, DC, MC, V. EP,
MAP, FAP, All-inclusive. Very Expensive.*

★ **Sandals Royal Caribbean.** Another all-inclusive resort for couples
only, the Royal Caribbean is enlivened by Jamaican-style architecture arranged in a semicircle around attractive gardens. It's a sister
in both theme and quality to other Sandals resorts; the renovated
rooms feature king-size beds, hair dryers, safes, clock radios, and
satellite TVs. While sportive and activity-laden, this property is a
bit quieter and more genteel than the other Sandals and draws a
nicely mixed international crowd. *Box 167, Montego Bay, tel. 809/
953–2231 or 800/SANDALS, fax 809/953–2788. 190 rooms. Facilities: 4 restaurants, 3 bars, 3 pools, 4 Jacuzzis, gym, body shop,
disco, private offshore island, beach, 2 lighted tennis courts, putting green, satellite TV. AE, DC, MC, V. All-inclusive. Expensive.*

Sandals Montego Bay. The largest private beach in Montego Bay is
the spark that lights Sandals, one of the most popular couples resorts in the Caribbean. The all-inclusive format includes airport
transfers, all taxes and tips, a plethora of water and land sports, including scuba diving and golfing (greens fees included), all sports
equipment and lessons, aerobics classes, meals, theme parties, and
other entertainment. It's a bit like a cruise ship that remains in port,
with rooms overlooking the bay. The revelers don't seem to mind the
zooming planes (the airport is next door), and the atmosphere here
remains one of a great big fun party. *Box 100, Montego Bay, tel. 809/
952–5510 or 800/SANDALS, fax 809/952–0816. 243 rooms. Facilities: 3 restaurants, 4 bars, 2 pools, swim-up bar, 4 Jacuzzis, gym,
body shop, water-sports center, 4 lighted tennis courts, 1 racquetball court, nightclub, satellite TV. AE, DC, MC, V. All-inclusive.
Moderate–Expensive.*

Holiday Inn Rose Hall. Here the great equalizer of hotel chains has
done much to raise a run-down campground to the level of a full-
service property with activities day and night and many tour facilities. It's big and noisy, with drab hallways and public areas, though
the rooms are cheerful enough. The quietest rooms are those farthest from the pool. The beach is just a sliver, but there's live entertainment nightly. *Box 480, Montego Bay, tel. 809/953–2485 or 800/
352–0731 or 800/HOLIDAY, fax 809/953–2840. 516 rooms, 5 suites.
Facilities: 3 restaurants, 4 bars, pool, water-sports center, exercise
room, 4 tennis courts, game room, disco, shops. AE, DC, MC, V.
EP. Moderate.*

★ **Richmond Hill Inn.** The hilltop Richmond Hill Inn, a quaint, daintily
decorated 200-year-old great house originally owned by the Dewars
clan, attracts repeat visitors by providing spectacular views of the
Caribbean and a great deal of peace in the midst of MoBay's hustle.
*Union St., Box 362, Montego Bay, tel. 809/952–3859 or 800/423–
4095. 23 rooms, 5 suites. Facilities: terrace dining room, coffee
shop, bar, pool, free beach shuttle. AE, MC, V. EP, MAP. FAP.
Moderate.*

Wyndham Rose Hall. The veteran Wyndham Rose Hall, a self-contained resort built on the 400-acre Rose Hall Plantation, mixes recreation with a top-flight conference setup. A typical bustling
business hotel popular with groups, it has all the amenities and completed a $30 million renovation in 1993. A "Kid's Klub" with daily
supervised activities was also added. *Box 999, Montego Bay, tel.
809/953–2650 or 800/996–3426, fax 809/953–5617. 489 rooms, 19
suites. Facilities: 4 restaurants, coffee shop, 3 pools, water sports, 6
tennis courts, golf course, nightclub, lounge, 8 meeting rooms, audiovisual equipment, fitness center, laundry service, shopping arcade. AE, DC, MC, V. EP, MAP, All-inclusive. Moderate.*

Fantasy Resort. After a brief stint as an all-inclusive resort, this property has gone back to normal hotel status. The resort sports high-rise design and a Mediterranean flair. All nine stories have terraces with ocean views. A small beach is across the street. Efficient and pleasant, Fantasy is a good buy, usually booked solid with tour groups. *Opposite Cornwall Beach, Box 161, Montego Bay, tel. 809/952–4150 or 800/223–9815, fax 809/952–3637. 119 rooms. Facilities: dining room, open-air bar, pool, disco, shopping arcade. AE, DC, MC, V. EP. Inexpensive.*

Reading Reef Club. Four miles west of Montego Bay airport, this owner-operated resort is ideal for families and budget-minded honeymooners. Another of Jamaica's fine small-hotel values, it offers simply but tastefully furnished rooms and an excellent pasta and seafood restaurant, the Safari. Golf and horseback riding can be arranged. *Box 225, Reading, Montego Bay, tel. 809/952–5909 or 800/223–6510, fax 809/952–7217. 30 rooms, suites and apartments. Facilities: gourmet restaurant, private beach, pool, dive shop, water sports. AE, MC, V. EP, CP, BP, MAP. Inexpensive.*

Sandals Inn. The Inn is less expensive than the other couples-only Sandals resorts, because it's the only one not on a private beach. It is more intimate than the other Sandals—managed more like a small hotel than a large resort. The charming rooms are smallish, but have balconies facing the pool. There's plenty to do here, but couples in search of more action can enjoy the other two MoBay Sandals by hopping aboard the free hourly shuttle. The in-town location makes the Inn convenient to shopping and tours. *Box 412, Montego Bay, tel. 809/952–4140 or 800/SANDALS; fax 809/952–6913. 52 rooms. Facilities: beach privileges, pool, 2 restaurants, pub, satellite TV, gift shop, 1 lighted tennis court, fitness center. AE, DC, MC, V. All-inclusive. Inexpensive.*

Negril **Grand Lido.** The opening of the SuperClubs' all-inclusive Grand
★ Lido in 1989 broke new ground by extending this popular concept to the upper-income bracket. The dramatic entrance of marble floors and columns sets a tone of striking elegance. The well-appointed oceanfront rooms (split-level and arguably the most spacious and stylish of the all-inclusives), sports facilities, and 24-hour room service follow up in high style. For some, the pièce de résistance is a sunset cruise on the resort's 147-foot yacht, *Zien*, which was a wedding gift from Aristotle Onassis to Prince Rainier and Princess Grace of Monaco and is now captained by Wynn Jones. Grand Lido attracts a slightly more mature and settled crowd than does the usual Negril resort. The gourmet restaurant, Piacere, is one of Jamaica's best, and an atmosphere of cool elegance prevails throughout. *Box 88, Negril, tel. 809/957–4010 or 800/859–7873, fax 809/957–4317. 200 suites. Facilities: 3 specialty restaurants, satellite TV, 24-hour room service, water-sports center including scuba diving, pools, clothed and nude beaches, 4 tennis courts (2 lighted), gym, beauty salon. AE, DC, MC, V. All-inclusive. Very Expensive.*

Sandals Negril. Sandals, built from the best parts of the old Sundowner and Coconut Cove resorts on one of the best stretches of Negril's 7-mile beach, was designed for fun-loving couples seeking an upscale, sportive getaway on a fabulous beach and a casual atmosphere (you can wear shorts to dinner) within an exclusive environment. Water sports, including scuba diving, are emphasized here; and the capable staff is happy to both teach neophytes and take out guests who are already certified. There's an offshore island, a huge swim-up pool bar, and a range of spacious accommodations. Both rooms and staff are sunny and appealing. *Negril, tel. 809/957–4216 or 800/SANDALS; Unique Vacations, 7610 S.W. 61st St., Miami, FL 33143. 199 rooms. Facilities: 3 restaurants, 2 pools, swim-up* *bar, private island, water-sports center including scuba diving, squash and racquetball courts, 4 tennis courts, croquet lawn, waterskiing, Jacuzzis, saunas, fitness center, movies, satellite TV, disco, piano bar. AE, DC, MC, V. All-inclusive. Expensive.*

★ **Swept Away.** One of the newer and better all-inclusive resorts, Swept Away opened in early 1990 and is geared toward fitness and health-conscious couples, with an emphasis on sports and healthy cuisine. There are 130 suites in 26 cottages; all have a private inner-garden atrium. There are also four two-bedroom villas spread out along a half-mile of "drop-dead" beach. The 10-acre sports complex across the road outclasses the competition by a long shot; the Feathers Continental Restaurant here is open to nonguests. The compound's chefs concentrate on healthful dishes with lots of fish, white meat, fresh fruits, and veggies. *Long Bay, Negril, tel. 809/957–4061 or 800/545–7937; fax 809/957–4060. 138 rooms. Facilities: 2 restaurants, 2 bars, 10 lighted tennis courts, 2 squash courts, 2 racquetball courts, fitness center, steam rooms and saunas, Jacuzzis, pool with lap lines. Full water-sports center including scuba diving. AE, MC, V. All-inclusive. Expensive.*

★ **Hedonism II.** Here is the resort that introduced the Club Med–style all-inclusive to Jamaica a little over 16 years ago. Still wildly successful, Hedonism appeals most to vacationers who like a robust mix of physical activities, all listed daily on a chalkboard. A $2 million refurbishment in 1993 spruced up the public areas; the rooms are modern and handsome, with a lot of blond woods (but the 60% single clientele spends little time in them). *Box 25, Negril, tel. 809/957–4200 or 800/859–7873, fax 809/957–4289. 280 rooms. Facilities: open-air buffet dining room, disco, and bar; water-sports center, including scuba diving; fitness center and trapeze and trampoline clinics; horseback riding; 6 lighted tennis courts; shuffleboard; volleyball; squash. AE, MC, V. All-inclusive. Moderate–Expensive.*

★ **Charela Inn.** Intimacy is special at the Charela Inn, where each of the quiet, elegantly appointed rooms offers a balcony or a covered patio. The owners' French-Jamaican roots find daily expression in the kitchen, and there's an excellent selection of wines. *Box 33, Negril, Westmoreland, tel. 809/957–4277 or 800/423–4095, fax 809/957–4414. 38 air-conditioned rooms, 1 apartment. Facilities: restaurant, pool, beach. DC, MC, V. EP, MAP. Moderate.*

Negril Gardens. A study in colonial pink and white, with half the rooms beachside and half across the street overlooking the pool. At press time, all of the rooms were in the midst of being refurbished, and a fitness center was being added. *Negril, Westmoreland, tel. 809/957–4408 or 800/752–6824, fax 809/957–4374. 54 rooms. Facilities: terrace restaurant, tennis, beach, pool, water sports, disco. AE, MC, V. EP. Moderate.*

Negril Inn. The rooms in this all-inclusive inn are air-conditioned, and each has a garden view and a patio or balcony. Air-conditioning is about the only modern convenience in this simple place, since rooms do not have phones or televisions. If you don't mind this bit of isolation, you can enjoy the inn's beach—one of the prettiest palm-speckled sandy beaches in Jamaica. *Negril, tel. 809/957–4370 or 800/634–7456, fax 809/957–4365. 46 rooms. Facilities: restaurant, dancing, entertainment, lounge, disco, 2 tennis courts, pool, Jacuzzi, water-sports center. AE, MC, V. All-inclusive. Moderate.*

Negril Cabins. The 12 timber cottages are nestled amid lush vegetation and towering royal palms. The rooms are unadorned, but warm and snug, with a fresh, natural look. The gleaming beach is right across the road. A most convivial place, highly popular with young Europeans. *Negril, tel. 809/957–4350 or 800/423–4095, fax 809/957–*

4381. 24 rooms. Facilities: restaurant, bar. AE, MC, V. EP. Inexpensive.

Ocho Rios **Jamaica Inn.** This vintage property is a special favorite of the privi-
★ leged from both the United States and Europe, a clientele fascinated
by the combination of class and quiet. There are weeks in season
when every single guest is on at least his or her second visit. Each
room has its own veranda (larger than most hotel rooms) on the powdery champagne-color beach. This is the kind of retreat that makes
Americans yearn to be colonists again, happily discussing the royals'
latest trials. The owning Morrow brothers are committed to making
everything perfect; they're not far off. *Box 1, Ocho Rios, tel. 800/
243–9420 or 809/974–2514, fax 809/974–2449. 45 rooms. Facilities:
restaurant, bar, pool, golf, tennis and horseback riding nearby. No
children under 14. AE, MC, V. EP, MAP, FAP. Very Expensive.*

Plantation Inn. This plantation actually looks like one—the Deep
South variety à la *Gone with the Wind.* The whole place serves up a
veranda-soft existence. All the rooms come with private balconies,
and each has a dramatic view down to the sea. *Box 2, Ocho Rios, tel.
809/974–5601 or 800/752–6824, fax 809/974–5912. 77 rooms. Facilities: dining and dancing by candlelight, shops, 2 lighted tennis
courts, health club, afternoon tea, entertainment twice weekly. No
children under 12. AE, DC, MC, V. EP, MAP, FAP, All-inclusive.
Very Expensive.*

★ **Sans Souci Lido.** The newest acquistion of the SuperClubs, this pas-
tel-pink cliffside fantasyland looks and feels like a dream, if indeed
the dreamer had absolute taste and no need to fret over the bill (unlike the owners, who recently completed a $7 million renovation).
Cuisine at the Casanova Restaurant delights resort guests, as does
the pampering they get at Charlie's Spa in the form of a complimentary massage, facial, manicure, and pedicure. This elegant, exclusive property is first-rate. A wonderfully luxurious experience.
*Ocho Rios, tel. 809/974–2353 or 800/859–7873, fax 809/974–2544. 13
rooms, 98 suites. Facilities: 2 restaurants, full-service health spa
and fitness center, freshwater and mineral pool, 3 lighted tennis
courts, scuba diving, water-sports center. AE, DC, MC, V. All-inclusive. Very Expensive.*

Ciboney, Ocho Rios. A Radisson Villa, Spa and Beach Resort, this
stately plantation property opened its doors in winter 1991. The $46
million project has 36 rooms in a plantation-style great house and
264 spacious one-, two-, and three-bedroom villa suites on 45 lush
hillside acres overlooking the Caribbean. It is operated as a luxury
all-inclusive geared toward affluent adults, both singles and couples;
no children under the age of 16 are allowed. Outstanding features
are the European-style spa and four signature restaurants, including the Orchids restaurant, whose menu was developed by the Culinary Institute of America. Every villa has a private attendant and
pool, giving guests the ultimate in privacy and pampering. All
guests receive complimentary massage, foot reflexology, manicure,
and pedicure. *Box 728, Main St., Ocho Rios, tel. 809/974–1027 or
800/333–3333, fax 809/974–5838. 264 1-, 2-, and 3-bedroom suites, 36
rooms. Facilities: 4 restaurants, 2 pools with swim-up bars, 6 tennis
courts, full-service spa, steam room, sauna, hot tubs, cold plunges,
golf greens fees and transportation, 3 bars, 2 squash courts, racquetball court, water-sports center including scuba diving, beach
shuttle to private beach club, disco, boutique, beauty salon, jogging
track, nightly entertainment, conference facilities. All-inclusive.
Expensive–Very Expensive.*

★ **Boscobel Beach.** Boscobel Beach is a parent's dream for a Jamaican
vacation, an all-inclusive that makes families feel welcome. Every-

body is kept busy all week for a single package price, and everyone leaves happy. The cheery day-care centers, divided by age group, should be a model for the rest of the Caribbean. Thoughtfully, there is an "adults only" section (for when the kids want to get away). *Box 63, Ocho Rios, tel. 809/974–3291 or 800/859–7873, fax 809/975–3270. 208 rooms, half of them junior suites. Facilities: 3 restaurants, 5 bars, satellite TV, gym, Jacuzzi, windsurfing, scuba diving, sailing, snorkeling, 2 pools, disco, day-care center, boutique, 4 lighted tennis courts, volleyball, golf at Jamaica, Jamaica/Runaway Bay. AE, DC, MC, V. All-inclusive. Expensive.*

Chukka Cove. The battle cry at Chukka Cove is "Saddle Up." Chukka Cove earns its horse feed by maintaining some of the best equestrian facilities in the Western Hemisphere. In addition to polo, experienced riders will want to investigate Chukka Cove's Jamaican Riding Holiday, an exploration of the north coast on horseback. Less-dedicated riders have a choice of trail rides, mountain trail rides, beach rides, or an overnight escorted ride to the Lillyfield Great House. *Box 160, Ocho Rios, tel. 809/974–2593, fax 809/974–5568. 6 villas with 12 sets of private suites, with cook and maid. Facilities: stables, equestrian instruction (all levels), cooks to prepare meals in villas, swimming from rocks. No credit cards. EP, MAP, FAP. Expensive.*

The Enchanted Garden. Set on 20 acres in the former Carinosa Gardens, this all-inclusive resort opened its doors in the winter of 1991–1992. The gardens have been maintained and are stunning with tropical plants, flowers, and a dramatic series of streams and waterfalls. There is an aviary and a seaquarium where you can enjoy a delicatessen lunch or tea surrounded by tanks of fish and hanging orchids. The futuristic pink cinderblock villas regrettably seem incongruous amid the natural splendor, but the rooms are comfortable and you're never far from the soothing sound of rushing water. *Box 284, Ocho Rios, tel. 809/974–5346 or 800/323–5655, fax 809/974–5823. 112 villa suites, 40 with private plunge pool. Facilities: 4 restaurants, spa, disco, gift shop, beauty parlor, satellite TV, aviary, hillside gardens, 2 lighted tennis courts, and golf and horseback riding nearby. Daily transportation and picnic to private beach. AE, MC, V. All-inclusive. Expensive.*

Jamaica Grande. Ramada bought the Americana (Divi-Divi) and Mallards Beach resorts and created Jamaica Grande, now the largest conference hotel in Jamaica. A major refurbishment and the addition of a conference center were completed in mid-1993 at a cost of more than $20 million. This property attracts families, couples, conference attendees, and incentive-travel winners, who enjoy the focal point—the fantasy pool with waterfall, swaying bridge, and swim-up bar. Accommodations in the south building are a bit roomier, whereas those in the north boast slightly better views. The staff is quite friendly for such a large, and rather overwhelming, beachfront property. Families enjoy the daily Club Mongoose children's program. *Box 100, Ocho Rios, tel. 809/974–2201 or 800/228–9898, fax 809/974–5378. 691 rooms, 21 suites. Facilities: 5 restaurants, 8 bars,water-sports center, fitness center, disco, 4 tennis courts, daily supervised children's program, secretarial services, 3 swimming pools, gaming parlor with slot machines, shopping arcade, beauty salon, 6 lighted tennis courts, 24-hour room service. AE, DC, MC, V. EP, MAP, All-inclusive. Expensive.*

★ **Sandals Dunn's River.** This luxury all-inclusive, couples-only resort in 23 acres of gardens opened its doors in winter 1991. A complete architectural reconstruction transformed the former Hilton/Eden II hotel into a Continental-Italian masterpiece. The accommodations are unusually spacious. This resort draws a well-heeled crowd in their thirties and forties and prides itself on catering to every guest's every whim. *Box 51, Ocho Rios, tel. 809/972-1610 or 800/ SANDALS, fax 809/972-1611. 256 rooms. Facilities: 4 restaurants, beach, 2 swimming-pool bars, 3 whirlpools, water sports including scuba diving, 9-hole pitch-and-putt golf green, jogging course, 4 tennis courts (2 lighted), gaming parlor, disco, air-conditioned nightclub, satellite TV in all rooms. AE, MC, V. All-inclusive. Expensive.*

Sandals Ocho Rios. The Sandals concept follows its successful formula at this couples-only, all-inclusive, 9-acre beachfront resort. The mix of white and sand colors contrasts nicely with the vegetation and the sea. The accommodations are airy and pleasant, with king-size beds, air-conditioning, satellite TV, direct-dial phones, hair dryers, and safety deposit boxes. The resort is popular with honeymooners and more mature duos, with meandering paths through lush foliage, hammocks for two strung between trees, and cozy benches nestled amid flower beds for private stargazing. Activities include scuba diving, greens fees at, and transportation to, nearby Sandals Golf Club, and an excursion to Dunn's River Falls. *Ocho Rios, tel. 809/974-5691 or 800/SANDALS, fax 809/974-5700. 237 units. Facilities: 3 restaurants, 4 bars, gift shop, 3 pools, 2 lighted tennis courts, disco, fitness center, satellite TV, watersports center with scuba diving, golf nearby, tours. AE, DC, MC, V. All-inclusive. Expensive.*

Couples. No singles, no children. The emphasis at Couples is on romantic adventure for just the two of you, and the all-inclusive concept eliminates the decision making that can intrude on social pleasure. Couples has the highest occupancy rate of any resort on the island—and perhaps the most suggestive logo as well. There may be a correlation. *Tower Isle, St. Mary, tel. 809/975-4271 or 800/ 859-7873, fax 809/975-4439. 172 rooms, 12 suites. Facilities: 3 restaurants, 3 bars, 2 pools, satellite TV, island for nude swimming, 3 lighted tennis courts, Nautilus gym, 2 air-conditioned squash courts, a water-sports center that includes scuba diving, horseback riding, nightly entertainment, golf at Runaway Bay, 7 Jacuzzis, shopping arcade. AE, DC, MC, V. All-inclusive. Moderate–Expensive.*

Shaw Park Beach Hotel. Another popular property, Shaw Park offers a pleasant alternative to downtown high rises. All rooms have water views, air-conditioning, and telephones. The grounds are colorful and well tended, while the Silks disco is a favorite for late-night carousing. *Cutlass Bay, Box 17, Ocho Rios, tel. 809/974-2552 or 800/243-9420, fax 809/974-5042. 118 rooms. Facilities: restaurant, water sports, disco, pool, massage. AE, DC, MC, V. CP. Moderate.*

★ **Hibiscus Lodge.** This gleaming white building with a blue canopy sits amid beautifully manicured lawns laced with trellises, not too far from its tiny private beach. The impeccably neat, cozy rooms all have at least a partial sea view, terrace, air-conditioning, and full bath. This German-run property may be Jamaica's best bargain, attracting a discriminating (and jubilant) crowd. *Box 52, Ocho Rios, tel. 809/974-2676 or 800/JAMAICA, fax 809/974-1874. 26 rooms. Facilities: restaurant, pool, piano bar, 1 lighted tennis court. AE, DC, MC, V. CP, MAP. Inexpensive.*

Jamel Continental. This spotless upscale tropical motel is set on its own beach in a relatively undeveloped area close to all the activities of Ocho Rios and Runaway Bay. The well-appointed units are spacious and breezy; all feature a balcony with sea view, full bath, phone, air-conditioning, and satellite TV. In addition to the usual floral prints and pastel hues, there are unexpected touches, such as mahogany writing desks and Oriental throw rugs. The moderately priced restaurant serves fine local dishes, and the staff is friendly and helpful. There's also a daily children's program, and the hotel is wheelchair-friendly. *2 Richmond Estate, Priory, St. Ann, tel. 809/ 972–1221, fax 809/972–0714. 21 rooms, 3 suites. Facilities: restaurant, bar, pool, Jacuzzi, gift shop. MC, V. MAP. Inexpensive.*

Port Antonio
★
Trident Villas and Hotel. If a single hotel had to be voted the most likely for coverage by "Lifestyles of the Rich and Famous," this would have to be it. Peacocks strut the manicured lawns; colonnaded walkways wind through whimsically sculpted topiary; and the pool, buried in a rocky bit of land jutting out into crashing surf, is a memory unto itself. The luxurious Laura Ashley–style rooms, many with turrets and bay windows, are awash in mahogany and lace. The truly gracious living will transport you back to the days of Empire. *Box 119, Port Antonio, tel. 809/993–2602 or 800/237–3237, fax 809/993– 2590. 11 rooms, 16 suites. Facilities: restaurant, water sports, boutique, tennis court, swimming pool. AE, MC, V. EP, MAP, FAP, All-inclusive. Very Expensive.*

Fern Hill Club. This is an all-inclusive hilltop property that's well run and usually full. The 16 new suites are bi-level and built into steep cliffs, with TVs, videos on request, small refrigerators, and a whirlpool-spa surrounded by a minigarden. The views are predictably spectacular. *Box 100, Port Antonio, tel. 809/993–3222 or 800/ 263–4354, fax 809/993–2257. 5 rooms, 16 suites, 5 1- and 2-bedroom apartments. Facilities: 3 swimming pools, 1 lighted tennis court, nightly entertainment, billiards, table tennis, shuffleboard, horseback riding (extra cost), transport to and from nearby San San beach, where scuba diving (extra cost) can be arranged. AE, MC, V. All-inclusive. Expensive.*

Goblin Hill. For a while this was known as the Jamaica Hill resort, but it is once again going by its original, evocative name. It's a lush 12-acre estate atop a hill overlooking San San cove. Each attractively appointed villa comes with its own dramatic view, plus a housekeeper-cook. Excellent villa and car-rental packages are available. *Box 26, Port Antonio, tel. 809/993–3286, fax 809/925–6248. 28 villas. Facilities: pool, beach, 2 tennis courts, water sports, reading and game room. AE, MC, V. EP. Expensive.*

Jamaica Palace. Errol Flynn might have loved this place for its sense of style and humor. Built to resemble an Edwardian mansion, this imposing five-year-old property rises in an expanse of white pillared marble, with the all-white theme continued on the interior, broken only by the black lacquer and gilded oversize furniture. Each room has a semicircular bed and original European objets d'art and Oriental rugs; some are more lavish than others. Although the hotel is not on the beach, there is a 114-foot swimming pool shaped like Jamaica. *Box 227, Port Antonio, tel. 809/993–2021 or 800/423–4095, fax 809/ 993–3459. 54 rooms, 5 suites, 20 junior suites. Facilities: restaurant, 2 bars, swimming pool, baby-sitters on request, boutique. AE, MC, V. EP, MAP. Moderate.*

Bonnie View Plantation Hotel. Though the main appeal of this property is to the budget, it does have a few nice rooms with private verandas overlooking spectacular scenery. Its restaurant atop a 600-foot hill offers the finest view of all. *Box 82, Port Antonio, tel. 809/ 993–2752 or 800/423–4095, fax 809/993–2862. 20 rooms. Facilities: restaurant, pool, sun deck. AE, DC, MC, V. EP. Inexpensive.*

DeMontevin Lodge. This historic place offers the ambience of a more genteel time. The rooms are basic and spotless, with circular fans overhead. Outsiders are welcome for very tasty home-cooking at lunch or dinner, with prior reservations. *Fort George St. on*

Titchfield Hill, Port Antonio, tel. 809/993–2604. 15 rooms. Facilities: restaurant, bar. AE. EP. Inexpensive.

Runaway Bay
★

FDR, Franklyn D. Resort. Jamaica's first all-suite, all-inclusive resort for families, this fabulous answer to parents' prayers opened in 1990. Upscale yet unpretentious, the pink buildings house spacious and well-thought-out one-, two-, and three-bedroom villas and are grouped in a horseshoe around the swimming pool. Best of all, a "girl Friday" comes with each suite, filling the role of nanny, housekeeper, and (when desired) cook. She'll even baby-sit at night for a small charge. Most parents are so impressed that they wish they could take their girl Friday home with them when they leave. Children and teens are kept busy with day-long supervised activities and sports, while parents are free to join in, lounge around the pool, play golf, go scuba diving, or just enjoy uninterrupted time together getting reacquainted. *Runaway Bay, tel. 809/973–3067 or 800/654–1FDR, fax 809/973–3071. 67 suites. Facilities: restaurant, pool, water sports including scuba diving, beach, gym, satellite TV, lighted tennis court, golf, disco, piano bar, miniclub for children with supervised activities, petting zoo, piano bar, beach across the street, glass-bottom-boat tour. AE, MC, V. All-inclusive. Expensive–Very Expensive.*

Jamaica, Jamaica. This all-inclusive was a pioneer in emphasizing the sheer Jamaican-ness of the island. The cooking is particularly first-rate, with an emphasis on Jamaican cuisine and fresh seafood. Lodgings are rather spartan, resembling tropical dorm rooms, but comfortable, with amenities that include hair dryers and safety deposit boxes. The happy campers don't mind; Germans, Italians, and Japanese flock here for the psychedelically colored reef surrounding the beach and the superb golf school (plans are afoot to make the already excellent course more challenging). Those seeking more upscale accommodations should request the beachfront one-bedroom suites, which were renovated in 1993. *Box 58, Runaway Bay, tel. 809/973–2436 or 800/859–7873, fax 809/973–2352. 238 rooms, 4 suites. Facilities: 2 restaurants, 2 bars, water-sports center, 2 lighted tennis courts, horseback riding, PADI 5-star dive center, gym, sundry shop, sightseeing tours, disco, nightly entertainment, 3 Jacuzzis, 18-hole golf course with golf school nearby. Guests must be over 16. AE, DC, MC, V. All-inclusive. Expensive.*

Club Caribbean. This resort reopened its doors in winter 1990 after a $3 million renovation and became all-inclusive in 1992, catering to families on a budget. A series of 128 typically Caribbean cottages, 68 with kitchenette, lines the long but narrow beach. The rooms are simple but clean, with rattan furnishings and floral prints. Very popular with European families (children under 7 stay free, and 60 cottages feature bunk beds instead of kitchenettes). While most water sports are included, scuba diving costs extra. *Box 65, Runaway Bay, tel. 809/973–3507 or 800/223–9815, fax 809/973–3509. 128 rooms. Facilities: 2 restaurants, pool, shopping arcade, PADI 5-star dive center, water-sports center, 2 tennis courts, massage and exercise, day-care center with children's program. AE, MC, V. All-inclusive. Inexpensive.*

H.E.A.R.T. Country Club. It's a shame more visitors don't know about this place, perched above Runaway Bay and brimming with Jamaica's true character. While training young islanders interested in the tourism industry—H.E.A.R.T. stands for Human Employment And Resource Training—it also provides a remarkably quiet and pleasant stay for guests. The employees make an effort to please. Accommodations have air-conditioning and private baths and either an ocean or garden view. The tranquil restaurant serves

Updated by
Joseph
Sponholz

Not for naught did the Arawaks name Martinique *Madinina*, which means "Island of Flowers." This is one of the most beautiful islands in the Caribbean, lush with exotic wild orchids, frangipani, anthurium, jade vines, flamingo flowers, and hundreds of vivid varieties of hibiscus. Trees bend under the weight of such tropical treats as mangoes, papayas, bright red West Indian cherries, lemons, limes, and bananas. Acres of banana plantations, pineapple fields, and waving green seas of sugarcane show the bounty of the island's fertile soil.

The towering mountains and verdant rain forest in the north lure hikers, while underwater sights and sunken treasures attract snorkelers and scuba divers. Martinique appeals as well to those whose idea of exercise is turning over every 10 or 15 minutes to get an even tan or whose adventuresome spirit is satisfied by finding booty in a duty-free shop. Francophiles in particular will find the island enchanting.

This 425-square-mile island, the largest of the Windward Islands, is 4,261 miles from Paris, but its spirit (and language) is French, with more than a mere soupçon of West Indian spice. Tangible, edible evidence of that fact is the island's cuisine—a tempting blend of classic French and Creole dishes.

Columbus sailed near Martinique in 1493, but it was not until his fourth voyage, in 1502, that he came ashore at Le Carbet. He paused long enough to remark, "My eyes would never tire of contemplating such vegetation," and to put ashore a number of goats to provide fresh meat for future visits. His eyes very quickly tired of the snakes he saw slithering about in his newfound Eden, so he weighed anchor and put water between him and them, never to return.

By the time Columbus made his way to Martinique, the cannibalistic Caribs had long since arrived on the island and eaten the Island of Flowers's Arawaks. Carib arrows kept outsiders at bay until 1635, when Pierre Belain d'Esnambuc, a Norman nobleman and adventurer, landed with a group of 100 settlers at the mouth of the Roxelane River. The French promised the Caribs the western half of the island, but instead polished them off and imported African slaves to work their sugarcane plantations.

By the mid-17th century, Martinique was an important sugar-producing island. Britain wanted to pluck the pearl away from the French, and the two nations fought over the island until the early 19th century. In 1815, the island was ceded by treaty to France, and French it has remained ever since.

Martinique became an overseas department of France in 1946 and a *région* in 1974, a status not unlike that of an American state vis-à-vis the federal government. The Martinicans vote in French national elections and have all the benefits of France's social and economic systems. The island is governed by a prefect who is appointed by the French minister of the interior. Martinique has one of the highest standards of living in the Caribbean.

Though the majority of tourists are from France, Martinique is encouraging North Americans to visit the island. Efforts are being made to teach taxi drivers a few important words in English; the tourist office has a number of free guide booklets written in English; and most hotels, restaurants, and shops have English-speaking staff.

Before You Go

Tourist Information — For information contact the **French West Indies Tourist Board** by calling France-on-Call at 900/990–0040 (50¢ per minute), or write to the **French Government Tourist Office,** 610 5th Ave., New York, NY 10020; 9454 Wilshire Blvd., Beverly Hills, CA 90212, tel. 310/271–2358; 676 N. Michigan Ave., Chicago, IL 60611, tel. 312/751–7800; 2305 Cedar Spring Rd., Dallas TX 75201, tel. 214/720–4010. In Canada contact the French Government Tourist Office, 1981 McGill College Ave., Suite 490, Montreal, Québec H3A 2W9, tel. 514/288–4264; or 1 Dundas St. W, Suite 2405, Toronto, Ontario M5G 1Z3, tel. 416/593–4723 or 800/361–9099. In the United Kingdom the tourist office can be reached at 178 Piccadilly, London, United Kingdom W1V 0AL, tel. 089/124–4123.

Arriving and Departing By Plane — The most frequent flights from the United States are on **American Airlines** (tel. 800/433–7300), which has year-round daily service from more than 100 U.S. cities to San Juan. From there, the airline's American Eagle flies on to Martinique with a stop first at Guadeloupe. **Air France** (tel. 800/237–2747) flies direct from Miami and San Juan; **Air Canada** (tel. 800/422–6232) has service from Montreal and Toronto; **LIAT** (tel. 809/462–0700), with its extensive coverage of the Antilles, flies in from Antigua, St. Maarten, Guadeloupe, Dominica, St. Lucia, Barbados, Grenada, and Trinidad and Tobago.

From the Airport — You'll arrive at Lamentin International Airport, which is about a 15-minute taxi ride from Fort-de-France and about 40 minutes from the Trois-Ilets peninsula, where most of the hotels are located.

Passports and Visas — U.S. and Canadian citizens must have a passport (an expired passport may be used as long as the expiration date is no more than five years ago) or proof of citizenship, such as an original (not photocopied) birth certificate or a voter registration card accompanied by a government-authorized photo identification. British citizens are required to have a passport. In addition, all visitors must have a return or ongoing ticket.

Language — Many Martinicans speak Creole, which is a mixture of Spanish and French. Try *sa ou fe* for hello. In major tourist areas you'll find someone who speaks English, but the courtesy of using a few French words, even if it is *Parlez-vous anglais*, is appreciated. The people of Martinique are extremely courteous and will help you through your French. Even if you do speak fluent French, you may have a problem understanding the accent of the country people. Most menus are written in French, so a dictionary is helpful.

Precautions — Exercise the same safety precautions you would in any other big city: Leave valuables in the hotel safe-deposit vault and lock your car, with luggage and valuables stashed out of sight. Also, don't leave jewelry or money unattended on the beach.

Beware of the *mancenillie* (manchineel) trees. These pretty trees with little green fruits that look like apples are poisonous. Sap and even raindrops falling from the trees onto your skin can cause painful, scarring blisters. The trees have red warning signs posted by the Forestry Commission.

If you plan to ramble through the rain forest, be careful where you step. Poisonous snakes, cousins of the rattlesnake, slither through this lush tropical Eden.

Except for the area around Cap Chevalier, the Atlantic waters are rough and should be avoided by all but expert swimmers.

Staying in Martinique

Important Addresses

Tourist Information: The **Martinique Tourist Office** (Blvd. Alfassa, tel. 596/63–79–60) is open Monday–Thursday 8:00–5:00, Friday 7:30–5:00, Saturday 8–noon. The Tourist Information Booth at Lamentin International Airport is open daily until the last flight has landed.

Emergencies

Police: Call 17. **Fire:** Call 18. **Ambulance:** Call 70–36–48 or 71–59–48. **Hospital:** There is a 24-hour emergency room at **Hôpital La Meynard** (Châteauboeuf, just outside Fort-de-France, tel. 596/55–20–00). **Pharmacies:** Pharmacies in Fort-de-France include **Pharmacie de la Paix** (corner rue Victor Schoelcher and rue Perrinon, tel. 596/71–94–83) and **Pharmacie Cypria** (Blvd. de Gaulle, tel. 596/63–22–25).

Currency

The coin of the realm is the French franc, which consists of 100 *centimes* (for example, the cost of an airmail stamp is 4.40F: 4 francs, 40 centimes). At press time, the rate was 5.86F to U.S. $1, but check the current exchange rate before you leave home. U.S. dollars are accepted in some of the tourist hotels, but for convenience, it's better to convert your money into francs. Banks give a more favorable rate than do hotels. A currency exchange service, **Change Caraibes,** is located at the Arrivals Building at Lamentin International Airport (tel. 596/51–57–91; open weekdays 7 AM–9:00 PM, Sat. 8:30–2) and at the Galerie des Flibustiers in Fort-de-France (tel. 596/60–28–40; open weekdays 8–7:00, Sat. 8:00–12:30, closed Sun.). Note: Prices quoted here are in U.S. dollars unless indicated otherwise.

Major credit cards are accepted in hotels and restaurants in Fort-de-France and the Pointe du Bout areas; few establishments in the countryside accept them. There is a 20% discount on luxury items paid for with traveler's checks or with certain credit cards.

Taxes and Service Charges

A resort tax varies from hotel to hotel; the maximum is $1.50 per person per day. Rates quoted by hotels usually include a 10% service charge; some hotels add 10% to your bill. All restaurants include a 15% service charge in their menu prices.

Guided Tours

For a personalized tour of the island, ask the tourist office to arrange a tour with an English-speaking taxi driver. There are set rates for tours to various points on the island, and if you share the ride with two or three other sightseers, the price will be whittled down.

Madinina Tours (tel. 596/61–49–49) offers half- and full-day jaunts, with lunch included in the all-day outings. Boat tours are also available, as are air excursions to the Grenadines and St. Lucia. Madinina has tour desks in most of the major hotels.

Parc Naturel Regional de la Martinique (Regional Nature Reserve, tel. 596/73–19–30) organizes inexpensive guided hiking tours year-round. Descriptive folders are available at the tourist office.

Getting Around

Taxis

Taxi stands are located at Lamentin International Airport, in downtown Fort-de-France, and at major hotels. They are expensive. Rates are regulated by the government, but local taxi drivers are an independent lot, and prices often turn out to be higher than the minimum "official" rate. The official rate is established at the beginning of each year and is listed in the tourist brochures, which you can get on your arrival at the tourist office at the airport. When taxi drivers overcharge, passengers have little recourse. You can either cause a fuss by contacting the police or show the driver the "officially quoted rate" in the brochure and hope that he accepts it. The cost from the airport to Fort-de-France is about 70F; from the airport to Pointe du

Bout, about 150F. A 40% surcharge is in effect between 8 PM and 6 AM. This means that if you arrive at Lamentin at night, depending on where your hotel is, it may be cheaper to rent a car from the airport and keep it for 24 hours than to take a one-way taxi to your hotel.

Buses Public buses and eight-passenger minivans (license plates bear the letters TC) are an inexpensive means of getting from point to point around the island. Buses are always crowded and are not recommended for the timid traveler. In Fort-de-France, the main terminal for the minivans is at Pointe Simon on the waterfront. There are frequent departures from early morning until 8 PM; fares range from $1 to $5.

Ferries Weather permitting, *vedettes* (ferries) operate daily between Fort-de-France and the Marina Méridien in Pointe du Bout and between Fort-de-France and Anse-Mitan and Anse-à-l'Ane. The Quai d'Esnambuc is the arrival and departure point in Fort-de-France. At press time, the one-way fare was 12F; round-trip, 20F. The trip takes 20 minutes.

The **Caribbean Express** (tel. 596/60–12–38) offers daily, scheduled interisland service aboard a 128-foot, 227-passenger motorized catamaran, linking Martinique with Guadeloupe and Dominica. Fares run approximately 25% below economy airfares.

Bicycles and Motorbikes Bikes and motorbikes can both be rented from **Vespa** (tel. 596/71–60–03), **Funny** (tel. 596/63–33–05), or **T. S. Location Sarl** (tel. 596/63–42–82), all of which are located in Fort-de-France.

Rental Cars Having a car will make your stay in Martinique much more pleasurable. You will be limited to the environs of your hotel otherwise, and most of the better beaches are away from the hotel complexes. Martinique has about 175 miles of well-paved and well-marked roads (albeit with international signs). Streets in Fort-de-France are narrow and clogged with traffic; country roads are mountainous with hairpin curves. The Martinicans drive with aggressive abandon, but are surprisingly courteous and will let you into the flow of traffic. When driving up-country, take along the free map supplied by the tourist office and you will have no trouble finding your way. If you want a detailed map, the *Carte Routière et Touristique* is available at bookstores. There are plenty of gas stations in the major towns, but a full tank of gas will get you all the way around the island with gallons to spare.

If you book a rental car from the United States at least 48 hours in advance, you can qualify for a hefty discount.

A valid driver's license is needed to rent a car for up to 20 days. After that, you'll need an International Driver's Permit. Major credit cards are accepted by most car-rental agents. Rates are about $60 per day (unlimited mileage). Lower daily rates with per-mile charges, which usually turn out to be higher overall rates, are sometimes available. Question agents closely. Among the many agencies are **Avis** (tel. 596/70–11–60 or 800/331–1212), **Budget** (tel. 596/63–69–00 or 800/527–0700), and **Hertz** (tel. 596/60–64–64 or 800/654–3131).

Telephones and Mail To call Martinique station-to-station from the United States, dial 011 plus 596 plus the local six-digit number.

It is not possible to make collect or credit calls from Martinique to the United States. There are few coin telephone booths on the island, and those are usually in hotels and restaurants. Most public telephones now use the Telecarte. Units are deducted from your card according to how long and far a phone call you make. Telecartes may be purchased from post offices, café-tabacs, and hotels. Long-distance calls made with Telecartes are less costly than are operator-assisted calls.

To place an interisland call, dial the local six-digit number. To call the United States from Martinique, dial 19–1, area code, and the local number. For Great Britain, dial 19–44, area code (without the first zero), and the number.

Airmail letters to the United States cost 4.40F for up to 20 grams; postcards, 3.80F. For Great Britain, the cost is 3.80F and 3.00F, respectively. Stamps may be purchased from post offices, café-tabacs, or hotel newsstands.

Opening and Closing Times Stores that cater to tourists are generally open weekdays 8:30–6; Saturday 8:30–1. Banking hours are weekdays 7:30–noon and 2:30–4.

Exploring Martinique

Numbers in the margin correspond to points of interest on the Martinique map.

The starting point of the tour is the capital city of Fort-de-France, where almost a third of the island's 320,000 people live. From here, we'll tour St-Pierre, Mont Pelée, and other points north; go along the Atlantic coast; and finish with a look at the sights in the south.

Fort-de-France **Fort-de-France** lies on the beautiful Baie des Flamands on the is-
❶ land's Caribbean (west) coast. With its narrow streets and pastel buildings with ornate wrought-iron balconies, the capital city is reminiscent of the French Quarter in New Orleans. However, where New Orleans is flat, Fort-de-France is hilly. Public and commercial buildings and residences cling to its hillsides behind downtown.

Stop first at the **tourist office**, which shares a building with Air France on the boulevard Alfassa, right on the bay near the ferry landing. English-speaking staffers provide excellent, free material, including detailed maps and an 18-page booklet in English with a series of seven self-drive tours that are well worth your while.

Thus armed, walk across the street to **La Savane.** The 12½-acre landscaped park is filled with gardens, tropical trees, fountains, and benches. It's a popular gathering place and the scene of promenades, parades, and impromptu soccer matches. A statue of Pierre Belain d'Esnambuc, leader of the island's first settlers, is upstaged by Vital Dubray's flattering white Carrara marble statue of the empress Joséphine, Napoléon's first wife. Sculpted in a high-waisted Empire gown, Joséphine gazes toward Trois-Ilets across the bay, where in 1763 she was born Marie-Joseph Tascher de la Pagerie. Near the harbor is a **marketplace** where high-quality local crafts are sold. On the edge of the Savane, you can catch the **ferry** for the beaches at Anse-Mitan and Anse-à-l'Ane and for the 20-minute run across the bay to the resort hotels of Pointe du Bout. The ferry is more convenient than a car for travel between Pointe du Bout and Fort-de-France.

Rue de la Liberté runs along the west side of La Savane. Look for the main post office (rue de la Liberté, between rue Blénac and rue Antoine Siger). Just across rue Blénac from the post office is the **Musée Departementale de Martinique,** which contains exhibits pertaining to the pre-Columbian Arawak and Carib periods. On display are pottery, beads, and part of a skeleton that turned up during ex-

Exploring

Ajoupa-Bouillon, **10**
Balata, **9**
Bellefontaine, **3**
Diamond Rock, **18**
Dubuc Castle, **15**
Forêt de
Montravail, **19**
Fort-de-France, **1**
La Trinité, **14**
Le Carbet, **4**
Le François, **23**
Le Morne Rouge, **8**
Le Prêcheur, **7**
Le Vauclin, **22**
Les Trois-Ilets, **16**
Leyritz Plantation, **11**
Macouba, **12**
Musée Gauguin, **5**
Petrified Forest, **21**
Pointe du Bout, **17**
St-Pierre, **6**
Ste-Anne, **20**
Ste-Marie, **13**
Schoelcher, **2**

Dining

Athanor, **68**
Auberge de la
Montagne Pelée, **28**
Aux Filets Bleus, **66**
Bambou
Restaurant, **45**
Bidjoul, **56**
Chez Gaston, **38**
Club Nautique, **42**
L'Ami Fritz, **30**
L'Amphore, **51**
La Biguine, **33**
La Dunette, **67**
La Factorérie, **29**
La Fontane, **35**
La Grand' Voile, **36**
La Matadore, **52**
La Petite
Auberge, **63**
La Villa Creole, **53**
Le Bristol, **34**
Le Colibri, **26**
Le Coq Hardi, **37**
Le Crew, **39**
Le Diam's, **58**
Le Lafayette, **41**
Le Verger, **44**
Leyritz Plantation, **25**
Relais Caraibes, **62**
Restaurant Chez
Mally, **24**
Tamarin Plage
Restaurant, **57**

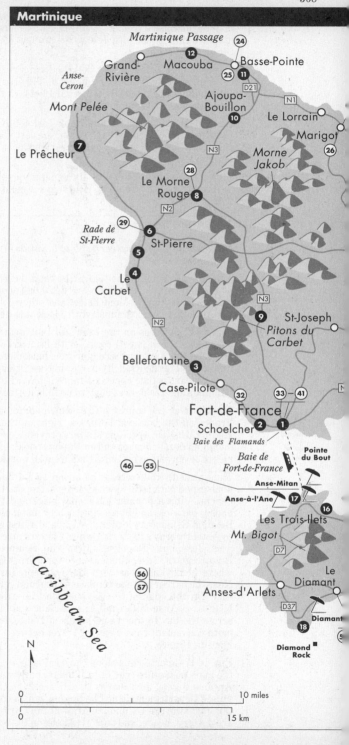

Martinique

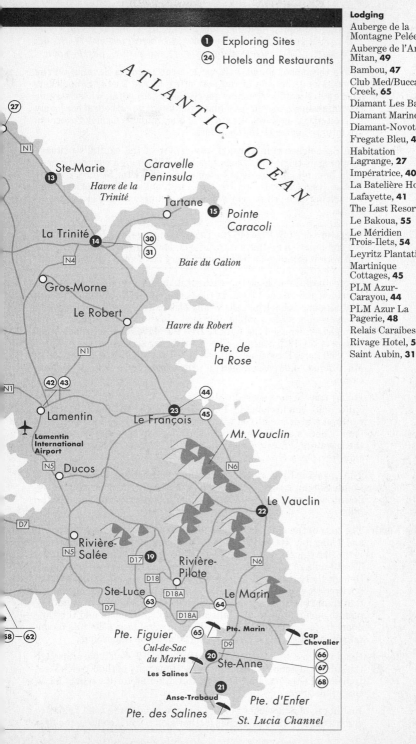

① Exploring Sites

㉔ Hotels and Restaurants

Lodging

Auberge de la Montagne Pelée, **28**

Auberge de l'Anse-Mitan, **49**

Bambou, **47**

Club Med/Buccaneer's Creek, **65**

Diamant Les Bains, **60**

Diamant Marine, **61**

Diamant-Novotel, **59**

Fregate Bleu, **47**

Habitation Lagrange, **27**

Impératrice, **40**

La Batelière Hotel, **32**

Lafayette, **41**

The Last Resort, **64**

Le Bakoua, **55**

Le Méridien Trois-Ilets, **54**

Leyritz Plantation, **25**

Martinique Cottages, **45**

PLM Azur-Carayou, **44**

PLM Azur La Pagerie, **48**

Relais Caraibes, **62**

Rivage Hotel, **50**

Saint Aubin, **31**

cavations in 1972. One exhibit examines the history of slavery; costumes, documents, furniture, and handicrafts from the island's colonial period are on display. *9 rue de la Liberté, tel. 596/71–57–05. Admission: 15F. Open weekdays 8:30–1 and 2:30–5, Sat. 9–noon.*

Leave the museum and walk west (away from La Savane) on rue Blénac along the side of the post office to rue Victor Schoelcher. There you'll see the Romanesque **St-Louis Cathedral,** whose steeple rises high above the surrounding buildings. The cathedral has lovely stained-glass windows. A number of Martinique's former governors are interred beneath the choir loft.

Rue Schoelcher runs through the center of the capital's primary shopping district, which consists of a six-block area bounded by rue de la République, rue de la Liberté, rue de Victor Severe, and rue Victor Hugo. Stores feature Paris fashions (at Paris prices) and French perfume, china, crystal, and liqueurs, as well as local handicrafts.

Time Out **Drugstore de la Galerie** (46 rue Ernest Duproge, tel. 596/73–90–85) is a combination restaurant, cafeteria, and tearoom, where you can rest your feet and get a light repast every day from 7 AM to midnight.

Three blocks north of the cathedral, make a right turn on rue Perrinon and go one block. At the corner of rue de la Liberté is the **Bibliothèque Schoelcher,** the wildly elaborate Byzantine-Egyptian-Romanesque–style public library. It's named after Victor Schoelcher, who led the fight to free the slaves in the French West Indies in the 19th century. The eye-popping structure was built for the 1889 Paris Exposition, after which it was dismantled, shipped to Martinique, and reassembled piece by ornate piece on its present location.

Follow rue Victor Severe five blocks west, just beyond the Hôtel de Ville, and you'll come to Place Jose-Marti. The **Parc Floral et Culturel** will acquaint you with the variety of exotic flora on this island. There's also an aquarium showing fish that can be found in these waters. *Place Jose-Marti, Sermac, tel. 596/71–66–25. Admission free. Open Mon.–Sat. 9–noon and 3–6.*

The Levassor River meanders through the park and joins the bay at **Pointe Simon,** where yachts can be chartered. The river divides the downtown area from the ritzy residential district of Didier in the hills.

The North The tour of the north is divided into two sections: a short day's trip and a long day's (even overnight) excursion. Martinique's "must do" is the drive north along the coast from Fort-de-France to St-Pierre. The 40-mile round-trip to St-Pierre can be made in an afternoon, although there is enough to see to fill an entire day. The drive to the north coast will appeal primarily to nature lovers, hikers, and mountain climbers. If you are interested in climbing Mont Pelée or hiking, plan to spend at least a night on the road (*see* Sports and the Outdoors, *below,* for guided hikes). Bear in mind that a 20-mile mountain drive takes longer than driving 20 miles on the prairie.

Tour 1 Head west out of Fort-de-France on Route N2. You'll pass through
❷ the suburb of **Schoelcher,** home of the University of the French West Indies and Guyana. La Batelière Hotel, noted for its sports facilities, is also here.

Just north of Schoelcher is Fond-Lahaye, where the road begins to climb sharply. About 4½ miles farther along, you'll come to the fishing village of **Case-Pilote,** named after a Carib chief to whom the French took kindly and called Pilote.

③ Continuing along the coastal road, you'll see red-roof houses clinging to the green mountainside on the way to **Bellefontaine,** 4 miles north. This is another fishing village, with pastel houses on the hillsides and colorful *gommier* canoes (fishing boats made from the gum tree) bobbing in the water. One of the houses here is built in the shape of a boat.

④ Continue north along the coast until you get to **Le Carbet.** Columbus is believed to have landed here on June 15, 1502. In 1635, Pierre Belain d'Esnambuc arrived here with the first French settlers.

Le Carbet is home to the **Zoo de Carbet,** also called the Amazona Zoo, which features animals from the Caribbean, Amazonas, and Africa, including rare birds, snakes, wildcats, and caimans. *Le Coin, Le Carbet, tel. 596/78–00–64. Admission: 15F adults, 10F children. Open daily 9–6.*

Just north of Carbet is **Anse-Turin,** where Paul Gauguin lived for a short time in 1887 with his friend and fellow artist, Charles Laval. ⑤ The **Musée Gauguin** traces the history of the artist's Martinique connection through documents, letters, and reproductions of some of the paintings he did while on the island. There is also a display of Martinican costumes and headdresses. *Anse Turin Le Carbet, tel. 596/78–22–66. Admission: 10F. Open daily 10–5.*

⑥ **St-Pierre,** the island's oldest city, now has a population of about 6,000. At the turn of this century, St-Pierre was a flourishing city of 30,000 and was called the Paris of the West Indies. In spring 1902, Mont Pelée began to rumble and spit out ash and steam. By the first week in May, all wildlife had wisely vacated the area. City officials, however, ignored the warnings, needing voters in town for an upcoming election. At 8 AM on May 8, 1902, the volcano erupted, belching forth a cloud of burning ash with temperatures over 3,600°F. In the space of three minutes, Mont Pelée transformed the Paris of the West Indies into Martinique's Pompeii. The entire town was destroyed, and its inhabitants were instantly calcified. There was only one survivor, a prisoner named Siparis, who was saved by the thick walls of his underground cell. (He was later pardoned and for some years afterward was a sideshow attraction at the Barnum & Bailey Circus.) You can wander through the site to see the ruins of the island's first church, built in 1640; the theater; the toppled statues; and Siparis's cell.

The **Musée Vulcanologique** was established in 1932 by American volcanologist Franck Perret. His collection includes photographs of the old town, documents, and a number of relics excavated from the ruins, including molten glass, melted iron, and contorted clocks stopped at 8 AM, the time of the disaster. *St-Pierre, tel. 596/78–15–16. Admission: 10F adults, 5F children. Open daily 9–5.*

In St-Pierre, Route N2 turns inland toward Morne Rouge, but before going there, you may want to follow the coastal road 8 miles ⑦ north to **Le Prêcheur.** En route, you'll pass what is called the Tomb of the Carib Indians. The site is actually a formation of limestone hills from which the last of the Caribs are said to have flung themselves to avoid capture by the French. The village of Le Prêcheur was the childhood home of Françoise d'Aubigné, later to become the Marquise de Maintenon and the second wife of Louis XIV.

⑧ Return to St-Pierre and drive 4 miles east on Route N2 to reach **Le Morne Rouge.** Lying on the southern slopes of Mont Pelée, the town of Morne Rouge, too, was destroyed by the volcano. It is now a popular resort spot, with spectacular mountain scenery. This is the starting point for a climb up the 4,600-foot mountain, but you must have a guide (*see* Sports and the Outdoors, *below*).

At this point, you have the option of returning to Fort-de-France or continuing on for a tour of the north and Atlantic coasts.

If you choose to return to the capital, take the Route de la Trace (Rte. N3) south from Le Morne Rouge. The winding, two-lane paved road is one of the island's great drives, snaking through dense tropical rain forests.

⑨ La Trace leads to **Balata,** where you can see the **Balata Church,** an exact replica of Sacré-Coeur Basilica in Paris, and the **Jardin de Balata** (Balata Gardens). Jean-Philippe Thoze, a professional landscaper and devoted horticulturist, spent 20 years creating this collection of thousands of varieties of tropical flowers and plants. There are shaded benches where you can relax and take in the panoramic views of the mountains. *Rte. de Balata, tel. 596/72–58–82. Admission: 30F adults, 10F children. Open daily 9–5.*

From Balata, Route N3 continues 8 miles south to the capital city.

If you've opted to continue exploring the north and Atlantic coasts, take Route N3 north from Morne Rouge. You'll pass through Petite Savane and wind northeast to the flower-filled village of **⑩** **Ajoupa-Bouillon,** a 17th-century settlement in the midst of pineapple fields.

A mile and a half east of Ajoupa-Bouillon, Route N3 dead-ends at Route 1, which runs north–south. Turn left and drive 3 miles through sugarcane, pineapple, and banana fields to **Basse-Pointe,** which lies at sea level on the Atlantic coast. Just before reaching Basse-Pointe you'll pass a Hindu temple, one of the relics of the East Indians who settled in this area in the 19th century. The view of the eastern slope of Mont Pelée is lovely from here.

On the approach to Basse-Pointe, you'll see a small road (D21) off to **⑪** the left. This road leads to the estimable **Leyritz Plantation,** which has been a hotel for several years. Guests have the questionable pleasure of staying in the converted slave cabins. Recently, the property was acquired by new owners, who have expanded the tourist attractions to include a boutique, conference/seminar dining room, and spa-fitness center. When tour groups from the cruise ships are not swarming over the property, the rustic setting, complete with sugarcane factory and gardens, is delightful. Visit the plantation's **Musée de Poupées Végétales,** which contains a collection of exotic "doll sculptures," in which a local plant is shaped into a figurine. The creative results, which depict famous women of French history, are made entirely of plants and leaves. They are the work of local artisan Will Fenton. *Musée de Poupées Végétales, Leyritz Plantation, tel. 596/78–53–92. Admission: 15F. Open daily 7–5:30.*

⑫ Three miles along, you'll come to **Macouba** on the coast. From here, the island's most spectacular drive leads 6 miles to **Grand-Rivière,** on the northernmost point. Perched on high cliffs, this village affords magnificent views of the sea, the mountains, and, on clear days, the neighboring island of Dominica. From Grand-Rivière, you can trek 11 miles on a well-marked path that leads through lush tropical vegetation to the beach at Anse-Ceron on the northwest coast. The beach is lovely and the diving is excellent, but the currents are very strong and swimming is not advised.

Time Out Stop in at **Chez Vava** (Rte. 1 on the eastern edge of Grand-Rivière, tel. 596/55–72–72) for a rum punch and a lunch of seafood and Creole dishes including an excellent fish soup and a tasty fricassee of crayfish.

From Grand-Rivière, backtrack 13 miles to the junction of Routes N1 and N3.

From the junction, continue 10 miles on Route 1 along the Atlantic coast, driving through the villages of Le Lorrain and Marigot to ⑬ **Ste-Marie**, a town of about 20,000 Martinicans and the commercial capital of the island's north. There is a lovely mid-19th-century church in the town and, on a more earthy note, a rum distillery.

The **Musée du Rhum**, operated by the St. James Rum Distillery, is housed in a graceful galleried Creole house. Guided tours of the museum take in displays of the tools of the trade and include a visit to the distillery. And, yes, you may sample the product. *Ste-Marie, tel. 596/69–30–02. Admission free. Open weekdays 9–6, weekends 9–1.*

⑭ **La Trinité**, a northern subprefecture, is 6 miles to the south in a sheltered bay. From La Trinité, the **Caravelle Peninsula** thrusts 8 miles into the Atlantic Ocean. Much of the peninsula is under the auspices of the Regional Nature Reserve and offers places for trekking, swimming, and sailing. This is the home of the **Morne Pavilion**, an open-air sports and leisure center operated by the nature reserve (*see* Sports and the Outdoors, *below*). To reach it, turn right before Tartane on the Spoutourne Morne Pavilion road. Tartane has a popular beach with cool Atlantic breezes. Across the road from the brown-gold sand are numerous local restaurants, including **Le Dubuc** (tel. 596/58–60–81) for good Creole food and the **Madras Hotel and Restaurant** (tel. 596/58–33–95) for air-conditioned comfort, good dining, and clean comfortable lodging.

At the eastern tip of the peninsula, you can root through the ruins of ⑮ the **Dubuc Castle.** This was the home of the Dubuc de Rivery family, who owned the peninsula in the 18th century. According to legend, young Aimée Dubuc de Rivery was captured by Barbary pirates, sold to the Ottoman Empire, became a favorite of the sultan, and gave birth to Mahmud II.

Return to La Trinité and take Route N4, which winds about 15 miles through lush tropical scenery to Lamentin. There you can pick up Route N1 to Fort-de-France or Route N5 to D7 and the southern resort areas.

Tour 2 The loop through the south is a round-trip of about 100 miles. This excursion will include the birthplace of the empress Joséphine, Pointe du Bout and its resort hotels, a few small museums, and many large beaches. You can spend an afternoon, a day, or a couple of weeks exploring this region, depending on the time at your disposal and your frame of mind.

From Fort-de-France, take Route N1 to Route N5, which leads south through Lamentin, where the airport is located. A 20-mile drive will bring you to Rivière-Salée, where you'll make a right turn ⑯ on Route D7 and drive 4½ miles to the village of **Les Trois-Ilets.**

Time Out **Euromarche** (Lamentin) is one of the most complete supermarkets in the Western Hemisphere. For under $15, two of you can stagger out with hot French breads, pâtés, cheeses, and salmon flown in from Europe. Add some Creole boudin from the deli counter and a chilled bottle of wine or the local dark Rhum St. James, and have a gourmet picnic. *Closed Sun.*

Les Trois-Ilets, named after the three rocky islands nearby, is a lovely little village with a population of about 3,000. It's known for its pottery, straw, and wood works and as the birthplace of Napoléon's Empress Joséphine. On the village square, you can visit the simple church where she was baptized Marie-Joseph Tascher de la Pagerie. To reach the museum and the old sugar plantation on which she was born, drive a mile west on Route D7 and turn left on Route D38.

A stone building that held the kitchen of the estate is now home to the **Musée de la Pagerie.** (The main house blew down in the hurricane of 1766, when Joséphine was three.) It contains an assortment of memorabilia pertaining to Joséphine's life and loves (she was married at 16 in an arranged marriage to Alexandre de Beauharnais). There are family portraits; documents, including a marriage certificate; a love letter written to her in 1796 by Napoleon; and various antique furnishings, including the bed she slept in as a child. *Trois-Ilets, tel. 596/68–38–34. Admission: 15F adults, 3F children. Open Tues.–Sun. 9–5.*

The **Maison de la Canne** will teach you everything you ever wanted to know about sugarcane. Exhibits take you through three centuries of sugarcane production, with displays of tools, scale models, engravings, and photographs. *Trois-Ilets, tel. 596/68–32–04. Admission: 15F. Open Tues.–Sun. 9–5:30.*

17 You can reach **Pointe du Bout** and the beach at **Anse-Mitan** by turning right on Route D38 west of Trois-Ilets and just past the **Golf de Impératrice Joséphine** (a golf course). This area is filled with resort hotels, among them the Bakoua and the Méridien. The Pointe du Bout marina is a colorful spot where a whole slew of boats are tied up. The ferry to Fort-de-France leaves from this marina. More than anywhere else on Martinique, Pointe du Bout caters to the vacationer. A cluster of boutiques, ice-cream parlors, and rental-car agencies forms the hub from which restaurants and hotels of varying caliber radiate. If you are looking for resort life and action, what little there is in Martinique will be found here.

When you return to Route D7, turn right and head west. Less than five miles down the road you will reach **Anse-à-l'Ane,** where there is a pretty white-sand beach complete with picnic tables. There are also numerous small restaurants and inexpensive guest-house hotels for the budget traveler.

South from Anse-à-l'Ane, Route D7 turns into a 10-mile roller coaster en route to **Anse-d'Arlets,** a quiet backwater fishing village. You'll see fishermen's nets strung up on the beach to dry and pleasure boats on the water. In recent years, the activity has centered on the restaurants and small shops lining the shore. The popular gathering spot for Sunday brunch is **Ti Sable** (tel. 596/68–62–44), a restaurant on the beach at the northern edge of the village that offers a fixed menu at 180F. Another good place, especially to view the sunsets, is **Bidjoul** in the center of the village (*see* Dining, *below*).

From the center of town, take Route D37 along the coast down to Morne Larcher and on to **Le Diamant.** The road—narrow, twisting, and hilly—offers some of the best shoreline views in Martinique. Be sure to pull to the side at a scenic spot from which you can stare out **18** at **Diamond Rock,** a mile or two offshore.

In 1804, during the squabbles over possession of the island between the French and the English, the latter commandeered the rock, armed it with cannons, christened it HMS *Diamond Rock*, and proceeded to use it as a warship. For almost a year and a half, the British held the rock, bombarding any French ships that came along. The French got wind of the fact that the British were getting cabin fever on their isolated ship-island and arranged a supply of barrels of rum for those on the rock. The French easily overpowered the inebriated sailors, ending one of the most curious engagements in naval history.

Le Diamant is a small, friendly village with a little fruit-and-vegetable market on its town square. Next to the town square is **Longchamp** (tel. 596/76–25–47), an ice-cream/pizza restaurant (a more elaborate menu is offered in the second-floor dining room), but the adventurous will want to cross the street and enter a dark, wood-tabled bar called **Maully's** (no tel.). You'll be the only tourist here, but by your second *'ti punch*, the locals will warm to you. This town also offers the reasonable and accommodating **Diamant Les Bains** hotel.

Just out of town, heading toward Rivière-Salée, you'll see on the right-hand side a small shop, **Atelier Ceramique** (tel. 596/76–42–65), that sells ceramics. The owners and talented artists, David and Jeannine England, have lived in the Caribbean for more than a decade and are members of the small British expatriate community on the island. Whether or not you like their products—ceramics, paintings, and miscellaneous souvenirs—it's a rare chance to brush up on your English.

A mile farther along the road to Rivière-Salée is the turnoff for the **Diamant-Novotel**, the **Diamant Marine** hotel, and the **Relais Caraibes** (tel. 596/76–44–65), one of Martinique's better dining establishments.

Back on the road (D7), it's about 5 miles to the junction of the island's main highway to the south (N5). If you go to the north, you'll be back in Fort-de-France within a half hour. Instead, go south along the coast.

Some 10 miles down the coastline lies **Ste-Luce,** another fishing village with a pretty white beach. From Ste-Luce, you can take Route D17 north 1 mile to the **Forêt de Montravail,** where arrows point the way to Carib rock drawings.

Time Out **La Vogue du Sud** (rue Schoelcher, Ste-Luce, tel. 596/62–44–96) is an unpretentious little eatery serving seafood.

The recent repaving and straightening of the highway can quickly take you through to Ste-Anne, or you can say good-bye to Route D7 in Ste-Luce and hook up with Route D18, which will take you northeast 4 miles to **Rivière-Pilote,** a town of about 12,000 people. From there, Route D18A trickles down south to **Pointe Figuier,** where the scuba diving is excellent. Stay with Route D18A and curve around the beautiful Cul-de-Sac inlet through **Le Marin.** Just east of Le Marin, turn right on Route D9 and drive all the way down to the sea. En route you'll pass the turnoff to Buccaneer's Creek/Club Med and the pretty village of **Ste-Anne,** where a Roman Catholic church sits on the square facing a lovely white beach. Not far away, at the southernmost tip, is the island's best beach, **Les Salines.** It's 1½ miles of soft white sand, calm waters, and relative seclusion (except on weekends).

In sharp contrast to the north, this section of the island is dry. The soil does not hold moisture for long. A rutted track—suitable for vehicles but not for queasy stomachs—leads all the way to **Pointe des Salines** and slightly beyond. The gnarled, stubby trees have given **㉑** the area the name **Petrified Forest,** in part because the sight is unexpected in a place known as the Island of Flowers.

Though there is a restaurant, **Aux Delices de la Mer** (tel. 596/62–50–12), near the point facing the channel that separates Martinique from St. Lucia, many people bring their own refreshments and picnic in the shade of the palms.

Backtrack 9 miles to Le Marin. The adventuresome should take a detour a mile before reaching town. Take the small road on your right that leads to **Cap Chevalier.** After less than 2 miles, the road forks. The road to the left dead-ends at a small community and does not justify the 4 miles of driving. The fork to the right, however, runs for about 4 miles to a tiny cove with five or six one-man fishing boats and racks where the fishermen dry their nets. The scene is definitely worth a photograph. Facing the cove is a small Creole restaurant, the **Gracieuse** (tel. 596/76–93–10). Choose the terrace and order the catch of the day or a grilled lobster. The cooking is quite good; this remains one of the undiscovered bargains on Martinique.

If you retrace your steps for half a mile, you will come to a turnoff on the right. Less than a mile down this road there is a long, empty beach that rarely has more than four or five couples taking sun and a cool dip in the Atlantic waters.

To get out of Cap Chevalier, you must go back toward Le Marin. On the outskirts of Le Marin, Route N6 branches off to the right and **㉒** goes north 7 miles to **Le Vauclin,** skirting the highest point in the south, **Mt. Vauclin** (1,654 feet). Le Vauclin is an important fishing port on the Atlantic coast, and the return of the fishermen shortly before noon each day is a big event.

㉓ Continue north 9 miles on Route N6 to **Le François,** a sizable city of some 16,000 Martinicans. This is a great place for snorkeling. Offshore are a number of shallow basins with white-sand bottoms between the reefs.

There is a lovely bay 6 miles farther along at **Le Robert.** You'll also come to the junction of Route N1, which will take you west to Fort-de-France, 12½ miles away.

Beaches

All Martinique's beaches are open to the public, but hotels charge a fee for nonguests to use changing rooms and facilities. There are no official nudist beaches, but topless bathing is prevalent at the large resort hotels. Unless you're an expert swimmer, steer clear of the Atlantic waters, except in the area of Cap Chevalier and the Caravelle Peninsula. The soft, white-sand beaches begin south of Fort-de-France and continue; to the north the beaches are made up of hard-packed gray volcanic sand.

The soft white beaches of **Pointe du Bout** are man-made, superb, and lined with luxury resorts, among them the Méridien and the Bakoua.

Anse-Mitan was created by Mother Nature, who placed it just to the south of Pointe du Bout and sprinkled it with white sand. The waters around this beach offer superb snorkeling opportunities. Small, family-owned bistros are half hidden in palm trees nearby.

On the beach at **Anse-à-l'Ane,** you can spread your lunch on a picnic table, browse through the nearby shell museum, and cool off in the bar of the Le Calalou hotel.

Diamant, the island's longest beach (2½ miles), has a splendid view of Diamond Rock, but the waters are sometimes rough and the currents are strong. This area is home to the Diamant-Novotel, Diamant Les Bains, Diamant Marine, and Relais Caraibes hotels.

Anse-Trabaud is on the Atlantic side, across the southern tip of the island from Ste-Anne. There is nothing here but white sand and the sea.

Les Salines is a 1½-mile cove of soft white sand lined with coconut palms. A short drive south of Ste-Anne, Les Salines is awash with families and children during holidays and on weekends, but quiet and uncrowded during the week—even at the height of the winter season. This beach, especially the far end, is the most peaceful and beautiful. Take along a picnic, including plenty of liquids; there is only one restaurant, Aux Delices de la Mer (tel. 596/62–50–12), close to Pointe des Salines.

Near Les Salines, **Pointe Marin** stretches north from Ste-Anne. A good windsurfing and waterskiing spot, it also has restaurants, campsites, sanitary facilities, and a 10F admission charge. Club Med occupies the northern edge, and Ste-Anne, with several good restaurants, is near at hand.

Sports and the Outdoors

Bicycling The **Parc Naturel Regional de la Martinique** (tel. 596/64–42–59) has designed biking itineraries off the beaten track. Bikes can be rented from **Funny** (tel. 596/63–33–05) and **T. S. Location Sarl** (tel. 596/63–42–82), both in Fort-de-France. In Ste-Luce, try **Marquis Moto** (no tel.). Mountain biking is popular in mainland France. Now it has reached Martinique. VTT (Vélo Tout Terrain) bikes specially designed with 18 speeds to handle all terrains may be rented from **V.T.Tilt** (Anse-Mitan, tel. 596/66–01–01).

Boating For boat rentals and yacht charters, check with **Ship Shop** (6 rue Joseph-Compère, Fort-de-France, tel. 596/71–43–40), **Carib Charter** (Habitation Croix du Sud, Pointe de Jaham, Schoelcher, tel. 596/73–08–80), **Soleil et Voile** (Marina Pointe du Bout, tel. 596/66–07–74 or 596/66–07–87), **Caraibes Nautique** (Le Bakoua, Trois-Ilets, tel. 596/66–06–06), **Captains Shop** (Marina Pointe du Bout, tel. 596/66–06–77), and **Somatour** (14 rue Blénac, tel. 596/71–31–68).

Deep-Sea Fishing Fish cruising these waters include tuna, barracuda, dolphin, kingfish, and bonito. For a day's outing on the 37-foot *Egg Harbor*, with gear and breakfast included, contact **Bathy's Club** (Méridien, tel. 596/66–00–00). Charters of up to five days can be arranged on Captain Réné Alaric's 37-foot *Rayon Vert* (Auberge du Vare, Case-Pilote, tel. 596/78–80–56).

Golf At **Golf de l'Impératrice Joséphine** (tel. 596/68–32–81) there is an 18-hole Robert Trent Jones course with an English-speaking pro, fully equipped pro shop, a bar, and restaurant. Located at Trois-Ilets, a mile from the Pointe du Bout resort area and 18 miles from Fort-de-France, the club offers special greens fees for hotel guests and cruise-ship passengers.

Hiking Inexpensive guided excursions are organized year-round by the Parc Naturel Regional de la Martinique (Regional Nature Reserve, Caserne Bouille, Fort-de-France, tel. 596/73–19–30).

Horseback Riding Excursions and lessons are available at **Ranch Jack** (near Anse-d'Arlets, tel. 596/68-37-67), the **Black Horse Ranch** (near La Pagerie in Trois-Ilets, tel. 596/68-37-80), and **La Cavale** (near Diamant on the road to the Novotel hotel, tel. 596/76-22-94).

Sailing Hobie Cats, Sunfish, and Sailfish can be rented by the hour from hotel beach shacks. Also check **Club Nautique du Marin** (tel. 596/74-92-48), **Cercle Nautique de Schoelcher** (Anse Madame, tel. 596/61-15-21), **Hotel Frantel** (tel. 596/66-04-04), and **ATM Yachts** (Club Nautique du Marin, tel. 596/74-98-17; in the U.S., tel. 909/678-2250 or 800/227-5317).

Scuba Diving To explore the old shipwrecks, coral gardens, and other undersea sites, you must have a medical certificate and insurance papers. Among the island's dive operators are **CSCP** (Le Port, Case-Pilote, tel. 596/78-73-75), **Cressma** (Fort-de-France, tel. 596/61-34-36), **Bathy's Club** (Méridien, tel. 596/66-00-00), **Planete Bleue** (La Marina, Trois-Ilets, tel. 596/66-08-79), **Sub Diamant Rock** (Novotel, tel. 596/76-42-42), and **Oxygene Bleu** (Longpre, Lamentin, tel. 596/50-25-78).

Sea Excursions and Snorkeling The *Aquarium* (Fort-de-France, tel. 596/61-49-49) is a glass-bottom boat that does excursions. For information on other sailing, swimming, snorkeling, and beach picnic trips, contact **Affaires Maritimes** (tel. 596/71-90-05).

Sports Center The **Morne Pavilion** (tel. 596/73-19-30), on the Caravelle Peninsula, is an open-air sports and leisure center offering sailing, tennis, and other activities.

Tennis In addition to its links, the **Golf de l'Impératrice Joséphine** (Trois-Ilets, tel. 596/68-32-82) has three lighted tennis courts. There are also two courts at the **Le Bakoua** (tel. 596/66-02-02); six courts at **La Batelière Hotel** (tel. 596/61-49-49); seven courts at **Buccaneer's Creek/Club Med** (tel. 596/76-74-52); two courts at **Diamant-Novotel** (tel. 596/76-42-42); one court at the **Leyritz Plantation** (tel. 596/78-53-92); and two courts at the **Méridien Hotel** (tel. 596/66-00-00). Other hotels with tennis courts are **Hotel PLM Azur Carayou** (tel. 596/66-04-04), **Le Calalou** (tel. 596/68-31-67), **Relais Caraibes** (tel. 596/74-44-65), **La Caravelle** (tel. 596/58-37-32), **Diamant Bleu** (tel. 596/76-42-15), **Rivage Hotel** (tel. 596/66-00-53), **La Margelle** (tel. 596/76-40-19), and **Brise Marine** (tel. 596/62-46-94). For additional information about tennis on the island, contact **La Ligue Regionale de Tennis** (Petit Manoir, Lamentin, tel. 596/51-08-00).

Shopping

French fragrances and designer scarves, fine china and crystal, leather goods, and liquors and liqueurs are all good buys in Fort-de-France. Purchases are further sweetened by the 20% discount on luxury items when paid for by traveler's checks and major credit cards. Among local items, look for Creole gold jewelry, such as loop earrings, heavy bead necklaces, and slave bracelets; white and dark rum; and handcrafted straw goods, pottery, and tapestries. In addition, U.S. Customs allows you to bring some of the local flora into the country.

Shopping Areas The area around the cathedral in Fort-de-France has a number of small shops carrying luxury items. Of particular note are the shops on **rue Victor Hugo, rue Moreau de Jones, rue Antoine Siger,** and **rue Lamartine.** There is also a duty-free shop at the airport. On the outskirts of Fort-de-France, shopping malls include **Centre Commer-**

cial de Cluny, **Centre Commercial de Dillon, Centre Commercial de Bellevue,** and more than 60 boutiques at **La Galleria** in Le Lamentin.

Good Buys Look for Lalique, Limoges, and Baccarat at **Cadet Daniel** (72 rue
China and Antoine Siger, Fort-de-France, tel. 596/71–41–48) and **Roger Albert**
Crystal (7 rue Victor Hugo, Fort-de-France, tel. 596/71–71–71).

Flowers Anthuriums, torch lilies, and lobster claws are packaged for shipment at **MacIntosh** (31 rue Victor Hugo, Fort-de-France, tel. 596/70–09–50, and at the airport, tel. 596/51–51–51) and **Les Petites Floralies** (75 rue Blénac, Fort-de-France, tel. 596/71–66–16).

Local The **Galerie d'Art** (89 rue Victor Hugo, tel. 596/63–10–62) has some
Handicrafts unusual and excellent Haitian art—paintings, sculptures, ceramics, and intricate jewelry cases—at reasonable prices.

Perfumes Dior, Chanel, and Guerlain are among the popular scents at **Roger Albert** (7 rue Victor Hugo, Fort-de-France, tel. 596/71–71–71). Airport minishops sell the most popular scents at in-town prices, so there's no need to carry purchases around.

Rum Rum can be purchased at the various distilleries, including **Duquesnes** (Fort-de-France, tel. 596/71–91–68), **St. James** (Ste-Marie, tel. 596/69–30–02), and **Trois Rivières** (Ste-Luce, tel. 596/62–51–78).

Dining

It used to be argued that Martinique had the best food in all the Caribbean, but many believe this top-ranking position has been lost to some of the other islands of the French West Indies—Guadeloupe, St. Barts, even St. Martin. Nevertheless, Martinique remains an island of restaurants serving classic French cuisine and Creole dishes, its wine cellars filled with fine French wines. Some of the best restaurants are tucked away in the countryside, and therein lies a problem. The farther you venture from tourist hotels, the less likely you are to find English-speaking folk. But that shouldn't stop you from savoring the countryside cuisine. The local Creole specialties are *colombo* (curry), *accras* (cod or vegetable fritters), *crabes farcis* (stuffed land crab), *écrevisses* (freshwater crayfish), *boudin* (Creole blood sausage), *lambi* (conch), *langouste* (clawless Caribbean lobster), *soudons* (sweet clams), and *oursin* (sea urchin). The local favorite libation is *le 'ti punch*, a "little punch," concocted of four parts white rum, one part sugarcane syrup (some people like a little more syrup), and a squeeze of lime.

As in Guadeloupe, people dress for dinner in casual resort wear. Men don't wear a jacket, but do sport a new shirt bought for their vacation. Women wear dresses that show off their suntan, but fashion here is practical not Parisian.

Highly recommended restaurants are indicated by a star ★.

Category	Cost*
Expensive	over $50
Moderate	$30–$50
Inexpensive	under $30

**per person, excluding drinks*

Anse-d'Arlets **Tamarin Plage Restaurant.** The lobster *vivier* in the middle of the room gives you a clue to the specialty here, but there are other recommendable offerings as well. Fish soup or Creole boudin are good starters, then consider court bouillon, chicken fricassee, and curried mutton. The beachfront bar is a popular local hangout. *Anse-d'Arlets, tel. 596/68–67–88. Reservations accepted. No credit cards. Moderate.*

Bidjoul. The small side street off the main road is Anse-d'Arlets's main drag, with numerous modest restaurants on either side. The latest addition is the small Bidjoul, with tables on the sand under a canopy and across the road a tiny indoor dining room. The salads are huge and the grilled fish as fresh as could be. So, too, is the fish at the neighboring restaurants, but the enthusiasm of the owner makes this one stand out and become the popular gathering spot to watch the sun set into the Caribbean Sea. *Anse-d'Arlets, tel. 596/ 68–65–28. No reservations. MC, V. Inexpensive.*

Anse-Mitan/ Pointe du Bout

La Matadore. Fresh flowers adorn each table in this simply furnished terrace restaurant. Creole boudin, quiche, or sea urchins are good for openers. Main dishes include turtle steak, Creole bouillabaisse, lobster thermidor, and fillet of beef with port wine and mushrooms. This pretty restaurant with checkered tablecloths would be more enjoyable if it had a view of the sea instead of the road and the Bambou Hotel. *Anse-Mitan, tel. 596/66–05–36. Reservations suggested in high season. AE, DC, MC, V. Closed Wed. Moderate.*

L'Amphore. Dining is either on the front terrace, where there's a nice view of the bay, or in a gas-lit garden. Lobster, selected from a tank, is the menu's highlight, but there are Creole specialties and classic French dishes as well. During dinner, a guitarist strums and sings in several languages. *Anse-Mitan, tel. 596/66–03–09. Reservations accepted. MC, V. Closed Mon. No lunch Tues. Moderate.*

★ **La Villa Creole.** The steak béarnaise, curries, conch, court bouillon, and other dishes are all superb. However, the real draw here is owner Guy Dawson, a popular singer and guitarist who entertains during dinner, either solo or en duo with Roland Manere or Guy Vadeleux. The setting is romantic, with oil lamps flickering in the lush back garden of this very popular place. *Anse-Mitan, tel. 596/ 66–05–53. Reservations essential. AE, DC, V. No lunch. Closed Sun. Moderate.*

Bambou Restaurant. This casual place, right on the beach, serves omelets and salads, as well as lamb cutlets, curried chicken, steak au poivre, codfish pie, and sole meunière. For dessert there's coconut flan or banana or pineapple flambé. *Bambou Hotel, Anse-Mitan, tel. 596/66–01–39. Reservations accepted. AE, DC, MC, V. Inexpensive.*

Basse-Pointe
★

Leyritz Plantation. The pride of Martinique is *the* place all the cruise passengers head to as soon as they disembark. The restored 18th-century plantation has the ambience of a country inn and a dramatic view of Mont Pelée. The menu is mostly Creole, featuring boudin, chicken with coconut, and several curried dishes. *Basse-Pointe, tel. 596/78–53–92. Reservations essential. DC, MC V. Moderate–Expensive.*

Restaurant Chez Mally. Unpretentious and popular, Mally Edjam's home has a few tables inside and only four on the side porch under an awning. The lady is a legend on the island, and you'll be rewarded with the likes of papaya soufflé, spicy Creole concoctions such as curried pork and stuffed land crabs, and fresh local vegetables. Her exotic confitures of guava, pineapple, and cornichon top off the feast, along with a yogurt or light coconut cake. *Rte. de la Côte Atlantique, tel. 596/78–51–18. Reservations required. V. Inexpensive.*

Fort-de-France **La Fontane.** In a pastoral setting on the road to Balata, this lovely
★ gingerbread house with a wraparound veranda is shaded by mango
trees. Inside you'll find Oriental rugs, fresh flowers, and a display of
antiques that includes a handsome gramophone and a grandmoth-
er's clock. *Le Bambou de la Fontane* is a mixed salad with fish, tomato, corn, melon, and crayfish. Other dishes served here are cream
soup with crabs, crayfish bisque, red snapper with lemon-lime
sauce, *magret de canard* (breast of duck), and steak au poivre. *Km 4,
Rte. de Balata, tel. 596/64–28–70. Reservations essential. Jacket
and tie required. AE. Closed Sun. and Mon. Expensive.*

La Grand' Voile. Crisp white cloths, fine china and crystal, and lots
of windows overlooking the harbor contribute to a lovely dining
room. Starters include chilled chicken liver mousse and fresh
steamed mussels. Main dishes include lobster in Creole sauce and fillet of beef Creoline. The *menu dégustation* (a variety of sample-size
portions) is a practical way to savor the restaurant's specialties.
Service here is sometimes on the slow side. *Pte. Simon, tel. 596/70–
29–29, fax 596/61–85–02. Reservations suggested. Jacket suggested. AE, MC, V. Closed Sun. Expensive.*

Le Bristol. Selecting from a long list of rum drinks is the first order
of business in this handsome terrace restaurant. The menu changes
monthly, but you may find gazpacho or escargots in garlic butter for
starters, and such main dishes as lobster fricassee and magret de
canard, as well as a variety of beef and fish dishes. Hot apple tarts
and feathery coconut soufflés are usually on the dessert list. *Km 0.2,
rue Martin Luther King, tel. 596/72–69–02. Reservations required
for dinner. Jacket required for dinner. AE. Expensive.*

★ **Le Lafayette.** This is a true "salon" on the second story of a renovated hotel of the same name. Clusters of indoor greenery combine
with white latticework and rich Haitian paintings as the setting for
what may be the finest dining room in Fort-de-France. Begin the
day with a chocolate brioche for breakfast, continue to a light fondue
and salad for lunch, and end with a perfectly grilled lobster in a
spicy sauce or perhaps with imported sirloin in a black-pepper
sauce. Dessert is something simple, such as banana flambé in 20-
year-old rum. *Lafayette Hotel, 5 rue de la Liberté, tel. 596/73–80–
50. Reservations required. AE, MC, V. Closed Sun. Expensive.*

La Biguine. Downstairs is a cozy, casual café with red-and-white
check cloths; upstairs, a more formal candlelit dining room. Local
fish poached in Creole sauce, shark cooked in tomato sauce, and duck
fillet with pineapple or orange sauce are among the à la carte offerings, with homemade tarts for dessert. It's a convenient place for
lunch. *11 Rte. de la Folie, tel. 596/71–47–75. Reservations required
for dinner. Jacket required for dinner. V. No lunch Sat.; closed
Sun. Moderate.*

★ **Le Coq Hardi.** Crowds flock here for the best steaks and grilled
meats in town. You can pick out your own steak and feel confident
that it will be cooked to perfection. Steak tartare is the house specialty, but there are tournedos Rossini (with artichoke hearts, foie
gras, truffles, and Madeira sauce), entrecôte Bordelaise, prime rib,
and T-bone steaks among the wide selection of beef offerings. For
dessert, there's a selection of sorbets, profiteroles, and pear Belle
Hélène. *Km 0.6, rue Martin Luther King, tel. 596/71–59–64. Reservations suggested. AE, MC, V. Closed Wed. Moderate.*

Chez Gaston. This cozy upstairs dining room, very popular with local residents, has a Creole menu that includes such items as ox-foot
soup, conch kebabs, and simmered sea urchins. The brochettes are
especially recommended. The kitchen stays open late, and there's a
small dance floor. The downstairs section serves snacks all day. A
French phrase book will be very helpful. *10 rue Felix Eboue, tel.*

596/71–59–71. Reservations accepted. No credit cards. Inexpensive.

Le Crew. The meals here are served family-style in rustic dining rooms, where the bill of fare includes a few Creole dishes and lots of typical French bistro dishes: fish soup and stuffed mussels, snails, country pâté, frogs' legs, tripe, grilled chicken, and steak. The portions are ample, and there's a daily 60F three-course tourist menu that simplifies ordering. *42 rue Ernst Deproge, tel. 596/73–04–14. Reservations accepted. No credit cards. No dinner Sat. Closed Sun. Inexpensive.*

Lamentin **Le Verger.** An orchard is the setting for this green-and-white coun-
★ try house, not far from the airport. Pheasant, duck, and other game are on the extensive menu along with classic French and Creole dishes. Follow the signs for La Trinité; the entrance to the restaurant is on the right immediately after the Esso and Shell stations. *Place d'Armes, tel. 596/51–43–02. Reservations suggested. AE, DC, MC, V. No lunch Sat.; no dinner Sun. Moderate–Expensive.*

La Trinité **L'Ami Fritz.** Named after the popular Weinstub in Strasbourg, this
★ is where locals flock for Muenster cheese, game, sauerkraut, and fine wines. The cuisine is Alsatian, but the chef uses local produce to create an interesting repertoire of dishes, from grilled lobster with a gratin Creole to "Royal Sauerkraut." The lovely country mansion nestles in rolling hills, surrounded by flowers and greenery. *Brin d'Amour, tel. 596/58–20–81. Reservations suggested. Jacket and tie required. V. Closed Mon. Expensive.*

Le Diamant **Relais Caraibes.** Parisians Monsieur and Madame Senez have
★ opened this individual bungalow colony *avec* restaurant but still manage to spend enough time in Paris to gather original objets d'art for decor and for sale. Dishes include chicken Antilloise, a half lobster in two sauces, fresh-caught fish in a basil sauce, and fricassee of country shrimp. The crisply decorated dining room, always awash in fresh flowers, commands an always-clear view of Diamond Rock. *La Cherry, Diamant, tel. 596/76–44–65. Open for lunch and dinner. AE, MC, V. Closed Mon. Expensive.*

Le Diam's. For an inexpensive meal that may consist of crisp and tasty pizzas or a grilled fish of the day, this casual, open-sided restaurant facing the village square is hard to beat. Checkered tablecloths and wicker furniture are the only decor; the overhead fan helps to keep a breeze going through the dining room. *Place de l'Eglise, tel. 596/76–23–28. No reservations. MC, V. Closed Tues. Inexpensive.*

Le François **Club Nautique.** While this little place is not going to turn up in *Ar-*
★ *chitectural Digest*, the food that comes fresh daily out of the sea is exquisitely prepared. Have a couple of rum punches, then dig into turtle steak or charcoal-broiled lobster. The restaurant is right on the beach, and boat trips leave here for snorkeling in the nearby coral reefs. *Le François, tel. 596/54–31–00. Reservations accepted. V. Inexpensive.*

Le Morne **Auberge de la Montagne Pelée.** This restaurant is open for dinner by
Rouge reservation only, but the real treat is lunch on a clear day, when you can see Mont Pelée's summit from the terrace. Creole and French dishes are featured, including a Caribbean-style pot-au-feu, with whitefish, scallops, salmon, crayfish, and tiny vegetables. *Rte. de l'Aileron, tel. 596/52–32–09. Reservations essential. MC, V. Moderate.*

Morne-des- **Le Colibri.** In the northwestern reaches of the island, this is the do-
Esses main of Clotilde Palladino, who presides over the kitchen while her

So, you're getting away from it all.

Just make sure you can get back.

AT&T Access Numbers
Dial the number of the country you're in to reach AT&T.

ANGUILLA	1-800-872-2881	**COLOMBIA**	**980-11-0010**	JAMAICA††	0-800-872-2881
ANTIGUA (Public Card Phones)	#1	*COSTA RICA	114	MEXICO◊◊◊	95-800-462-4240
ARGENTINA♦	001-800-200-1111	**CURACAO**	**001-800-872-2881**	MONTSERRAT†	1-800-872-2881
BAHAMAS	**1-800-872-2881**	DOMINICA	1-800-872-2881	**NICARAGUA**	**174**
BELIZE♦	555	DOMINICAN REP.††	1-800-872-2881	PANAMA	109
BERMUDA†	1-800-872-2881	ECUADOR†	119	PARAGUAY†	0081-800
*BOLIVIA	0-800-1112	*EL SALVADOR	190	PERU†	191
BONAIRE	**001-800-872-2881**	GRENADA†	1-800-872-2881	ST. KITTS/NEVIS	1-800-872-2881
BRAZIL	**000-8010**	*GUATEMALA	190	**ST. MAARTEN 001-800-872-2881**	
BRITISH V.I.	1-800-872-2881	*GUYANA††	**165**	**SURINAME**	**156**
CAYMAN ISLANDS	1-800-872-2881	HAITI†	001-800-972-2883	URUGUAY	00-0410
CHILE	**00◊-0312**	HONDURAS†	123	*VENEZUELA	80-011-120

Countries in bold face permit country-to-country calling in addition to calls to the U.S. **World Connect℠** prices consist of **USADirect®** rates plus an additional charge based on the country you are calling. Collect calling available to the U.S. only. *Public phones require deposit of coin or phone card. †May not be available from every phone. ††Collect calling only. ♦Not available from public phones. ◊Await second dial tone. ◊◊◊When calling from public phones, use phones marked "Ladatel." ©1994 AT&T.

Here's a travel tip that will make it easy to call back to the States. Dial the access number for the country you're visiting and connect right to AT&T. It's the quick way to get English-speaking AT&T operators and can minimize hotel telephone surcharges.

If all the countries you're visiting aren't listed above, call **1 800 241-5555** for a free wallet card with all AT&T access numbers. Easy international calling from AT&T. **TrueWorld Connections.**

AT&T

American Express offers Travelers Cheques built for two.

Cheques *for Two*^{SM} from American Express are the Travelers Cheques that allow either of you to use them because both of you have signed them. And only one of you needs to be present to purchase them.

Cheques *for Two* are accepted anywhere regular American Express Travelers Cheques are, which is just about everywhere. So stop by your bank, AAA* or any American Express Travel Service Office and ask for Cheques *for Two*.

children serve. Choice seating is at one of the seven tables on the back terrace. For starters, try *buisson d'écrevisses*, six giant fresh-water crayfish accompanied by a tangy tomato sauce flavored with thyme, scallions, and tiny bits of crayfish. Stuffed pigeon, lobster omelets, suckling pig, and coconut chicken are among the main dishes. *Morne-des-Esses, tel. 596/69–91–95. Reservations essential. AE, DC, MC, V. Moderate–Expensive.*

Ste-Anne **Aux Filets Bleus.** This breezy open-air eatery is right on the beach, and you can go for a swim before or after dining. Turtle or fish soup, stuffed crab, and avocado vinaigrette are all good opening bids. In addition to an assortment of lobster entrées, there is grilled or steamed fish and octopus with red beans and rice. Prices are slightly above what you'd expect for basically straightforward cooking and beachfront ambience. *Pointe Marin, tel. 596/76–73–42. Reservations essential. No credit cards. Closed Mon. Expensive.*

Athanor. Replacing the L'Arbre à Pain, the new owners offer an ambitiously extensive menu that includes pizzas, grilled fish, creole dishes, and meats with French sauces. However, the grilled lobster is the real treat. Choose a table either in a plant-filled room or in the small garden at the back. *Rue de Bord de Mer, Ste-Anne, tel. 596/ 76–72–93. MC, V. Inexpensive–Moderate.*

La Dunette. Dinner at this restaurant, in the small Ste-Anne hotel of the same name, is served on a plant-hung terrace overlooking the sea. Wrought-iron chairs and tables and bright blue awnings add to the refreshing garden atmosphere. Your choices for lunch or dinner include fish soup, grilled fish or lobster, poached sea urchins, pork en brochette with pineapple, and several curried dishes. *Ste-Anne, tel. 596/76–73–90. Reservations suggested in high season. MC, V. Closed Wed. Inexpensive.*

Ste-Luce **La Petite Auberge.** This country inn is hidden behind a profusion of tropical flowers, just across the main road from the beach. Fresh seafood is turned into such dishes as *filet de poisson aux champignons* (fish cooked with mushrooms), *crabe farci*, and fresh langouste in a Creole sauce. Or sample *canard à l'ananas* (duck with pineapple), *poulet Creole* (chicken Creole), or entrecôte Creole. They're all winners. *Plage du Gros Raisins, Ste-Luce, tel. 596/62– 47–26. No credit cards. Moderate.*

St-Pierre **La Factorérie.** The food is pleasant and the view outstanding at this open-air restaurant alongside the ruins of the Eglise du Fort. Fresh vegetables grown by students at the nearby agricultural training school accompany such dishes as grilled langouste, grilled chicken in a piquant sauce, *fricassee de lambi* (conch), and the fresh catch of the day. This is a convenient spot to have lunch when visiting St-Pierre, but it is not worth a special trip. *Quartier Fort, St-Pierre, tel. 596/78–12–53. No credit cards. No dinner Sat. and Sun. Inexpensive.*

Lodging

Martinique's range of accommodations runs from tiny French inns called Relais Creoles to splashy tourist resorts, with an 18th-century plantation to round things out. The majority of the hotels are clustered in Pointe du Bout and Anse-Mitan on the Trois-Ilets peninsula across the bay from Fort-de-France, but Le Diamant and Ste-Anne are becoming rival resort areas. You will also find other notable lodgings scattered around the island. Attractive packages are offered by many of the hotels during the year, and it's a good idea to ask what's available when you call to reserve. Martinique is not an island distinguished for its hotels. Expect functional accommodations and friendly but laid-back service. Most of the major hotels include a large buffet breakfast in their tariff or will arrange a MAP plan. Perhaps because there are so many good restaurants on the island, hotels have refrained from developing all-inclusive packages.

Highly recommended lodgings are indicated by a star ★.

Category	Cost*
Very Expensive	over $220
Expensive	$150–$220
Moderate	$85–$150
Inexpensive	under $85

All prices are for a standard double room for two with Continental breakfast, excluding $1.50 per person per night tax and 10% service charge.

Hotels
Anse-Mitan/
Pointe du Bout
★

Le Bakoua. This hotel was thoroughly renovated in 1990. Now, under the stewardship of the Sofitel chain, Le Bakoua is the best of Martinique's resort hotels. Located in Pointe du Bout, the hotel has accommodations in three hillside buildings and a fourth on its manmade white-sand beach. The decor is cushy-cum-rustic, with wooden furnishings and tile floors. All rooms have a balcony or patio, TV, radio, king-size bed, direct-dial phone, and air-conditioning. The rooms are relatively small, given the $250-a-night tariff, and the price is higher if they face the sea rather than the garden. The beach is compact and adjoins that of the Méridien. The pool, referred to as a *piscine trompe de l'oeil*, is above the beach, and the water flows over one side, giving the impression that the pool is part of the ocean. Entertainment consists of live music and shows nightly, including dinner, dancing, limbo, and Friday-night performances of Les Grands Ballets de la Martinique. Most of the staff speaks commendable English. Be sure to inquire about special package deals. *Box 589, Fort-de-France, tel. 596/66–02–02 or 800/221–4542, fax 596/66–00–41; in the United Kingdom, 071/730–7144. 140 rooms, including 2 1-bedroom suites. Facilities: 2 restaurants, bar, pool, 2 lighted tennis courts, boutique, beauty salon, water-sports center. AE, DC, MC, V. CP. Very Expensive.*

Le Méridien Trois-Ilets. There is a great deal of activity here, even in the low season, much of it revolving around the pool, the strip of white-sand beach, and the Air France flight crews who stay here. But the hotel has aged, and despite sporadic redecorations, the small rooms remain patchworked with repairs. New sand has been brought in to replace that lost to hurricanes, but the beach can become congested during peak season. All rooms are air-conditioned, with wall-to-wall carpeting, built-in hair dryers, and boat-size tubs; some have balconies with a splendid view of the bay and of Fort-de-France. Dinner at La Case Créole offers some of the better hotel dining on the island. English is spoken well here, and there's live entertainment nightly. *Trois-Ilets 97229, tel. 596/66–00–00 or 800/ 543–4300, fax 596/66–00–74; in NY, 212/245–2920. 295 rooms, 2 luxury suites, 4 1-bedroom suites. Facilities: 2 restaurants, bar, casino, pool, 2 lighted tennis courts, duty-free shops, marina, car-rental desk, tour desk, water-sports center. AE, DC, MC, V. BP. Very Expensive.*

PLM Azur-Carayou. The style here is definitely tropical. The reception area has rattan furniture and, overhead, quaint wood rafters.

The rooms, built around the large swimming pool in the garden, are air-conditioned and equipped with TVs, direct-dial phones, and well-stocked minibars. There are lots of sporting options for daytime activity, and a popular disco, Le Vésou, for evening. Located on the other side of the marina to Le Bakoua, the hotel has its own small but pleasant beach. The hotel is well run, and the staff is helpful and friendly. *Pointe du Bout 97229, tel. 596/66–04–04 or 800/221–4542, fax 596/66–00–57. 190 double rooms. Facilities: 3 restaurants, 2 bars, 2 tennis courts, pool, scuba diving, fishing, waterskiing, sailing. AE, DC, MC, V. MAP. Moderate–Expensive.*

Bambou. This resort is a complex of rustic A-frame "chalets" with shingled roofs. The rooms are paneled in pink; they are tiny and Spartan, albeit with such modern conveniences as air-conditioning, phones, and shower baths. The hotel is open year-round, and during high season, entertainment is featured five nights a week. *Anse-Mitan 97229, tel. 596/66–01–39 or 800/224–4542, fax 596/66–05–05. 118 rooms. Facilities: restaurant and bar, pool, water-sports center. AE, DC, MC, V. CP, MAP. Moderate.*

★ **PLM Azur La Pagerie.** La Pagerie looks as if it were plucked out of southern Louisiana and planted near the marina in Pointe du Bout. Fully air-conditioned, the hotel has small rooms and studios, some with kitchenettes, all with private baths. Although the hotel has no beach or water-sports activities, it is within a short stroll of the resort hotels, restaurants, and activity. Lunch and dinner are served alfresco by the pool. On an island not known for the attractiveness of its hotels, this exception draws the local expatriate and sailing crowd for a round of evening cocktails. *Pointe du Bout 97229, tel. 596/66–05–30, fax 596/66–00–99. U.S. reservations, 800/221–4542; in NY, 212/757–6500. 98 rooms. Facilities: restaurant, bar, pool. AE, MC, V. EP. Inexpensive–Moderate.*

Auberge de l'Anse-Mitan. This beachfront hotel, established in 1930, is the island's oldest family-run inn. The rooms are spartan, but all are air-conditioned and have a shower bath. Views are either of the bay or the tropical garden at the back, and some rooms have balconies. Informal meals are served on the terrace for guests. At the end of the road along the beachfront, things are peaceful and quiet here—even more so if you don't speak French. *Anse-Mitan 97229, tel. 596/66–01–12, fax 596/66–01–05; in Canada, 800/468–0023; in NY, 212/251–1800. 26 rooms. Facilities: restaurant, bar. AE, DC. CP. Inexpensive.*

Rivage Hotel. Maryelle and Jean Claude Riveti's garden studios have kitchenettes, air-conditioning, TVs, phones, and private baths. The hotel is right across the road from the beach. Breakfast and light meals are served in the friendly, informal snack bar. You get good value for your money, and you should have no difficulty communicating: English, Spanish, and French are spoken. *Anse-Mitan 97229, tel. 596/66–00–53, fax 596/66–06–56. 17 rooms. Facilities: snack bar, pool. MC, V. EP. Inexpensive.*

Basse-Point **Leyritz Plantation.** Sleeping on a former sugar plantation in either
★ the old-fashioned furnished rooms at the manor house or in one of the restored former slave cabins is a novelty that may appeal to you. The place is authentic—and isolated in the northern part of the island on 16 acres of lush vegetation. Except for when tour buses carrying cruise-ship passengers pass through, it is very quiet here—a sharp contrast to the frenzied level of activity at the hotels in Pointe du Bout. The new owners are improving the property and have installed a health spa with a nutrition and fitness program, a swimming pool, a meeting room, and an enlarged boutique. Most people won't want to spend their entire vacation here, but it makes for an

interesting overnight stay while visiting the northern part of the island. There's free transportation to the beach, which is about 30 minutes away. *Basse-Pointe 97218, tel. 596/78–53–92, fax 596/78–92–44. 53 rooms. Facilities: restaurant, bar, spa, health-and-fitness center, horseback riding, tennis court, pool. DC, MC. CP. Moderate–Expensive.*

Fort-de-France **Impératrice.** Overlooking La Savane park in the center of the city, the Impératrice's air-conditioned rooms are in a 1950s five-story building (with an elevator). The rooms in the front are either the best or the worst, depending upon your sensibilities: They are noisy, but they overlook the city's center of activity. All rooms have a TV and a private bath; 20 have balconies. Children under 8 stay free in the room with their parents, children 8–15 stay at 50% of the room rate. The hotel also has a popular sidewalk café. The owners recently opened **L'Impératrice Village** at Anse-Mitan. It is a cluster of small bungalows in a meadow off a rutted track and a good 10-minute hike from the nearest beach. It is not worth the $120-a-night tab. *Fort-de-France 97200, tel. 596/63–06–82 or 800/223–9815, fax 596/72–66–30; in Canada, 800/468–0023; in NY, 212/251–1800. 24 rooms. Facilities: restaurant, café, bar. AE, DC, MC, V. CP. Moderate.*
Lafayette. This hotel's claim to fame is its superb second-story dining room overlooking the Savane. For those who want to be right in the heart of town, this place is a real find. The choicest rooms are those with French windows. *5 rue de la Liberté, Fort-de-France, tel. 596/73–80–50 or 800/223–9815, fax 596/60–97–75. 24 rooms with TV, telephone, telex, and fax services. Facilities: restaurant, bar, complimentary use of Le Bakoua hotel beach facilities. AE, DC, V. EP. Inexpensive.*

Lamentin **Martinique Cottages.** These garden bungalows in the country-side have kitchenettes, cable TVs, and phones. The restaurant here, La Plantation, is a gathering spot for gourmets. The beaches are about a 15-minute drive away. The cottages are difficult to find, and you should take advantage of the property's airport transfers. *Lamentin 97232, tel. 596/50–16–08, fax 596/50–26–83. 8 rooms. Facilities: restaurant. AE, MC, V. EP. Inexpensive.*

La Trinité **Saint Aubin.** This restored colonial house is in the countryside above the Atlantic coast. The rooms are modern, with air-conditioning, TVs, phones, and private baths. This is a peaceful retreat, and only 3 miles from La Trinité, 2 miles from the Spoutourne sports center and the beaches on the Caravelle Peninsula. The inn's restaurant is reserved for hotel guests and is closed during June and October. *Box 52, La Trinité, 97220, tel. 596/69–34–77 or 800/223–9815; in Canada, 800/468–0023; in NY, 212/840–6636, fax 596/69–41–14. 15 double rooms. Facilities: restaurant, bar, pool. AE, DC, MC, V. CP. Moderate.*

Le Diamant **Diamant-Novotel.** This self-contained resort occupies half an island in an ideal windsurfing location. Just beyond the registration area, a footbridge spans a large pool on the way to the air-conditioned, spacious guest rooms, each of which has a small balcony facing either the sea or the pool. Furnishings are cane and wickerwork painted pastel peach and green, and the floors are tile. The four beaches on the 5-acre property are small. The dining room is large and unromantic, set up to accommodate groups, but there is a pleasant terrace bar where a local band plays on most nights. A smaller, more formal restaurant is open during peak season. Scuba packages are offered. The staff speaks English. *Le Diamant 97223, tel. 596/76–42–42 or 800/221–4542, fax 596/76–22–87. 180 rooms. Facilities: 2 restaurants, 3 bars, 2 tennis courts, pool, dive shop, car-rental*

*desk, water-sports center. AE, DC, MC, V. CP, MAP. Expensive–
Very Expensive.*

★ **Diamant Les Bains.** Although manager Hubert Andrieu and his
family go all out to make their guests comfortable, you won't feel
quite at home unless you speak at least a little French. A few of the
rooms are in the main house, where the restaurant is located, but
most are in bungalows, some just steps away from the sea. All rooms
are air-conditioned, with private baths, TVs, and phones; eight
have small refrigerators. *Le Diamant 97223, tel. 596/76–40–14 or
800/223–9815; in Canada, 800/468–0023; in NY, 212/251–1800, fax
596/76–27–00. 26 rooms. Facilities: restaurant, bar, pool, water-
sports center. MC. CP, MAP. Closed Sept. Moderate.*

Diamant Marine. Here you'll find self-contained miniapartments
(sleeping room with kitchenette and balcony) in a pristine stucco
building, where the motel-style rooms are painted in pastel colors.
The main part of the hotel is some 100 feet above the beach, and rows
of dwelling units are tiered on the hillside down to the shore. The
pool is just above the beach. Although this arrangement is visually
attractive and the walk down is easy, the climb up the steps from the
pool and beach to the main house and restaurant is strenuous. The
hotel attracts French families. *Point de la Chery, near Diamant,
tel. 596/76–46–00 or 800/221–4542, fax 596/76–25–99. 149 rooms.
Facilities: restaurant, 2 bars, 2 pools (1 for children), water sports,
deep-sea fishing, 2 tennis courts. AE, DC, MC, V. CP. Moderate.*

★ **Relais Caraibes.** This is a colony of bungalows on manicured
grounds, with Diamond Rock dominating the seascape. Each of the
12 bungalows has a bedroom, a small salon with a sofa bed, and a
bathroom. The decorations are objects the owner has brought from
trips to her native Paris. There are also three standard rooms in the
main house. The pool is perched at the edge of the cliff that drops to
the sea—a very dramatic setting. Of all the hotels on Martinique,
this one comes closest to having an individuality and the authentici-
ty of a country inn with good food and attractive accommodations.
*Point de la Chery, Diamant 97223, tel. 596/76–44–65 or 800/223–
9815, fax 596/76–21–20. 15 rooms. Facilities: restaurant, bar, pool,
private beach, boat, scuba instruction. AE, MC, V. CP. Moderate.*

Marigot **Habitation Lagrange.** This unexpected find, an 18th-century manor
house, stands amid a rambling former sugar plantation scattered
with crumbling stone buildings 1½ miles off the main road north of
Marigot. High ceilings, austere furnishings, and polished wood
floors set a degree of colonial formality that may not appeal to all,
but Habitation Lagrange is Martinique's only hotel with a vestige of
the island's cultivated past. The mood continues in the three master
bedrooms, with high canopy beds on bare wood floors and ceiling
fans. Bathrooms have modern fixtures but keep to the 18th-century
style, from the gold-plated taps to the bathtubs encased in wood.
Two new two-story buildings house 12 rooms with gabled ceilings.
Three more rooms are in an original stone building facing the pool
and are decorated rather sparsely with little more than a canopy bed
on white parquet floors. Dinner is served at polished tables in the
dining room, followed by a brandy in the small library. The young
owners are extremely enthusiastic, but you may need a little French
to appreciate their hospitality. *97225 Marigot, tel. 596/53–60–60,
fax 596/53–50–58. 17 rooms, 1 suite. Facilities: dining room, bar,
library, pool, tennis court. MC, DC, V. BP. Very Expensive.*

Le Marin **The Last Resort.** John and Véronique Deschamps' bed-and-breakfast on rue Osman Duquesnay is in the former gendarmerie annex.
Language will be no problem here, since the Deschampses once
lived in Sausalito, but you'll have to be flexible enough to share a

bathroom with the other guests on your floor. A small communal kitchen is available, and an excellent family-style dinner is served nightly. *Le Marin 97290, tel. 596/74–83–88, fax 596/74–76–41. 5 rooms. Facilities: restaurant. MC, V. CP. Inexpensive.*

Le Morne Rouge   **Auberge de la Montagne Pelée.** There are three rooms and six studios with kitchenettes in this hillside inn that faces the famed volcano. Accommodations are simple; the view from the restaurant terrace is spectacular. The inn was closed for repairs and renovations at press time, but should reopen for the 1994–95 season. *Le Morne Rouge 97260, tel. 596/52–32–09, fax 596/73–20–75. 12 rooms. Facilities: restaurant. No credit cards. EP. Inexpensive.*

Schoelcher   **La Batelière Hotel.** This beachfront property boasts the island's largest rooms, and arguably the best tennis courts. But before you rush to stay here, consider the location—north of Fort-de-France and away from most of the island's resort activity (although, for some that would be a plus). The hotel overlooks the sea, and all rooms are air-conditioned, with direct-access phone, cable TV, radio, and private balcony or patio. The rooms have new furniture and marble-tiled bathrooms, and suites have canopy beds. Recent renovations have created a smart, if sober, reception area with a lounge facing the sea. One level below the lounge is the semicircular pool and pool bar, and below that is a small beach sheltered from the waves by a breakwater. With these upgraded facilities and its proximity to Fort-de-France, the hotel should be attractive to businessmen. Ask about the scuba and honeymoon packages. *Schoelcher 97233, tel. 596/61–49–49 or 800/223–6510, fax 596/61–70–57. 192 rooms, 5 duplexes, and 2 suites. Facilities: 2 restaurants, 2 bars, pool, 6 lighted tennis courts, shopping arcade, conference rooms, water-sports center. AE, DC, MC, V. CP. Expensive–Very Expensive.*

Ste-Anne   **Club Med/Buccaneer's Creek.** Occupying 48 landscaped acres, Martinique's Club Med is an all-inclusive village with plazas, cafés, restaurants, boutique, and a small marina. Air-conditioned pastel cottages contain twin beds and private shower bath. The only money you need spend here is for bar drinks, personal expenses, and excursions into Fort-de-France or the countryside. There's a white-sand beach, a plethora of water sports, and plenty of nightlife. *Pointe Marin 97180, tel. 596/76–72–72 or 800/CLUBMED; in NY, 212/750–1670; fax 596/72–76–02. 300 rooms. Facilities: 2 restaurants and bars, 6 tennis courts (4 lighted), fitness and water-sports center, nightclub, disco. AE, V. All-inclusive (drinks not included). Moderate–Expensive.*

St-François   **Fregate Bleu.** The owner, Madame De Lucie, left the management of Leyfritz Plantation because she wanted the quiet life. In 1991 she opened the Fregate Bleu, an eight-room glorified bed-and-breakfast. Five of the rooms are delightful—their spaciousness accentuated by off-white furnishings, patterned carpets, and the occasional antique. All of these five rooms have a balcony overlooking Les Islets de l'Impératrice. (The other two rooms do not have a balcony or this view.) All rooms have a small kitchenette and modern bathrooms with such niceties as bathrobes. Only *petit déjeuner* (breakfast) is served, so if you decline to use your kitchenette you must negotiate the rutted road to the highway and drive at least 20 minutes to a restaurant. Though the sea is a stone's throw away, there is no beach nearby and the Fregate Bleu's pool is small. You are paying for what Madame De Lucie wanted—peace and quiet in very comfortable surroundings. *Le François 97240 (5 mi south of St-François on Vauclin Rd.), tel. 596/54–54–66 or 800/633–7411, fax*

596/54–78–48. 7 rooms. Facilities: small pool. MC, V. BP. Expensive.

Home and The **Villa Rental Service** of the Martinique Tourist Office (tel. 596/
Villa Rentals 63–79–60) can assist with rentals of homes, villas, and apartments. Most are in the south of the island near good beaches and can be rented on a weekly or monthly basis.

The Arts and Nightlife

The island is dotted with lively discos and nightclubs, but entertainment on Martinique is not confined to partying.

Discos Your hotel or the tourist office can put you in touch with the current "in" places. It's also wise to check on opening and closing times and admission charges. For the most part, the discos draw a mixed crowd of locals and tourists, the young and the not so young. Some of the currently popular places are **Le New Hippo** (24 blvd. Allegre, Fort-de-France, tel. 596/71–74–60), **Le Sweety** (rue Capitaine Pierre Rose, Fort-de-France, no tel.), **Le Vésou** (Carayou-PLM Azur, tel. 596/66–04–04), **VonVon** (Méridien, tel. 596/66–00–00), **La Cabane de Pêcheur** (Diamant-Novotel, tel. 596/76–42–42), **L'Oeil** (Petit Cocotte, Ducos, tel. 596/56–11–11), and **Zipp's Dupe Club** (Dumaine, Le François, tel. 596/54–47–06).

Zouk and Jazz Currently the most popular music is the zouk, which mixes the Caribbean rhythm and an Occidental tempo with Creole words. Jacob Devarieux (Kassav) is the leading exponent of this style and is occasionally on the island. More likely, though, you will hear zouk music played by one of his followers at the hotels and clubs. Jazz musicians, like the music, tend to be informal and independent. They rarely hold regular gigs. In season, you'll find one or two combos playing at clubs and hotels, but it is only at **Coco Lobo** (tel. 596/63–63–77, located next to the tourist office in Fort-de-France), that there are regular jazz sessions.

Casinos The island's two casinos are open from 9 PM to 3 AM Monday to Saturday. You have to be at least 21 (with a picture ID); jacket and tie are not required. The **Casino Trois-Ilets** (Méridien, tel. 596/66–00–00) has American and French roulette, blackjack, and an admission charge of 70F. The other casino, at La Batelière, offers American roulette, blackjack, and craps with similar restrictions and a 60F admission.

16 Montserrat

Updated by
Laurie S.
Senz

Christopher Columbus sailed by the leeward coast of this Caribbean island in 1493, and, seeing the jagged mountains, he named it Montserrat, after the Santa Maria de Montserrate monastery near Barcelona, which is surrounded by similar terrain.

The Carib Indians who inhabited the island then were still there in 1632, when dissident Irish Catholics arrived from nearby St. Kitts, from which they were escaping persecution. These new settlers found an island whose topography strongly resembled that of their native Ireland, prompting Montserrat's nickname, "the Emerald Isle of the Caribbean." Today the Irish influence is much diminished. Still, your passport is stamped with a shamrock upon arrival, the phone book is loaded with Irish places and surnames, and St. Patrick's Day is celebrated enthusiastically (albeit to commemorate a major 18th-century slave uprising).

Actually, the African influence is more pronounced, thanks to Montserrat's comparatively low profile. Newborns are still given "jumbie" nicknames to fool the evil spirits, and the related jumbie dances, designed to ward off or propitiate those spirits, are lusty and vibrant. The rollicking Carnival, held during the Christmas season, is a riot of color in traditional authentic costumes.

On the map Montserrat looks like a flint-ax head with the sharp end pointing north. The island is divided along the center by a range of switchback hills, the highest of which is Chance's Peak in the south, which rises to a height of 3,002 feet. Also in the southern hills is the volcano known as Galway's Soufrière. It is long extinct, but steam pouring from vents in the dramatic yellow-and-pink rock and the lush tropical vegetation circling the rim of the crater make this a powerful, evocative sight.

Measuring only 11 miles by 7 miles, Montserrat is a small, friendly island that has escaped much of the large-scale development common in other parts of the Caribbean. It tends to attract independent travelers who want a low-key, away-from-it-all vacation. If you want to pump iron, drink piña coladas, and boogie till dawn, you'll probably be bored. If you like seclusion, nature, and peace and quiet, you'll love it.

Most visitors arrive at Blackburn Airport on the Atlantic (east) coast of the island and then drive to the Caribbean (west) coast. Since there are no roads that traverse the island from east to west or circle it to the south, this will mean a trip around the northern tip. On the way, you will notice that the landscape changes considerably. The Atlantic coast is rockier, more windswept, and less fertile. Steep cliffs make most of the beaches on that side of the island inaccessible.

The best beaches, as well as the capital, Plymouth, and most of the villas and hotels are concentrated in a small area, measuring about five miles by two miles, on the Caribbean coast. Here Montserrat's lush vegetation is at its most luxuriant. Hibiscus and bougainvillea, giant philodendron and avocado trees, mango trees, christophines, and many others all thrive on the terracelike hills that slope down to the water. There are also spectacular views across the Caribbean to the mysterious island of Rodondo and St. Kitts, a sequence of indigo blue peaks on the horizon.

Nearly all Montserratians have harrowing tales of how they spent a night in September 1989 cowering in cellars or hiding in clothes cupboards as a wild vortex of wind and water ripped off roofs, defoliated trees, and sent cars hurtling through the air like tin cans.

Amazingly—and it is a tribute to the islanders' tenacity and courage—few traces of Hurricane Hugo remain today. The vegetation has grown back. The infrastructure has been repaired and, in many cases, upgraded. Thanks to Hugo, Montserrat also has a brand-new $30 million seaport.

Before You Go

Tourist Information You can get information about Montserrat through the **Caribbean Tourism Organization** (20 East 46th St., New York, NY 10017, tel. 212/682–0435).

Arriving and Departing
By Plane Although Antigua is not the only gateway, it's the best way to reach Montserrat. **BWIA** (tel. 800/538–2942) has three weekly nonstop flights to Antigua from New York and two from Miami; it also has regularly scheduled nonstop service from Toronto, Canada, and Heathrow Airport, London. **American Airlines** (tel. 800/433–7300) has connecting service from a number of U.S. cities through San Juan, Puerto Rico. **Air Canada** (tel. 800/776–3000) offers service from Toronto; **British Airways** (tel. in Britain, 081/897–4000; in the United States, 800/247–9297) from Gatwick Airport, London; and **Lufthansa** (tel. 800/645–3880 in the United States) transports visitors from Frankfurt via Puerto Rico.

From Antigua's V. C. Bird International Airport, you can make your connections with **LIAT** (tel. 800/253–5011 or 809/491–2200) or **Montserrat Airways** (tel. 809/491–5342 or 809/491–6494) for the15-minute flight to Montserrat.

You will land on the 3,400-foot runway at Blackburne Airport, on the Atlantic coast, about 11 miles from Plymouth.

From the Airport Taxis meet every flight; the government-regulated fare from the airport to Plymouth is E.C.$29 (U.S.$11).

Passports and Visas U.S. and Canadian citizens only need proof of citizenship, such as a passport, a notarized birth certificate, or a voter registration card plus a photo ID, such as a driver's license. British citizens must have a passport; visas are not required. All visitors must hold an ongoing or return ticket.

Language It's English with more of a lilt than a brogue. You'll also hear a patois that's spoken on most of the islands.

Precautions Ask for permission before taking pictures. Some residents may be reluctant photographic subjects, and they will appreciate your courtesy.

Most Montserratians frown at the sight of skimpily dressed tourists; do not risk offending them by strolling around town in shorts and swimsuits.

Staying in Montserrat

Important Addresses Tourist Information: The Montserrat Department of Tourism (Church Rd., Plymouth, tel. 809/491–2230) is open weekdays 8–noon and 1–4.

Emergencies **Police:** tel. 999 or 809/491–2555. **Hospital:** There is a 24-hour emergency room at **Glendon Hospital** (Plymouth, tel. 809/491–2552). **Pharmacies:** **Lee's Pharmacy** (Evergreen Dr., Plymouth, tel. 809/491–3274) and **Daniel's Pharmacy** (George St., Plymouth, tel. 809/491–2908).

Currency The official currency is the Eastern Caribbean dollar (E.C.$), often called beewee. At press time, the exchange rate was E.C.$2.70 to U.S.$1. U.S. dollars are readily accepted, but you'll often receive change in beewees. Note: Prices quoted here are in U.S. dollars unless noted otherwise.

Taxes and Service Charges Hotels collect a 7% government tax. The departure tax is E.C.$20 (about U.S.$7.50). Hotels add a 10% service charge. Most restaurants add a 10%–15% service charge. If restaurants do not add the service charge, it's customary to leave a 10% or 15% tip. Taxi drivers are tipped on a voluntary basis only.

Guided Tours Several local companies offer tours of the island, either in minivans or sedans. **Runaway Tours** (tel. 809/491–2776 or 809/491–2800) offers a day tour of the island that includes Galway's Soufrière, St. George's Fort, and the Fox's Bay Bird Sanctuary. The price of $122 per person includes refreshments and a meal, usually at the Emerald Café. The tour lasts five hours, and sturdy walking shoes are recommended. Other companies include **Carib World Tours** (tel. 809/491–2713) and **Best Foot Forward** (tel. 809/491–5872).

The Rotary Club of Montserrat (tel. 809/491–2520 or 809/491–5822) conducts garden tours from December through April. The cost is $30 per person and includes drinks at the Vue Point Hotel.

A number of taxi drivers also do tours of the island. Of these, the best is run by **James Frith,** known to everyone simply as Mango (tel. 809/491–2134), an enormously likable Montserratian. Also recommended are **John Ryner** (tel. 809/491–2190) and the aptly named **Be-Beep Taylor** (tel. 809/491–3787). Prices (fixed by the Department of Tourism) are E.C.$30 per hour (U.S. $12) or E.C.$130–$150 (U.S. $50–$58) for a five-hour day tour. Refreshments are extra. For further information, contact the Department of Tourism.

Getting Around **Taxis** Taxis, private vehicles, or the M11 (a play on the local registration numbers, meaning your own two legs) are the main means of transport on the island. A loosely organized network of minibuses travels between the villages and Plymouth, but schedules are erratic and unreliable. Taxis are always available at the airport, the main hotels, and the taxi stand in Plymouth (tel. 809/491–2261). The Department of Tourism publishes a list of taxi fares to most destinations.

Car Rentals The island has more than 115 miles of good paved roads. Unless you're uncomfortable about driving on the left, you won't have any trouble exploring. You'll need a valid driver's license, plus a Montserrat license, which is available at the airport or the Treasury Department on Strand Street in Plymouth. The fee is E.C.$30 (U.S.$12). Rental cars cost about $35–$40 per day. The smaller companies, whose prices are generally 10%–25% cheaper, will negotiate, particularly off-season. **Pauline Car Rentals** (Plymouth, tel. 809/491–2345) is a local rental company. Other agencies are **Jefferson's Car Rental** (Dagenham, tel. 809/491–2126), **Budget** (Blackburne Airport, tel. 809/491–6065), **Reliable** (Marine Dr., Plymouth, tel. 809/491–6990), and **Fenco** (Plymouth, tel. 809/491–4901).

Telephones and Mail To call Montserrat from the United States, dial area code 809 and access code 491 plus the local four-digit number. International direct dial is available on the island; both local and long-distance calls come through clearly. To call locally on the island, you need to dial the seven-digit number, the first three digits of which are always 491.

Airmail letters and postcards to the United States and Canada cost E.C.$1.15 each. Montserrat is one of several Caribbean islands whose stamps are of interest to collectors. You can buy them at the main post office in Plymouth (open Mon., Tues., Thurs., Fri. 8:15–3:55, Wed. and Sat. 8:15–11:25 AM).

Opening and Most shops are open Monday to Saturday 8–5. Banking hours are
Closing Times Monday to Thursday 8–3 and Friday 3–5.

Exploring Montserrat

Numbers in the margin correspond to points of interest on the Montserrat map.

Plymouth About a third of the island's population of 11,000 lives in the capital
① city of **Plymouth,** which faces the Caribbean on the southwest coast. The town is neat and clean, its narrow streets lined with trim Georgian structures built mostly of stones that came from Dorset as ballast on old sailing vessels. Most of the town's sights are located right along the water. On the south side, a bridge over Fort Ghaut ("gut," or ravine) leads to Wapping, where most of the restaurants are located.

We'll begin at **Government House,** on the south side of town just above Sugar Bay. The frilly Victorian house, decorated with a shamrock, dates from the 18th century. Beautifully landscaped gardens surround the building, but unfortunately the house is no longer open to the public. The grounds, however, are open to visitors Monday, Tuesday, Thursday, and Friday, from 10:30 AM to 12:30 PM and are worth a visit.

Follow Peebles Street north and cross the bridge. Just over the bridge, at the junction of Harney, Strand, and Parliament streets, you'll see the **market,** where islanders bring their produce on Friday and Saturday mornings—a very colorful scene.

From the market, walk along Strand Street for one block to the tall, white **war memorial** with a bell turret. The memorial is a tribute to the soldiers of both world wars. Next to the monument is the **post office and treasury,** a galleried West Indian–style building by the water, where you can buy stamps that make handsome souvenirs.

Walk away from the water on George Street, which runs alongside the war memorial. The town's main thoroughfare, Parliament Street, cuts diagonally north–south through the town. A left turn onto Parliament Street, at the corner of George Street, will take you to the Methodist church and the courthouse. If you continue straight on George Street, you'll come to the Roman Catholic church. From back in Plymouth, if you cross the bridge heading east towards Amersham, you will come across the **American University of the Caribbean,** a medical school with many American students.

Elsewhere on From here on, you'll need wheels. Take Highway 2, the main road
the Island north out of Plymouth. On the outskirts of town there's a stone marker that commemorates the first colony in 1632.

Tour 1 **St. Anthony's Church,** which is just north of town, was consecrated
② sometime between 1623 and 1666. It was rebuilt in 1730 following one of the many clashes between the French and the English in the area. Two silver chalices displayed in the church were donated by freed slaves after emancipation in 1834.

③ Richmond Hill rises north of town. Here you will find the **Montserrat Museum** in a restored sugar mill. The museum contains maps, historical records, artifacts, and all sorts of memorabilia pertaining to the island's growth and development. *Richmond Hill, tel. 809/491–5443. Admission free (donations accepted). Open Sun. and Wed. 2:30–5 (but telephone to be sure).*

④ Take the first left turn past the museum to Grove Road; it will take you to the **Fox's Bay Bird Sanctuary,** a 15-acre bog area. Marked trails lead into the interior, which is aflutter with egrets, herons, coots, and cuckoo birds.

The **Bransby Point Fortification** is also in this area and contains a collection of restored cannons.

⑤ Backtrack on Grove Road to Highway 2, drive north, and turn right on Highway 4 to **St. George's Fort.** It's overgrown and of little historical interest, but the view from the hilltop is well worth the trip.

Highway 2 continues north past the Belham Valley Golf Course to **Vue Pointe Hotel,** on the coast at Old Road Bay. Head east to the green slopes of Centre Hills, almost in the center of the island, for
⑥ **Air Studios,** a recording studio founded in 1979 by former Beatles producer George Martin. Sting, Boy George, and Paul McCartney have all cut records here, but following Hugo, Martin closed up shop.

⑦ About 1½ miles farther north, a scenic drive takes you along **Runaway Ghaut.** Over two centuries ago, this peaceful green valley was the scene of bloody battles between the French and the English. Local legend has it that "those who drink its water clear they spellbound are, and the Montserrat they must obey." **Carr's Bay, Little Bay,** and **Rendezvous Bay,** the island's three most popular beaches, are along the northwest coast.

Tour 2 The next tour of the island will be considerably more arduous, taking in the mountains, rain forests, and *soufrières* (volcanic craters with sulfuric springs) to the south and east of Plymouth. To hire a knowledgeable guide, contact the Department of Tourism or ask at your hotel. The guide's fee will be about $6 (E.C.$15) per person to the waterfall. Wear rubber-soled shoes.

⑧ A 15-minute drive south of Plymouth on Old Fort Road will bring you to the village of **St. Patrick's.** From there, a scenic drive takes you to the starting point of the moderately strenuous 30- to 45-minute hike through thick rain forests to **Great Alps Waterfall.** The falls cascade 70 feet down the side of a rock and splash into a shallow pool, where you can see a rainbow in the mist.

⑨ A rugged road leads eastward to **Galway's Soufrière,** where another hike is involved, this one lasting about a half hour. Once there, you'll see volcanic rock, boiling water, and small vents of gurgling, molten sulfur. City people are fond of complaining in the summertime of streets so hot you could fry an egg on them. Here your guide will almost certainly fry an egg to demonstrate the intense heat of the rocks.

⑩ The island's highest point, **Chance's Peak,** pokes up 3,002 feet through the rain forests. Your best bet is to walk up the 2,003 steps built into the side of the mountain, as an over-the-terrain climb to the top is arduous—and shouldn't be attempted without a guide. The hike may be tiring, but if you do make it to the top, what little breath you may have left will be taken away by the view.

Also in this area is the old **Galway's Estate,** a plantation built in the late 17th century by the prosperous Irishmen John and Henry Blake, who came to Montserrat from Galway. All that now remains

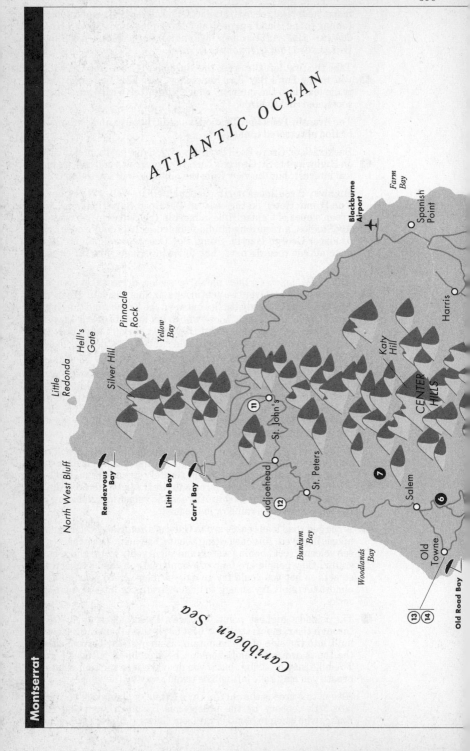

Montserrat

ATLANTIC OCEAN

Caribbean Sea

Little
Redonda

North West Bluff

Hell's
Gate

Pinnacle
Rock

Silver Hill

Yellow
Bay

Blackburne
Airport

Farm
Bay

Spanish
Point

Harris

Katy
Hill

CENTER
HILLS

Rendezvous
Bay

Little Bay

Carr's Bay

⑪
St. John's

Cudjoehead

⑫
St. Peters

Bunkum
Bay

Woodlands
Bay

⑦

Salem

⑥

Old
Towne

⑬ ⑭
Old Road Bay

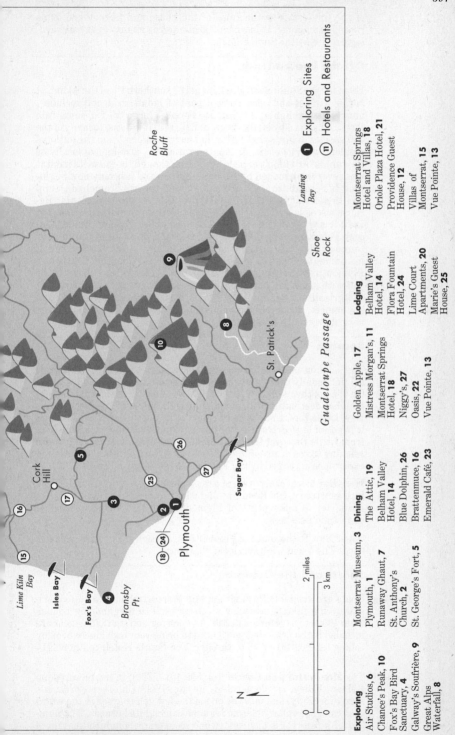

Exploring
Air Studios, **6**
Chance's Peak, **10**
Fox's Bay Bird
Sanctuary, **4**
Galway's Soufrière, **9**
Great Alps
Waterfall, **8**

Montserrat Museum, **3**
Plymouth, **1**
Runaway Ghaut, **7**
St. Anthony's
Church, **2**
St. George's Fort, **5**

Dining
The Attic, **19**
Belham Valley
Hotel, **14**
Blue Dolphin, **26**
Brattenmuce, **16**
Emerald Café, **23**

Golden Apple, **17**
Mistress Morgan's, **11**
Montserrat Springs
Hotel, **18**
Niggy's, **27**
Oasis, **22**
Vue Pointe, **13**

Lodging
Belham Valley
Hotel, **14**
Flora Fountain
Hotel, **24**
Lime Court
Apartments, **20**
Marie's Guest
House, **25**

Montserrat Springs
Hotel and Villas, **18**
Oriole Plaza Hotel, **21**
Providence Guest
House, **12**
Villas of
Montserrat, **15**
Vue Pointe, **13**

1 Exploring Sites

11 Hotels and Restaurants

of the fine estate is the ruins of the house and factory and some rusted machinery. It has been earmarked as an important archaeological site by the Smithsonian.

Off the Beaten Track

Head for the **South Soufrière Hills** at the southern tip of the island. It is the wildest and least spoiled part of Montserrat and includes, among its highlights, the **Bamboo Forest,** a large tract of semi–rain forest inhabited by birds, frogs, and plants. It is home to many of the 100 species of birds that visit Montserrat, among them the national emblem, *iaterus oberi,* or Montserrat oriole, also known locally as the tannia bird (don't expect to see one, though, because its habitat was severely damaged by Hurricane Hugo and it is only now beginning to reestablish itself). What you will see are bromeliads, tulip and breadfruit trees, and a plethora of other tropical plants. Because no roads lead into the area and there are no marked paths, you are advised to go with a guide. The most knowledgeable guide is **Joseph Peters,** a young man who will take you on a two- to three-hour tour and fill you in on the wildlife and botany. He can be reached at his home (tel. 809/491–6850) or via the Department of Tourism in Plymouth. James Daley, one of the forest rangers, can also provide you with helpful information. He can be reached at the **Department of Agriculture** (tel. 809/491–2546). Plans are afoot for some sort of low-impact, ecotourism development in the area, but things move very slowly on Montserrat.

Beaches

The sand on the beaches on Montserrat's south coast is of volcanic origin; usually referred to as black, it's actually light to dark gray. On the northwest coast, the sand is beige or white. The three most popular destinations for swimming and sunning are **Rendezvous Bay, Little Bay,** and **Carr's Bay,** all on the northwest coast. Though it is possible to drive to both Carr's Bay and Little Bay and to hike from Little Bay over the hill to Rendezvous Bay, it is certainly more relaxing to reach any of these beaches via the sailing and snorkeling excursions arranged by the **Vue Pointe Hotel** (tel. 809/491–5210).

Fox's Bay has a lovely strip of gray sand on the bay just north of the bird sanctuary. **Old Road Bay** and **Isles Bay** are on the coast north of Fox's Bay (4 miles north of Plymouth) and also have stretches of gray-sand beaches.

Sugar Bay, to the south of Plymouth, is a beach of fine gray volcanic sand. The Yacht Club overlooks this beach.

Sports and the Outdoors

Boating Boats are available through **Captain Martin,** who has a 46-foot trimaran and takes guests for a full-day sail to neighboring islands from 10 AM to 5 PM for about $45. An open bar and snorkeling gear are included in the price, but you'll need to bring your own lunch (book by calling tel. 809/491–5738 or through **Vue Pointe Hotel,** tel. 809/491–5210).

Golf The **Montserrat Golf Course** (tel. 809/491–5220), in the picturesque Belham Valley, is "slope rated" by the USGA (in other words, it's incredibly hilly) and must be one of the few golf courses in the world that can list gopher holes and iguanas among its hazards. The number of holes (11) is also somewhat eccentric, though by playing a number of them twice, you can get your 18. Four fairways run along the ocean. The rest are up hill and down dale. Watch out for the iguanas—they collect golf balls.

Mountain Biking Montserrat is perfect mountain-bike country: small, relatively traffic-free roads with lots of challenging hills to try out all those gears. An excellent addition to the island's facilities is the fleet of cross-terrain and mountain bikes available from **Island Bikes** (tel. 809/491–5552 or 809/491–4696) in Harney Street, Plymouth. Rentals run at $25 per day or $110 per week. Guided tours, which include refreshments and a support vehicle for the faint of heart, are available.

Sailing, Snorkeling, and Scuba Diving Snorkeling equipment is provided on the day cruises to the whitesand coves on the west coast; boats usually have an open bar. Arrangements can be made through the **Vue Pointe Hotel** (tel. 809/491–5210) or **Captain Martin** (tel. 809/491–5738).

Sea Wolf Diving School (tel. 809/491–7807) in Plymouth is currently the only dive operation on the island offering one- or two-tank dives, night dives, and instruction from a PADI-certified teacher. Costs are about $40 for a one-tank dive and $60 for a two-tank dive.

Danny Water Sports (tel. 809/491–5645), operating out of the Vue Pointe Hotel, rents snorkel equipment and Windsurfers and also offers fishing, Sunfish sailing, and waterskiing.

Tennis There are lighted tennis courts at the **Vue Pointe Hotel** (tel. 809/491–5210) and the **Montserrat Springs Hotel** (tel. 809/491–2481). Daylight-only courts are also available at the **Montserrat Golf Club** (tel. 809/491–5220).

Windsurfing Contact **Danny Water Sports** (tel. 809/491–5645) to rent boards (about $10 per 45 minutes).

Spectator Sports Cricket is the national passion. Cricket and soccer matches are held from February through June in **Sturge Park. Shamrock Car Park** is the venue for netball and basketball games. Contact the Department of Tourism (tel. 809/491–2230) for schedules.

Shopping

Montserrat's sea-island cotton is famous for its high quality. Unfortunately, only a limited amount could be grown, and that was *before* Hurricane Hugo. Since then, the supply has been even more limited. Several new boutiques have opened, however, and there are also always good buys on hand-turned pottery, straw goods, and jewelry bits made from shells and coral. Montserratian stamps can be purchased at the post office or at the Philatelic Bureau, just across the bridge in Wapping. Two lip-smacking local food products are Cassell's hot sauce, available at most supermarkets, and Perk's Punch, an effervescent rum-based concoction manufactured by **J. W. R. Perkins, Inc.** (tel. 809/491–2596).

Good Buys
Clothes **Jus' Looking** (George St., Plymouth, tel. 809/491–4076) is a boutique that opened in 1989 featuring "sculpted," hand-painted pillows from Antigua; painted and lacquered boxes from Tortola; Sunny Caribbee's jams, jellies, and packaged spices from the British West Indies (including an Arawak love potion and a hangover cure); special teas; and Caribelle Batik's line of richly colored fabrics, shirts, skirts, pants, and dressesfor him and her. (These batiks originated in St. Kitts.) The shop also has an excellent selection of local poetry and history books. **Montserrat Shirts** (Parliament St., tel. 809/491–2892) has a good selection of T-shirts and sandals. **Etcetera** (John St., tel. 809/491–3299) has American-imported

dresses and a small, but fine, selection of local crafts. If you're lucky, you may see someone making a hat of coconut palm fronds.

The **Montserrat Sea Island Cotton Co.** (corner of George and Strand Sts., Plymouth, tel. 809/491–7009) has long been famous for its cotton creations. Should you really need to purchase a T-shirt, stop in at **Sea Isle Style** (Parliament St., Plymouth, tel. 809/491–2892).

Crafts The **Tapestries of Montserrat** (Parliament St., tel. 809/491–2520), located on the second floor of the John Bull Shop, offers a floor-to-ceiling display of hand-tufted creations—from wall hangings and pillow covers to tote bags and rugs—all with fanciful yarn creations of flowers, carnival figures, animals, and birds. Owners Gerald and Charlie Handley will even help you create your own design for a small additional fee. **Carol's Corner** (Vue Pointe Hotel, tel. 809/491–5210) has finds by Carol Osborne that are first-rate: copper bookmarks and books ranging from the *Montserrat Cookbook* to Frane Lessac's books of prose and paintings. Drop by **Dutcher's Studio** (Olveston, tel. 809/491–5253) to see hand-cut, hand-painted objects made from glass, ceramics, and old bottles. If Paula Dutcher is there, ask about the morning iguana feeding at her house. Anywhere from 5 to 50 reptiles converge on her lawn, sunning themselves and eating hibiscus from your hand. **Island House,** (tel. 809/491–3938) on John Street, stocks Haitian art, Caribbean prints, and clay pottery.

Dining

Despite its size, Montserrat offers a variety of dining options to fit all budgets. Most of the more inexpensive eateries are found in small cafes, some of which look like the proverbial hole-in-the-wall. Don't be deceived, as most offer delicious Caribbean home-cooking. The island also has a lively assortment of rum shops—the Caribbean version of local bars—packed with islanders on Friday nights; you can join in and get a drink and a simple meal.

Montserrat's national dish is goatwater stew, made with goat meat and vegetables and similar to Irish stew. Goat meat is reminiscent of mutton. Mountain "chicken" (actually enormous frogs) is also a great favorite. Yams, breadfruit, christophine (a green vegetable), limes, mangoes, papayas, and a variety of seafood are served in most restaurants. Home-brewed ginger beer, one of the finest traditional drinks of the West Indies, is widely available.

Highly recommended restaurants are indicated by a star ★.

Category	Cost*
Expensive	over $30
Moderate	$20–$30
Inexpensive	under $20

per person, excluding drinks and service. If the service charge is not added to the bill, leave a 10%–15% tip.

Montserrat Springs Hotel. The split-level dining room, enclosed on three sides, faces a large pool and a sun deck and has views of the ocean. The menu features Caribbean cuisine that makes use of local fruits and vegetables. Broiled snapper and grilled tenderloin steak are two specialties, and there are several chicken and seafood dishes. *Richmond Hill, Plymouth, tel. 809/491–2481. Reservations suggested in season. AE, MC, V. Expensive.*

★ **Vue Pointe.** Candlelit dining in the hotel's restaurant overlooking the sea makes this a very romantic place, and with 60% of the roster made up of return guests, the atmosphere is that of a house party. The menu may include West Indian curried chicken, beef Wellington, red snapper with Creole sauce, and for dessert, a luscious lime pie or cheesecake. The Wednesday-night barbecue, accompanied by music from a steel band, is a popular island event. *Old Towne, tel. 809/491–5210. Reservations suggested for dinner. AE, MC, V. Expensive.*

★ **Belham Valley Hotel.** The best tables at this romantic candlelit restaurant are on the open-air terrace. Hung with ferns and croton plants, it looks down over picturesque Belham Valley and the lights of Isle Bay Hill opposite. The sound of tree frogs and the splash of the ocean mingle with the clink of glasses and the music of Stan Getz and Astrud Gilberto. Hibiscus tumbles over stone walls and sprouts from table vases; ceilings and floors are timbered—all this as you enjoy one of the best menus on the island. Appetizers include conch fritters and liver pâté. Main dishes include Seafood Delight (sautéed lobster, red snapper, and sea scallops in a vermouth sauce) and broiled baby lobster tails. Scrumptious desserts are mango or lime mousse, lemon cake, and a tropical fruit sundae with a ginger sauce. At lunchtime, the offerings are lighter: omelets, salads, and sandwiches. On Thursdays a good Chinese menu is offered. *Old Towne, tel. 809/491–5553. Reservations required for dinner. AE, MC, V. No lunch weekends; closed Mon. Moderate–Expensive.*

Emerald Café. Dining is relaxed at 10 tables inside and on the terrace, where there are white tables shaded by blue umbrellas. Burgers, sandwiches, salads, and grilled-plate lunches are served at lunchtime. Dinner dishes include tournedos sautéed in spicy butter, broiled or sautéed Caribbean lobster, T-bone steak, mountain chicken Diable, and kingfish, broiled or sautéed. The homemade pastries, such as Island Coconut Pie, are superb. There's also an ample list of liqueurs and wines, a full bar, and entertainment on weekends. *Wapping, Plymouth, tel. 809/491–3821. Dinner reservations suggested in season. MC. Closed Sun. Moderate.*

Oasis. A 200-year-old stone building houses this restaurant, where you can dine outdoors on the patio. Entrées include mountain chicken, jumbo shrimp Provençale, and red snapper with lime butter. Owners Eric and Mandy Finnamore, well known for their fish-and-chips, will also cook to order with proper notice. *Wapping, Plymouth, tel. 809/491–2328. Reservations suggested in season. No credit cards. Closed Wed. Moderate.*

The Attic. For breakfast, lunch, and dinner, the 12 busy tables of this second-floor restaurant supply townsfolk with specialties of *roti* (West Indian sandwiches); chicken, vegetable, or shrimp quesadilla; ocean perch; pork chops with "pantry" sauce (the chef mixes whatever's in the cupboard!); breaded shrimp; and lobster tail. *Marine Dr., Plymouth, tel. 809/491–2008. No credit cards. Inexpensive.*

★ **Blue Dolphin.** The inside is short on ambience—the chairs are Naugahyde, and the menu is scrawled on a blackboard without prices or descriptions—but the seductive aromas wafting from the kitchen announce that the Blue Dolphin serves some of the best food on the island, including luscious pumpkin fritters, mouth-watering lobster, and meltingly tender mountain chicken. And this hilltop-perched eatery has a fabulous view of the town and sea. *Amersham, tel. 809/491–3263. No credit cards. Inexpensive.*

Brattenmuce. About 10 minutes by car above the road from Plymouth to Belham Valley, you can't miss the canary yellow facade and brightly colored croton bushes of this restaurant. The name is a play on the name of the owners, Matt Hawthorne and Bruce Munro, two Toronto exiles who have been in Montserrat since 1985. They serve no-frills, North American cuisine—meat loaf and creamed potatoes, curried pork chops, and chicken cordon bleu. On Wednesday nights they have a Games Night, which is popular with "the snow birds," retirees from the North. A three-course meal for E.C.$25 includes free use of the Scrabble boards and Trivial Pursuit. For those who want to stay over, Rogie's, above the restaurant, has simple rooms to let. In the off-season Brattenmuce is open on Wednesday, Friday, and Saturday in the evening. In season, it closes only on Mondays. *Belham Valley, tel. 809/419–7564. Reservations suggested. No credit cards. Inexpensive.*

Golden Apple. In this large, galleried stone building, you'll be served huge plates of good, local cooking: the restaurant's special goatwater stew (weekends only) cooked outside over an open fire; souse; *pelau* (chicken-and-rice curry); conch, stewed or curried; and mountain chicken. Tables are covered with cheerful red-and-white-checked tablecloths; families will appreciate the relaxed atmosphere. There's also a grocery store attached. Fun and funky. *Cork Hill, tel. 809/491–2187. No credit cards. Inexpensive.*

Mistress Morgan's. Saturday is goatwater-stew day at Mistress Morgan's, and from 11:30 onward you can join the carloads of locals who make the trek up here to the north of the island to eat their fill. A hearty bowl of the stew costs E.C.$8 (U.S.$3.50), and diners eat at four picnic tables in a simple, unadorned room with seafoam walls. The food is definitely down-home: souse, baked chicken, and the increasingly hard-to-find goatwater stew that's served just the way it should be—with the flesh falling off the bone, brimming with dumplings and innards. If you like that sort of thing, you'll find yourself coming back. *Airport Rd., St. John's, tel. 809/491–5419. No credit cards. Inexpensive.*

★ **Niggy's.** In his previous life, the owner was a British character actor in Hollywood for many years before he decided to trade the smell of greasepaint and the roar of the crowd for a place behind the bar in this simple, but attractive, restaurant. When it opened in the fall of 1992, Niggy's immediately became one of the island's best-kept secrets (the British governor eats here regularly). It doesn't look like much from the outside—a simple clapboard cottage with yellow bella flowers trailing over the gate—but the food, served at picnic-style benches under a trellis of flowering plants, is excellent and a good value. Inside at the bar, an ingeniously converted fishing boat, the owner will regale you with tales of Hollywood —and the whole place feels like a set for a Caribbean remake of *Casablanca*. For those who want to stay over, there are two simple but clean rooms in the back. *Kinsale, tel. 809/491–7489. No credit cards. Inexpensive.*

Lodging

Accommodations on Montserrat are limited. The two largest hotels—the Vue Point and Montserrat Springs—are also the island's only real resorts. Small hotels that cater to businesspeople, guest houses, and a few bed-and-breakfasts are also available. Be aware that most hotels are still "tropical breeze–cooled": Only a few have rooms that are air-conditioned.

Villas are not only affordable here; given their comforts and conveniences, they're preferable to the hotels. You can even request the properties where your favorite rock stars—from Sting to Elton John—relaxed.

Most of Montserrat's hotels operate on the Modified American Plan (MAP: breakfast and dinner are included in the rate).

Highly recommended lodgings are indicated by a star ★.

Category	Cost*
Expensive	over $145
Moderate	$75–$145
Inexpensive	under $75

All prices are for a standard double room for two in winter, excluding 7% tax and 10% service charge.

Hotels   **Montserrat Springs Hotel and Villas.** This hotel, even though it underwent substantial renovation after Hurricane Hugo, has lost some of its allure. The sweeping view—ocean in one direction, Chance's Peak in the other—from the terrace surrounding the beautiful outdoor swimming pool (at 70 feet, the largest in Montserrat) is still one of the island's highlights, though. The rooms, in a wing of the main building and in cottages along the steep hillside sloping down to the beach, are air-conditioned, spacious, and well appointed. All the rooms have private balconies, phones, hair dryers, and cable TV. There are two lighted tennis courts, and the beach bar with a whirlpool filled with piping hot mineral water direct from a soufrière is a special treat. But the breakfasts are overpriced and miserly and the staff and service rather below standard for a hotel of its class. *Box 259, Plymouth, tel. 809/491–2482 or 800/253–2134, fax 809/491–4070. 40 rooms and 6 suites. Facilities: restaurant, 2 bars, room service, pool, hot/cold mineral-water Jacuzzi, beach, 2 lighted tennis courts, AE, MC, V. EP, MAP. Expensive.*

★   **Villas of Montserrat.** If you've ever wanted to do an island in style, this is the way to do it. After you're chauffeured to your villa, you'll be treated to a cold lobster and champagne supper. The next morning, a maid will serve you breakfast on your patio, give you a familiarization tour, and take you grocery shopping (you can cook yourself or pay extra to have a chef prepare your meals). The rate of $1,500 to $2,000 a week in high season is for up to six people and includes all of the above, as well as daily maid service. Each three-bedroom, ceiling fan– and tropical breeze–cooled villa is decorated island-style with upholstered rattan furnishings and has a color TV, microwave oven, dishwasher, three bathrooms, a whirlpool bathtub, and a private swimming pool. The cluster of villas overlooks Isle Bay and the Caribbean. *Box 421, Plymouth, tel. 809/491–5513 or 408/685–3498. 3 villas. Facilities: pool, full kitchen. No credit cards. EP. Expensive.*

★   **Vue Pointe.** The moment you arrive here you feel as though both the staff and the owners, Cedric and Carol Osborne, really care about your well-being. The gracious Monday-night cocktail parties that the Osbornes host at their house, with drinks, delicious homemade hors d'ouevres, and good conversation, are a perfect example. (Cedric Osborne comes from one of the island's first families and is a mine of information about local goings-on). The breeze-cooled accommodations include 12 rooms in the main building and 28 hexagonal rondavels that spill down to the gray-sand beach on Old Road Bay. Each rondavel has a large bedroom, great view, cable TV, phone, hair dryer, minifridge, and spacious bathroom. In the main building a large lounge and bar overlook the pool; the Wednesday night barbecue, with steel bands and other entertainment, is an event wellattended by locals and guests alike. In the adjacent sea-view restaurant, you can have a candlelight dinner of local and international specialties (the chef is one of the most skilled on the island). A 150-seat conference center serves as a theater and disco, and for water-sports enthusiasts, there is scuba diving, snorkeling, and fishing. What more could you want? *Box 65, Plymouth, tel. 809/491–5210 or 800/235–0709; fax 809/491–4813. 12 rooms, 28 rondavels. Facilities: restaurant, bar, gift shop, pool, 2 lighted tennis courts, water-sports center. AE, MC, V. EP, MAP. Closed Sept. Moderate–Expensive.*

Flora Fountain Hotel. This is a hotel for people coming on business (only 35% of the clientele are tourists) or for those who appreciate an old, rambling hotel in the heart of town. The two-story structure has been created around an enormous fountain that's sometimes lighted at night, with small tables scattered in the inner courtyard. There are 18 serviceable rooms, all with tile bath, air-conditioning, and phone, and most with balconies. The restaurant has a chef from Bombay who serves simple sandwiches and fine Indian dishes, particularly on Friday night, which is Indian buffet night: several meat and fish dishes, at least two kinds of rice, vegetable and pork dishes with spices and *raita* (a yogurt sauce), and *samosa* (spicy meat patties). *Box 373, Church Rd., Plymouth, tel. 809/491–6092, fax 809/491–2568. 18 rooms. Facilities: restaurant, bar. AE, D, MC, V. EP, CP, MAP. Moderate.*

★ **Providence Guest House.** On an island where it is almost impossible to find good bed-and-breakfast accommodations, this guest house, perched on a bluff high above the ocean with spectacular views of St. Kitts and Redonda, stands out. Formerly a plantation house, this beautiful stone-and-wood building, with its spider-box balustrade, wraparound veranda, and gleaming swimming pool edged with tiles from Trinidad, has been lovingly restored by its present owners. It now ranks as one of the finest examples of traditional Caribbean architecture on the island. In its day, it was host to such luminaries as Paul McCartney, Stevie Wonder, and Carl Perkins. The two guest rooms—one has a bath as well as a shower and is considerably larger—are on the ground floor and open directly onto the pool area. Both have the original timbered ceilings and massive stone walls, which keep them cool in the summer, and are decorated with red quarry tiles and attractive pastel fabrics. If there is any drawback to this idyll, it is the location. The nearest restaurant is three miles away in Belham Valley, and the nearest beach is a hike down the hillside. But the owners are willing to make evening meals on request, and they have also provided a kitchenette by the pool where guests can prepare their own meals. *Providence Estate House, Montserrat, tel. 809/491–6476. 2 rooms. Facilities: swimming pool, kitchenette, cable TV. No credit cards. CP. Inexpensive–Moderate.*

Belham Valley Hotel. On a hillside overlooking Belham Valley and the Belham Valley River, this hotel has three non-air-conditioned, self-catering units: a cottage and two apartments (a studio and a newer two-bedroom), all with stereo, cable TV, fully equipped kitchen, and phone. It's the restaurant here that's the big draw, with its lovely views and great food. The beach is an eight-minute walk away. *Box 409, Plymouth, tel. 809/491–5553. 3 units. Facilities: restaurant, maid service. AE, MC. EP. Inexpensive.*

Lime Court Apartments. This slightly run-down, large white colonial-style apartment building is right in the center of town opposite the Parliament building. The downstairs apartments tend to be dark and airless, and with the sound of the generator and the puttering of the fridges, not that peaceful. But the large, well-equipped, two-bedroom, two-bath "penthouse," up a flight of steps at the top of the building, has a fine view from the balcony over the town's red rooftops to the sea beyond. It can sleep two couples and is reasonable at $45 per night. All apartments come with kitchenettes, including a stove and microwave, and have private bathrooms (showers only). *Box 250, Parliament St., Plymouth, tel. 809/491–3656. 8 apartments. Facilities: maid service, cable TV. AE, MC, V. EP. Inexpensive.*

Marie's Guest House. This well-kept modern bungalow, set on a half acre of garden, is half a mile from Plymouth on the main road north. Marie, a soft-spoken islander with a reserved manner, keeps the place neat and tidy, and the rooms, with their mosquito nets, tasteful fabrics, good, solid furniture, and clean, tiled bathrooms are a good value, running only $30 a night year-round. At the front of the house there is a communal living-dining area, where guests can make their own simple meals. *The Groves, Plymouth, tel. 809/419–2745. 4 rooms. Facilities: maid service. No credit cards. EP. Inexpensive.*

Oriole Plaza Hotel. Right in the center of town, about five minutes' walk from the post office and from Wapping Beach, the town's only beach, this simple but well-kept hotel was substantially refurbished after Hugo and now caters mostly to businesspeople. Rooms off a long corridor upstairs have either two twin beds or one queen-size bed. Some also have a balcony. All rooms have ceiling fans, private bathroom (shower only), cable TV, and phone. The three rooms at the back of the building are simpler—and cheaper—but have the advantage of opening onto a sunny wooden landing from which you can see Chance's Peak. BB's, the restaurant in the downstairs foyer, serves marlin, lobster, and mountain chicken at reasonable prices. *Parliament St., Box 250, Plymouth, tel. 809/491–6982, fax 809/491–6690. 12 rooms with ceiling fans. Facilities: restaurant, bar. AE, MC, V. EP. Inexpensive.*

Villas and Condominiums Villas at the top end of the market is a niche that Montserrat decided, back in the 1980s, that it was going to fill. The result is a great range of accommodations catering to those who want to do it themselves on the island. All the villa developments are on the west coast of the island, within 20 minutes of Plymouth by car. The majority are in the districts of Old Towne, Olveston, and Woodlands. The latter, with its steep hillsides covered in luxuriant vegetation and magnificent views of the ocean, is especially noteworthy. Prices start at about $350 per week and spiral quickly up to $2,000 (for which you will get a luxurious villa that can sleep 6 people). Off-season rates are as much as 50% lower (and usually negotiable), and some excellent bargains can be picked up by summer travelers. All come with maid service, and most come with pools.

Caribbean Connection Plus (tel. 203/261–8603) is a Stateside reservation service for about 50 villas and apartments. They also have an on-island representative to ensure that all goes well. **Montserrat Enterprises Ltd** (Box 58, Marine Dr., Plymouth, tel. 809/491–2431 [ask for Mr. Edwards], fax 809/491–4660) has 22 villas in Old Towne, Woodlands, and Isles Bay. **Neville Bradshaw Agencies** (Box 270, Plymouth, tel. 809/491–5270, fax 809/491–5069) has a wide range of villas, mostly in Old Towne and Isles Bay. **Isles Bay Plantation** (Box 64, Plymouth, tel. 809/491–5248, fax 890/491–5016; in London, tel. and fax 071/482–1071), known locally as the Beverly Hills of Montserrat, has the crème de la crème of Montserrat's villas. **Shamrock Villas** (Box 180, Plymouth, tel. 809/491–2974) are one- and two-bedroom apartments and town-house condominiums in a hillside development minutes from Plymouth.

Nightlife

The hotels offer regularly scheduled barbecues and steel bands, and the small restaurants feature live entertainment in the form of calypso, reggae, rock, rhythm and blues, and soul.

The Yacht Club (Wapping, tel. 809/491–2237) has live island music on Friday, while the **Plantation Club** (Wapping, upstairs over the Oasis, tel. 809/491–2892) is a lively late-night place with taped rhythm and blues, soul, and *soca* (Caribbean music). **La Cave** (Evergreen Dr., Plymouth, no tel.), featuring West Indian–style disco and Caribbean and international music, is popular among the young locals. **Nepcoden** (Weekes, no tel.), with its ultraviolet lights, peace signs, and black walls, is a throwback to the '60s. In this cellar restaurant you can eat rotis or chicken for $6. **Jazzy's** (Parliment St., Plymouth, no tel.) features live jazz on weekend nights. **Colors** (Fox's Bay, no tel.) is the island's newest and currently most popular nightclub, with live bands and lots of dancing on weekends.

The Village Place. In its heyday this funky bar and disco on a hillside outside Plymouth was *the* hangout for rock glitterati like Eric Clapton, Sting, and Elton John while they recorded at Monserrat's legendary Air Studios, founded by George Martin of Beatles fame. Mick Jagger is even known to have eaten owner Andy Lawrence's secret chicken spiced with paprika and thyme. These days, though, Andy's allure is just a little faded—the local bands trying out are rarely that good; the drinking is heavy-duty; and on Saturdays, it is full and loud. A must for rock nostalgics; others may want to pass. *Salem, tel. 809/491–5202. No credit cards. Open 6–midnight. Closed Tues.*

17 Puerto Rico

Updated by
Jordan
Simon

No city in the Caribbean is as steeped in Spanish tradition as Puerto Rico's Old San Juan. Originally built as a fortress enclave, the old city's myriad attractions include restored 16th-century buildings, museums, art galleries, bookstores, and 200-year-old houses with balustraded balconies of filigreed wrought iron overlooking narrow cobblestone streets. This Spanish tradition also spills over into the island's countryside, from its festivals celebrated in honor of various patron saints in the little towns to the *paradores*, those homey, inexpensive inns whose concept originated in Spain.

Puerto Rico boasts hundreds of beaches with every imaginable water sport available, acres of golf courses, and miles of tennis courts. It has, in San Juan's sophisticated Condado and Isla Verde areas, glittering hotels; flashy, Las Vegas–style shows; casinos; and frenetic discos. It has the ambience of the Old World in the seven-square-block area of the old city and in its quiet colonial towns. Out in the countryside lie its natural attractions including the extraordinary, 28,000-acre Caribbean National Forest, more familiarly known as the El Yunque rain forest, with its 100-foot-high trees (more than 240 species of them) and its dramatic mountain ranges. You can also hike through forest reserves laced with trails, go spelunking in vast caves, and explore coffee plantations and sugar mills. Having seen every sight on the island, you can then do further exploring on the islands of Culebra, Vieques, Icacos, and Mona, where aquatic activities, such as snorkeling and scuba diving, prevail.

Puerto Rico, 110 miles long and 35 miles wide (about the size of Connecticut), was populated by several tribes of Indians when Columbus landed on the island on his second voyage in 1493. In 1508, Juan Ponce de León, the frustrated seeker of the Fountain of Youth, established a settlement on the island and became its first governor, and in 1521, he founded Old San Juan. For three centuries, the French, Dutch, and English tried unsuccessfully to wrest the island from Spain. In 1897, Spain granted the island dominion status. Two years later, Spain ceded the island to the United States, and in 1917, Puerto Ricans became U.S. citizens. In 1952, Puerto Rico became a semiautonomous commonwealth territory of the United States.

As such, if you're a U.S. citizen, you need neither passport nor visa when you land at the bustling Luis Muñoz Marín International Airport, outside San Juan. You don't have to clear customs, and you don't have to explain yourself to an immigration official. English is widely spoken, though the official language is Spanish.

Before You Go

Tourist
Information

Contact the **Puerto Rico Tourism Company** (tel. 800/223–6530 or 800/866–STAR). Other branches: 575 5th Ave., 23rd Floor, New York, NY 10017, tel. 212/599–6262, fax 212/818–1866; 3575 W. Cahuenga Blvd., Suite 560, Los Angeles, CA 90068, tel. 213/874–5991, fax 213/874–7257; 901 Ponce de Leon Blvd, Suite 604, Coral Gables, FL 33134, tel. 305/445–9112 or 800/815–7391, fax 305/445–9450.

Addresses of representatives in other cities can be obtained by calling the toll-free numbers above.

Arriving and
Departing
By Plane

The Luis Muñoz Marín International Airport (tel. 809/462–3147), east of downtown San Juan, is the Caribbean hub for **American Airlines** (tel. 800/433–7300). American has daily nonstop flights from New York, Newark, Miami, Boston, Philadelphia, Chicago, Nashville, Los Angeles, Dallas, Baltimore, Hartford, Raleigh-Durham,

Washington, D.C., and Tampa. **Delta** (tel. 800/221–1212) has non-stop service from Atlanta and Orlando, as well as connecting service from other major cities. **Northwest** (tel. 800/447–4747) has recently added nonstop flights from Detroit to San Juan. **TWA** (tel. 800/892–4141) flies nonstop from New York and Miami. **United** (tel. 800/241–6522) flies nonstop from Washington, D.C., and Chicago. **USAir** (tel. 800/428–4322) offers daily nonstop flights from Philadelphia and Charlotte. Puerto Rico–based **Carnival Airlines** (tel. 800/437–2110) operates weekly nonstop flights from New York, Newark, Miami, and Orlando to San Juan, Ponce, and Aguadilla.

Foreign carriers include **Air France** (tel. 800/237–2747), **British Airways** (tel. 800/247–9297), **BWIA** (tel. 800/538–2942), **Iberia** (tel. 800/772–4642), **LACSA** (tel. 800/225–2272), **LIAT** (tel. 809/791–3838), and **Lufthansa** (tel. 800/645–3880).

Connections between Caribbean islands can be made through **Air Jamaica** (tel. 809/791–3870 or 800/523–5585), **Dominicana Airline** (tel. 809/724–7100), and **Sunaire Express** (tel. 809/791–4755 or 800/595–9501).

From the Airport **Airport Limousine Service** (tel. 809/791–4745) provides minibus service to hotels in the Isla Verde, Condado, and Old San Juan areas at basic fares of $2.50, $3.50, and $4.50, respectively; the fares, which are set by the Public Service Commission, can vary, depending on the time of day and number of passengers. Limousines of **Dorado Transport Service** (tel. 809/796–1214) serve hotels and villas in the Dorado area for $8 per person. Taxi fare from the airport to Isla Verde is about $6–$10; to the Condado area, $12–$15; and to Old San Juan, $15–$18. Be sure the taxi driver starts the meter, or agree on a fare beforehand.

Passports and Visas Puerto Rico is a commonwealth of the United States, and U.S. citizens do not need passports to visit the island. British citizens must have passports. Canadian citizens need proof of citizenship (preferably a passport).

Language Puerto Rico's official language is Spanish, and although English is widely spoken, you will probably want to take a Spanish phrase book along if you rent a car to travel around the island.

Precautions San Juan, like any other big city and major tourist destination, has its share of crime, so guard your wallet or purse on the city streets. Puerto Rico's beaches are open to the public, and muggings occur at night even on the beaches of the posh Condado and Isla Verde tourist hotels. Don't leave anything unattended on the beach. Leave your valuables in the hotel safe, and stick to the fenced-in beach areas of your hotel. Always lock your car and stash valuables and luggage out of sight. Avoid deserted beaches day or night.

Staying in Puerto Rico

Important Addresses The government-sponsored **Puerto Rico Tourism Company** (Paseo la Princesa, Old San Juan, Puerto Rico 00902, tel. 809/721–2400) is an excellent source for maps and printed tourist materials. Pick up a free copy of *¿Qué Pasa?*, the official visitors' guide.

Information offices are also found at **Luis Muñoz Marín International Airport,** Isla Verde (tel. 809/791–1014 or 809/791–2551); **301 Calle San Justo,** Old San Juan (tel. 809/723–3135 or 809/723–0017); and **La Casita,** near Pier 1 in Old San Juan (tel. 809/722–1709). Out on the island, information offices are located in **Ponce** (Casa Armstrong-Poventud, Plaza, Las Delicias, tel. 809/840–5695); **Aguadilla** (Rafael

Hernandez Airport, tel. 809/890–3315); and in each town's city hall on the main plaza. Offices are open weekdays from 8 to noon and 1 to 4:30.

Emergencies **Police, fire, and medical emergencies:** Call 911. **Hospitals:** Hospitals in the Condado/Santurce area with 24-hour emergency rooms are **Ashford Community Hospital** (1451 Av. Ashford, tel. 809/721–2160) and **San Juan Health Centre** (200 Av. De Diego, tel. 809/725–0202). **Pharmacies:** In San Juan, **Walgreens** (1130 Av. Ashford, tel. 809/ 725–1510) operates a 24-hour pharmacy; in Old San Juan, try **Puerto Rico Drug Company** (157 Calle San Francisco, tel. 809/725–2202). Walgreens operates more than 20 pharmacies on the island.

Currency The U.S. dollar is the official currency of Puerto Rico.

Taxes and Service Charges The government tax on room charges is 7% (9% in hotels with casinos). There is no departure tax. Some hotels automatically add a 10%–15% service charge to your bill. In restaurants, a 15%–20% tip is expected.

Guided Tours Old San Juan can be seen either on a self-guided walking tour or on the free trolley. To explore the rest of the city and the island, consider renting a car. (We do, however, recommend a guided tour of the vast El Yunque rain forest.) If you'd rather not do your own driving, there are several tour companies you can call. Most San Juan hotels have a tour desk that can make arrangements for you. The standard half-day tours (at $15–$25) are of Old and New San Juan, Old San Juan and the Bacardi Rum Plant, Luquillo Beach and El Yunque rain forest. All-day tours ($25–$40) can include a trip to Ponce, a day at El Comandante Racetrack, or a combined tour of the city and El Yunque rain forest.

Leading tour operators include **Loose Penny Tours** (tel. 809/261–3333), **Gray Line of Puerto Rico** (tel. 809/727–8080), **Normandie Tours, Inc.** (tel. 809/725–6990 or 809/722–6308), **Rico Suntours** (tel. 809/722–2080 or 809/722–6090), and **United Tour Guides** (tel. 809/ 725–7605 or 809/723–5578). **Cordero Caribbean Tours** (tel. 809/780–2442; open 24 hours) does tours at hourly rates out on the island in air-conditioned limousines.

Getting Around Roads in Puerto Rico are generally well marked; however, a good road map is helpful when traveling to more remote areas on the island. Some car-rental agencies distribute free maps of the island when you pick up your car. Good maps are also found at **The Book Store** (257 Calle San José, Old San Juan, tel. 809/724–1815).

Taxis Metered cabs authorized by the **Public Service Commission** (tel. 809/ 751–5050) start at $1 and charge 10¢ for every additional ¹⁄₁₀ mile, 50¢ for every suitcase, and $1 for home or business calls. Waiting time is 10¢ for each 45 seconds. Be sure the driver begins the meter. You can also call **Major Taxicabs** in San Juan (tel. 809/723–2460) and **Ponce Taxi** (tel. 809/840–0088).

Buses The **Metropolitan Bus Authority** (tel. 809/767–7979) operates *guaguas* (buses) that thread through San Juan. The fare is 25¢, and the buses run in exclusive lanes, *against the traffic* on major thoroughfares, stopping at upright yellow posts marked *Parada* or *Parada de Guaguas*. The main terminals are Intermodal Terminal, Calles Marina and Harding, in Old San Juan, and Capetillo Terminal in Rio Piedras, next to the central business district.

Públicos *Públicos* (public cars), with yellow license plates ending in "P" or "PD," scoot to towns throughout the island, stopping in each town's main plaza. The 17-passenger cars operate primarily during the day, with routes and fares fixed by the Public Service Commission. In San Juan, the main terminals are at the airport and at Plaza Colón on the waterfront in Old San Juan.

Trolleys If your feet fail you in Old San Juan, climb aboard the free open-air trolleys that rumble and roller-coast through the narrow streets. Departures are from La Puntilla and from the marina, but you can board anywhere along the route.

Linéas *Linéas* are private taxis you share with three to five other passengers. There are over 20 companies, each usually specializing in a certain region. Most will arrange door-to-door service. Check local yellow pages listings under Linéas. They're a cheaper method of transport and a great way to meet people, but be prepared to wait: they usually don't leave until they have a full load.

Motor Coaches The **Puerto Rico Motor Coach Co.** (tel. 809/725–2460) offers charter service and 50-passenger buses for conventions.

Ferries The ferry between Old San Juan and Catano costs a mere 50¢ one-way. The ferry runs every half hour from 6:15 AM to 10 PM. The 400-passenger ferries of the **Fajardo Port Authority** (tel. 809/863–0705) make the 80-minute trip twice daily between Fajardo and Vieques (one-way $2 adults, $1 children 3–12) and the one-hour run between Fajardo and Culebra daily (one-way $2.25 adults, $1 children).

Rental Cars U.S. driver's licenses are valid in Puerto Rico for three months. All major U.S. car-rental agencies are represented on the island, including **Avis** (tel. 809/721–4499 or 800/331–1212), **Hertz** (tel. 809/791–0840 or 800/654–3131), and **Budget** (tel. 809/791–3685 or 800/527–0700). Local rental companies, sometimes less expensive, include **Caribbean Rental** (tel. 809/724–3980) and **L & M Car Rental** (tel. 809/725–8416, fax 809/725–8307). Prices start at about $30 (plus insurance), with unlimited mileage. Discounts are offered for long-term rentals, and insurance can be waived for those who rent with American Express credit cards. Some discounts are offered for AAA or 72-hour advance bookings. Most car rentals have shuttle service to or from the airport and the pickup point. If you plan to drive across the island, arm yourself with a good map and be aware that there are many unmarked roads up in the mountains. Many service stations in the central mountains do not take credit cards. Speed limits are posted in miles, distances in kilometers, and gas prices in liters.

Planes **Vieques Air-Link** (tel. 809/722–3736) flies from the Isla Grande Airport to Vieques for about $28 one-way, and **Flamenco Airways** (tel. 809/725–7707) flies to Culebra for $25 one-way.

Telephones and Mail The area code for Puerto Rico is 809. Puerto Rico uses U.S. postage stamps and has the same mail rates (19¢ for a postcard, 29¢ for a first-class letter). Post offices in major Puerto Rican cities offer Express Mail next-day service to the U.S. mainland and to Puerto Rican destinations.

Opening and Closing Times Shops are open from 9 to 6 (from 9 to 9 during Christmas holidays). Banks are open weekdays from 8:30 to 2:30 and Saturday from 9:45 to noon.

Exploring Puerto Rico

Numbers in the margin correspond to points of interest on the Old San Juan Exploring map.

Old San Juan   Old San Juan, the original city founded in 1521, contains authentic and carefully preserved examples of 16th- and 17th-century Spanish colonial architecture, some of the best in the New World. More than 400 buildings have been beautifully restored in a continuing effort to preserve the city. Graceful wrought iron balconies, decorated with lush green hanging plants, extend over narrow streets paved with blue gray stones (*adequines*, originally used as ballast for Spanish ships). The old city is partially enclosed by the old walls, dating from 1633, that once completely surrounded it. Designated a U.S. National Historic Zone in 1950, Old San Juan is chockablock with shops, open-air cafés, private homes, tree-shaded squares, monuments, plaques, pigeons, and people. The traffic is awful. Get an overview of the inner city on a morning's stroll (bearing in mind that this "stroll" includes some steep climbs). However, if you plan to immerse yourself in history or to shop, you'll need two or three days.

El Morro and Fort San Cristóbal are described in our walking tour: You may want to set aside extra time to see them, especially if you're an aficionado of military history. UNESCO has designated each fortress a World Heritage Site; each is also a National Historic Site. Both are administered by the National Park Service; you can take one of its tours or wander around on your own.

1   Sitting on a rocky promontory on the northwestern tip of the old city is **Fuerte San Felipe del Morro** ("El Morro"), a fortress built by the Spaniards between 1540 and 1783. Rising 140 feet above the sea, the massive six-level fortress covers enough territory to accommodate a nine-hole golf course. It is a labyrinth of dungeons, ramps and barracks, turrets, towers, and tunnels. Built to protect the port, El Morro has a commanding view of the harbor. Its small, air-conditioned museum traces the history of the fortress. *Calle Norzagaray, tel. 809/729–6960. Admission free. Open daily 9:15–6.*

2   San José Plaza is two short blocks from the entrance to El Morro, but for the moment we'll bypass it and head for the **San Juan Museum of Art and History,** which is a block east of the tour's path but a must. A bustling marketplace in 1855, this handsome building is now a modern cultural center that houses exhibits of Puerto Rican art. Multi-image audiovisual shows present the history of the island; concerts and other cultural events take place in the huge courtyard. *Calle Norzagaray, at the corner of Calle MacArthur, tel. 809/724–1875. Admission free. Open weekdays 8–noon and 1–4.*

3   Turn back west toward San José Plaza to **La Casa de los Contrafuertes,** on Calle San Sebastián. This building is also known as the Buttress House because wide exterior buttresses support the wall next to the plaza. The house is one of the oldest remaining private residences in Old San Juan. Inside is the Pharmacy Museum, a recreation of an 18th-century apothecary shop. *101 Calle San Sebastián, Plaza de San José, tel. 809/724–5949. Admission free. Open Wed.–Sun. 9–4:30.*

4   The **Pablo Casals Museum,** a bit farther down the block, contains memorabilia of the famed cellist, who made his home in Puerto Rico for the last 16 years of his life. The museum holds manuscripts, photographs, and his favorite cellos, in addition to recordings and videotapes of Casals Festival concerts (the latter shown on request). *101 Calle San Sebastián, Plaza de San José, tel. 809/723–9185. Admission free. Open Tues.–Sat. 9:30–5:30, Sun. 1–5, closed Mon.*

5   In the center of the plaza, next to the museum, is the **San José Church.** With its series of vaulted ceilings, it is a splendid example of 16th-century Spanish Gothic architecture. The church, which is one of the oldest Christian houses of worship in the Western Hemisphere, was built in 1532 under the supervision of the Dominican friars. The body of Ponce de León, the Spanish explorer who came to the New World seeking the Fountain of Youth, was buried here for almost three centuries before being removed in 1913 and placed in the San Juan Cathedral. *Calle San Sebastián, tel. 809/725–7501. Admission free. Open Mon.–Sat. 8:30–4; mass Sun. at 12:15 PM.*

6 Next door is the **Dominican Convent.** Built by Dominican friars in 1523, the convent often served as a shelter during Carib Indian attacks and, more recently, as headquarters for the Antilles command of the U.S. Army. Now home to the Institute of Puerto Rican Culture, the beautifully restored building contains an ornate 18th-century altar, religious manuscripts, artifacts, and art. Classical concerts are occasionally held here. *98 Calle Norzagaray, tel. 809/ 724–0700. Admission free. Chapel museum open Wed.–Sun. 9– noon and 1–4:30.*

7 From San José Plaza, walk west on Calle Beneficencia to **Casa Blanca.** The original structure on this site, not far from the ramparts of El Morro, was a frame house built in 1521 as a home for Ponce de León. But Ponce de León died in Cuba, never having lived in it, and it was virtually destroyed by a hurricane in 1523, after which Ponce de León's son-in-law had the present masonry home built. His descendants occupied it for 250 years. From the end of the Spanish-American War in 1898 to 1966, it was the home of the U.S. Army commander in Puerto Rico. A museum devoted to archaeology is on the second floor. The lush surrounding gardens, cooled by the spraying fountains, are a tranquil spot for a restorative pause. *1 Calle San Sebastián, tel. 809/724–4102. Admission free. Open Wed.–Sun. 9–noon and 1–4.*

8 Head east on Calle Sol and down Calle Cristo to **San Juan Cathedral.** This great Catholic shrine of Puerto Rico had humble beginnings in the early 1520s as a thatch-topped wood structure. Hurricane winds tore off the thatch and destroyed the church. It was reconstructed in 1540, when the graceful circular staircase and vaulted ceilings were added, but most of the work on the church was done in the 19th century. The remains of Ponce de León are in a marble tomb near the transept. *153 Calle Cristo, tel. 809/722–0861. Open daily 8:30–4. Masses: Sat. 7 PM, Sun. 9 AM and 11 AM, weekdays 12:15 PM.*

Time Out   Stop in at **Kambalache, First House of Tea** (252 Calle Cristo, tel. 809/ 724–5654) for coffee and exotic teas from around the world; try vanilla rum, dragon well, cinnamon bark, or Taiwan broken leaf tea. Seating is inside or at the busy streetside café.

Across the street from the cathedral you'll see the Gran Hotel El Convento, which was a Carmelite convent more than 300 years ago. Go west alongside the hotel on Caleta de las Monjas toward the city
9 wall to the **Plazuela de la Rogativa.** In the little plaza, statues of a bishop and three women commemorate a legend, according to which the British, while laying siege to the city in 1797, mistook the flaming torches of a *rogativa* (religious procession) for Spanish reinforcements and beat a hasty retreat. The monument was donated to the city in 1971 on its 450th anniversary.

10 One block south on Calle Recinto Oeste you'll come to **La Fortaleza,** which sits on a hill overlooking the harbor. La Fortaleza, the Western Hemisphere's oldest executive mansion in continual use and official residence of the present governor of Puerto Rico, was built as a fortress. The original primitive structure, built in 1540, has seen nu-

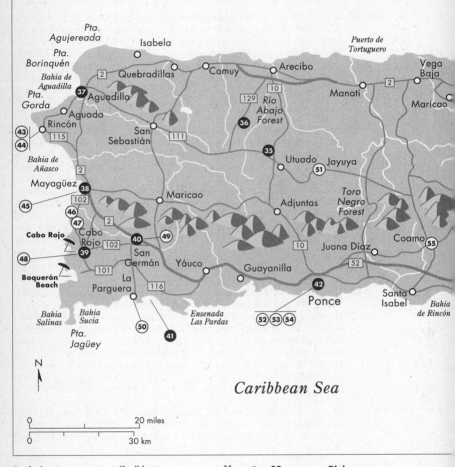

Pta.
Agujereada

Isabela

Puerto de
Tortuguero

Pta.
Borinquén

Bahía de
Aguadilla

2 Quebradillas

Camuy

Arecibo

Vega
Baja

Pta.
Gorda

37 Aguadilla

129 Río
Abajo
Forest

Manati

2

Maricao

43
44

Aguada
Rincón

Aguada

115

San
Sebastián

111

36

10

35

Utuado

Jayuya

51

Bahía de
Añasco

2

Mayagüez

38

Maricao

Toro
Negro
Forest

45

102

Adjuntas

46

47

2

40

49

Coamo

55

Cabo Rojo

Cabo
Rojo

102

Juana Díaz

48

39

San
Germán

Yáuco

Guayanilla

10

52

Boquerón
Beach

101

La
Parguera

116

42

Santa
Isabel

Bahía de
Rincón

Bahía
Salinas

Bahía
Sucia

Ensenada
Las Pardas

52 53 54

Ponce

Pta.
Jagüey

50

41

N

Caribbean Sea

0   20 miles
0   30 km

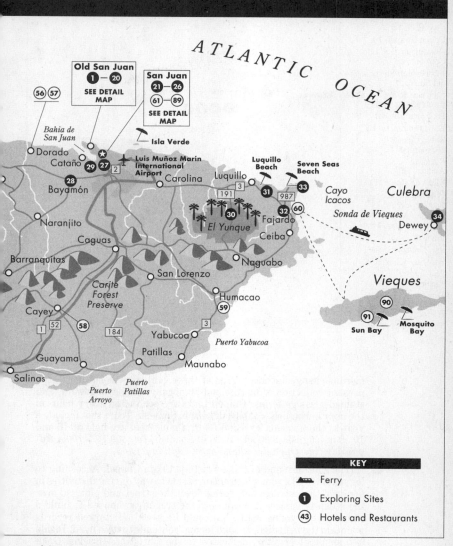

ATLANTIC OCEAN

Old San Juan
1 — 20
SEE DETAIL MAP

San Juan
21 — 26
61 — 89
SEE DETAIL MAP

56 57

Bahia de San Juan

Dorado   Cataño

Isla Verde

29 27

Luis Muñoz Marín International Airport

2

28

Bayamón

Carolina

3

Luquillo

Luquillo Beach

31

Seven Seas Beach

33

Cayo Icacos

Culebra

Naranjito

191

30

El Yunque

987

32   60

Sonda de Vieques

Dewey

34

Caguas

Fajardo

Barranquitas

Ceiba

Naguabo

Carite Forest Preserve

San Lorenzo

Vieques

Cayey

Humacao

59

90

1   52   58

184

Yabucoa

3

91

Sun Bay

Mosquito Bay

Guayama

Patillas

Puerto Yabucoa

Salinas

Maunabo

Puerto Arroyo

Puerto Patillas

KEY

Ferry

1 Exploring Sites

43 Hotels and Restaurants

Lodging
Casa del Francés, **91**
El Conquistador
Resort and Country
Club, **60**
Hilton International
Mayagüez, **45**
Horned Dorset
Primavera, **43**
Hyatt Dorado

Beach, **57**
Hyatt Regency
Cerromar Beach, **56**
Palmas del Mar, **59**
Parador Baños de
Coamo, **55**
Parador Boquemar, **48**
Parador Hacienda
Gripinas, **51**

Parador Oasis, **49**
Parador Villa
Parguera, **50**
Ponce Hilton
Hotel and Casino, **53**
Sea Gate (Vieques), **90**

Old San Juan Exploring

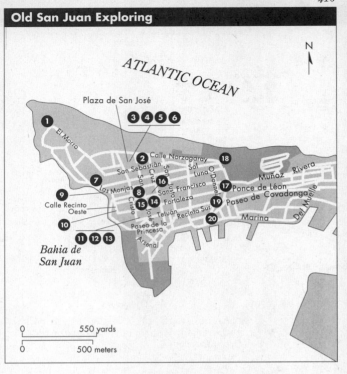

merous changes over a period of three centuries, resulting in the present collection of marble and mahogany, medieval towers, and stained-glass galleries. Guided tours are conducted every hour on the hour in English, on the half hour in Spanish. Tours that include a visit to the mansion's second floor, a must-see, are held at 10 and 10:50 in English, 9:30 and 10:30 in Spanish. *Tel. 809/721–7000. Admission free. Open weekdays (except holidays) 9–4.*

11 At the southern end of Calle Cristo is **Cristo Chapel.** According to legend, in 1753 a young horseman, carried away during festivities in honor of the patron saint, raced down the street and plunged over the steep precipice. A witness to the tragedy promised to build a chapel if the young man's life could be saved. Historical records maintain the man died, though legend contends that he lived. Inside is a small silver altar, dedicated to the Christ of Miracles. *Open Tues. 10–4 and on most Catholic holidays.*

12 Across the street from the chapel, the 18th-century **Casa del Libro** has exhibits devoted to books and bookbinding. The museum's 5,000 books include rare volumes dating back 2,000 years; more than 200 of these books—40 of which were produced in Spain—were printed before the 16th century. *255 Calle Cristo, tel. 809/723–0354. Admission free. Open Tues. 11–4:30 and 7:30–10 PM, Wed.–Sat. (except holidays) 11–4:30.*

13 The **Popular Arts and Crafts Center** (253 Calle Cristo, tel. 809/723–2320), in a lovely colonial building next door, is a superb repository of island craftwork.

Follow the wall east one block and head north on Calle San José two **14** short blocks to **Plaza de Armas,** the original main square of Old San

Juan. The plaza, bordered by Calles San Francisco, Fortaleza, San José, and Cruz, has a lovely fountain with 19th-century statues representing the four seasons.

⑮ West of the square stands **La Intendencia,** a handsome three-story neoclassical building. From 1851 to 1898, it was home to the Spanish Treasury. Recently restored, it is now the headquarters of Puerto Rico's State Department. *Calle San José, at the corner of Calle San Francisco, tel. 809/722–2121, ext. 230. Admission free. Tours at 2 and 3 in Spanish, 4 in English. Open weekdays 8–noon and 1–4:30.*

⑯ On the north side of the plaza is **City Hall,** called the *Alcaldía.* Built between 1604 and 1789, the alcaldía was fashioned after Madrid's city hall, with arcades, towers, balconies, and a lovely inner courtyard. A tourist information center and an art gallery are on the first floor. *Tel. 809/724–7171, ext. 2391. Open weekdays 8–noon and 1–4.*

Time Out **La Bombonera** (259 Calle San Francisco, tel. 809/722–0658), established in 1903, is known for its strong Puerto Rican coffee and *Mallorca*—a Spanish pastry made of light dough, toasted, buttered, and sprinkled with powdered sugar. Breakfast, for under $5, is served until 11. It's a favorite Sunday-morning gathering place in Old San Juan.

Four blocks east, on the pedestrian mall of Calle Fortaleza, you'll
⑰ find **Plaza de Colón,** a bustling square with a statue of Christopher Columbus atop a high pedestal. Originally called St. James Square, it was renamed in honor of Columbus on the 400th anniversary of the discovery of Puerto Rico. Bronze plaques in the base of the statue relate various episodes in the life of the great explorer. On the north side of the plaza is a terminal for buses to and from San Juan.

Walk two blocks north from Plaza de Colón to Calle Sol and turn
⑱ right. Another block will take you to **San Cristóbal,** the 18th-century fortress that guarded the city from land attacks. Even larger than El Morro, San Cristóbal was known as the Gibraltar of the West Indies. *Tel. 809/724–1974. Admission free. Open daily 9:15–6.*

⑲ Just south of Plaza de Colón is the magnificent **Tapia Theater** (Calle Fortaleza at Plaza de Colón, tel. 809/722–0407), named after the famed Puerto Rican playwright Alejandro Tapia y Rivera. Built in 1832 and remodeled in 1949 and again in 1987, the municipal theater is the site of ballets, plays, and operettas. Stop by the box office to see what's showing and find out if you can get tickets.

⑳ Stroll from Plaza de Colón down to the **port,** where the **Paseo de la Princesa** is spruced up with flowers, trees, and street lamps. Across from Pier 3, where the cruise ships dock, local artisans display their wares at the Plazoleta del Puerto. At the marina, pay 50¢ and board a ferry for a one-way ride to Catano.

San Juan *Numbers in the margin correspond to points of interest on the San Juan Exploring, Dining, and Lodging map.*

You'll need to resort to taxis, buses, públicos, or a rental car to reach the points of interest in "new" San Juan.

Avenida Muñoz Rivera, Avenida Ponce de León, and Avenida Fernández Juncos are the main thoroughfares that cross Puerta de Tierra, just east of Old San Juan, to the business and tourist districts of Santurce, Condado, and Isla Verde.

㉑ In Puerta de Tierra is Puerto Rico's **Capitol,** a white marble building that dates from the 1920s. The grand rotunda, with mosaics and

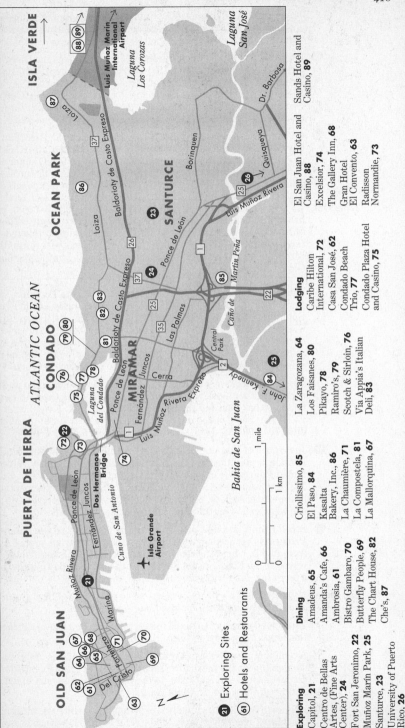

San Juan Exploring, Dining, and Lodging

ATLANTIC OCEAN

ISLA VERDE

OCEAN PARK

CONDADO

PUERTA DE TIERRA

MIRAMAR

SANTURCE

OLD SAN JUAN

Luis Muñoz Marín International Airport

Laguna Los Corozas

Laguna San José

Laguna del Condado

Bahía de San Juan

Isla Grande Airport

Dos Hermanos Bridge

Caño de San Antonio

Caño de Martín Peña

Loíza

Baldorioty de Casto Expreso

Ponce de León

Muñoz Rivera

Fernández Juncos

Los Palmas

Luis Muñoz Rivera Expreso

John F. Kennedy

Central Park

Cerra

Del Cristo

Fortaleza

Marina

Dr. Barbosa

Quisqueya

Borinquen

Martín Peña

1 mile

1 km

21 Exploring Sites

61 Hotels and Restaurants

Exploring

Capitol, **21**
Centro de Bellas Artes, (Fine Arts Center), **24**
Fort San Jeronimo, **22**
Muñoz Marín Park, **25**
Santurce, **23**
University of Puerto Rico, **26**

Dining

Amadeus, **65**
Amanda's Cafe, **66**
Ambrosia, **61**
Bistro Gambaro, **70**
Butterfly People, **69**
The Chart House, **82**
Che's, **87**

Criollissimo, **85**
El Paso, **84**
Kasalta Bakery, Inc., **86**
La Chaumière, **71**
La Compostela, **81**
La Mallorquina, **67**

La Zaragozana, **64**
Los Faisanes, **80**
Pikayo, **78**
Ramiro's, **79**
Scotch & Sirloin, **76**
Via Appia's Italian Deli, **83**

Lodging

Caribe Hilton International, **72**
Casa San José, **62**
Condado Beach Trio, **77**
Condado Plaza Hotel and Casino, **75**

El San Juan Hotel and Casino, **88**
Excelsior, **74**
The Gallery Inn, **68**
Gran Hotel El Convento, **63**
Radisson Normandie, **73**

Sands Hotel and Casino, **89**

friezes, was completed a few years ago. The seat of the island's bicameral legislature, the Capitol contains Puerto Rico's constitution and is flanked by the modern buildings of the Senate and the House of Representatives. There are spectacular views from the observation plaza on the sea side of the Capitol. Pick up a booklet about the building from the House Secretariat on the second floor. Guided tours are by appointment only. *Av. Ponce de León, tel. 809/721–7305 or 809/721–7310. Admission free. Open weekdays 8:30–5.*

㉒ At the eastern tip of Puerta de Tierra, behind the splashy Caribe Hilton, the tiny **Fort San Jeronimo** is perched over the Atlantic like an afterthought. Added to San Juan's fortifications in the late 18th century, the structure barely survived the British attack of 1797. Restored in 1983 by the Institute of Puerto Rican Culture, it is now a military museum with displays of weapons, uniforms, and maps. *Tel. 809/724–5949. Admission free. Open Wed.–Sun. 9:30–noon and 1:30–4:30.*

Dos Hermanos Bridge connects Puerta de Tierra with Miramar, Condado, and Isla Grande. Isla Grande Airport, from which you can take short hops, is on the bay side of the bridge.

On the other side of the bridge, the Condado Lagoon is bordered by Avenida Ashford, which threads past the high-rise Condado hotels and El Centro Convention Center, and Avenida Baldorioty de Castro Expreso, which barrels all the way east to the airport and beyond. Due south of the lagoon is Miramar, a primarily residential area with fashionable turn-of-the-century homes and a cluster of hotels and restaurants.

㉓ **Santurce,** which lies between Miramar on the west and the Laguna San José on the east, is a busy mixture of shops, markets, and offices. The classically designed **Sacred Heart University** is the home of the **Museum of Contemporary Puerto Rican Art,** which showcases the works of such modern masters as Rodon, Campeche, and Oller. *Tel. 809/268–0049. Admission free. Open Mon.–Fri. 9–4.*

㉔ Internationally acclaimed performers appear at the **Centro de Bellas Artes** (Fine Arts Center). This completely modern facility, the largest of its kind in the Caribbean, has a full schedule of concerts, plays, and operas. *Corner of Av. De Diego and Av. Ponce de León, tel. 809/724–4751.*

South of Santurce is the "Golden Mile"—Hato Rey, the city's bustling new financial hub. Isla Verde, with its glittering beachfront hotels, casinos, discos, and public beach, is to the east, near the airport.

Time Out **Pescadería Atlántica** (81 Calle Loiza, tel. 809/726–6654) is a combination seafood restaurant and retail store. Stop in for a cool drink at the bar and a side dish of *calamares*, lightly breaded squid in a hot, spicy sauce.

Las Américas Expressway, heading south, goes by Plaza Las Américas, the largest shopping mall in the Caribbean, and takes you

㉕ to the new **Muñoz Marín Park,** an idyllic tree-shaded spot dotted with gardens, lakes, playgrounds, and picnic areas. Cable cars connect the park with the parking area. *Next to Las Américas Expressway, west on Av. Piñero, tel. 809/763–0568 or 809/763–0787. Admission free; parking $1 per vehicle. Open Tues.–Sun. 9–5:30; closed Mon.*

Río Piedras, a southern suburb of San Juan, is home to the
②⑥ University of Puerto Rico, located between Avenida Ponce de León
and Avenida Barbosa. The university's campus is one of two sites for
performances of the Puerto Rico Symphony Orchestra. Theatrical
productions and other concerts are also scheduled here throughout
the year. The University Museum has permanent archaeological and
historical exhibits and occasionally mounts special art displays.
*Next to the university's main entrance on Av. Ponce de León, tel.
809/764–0000, ext. 2452 or 2456. Open weekdays 9–9, Sat. 8–3:30;
closed Sun. and holidays.*

The university's main attraction is the **Botanical Garden,** a lush garden with more than 200 species of tropical and subtropical vegetation. Footpaths through the thick forests lead to a graceful lotus
lagoon, a bamboo promenade, an orchid garden, and a palm garden.
*Intersection of Rtes. 1 and 847 at the entrance to Barrio Venezuela,
tel. 809/763–4408. Admission free. Open Tues.–Sun. 9–5; when
Mon. is a holiday, it is open Mon. and closed Tues.*

San Juan *Numbers in the margin correspond to points of interest on the Puer-*
Environs *to Rico map.*

From San Juan, follow Route 2 west toward Bayamón, and you'll
②⑦ spot the **Caparra Ruins,** where, in 1508, Ponce de León established
the island's first settlement. The ruins are that of an ancient fort. Its
small **Museum of the Conquest and Colonization of Puerto Rico** contains historical documents, exhibits, and excavated artifacts. (You
can see the museum's contents in less time than it takes to say the
name.) *Km 6.6 on Rte. 2, tel. 809/781–4795. Admission free. Open
weekdays 9–5, weekends and holidays 10–6.*

②⑧ Continue on Route 2 to **Bayamón.** In the central park, across from
Bayamón's city hall, there are some historical buildings and a 1934
sugarcane train that runs through the park (open daily 8 AM–10 PM).
On the plaza, in the city's historic district, stands the 18th-century
Catholic church of Santa Cruz and the old neoclassical city hall, which
now houses the **Francisco Oller Art and History Museum.** *Tel. 809/
798–8191. Admission free. Open weekdays 8–noon and 1–4.*

②⑨ Along Route 5 from Bayamón to Catano, you'll see the **Barrilito Rum
Plant.** On the grounds are a 200-year-old plantation home and a 150-
year-old windmill, which is listed in the National Register of Historic Places.

The **Bacardi Rum Plant,** along the bay, conducts 45-minute tours of
the bottling plant, museum, and distillery, which has the capacity to
produce 100,000 gallons of rum a day. (Yes, you'll be offered a sample.) *Km 2.6 on Rte. 888, tel. 809/788–1500. Admission free. Tours
Mon.–Sat., except holidays, 9:30–3:30; closed Sun.*

Out on the Puerto Rico's 3,500 square miles is a lot of land to explore. While you
Island can get from town to town via público, we don't recommend traveling that way unless your Spanish is good and you know exactly
where you're going. The public cars stop in each town's main square,
leaving you on your own to reach the beaches, restaurants,
paradores, and sightseeing attractions. You'll do much better if you
rent a car. Most of the island's roads are excellent. However, there is
a tangled web of roads through the mountains, and they are not always well marked. It helps to buy a good road map.

East and South Our first excursion out on the island will take us east, down the coast
to the south, and back up to San Juan. The first leg of the trip—to
③⓪ Luquillo Beach and the nearby **Caribbean National Forest,** commonly known as **El Yunque,** can easily be done in a day. (There will be

heavy traffic and a crowded beach on weekends, when it seems as if the whole world heads for Luquillo.) The full itinerary will take two to three days, depending upon how long you loll on the beach and linger over the mountain scenery.

To take full advantage of the 28,000-acre El Yunque rain forest, go with a tour. Dozens of trails lead through the thick jungle (it sheltered the Carib Indians for 200 years), and the tour guides take you to the best observation points, bathing spots, and waterfalls. Some of the trails are slippery, and there are occasional washouts.

However, if you'd like to drive there yourself, take Route 3 east from San Juan and turn right (south) on Route 191, about 25 miles from the city. The **Sierra Palm Visitor Center** is on Route 191, Km 11.6 (open daily 9:30–5). Nature talks and programs at the center are in Spanish and English and by appointment only—another good reason to go with a tour group.

El Yunque, named after the good Indian spirit Yuquiyu, is in the Luquillo mountain range. The rain forest is verdant with feathery ferns, thick ropelike vines, white tuberoses and ginger, miniature orchids, and some 240 different species of trees. More than 100 billion gallons of rainwater fall on it annually. Rain-battered, wind-ravaged dwarf vegetation clings to the top peaks. (El Toro, the highest peak in the forest, is 3,532 feet.) El Yunque is also a bird sanctuary and the base of the rare Puerto Rican parrot. Millions of tiny, inch-long *coquis* (tree frogs) can be heard singing (or squawking, depending on your sensibilities). *For further information call the Catalina Field Office, tel. 809/887–2875 or 809/766–5335; or write Caribbean National Forest, Box B, Palmer, PR 00721.*

③① To reach **Luquillo Beach,** take Route 191 back to Route 3 and continue east 5 miles to Km 35.4. One of the island's best and most popular beaches, Luquillo was once a flourishing coconut plantation. Coral reefs protect its calm, pristine lagoon, making it an ideal place for a swim. The entrance fee is $1 per car, and there are lockers, showers, and changing rooms, as well as stands selling savory Puerto Rican delicacies *(see* Beaches, *below).*

③② If you want to continue exploring, get back on Route 3 and drive 5 miles to **Fajardo,** a major fishing and sailing center with thousands of boats tied and stacked in tiers at its three large marinas. Boats can be rented or chartered here, and the *Spread Eagle* catamaran can take you out for a full day of snorkeling, swimming, and sunning. Fajardo is also the embarkation point for ferries to the islands of Culebra (a $2.25 fare) and Vieques ($2).

③③ North of Fajardo on Route 987, just past the Seven Seas Recreational Area, is the entrance to **Las Cabezas de San Juan Nature Reserve.** Opened in 1991, the reserve contains mangrove swamps, coral reefs, beaches, a dry forest, and thalassia beds—all of Puerto Rico's natural habitats rolled into a microcosmic 316 acres. Nineteenth-century El Faro, one of the island's oldest lighthouses, is restored and still functioning; its first floor contains a small nature center that has an aquarium and other exhibits. The reserve is open to the general public on Friday and weekends and to tour groups, by reservation, Monday–Thursday. *Rte. 987, tel. 809/722–5882; weekends, 809/722–5882. Admission: $4 adults, $1 children under 12. Open to the general public Fri.–Sun., except holidays; tours at 9:30, 10:30, and 1:30.*

③④ **Culebra** has lovely white-sand beaches, coral reefs, and a wildlife refuge. In the sleepy town of Dewey, on Culebra's southwestern side, check at the visitor information center at city hall (tel. 809/

742–3291) about boat rentals. On **Vieques,** Sun Bay public beach has picnic facilities; Blue Beach is superb for snorkeling; and Mosquito Bay is luminous even on moonless nights, thanks to the millions of bioluminescent organisms that glow when disturbed—it's like swimming in a cloud of fireflies. Seventy percent of Vieques is owned by the U.S. Navy, ensuring it will remain unspoiled. The deserted beaches—Green, Red, Blue, Navia, and Media Luna—are among the Caribbean's loveliest; you might see a wild *paso fino* horse galloping in the surf. Both islands are havens for colorful "expatriates" escaping the rat race Stateside. This is pure old-time Caribbean: fun and funky, the kind of getaway that is fast disappearing.

Resume your ramble on Route 3, heading south past the U.S. Naval Base, and ride through the sugarcane fields to Humacao. South of Humacao (take Route 906) is the 2,700-acre Palmas del Mar, the island's largest residential resort complex.

Stay on Route 3 through Yabucoa, tucked up in the hills, and Maunabo and Patillas, where you can pick up routes that will take you through the Cayey Mountains. Route 184 north skirts Lake Patillas and cuts smack through the Carite Forest Reserve. Stay on Route 184 until it meets Route 1, where you'll shoot northward back to San Juan.

Western Island If you're short of time, drive the 64 miles from San Juan to Ponce in 90 minutes. Take the Las Américas Expressway, Route 52, which cuts through the splendid mountains of Cordillera Central.

If time is not a problem, take a three- or four-day tour exploring the western regions of the island. This route covers Aguadilla, Rincón, Mayagüez, San Germán, and Ponce. There's much to see along the way—caves and coves, karst fields and coffee plantations, mountains, beaches, and even a zoo.

Start out going west on Route 2. Arecibo is home to one of the world's largest telescopes. You can take a self-guided tour of the Arecibo Observatory, where groundbreaking work in astronomy, including SETI (the search for intelligent life in the universe) continues. *Route 625, tel. 809/878–2612. Admission free. Open Tues.– Fri. 12–3, Sun. 1–4.*

In Arecibo pick up Route 10 and go south. Make a right on Route **35** 111, and you'll find the **Caguana Indian Ceremonial Park,** used 800 years ago by the Taino tribes for recreation and worship. Mountains surround a 13-acre site planted with royal palms and guava. According to Spanish historians, the Tainos played a game similar to soccer, and in this park there are 10 courts bordered by cobbled walkways. There are also stone monoliths, some with colorful petroglyphs; a small museum; and a souvenir shop. *Rte. 111, Km 12.3, tel. 809/894–7325. Admission free. Open daily 8:30–4:30.*

Drive west on Route 111 and then north on Route 129 through the spectacular karst country, an alien landscape of collapsed limestone **36** sinkholes, to Km 18.9, where you'll find the **Río Camuy Cave Park,** a 268-acre reserve that contains one of the world's largest cave networks. Guided tours take you on a tram down through dense tropical vegetation to the entrance of the cave, where you continue on foot over underground trails, ramps, and bridges. The caves, sinkholes, and subterranean streams are all spectacular (the world's second-largest underground river runs through here), but this trip is not for those with claustrophobia. Be sure to call ahead; the tours allow only a limited number of people. *Rte. 129, Km 18.9, tel. 809/898–3100 or*

809/756–5555. Admission: $6 adults, $4 children. Parking $1. Open Wed.–Sun. and holidays 8–4. Last tour starts at 3:50.

㊲ Backtrack to Route 111, which twists westward to **Aguadilla** on the northwest coast. In this area, somewhere between Aguadilla and Añasco, south of Rincón, Columbus dropped anchor on his second voyage in 1493. Both Aguadilla and **Aguada,** a few miles to the south, claim to be the spot where his foot first hit ground, and both towns have plaques to commemorate the occasion.

Route 115 from Aguadilla to **Rincón** is one of the island's most scenic drives, through rolling hills dotted with pastel-colored houses. Rincón, perched on a hill, overlooks its beach, which was the site of the World Surfing Championship in 1968. Skilled surfers flock to Rincón during the winter, when the water is rough and challenging.

㊳ Pick up Route 2 for the 6-mile drive to **Mayagüez,** Puerto Rico's third-largest city, with a population approaching 100,000. Although bypassed by the mania for restoration that saw Ponce and Old San Juan spruced up for the Columbus quincentennial, Mayagüez is graced by some lovely turn-of-the-century architecture, such as the landmark Art Deco Teatro Yagüez and the Plaza Colon.

North of town visit the **Mayagüez Zoo,** a 45-acre tropical compound that's home to about 500 animals. In addition to Bengal tigers, reptiles, and birds, there's a lake and a children's playground. *Rte. 108 at Barrio Miradero, tel. 809/834–8110. Admission: $1 adults, 50¢ children. Parking $1. Open Tues.–Sun. 9–4.*

㊴ Due south of Mayagüez, via the coastal section of Route 102, is **Cabo Rojo,** once a pirates' hangout and now a favorite resort area of Puerto Ricans. The area has long stretches of white-sand beaches on the clear, calm Caribbean Sea, as well as many seafood restaurants. There are also several paradores in the region. **Boquerón,** at the end of Route 101, has one of the best beaches on the island, as well as two-room cabins for rent. Parking is $1 per car.

㊵ From Cabo Rojo continue east on Route 102 to delightfully quaint **San Germán,** a quiet Old World town that's home to the oldest intact church under the U.S. flag. Built in 1606, Porta Coeli (Gates of Heaven) overlooks one of the town's two plazas (where the towns-people continue the Spanish tradition of promenading at night). The church is now a museum of religious art, housing 18th- and 19th-century paintings and statues. *Tel. 809/892–5845. Admission free. Open Wed.–Sun. 8:30–noon and 1–4:30.*

㊶ The fishing village of **La Parguera,** an area of simple seafood restaurants, mangrove cays, and small islands, lies south of San Germán at the end of Route 304. This is an excellent scuba-diving area, but the main attraction is **Phosphorescent Bay.** Boats tour the bay, where microscopic dinoflagellates (marine plankton) light up like Christmas trees when disturbed by any kind of movement. The phenomenon can be seen only on moonless nights. Boats leave for the hour-long trip nightly between 7:30 and 12:30, depending on demand, and the trip costs $8 per person. You can also rent or charter a small boat to explore the numerous cays.

㊷ From San Germán, Route 2 traverses splendid peaks and valleys; pastel houses cling to the sides of steep green hills. East of Yauco, the road dips and sweeps right along the Caribbean and into **Ponce.**

Puerto Rico's second-largest city (population 300,000) is undergoing a massive restoration in anticipation of the 300th anniversary in 1996 of the city's first settlement. The town's 19th-century style has been recaptured with pink marble-bordered sidewalks, gas lamps, painted trolleys, and horse-drawn carriages. Another reminder of gracious turn-of-the-century living is the restored La Guancha boardwalk fronting the sea, where couples still promenade weekend nights, enjoying open-air concerts and the aroma of barbecue wafting from the *kioskos*. You have not seen a firehouse until you've seen the red-and-black **Parque de Bombas,** a structure first built in 1882 for an exposition and converted to a firehouse the following year. The city hired architect Pablo Ojeda O'Neill to restore it, and it reopened as a museum in July 1990.

Ponce's charm stems from a combination of neoclassical, Ponce Creole, and art deco styles. Stop in and pick up information about this seaside city at the columned **Casa Armstrong-Poventud,** the home of the Institute of Puerto Rican Culture and Tourism Information Office (open Mon.–Fri. 8–12 and 1–4:30; use the side entrance). Stroll around the **Plaza Las Delicias,** with its perfectly pruned India-laurel fig trees, graceful fountains, gardens, and park benches. View **Our Lady of Guadelupe Cathedral,** and walk down Calles Isabel and Christina to see turn-of-the-century wooden houses with wrought iron balconies. Two superlative examples house the new Ponce History Museum, whose 10 rooms vividly recreate Ponce's golden years, providing especially fascinating glimpses into the worlds of culture, high finance, and journalism during the 19th century. *Calle Isabel, tel. 809/844–7071. Admission: $3 adults, $2 seniors, $1 children under 12. Open Mon. and Wed.–Fri. 10–5, Sat. 10–9, Sun. 1–5.; closed Tuesday.*

Continue as far as Calles Mayor and Christina to the white stucco **La Perla Theater,** with its Corinthian columns. Be sure to allow time to visit the **Ponce Museum of Art.** The architecture alone is worth seeing: The two-story modern building designed by Edward Durell Stone (who designed New York's Museum of Modern Art) has seven interconnected hexagons, glass cupolas, and a pair of curved staircases. The collection includes late Renaissance and Baroque works from Italy, France, and Spain, as well as contemporary art by Puerto Ricans. *Av. Las Américas, tel. 809/840–0511 or 809/848–0505. Admission: $3 adults, $2 children under 12. Open Mon. and Wed.–Fri. 9–4, Sat. 10–4, Sun. 10–5.*

Another fine museum is **Castillo Serralles,** a splendid Spanish Revival mansion perched on El Vigia Hill with smashing views of Ponce and the Caribbean. This former residence of the Serralles family, owners of the Don Q rum distillery, has been restored to its former glory with a mix of original furnishings and antiques that recall the era of the sugar barons, including a baronial dining room with heavy carved mahogany and wrought iron doors. A short film details the history of the sugar and rum industries. The unusual, rather ugly 100-foot-tall cross looming behind the museum is under renovation; when finished, visitors will be able to climb to its observation tower. *El Vigia Hill, tel. 809/259–1774. Admission: $3 adults, $1.50 children under 12. Open Tues.–Thurs. 9:30–4:30, Fri.–Sun. 10–5.*

There are two intriguing historical sights just outside the city. **Hacienda Buena Vista** is a 19th-century coffee plantation, recently restored by the Conservation Trust of Puerto Rico, with much of the authentic machinery and furnishings intact. *Route 10, north of Ponce, tel. 809/722–5882. Admission: $4 adults, $1 children under 12. Open Fri.–Sun.; call for tour schedule.*

The **Tibes Indian Ceremonial Center** is the oldest cemetery in the Caribbean. It is a treasure trove of pre-Taino ruins and burials, dating from AD 300 to AD 700. Some archaeologists, noting the symmetrical arrangement of stone pillars, surmise the cemetery may have been of great religious significance. The complex includes a detailed recreation of a Taino village. *Rte. 503, Km 2.7, tel. 809/840–2255. Admission: $2 adults, $1 children. Open Tues.–Sun. 8–4.*

What to See and Do with Children

El Morro and **San Cristóbal** forts.
El Yunque rain forest.
The **Ponce Hilton, Hyatt Regency Cerromar Beach,** and **Hyatt Dorado Beach** offer chaperoned camps for children on weekends, during the summer, and during the Christmas and Easter holidays.
Las Cabezas de San Juan Nature Reserve, near Fajardo.
Mayagüez Zoo, Mayagüez.
Muñoz Marín Park, San Juan.
Río Camuy Caves, near Utuado.
Trolleys, Old San Juan.
Villa Coqui Wet N'Slide. A recreational park with pools, water slides, paddleboats, and canoes. *Rte. 763, Km 6, Caqua, tel. 809/747–4747. Open weekends and holidays 9–5.*

Off the Beaten Track

Mona Island, situated west of Puerto Rico in the turbulent shark-infested Mona Passage, is nicknamed the Galápagos of the Caribbean, thanks to the plethora of endangered and virtually unique indigenous species that call it home. The variety of marine and bird life is especially breathtaking. The coastline is rimmed with imposing limestone cliffs pocked with caves that are said to contain buried treasure; the many perfectly preserved Taino hieroglyphs and rock paintings there are certainly of great archaeological value.

Access to the island is only via private plane or boat. Very limited camping facilities are available on the pristine beaches. Call the Department of Natural Resources for information and camping reservations (tel. 809/724–3647).

Beaches

By law, all Puerto Rico's beaches are open to the public (except for the Caribe Hilton's man-made beach in San Juan). The government runs 13 *balnearios* (public beaches), which have lockers, showers, picnic tables, and in some cases playgrounds and overnight facilities. Admission is free, parking $1. Most balnearios are open Tuesday through Sunday 9–6 in the winter, 8–5 in the summer. Listed below are some major balnearios.

Boquerón Beach is a broad beach of hard-packed sand fringed with coconut palms. It has picnic tables, cabin rentals, bike rentals, basketball court, minimarket, scuba diving, and snorkeling. *On the southwest coast, south of Mayagüez, Rte. 101, Boquerón.*

A white sandy beach bordered by resort hotels, **Isla Verde** offers picnic tables and good snorkeling, with equipment rentals nearby. It's a lively beach popular with city folk. *Near metropolitan San Juan, Rte. 187, Km 3.9, Isla Verde.*

Crescent-shape **Luquillo Beach** comes complete with coconut palms, picnic tables, and tent sites. Coral reefs protect its crystal-clear lagoon from the Atlantic waters, making it ideal for swimming. Although it gets crowded on weekends, it's one of the largest and most well-known beaches. *30 mi east of San Juan, Rte. 3, Km 35.4.*

An elongated beach of hard-packed sand, **Seven Seas** is always popular with bathers. It has picnic tables and tent and trailer sites; snorkeling, scuba diving, and boat rentals are nearby. *Rte. 987, Fajardo.*

Sun Bay, a white-sand beach on the island of Vieques, has picnic tables and tent sites and offers such water sports as snorkeling and scuba diving. Boat rentals are nearby. *Rte. 997, Vieques.*

Surfing The best surfing beaches are along the Atlantic coastline from Borinquén Point south to Rincón, where there are several surf shops; surfing is best from October through April. Aviones and La Concha beaches in San Juan and Casa de Pesca in Arecibo are summer surfing spots; all have nearby surf shops.

Sports and the Outdoors

Bicycling The broad beach at Boquerón makes for easy wheeling. You can rent bikes at **Boquerón Balnearios** (Rte. 101, Boquerón, Dept. of Recreation and Sports, tel. 809/722–1551). In the Dorado area on the north coast, bikes can be rented at the **Hyatt Regency Cerromar Beach Hotel** (tel. 809/796–1234) or the **Hyatt Dorado Beach Hotel** (tel. 809/796–1234).

Boating Virtually all the resort hotels on San Juan's Condado and Isla Verda strips rent paddleboats, Sunfish, Windsurfers, and the like. Contact **Condado Plaza Hotel Watersports Center** (tel. 809/721–1000, ext. 1361), **Caribbean School of Aquatics** (La Concha Hotel, Av. Ashford, Condado, tel. 809/723–4740), or **Castillo Watersports** (ESJ Towers, Isla Verde, tel. 809/791–6195). Sailing and boat rentals are also available at **Playita Boat Rental** (1010 Av. Ashford, Condado, tel. 809/722–1607).

Fishing Half-day, full-day, split charters, and big- and small-game fishing can be arranged through **Benitez Deep-Sea Fishing** (Club Náutico de San Juan, Stop 9½, Av. Fernández Juncos, Miramar, tel. 809/723–2292 or 809/724–6265), **Castillo Watersports** (ESJ Towers, Isla Verde, tel. 809/791–6195 or evenings 809/726–5752), and **San Juan Fishing Charters** (Stop 10, Av. Fernández Juncos, Miramar, tel. 809/723–0415).

Golf There are four Robert Trent Jones–designed 18-hole courses shared by the **Hyatt Dorado Beach Hotel** and the **Hyatt Regency Cerromar Beach Hotel** (Dorado, tel. 809/796–1234, ext. 3238 or 3013). You'll also find 18-hole courses at **Palmas del Mar Resort** (Humacao, tel. 809/852–6000, ext. 54), **Club Ríomar** (Río Grande, tel. 809/887–3964), and **Punta Borinquén** (Aguadilla, tel. 809/890–2987).

Hiking Dozens of trails lace **El Yunque** (information is available at the Sierra Palm Visitor Center, Rte. 191, Km 11.6). You can also hit the trails in **Río Abajo Forest** (south of Arecibo) and **Toro Negro Forest** (east of Adjuntas). Each reserve has a ranger station.

Horseback Riding Beach-trail rides can be arranged at **Palmas del Mar Equestrian Center** (Palmas del Mar Resort, Humacao, tel. 809/852–6000, ext. 12721). Take to the trails in the foothills of the rain-forest foothills, as well as to the beaches, through **Hacienda Carabali** (tel. 809/889–5820).

Sailing Sailing instruction and trips are offered by **Palmas Sailing Center** (Palmas del Mar Resort, Humacao, tel. 809/852–6000, ext. 10310), **Calypso Watersports** (Sands Hotel, San Juan, tel. 809/791–6100), Caribbean School of Aquatics (La Concha Hotel, Av. Ashford, Condado, tel. 809/723–4740), Caribe Aquatic Adventure (Radisson Normandie Hotel, tel. 809/724–1882), and Castillo Watersports (ESJ Towers, Isla Verde, tel. 809/791–6195).

Snorkeling and Scuba Diving Snorkeling and scuba-diving instruction and equipment rentals are available at Caribbean School of Aquatics and Calypso Watersports (*see* Sailing, *above*), Coral Head Divers (Marina de Palmas, Palmas del Mar Resort, Humacao, tel. 809/850–7208 or 800/221–4874), La Cueva Submarina Training Center (Plaza Cooperativa, Isabela, tel. 809/872–3903 or evenings 809/872–1094), Caribe Aquatic Adventure (*see* Sailing, *above*), Castillo Watersports (*see* Sailing, *above*), and Parguera Divers Training Center (Road 304, MM3-2, Lajas, tel. 809/899–4171).

Caution: Puerto Rico's coral-reef waters and mangrove areas can be dangerous to novices. Unless you're an expert or have an experienced guide, avoid unsupervised areas and stick to the water-sports centers of major hotels.

Tennis There are 17 lighted courts at San Juan Central Park (Calle Cerra exit on Rte. 2, tel. 809/722–1646); 6 lighted courts at the Caribe Hilton Hotel (Puerta de Tierra, tel. 809/721–0303, ext. 1730); 8 courts, 4 lighted, at Carib Inn (Isla Verde, tel. 809/791–3535, ext. 6); and 2 lighted courts at the Condado Plaza Hotel (Condado, tel. 809/721–1000, ext. 1775). Out on the island, there are 14 courts, 2 lighted, at Hyatt Regency Cerromar Beach Hotel (Dorado, tel. 809/796–1234, ext. 3040); 7 courts, 2 lighted, at the Hyatt Dorado Beach Hotel (Dorado, tel. 809/796–1234, ext. 3220); 20 courts, 4 lighted, at Palmas del Mar Resort (Humacao, tel. 809/852–6000, ext. 51); 3 lighted courts at the Mayagüez Hilton Hotel (Mayagüez, tel. 809/831–7575, ext. 2150); 4 lighted courts at the Ponce Hilton (Ponce, tel. 809/259–7676); and 4 lighted courts at Punta Borinquén (Aguadilla, tel. 809/891–8778).

Windsurfing Windsurfing rentals are available at Caribbean School of Aquatics, Castillo Watersports, Palmas Sailing Center, Playita Boat Rental (*see* Boating and Sailing sections, *above*, for all information), and Lisa Penfield Windsurfing Center (El San Juan Hotel, tel. 809/726–7274).

Spectator Sports

Horse Racing Thoroughbred races are run year-round at El Comandante Racetrack. On race days the dining rooms open at 12:30 PM. *Rte. 3, Km 15.3, Canovanas, tel. 809/724–6060. Open Wed., Fri., Sun., and holidays.*

Baseball If you have a post–World Series letdown, you can fly down to the island, where the season runs October–April. Many major-league ballplayers in the United States got their start in Puerto Rico's baseball league, and some return in the off-season to hone their skills. Stadiums are in San Juan, Santurce, Ponce, Caguas, Arecibo, and Mayagüez. Contact the tourist office for details or call Professional Baseball of Puerto Rico (tel. 809/765–6285).

Shopping

San Juan is not a free port, and you won't find bargains on electronics and perfumes. You can, however, find excellent prices on china, crystal, fashions, and jewelry.

Shopping for local Caribbean crafts can be great fun. You'll run across a lot of tacky things you can live without, but you can also find some treasures, and in many cases you'll be able to watch the artisans at work. (For guidance, contact the Tourism Artisan Center, tel. 809/721–2400, ext. 229, or the Fomento Crafts Project, tel. 809/ 758–4747, ext. 2291).

Popular souvenirs and gifts include *santos* (small, hand-carved figures of saints or religious scenes), hand-rolled cigars, handmade *mundillo* lace from Aguadilla, carnival masks (papier-mâché from Ponce and fierce *veijigantes* made from coconut husks in Loiza, an African-American enclave near San Juan), and fancy men's shirts called *guayaberas*. Also, some folks swear that Puerto Rican rum is the best in the world.

Shopping Districts Old San Juan is full of shops, especially on Cristo, Fortaleza, and San Francisco streets. The **Las Américas Plaza** south of San Juan is the largest shopping mall in the Caribbean, with 200 shops, restaurants, and movie theaters. Other malls out on the island include **Plaza del Caribe** in Ponce, **Plaza del Carmen** in Caguas, and the **Mayagüez Mall.**

Good Buys
Clothing You can get discounts on Hathaway shirts and Christian Dior clothing at **Hathaway Factory Outlet** (203 Calle Cristo, tel. 809/723–8946); discounts on Ralph Lauren apparel at the **Polo Factory** (201 Calle Cristo, tel. 809/722–2136); and reductions on men's, women's, and children's raincoats at the **London Fog Factory Outlet** (156 Calle Cristo, tel. 809/722–4334). Try the **Bikini Factory** (3 Palmar Norte, Isla Verde, tel. 809/726–0016) for stylish men's and women's swimwear.

Jewelry There is gold, gold, and more gold at **Reinhold** (201 Calle Cristo, tel. 809/725–6878) and brand-name watches at the **Watch and Gem Palace** (204 Calle San José, Old San Juan, tel. 809/722–2136).

Local Crafts For one-of-a-kind buys, head for **Puerto Rican Arts & Crafts** (204 Calle Fortaleza, Old San Juan, tel. 809/725–5596), **Plazoleta del Puerto** (Calle Marina, Old San Juan, tel. 809/722–3053), and the artisan markets in **Sixto Escobar Park** (Puerta de Tierra, tel. 809/ 722–0369) and **Luis Muñoz Marín Park** (next to Las Américas Expressway west on Piñero Ave., Hato Rey, no tel.). In Ponce, consult the **Casa Paoli Center of Folkloric Investigations** (14 Calle Mayor, tel. 809/840–4115).

Paintings and Sculptures **Galería Palomas** (207 Calle Cristo, Old San Juan, tel. 809/724–8904) is popular. **Galería Botello** (208 Calle Cristo, Old San Juan, tel. 809/ 723–9987) features a display of antique *santos* (religious sculptures).

Other galleries worth visiting are **Galería San Juan** (204–206 Calle Norzagaray, Old San Juan, tel. 809/722–1808 or 809/723–6515) and **Corinne Timsit International Galleries** (104 Calle San Jose, Old San Juan, tel. 809/724–1039 or 809/724–0994).

Dining

The quality of restaurants on the island is uniformly excellent. In San Juan, you'll find everything from Italian to Thai, as well as superb local eateries serving *comidas criollas* (traditional Caribbean-Creole meals). Hotel food in Puerto Rico sets a standard for the Caribbean. Consult the lodging listings for additional recommendations. Wherever you go, dress is casual to casually elegant; few establishments require a jacket.

One unique aspect of Puerto Rican cooking is its generous use of local vegetables: Plantains are cooked a hundred different ways— *tostones* (fried green), *amarillos* (baked ripe), and chips. Rice and beans with tostones or amarillos are basic accompaniments to every dish. Locals cook white rice with *achiote* (annatto seeds) or saffron, brown rice with *gandules* (pigeon peas), and black rice with *frijoles* (black beans). *Garbanzos* (chickpeas) and white beans are served in many daily specials. A wide assortment of yams is served baked, fried, stuffed, boiled, mashed, and whole. *Sofrito*—a garlic, onion, sweet pepper, coriander, oregano, and tomato puree—is used as a base for practically everything.

Beef, chicken, pork, and seafood are all rubbed with *adobo*, a garlic-oregano marinade, before cooking. *Arroz con pollo* (chicken with rice), *sancocho* (beef and tuber soup), *asopao* (a soupy rice with chicken or seafood), *empanada* (breaded cutlet), and *encebollado* (steak smothered in onions) are all typical plates.

Fritters, also popular, are served in snack places along the highways as well as at cocktail parties. You may find *empanadillas* (stuffed fried turnovers), *surrullitos* (cheese-stuffed corn sticks), *alcapurias* (stuffed green banana croquettes), and *bacalaitos* (codfish fritters).

Local *pan de agua* is an excellent French loaf bread, best hot out of the oven. It is also good toasted and should be tried in the *Cubano* sandwich (roast pork, ham, Swiss cheese, pickles, and mustard).

Local desserts include flans, puddings, and fruit pastes served with native white cheese. Home-grown mangoes and papayas are sweet, and *pan de azucar* (sugar bread) pineapples make the best juice on the market. Fresh *parcha* (passion fruit) juice fresh *guarapo* (sugarcane) juice, and fresh *guanabana* (a fruit similar to papaya) juice are also sold cold from trucks along the highway. Puerto Rican coffee is excellent served espresso-black or generously cut *con leche* (with hot milk).

To sample local cuisine, consult the the listing of *mesones gastronomicos* in the *¿Qué Pasa?* guide. These are restaurants cited by the government for preserving island culinary traditions and maintaining high standards.

The best frozen piña coladas are served at the Caribe Hilton Hotel and Dorado Beach Hotel, although local legend has it that the birthplace of the piña colada is the Gran Hotel El Convento. Rum can be mixed with cola (known as a *cuba libre*), soda, tonic, juices, water, served on the rocks, or even up. Puerto Rican rums range from light white mixers to dark, aged sipping liqueurs. Look for Bacardi, Don Q, Ron Rico, Palo Viejo, and Barillito.

Highly recommended restaurants are indicated by a star ★.

Category	Cost*
Very Expensive	over $45
Expensive	$30–$45
Moderate	$15–$30
Inexpensive	under $15

per person, excluding drinks and service

Old San Juan **La Chaumière.** Reminiscent of an inn in the French provinces, this intimate restaurant with black-and-white floors, heavy wood beams, and floral curtains serves respected onion soup, oysters Rockefeller, rack of lamb, scallops Provençale, and veal Oscar (layered with lobster and asparagus in béarnaise sauce) in addition to daily specials. *367 Calle Tetuan, tel. 809/722-3330. Reservations advised. AE, DC, MC. Closed Sun. Expensive–Very Expensive.*

La Zaragozana. One of the oldest restaurants around, this adobe hacienda recreates an old Spanish atmosphere. The ambience is pleasant, with strolling musicians, cast iron street lamps, a cool stone fountain, murals, and vaulted white stucco archways. The menu offers black-bean soup, steaks, lobster, paella, and flan. *356 Calle San Francisco, tel. 809/723-5103 and 809/725-3262. Reservations advised. AE, DC, MC, V. Expensive.*

★ **Amadeus.** In an atmosphere of gentrified Old San Juan, this charming stone-and-brick restaurant offers a nouvelle Caribbean menu. The roster of appetizers includes tostones (fried green plaintains) with sour cream and caviar or fish mousse, marlin ceviche, and crabmeat tacos. Entrées range from shrimp cassoulet (with black beans and chorizo) and grilled dolphin (with coriander butter) to chicken lasagna and tuna- or egg-salad sandwiches. *106 Calle San Sebastián, tel. 809/722-8635 or 809/721-6720. Reservations required. AE, MC, V. Closed Mon. Moderate.*

Amanda's Cafe. This airy café, on the north side of the city, offers seating inside or out, with a view of the Atlantic and the old city wall. The cuisine is Mexican, French, and Caribbean, and the nachos, refreshing fruit frappés, and margaritas are the best in town. *424 Calle Norzagaray, tel. 809/722-1682. AE, MC, V. Moderate.*

Bistro Gambaro. This serene, unpretentious spot instantly transports you from the hustle and bustle of Old San Juan. A virtual shrine to the creative impulse, it sports whimsically carved and painted chairs and tables draped with colorful textiles. The food is equally imaginative, running from an impeccable pasta pesto to chicken in mango-cognac sauce. The three-course fixed-price menus are an excellent buy. *320 Fortaleza, tel. 809/724-4592. AE, MC, V. Closed for lunch Sat. and Mon. Moderate.*

La Mallorquina. The Old World atmosphere here—accentuated by pale pink walls and whirring ceiling fans and a friendly, nattily attired waitstaff— is better than the food, which is good, but basic, Puerto Rican and Spanish fare such as asopao and paella. *207 Calle San Justo, tel. 809/722-3261. AE, DC, MC, V. Moderate.*

The Butterfly People. The tables in this restored mansion look onto a lush tropical indoor courtyard. The food is simple and well prepared, including basics such as asopao as well as sautéed plantains stuffed with spiced beef and kingfish grilled in olive oil and green peppercorns. But the real reason for visiting is the gallery, which boasts the largest collection of iridescent rainbow-hued butterflies in the world. *152 Fortaleza, tel. 809/732-2432. AE, D, DC, MC, V. Open Mon.–Sat. 11–5 (gallery open 10–6). Inexpensive–Moderate.*

Ambrosia. At the bottom of Calle Cristo, this restaurant serves frozen drinks made with fresh fruit at the bar, while the menu features pastas, veal, and chicken. The daily lunch specials usually include quiche and lasagna served with large mixed salads for good value. *205 Calle Cristo, tel. 809/722-5206. AE, MC, V. Inexpensive.*

San Juan **La Compostela.** Contemporary Spanish food and a serious 9,000-bot-
★ tle wine cellar are the draws to La Compostela. Specialties include mushroom pâté and Port *pastelillo* (meat-filled pastries), grouper fillet with scallops in salsa verde, rack of lamb, duck with kiwi sauce, and paella. This is a favorite restaurant with the local dining elite, and it is honored yearly in local competitions. *106 Av. Condado, Santurce, tel. 809/724-6088. Reservations advised. AE, DC, MC, V. Very Expensive.*

★ **Ramiro's.** Step into a soft sea green dining room serving imaginative Castilian cuisine. Chef-owner Jesus Ramiro describes his food as *cocina imaginativa* (imaginative cuisine), and each of his dishes is artfully arranged and decorated. Specialties include flower-shape peppers filled with fish mousse; a seafood fantasy caught under a vegetable net; roast duckling with sugarcane honey; and, if you can stand more, a syrupy kiwi dessert arranged to resemble twin palms. *1106 Av. Magdalena, Condado, tel. 809/721-9049. Reservations advised. AE, DC, MC, V. Very Expensive.*

★ **Los Faisanes.** This Continental stunner is one of San Juan's most distinguished eateries. Mahogany doorways, faux-Tiffany lamps, crisp white and ecru napery, and Bernadaud china set a refined tone, carried through by the equally elegant cuisine. Feast on such sumptuous fare as pheasant with champagne and prunes, a sublime roast suckling pig, and wonderfully light soufflés. *1108 Av. Magdalena, Condado, tel. 809/725-2801. Reservations advised. AE, DC, MC, V. Expensive–Very Expensive.*

The Chart House. Set in a restored Ashford mansion laced with graceful tropical verandas perfect for cocktails, the bar offers good drinks to a lively mix of people. Open-air dining rooms are upstairs, set at different levels and splashed with bright marine-themed artworks. The menu includes prime rib, steak, shrimp teriyaki, Hawaiian chicken, and the signature dessert: mud pie. *1214 Av. Ashford, Condado, tel. 809/728-0110. Reservations required. AE, DC, MC, V. Expensive.*

Pikayo. Chef Wilo Benet is the new darling in the foodie firmament, thanks to his artful fusion of classic French, Caribbean Creole, and California nouvelle cuisine. The beautifully presented dishes, which change regularly, are a feast for the eye as well as the palate. Your meal might consist of popcorn shrimp in an apple-ginger remoulade, followed by fillet of beef with roquefort in a red wine sauce. The decor is smartly contemporary, with lots of black and white accents and comfortable banquettes. *Tanama Princess Hotel, 1 Joffre Street, Condado, tel. 809/724-4160. Reservations advised. AE, MC, V. Expensive.*

★ **Criollissimo.** A battalion of formally attired waiters attends to the needs of a distinguished clientele—present and former governors, corporate sharks, and the like—in this airy green and white dining room. They return regularly for what is arguably the finest Puerto Rican food in the capital. Choose from sublime *mofongos* (a shell of fried and mashed green plantains filled with chicken, lobster, or beef), thick sultry asopaos, and beef *criollissimo* (smothered in green peppers, ham, tomatoes, and onions). *300 Av. F. D. Roosevelt, Hato Rey, tel. 809/767-3343. Reservations advised. AE, DC, MC, V. Moderate–Expensive.*

Che's. The most established and casual of three Argentinian restaurants within a few blocks of one another, Che's features juicy *churrasco* (barbecued) steaks, lemon chicken, and grilled sweetbreads. The hamburgers are huge and the french fries are fresh. The Chilean and Argentinian wine list is also decent. *35 Calle Caoba, Punta Las Marias, tel. 809/726-7202. AE, DC, MC, V. Moderate.*

★ **Scotch & Sirloin.** Tucked back among the tropical overgrowth overlooking the lagoon, the Scotch & Sirloin has been San Juan's most consistently fine steak house. Dine either on the terrace, hung with twinkling lights, or in the dim bar, which is illuminated by aquariums. Steaks are aged in-house and cooked precisely to order, there's a salad bar stocked with lots of fresh ingredients, and baskets of delicious moist banana bread are served with every meal. Live jazz is now offered Sunday brunch and Saturday evening. *La Rada Hotel,*

1020 Av. Ashford, Condado, tel. 809/722–3640. Reservations required. AE, DC, MC, V. Moderate.

El Paso. This family-run restaurant serves genuine Creole food seasoned for a local following. Specialties include asopao, pork chops, and breaded empanadas. There's always tripe on Saturday and arroz con pollo on Sunday. *405 Av. De Diego, Puerto Nuevo, tel. 809/ 781–3399. AE, DC, MC, V. Inexpensive.*

★ **Kasalta Bakery, Inc.** Make your selection from row upon row of display cases offering a seemingly endless array of tempting treats. Walk up to the counter and order an assortment of sandwiches (try the Cubano), meltingly tender octopus salad, savory *caldo gallego* (a soup jammed with fresh vegetables, sausage, and potatoes), cold drinks, strong café con leche, and luscious pastries. *1966 Calle McLeary, Ocean Park, tel. 809/727–7340. No credit cards. Inexpensive.*

Via Appia's Italian Deli. The only true sidewalk café in San Juan, this eatery serves pizzas, sandwiches, cold beer, and pitchers of sangria. It is a good place to people-watch. *1350 Av. Ashford, Condado, tel. 809/725–8711. AE, MC, V. Inexpensive.*

Out on the Island

The Black Eagle. Literally on the water's edge, you dine outside on the restaurant's veranda listening to the lapping waves under the stars. Under new management, the restaurant has been upgraded and the menu improved. House specialties include breaded conch fritters, fresh fish of the day, lobster, and prime meats that are imported by the owner. *Hwy. 413, Km 1, Barrio Ensenada, Rincón, tel. 809/823–3510. AE, DC, MC, V. Moderate.*

La Casona de Serafin. This informal, oceanside bistro, with blanched walls and mahogany furniture, specializes in steaks, seafood, and Puerto Rican *criolla* (Creole) dishes. Sample the tostones, asopao, and surrullitos. *Hwy. 102, Km 9, Cabo Rojo, tel. 809/851–0066. AE, MC, V. Moderate.*

Restaurant El Ancla. This relaxed spot by the water serves seafood and Puerto Rican specialties with courteous service. Entrées are served with tostones, *papas fritas* (french fries), and garlic bread. The menu ranges from lobster and shrimp to chicken, beef, and asopao. The piña coladas, with or without rum, and the flan are especially good. *Av. Hostos Final 9, Playa-Ponce, tel. 809/840–2450. AE, DC, MC, V. Moderate.*

Sand and the Sea. Looking down onto Guayama and out across the sea, this mountain cottage is a retreat into Caribbean living. The menu leans toward steaks and barbecues with a good carrot vichyssoise and excellent baked beans. Bring a sweater—it cools down to 50°F at night. *Hwy. 715, Km 5.2, Cayey, tel. 809/745–6317. AE, DC, MC, V. Moderate.*

Anchor's Inn. This unadorned seaside eatery has a fine view of the Fajardo harbor, where you can watch the flotillas of brightly colored yachts and fishing boats at play. The latter must head straight for the restaurant with their catch, for the seafood is as fresh and succulent as it gets. A *meson gastronomico*, Anchor's Inn specializes in such Puerto Rican specialties as surrullitos, asopao, and lobster mofongo. *Route 987, Km 2.4, Fajardo, tel. 809/863–7200. AE, MC, V. Inexpensive–Moderate.*

El Bohio. Serving fresh seafood in an informal setting overlooking the sea, a 10- to 15-minute drive south of Mayagüez, this restaurant reveals how the locals enjoy a meal. Selections range from red snapper to lobster and shrimp. *Hwy. 102, Playa Joyuda, Cabo Rojo, tel. 809/851–2755. AE, DC, MC, V. Inexpensive–Moderate.*

Lupita's. A fine mariachi band patrols the mezzanine and courtyard of this festive Mexican restaurant Thursday through Sunday nights.

The handsome arched dining room features Aztec decor, with panchos and serapes hung on the walls for added color. The food—Mexican-American standards like nachos, tacos, and chicken mole—is quite good, the margaritas and shooters even better, and the ambience festive. *Calle Isabel 60, Ponce, tel. 809/848–8808. AE, MC, V. Inexpensive.*

Lodging

Accommodations on Puerto Rico come in all shapes and sizes. Self-contained luxury resorts cover hundreds of acres. San Juan's high-rise beachfront hotels likewise cater to the epicurean; several target the business traveler. Out on the island, the government-sponsored paradores are country inns modeled after Spain's successful parador system. They are required to meet certain standards, such as proximity to a sightseeing attraction or beach and a kitchen serving native cuisine. (Parador prices range from $50 to $90 for a double room. Reservations for all paradores can be made by calling 800/443–0266 or 809/721–2884 in Puerto Rico.) They are a phenomenal bargain—but tend to get noisy and raucous on weekends, when families descend from the cities for a minivacation.

Most hotels in Puerto Rico operate on the European Plan. In some larger hotels, however, packages are available that include several or all meals, while others offer all-inclusive deals.

Highly recommended lodgings are indicated by a star ★.

Category	Cost*
Very Expensive	over $225
Expensive	$150–$225
Moderate	$75–$150
Inexpensive	under $75

*All prices are for a standard double room for two, excluding 7% tax (9% for hotels with casinos) and 10% service charge.

Old San Juan
★

Casa San José. Unassuming elegance defines the character of the newest Old San Juan hotel. Black-and-white marble floors decorate the foyer, and each of the 10 rooms, individually stylized with hand-picked Spanish, French, and English Colonial antiques, opens onto an interior patio filled with tropical plants. The second-floor salon is equipped with a small library and grand piano. Children under 12 are not accommodated. *159 Calle San José, 00901, tel. 809/723–1212, fax 809/723–7620. 4 1-bedroom suites, 1 2-bedroom suite, 4 doubles. Facilities: restaurant. AE, DC, MC, V. CP. Expensive–Very Expensive.*

The Gallery Inn. Owners Jan D'Esopo and Manuco Gandia restored one of the oldest private residences in the area and turned it into a rambling, classically Spanish guest house with winding, uneven stairs, private balconies, individually decorated rooms, and gardens hidden throughout. This small inn and art gallery (Galería San Juan) overlooks the Atlantic along the north wall of Old San Juan. With its views of El Morro and San Cristóbal forts, the inn has a compelling and singular panorama that is one of the best in the old city. The gallery is also a working studio, and you may run into models posing in any of the suites in the house. The gallery features work by the likes of Jan D'Esopo, Bruno Lucchesi, and Burton Silverman. The inn even offers a package that combines a five-night stay with the creation of your portrait bust. *204–206 Calle Norzagaray, 00901, tel. 809/722–1808, fax 809/724–7360. 3 suites and 5 guest rooms. Facilities: self-service bar, restaurant for guests only. AE, MC, V. EP. Moderate–Expensive.*

Gran Hotel El Convento. This is one of Puerto Rico's most famous hotels. On Calle Cristo right across from the San Juan Cathedral, the light brown stucco building, with its dark wood paneling and arcades, was a Carmelite convent in the 17th century. Alas, the heavy dour furnishings seem not to have been refurbished since. All the rooms are air-conditioned, with twin beds and wall-to-wall carpeting. Fourteen rooms have balconies (ask for one with a view of the bay). *100 Calle Cristo, 00902, tel. 809/723–9020 or 800/468–2779, fax 809/721–2877. 99 rooms. Facilities: 2 restaurants and bar, pool, free transport to beach. AE, D, DC, MC, V. EP. Moderate–Expensive.*

San Juan

★ **El San Juan Hotel and Casino.** An immense chandelier shines over the hand-carved wood paneling and rose marble of the lobby in this sprawling 22-acre resort on the Isla Verde beach. You'll be hard pressed to decide if you want a spa suite in the main tower with whirlpool and wet bar; a garden lanai room, with private patio and spa; or a custom-designed casita with sunken Roman bath. (Some of the tower rooms have no view; your best bet is an oceanside lanai, with or without spa.) In any case, all rooms are air-conditioned, with three phones, remote-control TVs with VCRs, hair dryers, minibars, and many other amenities. The posh Dar Tiffany restaurant, an oasis of potted palms, etched glass, and yes, Tiffany lamps, serves impeccable Continental fare. The intimate romantic La Piccola Fontana is one of San Juan's better Italian restaurants. *Av. Isla Verde, Box 2872, San Juan 00902, tel. 809/791–1000 or 800/468–2818, fax 809/791–0390. 392 rooms. Facilities: 5 restaurants, 2 snack bars, 8 cocktail lounges, supper club, 2 pools, children's pool, disco, casino, 3 lighted tennis courts with pro shop, activity center, water-sports center, shopping arcade, health club, no-smoking floor, facilities for people with disabilities, complimentary shuttle bus to Condado Plaza Hotel, courtyard Jacuzzi, concierge, valet parking. AE, DC, MC, V. EP. Very Expensive.*

★ **Sands Hotel and Casino.** One of Puerto Rico's largest casinos glitters just off the lobby, stunning artworks from around the world grace the public rooms, and a huge free-form pool lies between the hotel and its beach. The air-conditioned hotel has rooms with private balconies (ask for one with an ocean view), minibars, and many frills. The exclusive Plaza Club section is that rare executive level worth the added expense, offering garden suites, a masseuse, private spas, and other enticements. *Box 6676, Calle Isla Verde 187, Isla Verde 00913, tel. 809/791–6100 or 800/468–9076, fax 809/791–8525. 418 rooms. Facilities: 5 restaurants, pool, lounge, casino, concierge, 24-hr room service, facilities for people with disabilities, nightclub, water-sports center, business center, valet parking. AE, D, DC, MC, V. EP. Very Expensive.*

★ **Caribe Hilton International.** Built in 1949, this property occupies 17 acres on Puerta de Tierra and completed (in early 1991) a $40 million renovation that modernized rooms, giving them a crisp, pastel decor. The spacious atrium lobby is decorated with rose marble, waterfalls, and lavish tropical plants. The hotel boasts San Juan's only private, palm-fringed swimming cove complete with a boardwalk and a bar to serve you as you swim by. The airy guest rooms have balconies with ocean or lagoon views. Three executive levels provide services and amenities for the business traveler. *Box 1872, San Juan 00902, tel. 809/721–0303 or 800/468–8585, fax 809/722–2910. 668 rooms and suites. Facilities: 5 restaurants, pastry shop, private* *beach, 2 pools, 6 lighted tennis courts, workout area, air-conditioned squash and racquetball courts, executive business center. AE, D, DC, MC, V. EP. Expensive–Very Expensive.*

Condado Plaza Hotel and Casino. Nestled between the Atlantic Ocean and the Condado Lagoon, this stunning resort is two hotels in one, with a Lagoon Wing and an Ocean Wing. Standard rooms have walk-in closets and separate dressing areas. There is a variety of suites (including spa suites with whirlpools) and a fully equipped executive service center. If that isn't posh enough, you can check into the Plaza Club, which has 24-hour concierge service. L. K. Sweeney & Son Ltd. overlooks the lagoon and serves superb seafood. *Box 1270, 999 Av. Ashford, Condado 00907, tel. 809/721–1000 or 800/ 468–8588, fax 809/721–4613. 580 rooms and suites. Facilities: 5 pools (1 saltwater); casino; disco; 2 lighted tennis courts; 6 restaurants; 7 bars and lounges; fitness, water sports, and business centers. AE, D, DC, MC, V. EP. Expensive–Very Expensive.*

★ **The Condado Beach Trio.** Carnicom is combining the venerable Condado Beach Hotel, the family-oriented La Concha Hotel, and the El Centro Convention Center into a megacomplex sure to be a top choice for business travelers. Both hotels are undergoing extensive renovations. Built in 1919 by Cornelius Vanderbilt, the Condado Beach hotel has a pale pink lobby adorned with bouquets of flowers, a sweeping double staircase, and Victorian furnishings. Guest rooms, each decorated in the Spanish Colonial style of the 1920s, have either an ocean, lagoon, or city view. The Vanderbilt Club floors, reached by private elevator, provide all manner of pampering. Vivas offers delectable New World cuisine, and Café del Arté has become a hip gathering spot in the early evening. Looking like a large pink seashell, the La Concha completed extensive renovations in 1993. Its individually air-conditioned rooms all face the ocean and are furnished in fresh contemporary pastels. The ritzy Sirenas disco, built in the shape of a conch shell, is perched right over the water. *La Concha Hotel, Box 4195, Condado 00905, tel. 809/721– 6090 or 800/468–2822, fax 809/721–3200. 236 oceanfront rooms. Facilities: 2 restaurants and lunges, activity center, water-sports center, 2 lighted tennis courts, volleyball court on the beach, pool, poolside bar, disco, facilities for people with disabilities, shopping arcade. Condado Beach Hotel, Box 41226, Minillas Station, Condado 00940, tel. 809/721–6090 or 800/468–2775, fax 809/722– 5062. 245 rooms, including 18 junior suites, 2 1- and 2-bedroom suites, and a presidential suite. Facilities: 3 restaurants and lunges, cable TV, 3rd-level pool, facilities for people with disabilities. AE, D, DC, MC, V. EP. Expensive.*

Radisson Normandie. Built in 1939 in the shape of the fabled ocean liner of the same name, this oceanfront hotel reopened in late 1988 under the Radisson banner. It's a national historic landmark, done up in art-deco style, and each room comes with sun room, minibar, and cable TV. Additional frills and pampering can be found at the seventh-floor executive club. *Corner of Av. Muñoz Rivera and Av. Rosales, Puerta Tierra, Box 50059, San Juan 00902, tel. 809/729– 2929 or 800/333–3333; fax 809/729–3083. 180 air-conditioned rooms. Facilities: 2 restaurants, outdoor pool, lounge, business center, health club, water-sports center. AE, D (for payment only), MC, V. EP, MAP. Expensive.*

Excelsior. Recently spruced up with English carpets in the corridors and new sculptures in the lobby, this hotel is home to the estimable restaurant Augusto's Cuisine in Ali-Oli. Each room has a private bath with phone and hair dryer. Although the decor is standard, this hotel is a very good value for its price range. Complimentary coffee, newspaper, and shoeshine are offered each morning. *801*

Av. Ponce de León, Miramar 00907, tel. 809/721–7400 or 800/223–9815, fax 809/723–0068. 140 rooms, 60 with kitchenette. Facilities: cocktail lounge, restaurants, pool, fitness rooms, free parking and free transportation to the beach. AE, MC, V. EP. Moderate.

Out on the Island
Cabo Rojo

Parador Boquemar. Located on Route 101 near the beach in a small, unpretentious fishing village, this parador has comfortable air-conditioned rooms, all with cable TV, minifridge, and private bath and decorated in standard tropical prints and rattans. La Cascada is well known for its scrumptious traditional native cuisine. *Box 133, 00622, tel. 809/851–2158 or 800/443–0266. 64 rooms. Facilities: restaurant, pool. AE, DC, MC, V. EP. Moderate.*

Coamo

Parador Baños de Coamo. On Route 546, Km 1, northeast of Ponce, this mountain inn is located at the hot sulfur springs that are said to be the Fountain of Youth of Ponce de León's dreams. Rooms open onto latticed wooden verandas and feature a pleasing blend of contemporary and period furnishings. The parador can make arrangements for guests to ride Puerto Rico's glorious, unique paso fino horses. *Box 540, 00640, tel. 809/825–2186 or 800/443–0266. 48 rooms. Facilities: restaurant, lounge, pool, horseback riding. AE, D, DC, MC, V. EP. Inexpensive.*

Dorado
★

Hyatt Regency Cerromar Beach. Located 22 miles west of San Juan at Route 693, Km 11.8, smack on the Atlantic, the Cerromar not only has a lovely reef-protected beach, it also claims that its $3 million river pool—with 4 waterfalls, an underwater Jacuzzi, a swim-up bar, and a three-story-high water slide—is the world's longest freshwater pool. It's a fitting crown to one of the best sports-oriented resorts in the Caribbean. The modern seven-story hotel, done up in tropical style, has tile floors, marble baths, air-conditioning, and rooms with a king-size or two double beds. (You'll find quieter rooms on the west side, away from the pool activity.) Guests at the Cerromar and its sister facility, the Hyatt Dorado Beach a mile down the road, have access to the facilities of both resorts, and colorful red trolleys (free, of course) make frequent runs between the two. Sushi Wong's serves delicious pan-Asian cuisine, and Medici's is an ultra-sophisticated Northern Italian eatery. *Dorado 00646, tel. 809/796–1234 or 800/233–1234, fax 809/796–4647. 504 rooms. Facilities: 4 restaurants, 3 bars, airport limo, casino, disco, 2 18-hole Robert Trent Jones golf courses, 14 tennis courts (2 lighted), pool, spa and health club, horseback riding, bike rentals, jogging and hiking trails. AE, D, DC, MC, V. EP. Very Expensive.*

★

Hyatt Dorado Beach. The ambience is a bit more subdued and family oriented at the Cerromar's sophisticated sister, where a variety of elegant accommodations are in low-rise buildings scattered over 1,000 lavishly landscaped acres. Most rooms have private patios or balconies, and all have polished terra-cotta floors, marble baths, air-conditioning, and many frills. Upper-level rooms in the Oceanview Houses have a view of the two half-moon beaches. *Rte. 693, 00646, tel. 809/796–1234 or 800/233–1234, fax 809/796–2022. 298 rooms. Facilities: 3 restaurants, 2 lounges, 2 18-hole Robert Trent Jones golf courses, 7 tennis courts, horseback riding, hiking and jogging trails, 2 pools, wading pool, casino, water-sports center. AE, D, DC, MC, V. EP. Very Expensive.*

Humacao
★

Palmas del Mar. This is an already luxurious but still developing resort community, on 2,750 acres of a former coconut plantation on the sheltered southeast coast (about an hour's drive from San Juan). Two hotels, the elegant 23-suite Palmas Inn and 102-room Candelero Hotel, are the centerpieces of the complex. In the rustic yet elegant Candelero, rooms are airy and spacious, with cathedral ceilings. The Palmas Inn suites, all with stunning sea or mountain views, evoke luxurious Mediterranean villas, with pastel pink connecting walkways, cobblestone plazas, and fountains adorned with hand-painted tilework. In addition, the resort includes private homes and condominium villas. *Box 2020, Rte. 906, 00792, tel. 809/ 852–6000, 800/221–4874, or in NY, 212/983–0393; fax 212/949–8084. 102 rooms; 85 villas; 23 1-, 2-, and 3-bedroom suites. Facilities: 10 restaurants, beach, 18-hole Gary Player golf course, 20 tennis courts (4 lighted), casino, equestrian center, 6 pools, bike rentals, fitness center, water-sports center, golf, tennis, and honeymoon packages. AE, DC, MC, V. EP. Expensive–Very Expensive.*

Jayuya **Parador Hacienda Gripinas.** This is a white hacienda with polished
★ wood, beam ceilings, a spacious lounge with rocking chairs, a porch with hammocks, and splendid gardens. The large airy rooms are decorated with native crafts—a very romantic hideaway. Your morning coffee was grown on the adjacent working plantation. Its aroma seems to fill the grounds, as does the inimitable chirp of the ubiquitous coquis (tree frogs). *Rte. 527, Km 2.5, Box 387, 00664, tel. 809/828–1717, 809/721–2884, or 800/443–0266. 19 rooms. Facilities: restaurant, lounge, pool, hiking and horseback-riding trails. AE, MC, V. EP. Inexpensive.*

La Parguera **Parador Villa Parguera.** This parador is a stylish hotel on Phosphorescent Bay, with large, colorfully decorated, air-conditioned rooms. A spacious dining room, overlooking the swimming pool and the bay beyond, serves excellent native and international dishes. *Rte. 304, Box 273, Lajas 00667, tel. 809/899–3975 or 809/443–0266. 50 rooms. Facilities: restaurant, lounge, saltwater pool, some facilities for people with disabilities. AE, D, DC, MC. EP. Moderate.*

Las Croabas **El Conquistador Resort and Country Club.** This new $250 million complex is a world unto itself, divided into five self-contained hotels perched dramatically atop a 300-foot bluff overlooking the Caribbean, the Atlantic, and the El Yunque rain forest. The architecture is a harmonious blend of Moorish and Spanish colonial: cobblestone streets, white stucco and terra-cotta buildings, open-air plazas with tinkling fountains, tiled benches, and gas lamps, all reminiscent of Old San Juan or an Andalusian fishing village. One of the five hotels, Las Olas, is actually built into the cliff face. The stylish decor runs toward the ubiquitous Caribbean rattan and pastels, spiced with native crafts and artworks. The pampering begins at LMM International Airport: The resort is currently the only one on the island to operate a private lounge and its own deluxe motorcoach transfers. *Fajardo 00738, tel. 809/863–1000 or 800/468–8365, fax 809/863–6500. 924 rooms and suites. Facilities: 16 restaurants and lounges, casino, convention center, nightclub, marina, water-sports center, 5 pools, 7 tennis courts, 18-hole golf course (with another scheduled for completion in 1995), fitness center, shopping arcades. Very Expensive.*

Mayagüez **Hilton International Mayagüez.** Built on 20 acres overlooking the Mayagüez harbor, this resort on the island's west coast is about a 2½-hour drive from San Juan. The casino, one of the executive floors, and the superb Rotisserie restaurant (known for its lavish theme buffets and top-notch steaks and seafood) were recently renovated, as was the pool. The hotel is 2 miles from the town of Mayagüez. Also close by are the Boquerón swimming beach, Punta Higuero surfing beach, the Mayagüez Marina for deep-sea fishing, seven excellent skin-diving spots, and two golf courses. *Rte. 2, Km 152.5, Box 3629, 00709, tel. 809/831–7575, 800/445–8667, or in Puerto Rico, 800/462–3954; fax 809/834–3475. 141 air-conditioned rooms*

*and suites. Facilities: restaurant, lounge, Olympic-size pool, 3
lighted tennis courts, casino, disco. AE, D, DC, MC, V. EP. Expensive–Very Expensive.*

Ponce **Ponce Hilton Hotel and Casino.** By far the class hotel act on the south
★ coast, this splashy resort nestled amid 80 acres of landscaped gardens opened in 1992. Completely self-contained, it offers three fine
restaurants (La Hacienda duplicates an old coffee plantation; the delightfully quaint La Cava can be reserved for a private dinner with
chef Mark French), a man-made lagoon and beach, casino, shopping
arcade, free-form pool, and four tennis courts. The huge rooms are
decorated in cool pastels—sky blue, teal, and peach—with bright
tropical spreads. All feature minibar, safe, cable TV, balcony, and
hair dryer. The only drawback is its out-of-town location (a ten-minute cab ride from town). *Box 7149, 00732, tel. 809/259–7676 or 800/
HILTONS, fax 809/259–7674. 156 rooms. Facilities: 3 restaurants, 2
bars, casino, pool, 4 lighted tennis courts, business center, fitness
room, shopping arcade, beauty salon. AE, D, DC, MC, V. EP.
MAP. Moderate–Expensive.*

Rincón **Horned Dorset Primavera.** Nestled amid lush landscaping with a dra-
★ matic view of the sea, this tranquil resort features 24 suites with private balconies and exquisite antique furnishings, including
handsome mahogany four-poster beds. The architecture here is
Spanish, and the location—on the west coast, north of Mayagüez—
promises privacy. The resort's beach is long and secluded. The elegant restaurant serves stylish, definitively Continental cuisine in
surroundings befitting royalty. *Rte. 429, Km 3, Box 1132, 00743, tel.
809/823–4030 or 809/823–4050, fax 809/823–5580. Facilities: restaurant, pool, lounge. AE, MC, V. EP. Very Expensive.*

San Germán **Parador Oasis.** The Oasis, not far from the town's two plazas, was a
family mansion 200 years ago. You'll get a better taste for its history
in the older front rooms charmingly painted peppermint pink and
crammed with antiques and family heirlooms; rooms in the new section in the rear are small and somewhat motelish. *72 Calle Luna,
Box 144, 00753, tel. 809/892–1175 or 800/443–0266. 50 rooms. Facilities: restaurant, pool, Jacuzzi, lounge, gym, sauna. AE, DC, MC,
V. EP. Moderate.*

Vieques **Casa del Francés.** Self-professed curmudgeon Irving Greenblatt, a
refugee from Boston, runs this atmospheric guest house in a restored French sugar plantation great house. Rooms are rather plain
but enormous, with vaulting 17-foot ceilings. The food is good, the
pool inviting, the guests an eclectic fascinating mix, and Irving a
true character who will regale you with horror stories of running a
Caribbean hotel. *Box 458, Esperanza, 00765, tel. 809/741–3751. 8
rooms. Facilities: restaurant, pool. AE, MC, V. EP, MAP. Moderate.*

Sea Gate. Occupying 2 acres of a hilltop on the island of Vieques, this
whitewashed hotel is a family-run operation. Friendly, helpful proprietors John, Ruthye, and Penny Miller will meet you at the airport
or ferry, drive you to the beaches, arrange scuba-diving and snorkeling trips, and give you a complete rundown on their adopted
home. Accommodations include three-room efficiencies with full
kitchens and terraces. *Box 747, 00765, tel. 809/741–4661. 16 units.
No credit cards. No restaurant. Inexpensive.*

The Arts and Nightlife

¿Qué Pasa?, the official visitors' guide, has current listings of events
in San Juan and out on the island. Also, pick up a copy of the *San*

Juan Star, Quick City Guide, or *Sunspots*, and check with the local tourist offices and the concierge at your hotel to find out what's doing.

Music, Dance, and Theater LeLoLai is a year-round festival that celebrates Puerto Rico's Indian, Spanish, and African heritage. Performances take place each week, moving from hotel to hotel, showcasing the island's music, folklore, and culture. Because it is sponsored by the Puerto Rico Tourism Company and major San Juan hotels, passes to the festivities are included in some packages offered by participating hotels. Others can purchase tickets for $8 (adults) and $6 (children) for the series. *Contact the El Centro Convention Center, tel. 809/723–3135. Reservations can be made by telephoning 809/722–1513.*

La Tasca del Callejon (Calle Fortaleza 317, tel. 809/721–1689) is renowned for its tapas bar and the cabaret show (usually including flamenco guitar) performed by its engaging, talented staff.

Bars The Blue Dolphin (2 Calle Amapola, Isla Verde, tel. 809/791–3083) is a hangout where you can rub elbows with some offbeat locals and enjoy some stunning sunset happy hours. While strolling along the Isla Verde beach, just look for the neon blue dolphin on the roof—you can't miss it.

El Patio de Sam (102 Calle san Sebastián, tel. 809/723–1149) is an Old San Juan institution whose expatriate clientele claims it serves the best burgers on the island. The dining room is awash in potted plants and strategically placed canopies that create the illusion of dining on an outdoor "patio." After a few happy hour drinks, patrons claim they *are* drinking alfresco.

Casinos By law, all casinos are in hotels, primarily in San Juan. The government keeps a close eye on them. Dress for the larger casinos tends to be on the formal side, and the atmosphere is refined. The law permits casinos to operate noon–4 AM, but individual casinos set their own hours.

Casinos are located in the following San Juan hotels (*see* Lodging, *above*): **Condado Plaza Hotel, Caribe Hilton, Carib Inn, Clarion Hotel, Ramada, Dutch Inn, Sands,** and **El San Juan.** Elsewhere on the island, there are casinos at the **Hyatt Regency Cerromar** and **Hyatt Dorado Beach hotels,** and at **Palmas del Mar,** the **Ponce Hilton,** the **El Conquistador,** and the **Hilton International Mayagüez.**

Discos In San Juan, young people flock to **Krash** (1257 Av. Ponce de León, Santurce, tel. 809/722–1390) and **Lazers** (251 Calle Cruz, tel. 809/721–4479).

In Puerta de Tierra, Condado, and Isla Verde, the thirty-something crowd heads for **Juliana's** (Caribe Hilton Hotel, tel. 809/ 721–0303), **Isadora's** (Condado Plaza Hotel, tel. 809/721–1000), **Mykonos** (La Concha Hotel, tel. 809/721–6090), and **Amadeus** (El San Juan Hotel, tel. 809/791–1000).

Nightclubs The Sands Hotel's **Players Lounge** brings in such big names as Joan Rivers, Jay Leno, and Rita Moreno. El San Juan's **Tropicoro** presents international revues, occasional top-name entertainers, and a flamenco show four times a week. Try El San Juan's **El Chico** to dance to Latin music in a western saloon setting. The Condado Plaza Hotel has the **Copa Room,** and its **La Fiesta** sizzles with steamy Latin shows. The El Centro Convention Center offers the festive **Olé**

Latino (tel. 809/721–1880). In Old San Juan, the Hotel El Convento's **Ponce de León Salon** (tel. 809/723–9020) puts on flamenco shows. Young professionals gather at **Peggy Sue** (1 Av. Roberto H. Todd, tel. 809/722–4664), where the design is 1950s and the music includes oldies and current dance hits.

18 Saba

Updated by
Jordan
Simon

This 5-square-mile fairy-tale isle is not for everybody. If you're look-ing for exciting nightlife or lots of shopping, forget Saba, or take the one-day trip from St. Maarten. There are only a handful of shops, even fewer inns and eateries, and only 1,200 friendly, but shy, inhab-itants. Beach lovers should also take note that Saba is a beachless volcanic island, ringed with steep cliffs that plummet sharply to the sea.

So, why Saba? Saba is a perfect hideaway, a challenge for adventur-ous hikers (Mt. Scenery rises above it all to a height of 2,855 feet), a longtime haven for divers, and, for Sabans, heaven on water. It's no wonder that they call their island the Unspoiled Caribbean Queen.

The capital of Saba (pronounced *SAY*-ba) is The Bottom, which is at the top, not the bottom, of a hill. Meandering goats have the right of way on The Road (there's only one); chickens cross at their own risk. In tiny, toylike villages, narrow paths are bordered by flower-draped walls and neat picket fences. Tidy houses with red roofs and gingerbread trim are planted in the mountainside among the bromeliads, palms, hibiscus, orchids, and Norwegian pines. Saba may be the prettiest island in the Caribbean; it's certainly the most immaculate, with a "once upon a time" storybook enchantment. De-spite such recent modern additions as televisions sets (since 1965) and 24-hour electricity (installed in 1970), the island's uncompli-cated lifestyle has persevered. Saban ladies still hand-embroider the very special, delicate Saba lace—a reminder of Saban gentility that has flourished since the 1870s—and brew the potent rum-based liquor, Saba Spice, sweetened with secret herbs and spices. Fami-lies still follow the generations-old tradition of burying their dead in their neatly tended gardens.

Saba is part of the Netherlands Antilles Windward Islands, 28 miles—a 15-minute flight—from St. Maarten. The island is a volca-no that has been extinct for 5,000 years (no one even knows where the crater was). Carib Indians may have hung out here around AD 800; Columbus spotted the little speck in 1493, but somehow Saba remained uninhabited until the first Dutch settlers arrived from Statia in 1640. In the 17th, 18th, and early 19th centuries the French, Dutch, English, and Spanish vied for control of the island. Saba changed hands 12 times before permanently raising the Dutch flag.

Sabans are a hardy lot. To get from Fort Bay to The Bottom, the ear-ly Sabans carved 900 steps out of the mountainside. Everything that arrived on the island, from a pin to a piano, had to be hauled up. Those rugged steps remained the only way to get about the island until The Road was built by Josephus Lambert Hassell (a carpenter who took correspondence courses in engineering) in the 1940s. An extraordinary feat of engineering, the handmade road took 20 years to build, and if you like roller coasters, you'll love it. The 6½-mile, white-knuckle route begins at sea level in Fort Bay, zigs up to 1,968 feet, and zags down to 131 feet above sea level at the airport, con-structed on the island's only flat point called (what else?) Flat Point.

Before You Go

Tourist For help planning your trip, contact the **Caribbean Tourism Organi-**
Information **zation** (20 E. 46th St., New York, NY 10017–2452, tel. 212/682–0435) or, in Canada, **New Concepts in Travel** (410 Queens Quai W, Suite 303, Toronto, Ontario M5V 2Z3, tel. 416/362–7707).

Book reservations through a travel agent or over the telephone because mail can take a week or two to reach the island.

Arriving and Unless you parachute in, you'll arrive from St. Maarten via **Wind-**
Departing **ward Islands Airways** (tel. 599/5–42255 or 599/5–44237). The ap-
By Plane proach to Saba's tiny airstrip is the stuff of which nightmares are made. The strip is only 1,312 feet long, but the STOL (Short Takeoff and Landing) aircrafts are built for it, and the pilot needs only half of it. Try not to panic; remember that the pilot knows what he is doing and wants to live just as much as you do. (If you're nervous, don't sit on the right. The wing just misses grazing the cliffside on the approach.) Once you've touched down on the airstrip, the pilot taxis an inch or two, turns, and deposits you just outside a little shoebox called the Juancho E. Yrausquin Airport.

By Boat *Style*, an open-air vessel with an open bar, departs St. Maarten's Great Bay Marina, Phillipsburg, three times weekly at 9 AM and returns at 3 PM. The trip to Saba's Fort Bay takes an hour, and the round-trip fare is $45 (tel. 599/5–22167 in St. Maarten). If you take the watery way, however, you'll have lost more than an hour of sightseeing time on Saba.

Passports U.S. citizens need proof of citizenship. A passport is preferred, but
and Visas a birth certificate or voter registration card will do (a driver's license will *not*). British citizens must have a British passport. All visitors must have an ongoing or return ticket.

Language Saba's official language is Dutch, but everyone on the island speaks English.

Precautions Everyone knows everyone else on the island, and crime is virtually nonexistent. Take along insect repellent, sunscreen, and sturdy, nononsense shoes that get a good grip on the ground.

Staying in Saba

Important **Tourist Information:** The amiable Glenn Holm is at the helm of the
Addresses **Saba Tourist Office** (Windwardside, tel. 599/4–62231, fax 599/4–62350) weekdays 8–noon and 1–5. If needed, the tourist office will help secure accommodations in guest houses.

Emergencies **Police:** Call 599/4–63237. **Hospital:** The **A. M. Edwards Medical Center** (The Bottom, tel. 599/4–63288) is a 10-bed hospital with a full-time physician and various clinics. **Pharmacy:** The **Pharmacy** (The Bottom, tel. 599/4–63289).

Currency U.S. dollars are accepted everywhere, but Saba's official currency is the Netherlands Antilles florin (NAf; also called the guilder). The exchange rate fluctuates but is around NAf1.80 to U.S.$1. Prices quoted here are in U.S. dollars unless noted otherwise. **Barclays Bank** in Windwardside is the island's only major bank; it's open weekdays 8:30–2.

Taxes and Hotels collect a 5% government tax. Most hotels and restaurants
Service add a 10%–15% service charge to your bill. The departure tax is $2
Charges from Saba to St. Maarten or St. Eustatius.

Guided Tours All 10 of the taxi drivers who meet the planes at Yrausquin Airport also conduct tours of the island. The cost for a full-day tour is $8 per person with a minimum of four people. If you're just in from St. Maarten for a day trip, have your driver make lunch reservations for you at **the Serving Spoon** or the **Captain's Quarters** (*see* Dining, *below*) before starting the tour. After a full morning of sightseeing, your driver will drop you off for lunch, complete the tour afterward, and return you to Yrausquin in time to make the last flight back to St. Maarten. Guides are available for hiking. Arrangements may be made through the tourist office.

Getting Around
Rental Cars

Saba's one and only road—The Road—is a serpentine affair with many a hairpin (read hair-raising) curve. However, if you dare to make your way about by car, there are nine rental cars at **Doc's Car Rentals** (Windwardside, tel. 599/4–62271). Cars can also be rented at **Scout's Place** (Windwardside, tel. 599/4–62205) and at **Juliana's** (Windwardside, tel. 599/4–62269). A car rents for about $35 per day, with a full tank of gas and unlimited mileage. (If you run out of gas, call the island's only gas station, down at Fort Bay, tel. 599/4–63272. It closes at noon.) Scooters can be rented at **Steve's** (tel. 599/4–62507), next to Sandra's Salon & Boutique, for $30–$35 per day, less by the week.

Hitchhiking

Carless Sabans get around the old-fashioned ways—walking and hitchhiking (very popular and safe). If you choose to get around by thumbing rides, you'll need to know the rules of The Road. To go from The Bottom (which actually is near the top of the island), sit on the wall opposite the Anglican church; to go from Fort Bay, sit on the wall opposite Saba Deep dive center, where the road begins to twist upward.

Telephones and Mail

To call Saba from the United States, dial 011/599/4 followed by the five-digit number, which always begins with a 6. On the island, it is only necessary to dial the five-digit number. Telephone communications are excellent on the island, and direct-dial long distance is in effect.

To airmail a letter to the United States costs NAf1.30; a postcard, NAf.60.

Opening and Closing Times

Businesses and government offices on Saba are open weekdays 8 AM to 5 PM.

Exploring Saba

Numbers in the margin correspond to points of interest on the Saba map.

Begin your driving tour with a trip from Flat Point, at the airport, up to Hell's Gate. Because there is only one road, we'll continue along its hairpin curves up to Windwardside and then on to The Bottom and down to Fort Bay. This cross-island tour will give you a quick overview of tiny Saba, its limited cultural sights, and varied natural settings.

❶ There are 20 sharp curves on The Road between the airport and Hell's Gate. On one of these curves, poised on Hell's Gate's hill, is the stone **Holy Rosary Church,** which looks medieval but was built in 1962. In the **community center** behind the church, village ladies sell blouses, handkerchiefs, tablecloths, and tea towels embellished with the very special and unique Saba lace. These same ladies also turn out innocent-sounding Saba Spice—each according to her old family recipe—a rum-based liqueur that will knock your proverbial socks off.

❷ The Road spirals past banana plantations, oleander bushes, and stunning views of the ocean below. In **Windwardside,** the island's second-largest village, teetering at 1,968 feet, you'll see rambling lanes and narrow alleyways winding through the hills and a cluster of tiny, neat houses and shops.

On your right as you enter the village is the **Church of St. Paul's Conversion,** a colonial building with a red-and-white steeple. Your next stop should be the **Saba Tourist Office** (just down the road), where you can pick up brochures and books about Saba. You may then want to spend some time browsing through the **Square Nickel,** the **Breadfruit Gallery,** the **Weaver's Cottage, Saba Tropical Arts,** and the **Island Craft Shop** (*see* Shopping, *below*).

The **Saba Museum,** surrounded by lemongrass and clover, lies just behind the Captain's Quarters. There are small signs marking the way to the 150-year-old house that has been set up to look much as it did when it was a sea captain's home. Its furnishings include a handsome mahogany four-poster bed with pineapple design, an antique organ, and, in the kitchen, a rock oven and a hearth. Among the old documents on display is a letter a Saban wrote after the hurricane of 1772, in which he sadly says, "We have lost our little all." The first Sunday of each month, the museum holds croquet matches on its grounds; all-white attire is requested at this formal but fun social event. *Windwardside, no tel. Admission: $1 donation requested. Open weekdays 10–12:30 and 1–3.*

③ Near the museum are the stone and concrete steps—1,064 of them—that rise to **Mt. Scenery.** The steps lead past giant elephant ears, ferns, begonias, mangoes, palms, and orchids up to a mahogany grove at the summit: six identifiable ecosystems in all. New, helpful signs have been posted naming the trees, plants, and shrubs. On a cloudless day the view is spectacular. For a breathtaking journey, have your hotel pack a picnic lunch, wear nonslip shoes, take along a jacket and a canteen of water, and hike away. The round-trip excursion will take about a half day and is best begun in the early morning.

Time Out The **Corner Deli and Gourmet Shop,** opened by native New Yorker Alan Slatky, who spent 20 years as executive chef at four-star hotels before escaping the rat race, is *the* place to pick up picnic provisions and local gossip. It offers fresh salads, homemade breads, roast chicken, charcuterie, and a little bit of Soho in Saba.

④ You'll be zigzagging downhill, past the small settlement of St. John's, from Windwardside to **The Bottom,** which sits in its bowl-shape valley 820 feet above the sea. The Bottom is the seat of government and the home of the lieutenant governor. The large house next to Wilhelmina Park has fancy fretwork, a high-pitched roof, and wraparound double galleries.

On the other side of town is the **Wesleyan Holiness Church,** a small stone building dating from 1919 with bright white fretwork. Stroll by the church, beyond a place called The Gap, and you'll come to a **lookout point** where you can see the rough-hewn steps leading down to Ladder Bay. Ladder Bay, with 524 steps, and Fort Bay, with its 200 steps, were the two landing sites from which Saba's first settlers had to haul themselves and their possessions. Sabans sometimes walk down to Ladder Bay to picnic. Think long and hard before you do, bearing in mind that it's 524 steps back *up* to The Road. (Hitchhiking from down there will get you nowhere!)

⑤ The last stop on The Road is **Fort Bay,** which is the jumping-off place for two of the island's dive operations (*see* Scuba Diving and Snorkeling, *below*) and the St. Maarten ferry docks. There's also a gas station, a 277-foot deep-water pier that accommodates the tenders from ships that call here, and the information center for the **Saba Marine Park** (*see* Scuba Diving and Snorkeling, *below*). The damage

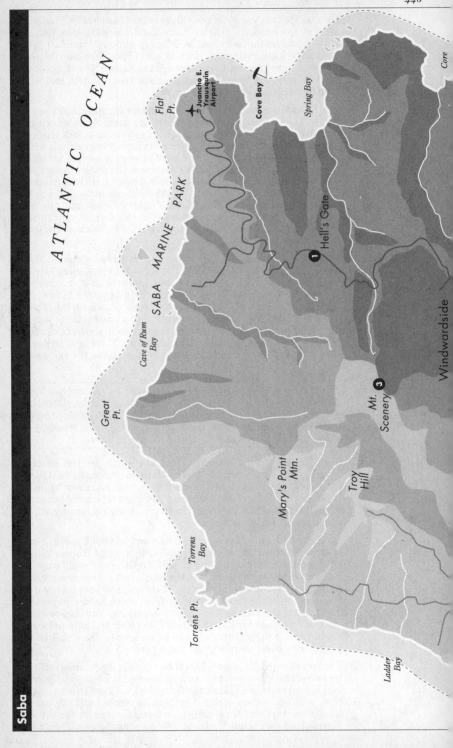

Saba

ATLANTIC OCEAN

Flat Pt.

Juancho E. Yrausquin Airport

Cove Bay

Spring Bay

Core

SABA MARINE PARK

Cave of Rum Bay

Great Pt.

Hell's Gate

1

Windwardside

Mary's Point Mtn.

Mt. Scenery

3

Torrens Bay

Troy Hill

Torrens Pt.

Ladder Bay

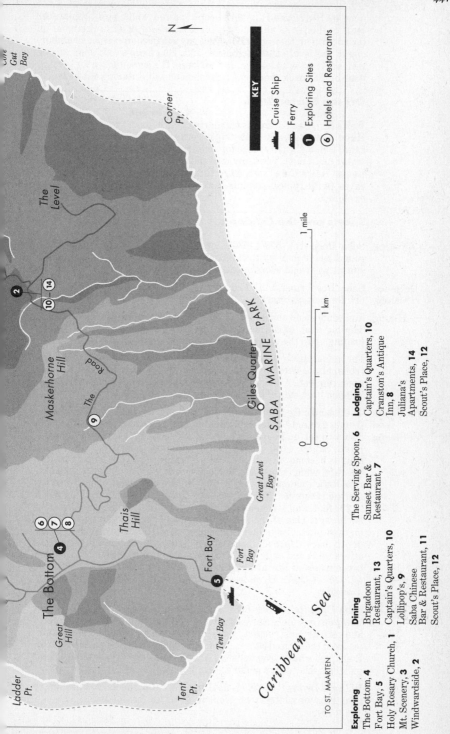

447

KEY

🚢 Cruise Ship

⛴ Ferry

① Exploring Sites

⑥ Hotels and Restaurants

TO ST. MAARTEN

Caribbean Sea

Ladder Pt.

Great Hill

The Bottom

Tent Pt.

Tent Bay

Fort Bay

Thais Hill

Great Level Bay

The Road

Maskerhorne Hill

The Level

Corner Pt.

Core Gut Bay

Giles Quarter

SABA MARINE PARK

Fort Bay

N

0   1 km

0   1 mile

Exploring

The Bottom, **4**
Fort Bay, **5**
Holy Rosary Church, **1**
Mt. Scenery, **3**
Windwardside, **2**

Dining

Brigadoon Restaurant, **13**
Captain's Quarters, **10**
Lollipop's, **9**
Saba Chinese Bar & Restaurant, **11**
Scout's Place, **12**
The Serving Spoon, **6**
Sunset Bar & Restaurant, **7**

Lodging

Captain's Quarters, **10**
Cranston's Antique Inn, **8**
Juliana's Apartments, **14**
Scout's Place, **12**

done by Hurricane Hugo has been repaired, and a new breakwater built to shelter small boats makes it easier for divers to clamber on board with all their gear. On the quay is a decompression chamber, one of the few in the Caribbean, and **Saba Deep's** dive shop, above which is its new snack bar, **In Two Deep.** It's a good place for getting your breath back over some refreshment while staring out to sea!

Off the Beaten Track

Well's Bay, Saba's famous wandering beach, hasn't reappeared since Hugo. **Cove Bay,** a 20-foot strip of rocks and pebbles laced with gray sand, is now the only place for sunning (and moonlit dips after a Saturday night out). The truly intrepid can then take The Road back to Lower Hell's Gate, where the Old Sulphur Mine Walk leads to bat caves (with typical sulphuric stench) that can—with caution—be explored.

Sports and the Outdoors

Boating   **Saba Deep** (tel. 599/4–63347 or 599/4–62201) conducts one-hour, round-island cruises that include cocktails, hors d'oeuvres, and a sunset you won't soon forget.

Deep-Sea Fishing   **Saba Deep** runs half- and full-day charters that include lunch, drinks, bait, and tackle.

Hiking   You can't avoid some hiking, even if you just go to mail a postcard. The big deal, of course, is Mt. Scenery, with 1,064 slippery steps leading up to the top (*see* Exploring Saba, *above*).

For information about Saba's 18 recommended botanical hiking trails, check with the Tourist Office. Botanical tours are available upon request. A guided strenuous full-day hike through the undeveloped back side of Mt. Scenery will cost about $50.

Scuba Diving and Snorkeling   The island's first settlers probably found the **Saba Bank** (a fertile fishing ground 3 miles southwest of Saba) a crucial point in their decision to set up house here. In more recent times, divers have enjoyed Saba's coral gardens and undersea mountains. As other islands become "dived out," Saba is dedicated to preserving its marine life, which more than 3,000 divers explore each year. **Saba Marine Park** was established in 1987 to preserve and manage Saba's marine resources. The park circles the entire island, dipping down to 200 feet, and is zoned for diving, swimming, fishing, boating, and anchorage. One of the unique features of Saba's diving is the submerged pinnacles (islands that never made it!) at about the 70-foot depth mark. Here all forms of sea creatures rendezvous. The park offers talks and slide shows for divers and snorkelers and provides brochures and literature on marine life. *Harbor Office, Fort Bay, tel. 599/4–63295. Open weekdays 8–5. Call first to see if anyone's around.*

Saba Deep (tel. 599/4–63347) and **Sea Saba** (tel. 599/4–62246) will take you to explore Saba's 25 dive spots. Both offer rental equipment and certified instructors, as well as hotel-dive packages. For inquiries from the United States, direct dial 599/4–63347. Sea Saba's Joan Bourque, whose accomplished photographs are displayed at island galleries, also offers underwater photography lessons.

Wilson's Diving (tel. 599/4–63410) in Fort Bay specializes in shorter dive trips for visitors over from St. Maarten for the day.

Shopping

Gift Ideas The island's most popular purchases are Saba lace and Saba Spice. The history of Saba lace (also called Spanish lace) goes back more than a century to Saban Gertrude Johnson, who attended a Caracas convent school where she learned the art of drawing and tying threads to adorn fine linens. When she returned home in the 1870s, she taught lacemaking to other Saban ladies, and the art has endured ever since. Every weekday Saban ladies display and sell their creations at the community center in Hell's Gate. Many also sell their wares from their houses; just follow the signs. Collars, tea towels, napkins, and other small items are relatively inexpensive, but larger items, such as tablecloths, can be pricey. You should also know that the fabric requires some care—it is not drip-dry.

Saba Spice may *sound* as delicate as Saba lace, and the aroma is as sweet as can be. However, the base for the liqueur is 151-proof rum, and all the rest is window dressing.

Shops Saba's famed souvenirs can be found in almost every shop. In Windwardside, stop in at **Saba Tropical Arts,** the **Square Nickel, Island Craft Shop, Piggy's Boutique, Lynn's Gallery,** and the **Breadfruit Gallery** downstairs from the Tourist Office. Ruth Buchanan's especially lovely clothing designs are available at local galleries and at her own **Weaver's Cottage.** In The Bottom, the **Saba Artisan Foundation** (tel. 599/4–63260) turns out hand-screened fabrics that you can buy by the yard or already made into resort clothing for men, women, and children. Look also for the superlative *Saban Cottages: A Book of Watercolors,* sold at the Tourist Office and several stores.

Dining

In most of Saba's restaurants you pretty much have to take potluck. If you don't like what's cooking in one place, you can check out the other restaurants. However, it won't take you long to run out of options, and nowhere will you find gourmet-style cooking. It follows, then, that dress here is quite casual wherever you go.

Category	Cost*
Expensive	over $25
Moderate	$20–$25
Inexpensive	under $20

per person, excluding drinks and service

Captain's Quarters. Dining is comfortable on a cool porch surrounded by flowers and mango trees. Under new and enthusiastic ownership, the quality of food has considerably improved, thanks to the new chef, Manuela, whose cuisine artfully blends Dutch, Indonesian, French, and Creole influences. Her $18 three-course Saba menu and $20 chef's menu are wonderful bargains. *Windwardside, tel. 599/4–62201. Reservations required. AE, MC, V. Closed Sept. Moderate–Expensive.*
Brigadoon Restaurant. From the first floor of a colonial building, one can enjoy the street scene passing before this new, open-front restaurant. Fresh fish grilled with a light Creole sauce is the specialty, but there are also chicken and steak dishes, lobster, and unusual creations like shrimp encrusted with salt and pepper. For light

snacks, sandwiches are also offered. *Windwardside, tel. 599/4–62380. Closed lunch. AE, D, MC, V. Moderate.*

Lollipop's. Lollipop is the affectionate nickname of Carmen, the owner, celebrated for her "sweet" disposition. The outdoor terrace, with stonework and a charming aqua-and-white trellis, is a tranquil place to sample her fine land crab, goat, and fresh grilled fish. *St. John's, tel. 599/4–63330. No credit cards. Inexpensive–Moderate.*

Scout's Place. Here Diana Medero cooks up her version of chicken cordon bleu, braised steak with mushrooms, and curried goat. You can also opt simply to order a sandwich—the crab is best. Wednesday breakfast serves as the unofficial town meeting for expatriate locals, offering the visitor a slice of Saba life. *Windwardside, tel. 599/4–62295. Reservations required. Dinner is at 7:30. MC, V. Inexpensive–Moderate.*

Saba Chinese Bar & Restaurant. This restaurant is a plain house with plastic tablecloths where you can get, among other things, sweet-and-sour pork or chicken, cashew chicken, and some curried dishes. *Windwardside, tel. 599/4–62268. Reservations advised. No credit cards. Closed Mon. Inexpensive.*

The Serving Spoon. Queenie Simmons's house adjoins the sky-blue eight-table restaurant, where plates come heaped with huge portions. Stop by and ask her what she's preparing for the day: She'll start cooking to order. It might be meatballs with rice, baked onion chicken, or curried goat with butter. Eighteen dollars (you can haggle) buys all you can eat and then some. *The Bottom, tel. 599/4–63225. Reservations required. No credit cards. Inexpensive.*

Sunset Bar & Restaurant. Artificial flowers and colorful place mats enliven this humble, homey place, serving authentic Creole food, including heavenly johnnycakes, bread tart pudding, and lip-smacking ribs. *The Bottom, tel. 599/4–63332. No credit cards. Inexpensive.*

Lodging

Like everything else on Saba, the guest houses are tiny and tucked into tropical gardens. The selection is limited, and because most restaurants are located in the guest houses, you would do well to take advantage of meal plans. Accommodations are invariably neat and quite reasonably priced; only three properties raise rates in "high" season. Saba has experienced a (relative) boom in hotel development of late. Four new properties are scheduled to open during 1994. Two are between Windwardside and The Bottom, off a newly constructed road up the shoulder of Mt. Scenery. The 20-room Queens Gardens Resort, in 8 acres of tropical gardens, will have a restaurant, bar, and swimming pool. An additional 30 units are planned. Saba Villas is planning some 50 luxury villas on 30 acres above the Queens Gardens Resort, which may be available for rental, but they are unlikely to be completed anytime soon. Elsewhere on the island, Willards, a luxurious 10-room hideaway with stunning panoramic vistas of the Caribbean, was slated to open in mid-1994. Spacious rooms and bungalows will all boast a private bath and balcony. There will be a tennis court, swimming pool, and Jacuzzi on the grounds. Also to open by mid-1994 is the Cottage Club, 10 gingerbread bungalows nestled amid rainbow-hued tropical gardens on a ridge overlooking the tiny settlement of English Quarter. The bungalows—each with its own kitchen, bath, balcony, and cable TV—will surround a stone colonial-style main building.

Highly recommended lodgings are indicated by a star ★.

Category	Cost*
Expensive	over $125
Moderate	$75–$125
Inexpensive	under $75

All prices are for a standard double room for two with breakfast and dinner, excluding 5% tax and 10%–15% service charge.

Hotels **Captain's Quarters.** All the recently refurbished rooms here are spa-
★ cious and airy, with antique Victorian furnishings (including four-
poster beds) and views of the tiny pool that's perched 1,500 feet
above the sea. Four choice bedrooms are in a small house that was
built by a Saban sea captain in 1832. Adjacent to the main house is a
long bungalow unit with six rooms—numbers 9 and 10 are slightly
larger than the others. Dining is in a shaded garden pavilion surrounded by hibiscus, poinsettia, and papaya trees. New owners, a
local Saban family of Scottish descent, have taken over and cheerfully renovated the property. Their love for the island is manifest
throughout the hotel; plans are set for expansion through 1995/96 including 15 more guest rooms, a conference center, spa, new dining
area, and pool. *Windwardside, tel. 599/4–62201 or 800/468–0023. 10
rooms with bath. Facilities: pool, restaurant, gift shop, bar, and
lounge. AE, MC, V. EP, MAP. Expensive.*

Juliana's Apartments. Near the Captain's Quarters, Mrs. Juliana
Johnson offers eight comfortable, tidy studios and a 2½-room apartment with private bath, balcony, kitchenette, living/dining room,
bedroom, and a large porch facing the sea. Across the street a pool
has been added to the Juliana's complex, along with a café, Tropics,
for breakfast and light meals; the views of the Caribbean are truly
inspiring. *Windwardside, tel. 599/4–62269; in the United States,
800/223–9815; in Canada, 800/468–0023. 8 rooms, 1 1-bedroom
apartment. Facilities: restaurant, pool. AE, MC, V. EP. Moderate.*

Scout's Place. Billed as "Bed 'n Board, Cheap 'n Cheerful," Scout's
Place, near the post office and within walking distance of Sea Saba
dive center, was originally the government guest house. "Scout" is
retired owner Scout Thirkield, who turned his place over to his longtime cook Diana Medero, and who is still very much in evidence. Ten
new rooms, all with four-poster beds; reproductions of antiques; private balconies; and private baths with hot water have been added to
the original four plain rooms, which have *no* hot water. There's a
small breakfast room where you can have cheese omelets, bacon, and
coffee. *Windwardside, tel. 599/4–62205. 14 rooms, 12 with private
bath. Facilities: restaurant, pool, bar, and gift shop. D, MC, V. EP,
MAP. Inexpensive–Moderate.*

Cranston's Antique Inn. There are six cozy rooms with elegant hardwood floors, most with four-poster beds, in this casual spot popular
with the surfing set. The pool bar often rocks with live music on
weekends. *The Bottom, tel. 599/4–63203. 6 rooms, 1 with private
bath. Facilities: restaurant, pool, bar. No credit cards. EP. Inexpensive.*

Apartment Twenty apartments and wood cottages, all with hot water and mod-
Rentals ern conveniences, are available for weekly and monthly rentals. For
a listing of all rental properties, check with the **Saba Tourist Office**
(*see* Important Addresses, *above*).

Nightlife

Guido's Pizzeria (Windwardside, tel. 599/4–62330) is transformed into the Mountain High Club and Disco on Saturday night, and you can dance till 2 AM on Sunday. Do the nightclub scene at the **Lime Tree Bar & Restaurant** (The Bottom, tel. 599/4–63256) and the **Birds of Paradise,** aka the **Cozy Corner Club** (The Bottom, tel. 599/4–62240), or just hang out at **Scout's Place** or the **Captain's Quarters.** Consult the bulletin board in each village for a listing of the week's events.

19 St. Barthélemy

Updated by
Pamela
Acheson

St. Barthélemy's magic lies in the way this tiny tropical isle blends the essence of the Caribbean with the essence of France. You can spend the day on a deserted beach lying under a palm tree, then shower and choose from over 50 excellent restaurants for an elegant meal. When you tire of the sun, you can easily drive all over the island, taking in the vistas and the soft breezes, and then stop off for an exquisitely prepared gourmet lunch. Or you can head to one of the three shopping areas for duty-free French perfumes and the latest in French fashion.

The island itself is a mere 10 square miles, with lots of hills and sheltered inlets. Gustavia, the only real town, wraps itself neatly around a lilliputian harbor. Red-roof bungalows dot the hillsides. And beaches that run the gamut from calm to "surfable," shell to fine white sand, and crowded to deserted encircle the island. The French cuisine here is tops in the Caribbean, and gourmet lunches and dinners are rallying points of island life. A French *savoir vivre* pervades, and the island is definitely for the style conscious—casual but always chic. This is no place for the beach-bum set.

Rothschild owns property and Rockefeller built an estate here, and for a long time the island, 15 miles from St. Martin in the French West Indies, was the haunt of the well-heeled and well-informed. In the past decade, the tourist base has expanded, and last year more than 120,000 visitors stopped by, including day-trippers from nearby islands and passengers from the occasional cruise ships that now anchor just outside the harbor.

Longtime visitors speak wistfully of the old, quiet St. Barts. While development *has* quickened the pace, the island has not been overrun with prefab condos or glitzy resorts. The largest hotel has fewer than 100 rooms, and the remaining 650 rooms are scattered in about 40 small hotels around the island; no high rises are allowed. The tiny airport accommodates nothing bigger than 19-passenger planes (and these only during daylight hours), and there aren't any casinos or flashy late-night attractions. Moreover, St. Barts is generally not a destination for the budget-minded. Development has largely been in luxury lodgings and gourmet restaurants, and, with the decline in the dollar, in recent years prices have increased sharply throughout the island.

When Christopher Columbus "discovered" the island in 1493, he named it after his brother, Bartholomeo. A small group of French colonists arrived from nearby St. Kitts in 1656 but were wiped out by the fierce Carib Indians who dominated the area. A new group from Normandy and Brittany arrived in 1694. This time the settlers prospered—with the help of French buccaneers, who took full advantage of the island's strategic location and well-protected harbor. In 1784 the French traded the island to King Gustav III of Sweden in exchange for port rights in Göteborg. He dubbed the capital Gustavia, laid out and paved streets, built three forts, and turned the capital into a prosperous free port. The island thrived as a major shipping and commercial center until the 19th century, when earthquakes, fire, and hurricanes brought financial ruin. Many residents fled for newer lands of opportunity, and in 1878 France agreed to repurchase its beleaguered former colony.

Today the island is still a free port, and, as a dependency of Guadeloupe, is part of an overseas department of France. Dry, sunny, and stony, St. Barts was never one of the Caribbean's "sugar islands," and thus never developed an industrial slave base. Most natives are descendants of those tough Norman and Breton settlers of three centuries ago. They are feisty, industrious, and friendly but insular. However, you will find many new, young French arrivals—predominantly from northwestern France—who speak English well.

You may hear some old-timers speak the old Norman patois of their ancestors or see the older women dressed in the traditional garb of provincial France. They have prospered with the tourist boom, but some are worried that the upward swing of prices may threaten business, especially tour groups and families. So far, though, this gem of an island continues to draw an ever-widening circle of fans.

Before You Go

Tourist Information
For information contact the **French West Indies Tourist Board** by calling France-on-Call at 900/990–0040 (50¢ per minute) or write to the **French Government Tourist Office**, 610 5th Ave., New York, NY 10020; 9454 Wilshire Blvd., Beverly Hills, CA 90212; 645 N. Michigan Ave., Chicago, IL 60611; 2305 Cedar Spring Rd., Dallas TX 75201. In Canada contact the French Government Tourist Office, 1981 McGill College Ave., Suite 490, Montreal, Québec H3A 2W9, tel. 514/288–4264, or 1 Dundas St. W, Suite 2405, Toronto, Ontario M5G 1Z3, tel. 416/593–4723 or 800/361–9099. In the United Kingdom the tourist office can be reached at 178 Piccadilly, London W1V 0AL, tel. 071/499–6911.

Arriving and Departing
By Plane
The principal gateway from North America is St. Maarten's Juliana International Airport. Although it is only 10 minutes by air to St. Barts, the last 2 may take your breath away. Don't worry when you see those treetops out your window. You're just clearing a hill before dropping down to the runway. Flights leave at least once an hour between 7:30 AM and 5:30 PM on either **Windward Islands Airways** (tel. 590/27–61–01) or **Air St. Barthélemy** (tel. 590/27–71–90). **Air Guadeloupe** (tel. 590/27–61–90) and **Air St. Barthélemy** offer daily service from Espérance Airport in St. Martin, the French side of the same island. Air Guadeloupe also has direct flights to St. Barts from Guadeloupe and San Juan, while **Virgin Air** (tel. 590/27–71–76) operates daily flights between St. Barts and both St. Thomas and San Juan. You must reconfirm your return interisland flight, even during off-peak seasons, or you may very well lose your reservation. Windward, Air St. Barthélemy, and Virgin Air also offer charter service.

From the Airport
Airport taxi service costs $5–$15 (to the farthest hotel). Since the cabs are unmetered, you may be charged more if you make stops on the way. Cabs meet some flights, and a taxi dispatcher (tel. 590/37–66–31) is there some of the time, but if you plan to rent a car, which most people do, it's really easiest to do it at the airport. Many hotels offer free pickup and drop-off.

By Boat
Catamarans leave Philipsburg in St. Maarten at 9 AM daily, arriving in Gustavia's harbor around 11 AM. These are one-day, round-trip excursions (about $50, including open bar), with departures from St. Barts at 3:30 PM. If there's room, one-way passengers ($25) are often taken as well. Beware that the seas can be choppy and it is not uncommon for passengers to get seasick (although, perhaps because everyone is on vacation, no one seems to really mind). Contact **Bobby's Marina** in Philipsburg (tel. 599/5–23170) for reservations. The *St. Barth Express,* and *La Dame du Coeur* leave Gustavia at 7:30 AM and 3:30 PM on a varying daily schedule. The crossing to Marigot, St. Martin, takes one hour. The boat departs from Marigot at 9 AM and 3:45 PM on the same varying schedule and goes directly to St. Barts. One-way fare is

$30 and round-trip $60. The **Yacht Charter Agency** (tel. 590/27–62–38) and **La Marine Service** (tel. 590/27–70–34) in Gustavia have boats for private charter.

Passports and Visas U.S. and Canadian citizens need either a passport (one that expired no more than five years ago will suffice) or other proof of citizenship, such as a notarized birth certificate with a raised seal or a voter registration card, both accompanied by photo identification. A visa is required for stays of more than three months. British citizens need a valid passport.

Language French is the official language, though a Norman dialect is spoken by some longtime islanders. Most hotel and restaurant employees speak some English—at least enough to help you get or find what you want or need.

Precautions Roads are frequently unmarked, so be sure to get a map. Instead of road signs, look for signs pointing to a destination. These will be nailed to posts at all crossroads. Roads are narrow and sometimes very steep, so check the brakes and gears of your rental car *before* you drive away. St. Barts drivers seem to be in some kind of unending grand prix and keep their minimokes (the car of choice on this island) maxed out at all times. Prepare yourself for cars charging every which way, making sudden changes in direction while honking wildly, and backing up at astonishingly high speeds. They pause for no one. Some hillside restaurants and hotels have steep entranceways and difficult steps that require a bit of climbing or negotiating. If this could be a problem for you, ask about accessibility ahead of time.

Staying in St. Barthélemy

Important Addresses Tourist Information: The **Office du Tourisme** (tel. 590/27–87–27) is in a white building on the Gustavia pier; the people who work there are most eager to please. Hours are Monday through Thursday from 10:30–12:30 and 3–7 and Friday from 8:30–10:30.

Emergencies **Hospital: Gustavia Clinic** (tel. 590/27–60–35 or 590/27–60–00) is on the corner of rue Jean Bart and rue Sadi Carnot. For the doctor on call, dial 590/27–76–03. **Pharmacies:** There is a pharmacy in Gustavia on rue de la République (tel. 590/27–61–82), and one in St. Jean (tel. 590/27–66–61).

Currency The French franc is legal tender. Figure about 5.5F to the U.S. dollar. U.S. dollars are accepted in most establishments, but you will receive change in francs. Credit cards are accepted at most shops, hotels, and restaurants. Note: Prices quoted here are in U.S. dollars unless indicated otherwise.

Taxes and Service Charges A 10F departure tax is charged for departure to other French islands and a 16F departure tax is charged to all other destinations. Some hotels add a 10%–15% service charge to bills; others include it in their tariffs. All restaurants are required to include a 15% service charge in their published prices. It is especially important to remember this when your credit-card receipt is presented to be signed with the tip space blank (just draw a line through it), or you could end up paying a 30% service charge.

Most taxi drivers own their vehicles and do not expect a tip.

Guided Tours Tours are by minibus or taxi. An hour-long tour costs about $40 for up to three people and $50 for up to eight people. A five-hour island tour costs about $100 per vehicle. Itineraries are negotiable; other officially recommended tours (of 45 and 90 minutes) are available. Tours can be arranged at hotel desks and through the tourist office.

Getting Taxis are expensive and not particularly easy to arrange, especially
Around in the evening. You may arrange cab service by calling 590/27–66–
Taxis 32, 590/27–60–59, or 590/27–63–12. Note: Fares are 50% higher from 8 PM to 6 AM and on Sundays and holidays.

Rental Cars Most people opt to rent cars. There are excellent beaches, restaurants, and vistas all around the island. Beware the steep, curvy, haphazardly paved roads; get a map; and check the rental car's brakes before you drive away. The most common rental car is a minimoke, a small open-air vehicle without frills. **Avis** (tel. 590/27–71–43), **Budget** (tel. 590/27–67–43), and **Europcar** (tel. 590/27–73–33) are represented at the airport, among others. Check with several of the rental counters for the best price. All accept credit cards. You must have a valid driver's license, and in high season there may be a three-day minimum (or no cars available). In February especially, arrange for your car rental ahead of time. Your choices will most likely be limited to minimokes, Suzuki Jeeps, and open-sided Gurgels (VW Jeep)—all with stick shift only, which rent in season for $40–$45 a day, with unlimited mileage and limited collision insurance. You may find a Jeep, which is sturdier, preferable to the chic but rickety minimokes. A few hotels have their own car fleets, and a car should be rented at the time you make your room reservation. The choice of vehicles may be limited, but many hotels offer 24-hour emergency road service, which most rental companies do not. Note that there are only two gas stations on the island, one near the airport and one in Lorient. They are not open on Sunday or after 5 PM, but you can purchase a magnetized card at the one near the airport and use this after hours.

Motorbikes Motorbike companies rent motorbikes, scooters, mopeds, and mountain bikes. Motorbikes go for about $25 per day and require a $100 deposit. Call **Rent Some Fun** (tel. 590/27–70–59).

Telephones To phone St. Barts from the United States, dial 011–590 and the lo-
and Mail cal six-digit number. To call the United States from St. Barts, dial 19–1, the area code, and the local number. For St. Martin, dial just the six-digit number; for St. Maarten, dial 3 plus the five-digit number. For local information, dial 12. Public telephones do not accept coins; they accept Telecartes, a type of prepaid credit card that you can purchase from the post offices at Lorient and Gustavia as well as at the gas station next to the airport. Making an international call with a Telecarte is less expensive than making the call from your hotel.

Mail is slow. It can take up to three weeks for correspondence between the United States and the island. Post offices are in Gustavia and Lorient. It costs 3.10F to mail a postcard to the United States, 3.90F to mail a letter.

Opening and Businesses and offices close from noon to 2 during the week and are
Closing Times closed on Saturday and Sunday. Shops are generally open weekdays 8:30–noon and 2–5, and Saturday 8:30 to noon. Some of the shops across from the airport and in St. Jean also open on Saturday afternoon and until 7 PM on weekdays. The banks are open weekdays 8–noon and 2–3:30.

Exploring St. Barthélemy

Numbers in the margin correspond to points of interest on the St. Barthélemy map.

Gustavia and the West ❶ With just a few streets on three sides of its tiny harbor, **Gustavia** is easily explored in a two-hour stroll. Here you will find excellent shopping, many restaurants and cafés, and a museum. Remember that most shops close from noon to 2, so you might want to combine shopping with an enjoyable lunch at one of the restaurants overlooking the harbor.

A good place to park your car is harborside on the rue de la République, where flashy catamarans, yachts, and sailboats are moored. If you haven't gotten a map or have some questions, head to the **tourist office** right on the pier, where you can pick up an island map and a free copy of *St. Barth Magazine,* a monthly publication on island happenings. If you feel like stopping for a café au lait and a croissant, settle in at either **Le Repaire** or **Gustavia's Le Select** (*see* Nightlife, *below*), two cafés just a few steps away.

As you stroll through the little streets, you will notice that plaques sometimes spell out names in both French and Swedish, a reminder of the days when the island was a Swedish colony. Small shops along **rue du Roi Oscar II, rue de la France, rue du Bord de Mer,** and **rue du Général de Gaulle** sell French perfumes, the latest in French and Italian designer wear for men and women, resortwear, crystal, gold jewelry, and other luxury items.

If you feel like a swim, drive to the end of the harbor, turn onto **rue Victor Hugo,** turn right on **rue de l'Eglise,** and follow the road to **Petit Anse de Galet.** This quiet little *plage* is also known as Shell Beach because of the tiny shells heaped ankle-deep in some places.

On the far side of the harbor, known as **Le Pointe,** is the charming **Municipal Museum,** where you will find watercolors, portraits, photographs, and historic documents detailing the island's history as well as displays of the island's flowers, plants, and marine life. *No tel. Admission: 10F. Open Mon.–Thurs. 8–noon and 1:30–5:30, Fri. 1:30–5:30, Sat. 8:30–noon. Closed Sun.*

For a good beach and some spectacular vistas, head south out of town, following the signs to Lurin. (You'll head up the hill past the Carl Gustaf Hotel.) The views of the harbor get better and better the higher up you go. After about five minutes, look for a sign to Plage du Gouverneur. A small rocky route off to the right will take you bumping and grinding down a steep incline to **Anse du Gouverneur,** one of St. Barts's most beautiful beaches, where pirate's treasure is said to be buried. If the weather is clear, you will be able to see the islands of Saba, St. Eustatius, and St. Kitts.

Time Out The hilltop **Sante Fe Restaurant** (Morne Lorne, at the turnoff to Gouverneur's Beach, tel. 590/27–61–04) is a popular spot for sundowners, sunsets, and American-style hamburgers. Sunday afternoons find it jammed with Americans and Brits cheering their favorite teams on the closed-circuit TV.

Corossol, Colombier, Flamands ❷ Starting at the intersection on the hilltop overlooking the airport (known as Tourmente), take the road to Public Beach and on to **Corossol,** a two-street fishing village with a little beach. Corossol is where the island's French provincial origins are most evident. Residents speak an old Norman dialect, and some of the older women still wear traditional garb—ankle-length dresses, bare feet, and starched white sunbonnets called *quichenottes* (kiss-me-not hats). The women don't like to be photographed. However, they are not shy about selling you some of their handmade straw work—handbags, baskets, broad-brim hats, and delicate strings of birds—made from lantana palms. The palms were introduced to the island 100 years ago by foresighted Father Morvan, who planted a grove in Corossol and Flamands, thus providing the country folk with a living that is still pursued today. Here, too, is the **Inter Oceans Museum,** which features over 7,000 seashells from around the world. *Tel. 590/27–62–97. Admission: 20F. Open daily 10–5.*

③ From Corossol, head down the main road about a mile to **Anse des Flamands,** a wide beach with several small hotels, including the St. Barth Isle de France, and many rental villas. From here, take a brisk hike to the top of what is believed to be the now-extinct volcano that gave birth to St. Barts. From the peak you can take in the gorgeous view of the islands.

A drive to the end of Flamands Road brings you to a rocky footpath that leads to the island's most remote beach, **Anse de Colombier.** If you're not up to the 30-minute hike, take a 3 PM sail from Gustavia (*see* Sports and the Outdoors, *below*). You'll have time for a swim and refreshments before the sunset sail back to the harbor.

St. Jean, Grand Cul de Sac, Saline ④ Brimming with bungalows, bistros, sunbathers, and windsurfing sails, the half-mile crescent of sand at **St. Jean** is the island's most popular beach. Informal restaurants are scattered here and there along the shore, and windsurfers skim along the water, catching the strong breezes. If you walk as far to the west as possible, you can get a close look at the little planes taking off from the airport. For respite from the sun, cross the street near Eden Rock and you will find many branches of Gustavia boutiques and several restaurants.

⑤ Leaving St. Jean, take the main road to **Lorient.** On your left are the royal palms and rolling waves of Lorient Beach. Lorient, site of the first French settlement, is one of the island's two parishes, and a newly restored church, historic headstones, a school, post office, and gas station mark the spot.

Turn right before the gleaming white Lorient cemetery. In a short while you'll reach a dusty cutoff to your right. The pretty little Creole house on your left is home to Ligne de Cosmetiques M (*see* Shopping, *below*). Behind it is one of St. Barthélemy's treasured secrets, **Le Manoir.** The 1610 Norman manor was painstakingly shipped from France and reconstructed here in 1984 by the charming Jeanne Audy Rowland in tribute to the island's Viking forebears. The tranquil surrounding courtyard and garden contain a waterfall and a lily-strewn pool. Madame Rowland graciously allows visitors. The manor (and its cottage) are also available at a reasonable weekly rent, "but you must have an artist's soul," she requests sweetly and earnestly.

Retrace your route back to Lorient and continue along the coast. Turn left at the Mont Jean sign. Your route rolls around the island's pretty windward coves, past **Pointe Milou,** an elegant residential colony, and on to **Marigot,** where you can pick up a bottle of fine wine at **La Cave.** The bargain prices may surprise you (*see* Shopping, *below*).

The winding road passes through the mangroves, ponds, and beach of **Grand Cul de Sac,** where there are plenty of excellent beachside restaurants and water-sports concessions.

Time Out **Chez Pompi** (Petit Cul de Sac, tel. 590/27–75–67), on the road to Toiny, is a delightful cottage straight from a Cézanne painting. Pompi (aka Louis Ledee) is an artist of some repute, whose naive, slightly abstract artwork clutters the walls of his tiny studio. You

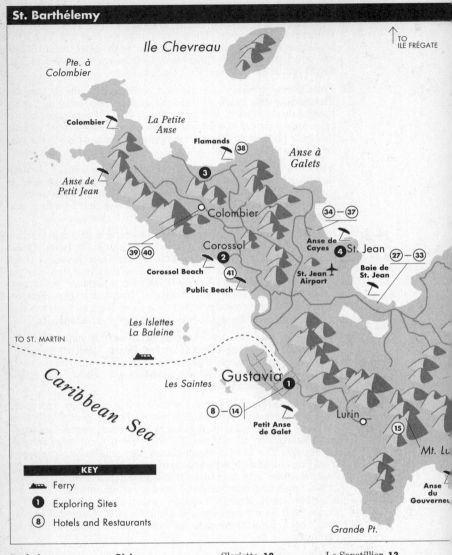

TO
ILE FRÉGATE

Ile Chevreau

Pte. à
Colombier

Colombier

La Petite
Anse

Flamands **38**

3

Anse à
Galets

Anse de
Petit Jean

Colombier

39 40

Corossol

2

Corossol Beach

41

Public Beach

Anse de
Cayes

34 — 37

4 St. Jean

St. Jean
Airport

Baie de
St. Jean

27 — 33

Les Islettes
La Baleine

TO ST. MARTIN

Les Saintes

Gustavia

1

8 — 14

Petit Anse
de Galet

Lurin

15

Mt. Lu

Caribbean Sea

Anse
du
Gouvernei

Grande Pt.

KEY

🛳 Ferry

1 Exploring Sites

8 Hotels and Restaurants

Exploring

Anse des Flamands, **3**
Corossol, **2**
Grande Saline, **7**
Gustavia, **1**
Lorient, **5**
St. Jean, **4**
Toiny coast, **6**

Dining

Adam, **27**
Brasserie
La Creole, **28**
Carl Gustav, **12**
Club Lafayette, **17**
Eddy's Ghetto, **11**
François
Plantation, **39**

Gloriette, **18**
L'Escale, **8**
La Toque
Lyonnaise, **19**
Le Flamboyant, **20**
Le Gaiac, **16**
Le Patio, **36**
Le Repaire, **9**

Le Sapotillier, **13**
Marigot Bay Club, **22**
Maya's, **41**
New Born, **34**
Pasta in Paradise, **10**
Topolino, **30**
Wall House, **14**

TO
ILE TOC VERS

ATLANTIC OCEAN

Les Grenadiers

La Tortue

Pte. Milou (24)

(25) (26) Lorient

Marigot Marechal
Beach

(21)

Lorient (22)
Marigot Grand
Cul de Sac

(17) — (20)

Lorient

(5) Petit
Cul de Sac

(23) Vitet
Toiny

Mt. du
Grand Fond Morne Vitet (16) (6)

Morne de
Grand Fond Pt. à Toiny

Grande
Saline (7)

Anse de
Grand Fond N

rin Grande
Saline

0   1 mile

0   1 km

r

Pt. du Gouverneur

Lodging

Baie des Flamands, **38**
Carl Gustaf, **12**
Castelets, **15**
Eden Rock, **29**
El Sereno Beach
Hotel and Villas, **19**
Filao Beach, **31**

François
Plantation, **39**
Guanahani, **21**
Hostellerie des Trois
Forces, **23**
Hotel La Banane, **25**
Hotel Christopher, **24**
Hotel Manapany
Cottages, **35**

Hotel Yuana, **37**
La Normandie, **26**
Le P'tit Morne, **40**
Le Toiny, **16**
St. Barth Isle de
France, **38**
Tropical Hotel, **32**
Village St. Jean, **33**

can browse and chat with the amiable Monsieur Pompi while enjoy-ing his fine Creole and country French cuisine.

Over the hills beyond Grand Cul de Sac is the much photographed **⑥ Toiny coast.** Drystone fences crisscross the steep slopes of Morne Vitet along a rocky shoreline that resembles the rugged coast of Normandy. The road turns inland and up the slopes of Morne de Grand Fond. At the first fork (less than a mile), the road to the right leads back to Lorient. A left-hand turn at the next intersection will **⑦** bring you within a few minutes to a dead end at **Grande Saline.** Ten years ago the big salt ponds of Grande Saline were shut down after a half-century of operation. The place looks desolate, but climb the short hillock behind the ponds for a surprise—the long arc of **Anse de Grande Saline.**

Beaches

There are nearly 20 *plages* (beaches), scattered around the island, each with a distinctive personality and all of them public. Even in season, it is possible to find a nearly empty beach. Topless sunbath-ing is common, but nudism is forbidden. Here are the main attrac-tions:

St. Jean is like a mini Côte d'Azur—beachside bistros, bungalow ho-tels, bronze beauties, windsurfing, and lots of day-trippers. The reef-protected strip is divided by Eden Rock promontory, and there's good snorkeling west of the rock. **Lorient** is popular with St. Barts's families and surfers, who like its rolling waves. **Marigot** is a tiny, calm beach with good snorkeling along the rocky far end. Shal-low, reef-protected **Grand Cul de Sac** is especially nice for small chil-dren and windsurfers; it has excellent lunch spots and lots of pelicans. Around the point, next to the Guanahani Hotel, is tiny **Marechal Beach,** which offers some of the best snorkeling on the is-land. Secluded **Grande Saline,** with its sandy ocean bottom, is just about everyone's favorite beach and is great for swimmers. Despite the law, young and old alike go nude on this beach. It can get windy here, so go on a calm day. **Anse du Gouverneur** is even more secluded and equally beautiful, with good snorkeling and views of St. Kitts, Saba, and St. Eustatius.

A five-minute walk from Gustavia is **Petit Anse de Galet,** named after the tiny shells on its shore. Both **Public Beach** and **Corossol Beach** are best for boat- and sunset-watching. The beach at **Colombier** is the least accessible but the most private; you'll have to take either a rocky footpath from La Petite Anse or brave the 30-minute climb down a cactus-bordered trail from the top. **Flamands** is the most beautiful of the hotel beaches—a roomy strip of silken sand.

Sports and the Outdoors

Boating   St. Barts is a popular yachting and sailing center, thanks to its loca-tion midway between Antigua and St. Thomas. Gustavia's harbor, 13 to 16 feet deep, has mooring and docking facilities for 40 yachts, with good anchorages available at Public, Corossol, and Colombier. **Loulou's Marine** (tel. 590/27–62–74) is the place for yachting infor-mation and supplies. **Marine Service** (tel. 590/27–70–34), operated by Henri and Dominique Jouan, offers full-day outings on a 40-foot catamaran to the uninhabited Ile Fourchue for swimming, snorkel-ing, cocktails, and lunch at $90 per person. Marine Service also ar-ranges deep-sea fishing trips, with a full-day charter of a 32-foot crewed cabin cruiser running $800. You can take an hour's cruise on the glass-bottom boat *L'Aquascope* by contacting Marine Service, and the **Yacht Charter Agency** (tel. 590/27–62–38) offers sunset and half- and full-day sails. Marine and **La Maison de la Mer** (tel. 590/27–81–00) also have unskippered motor rentals for about $260 a day.

Diving and Deep-Sea Fishing Deep-sea fishing can be arranged through **La Maison de la Mer** (tel. 590/27–81–00), **Yacht Charter Agency** (tel. 590/27–62–38), **Marine Service** (tel. 590/27–70–34), or with **Pierre Choisy** (tel. 590/27–61–22) on his *Bertram*. Marine Service also operates a PADI (Professional Association of Diving Instructors) diving center, with scuba-diving trips for about $50 per person, gear included. **Club La Bulle** (tel. 590/27–68–93) and PADI-certified **Dive with Dan** (tel. 590/27–64–78) are other scuba options.

Horseback Riding Laure Nicolas leads two-hour excursions for $35 per person from **Ranch des Flamands** (Anse des Flamands, tel. 590/27–80–72).

Tennis There are two tennis courts at the **Guanahani** (tel. 590/27–66–60), **Le Flamboyant Tennis Club** (tel. 590/27–69–82), and the **Sports Center of Colombier** (tel. 590/27–61–07). There is one court each at the **Manapany** (tel. 590/27–66–55), the **Taiwana** (tel. 590/27–65–01), **Les Ilets de la Plage** (tel. 590/27–62–38), the **St. Barths Beach Hotel** (tel. 590/27–62–73), and the **St. Barth Isle de France** (tel. 590/27–61–81), which also has the island's only squash court.

Windsurfing Windsurfing fever has definitely caught on here. Boards can be rented for about $20 an hour at water-sports centers along St. Jean and Grand Cul de Sac beaches. Lessons are offered for about $40 an hour at **St. Barth Wind School** (St. Jean, tel. 590/27–71–22) and at **Wind Wave Power** (St. Barths Beach Hotel, tel. 590/27–62–73), which also has parasailing.

Shopping

St. Barts is a duty-free port, and there are especially good bargains in jewelry, porcelain, imported liquors, and French perfumes, cosmetics, and designer resortwear.

Shopping Areas Shops are clustered in **Gustavia, La Savane Commercial Center,** which is across from the airport, and **La Villa Creole,** an appealing shopping complex in St. Jean. A gourmet supermarket is located across from the airport, and there is a second one just east of the airport that specializes in fresh fruits and vegetables.

Good Buys
Clothing A number of boutiques in all three shopping areas carry the latest in French and Italian sportswear and haute couture fashion items. The price tags may astound you (even after you divide by 5.5 to convert the francs to dollars you may still be in high three-figures), but these prices are actually well below the Paris price for the same item, and so they are considered bargains by some. Shops to look for include Stéphane & Bernard, Kokonuts, Libertine, and Black Swan, all of which are in Gustavia and have branches either across from the airport or in St. Jean or both; but there are many other stores and boutiques to be found. At both St. Jean's La Villa Creole and La Savane (across from the airport), it is worth working your way from one end of the shopping complex to the other.

Island Crafts Stop in Corossol to pick up some of the intricate straw work (wide-brim beach hats, mobiles, handbags) that the ladies of Corossol create by hand (*see* Exploring St. Barthélemy, *above*). In Gustavia, look for hand-turned pottery at **St. Barts Pottery** (tel. 590/27–62–74) and exotic coral and shark's tooth and shell jewelry at the **Shell Shop** (no tel.). In Colombier (just follow the signs up and up the hill) you'll find the studio of **Jean-Yves Froment,** who creates brilliantly colored patterns and designs on cotton and silk fabrics. Stop here for yards of beautiful fabrics as well as ready-made skirts, dresses, bikinis, hats, and pareus. Superb local skin-care products are available at **Ligne de Cosmetiques M** (tel. 590/27–82–63; *see* Exploring St. Barthélemy, *above*).

Wine and Gourmet Shops — Wine lovers will enjoy **La Cave** (Marigot, tel. 590/27–63–21), where an excellent collection of French vintages is stored in temperature-controlled cellars. Also check out **La Cave du Port Franc** (tel. 590/27–71–75), on the far side of the harbor, for vintage wines, contemporary paintings, and objets d'art.

For exotic groceries or picnic fixings, stop by one of St. Barts's fabulous gourmet delis—**La Rotisserie** (tel. 590/27–63–13) on rue du Roi Oscar II (branches in St. Jean and Pointe Milou).

Dining

The French reverence for food is evident everywhere on St. Barts, from the most expensive classic French restaurant to the simplest beachside cafe. If you enjoy exquisitely prepared cuisine served at an enjoyable pace (and don't mind paying for it), then you may never want to leave St. Barts. A la carte prices at the well-known French restaurants are very high, but many offer a prix fixe menu for a very reasonable price–a nice way to sample the cuisine. Lunch prices are usually cheaper than evening prices, and Italian, Creole, and French-Creole restaurants tend to be less expensive day and night. Beware that restaurants here typically charge for drinking water (a French custom), which comes by the bottle, both bubbly and flat, and costs about $4. Jackets are rarely required, but this is a tony island and people here are fashionably dressed. In a way, anything goes as long as it is tasteful. *Accras* (salt cod fritters) with Creole sauce (minced hot peppers in oil), spiced christophine (a kind of squash), *boudin Créole* (a very spicy blood sausage), and a lusty *soupe de poissons* (fish soup) are some of the delicious and ubiquitous Creole dishes.

Highly recommended restaurants are indicated by a star ★.

Category	Cost*
Very Expensive	over $60
Expensive	$45–$60
Moderate	$30–$45
Inexpensive	under $30

per person, excluding drinks, service, and 4% sales tax

Carl Gustaf. Not even the sweeping views of the harbor can detract from the sublime creations of Patrick Gateau. Monsieur Gateau, who trained at the Crillon in Paris, deftly weaves tropical influences into his classical cuisine. Among his standouts are a warm scallop salad with mango vinaigrette, grilled tuna with anise rice, beef with a potato–cheese gâteau, chicken Provençale, and a delectable crème brûlée. The $27 prix fixe lunch menu is an amazing bargain. *Rue des Normands, Gustavia, tel. 590/37–82–83. Reservations required. AE, D, MC, V. Very Expensive.*

Le Gaiac. Cool breezes waft through this refined open-air restaurant at the elegant, out-of-the-way Le Toiny. Jean Christophe

Perrin studied with the Troisgros brothers and Michel Rostang. Their influence is clear in his elegant preparations, which are innovative blends of traditional French and Creole cuisines. Among his latest creations are ravioli filled with scallops and wild mushrooms, roast saddle of rabbit stuffed with onions and ham, and a gratin of lobster tails in coconut milk. The lunch menu has lighter, equally exquisite fare, including christophine and pumpkin salad served with stuffed crabs, emincé of chicken sautéed with almonds, and an excellent lobster club sandwich. *Anse de Toiny, tel. 590/27–88–88. Reservations required. AE, MC, V. Closed Sept.–mid-Oct. Expensive–Very Expensive.*

Adam. In 1990, Vincent Adam, a graduate of the Culinary Academy of France, opened this haute cuisine gem in the hills just off St. Jean beach. There are both an à la carte menu and a very reasonably priced prix fixe menu with wonderful choices. Offerings include lobster tabouli, salmon tartare with caviar and oysters, terrine of sweetbreads, and fillet of beef. *St. Jean, tel. 590/27–84–56. AE. Dinner only. Closed Tues. Expensive.*

Club Lafayette. Despite outrageous prices, this lunch-only, beachside bistro is such an in-season "in" spot that reservations are necessary if you want to eat between noon and 2. Expect to pay about $14 for a green salad with bacon and croutons or goat cheese and sliced tomatoes; $30 and up for grilled local fish, fillet of duck, shrimp with fresh pasta, and grilled lobster. *Grand Cul de Sac, tel. 590/27–62–51. Reservations suggested. No credit cards. Closed May–mid-Nov. Expensive.*

★ **François Plantation.** A flower-draped, lantern-hung arborway leads to this elegant restaurant with mahogany tables and chairs and beautiful plants. Chef Christophe Picard's cuisine legère, a lighter version of classic French cuisine, draws guests from all over the island. Try his shrimp cooked in spicy carrot juice, tournedos of lamb sautéed with bacon and juniper and served with horseradish flan, cheese soup, and red mullet steamed in vanilla bourbon and dancing in pesto. You can also order the rare Coutancie beef: the cattle must drink three liters of beer and receive a 20-minute rubdown daily, among other strict guidelines, to qualify. Dessert specials include a remarkable celery-flavored ice cream. *Colombier, tel. 590/27–61–26. Reservations essential. AE, V. Dinner only. Closed Sept. and Oct. Expensive.*

★ **La Toque Lyonnaise.** At this pleasant outdoor dining spot at El Sereno Beach Hotel and Villas, chef Michel Fredric (who apprenticed with masters Bocuse, Troisgros, and Veras) wows diners with his ability to adapt classic recipes to enhance local ingredients. À la carte choices include marinated salmon in ginger cream, grilled lobster flavored with vanilla beans, and rack of lamb in tapenade. He also creates a three-course *menu dégustation* for 240F (about $43). Courses vary, but might start with a roquefort terrine with pears poached in Sauternes, followed by a salmon steak in a mustard sauce and a warm apple tart with cinnamon. *El Sereno Beach Hotel and Villas, Grand Cul de Sac, tel. 590/27–64–80. Reservations suggested. Dinner only. AE, DC, MC, V. Closed June–Aug. Expensive.*

★ **Le Sapotillier.** Dining in this cozy boîte or in the courtyard under a grand old sapodilla tree will make you feel like guests in the owners' house—yet, their food is anything but down-home. This long-established French restaurant serves fresh local fish provençale style, veal stew with roquefort and vegetables, red snapper in ginger sauce with gnocchi, and young rabbit in puff pastry. Their sumptuous black-and-white-chocolate mousse is a house favorite. *Rue de*

Centenaire, Gustavia, tel. 590/27–60–28. Reservations required. MC, V. Closed May–mid-Oct. Expensive.

Le Flamboyant. In the hills above Grand Cul du Sac is this small restaurant famous for its French and Creole cuisine. The menu is not extensive but includes duck, beef, and local seafood, and there is always a Creole plat du jour. One can dine inside, but most opt for the breezy terrace with a fine view of the countryside and the sea in the distance. *Grand Cul de Sac, tel. 590/27–75–65. AE, V. Closed Mon. Dinner only. Moderate–Expensive.*

Maya's. Locals and visitors keep returning to this informal, open-air restaurant just outside of Gustavia on the north end of Public Beach. Relaxing in colorful deck chairs, diners watch the boats heading in and out of Gustavia's harbor as they contemplate the Creole, Oriental, Vietnamese, and Thai menu. You choose from five selections for each of three courses. Selections change nightly, but you might find christophine au gratin, several fresh salads, canard à l'orange, salmon teriyaki, and shrimp curry. The lunch menu is lighter and features à la carte hamburgers, grilled seafood, and Creole specials. *Public Beach, tel. 590/27–73–61. Reservations suggested. AE, D, MC, V. Closed Sun. and June–Oct. Moderate–Expensive.*

Wall House. Consistently excellent French cuisine is the hallmark of this restaurant set at the far end of the far side of Gustavia's harbor. The interior is glistening white—shiny white wicker furniture, white tile floors, white tablecloths and walls—with pots of greenery here and there. Owner Gerard Began is unobtrusively on-site most evenings, helping out in the kitchen and at the bar and seeing that all goes well. Appetizers might include lobster ravioli on a bed of celery cream sauce, gazpacho, mahimahi over sliced cucumbers, foie gras, and cold eggplant mousse. Entrées include yellowtail snapper with pimentos, sautéed salmon with mushrooms and tomatoes, and breast of duck with julienne of celery and oranges. Raspberry custard and crème brûlée are house specialties. *Gustavia, tel. 590/27–71–83. MC, V. Moderate–Expensive.*

★ **Le Patio.** Dine by candlelight inside or on the terrace at this pleasant hillside restaurant that serves some of the best Italian food on the island. For dinner, choose from ravioli stuffed with lobster, spaghetti bolognese, *poulet incappuciate* (chicken breast with artichoke hearts, mushrooms, and garlic), a variety of gourmet pizzas, and many more veal, chicken, beef, and pasta dishes. Lunch, available only in season, includes sandwiches, hamburgers, and salads. The atmosphere here is romantic and the service unhurried, despite the remarkably reasonable prices. *St. Jean, tel. 590/27–61–39. MC, V. Closed Wed. and June and Oct. Moderate.*

Marigot Bay Club. Sailboats lie just offshore at this intimate spot. The owner loves to fish, and the catch of the day is whatever he caught. It might be grouper, tuna, red snapper, or yellowtail, served with a Creole sauce. Other specials here include veal sautéed with mushrooms and wine, filet mignon, chicken breast in creamy lime sauce, and fresh local lobster baked in the shell with Gruyère cheese. In season, lunch is also served. *Marigot, tel. 590/27–75–45. Reservations required. AE, V. Closed Sun. and Sept. and Oct. Open for lunch, except Mon., in season. Moderate.*

New Born. For authentic Creole cuisine, head to this unadorned but pleasant restaurant that is down the bumpy road that leads to the Hotel Manapany. The fresh seafood is caught right at the beach steps away. This is the place to sample such Creole specialties as accras, callaloo soup, boudin, curried goat or shrimp, and salt cod salad. For dessert try the coconut flan or bananas flambées. *Anse des Cayes, tel. 590/27–67–07. Reservations suggested. MC, V. Moderate.*

★ **Eddy's Ghetto.** The combination of imaginatively prepared, modestly priced fare—crab salad, ragout of beef, crème caramel—served in a disarmingly fun-loving atmosphere turned Edward Stakelborough's restaurant into an instant success when it opened in 1989. The crowd is lively, the wine list impressive, and the restaurant is still as popular as ever. *Gustavia, just off rue du Général de Gaulle. No tel. No credit cards. Inexpensive–Moderate.*

Le Repaire. This busy brasserie looks out over Gustavia's harbor and is open from early morning until well into the evening. The 10-page menu includes everything from bacon and eggs and cheeseburgers to very French foie gras and grilled local fish and lobster. There is a billiards table and live music on weekends. This is a popular spot from early breakfast to cocktails at sunset–and on into the evening. *Gustavia (Quai de la République), tel. 590-27-72-48. Open daily 6 AM–midnight. MC, V. Inexpensive–Moderate.*

★ **L'Escale.** This popular open-air restaurant is set at the water's edge on the far side of Gustavia's harbor. Locals and visitors alike head here for the ambience, the views, and the excellent fare. The varied menu includes a wide range of pasta (lasagna, tortellini, ravioli, plus spaghetti with marinara, bolognese, and other sauces), as well as fresh local fish, veal scallopini in an assortment of sauces, beef, chicken, and 12 kinds of pizza. Many dishes are cooked in a wood-burning oven. *Gustavia, tel. 590/27-81-06. MC, V. Inexpensive–Moderate.*

Topolino. This lesser-known but excellent (and very reasonably priced) Italian restaurant is set back from the road, within easy walking distance from St. Jean beach. Linen tablecloths, freshly cut flowers, and dim lighting create a romantic evening atmosphere. The open-air dining room looks out over a pool, and many guests come for lunch and a dip. The menu includes local fresh seafood, grilled chicken and steaks, various veal dishes, a number of pasta choices, and thin-crusted pizzas. There are also specials that change daily and a variety of luncheon salads. The wine list has a number of fine, inexpensive choices. *St. Jean, tel. 590/27-70-92. MC, V. Inexpensive–Moderate.*

Brasserie La Creole. Right in the center of the St. Jean shopping aracade is this casual brasserie with indoor seating, a comfortable bar, and outdoor umbrella tables. Drop by here in the morning for freshly baked croissants and magnificent coffee. At lunch try the croque-monsieur (a thin-sliced-ham sandwich on a French baguette). There is a full breakfast menu, and from noon until late in the evening the restaurant serves sandwiches, salads, and various beef, chicken, and fish entrées. *St. Jean, tel. 590/27-68-09. Open daily 7 AM–midnight. AE. Inexpensive.*

Gloriette. This beachside lunch spot serves delicious local Creole dishes such as crunchy accras and grilled red snapper with Creole sauce, as well as light salads. *Grand Cul de Sac, tel. 590/27-75-66. No credit cards. Lunch only. Closed Sun. Inexpensive.*

Pasta in Paradise. This newcomer, in the historic building formerly occupied by La Citronelle, offers homemade pasta (eight kinds daily) served with many different sauces, such as carbonara and bolognese. There are other items on the menu, including grilled local fish and lobster and filet mignon in a shallot sauce. Sit in the air-conditioned indoor dining room or on the breezy, open-air terrace. *Gustavia (rue du Roi), tel. 590/27-80-78. No lunch Sun. MC, V. Inexpensive.*

Lodging

Expect to be shocked at the prices that you must pay for accommodations. You pay for the privilege of staying on the island rather than for the hotel. Even at $500 a night, bedrooms tend to be small, but that does not detract from the lure of St. Barts for those who can afford it. Away from the beaches are a number of small hotels and a multitude of rental bungalows that offer less expensive accommodations. Most hotels offer either CP or EP, though MAP is sometimes available.

Highly recommended lodgings are indicated by a star ★.

Category	Cost*
Very Expensive	$400–$550
Expensive	$300–$400
Moderate	$200–$300
Inexpensive	under $200

All prices are for a standard double room for two, excluding a 10%–15% service charge; there is no government room tax.

Hotels

★ **Carl Gustaf.** Red tile–roofed buildings spill down the hillside setting of this very expensive, small luxury resort at the head of Gustavia Harbour. Each one- and two-bedroom suite looks out—across a deck with a small, private plunge pool—to spectacular views of the harbor dotted with sailboats, the quaint town of Gustavia, and the hilly coastline of the island. Units have spacious, gleaming-white bedrooms and living rooms stylishly highlighted with pastel prints, plus marble floors, high ceilings, tiny but state-of-the-art kitchens, fax machines, two TVs, two stereos, ceiling fans, and air-conditioning. The glittering nighttime view from the piano bar lounge and elegant, open-air restaurant (known for its classic French cuisine) is one of the most spectacular on the island. *Box 700, Rue des Normands, Gustavia 97133, tel. 590/27–82–83 or 800/932–3222, fax 590/27–82–37. 14 1- and 2-bedroom suites. Facilities: restaurant, pool, private plunge pools, fitness club, sauna. AE, DC, MC, V. CP. Very Expensive.*

Filao Beach. Set on one of St. Barts's most popular beaches, this casual resort has many repeat guests who come back for the service. Rooms are in two-unit bungalows scattered back from the beach, and though simple and smallish, they are brightly decorated and air-conditioned. Banks of sea grapes make some patios more private than others. Bathrooms are compact but neat, and include toiletries. Rooms closer to the beach rise accordingly in price, but the "garden rooms" are still only steps away from the sands. Breakfast is served in the rooms. A restaurant, open only for lunch, is on the raised wooden deck that surrounds the pool. *Box 167, St. Jean 97133, tel. 590/27–64–84 or 800/372–1323, fax 590/27–62–24. 30 rooms. Facilities: restaurant (lunch only), bar, pool. CP. Very Expensive.*

Guanahani. This elegant 7-acre resort, the island's largest, is set between two beaches, one sheltered and one open to ocean waves. Rooms and one-bedroom suites are in tightly clustered bungalows (some much more secluded than others) and are expensively furnished in bright tropical fabrics and Georgian-style furniture. Suites have either private pools or Jacuzzis. Units vary tremendously in terms of privacy, views, and distance from activities. To avoid disappointment, be sure to make your preferences known when making your reservation. A poolside restaurant is open for lunch and dinner, and there is a more formal restaurant open for dinner that serves classic French cuisine and has both indoor and garden seating. The resort is a member of the Leading Hotels of World. *Box 609, Grand Cul de Sac 97098, tel. 590/27–66–60 or 800/372–1323, fax 590/27–70–70. 17 double rooms, some with ocean views; 33 deluxe doubles; 3 spa suites with Jacuzzis; 27 1-bedroom suites with private pool and kitchens. Facilities: 2 restaurants, 2 lighted tennis courts, 2 pools, 1 with Jacuzzi, 2 beaches, water-sports center, dive shop, beauty salon. AE, MC, V. CP. Very Expensive.*

Hotel La Banane. This intimate and appealing hideaway has nine wonderfully unique units, decorated with plants, antique furniture, and a bit of whimsy. There are four-poster beds, sunken bath areas, all kinds of antiques, Haitian artwork, and unusual pottery. Rooms look out to dense tropical greenery. There are two small swimming pools (one with a waterfall), and it's a three-minute walk to the beach. This is a place for people seeking true privacy—guests keep to themselves here. The restaurant is open only to hotel guests for breakfast and lunch. Visitors come from around the island for dinner, served alfresco around the pool, and for the nightly after-dinner show in which the entire staff participates, including owner Jean-Marie Rivière, a Parisian cabaret producer. *Quartier Lorient 97133, tel. 590/27–68–25, fax 590/27–68–44. 9 rooms. Facilities: restaurant, 2 pools, Jacuzzi. AE. CP. Very Expensive.*

★ **Le Toiny.** This luxuriously comfortable little hideaway is tucked into the hillside at a remote end of the island. Twelve spacious, green-roofed villas, each with a private pool (10 x 20 feet), are arranged for maximum privacy. The units are exquisitely appointed, with four-poster mahogany beds and armoires, Chinese porcelain vases, Italian fabrics, and fine linens; and each has a minibar, two TVs, VCR, hair dryer, fax, safe, stereo, air-conditioning, and three direct-dial telephones. There is a walk-in shower as well as a tub, and each villa has a large patio. The elegant, alfresco restaurant overlooks the Italian tiled communal swimming pool and offers sweeping views of the distant ocean. A windy beach is a five-minute walk away. *Anse Toiny 97133, tel. 590/27–88–88, fax 590/27–89–30. 12 1-bedroom cottages. Facilities: restaurant, bar, pool. AE, MC, V. EP. Very Expensive.*

Hotel Christopher. Sofitel Resorts manages this full-service hotel. Overlooking the water (but not on the beach), four two-story Colonial-style buildings offer smartly furnished, air-conditioned rooms with panoramic views of St. Martin and nearby islets. Each room has a sitting area, private terrace or balcony, minibar, and contemporary bathroom; some bathrooms open onto small gardens. There is a giant (4,500 sq. ft.) swimming pool—by far the largest on the island—with islands and footbridges. L'Orchidee serves French and Creole cuisine at dinner, and the poolside restaurant, Le Mango, has a lunch menu that includes selections for the calorie-conscious. Many packages are available. *Pointe Milou 97133, tel. 590/ 27–63–63 or 800/435–5567, fax 590/27–92–92. 40 suites. Facilities: 2 restaurants, complimentary afternoon tea, pool, shuttle service to every beach on the island, room service, fitness center, tennis court. AE, MC, V. FAP. Expensive–Very Expensive.*

St. Barth Isle de France. This intimate luxury enclave is set on one of the island's prettiest beaches. Enormously spacious units are either beachfront, in the two-story clubhouse, or across the street, in bungalows facing gardens and one of the hotel's two pools. Suites and rooms are decorated with mahogany furniture, island prints, and white cotton bedspreads and have patios or balconies. All units feature a private bath (with two sinks and a tub), a safe, a cable TV, and a phone. Garden bungalows include kitchenettes. Lunch and dinner are served in the hotel's restaurant, which is in a charming St. Bartian house next door to the main building. *Box 612, Baie des Flamands 97098, tel. 590/27–61–81, fax 590/27–86–83. 24 rooms, 5 1-bedroom suites. Facilities: restaurant, bar, 2 pools, beach, tennis. AE, MC, V. CP. Expensive–Very Expensive.*

Eden Rock. Set on a craggy bluff that abruptly splits St. Jean Beach is St. Barts's first hotel, opened in the '50s by Rémy de Haenen and now lovingly restored by his granddaughter. Six rooms have been spiffed up with four-poster beds, new tropical print fabrics, and minibar. The rooms have the original terra-cotta floors and, of course, their original stunning views of St. Jean Bay. The open-air bar and French Creole restaurant, which stretch along the top of the rock, are a great place to enjoy the sea breezes and watch the frigates dive-bomb for fish. *St. Jean 97133, tel. 590/27–72–94, fax 590/27–88–37. 6 rooms. Facilities: restaurant, bar. AE, MC. CP. Expensive.*

Hotel Manapany Cottages. A ramshackle entry road ends at this luxury enclave of closely spaced units that stretch back from a narrow and not very swimmable beach. Accommodations vary from rather snug St. Barts–style cottages and suites tucked into the hillside to much-in-demand beachfront suites with marble baths and four-poster beds. Bronze bodies line the pretty but small pool, and outsiders drop in regularly to dine at the hotel's two restaurants. The atmosphere here is sophisticated and cosmopolitan, and there are many repeat guests; but the facilities are somewhat cramped compared to the newer properties on the island. *Box 114, Anse des Cayes 97133, tel. 590/27–66–55; in the U.S., 212/757–0225; fax 590/27–75–28. 20 cottages and 12 club suites. Facilities: 2 restaurants, 2 bars, pool, Jacuzzi, beach, exercise room, boutique, lighted tennis court, water-sports center. AE, MC, V. CP. Expensive.*

Castelets. After a brief stint as Sapore di Mare, Madame Jouany's hotel is back to its former self. At this exclusive retreat the antiques-furnished rooms are in terraced chalets (with the exception of two in the main house) that are connected by steep paths. These rooms vary in size in direct relation to their price, and while the hotel is listed as Moderate–Expensive, the smaller rooms have an Inexpensive and the suites an Expensive–Very Expensive price tag. The pool is small, but the views from this property, situated atop Morne Lurin, are breathtaking. Since the hotel is inland and off by itself, you will need a car (it's a very steep seven-minute drive down to Gustavia or the nearest beach). The hotel restaurant now features lighter (and less expensive) fare than in the past. *Box 60, Morne Lurin 97133, tel. 590/27–61–73 or 800/223–1108, fax 590/27–85–27. 10 rooms, 1 2-bedroom suite. Facilities: restaurant, small pool. AE, MC, V. CP. Moderate–Expensive.*

François Plantation. A colonial-era graciousness pervades this elegant complex of hilltop West Indian–style cottages owned and managed by longtime island habitués Françoise and François Beret. Monsieur Beret is a passionate gardener, and the grounds are an intensely colorful display of tropical flowers and greenery. Rooms are air-conditioned, furnished with antique queen-size four-poster beds, and decorated with brightly colored fabrics. They all have refrigerators and satellite TV. The pool is spectacularly placed at the very top of the hill, with stunning views of the beach below, the hills of St. Barts, and nearby islets. You'll need a car for the beach (and for lunch; the restaurant is open only for breakfast and dinner) and reservations for its smart and gourmet restaurant. *Colombier 97133, tel. 590/27–78–82; in the U.S., 800/932–3222; fax 590/27–61–*

26. 4 garden and 8 sea-view rooms. Facilities: restaurant, pool. AE, V. CP. Moderate–Expensive.

★ **El Sereno Beach Hotel and Villas.** A quiet, casually chic ambience pervades this compact resort, which attracts many repeat guests. The small, simply furnished rooms, with whitewashed walls and blue beams, are arranged around a central courtyard. They don't get much of a breeze, but they are air-conditioned and have a minifridge, satellite TV, and patio. High walls and plants provide needed privacy. The exceptionally calm beach is just steps away. The addition of nine modern, comfortably furnished one-bedroom suites, in three new gingerbread-trimmed villas, makes this one of the better-value hotels on this end of the island. The restaurant suffered a decline in recent years but now has a new chef and the food is, once again, outstanding. *Box 19, Grand Cul de Sac 97133, tel. 590/ 27–64–80, fax 590/27–75–47. 20 rooms (3 sea-view), 9 1-bedroom villas. Facilities: 2 restaurants, bar, pool, beach with water-sports center, boutique. AE, DC, MC, V. EP. Moderate.*

Baie des Flamands. Upper-level rooms have balconies, and lower-level ones have terrace kitchenette units in this well-kept-up but very motel-style hotel. One of the first hotels on the island, it is still run by a St. Barts family, with a gentle laid-back island ambience, and is popular with families and tour groups. It has an excellent restaurant, Le Frigate, and a fine beach location. *Box 68, Anse des Flamands 97133, tel. 590/27–64–85, fax 590/27–83–98. 24 rooms with baths. Facilities: restaurant, bar, beach, pool, TV/library room, rental cars. AE, MC, V. CP. Inexpensive–Moderate.*

Hotel Yuana. Green-roofed West Indian–style cottages are strung along a flowery hillside at this small complex overlooking Anse des Cayes. Appealing rooms have white walls, white tile floors, painted wicker furniture, floral print fabrics, a kitchenette, and a wide terrace overlooking the ocean. Each unit has both a ceiling fan and air-conditioning, plus a TV and VCR. *Anse des Cayes 97133, tel. 590/ 27–80–84 or 800/633–7411, fax 590/27–78–45. 12 rooms. Facilities: pool, Continental breakfast available for a charge. AE, MC, V. Inexpensive–Moderate.*

Tropical Hotel. This simple, well-maintained complex is straight up the hill from St. Jean Beach. Rooms are in a motel-like, one-story, L-shape building and open out to patios and views of either the ocean or thick tropical foliage. Furnishings are modest, but white walls keep the rooms bright, and air-conditioning keeps them cool. A gingerbread-trimmed building houses reception, a TV/game room, and an appealing open-air bar and lounge. *Box 147, St. Jean 97133, tel. 590/27–64–87, fax 590/27–81–74. 20 rooms. Facilities: restaurant, reception bungalow with bar and wide-screen video lounge, pool. AE, MC, V. CP. Inexpensive–Moderate.*

★ **Village St. Jean.** The second generation of the Charneau family now runs this popular cottage colony, which has acquired a strong following over the years. The accent is on service and affordability, and this is one of the best values on the island. Air-conditioned cottages are spacious, although a bit sparsely furnished (except for the newly refurbished two-bedroom cottages), and have open-air kitchenettes and patios. There are also six hotel rooms without kitchenettes but with refrigerators. Units have a variety of views, from full ocean to almost none, and the units closest to the road are subject to the ongoing noise of minimoke engines struggling with the steep terrain. The open-air restaurant serves excellent Italian fare. From the hotel it is an easy five-minute walk down to popular St. Jean Beach and to a variety of stores and restaurants (the walk back up is a bit more strenuous). *Box 623, St. Jean 97133, tel. 590/27–61–39 or 800/633– 7411, fax 590/27–77–96. 6 rooms, 20 studio, one-, and two-bedroom* *cottages. Facilities: restaurant, bar, pool, small grocery, boutique, games room, library. MC, V. EP. Inexpensive–Moderate.*

★ **Hostellerie des Trois Forces.** This rustic, fairly isolated mountaintop inn is an idiosyncratic delight, with a string of tiny, gingerbread-trimmed West Indian–style cottages charmingly decorated according to astrological color schemes (Libra is soft blue; Leo, bright red; etc.). All feature a minibar, a terrace with a breathtaking ocean view, and air-conditioning or a ceiling fan. Most have four-poster beds. The tinkle of chimes floats through the pleasant restaurant. Astrologer Hubert de la Motte (he's a Gemini, by the way) is the personable owner (and also the talented chef), and he may even arrange a reading for you. *Morne Vitet, tel. 590/27–61–25, fax 590/27–81–38. 12 rooms. Facilities: restaurant, bar, pool. AE, MC, V. CP. Inexpensive.*

La Normandie. This small, family-run inn offers reasonably priced, very modestly furnished rooms that are far from the beach but extremely inexpensive. Two of the rooms are air-conditioned, and the rest are cooled by ceiling fan. *Lorient 97133, tel. 590/27–61–66, fax 590/27–68–64. 8 rooms. Facilities: pool. No credit cards. EP. Inexpensive.*

★ **Le P'tit Morne.** There is excellent value in these mountainside studios, each with a private balcony, air-conditioning, and panoramic views of the coastline below. A snack bar serving breakfast and light lunches recently opened, but each room has a kitchenette that is small but adequate for creating light meals or making picnic lunches. *Box 14, Colombier 97133, tel. 590/27–62–64, fax 590/27–84–63. 14 rooms with kitchens. Facilities: snack bar, pool, reading room. AE, MC, V. CP. Inexpensive.*

Villas, Condos, Apartments
On St. Barthélemy, "villa" is used generically to describe anything from a small cottage to a truly luxurious house with a cook, a maid, and a pool. You get what you pay for. In-season rates range from $700 to $7,000 a week. For the price of a moderately expensive hotel room, you can get a condo or a small cottage; and for the price of a room at one of the really expensive hotels, you can get a villa with a number of bedrooms and your own swimming pool. These can turn out to be a bargain if shared with friends. How to choose between a villa and a hotel? Some people want the full kitchen that comes with a villa, since so many of the restaurants are expensive. Others want to eat out all the time because the food is so exceptional. (Remember that one can make light meals easily in the kitchenettes found in many St. Barts hotel rooms.) Whether you stay in a villa or a hotel you will almost always want to rent a car, so be sure to figure this as part of your budget, no matter where you stay.

Villas, apartments, and condos can be rented through **SIBARTH** (tel. 590/27–62–38), which handles about 200 properties. **WIMCO** (tel. 800/932–3222) is the agency's representative in the United States. Rents range from $700–$2,700 per week for one-bedroom villas, $1,600–$7,000 for two- and three-bedroom villas. **Villa Caraibe** (tel. 800/743–8270) has about 80 properties.

Nightlife

St. Barts is a mostly in-bed-by-midnight island. There are many special places to go for the cocktail hour, and some of the hotels and restaurants provide late-night fun. Cocktail hour finds a crowd at **Le Repaire** (tel. 590/27–72–48). The barefoot boating set gathers in the boisterous garden of **Gustavia's Le Select** (tel. 590/27–86–87). Those in search of quiet conversation and some gentle piano at the day's end head up the hill to the **Carl Gustaf** (tel. 590/27–82–83), which has supplanted the much-missed L'Hibiscus as Gustavia's sunset-watching spot. Both the **Manapany** (tel. 590/27–66–55) and the **Guanahani** (tel. 590/27–66–60) also have piano bars. After dinner, the locals head to **Le Pelican** (tel. 590/27–64–64) and **L'Escale**'s retro hip (there's a 1968 Cadillac Eldorado outside and lots of neon inside) **American Bar-Video** (tel. 590/27–86–07). Jean-Marie Rivière, owner of **La Banane** (tel. 590/27–68–25) hotel and restaurant, and his entire restaurant staff perform an amusing after-dinner revue. For real late-night activity, head to Gustavia's **Le Petit Club** (no tel.) and **Bar de l'Oubli** (no tel.), or **Club Hurricane** (no tel.) in St. Jean.

20 St. Eustatius

Updated by
Jordan
Simon

The flight approach to the tiny Dutch island of St. Eustatius, commonly known as Statia (pronounced *STAY-sha)* in the Netherlands Antilles, is almost worth the visit itself. The plane circles the Quill, a 1,968-foot-high extinct volcano that encloses a stunning primeval rain forest within its crater. Here you'll see giant elephant ears, ferns, flowers, wild orchids, fruit trees, wildlife, and birds hiding in the trees. The entire island is alive with untended greenery and abloom with flowers—bougainvillea, oleander, and hibiscus.

Little 12-square-mile Statia, past which Columbus sailed in 1493, prospered almost from the day the Dutch Zeelanders colonized it in 1636. In the 1700s, a double row of warehouses crammed with goods stretched for a mile along the bay, and there were sometimes as many as 200 ships tied up at the duty-free port. The island was called the "Emporium of the Western World" and "Golden Rock." There were almost 8,000 Statians on the island in the 1790s (today, there are about 1,700). Holland, England, and France fought one another for possession of the island, which changed hands 22 times. In 1816, it became a Dutch possession and has remained so to this day.

During the American War of Independence, when the British blockaded the North American coast, food, arms, and other supplies for the American revolutionaries were diverted through the West Indies, notably through neutral Statia. (Benjamin Franklin had his mail routed through Statia to ensure its safe arrival in Europe.) On November 16, 1776, the brig of war *Andrew Doria,* commanded by Captain Isaiah Robinson of the Continental Navy, sailed into Statia's port flying the Stars and Stripes and fired a 13-gun salute to the Royal Netherlands standard. Governor Johannes de Graaff ordered the cannons of Fort Oranje to return the salute, and that first official acknowledgment of the new American flag by a foreign power earned Statia the nickname "America's Childhood Friend." Ironically, Statia's prosperity ended partly because of the success of the American Revolution. The island was no longer needed as a transshipment port, and its bustling economy gradually came to a stop.

Statia is in the Dutch Windward Triangle, 178 miles east of Puerto Rico and 35 miles south of St. Maarten. Oranjestad, the capital and only "city" (note quotes), is on the western side facing the Caribbean. The island is anchored at the north and the south by extinct volcanoes, like the Quill, that are separated by a central plain.

Statia is a wonderful playground for hikers and divers. Myriad ancient ships rest on the ocean floor alongside 18th-century warehouses that were slowly buried in the sea by storms. Much of the aboveground activity has to do with archaeology and restoration. Students from William and Mary's College of Archaeology converge on the island each summer; the University of Leiden in the Netherlands has a pre-Columbian program; and the island's Historical Foundation is actively engaged in restoring Statian landmarks.

Most visitors will be content with a day visit from nearby St. Maarten, exploring some of the historical sights and enjoying a relaxed meal at the Old Gin House. Those who stay longer tend to be collectors of unspoiled islands with a need to relax and a taste for history. But Statia is mindful of the potential gold mine of tourism and is spending several million dollars reconstructing the harbor and pier, which were severely damaged by Hurricane Hugo, in hopes of attracting cruise business.

Before You Go

Tourist Information Contact the **Caribbean Tourism Organization** (20 E. 46th St., New York, NY 10017–2452, tel. 212/682–0435). You may also contact the **tourist board** on the island (Oranjestad, St. Eustatius, Netherlands Antilles, tel. 599/38–2433) which is very willing to advise and reserve guest-house accommodations. Although telephone communications are good, it can take several weeks for mail to get through.

Arriving and Departing **Windward Islands Airways** (tel. 599/5–44230 or 599/5–44237) makes the 20-minute flight from St. Maarten four times a day, the 10-minute flight from Saba daily, and the 15-minute flight from St. Kitts daily. **LIAT** (tel. 809/462–0700) has twice-weekly flights from St. Kitts.

By Plane

From the Airport Planes put down at the **Franklin Delano Roosevelt Airport,** where taxis meet all flights and charge about $4 for the drive into town.

Passports and Visas All visitors must have proof of citizenship. A passport is preferred, but a birth certificate or voter registration card will do. (A driver's license will *not* do.) British citizens need a valid passport. All visitors need a return or ongoing ticket.

Language Statia's official language is Dutch (it's used on government documents), but everyone speaks English. Dutch is taught as the primary language in the schools, and street signs are in both Dutch and English.

Staying in St. Eustatius

Important Addresses **Tourist Office:** The **St. Eustatius Tourist Office** is at the entrance to Fort Oranje (3 Fort Oranjestraat, tel. 599/38–2433). Office hours are weekdays 8–noon and 1–5.

Emergencies **Police:** tel. 599/38–2333. **Hospital: Queen Beatrix Medical Center** (25 Prinsesweg, tel. 599/38–2211 and 599/38–2371) has a full-time licensed physician on duty.

Currency U.S. dollars are accepted everywhere, but legal tender is the Netherlands Antilles florin (NAf). Florins are also referred to as guilders, and you shouldn't be surprised to receive change in them. The exchange rate fluctuates but is about NAf1.80 to U.S.$1. Prices quoted here are in U.S. dollars unless noted otherwise.

Taxes and Service Charges Hotels collect an 8% government tax and a 10% service charge. The departure tax is $3 for flights to other islands of the Netherlands Antilles and $5 to foreign destinations. In addition, you'll probably be asked to contribute your leftover guilders to the latest cause.

All hotels and restaurants add a 10%–15% service charge.

Guided Tours All 10 of Statia's taxis are available for island tours. A full day's outing costs $35 per vehicle, usually including airport pickup.

Getting Around To explore the island (and there isn't very much), car rentals are available through the **Avis** outlet at the airport (tel. 599/38–2421 and 800/331–1084) at a cost of $40–$45 per day. **Rainbow Car Rental** (tel. 599/38–2586) has several Hyundais for rent. **Brown's** (tel. 599/38–2266) and **Lady Ama's Services** (tel. 599/38–2451) rent cars and Jeeps; rentals are also available through the island's taxi drivers. A taxi driver with a broad knowledge of the island and its folklore is Mr. Daniel. Statia's roads are pocked with potholes and the going is slow and bumpy. Goats and cattle have the right of way.

Telephones and Mail Statia has microwave telephone service to all parts of the world. To call Statia from the United States, dial 011–599/38 + the local number. When calling interisland, dial only the four-digit number. Direct dial is available. Airmail letters to the United States are NAf1.30; postcards NAf60/.

Opening and Closing Times Most offices are open weekdays 8–noon and 1–4 or 5. **Barclays Bank** (the only bank on the island) is open Monday–Thursday 8:30–1, Friday 8:30–1 and 4–5.

Exploring St. Eustatius

Numbers in the margin correspond to points of interest on the St. Eustatius map.

Oranjestad Statia's capital and only town, **Oranjestad** sits on the western coast ❶ facing the Caribbean. It's a split-level town: Upper Town and Lower Town. History buffs will enjoy poking around the ancient Dutch Colonial buildings, which are being restored by the historical foundation, while hikers will want to head for the hills of the Quill. Both Upper Town and Lower Town are easily explored on foot.

The first stop is the **tourist office,** which is right at the entrance to Fort Oranje. You can pick up maps, brochures, and friendly advice, as well as a listing of 12 marked hiking trails. You can also arrange for guides and guided tours.

❷ When you leave the tourist office, you will be at the entrance to **Fort Oranje.** With its three bastions, the fort has clutched these cliffs since 1636. In 1976, Statia participated in the U.S. bicentennial celebration by restoring the old fort, and now gleaming black cannons point out over the ramparts. In the parade grounds a plaque, presented in 1939 by Franklin D. Roosevelt, reads, "Here the sovereignty of the United States of America was first formally acknowledged to a national vessel by a foreign official." A few government offices are within the fort, and restoration continues.

From the fort, cross over to Wilhelminaweg (Wilhelmina Way) in the center of Upper Town. The **St. Eustatius Historical Foundation Museum** is in the Doncker/de Graaff house, a lovely building with slim columns and a high gallery. British Admiral Rodney is believed to have lived here during the American Revolution, while he was stealing everything from gunpowder to port in retaliation for Statia's gallant support of the fledgling country. The house, acquired by the foundation in 1983 and completely restored, is Statia's most important intact 18th-century dwelling. Exhibits trace the island's history from the 6th century to the present. The most recent addition is a pre-Columbian annex across the street. Statia is the only island thus far where ruins and artifacts of the Saladoid, a newly discovered tribe, have been excavated. *12 Van Tonningenweg, tel. 599/38–2288. Admission: $1 adults, 50¢ children. Open weekdays 9–5, weekends 9–noon.*

Return to Fort Oranjestraat (Fort Orange St.) and turn left. Continue to 4 **Fort Oranjestraat,** at the corner of Kerkweg (Church Way). The big yellow house, with a stone foundation, shingled walls, and gingerbread trim, is typical of the houses built in the West Indies around the turn of the century. Just behind it is **Three Widows Corner,** a tropical courtyard where you'll see two more examples of Statian architecture in a town house and another gingerbread house.

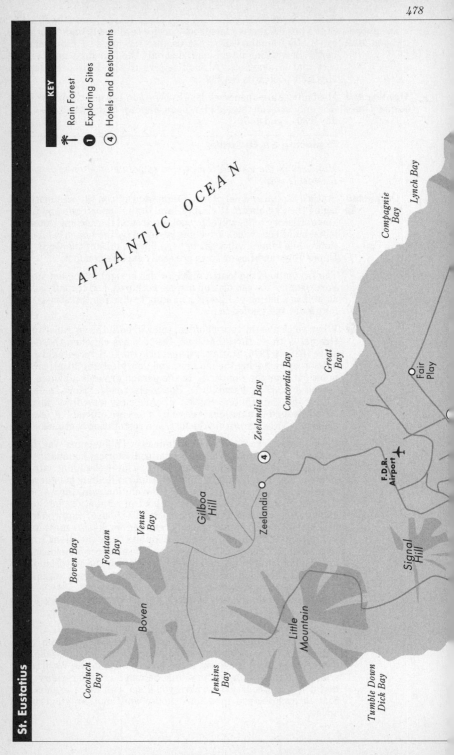

479

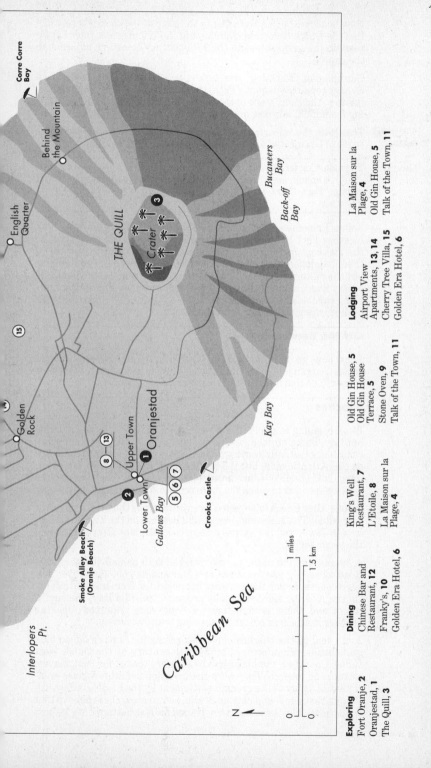

Now head west down Kerkweg to the edge of the cliff, where you'll find the **Dutch Reformed church,** built in 1775. Ancient tales can be read on the gravestones in the 18th-century cemetery adjacent to the church.

Continue on Kerkweg and take the next two left turns onto Synagogepad (Synagogue Path) to **Honen Dalim** ("She Who Is Charitable to the Poor"), one of the Caribbean's oldest synagogues. Dating from 1738, it is now in ruins but is slated for restoration.

❸ The Quill, the volcanic cone rising in the southern sector, is 3 miles south of Oranjestad on the main road (*see* Hiking, *below*).

Time Out The **Cool Corner,** just up from the tourist office, is a cool spot to have a beer, a snack, and shoot the breeze if you want to catch up on island gossip. *Fort Oranjestraat, tel. 599/38-2523. Open Mon.–Sat. 7 AM–2 AM.*

Follow Prinsesweg back to the main square and zigzag down the cobblestone Fort Road to Lower Town. Warehouses and shops that in the 18th century were piled high with European imports are now either abandoned or simply used to store local fishermen's equipment, but the restoration of the 18th-century cotton mill, on the land side of Bay Road, now the **Old Gin House,** is impressive. The palms, flowering shrubs, and park benches along the water's edge are the work of the historical foundation members.

Off the Beaten Path

Local boys go up to the Quill by torchlight to catch delectable sand crabs. You can join them and ask your hotel to prepare your catch for dinner. The tourist board will make arrangements.

Beaches

Beachcombing is a sport for the intrepid: The beaches are pristine but tiny, unmaintained, and occasionally rocky. Sand is mainly volcanic black (actually varying shades of gray). The nicest strands are on the Atlantic side, but the surf is generally too rough for swimming. It is possible to hike around the coast at low tide, though a car is recommended to reach the more remote Atlantic stretches.

Smoke Alley Beach (also called **Oranje Beach**) is the nicest and most accessible. The beige-and-black-sand beach is on the Caribbean, off Lower Town, and is relatively deserted until late afternoon, when the locals arrive.

A 30-minute hike down an easy marked trail behind the Mountain Road will bring you to **Corre Corre Bay** and its gold-sand beach. Two bends north, **Lynch Bay** is somewhat protected from the wild swells. On the Atlantic side, especially around Concordia Bay, the surf is rough and there is sometimes a dangerous undertow, making beaches in this area better for sunning than swimming.

A big deal on the beaches here is searching for Statia's famed blue glass beads. Manufactured in the 17th century by the Dutch West Indies Company, the blue glass beads were traded for rum, slaves, cotton, and tobacco. They were also awarded to faithful slaves or included as a part of the groom's settlement by the bride's father. Although they are found only on Statia, some researchers believe that it was beads like these that were traded for Manhattan. They're best unearthed after a heavy rain, but as the locals chuckle, "If you find one, it's a miracle, man."

Sports and the Outdoors

Fishing Dive Statia (tel. 599/38–2435) has a 31-foot Chris-Craft available for deep-sea fishing. It also rents fishing gear.

Hiking Trails range from the easy to the "Watch out!" The big thrill here is the Quill, the 1,968-foot extinct volcano with its crater full of rain forest. Give yourself two to three hours to make the climb and the return. The tourist office has a list of 12 marked trails and can put you in touch with a guide (whose fee will be about $20). Wear layers: it can be cool on the summit and steamy in the interior.

Scuba Diving If you've never gone to an undersea supermarket, here's your chance. The "supermarket" is actually two parallel shipwrecks less than 50 yards apart that are "stocked" with lots of marine life. It's but one of the many wrecks and 18th-century submerged seaports you can see. **Dive Statia** (tel. 599/38–2435), a fully equipped dive shop offering certification courses, is operated by Americans Mike and Judy Brown out of a warehouse just down the road from the Old Gin House. Most of the hotels offer dive packages with Dive Statia.

Snorkeling Crooks Castle has several stands of pillar coral, giant yellow sea fans, and sea whips. Jenkins Bay and Venus Bay are other favorites with snorkelers. For equipment rental, contact **Dive Statia** (*see* Scuba Diving, *above*). Equipment rentals are $5–$10.

Tennis There's a lone tennis court at the **community center** that's even lighted at night. It has changing rooms, but you'll have to bring your own rackets and balls. The cost is $2 (check with the tourist office for more information).

Shopping

Though shopping on Statia is duty-free, it is also somewhat limited. A handful of shops do offer unusual items, however. **The Old Gin House** (tel. 599/38–2319) features handicrafts from around the Caribbean, as well as cottons silk-screened with traditional Statian motifs, sold both by the yard and made up into attractive resort wear. Barbara Lane shows her own sophisticated ceramic pieces, together with paintings and woven sculptures by local artists at **the Park Place Gallery** (tel. 599/38–2452) across from the Cool Corner in the center of town. **Mazinga Gift Shop** on Fort Oranjestraat in Upper Town (tel. 599/38–2245) is a small department store of sorts. It has duty-free jewelry, cosmetics, and liquor, in addition to beachwear, sports gear, stationery, books, and magazines.

Dining

The variety of cuisines here is surprising, given the size of the island. Besides the traditional West Indian fare, you can find French and Chinese cuisine. Also, it's supercasual here; a beach wrap or a bathing suit will do.

Highly recommended restaurants are indicated by a star ★.

Category	Cost*
Expensive	over $25
Moderate	$15–$25
Inexpensive	under $15

per person, excluding drinks and service

★ **Old Gin House.** Here you'll find the most sophisticated dining on the island, even though it's lost some of its past flair. Your four-course, fixed-price feast will probably begin with warm grapefruit soup or a salad of smoked red snapper. The main course could be chateaubriand Dijonnaise, roast duck with sweet-and-sour sauce, or lobster mousse with caviar and horseradish. Two wines are included with the dinner. The poolside setting is elegantly rustic, with old-brick walls, candlelight, pewter, and gleaming crystal. *Old Gin House, Lower Town, Oranjestad, tel. 599/38–2319. Reservations suggested. AE, D, MC, V. Expensive.*

Golden Era Hotel. The restaurant and bar of this establishment are somewhat stark, but the Creole food is good and the setting is right on the water. Sunday-night buffets, a steal at $14.50, are popular, served outside by the pool and ocean, with a local band providing entertainment. *Golden Era Hotel, Lower Town, Oranjestad, tel. 599/ 38–2345. AE, D, MC, V. Moderate.*

King's Well Restaurant. "Good food, cold drinks and easy prices" reads the hand-painted sign at this breezy terrace eatery overlooking the sea, run by a fun-loving expatriate couple. Fine grilled chicken and fish and authentic *rostbraten* and schnitzels are featured. The owners now offer three spacious, attractive rooms for rent, with promises of a full spa facility to come. *Bay Rd., Lower Town, Oranjestad, tel. 599/38–2538. No credit cards. Moderate.*

La Maison sur la Plage. The view here is of the Atlantic, the cloths are crisp and white, and the fare is classic bistro French. For dinner, openers include fish soup and quiche Lorraine. Among the entrées are duck breast with green-peppercorn sauce and *entrecôte forestière* (sirloin with mushrooms, cream, and red wine). Try the *crêpes à l'orange* for dessert. *Zeelandia, tel. 599/38–2256. Reservations required. AE, MC, V. Moderate.*

★ **Old Gin House Terrace.** Dining is delightful on the oceanside terrace of this hotel. The menu may include peanut soup, fillet of orange roughy fish, lobster Antillean (lobster chunks stewed with onions, red wine, Pernod, and a dash of hot pepper), plain burgers and dillyburgers (with sour cream and dill sauce), lobster salad, and sandwiches. Lunch is more casual and offers lighter fare than dinner. *Old Gin House, Lower Town, Oranjestad, tel. 599/38–2319. Reservations suggested. AE, D, MC, V. Moderate.*

Talk of the Town. Breakfast, lunch, and dinner are served at this pleasant restaurant midway between the airport and town. Magenta and white tablecloths, an abundance of hanging plants, and softly seductive calypso music in the background weave a romantic spell. Caribbean, Oriental, and American dishes are offered, with seafood (predictably) the standout. *L. E. Sadlerweg, near Upper Town, tel. 599/38–2236. MC, V. Moderate.*

Chinese Bar and Restaurant. Owner Kim Cheng serves up tasty Oriental and Caribbean dishes—*Bamigoreng* (Indonesian chow mein), pork chops Creole—in hearty portions at his unpretentious establishment. Dining indoors can be slightly claustrophobic, but just ask your waitress if you may tote your Formica-top table out onto the terrace. She'll probably be happy to lend a hand and then serve you under the stars. *Prinsesweg, Upper Town, Oranjestad, tel. 599/38–2389. No credit cards. Inexpensive.*

★ **Franky's.** Come here for good local barbecue: ribs, chicken, lobster, and fish served later than at most other places on Statia. Try the bullfoot soup and goatwater stew. The less adventurous can get pizza on the weekend, when there is live music. *Ruyterweg, Upper Town, Oranjestad, tel. 599/38–2575. Inexpensive.*

L'Etoile. West Indian dishes, such as spicy stuffed land crab and goat meat, are prepared by Caren Henriquez in a simple snack bar/restaurant. You can also get hot dogs, hamburgers, and spareribs. *Heiligerweg, Upper Town, Oranjestad, tel. 599/38–2299. No credit cards. Inexpensive.*

Stone Oven. Such West Indian specialties as goatwater stew are featured here. You can eat either indoors in the little house or outside on the palm-fringed patio. *16A Feaschweg, Upper Town, Oranjestad, tel. 599/38–2247. Reservations required. No credit cards. Inexpensive.*

Lodging

Accommodations, already scarce, are even harder to find because of the influx of Dominicans and Jamaicans seeking work. You may also compete for a room with young Dutch on driver's-license vacation packages, here to avoid the excessive length and cost of lessons back home. There are only three full-service hotels and a few apartment rentals on the island, usually on EP. Only one property can actually claim to be *on* a beach. On the plus side, hotels here are among the cheapest in the Caribbean; all but the three priciest properties offer the same rates year-round.

Highly recommended lodgings are indicated by a star ★.

Category	Cost*
Very Expensive	over $125
Expensive	$100–$125
Moderate	$75–$100
Inexpensive	under $75

All prices are for a standard double room for two, excluding 8% tax and 10% service charge.

Hotels **Old Gin House.** This once-proud property, fashioned by American expatriate John May out of the ruins of an 18th-century cotton-gin factory and warehouse, is living off its faded glory. The cluster of buildings includes one that is two stories high, its bougainvillea-swathed double balconies overlooking a secluded tropical courtyard and pool; the highly acclaimed Old Gin House Restaurant; a terrace restaurant and bar by the sea; and an additional six rooms in a two-story building with high ceilings, custom-made furnishings, and balconies that jut out over the ocean. The comfortable, individually decorated rooms are relatively spacious with superb Haitian artwork and antiques for furnishings. Regrettably, over the last few years, enthusiasm for and upkeep of the hotel's facilities have declined. *Box 172, Oranjestad, tel. 599/38–2319; in U.S., 800/223–5581. 20 rooms with bath. Facilities: 2 restaurants, bar, lounge, pool, library, boutique. AE, DC, MC, V. EP, MAP. Very Expensive.*

Golden Era Hotel. This is a harborfront hotel whose rooms are neat, small, air-conditioned, and motel-modern. All have little terraces, but only half have a full or partial view of the sea. The other rooms look out over concrete or down onto the roof of the restaurant. There is little that is aesthetically attractive about this hotel, but at least it is central, by the water, and enjoys a cheerful clientele. *Box 109, Oranjestad, tel. 599/38–2345 or 800/223–6510. 19 rooms, 1 suite; all with private bath. Facilities: restaurant, bar, pool. AE, D, MC, V. EP. Moderate.*

La Maison sur la Plage. The *plage* is a 2-mile crescent of gray sand slapped by the wild waters of the Atlantic. The undertow here can be dangerous, so you should do your swimming in the pool. A cozy lobby has rattan furnishings, a checkerboard on the coffee table, and shelves filled with books. There's a stone-and-wood bar, and a *très* French dining room bordered by a trellis and greenery. French-born Michelle Greca's *maison* (house) is actually five spartan cottages, where you have a choice of twin, double, or king-size beds. Every cottage has two bedrooms, each with a bath and a private veranda where a Continental breakfast is served. Repairs from recent hurricanes, however, have so far been makeshift rather than improvements. The main attraction of this isolated area is the Atlantic. *Box 157, Zeelandia, tel. 599/38–2256 or 800/845–9504. 10 rooms with bath. Facilities: restaurant, bar, lounge, pool. AE, MC, V. EP. Moderate.*

★ **Talk of the Town.** These simple but bright rooms are decorated with locally handcrafted furnishings. Four cottages, with a total of nine rooms, were recently added. All rooms feature air-conditioning, private bathroom with shower, cable TV, and direct-dial phone. There is a new swimming pool, a deck with lounge chairs for use by guests, and a restaurant downstairs. The hotel is on the road between the airport and town, a perfect choice for those who don't need a view. *L. E. Saddlerweg, tel. 599/38–2236. 18 rooms. Facilities: restaurant, bar, pool. MC, V. EP. Inexpensive.*

Apartment Rentals Statia has only a handful of apartments, though a spate of small developments and guest houses have gone up recently to meet demand. As a general rule, figure $50 and under per night and don't expect much beyond a bathroom and kitchenette. The only luxury accommodation is **Cherry Tree Villa** (tel. 800/325–2222 or 813/787–2579), which sprawls over 17 lush acres. The moderately priced two-bedroom villa sleeps four, and its luxe touches include a Cuisinart, dishwasher, microwave oven, outdoor Jacuzzi facing the sea, and the use of a car. A Hobie Cat and a 32-foot skippered yacht are available for an extra charge.

★ The **Airport View Apartments** (tel. 599/38–2299), near the airport, are inexpensive studios with carpeted floors, small refrigerators, TVs, air-conditioning, coffeemakers, private baths, and either two double or twin beds. There's an outdoor patio with a barbecue pit and a meeting room that can accommodate 12. The Airport View also has a vastly inferior in-town location.

Check with the tourist office for information about these and other apartment rentals in Oranjestad.

Nightlife

Statia's five local bands stay busy on weekends. **Talk of the Town** (*see* Lodging, *above*) is the place to be for live music on Friday night. Saturday nights **Cool Corner** (*see* Exploring St. Eustatius, *above*) and the **Chinese Bar and Restaurant** (*see* Dining, *above*) offer live music, and occasionally the **community center** (*see* Sports and the Outdoors, *above*) has a dance. Sunday nights find everyone at the **Golden Era Hotel** (*see* Lodging, *above*). Crowds are found all weekend at **Franky's** (*see* Dining, *above*) and the **Lago Heights Club and Disco** (at the shopping center in Chapelpiece, no tel.), known to all as Gerald's, which has dancing and a late-night barbecue.

21 St. Kitts and Nevis

*Updated by
Pamela
Acheson*

For years, visitors to St. Kitts and Nevis have tended to be self-suffi-cient types who know how to amuse themselves and appreciate the warmth and character of country inns. The Frigate Bay area of St. Kitts is the only area with a few larger hotels and condominium developments. However, big hotels are heading this way, and these islands will soon be attracting a broader clientele. The Four Seasons opened a resort in 1991 on tiny Nevis. Now several brand-name hotels are in the early stages of development on St. Kitts's South East Peninsula.

Tiny though it is, mountainous St. Kitts, the first English settlement in the Leeward Islands, crams some stunning scenery into its 65 square miles. Vast, brilliant green fields of sugarcane sweep down to the sea. The island is fertile and lush with tropical flora and has some fascinating natural and historical attractions: a rain forest, replete with waterfalls, thick vines, and secret trails; a central mountain range, dominated by the 3,792-foot Mt. Liamuiga, whose crater has been long dormant; and Brimstone Hill, the Caribbean's most impressive fortress, which was known in the 17th century as the Gibraltar of the West Indies.

The island is home to 35,000 people and hosts some 60,000 visitors annually. The shape of St. Kitts has been variously compared to a whale, a cricket bat, and a guitar. It's roughly oval, 19 miles long and 6 miles wide, with a narrow peninsula trailing off toward Nevis, 2 miles southeast across the strait.

The island is known as the mother colony of the West Indies because it was from here that the English settlers sailed to Antigua, Barbuda, Tortola, and Montserrat, and the French dispatched colonizing parties to Martinique, Guadeloupe, St. Martin, St. Barts, La Désirade, and Les Saintes. The French, who inexplicably brought a bunch of monkeys with them, arrived on St. Kitts a few years after the British.

In 1493, when Columbus spied a cloud-crowned volcanic isle during his second voyage to the New World, he named it *Nieves*, the Spanish word for "snows." It reminded him of the snowcapped peaks of the Pyrenees. Nevis (pronounced *NEE-vis*) rises out of the water in an almost perfect cone, the tip of its 3,232-foot central mountain smothered in clouds. It's less developed than its sister island, St. Kitts.

Nevis is known for its natural beauty—long beaches with white and black sand, lush greenery—for a half-dozen mineral spa baths, and for the restored sugar plantations that now house small, charming inns. In 1628, settlers from St. Kitts sailed across the 2-mile channel that separates the two islands. At first they grew tobacco, cotton, ginger, and indigo, but with the introduction of sugarcane in 1640, Nevis became the island equivalent of a boomtown. As the mineral baths were drawing crowds, the island was producing an abundance of sugar. Slaves were brought from Africa to work on the magnificent estates, many of them nestled high in the mountains amid lavish tropical gardens.

The restored plantation homes that now operate as inns are the island's most sybaritic lures for the leisurely life. There is plenty of activity for the energetic—mountain climbing, swimming, tennis, horseback riding, snorkeling. But the going is easy here, with hammocks for snoozing, lobster bakes on palm-lined beaches, and candlelit dinners in stately dining rooms and on romantic verandas.

As rich in history as it is fertile and lush with tropical flora, St. Kitts is just beginning to develop its tourism industry, and this quiet member of the Leeward group has that rare combination of natural and historic attractions and fine sailing, island hopping, and watersports options offshore.

Nevis is linked with St. Kitts politically. The two islands, together with Anguilla, achieved self-government as an Associated State of Great Britain in 1967. In 1983, St. Kitts and Nevis became a fully independent nation. Nevis papers sometimes run fiery articles advocating independence from St. Kitts, and the sister islands may separate someday. However, it's not likely that a shot will be fired, let alone one that will be heard around the world.

What It Will Cost These sample prices, meant only as a general guide, are for the high season. On St. Kitts, an expensive hotel room will be about $250 a night, an inexpensive hotel about $150 a night. On Nevis, a room at a restored plantation inn will cost about $230. Dinner at an expensive restaurant on either island can run about $70 for two people. A rum punch is $3–$4 on either island; a beer is about $2.50. You'll spend $35–$45 a day for a car or four-wheel drive rental. On St. Kitts, cab fare from the airport to Basseterre is only about $6, fare to the Frigate Bay hotels is about $10, and to the most distant hotels about $20. On Nevis, cab fare from the airport to Charlestown or the Four Seasons Resort is about $14, and to Montpelier Plantation it's about $17. A single-tank dive on both islands costs around $45; snorkel equipment rents for about $10.

Before You Go

Tourist Information Contact the **St. Kitts & Nevis Tourist Board** (414 E. 75th St., New York, NY 10021, tel. 800/582–6208 or 212/535–1234, fax 212/734–6511), **St. Kitts & Nevis Tourist Office** (11 Yorkville Ave., Suite 508, Toronto, Ontario, Canada M4W 1L3, tel. 416/921–7717), **St. Kitts & Nevis Tourist Office** (10 Kensington Ct., London W8 5DL, tel. 071/376–0881, fax 071/937–3611), and **St. Kitts & Nevis Tourist Office** (President's Plaza II, 8700 Bryn Mawr, Suite 800 S, Chicago, IL 60631, tel. 312/714–5015, fax 312/714–4910).

Arriving and Departing
By Plane **American** (tel. 800/433–7300) and **Delta** (tel. 800/221–1212) fly from the United States to Antigua, St. Croix, St. Thomas, St. Maarten, and San Juan, Puerto Rico, where connections to St. Kitts (and to a lesser extent, to Nevis) can be made on regional carriers such as **American Eagle,** part of the **American Airlines** system (tel. 800/433–7300); **LIAT** (tel. 809/465–2511); and **Windward Island Airways** (tel. 809/465–0810). LIAT has two flights daily between St. Kitts and Nevis. **British Airways** (tel. 800/247–9297) flies from London to Antigua, and **Air Canada** (tel. 800/422–6232) flies from Toronto to Antigua. **Air St. Kitts-Nevis** (tel. 809/465–8571) and **Carib Aviation** (in St. Kitts, tel. 809/465–3055; in Nevis, 809/469–9295; fax 809/469–9185) are reliable air-charter operations providing service between St. Kitts and Nevis and other islands.

From the Airport Taxis meet every flight at the airports on both islands. The taxis are unmetered, but fixed rates, in E.C. dollars, are posted at the airport and at the jetty. On St. Kitts the fare from the airport to the closest hotel in Basseterre is E.C.$16; to the farthest point, E.C.$52. On Nevis some sample fares are from the ferry slip to Nesbit Plantation, E.C.$17, and to Golden Rock, E.C.$40. (The current exchange rate is E.C.$2.70 for U.S.$1.) Be sure to clarify whether the rate quoted is in E.C. or U.S. dollars.

By Boat The 150-passenger government-operated ferry MV *Caribe Queen* makes the 45-minute crossing from Nevis to St. Kitts daily except Thursday, which is maintenance day, and Sunday. The schedule is a bit erratic, so confirm departure times with the tourist office. Round-trip fare is U.S.$8. A new, air-conditioned, 110-passenger ferry, MV *Spirit of Mount Nevis*, makes the run twice daily except Monday and Wednesday. The fare is U.S.$12 round-trip. Call **Nevis Cruise Lines** (tel. 809/469–9373) for information and reservations. Sea-taxi service between the two islands is operated by dive master Kenneth Samuel (tel. 809/465–2670) and by Auston MacLeod of Pro-Divers (tel. 809/465–2754) for U.S.$20 (summer), $25 (winter).

Passports and Visas Although it is always wiser to travel in the Caribbean with a valid passport, U.S. and Canadian citizens need only produce proof of citizenship in the form of a voter registration card or birth certificate (a driver's license will not suffice). British citizens must have a passport; visas are not required. All visitors must have a return or ongoing ticket.

Language English with a strong West Indian lilt is spoken here.

Precautions Visitors, especially women, are warned not to go jogging on long, lonely roads.

St. Kitts

Staying in St. Kitts

Important Addresses **Tourist Information: St. Kitts/Nevis Department of Tourism** (Pelican Mall, Bay Rd., Box 132, Basseterre, tel. 809/465–2620 and 809/465–4040, fax 809/465–8794) and the **St. Kitts-Nevis Hotel Association** (Box 438, Basseterre, tel. and fax 809/465–5304).

Emergencies **Police:** Call 911. **Hospital:** There is a 24-hour emergency room at the **Joseph N. France General Hospital** (Basseterre, tel. 809/465–2551). **Pharmacies:** In Basseterre, **Skerritt's Drug Store** (Fort St., tel. 809/465–2008) is open Monday–Wednesday 8–5, Thursday 8–1, Friday 8–5:30, and Saturday 8–6; closed Sunday; **City Drug** (Fort St., Basseterre, tel. 809/465–2156) is open Monday–Wednesday, Friday–Saturday 8–7; Thursday 8–5, Sunday 8–10 AM; and **City Drug** (Sun 'n' Sand, Frigate Bay, tel. 809/465–1803) is open Monday–Saturday 8:30–8, Sunday 8:30–10:30 AM and 4–6 PM.

Currency Legal tender is the Eastern Caribbean (E.C.) dollar. At press time, the rate of exchange was E.C.$2.70 to U.S.$1. U.S. dollars are accepted practically everywhere, but you'll almost always get change in E.C.s. Prices quoted here are in U.S. dollars unless noted otherwise. Most large hotels, restaurants, and shops accept major credit cards, but small inns and shops usually do not. It's always a good idea to check current credit-card policies before you turn up with only plastic in your pocket.

Taxes and Service Charges Hotels collect a 7% government tax. The departure tax is $8. (There is no departure tax from St. Kitts to Nevis, or vice versa.) All hotels add a 10% service charge to your bill. In restaurants, a tip of 10%–15% is appropriate.

Guided Tours **Tropical Tours** (tel. 809/465–4167) can run you around the island and take you to the rain forest. **Kantours** (tel. 809/465–2098) also offers a variety of island tours. **Kriss Tours** (tel. 809/465–4042) and **Greg Pereira** (tel. 809/465–4121) both specialize in rain-forest and volcano tours.

Getting
Around
Taxis

Taxis rates are government regulated, and the rates are posted at the airport and the dock and in the free **Traveller** tourist guide. There are fixed rates to and from all the hotels and to and from major points of interest. Taxi drivers are also happy to give tours. Stop by the **St. Kitts/Nevis Department of Tourism** in Basseterre or the front desk of your hotel to arrange for a tour. Expect to pay approximately $50 for a 3½-hour island taxi tour.

Buses

A privately owned minibus circles the island. Check with the tourist office about schedules.

Rental Cars
and
Scooters

You'll need a local driver's license, which you can get by presenting yourself, your valid driver's license, and E.C.$30 (U.S.$12) at the police station, Cayon Street, Basseterre. Rentals are available at **Holiday** (tel. 809/465–6507) and **Caines** (tel. 809/465–2366). Delise Walwyn (tel. 809/465–8449) operates **Economy Car,** which also rents scooter bikes. **TDC Rentals** (tel. 809/465–2991) has a wide selection of vehicles and the best service. Car rentals run about U.S.$35 per day. At press time, the price of gas was U.S.$1.70 per gallon. Remember to drive on the left!

Telephones
and Mail

To call St. Kitts from the United States, dial area code 809, then access code 465 and the local 4-digit number. Caribbean Phone Cards, which can be purchased in denominations of $5, $10, and $20, are handy for making local phone calls, calling other islands, and accessing USA Direct lines. To make an intraisland call, simply dial the seven-digit number.

Airmail letters to the United States and Canada cost E.C.80/ per half ounce; postcards require E.C.50/. Mail takes at least 7–10 days to reach the United States. St. Kitts and Nevis issue separate stamps, but each also honors the other's. The beautiful stamps are collector's items, and you may have a hard time pasting them on postcards.

Opening and
Closing Times

Although shops typically used to close for lunch from 12 to 1, more and more establishments are remaining open Monday–Saturday 8–4. Some shops close earlier on Thursday. Hours vary somewhat from bank to bank but are typically Monday–Thursday 8–3; Friday 8–5. St. Kitts & Nevis National Bank is also open Saturday 8:30–11.

Exploring St. Kitts

Numbers in the margin correspond to points of interest on the St. Kitts map.

Basseterre
1

The capital city of **Basseterre,** set in the southern part of the island, is an easily walkable town. It is graced with tall palms, and although many of the buildings appear run-down and in need of paint, you will find interesting shopping areas, excellent art galleries, and some beautifully maintained houses. You can see the main sights of the capital city in a half hour or so; allow three to four hours for an island tour.

If you don't have a map, pick one up at the **St. Kitts Tourist Board** (Tourism Complex, Bay Rd.). Turn left when you leave there and walk past the handsome Treasury Building. It faces the octagonal **Circus,** which is built in the style of London's famous Piccadilly Circus. Duty-free shops can be found along the streets and courtyards leading off from around the Circus. The **St. Kitts Philatelic Bureau** (open weekdays 8–4) is nearby on the second floor of the Social Security Building (Bay Rd.).

The colorful **Bay Road produce market** is open on weekends only. On the waterfront, next to the Treasury Building, is the air-conditioned **Shoreline Plaza,** with its tax-free shops, and nearby is the landing for the ferries to Nevis.

Time Out **Chef's Place** (Upper Church St., tel. 809/465–6176) is a lively place with an outdoor patio where local businesspeople go for spicy chicken platters and mutton curry. The Kittitian owner used to live in Brooklyn.

From the Circus, Bank Street leads to **Independence Square,** with lovely gardens on the site of a former slave market. The square is surrounded on three sides by Georgian buildings, including the popular **Georgian House** restaurant.

Walk up West Square Street, away from the bay, to Cayon Street, turn left, and walk one block to **St. George's Anglican Church.** This handsome stone building with crenellated tower was built by the French in 1670 and called Nôtre Dame. The British burned it down in 1706 and rebuilt it four years later, naming it after the patron saint of England. Since then, it has suffered fire, earthquake, and hurricanes and was once again rebuilt in 1859.

Elsewhere on Main Road traces the perimeter of the large, northwestern part of
the Island the island. Head west on it out of Basseterre, and be prepared for some stunning scenery. For the most part, you'll always have the sea in view as you drive through acres of sugar fields that encircle the island's mountain range. Here and there you'll see tiny villages with tiny houses of stone and weathered wood.

② Just outside Challengers is **Bloody Point,** where, in 1629, French and British soldiers joined forces to repel a mass attack by the Caribs. Be on the lookout for signs for **Old Road Town;** follow the road
③ until you see signs for the turnoff for the rain forest and **Romney Manor,** where batik fabrics are printed at **Caribelle Batik** (*see* Shopping, *below*). The house is set in six acres of gardens, with exotic flowers, an old bell tower, and a 350-year-old saman tree (sometimes called a rain tree). Inside, you can watch artisans hand-printing fabrics by the 2,500-year-old Indonesian process known as *batik*.

④ The village after Old Road Town is **Middle Island,** where Thomas Warner, the "gentleman of London" who brought the first settlers here, died in 1648 and is buried beneath a green gazebo in the churchyard of **St. Thomas Church.**

The road continues through the village of Half-Way Tree to well-re-
⑤ stored **Brimstone Hill,** a 38-acre fortress that is the most important historic site on St. Kitts. From the parking area it's quite a walk up to the top of the fort, but it's well worth it if military history and/or spectacular views interest you. After routing the French in 1690, the English erected a battery on top of Brimstone Hill, and by 1736, there were 49 guns in the fortress. In 1782, the French lay siege to the fortress, which was defended by 350 militia and 600 regular troops of the Royal Scots and East Yorkshires. A plaque in the old stone wall marks the place where the fort was breached. When the English finally surrendered, the French allowed them to march from the fort in full formation out of respect for their bravery. (The English afforded the French the same honor when they surrendered the fort a mere year later.) A hurricane did extensive damage to the fortress in 1834, and in 1852 it was evacuated and dismantled.

The citadel has been partially reconstructed and its guns remounted. You can see what remains of the officers' quarters, the re-

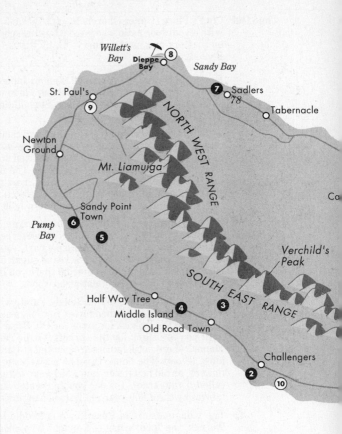

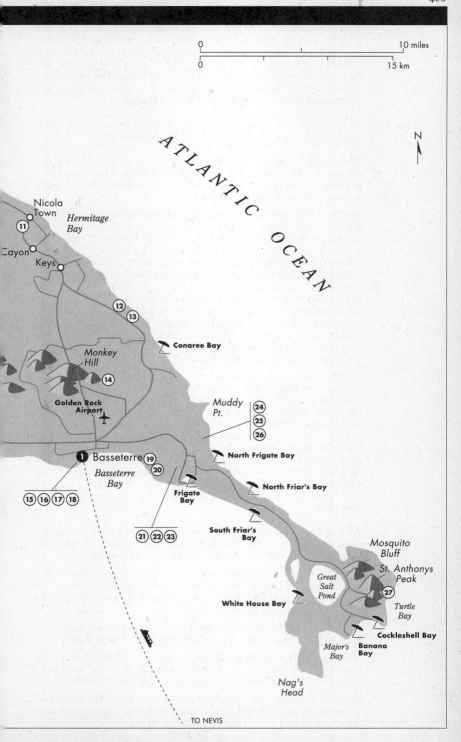

0   10 miles

0   15 km

ATLANTIC OCEAN

N

Nicola Town

⑪

Hermitage Bay

Cayon

Keys

⑫ ⑬

Monkey Hill

Conaree Bay

⑭

Golden Rock Airport

Muddy Pt.

㉔
㉕
㉖

❶ Basseterre ⑲
⑳

North Frigate Bay

Basseterre Bay

⑮⑯⑰⑱

Frigate Bay

North Friar's Bay

㉑㉒㉓

South Friar's Bay

Mosquito Bluff

St. Anthonys Peak

Great Salt Pond

㉗

Turtle Bay

White House Bay

Cockleshell Bay

Major's Bay

Banana Bay

Nag's Head

TO NEVIS

doubts, barracks, the ordnance store, and the cemetery. Its museums display, among other things, weaponry, uniforms, photographs, and old newspapers. In 1985, Queen Elizabeth visited Brimstone Hill and officially opened it as part of a national park. There's a splendid view from here that includes Montserrat and Nevis to the southeast, Saba and Statia to the northwest, and St. Barts and St. Maarten to the north. *Main Rd., Brimstone Hill. Admission: $5; children, $2.50. Open daily 9:30–5:30.*

Time Out　　**J's Place** (tel. 809/465–6264) across from the entrance to the fort is ideal for a drink, a sandwich, or a full West Indian meal.

❻　Continuing on through seas of sugarcane, past breadfruit trees and old stone walls, you'll come to **Sandy Point Town.** The houses here are West Indian–style raised cottages. The **Roman Catholic Church** has lovely stained-glass windows.

Farther along, just outside the village of **Newton Ground,** are the remains of an old sugar mill and some ancient coconut palms. Outside the village of **St. Paul's** is a road that leads to **Rawlins Plantation,** a restored sugar plantation that's popular for dining and lodging. The fishing town of **Dieppe Bay** is at the northernmost point of the island. Its tiny black-sand beach is backed by the **Golden Lemon,** one of the **❼**　Caribbean's most famous inns (*see* Lodging, *below*). **Black Rocks** on the Atlantic coast just outside the town of Sadlers, in Sandy Bay, are lava deposits, spat into the sea ages ago when the island's volcano erupted. They have since been molded into fanciful shapes by centuries of pounding surf. The drive back to Basseterre around the other side of the island is a pleasant one, through small, neat villages with centuries-old stone churches and pastel-colored cottages.

But perhaps the most spectacular drive is yet ahead of you. Go south through the **Frigate Bay** area (home to many hotels) and take the splendid $12 million Dr. Kennedy Simmonds Highway to the tip of the **South East Peninsula.** Reminiscent of California's famed Highway 1, this ultrasleek modern road twists and turns through the grassy hills (as yet virtually undeveloped) that rise between the calm Caribbean sea and the windswept Atlantic. At the far end, once you're back to sea level, follow the signs to Turtle Bay Beach for great views of Nevis and the OTI Turtle Beach Bar and Grill (*see* Dining, *below*).

Beaches

All beaches on the island are free and open to the public, even those occupied by hotels. The powdery white-sand beaches are all in the Frigate Bay area of the island or on the lower peninsula.

Two of the island's best beaches are the twin beaches of **Banana Bay** and **Cockleshell Bay,** which together cover more than 2 miles at the southeastern tip of the island. Several large hotels are currently in the very early stages of construction here.

Other good peninsula beaches are **Friar's Bay** (on both the Atlantic and the Caribbean sides), **Turtle Bay,** and **White House Bay.**

North of these beaches is talcum-powder-fine **Frigate Bay,** on the Caribbean. On the Atlantic, **North Frigate Bay** is 4 miles wide and a favorite with horseback riders (*see* Sports and the Outdoors, *below*).

Beaches elsewhere on the island are of gray-black volcanic sand. **Conaree Bay** on the Atlantic side is a narrow strip of gray-black sand where the water is good for body surfing (no facilities). Snorkeling and windsurfing are good at **Dieppe Bay,** a black-sand beach on the north coast, where the Golden Lemon Hotel is located.

Sports and the Outdoors

Boating Sunfish can be rented at **Tropical Surf** in Turtle Bay (tel. 809/496–9086) and Hobie Cats at **R. G. Watersports** in Frigate Bay (tel. 809/465–8050).

Deep-Sea Fishing Angle for yellowtail snapper, wahoo, mackerel, tuna, dolphin, and barracuda with **Tropical Tours** (tel. 809/465–4167) or **Pelican Cove Marina** (tel. 809/465–2754).

Golf The **Royal St. Kitts Golf Club** (tel. 809/465–8339) is an 18-hole championship course in the Frigate Bay area.

Hiking Trails in the central mountains vary from easy to don't-try-it-by-yourself. Monkey Hill and Verchild's Mountain are not difficult, although the Verchild's climb will take the better part of a day. Don't attempt Mt. Liamuiga without a guide. You'll start at Belmont Estates on horseback, then proceed on foot to the lip of the crater at 2,600 feet. You can go down into the crater, clinging to vines and roots. **Greg Pereira** (tel. 809/465–4121) takes groups on half-day trips into the rain forest and on full-day hikes up the volcano. **Kriss Tours** (tel. 809/465–4042) takes small groups into the crater and to Dos d'Anse Pond on Verchild's Mountain.

Horseback Riding Frigate Bay and Conaree Beach are great for riding. Guides from **Trinity Stable** (tel. 809/465–3226) will lead you into the hills at a leisurely gait. **Royal Stables** (tel. 809/465–2222) offers sunset beach rides and tours into the rain forest on horseback.

Scuba Diving and Snorkeling Kenneth Samuel of **Kenneth's Dive Centre** (tel. 809/465–7043 or 809/465–2670) is a PADI-certified dive master who takes small groups of divers with C cards to nearby reefs. Auston MacLeod, a PADI-certified dive master/instructor and owner of **Pro-Divers** (tel. 809/465–3223 or 809/465–2754), offers resort and certification courses. He also has Nikonos camera equipment for rent.

Sea Excursions **Leeward Island Charters** (tel. 809/465–7474) offers day and overnight charters on two catamarans—the 47-foot *Caona* or the 70-foot *Spirit of St. Kitts.* Day sails are from 9:30 to 4:30 and include barbecue, open bar, and snorkeling equipment. **Tropical Tours** (tel. 809/465–4039) offers moonlight cruises on the 52-foot catamaran *Cileca III* and glass-bottom-boat tours. *Tropical Dreamer* (tel. 809/465–8224) is another catamaran available for day and sunset cruises. For the ultimate underwater trip, call **Blue Frontier Ltd.** (tel. 809/465–4945); owner Lindsey Beck will take even nondivers for a half-hour ride off Frigate Bay in his two-man submarine. **Kantours** (tel. 809/465–2098) will take you on a Banana Bay Beach Safari for a day of snorkeling and swimming and an evening barbecue.

Tennis There are two lighted courts at **Jack Tar Village/Royal St. Kitts** (tel. 809/465–2651) and a functional grass court at **Rawlins Plantation** (tel. 809/465–6221).

Waterskiing and Windsurfing **Tropical Surf** (tel. 809/469–9086) at Turtle Bay rents Windsurfers, surfboards, and boogie boards. **R. G. Watersports** (tel. 809/465–8050) has windsurfing and waterskiing equipment.

Spectator Sports **Cricket** matches are played in Warner Park from January to July, **soccer** from July to December, **softball** from January to August. Contact the tourist board (tel. 809/465–4040) for schedules.

Shopping

St. Kitts has limited shopping, but there are a few duty-free shops where you can find some good buys in jewelry, watches, perfume, china, and crystal. Excellent painting and sculptures can be found at several galleries around the island. Among the island crafts, the best-known are the batik fabrics, scarves, caftans, and wall hangings of Caribelle Batik. There are also locally produced jams, jellies, herb teas, and handcrafts of local shell, straw, and coconut. And CSR (Cane Spirit Rothschild) is a "new cane spirit drink" that's distilled from fresh sugarcane right on St. Kitts.

Shopping Districts
Most shopping plazas are near the Circus in downtown Basseterre. Some shops have tiny branches in other areas, particularly in Dieppe Bay. The **Pelican Mall,** opened in 1991, has 26 stores, a restaurant, tourism offices, and a bandstand. This shopping arcade is designed to look like a traditional Caribbean street. **TDC Mall** is just off the Circus in downtown Basseterre. **Shoreline Plaza** is next to the Treasury Building, right on the waterfront in Basseterre. **Palms Arcade** is on Fort Street, also near the Circus.

Good Buys
TDC (TDC Plaza, on Bank St., tel. 809/465–2511) carries fine china and crystal, along with cameras and other imports.

Slice of the Lemon (Palms Arcade, tel. 809/465–2889) carries fine perfumes, but is better known for its elegant jewelry. **Lemonaid** (Dieppe Bay, tel. 809/465–7359) has select Caribbean handicrafts, antiques, and clothing by John Warden.

Caribelle Batik (Romney Manor, tel. 809/465–6253), **The Kittitian Kitchen** (Palms Arcade, Basseterre, and at the Golden Lemon, Dieppe Bay, no tel.), and **Palm Crafts** (also in Palms Arcade, tel. 809/465–2599) all sell that special something (island crafts, jams and jellies, batik) to take home as gifts and souvenirs. **Spencer Cameron Fabrics** (Ballaho Bldg., The Circus) has silk, cotton, and muslin fabrics hand-painted with clever, colorful designs that include monkeys and tropical flowers. **Spencer Cameron Art Gallery** (South Square St., tel. 809/465–4047) has historical reproductions of Caribbean island charts and prints, in addition to owner Rosey Cameron's popular Carnevale clown prints and a wide selection of exceptional artwork by Caribbean artists. They will mail anywhere, so you don't have to lug home something that catches your eye. **Splash** (tel. 809/465–9279,) in the Pelican Mall, carries colorful ceramics, including eye-catching work by local artist Paula Fiorel.

Dining

St. Kitts restaurants range from funky little beachfront bistros to small, elegant plantation dining rooms; and there is an interesting variety of cuisine to sample, most tinged, one way or another, with the flavors of the Caribbean. Many restaurants offer the visitor a chance to try a variety of West Indian specialties that are popular on St. Kitts, such as curried mutton, Arawak chicken (seasoned rice and almonds served on breadfruit leaf), pepper pot, and honey-glazed garlic spare ribs.

Highly recommended restaurants are indicated by a star ★.

Category	Cost*
Very Expensive	over $35
Expensive	$25–35
Moderate	$15–$25
Inexpensive	under $15

*per person, excluding drinks and service. There is no sales tax on St. Kitts.

The Patio Restaurant. Owner Peter Mallalieu and his daughter Helen, a graduate of the Culinary Institute of America, prepare a full à la carte menu with complimentary wine and liqueur, by reservation only, in his flower-filled home. Try the flame-broiled mahimahi with shrimp, or treat yourself to a sampling of traditional local dishes, including *conki* (a coconut side dish) and pepper pot. Piña colada gâteau and tropical fruit mousses are tempting desserts. *Frigate Bay Beach, tel. 809/465–8666. Reservations required. Dress: casual elegant, no shorts. MC, V. Very Expensive.*

★ **Rawlins Plantation.** Elegant dinners are served in a lovely room with fieldstone walls and high, vaulted ceilings. The fixed-price (U.S.$38 per person) meal features local ingredients and may include callaloo or fresh tomato soup, smoked salmon salad, shrimp in orange butter, and chocolate terrine with passion-fruit sauce. The menu for the four-course meal is set, but changes nightly. This is also a popular lunch spot, where you will find a bountiful buffet (U.S.$20) of such items as breadfruit salad, flying fish fritters, or *bobote* (ground beef, eggplant, spices, curry, and homemade chutney). *Mt. Pleasant, tel. 809/465–6221. Reservations required by noon. No credit cards, but personal checks are accepted. Closed for dinner on Sun. Very Expensive.*

The White House. Lunch is served on the garden terrace, and dinner is served in the elegant, antiques-filled dining room. The chef prepares a four-course dinner each night that may include such dishes as pumpkin or crab soup, Cornish game hen with banana stuffing, or fresh broiled local seafood. Afternoon tea is also served here. *St. Peter's, tel. 809/465–8162. Reservations required. AE, MC, V. Very Expensive.*

The Golden Lemon. Owner Arthur Leaman creates the recipes himself for the West Indian, Continental, and American cuisines served in his hotel, and he never repeats them more than once in a two-week period. The evening begins with cocktails and hors d'oeuvres on the patio. The three-course dinner, with its fixed menu, is served in an elegant room decorated with crystal chandeliers and antiques; graceful arched doorways welcome the island breezes. The patio, lush with bougainvillea and ferns, is a popular spot for Sunday brunch, which can include banana pancakes, rum beef stew, and curried conch fritters. *Dieppe Bay, tel. 809/465–7260. Reservations required. Dress: casual elegant. AE, MC, V. Expensive.*

The Lighthouse Gourmet Restaurant. Overlooking the harbor of Basseterre and close to town, this restaurant offers panoramic views and both West Indian and Continental cuisines. *Deepwater Port Rd., tel. 809/465–8914. AE, MC, V. Closed Sun. and Mon. Expensive.*

Ocean Terrace Inn. This is one of the most popular spots for the local elite. Dinner is by candlelight, in the inn's dining room or on a small balcony or terrace overlooking the bay. Lobster is the specialty here—grilled, broiled, and thermidor. At the Friday-night buffet, a lobster and steak barbecue alternates with West Indian specialties.

Dinner is followed by entertainment and dancing. *Fortlands, Basseterre, tel. 809/465–2754. Reservations advised. AE, MC, V. Expensive.*

★ **The Royal Palm.** Set beside the pool at Ottley's Plantation, this is a restaurant to experience at night, under the latticed roof, gazing across manicured lawns to the lights of the elegantly restored great house. The menu has an eclectic mix of California–Caribbean dishes and some classic Italian, French, and Chinese items. Start with baked brie or creole pumpkin soup and then have grilled sea scallops with Kittitian salsa, lobster with fruit and herb stuffing, or veal medallions. For dessert, try banana fritters l'antillaise or mango mousse with raspberry sauce. *Ottley's Plantation Inn, tel. 809/645–7234. Reservations required. AE, D, MC, V. Expensive.*

The Atlantic Club. After a morning of exploring, stop at this hillside, ocean-view eatery for a West Indian meal, seafood dishes, or club sandwiches and hamburgers, accompanied by divine piña coladas. Glenford Gumbs, a Nevisian who worked at the Golden Lemon for 15 years, opened this restaurant and bar next to his Morgan Heights Condominiums in 1992. He aims to please patrons and knows how: The portions are hearty and the prices can't be beat. *Morgan Heights Condominiums, Main Rd. near Basseterre, tel. 809/465–8633. AE, D, MC, V. Closed Sun. Moderate.*

★ **Fisherman's Wharf.** Part of the Ocean Terrace Inn (head straight rather than up the hill to the hotel's main building), this extremely casual waterfront eatery serves very fresh grilled lobster and seafood and excellent conch chowder in the evening. The tables are long, wooden affairs and it's generally lively, especially on weekend nights. *Fortlands, Basseterre, tel. 809/465–2754. Dinner only. No credit cards. Moderate.*

Blue Horizon. On the cliffs of Bird Rock, this unassuming restaurant affords a panoramic, waterfront view of Basseterre and of spectacular sunsets. The charming menu is written in five different languages (including English) on dinner plates, and the tables, with red-and-white checked tablecloths, are set to catch the breezes. The chef is Austrian, so specials such as Wiener schnitzel are often found on the menu alongside fresh local fish dishes. The lobster bisque is outstanding. *Bird Rock (just outside Basseterre, tel. 809/465–5863. Reservations advised. AE, MC, V. Inexpensive–Moderate.*

Coconut Cafe. This restaurant offers casual beachfront dining— breakfast, lunch, and dinner—at the Colony's Timothy Beach Resort on Frigate Bay. Featuring fresh grilled seafood, plus teriyaki shrimp, baby back ribs, calypso chicken, flying fish, and homemade soups, this is a perfect place from which to watch the sunset. *Frigate Bay, tel. 809/465–3020. AE, D, MC, V. Inexpensive–Moderate.*

OTI Turtle Beach Bar and Grill. This informal restaurant, set on an isolated beach at the south end of the South East Peninsula Road (look for the signs), is an excellent daytime watering hole (dinner served Saturday only). It offers water sports in addition to creating delicious cuisine by using solar panels for hot water, wind generators for electricity, and charcoal for cooking. Taste treats include their honey mustard ribs, calypso chicken, coconut shrimp salad, and grilled, stuffed lobster. *Turtle Beach, tel. 809/469–9086. Deep-sea fishing, kayaks, windsurfing, mountain bikes, all for a fee. Dinner Saturday only. AE, MC, V. Inexpensive–Moderate.*

★ **Ballahoo.** This second-floor terrace restaurant is in the heart of downtown, overlooking the Circus. It draws a crowd of locals and tourists for breakfast, lunch, and dinner. Specialties include conch simmered in garlic butter, beef Stroganoff, lobster and shrimp in a light creamy sauce, and (it's true) their rum and banana toasted sandwich. *Fort St., Basseterre, tel. 809/465–4197. AE, MC, V. Closed Sun. Inexpensive.*

Chef's Place. This is a great place to have an inexpensive West Indian meal and meet the local businesspeople. The best seats are on the outdoor, white veranda; try the local version of jerk chicken, moist rather than dry, or the goat stew. *Upper Church St., Basseterre, tel. 809/465–6176. No credit cards. Closed Sun. Inexpensive.*

PJ's Pizza. This casual spot, which borders the golf course, is hung with tropical greenery, open to the breezes, and famous for its "garbage" pizza—topped with everything but the kitchen sink. There are 10 other varieties of pizza, or you can create your own. Lasagna and a moist rum cake are house specialties. Other Italian dishes are served, as are sandwiches. *Frigate Bay, tel. 809/465–8373. AE, MC, V. Closed Sun. and Sept. Inexpensive.*

Lodging

St. Kitts has an appealing variety of places to stay. Here you'll find beautifully restored plantation inns, full-service hotels, condominium complexes, simple beachfront cottage colonies, and an all-inclusive hotel.

Highly recommended lodgings are indicated by a star ★.

Category	Cost*
Very Expensive	over $275
Expensive	$200–$275
Moderate	$125–$200
Inexpensive	under $125

*All prices are for a standard double room for two, excluding 7% tax and 10% service charge.

Hotels
★ **The Golden Lemon.** Arthur Leaman, a former decorating editor of *House and Garden*, created, and runs, this internationally famous, quiet retreat at the isolated north end of the island. There are nine rooms in the restored 17th-century great house, each one differently, and impeccably, decorated. There are canopied, wrought-iron, and four-poster beds, armoires, chaise longues, rocking chairs, and a variety of stunning fabrics. Accommodations are also found in one- or two-bedroom town houses (some with private pools), which are also exquisitely decorated. The cool, dark, well-appointed bar and lounge offer a peaceful respite from the bright sun, and the restaurant is one of the very best on the island. The hotel allows no children under 18. *Box 17, Dieppe Bay, tel. 809/465–7260 or 800/633–7411, fax 809/465–4019. 34 rooms and suites. Facilities: restaurant, beach, pool, duty-free shop, free laundry service, 1 tennis court. AE, MC, V. MAP (including afternoon tea). Very Expensive.*

The White House. This small, secluded property is located in the foothills above Basseterre and overlooks the Caribbean—from a distance. The beautifully restored plantation great house and rebuilt stable and carriage house are set on three radiant acres of flowering gardens and manicured green lawns. The bedrooms, each one different, have hardwood floors and are beautifully decorated with 19th-century antiques, mahogany beds (many are four-poster), and Laura Ashley fabrics. There is no air-conditioning, but all rooms have ceiling fans, and the cross-ventilation here is particularly good. There is a grass tennis court. Transportation is provided to the beach, about ten minutes away. The restaurant is considered among the best on the island; dinner is served by candlelight in the main dining room or outside under a marquee tent. *Box 436, St. Peter's, tel. 809/465–8162 or 800/223–1108, fax 809/465–8275. 10 rooms. Facilities: restaurant, bar, pool, tennis court, croquet, laundry service, shuttle to beach/town. AE, MC, V. MAP (including afternoon tea). Very Expensive.*

★ **Ocean Terrace Inn.** Referred to locally as OTI, this is one of the island's most upscale, Stateside-like hotels. It is not on the beach and is often used by business travelers, who appreciate its excellent service and its closeness to town. The main building, which houses the fancier restaurant, reception, a bar (which one can also swim up to), and many of the rooms, is set high on a hill overlooking the ocean. Condominium units are located farther down the hill but also have water views. All units are air-conditioned and have cable TV; they range in size from standard rooms to luxury suites to one- and two-bedroom condos with full kitchens. Fisherman's Wharf, waterfront at the bottom of the hill, is a casual seafood restaurant. The hotel's Pelican Cove Marina has its own fleet of boats. There is a shuttle daily to the hotel's beach (a good 20 minutes away) at pretty Turtle Bay, where you'll find a restaurant/bar (also owned by OTI) and all water sports. *Box 65, Basseterre, tel. 809/465–2754, 800/223–5695, or 800/524–0512, fax 809/465–1057. 52 rooms. Facilities: 2 restaurants, 2 bars, beach (20 minutes away), 2 pools, outdoor Jacuzzi, cable TV, fleet of boats, water-sports center. AE, MC, V. EP, MAP. Expensive.*

★ **Ottley's Plantation Inn.** This former sugar plantation has been transformed into a spectacularly elegant inn. Set on 35 manicured acres at the edge of a rain forest, at the foot of Mt. Liamuiga, this fairly isolated spot has views that sweep out to the wild Atlantic. The beautifully restored 18th-century English colonial–style great house and cut-stone cottages hold the inn's 15 guest rooms. All rooms are spacious, many with high ceilings, and they are decorated with an eclectic mix of white wicker, authentic antiques, and floral print fabrics. The large, 65-foot, spring-fed pool stretches out from the remaining walls of the sugar factory with an open-air bar at one end and the open-air Royal Palm restaurant along one side. Take a stroll on the property's rain-forest trail. *Ottley's Plantation Inn, Box 345, Ottley's, tel. 809/465–7234 or 800/772–3039, fax 809/465–4760. 15 rooms. Facilities: restaurant, bar, pool, shuttle to beach/town. AE, MC, V. EP, MAP. Expensive.*

★ **Rawlins Plantation.** This small, fairly isolated, but very lovely inn is set 350 feet above sea level on 12 acres of a former sugar plantation on the northern end of the island. On one side of the inn, the view stretches up across lush greenery to the peak of Mt. Liamuiga, which is nearly 4,000 feet high. On the other side, the view sweeps out to the Caribbean sea and the island of Statia. Accommodations are scattered across the grounds in various restored buildings of the old estate; each is unique. You'll find mahogany four-poster beds, wicker chairs, and fabrics in soft pastel prints. Some might consider the furnishings a bit spare. There is no air-conditioning, but all units have ceiling fans and good cross-ventilation. The restaurant, well-known on the island for its Continental-Caribbean cuisine, is decorated with antiques. This is a place for people who really want to get away from it all. *Box 340, Mt. Pleasant, tel. 809/465–6221 or 800/621–1270, fax 809/465–4954. 10 rooms. Facilities: restaurant, pool, tennis court, croquet, and complimentary laundry service. No credit cards, but personal checks are accepted. MAP (including afternoon tea). Expensive.*

Jack Tar Village Beach Resorts and Casino. A $2 million renovation has put this hotel back into shape, and it's now an appealing, very lively, all-inclusive vacation destination. Grounds are nicely landscaped, and guest rooms are newly decorated in pale pastel prints. One price covers all the activities, including the greens fees for the golf course. Two pools fit everyone's needs—those who want splashing, aerobics, or volleyball head one way, while the others can have a quiet, relaxing dip at the other. In addition to the sports activities listed below, there are daily contests and scheduled events and supervised activities for kids. Nightly live entertainment, a disco, and the island's only casino keep the action going late into the night. *Box 406, Frigate Bay, tel. 809/465–8651 or 800/999–9182, fax 809/465–8651. 240 rooms, 2 suites. Facilities: 2 restaurants, bars and lounges, casino, 2 pools, 2 lighted tennis courts, shuffleboard, ping-pong, basketball, scuba lessons, exercise and aerobic classes, facilities for people with disabilities, water-sports center, access to golf course. AE, MC, V. All-inclusive. Moderate–Expensive.*

Bird Rock Beach Resort. Perched on a bluff overlooking its own beach a few miles from the airport and downtown, this rather plain-looking resort has just added 16 new rooms and a second swimming pool, widened its crescent beach, and expanded its restaurant. Two-story buildings contain air-conditioned rooms and suites with direct-dial telephone, cable TV, and balcony. The tile-floored rooms are simply furnished with rattan furniture and floral fabrics. There is an informal dining room next to the pool and shuttle service to the gourmet Lighthouse Restaurant, which is owned by the hotel. There is particularly excellent snorkeling and diving in the waters just off the resort's golden-sand beach. Golf and the larger Frigate Bay beaches are just five minutes away. *Box 227, Basseterre, tel. 809/465–8914 or 800/621–1270, fax 809/465–1675. 40 rooms. Facilities: 2 restaurants, bar, 2 pools (one with swim-up bar), beach, tennis court, shuttle service to golf. AE, MC, V. EP, MAP. Moderate.*

★ **Colony's Timothy Beach Resort.** Set at the end of the Frigate Bay beach, this casual hotel overlooks the Caribbean. Simple white stucco buildings hold comfortable, adequately funished rooms and suites. Larger units have kitchens and multiple bedrooms; the best units sit right over the beach. Guests can participate in a wide variety of water and land activities, including nearby golf. The hotel's Coconut Cafe (*see* Dining, *above*) is a local favorite. The management is attentive and friendly. For couples and families who don't mind trading some atmosphere for modern comfort at a good price, this could well be the ideal spot for a beach-oriented vacation. Rates here are based on EP, so guests can feel free to sample the cuisine around St. Kitts. *Box 81, Frigate Bay, tel. 809/465–8597 or 800/621–1270, fax 809/465–7723; Colony Reservations Worldwide, 800/777–1700. 60 rooms. Facilities: restaurant, pool, beach, water activities, nearby golf, shopping, and other conveniences. AE, MC, V. EP. Moderate.*

Inter Grande Frigate Bay Beach Hotel. The owners of this property, formerly known as the Frigate Bay Beach Hotel, have just finished spending three-quarters of a million dollars on a much-needed cosmetic overhaul of the rooms. Walls have been repainted, furniture has been replaced, and there are new pastel print bedspreads and draperies. The third fairway of the island's golf course adjoins the property, and the two nearby beaches—Caribbean and Atlantic—are reached by complimentary shuttle buses (the Caribbean beach is also easily reached by following the path from the far end of the pool, along the edge of the golf course). The whitewashed, air-conditioned buildings contain standard rooms as well as condominium units with fully equipped kitchens. There are hillside and poolside units; the latter are preferable. Standard rooms are large but simply furnished, with tile floors and sliding glass doors leading to a terrace or balcony. There's an Olympic-size pool with swim-up bar and a terraced restaurant overlooking the pool. Packages of all sorts are available. *Box 137, Basseterre, tel. 809/465–8936, 809/465–8935, or 800/223–9815, fax 809/465–7050. 64 rooms. Facilities: restaurant, bar, pool. AE, D, MC, V. EP, MAP. Moderate.*

Sun 'n' Sand Beach Village. This simple complex is on the beach at Frigate Bay, on the Atlantic side of the island. These studio and two-bedroom, self-catering units are in cottages and two rows of two-story apartments that stretch back from the beach. Furnishings are simple and tropical, with tile floors, terraces, twin or queen-size beds, and private baths (shower only). Studios are air-conditioned; apartments have window air conditioners in bedrooms and ceiling fans in living rooms. Bedroom apartments have convertible sofas in living rooms and fully equipped kitchens with microwave ovens and full-size refrigerators. *Box 341, Frigate Bay, tel. 809/465–8037, 800/621–1270, or 800/223–6510, fax 809/465–6745. 32 studios, 18 2-bedroom cottages. Facilities: restaurant, beach, pool, children's pool, 2 lighted tennis courts, grocery store, nearby drugstore, gift shop. AE, D, MC, V. CP. Moderate.*

Fairview Inn. The main building of this old, quiet, and rather simple inn is an 18th-century great house, with graceful white verandas and Oriental rugs on hardwood floors. The rooms are in little cottages sprinkled around the backyard, which happens to be at the beginning of a mountain of considerable size. The rooms are tiny and have functional furnishings (they look rather like a U.S. motel room you might find in the middle of nowhere), with either twin or double beds, private patios, and radios. All have simple private baths with showers or bathtubs. Some have air-conditioning, some fans, some neither. The hotel restaurant serves West Indian cuisine. *Box 212, Basseterre, tel. 809/465–2472 or 800/223–9815, fax 809/465–1056. 30 rooms. Facilities: restaurant, 2 bars, pool. AE, D, MC, V. EP. Inexpensive.*

Fort Thomas Hotel. This hotel, which has long been popular with business travelers and tour groups, reopened in late 1993 after extensive refurbishing. It's built on the site of an old fort, on a hillside overlooking Basseterre and the harbor, and is across from (and a sort of a cheaper version of) the Ocean Terrace Inn. The building looks like a Stateside motel, but the rooms are spacious; all have two double beds, telephone, private bath, air-conditioning, and radio, and TVs can be rented. There's a free shuttle bus to the Frigate Bay beaches, and you can walk to town and to the stores at Pelican Mall. *Box 407, Basseterre, tel. 809/465–2695, fax 809/465–7518. 64 rooms. Facilities: restaurant, bar, pool, games room. AE, D, MC, V. EP. Inexpensive.*

Morgan Heights Condominiums. Glenford Gumbs left the Golden Lemon after 15 years to build Morgan Heights along the Atlantic coast (although it's not on the beach) 10 minutes from Basseterre. Built in 1992, these rooms are clean and comfortable—perfect for someone who wants a laid-back atmosphere and reasonable prices. The rooms are simple but contemporary, with ceramic tile floors, shell motifs, and white wicker furniture. All are air-conditioned and have direct-dial phones, fully equipped kitchens, cable TV, and private bath. Their covered patios overlook the water. Gumbs plans to add 10 units by winter 1994. *Box 536, Basseterre, tel. 809/465–8633 or 809/465–9210, fax 809/465–9272. 5 2-bedroom units that can be rented as 1-bedroom units. Facilities: restaurant, freshwater pool, beach shuttle. AE, D, MC, V. EP. Inexpensive.*

| Condos and Guest Houses | This little island has a number of condominiums and guest houses available to visitors. For information, contact the St. Kitts Tourist Board (Box 132, Basseterre, St. Kitts, tel. 809/465–2620). |

Nightlife

Most of the Kittitian nightlife revolves around the hotels, which host such live entertainment as folkloric shows, calypso music, and steel bands.

| Casinos | The only game in town is at the **Jack Tar Village Casino** (*see* Lodging, *above*), where you'll find blackjack tables, roulette wheels, craps tables, and one-armed bandits. Dress is casual, and play continues till the last player leaves. Note: You do not need to purchase Jack Tar passes to play, even though the casino entrance is in the hotel lobby. |

| Discos | On Saturday night head for the **Turtle Beach Bar and Grill** (Turtle Bay, tel. 809/496–9086), where there is a beach dance-disco. Play volleyball into the evening, then dance under the stars into the night. At **J's Place** (across from Brimstone Hill, tel. 809/465–6264), you and the locals can dance the night away on Friday and Saturday. **Reflections Night Club** (tel. 809/465–7616), upstairs at Flex Fitness Center, is a hot Kittitian night spot. It's open Tuesday through Sunday from 9 until well past midnight. Cover charge is E.C.$10 Thursday, Friday, and Saturday nights. |

Nevis

Staying in Nevis

| Important Addresses | **Tourist Information:** The **tourism office** (tel. 809/469–5521) is on Main Street in Charlestown. The office is open Monday and Tuesday 8–4:30 and Wednesday–Friday 8–4. |

| *Emergencies* | **Police:** Call 911. **Hospital:** There is a 24-hour emergency room at **Alexandra Hospital** (Charlestown, tel. 809/469–5473). **Pharmacies:** **Evelyn's Drugstore** (Charlestown, tel. 809/469–5278) is open weekdays 8–5, Saturday 8–7:30, and Sunday 7 AM–8 PM; the **Claxton Medical Centre** (Charlestown, tel. 809/469–5357) is open Monday–Wednesday and Friday 8–6, Thursday 8–4, Saturday 7:30–7, and Sunday 6–8 PM. |

| Currency | Legal tender is the Eastern Caribbean (E.C.) dollar. The rate of exchange fluctuates but hovers around E.C.$2.60 to U.S.$1. The U.S. dollar is accepted everywhere, but you'll almost always get change in E.C.s. Prices quoted here are in U.S. dollars unless noted otherwise. Credit cards are accepted at several hotels and quite a few of the restaurants on the island, though some of the inns and hotels will take only personal checks, and some of the restaurants will only take cash. |

| Taxes and Service Charges | Hotels collect a 7% government tax. The departure tax is $8. Most hotels add a 10% service charge to your bill. In restaurants, a 15% gratuity is the norm, provided that the service was satisfactory. Taxi drivers typically receive a 10% tip. |

| Guided Tours | The **taxi driver** who picks you up will probably offer to act as your guide to the island. Each driver is knowledgeable and does a three-hour tour for $50. He can also make a lunch reservation at one of the plantation restaurants, and you can incorporate this into your tour. |

All Seasons Streamline Tours (tel. 809/469–5705 or 809/469–1138, fax 809/469–1139) has a fleet of air-conditioned, 14-seat vans and uniformed drivers to take you around the island at a cost of $75 for three hours.

Another tour option is **Jan's Travel Agency** (Arcade, Charlestown, tel. 809/469–5578), which arranges half- and full-day tours of the island.

Getting Around
Rental Cars
Arrive in Nevis with a valid driver's license, and your car-rental agency will help you obtain a local license at the police station. The cost is E.C.$30 (U.S.$12), and it is valid for one year.

Beware: The island's roads are pocked with crater-size potholes; driving is on the left and, to make it more difficult, you may be given a right-drive vehicle); goats and cattle crop up out of nowhere to amble along the road; and if you deviate from Main Street, you're likely to have trouble finding your way around, although the island is small enough so that you can't get horribly lost. **TDC Rentals, Ltd.** (Charlestown, tel. 809/469–5690), known for their exceptional service, rents a wide range of vehicles, has offices on St. Kitts, and offers a three-day rental that includes a car on both islands. **Skeete's Car Rental** (Newcastle Village, at the airport, tel. 809/469–9458) has Toyota Corollas, Suzuki Jeeps, and Mitsubishi Lancers; **Striker's Car Rental** (Hermitage, tel. 809/469–2654) has minimokes (simple open-air vehicles) and compacts; **Nisbett Rentals Ltd.** (tel. 809/469–1913 or 809/469–6211) rents cars, minimokes, and Jeeps. None of them charges for mileage, and all of them accept major credit cards.

Taxis
Taxi service is available at the airport and in Charlestown, down by the dock. You can also arrange for a taxi through your hotel.

Telephones and Mail
To call Nevis from the United States, dial area code 809, followed by 469 and the local 4-digit number. Communications are excellent, both on the island and with the United States, and direct-dial long distance is in effect.

Airmail letters to the United States and Canada require E.C.80¢ per half ounce; postcards, E.C.50¢. It will take at least a week to 10 days for mail to reach home. Nevis and St. Kitts have separate stamp-issuing policies, but each honors the other's stamps, and stamps from both islands are beautiful.

Opening and Closing Times
Shops are open Monday–Friday 8–noon and 1–4 and some are open on Saturday. Banking hours vary but are generally Monday–Thursday 8–2; Friday 8–5. **St. Kitts-Nevis-Anguilla National Bank** and the **Bank of Nevis** are open Saturday 8:30–11 AM.

Exploring Nevis

Numbers in the margin correspond to points of interest on the Nevis map.

Charlestown
❶
About 1,200 of the island's 9,300 inhabitants live in **Charlestown,** the capital of Nevis. It faces the Caribbean, about 12½ miles south of Basseterre in St. Kitts. If you arrive by ferry, as most people do, you'll walk smack onto Main Street from the pier. You can tour the capital city in a half hour or so, but you'll need three to four hours to explore the entire island.

Turn right on Main Street and look for the **Nevis Tourist Office** (on your right as you enter the main square). Pick up a copy of the Nevis Historical Society's self-guided tour of the island and stroll back onto Main Street.

While it is true that tiny Charlestown has seen better days—it was founded in 1660—it's easy to imagine how it must have looked in its heyday. The buildings may be weathered and a bit worse for wear now, but there is still evidence of past glory in their fanciful galleries, elaborate gingerbread, wood shutters, and colorful hanging plants.

The stonework building with the clock tower at the corner of Main and Prince William streets houses the **courthouse** and **library.** A fire in 1873 severely damaged the building and destroyed valuable records; the current building dates from the turn of the century. You're welcome to poke around the second-floor library (open Mon.–Sat. 9–6), which is one of the coolest places on the island.

If you intend to rent a car, the **police station** across from the courthouse is the place to go to for your local driver's license.

The little park opposite the courthouse is **Memorial Square,** dedicated to the fallen of World Wars I and II.

Time Out Drop into the **Courtyard Cafe** (across the street from the tourist office, tel. 809/469–5685), Caribbean Confections's lush, foliage-filled outdoor restaurant, for coffee and homemade pastries. There are also sandwiches, peanut-butter cookies, and popcorn.

When you return to Main Street from Prince William Street, turn right and go past the pier. Main Street curves and becomes Craddock Road, but keep going straight and you'll be on Low Street. The **Alexander Hamilton Birthplace,** which contains the **Museum of Nevis History,** is on the waterfront, covered in bougainvillea and hibiscus. This Georgian-style house is a reconstruction of the statesman's original home, which was built in 1680 and is thought to have been destroyed during an earthquake in the mid-19th century. Hamilton was born here in 1755. He left for the American colonies 17 years later to contrive his education; he became secretary to George Washington and died in a duel with political rival Aaron Burr. The **Nevis House of Assembly** sits on the second floor of this building, and the museum downstairs contains Hamilton memorabilia and documents pertaining to the island's history. *Low St., no tel. Admission free. Open weekdays 8–4, Sat. 10–noon. Closed Sun.*

Elsewhere on the Island The main road makes a 20-mile circuit, with various offshoots bumping and winding into the mountains. Take the road south out of Charlestown, passing **Grove Park** along the way, where soccer and cricket matches are played.

❷ About ¼ mile from the park you'll come to the ruins of the **Bath Hotel** (built by John Huggins in 1778) and **Bath Springs.** The springs, with temperatures of 104–108°F, emanate from the hillside. Huggins's 50-room hotel, the first hotel in the Caribbean, was adjacent to the waters. Eighteenth-century accounts reported that a few days of imbibing in these waters resulted in miraculous cures. It would take a minor miracle to restore the decayed hotel to anything like grandeur—it closed down in the late-19th century—but the Spring House has been partially restored and some of the springs are still as hot as ever. *Bathing costs $2. Open weekdays 8–noon and 1–3:30, Sat. 8–noon. Closed Sun.*

❸ On Bath Road is the **Nelson Museum,** worth a visit for the memorabilia of Lord Nelson, including letters, documents, paintings, and even furniture from his flagship. Nelson was based in Antigua, but returned often to court, and eventually marry, Frances Nisbet, who lived on a 64-acre plantation here. *Bath Rd., tel. 809/469–0408. Ad-*

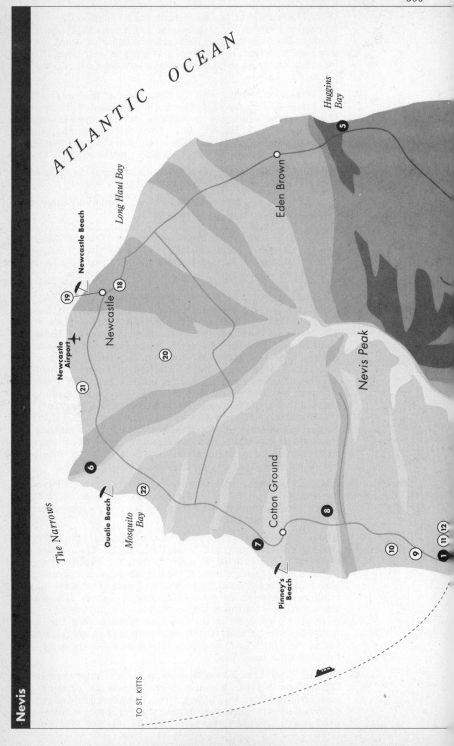

Nevis

ATLANTIC OCEAN

Huggins Bay

Eden Brown

⑤

Long Haul Bay

Newcastle Beach

⑲ ⑱

Newcastle

Newcastle Airport

⑳

㉑

Nevis Peak

⑥

Oualie Beach

Mosquito Bay

㉒

Cotton Ground

⑧

The Narrows

⑦

Pinney's Beach

⑩

⑨

① ⑪ ⑫

TO ST. KITTS

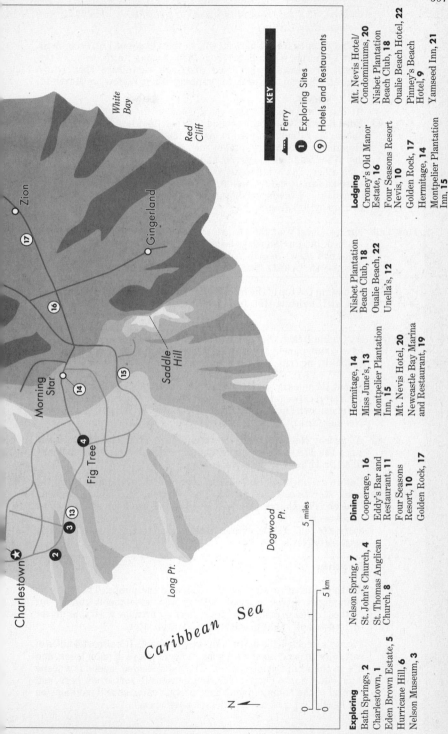

Exploring
Bath Springs, **2**
Charlestown, **1**
Eden Brown Estate, **5**
Hurricane Hill, **6**
Nelson Museum, **3**

Nelson Spring, **7**
St. John's Church, **4**
St. Thomas Anglican
Church, **8**

Dining
Cooperage, **16**
Eddy's Bar and
Restaurant, **11**
Four Seasons
Resort, **10**
Golden Rock, **17**

Hermitage, **14**
Miss June's, **13**
Montpelier Plantation
Inn, **15**
Mt. Nevis Hotel, **20**
Newcastle Bay Marina
and Restaurant, **19**

Nisbet Plantation
Beach Club, **18**
Oualie Beach, **22**
Unella's, **12**

Lodging
Croney's Old Manor
Estate, **16**
Four Seasons Resort
Nevis, **10**
Golden Rock, **17**
Hermitage, **14**
Montpelier Plantation
Inn, **15**

Mt. Nevis Hotel/
Condominiums, **20**
Nisbet Plantation
Beach Club, **18**
Oualie Beach Hotel, **22**
Pinney's Beach
Hotel, **9**
Yamseed Inn, **21**

KEY

Ferry
1 Exploring Sites
9 Hotels and Restaurants

mission: U.S.$2. Open Mon.–Wed. 8–4:30, Thurs.–Fri. 8–4, Sat. 8–noon. Closed Sun.

4 About 2 miles from Charlestown, in the village of Fig Tree, is **St. John's Church,** which dates from 1680. Among its records is a tattered, prominently displayed marriage certificate that reads: "Horatio Nelson, Esquire, to Frances Nisbet, Widow, on March 11, 1787."

At the island's east coast, you'll come to the government-owned **5** **Eden Brown Estate,** built around 1740 and known as Nevis's haunted house, or, rather, haunted ruins. In 1822, apparently, a Miss Julia Huggins was to marry a fellow named Maynard. However, on the day of the wedding the groom and his best man had a duel and killed each other. The bride-to-be became a recluse, and the mansion was closed down. Local residents claim they can feel the presence of . . . someone . . . whenever they go near the old house. You're welcome to drop by. It's free.

Time Out For real, local West Indian fare, stop at **Clà-Cha-Del.** The specialty is seafood, but on Saturdays be adventurous and try the goatwater or bull-head stew. *Shaw's Rd., Newcastle, tel. 809/469–9640. Open Tues.–Sat. 9 AM–11 PM, Sun. 6–11 PM. Closed Mon.*

Rounding the top of the island, west of Newcastle Airport, you'll ar- **6** rive at **Hurricane Hill,** from which there is a splendid view of St. Kitts.

Time Out At **Oualie Beach Club** (Mosquito Bay, tel. 809/469–9518), you can have a rum punch, swim in the sea, and sign up for a snorkeling or scuba-diving trip. Try the Sunday barbecue.

About 1½ miles farther along the Main Road, **Fort Ashby,** overgrown with tropical vegetation, overlooks the place where the settlement of Jamestown fell into the sea after a tidal wave hit the coast in 1680. Needless to say, this is a favored target of scuba divers.

7 At nearby **Nelson Spring,** the waters have considerably decreased since the 1780s, when young Captain Horatio Nelson periodically filled his ships with fresh water here.

Before driving back into Charlestown, a little over a mile down the **8** road, stop to see the island's oldest church, **St. Thomas Anglican Church.** The church was built in 1643 and has been altered many times over the years. The gravestones in the old churchyard have stories to tell, and the church itself contains memorials to the early settlers of Nevis.

Beaches

All the beaches on the island are free to the public. There are no changing facilities, so you'll have to wear a swimsuit under your clothes. If you're doing a cab tour, you may arrange with your driver to drop you off at the beach and pick you up later.

Pinney's Beach is the island's showpiece beach. It's almost 4 miles of soft, golden sand lined with a magnificent grove of palm trees, and it's on the calm Caribbean Sea. The palm-shaded lagoon is a scene right out of *South Pacific*. The Four Seasons Resort is now here, and several of the mountain inns have private cabanas and pavilions on the beach, but it is, nevertheless, a public beach.

Oualie Beach, at Mosquito Bay, just north of Pinney's, is a black-sand beach where Oualie Beach Club (tel. 809/469–9518) can mix you a drink and fix you up with water-sports equipment.

Newcastle Beach is the beach location of Nisbet Plantation. Popular among snorkelers, it's a broad beach of soft, white sand shaded by coconut palms on the northernmost tip of the island, on the channel between St. Kitts and Nevis.

Sports and the Outdoors

Boating   Hobie Cats and Sunfish can be rented from **Oualie Beach Club** (tel. 809/469–9518). **Newcastle Bay Marina** (Newcastle, tel. 809/469–9373) has Phantom sailboats, a 23-foot KenCraft powerboat, and several inflatables with outboards available for rent. **Frank Morse** (Oualie Beach, tel. 809/469–9735) has a 65-foot aluminum sloop, *Never Say Never,* on which he takes guests for day sails.

Deep-Sea Fishing   The game here is kingfish, wahoo, grouper, tuna, and yellowtail snapper. If you want local knowledge, call **Captain Valentine Glasgow** (tel. 809/469–1989), who has a 31-foot Ocean Master, *Lady James,* to take you in search of the big ones. **Jans Travel Agency** (tel. 809/469–5578) arranges deep-sea fishing trips.

Hiking   The center of the island is Nevis peak, which soars up to 3,232 feet, flanked by Hurricane Hill on the north and Saddle Hill on the south. If you plan to scale Mt. Nevis, a daylong affair, it is highly recommended that you go with a guide. Your hotel can arrange it for you; you can also ask the hotel to pack a picnic lunch. The **Nevis Academy** (tel. 809/469–2091, fax 809/469–2113), headed by David Rollinson, offers ecorambles (slower tours) and hikes. Three-hour rambles or hikes are $20 per person.

Horseback Riding   You can arrange for mountain-trail and beach rides through **Cane Gardens** (tel. 809/469–5648) and Ira Dore at **Garner's Estate** (tel. 809/469–5528).

Scuba Diving and Snorkeling   The village of **Jamestown** was washed into the sea around Fort Ashby; the area is a popular spot for snorkeling and diving. Reef-protected **Pinney's Beach** offers especially good snorkeling. Try **SCUBA Safaris** (tel. 809/468–9518) at Oualie Bay for everything from a resort course to full certification.

Tennis   There are 10 tennis courts at the **Four Seasons Resort Nevis** (tel. 809/469–1111), two at **Pinney's Beach Hotel** (tel. 809/469–5207), and one court each at **Nisbet** (tel. 809/469–9325), **Montpelier** (tel. 809/469–3462), and **Golden Rock** (tel. 809/469–3346).

Water Sports   **Montpelier Plantation** (tel. 809/469–5462) has a 17-foot Boston whaler for scuba, snorkeling, and waterskiing trips. Snorkeling and waterskiing trips can also be arranged through **Oualie Beach** (tel. 809/469–9518) and **Newcastle Bay Marina** (tel. 809/469–9373). Windsurfers can also be rented at both places.

Windsurfing   For windsurfing, **Winston Crooke** (tel. 809/469–9615) rents equipment and teaches classes. A two-hour beginners class is $40 per person. If you rent equipment only, it's $12 an hour per person.

Spectator Sports   Grove Park is the venue for cricket (Jan.–July) and soccer (July–Dec.). Your hotel or the tourist board can fill you in on dates, times, and grudge matches of particular interest between Kittitians and Nevisians.

Shopping

Nevis is certainly not the place for a shopping spree, but there are unique and wonderful surprises here, notably the island's stamps, batik and hand-embroidered clothing, and the artwork of Dame Eva Wilkins, who died in 1989.

For more than 50 years Wilkins painted island people, flowers, and landscapes. An Eva Wilkins mural hangs over the bar at the Golden Rock (*see* Dining, *below*). Her originals sell for $100 and up, and prints are available in some of the local shops.

For dolls and baskets hand-crafted in Nevis, visit the **Sandbox Tree** (tel. 809/469–5662) in Evelyn's Villa, Charlestown. Among other items available here are hand-painted chests. This is an appealing shop even if you are only browsing. The **Nevis Handicraft Co-op Society** (tel. 809/469–5509), next door to the Tourism Office, offers work by local artisans, including clothing, woven goods, and homemade jellies. Heading out of town, just past Alexander Hamilton's birthplace, you'll see the **Nevis Crafts Studio Cooperative.** Here Alvin Grante, a multitalented Nevisian artisan, displays his works and those of Ashley Phillips: hand-blocked prints and watercolors of the local landscape and architecture, hand-painted T-shirts, and baskets.

Stamp collectors should head for the **Philatelic Bureau,** just off Main Street opposite the tourist office. St. Kitts and Nevis are famous for their decorative, and sometimes lucrative, stamps. An early Kittitian stamp recently brought in $7,000.

Other local items of note are the batik caftans, scarves, and fabrics found in the Nevis branch of **Caribelle Batik** (in the Arcade of downtown Charlestown, tel. 809/469–1491).

Dining

Dinner options on Nevis include the elegance of the dining room at the Four Seasons Resort, intimate dinners at plantation guest houses where guests mingle before dinner in the library or parlor (and where the menu is often set), and a variety of more casual eateries. Seafood is ubiquitous, and there are many places in which to sample excellent, authentic West Indian fare.

Highly recommended restaurants are indicated by a star ★.

Category	Cost*
Very Expensive	over $35
Expensive	$25–$35
Moderate	$15–$25
Inexpensive	under $15

per person, excluding drinks and service

Four Seasons Resort. This elegant dining room, paneled in imported South American hardwood, has tables set with glistening silver and china, and graceful, 12-foot-high doors that open to the breezes and sweeping views of Pinney's Beach and the sea beyond. Cuisine is nouvelle with a Caribbean flair, such as grilled Norwegian salmon with a spicy but light Creole Hollandaise or grilled local snapper with a cumin broth. There is a weekly Caribbean buffet with a full steel band. *Pinney's Beach, tel. 809/469–1111. Reservations required. AE, D, MC, V. Very Expensive.*

Miss June's. Dinner with Miss June Mestier, a lady from Trinidad, could never be called ordinary. While she prepares the fare, her son serves beverages to the guests (limited to 20) on the veranda. Promptly at 8:30 everyone heads to the dining room, where several tables are set with fine china and crystal. The first course is a soup of Miss June's creation, usually something spicy. Then guests turn to the buffet table laden with at least 18 dishes. Selections change nightly but always include curries; dishes made with local vegetables, such as christophine in fruit sauce; and local seafood, such as conch simmered with garlic; all adapted by Miss June from Trinidadian recipes. At the meal's end, Miss June joins the guests for coffee and brandy. *Stony Grove Plantation Ruins, tel. 809/469–9330. Reservations required. MC, V. Very Expensive.*

Nisbet Plantation Beach Club. The antiques-filled dining room in the great house at Nisbet has long been a popular place for lunch and dinner. There are also tables on the screened-in veranda, where there's a view down the palm tree–lined fairway to the sea. The five-course menu is unusually varied for Nevis; the combination of Continental and Caribbean cuisines is prepared with many local ingredients. Lighter fare (sandwiches, salads, hamburgers) is served at lunch at the beach restaurant, Coconuts. *Nisbet Plantation, tel. 809/469–9325. Reservations required. AE, MC, V. Very Expensive.*

Golden Rock. Tables are set with pink tablecloths and arranged in a romantic, dimly lit room with walls of fieldstone dating back to when this was a plantation house. Local Nevisian cuisine is the specialty here; house favorites include chicken in a raisin curry, grilled local snapper with tania (a type of tuber) fritters, and green papaya pie. *Golden Rock, tel. 809/469–3346. Reservations required. AE, MC, V. Closed Sun. Expensive.*

Hermitage. Dinner is served at one long table on the outside veranda after cocktails in the antiques-filled parlor. The four-course menu is pre-set and always features local ingredients. Selections might include carrot and tarragon soup, West Indian red snapper in ginger sauce, fried conch steak, and a rum soufflé. *Hermitage Plantation, tel. 809/469–3477. Reservations required. AE, MC, V. Personal checks accepted. Expensive.*

Montpelier Plantation Inn. Cocktails and hors d'oeuvres are served amid the antiques in the parlor of the great house. Dinner is by candlelight on the white terrace. Your feast may include cream of avocado and coconut soup, lobster, red snapper, chicken calypso, sirloin steak Bordelaise, or even roast beef and Yorkshire pudding. Many of the ingredients are truly homegrown. The inn has its own farm and orchard, and produces everything from berries to suckling pigs. *Montpelier Plantation, tel. 809/469–3462. Reservations required. AE, MC, V. Closed late Aug. through early Oct. Expensive.*

★ **Cooperage.** An old stone dining room provides an elegantly rustic setting. Among the specialties here are green-pepper soup, curried chicken breasts, coconut shrimp, and sorbets. An à la carte menu has been added; lobster for $19.50 is the most expensive item, making this a good bet. *Croney's Old Manor Estate, tel. 809/469–3445. Reservations required. AE, D, MC, V. Moderate–Expensive.*

Mt. Nevis Hotel. The airy 60-seat dining room, where tables are set with fine china and silver, opens onto the terrace and pool, beyond which there is a splendid daytime view of St. Kitts in the distance. Starters include fish chowder and lobster bisque. Entrées may include red snapper, lobster, or sirloin steak embellished with mushrooms and onions. *Mt. Nevis Hotel/Condominiums, Newcastle, tel. 809/469–9373. Reservations suggested. AE, D, MC, V. Moderate.*

Eddy's Bar and Restaurant. This white-on-white decorated, second-story restaurant, set on a veranda overlooking Memorial Square in the center of Charlestown, is popular day and night. You'll find fine stir-fried dishes and local West Indian specialties, such as conch chowder and conch fritters. Stop by between 5 and 8 on Wednesday for happy hour; drinks are half price, snacks are free. *Main St., Charlestown, tel. 809/469–5958. Reservations advised. AE, MC, V. Closed Thurs., Sun., and Sept. Inexpensive–Moderate.*

Unella's. The atmosphere is nothing fancy, just simple tables set on a second-floor porch overlooking the waterfront in Charlestown, but the fare is authentic West Indian. Stop here for exceptional lobster, as well as curried lamb, island-style spare ribs, and steamed conch, all served with local vegetables, rice, and peas. Unella opens shop around 9 in the morning, when locals and boaters appear waiting for breakfast; she stays open all day. *Waterfront, Charlestown, tel. 809/469–5574. Inexpensive–Moderate (Expensive, lobster only).*

Newcastle Bay Marina and Restaurant. The pizza here is excellent, but even non-pizza lovers will enjoy sitting back on the deck and looking out to sea. Try the conch chowder, a sandwich, or a salad. *Newcastle Bay Marina, tel. 809/469–9373. AE, D, MC, V. Inexpensive.*

Oualie Beach. This low-key, casual bar and restaurant on Oualie Bay is the perfect stop for authentic Nevisian fare after a long day on the beach. Try the delicious homemade soups, including ground-nut or breadfruit vichyssoise. Then move on to Creole conch stew, lobster crêpes, or snapper in dill sauce garnished with local vegetables. *Oualie Beach, tel. 809/469–9735. AE, MC, V. Inexpensive.*

Lodging

With the exception of the Four Seasons Resort, most hotels on Nevis are beautifully restored manor or plantation houses. Typically, the owners of the inn live there with their families. Visitors are received warmly and graciously, almost like friends, and it is easy to begin thinking you have been personally invited down for a visit. In the evening, before dinner, it is common for the family, inn guests, and those visitors who have come to eat at the restaurant to gather in a drawing room or on a terrace for cocktails and to exchange stories of the day. Most of the inns operate on the MAP.

Highly recommended lodgings are indicated by a star ★.

Category	Cost*
Very Expensive	over $300
Expensive	$225–$300
Moderate	$150–$225
Inexpensive	under $150

All prices are for a standard double room for two, MAP, excluding 7% tax and 10% service charge.

★ **Four Seasons Resort Nevis.** This prestigious Canadian company's first foray into the Caribbean is a real winner. The 196-room property manages to combine world-class elegance with West Indian ambience and hospitality. Situated on a stunning stretch of Pinney's Beach, with a spectacular view of St. Kitts in the distance, the hotel offers a complete range of water activities, along with clay and all-weather tennis courts, an attractive free-form pool, a challenging

18-hole golf course designed by Robert Trent Jones II, and a full-service health club. Spacious guest rooms are richly furnished with mahogany armoires and headboards and cushioned rattan sofas and chairs, and have large indoor and veranda seating areas, which can be used for private dining. Contemporary bathrooms feature marble double sinks, a stall shower, and a soaking tub. Rooms have both ceiling fans and air-conditioning, ice-maker, fully stocked refrigerated bar, and a multichannel cable TV/VCR. There are two outstanding restaurants, one of which is fairly formal (although jacket and tie are not required). Special activities for children are regularly scheduled. Note: Four Seasons usually offers good-value sports and romantic packages even during the high season. *Box 565, Charlestown, tel. 809/469–1111; in the U.S., 800/332–3442; in Canada, 800/268–6288; fax 809/469–1112. 196 rooms. Facilities: 2 dining rooms, pub, casual outdoor dining, pool, beach, water sports, catamaran rentals, fitness center, free daily aerobics, 10 tennis courts, 18-hole golf course, children's program, baby-sitting, laundry service and free washer/dryers, 2 boutiques. AE, D, MC, V. EP, MAP, FAP. Very Expensive.*

★ **Hermitage.** A 250-year-old great house, said to be the oldest wooden house on the island, houses the restaurant and forms the core of this appealing inn set in the hills. The duplex guest cottages have some of the prettiest accommodations on the island. Rooms are furnished with antiques, including four-poster canopy beds (mostly king-size), and have patios or balconies; some also have lovely views of the distant ocean, and some have full kitchens. Also available is a two-bedroom replica of a manor house, with its own private pool. The beach is 15 minutes away, and if you haven't got a car, transportation will be arranged. But many guests simply relax in a hammock or spend the day by the pool at this peaceful retreat. *St. Johns, Fig Tree Parish, tel. 809/469–3477, fax 809/469–2481. 12 suites. Facilities: restaurant, pool. AE, MC, V. Personal checks accepted. EP, MAP. Expensive.*

Montpelier Plantation Inn. Iron gates provide a majestic entrance to this intimate and charming inn set on 100 beautifully landscaped hillside acres. Reception, evening cocktails, and dinner take place in and around the great house, an imposing fieldstone structure furnished with antiques. Accommodations are in simple cottages scattered along the hillside. The floors of all the rooms have just been redone with Italian ceramic tile; and the bathrooms have been completely refurbished and now have bathtub, shower, and full-length mirror. Each cottage has two patios and is adequately but sparely furnished. The pool is large and pretty, but beach-lovers can head (via complimentary transportation) to Pinney's Beach, where the estate has a new 3-acre private section of beach and a pavilion. The estate also has a 17-foot Boston whaler for waterskiing, snorkeling, and fishing. *Box 474, Charlestown, tel. 809/469–3462 or 800/243–9420, fax 809/469–2932. 17 rooms. Facilities: restaurant, bar, pool, beach (away from hotel), tennis court. No credit cards. Closed late Aug. through early Oct. BP, MAP. Expensive.*

★ **Nisbet Plantation Beach Club.** From the manor house of this 18th-century plantation you can see the beach at the end of a long avenue of coconut palms, and from the bar, you look out over an old sugar mill covered with hibiscus, cassia, frangipani, and flamboyants. Well-maintained Nisbet offers a range of accommodations, from plantation-style cottages to lanai suites, all simply but tastefully appointed in whitewashed rattan and tropical prints and situated along an avenue of palms that leads to a blinding white-sand beach and the ocean. *Newcastle Beach, tel. 809/469–9325; in the U.S., 800/344–2049; fax 809/469–9864. 38 rooms. Facilities: 2 restaurants, 2* *bars, beach, pool,tennis court, croquet, free laundry, boutique, free snorkeling gear. AE, MC, V. EP, MAP. Expensive.*

Croney's Old Manor Estate. Vast tropical gardens surround this restored sugar plantation. Many guest rooms have high ceilings, king-size 4-poster beds, and colonial reproductions, but some units are a bit gloomy and dark. The outbuildings, such as the smokehouse and jail, have been imaginatively restored, and the old cistern is now the pool. This is the home of the Cooperage, a well-respected restaurant (*see* Dining, *above*). There's transportation to and from the beach. The hotel is not recommended for children under 12. *Box 70, Charlestown, tel. 809/469-3445; in the U.S., 800/223-9815 or 800/892-7093; fax 809/469-3388. 14 rooms. Facilities: 2 restaurants, 2 bars, pool. AE, MC, V. EP, MAP. Moderate.*

★ **Golden Rock.** Co-owner Pam Barry runs this inn, which was built by her great, great, great grandfather over 200 years ago. She has decorated the 16 units with 4-poster beds of mahogany or bamboo, native grass rugs, rocking chairs, and island-made floral-print fabrics. All rooms have private baths and a patio. The restored sugar mill is a two-level suite for honeymooners or families, and the old cistern is now a spring-fed swimming pool. The estate covers 150 mountainous acres and is surrounded by 25 acres of lavish tropical gardens, including a sunken garden. Enjoy the Atlantic view and cooling breeze from the bar. The Saturday night West Indian buffet is very popular, December through June. Environmentalist Barry organizes historical and nature hikes. *Box 493, Gingerland, tel. 809/469-3346 or 800/223-9815, fax 809/469-2113. 16 rooms. Facilities: restaurant, bar, beach (away from hotel), pool, tennis court, educational activities. AE, MC, V. Personal checks accepted. EP, MAP. Moderate.*

Mt. Nevis Hotel/Condominiums. Standard rooms and suites at this hotel are done up with handsome white wicker furnishings, glass-top tables, and colorful island prints. Suites have full, modern kitchens and dining areas; all units have a balcony, direct-dial phone, cable TV, and VCR. The main building houses the casual restaurant and bar, which open onto the terrace, with a view that overlooks the pool and, beyond, to St. Kitts. Shuttle service is provided to the water-sports center at Newcastle Beach, replete with a boutique and outdoor restaurant-bar. The hotel also has its own ferry, which is used for moonlight cruises when it's not ferrying passengers to and from St. Kitts. *Box 494, Newcastle, tel. 809/469-9373 (collect), fax 809/469-9375. 32 rooms. Facilities: restaurant, bar, pool,water sports, beach club. AE, D, MC, V. EP, MAP. Moderate.*

Oualie Beach Hotel. Every few years this beachside spot builds a few more charming West Indian–style cottages, and there are now 22 rooms, including deluxe rooms with mahogany four-poster canopy beds and marble vanities. All rooms look across the water to stunning views of neighboring St. Kitts. The rooms are bright, airy, and simply furnished, and all have refrigerators. There is a full dive shop here offering NAUI-certified instruction, and dive packages are available. Sunfish and Windsurfers may be rented, and the hotel just introduced Skimmer waterborne rowing machines. Breakfast, lunch, and dinner are served at an informal restaurant and bar. *Oualie Beach, tel. 809/469-9735, fax 809/469-9176. 22 rooms. Facilities: restaurant, bar, beach, water-sports and dive center. MC, V. EP, MAP. Inexpensive.*

Pinney's Beach Hotel. Though these bungalows and rooms are smack on Pinney's Beach, don't expect more than just a basic room and you won't be disappointed. All rooms are air-conditioned, all have private baths, and some of the cottages are set around a garden. You'll be more comfortable in one that opens directly onto the beach. *Pinney's Beach, tel. 809/469–5207; in the U.S., 312/699–7570. 36 rooms. Facilities: 2 restaurants, 2 bars, beach, 2 tennis courts, pool. AE, MC, V. EP. Inexpensive.*

Yamseed Inn. If you want a place with its own private beach, hidden away from resort and plantation hotels, stay at this pale yellow bed-and-breakfast overlooking St. Kitts, a few minutes' drive from Newcastle Airport in the northernmost part of Nevis. Friendly innkeeper Sybil Siegfried officially opened Yamseed in January 1992 and operates it as a bed-and-breakfast. All four rooms are in her house right by the sea. *On the beach, Newcastle, tel. 809/469–9361. 4 rooms. 3-night minimum. No credit cards. BP. Inexpensive.*

Nightlife

In season, it is usually easy to find a local calypso singer or a steel or string band performing at one of the hotels on weekends. You can count on entertainment at the **Four Seasons Resort** (tel. 809/469–1111) on both Friday and Saturday nights. On Friday night the Shell All-Stars steel band entertains in the gardens at **Croney's Old Manor** (tel. 809/469–3445). The **Golden Rock** (tel. 809/469–3346) brings in David Freeman's Honeybees String Band to jazz things up for the Saturday-night buffet. You can have dinner and a dance on Wednesday nights at **Pinney's Beach Hotel** (tel. 809/469–5207).

Apart from the hotel scene, there are a few places where young locals go for late-night calypso, reggae, and other island music. **Club Trenim** (no tel.) on Government Road in Charlestown has disco dancing starting at 8:30 every night except Tuesday. **Dick's Bar** (no tel.) in Brickiln has live music or a DJ on Friday and Saturday evenings.

22 St. Lucia

Updated by
Andrew
Collins

Contrary to popular folklore, Columbus never set foot on St. Lucia; until recently, neither did most Americans. A boom in all-inclusive resort construction has suddenly drawn increasing droves of Yankees—a bit to the dismay of Brits and Europeans who've cherished this lush, oval island for decades. St. Lucia, a 238-square-mile island toward the southern end of the Windwards, has honey-colored sand beaches and fancy hotels in the north. In the south, striking natural attractions dominate: The island's twin peaks, the Pitons (Petit and Gros), rise straight out of the sea to more than 2,400 feet; a dense rain forest permeates much of the topography; and bubbling sulfur springs gurgle at the mouth of a low-lying volcano that erupted thousands of years ago and now produces highly acclaimed curative waters.

On this ruggedly beautiful island, mountains tower over lush green valleys and acres of banana plantations. Yachtsmen put in at Marigot Bay, one of the Caribbean's most beautiful secluded harbors. The diving is good, and so is the liming—the St. Lucian term for "hanging out."

St. Lucians still celebrate December 13, 1502 as Discovery Day, but historians now think the island was sighted in 1499 by Juan de la Cosa, Columbus's navigator. In any case, its true first inhabitants, the Arawaks, paddled up from South America sometime before AD 200. The warlike Caribs followed and conquered around AD 800, and were still here when the first Europeans attempted to set up camp.

In 1605, 67 English settlers bound for Guiana blew off course and landed near Vieux Fort. Within a few weeks the Caribs had killed all but 19, who escaped in a canoe. Another group of English settlers dropped by 30 years later but were met with a similar lack of hospitality. Finally, the French signed a treaty with the Caribs in 1660 and took control of the island.

Thus began a 150-year period of battles between the French and the English that saw a dizzying 14 changes in power before the British took permanent possession in 1814. During those battle-filled years, Europeans colonized the island. They developed sugar plantations, using slaves from West Africa to work the fields. By 1838, when slaves were emancipated, more than 90% of the island consisted of African descendants, and this is still largely true of today's 140,000 St. Lucians. The coal industry was begun on the island in 1883, and until about 1920, Castries, the capital, was a leading coal port in the West Indies. Sugarcane became the next major money crop, followed by bananas during the 1960s.

On February 22, 1979, St. Lucia became an independent state within the British Commonwealth of Nations, with a resident governor-general appointed by the Queen. Still, there are many relics of French occupation, notably in the island patois, the Creole cuisine, and the names of the places and the people.

With the strengthening of Britain's economic ties with the European Economic Community, the export of bananas to Britain, once a major importer, has become less secure; tourism surpassed bananas in revenue for the first time in 1993. The trend now is to diversify agriculturally, thereby reducing the need to import most fruits and vegetables and expanding St. Lucia's export base. Where tourist development is concerned, the island has seen how other Caribbean destinations overbuilt, and is now working hard to balance growth with the preservation of St. Lucia's unrivaled natural beauty.

Before You Go

Tourist Information Contact the **St. Lucia Tourist Board** (820 2nd Ave., 9th Floor, New York, NY 10017, tel. 212/867–2950 or 800/456–3984, fax 212/370–7867). In Canada: 4975 Dundas St. W, Ste. 457, Etobicoke D, Islington, Ontario M9A 4X4, tel. 416/236–0936 or 800/456–3984. In the United Kingdom: 421A Finchley Rd., London NW3 6HJ, tel. 071/431–4045.

Arriving and Departing
By Plane
There are two airports on the island. Wide-body planes use Hewanorra International Airport, on the southern tip of the island. Vigie Airport, near Castries, handles interisland and charter flights. **BWIA** (tel. 800/327–7401) has direct service from Miami and, on Sundays, New York. **American** (tel. 800/433–7300) has daily service from most major U.S. cities, with a transfer in San Juan. (**American Eagle** flights from San Juan land at Vigie Airport.) **Air Canada** (tel. 800/776–3000; in Canada, 800/268–7240) has direct weekend service from Toronto. **British Airways** (tel. 081/897–4000) has service from London to St. Lucia with a stop in Antigua on Thursdays, Saturdays, and Sundays. **LIAT's** (tel. 809/462–0701) small island-hoppers fly into Vigie Airport, linking St. Lucia with Barbados, Trinidad, Antigua, Martinique, Dominica, Guadeloupe, and other islands.

From the Airport
Taxis are unmetered, and the government's list of suggested fares is not binding. Negotiate with the driver *before* you get in, and be sure that you both understand whether you've agreed upon E.C. or U.S. dollars. The drive from Hewanorra to Castries takes about 75 minutes and costs $47.

Many guests to northern St. Lucia opt for the expensive but quick means of helicopter transportation. The cost from Castries is $90 per person, including luggage, and the flight takes 10–15 minutes. Aside from Vigie Airport, there are helipads at Pointe Seraphine, Windjammer Landing, Jalousie Plantation, and several other locations. Contact **Eastern Caribbean Helicopters** (tel. 809/453–6952) or **St. Lucia Helicopters** (tel. 809/453–6950). Both of these companies arrange sightseeing tours, too.

Passports and Visas U.S., Canadian, and British citizens must produce a driver's license or passport and a return or ongoing ticket.

Language The official language is English, but you'll also hear the local French Creole patois.

Precautions Bring along insect repellent to ward off mosquitoes and sand flies. Beware that sea urchins live among the rocks on the coastline; should one's long black spines lodge under your skin, don't try to pull them out. Apply an ammonia-based liquid and the spine will retreat, allowing you to ease it out. Manchineel trees have poisonous fruit and leaves that can cause skin blisters on contact. Even raindrops falling off the trees can cause blisters; these trees are usually marked when on hotel property. Do not swim on the rough ocean side of the island.

Staying in St. Lucia

Important Addresses **Tourist Information: St. Lucia Tourist Board** is based at the Pointe Seraphine duty-free complex on Castries Harbor (tel. 809/452–4094 or 809/452–5968). The office is open weekdays 8–4:30. There are also offices in downtown Castries (Jeremie St., tel. 809/452–2479), Soufrière (Bay St., tel. 809/459–7200), at Vigie Airport (tel. 809/452–2596), and at Hewanorra International Airport (tel. 809/454–6644).

Emergencies **Police:** Call 999. **Hospitals:** Hospitals with 24-hour emergency rooms are **Victoria Hospital** (Hospital Rd., Castries, tel. 809/452–2421) and **St. Jude's Hospital** (Vieux Fort, tel. 809/454–6041), a privately endowed hospital run by nuns, which is said to have the better equipment. **Pharmacies:** Try **Williams Pharmacy** (Williams Bldg., Bridge St., Castries, tel. 809/452–2797) or **M&C's Drugstore** (Gablewoods Mall, Gros Islet Hwy., north of Castries, tel. 809/451–7808).

Currency The official currency is the Eastern Caribbean dollar (E.C.$). Figure about E.C.$2.70 to U.S.$1. U.S. dollars are readily accepted, but you'll usually get change in E.C. dollars. Major credit cards are widely accepted, as are traveler's checks. Prices quoted here are in U.S. dollars unless indicated otherwise.

Taxes and Hotels collect an 8% government tax. The departure tax is $11 or
Service E.C.$27. Hotels and most restaurants add a 10% service charge.
Charges Taxi drivers appreciate a 10% tip.

Guided Tours **Taxi drivers** generally know the island and can give you a full tour. Expect to pay $120 for up to four people (add $20 per person thereafter) not including tip. It will take about six hours. The cost of hiring a taxi by the hour is $20.

The **Carib Touring Company** (tel. 809/452–6791) and **Sunlink International** (tel. 809/452–8232) offer a variety of half- and full-day tours. **Barnards Travel** (Micoud St., Castries, tel. 809/452–2214) also offers a full range of half- and full-day island tours, as well as excursions to Dominica, Martinique, St. Vincent, and the Grenadines. **St. Lucia Representative Services Ltd.** (tel. 809/452–3762) offers a full range of half- and full-day island tours, as well as excursions to a number of neighboring islands.

Eastern Caribbean Helicopters (tel. 809/453–6952) and **St. Lucia Helicopters** (tel. 809/453–6950) give sightseeing tours of the island.

Getting This is a cheap, though not always dependable, means of transporta-
Around tion. Minivans cruise the island and, like taxis, will stop when
Buses hailed. You can also catch a minivan in Castries at the corner of Micoud and Bridge streets.

Taxis Taxis are always available at the airport, the harbor, and in front of the major hotels, although they are expensive and do not have meters. Most hotels post the names and phone numbers of drivers and a table of fares suggested by the taxi commission. Learn the fare before you get in. The cost from Hewanorra International Airport to Castries, for example, is $47; from Vigie Airport to most resorts in the north, it's $7–$15.

Rental Cars To rent a car, you have to be 25 years or older and hold a valid driver's license. You must buy a temporary St. Lucian license at the airports or police headquarters (Bridge St., Castries); however, most resorts have their own branches of major agencies, which will obtain the temporary license for you—it costs $16. Rates begin at about $45 per day or $270 per week. Rental agencies include **Avis** (tel. 809/452–2700 or 800/331–1212), **Budget** (tel. 809/452–0233 or 800/527–0700), **National** (tel. 809/450–8721 or 800/328–4567), and **Dollar** (tel. 809/452–0994 or 800/800–4000). Driving in St. Lucia is on the left.

By Ferry The **Rodney Bay Ferry** (tel. 809/452–0203) has ferry service three times daily from Rodney Bay (right by the Lime Restaurant) to Pigeon Island ($10 per person). Service from Pointe Seraphine to Castries (when cruise ships are in port) was added in 1994.

Telephones, Electricity, and Mail To call St. Lucia from the United States, dial area code 809, access code 45, and the local five-digit number. You can make direct-dial long-distance calls from the island, and the connections are excellent. To place interisland calls, dial the local five-digit number.

Electric voltage is 220/240 AC, 50 cycles. American appliances require an adaptor.

Postage for airmail letters to the United States and Canada is E.C.$1 and to Great Britain up to one ounce; postcards are E.C.75¢ and E.C.85¢, respectively.

Opening and Closing Times Shops are open weekdays 8–4, Saturday 8–noon. Banks are open Monday–Thursday 8–3, Friday 8–5, and, at a few branches in Rodney Bay, Saturdays 9–noon.

Exploring St. Lucia

Numbers in the margin correspond to points of interest on the St. Lucia map.

Castries **Castries,** on the northwest coast, is a busy commercial city of about **①** 60,000. Though the city itself is not especially picturesque, it lies in a sheltered bay surrounded dramatically by green Morne Fortune. Ships carrying bananas, coconut, cocoa, mace, nutmeg, and citrus fruits for export leave from **Castries Harbour,** one of the busiest ports in the Caribbean.

Cruise ships dock across the harbor at **Pointe Seraphine,** about a 20-minute walk or short cab ride from the city center—or you can take the shuttle boat, available when ships are in port. Spanish-style Pointe Seraphine has 23 mostly upscale duty-free shops, a tourist information center where you can get island maps, and a taxi stand. This is the starting point for many of the island tours.

Morne Fortune (the Hill of Good Luck) has had more than its share of bad luck over the years, including devastating hurricanes and four fires. As a result, Castries lacks the colorful colonial architecture found in other island capitals. It is stark, modern, and has only a few sights of historical note.

Head first to **Derek Walcott Square,** a green oasis ringed by Brazil, Laborie, Micoud, and Bourbon streets. Formerly Columbus Square, it was renamed in 1993 after Nobel poet and St. Lucian son Derek Walcott—one of two Nobel laureates from the island, the other being the late economist Sir Arthur Lewis. At the corner of Laborie and Micoud streets there is a 400-year-old saman tree. A favorite local story is of the English botanist who came to St. Lucia many years ago to catalogue the flora. Awestruck by this huge old tree, she asked a passerby what it was. "Massav," he replied, and she gratefully jotted that down in her notebook, unaware that "massav" is patois for "I don't know." Directly across the street is the Roman Catholic **Cathedral of the Immaculate Conception,** which was built in 1897. Some of the 19th-century buildings that managed to survive fire, winds, and rains can be seen on Brazil Street, the southern border of the square.

Time Out In the courtyard of the Victorian building that houses Rain restaurant (*see* Dining, *below*), the **Pizza Park** (Derek Walcott Sq., tel. 809/452–3022) sells takeout or eat-in pizza all day.

Head north on Laborie Street and walk past the government buildings on your right. On the left, William Peter Boulevard is one of

Castries's shopping areas. "The Boulevard" connects Laborie Street with Bridge Street, which is another shopping street. The shopping here is of mostly local appeal, however; die-hard shoppers will be happier at Pointe Seraphine.

Continue north for one more block on Laborie Street and you'll come to Jeremie Street. Turn right, and head a few blocks to the **market** on the corner of Jeremie and Peynier streets. This dusty, bustling all-day affair is most crowded on Saturday mornings, when farmers bring their produce to town.

Elsewhere on the Island

Morne Fortune

To reach **Morne Fortune,** head due south on Bridge Street, turning right onto Government House Road. The drive will take you past the **Government House,** the official residence of the governor-general of St. Lucia and one of the island's few remaining examples of Victorian architecture.

Driving up the Hill of Good Fortune, you'll see some of the Caribbean's most beautiful tropical plants—frangipani, lilies, bougainvillea, hibiscus, and oleander—along the road. From the top of the hill, at **Fort Charlotte,** you'll see Martinique to the north and the twin peaks of the Pitons to the south.

Fort Charlotte was begun in 1764 by the French as the *Citadelle du Morne Fortune.* It was completed after 20 years of battling and changing hands. Its old barracks and batteries have now been converted to government buildings and local educational facilities, but you can drive around and look at the remains, including redoubts, a guard room, stables, and cells. At the end of the road you can also walk up to the Inniskilling Monument, a tribute to one of the most famous battles, fought in 1796, when the 27th Foot Royal Inniskilling Fusiliers wrested the Hill of Good Fortune from the French. Stop also in the Military Cemetery, which was first used in 1782; faint inscriptions on the tombstones tell the tales of the French and English soldiers who died here. Six former governors of the island are buried here as well.

South of Castries

The road from Castries to Soufrière travels through beautiful country. The entire West Coast road has been undergoing a widening face-lift since 1992. As of 1995, it should be complete through Soufrière, but may be fully or partially closed to Vieux Fort. Be sure to check on the road's status before you set out anywhere on the west coast. And remember, you'll be handling a right-hand drive vehicle on the left side of a sharply curving road. It takes about three hours to drive the whole loop from Castries down the west coast, back up the east coast, and across the Barre de L'Isle Ridge—and that's with ideal conditions and no stops.

A few miles south of Castries, stop by **Marigot Bay,** one of the most beautiful natural harbors in the Caribbean. In 1778, British Admiral Samuel Barrington took his ships into this secluded bay within a bay and covered them with palm fronds to hide them from the French. The resort community today is a great favorite of yachtspeople. Parts of *Dr. Doolittle* were filmed here 30 years ago. You can arrange to charter a yacht, swim, snorkel, or lime with the yachting crowd at one of the bars. A 24-hour water taxi connects the various points on the bay.

Time Out

Stop for rum punch, lunch, and atmosphere at the **Rusty Anchor** (Hurricane Hotel, tel. 809/453–4230), a happy haunt of boaters.

If you continue south, you'll be in the vicinity of one of the island's two rum distilleries. Major production of sugar ceased here in

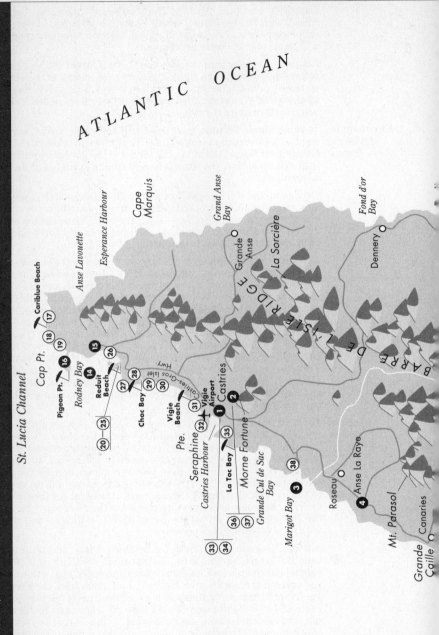

ATLANTIC OCEAN

Cape Marquis

Grand Anse Bay

Fond d'or Bay

Esperance Harbour

Anse Lavouette

Grande Anse

La Sorcière

Dennery

Cariblue Beach

⑰

⑱

⑲

Cap Pt.

Pigeon Pt. ⑯

⑮ ㉖

⑭

St. Lucia Channel

Rodney Bay

Reduit Beach

㉗ ㉘

⑳—㉕

Choc Bay

㉙ ㉚

Castries-Gros Islet Hwy.

BARRE DE L'ISLE RIDGE

Castries ①

㉛

Vigie Beach

Pte.

Vigie Airport

②

㉜

㉟

Morne Fortune

Seraphine

Castries Harbour

㉝ ㉞

La Toc Bay

㊱ ㊲

Grande Cul de Sac Bay

㊳

③

Marigot Bay

Roseau

Anse La Raye

④

Mt. Parasol

Grande Caille

Canaries

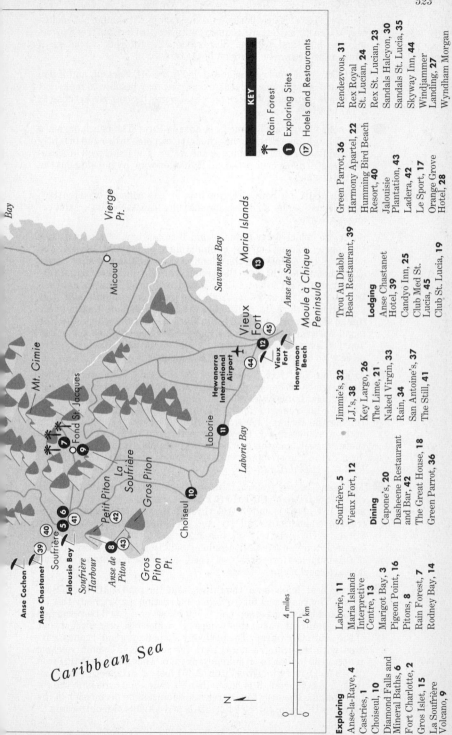

KEY

* Rain Forest

✳ Exploring Sites

① Hotels and Restaurants

Bay

Vierge Pt.

Micoud

Mt. Cimie

Fond St. Jacques

Savannes Bay

Maria Islands

13

Vieux Fort

Anse de Sables

Moule à Chique Peninsula

45

44

12

Hewanorra International Airport

Vieux Fort

Honeymoon Beach

Laborie

11

Laborie Bay

Soufrière

La Soufrière

Petit Piton

Gros Piton

Choiseul

10

5 6

41

40

39

8 43

42

Anse de Piton

Gros Piton Pt.

Anse Cochon

Anse Chastanet

Soufrière Bay

Jalousie Bay

Soufrière Harbour

7

9

Caribbean Sea

N

0   4 miles

0   6 km

Exploring
Anse-la-Raye, **4**
Castries, **1**
Choiseul, **10**
Diamond Falls and
Mineral Baths, **6**
Fort Charlotte, **2**
Gros Islet, **15**
La Soufrière
Volcano, **9**

Laborie, **11**
Maria Islands
Interpretive
Centre, **13**
Marigot Bay, **3**
Pigeon Point, **16**
Pitons, **8**
Rain Forest, **7**
Rodney Bay, **14**

Soufrière, **5**
Vieux Fort, **12**

Dining
Capone's, **20**
Dasheene Restaurant
and Bar, **42**
The Great House, **18**
Green Parrot, **36**

Jimmie's, **32**
J.J.'s, **38**
Key Largo, **26**
The Lime, **21**
Naked Virgin, **33**
Rain, **34**
San Antoine's, **37**
The Still, **41**

Trou Au Diable
Beach Restaurant, **39**

Lodging
Anse Chastanet
Hotel, **39**
Candyo Inn, **25**
Club Med St.
Lucia, **45**
Club St. Lucia, **19**

Green Parrot, **36**
Harmony Apartel, **22**
Humming Bird Beach
Resort, **40**
Jalouisie
Plantation, **43**
Ladera, **42**
Le Sport, **17**
Orange Grove
Hotel, **28**

Rendezvous, **31**
Rex Royal
St. Lucian, **24**
Rex St. Lucian, **23**
Sandals Halcyon, **30**
Sandals St. Lucia, **35**
Skyway Inn, **44**
Windjammer
Landing, **27**
Wyndham Morgan

around 1960, and distilleries now make rum with imported molasses. You're still in banana country, with acres of banana trees covering the hills and valleys. More than 127 different varieties of bananas are grown on the island.

In the mountainous region ahead you'll see **Mt. Parasol,** and if you look hard enough through the mists, you may be able to make out **Mt. Gimie** (pronounced "Jimmy"), St. Lucia's highest peak, rising to 3,117 feet.

❹ The next village you'll come to is **Anse-la-Raye.** The beach here is a colorful sight, with fishing nets hanging on poles to dry and brightly painted fishing boats bobbing in the water. The fishermen of Anse-la-Raye still make canoes the old-fashioned way, by burning out the center of a log.

Soufrière As you approach **Soufrière,** you'll be in the island's breadbasket, **❺** where most of the mangoes, breadfruit, tomatoes, limes, and oranges are grown.

Soufrière, which dates from the mid-18th century, was named after the nearby volcano and has a population of about 9,000 people. The harbor is the deepest on the island, accommodating smaller cruise ships that nose right up to the wharf. A nearby jetty contains an excellent small-crafts center. The **Soufrière Tourist Information Centre** (Bay St., tel. 809/459–7200) provides information about area attractions, which, in addition to the Pitons, include La Soufrière (billed as the world's only drive-in volcano), sulfur springs, the Diamond Mineral Baths, and the rain forest. You can also ask at the Tourist Centre about Soufrière Estate, on the east side of town, replete with botanical gardens and a minizoo.

❻ Adjoining Soufrière Estate are the **Diamond Falls and Mineral Baths,** which are fed by an underground flow of water from the sulfur springs. Louis XVI provided funds for the construction of these baths for his troops to "fortify them against the St. Lucian climate." During the Brigand's War, just after the French Revolution, the baths were destroyed. They were restored in 1966, and you can see the waterfalls and the gardens before slipping into your swimsuit for a dip in the steaming curative waters. *Soufrière. Admission: E.C.$5. Open daily 10–5.*

❼ The island's dense tropical **rain forest** is most easily accessible to the east of Soufrière on the road to Fond St. Jacques. It actually covers about 10% of the island. A trek through the lush landscape can take from three hours to a full day, and you'll need a guide (contact the Forestry Division, tel. 809/452–3231) and plenty of stamina. Mt. Gimie, Piton Canaries, Mt. Houlom, and Piton Tromasse are all part of this immense forest reserve. The views of the mountains and valleys are spectacular.

❽ For the best land view of the **Pitons,** take the road south out of Soufrière. The road is awful (though construction may remedy this by 1995) and leads up a steep hill; if you persevere, you'll be rewarded by a magnificent look at the twin peaks, which rise precipitously out of the azure Caribbean. The perfectly shaped pyramidal cones, covered with tropical greenery, were formed of lava from a volcanic eruption 30 million to 40 million years ago. The tallest is Petit Piton (2,619 feet); its twin, Gros Piton (2,461 feet) is so named because although it is shorter, it is fatter than its twin. You can climb the Pitons, but it's one very tough trek and requires the permission of the Forestry Division (tel. 809/452–3231) and a knowledgeable guide.

9 To the south of Soufrière, your nose will note the left turn that takes you to **La Soufrière,** the drive-in volcano, and its **sulfur springs.** Here are more than 20 pools of black, belching, smelly sulfurous waters and yellow-green sulfur baking and steaming. Though the sign announces that this is the world's only drive-in volcano, it is not; moreover, it is not strictly a volcano, but a fault in the substratum rock. This is an interesting, but hardly thrilling, stop. It won't take more than 20 minutes, and a tour is included in admission. *La Soufrière. Admission: E.C.$3. Open daily 9–5.*

10 Follow the road farther south and you'll come next to the coastal town of **Choiseul,** home to wood-carving and pottery shops. At the turn of the road past the Anglican Church, built in 1846, a bridge crosses the river Dorée, so named because the riverbed is blanketed with fool's gold. In La Fargue, just to the south, the **Choiseul Art & Craft Centre** (tel. 809/459–3226) sells superb traditional Carib handicrafts, including pottery, wickerwork, and braided khuskhus grass mats and baskets.

11 The next stop is **Laborie,** the prototypical St. Lucian fishing village, little changed over the centuries. There's not much to see here, but you can stop to buy some local bread and fresh fish.

12 Now drive along the southern coast of the island to **Vieux Fort,** St. Lucia's second-largest city and home of the Hewanorra International Airport. Drive out on the **Moule à Chique Peninsula,** the southernmost tip of the island. From here you can see all of St. Lucia to the north and St. Vincent 21 miles south. Looking straight down, you can see where the clear waters of the Caribbean blend with the bluer Atlantic waters.

Time Out | **Chak Chak** (Beanfield Rd., Vieux Fort, tel. 809/454–6260) is a casual, airy restaurant that serves Creole dishes.

13 The **Maria Islands Nature Reserve,** which has its own interpretive center, consists of two tiny islands in the Atlantic off the southeast coast. The 25-acre Maria Major and its little sister, 4-acre Maria Minor, are inhabited by rare species of lizards and snakes that share their home with frigate birds, terns, doves, and other wildlife. *Moule à Chique, tel. 809/454–5014. Admission: Wed.–Sat. E.C.$3, Sun. E.C.$.50. Open Wed.–Sun. 9:30–5.*

A good road leads from Vieux Fort through the towns on the Atlantic coast. The road will take you past **Honeymoon Beach,** a wide, grassy, flat Anse l'Islet peninsula jutting into the ocean. Drive through Micoud and, a few miles farther north, Dennery, both of which are residential towns overlooking the Atlantic. At Dennery the road turns west and climbs across the Barre de l'Isle Ridge, through the northern tip of St. Lucia's rain forest with its dense vegetation. There are trails along the way that lead to lookout points where you can get a view of the entire National Forest Preserve, to the south. This bumpy road leads back to Castries.

The North End and Gros Islet The west coast north of Castries is the most developed part of the island and is easy and safe to navigate. Take the John Compton Highway north toward the Vigie Airport. This whole stretch is of far more interest to the hedonist than to the historian, but it features some of the island's best beaches and resort hotels.

14 About 15 minutes north of Castries, **Rodney Bay,** named after Admiral Rodney, is an 80-acre man-made lagoon packed with hotels, restaurants, and tourists—the bulk of them European. The Rex St. Lucian Hotel and Rex Royal St. Lucian are in this area, as are

Capone's, Lime, and several other popular eateries. North of the lagoon, **Gros Islet** is a quiet little fishing village not unlike Anse-la-Raye to the south. But on Friday nights, Gros Islet springs to life with a wild and raucous street festival to which everyone is invited (*see* Nightlife, *below*).

Pigeon Point **Pigeon Point,** jutting out on the northwest coast, was Pigeon Island until a causeway was built several years back, connecting it to the mainland. Tales are told of the pirate Jambe de Bois (Wooden Leg), who used to hide out here. This 40-acre hilltop island, a strategic point during the struggles for control of the island, is now a national park, with long sandy beaches, calm waters for swimming, and areas for picnicking. On the grounds you'll see ruins of barracks, batteries, and garrisons dating from the French and English battles. *Pigeon Point, no tel. Admission: E.C.$3. Guided tours cost E.C.$10. Open Mon.–Sat. 9–4.*

Off the Beaten Track

If you want a close-up of a working banana plantation and are willing to get a little wet and muddy in the process, you can tour the island's largest—the **Marquis Plantation. St. Lucia Representative Services Ltd.** (*see* Guided Tours, *above*) will pick you up at your hotel in an air-conditioned bus. Wear your most casual clothes, and be prepared to rough it.

Beaches

Beaches are all public, and many are flanked by hotels, where you can rent water-sports equipment and have a rum punch. On the other hand, some are difficult to reach because they abut resort property. There are also secluded beaches, accessible only by water, to which hotels can arrange boat trips. Don't swim along the windward (east) coast; the Atlantic waters are rough and sometimes dangerous.

Pigeon Point, part of the Pigeon Island National Historic Park (admission E.C.$3), has a long white-sand beach and a small restaurant; it's great for picnicking and swimming.

Reduit Beach is a long stretch of beige sand facing Rodney Bay and is home to the Rex St. Lucian and Rex Royal St. Lucian hotels, which offer numerous water sports.

Anse Cochon, an uncrowded cove south of Anse-la-Raye, is a black-sand beach most easily reached by boat. The waters are superb for swimming and snorkeling.

Anse Chastanet is a gray-sand beach just north of Soufrière with a backdrop of green hills and the island's best reefs for snorkeling and diving. The wooden gazebos of the Anse Chastanet Hotel are nestled among the palms, with a dive shop and bar on the beach (*see* Dining and Lodging, *below*).

Black-sand **Anse des Pitons,** south of Soufrière in Jalousie Bay, sits directly between the Pitons and is accessible through Jalousie Plantation (*see* Lodging, *below*) or by boat; it offers great snorkeling and diving.

Vieux Fort, at the southernmost tip of St. Lucia, has a long secluded stretch of white sand and waters protected by reefs. **Honeymoon Beach,** just west of Vieux Fort, is another sandy escape.

Sports and the Outdoors

Most hotels offer Sunfish, water skis, fins, masks, and other water-sports equipment free to guests and for a fee to nonguests.

Boating Cat Inc. (Castries, tel. 809/450–8651) takes revelers on a journey along the Caribbean coast aboard the 56-foot-long catamarans *Endless Summer I* and *II*. Bare-boat or skippered yacht charters are available through **Sunsail Stevens** (Castries, tel. 809/452–8648), which has a fleet of 39- to 56-foot sailing yachts; **Trade Wind Yacht Charters** (Rodney Bay, tel. 809/452–8424); and the **Moorings Yacht Charter** (Marigot Bay, tel. 809/451–4256 or 800/535–7289).

Deep-Sea Fishing Among the sea creatures in these waters are dolphin, Spanish mackerel, barracuda, and white marlin. Contact **Captain Mike's** (tel. 809/452–7044) or **Mako Watersports** (tel. 809/452–0412) to steer you in the right direction.

Fitness Centers If your resort lacks the kind of equipment you'd expect for what you're paying—and many do—try the **St. Lucia Racquet Club** (Cap Estate, tel. 809/450–0551), which has Nautilus equipment, exercise machines, aerobics and step aerobics, and professional instruction. It's the best gym on the island. Day-passes are also available to **Jalousie Plantation** (Sourfrière, tel. 809/459–7666) and **Le Sport** (Cap Estate, tel. 809/452–8551), which have excellent facilities.

Golf There are 9-hole courses at **Sandals St. Lucia** (tel. 809/452–3081) and **Cap Estate Golf Club** (tel. 809/452–8523). A caddy is required at the former; greens fees are $15–$20 at either for 18 holes. Club rentals are another $10. These courses are scenic and good fun, but they're not of professional caliber.

Hiking The island is laced with trails, but you should not attempt the challenging peaks on your own. Your hotel, the tourist board, or the **Forestry Division** (tel. 809/452–3231) can provide you with a guide. **The St. Lucia National Trust** (tel. 809/452–5005), established to preserve the island's natural and cultural heritage, tours several sites, including Pigeon Island, the Maria Islands, and Fregate Island.

Horseback Riding For trail rides on the beach, contact **Trim's Riding School** (Gros Islet, tel. 809/452–8273), **North Point Riding Stables** (tel. 809/450–8853), or **Jalousie Plantation** (tel. 809/459–7666).

Jogging You can jog on the beach by yourself or team up with the **Roadbusters** (tel. Jimmy at 809/452–5142 or evenings at 809/452–4790).

Parasailing Contact the **Rex St. Lucian hotel** (tel. 809/452–8351).

Scuba Diving **Scuba St. Lucia** (tel. 809/459–7355) is a PADI five-star training facility, with dive shops at Anse Chastanet and the Rex St. Lucian Hotel, that offers daily beach and boat dives, resort courses, underwater photography, and day trips. Trips are also arranged through **Buddies Scuba** (tel. 809/452–5288), **Dive Jalousie** (tel. 809/459–7666), the **Moorings Scuba Centre** (tel. 809/451–4357), and **Windjammer Diving** (tel. 809/452–0913)

Sea and Snorkeling Excursions The 140-foot square-rigger *Brig Unicorn* (tel. 809/452–6811) sails to Soufrière, with steel bands, a swim stop, rum punch, and soda. **Captain Mike's** (tel. 809/452–0216) does swimming and snorkeling cruises. Sea and snorkeling excursions can also be arranged through **Mako Watersports** (tel. 809/452–0412) and the **Surf Queen** (tel. 809/452–8351, ext. 515) or through your hotel.

Squash The **St. Lucia Racquet Club** (adjacent Club St. Lucia, tel. 809/450–0551) has one court and its own pro, who gives lessons and clinics. It is not air-conditioned, however. **Jalousie Plantation** (tel. 809/459–7666) also has a squash court open to nonguests.

Tennis All the major hotels have their own tennis courts, but many restrict use to their own guests. The **St. Lucia Racquet Club** (adjacent Club St. Lucia, tel. 809/450–0551) opened in 1991 and is one of the top tennis facilities in the Caribbean—probably the best in the Lesser Antilles. Apart from hosting many tour events, its seven floodlit courts are in perfect shape, the pro shop is extensive, and the staff knowledgeable. **Jalousie Plantation** (tel. 809/459–7666) has four lighted courts open to nonguests.

Waterskiing Contact **Mako Watersports** (tel. 809/452–0412). Rentals are also available at most of the hotels.

Windsurfing The **Rex St. Lucian hotel** is the local agent for Mistral Windsurfers (tel. 809/452–8351). Also contact **Marigot Bay Resort** (tel. 809/453–4357) and **Mako Watersports** (tel. 809/452–0412). Most hotels rent Windsurfers to nonguests.

Spectator Sports Cricket and soccer, the two national pastimes, are played at **Mindoo Philip Park** in Marchand, 2 miles east of Castries. **The St. Lucia Racquet Club** (tel. 809/450–0551), which hosted the Davis Cup in 1994, is the frequent site of major and regional **tennis** events.

Contact the tourist board (tel. 809/452–4094) for specific information regarding schedules.

Shopping

Shopping on St. Lucia has been traditionally low-key, but as tourism is increasing, so are the options for shopping. The island's best-known products are the unique hand-silk-screened and hand-printed designs of Bagshaw Studios, which are designed, printed, and sold only on St. Lucia. The island is also home to Windjammer Clothing, which is sold on virtually every Caribbean island. Apart from those indigenous products, there are native-made wood carvings, pottery, and straw hats and baskets.

Shopping Areas For a duty-free spree, visit **Pointe Seraphine,** a Spanish-style complex by the harbor, where 23 shops sell designer perfumes, china and crystal, jewelry, watches, leather goods, liquor, and cigarettes. Native crafts are also sold in the shopping center. Though Castries has a number of shops, mostly on **Bridge Street** and **William Peter Boulevard,** selling locally made souvenirs, you can find the same items at the crafts stands and shopping arcades at virtually every resort; the **Rex St. Lucian hotel** has one of the best selections. **Gablewoods Mall** (Gros Islet Hwy., north of Castries), which opened in 1993, has about 25 shops selling groceries, spirits and wines, jewelry, clothing, local crafts, foreign newspapers, books, music, and household goods.

Good Buys Duty-Free In Pointe Seraphine, look for designer perfumes at **Images** (tel. 809/452–6883). **Little Switzerland** (tel. 809/452–7587) carries fine china and crystal. **A Touch of Class** (tel. 809/452–7443) is the place for Caribbean literature and local souvenirs. Leather handbags, jewelry, crystal, and perfumes can be found at **Meli's Boutique** (tel. 809/452–7587). Be sure to bring your passport and airline ticket to get duty-free prices.

Fabrics and Clothing Bagshaw's silkscreened fabrics and clothing can be found at their studio at La Toc Bay and their shop at Pointe Seraphine. **Windjam-**

mer Clothing Company (tel. 809/452–1041) has its main store at Vigie Cove and an outlet at Pointe Seraphine. **Caribelle Batik** (Old Victoria Rd., the Morne, Castries, tel. 809/452–3785) creates batik clothing and wall hangings. Visitors are welcome to watch the craftspeople at work. **The Batik Studio** at Humming Bird Beach Resort (Soufrière, tel. 809/459–7232) offers superb sarongs, scarves, and wall panels.

Native Crafts Trays, masks, and figures are carved from mahogany, red cedar, and eucalyptus trees in the studio adjacent to **Eudovic Art Studio** (Morne Fortune, tel. 809/452–2747). Hammocks, straw mats, baskets and hats, and carvings, as well as books and maps of St. Lucia, are at **Noah's Arkade** (Jeremie St., Castries, and Pointe Seraphine, tel. 809/452–2523). **Artsibit** (corner Brazil and Mongiraud Sts., tel. 809/452–7865) features works by top St. Lucian artists.

Dining

If you stop by the Castries market (*see* Exploring St. Lucia, *above*) on a Saturday, you'll see the riches produced in this fertile volcanic soil. Mangoes, plantains, breadfruits, limes, pumpkins, cucumbers, pawpaws (pronounced *poh-poh* here, known as papaya elsewhere), yams, christophines (a green vegetable), and coconuts are among the fruits and vegetables that appear on menus throughout the island. Every menu lists the catch of the day (most often flying fish), along with the ever-popular lobster. Chicken, pork, and barbecues are also big-time here. Most of the meats are imported—beef from Argentina and Iowa, lamb from New Zealand. The French influence is strong in St. Lucian restaurants, and most chefs cook with a Creole flair, pre–nouvelle cuisine. **Gablewoods Mall** (*see* Shopping, *above*) has a food court selling Mexican, Caribbean, Southeast Asian, Californian, and Italian meals.

Category	Cost*
Very Expensive	over $40
Expensive	$25–$40
Moderate	$15–$25
Inexpensive	under $15

**per person, excluding drinks and service*

★ **Dasheene Restaurant and Bar.** Part of the fanciful Ladera resort (*see* Lodging, *below*), Dasheene is a small, casual mountaintop retreat with breathtaking views of the Pitons and the clear Caribbean sea between them. This is some of the best food in St. Lucia and definitely the most creatively presented. The menu changes often but centers on Caribbean specialties with New American and Continental accents: Smoked kingfish wrapped in crepes makes a nice appetizer, and the spicy seafood gazpacho will make your mouth water, if not your eyes. A tender tuna steak might come swimming in a delicate coconut-avocado cream sauce; chicken breast comes in a mango sauce some nights, a pecan-and-peanut sauce on others. For dessert, the chocolate crème brûlée flambé takes about five minutes to cool down but is well worth the wait. There's live entertainment many nights and soft, jazzy tunes playing otherwise. This is the stuff of wedding anniversaries and very special occasions. *Soufrière, tel. 809/454–7323. Reservations advised. Dress: casual. AE, MC, V. Very Expensive.*

The Great House. Perched on a hill overlooking Anse Becune Bay and Martinique in the distance, this romantic spot is run by the owners of Club St. Lucia and is thus very popular with guests of that resort. The menu changes often, but for starters you might try the warm goat cheese on a bed of greens or pumpkin soup with glazed leeks. The better entrées utilize St. Lucia's local offerings: baked red snapper in a chive sauce, Antillean shrimp sautéed in a garlic-and-parsley butter, or curried goat. The food is good, but you really come here to enjoy the view and elegant setting. *Cap Estate, tel. 809/450-0450 or 809/450-0211. Reservations advised. Jacket advised. AE, DC, MC, V. No lunch. Very Expensive.*

San Antoine's. High on the Morne, with splendid views of Castries below and Martinique in the distance, this restored historic building was originally the great house of the San Antoine Hotel, built in the late 1800s and destroyed by fire in 1970. This is one of the most elegantly appointed restaurants in the Caribbean, although the food doesn't always match the service and decor. The streamlined menu features such classic standouts as *escargot en brioche* and *filet au poivre.* All in all, it's a memorable experience. *Morne Fortune, tel. 809/452-4660. Reservations suggested. Jacket recommended. AE, MC, V. Closed Sun. Very Expensive.*

Green Parrot. The Green Parrot comes complete with sommelier and crisp napery. The Continental menu includes poached fish fillet with mushroom cream and white-wine sauce glaze; *tournedos cordon rouge* (steak fillet topped with foie gras and Madeira sauce); and *escalope de volaille Viennese* (chicken breast grilled and served with mushrooms). There is lively entertainment on Wednesday and Saturday nights, with limbo and belly dancers, but the best reason for dining here is the view over Castries and the harbor. It rivals a similar view from the more expensive San Antoine's restaurant. *Red Tape La., Morne Fortune, tel. 809/452-3399. Reservations essential. Jacket recommended. AE, MC, V. Expensive.*

★ **Capone's.** The gang here does a skillful job of blending the tropics, the Jazz Age, and art deco touches. There are black-and-white tile floors, a polished wood bar, and a player piano. Waiters and waitresses dressed like gangsters serve rum drinks called Valentine's Day Massacre and Mafia Mai Tai and bring your check in a violin case. The pasta is fresh, and the meat dishes include *osso buco alla Milanese* (veal knuckle) and chicken rotisserie. The **Pizza Parlour** (open from 11 AM–midnight) turns out burgers and sandwiches, as well as pizza. The management also runs **Sweet Dreams** across the street, with more than 150 tempting dessert options. *Rodney Bay, across from the Rex St. Lucian Hotel, tel. 809/452-0284. Reservations advised. AE, MC, V. No lunch; closed Mon. Moderate–Expensive.*

Jimmie's. The bar here is a popular meeting place, and the restaurant is a romantic spot for dinner. Specialties include Madras fish, seafood risotto, and a lip-smacking saltfish and green fig (the national dish—and an acquired taste). There's also a wide choice of seafood, meat, chicken, and vegetable dishes. *Vigie Cove, Castries, tel. 809/452-5142. No reservations. AE, MC, V. Moderate–Expensive.*

Naked Virgin. Tucked away in the quiet Castries suburb of Marchand (just opposite the local post office—keep asking), this pleasant hangout offers terrific Creole cuisine—and every guest leaves with a free T-shirt. The owner, Mr. Paul John, has worked in many of the island's major hotels and his concoction, the Naked Virgin, could be the best punch you've ever tasted. Shrimp Creole and fried flying fish are highly recommended. *Marchand Rd., tel. 809/*

452–5594. Reservations advised. AE, MC, V. Moderate–Expensive.

★ **Rain.** This restaurant is in a Victorian building, and the balcony overlooking Derek Walcott Square is a favored spot. It's usually crowded and the tables are a tad too close together, but you can still soak up the atmosphere, especially after a few Downpours—their knockout tropical punches and frozen concoctions. Lunchtime offerings include Creole soup, *crabe farcie,* rainburgers, quiches, and salads; Creole chicken is a specialty. At night, the "Champagne Buffet of 1885" is a lavish but moderately priced seven-course feast. For dessert there's old-fashioned, hand-cranked ice cream. You can browse in the downstairs boutique. *Derek Walcott Sq., Castries, tel. 809/452–3022. Reservations advised. AE, MC, V. Moderate–Expensive.*

★ **The Lime.** Across the street from Capone's, the Lime is a favorite place for "liming," or hanging out. A casual place with lime-colored gingham curtains, straw hats decorating the ceiling, and hanging plants, it offers a businessman's three-course lunch. Starters may include homemade pâté or stuffed crab back. Entrée choices may be medallions of pork fillet with the chef's special orange-and-ginger sauce, stewed lamb, or fish fillet poached in white wine and mushroom sauce. The prices are more reasonable than neighboring Capone's, which is perhaps why the ex-patriates and locals gather here in the evenings. *Rodney Bay, tel. 809/452–0761. Reservations advised for dinner. MC, V. Closed Tues. Moderate.*

The Still. For visitors to Diamond Falls, lunching at the Still is not so much an option as it is an inevitability. This mammoth hall seats up to 400 and is popular with tour groups and cruise passengers. The emphasis is on local foods—christophines, breadfruits, yams, and callaloo, as well as seafood, pork chops, and beef dishes. *Soufrière, tel. 809/454–7224. Reservations suggested. MC, V. No dinner. Moderate.*

★ **Trou Au Diable Beach Restaurant.** This beachside open-air lunch spot at the Anse Chastanet resort (*see* Lodging, *below*) is the perfect place to break from a day of diving or sunbathing. The West Indian cuisine is delicious, and many specialties are prepared right before your eyes on a barbecue grill. The rotis (Caribbean-style burritos) here are mouth-watering, served with a sweet side of mango chutney. Try also the chicken or beef satays served in a peanut sauce; the island pepper pot—pork, beef, or lamb simmered in a medley of local veggies and spices; or a good old tuna melt in case you're homesick. Dessert always features an unusual flavor of ice cream, maybe soursop or anise seed; try it! There's always a young and lively crowd here, and although the restaurant caters mostly to the resort's guests, everyone is quite welcome. *Anse Chastanet, Soufrière, tel. 809/459–7000. Reservations not necessary. Dress: casual. AE, DC, MC, V. No dinner. Moderate.*

Key Largo. Brick-oven gourmet pizzas that recall California more than they do Italy are the specialty at this casual eatery across the lagoon from Rodney Bay's many hotels. You're welcome simply to stop in for an espresso or cappuccino, but the popular Pizza Key Largo—topped with shrimp, artichokes, and what seems like a few pounds of mozzarella—is tough to pass up. *Rodney Bay, tel. 809/452–0282. Reservations not necessary. Dress: casual. MC, V. Inexpensive–Moderate.*

J.J.'s. Not only are the prices right here, but the food is some of the best on the island. Superbly grilled fish with fresh vegetables is tops. Tables are on a terrace above the road, and the welcome is friendly and casual. On Friday nights the music blares, and the locals come for liming and dancing in the street. *Marigot Bay Rd. (3*

*mi before the bay), Marigot, tel. 809/453–4076. No reservations. No
credit cards. Inexpensive.*

Lodging

St. Lucia is beginning to rival Jamaica in the number of all-inclusives
and large resorts dotting the island. Sandals opened two couples-
only compounds here in 1993 and 1994, respectively. Wyndham's all-
inclusive debuted in 1992, Anse Chastanet added a small resort to its
25-year-old property in 1994, and Jalousie Plantation and Ladera
opened between the Pitons in 1992. Additionally, a few small and inexpensive lodgings have popped up around Rodney Bay—offering
bright, clean modern suites at bargain prices. Virtually all of the development, except Club Med in Vieux Fort, is along the calm Caribbean coast—either around Soufrière to the south or from Castries
to Cap Estate in the north.

Fortunately, there is not a glut of resorts or hotels in any one price
range or catering to any one type of tourist. You'll find some that
draw principally Europeans, others Americans. Some are lavish,
others laid-back and less costly. Some have all-inclusive meal plans;
just as many are MAP or EP. And many cater to honeymooners: St.
Lucian law requires residence for only three days for couples to ac-
quire a marriage license.

Just about every resort has friendly, accommodating service and is
located in a fairly secluded cove or along an unspoiled beach. Keep in
mind that the all-inclusives in this section will save each guest from
$50 to $100 daily on meals and drinks, meaning, for example, that a
one-week stay at Le Sport—listed below as Very Expensive—may
actually cost you less than a week at the Rex Royal St. Lucian or at
Windjammer Landing—which are priced in lower categories because they don't cover meals. Also, consider spending the final night
or two of your stay at one of the lodgings in Soufrière—about 35 minutes from Hewanorra International Airport—or at the new Skyway
Inn—just across the street from the airport. The foremost complaint of visitors to St. Lucia is the 60- to 90-minute topsy-turvy
sickness-inducing drive from their hotel to Hewanorra; it pays to
break up the long drive in any way possible. For winter, reserve at
least four months in advance.

Highly recommended lodgings are indicated by a star ★.

Category	Cost*
Very Expensive	over $350
Expensive	$200–$350
Moderate	$125–$200
Inexpensive	under $125

**All prices are for a standard double room for two, excluding 8% tax
and 10% service charge.*

Hotels **Jalousie Plantation.** This fancy all-inclusive resort opened in late
1992 and has suffered some under the harsh glare of controversy.
Some of the early criticism about disorganization was probably fair,
but a new general manager took over in 1993, and the staff now
seems professional, friendly, and quite together. Building a resort
in this dramatic setting, between the Pitons, angered some locals
who felt this land should never have been developed—but you can't

not love this location. Brown wood cottages tumble down the steep hillside to a small bay, and tropical gardens lead down from the main buildings, with restaurants and lounges, to the oval pool, water-sports facilities, and gray-sand beach. People-movers shuttle guests around the resort. Public areas are designed and decorated with the formality of a palazzo, the cottages crowd together a bit, and the smaller of the two types of plunge pools is lilliputian. But otherwise, this is everything you would expect from a luxury resort: Larger cottages have an extra shower and a large sitting area; all rooms have a stocked refrigerator, air-conditioning, cable TV, elegant dark-wood furniture, and plenty of closet space. The sports and beauty facilities are excellent, and the wealth of space and amenities ensures that you'll seldom have to battle crowds—whether at dinner or when reserving a tennis court. *Box 251, Soufrière, tel. 809/459-7566 or 800/877-3643, fax 809/459-7667. 103 cottages, 12 suites. Facilities: 4 restaurants, 3 bars/lounges, tennis, squash, water sports and scuba diving (offshore scuba diving is extra), horseback riding (extra), massage, spa and beauty treatments, deep-sea-fishing charters, boat shuttle to Soufrière and Castries (extra). AE, DC, MC, V. All-inclusive. Very Expensive.*

★ **Le Sport.** If you've been dying to dip into thalassotherapy (seawater massages, thermal jet baths, and the like), this is the place for you. The Oasis, a $3.5 million health and beauty temple, looms over the resort from a hilltop, beckoning you to experience beauty treatments, eucalyptus inhalations, and seaweed nutrient wraps. And a daily program involves everything from aerobics to yoga—though the exercise room is surprisingly primitive. Still, with an un-rivaled location and horseshoe-shape beach, guests are just as free to lie around, eat, and feel pampered. The architecture is a hand-some variety of styles, from Moorish to Mediterranean, in every hue from mauve to mint. Rooms have central air, queen-size beds, mar-ble baths, phones, and fridges. The costlier rooms were redone in 1993 and have wall sconces, four-poster beds, and marble floors. The less-expensive rooms have an ugly swath of carpeting beneath the beds but are otherwise just as luxurious as the others. A band plays nightly, and there's a piano bar. Food here is unusually good for an all-inclusive. *Box 437, Cariblue Beach, tel. 809/450-8551 or 800/544-2883, fax 809/452-0368. 100 rooms, 2 suites, 1 plantation house. Facilities: restaurant, 2 bars, 2 pools, bicycles, lighted tennis court, archery, 9-hole golf course nearby, water-sports center, thalassotherapy, laundry, beauty salon, beauty and rejuvenation treatments, Jacuzzi, Turkish baths, exercise rooms, health shop, boutique, bank, medical facilities. AE, DC, MC, V. All-inclusive. Very Expensive.*

Wyndham Morgan Bay Resort. The expanding Wyndham Hotel group took over this property from the Hotel Pullman in 1992, to offer another all-inclusive property on St. Lucia—this one more popular with Europeans than Americans. Despite such Caribbean-style touches as open-air public areas and pastel colors, the architecture has a stark, new look that contrasts with the luxuriant vegetation of the island. Rooms, with floral linens and peach wicker furniture, offer partial and angled sea views from each of the eight three-story buildings, lined up on a small rise above the pool and restaurant area. All have air-conditioning, cable TV, phone, and hair dryer. Party goers are apt to be happiest here because drinks are generous and free flowing, and the guests, though fairly laid-back, spend most of their time at the bar and pool area. Cuisine is unspectacular, but the nightly entertainment is quite good. The beach—small, with cloudy water—is the biggest disappointment. *Box 2216, Gros Islet, tel. 809/450-2511, fax 809/450-1050. 240 rooms. Facilities: 2* restaurants, 2 bars, beach grill, boutique, 4 tennis courts, pool, games room, Jacuzzi, exercise room, sauna, water-sports center. AE, D, MC, V. All-inclusive. Very Expensive.

★ **Anse Chastanet Hotel.** The theme at this 25-year-old resort is individuality. Every room is enormous and furnished differently—many with curved, louvered, or even open walls affording guests spectacular sweeping vistas of the Pitons and the Caribbean. Furnishings add to the sophistication with many items individually built by local craftsmen. The Canadian owner and architect has been careful to fit this development in closely with the lush environment—Robinson Crusoe would have been very much at home here. The older rooms, in a cluster of octagonal gazebos, are least interesting but most affordable. The beachside rooms are much classier, and the newer suites are truly striking. All accommodations have ceiling fans and verandas. The hotel is on a 500-acre estate near Soufrière and the Pitons. From the Trou Au Diable Beach Restaurant (*see* Dining, *above*), 125 steps lead to a lovely black-sand crescent, where there is another restaurant, a thatch-roof bar, and a dive shop. Sunfish and Windsurfers are gratis to guests. The restaurants serve fine West Indian fare. The hotel is quiet (no TVs), peaceful, and secluded, reached by a rough, pot-holed road from Soufrière or a launch from Castries. Be prepared to walk up plenty of steps and hills—this is a truly vertical resort. *Box 7000, Soufrière, tel. 809/459-7000, fax 809/454-7067. 36 rooms and 12 suites. Facilities: 2 restaurants, 2 bars, tennis court, dive shop, water-sports center. AE, DC, MC, V. EP, MAP. Expensive–Very Expensive.*

Club St. Lucia. Refurbished bit by bit over the past 12 years, this bustling, friendly resort is the island's largest. Of the all-inclusives, this is the least expensive; it's not particularly luxurious. It caters mostly to Brits, but tennis enthusiasts come here to be close to the adjacent St. Lucia Racquet Club (*see* Sports, *above*), which is available to guests for a nominal fee. Others come here to get hitched; expect to see three to five weddings per day. The resort sits on 50 acres, with rooms and suites in bungalows scattered over the hillside, and has two beaches. Accommodations are spacious, with king-size beds (twins on request), tile floors, patios, baths with tubs and showers, and air-conditioning in all but the standard rooms, which have ceiling fans. There are clock radios in all the rooms, but no phones. Live entertainment is scheduled nightly. Though the food is adequate at best, guests receive a discount and free transportation to the Great House Restaurant (*see* Dining, *above*). A pizza parlor and 40 rooms were added in 1994. *Box 915, Smugglers Village, Castries, tel. 809/452-0551 or 800/223-9815, fax 809/452-0281. 352 rooms and suites. Facilities: restaurant, pizza parlor, 2 bars, pool, tennis, disco, minimart, several shops, Jacuzzi, water-sports center, transport to stables, laundry, golf nearby, tennis club and fitness center nearby. AE, DC, MC, V. All-inclusive. Expensive–Very Expensive.*

★ **Ladera.** This quiet, luxurious hideaway is nestled amid lush botanical gardens overlooking the Pitons, the Caribbean sea, and Jalousie Plantation down below. It opened in 1992 and has immediately become one of the most exclusive and unusual small resorts in the Caribbean—a home away from home for rock stars, corporate VIPs, and honeymooners. Most guests are North American, and many stay for the last night or two of a longer vacation at a larger resort. The two-story suites and three-bedroom villas, furnished with a harmonious blend of French colonial antiques and local crafts, feature a completely open western wall to afford dazzling unobstructed views. Many units have sizable plunge pools, and some have a Jacuzzi. You may have a banana tree in your living room, salamanders fleeting across your kitchen counter, or even the odd bat (remember, they eat the mosquitoes!) fluttering under your rafters—so expect the unexpected. Staying here is for many a once-in-a-lifetime treat. Reserve your room at least six months in advance. Four suites were added late in 1993. *Box 255, Soufrière, tel. 809/454–7323. 7 villas, 12 suites. Facilities: restaurant, bar, pool, gift shop. AE, MC, V. MAP. Expensive–Very Expensive.*

Rendezvous. Formerly Couples, this all-inclusive resort on Malabar Beach is still for couples only. Things tend to be quite active, with volleyball in the pool and on the beach, aerobics, and water exercises. The activities desk can arrange anything, including a wedding. Accommodations have pink marble floors, king-size four-poster beds, a balcony or terrace, and air-conditioning—but no TVs. There is nightly live music for dancing, and a piano bar that's open until the last couple leaves. *Box 190, Malabar Beach, tel. 809/452–4211 or 800/221–1831, fax 809/452–7419. 84 rooms, 8 suites, 8 cottages. Facilities: 2 restaurants, 3 bars, 2 pools, lighted tennis court, sauna, Jacuzzi, exercise room, bicycles, horseback riding, water-sports center, dive shop, catamaran. AE, MC, V. All-inclusive. Expensive–Very Expensive.*

Rex Royal St. Lucian. This property caters to your every whim. The colonnaded reception area is stunning—an Italian palazzo with cool marble, a gurgling fountain, and a sweeping grand staircase. However, the russet-roofed white buildings form an uninspired "U" in the pristine landscaped grounds. The large, rambling pool is laced with Japanese bridges and has a natural rock waterfall. The split-level ocean-view suites are sumptuous, featuring a soothing pastel color scheme, cable TV, air-conditioning, three phones, a minibar, and a jet shower. Guests, which tend toward European, may use the tennis and water-sports facilities at the adjacent sister property, the St. Lucian. Not the most authentic Caribbean experience in St. Lucia, the food, service, and decorating is nevertheless stellar. *Box 977, Castries, tel. 809/452–0999 or 800/225–5859, fax 809/452–9639. 98 suites. Facilities: 2 restaurants, 2 bars, pool. AE, DC, MC, V. EP, MAP. Expensive–Very Expensive.*

Sandals Halcyon. Sandals's renovation of the 170-room Halcyon Beach Club in Choc Bay was nearing completion at press time. This is the second Sandals resort on St. Lucia and has the same couples-only, all-inclusive policy as Sandals St. Lucia. Guests at both resorts will have reciprocal entertainment and recreation privileges. The new resort is on 1,200 yards of white-sand beach at Choc Bay, 4 miles from Castries, 3 miles from Vigie Airport, and a 75-minute drive from Hewanorra International Airport. Each room has air-conditioning, king-size bed, hair dryer, clock radio, direct-dial telephone, cable TV, safe, and either a patio or a balcony. Three restaurants will serve Continental, Italian, and island cuisine. *Box GM 910, Castries, tel. 809/453–0222, fax 809/451–8435. 170 rooms. Facilities: 3 restaurants, 7 bars (including piano bar and two swim-up bars), 2 pools, 2 lighted tennis courts, 9-hole golf course at Sandals St. Lucia, water-sports center, fitness center. AE, DC, MC, V. All-inclusive. Expensive–Very Expensive.*

Sandals St. Lucia. Sandals debuted here in April 1993 and has been a smashing success. Previously, the hotel was the Cunard Hotel La Toc and La Toc Suites, a combination of high-rise hotel and luxury villa suites. But in the past few years the resort fell into disrepair. Sandals, a couples-only resort, came in and restored this secluded 155-acre resort, within a 10-minute drive of Castries, to its original splendor. They kept the best —private plunge pools, a quarter-acre swimming pool, a lovely beach, a nine-hole golf course, and four floodlit tennis courts—and added restaurants serving Oriental,

Continental, and Caribbean cuisine, an outstanding fitness center, and whirlpools around the property. Guest rooms, done in mahogany furnishings with king-size four-poster beds, all have air-conditioning, hair dryers, direct-dial telephones, and cable TV. Most important, guests, who are mostly American, seem to have a blast—thanks in part to a young, raucous, and fun-loving staff. *La Toc Rd., Castries, tel. 809/452–3081, fax 809/453–7089. 213 rooms, 60 suites. Facilities: 4 restaurants, 5 bars, 5 tennis courts, 9-hole golf course, water-sports center, fitness center. AE, DC, MC, V. All-inclusive. Expensive–Very Expensive.*

Club Med St. Lucia. This four-story air-conditioned hotel is on a 95-acre beachfront property on the southeast coast, where the Atlantic waters are rough. All the usual Club Med activities are here, including nightly entertainment. Hewanorra International Airport is five minutes away. *Vieux Fort, tel. 809/455–6001 or 800/CLUBMED, fax 809/452–0958. 256 rooms. Facilities: restaurant, bar, boutique, fitness center, 8 tennis courts, pool, horseback riding, water-sports center. AE, DC, MC, V. All-inclusive (except drinks). Expensive.*

★ **Windjammer Landing.** This sun-kissed resort, with sweeping prospects of one of St. Lucia's prettiest bays, fulfills anyone's beachcombing fantasies: White stucco villas crowned with tile alternate with a porticoed reception area and thatch-hut public rooms. Villas are huge and tastefully decorated in the ubiquitous island pastels and rattan furnishings. All villas have air- conditioning, a VCR and cable TV, a stereo, microwave, coffeemaker, and blender; and you can arrange to have dinner prepared in your kitchen and served on your terrace. The ambience is rustic simplicity with painted natural wood timbers, tile floors, wicker chairs, and straw mats. Guests tend toward young, and most are American and love the energetic staff. A people-mover transports guests to their villas up the steep hill from the main building and the shops. This is truly an idyllic spot. Though expensive for one couple, six guests in a three-bedroom villa will find Windjammer a steal. *Box 1504, Labrelotte Bay, Castries, tel. 809/452–0913, fax 809/452–9454. 114 1-, 2-, and 3-bedroom villas. Facilities: 3 restaurants, 2 bars, picnic meals, tennis, 3 pools, minimarket, 3 boutiques, water sports, laundry. AE, MC, V. EP, MAP. Expensive.*

Harmony Apartel. On Rodney Bay Marina, this clean, two-story all-suite hotel was completely overhauled in 1993. Reduit Beach is just 200 yards away. The 22 suites have air-conditioning, a red-tile balcony or terrace with marina or pool views, wet bar, direct-dial phones, refrigerator, cable TV, and coffeemaker; four of these suites have kitchenettes. The eight VIP suites have additional 10-foot sundecks, a whirlpool bath, a four-poster bed, Australian sheepskin throw rugs, but no kitchen. A rarity: the terrace furniture is not the plastic junk the Caribbean is notorious for, consisting instead of comfortable, cushioned chaise longues. This is a nice alternative to the mega-resort scene, and the adjacent minimarket—one of the best-stocked on the island—makes the kitchenette suites ideal for long-term stays. The Mortar and Pestle restaurant is right on the bay, and serves excellent food, including Malaysian, Indian, and Chinese specialties. *Box 155, Castries, tel. 809/452–8756 or 800/ 223–6510, fax 809/452–8677. 30 units. Facilities: restaurant, bar, minimarket, pool, water sports, laundry. MC, V. EP, MAP. Moderate–Expensive.*

Green Parrot. There are green velvet chairs in the small reception room, in the first and lowest of three rows of buildings that are stacked on the hillside high up in the Morne above Castries. The large, motel-like rooms have a patio, phone, air-conditioning, and bath with tub/shower and vanity. Though there is a restaurant for nonguests, hotel guests have a separate dining room with a popular sunken bar. The hotel arranges boat trips to Jambette Beach for barbecue and snorkeling and a free bus scoots you to town and the beach. *Box 648, Castries, tel. 809/452–3399, fax 809/453–2272. 60 rooms. Facilities: 2 restaurants, bar, games room, pool, nightclub. AE, MC, V. EP, MAP. Moderate.*

Rex St. Lucian. The lobby is broad, white, and informal, with potted plants and upholstered sofas, from which a corridor leads to the gardens, pool area, and beach. This was once two hotels, and the rooms are spread out over considerable acreage, some on Reduit Beach, some in gardens. All have double or king-size beds, clock radios, direct-dial phones, and patios or terraces. Most have air-conditioning and tubs; 36 have ceiling fans and showers. Discounted package tours from Britain have taken their toll on this resort and the furnishings have that well-worn, drab look, but there is lots of action to distract you. This is the home of Splash, one of the island's hottest discos, and the local agent for Mistral Windsurfers. Many of the water sports are free to hotel guests. *Box 512, Reduit Beach, Castries, tel. 809/452–8351, fax 809/452–8331. 260 rooms. Facilities: 2 restaurants, 3 bars, disco, pool, laundry/dry cleaning, lighted tennis court, dive shop, boutiques, ice-cream parlor, beauty salon, minimarket, water-sports center. AE, DC, MC, V. EP, MAP. Moderate.*

★ **Candyo Inn.** This small pink hotel, which opened in 1992 in the heart of Rodney Bay, is one of the best buys in the Caribbean. It's a five-minute walk to beaches and several good restaurants, and has a small pool and lanai decked with the usual plastic lawn furniture and potted palms; nearby, a small outdoor bar serves drinks and snacks. The two-story building and its lush green grounds are carefully looked after and spotless. All 12 rooms have air-conditioning, cable TV, clock radio, direct-dial phone, veranda, white-tile floors, and white contemporary furniture with floral upholstery. The eight suites have kitchenettes, larger sitting areas, and tubs; they're worth the extra $15 a night. A small atrium lobby has a small convenience shop, and the staff is delightful. *Box 386, Rodney Bay, tel. 809/452–0712, fax 809/452–0774. 4 rooms, 8 suites. Facilities: drink/snack bar, minimarket, pool. AE, MC, V. EP. Inexpensive.*

Humming Bird Beach Resort. A wide range of accommodations is available at this charming spot at the edge of Soufrière. Four-poster beds and African sculpture adorn many rooms; however, they are a bit dark and would fare better without the dingy carpeting. The highly regarded restaurant is a favorite hangout of locals and expatriates. Joyce Alexander, the owner, is a marvelous, dynamic hostess who, when not making improvements to her small hotel, designs batiks for the adjoining boutique. *Box 280, Soufrière, tel. 809/454–7232. 10 units. Facilities: restaurant, bar, pool. D, MC, V. EP, MAP. Inexpensive.*

Orange Grove Hotel. Up a long hill off the road to Windjammer Landing you'll come upon this hilltop motel with a nondescript exterior. It looks like a budget accommodation and it is one. Surprisingly, the rooms—which are large, light, and clean—are packed with all the conveniences you'd expect at a large resort: two phones, two cable TVs, air-conditioning, full baths, white-tile floors, and new but typical Caribbean-style furniture. All have separate sitting areas and balconies or patios overlooking the hillside. And although you're away from the beach, guests are welcome to use the beach facilities at Club St. Lucia 15 minutes away—free transportation is available. Forty rooms are to be added in 1994; maybe then more Americans will discover these bargain rooms that rent for just $45–$60 per night. The restaurant serves West Indian cuisine for similarly low

prices. *Box 98, Castries, tel. 809/452–8213. 22 rooms. Facilities: restaurant, bar, pool. AE, MC, V. EP, MAP. Inexpensive.*
The Skyway Inn. Opened in 1992, this is the ideal spot if you're staying in the north but have an early flight to catch from Hewanorra in the morning—it's just 100 yards from the airport, and minutes from Vieux Fort and its beaches. The inn is clean and comfortable with air-conditioned rooms, cable TV, meeting facilities, and a free shuttle to the beach. There's an open-air restaurant and bar on the roof and a pool down below. You don't want to spend a week here, but as far as airport hotels go, it's quite impressive. *Box 353, Vieux Fort, tel. 809/454–7111, fax 809/454–7116. 32 rooms, 1 suite. Facilities: restaurant, bar, gift shop. AE, MC, V. Inexpensive.*

Home Rentals   For private-home rentals, contact **Happy Homes** (Box 12, Castries, St. Lucia) or **Tropical Villas** (Box 189, Castries, tel. 809/452–8240).

Nightlife

Most of the action is in the hotels, which feature entertainment of the island variety—limbo dancers, fire-eaters, calypso singers, and steel band jump-ups. Many offer entertainment packages, including dinner, to nonguests.

The **Splash Disco** (Rex St. Lucian Hotel, tel. 809/452–8351) has a good dance floor and splashy lighting effects. It's open Monday–Saturday from 9 PM.

On weekends, locals usually hang out at the **Lime** (Rodney Bay, tel. 809/452–0761); **Capone's** (Rodney Bay, tel. 809/452–0284), an art deco place right out of the Roaring '20s—with a player piano and rum drinks—or **A-Pub** (tel. 809/452–8725), a lounge in an A-frame building overlooking Rodney Bay. The **Charthouse** (Rodney Bay, tel. 809/452–8115) has a popular bar, jazz on stereo, and live music on Saturday. Young boaters tie up at the **Bistro** (Rodney Bay, tel. 809/452–9494) for drinks, chess, darts, and backgammon. The **Green Parrot** (the Morne, tel. 809/452–3399) is in a class all by itself. Chef Harry Edwards hosts the floor show, which features limbo dancers. Harry has been known to shimmy under the pole himself. There are also belly dancers. Great fun; semiformal attire.

On Friday nights, sleepy Gros Islet becomes sin city, Bourbon Street during Mardi Gras, as the entire village is transformed into a street fair. At the far end of the street, mammoth stereos loudly beat out sounds as locals and strangers let their hair down. **Club Society** (Grande Rivière, Gros Islet, tel. 809/453–0312) is probably the best spot for meeting locals. **The Banana Split** (St. Georges St., Gros Islet, tel. 809/450–8125) offers entertainment and special theme nights, with a perpetual "spring break" atmosphere. It can get rowdy, so it's best to travel in a group and keep your wits about you. But then Friday night is *the* night to hang, party, lime. Worried about crashing the party? Just roll down your window and ask: You'll know if you're invited. Another Friday night street scene and a popular alternate venue for liming can be found just before you enter Marigot Bay. The music is supplied by **J. J.'s** restaurant (tel. 809/451–4076), and the popular fare is curried goat. More and more locals are choosing to come here instead of the more touristy Gros Islet happening.

23 St. Martin St. Maarten

*Updated by
Jordan
Simon*

There are frequent nonstop flights from the United States to St.
Martin/St. Maarten, so you don't have to spend half your vacation
getting here—a critical advantage if you have only a few days to enjoy the sun. The 37-square-mile island is home to two sovereign nations, St. Maarten (Dutch) and St. Martin (French), so you can
experience two cultures for the price of one. However, the Dutch
side has lost much of its European flavor.

The island, particularly the Dutch side, is ideal for people who like
to have lots of things to do. Whatever can be done in or on the water—snorkeling, windsurfing, waterskiing—is available here;
there is golf and tennis as well. Especially on the French side, there
are enough good-quality restaurants for serious diners to try a different one each night, even on a two-week stay. The duty-free shopping is as good as anywhere else in the Caribbean, except perhaps in
the U.S. Virgin Islands. There's an active nightlife, with discos and
casinos. Water-sports enthusiasts will love Simpson Bay Lagoon,
the largest inland body of water in the Caribbean. Day trips can be
taken by ship or plane to the nearby islands of Anguilla, Saba, St.
Eustatius, and St. Barthélemy. There are hotels for every taste and
budget—from motel-type units for the package tour trade to some
of the most exclusive resorts in the Caribbean. The standard of living is one of the highest in the Caribbean, so the islanders can afford
to be honest and to treat visitors as welcome guests. Corruption and
crime, which had been on the rise, have decreased dramatically in
the '90s, thanks to an exemplary cooperative effort between the two
governments.

On the negative side, St. Martin/St. Maarten has been thoroughly
discovered and developed; unless you stay in an exclusive resort, you
are likely to find yourself sharing beachfronts with tour groups or
conventioneers. Yes, there is gambling, but the table limits are so
low that hard-core gamblers will have a better time gamboling on
the beach. It can be fun to shop, and there's an occasional bargain,
but many goods, particularly electronics, are cheaper in the United
States.

Perhaps what makes this island unique is the opportunity it affords
the visitor to lead an active life one moment and to come to a complete halt the next. For all its bustle, St. Martin/St. Maarten is still a
Caribbean island brushed by gentle trade winds. You can do nothing
at all and enjoy yourself immensely.

Before You Go

**Tourist
Information**
For information about the Dutch side, contact the **St. Maarten Tourist Office** (275 7th Ave., New York, NY 10001, tel. 212/989–0000) or
the **St. Maarten Information Office** (243 Ellerslie Ave., Willowdale,
Toronto, Ontario, Canada M2N 1Y5, tel. 416/223–3501). Information about French St. Martin can be obtained through the **French
West Indies Tourist Board** by calling France-on-Call at 900/990–0040
(50¢ per minute). You can also write to the **French Government Tourist Office** at 610 5th Ave., New York, NY 10020; 9454 Wilshire Blvd.,
Beverly Hills, CA 90212; 645 N. Michigan Ave., Chicago, IL 60611;
or 2305 Cedar Spring Rd., Dallas TX 75201. In Canada contact the
French Government Tourist Office, 1981 McGill College Ave., Suite
490, Montreal, Québec H3A 2W9, tel. 514/288–4264, or 1 Dundas St.
W, Suite 2405, Toronto, Ontario M5G 1Z3, tel. 416/593–4723 or 800/
361–9099. In the United Kingdom the tourist office can be reached
at 178 Piccadilly, London W1Z OAL, tel. 071/493–6594.

Arriving and Departing
By Plane
There are two airports on the island. L'Espérance on the French side is small and handles only island-hoppers. Bigger planes fly into Juliana International Airport on the Dutch side. The most convenient carrier from the United States is **American Airlines** (tel. 800/433–7300), with daily nonstop flights from New York and Miami, as well as connections from more than 100 U.S. cities via its San Juan hub. **Continental Airlines** (tel. 800/231–0856) has daily flights from Newark. **LIAT** (tel. 809/462–0701) flies from Antigua; **ALM** (tel. 800/327–7230) from Aruba, Bonaire, Curaçao, the Dominican Republic, and from Atlanta and Miami via Curaçao. ALM also offers a Visit Caribbean Air Pass, which offers savings for traveling to several Caribbean islands. BWIA (tel. 800/327–7401) offers twice-weekly service from Miami; **Air Martinique** (tel. 596/51–08–09) connects the island with Martinique twice a week. **Windward Islands Airways** (Winair, tel. 599/54–42–30), which is based on St. Maarten, has daily scheduled service to Saba, St. Eustatius, St. Barts, Anguilla, St. Thomas, and St. Kitts/Nevis. **Air Guadeloupe** (tel. 590/90–37–37) has several flights daily to St. Barts and Guadeloupe from both sides of the island. **Air St. Barthélemy** (tel. 590/27–71–90) has frequent service between Juliana and St. Barts. Tour and charter services are available from Winair and **St. Martin Helicopters** (Dutch side, tel. 599/5–4287).

By Boat
Motorboats zip several times a day from Anguilla to the French side at Marigot, three times a week from St. Barts. Catamaran service is available daily from the Dutch side to St. Barts. The 50-passenger *Style* (tel. 599/5–22167) slaps across from Saba three times a week.

Passports and Visas
U.S. citizens need proof of citizenship. A passport (valid or not expired more than five years) is preferred. An original birth certificate with raised seal (or a photocopy with notary seal), or a voter registration card is also acceptable. All visitors must have a confirmed room reservation and an ongoing or return ticket. British and Canadian citizens need valid passports.

Language
Dutch is the official language of St. Maarten and French is the official language of St. Martin, but almost everyone speaks English. If you hear a language you can't quite place, it's Papiamento, a Spanish-based Creole of the Netherlands Antilles.

Staying in St. Martin/St. Maarten

Important Addresses
Tourist Information: On the Dutch side, the **Tourist Information Bureau** is on Cyrus Wathey (pronounced *watty*) Square in the heart of Philipsburg, at the pier where the cruise ships send their tenders. The executive office is on Walter Nisbeth Road 23 (Imperial Building) on the third floor. *Tel. 599/5–22337. Open weekdays 8–noon and 1–5, except holidays.*

On the French side, there is the smart and very helpful **Tourist Information Office** on the Marigot pier. *Tel. 590/87–57–21. Open weekdays 8:30–1 and 2:30–5:30; Sat. 8–noon. Closed holidays and the afternoon preceding a holiday.*

Emergencies
Police: Dutch side (tel. 599/5–22222), French side (tel. 590/85–50–16). **Ambulance:** Dutch side (tel. 599/5–22111), French side (tel. 590/87–50–06). **Hospital: St. Maarten Medical Center** (Cay Hill, tel. 599/5–31111) is a fully equipped hospital. **Pharmacies:** Pharmacies, which are open Monday–Saturday 7–5, include the **Central Drug Store** (Philipsburg, tel. 599/5–22321), **Mullet Bay Drug Store** (tel. 599/5–42801, ext. 342), and **Pharmacie** (Marigot, tel. 590/87–50–79).

Currency   Legal tender on the Dutch side is the Netherlands Antilles florin (guilder), written NAf; on the French side, the French franc (F). The exchange rate fluctuates, but in general it is about NAf 1.78 to U.S.$1 and 5F to U.S.$1. On the Dutch side, prices are usually given in both NAf and U.S. dollars, which are accepted all over the island, as are credit cards. Note: Prices quoted here are in U.S. dollars unless otherwise noted.

Taxes and   On the Dutch side, a 5% government tax is added to hotel bills. On
Service   the French side, a *taxe de séjour* (visitor's tax) is tacked onto hotel
Charges   bills (the amount differs from hotel to hotel, but the maximum is $3 per day, per person). Departure tax from Juliana airport is $5 to destinations within the Netherlands Antilles and $10 to all other destinations. It will cost you 15 French francs to depart by plane from l'Espérance Airport or by ferry to Anguilla from Marigot's pier.

In lieu of tipping, service charges are added to hotel bills all over the island, and, by law, are included in all menu prices on the French side. On the Dutch side, most restaurants add 10%–15% to the bill.

Hotels on the Dutch side add a 15% service/energy charge to the bill. Hotels on the French side add 10%–15% for service.

Taxi drivers expect a 10% tip.

Guided Tours   A 2½-hour taxi tour of the island costs $35 for one or two people, $10 for each additional person. Your hotel or the tourist office can arrange it for you. Best bets are **St. Maarten Sightseeing Tours** (Philipsburg, tel. 599/5–22753) and **Calypso Tours** (Philipsburg, tel. 599/5–42858), which offer, among other options, a 2½-hour island tour for $15 per person. You can tour in deluxe comfort with **St. Maarten Limousine Service** (tel. 599/5–24698 or 599/5–22698) for $40–$50 per hour with a three-hour minimum. Fully equipped Lincoln Continentals accommodate up to six people and are furnished with stereo, fully stocked bar, and air-conditioning. The limo service also offers transportation to and from Juliana airport at rates ranging from $30 to $65 one-way. (This includes one hour of waiting time free of charge for late arrivals.) On the French side, **Société Touristique de St. Martin** (tel. 590/87–56–20) also runs excellent islandwide tours.

Getting   Taxi rates are government regulated, and authorized taxis display
Around   stickers of the St. Maarten Taxi Association. There is a taxi service
Taxis   at the Marigot port near the Tourist Information Bureau. Fixed fares apply from Juliana International Airport and the Marigot ferry to the various hotels and around the island. Fares are 25% higher between 10 PM and midnight, 50% higher between midnight and 6 AM.

Buses   One of the island's best bargains at 80¢ to $2.00, depending on your destination, buses operate frequently between 7 AM and 7 PM and run from Philipsburg through Cole Bay to Marigot.

Rental Cars   You can book a car at Juliana International Airport, where all major rental companies have booths, but to give taxi drivers work, you must collect the car at the rental offices located off the airport complex. (The Hertz office is closest to the airport, just a quarter of a mile away.) There are also rentals at every hotel area. Rental cars are inexpensive—approximately $35–$45 a day for a subcompact car plus collision damage waiver. All foreign driver's licenses are honored, and major credit cards are accepted. **Avis** (tel. 800/331–1212), **Budget** (tel. 800/527–0700), **Dollar** (tel. 800/421–6868), **Hertz** (tel. 800/654–3131), and **National** (tel. 800/328–4567) all have offices on the island. Scooters rent for $25–$30 a day at **Honda** (Pondfill, Philipsburg, tel. 599/5–25712) and **Rent 2 Wheels** (Nettle Bay, tel. 590/87–20–59).

Telephones and Mail To call the Dutch side from the United States, dial 011–599 + local number; for the French side, 011–590 + local number. To phone from the Dutch side to the French, dial 06 + local number; from the French side to the Dutch, 3 + local number. Keep in mind that a call from one side to the other is an overseas call, not a local call. Telephone communications, especially on the Dutch side, leave something to be desired. At the Landsradio in Philipsburg, there are facilities for overseas calls and an AT&T USADIRECT telephone, where you are directly in touch with an AT&T operator who will accept collect or credit-card calls. On the French side, it is not possible to make collect calls to the United States, and there are no coin phones. If you need to use public phones, go to the special desk at Marigot's post office and buy a Telecarte (it looks like a credit card), which gives you 40 units for around 31F or 120 units for 93F. There is a small kiosk next to the tourist office in Marigot where you can make credit card–phone calls. The operator will assign you a PIN (Personal Identification Number) number, valid for as long as you specify. Calls are $4 per minute to the United States.

Letters from the Dutch side to the United States and Canada cost NAf1.30; postcards, NAf.60. From the French side, letters up to 20 grams, 4.10F; postcards, 3.50F.

Opening and Closing Times Shops on the Dutch side are open Monday–Saturday, 8–noon and 2–6; on the French side, Monday–Saturday 9–noon or 12:30, and 2–6. Some of the larger shops on both sides of the island open Sunday and holidays when the cruise ships are in port. Some of the small Dutch and French shops set their own capricious hours.

Banks on the Dutch side are open Monday–Thursday 8–1 and Friday 4–5. French banks are open weekdays 8:30–1:30 and 2–3 and close afternoons preceding holidays.

Exploring St. Martin/St. Maarten

Numbers in the margin correspond to points of interest on the St. Martin/St. Maarten map.

Philipsburg The Dutch capital of **Philipsburg,** which stretches about a mile along ❶ an isthmus between Great Bay and the Salt Pond, has three more or less parallel streets: Front Street, Back Street, and Pondfill. Front Street has been recently recobbled, cars are discouraged from using it, and the pedestrian area has been widened. Shops, restaurants, and casinos vie for the hordes coming off the cruise boats. Head for **Wathey Square** and stroll out on the pier. **Great Bay** is rolled out before you, and the beach stretches alongside it for about a mile. The square bustles with vendors, souvenir shops, and tourists. There's a taxi stand, where you can arrange for a driver to take you around if you'd rather not rent a car. Philipsburg should be explored on foot, but you'll need wheels to get around the island.

Directly across the street from Wathey Square, you'll see a striking white building with a cupola. It was built in 1793 and has since served as the commander's home, a fire station, and a jail. It now serves as the town hall, court house, and the post office.

The square is in the middle of the isthmus on which Philipsburg sits. To your right and left the streets are lined with hotels, duty-free shops, fine restaurants, and cafés, most of them in pastel-colored

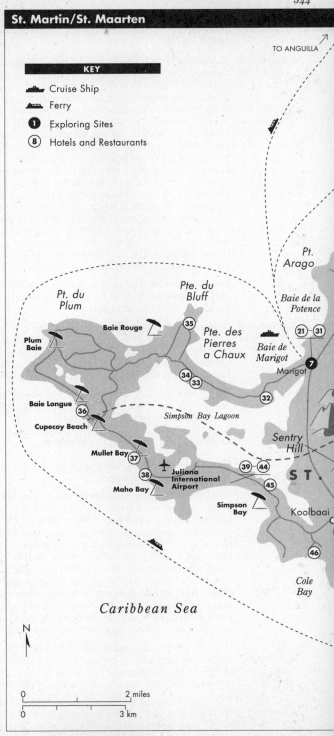

St. Martin/St. Maarten

West Indian cottages gussied up with gingerbread trim. Narrow alleyways lead to arcades and flower-filled courtyards where there are yet more boutiques and eateries.

A half-block away across the street, Simart'n Museum, in a restored 19th-century West Indian house, hosts rotating cultural exhibits and the permanent historical display entitled "Forts of St. Maarten/ St. Martin," featuring artifacts ranging from Arawak pottery shards to articles salvaged from the wreck of HMS *Proselyte*. (Open Mon.–Sat. 10–6, Sun. 9:30–noon. Admission: $1. 119 Front Street, Philipsburg, tel. 599/5–32125.) If you'd like to clamber through the ruins themselves, take the dirt path at the Great Bay Hotel parking lot to Fort Willem for a spectacular view of Philipsburg and the surrounding islands.

Little lanes called *steegjes* connect Front Street with Back Street, which is considerably less congested because it has fewer shops.

Our drive begins at the western end of Front Street. The road (it will become Sucker Garden Road) leads north along Salt Pond and begins to climb and curve just outside of town. Take the first right to ② **Guana Bay Point**, from which there is a splendid view of the island's east coast, tiny deserted islands, and small St. Barts, which is anything but deserted.

Sucker Garden Road continues north through spectacular scenery. Continue along a paved roller-coaster road down to **Dawn Beach**, one of the island's best snorkeling beaches.

③ **Oyster Pond** is the legendary point where two early settlers, a Frenchman and a Dutchman, allegedly began to pace in opposite directions around the island to divide it between their respective countries. Local legend maintains that the obese sweaty Hollander stopped frequently to refresh himself with gin—the reason why the French side is nearly twice the size of the Dutch. (The official boundary marker is on the other side of the island.)

Elsewhere on the Island From Oyster Pond, follow the road along the bay and around Etang aux Poissons (Fish Lake), all the way to **Orléans.** This settlement, ④ which is also known as the French Quarter, is the oldest on the island. Noted local artist Roland Richardson makes his home here. He holds open studio on Thursdays from 10 to 6 to sell his art. He's a proud islander ready to share his wealth of knowledge about the island's cultural history.

A rough dirt road leads northeast to **Orient Beach,** the island's best-known nudist beach. There's even a pricey rustic resort catering to "naturists." Offshore, little **Ilet Pinel** is an uninhabited island that's fine for picnicking, sunning, and swimming.

⑤ Farther north you'll come to **French Cul de Sac,** where you'll see the French colonial mansion of St. Martin's mayor nestled in the hills. Little red-roof houses look like open umbrellas tumbling down the green hillside. The scenery here is glorious, and the area is great for hiking. There is a lot of construction, however, as the surroundings are slowly being developed. From the beach here, three shuttle boats make the five-minute trip ($5) to Ilet Pinel.

The road swirls south through green hills and pastures, past flower-entwined stone fences. Past L'Espérance Airport is the town of ⑥ **Grand Case.** Though it has only one mile-long main street, it's known as the "Restaurant Capital of the Caribbean": More than 20 restaurants serve French, Italian, Indonesian, and Vietnamese fare, as well as fresh seafood. The budget-minded will appreciate the "lolos"—savory barbecue stands along the waterfront. **Grand Case Beach Hotel** is at the end of this road and has two beaches to choose from for a short dip. Better yet, travel down the road about 5 miles toward Marigot, and on the right is a turnoff to **Friar's Beach,** a small, picturesque cove that attracts a casual crowd of locals. A small snack bar, **Kali's,** owned by a welcoming gentleman wearing dreadlocks, serves refreshments. From here, you can turn inland and follow a bumpy tree-canopied road to Pic du Paradis, at 1,278 feet the highest point on the island, affording breathtaking vistas of the Caribbean.

❼ Just before entering the French capital of **Marigot,** you will notice a shopping complex on the left. At the back of it is **Match** (tel. 590/87–92–36), the largest supermarket on the French side, carrying a broad selection of tempting picnic makings—from country pâté to foie gras—and a vast selection of wines.

If you are a shopper, a gourmet, or just a Francophile, you'll want to tarry awhile in Marigot. Marina Port La Royale is the shopping complex at the port, but Rue de la République and Rue de la Liberté, which border the bay, are also filled with duty-free shops, boutiques, and bistros. The harbor area has stalls selling anything from fruits and vegetables to handmade crafts. Across from these stalls on the pier road leading to the ferries for Anguilla is the helpful **French tourist office,** where you may collect an assortment of free maps and brochures.

Time Out With a roguish glint in his eye, owner Roger Drovin proclaims the melt-in-your-mouth croissants at **Cafe Terrasse Mastedana** (Rue de la Liberté, no tel.) to be "zee best." This humble little establishment along the main road by Port La Royale, bedecked with pennants from around the world, is perfect for a light breakfast or snack.

You are likely to find more creative and fashionable buys in Marigot than in Philipsburg, and if you are not a shopper, there is less bustle and the open-air cafés are tempting places in which to stop for a rest. Also, unlike Philipsburg, Marigot does not die at night, so you may wish to return in the evening. **Le Bar de la Mer** (tel. 590/87–81–79) on the harbor is a popular gathering spot in the early evening, though the bar and restaurant are open all day.

The road due south of Marigot to Philipsburg passes the official boundary, where a simple border marker, erected by the Dutch and French citizenry to commemorate 300 years of peaceful coexistence, bears the dates "1648 to 1948." Straddling the border is a mammoth condominium hotel complex, the Port de Plaisance, where Sheraton has constructed the extravagant Mont Fortune casino adjacent to the hotel.

At the airport, the road from Marigot to the north and Simpson Bay to the west join together and lead to Philipsburg, passing the cutoff to Divi Little Bay Beach Resort.

The other road from Marigot leads west and hugs the coastline to cross a small bridge to Sandy Ground and then along Baie Nettlé, with its many reasonably priced hotels. Soon thereafter, on the right, you'll come to the Mediterranean-style village resort of **La Belle Creole,** commanding Pointe du Bluff. Then you'll begin to see some of the island's best beaches—**Baie Rouge, Plum Baie,** and **Baie Longue**—clinging to its westernmost point. They are all accessible down bumpy but short dirt roads and perfect for swimming and picnicking.

At the end of Baie Longue and running eastward along the south coast is **La Samanna,** the fashionable jet set resort. Just after this hotel you'll reenter Dutch territory at **Cupecoy Beach.** You'll have to endure the huge, garish vacation condo-hotel complexes of Mullet Bay and Maho Bay before you reach Juliana International Airport and Philipsburg.

What to See and Do with Children

The St. Maarten Zoo and Botanical Garden. This ambitious development, the labor of love of a local policeman, features plants and animals indigenous to the Caribbean basin and South America, including coatimundis, ocelots, peccaries, and boa constrictors. The two large walk-through aviaries, petting zoo, and playground should delight children of all ages. *Madame Estate, tel. 599/5–32030. Admission: $4 adults, $2 children. Open Wed.–Fri. 9–5, weekends 10–6.*

Off the Beaten Track

Ocean Explorers Sea Walk. Uniquely designed helmets enable you to breathe normally underwater as guides point out the profusion of riotously colored marine life in Simpson Bay. Swimming ability is not required, just curiosity and a bathing suit. The cost is $35 per person. *Simpson Bay, tel. 599/5–45252.*

Beaches

The island's 10 miles of beaches are all open to the public. Beaches occupied by resort properties charge a small fee (about $3) for changing facilities, and water-sports equipment can be rented in most of the hotels. You cannot, however, enter the beach via the hotel unless you are a paying guest. Some of the 37 beaches are secluded, some are located in the thick of things. Topless bathing is virtually de rigueur on the French side, where the beaches are generally better than on the Dutch side. If you take a cab to a remote beach, be sure to arrange a specific, clearly understood time for your driver to return to pick you up, and don't leave valuables unattended on the beach.

Hands down, **Baie Longue** is the best beach on the island. It's a beautiful, mile-long curve of white sand on the westernmost tip of the island. This is a good place for snorkeling and swimming, but beware of a strong undertow when the waters are rough. You can sunbathe in the buff, though only a few do. Pack a lunch. There are no facilities.

Beyond Baie Longue is **Plum Baie,** where the beach arcs between two headlands and the occasional sunbather discloses all.

Baie Rouge is one of the most secluded beaches on the island. This little patch of sand is located at the base of high cliffs and is backed by private homes rather than by hotels. Some rate it the prettiest beach on the island, although it can have rough waves. A small snack and soda stand is located at the entrance.

Orient Beach is the island's best-known "clothes optional" beach—it's on the agenda for voyeurs from visiting cruise ships. You can enter from the parking area or through the **Club Orient** (tel. 590/87–33–85), which has chalet self-catering bungalows for rent, in addition to shops and rental water-sports equipment.

You have to approach the **Dawn Beach–Oyster Pond** area through the Dawn Beach Hotel. This long white-sand beach is partly protected by reefs (good for snorkeling), but the waters are not always calm. When the waves come rolling in, this is the best spot on the island for bodysurfing.

Ilet Pinel is a little speck off the northeast coast, with about 500 yards of beach, where you can have picnics and privacy. There are no facilities. Putt putts are available to take you from Orient Beach.

Simpson Bay is a long half-moon of white sand near Simpson Bay Village, one of the last undiscovered hamlets on the island. In this small fishing village you'll find refreshments, **Ocean Explorers Dive Shop** (*see* Sports and the Outdoors, *below*) for water-sports rentals, and neat little ultra-Caribbean town homes.

Ecru-color sand, palm and sea-grape trees, calm waters, and the roar of jets lowering to nearby Juliana International Airport distinguish the beach at **Maho Bay.** Concession stand, beach chairs, and facilities are available.

At **Mullet Bay,** the powdery white-sand beach is crowded with guests of the Mullet Bay Resort.

Cupecoy Beach is a small shifting arc of white sand fringed with eroded limestone cliffs, just south of Baie Longue on the western side of the island, near the Dutch-French border. On the first part of the beach, swimwear is worn, but farther up, sun worshipers start shedding their attire. There are no facilities, but a truck is often parked at the entrance, with a vendor who sells cold sodas and beers.

Sports and the Outdoors

All the resort hotels have activities desks that can arrange virtually any type of water sport.

Boating Motorboats, speedboats, Dolphins, pedal boats, sailboats, and canoes can be rented at **Lagoon Cruises & Watersports** (tel. 599/5–52801, ext. 1873) and **Caribbean Watersports** (tel. 599/5–42801).

Sun Yacht-Charters (tel. 800/772–3500), based in Oyster Pond, has a fleet of 30 Centurion sailboats for hire. The cost of a week's bareboat charter for a 36-foot Centurion with six berths runs $2,590 in peak winter season. Also in Oyster Pond, the **Moorings** (tel. 800/535–7289 or 590/87–32–55) has a fleet of Beneteau yachts, 38–50 feet in length. **Dynasty** (Marigot's Port La Royale Marina, tel. 590/87–85–21) offers an excellent fleet of Dynamique yachts.

Deep-Sea Fishing Angle for yellowtail, snapper, grouper, marlin, tuna, and wahoo on half-day deep-sea excursions, including bait and tackle, instruction for novices, and an open bar. Contact **Wampum** (Bobby's Marina, Philipsburg, tel. 599/5–22366) or **Sailfish Caraibes** (Port Lonvilliers, tel. 590/87–31–94).

Fitness **Le Privilege** (tel. 590/87–37–37), a sports complex at Anse Marcel above Meridien L'Habitation, features a full range of exercise equipment. **Fitness Caraibes** (tel. 590/87–97–04), a toning center run by Marc Bozzetto, is at Nettle Bay. **Club Crazy** (Marigot, tel. 590/87–05–94) offers weight training and aerobics classes. On the Dutch side, **Life Styles** (Pt. Pirouette Hotel, tel. 599/5–54207, ext. 610) has everything from Lifecycles to treadmills. **L'Aqualigne** at the Pelican Resort (tel. 599/5–54330) is a health spa with gym, sauna, and beauty and weight-loss treatments, among other things.

Golf **Mullet Bay Resort** (tel. 599/5–42081) has an 18-hole championship course.

Horseback Contact **Crazy Acres Riding Center** (Wathey Estate, Cole Bay, tel.
Riding 599/5–42793), **Bayside Riding Club** (Orient Bay, 590/87–33–85) or **O.K. Corral** (Oyster Pond, tel. 590/87–40–72).

Jetskiing and Rent equipment through **Caribbean Watersports** (tel. 599/5–42801 or
Waterskiing 599/5–44363) and **Maho Watersports** (tel. 599/5–44387). On the French side, try **Orient Bay Watersports** (tel. 590/87–33–85).

Parasailing A great high can be arranged through **Lagoon Cruises & Watersports** (tel. 599/5–52898).

Running The **Road Runners Club** (Pelican Resort Activities Desk, tel. 599/5–42503) meets weekly for its 5K or 10K run.

Scuba Diving On the Dutch side is Proselyte Reef, named for the British frigate HMS *Proselyte*, which sank south of Great Bay in 1802. In addition to wreck dives, reef, night, cave, and drift dives are popular. Off the northeast coast of the French side, dive sites include Ilet Pinel, for good shallow diving; Green Key, a prolific barrier reef; and Flat Island (also known as Ile Tintamarre) for sheltered coves and undersea geologic faults. NAUI- and PADI- certified dive centers offer instruction, rentals, and trips at **Tradewinds Dive Center/Maho Watersports** (tel. 599/5–54387), **St. Maarten Divers** (tel. 599/5–22446), **Leeward Island Divers** (tel. 599/5–42268), and **Ocean Explorers Dive Shop** (599/5–45252). On the French side, PADI-certified **Lou Scuba** (tel. 590/87–22–58) has opened at the Marine Hotel at Nettle Bay. **Blue Ocean** (tel. 590/87–66–89) is PADI and CMAS certified.

Sea You can take a day-long picnic sail to nearby islands or secluded
Excursions coves aboard the 45-foot ketch *Gabrielle* (tel. 599/5–23170), the 41-foot ketch *Pretty Penny* (tel. 599/5–2167), or the 60-foot schooner *Gandalf*. The catamaran *Bluebeard II* (tel. 599/5–42801 or 599/5–42898), moored in Marigot, sails around Anguilla's south and northwest coasts to Prickley Pear, where there are excellent coral reefs for snorkeling and powdery white sands for sunning. The *Lady Mary* (tel. 599/5–70145) sails around the island Tuesday–Saturday evenings from La Palapa Center, Simpson Bay; $60 per person includes dinner, open bar, and live calypso. The *Laura Rose* (tel. 599/5–23605) offers a variety of half- and full-day sails. The *Karib One* glass-bottom boat (tel. 590/87–89–73) offers three cruises daily, including dinner-and-disco trips.

The luxurious 75-foot motor catamaran *White Octopus* (tel. 599/5–23170) does full-moon and cocktail cruises, complete with calypso music. During the day the *White Octopus* makes the run to St. Barts, departing at 9 AM from Bobby's Marina and returning at 5 PM. In St. Martin, sailing, snorkeling, and picnic excursions to nearby islands can be arranged through **Orient Watersports** (Club Orient, tel. 590/87–33–85), **L'Habitation** (tel. 590/87–33–33), **La Belle Creole** (tel. 590/87–58–66), and **La Samanna** (tel. 590/87–51–22).

Snorkeling Coral reefs teem with marine life, and clear water allows visibility of up to 200 feet. Some of the best snorkeling on the Dutch side can be had around the rocks below Fort Amsterdam off Little Bay Beach, the west end of Maho Bay, Pelican Key and the rocks near the Caravanserai Hotel, and the reefs off Dawn Beach and Oyster Pond. On the French side, the area around Orient Bay, Green Key, Ilet Pinel, and Flat Island (or Tintamarre) is especially lovely for snorkeling, and has been officially classified a regional underwater nature reserve. Arrange rentals and trips through **Watersports Unlimited**

(tel. 599/5–23434), **Red Ensign Watersports** (tel. 599/5–22929), **Ocean Explorers** (tel. 599/5–45252), and **Orient Bay Watersports** (tel. 590/87–33–85).

Tennis There are four lighted courts at **Dawn Beach Hotel** (tel. 599/5–22944); four lighted courts at **Pelican Resort** (tel. 599/5–42503); three asphalt courts at **Little Bay and Belair Beach Resorts** (tel. 599/5–22333 or 599/5–23362); four courts at **Maho Reef & Beach** (tel. 599/5–42115); six lighted courts at **Le Privilege** (Anse Marcel, tel. 590/87–59–28), which also has squash and racquetball courts; 14 lighted courts at **Port de Plaisance** (tel. 599/5–45222); four lighted Omni courts at **La Belle Creole** (tel. 590/87–58–66); three lighted courts at **Nettle Bay Beach Club** (tel. 590/87–97–04); two lighted courts at **Mont Vernon Hotel** (tel. 590/87–62–00) and at **Simpson Beach Marine Hotel** (tel. 590/87–54–54); and 16 all-weather courts at **Mullet Bay Resort** (tel. 599/5–42081).

Windsurfing Rental and instruction are available at **Little Bay Beach Hotel** (tel. 599/5–22333, ext. 186), **Maho Watersports** (tel. 599/5–44387), **Orient Watersports** (590/87–33–85), and **Red Ensign Watersports** (tel. 599/5–22929).

Shopping

About 180 cruise ships call at St. Maarten each year, and they do so for about 500 reasons. That's roughly the number of duty-free shops on the island.

Prices can be 25%–50% below those in the United States and Canada on French perfumes, liquor, cognac and fine liqueurs, cigarettes and cigars, Swedish crystal and Finnish stoneware, Irish linen, Italian leather, German cameras, European designer fashions, plus thousands of other things you never knew you wanted. But check prices before you leave home, especially if you live in the New York City area—Manhattan's prices for cameras and electronic equipment are hard to beat anywhere. In general, you will find more fashion on the French side in Marigot, although stalwarts like Polo Ralph Lauren and Benetton have Philipsburg outlets.

St. Maarten's best-known "craft" is its guavaberry liqueur, made from rum and the wild local berries (not to be confused with guavas) that grow only on this island's central mountains.

Prices are quoted in florins, francs, and dollars; shops take credit cards and traveler's checks. Most shopkeepers, especially on the Dutch side, speak English. (If more than one cruise ship is in port, avoid Front Street. It's so crowded you won't be able to move.) Although most merchants are reputable, there are occasional reports of inferior or fake merchandise passed off as the real thing. As a rule of thumb, if you can bargain excessively, it's probably not worth it.

Shopping Areas In St. Maarten: **Front Street,** Philipsburg, is one long strip lined with sleek boutiques and cozy shops gift wrapped in gingerbread. **Old Street,** near the end of Front Street, has 22 stores, boutiques, and open-air cafés. There are almost 100 boutiques in **Mullet** and **Maho** shopping plazas, as well as at the Simpson Bay Yacht Club complex.

In St. Martin: Wrought-iron balconies, colorful awnings, and gingerbread trim decorate Marigot's smart shops, tiny boutiques, and bistros in the **Marina Port La Royale; Galerie Perigourdine;** and on the main streets, **Rue de la Liberté** and **Rue de la République.**

Good Buys **Little Switzerland** (Marigot and Philipsburg, tel. 590/52–25–23) and **Spritzer and Fuhrmann** (Marigot, tel. 590/87–59–62; Philipsburg, tel. 599/5–44381) handle the finest in crystal and china.

Jewelry and watches can be found at **Oro del Sol** (Marigot, tel. 590/87–56–51), **Carat** (Marigot, tel. 590/87–73–40; Philipsburg, tel. 599/5–22180), **Little Europe** (Philipsburg, tel. 599/5–23062), and **H. Stern** (Philipsburg, tel. 599/5–23328).

Pick up a bottle of wine for your picnic at **La Cave du Savour Club** (Marigot, tel. 590/87–58–51).

Lipstick (Marigot, tel. 590/87–73–24) and **Oro del Sol** (Marigot, tel. 590/87–57–02) carry perfumes and cosmetics.

For designer fashions head to **La Romana** (2 locations on Front St., tel. 599/5–22181) and **Havane** (Marigot, tel. 590/87–70–39).

New Amsterdam Store (Philipsburg, tel. 599/5–22787) and **The Yellow House** (Philipsburg, tel. 599/5–23438) handle fine linens and porcelain.

The Lil' Shoppe (Philipsburg, tel. 599/5–2177) carries eel-skin wallets, handbags, perfumes, and a large selection of swimwear. Shoes, belts, and handbags are also sold at **Maximoflorence** (Philipsburg, tel. 599/5–23735).

Island Specialties Caribelle batik, hammocks, handmade jewelry, the local guavaberry liqueur, and herbs and spices are stashed at **The Shipwreck Shop** (Philipsburg, tel. 599/5–22962 and Port La Royale, tel. 590/87–27–37). T-shirts, beach towels, native dolls, Indian glass bangles, and hand-painted delft souvenirs can all be found at **Sasha's** (Philipsburg, tel. 599/5–24331). Excellent galleries showcasing local artists include **Le Poisson D'Or** (Marigot, tel. 590/87–72–45), **ABC Art Gallery** (Marigot, tel. 590/87–96–00), **Gingerbread** (Port La Royale, tel. 590/87–73–21), **Galerie Lynn** (Grand Case, no tel.), **Minguet** (Rambaud Hill, 590/87–76–06), **Greenwith Galleries** (Philipsburg, tel. 599/5–23842), and **Calabash** (Philipsburg, tel. 599/5–25221).

Dining

It may seem that this island has no monuments. Au contraire, there are many of them, all dedicated to gastronomy. You'll scarcely find a touch of Dutch; the major influences are French and Italian. This season's "in" eatery may be next season's remembrance of things past, as things do have a way of changing rapidly. The generally steep prices reflect both the island's high culinary reputation and the difficulty of obtaining fresh ingredients. Not surprisingly, the hotel restaurants on the French side are usually more sophisticated, but at prices that would make almost anyone but a Rockefeller go Dutch. (*See* Lodging, *below*.) There's a big range of attire on this island, although a sports jacket or cocktail dress is de rigueur in fancier restaurants. In high season, unless otherwise noted in our text, be sure to make reservations, and call to cancel if you can't make it. Many restaurants close during August and/or September.

Highly recommended restaurants are indicated by a star ★.

Category	Cost*
Very Expensive	over $50
Expensive	$35–$50

Moderate	$25–$35
Inexpensive	under $25

per person, excluding drinks and service

Dutch Side   **Antoine's.** This is an elegant, airy terrace overlooking Great Bay. You might start your meal, which is served by candlelight, with French onion soup, then move on to steak au poivre, veal scallopini in vermouth sauce with grapes, or lobster thermidor. For dessert, try the sublime grand marnier soufflé. *Front St., Philipsburg, tel. 599/5–22964. AE, MC, V. Closed Sun. Expensive.*

Felix. This classy little beachside eatery serves dinner by candlelight. At lunchtime, take a dip before feasting on salad Felix (an imaginative concoction of bananas, sweet potatoes, and avocado), rack of lamb Provençal, or steak au poivre. The restaurant is on the road to Pelican Resort. *Pelican Key, tel. 599/5–45237. AE. Closed Tues. Expensive.*

Le Bec Fin. To reach the well-known upstairs restaurant, you stroll through a flowery courtyard where La Coupole's croissants and cakes are baked daily (a nice thing to bear in mind come breakfast time). Despite the rotation of chefs, the classical French cuisine remains professional, if inconsistent. Starters include vol-au-vent (pastry) bursting with escargots in fennel cream sauce and tagliatelle with shrimp in ginger. Fish, such as red snapper fillet in rum butter sauce, is your best bet for a main course. The meringue swan with mint ice cream is as delightful to the eye as it is to the palate. The breezy downstairs café annex serves breakfast and lunch with great crepes (try the seafood) and salads. *119 Front St., Philipsburg, tel. 599/5–22976. AE. Expensive.*

Le Perroquet. In striking contrast to the restaurant's setting in a cool green-and-white West Indian–style house overlooking the peaceful lagoon, with rattan furnishings and crisp white napery, are the exotic specialties prepared by its chef, Pierre Castagna. One example is grilled breast of ostrich in a Bordelaise sauce. *Airport Rd., Simpson Bay, tel. 599/5–44339. AE, MC, V. Closed Mon. Expensive.*

★ **Oyster Pond Hotel.** A more genteel evening on St. Maarten is hard to find. You'll enjoy fine linens and china, fresh flowers, and a delightful terrace with wonderful sea views. Specialties include lobster medallions dancing in a truffle, tomato, and basil sauce; fillet of red snapper in sauce piquante; and sweet, billowy soufflés for dessert. The hotel's guests have priority in this romantic dining room, so you should reserve well in advance. *Oyster Pond, tel. 599/5–22206 or 599/5–23206. Reservations advised. AE, MC, V. Expensive.*

★ **Saratoga.** The handsome mahogany-outfitted dining room in the Yacht Club's stucco and red tile building has views of the Simpson Bay Marina. The menu changes daily, according to the whim of owner and chef John Jackson, who trained at the Culinary Institute of America; everything is flown in fresh. He dubs his cuisine "freestyle creative contemporary," merrily borrowing from various influences, from Asian to Southwestern. You might start with Malpeque oysters with balsamic-horseradish mignonette or seven-seaweed salad with sea beans, daikon, and sesame, then segue into crispy fried roundhead snapper in fermented black bean sauce or grilled chicken breast in a cumin-gouda crust. The wine list is admirably balanced and even better priced, with 10–12 wines offered by the glass. *Simpson Bay Yacht Club, Airport Rd., tel. 599/5–42421. Reservations advised. AE, MC, V. Dinner only. Closed Sun. Expensive.*

Spartaco. Northern Italian cuisine is served in this 200-year-old stone plantation house. Everything here is either homemade or imported from Italy. Some of the specialties are black angel-hair pasta with shrimp and garlic; swordfish baked with pink pepper and rosemary, served over linguine; and veal Vesuviana, with mozzarella, oregano, and tomato sauce. *Almond Grove, Cole Bay, tel. 599/5-45379. No lunch. MC, V. Expensive.*

L'Escargot. A lovely 19th-century house wrapped in verandas is home to one of St. Maarten's oldest French restaurants. Starters include baked brie en croûte in kiwi sauce. There is also, of course, a variety of snail dishes. For an entrée, try red snapper grilled on a bed of red beets. There's a fun cabaret Sunday nights; no cover charge with dinner. *76 Front St., Philipsburg, tel. 599/5-22483. AE, MC, V. Moderate.*

Wajang Doll. Indonesian dishes are served in the garden of this West Indian–style house. *Nasi goreng* (fried rice), satay with peanut sauce, and red snapper in a sweet soy glaze are standouts; but the specialty is *rijsttafel*, the Indonesian rice table that offers 14 or 19 dishes in a complete dinner. *137 Front St., Philipsburg, tel. 599/5-22687. AE, MC, V. Inexpensive–Moderate.*

Chesterfield's. Burgers and salads are served at lunch, but menus are more elaborate for dinner at this nautically themed indoor-outdoor terrace restaurant overlooking the marina. Menu offerings include French onion soup, roast duckling with fresh pineapple and banana sauce, and chicken cordon bleu. The Mermaid Bar is a popular spot with yachtsmen, with a predictably raucous and rousing happy hour. *Great Bay Marina, Philipsburg, tel. 599/5-23484. AE, MC, V. Inexpensive.*

Harbour Lights. This modest family-run spot is in a historic building built in 1870. The decor is warm, with peach and coral walls and native-print tablecloths. Choose among excellent rotis and pilaus and even better stewed or curried chicken, meats, and seafood. Try one of the knockout cocktails, all made with the local guavaberry liqueur. *30 Back St., Philipsburg, tel. 599/5-23504. AE, MC, V. Inexpensive.*

Shiv Sagar. Authentic East Indian cuisine, emphasizing Kashmiri and Mogul specialties, is served in this small mirrored room fragrant with cumin and coriander. Marvelous tandooris and curries are offered, but try one of the less-familiar preparations like Amritsari fish. There's also a large selection of vegetarian dishes. *3 Front St., Philipsburg, tel. 599/5-22299. AE, D, MC, V. Inexpensive.*

★ **Turtle Pier Bar & Restaurant.** Chattering monkeys and squawking parrots greet you at the entrance to this classic Caribbean hangout, teetering over the lagoon and festooned with creeping vines. There are 200 animals in this informal zoo, but that's nothing compared to the menagerie hanging out at the bar during happy hour. The genial owner Sid Wathey, whose family is one of the island's oldest, leaves most of the business details to his American wife, Lorraine. They've fashioned one of the funkiest, most endearing places in the Caribbean, with cheap beer on draft, huge American breakfasts, all-you-can-eat ribs dinners for $9.95, and eclectic live music several nights a week. *Airport Rd., tel. 599/5-52230. No credit cards. Inexpensive.*

French Side **Alizéa.** Many who have tried this terrace restaurant have come away ★ claiming that the cuisine is the best on the island. The refined contemporary cuisine respects tradition. The menu changes constantly, but some outstanding dishes have been scrambled eggs and seaweed blinis, lobster savarin with caraway, and breast of quail stuffed with pistachios in black-currant sauce. Try an iced soufflé for dessert.

Alizéa Hotel, Mont Vernon 25, tel. 590/87–33–42. Reservations suggested. AE, MC, V. Very Expensive.

Chez Martine. A charming, globe-trotting French couple, Eliane and Jean-Pierre, have made this small hotel into a personable hostelry with a gastronomic restaurant. Dine by the water's edge in an intimate room with polished silverware and sparkling glasses. The chef, Thierry de Launay, studied under Joel Robuchon, whom many consider the world's greatest chef. You might begin with a superb velvety lobster velouté, then segue into roast lamb on a bed of eggplant and spinach in corn sauce or lobster in puff pastry. The wine list is well selected even if a bit overpriced, but for 150F you can select a drinkable wine. *140 blvd. Grand Case, Grand Case 97150, tel. 590/87–51–59, fax 590/87–87–30. Dinner only. Reservations suggested. AE, MC, V. Very Expensive.*

La Samanna. This restaurant has an exquisite setting in the celebrated hotel; you'll dine by candlelight on a tented terrace surrounded by bougainvillea. The clientele is chic, international, and often famous. Innovative chef Mark Ehrler might seduce the palate with air-dried Creole squab in fig sauce and polenta of grilled foie gras. The kitchen is still feeling its "hautes," and dinner for two (with wine) can easily set you back $250. The superb wine cellar boasts over 25,000 bottles. *Baie Longue, tel. 590/87–51–22. Jacket suggested. Reservations required. AE, DC, MC, V. Very Expensive.*

★ **Le Santal.** The approach to this dazzler, through a working-class suburb of Marigot, is forbidding. The exterior appears ramshackle, but the interior is transformed by soft lighting, china, and crystal. Dine on lobster soufflé on a bed of eggplant and spinach, foie gras sauteed in cassis, or lacquered duck. The owners also run the excellent Jean Dupont and Asia, but this is their showplace. *Sandy Ground, tel. 590/87–53–48. Reservations suggested. AE, MC, V. Very Expensive.*

★ **Le Poisson d'Or.** Posh and popular, this restaurant is in a restored stone house with a 20-table terrace. You can feast on a constantly changing menu of dishes such as terrine of foie gras with poached pear in Sauternes jelly, grilled tuna with sun-dried tomatoes and risotto in mustard sauce, and lobster medallions over linguini in an asparagus champagne velouté. The young chef, François Julien, cooks with enthusiasm, but his cuisine has stiff competition from the setting—the waters of the bay lapping the terrace. The space also doubles as a gallery exhibiting works of top-notch Caribbean artists. *Rue d'Anguille on the sea, Marigot, tel. 590/87–72–45. Reservations suggested. AE, MC, V. Closed for lunch May–Oct. and Tues. for lunch in high season. Expensive–Very Expensive.*

★ **Rainbow.** This split-level eatery is strikingly simple in cobalt blue and white and highly romantic, thanks to lapping waves and murmuring guests. Fleur and David are the stylish, energetic hosts, and chef Mario Tardif is from one of the world's gastronomic capitals, Quebec City. Don't miss his fettucine with smoked salmon and capers; sweetbreads galette with port, pine nuts, and rosemary; or duck *magret* (breast meat served with its skin). Dishes are dressed with fanciful touches like red cabbage crisps. Finish the meal off with the sublime orange, honey, and ginger soufflé. One of the first and still one of the best restaurants in this town of splendid seaside boîtes. *Grand Case, tel. 590/87–55–80. Reservations suggested. MC, V. Expensive–Very Expensive.*

Deep Blue. This expansive seaside restaurant is a favorite of visiting celebrities who enjoy classic French and Swiss creations as they are prepared with Caribbean flair by talented chef Christopher Terrasse. You can luxuriate in the sensuously textured tartare of

Balik smoked salmon or foie gras sautéed with apples and balsamic vinegar, or opt for the perfect raclette. *Grand Case, tel. 599/87-02-02. Reservations suggested. AE, MC, V. Dinner only. Expensive.*

La Vie En Rose. Prices here have escalated, based as much on the restaurant's past fame as on its present culinary art. The menu rewards adventurous eaters with mint-flavored vichyssoise with mussels, lobster salad with celery and truffles, breaded sautéed foie gras with pears, and sliced breast of duck in lemon-ginger sauce. Save room for chocolate mousse cake topped with vanilla sauce. The ground-floor tearoom and pastry shop serve an excellent luncheon with wine for $20. *Blvd. de France, Marigot, tel. 590/87-54-42. AE, MC, V. Expensive.*

Le Tastevin. The setting at this terrace restaurant is elegant: A chic pavilion, with tropical plants and ceiling fans, overlooks the water. Chef Daniel Passeri, a native of Burgundy, also founded the homey Auberge Gourmande across the street. The menu here is more ambitious, including foie gras scaloppine in Lillet sauce, duck breast in banana-lime sauce, and red snapper poached in vanilla. *Grand Case, tel. 590/87-55-45. MC, V. Expensive.*

Cas' Anny. Creole cooking is the specialty of Anne-Marie Boissard's appealing seaside terrace restaurant. She turns out delectably seasoned Creole boudin, crab farci, and lambi (conch) Provençal. *Rue d'Anguille, tel. 599/87-53-38. AE, MC, V. Moderate.*

★ **Cha Cha Cha Caribbean Cafe.** Pascal and Christina Chevillot's culinary pedigree is impeccable: His uncle Charles owns New York's La Petite Ferme. So what do they do? They create a chichi dive with Japanese gardens, gaudy colors, and a gaudier clientele who have made this the island's hot spot. Everyone eventually seems to end up here. (The mouth-watering haute Caraibes cuisine and reasonable prices don't hurt.) Try the giant prawns in passion-fruit butter or the grilled snapper with avocado, then wash it down with a "Grand Case Sunset." *Grand Case, tel. 590/87-53-63. MC, V. Moderate.*

Don Camillo da Enzo. Country-style decor and excellent service distinguish this small eatery. Both northern and southern Italian specialties are featured. Some favorites are the carpaccio, green gnocchi in Gorgonzola cream sauce, and veal medallions in marsala sauce. *Port La Royale, Marigot, tel. 590/87-52-88. AE, MC, V. Moderate.*

Maison sur le Port. Watching the sunset from the palm-fringed terrace is not the least of the pleasures in this old West Indian house, which boasts its own romantically lit fountain. Try the sautéed duck fillet in mango sauce or red snapper steamed with leeks and champagne. There is also a tempting three-course fixed-price menu. Chef Jean-Paul Fahrner's imaginative salads are lunchtime treats. *On the port, Marigot, tel. 590/87-56-38. AE, D, MC, V. Moderate.*

Mini Club. The popular upstairs terrace is virtually a treehouse nestled in the coconut palms. A pleasant eatery anytime, but especially Wednesday and Saturday, when there is a sumptuous buffet of almost 35 dishes—salads, roast pork, suckling pig, beef, fish, lobster—all for $45 per person, with wine. *Rue d'Anguille, Marigot, tel. 590/87-50-69. AE, MC, V. Moderate.*

Bistrot Nu. This friendly and enormously popular late-night spot serves traditional brasserie-style food, from coq au vin to fish soup, snails, pizza, and seafood, until 2 AM. For simple, unadorned fare at a reasonable price, this may be the best spot on the island. *Rue de Hollande, Marigot, tel. 590/87-77-39. MC, V. Inexpensive-Moderate.*

Le Marocain. This exotic oasis in the middle of Marigot resembles a pasha's posh digs, with lush potted plants, intricate mosaics, hand-painted tiles, and wood carvings. The food is as colorful and enticing as the ambience and decor, with wonderfully perfumed *tajines* (casseroles of chicken or meat) and *pastillas* (fragrant pastries filled with spices, raisins, and meat or chicken) among the standouts. *Rue de Hollande, Marigot, tel. 590/87–83–11. No credit cards. No lunch. Closed Mon. Inexpensive–Moderate.*

Le Plaisance. There are several fine ultracasual eateries at Port La Royale, all offering simple, appetizing food, fixed-price menus, and happy hours. The cool strains of jazz waft through this lively open-air brasserie as you sample terrific salads (try the niçoise or *landaine*—duck, smoked ham, croutons, and fried egg), pizzas (wonderful lobster), pastas (garlic and basil pistou), and fresh grilled seafood at unbeatable prices. *Port La Royale, Marigot, tel. 590/87–85–00. AE, MC, V. Inexpensive.*

Mark's Place. This barnlike restaurant is an institution on Sundays. You may start with pumpkin soup or stuffed crab, then follow with linguine bolognese or curried goat. Scrumptious daily specials, including homemade pies and pastries, are posted on a blackboard. Groups of 6–12 can eat a five-course meal in the snug wine cellar with their own chef and staff for $50 per person. All Mark needs to whip up a gourmet repast just for you is 24-hours' notice. *French Cul de Sac, tel. 590/87–34–50. AE, MC, V. Inexpensive.*

★ **Yvette's.** The attempts at romance couldn't be more endearing: Classical music plays softly, and the room is a symphony in Valentine red, from curtains and tablecloths and roses to hot pepper sauce. But kindly Yvette herself couldn't be more down-home, nor her food more delicious. Plates are piled high with smashing lip-smacking Creole specialties like *acras* (spicy fish fritters), stewed chicken with rice and beans, or conch and dumplings. This is the kind of place that is so good you're surprised to see other tourists—but word gets around. *Orleans, tel. 590/87–32–03. AE (5% surcharge). Inexpensive.*

Lodging

Until recently, the Dutch side commanded all the big, splashy resorts. The casinos are still to be found exclusively on the Dutch side—gambling is illegal on the French side. However, St. Martin is having something of a building boom, especially in the area around Nettle and Orient bays. All the hotels on the French side have an English-speaking staff. There are also small inns and Mediterranean-style facilities on both sides of the island. Many of the hotels offer enticing packages that are worth investigating. You'll also save substantially if you travel off-season; the downside of this is that many hotels and restaurants are closed for refurbishing or just plain recovering from the winter onslaught. In general, the French resorts are more intimate and romantic, but what the Dutch properties lack in ambience, they compensate for in clean, functional, comfortable rooms with all the "extras." Most of the larger Dutch resorts feature time-share annexes; the units are often available for rental for those who prefer the condo lifestyle at comparable rates.

As a rule, rooms on the beach command the highest prices. Most properties are EP or CP (the latter usually only in season), though meal plans are sometimes available.

Highly recommended lodgings are indicated by a star ★.

Category	Cost*
Very Expensive	over $300
Expensive	$225–$300
Moderate	$150–$225
Inexpensive	under $150

All prices are for a standard double room for two, excluding 5% tax (Dutch side), a taxe de séjour (set by individual hotels on the French side), and a 10%–15% service charge.

Hotels
Dutch Side

Port de Plaisance. If you're going to build a huge complex, this is the way to do it. Situated on its own island, this resort complex has 88 luxurious studios and one- and two-bedroom apartments; plans for an additional 550-room Sheraton are currently on hold. Nothing is left to chance or the imagination. All the units are fully equipped with air-conditioning, kitchen (including dishwasher and microwave), safe, satellite TV, direct-dial phones, and even a trouser press. The decor is in soft soothing seashell hues; the views are of either the lagoon or the marina. One pool is carved out of rock with a majestic waterfall. The polished marble entrance to the gleaming casino is dominated by a 25-foot bronze mermaid astride four dolphins. You receive one free ride in a stretch limo during your stay. The gourmet restaurant La Terrasse is playpen of stellar chef Nicolas Maire, who apprenticed with renowned chefs Paul Bocuse, Alain Senderens, and Michel Guerard. If there is a drawback, it's the lack of a beach—or even beach shuttle. *Box 2089, Simpson Bay, tel. 599/5–45222 or 800/732–9480, fax 599/5–42428. 88 apartments. Facilities: 2 restaurants, 4 bars, casino, fitness center, health bar, 2 pools, marina, water-sports center, 14 lighted tennis courts, 2 shopping arcades, 2 boats, car rental, disco. AE, D, MC, V. EP. Very Expensive.*

Dawn Beach Hotel. The rooms are air-conditioned and are located on the hillside or on the beach. All are spacious, with handsome rattan furnishings, combination living room/bedroom with king-size bed, kitchenette, closed-circuit color TV, radio, and private patio. (If you prefer tubs to showers, opt for the hillside villa.) The pool has a waterfall and the white-sand beach is one of the island's best for snorkeling, but the breeze is often strong and can whip up the waves. Since the hotel is off by itself, there's bus service to town twice daily. *Box 389, Philipsburg, tel. 599/5–22929; in the U.S., 800/223–9815; in Canada, 800/468–0023; fax 599/5–24421. 155 rooms. Facilities: restaurant, 2 beach bars, pool, 2 lighted tennis courts, car-rental desk, water-sports center. AE, DC, MC, V. EP. Expensive.*

Great Bay Beach Hotel and Casino. One of the island's few all-inclusive properties, this resort, just outside Philipsburg, has terrific views of the bay and its own stretch of beach. The white stucco and black tile lobby is more striking than the rooms, which are furnished in typical muted pastels and feature the usual amenities, including a balcony or terrace, satellite TV, and direct-dial phones. *Box 310, Great Bay, tel. 599/5–22446, fax 599/5–23859. 285 rooms, 5 1-bedroom suites. Facilities: 2 restaurants, bar, 2 pools, casino, nightclub, disco, water-sports center, 1 lighted tennis court, car rental. AE, DC, MC, V. EP, All-inclusive. Expensive.*

Maho Beach Hotel & Casino. A variety of accommodations are available at this facility, which is kept scrupulously shipshape and spic-and-span. All have two double beds or a king-size bed and a private balcony. The Casino Royale is the island's largest casino, and the open-air La Luna disco is currently the rage. The trick here is to get a room far enough away from the airport's landing strip (those behind the main lobby are the quietest); the roaring engines drown out the surf at the otherwise lovely beach. Built in 1992, a new tower has added 433 airy, spacious rooms with cathedral ceilings and light pastel and deep ocean-colored decors. The addition also includes 33 shops, five restaurants, the island's largest pool, and several banquet rooms. The complex may be likened to a minicity in an already congested hotel area near the airport. *Maho Bay, tel. 599/5–52115 or 800/835–6246, fax 599/5–53180. 688 rooms. Facilities: 10 restaurants, 3 bars, casino, disco, 2 pools, boutiques, 4 lighted tennis courts, 75 shops, all water sports. AE, DC, MC, V. EP, MAP. Expensive.*

Mullet Bay Resort and Casino. Of the self-contained mega-resorts, this is probably the least intrusive and most private, because it's spread out over a large area (easily negotiable by the ubiquitous golf carts), rather than condensed in high rises. There are an excellent championship 18-hole golf course; a gleaming crescent of sand; water sports galore; and comfortable, well-maintained accommodations, with standard but pleasing pastel decor and rattan furnishings. For those who like constant activity and variety, Mullet Bay is the place. *Box 309, Mullet Bay, tel. 599/5–52801 or 800/642–6401, fax 599/5–54281. 300 rooms and 300 1-bedroom suites. Facilities: 6 restaurants, 2 bars, 2 pools, 14 lighted tennis courts, 18-hole championship golf course, water-sports center, disco, shopping arcade, medical center, bank, food mart. AE, D, MC, V. EP, MAP. Expensive.*

Pelican Resort & Casino. Walk into the reception area and one-armed bandits and gaming tables greet you. On the lower level is a sales office enticing guests to buy into this hotel-condo complex. An assortment of white stucco buildings house the resort's air-conditioned apartments, suites, and deluxe studios, all of which have a sweeping view of the Caribbean. Each has a fully equipped kitchen (including hibachi and microwave), satellite TV, king-size beds, rattan furniture, and many frills (some have hot tubs). The resort has 1,400 feet of ocean frontage, though not good for bathing, and its own 60-foot catamaran, *El Tigre*, which is available for charters. *Simpson Bay, tel. 599/5–42503 or 800/327–3286, fax 599/5–42133. 660 suites and studios. Facilities: 2 restaurants, 6 bars, casino, 8 pools, health spa, Jacuzzi, 6 lighted tennis courts, car rental, medical center, children's playground, grocery store and shopping area, water-sports center. AE, DC, MC, V. EP. Expensive.*

★ **Horny Toad Guesthouse.** This is one of the most charming properties on the island, thanks to the caring touch of owners Bette and Earle Vaughn, who keep things as immaculate as if it were their own home (which it is most of the year). Each of the eight apartments on the beach is individually and thoughtfully decorated and fully equipped; many repeat guests request the same room. The blue-and-white sun terrace duplicates the patterns of delft china, chirping birds and fresh flowers greet you every morning, and Bette and Earle always treat you like family. *Simpson Bay, tel. 599/5–54323, fax 599/5–53316. 2 studios, 6 1-bedroom apartments. Facilities: library, barbecue. No credit cards. EP. Moderate–Expensive.*

Divi Little Bay Beach Resort. After new ownership experienced financial turmoil and shut down temporarily, this fine property reopened with a slight face-lift in 1993. The quaint, red-tile whitewashed buildings are nestled on an emerald hill overlooking the bay and ecru-sand beach. All the spacious rooms boast dazzling ocean views, terrace or balcony, cable TV, air-conditioning, and minifridge. The decor is pleasing, with aquamarine or terra-cotta tile floors and fresh-looking floral upholstery. The Papagayo restau-

rant is a restorative vision in blues, serving simple but deftly prepared grilled items. It may go all-inclusive for 1994/95. *Box 61,
Philipsburg, tel. 599/5–22333 or 800/367–3484, fax 599/5–23911. 163
rooms. Facilities: 3 restaurants, 3 bars, 2 pools, car-rental desk,
water-sports center, 3 lighted tennis courts, shops, casino. AE, DC,
MC, V. EP, MAP. Moderate.*

La Vista. All the accommodations are air-conditioned time-share
suites with cable TVs, direct-dial phones, balconies, and lovely
white iron queen-size beds. Guests have the use of the facilities at
the adjacent Pelican Resort. The service is personalized at this intimate property of quaint Antillean buildings connected by brick
walkways lined with just barely contained hibiscus and
bougainvillea. *Box 40, Pelican Key, tel. 599/5–43005 or 800/365–
8484, fax 599/5–43010. 24 suites. Facilities: restaurant, horseback
riding, pool, tennis. AE, MC, V. EP. Moderate.*

★ **Oyster Pond Hotel.** The refined, low-key quality of this hotel is quite
out of character with the rest of St. Maarten. Built around a courtyard, each of the two towers has two split-level suites and individually decorated rooms with terra-cotta floors, white wicker
furnishings, ceiling fans, and pastel French cottons. All these rooms
have a secluded balcony or terrace and a view of the ocean, the courtyard, or the yacht basin. The rooms have screened louvers for those
who prefer sea breezes to air-conditioning. The new, adjacent building offers larger rooms with subdued furnishings and balconies facing the sea. The hotel is on a mile-long beach that's excellent for
snorkeling, though not for sunbathing or lazy swimming. The dining
room opens onto the Atlantic Ocean; the pool is perched right on the
ocean's edge. You'll find hammocks instead of TVs, and the hotel's
only phone is manned by a staff member at the front desk. *Box 239,
Philipsburg, tel. 599/5–22206, 599/5–23206, or 800/374–1323; fax
599/5–25695. 40 rooms. Facilities: restaurant, bar, saltwater pool, 2
tennis courts, water-sports center. AE, MC, V. EP, MAP. Moderate.*

Holland House. This is a centrally situated hotel, with the shops of
Front Street at its doorstep and a mile-long backyard called Great
Bay Beach, which, unfortunately, is slightly polluted from the
cruise ships and freighters anchored in the bay. Rooms 104 through
107 open directly onto the beach. Each room has contemporary tropical furnishings, balcony, kitchenette, satellite cable TV, and air-
conditioning. The delightful open-air restaurant overlooking the
water serves reasonably priced dinners. *Box 393, Philipsburg, tel.
599/5–22572 or 800/223–9815; in NY, 212/840–6636; fax 599/5–
24673. 52 rooms, 2 suites. Facilities: restaurant, lounge, gift shop.
AE, DC, MC, V. EP. Inexpensive–Moderate.*

★ **Passangrahan Royal Guest House.** It's entirely appropriate that the
bar here is named Sidney Greenstreet. This is the island's oldest inn,
and it looks like a set for an old Bogie-Greenstreet film. The building
was once Queen Wilhelmina's residence (there's a picture of her in
the lobby) and the government guest house. Wicker peacock chairs,
slowly revolving ceiling fans, balconies shaded by tropical greenery,
king-size mahogany four-poster beds, and a broad tile veranda are
some of the hallmarks of this guest house. Afternoon tea is served.
There are no TVs or phones in the guest house, and it offers just a
sliver of Great Bay Beach. *Box 151, Philipsburg, tel. 599/5–23588,
fax 599/5–22885. 30 rooms and suites. Facilities: bar, restaurant,
Great Bay Beach, rental bikes. AE, MC, V. EP. Inexpensive–Moderate.*

Seaview Hotel & Casino. This is another good buy on Front Street
and Great Bay Beach. The air-conditioned, twin-bed rooms are modest, cheerful, and clean. All rooms have baths (some with showers

only), satellite TV, and phones. The four rooms above the sea have the best views. *Box 65, Philipsburg, tel. 599/5–22323 or 800/223–9815; in NY, 212/545–8469; in Canada, 800/468–0023; fax 599/5–24356. 45 rooms. Facilities: breakfast room, casino. AE, MC, V. EP. Inexpensive.*

French Side **Esmeralda Resort.** It looks like a housing development in the Sun Belt, but the interiors of these deluxe villas are tastefully decorated. The 54 rooms and suites in 15 villas can be combined any way you like, from studio to 5-bedroom palatial digs. All feature satellite TV, fully equipped kitchenette, direct-dial phone, and private terrace. L'Astrolabe has become a hot disco. *Box 541, Orient Bay, tel. 590/87–36–36 or 800/622–7836, fax 590/87–35–18. 15 villas. Facilities: 5 restaurants, pool, water-sports center, lighted tennis court, Jacuzzi. AE, MC, V. CP. Very Expensive.*

★ **La Belle Creole.** This 25-acre re-creation of an old Mediterranean village is replete with a stone central plaza. The enormous rooms and suites have every modern convenience, including air-conditioning, direct-dial phones, cable TVs, marble and tile bathrooms, and minibars. Accommodations (king-size or two double beds) are in 27 one- to three-story villas linked by stone-paved streets and graceful courtyards. Most villas have private balconies with a view of the ocean, the island, or Marigot Bay. Grand as it is, La Belle Creole has a casual, relaxed atmosphere even when it's crowded. A new water-sports complex has been added, the tennis program is the island's finest, and there are plans to link the two beach areas. Though it is on its own estate, the hotel has the advantage of quick and easy access to Marigot and the island's best beaches. La Provence is a fine gourmet restaurant, with especially popular weekly seafood and barbecue buffets. Mindful of the exorbitant cost of eating out, the management added a casual patio bistro. *Box 118, Marigot 97150, tel. 590/87–58–66 or 800–HILTONS, fax 590/87–56–66. 138 rooms and 18 1-bedroom suites. Facilities: activities desk, shopping arcade, free-form pool, 4 lighted tennis courts, fitness/beauty center, 2 restaurants, 2 bars, 5 rooms with facilities for people with disabilities, water-sports center. AE, DC, MC, V. CP. Very Expensive.*

Le Meridien L'Habitation. A white-knuckle road leads down to this huge, sleek, everything-you-could-ask-for enclave that sits amid beautifully landscaped gardens on enchanting Marcel Cove, with 1,600 feet of white-sand beach. The two-story main building is a white-column structure with red-tile roof and graceful galleries. All the air-conditioned rooms, suites, and apartments have spacious baths, balconies, wall safes, TVs, direct-dial phones, and fridges. One-bedroom apartments on the marina have fully equipped kitchens and private patios. Guests have complimentary access to the facilities of Le Privilege, a sports and entertainment complex on the hill (a minibus makes frequent trips to it). La Belle France is a typically solid and très cher gourmet restaurant. Another couple of two-story buildings, called "Le Domaine," were recently added to provide an additional 125 rooms, 20 suites, and an Italian restaurant. The rooms in Le Domaine are smaller and pricier, yet brighter and more tropical. But wherever you stay on the compound, few units boast an ocean view, the ambience is lacking, the service is polite but impersonal, and French Muzak blares throughout. There are better—or at least more chic—bargains on the island, yet this bustling resort remains wildly popular with tour groups and families seeking a "safe" vacation. *Box 581, Marcel Cove 97150, tel. 590/87–33–33 or 590/87–78–80; in the U.S., 800/543–4300; fax 590/87–30–38. 314 rooms, 82 suites. Facilities (including Le Privilege): 4 restaurants, 4 bars, beach, boutiques, aerobics, car rental, disco, 6 lighted tennis* *courts, minigolf, 2 pools, 2 squash courts, 1 racquetball court, 100-slip marina, water-sports center. AE, DC, MC, V. EP. Very Expensive.*

★ **La Samanna.** This luxurious, secluded hotel looks as if it were transported to St. Martin from Morocco. The hotel is set in a tropical garden on a slope overlooking the ravishing beach called Baie Longue. Red hibiscus is everywhere. There is a rich (the word is used advisedly) variety of accommodations from which to choose. Studios and one- and two-bedroom villas all feature private patio, minibar, full bath, and such thoughtful touches as potpourri and fresh flowers daily. The new, distinctive decor is stunning: cool mint, apricot, and teal fabrics; unusual ceramic work; painted tiles; and clever variations on traditional Caribbean wicker and rattan. It is a model of how to refurbish a classic property. *Box 159, Marigot 97150, tel. 590/87–51–22 or 800/854–2252, fax 590/87–87–86. 25 rooms, 30 1-bedroom suites and 30 2-bedroom suites. Facilities: restaurant, lounge, pool, fitness center, 3 tennis courts, library, TV room, boutique, water-sports center. AE. CP. Very Expensive.*

Grand Case Beach Club. This informal condo complex is situated on Grand Case's crescent-shape beach, with another "secret" strand two minutes' walk away. Air-conditioned studios and one- and two-bedroom apartments all have balconies or patios and kitchenettes. The 62 oceanfront units are much in demand, despite their undistinctive pastel decor. There are lots of repeat guests, so reserve well in advance. Attractive packages are offered. The kitchen at the aptly named Café Panoramique restaurant has been upgraded since it spirited chef Alain Billard, away from Le Bec Fin. *Box 339, Grand Case 97150, tel. 590/87–51–87 or 800/223–1588, fax 590/87–59–93. 40 studios and 33 1- and 2-bedroom apartments. Facilities: restaurant, lounge, 1 lighted tennis court, billiards, car rental, catamaran. AE, MC, V. CP. Expensive.*

Mont Vernon. This rambling hotel has a gingerbread, almost lacelike architecture and sits on a bluff overlooking Orient Bay, usually swept by a cooling sea breeze. The light, airy quality is maintained as you enter the large, open reception area. Each room has either a king-size bed or twin beds and a private balcony. The bathrooms are equipped with hair dryers, the sitting area with satellite TV. The rooms in the buildings on the crest facing the ocean have the best views and are slightly larger than the others. The other choice rooms are in the buildings down by the pools and beach. This is a big resort that lures package-tour groups as well as business seminars to its 20 15-people boardrooms and large parties to fill a 250-person banquet room. *Chevrise Baie Orientale, BP 1174, 97150, tel. 599/87–42–00 or 800/543–4300, fax 590/87–37–27. 370 rooms, 28 2-bedroom suites. Facilities: 2 restaurants, 2 bars, pool, 2 tennis courts, water sports. Free minibus to Marigot, Philipsburg, and casinos. AE, DC, MC, V. CP. Expensive.*

Anse Margot. The stretch divided by the sea and Simpson's Bay, known as Baie Nettlé, has become a row of hotels. While next door Le Flamboyant Bounty offers the all-inclusive packages, Anse Margot offers very reasonable room-only (EP) rates for attractive accommodations. The rooms are in eight three-story town-house buildings. Each room has a balcony, some with garden view and some with sea view, bathroom, and separate toilet. The furnishings are in light floral patterns. There are two pools, and the beach is on Simpson Bay. Entre Deux Mers is one of the better hotel restaurants. *Baie Nettlé 97150, tel. 590/87–92–01, fax 590/87–92–13; in the U.S., 800/333–1970, fax 590/87–92–13. 96 rooms, 35 1-bedroom suites. Facilities: restaurant, bar with nightly entertainment, 2 pools, meeting rooms. AE, MC, V. EP. Moderate–Expensive.*

★ **Captain Oliver's.** At Oyster Pond facing a beautiful horseshoe-shape bay, this small hotel, with bungalows featuring a view of the bay or garden, is for those who want to be away from the hustle of St. Maarten. The exceptionally clean, fresh, air-conditioned rooms—those facing the bay are the choicest—have their own patio decks, satellite TVs, minibars, direct-dial phones and kitchenettes. The property straddles the border: Stay in France, dine in the Netherlands (in the engaging open-air marina bistro). Sail-and-stay packages can be arranged by the friendly helpful staff. A great bargain. *Oyster Pond, 97150, tel. 590/87–40–26 or 800/223–9862; fax 590/87–40–84. 50 rooms. Facilities: restaurant, snack bar. AE, DC, MC, V. CP. Moderate–Expensive.*

Pavillon Beach Hotel. Every room of this small, new (1991) hotel faces the sea and comes with a private balcony. The spacious rooms with tile floors and warm-colored fabrics have clean bathrooms that come with a hair dryer and fixed-head shower (no tubs). On the balcony is a small but fully equipped kitchenette. The rooms on the ground level allow you to walk right onto the beach but do require that you close yourself in at night with sliding shutters: You may prefer the upper-story rooms, where you are not as exposed. The managers, Paul and Marie-Florence, are wonderfully warmhearted and helpful. *Plage de Grand Case, RN 7, Grand Case 97150, tel. 590/87–96–46, fax 590/87–71–04; in the U.S., tel. 800/223–9815. 17 rooms. Facilities: kitchenettes, in-room safes. MC, V. EP. Moderate–Expensive.*

Alizéa. The Alizéa is on Mont Vernon hill and offers splendid views over Orient Bay. Though there is a path for a 10-minute walk to the beach on Orient Bay, you will need a car to go elsewhere on the island. An open-air feeling pervades the hotel from its terrace restaurant, where the food is superb, to the 26 guest apartments done up with contemporary wood furnishings and pastel fabrics. Rooms vary in style and design, but all are tasteful and each has a large private patio balcony that makes breakfast a special treat. *Mont Vernon 25, 97150, tel. 590/87–33–42, fax 590/87–41–15. 8 1-bedroom bungalows, 18 studios. Facilities: restaurant, pool. AE, MC, V. CP. Moderate.*

★ **Marine Hotel Simpson Beach.** This may be the best buy on the hotel "strip" known as Nettle Bay. Rooms and duplex suites are cheerfully decorated, most with a view of the water, all with kitchenette, balcony, safe, cable TV, and direct-dial phone. The youthful fun-loving clientele make sure there's never a dull moment. Budget-conscious Europeans love this place because of the many extras, like a huge breakfast buffet and nightly local entertainment. *Box 172, Nettle Bay, tel. 590/87–54–54, fax 590/87–92–11. 120 studios, 45 1-bedroom duplexes. Facilities: restaurant, bar, beach, pool, watersports center, car and bike rental, minimart, laundromat, dive shop. AE, MC, V. BP. Inexpensive–Moderate.*

★ **Hevea.** This is a small, white guest house with smart awnings in the heart of Grand Case. The rooms are dollhouse small but will appeal to romantics. There are beam ceilings, washstands, and carved wood beds with lovely white coverlets and mosquito nets. The air-conditioned rooms, studios, and apartment are on the terrace level; fan-cooled studios and apartments are on the garden level. Hotel guests can get a special "house" dinner at the delightful gourmet restaurant for $30. *Grand Case 97150, tel. 590/87–56–85 or 800/423–4433, fax 590/87–83–88. 8 units. Facilities: restaurant. MC, V. EP. Inexpensive.*

★ **La Residence.** Located in Marigot and popular with business travelers, this soundproof hotel is an excellent choice. All the accommodations have baths (with showers only), phones, safes, cable TVs, minibars and air-conditioning. You've a choice among double rooms, studios, mezzanine loft beds, and apartments with or without kitchenette. The intimate restaurant offers a smashing $28 fixed-price three-course menu gastronomique. You'll have to take a cab to get to the beach. *Rue du Général de Gaulle, Marigot 97150, tel. 590/87–70–37, fax 590/87–90–44. 20 rooms. Facilities: restaurant, lounge, sundry shop. AE, MC, V. CP. Inexpensive.*

La Royale Louisiana. Located in downtown Marigot in the boutique shopping area, this upstairs hotel is pleasant and pretty. White and pale green galleries overlook the flower-filled courtyard. There's a selection of twin, double, and triple air-conditioned duplexes, all with private baths (tubs and showers), TVs, VCRs, and phones. You can reach the nearest beach by a 20-minute walk or by taxi. *Rue du Général de Gaulle, Marigot 97150, tel. 590/87–86–51, fax 590/87–86–51. 68 rooms. Facilities: restaurant, snack bar, beauty salon. AE, DC, MC, V. CP. Inexpensive.*

Home and Apartment Rentals
Both sides of the island offer a wide variety of homes, villas, condominiums, and housekeeping apartments. Information in the United States can be obtained through **Caribbean Home Rentals** (Box 710, Palm Beach, FL 33480, tel. 407/833–4454), **Jane Condon Corp.** (211 E. 43rd St., New York, NY 10017, tel. 212/986–4373), or **St. Maarten Villas** (707 Broad Hollow Rd., Farmingdale, NY 11735, tel. 516/249–4940). On the island, contact **Carimo** (tel. 590/87–57–58), **Ausar** (tel. 590/87–51–07), or **St. Maarten Rentals** (tel. 599/5–44330). **WIMCO** (Box 1461, Newport, RI 02840, tel. 800/932–3222) represents several higher-end properties, primarily on St. Martin.

Nightlife

To find out what's doing on the island, pick up any of the following publications: *St. Maarten Nights, What to Do in St. Maarten, St. Maarten Events,* or *St. Maarten Holiday*—all distributed free in the tourist office and hotels. *Discover St. Martin/St. Maarten,* also free, is a glossy magazine that includes articles about the island's history and the latest on shops, discos, restaurants, and even archaeological digs.

Each of the resort hotels has a Caribbean spectacular one night a week, replete with limbo and fire dancers and steel bands.

Casinos are the main focus on the Dutch side, but there are discos that usually start late and keep on till the fat lady sings.

Bars and Nightclubs
Cheri's Cafe (by the Maho Beach Hotel, tel. 599/5–53361) is a local institution, with cheap food and great live bands. **Turtle Pier Bar & Restaurant** (Airport Rd., tel. 599/5–52230) always hops with a lively crowd. **Coconuts Comedy Club** (Maho Plaza, tel. 599/5–52115) headlines top comedy acts Sunday–Friday. **David's** (Rue de la Liberté, Marigot, tel. 590/87–51–58) is run by an expatriate Brit; its raucous Tuesday and Friday trivia nights are legendary. **La Fiesta** (Rue de la Liberté, Marigot, tel. 590/87–99–41) pulsates to Brazilian rhythms, with occasional live magic and cabaret acts between sambas. In Grand Case, happy hours rock at the **Surf Club South** (no tel.). **Jimbo Lolo** (no tel.) stays open until midnight for French punks and American wannabes who then head over for a nightcap at **Cha Cha Cha Caribbean Café** (tel. 590/87–53–63).

Casinos
All the casinos have craps, blackjack, roulette, and slot machines. You must be 18 years old or older to gamble. The casinos are located at the **Great Bay Beach Hotel, Divi Little Bay Beach Resort, Pelican**

Resort, Mullet Bay Hotel, Seaview Hotel and the **Coliseum** in Philipsburg; **Port de Plaisance;** and **Casino Royal at Maho Beach.**

Discos **Last Stop** (A. T. Illidge Road, no tel.) and the **Tropics** (by Madame Estate in the Royal Inn Motel, no tel.) are hot, somewhat rowdy discos frequented by locals. There have been reports of drug activity at the latter. **Studio 7** (tel. 599/5–42115) attracts a young crowd in its ultramodern digs atop Casino Royale across from Maho Beach Hotel. Casino Royale also produces the splashy "Paris Revue Show." **Le Club** (Mullet Bay, tel. 599/5–42801) draws a mixed crowd of locals and tourists. French nationals and locals flock to **L'Atmosphere** (no tel.) on the second floor of L'Auberge de Mer in Marigot for the best in salsa and soca. **Night Fever** (Colombier, outside Marigot, no phone) attracts a young crowd of locals who gyrate to the latest Eurodisco beat.

24 St. Vincent and the Grenadines

Updated by
Kate Sekules

St. Vincent and the Grenadines form a necklace of lush, mountainous islands that beckon the traveler, sailor, and day-tripper who are more intrigued by blooming flowers than by Bloomingdale's. The fertile volcanic soil has helped to create the oldest botanical gardens in the Western Hemisphere, and rich aromatic valleys of bananas, coconuts, breadfruit, and arrowroot cover these relatively undeveloped islands.

St. Vincent, with a population of about 99,000, is only 18 miles long and 9 miles wide, but it delights those who have discovered its stunning natural beauty, both below and above its crystal seas. Equipped with little more than a snorkel and a sense of adventure, visitors can discover unrivaled underwater landscapes; a pair of comfortable shoes and a little stamina are enough to hike mountains that are as verdant as Hawaii's.

The Grenadines appeal to adventurous singles and couples who prefer active sports to glitz and gambling. Those looking for five-star amenities or designer shopping should go elsewhere. Hotels are small, the food is simple, and the residents' hospitality provides a peaceful, laid-back atmosphere. In contrast to St. Vincent's beaches of black volcanic sand, the Grenadines offer numerous powdery white bays and coves on both the calm leeward and surfy windward shores.

While the islands have their share of the poor and unemployed, the superfertile soil allows everyone to grow enough food to eat and trade for necessities. Since the locals haven't come to regard tourists as meal tickets, beggars are few. Recent progress (improved roads, Bequia's new airport), however, has its price; it is no longer entirely safe to hike alone along forest trails, and petty theft has become a reality.

Historians believe that in 4300 BC, long before King Tut ruled Egypt, the Ciboney Indians first inhabited St. Vincent. Unhampered by passports and political unrest, the Ciboney made their way to Cuba and Haiti, leaving St. Vincent to the Arawaks. Columbus sailed by in 1492, while the Arawaks were involved in intermittent skirmishes with the bellicose Caribs; though Columbus never actually stopped on St. Vincent, Discovery Day (or St. Vincent and the Grenadine's Day) is still commemorated on January 22.

Declared a neutral island by French and British agreement in 1748, St. Vincent became something of a political football in the years that followed. Ceded to the British in 1763, it was captured by the French in 1779 and restored to the British by the Treaty of Versailles in 1783. By the 19th century, St. Vincent was quite sure it was more British than French, and on October 27, 1979, it gained independence from Great Britain.

In contrast to their colorful history, the 32 islands and cays that make up the Grenadines seem timeless, as free from politics as the beaches are free from debris and crowds. Nine miles south of St. Vincent is Bequia, the second-largest Grenadine. Admiralty Bay is one of the finest anchorages in the Caribbean. With superb views, snorkeling, hiking, and swimming, the island has much to offer the international mix of backpackers and luxury-yacht owners who frequent its shores.

A two-hour sail (or ten-minute flight) south is the private island of Mustique. More arid than Bequia, Mustique does not need to tout itself for tourists, least of all those hoping for a glimpse of the rich and famous (Princess Margaret, Mick Jagger, David Bowie) who own houses here. The appeal of Mustique is seclusion and privacy.

Just over 3 square miles, Canouan is an unspoiled island that offers travelers an opportunity to relax, snorkel, and hike.

Numerous yachts and catamarans can be chartered for day sails from any of the Grenadines to the tiny uninhabited Tobago Cays. Avid snorkelers claim that the Cays have some of the best hard and soft coral formations found outside the Pacific Ocean. The beaches here are perfect for secluded picnics.

The tiny island of Mayreau has 182 residents, no phones, and one of the area's most beautiful beaches. The Caribbean is often mirror-calm, yet just yards away on the southern end of this narrow island is the rolling Atlantic surf.

John Caldwell has spent 20 years turning Palm Island from a mosquito-infested mangrove swamp into a small island paradise for couples and families. The Caldwell family also hosts day-tripping cruise passengers who come to lounge on the wide white beaches, which are dotted and fringed with palm trees.

Union Island isn't really a place for landlubbers: The island caters almost completely to French sailors, who keep very much to themselves. Surface transport is limited, and to see the island you need a boat. You won't find the laid-back friendliness of the other Grenadines here.

Petit St. Vincent is another private luxury-resort island, reclaimed from the jungle by manager Haze Richardson. It's actually possible to spend your entire vacation in one of the resort's widely spaced stone houses without ever seeing another human being.

Before You Go

Tourist Information
Contact the **St. Vincent and the Grenadines Tourist Office** (801 2nd Ave., 21st floor, New York, NY 10017, tel. 212/687–4981 or 800/729–1726, fax 212/949–5946; or 6505 Cove Creek Pl., Dallas, TX 75240, tel. 214/239–6451, fax 214/239–1002. In Canada: 100 University Ave., Suite 504, Toronto, Ontario M5J 1V6, tel. 416/971–9666, fax 416/971–9667. In the United Kingdom: 10 Kensington Court, London W8 5DL, tel. 071/937–6570, fax 071/937–3611). Ask for their visitor's guide, which is filled with useful, up-to-date information.

Arriving and Departing
By Plane
Most U.S. visitors fly via **American** (tel. 800/433–7300) into Barbados or St. Lucia, then take a small plane to St. Vincent's E.T. Joshua Airport or to Bequia, Mustique, Canouan, or Union.(Other destinations require a boat ride on either a scheduled ferry, a chartered boat, or your hotel's launch.) Other airlines that connect with interisland flights are **BWIA** (tel. 800/JET–BWIA), **British Airways** (tel. 800/247–9297), **Air Canada** (tel. 800/776–3000), and **Air France** (tel. 800/237–2747).

LIAT (Leeward Islands Air Transport, tel. 809/462–0700; in NY, 212/251–1717; elsewhere in the U.S., 800/253–5011), **Air Martinique** (tel. 809/458–4528), and **SVGAIR** (tel. 809/456–9246; in FL, 813/799–1858; elsewhere in the U.S., 800/677–3195;) fly interisland. Delays are common but usually not outrageous. A surer way to go is with **Mustique Airways** (tel. 809/458–4380). In the U.S., contact **Stratton Travel** (795 Franklin Ave., Franklin Lakes, NJ 07417, tel. 201/891–3456, or 800/223–0599). Its six- or eight-seat charter flights meet and wait for your major carrier's arrival even if it's delayed.

From the Taxis and buses are readily available at E.T. Joshua Airport, and
Airport are available, but rarer, on those Grenadine islands with airstrips.
A taxi from the airport to Kingstown will cost about $7 (E.C.$20);
bus fare is less than 50¢. If you have a lot of luggage, it might be best
to take a taxi—buses (actually minivans) are very short on space.

Passports and U.S., UK, and Canadian citizens must have a passport; all visitors
Visas must hold return or ongoing tickets. Visas are not required.

Language English is spoken everywhere in the Grenadines, often with a
Vincentian patois or dialect.

Precautions Insects are a minor problem on the beach during the day, but when
hiking and sitting outdoors in the evening, you'll be glad you brought
industrial-strength mosquito repellent.

Beware of the manchineel tree, whose little green apples look
tempting but are toxic. Even touching the sap of the leaves will
cause an uncomfortable rash. Most trees on hotel grounds are
marked with signs; on more remote islands, the bark may be painted
red. Hikers should watch for brazilwood trees/bushes, which look
and act similar to poison ivy.

When taking photos of market vendors, private citizens, or homes,
be sure to ask permission first and expect to give a gratuity for the
favor.

There's relatively little crime here, but don't tempt fate by leaving
your valuables lying around or your room or car unlocked.

Staying in St. Vincent and the Grenadines

Important **Tourist Information: The St. Vincent Board of Tourism** (tel. 809/457–
Addresses 1502) is located in a marked building on Egmont Street, on the second floor.

Emergencies **Police:** tel. 809/457–1211. **Hospital: Kingston General Hospital** (tel.
809/456–1185). **Pharmacies: Deane's** (tel. 809/456–2877) and **Reli-
ance** (tel. 809/456–1734), both in Kingstown; on Bequia, **Bequia
Pharmacy** (tel. 809/458–3296).

Currency Although U.S. and Canadian dollars are taken at all but the smallest
shops, Eastern Caribbean currency (E.C.$) is accepted and pre-
ferred everywhere. At press time, the exchange rate was fixed at
U.S.$1 to E.C.$2.67; hotels and shops generally give a rate of
U.S.$1 to E.C.$2.6.

Price quotes are normally given in E.C. dollars; however, when you
negotiate taxi fares and such, be sure you know which type of dollar
you're agreeing on. Note: Prices quoted here are in U.S. dollars unless indicated otherwise.

Taxes and The departure tax from St. Vincent and the Grenadines is $7.50
Service (E.C.$20), which must be paid in local currency. Restaurants and
Charges hotels charge a 5% government tax, and if a 10% service charge is
included in your bill, no additional tip is necessary.

Guided Tours Tours can be informally arranged through taxi drivers who double
as knowledgeable guides. Your hotel or the tourism board will recommend a driver, or call Kelvin Harry (tel. 809/457–1316), president of the Taxi Driver's Association, who will send one of the
Association's members, identifiable by a round yellow-and-blue
decal on the windshield. Always settle the fare first, in either U.S.
or E.C. dollars. The average cost is E.C.$35 per hour.

Grenadine Tours (St. Vincent, tel. 809/458–4818) arranges air, sea, and land excursions throughout the islands, as does **Barefoot Holidays** (tel. 809/456–9334; in the U.S., 800/677–3195).

Getting Around
Buses

Public buses come in the form of brightly painted minivans with names like "Easy Na," "Irie," and "Who to Blame." Bus fares run E.C.$1–$6 in St. Vincent, with the route direction indicated on a sign in the windshield. Just wave from the road, and the driver will stop for you. In Kingstown, buses leave from the Terminus in Market Square.

Smaller islands also have taxi-vans and pickup trucks with benches in the back and canvas covers for when it rains.

Rental Cars

Rental cars cost an average of $45–$50 per day; driving is on the left. Although major improvements are being made, many roads are not well marked or maintained. You may want to take a taxi instead of renting a car.

If you decide to rent a car, you'll need a temporary Vincentian license (unless you already have an international driver's license), which costs E.C.$20. Among the rental firms are **Johnson's U-Drive** (tel. 809/458–4864) at the airport and **Kim's Auto Rentals** (tel. 809/456–1884), which has a larger selection of slightly more expensive rental cars that must be rented by the week.

Telephones and Mail

The area code for St. Vincent and the Grenadines is 809. If you use Sprint or MCI in the United States, you may need to access an AT&T line to dial direct to St. Vincent and the Grenadines. From St. Vincent, you can direct dial to other countries; ask the hotel operator for the proper country code and the probable charge, surcharge, and government tax on the call. Local information is 118; international is 115.

When you dial a local number from your hotel in the Grenadines, you can drop the 45 prefix. Few hotels have phones in the rooms. Pay phones are E.C.25¢.

Mail between St. Vincent and the United States takes two to three weeks. Airmail postcards cost 45¢; airmail letters cost 65¢ an ounce.

Federal Express is located on Bay Street in Kingstown (tel. 809/456–1649) and at Solana's Boutique in Bequia (tel. 809/458–3554).

Opening and Closing Times

Stores and shops in Kingstown are open weekdays 8–4. Many close for lunch from noon to 1 or so. Saturday hours are 8–noon. Banks are open weekdays 8–1, 2, or 3, Friday from 3 to 5. The branch of National Commercial Bank of St. Vincent at the airport is also open Saturday 7–5.

St. Vincent

Exploring St. Vincent

Numbers in the margin correspond to points of interest on the St. Vincent map.

Kingstown's shopping and business district, cathedrals, and sights can easily be seen in a half-day tour, with a further half day for the Botanical Gardens. Outlying areas and the Falls of Baleine will each require a full day of touring, while trips to La Soufrière and the Vermont Trail are major undertakings, requiring a very early start and a full day's strenuous hiking. City maps are in the "Discover SVG" booklet, available everywhere.

Kingstown The capital and port of St. Vincent, **Kingstown** is at the southeastern
① end of the island. Begin your tour on Bay Street, near Egmont
Street. Kingstown's boutiques feature such local crafts as cotton batik hangings and clothing, floor mats, baskets, and black coral jewelry.

The **fish and vegetable market** on Bay Street is a hectic, lively place,
especially on Saturday before 11 AM. Note: Keep a tight grip on your
valuables in the market.

Unusual gifts for stamp collectors are at the **post office** on Granby
Street east of Egmont. St. Vincent is known worldwide for its particularly beautiful and colorful issues, which commemorate flowers,
undersea creatures, and architecture.

Follow Back Street (also called Granby Street) west past the Methodist Church to **St. George's Cathedral,** a yellow Anglican church
built in the early 19th century. The dignified Georgian architecture
includes simple wood pews, an ornate hanging candelabra, and
stained-glass windows. The gravestones tell the history of the island.

Across the street is **St. Mary's Roman Catholic Cathedral,** built in
1823 and renovated in the 1930s. The renovations resulted in a
strangely appealing blend of Moorish, Georgian, and Romanesque
styles in black brick.

A few minutes away by taxi or bus is St. Vincent's famous **Botanical
Gardens.** Founded in 1765, it is the oldest botanical garden in the
Western Hemisphere. Captain Bligh brought the first breadfruit
tree to this island, a direct descendant of which is in the gardens. St.
Vincent parrots and green monkeys are housed in cages, and unusual trees and bushes cover the well-kept grounds. Local guides offer
their services for $2–$4 an hour. *Information: c/o Minister of Agriculture, Kingstown, tel. 809/457–1003. Open weekdays 7–4, Sat. 7–
11 AM, Sun. 7–6.*

The tiny **National Museum** houses ancient Indian clay pottery found
by Dr. Earle Kirby, St. Vincent's resident archaeologist. Dr.
Kirby's historical knowledge is as entertaining as it is extensive.
Contact him for a guided tour, since the labels in the museum offer
little information. *Tel. 809/456–1787. Open Wed. 9–noon, Sat. 3–6.*

② Flag another taxi for the 10-minute ride to **Fort Charlotte,** built in
1806 to keep Napoleon at bay. The fort sits 636 feet above sea level,
with cannons and battlements perched on a dramatic promontory
overlooking the city and the Grenadines to the south, Lowman's
Beach and the calm east coast to the north. The fort saw little military action. Nowadays it is the island's women's prison. Next to it,
and visible from the water, is the old leper's colony.

Outside The coastal roads of St. Vincent offer panoramic views and insights
Kingstown into the island way of life. Life in the tiny villages has changed little
in centuries. This full-day driving tour includes Layou, Montreal
Gardens, Mesopotamia Valley, and the windward coast. Be sure to
drive on the left, and honk your horn before you enter the blind
curves.

Beginning in Kingstown, take the Leeward Highway about 45 minutes north through hills and valleys to **Layou,** a small fishing village.
③ Just north of the village are **petroglyphs** (rock carvings) left by the
Caribs 13 centuries ago. If you're seriously interested in archaeological mysteries, you'll want to stop here. Phone the tourism board
to arrange a visit with Victor Hendrickson, who owns the land. For

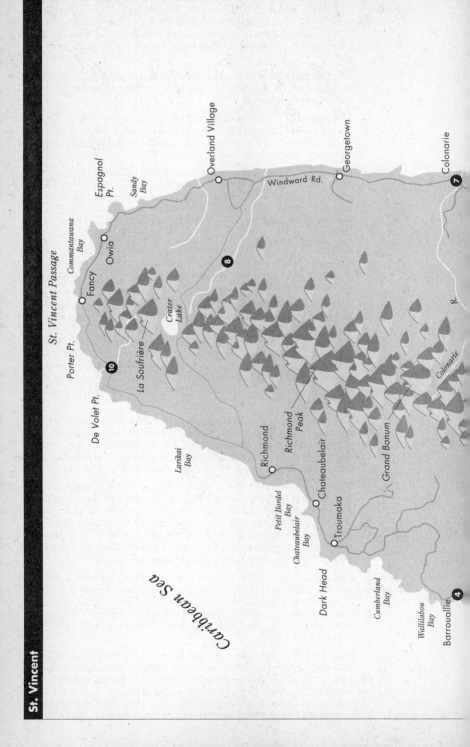

St. Vincent

St. Vincent Passage

Caribbean Sea

Porter Pt.

Commantawana Bay

Espagnol Pt.

Sandy Bay

Overland Village

Windward Rd.

Georgetown

Colonarie

7

Fancy

Owia

8

De Volet Pt.

10

La Soufrière

Crater Lake

Larikai Bay

Richmond

Richmond Peak

Chateaubelair

Grand Bonum

Colonarie R.

Petit Bordel Bay

Chateaubelair Bay

Troumaka

Dark Head

Cumberland Bay

Wallilabou Bay

Barrouallie

4

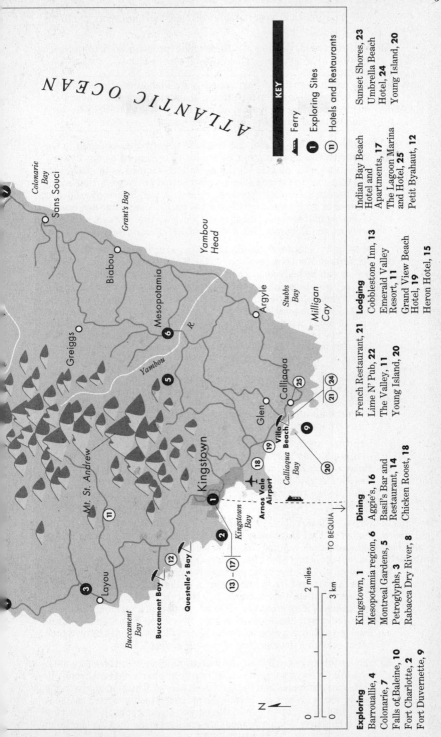

E.C.$5, Hendrickson or his wife will meet you and escort you to the site.

❹ Half an hour farther north is **Barrouallie** (pronounced *BAR-relly*), a onetime whaling village whose inhabitants now trawl for blackfish.

Time Out Ten minutes north of Barrouallie is **Wallilabou** (*wally-la-BOO*), a bay where you can stop for a picnic or simple lunch at the new yacht services building, sunbathe, and swim (there are no showers, but a small waterfall is a short, lovely stroll away).

Backtrack to Kingstown and continue toward Mesopotamia to the **❺** **Montreal Gardens,** another extensive collection of exotic flowers, trees, and spice plants. It's not as well maintained as the Botanical Gardens, but the aroma of cocoa powder and nutmeg wafting on the cool breeze is enticing. Spend an hour with well-informed guides or wander on your own along the narrow paths. Vincentian newlyweds often spend their honeymoon in the garden's tiny cottage, appropriately named Romance. *Tel. 809/458–5452. Open daily.*

Now drive southeast (roads and signs aren't the best, so ask directions at Montreal Gardens) to the **Mesopotamia region.** The rugged, ocean-lashed scenery along St. Vincent's windward coast is the perfect counterpoint to the lush, calm west coast. Mesopotamia is full of dense forests, streams, and bananas, the island's major export. The blue plastic bags on the trees protect the fruit from damage in high winds. Coconut, breadfruit, sweet corn, peanuts, and arrowroot grow in the rich soil here. St. Vincent is the world's largest supplier of arrowroot, which is used to coat computer paper.

Turn north on the Windward Highway up the jagged coast road toward Georgetown, St. Vincent's second-largest city. You'll pass **❼** many small villages and the town of **Colonarie.** In the hills behind the town are hiking trails. Locals are helpful with directions, because signs are limited.

Continue north to **Georgetown,** amid coconut groves and the long-defunct Mount Bentinck sugar factory. A few miles north is the **❽** **Rabacca Dry River,** a rocky gulch carved out by the lava flow from the 1902 eruption of La Soufrière. Here hikers begin the two-hour ascent to the volcano. Return south to Kingstown via the Windward Highway.

The Falls of Drive back to Villa Beach, south of Kingstown, in time to catch the
Baleine sunset at **Fort Duvernette,** the tiny island that juts up like a loaf of
and Fort pumpernickel behind Young Island Resort. Take the *African*
Duvernette *Queen*–style ferry for a few dollars from the dock at Villa Beach near
❾ Kingstown (call the boatman from the phone on the dock) and set a time for your return (60–90 minutes is plenty for exploring). When you arrive at the island, climb the 100 or more steps carved into the mountain. Views from the 195-foot summit are terrific, but avoid the overgrown house near the top, where you'll encounter (harmless) bats. Rusting cannons from the early 1800s are still here, aimed not at seagoing invaders but at the marauding Caribs.

❿ Impossible to get to by car, the **Falls of Baleine** are an absolute must to see on an escorted all-day boat trip or by chartered boat from Villa Beach (*see* Sports and the Outdoors, *below*). The ride offers scenic island views. When you arrive, be prepared to climb from the boat into shallow water to get to the beach. Local guides help visitors make the easy 5-minute sneakers-and-swimsuit trek to the falls.

Swim in the freshwater pool, climb under the 63-foot falls (they're chilly), and relax in this bit of utterly untouched Eden.

Beaches

Most of the hotels and white-sand beaches are near Kingstown; black-sand beaches ring the rest of the island. The placid west coast, site of **Villa Beach** (white sand) and adjacent **Indian Bay, Questelle's** (pronounced Keet–ells) **Bay** (black sand) next to the Camden Park Industrial Site, and tiny **Buccament Bay** (black sand), is good for swimming. The beaches at Villa and the CSY Yacht Club are small but safe, with dive shops nearby. The exposed Atlantic coast is dramatic, but the water is rough and unpredictable. No beach has lifeguards, so even experienced swimmers are taking a risk. The windward side of the island has no beachfront facilities.

Sports and the Outdoors

Hiking Dorsetshire Hill, about 3 miles from Kingstown, rewards you with a sweeping view of city and harbor; picturesque Queen's Drive is nearby. Mt. St. Andrew, on the outskirts of the city, is a pleasant climb through a rain forest on a well-marked trail. Buccament Valley contains two well-marked trails, including the Vermont Trail, where you may be lucky enough to see the rare St. Vincent parrot, *Amazona guidingii*, for which a 5 AM start is recommended.

But the queen of climbs is La Soufrière, St. Vincent's active volcano (which last erupted, appropriately enough, on Friday the 13th in 1979). Approachable from both windward and leeward coasts, this is *not* a casual excursion for inexperienced walkers; you'll need stamina and sturdy shoes for this climb of just over 4,000 feet. Be sure to check the weather before you leave; hikers have been sorely disappointed when they reached the top and found the view completely obscured by enveloping clouds.

Climbs are all-day affairs; a Land Rover and guide can be arranged through your hotel or a knowledgeable taxi driver. The four-wheel-drive vehicle takes you past Rabacca Dry River through the Bamboo Forest. From there it's a two-hour hike to the summit, and you can arrange in advance to come down the other side of the mountain to the Chateaubelair area.

Sailing and Charter Yachting The Grenadines are the perfect place to charter a sailboat or catamaran (bareboat or complete with captain, crew, and cook) to weave you around the islands for a day or a week. Boats of all sizes and degrees of luxury are available; the Lagoon Marina and Hotel (tel. 809/458–4308) in the Blue Lagoon area of St. Vincent has 44-foot crewed sloops from $200 per day. Hotels can also recommend charter yachts.

Water Sports The constant trade winds are perfect for windsurfing, and 80-foot visibility on numerous reefs means superior diving. Many experienced divers find St. Vincent and Bequia far less crowded and nearly as rich in marine life as Bonaire and the Caymans; snorkeling in the Tobago Cays is among the world's best.

Dive operations are small and often less luxurious than on other islands, but competent and professional. Many offer three-hour beginner "resort" courses, full certification courses, and excursions to nearby reefs, walls, and wrecks. Dive shops are on St. Vincent, Bequia, Mustique, Union, and Palm islands; individual island listings have full information. Most dive shops and larger hotels also rent Sunfish, Windsurfers, and snorkel gear.

Dive St. Vincent (tel. 809/457–4714), on Villa Beach, just across from Young Island, is where NAUI instructor Bill Tewes and his staff offer beginner and certification courses, and trips to the Falls of Baleine. A single-tank dive is about $50. Based at the Lagoon Marina Hotel, NAUI instructor Perry Hughes's **St. Vincent Dive Experience** (tel. 809/456–9741) offers all levels of training and certification, plus night dives, snorkeling, and tours. A single-tank dive is about $40.

Depending on the weather, Young Island has some of the area's most colorful snorkeling. If you're not a guest on this private island, phone the resort for permission to take the ferry and rent equipment from the resort's water-sports center (*see* Lodging, *below*).

Shopping

St. Vincent isn't a duty-free port, but appealing local crafts (batik, baskets) and resort wear can be found at **Noah's Arkade** (tel. 809/457–1513) on Bay Street. The best batiks are at **Batik Carib** (tel. 809/456–1666) and **Sprotties** (tel. 809/458–4749), also on Bay Street. The **St. Vincent Craftsmen Center** (tel. 809/457–1288), in the northwest end of Kingstown on James Street above Granby Street, sells grass floor mats and other woven items. Swiss watches, crystal, china, and jewelry can be found at **Stecher's** (tel. 809/457–1142) on Bay Street in the Cobblestone Arcade (a branch is at the airport).

Dining

West Indian food is the way to go in St. Vincent. You'll enjoy interesting local fare that is reasonably priced at all but the expensive hotels. Dishes include callaloo soup, made from the spinachlike vegetable, dasheen; goat stew; *rotis* (burritos filled with curried potatoes and meat or conch); seasonal seafood, including lobster, kingfish, snapper, and dolphin ("not Flipper," as everyone assures you, but dolphin *fish*); local vegetables such as christophines, breadfruit, and eddoes; and exotic fruit ranging from sugar apples and soursop to pineapple and papaya. Fried chicken and burgers are available everywhere, but look for the "imported beef" note on the menu; local beef is not aged, so it tends to be extremely chewy. The local lager, Hairoun, is brewed at Camden Park on the leeward coast, according to a German recipe.

Highly recommended restaurants are indicated by a star ★.

Category	Cost*
Expensive	over $20
Moderate	$10–$20
Inexpensive	under $10

per person, excluding drinks and 5% sales tax

★ **Basil's Bar and Restaurant.** This air-conditioned restaurant, downstairs in the Cobblestone Inn, is owned by the infamous Basil of Mustique, but has little else in common with that laid-back Grenadine glitterati hangout. This is the Kingstown power lunch venue, serving a daily buffet of local fish dishes, plus the likes of seafood pasta and chicken in fresh ginger and coconut milk, to local businessmen and yachties. The bar can get lively in the evenings, when dinner tables are candlelit; and there's a Chinese buffet on Fridays. *Bay St., Kingstown, tel. 809/457–2713. Reservations recommended. AE, MC, V. Expensive.*

★ **French Restaurant.** Referred to as "The French," this Caribbean institution on Villa Beach has long enjoyed its reputation as one of the best restaurants in the Windwards. Tables are on an elegant terrace overlooking Young Island, as well as the state-of-the-art lobster pool, from which you can observe the staff of somewhat unfriendly local girls fish for your supper—if you ordered from the Lobster Menu, that is. Those crustaceans come poached or broiled, in thermidor or bisque, or as surf and turf, and are never fresher. As befits a place run by a couple from Orléans, most dishes are the gallic version of local cuisine. Stuffed crab back, for instance, comes in a shell of pastry, not crab; steak—*au poivre*, with garlic butter, or béarnaise—is imported; onion soup and lemon tart are *comme il faut*; and bread is warm, fresh, real baguette. The inside bar, complete with eccentric, giggling, barman serves frothy cocktails and Martinique-style tea punch to yacht people who hang out here in the winter season. *Villa Beach, tel. 809/458–4972. Dinner reservations recommended. AE, V. Expensive.*

The Valley. It's a long drive to dinner, but this pretty, green-floored terrace hung with fishing nets is part of the Emerald Valley Resort, which includes the only casino in the Grenadines, and if it's Saturday (also some Fridays), a local band serenades diners too. The pride of the kitchen is river lobster, retrieved from the Vermont River, which runs through here; other dishes are a local-international mix: tomato, mozzarella and basil salad; baked red snapper with coconut stuffing; broiled poussin with local herbs. Get directions if you're driving, and call first—the restaurant has an unpredictable tendency to be closed. *Penniston Valley, tel. 809/456–7140. AE, MC, V. Expensive.*

Young Island. Five-course chef's-choice dinners of seafood, roast pig, beef, and chicken tend to be heavy and old-fashioned, except for the Lucullan Tuesday buffets and Saturday barbecues with steel band in attendance. Lunch is served buffet- or barbecue-style on the beach, and features fish and seafood, fresh fruits, salads and cold cuts, with an assortment of fresh breads. Tables are romantically pink-clothed and candlelit, and secreted individually in palm-thatched huts dotted around the beach, with more in the stone-floored terrace dining room. For both meals you must make reservations, unless you are a hotel guest. *Young Island, tel. 809/458–4826. Reservations required. AE, MC, V. Expensive.*

Lime N' Pub. Although this sprawling, waterfront, indoor-outdoor restaurant and bar is named after the *pursuit* of liming, its decor happens to feature a great deal of virulent green, which could prove painful after several cocktails. An eclectic menu caters to burger and pizza eaters as well as seafood fans, and even provides for hybrid diners if they're brave enough to order the smoked sailfish pizza. Good rotis and coconut shrimp go down well with Hairoun. Shop before dinner at the swimwear-and-batik boutique, or stay late and dance on weekends, when the place tends to resemble a singles bar. *Opposite Young Island, tel. 809/458–4227. AE. Inexpensive–Moderate.*

Aggie's. Up on the second floor opposite the Sardine Bakery on Grenville, the Kingstown shopping street, is this casual bar and restaurant, with a swimming-pool-blue ceiling and trellised arches. It serves local seafood dishes, like conch souse and kingfish steak, various soups, including callaloo and pumpkin, rotis, and salads, right

up to midnight. There's a Friday happy hour from 4 to 6. *Grenville St., Kingstown, tel. 809/456–2110. No credit cards. Inexpensive.*
Chicken Roost. This eatery is handy if you're waiting at the airport. The rotis, sandwiches (including shark), pizzas, and ice cream can't be beat. Open daily till 11 PM. *Opposite airport, tel. 809/456–4939. No credit cards. Inexpensive.*

Lodging

Luxury resorts require booking about six months in advance, but most St. Vincent hotels can squeeze you in with far less notice. There's a bit of a lull in January, between Christmas week and the February rush, when rooms are sometimes available on a day's notice. Many hotels offer MAP (Modified American Plan, with breakfast and dinner included).

Highly recommended lodgings are indicated by a star ★.

Category	Cost*
Very Expensive	over $200
Expensive	$130–$200
Moderate	$80–$130
Inexpensive	under $80

*All prices are for a standard double room for two, excluding 5% tax and 10% service charge.

Young Island
★

Young Island. A mere 200 yards from Villa beach lies a 25-acre island populated by prosperous couples who dream of being shipwrecked on a tropical island but don't want to get their feet wet. You arrive by ferry, are handed a rum punch crowned with a hibiscus blossom, and are conducted to your private domain. "Room" is not the word for the 29 houselets. Each has its own patio; fridge; king-size bed; ceiling fan; rattan, palm-weave, and cane decor; and a bathroom that opens into an open-air, but private, shower. Keys are optional, but you have a wall safe; phones are nonexistent, but messages are brought promptly; and there's dual voltage. "Superiors" are lower down, among the tumbling masses of flamboyant, nutmeg, almond, mango, ferns, coffee, breadfruit, etc., etc., while the more expensive deluxe and luxury cottages, with sitting area, are high over the sea; all are exactly halfway between the Swiss Family Robinson's tree house and the Ritz. The landscape conceals a lagoon pool, shaded hammocks, beach (it's tiny, but white-sand) loungers, tennis court, bar, swim-up Coconut Bar, restaurant, plus various bird families. Watch hummingbirds over a Creole French toast breakfast (made with banana bread) on your terrace, and you may feel like you've taken a five-minute boat to heaven. *Box 211, Young Island, tel. 809/458–4826, fax 809/457–4567. U.S. agent: Ralph Locke Islands, Box 800, Waccabuc, NY 10597, tel. 914/763–5526 or 800/223–1108. 29 rooms. Facilities: scuba diving, saltwater pool, watersports center, lighted tennis court, yacht charters. AE, D, MC, V. MAP, AP. Very Expensive.*

Emerald Valley

Emerald Valley Resort. The rural, rain-forested Penniston Valley, half an hour by road from Kingstown, is the unlikely setting for the Grenadines' only casino, which is, equally improbably, attached to this newly renovated family-friendly 5-acre resort. Two pairs of Brits toiled for two years to bring a run-down property up to very high standards, installing air-conditioning, fans, satellite TV,

VCRs and phones, locally made wood-frame king-size or twin beds, stone-floored terraces, and (stoveless) kitchenettes in the 12 chalets. In the garden grounds are an outdoor bar over a two-level pool, bisected by a wooden bridge and diving platform, a stage for local bands on weekends, a tennis court (pro lessons available), a nine-hole golf course (make sure this is finished before you book), and the pretty Valley restaurant (*see* Dining, *above*). What you don't get, of course, is a beach, and the nearest groceries are in Kingstown, but the Vermont Nature Trail is 2½ miles away, and you can gamble till the small hours if bored. *Penniston Valley, Box 1081, St. Vincent, tel. 809/456-7140, fax 809/456-7145. 12 chalets. Facilities: restaurant, casino with bar, 2 bars, 9-hole golf course, 2 tennis courts, grass volleyball court, croquet, pool. AE, MC, V. EP. Inexpensive.*

Villa Beach
★

Grand View Beach Hotel. The Sardine family's turn-of-the-century cotton plantation great house is now Tony and Heather Sardine's beautiful hotel, perched on a lookout point just east of Indian Bay, and freshly renovated. It manages to have both great facilities and down-home charm, set in 8 acres of landscaped grounds that feature not only the expected swimming pool (with swim-up bar) but also a fitness center and sauna, a tennis court, plus one of the island's few squash courts. Most of the simple white-walled rooms with hardwood floors enjoy the sweeping vista toward the Grenadines, and all have air-conditioning or fan, direct-dial phones and satellite TV. *Box 173, Villa Point, St. Vincent, tel. 809/458-4811, fax 809/457-4174. U.S. agent: Charms Caribbean Vacations, tel. 800/223-6510. 12 rooms. Facilities: restaurant, tennis and squash courts, fitness center, sauna, massage, pool, reading room, water-sports center nearby. AE, MC, V. CP, MAP. Expensive.*

Sunset Shores. This U-shape, lemon-colored low rise is the nearest thing on St. Vincent to a corporate hotel, which is not very near at all. There's a Caribbean news update board in the lobby, conference facilities for 100, and the Lions—the local Rotary Club—tend to hold their roisterous meetings here, attended by half the island and its family, but other than that, you won't be bothered by men in suits. In the center of the U is a large-enough pool, facing the sea at Indian Bay, which all rooms overlook. Basic rooms have air-conditioning and phones; superior ones have patios, carpets, and TVs too, and really are superior to the rest. The poolside Sunrunner Bar is nicely placed opposite the sunset. *Box 849, Villa Beach, St. Vincent, tel. 809/458-4411, fax 809/457-4800. 31 air-conditioned rooms. Facilities: restaurant, 2 bars, conference facilities, table tennis, pool, water-sports center nearby. AE, D, MC, V. EP, MAP. Moderate–Expensive.*

Umbrella Beach Hotel. If you're prepared to sacrifice gorgeous bedroom decor for the sake of your pocketbook but still want to be well-located, this very simple cluster of small apartment rooms may fit the bill. All are clean and equipped with ceiling fan, phone, kitchenette with fridge and Calor gas stove, and shower-only bathroom, but, make no mistake, they're dark and plain, with white walls, red marble-chip floors with a rush mat, and plastic chairs at a small Formica table. Steps away are Villa Beach, across from Young Island (ask permission to take the ferry over), the Lime N' Pub, and the French, where you could spend the cash you saved on the room. *Villa Beach, St. Vincent, tel. 809/458-4651, fax 809/457-4930. 9 rooms. Facilities: beach and water sports nearby. MC, V. EP. Inexpensive.*

Indian Bay Beach Hotel and Apartments. This pretty, whitewashed, two-story building sits on Indian Bay, with its small, sheltered, somewhat rocky, white-sand beach that's good for snorkelers. The simple apartments have either one or two bedrooms, air-conditioning and kitchenettes; the best overlook the Bay, with use of a large terrace on top of the restaurant, A La Mer—an airy space with white-trellised arches and a sapphire blue awning. Both baby-sitting and lower weekly rates are available, making this spot useful for families. *Box 538, Kingstown, St. Vincent, tel. 809/458–4001, fax 809/457–4777. 12 apartments. Facilities: restaurant, bar, beach, water sports nearby. AE, MC, V. EP, CP, MAP. Inexpensive.*

Petit Byahaut   **Petit Byahaut.** Sort of a Young Island for those with Swiss Family Robinson fantasies who *do* want to get their feet wet, this 50-acre valley resort accommodates its guests in tents, albeit permanent, wood-floored, 10-by-13-foot tents, complete with private deck, queen-size beds, and solar-heated showers. This adults' camp is accessible only by boat, which collects you from Kingstown (rates include this, as well as all meals), and there is a selection of other boats to play with once you're settled in, along with scuba and snorkeling equipment. In the grounds are a big, black-sand beach, hammocks, and some interesting Carib Indian finds. There's a boutique, excursions are easily arranged, and that's about the extent of the facilities, but then, you don't stay here unless you're reasonably adventuresome and interested in seclusion. *Petit Byahaut Bay, St. Vincent, tel. and fax 809/457–7008. 6 tents. Facilities: restaurant, bar, beach, gardens, solar-heated showers, water sports, ferry service. MC, V. FAP. Expensive.*

Blue Lagoon   **The Lagoon Marina and Hotel.** The only hotel overlooking sheltered
   ★   Blue Lagoon Bay may well be the friendliest hotel on the island. Thanks to its full-service yacht marina, complete with the best-equipped marine shop in St. Vincent, there are usually seafaring types liming in the terrace bar, and plenty of yacht traffic to watch from your big, comfortable balcony with its two couches. Sliding patio doors lead onto these from the tall wood-ceilinged, carpeted rooms; you can practically dive into the sea from numbers 1–9, which hang over the wooden quay and face the sunset; 10–20 overlook the narrow, curved, black-sand beach. Basic wooden furniture, twin beds, rather dim lighting, phones, tiled bathrooms and ceiling fans provide unpretentious comfort; about half the rooms have air-conditioning, too, for a few dollars extra. Sloping garden grounds contain a secluded two-level pool and the St. Vincent Dive Experience Headquarters, and there's a pretty, candlelit, terrace restaurant that was about to change hands at press time. *Box 133, Blue Lagoon, St. Vincent, tel. 809/458–4308, fax 809/457–4716. U.S. agent: Charms Caribbean Vacations, tel. 800/742–4276. 19 rooms. Facilities: restaurant, bar, yacht marina, yacht charter, beach, pool, conference room, scuba, and water sports. AE, V. EP. Moderate.*

Kingstown   **Cobblestone Inn.** Downtown in the city, as Vincentians call Kingstown (correctly, seeing as there's a cathedral), this 1814 stone-built onetime sugar warehouse has a delightful, sunny interior courtyard and arched passageways, which most rooms lead from, and a popular rooftop bar-restaurant for breakfast and soup-salad-burger lunches (come dinnertime, Basil's is downstairs). All the rooms have air-conditioning, phones, small, sparkling bathrooms, exposed stone walls painted white, and rattan furniture. Number 5 at the front is lighter and bigger than most of the other rooms, but noisier too, and many are rather dark, with a faint, not unpleasant, smell of dungeon emanating from the stones. Next to Basil's downstairs is an array of shops selling local craftwork and fashions. The staff is lackadaisical but efficient enough. *Box 867, Kingstown, St. Vincent, tel. 809/456–1937. 19 rooms. Facilities: bar, restaurant. AE, D, MC, V. CP. Inexpensive.*

Heron Hotel. Steps away from the Grenadines wharf, on the second floor above a Georgian plantation warehouse that now contains shops but once provided lodgings for the plantation bosses, the Heron now caters mostly to stopover island-hoppers. It has managed to retain an old-fashioned atmosphere, maybe due to the grouchy manageress, or the radio tuned faintly to a religious station, or the rooms themselves, which are straight out of a '50s boardinghouse, with thin, wine red or navy carpets, billowing faded floral drapes, single beds, bentwood chairs and tiny cream-painted bathrooms. These have air-conditioning and phones and fan out from a palm-filled central courtyard, with tables set on a veranda for breakfast (light lunches, drinks, and West Indian dinners are also available). There's also a corner TV lounge with rows of wooden armchairs, black floorboards and two giant ficus plants. *Box 226, Kingstown, St. Vincent, tel. 809/457–1631, fax 809/457–1189. 12 rooms. Facilities: dining room, courtyard, lounge. MC, V. CP. Inexpensive.*

Nightlife

Don't look for fire-eaters and limbo demonstrations on St. Vincent. Nightlife here consists mostly of hotel barbecue buffets and jump-ups, so called because the lively steel-band music makes listeners jump up and dance.

The Attic (on Grenville St., above the Kentucky Fried Chicken, tel. 809/457–2558), a jazz club with modern decor, features international artists and steel bands. There is a small cover charge; call ahead for hours and performers.

Vidal Browne, manager of **Young Island** (tel. 809/458–4826), hosts sunset cocktail parties with hors d'oeuvres once a week on Fort Duvernette, the tiny island behind the resort. On that night, 100 steps up the hill are lit by flaming torches and a string band plays. Reservations are necessary for nonguests.

The Emerald Valley Casino (tel. 809/456–7140) has the homey atmosphere of an English pub, but offers bar, food, and all the gaming of Vegas—three roulette tables (the only single-zero ones in the Caribbean), three blackjack, one Caribbean stud poker, one craps, five video slots, three slots—and is open daily except Tuesday 9 PM–3 AM; until 4 AM on Saturday.

The Grenadines

The Grenadines are wonderful islands to visit for fine diving and snorkeling opportunities, good beaches, and unlimited chances to laze on the beach with a picnic, waiting for the sun to set so you can go to dinner. For travelers seeking privacy, peace and quiet or active water sports and informal socializing, these are the islands of choice.

Bequia

Arriving and Departing
By Plane **Mustique Airways** (tel. 809/458–4380 or 809/458–4818) flies into Bequia's airport daily from Barbados. **Liat** (tel. 809/458–4841 or 800/253–5011) usually offers day-trip airfare to any three Grenadines and back to St. Vincent for around $170.

By Ferry The MV *Admiral I* and the MV *Admiral II* motor ferries leave Kingstown for Bequia Monday through Friday at 9 AM, 10:30 AM, 4:30 PM, and, depending on availability, 7 PM. Saturday departures are at 12:30 PM and 7 PM; Sunday, 9 AM and 7 PM. Schedules are subject to change, so be sure to check times upon your arrival. All scheduled ferries leave from the main dock in Kingstown. The trip takes 60 minutes and costs $4.

The MV *Snapper* mail boat travels south on Mondays and Thursdays at about 10:30 AM, stopping at Bequia, Canouan, Mayreau, and Union, and returns north on Tuesdays and Fridays, departing Bequia at 11 AM. The cost is under $10.

Weekday service between St. Vincent and Bequia is also available on the island schooner *Friendship Rose*, which leaves St. Vincent at about 12:30 PM. The *St. Vincent and the Grenadines Visitor's Guide*, available in hotels and at the airport, has complete interisland schedules.

Important Addresses **Tourist Information:** The **Bequia Tourism Board** (tel. 809/458–3286) is located on the main dock.

Emergencies **Police:** tel. 809/456–1955. **Medical emergencies:** tel. 999. **Hospital: Bequia Hospital** (tel. 809/458–3294).

Guided Tours To see the views, villages, and boatbuilding around the island, hire a taxi (Gideon, tel. 809/458–3760, is recommended) and negotiate the fare in advance. Water taxis, available from any dock, will also take you by Moonhole, a private community of stone homes with glassless windows, some decorated with bleached whale bones. The fare is about $11.

For those who prefer sailboats to motorboats, Arne Hansen and his catamaran *Toien* can be booked through the **Frangipani Hotel** (tel. 809/458–3255). Day sails to Mustique run $35–$40 per person, including drinks. An overnight snorkel/sail trip to the Tobago Cays costs about $150 for two people, including breakfast and drinks.

Beaches A half-hour walk from the Plantation House Hotel will lead you over rocky bluffs to **Princess Margaret Beach,** which is quiet and wide, with a natural stone arch at one end. Though it has no facilities, this is a popular spot for swimming, snorkeling, or simply relaxing under palms and sea-grape trees. Snorkeling and swimming are also excellent at **Lower Bay,** a wide, palm-fringed beach that can be reached by taxi or by hiking beyond Princess Margaret Beach; wear sneakers, not flip-flops. Facilities for windsurfing and snorkeling are here, as well as the **De Reef** restaurant.

Friendship Bay can be reached by land taxi and is well equipped with windsurfing and snorkeling, rentals and an outdoor bar.

Hope Beach, on the rougher Atlantic side, is accessible by a long taxi ride (about E.C.$20—every driver knows how to get there) and a mile-long walk downhill on a semipaved path. Your reward is a magnificent beach and total seclusion, and—if you prefer—nude bathing. Be sure to ask your taxi driver to return at a prearranged time. Bring your own lunch and drinks; there are no facilities, and swimming can be dangerous.

Industry Bay boasts towering palm groves, a nearly secluded beach, and a memorable view of several uninhabited islands. The tiny, three-room Crescent Bay Lodge is here; its huge bar offers drinks and late lunches (tel. 809/458–3400).

Sports and the Outdoors *Water Sports* Of Bequia's two dozen dive sites, the best are Devil's Table, a shallow dive rich in fish and coral; a sailboat wreck nearby at 90 feet; the 90-foot drop at The Wall, off West Cay; the Bullet, off Bequia's north point for rays, barracuda, and the occasional nurse shark; the Boulders for soft corals, tunnel-forming rocks, thousands of fish; and Moonhole, shallow enough in places for snorkelers to enjoy.

Dive Bequia (tel. 809/458–3504, fax 809/458–3886) and **Sunsports** (tel. 809/458–3577, fax 809/457–3031) offer one- and two-tank dives, night dives, and certified instruction, plus snorkel excursions and equipment rental.

For snorkeling on your own, take a water taxi to the bay at Moonhole and arrange a pickup time.

Shopping All Bequia's shops are along the beach and are open weekdays 10:30–5 or 6, Saturdays 10:30–noon.

Best Buys Handmade model boats (you can special-order a replica of your own yacht) are at **Mauvin's** (¼ mile down the road to the left of the main dock, no tel.). Along Admiralty Bay, hand-printed and batik fabric, clothing, and household items are sold at the **Crab Hole** (tel. 809/458–3290). You can watch the fabrics being made in the workshop out back. **Solana's** (tel. 809/458–3554) offers attractive beachwear, saronglike pareos, and handy plastic beach shoes. The **Bequia Bookshop** (tel.809/458–3905) has an exhaustive selection of Caribbean literature, plus cruising guides and charts, beach novels, souvenir maps, and exquisite hand-carved and -etched whalebone penknives. **Local Color** (tel. 809/458–3202), above the Porthole restaurant in town, has an excellent and unusual selection of handmade jewelry, wood carvings, and resort clothing. Next door is **Melinda's By Hand** (tel. 809/458–3409), with hand-painted cotton and silk clothing and accessories.

Dining Dining on Bequia ranges from West Indian to gourmet cuisine, and it's consistently good. Barbecues at Bequia's hotels mean spicy West Indian seafood, chicken, or beef (although it is usually tougher than Hulk Hogan), plus a buffet of spicy side dishes and sweet desserts. Restaurants are occasionally closed on Sundays; phone to check.

For price information on restaurants and hotels, see the price charts in the Dining and Lodging sections of St. Vincent, above.

★ **Le Petit Jardin.** This chalet-style restaurant serves gourmet lobster and fish prepared with West Indian ingredients, and according to French recipes. If you're missing your prime rib, the house specialty is steak imported from the U.S., which you can wash down with a bottle from the longer-than-average wine list. *Port Elizabeth, tel. 809/458–3318. Reservations necessary. No credit cards. Expensive.*

The Old Fort. Overlooking the Atlantic from Mt. Pleasant, this building dates from the mid-1700s. Otmar and Sonja Schaedle restored it to bougainvillea-shaded, stone-arched, candlelit beauty, and continue to serve food good enough to attract nonhotel guests up the newly paved road. Try a tuna steak, trendily *au point*, accompanied by fresh, homemade bread and a curry of pigeon peas, or a chargrilled whole snapper. *The Old Fort Hotel, Mt. Pleasant, tel. 809/458–3440. MC, V. Expensive.*

La Mezzaluna. Only a year or so old, this is an incongruously traditional Italian trattoria planted above Port Elizabeth, owned by its Roman chef, and useful for city dwellers with pasta withdrawal symptoms. Here, ravioli is more likely to be stuffed with local lobster than spinach and ricotta, but eggplant parmigiana, beef carpaccio and grissini they have got. *Above Port Elizabeth, tel. 809/457–3080. No credit cards. Moderate.*

De Reef. This duo of a restaurant and a café on Lower Bay is the essential feeding station for long, lazy beach days, with the restaurant taking over when the café closes at dusk, as long as you've made res-

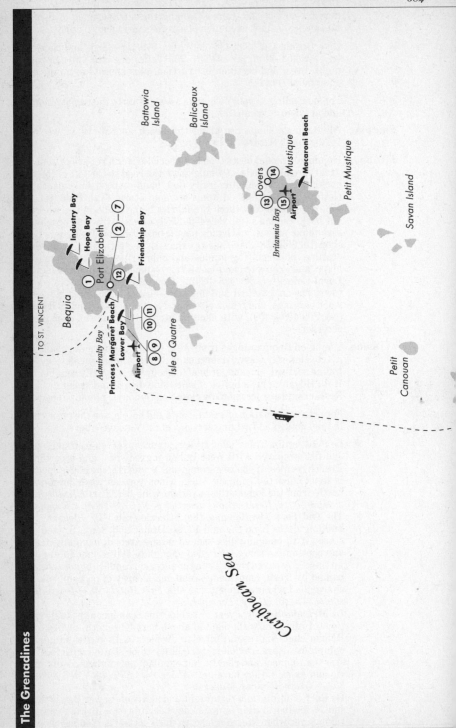

The Grenadines

Battowia Island

Baliceaux Island

Industry Bay

Hope Bay

Port Elizabeth

Friendship Bay

Bequia

TO ST. VINCENT

Admiralty Bay

Princess Margaret Beach

Lower Bay

Airport

Isle a Quatre

Dovers

Mustique

Macaroni Beach

Britannia Bay

Airport

Petit Mustique

Savan Island

Petit Canouan

Caribbean Sea

ATLANTIC OCEAN

N

KEY

Ferry

① Hotels and Restaurants

0   4 miles
0   6 km

Canouan

Friendship Bay

Charleston Bay

North Mayreau Channel

Tobago Cays

Sail Rock

Mayreau

Palm Island

Petit St. Vincent

Petit Martinique

Salt Whistle Bay Beach

Saline Bay Beach

Chatham Bay

Union Island

Clifton

Airport

Martinique Channel

Carriacou

TO CARRIACOU

Dining
Basil's Bar and
Restaurant, **13**
Dawn's Creole
Garden, **11**
De Reef, **8**
Dennis Hideaway, **20**
La Mezzaluna, **3**

Lambi's, **22**
Le Petit Jardin, **2**
Mac's Pizzeria, **4**
Salt Whistle Bay
Club, **19**
The Old Fort, **12**
Theresa's
Restaurant, **10**

Lodging
Anchorage Yacht
Club, **21**
Canouan Beach
Hotel, **18**
The Cotton House, **15**
Crystal Sands Beach
Hotel, **16**
Dennis Hideaway, **20**

Firefly House, **14**
The Frangipani
Hotel, **7**
Friendship Bay
Hotel, **13**
Isola and Julie's Guest
House, **6**
Keegan's Guest
House, **9**

The Old Fort
Hotel, **12**
Palm Island
Resort, **23**
Plantation House
Hotel, **5**
Salt Whistle Bay
Club, **19**
Spring on Bequia, **1**

Villa Le Bijou Guest
House, **17**

ervations. For lunch or dinner, conch, lobster, whelks and shrimp are treated the West Indian way, and the mutton curry is famous. For breakfast (from 7 AM), or light lunch, the café bakes its own breads, croissants, coconut cake and cookies, and blends fresh juices to accompany them. *Lower Bay, tel. 809/458–3484. No credit cards. Inexpensive–Moderate.*

Dawn's Creole Garden. The walk up the hill is worth the delicious West Indian lunches and dinners, especially the Saturday-night barbecue buffet and the major five-course, two-entrée dinners, including the fresh, local christophine and breadfruit accompaniments that Dawn's is known for. There's a wonderful view and live guitar entertainment most Saturday nights. *At the far end of Lower Bay beach, tel. 809/458–3154. Dinner reservations necessary. No credit cards. Inexpensive–Moderate.*

★ **Mac's Pizzeria.** The island's best lunches and casual dinners are enjoyed amid fuchsia bougainvillea on the covered outdoor terrace overlooking the harbor. Choose from mouth-watering lobster pizza, quiche, pita sandwiches, lasagna, home-baked cookies, and muffins. *On the beach, Port Elizabeth, tel. 809/458–3474. Dinner reservations necessary. No credit cards. Inexpensive–Moderate.*

★ **Theresa's Restaurant.** On Monday nights, Theresa and John Bennett offer a rotating selection of enormous and tasty Greek, Indian, Mexican, or Italian buffets. West Indian dishes are served at lunch and dinner the rest of the week. *At the far end of Lower Bay beach, tel. 809/458–3802. Dinner reservations necessary. No credit cards. Inexpensive–Moderate.*

Lodging **Plantation House Hotel.** The aptly named pale peach Plantation
★ House spills elegance and calm all over the beach—you can't help passing by here when strolling to Princess Margaret or Lower Bay. Set in 10 grassy acres of manicured gardens, dotted with palms, hammocks, loungers, and a raised pool, the house, with its five air-conditioned luxury rooms, is appended by 17 breeze-cooled cottages; there are also 3 deluxe beach cabanas for about $30 extra. Decor is in simple, wood-floored style, as befits the laid-back ambience. New this season are an Italian restaurant, a revamped cocktail bar in the garden with live music some nights, a boutique featuring Italian fashions and leather goods, and a health club, with weights, aerobics, and beauty treatments, augmenting the preexisting tennis and water-sports facilities. Why all the Italian stuff? Maybe General Manager Jim Fiore got homesick. *Box 16, Admiralty Bay, Bequia, St. Vincent, tel. 809/458–3425, fax 809/458–3612. U.S. agent: E & M Assoc., 211 E. 43 St., NY 10017, tel. 800/223–9832. 5 rooms, 20 cottages. Facilities: bar, restaurant, water sports, scuba diving, tennis, health club, boutique, pool. AE, MC, V. MAP. Very Expensive.*

Spring on Bequia. Spring is nestled in green hills overlooking groves of tall palms and grazing goats. The hotel is about a mile above town (a pretty walk, though you may want to take a taxi back uphill), and the nearest beach, lovely but too shallow and occasionally seaweedy for serious swimming, is a 10-minute stroll away. The large wood-and-stone rooms attract upscale travelers who want serenity and seclusion. The airy veranda bar is the site of manager Candy Leslie's deservedly famous Sunday curry lunch (reservations necessary). *Bequia, St. Vincent, tel. 809/458–3414. U.S. agent: Spring on Bequia, Box 19251, Minneapolis, MN 55419, tel. 612/823–1202. 10 rooms. Facilities: bar, restaurant, pool, tennis. AE, D, MC, V. EP. Expensive.*

Friendship Bay Hotel. This sprawling white house on a hill with large terraces and sweeping views overlooks another group of pretty, coral stone accommodations close to the beach. Friendship offers a beautiful curve of white-sand beach and tropical plant-filled grounds, and on Saturday nights around the Mau Mau Beach Bar, the liveliest barbecue and jump-up in the Caribbean. This is distinguished from the hundreds of beach bars you have known by its swing seats, cleverly built to keep you upright even after potent rum punches. *Box 9, Bequia, St. Vincent, tel. 809/458–3222, fax 809/458–3840. 27 rooms. Facilities: restaurant, 2 bars, water-sports center, tennis, boutique. AE, MC, V. CP. Moderate–Expensive.*

The Old Fort Hotel. A stunning setting on a cliff above the Atlantic, in a stone estate house built by the French 200 years ago, marks this property out from the others, and endows its rooms with some of the most panoramic Grenadine vistas around, plus the most cooling of trade-wind breezes, obviating any need for air-conditioning. There are only six rooms here, all done out like Captain Bligh's cabin crossed with a Provençale farmhouse, featuring chunky hardwoods and exposed stone. This modest scale, and the fact that the nearest beach, Ravine, is nearly 500 feet below, and a bit too rough for swimming, makes the Old Fort a getaway destination, rather than a lazy vacation base. There will, however, be a new pool sometime in 1995. Luckily, the restaurant (*see* Dining, *above*) is excellent, because it's a trek into town. *Mt. Pleasant, Bequia, St. Vincent, tel. 809/458–3440, fax 809/458–3824. 6 rooms. Facilities: restaurant, bar, hiking. MC, V. EP, MAP. Moderate–Expensive.*

★ **The Frangipani Hotel.** The Frangipani, which has gained the status of venerable institution partly because its owner is St. Vincent's prime minister, who lives here on Bequia, is a local gossip center for international yachties and tourists. Surrounded by flowering bushes, the garden units are built of stone, with private verandas and baths. Four simple, less expensive rooms are in the main house, only one with a private bath. A two-bedroom house with a patio and another apartment with a large bedroom and kitchen are nearby. Several more garden units and two-bedroom dwellings are planned. String bands appear on Mondays, with folksingers on Friday nights during tourist season. The Thursday-night steel-band jump-up at the beachfront bar is a must; the bar, with its huge, white-painted wooden armchairs facing the sunset, is probably the nicest around. *Box 1, Bequia, St. Vincent, tel. 809/458–3255, fax 809/458–3824. 13 rooms. Facilities: bar, restaurant, tennis, water-sports center, yacht excursions, boutique. MC, V. EP. Inexpensive–Moderate.*

Isola and Julie's Guest House. Right on the water in Port Elizabeth, these two separate buildings share a small restaurant and bar. Furnishings (which are few) run to early Salvation Army, but the food is great and the rooms are airy and light, with private baths; some have hot water. *Box 12, Bequia, St. Vincent, tel. 809/458–3304, 809/458–3323 or 809/458–3220. 25 rooms. Facilities: bar, restaurant. No credit cards. MAP. Inexpensive.*

Keegan's Guest House. This is the place for budget-minded beach lovers who want quiet, friendly surroundings. Located on Lower Bay, this *very* simple place offers family-style West Indian breakfasts and dinners for its guests. Rooms 3, 4, and 5 have a shared bath and are cheaper, although there is no hot water to be found (you really do get used to it). *Bequia, St. Vincent, tel. 809/458–3254 or 809/458–3530. 11 rooms. Facilities: dining room. No credit cards. MAP. Inexpensive.*

Nightlife As well as the various jump-ups at hotels, the newish **Harpoon Saloon,** clearly visible above the bay to port side as you sail into Bequia, regularly hosts local bands, and is the nearest thing to a nightclub for miles.

Canouan

Goat-herding is still a career option here, and organized activities are nil. Walk, loaf, swim, or snorkel; Canouan still lives in the 18th century. Unfortunately, the 18th-century hotels don't live up to their 21st-century prices.

Dining and Lodging **Canouan Beach Hotel.** This hotel, the only modern one on the island, caters to French people and French people only—even if all you want is a dinner reservation. You won't find laid-back island friendliness here. Simple white cottages, with air-conditioning, patios and bathrooms, tennis, a golf driving range, catamaran day-sails weekdays, and live music twice a week are what's offered here. *Canouan, St. Vincent, tel. 809/458–8888, fax 809/458–8875. 43 rooms. Facilities: bar, restaurant, marina, windsurfing, snorkeling, scuba, tennis, driving range. AE, MC, V. MAP. Very Expensive.*

Crystal Sands Beach Hotel. Run by a local family and extremely simple, Crystal Sands is located on Charleston Bay and has a veranda bar and dining area. Cottages share a connecting door for larger groups and have private baths and patios. Fishing, sailing, and great snorkeling can be found off the fine beach. Phone the managers to arrange for air pickup in St. Vincent. If you take the mail boat from Kingstown (*see* Arriving and Departing in Bequia, *above*), pack light and be prepared to climb from the large ferry into a small rowboat to get to shore. *Canouan, St. Vincent, tel. 809/458–8015. 10 rooms. Facilities: bar, dining area, snorkeling, fishing. No credit cards. EP. Moderate–Expensive.*

Villa Le Bijou Guest House. Up the hill and only a 10-minute walk from Friendship Bay (15 minutes from the airstrip; pack light—taxis are rarely available). Accommodations border on the primitive, and the electricity is often on vacation, but the view is stunning. *M. de Roche, Villa La Bijou, Canouan, St. Vincent, tel. 809/458–8025. 6 rooms. No hot water in the shared baths. Facilities: snorkeling, Sunfish, windsurfing, dining area. No credit cards. MAP. Moderate–Expensive.*

Nightlife Surprise: There's a bar and disco on weekends at **Le Bijou.**

Mayreau

Farm animals outnumber citizens on tiny Mayreau. Except for water sports and hiking, there's nothing to do, and visitors like it that way. This is the perfect place for a meditative or vegetative vacation.

Guided Tours You can swim and snorkel in the Cays or nearby islands on day trips with charter yachts arranged by the hotel. Contact **Undine Potter** at the Salt Whistle Bay Resort (from the U.S., tel. 800/263–2780; in the Grenadines, marine radio VHF channel 16 or 68). Note that the Salt Whistle Bay's snorkel equipment has seen better days. Buy or rent your own before you arrive.

Beaches Top honors go to **Salt Whistle Bay Beach**—the Caribbean's prettiest. The beach is an exquisite half-moon of powdery white sand, shaded by perfectly spaced palms and flowering bushes, with the rolling Atlantic a stroll away. Hike 25 minutes over Mayreau's mountain (wear shoes; bare feet or flip-flops are a big mistake) to a good photo opportunity at the stone church atop the hill and stunning views of the Cays. Then have a drink at Dennis Hideaway and enjoy a swim at beautiful **Saline Bay Beach.** No facilities; the mail boat's tender stops at the dock here.

Sports and the Outdoors Scuba diving can be arranged through **Grenadines Dive** (tel. 809/458–8138 or 809/458–8122; *see* Sports and the Outdoors, Union Island, *below*.)

Dining and Lodging **Salt Whistle Bay Club.** Set far back from the water, the roomy stone cottages at Mayreau's only hotel are so cleverly hidden that sailors need binoculars to be sure a hotel is there at all. With names like "Oleander" and "Ivora," the cottages sport round-stone, hot-water showers that look like large, medieval telephone booths. You can dry your hair on the breezy, shared second-story veranda atop each two-room building. The outdoor dining area has stone tables covered by thatched palms where guests enjoy turtle steak, duckling, lobster, and à la carte lunches. Music is on CD if you like; there used to be a jump-up, but guests preferred peace and quiet. *Write Salt Whistle Bay Club, Management Offices, 1020 Bayridge Dr., Kingston, Ontario, Canada K7P 2S2. Tel. in the U.S. 800/263–2780; outside the U.S., call collect 613/634–1963. Fax in the U.S. 800/263–2780; outside the U.S., 613/384–6300. In the Caribbean, marine radio VHF channel 16 or 68. 10 cottages, 4 refurbished suites. Facilities: bar, restaurant. windsurfing, snorkeling, catamaran charter. No credit cards. FAP. Very Expensive.*
Dennis Hideaway. It's practically the only place on the island, but that's no great hardship, since Dennis (who plays the guitar two nights a week) is a charmer, the food is great, the drinks are strong, and the view is heaven. The rooms are clean, but very simple: a bed, nightstand, chair, and a place to hang some clothes. *Saline Bay, tel. 809/458–8594. 3 rooms. Facilities: restaurant. Reservations recommended. No credit cards. Restaurant: Moderate–Expensive. Lodging (EP): Inexpensive–Moderate.*

Mustique

Princess Margaret put this 3 x 1½ mile former copra, cotton, and sugarcane estate on the map, once her compatriot, Colin Tennant (now Lord Glenconner) bought it. The company he formed in 1968 to develop Mustique into the glamorous hideaway island it still remains now has 37 shareholders and a House Rentals Department you'd need to contact about a year in advance if you wanted to rent the royal holiday home, Balliceaux, or another of the 40-odd luxury villas that pepper the northern half of the island. Some house-owners keep their villas empty in their absence, including Mustique's two most glittering habitués, Mick Jagger and David Bowie. Their villas are concealed behind Brobdingnagian fences, but anyone who insists on star-gawking will get to see whoever's "on island" at Basil's Bar, the unofficial social center, sooner or later.

Next to his bar, in a cluster of candy-colored houses that don't quite qualify as a town, Basil also runs a boutique crammed with clothes and accessories imported and specially commissioned from all over the world, a cornucopian delicatessen to feed residents fresh Brie and Moët, and a new antiques shop stocked with fabulous pieces for those fabulous houses. There's also a fish market, a grocery warehouse, a gas station—and a police station with nothing much to do. To some, that adds up to paradise; others *hate* it, but you pays yer money, you takes yer choice.

Beaches **Macaroni Beach** is Mustique's most famous stretch of sand, offering surfy swimming (no lifeguards, so be careful), powdery white sand, a few palm huts for shade, and picnic tables on a grassy garden behind. From the northern coast, working west, L'Ansecoy, Endeavour, and Britannia Bays are also fine, and much calmer, the latter being the best for day-trippers, with Basil's Bar adjacent for lunch. Further south, Gelliceaux Bay, by the Cotton House, provides the best snorkeling beach.

Sports and the Outdoors Water-sports facilities are available at the Cotton House, and most villas have equipment of various sorts. Scuba is best arranged through **Dive Mustique** (tel. 809/458–4621). There's a communal tennis court for those whose villa lacks its own, a cricket ground for the Brits, and motorbikes for trail-riding around the bumpy roads for rent at $35 per day. The best sport to indulge in on Mustique, however, is horseback riding, since this is one of the few islands where you can rent a decent animal. Rides leave Mon.–Sat. at 8 and 9 AM, 3 and 4 PM from the **Equestrian Centre** (tel. 809/458–4316), and rates are $40 per hour.

Dining **Basil's Bar and Restaurant.** Basil's is the only place to be seen on
★ Mustique, and only partly because it *is* the only place on Mustique, apart from the more formal, quieter Cotton House. Resembling many a beachside terrace restaurant, with its wooden deck built over the waves, palm-roofed at the edges with a central bar and dance floor open to the stars, there's something about the atmosphere that hints at happenings. Well, you never know who you may run into. . . . The food is simple and good—mostly fish hauled out of the water a hundred yards away, homemade ice cream, burgers and salads, great French toast, the usual cocktails, many unusual wines. The Wednesday barbecue is the regular party night, and there's live music Mondays. *Tel. 809/458–4621. Reservations suggested. AE, MC, V. Inexpensive–Expensive.*

Lodging **The Cotton House.** The island's only hotel centers around the stone-
★ and-coral 18th-century former estate warehouse, originally converted by the late Oliver Messel (the great British theater designer/decorator/architect, who was to Mustique as Haussmann was to Paris) and just recently revamped to his original designs. In fact, the whole place, including most guest-room cottages and the restaurant, has been totally overhauled during the past year, transforming an expensively underwhelming hostelry back to an hotel in the world's top rank. All rooms have elegant French windows onto balconies, louvered cedar and pastel decor, and new air-conditioning. Ten are "deluxe" rooms—the closest to standard there is here—at a good $80–$125 less per night than the Junior Suites. Numbers 1–4 are the rooms to pick, since they've had top-to-toe make-overs (the freshest Junior Suites are 9–11; Deluxe Suites, 12–16). Further guest cottages are due this year. The restaurant menu now includes low-fat cuisine and beach lunches as well as the perennially popular picnic coolers; and—hoorah—you can now get a sunset rum punch on one of the two beaches, after playing tennis, fish-peeping, a dip in the freshwater pool, and a browse through library and boutique. *Box 349, Mustique, St. Vincent, tel. and fax 809/456–4777. U.S. agent: Ralph Locke Islands, tel. 800/223–1108. 24 rooms. Facilities: restaurant, bar, pool, library, boutique, water sports, tennis, horseback riding. AE, D, MC, V. FAP. Very Expensive.*
Firefly House. Tiny and charming with just five rooms, this is the island's only budget choice, but it's still well located, above Britannia Bay, and the rooms have private baths, fridges, and picnic equipment, plus, for $5 extra, air-conditioning. There's an honor bar for guests' use. *Mustique, Box 349, tel. 809/456–3414. 5 rooms. Facilities: water sports, bar. No credit cards. CP. Inexpensive–Moderate.*

Villa Rentals Renting one of Mustique's privately owned villas is undoubtedly the best way to see the island, and not as expensive as it seems at first glance, since rates include a full staff, with cook but no groceries, laundry service, and a vehicle or two; rates are per house, not per person. Houses range from simple rusticity—if you can call ensuite bathrooms for every bedroom, at least one phone line, probably a pool, cable TV, VCR, CD, and even fax, rustic—to extravagant, expansive, faux-Palladian follies with resident butler; but all are designer-elegant and immaculately maintained. Rates start at $2,800 a week for the two-bed Pelican Beach off-season, and go way up to $13,000 a week for the palatial five-bed, five-person staff, two-Jeep, one-Jacuzzi Blackstone, during winter. Princess Margaret's three-bed place is surprisingly modest, at a mere $3,200 a week in summer. *House Rentals Dept., Mustique Co. Ltd., Box 349, tel. 809/ 458–4621, fax 809/456–4565. 42 villas. AE, DC, MC, V. FAP. Very Expensive.*

Palm Island

★ **Palm Island Resort.** A seafarer was shipwrecked, stranded on a desert island, reunited with his new wife, had two sons, found a swamp-ridden, mosquito-infested jungle called Prune Island, and toiled with his family for 25 years to turn it into a practically perfect resort. What is this? A Judith Krantz novel? A Sly Stallone movie? No, it's how Palm Island came to be, and you can read all about it over tea, delivered at 4 PM to your cabana terrace. Quite aside from its amazing history, Palm Island is a special place, to which most guests (50/50 American–European) are moved to return, craving more of that barefoot peace and quiet, big, white, empty beaches, and glassy seas. Cabanas have king-size beds, somewhat dribbly, but scenic, outdoor hot-water showers, room-width patio doors, minifridges, silent ceiling fans, every conceivable bug-destroying apparatus and lounger configuration, and views over the water. Numbers 12 through 18 face the sunset, and are closest to the ship's bell that announces dinner. There are games and books to borrow, the "Highway 90" fitness trail to follow, birds to watch, tennis, water sports, boat and fishing trips to indulge in, and hammocks to lounge in. There's also a yacht club next to the hotel area, with an alternative restaurant. Book early—this is many people's ideal island. *Palm Island, St. Vincent, tel. 809/458– 8224, fax 809/458–8804. U.S. agent: Paradise Found, tel. 800/776– PALM. 24 rooms, 15 self-catering villas. Facilities: open-air bar/ restaurant, fitness course, water sports (scuba at extra charge), games room, tennis, boutique, grocery, catered charter yacht sails, yacht provisioning. AE, MC, V. FAP. Very Expensive.*

Petit St. Vincent

Many upscale travelers consider Petit St. Vincent the finest private island in the Caribbean. The privacy is as perfect as the food, which is worthy of any four-star Manhattan restaurant—the ideal place to pretend you own an uninhabited (yet elegantly serviced) island. Hoisting a yellow flag outside your spacious, secluded stone-and-wood house invites a staff member to drive out and see what you want; after they take your order, don't confuse them by hoisting the red "leave me alone" flag.

Meals are also served in the expanded Pavilion, where you can hear a talented and unusual quintet from Carriacou on Wednesday nights, while a band from Petit Martinique serenades diners at the Saturday beach barbecue.

Beaches   Small, secluded beaches surround the island, now hidden from the jogging/fitness trail by skillful new landscaping. The hotel will drop you for the day at Mopion (also known as Petit St. Richardson), a tiny sandbar with one thatch-roof shelter for shade. There is good swimming all over.

Sports and the Outdoors Activities include tennis, croquet, windsurfing, waterskiing (small extra charge), snorkeling, sailing trips, and jogging on a 20-stop, 32-exercise fitness trail that runs along the beaches and around a wooded area. Shaded hammocks are strung up every 100 feet along the trail. *PSV, Box 12506, Cincinnati, OH 45212, tel. 513/242–1333, 800/654–9326, or 809/458–8801. 22 houses. No credit cards. Closed Sept. and Oct. FAP. Very Expensive.*

Union

Union's airstrip is right behind the Anchorage Yacht Club. Gorgeous from a distance, Union doesn't offer the charm or friendliness of other Grenadines.

Beaches The beach around Clifton Harbour is narrow, unattractive, rocky, and shadeless. Other beaches have no facilities and are virtually inaccessible without a boat; the desolate but lovely Chatham Bay offers good swimming.

Sports and the Outdoors **Grenadines Dive** (tel. 809/458–8138 or 809/458–8122), run by NAUI instructor Glenroy Adams, is the local operation, including Tobago Cays trips and wreck dives at the *Purina*, a sunken World War I English gunship.

Dining **Lambi's.** On the main street in Clifton, Lambi's offers good conch Creole and walls made from their shells. *Tel. 809/458–8549.* No credit cards. Moderate.

Lodging **Anchorage Yacht Club.** Between the airstrip and what little beach there is are rooms and bungalows with concealed outdoor showers and terraces facing the water, all comfortably refurbished, with water sports and yacht chartering galore for entertainment. The enormous bar area is fronted by a pool inhabited by dozens of nurse sharks so docile that a sign warns PLEASE DO NOT TOUCH THE SHARKS. *Union, St. Vincent, tel. 809/458–8221, fax 809/458–8365. 10 rooms, 6 bungalows. Facilities: restaurant, bar, water-sports center, boutique, air-conditioning, yacht provisioning and charters. AE, MC, V. CP. Moderate–Expensive.*

25 Trinidad and Tobago

Updated by
Kate Sekules

Trinidad and Tobago, the southernmost islands in the West Indies chain, could not be more dissimilar. Trinidad's cosmopolitan capital, Port-of-Spain, bustles with shopping centers, modern hotels, sophisticated restaurants, and an active nightlife. It is also home to a riotous Carnival, the birthplace of steel-band music, and a busy port. The 1.3 million Trinidadians know prosperity from oil (Trinidad is one of the biggest producers in the Western Hemisphere), a steel plant, natural gas, and a multiplicity of small businesses. Around 51,000 of them—Indians, Africans, Europeans, Asians, and Americans, each with their own language and customs—live in Port-of-Spain. The Trinidadians are heavy on cricket and horse racing. But you have to leave the capital to find a good beach. And because it is one of the most active commercial cities in the West Indies, most visitors are business travelers.

Tobago, 22 miles away, offers the lazier life most tourists seek. The Robinson Crusoe island is more laid-back; the pace is slower, with beautiful, near-deserted beaches, secluded bays, small hotels, and little fishing villages. Goats outnumber cars. Tobago is popular with snorkelers and divers; its Buccoo and Speyside reefs are underwater wonderlands.

Columbus reached these islands on his third voyage, in 1498. Three prominent peaks around the southern bay where he anchored prompted him to name the land La Trinidad, after the Holy Trinity. Trinidad was captured by British forces in 1797, ending 300 years of Spanish rule.

Tobago's history is more complicated. It was "discovered" by the British in 1508. The Spanish, Dutch, French, and British all fought for it until it was ceded to England under the Treaty of Paris in 1814. In 1962, both islands—T&T, as they're commonly called—gained their independence within the British Commonwealth, finally becoming a republic in 1976.

In 1986, the National Alliance for Reconstruction (NAR) won a landslide victory, toppling the People's National Movement (PNM), which had been in power for 30 years but had brought the country to the brink of economic ruin. Then, in the 1991 elections, the electorate presumably were not impressed by the NAR and returned power back to the PNM. The new government, especially because of the decline in oil prices, is now looking for ways to encourage tourist development.

Trinidad's capital may be noisy and its way of life somewhat frenetic, but its countryside is rich in flora and fauna, home to more than 400 species of birds and 700 varieties of orchids.

Before You Go

Tourist Information

Contact the **Trinidad and Tobago Tourism Development Authority.** In the United States: 25 W. 43rd St., Suite 1508, New York, NY 10036, tel. 212/719–0540 or 800/232–0082, fax 212/719–0988. In the United Kingdom: 8a Hammersmith Broadway, London W6 7AL, tel. 081/741–4466, fax 081/741–1013. In Canada: 40 Holly St., Suite 102, Toronto, Ontario M4S 3C3, tel. 416/486–4470 or 800/268–8986, fax 416/440–1899.

Arriving and Departing
By Plane

There are daily direct flights to Piarco Airport, about 30 minutes east of Port-of-Spain, from New York, Miami, and Toronto on **BWIA** (tel. 800/JET–BWIA), Trinidad and Tobago's national airline. You can also fly from one or more of these cities on **American** (tel. 800/433–7300) and **Air Canada** (tel. 800/422–6232). BWIA has flights three times a week from London and serves Boston and Baltimore once a week. There are flights from Amsterdam and Paramaribo via **KLM Royal Dutch Airlines** (tel. 800/777–5553). **ALM** (tel. 800/327–7230) flies from Atlanta and Miami via Curaçao. There are numerous interisland flights in the Caribbean by BWIA and **LIAT** (tel. 809/462–0701). All flights to Trinidad alight at Piarco Airport. BWIA and LIAT flights from Trinidad to Crown Point Airport in Tobago take about 15 minutes and depart about 6 to 10 times a day. For those wishing to circumvent Trinidad entirely, LIAT has direct service from Barbados to Tobago.

Package tours aren't generally touted as heavily as they are for other Caribbean islands, but there are bargains to be had, especially around Carnival. One particularly good agency in this regard is **Pan Caribe Tours** (Box 46 3223, Austin, TX 78764, tel. 512/267–9209 or 800/525–6896).

By Boat The Port Authority runs a ferry service between Trinidad and Tobago; the ferry leaves once a day, except for Saturday. The trip takes about six hours (flying is preferable); round-trip fare is TT$60, about U.S.$12; cabin fare is $22 (one-way double occupancy), with an extra charge for vehicles. Tickets are sold at offices in Port-of-Spain (tel. 809/625–4906) and at Scarborough, in Tobago (tel. 809/639–2181).

From the Taxis are readily available at Piarco Airport. The fare to Port-of-
Airport Spain is set at $20. By car, take Golden Grove Road north to Arouca, then follow Eastern Main Road west for about 10 miles.

Passports Citizens of the United States, the United Kingdom, and Canada who
and Visas expect to stay for less than two months may enter the country with a valid passport. A visa is required for a stay of more than two months.

Language The official language is English, although there is no end of idiomatic expressions used by the loquacious Trinis. You will also hear smatterings of French, Spanish, Chinese, and Hindi.

Precautions Insect repellent is a must during the rainy season (June–December) and is worth having around anytime. Trinidad is only 11 degrees north of the equator, and the sun here can be intense. Even if you tan well, it's a good idea to use a strong sunblock, at least for the first few days.

Staying in Trinidad and Tobago

Important **Tourist Information:** Information is available from the **Trinidad &**
Addresses **Tobago Tourism Development Authority** (134–138 Frederick St., Port-of-Spain, tel. 809/623–1932, fax 809/623–3848; Piarco Airport, tel. 809/664–5196). For Tobago, write to the **Tobago Division of Tourism** (N.I.B. Mall, Scarborough, tel. 809/639–2125, fax 809/639–3566) or drop in at its information booth at Crown Point Airport (tel. 809/639–0509).

Emergencies **Police:** Call 999. **Fire and ambulance:** Call 990. **Hospitals: Port-of-Spain General Hospital** is at 169 Charlotte Street (tel. 809/623–2951); **Tobago County Hospital** is on Fort Street in Scarborough (tel. 809/639–2551). **Pharmacies: Oxford Pharmacy** (tel. 809/627–4657) is at Charlotte and Oxford streets near the Port-of-Spain General Hospital; **Ross Drugs** (tel. 809/639–2658) is in Scarborough. For a complete list of other pharmacies, check the T&T Yellow Pages.

Currency The Trinidadian dollar (TT$) has been devalued twice in recent years. The current exchange rate is about U.S.$1 to TT$5.50. The

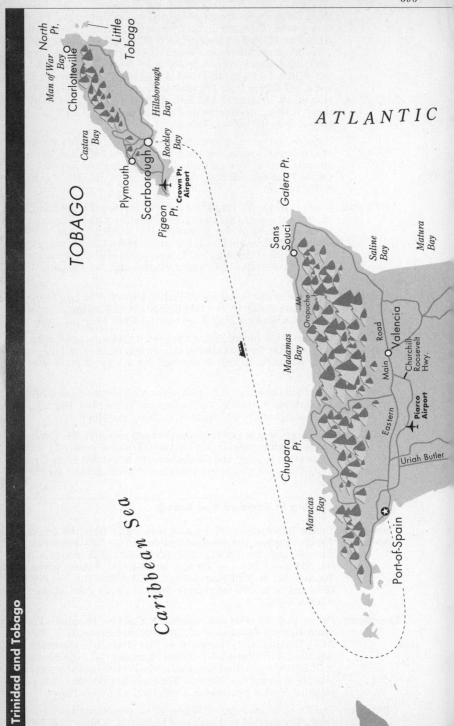

Trinidad and Tobago

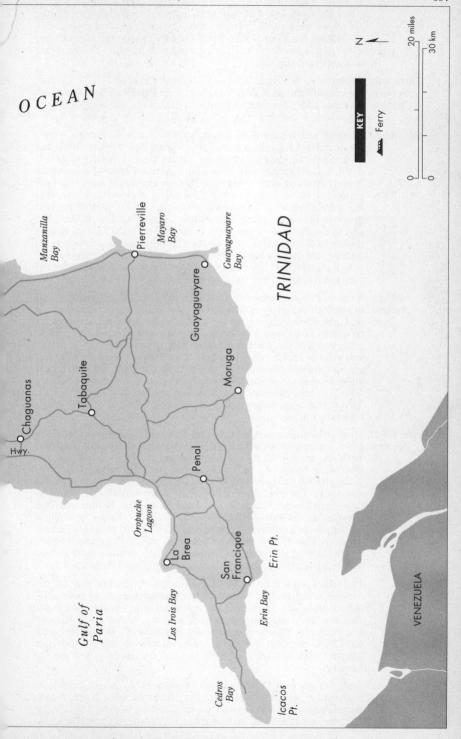

major hotels in Port-of-Spain have exchange facilities whose rates are comparable to official bank rates. Trinidad's best rate is found at the Hilton. Most businesses on the island will accept U.S. currency if you're in a pinch. Note: Prices quoted here are in U.S. dollars unless indicated otherwise.

Taxes and Service Charges Restaurants and hotels add a 15% value-added Tax (VAT). The airport departure tax is TT$50, or about U.S.$10. Many hotels and restaurants add a 10% service charge to your bill. If the service charge is not added, you should tip 10%–15% of the bill for a job well done.

Guided Tours **Trinidad and Tobago Sightseeing Tours** (Galleria Shopping Centre, Western Main Rd., St. James, Port-of-Spain, tel. 809/628–1051) has a variety of sightseeing packages, from a tour of the city to an all-day drive to the other side of the island. Another reputable agency is **Travel Trinidad and Tobago** (69 Independence Square, Port-of-Spain, tel. 809/625–2201 or 809/623–1980 on weekends), with everything from Trini nightlife crawls to Tobago by bike. Almost any **taxi driver** in Port-of-Spain will be willing to take you around the town and to the beaches on the north coast for around $70 for up to four people to Maracas Bay, plus $20 per hour extra if you decide to go farther, but you can haggle for a cheaper rate. For a complete list of tour operators and sea cruises, contact the tourism office. For nature guides, *see* Sports and the Outdoors, *below*.

Getting Around Taxis Taxis in Trinidad are easily identified by their license plates, which begin with the letter H. Passenger vans, called Maxi Taxis, pick up and drop off passengers as they travel and are color coded according to which of four areas they cover. They are easily hailed day or night along most of the main roads near Port-of-Spain. For longer trips you will need to hire a pri vate taxi. There are set rates, though they are not always observed, particularly at Carnival. Pick up a rate sheet from the tourism office. On the whole, the drivers are honest, friendly, and informative, and the experience of riding in a Maxi Taxi with a souped-up sound system during Carnival is worth whatever fare you pay.

Rental Cars/ Scooters If you are a first-time visitor to Port-of-Spain, where the streets are often jammed with traffic and drivers who routinely play "chicken" with one another, taxis are your best bet, though expensive if you plan to see everything on the island, and you may feel immobile. Nor is the city easy to negotiate on foot, though Maxi Taxis are plentiful and cheap. Car-rental services include **Auto Rentals** (tel. 809/675–2258), with eight locations, and **Lord Kalloo Car Rental and Taxi Service** (tel. 809/669–5673 or 809/645–5182). Mr. Kalloo goes out of his way to help, and is as friendly as his cars are reliable. Various tours are also offered, and rates are negotiable. All agencies require a credit card slip deposit, and in season you must make reservations well in advance of your arrival. Figure on paying $40–$60 per day.

In Tobago you will be better off renting a Jeep than relying on taxi service, which is less frequent and ultimately much more expensive. A four-wheel drive vehicle is far better and safer than a car for roads that are frequently bumpy, pitted, winding, and/or steep (though the main highways are smooth and fast). **Baird's Rental** (tel. 809/639–7054, or 2528) is reliable, and has new Suzuki Jeeps—plus Toyota Hilux minivans, motorbikes, and bicycles—at around $40 per day.

As befits one of the world's largest exporters of asphalt, Trinidad's roads are generally good, though you'll find road work in progress as major resurfacing work is carried out, starting in early 1994. In the outback, roads are still often narrow, twisting, and prone to washouts in the rainy season. Inquire about conditions before you take off, particularly if you're heading toward the north coast. Never drive into downtown Port-of-Spain during afternoon rush hour. Don't forget to drive on the left.

Telephones and Mail The area code throughout the two islands is 809. For telegraph, telefax, teletype, and telex, contact **Textel** (1 Edward St., Port-of-Spain, tel. 809/625–4431). Cables can be sent from the tourism office and major hotels.

To place an intraisland call, dial the local seven-digit number. To reach the United States by phone, dial 1, the appropriate area code, and the local number.

Postage for first-class letters to the United States is TT$2.25; postcards, TT$2.

Opening and Closing Times Most shops open Monday–Thursday 8–4, Friday 8–6, and Saturday 8–noon. Banking hours are Monday–Thursday 9–2 and Friday 9–12 and 3–5.

Carnival

Trinidad always seems to be either anticipating, celebrating, or recovering from a festival, the biggest of which is **Carnival.** Carnival occurs each year between February and early March. Trinidad's version of the pre-Lenten bacchanal is reputedly the oldest in the Western Hemisphere; there are festivities all over the country, but the most lavish is in Port-of-Spain.

Carnival officially lasts only two days, from *J'ouvert* (sunrise) on Monday to midnight the following day. If you're planning to go, it's a good idea to arrive in Trinidad a week or two early to enjoy the events leading up to Carnival. Not as overwhelming as its rival in Rio or as debauched as Mardi Gras in New Orleans, Trinidad's festival has the warmth and character of a massive family reunion.

Carnival is about extravagant costumes: Individuals prance around in imaginative outfits. Colorfully attired troupes—called *mas*—that sometimes number in the thousands march to the beat set by the steel bands. You can visit the various mas "camps" around the city where these elaborate costumes are put together—the addresses are listed in the newspapers—and perhaps join one that strikes your fancy. Fees run anywhere from $35 to $100; you get to keep the costume. Children can also parade in a Kiddie Carnival that takes place on Saturday morning a few days before the real thing.

Throwing a party is not the only purpose of Carnival; it's also a showcase for calypso performers. Calypso is music that mixes dance rhythms with social commentary, sung by characters with such evocative names as Shadow, the Mighty Sparrow, and Black Stalin. As Carnival approaches, many of these singers perform nightly in calypso tents, which are scattered around the city. You can also visit the pan yards of Port-of-Spain, where steel orchestras, such as the Renegades, Desperadoes, Catelli All-Stars, Invaders, and Phase II, rehearse their arrangements of calypso. Most can be heard practically year-round.

For several nights before Carnival, costume makers display their talents, and the steel bands and calypso singers perform in spirited competitions in the grandstands of the old racetrack in Queen's Park, where the Calypso Monarch was crowned until 1993, when the Dimanche Gras festivities moved to the National Stadium in the Cruise Ship Complex at the Port. At sunrise, or J'ouvert, the city starts filling up with metal-frame carts carrying steel bands, flatbed trucks hauling sound systems, and thousands of revelers who squeeze into the narrow streets. Finally, at the stroke of midnight on "Mas Tuesday," Port-of-Spain's exhausted merrymakers go to bed. The next day everybody settles back to business.

Exploring Trinidad

Numbers in the margin correspond to points of interest on the Trinidad map.

Port-of-Spain
❶

It is not really surprising that a sightseeing tour of **Port-of-Spain** begins at the port. (If you're planning to explore by foot, which will take two to four hours, start early in the day; by mid-afternoon Port-of-Spain can be hot and is always packed like Calcutta.) Though it is no longer as frenetic as it was during the oil boom of the 1970s, **King's Wharf** entertains a steady parade of cruise and cargo ships, a reminder that the city started from this strategic harbor. Across Wrightson Road is **Independence Square,** which is not a square at all: It's a wide, dusty thoroughfare crammed with pedestrians, car traffic, taxi stands, and peddlers of everything from shoes to coconuts— not a pleasant walk for lone females. Flanked by government buildings and the familiar twin towers of the Financial Complex (familiar because it adorns one side of all T&T dollar bills), the square is gloriously chaotic, loud, and confusing.

Walk all the way west along the square to Wrightson Road, where stands the Gothic-style Cathedral of the Immaculate Conception. On the south side is the Cruise Ship Complex, full of duty-free shops, forming an enclave of international anonymity with the Holiday Inn. Alternatively, head north up Frederick Street—the main shopping drag—at the midpoint of Independence Square, and, at the corner of Prince Street, look across **Woodford Square** toward the magnificent **Red House,** a Renaissance-style building that takes up an entire city block. Trinidad's House of Parliament takes its name from a paint job done in anticipation of Queen Victoria's Diamond Jubilee in 1897. Woodford Square has served as the site of political meetings, speeches, public protests, and occasional violence. The original Red House, in fact, was burned to the ground in a 1903 riot. The present structure was built four years later. The chambers are open to the public.

The view of the south side of the square is framed by the Gothic spires of **Trinity,** the city's other cathedral, and, on the north, by the impressive **public library** building, the **Hall of Justice** and **City Hall.**

Continue north along Pembroke Street and note the odd mix of modern and Colonial architecture, gingerbread and graceful estate houses, and stucco storefronts. After five blocks, Pembroke crosses Keate Street at **Memorial Park,** from which a short walk north leads to the greater green expanse of **Queen's Park,** more popularly called the **Savannah.**

Time Out

Buy a cool coconut water from any of the vendors operating out of flatbed trucks along the Savannah. For about 50¢, he'll lop the top off a green coconut with a deft swing of the machete and, when you've finished drinking, lop again, making a bowl and spoon of coconut shell for you to eat the young pulp—the texture of a boiled egg white. According to Trinis, "It'll cure anyt'ing dat ail ya, mon."

Proceeding west along the Savannah, you'll come to a garden of architectural delights: the elegant lantern-roof **George Brown House;** what remains of the **Old Queen's Park Hotel;** and a series of astonishing buildings constructed in a variety of 19th-century styles, known as the **Magnificent Seven.**

Notable among these buildings are **Killarney,** patterned after Balmoral Castle in Scotland, with an Italian-marble gallery surrounding the ground floor; **Whitehall,** constructed in the style of a Venetian palace by a cacao-plantation magnate and currently the office of the prime minister; **Roomor,** a flamboyantly baroque Colonial-period house with a preponderance of towers, pinnacles, and wrought-iron trim that suggests an elaborate French pastry; and the **Queen's Royal College,** in German Renaissance style, with a prominent tower clock that chimes on the hour.

The **racetrack** at the southern end of the Savannah is no longer a venue for horse racing, but it is still the setting for music and costume competitions during Carnival and, when not jammed with calypso performers, tends toward quietude.

The northern end of the Savannah is devoted to plants. A rock garden, known as the **Hollow,** and a fish pond add to the rusticity. The **Botanic Gardens,** across the street, date from 1820. The official residences of the president and prime minister are on these grounds.

Way east, on Picton Road in the scruffy, industrial district of Laventille, are **Fort Chacon** and **Fort Picton,** erected to ward off invaders by the Spanish and British regimes, respectively. The latter is a martello tower with a fine view of the gulf.

Out on the Island
The intensely urban atmosphere of Port-of-Spain belies the tropical beauty of the countryside surrounding it. It is truly stunning, but you will need a car, and three to eight (if you include the Caroni swamp) hours to find it. Begin by circling the Savannah—seemingly obligatory to get almost anywhere around here—to Saddle Road, the residential district of **Maraval.** After a few miles the road begins to narrow and curve sharply as it climbs into the Northern Range. Here you'll find undulating hills of lush, junglelike foliage. Stop at the **Lookout**—and have Keith Davis sing you an echt and hilarious calypso, complete with any biographical details you give him. (He's not allowed to ask, but a few T&T dollars are appreciated—and deserved.) Half an hour through this hilly terrain will lead you to **Maracas Bay,** the island's most popular beach, with smaller **Tyrico Bay** adjacent.

Time Out
Try a shark-and-bake from one of the huts ranged along the road at Maracas. It's a deep-fried pita-type-bread shark sandwich, served with hot sauce and cilantro-garlic salsa. Patsy's is considered the best. Wash it down with a grenadillo (like a giant passion fruit) juice from the stand on Patsy's right, if it's available.

About four miles along is **Las Cuevas Beach.** Follow the same road through tiny La Fillete for several miles, crossing the bridge over the Yarra River. Here, washerwomen hang their laundry out, which is how **Blanchisseuse** got its name.

In this town the road narrows again, winding through canyons of moist, verdant foliage, towering palms and "big bamboo" (it's so gigantic they wrote a calypso song about it), and mossy grottoes. As you painstakingly execute the hairpin turns, you'll begin to think you've entered a tropical rain forest. You have.

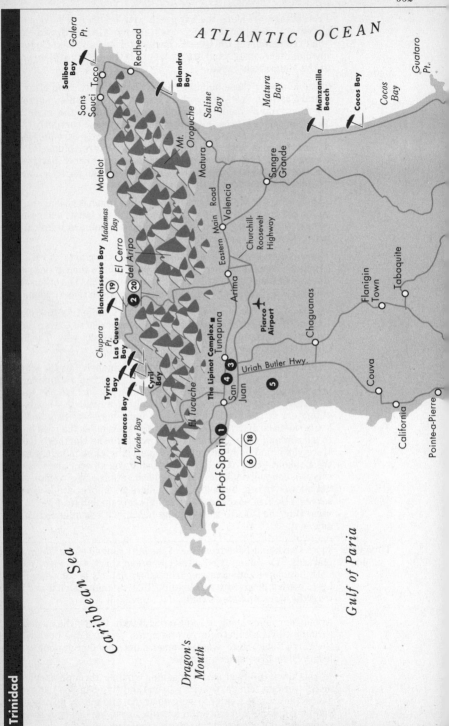

Trinidad

ATLANTIC OCEAN

Caribbean Sea

Galera Pt.

Salibea Bay

Redhead

Balandra Bay

Toco

Sans Souci

Saline Bay

Matura Bay

Manzanilla Beach

Cocos Bay

Cocos Bay

Guataro Pt.

Matelot

Mt. Oropuche

Madamas Bay

El Cerro del Aripo

Blanchisseuse Bay

Matura

Sangre Grande

⑲ ⑳ ②

Chupara Pt.

Las Cuevas Bay

Eastern Main Road

Valencia

Churchill-Roosevelt Highway

Tabaquite

Flanigin Town

Tyrico Bay

Cyril Bay

Arima

✈ Piarco Airport

Chaguanas

Maracas Bay

El Tucuche

The Lipinot Complex ■
Tunapuna

④ ③

Uriah Butler Hwy.

⑤

Couva

La Vache Bay

San Juan

① **Port-of-Spain**

⑥ — ⑱

California

Pointe-a-Pierre

Dragon's Mouth

Gulf of Paria

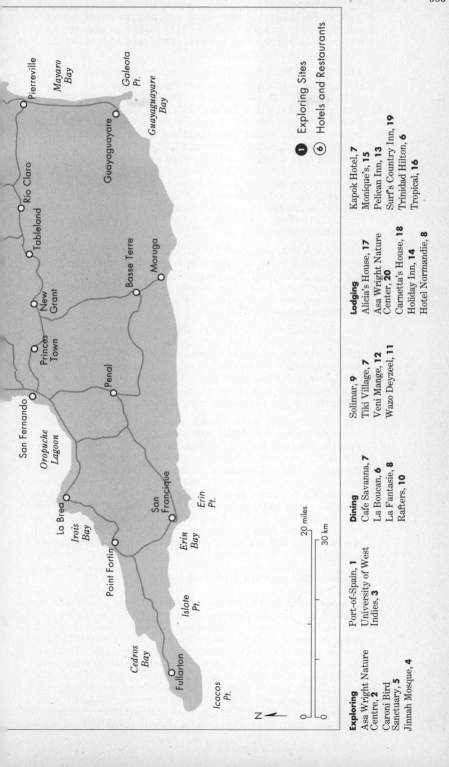

Pierreville

Mayaro Bay

Galeota Pt.

Guayaguayare

Guayaguayare Bay

Rio Claro

Tableland

Basse Terre

New Grant

Moruga

Princes Town

Penal

San Fernando

Oropuche Lagoon

La Brea

Irois Bay

San Francique

Erin Pt.

Erin Bay

Point Fortin

Islote Pt.

Cedros Bay

Fullarton

Icacos Pt.

N

0   20 miles
0   30 km

Exploring
Asa Wright Nature
Centre, **2**
Caroni Bird
Sanctuary, **5**
Jinnah Mosque, **4**

Port-of-Spain, **1**
University of West
Indies, **3**

Dining
Cafe Savanna, **7**
La Boucan, **6**
La Fantasie, **8**
Rafters, **10**

Solimar, **9**
Tiki Village, **7**
Veni Mange, **12**
Wazo Deyzeel, **11**

Lodging
Alicia's House, **17**
Asa Wright Nature
Center, **20**
Carnetta's House, **18**
Holiday Inn, **14**
Hotel Normandie, **8**

Kapok Hotel, **7**
Monique's, **15**
Pelican Inn, **13**
Surf's Country Inn, **19**
Trinidad Hilton, **6**
Tropical, **16**

● Exploring Sites

⑥ Hotels and Restaurants

Keep an eye out for vultures, parakeets, hummingbirds, toucans, and, if you're lucky, even red-bellied yellow-and-blue macaws. And, by the way, the mass of white cotton-candy substance on the rocks by the road hides tarantula nests.

About half an hour from Blanchisseuse, the road forks. Take the right, signposted to Arima, and another half hour on this road (and a *very* sharp right at the green hut) brings you to a bird-watcher's paradise, the **Asa Wright Nature Centre** (*see* Lodging, *below*). The grounds are festooned with a mass of plants, trees and multihued flowers, and the surrounding acreage is atwitter with more than 100 species of birds, from the gorgeous blue-green motmot to the rare nocturnal oilbird. The oilbirds' breeding grounds in Dunston Cave are included among the sights along the center's guided hiking trails. If you're not feeling too energetic, lounge on the veranda of the handsome estate house, which offers a panorama of the Arima Valley. You can also have lunch. *Tel. 809/667–4655. Admission: $6 adults, $4 children. Open daily 9–5. Guided tours at 10:30 and 1:30, reservations necessary.*

The descent to **Arima,** about 7 miles, is equally pastoral. The Eastern Main Road connecting Arima to Port-of-Spain is anything but: It's a busy, bumpy, and densely populated corridor full of roadside stands and businesses. Along the way you'll pass the **University of West Indies** campus in Curepe and the majestic turrets and arches of the **Jinnah Mosque** in St. Joseph.

Proceed west from Arima along the Churchill-Roosevelt Highway, a limited-access freeway that runs parallel to the Eastern Main Road a few miles to the south. Both avenues cross the Uriah Butler Highway just outside Port-of-Spain in San Juan; a few miles south on Butler Highway, take the turnoff for the **Caroni Bird Sanctuary.** Across from the sanctuary's parking lot is a sleepy canal with several boats and guides for hire; the smaller boats are best.

The Caroni is a large swamp with mazelike waterways bordered by mangrove trees, some plumed with huge termite nests. In the middle of the sanctuary are several islets that are home to Trinidad's national bird, the scarlet ibis. Just before sunset the ibis arrive by the thousands, their richly colored feathers brilliant in the gathering dusk, and, as more flocks alight, they turn their little tufts of land into bright Christmas trees. It's not something you see every day. Bring a sweater and insect repellent for your return trip. The boat fee is usually about $6–$15. Advance reservations can be made with boat operators Winston Nanan (tel. 809/645–1305) or David Ramsahai (tel. 809/663–2207). Nanan also arranges highly recommended bird-watching tours to Guyana and Venezuela.

What to See and Do with Children

Emperor Valley Zoo and the **Botanical Gardens** are a cultivated expanse of parkland just north of the Savannah, the site of the president's official residence. A meticulous lattice of walkways and local flora, the parkland was first laid out in 1820 and is a model of what a tropical garden should be. In the midst of this serene wonderland is the zoo, leisurely apportioned on eight acres and largely featuring birds and animals of the region—from the brilliantly plumed scarlet ibis to slithering anacondas and pythons; wild parrots breed in the area and can be seen (and heard) in the surrounding foliage. The zoo draws a quarter of a million visitors a year and more than half of them are children, so admission is priced accordingly—a mere

TT$3, or TT$1.50 for under-12s. *Botanical Gardens, Port-of-Spain, tel. 809/622–3530. Open daily 9:30–6.*

The **Water Park** at the Valley Vue Hotel is open to nonguests, and has the biggest, wettest slides in the West Indies—three 400-foot chutes leading to a shallow pool. *Ariapita Rd., St. Ann's, Port-of-Spain, tel. 809/624–0940. Admission: $5 adults, $4 children. Open daily 10–6.*

Junior Carnival (*see* Carnival, *above*).

Off the Beaten Track

The Lopinot Complex is a French settlement founded in the 19th century; there's a well-preserved estate house from a once-prosperous colonial coffee and cocoa plantation, complete with a museum and—so they say—Lopinot's ghost. (A guide is available from 10 to 6.) This is one of the main centers for Parang, a beautiful string-based folk music, which has become Trinidad's equivalent of Christmas carols. To get there, take the Eastern Main Road from Port-of-Spain to Arouca and look for the sign that points north.

Exploring Tobago

Numbers in the margin correspond to points of interest on the Tobago map.

A driving tour of Tobago, from Scarborough to Charlotteville and back, can be done in about four hours.

1 **Scarborough** is nestled around **Rockley Bay,** and it gives the feeling that not much here has changed since the area was settled two centuries ago. This is its charm.

The road east from Scarborough soon narrows as it twists through **2** **Mt. St. George,** a village that clings to a cliff high above the ocean. Fort King George is a lovely, tranquil spot commanding sweeping views of the bay, with a restored 18th-century English fort and barracks, a fine-arts center, and lush landscaped gardens.

The sea dips in and out of view as you pass through a series of small settlements and the town of Roxborough. About an hour's drive will **3** bring you to **King's Bay,** an attractive crescent-shape beach. Just before you reach the bay there is a bridge with an unmarked turnoff that leads to a gravel parking lot; beyond that, a landscaped path leads to a waterfall with a rocky pool where you can refresh yourself. You may meet enterprising locals who'll offer to guide you to the top of the falls, a climb that you may find not worth the effort.

After King's Bay the road rises dramatically; just before it dips **4** again there's a marked lookout with a vista of **Speyside,** a small fishing village, and several offshore islands.

Time Out **Jemma's Sea View Kitchen** (tel. 809/660–4066), along the main road in Speyside, offers tasty West Indian meals served in a house on stilts by the ocean. You'll find nothing fancy here, just delicious Tobagonian home cooking, including a wondrous baked chicken, and great views.

Past Speyside the road cuts across a ridge of mountains that separates the Atlantic side of Tobago from the Caribbean. On the far side **5** is **Charlotteville,** a remote fishing community, albeit the largest vil-

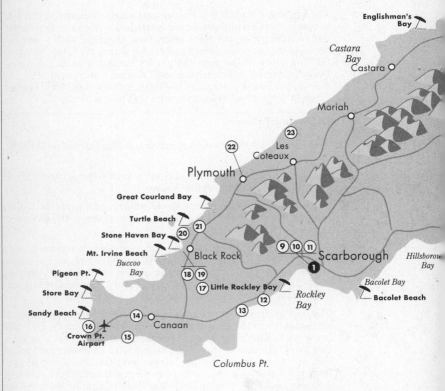

Caribbean Sea

Englishman's Bay

Castara Bay

Castara

Moriah

(23)

(22)

Les Coteaux

Plymouth

Great Courland Bay

Turtle Beach

Stone Haven Bay (20) (21)

Mt. Irvine Beach

Buccoo Bay

Black Rock

(9) (10) (11)

Scarborough

Hillsborough Bay

Pigeon Pt.

(18) (19)

(17) Little Rockley Bay

(1)

Store Bay

Sandy Beach

(16)

Crown Pt. Airport

(15)

(14) Canaan

(12) Rockley Bay

(13)

Bacolet Bay

Bacolet Beach

Columbus Pt.

Exploring
Charlotteville, **5**
Flagstaff Hill, **6**
King's Bay, **3**
Mt. St. George, **2**
Scarborough, **1**
Speyside, **4**

Dining
Blue Crab, **9**
Cocrico Inn, **22**
Dillon's, **14**
Grafton's, **20**
The Old Donkey Cart House, **10**

Papillon, **19**
Rouselles, **11**
The Village, **15**

Lodging
Arnos Vale Hotel, **23**
Blue Horizon Resort, **17**
Blue Waters Inn, **7**
Grafton Beach Resort, **20**

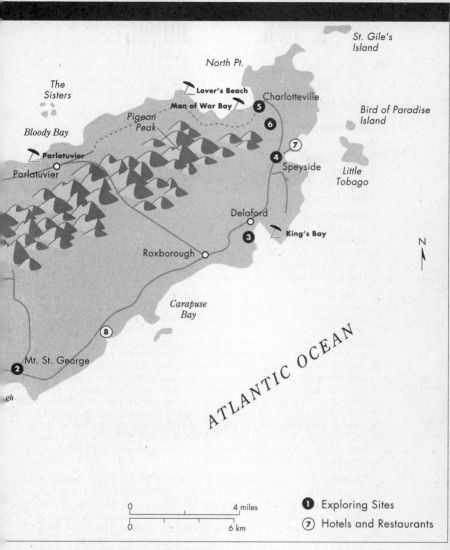

St. Gile's Island

North Pt.

The Sisters

Lover's Beach

Man of War Bay

Charlotteville

Bird of Paradise Island

Pigeon Peak

Bloody Bay

Parlatuvier

Parlatuvier

Speyside

Little Tobago

Delaford

King's Bay

Roxborough

Carapuse Bay

ATLANTIC OCEAN

Mt. St. George

gh

N

0		4 miles
0		6 km

1 Exploring Sites

7 Hotels and Restaurants

Kariwak Village, **15**
Mt. Irvine Bay Hotel, **18**
Ocean Point, **13**
Palm Tree Village, **12**
Richmond Great House, **8**

Sandy Point Beach Club, **16**
Turtle Beach Hotel, **21**

lage on the island. Fishermen here announce the day's catch (usually
flying fish, redfish, or bonito) by sounding their conch shells.

The paved road ends a few miles outside Charlotteville, in
Camberton. Returning to Speyside, take a right at the sign for
❻ Flagstaff Hill. Follow a well-traveled dirt road for about 1½ miles to
a radio tower. It's one of the highest points in Tobago, surrounded
by ocean on three sides and with a view of the hills, Charlotteville,
and Bird of Paradise Island in the bay.

Beaches

Trinidad   Contrary to popular notion, Trinidad has far more beaches than Tobago; the catch is that Tobago's beaches are close to hotels, and
Trinidad's are not. There are, however, some worthy sites within an
hour's drive of Port-of-Spain, spread out along the North Coast
Road.

Maracas Bay is a long stretch of sand with a cove and a fishing village
at one end. It's a local favorite, so it can get crowded on weekends.
Parking sites are ample, and there are snack bars and rest facilities.
Tyrico Bay, just past Maracas, is a small beach lively with surfers
who flock here to enjoy the excellent surfing. The strong undertow
may be too much for some swimmers.

A few miles farther along the North Coast Road **Las Cuevas Bay,** a
narrow, picturesque strip of sand named for the series of partially
submerged and explorable caves that ring the beach. A food stand
offers tasty snacks, and vendors hawk fresh fruit across the road.
It's less crowded here, and seemingly serene, although, as at Maracas, the current can be treacherous. About 8 miles east, along the
North Coast Road, is another narrow beach, palm-fringed
Blanchisseuse Bay. Facilities are nonexistent, but the beach is ideal
for a romantic picnic. You can haggle with local fishermen to take
you out in their boats to explore the coast. Two miles or so farther
along the North Coast Road, you come to **Marianne Beach,** the quietest and prettiest of all, with a natural freshwater lagoon at the
east end. Pay Vincent James TT$3 to park on his land; you can also
rent the three-room first floor of the house you see for TT$75—it's
very basic (tel. 809/674–7145 after 1 PM).

The drive to the northeast coast takes several hours. To get there you
must take the detour road to Arima, but "goin' behind God's back," as
the Trinis say, does reward the persistent traveler with gorgeous vistas and secluded beaches. **Balandra Bay,** sheltered by a rocky out-
cropping, is popular among bodysurfers. **Salibea Bay,** just past
Galera Point, which juts toward Tobago, is a gentle beach with shallows and plenty of shade—perfect for swimming. Snack vendors
abound in the vicinity. The road to **Manzanilla Beach** and **Cocos Bay**
to the south, nicknamed the Cocal, is lined with stately palms whose
fronds vault like the arches at Chartres. This is where many well-
heeled Trinis have vacation homes. Manzanilla has picnic facilities
and a postcard-pretty view of the Atlantic, though its water is occasionally muddied by the Orinoco River, which flows in from South
America.

Tobago   Traveling to Tobago without sampling the beaches is like touring
Burgundy in France without drinking the wine. So, starting from
the town of Plymouth and slowly gravitating counterclockwise,
we'll explore a dozen of the island's more memorable sand spots.

Great Courland Bay, near Fort Bennett, is a long stretch of clear,
tranquil water, bordered on one end by **Turtle Beach,** so named for

the turtles that lay their eggs here at night between April and May. (You can watch; the turtles don't seem to mind.) A short distance west, there's a side road that runs along **Stone Haven Bay,** a gorgeous beach that's across the street from Grafton Beach Resorts, a luxury hotel complex.

Mt. Irvine Beach, across the street from the Mt. Irvine Beach Hotel, is an unremarkable setting that has the best surfing in July and August. It's also ideal for windsurfing in January and April. There are picnic tables surrounded by painted concrete pagodas and a snack bar.

Pigeon Point is the locale inevitably displayed on Tobago travel brochures. It's the only privately owned beach on the island, part of what was once a large coconut estate, and you must pay a token admission (about $2) to enter the grounds. The beach is lined with royal palms, and there's a food stand, gift shop, and paddleboats for rent. The waters are calm.

Store Bay, where boats depart for Buccoo Reef, is probably the most socially convivial setting in the area. The beach is little more than a small sandy cove between two rocky breakwaters, but, ah, the food stands here: six shacks licensed by the tourist board to local ladies, featuring *roti* (an East Indian sandwich), *pelau* (rice and peas), and the world's messiest dish, crab and dumplings. Miss Jean's (tel. 809/ 639–0563) is the most popular; try Miss Esmie's crab, though. Farther west along Crown Point, **Sandy Beach** is abutted by several hotels. You won't lack for amenities around here.

Just west of Scarborough, take Milford Road off the main highway to the shores of **Little Rockley Bay.** The beach is craggy and not much good for swimming, but it is quiet and offers a pleasing view of Tobago's capital across the water.

After driving through Scarborough, continue south on Bacolet Street 4 miles to **Bacolet Beach,** a dark-sand beach that was the setting for the films *Swiss Family Robinson* and *Heaven Knows, Mr. Allison.*

The road from Scarborough to Speyside has plenty of swimming sites, of which **King's Bay Beach,** surrounded by steep green hills, is the most visually satisfying—the bay hooks around so severely that you feel as if you're swimming in a lake. It's easy to find because it's marked by a sign about halfway between Roxborough and Speyside.

Man of War Bay in Charlotteville is flanked by one of the prettiest fishing villages in the Caribbean. You can lounge on the sand and purchase the day's catch for your dinner. Farther west across the bay is **Lover's Beach,** so called because of its pink sand and because it can be reached only by boat. You can hire one of the locals to take you across.

Parlatuvier, on the north side of the island, is best approached via the road from Roxborough. The beach here is a classic Caribbean crescent, a scene peopled by villagers and local fishermen. The next beach over, **Englishman's Bay,** is equally seductive and completely deserted.

Sports and the Outdoors

Bird-watching Bird-watchers can fill up their books with notes on the variety of species to be found in Trinidad at the **Asa Wright Nature Centre,** the **Caroni Bird Sanctuary** (*see* Exploring Trinidad, *above*), and the **Pointe-à-Pierre Wild Fowl Trust,** which is located within the confines of a petrochemical complex (42 Sandown Rd., Pt. Cumana, tel. 809/ 637–5145). In Tobago, naturalist **David Rooks** offers walks inland and trips to offshore bird colonies (tel. 809/639–4276).

Deep-Sea Fishing The islands off the northwest coast of Trinidad offer excellent waters for deep-sea fishing; the ocean here was a favorite angling spot of Franklin D. Roosevelt. Members of the **Trinidad and Tobago Yacht Club** (Bayshore, tel. 809/637–4260) may be willing to arrange a tour.

On Tobago, **Dillon's Fishing Charter** (Pigeon Point, tel. 809/639– 8765) is the best for whole- and half-day trips for kingfish, barracuda, wahoo, dolphinfish, blue marlin etc., from $165 for four hours.

Golf There are nine golf courses in the country, the best of which are the **Mt. Irvine Golf Club** (tel. 809/639–8871) in Tobago and **St. Andrew's Golf Club** in Moka, Maraval (tel. 809/629–2314), just outside Port-of-Spain.

Horseback Riding **Palm Tree Village** (Tobago, tel. 809/639–4347) has (very) ex–race horses on which to amble along the beach at low tide.

Scuba Diving Tobago draws scuba-diving aficionados from around the world. You can get information, supplies, and instruction at **Dive Tobago** (tel. 809/639–3695), **Sean Robinson** (tel. 809/639–1279), **Man Friday Diving** (tel. 809/660–4676), and **Tobago Dive Experience** (tel. 809/639– 0191).

Snorkeling The best spots for snorkeling are on Tobago, of which **Buccoo Reef** is easily the most popular—perhaps too popular. Over the years the reef has been damaged by the ceaseless boat traffic and by the thoughtless visitors who take pieces of coral for souvenirs. Even so, it's still a trip worth experiencing, particularly if you have children. For about $8 (get tickets at any hotel, or try C. J. Johnson, tel. 809/ 639–8519, at Buccoo), you board a Plexiglas-bottom boat at either Store Bay or Buccoo Beach; the 15-minute trip to the reef, 2 miles offshore, is made only at low tide. Operators provide rubber shoes, masks, and snorkels but not fins, which are helpful in the moderate current.

There is also good snorkeling by the beach near the **Arnos Vale Hotel** and at **Blue Waters,** and the government is slowly developing reefs around Speyside that rival, if not surpass, Buccoo.

Tennis The following hotels have tennis courts: in Trinidad, the **Trinidad Hilton** (tel. 809/624–3211), the **Trinidad Country Club** (tel. 809/622– 3470), the **Tranquility Square Lawn Tennis Club** (Victoria Ave., Port-of-Spain, tel. 809/625–4182); on Tobago, **Arnos Vale** (tel. 809/ 639–2881), **Turtle Beach** (tel. 809/639–2851), **Mt. Irvine** (tel. 809/ 639–8817), and the **Blue Waters Inn** (tel. 809/660–4341).

Shopping

Thanks in large part to Carnival costumery, there's no shortage of fabric shops on the islands. The best bargains for Oriental and East Indian silks and cottons can be found in downtown Port-of-Spain, on **Frederick Street** and around **Independence Square.** Other good buys are such duty-free items as Angostura Bitters and Old Oak or Vat 19 rum, all widely available throughout the country.

Upscale boutiques at the **Hilton** and in the **Long Circular Mall** (Long Circular Rd., St James, tel. 809/622–4925) make for relaxed browsing. Luxury items are available in Port-of-Spain at **Y. de Lima,** with branches on High Street and at the West Mall; and at **Stecher's** at the Hilton Hotel, on Lady Young Street, in the Long Circular Mall, and in the Cruise Ship Complex (Wrightson Rd.). There are no real bargains, though.

Local Crafts The tourism office can provide an extensive list of local artisans who specialize in everything from straw and cane work to miniature steel pans. The **Village** (Nook Ave. by the Hotel Normandie) has several shops that specialize in indigenous fashions, crafts, jewelry, basketwork and ceramics. Around the corner is **Art Creators** (7 St. Ann's Rd., tel. 809/624–4369), a top-notch gallery. On Tobago, the **Hangover Cafe and Art Gallery** (Pigeon Point Gate, tel. 809/639–7940) sells watercolors, handicrafts, and T-shirts. The **Cotton House** (Bacolet and Windward Rds., tel. 809/639–3695) is a good bet for jewelry and imaginative batik work. Paula Young runs her shop like an art school. You can visit the upstairs studio; if it's not too busy, you can even try batiking at no charge.

Records For the best selection of calypso and soca music, check out **Rhyner's Record Shop** (54 Prince St., 809/623–5673, and at the Cruise Ship Complex, tel. 809/627–8717).

Dining

Trinidad Although you can find all manner of Oriental, European, East Indian and Caribbean food in the restaurants of Port-of-Spain, as well as fast-food outlets—including plenty of pizzerias (they're nothing like back home) and abundant KFCs—what is difficult to procure is anything that hasn't been fried. Even in upmarket restaurants sautéeing and deep-fat frying seem to be the preferred medium, and you won't find huge salads to order instead.

What you will usually find is *callaloo*, a soup or stew of dasheen leaves (similar to spinach) and okra (called *ochroes* hereabouts), flavored with anything from pork to coconut, and pureed. It's hard to believe anything this green and swampy-looking can taste so delicious. On the streets you'll see shacks everywhere serving "little foods"—the real Trinidadian menu. Try *doubles*, a bake (Trini for bread—this kind is like a small, fat, fried pita) filled with spicy chickpeas; *coocoo*, a dumpling of cornmeal and coconut (similar to polenta); *roti*, a bake filled with curried meat or vegetables, of East Indian origin; *pelau*, rice and peas cooked with meat, coconut and peppers; and tamarind ball, a dessert made from the sweet-sour tamarind.

No Trinibagan dining experience can be complete, of course, without a rum punch with fresh fruit and the legendary Angostura Bitters, made by the same company that produces the excellent Old Oak rum, but watch out for the fiendish sugar content. Light, refreshing Carib beer is the local lager; dark-beer aficionados can try Royal Extra Stout (R.E.), which is even sweeter than Guinness.

Tobago On Tobago, it's easier to find local food—as opposed to "international" versions—often cooked with love and imagination. Specialties are the same, except for crab and dumplings, coated with messy, freshly mixed curry paste and best from the Store Bay beach huts (try Miss Esmie's), and *bena balls*, sesame-seed sweetmeats.

Highly recommended restaurants are indicated by a star ★.

Category	Cost*
Expensive	over $25
Moderate	$15–$25
Inexpensive	under $15

per person, excluding drinks, service, and 15% tax

Trinidad
★ **Cafe Savanna.** Caribbean style, with bare wood walls and Sade on the sound system, this cozy den consistently serves the best fare on the island. The menu specializes in Trinidadian dishes with a distinctive flair, such as Bacchannal Woman—fillets of red snapper dipped in cinnamon and baked. The callaloo soup here sets the standard for other island delicacies. A three-course lunch menu gives you choices for TT$45. *Kapok Hotel, 16–18 Cotton Hill, Port-of-Spain, tel. 809/622–6441. AE, DC, MC, V. Closed Sun. Expensive.*

La Boucan. Geoffrey Holder's large mural of a social idyll in the Savannah dominates one wall of the room. The restaurant strives for elegance: silver service, uniformed waiters, candlelight, pink tablecloths, and the soft tinkling of a grand piano. The chef is less inventive than in the past, and meals here tend toward good-but-not-really-gourmet, suggesting an Anglicized French restaurant. *Trinidad Hilton, Lady Young Rd., Port-of-Spain, tel. 809/624–3211. Reservations recommended. Jacket recommended. AE, DC, MC, V. Expensive.*

La Fantasie. The Hotel Normandie's restaurant is pretty, pink, and glacially air-conditioned inside, with pink-clothed wrought iron tables on the terrace out front. Fancifully titled dishes belie the freshness of what they insist on calling Cuisine Créole Nouvelle. "Drunkin Parendero," for instance, is simply poached local fish in a wine-herb sauce, while "De Road to Malabar" is a 12-oz. rib eye cooked in red wine, onion, and mushrooms. Fish and seafood are best bets; the day's catch best of all: grilled snapper stuffed with shrimp in a tart tomato sauce, perhaps. People rave about the homemade ice cream here, but it's often unavailable. *Hotel Normandie, 10 Nook Ave., St. Ann's, Port-of-Spain, tel. 809/624–1181. AE, DC, MC, V. Expensive.*

Solimar. This is oddly, but not unpleasantly, like dining under the Caribbean, thanks to the huge turquoise-lit fish tank, jungle of greenery, and candlelight. The ex-Hilton chef offers a menu you'd do well to avoid at home, since it tries to travel the world in one meal—you can eat shrimp tempura, Irish smoked salmon, Hawaiian barbecued mahimahi, Greek salad, linguine Alfredo, or Zwiebel Schnitzel—all while listening to John Denver singing "I think I'd rather be a cowboy." Best bets are the day's specials—seafood mixed grill, perhaps (which is not, in fact, grilled, but fried like everything else on Trinidad), then hot chocolate soufflé with chilled coconut cream. Solimar is popular with expat types and tends toward dressiness. *6 Nook Ave., St. Ann's, Port-of-Spain, tel. 809/ 624–1459. AE, DC, MC, V. Moderate–Expensive.*

Rafters. Behind a stone facade with green rafters is a pub that has become an urban institution. Once it was a rum shop; currently it's a bar and a restaurant. The pub is the center of activity, especially Friday night. In late afternoons the place begins to swell with Port-of-Spainers ordering from the tasty selection of burgers and barbecue and generally loosening up. *6A Warner St., Port-of-Spain, tel. 809/628–9258. AE, DC, MC, V. Moderate.*

Tiki Village. Cosmopolitan Port-of-Spainers are as passionate about their Oriental food as New Yorkers and San Franciscans are. Everyone touts their favorite, but this eatery, a serious version of Trader

Vic's, is the most reliable. It's high under the rafters atop the Kapok Hotel, air-conditioned and sunlit. What it lacks in kitsch, it compensates for in fine Oriental food. There's even dim sum, which you order by checking off your picks on a multiple-choice card. *Kapok Hotel, 16–18 Cotton Hill, Port-of-Spain, tel. 809/622–6441. AE, D, DC, MC, V. Moderate.*

★ **Veni Mange.** The best lunches in town are served inside this small stucco house. Credit Allyson Hennessy, a Cordon Bleu–trained cook who has become a celebrity of sorts because of a TV talk show she hosts, and her sister-partner Rosemary Hezekiah. The cuisine here is Creole. *13 Lucknow St., St. James, Port-of-Spain, tel.809/ 622–7533. No credit cards. No dinner. Moderate.*

Wazo Deyzeel. Wazo ("oiseaux des isles"—get it?) is adored by all for its setting, high up in the hills of St. Ann's hills with Point-of-Spain spread out below; its live bands and dancing on weekends; its friendliness; its prizewinning cocktails (the cucumber-lime-rum-syrup Wazo Combo is essential); as well as its food. The Thursday night all-you-can-eat Caribbean buffet might include grouper, flying fish, red snapper, macaroni pie, coocoo, *bhajia* (East Indian spinach fritters), and savory pumpkin pie, and is probably the best bargain in the city at about $10. Other nights—note it's closed Monday to Wednesday—you could go for a seafood platter or a beef pot roast, all cooked by three Jamaican ladies. Candy-colored director's chairs, white walls, a big, open-air terrace for admiring the view, wining (a naughty dance style), and liming (hanging out) set the tone. *Carib Way, 23 Sydenham Ave., St. Ann's, Port-of-Spain, tel. 809/623–0115. MC, V. Closed Mon.–Wed. Inexpensive.*

Tobago **Dillon's.** Stanley Dillon's other career as a fishing-charter operator
★ guarantees the freshest catch at this air-conditioned seafood restaurant by the airport. White walls hung with local art, red plaid tablecloths, silver service waitstaff, and a menu mixing traditional favorites (shrimp cocktail, French onion soup, lobster thermidor, surf and turf) with Creole dishes (callaloo, stuffed kingfish, chunky fish broth with local herbs) create a soothing atmosphere halfway between homey and posh. *Airport Rd. near Crown Point, tel. 809/ 639–8765. AE, MC, V. Moderate–Expensive.*

Grafton's. The resort's main restaurant is a large open terrace overlooking the Caribbean, but with a clearer view of the hotel pool, bar, and evening's entertainment than of the waves. Attend one of the Grafton's all-you-can-eat buffets, including maybe chargrilled chicken, steak and pork, a suckling pig, Creole dolphinfish, curried blue crab, any amount of root vegetables, spaghetti, pelau, cauliflower cheese, a salad bar, and an array of desserts, and you'll wish you'd remembered to pack the Tums. *Grafton Beach Resort, Black Rock, tel. 809/639–0191. AE, DC, MC, V. Moderate–Expensive.*

Cocrico Inn. A café with a bar against one wall, the Cocrico offers delectable home-cooking. The three rotating chefs frequently use fresh fruits and vegetables grown in the neighborhood. They zealously guard their recipes, including a marvelous coocoo and lightly breaded, subtly spiced grouper. There is nothing fancy here, just warm and delicious food. *Corner of North and Commissioner Sts., Plymouth, tel. 809/639–2661. AE, V. Moderate.*

The Old Donkey Cart House. The name is something of a curiosity, since this attractive restaurant is set in and around a green-and-white colonial house, about a 2-mile drive south of Scarborough. There's outdoor dining in a garden with twinkling lights. The cuisine is standard Caribbean, nothing special, but German side dishes and an extensive selection of Rhine and Moselle wines set it apart. *Bacolet St., Scarborough, tel. 809/639–3551. AE, V. Moderate.*

Papillon. Named after one of the proprietor's favorite books, this seafood restaurant is a homey room with an adjoining patio. What was once reckoned to be Tobago's most adventurous menu now offers more conventional, well-prepared Caribbean fare with a few fanciful touches. *Buccoo Bay Rd., Mt. Irvine, tel. 809/639–0275. AE, DC, MC, V. Moderate.*

★ **Rouselles.** An enchanting terrace high above Scarborough Bay, with a big, congenial bar, Rouselles was just a liming spot until friends and regulars demanded proper food. Bet they didn't expect food that could compete with big-city cuisine, though. The small menu dons different accessories rather than changing completely, so you may find grouper, broiled and served with a fresh Creole sauce, and several vegetables—garlicky green beans, carrots with ginger, a raw bok choy salad, and potato croquette with spices and celery—or dolphinfish with white wine sauce, or lobster, steamed just so, which is very hard to procure. Whatever there is, you can trust that it'll be delicious. A sizable *amuse-gueule*, hot garlic bread, plus dessert (save space for pineapple pie or homemade ice creams) are included in the entrée price, and don't forgo the Rouselles punch. The recipe's a secret, but the lovely, welcoming co-owners Bobbie or Charlene will probably let you in on it. Don't miss this one. *Old Windward Rd., Bacolet, tel. 809/639–4738. Lunch by reservation only. AE, MC, V. Moderate.*

★ **The Village.** Steel-band music plays gently in the background at this romantic candlelit spot. Under a thatched roof, waitresses clad in colorful island prints recite the fixed-price four-course menu. Changing daily, it may include christophine soup, curried green fig, kingfish with shrimp sauce, and coconut cake. Whatever it is, co-owner and chef, Cynthia Clovis, will have used herbs and vegetables freshly picked from her own organic garden, and everything will be bursting with flavor. Saturday buffets here are a Tobagonian highlight. *Kariwak Village, Crown Point, tel. 809/639–8442. AE, DC, MC, V. Moderate.*

Blue Crab. Alison Sardinha is Tobago's most ebullient and kindly hostess, and her husband, Ken, one of its best chefs. He cooks "like our mothers cooked," serving the local food with heavy East Indian influence, a bit of Portuguese, and occasionally Oriental too. There might be rolled flying fish, *katchowrie* (spiced split pea patties, a little like falafel), curry chicken, or long-cooked suckling pig. There's always a callaloo, differently flavored on different days, fine rotis and coocoo, and sometimes a "cookup"—pelau-type rice, with *everything* in it. Wednesday and Friday are regular nights, though Miss Alison will open up even for one table, if you call in the morning. Weekend lunches likewise; you can usually just drop in during the week. The setting, on a wide, verdant, shady terrace overlooking the bay, is just about perfect, and there's a new bar for cocktails. Two guest rooms (the front one's a beauty) in the Sardinhas' home are also new this year. *Robinson St. at Main St., Scarborough, tel. 809/639–2737. No credit cards. Inexpensive–Moderate.*

Lodging

On Trinidad most lodging establishments are within the vicinity of Port-of-Spain, far from any beach. On Tobago, it's the opposite; nearly every establishment listed here is either on or within walking distance of the ocean. Carnival week is one of two times in the year for which you should book reservations far in advance (the other is Christmas); expect to pay twice the price charged during the rest of the year.

Most places do offer breakfast and dinner for an additional flat rate (MAP), but on the whole these offer less variety than you'll get if you strike out for meals on your own. If you're lodging on the east side of Tobago, however, MAP is almost essential because of the dearth of restaurants.

Highly recommended lodgings are indicated by a star ★.

Category	Cost*
Very Expensive	over $175
Expensive	$100–$175
Moderate	$60–$100
Inexpensive	under $60

All prices are for a standard double room for two, excluding 15% tax and 10% service charge.

Trinidad

★ **Trinidad Hilton.** Perched above Port-of-Spain, the Hilton radiates the feeling of comfort and competence. Each room either has a balcony, which opens to a fine view of Savannah Park, the city, and the sea beyond, or overlooks the equally inviting Olympic-size pool, shaded by trees harboring brightly crested cornbirds. This is Port-of-Spain's most stylish hotel, with prices to match. It frequently bustles with conventioneers, which may be its only drawback. The good news is that it's usually available for last-minute Carnival bookings. The rooms are comfortably uniform, and those on the Executive Floors have good working desks and a small sitting area. The rooms have no clocks, but if you're on "island time," perhaps it won't matter. *Lady Young Rd., Box 442, Port-of-Spain, tel. 809/624–3211, fax 624–4485. 394 rooms. Facilities: 2 restaurants, bar, conference rooms, satellite TV, pool, health club, tennis court, drugstore, gift shops, car rental, taxi service. AE, DC, MC, V. EP. Expensive–Very Expensive.*

Holiday Inn. This hotel is at the port and close to Independence Square, which affords lodgers a pastel view of the old town and of ships idling in the Gulf of Paria. All there is within walking distance is the Cruise Ship Complex, where the National Stadium now hosts the pre-Carnival Dimanche Gras, and crazy, traffic-clogged Independence Square. The rooms are in standard international mode, complete with rare Trinidadian sightings of the hair dryer. The hotel's rooftop restaurant, **La Ronde,** is a revolving bistro that offers a striking panorama of the city at night. This is a more moderate alternative to the swankier, but similar, Hilton. *Wrightson Rd., Box 1017, Port-of-Spain, tel. 809/625–3361, fax 809/625–4166. 235 rooms. Facilities: satellite TV, pool, health spa, conference rooms, beauty salon, taxi service. AE, DC, MC, V. BP. Expensive.*

★ **Hotel Normandie.** Built in the 1930s by French Creoles on the ruins of an old coconut plantation, the Normandie has touches of Spanish, English Colonial, and even postmodern architecture. The standard rooms, set around a pretty pool courtyard, have beige textured-vinyl walls, wood floorboards and fittings, very little light, TV, phone, and noisy but efficient air-conditioning. The 13 loft rooms are far better. For $25 more, you get a towering duplex with simple wood furniture, exposed eaves, and a bigger bathroom. Number 236 is especially bright and beautiful, with a big window upstairs, and 231 has extra space. These are great for families, since two under-12s can share for free. The Normandie's conference facilities ensure a steady flow of convention groups, who also like its quiet location, set back from residential St. Ann's Road in the center of an artsy mall of crafts and clothes shops and galleries, and its friendly, efficient service. La Fantasie (*see* Dining, *above*) provides room service until 11 PM. *10 Nook Ave., St. Ann's Village, Port-of-Spain, tel. and fax 809/624–1181. 61 rooms. Facilities: restaurant and bar, pool, meeting rooms, gallery, café, shops, car rental, taxi service. AE, DC, MC, V. EP, MAP. Moderate–Expensive.*

★ **Kapok Hotel.** Although now part of the Golden Tulip hotel chain, this hotel has been run by the Chan family for years and gleams with cheerful efficiency. Pink-and-white rooms are spotless, spacious, and sunlit, with rattan furniture and Polynesian prints the colors of highlighter pens. Front ones are best for the view over the Savannah—the Kapok is next to it, but away from the hubbub—and even better are the studios, with kitchenette included for the same price as a room. Request a refrigerator when you book, and a hair dryer, which are built into about a quarter of the bathrooms; all rooms boast quiet air-conditioning, HBO, CNN, and ESPN on TV, push-button phones with an extra fax-friendly jack, and full-length mirrors. Suites are vast, and fine for families, who will also like the laundromat and the birds and monkeys who live by the pool, with its recently expanded lounging terrace. The two restaurants, Cafe Savanna and Tiki Village (*see* Dining, *above*), are popular with locals. With facilities and ambience this sophisticated, you'd think the Kapok would cost far more. *16–18 Cotton Hill, St. Clair, Port-of-Spain, tel. 809/622–6441, fax 809/622–9677. 65 rooms, 6 suites. Facilities: 2 restaurants, shops, hair salon, laundromat, satellite TV, pool, taxi service. AE, DC, MC, V. EP. Moderate–Expensive.*

★ **Alicia's House.** The Govias managed to keep the family atmosphere when they converted their home for guests, so all here is welcoming and reassuring. The enormous, breezy floor-through lounge is full of squashy sofas, round tables, cane chairs, a piano, and a tank of fish; it leads into the dining area, where you may take breakfast, plus other meals if you ask. Rooms vary enormously. "Admiral Rooney" (a local flower) is a big one with mahogany furniture, a cute garden-view desk, and a giant bathtub; "The Back Room" is very small but also very bright, and boasts a private spiral staircase to the pool; "Alicia's Room" (she's the Govias' daughter) is a petite apartment with twin cherry red sofas, many windows, an acre of closets, a pink bathroom with another huge bath, and mirror tiles over the bed. Extras you shouldn't expect for the low rates, but get anyway, include a Jacuzzi and a water cooler by the pool, and 14-channel U.S. cable TV, air-conditioning, private bathrooms, and push-button phones in every room. Alicia's is a 10-minute walk from the Savannah, very near the Normandie. *7 Coblentz Gardens, St. Ann's, Port-of-Spain, tel. 809/623–2802, toll-free from airport, 223; fax 809/622–8560. 16 rooms. Facilities: cable TV, lounge, dining room, pool, Jacuzzi. MC, V. EP, CP, MAP. Inexpensive.*

Asa Wright Nature Centre. Set in a lush rain forest about 90 minutes east of Port-of-Spain, this handsome lodge, built in 1908 and straight out of a Somerset Maugham novel, attracts international legions of bird-watchers and nature photographers. There are impressive views of the verdant Arima Valley and the Northern Range from the veranda, where tea is served each afternoon. It leads off an elegant, comfortable lounge with black lacquered floorboards, bookcases, antiques and ornithological memorabilia. The two huge bedrooms that abut this share its romantic atmosphere, with fans turning slowly on tall ceilings, hardwood closets, and antique beds. All other rooms are in modern lodges near the house, simply outfitted with marble floors, spartan wood furniture, and private covered terraces. You'll feel you're miles from anywhere and, actually, you are, so you'll need the three meals a day and evening rum punch that are included in the rates, along with a center tour and trip to the Oilbird Cave for three days plus. A car is essential, unless bird-watching at the center and being alone are your sole aims, in which case airport transfers cost $40. (For more information about the center, *see* Exploring, *above*.) *Box 4710, Arima, Trinidad, tel. 809/ 667–4655, fax 809/667–0493. 23 rooms. Facilities: dining room, veranda, lounge, guided field trips. No credit cards. Inexpensive.*

Carnetta's House. When Winston Borrell retired as director of tourism for Trinidad and Tobago, he and his wife, Carnetta, opened up their suburban two-story house to guests. One guest room is on the upper floor of the two-story house and on the same level as the lounge and terrace dining room. The other four are on the ground floor, with the choice room, Le Flamboyant, opening on to the garden's patio. All rooms have a private bathroom with shower, telephones, radio and TV. And, although there is air-conditioning, cool breezes usually do the trick. Unfortunately, at night, the doors need to be shuttered for security reasons. Winston is a keen gardener, and his garden has a sampling of plants that are a fascinating introduction to tropical flowers and herbs. Carnetta uses the herbs in her cooking, and she can prepare some of the best dinners that you may find in Port-of-Spain. Equally important is the fund of information that both Carnetta and Winston can offer on what to see and do in Trinidad and the necessary arrangements they can make to do it. *28 Scotland Terrace, Andalusia, Maraval, Port-of-Spain, tel. 809/ 628–2732, fax 809/628–7717. 5 rooms. Facilities: lounge, dining room, laundry facilities, car-rental arrangements, airport transfers. AE, DC, MC, V. EP, BP, MAP. Inexpensive.*

★ **Monique's.** Mike and Monique Charbonné really *like* having guests, as they have been proving for over 10 years. In fact, they like it so much, they've built an annex close by with a further 10 rooms. The new ones have TV—request one in the main house—and kitchenettes, and, like the others, air-conditioning, phones, and bathrooms. Everyone breakfasts in the front parlor-like dining room, where you can request dinner too, and hangs out in an airy, marble-floored lounge—with the hosts often as not. Mike sometimes organizes a picnic to the couple's 100-acre plantation near Blanchisseuse, if it seems a good idea. Rooms are sizable, spotless, and, mostly, light. Numbers 25 and 26 are enormous and can sleep up to six. They're dark, but there's a little sunken red stone patio in front to take the sun. One room was designed for guests with disabilities. *114 Saddle Rd., Maraval, Port-of-Spain, tel. 809/628–3334, fax 809/ 622–3232. 21 rooms. Facilities: dining room, common-room area with TV. AE. EP, MAP. Inexpensive.*

Pelican Inn. Near the Hilton, and steps from the Savannah, is this new hotel, appended to a popular pub (*see* Nightlife, *below*). Rooms lead off a veranda that looks like a cricket pavilion, carpeted with Astroturf and festooned with white gingerbread trellis. They're monklike and pristine, with white-on-white decor and simple tiled bathrooms, not unlike boarding school. There's air-conditioning, but windows are too high up to see from, and there are no TVs (ask in advance, and you may get one) and no phones. However, you'll not lack for entertainment, with the pub on one side, and the Celebrations' Mas Camp on the other, an inexpensive terrace restaurant sharing the veranda, and the Pelican Squash Club by the car park. Rates are very low too. *2–4 Coblentz Gardens, St. Ann's, Port-of-Spain, tel. 809/627–6271, fax 809/623–0978. 23 rooms. AE, MC, V. EP. Inexpensive.*

Surf's Country Inn. Way off the beaten track in the village of Blanchisseuse is this tiny, picturesque inn. At press time there were plans to add four cottages—which should be ready by now, but don't forget, we are on island time here. In fact, the rooms weren't viewable at press time, but TV, phone, and private bathrooms are promised, rates are *very* low, and the setting, among coconut palms and mango trees, with about the only sea view from a Trinidad guest house, is idyllic. There's even a tiny beach a 10-minute walk down the hill. Useful if you don't want to trek back to town after a north coast jaunt, as well as for those who'd rather be away from it all on Trinidad. *North Coast Rd., Blanchisseuse, tel. 809/669-2475. 3 rooms. Facilities: restaurant, bar. No credit cards. EP, BP. Inexpensive.*

Tropical. A circular drive leads up some crazy-paved steps into the pretty reception area with a clicking ceiling fan, murmuring TV, pea green Lloyd Loom chairs, white arches and white wrought iron gates shielding a central cloister-like courtyard. That does it for facilities, apart from the small pool. Rooms, too, are spartan, if psychedelic, with their fuchsia-and-tomato drapes, bedcovers, and shower curtains. Most are big, and all have air-conditioning and bathrooms. Big pluses are the excellent restaurant-bar and club attached, serving local food, and the low rates. *6 Rookery Nook, Maraval, Port-of-Spain, tel. 809/622-5815, fax 809/622-3174. 30 rooms. Facilities: restaurant, pool. AE. EP. Inexpensive.*

Bed-and-Breakfasts The number of private homes in Trinidad and Tobago offering bed-and-breakfast accommodations is growing each year. This is an excellent, inexpensive option and a wonderful way to meet the friendly locals. Contact the **Trinidad and Tobago Bed and Breakfast Association** (Box 3231, Diego Martin, or Park Lane Court, Amethyst Dr., El Dorado, Tunapuna, tel. 809/663-5265). All members conform to the association's rigorous standards.

Tobago **Arnos Vale Hotel.** The most romantic spot on Tobago, this hotel
★ crosses Tobago horticulture with Mediterranean design; it's Italian-run, and often full of Italian guests to prove it. White stucco cottages are set on a hill that descends through a series of winding paths to a secluded beach, pool, and bar. Suite 20 down on the beach is a favorite, though others may prefer the more isolated suites on top of the hill. Standard rooms, at the base of the hill, face the pool and are near the beach. The elegant hilltop restaurant, with iron lattice tables, a chandelier, and a hand-painted piano, leads to a crescent-shape patio that offers a sweeping view of the sea. *Arnos Vale, Box 208, Scarborough, tel. 809/639-2881. 32 rooms. Facilities: bar, restaurant, pool, tennis, beach, snorkeling dive shop, disco, gift shop. AE, DC, MC, V. EP. Very Expensive.*

★ **Grafton Beach Resort.** This sparkling, Trinidadian-owned complex has the most international ambience of any Tobago hotel, from the huge, lobby-bar-restaurant-pool area—all within view of each other, and perched over the sea—to the top-class in-room facilities. These include, as well as the expected satellite TV, phone, balcony, full-length mirror and so on, a hair dryer, minibar, 24-hour room service, and inaudible air-conditioning. Solid teak furniture and terra-cotta tiled floors, subtle lighting, and marble bathrooms make up the decor. Cruise liner–style, the Neptune seafood restaurant and the bar, where local folk shows and bands perform nightly, are perched above and around the bigger-than-average pool, with Grafton's (*see* Dining, *above*) to one side. A walkway leads directly to a fine beach, with its own bar, and there are showers at the top where you can rinse off. You can also meet the manager at the "Meet the Manager" Friday evening cocktails, dance in the disco, learn to scuba, play squash, work out in the gym, go canoeing, sailing, windsurfing, or surfing—all inclusive in the rates. If you're looking for a true American-style resort, look no further. *Black Rock, Tobago, tel. 809/639–0191, fax 809/639–0030. 110 rooms, 2 suites. Facilities: 2 restaurants, bar, beach, pool and beach bar, water sports, scuba training, golf nearby, beauty shop, discotheque, live entertainment, satellite TV, shopping arcade, 2 squash courts, gym with sauna. AE, DC, MC, V. EP, MAP. Very Expensive.*

Mt. Irvine Bay Hotel. The advantage of this low-key, somewhat overpriced hotel is golf, on the 18-hole, par-72, 127-acre International Championship course, for which guests get special rates. The carpeted bedrooms aren't so special, although all amenities are on tap, from quiet air-conditioning, good-sized desks, full-length mirrors, and 24-hour room service, to HBO, Cinemax, and CNN on TV. Bathrooms boast hair dryers and the only robes on Tobago. 51 cottages set in an arc around the main building cost double the room rate, for which you get a private patio and a mottled marble floor, but no kitchenette or lounge. A 17th-century mill is the focal point of the main restaurant, and there are two more restaurants besides—a dressy French one, Le Beau Rivage, and the Jacaranda, plus Cocrico Bar, serving a local-international menu, when it's open. You can swim up to the bar at the largest of the island's hotel pools, play tennis on two floodlit courts, take the private track across the road to the beach, where there's another bar—or just play golf all day. *Mt. Irvine Bay, Box 222, Tobago, tel. 809/639–8871, fax 809/639–8800. 107 rooms, 5 suites, 51 cottages. Facilities: 3 restaurants (1 formal), 2 bars, golf course, pool, tennis courts, convention facilities, beach across the street, beauty parlor, shops, taxi service, sauna, health spa. AE, DC, MC, V. EP, CP, MAP. Very Expensive.*

★ **Richmond Great House.** Tobagonian Hollis Lynch, professor of African History at Columbia University, owns a museum-worthy collection of African art and artifacts, which he's been kind enough to install in his part-18th century hilltop plantation house on the windward side of the island. The house is as noteworthy as its contents, huge and breezy, with expanses of polished floorboards, a homey lounge (with library, TV, VCR, and stereo), squashy sofas, bentwood rocking chairs, many other fine non-African pieces, and panoramic views over the landscaped gardens. The pool is poised above the ocean—a 20-minute walk down the hill—near an outdoor bar, a tennis court, and a new room for socializing, with Ping-Pong, billiards, cards, and board games. Also brand-new are four east-facing, lower-level bedrooms. Of the five great house bedrooms, enormous #2 is the prize, with a sitting room facing due west for the sunset; #3 is similar, but no sunset. #4 has a locally made mahogany king-size four-poster, while 5 & 6 are smaller, carpeted rooms in a modern extension. A talented local chef cooks, and the professor's cousin is resident manager. *Belle Garden, Tobago, tel. 809/660–4467. 10 rooms. Facilities: 10-minute drive to beach, dining room, pool, TV, game room. No credit cards. CP, MAP. Moderate–Expensive.*

Turtle Beach Hotel. There's no lack of space at this well-maintained 24-year-old beachfront property, with its sprawling, wooden-ceilinged lobby, lounge, bar, and restaurant open to the sea and filled with plants and birdsong—especially given the plan (tentative, at press time) to add a further 100 rooms. Rates drop way down in the summer season, meaning occupancy is high year-round, though winter guests miss out on the turtles who use this beach to lay their eggs from March to August. Another good deal is the triple room—not the usual fold-down in the corner, but a small extra bedroom for $21 more. Bedroom balconies all overlook the sea and, as with all the leeside hotels (Grafton, Mt. Irvine Bay, Sandy Point Village, Blue Horizon), the fabulous sunset. Typical Tobagonian wooden ceilings, marble-chip floors, and textured white plaster walls make for a functional feel, some air-conditioning units are noisy, and there's no in-room TV, but otherwise Turtle Beach's popularity—especially among Americans and Germans—is not hard to understand. *Great Courland Bay, tel. 809/639–2851; write Box 201, Scarborough, Tobago; fax 809/639–1495. 125 rooms. Facilities: restaurant, 2 bars, beach, small pool, 2 tennis courts, water-sports center, bike rentals, gift shop. AE, DC, MC, V. EP, MAP. Moderate–Expensive.*

★ **Kariwak Village.** People fall helplessly in love with Allan and Cynthia Clovis's 12-year-old cabana village, which is to the average hotel as the scarlet ibis is to the city pigeon. You enter a bamboo, raw teak, and coral stone lobby, bar, and restaurant (the highly recommended Village, *see* Dining, *above*), which along with a cluster of palm-thatched huts, an air-conditioned recreation room with TV (the only one there is), VCR, books, games, and local art on the walls, forms the lounge area. Nine round cabanas in a semicircle around a pretty pool contain simple air-conditioned bedrooms, with loft-height dark wood ceilings, carpeted floors, and wicker armchairs, each with separate bathroom and dressing area, and little terraces outside the patio doors. Lush flora makes a fairly small site seem more spacious, and an herb-and-vegetable garden out back, which furnishes Cynthia's kitchen with ingredients, provides an extra stroll. The best breakfast around—fresh cocoa made with local chocolate, homemade yogurt, granola, whole-wheat bread and spice tea accompany the meal—plus the best rum punches and local bands playing on weekends make this a favored liming spot as well as a lively holiday base. It's very near the airport, Store Bay, and Pigeon Point. *Crown Point, Tobago, tel. 809/639–8442, fax 809/639–8441. Write Box 27, Scarborough, Tobago. 18 rooms. Facilities: restaurant, bar, shuttle service to beach, pool. AE, DC, MC, V. EP, MAP. Moderate.*

Palm Tree Village. Across the rural old coast road from Little Rockley Bay, a five minute drive from Scarborough, this place offers peace and quiet with a useful array of facilities. Choose either a superior room, facing the beach, with a hardwood floor and furniture, or a two- or four-bedroom villa set back from the Atlantic in the manicured, but barely landscaped, grounds. Standard rooms, in cottages close to the main building, feature small lounge areas and plenty of windows, but these—in a confusing lineup of packages and plans—are usually only available at TT$ rates to locals. Try negotiating for one, though. There can be a forlorn feeling here, perhaps due to the lack of trees on site, the narrowness of the 2-mile-long beach (except at low tide), or the tininess of the pool; but Phillies, the new German-run pub in a converted barn, could liven things up. *Box 327, Little Rockley Bay, Scarborough, tel. 809/639–4347, fax 809/639–4180. 18 villas, 20 rooms, 36 "standard rooms." Facilities: restaurant, bar, beach, pool, disco, piano room, conference center, tennis court, horseback riding, water sports. AE, DC, MC, V. EP, MAP. Moderate.*

Blue Horizon Resort. "Resort" is a misnomer for this compact, new, red-roofed apartment complex set above the Mt. Irvine golf course, since all it offers in the way of facilities are a small pool, which the apartments overlook, a barbecue pit, and an understocked minimart. However, it does offer peace and quiet and sunset views from the deluxe apartments, which are a far better deal than the first-floor, viewless standards. Decor is basic—small, straight-backed plaid sofas and chairs around the satellite TV are the only lounge furniture—with pine-fitted kitchens and utility-tiled bathrooms. Deluxe apartments have spiral staircases leading to galleried lofts that children will adore–though little ones could easily fall from them. Balconies overlook each other, except for that in the single "luxurious" apartment; its "luxury" comprising an extra bedroom and tons of space. Free airport transfers are provided, and there's no charge for children under 12, making this a good budget family pick. *Jacamar Drive, Mt. Irvine, Tobago, tel. 809/639–0433, fax 305/592–4935. 13 apartments. Facilities: pool, minimart. AE, MC, V. EP. Inexpensive–Moderate.*

Blue Waters Inn. A good ninety minutes' drive from Scarborough and a bumpy driveway brings you to this beach hotel and villas on the northeast Atlantic coast, set in 46 acres of bird-infested greenery. Evidently, seclusion is the selling point here, with Little Tobago island over Batteaux Bay the only sight from the second-floor bedroom balconies, and the mango-and-palm-tree-fringed beach a step away from the apartment and suite patios. The latter are far nicer than the utilitarian bedrooms, which have cramped bathrooms, lit by a bare bulb, and partitioned by walls that don't reach the ceiling, and no air-conditioning or TV. Confusingly, the four-person "self-catering" apartments have no kitchens, while the two- or four-person suites do, along with air-conditioning. Shopping for the kitchen is a problem, with the nearest (small) supermarket a half-hour drive away. The terrace restaurant-bar is done out with ship paraphernalia, but is by no means open all hours off-season; neither is the staff very helpful. However, the newly-decorated suites (note these fall in the Expensive category) are great for peace-and-quiet fiends, as long as they can drive. *Batteaux Bay, Speyside, Tobago, tel. 809/660–4341, fax 809/660–5195. 23 rooms, 4 apartments, 3 suites. Facilities: restaurant, bar, tennis court, beach, dive instruction. AE, MC, V. EP, CP, FAP, MAP. Inexpensive–Expensive.*

Ocean Point. Less than two years old, this friendly "condo hotel," as owner-manager Dewan Kalliecharan, dubs it, is a resort in miniature, complete with tiny kitsch fountain, a quartet of parakeets and Raj the macaw, a barbecue pit, and a palm-thatched bar-restaurant (East Indian food is the specialty) at one end of the child-size, kidney-shape pool. Five studios with five split-level loft apartments above them constitute the living quarters, all sparkly white, with pine fittings and terra-cotta floors, big showers in the bathrooms, plus a welcome hammock in the balcony (upstairs) or porch (downstairs). All apartments have kitchenettes, TVs, and air-conditioning (though signs reading "Ocean Breeze! Pure and Natural. It's Healthier!!" seem to discourage its use), and, from the lofts, views of the sunrise over the ocean. Studios are viewed by pool users, but these are few, since an extension of Little Rockley beach (narrow and rough and not the best for bathing) is a minute's walk, with Store Bay a ten-minute drive. A free shuttle to the airport, supermarket, and golf course is provided. *Milford Rd., Lowlands, Tobago, tel. and fax 809/639–0973. 5 studios, 5 apartments. Facilities: restaurant/bar, airport/supermarket shuttle, pool. No credit cards. EP. Inexpensive–Moderate.*

★ **Sandy Point Beach Club.** This friendly, well-run complex near the airport might be the island's bargain. A bewildering selection of rooms run from perfectly cute ship's cabin–style hideaways with two sets of wooden bunk beds and private patios (116, 117, and 119 have a sea view), through several sizes of duplex suites with open loft-style gallery bedrooms, to family-sized suites and apartments. Decor features stone walls, lots of wood beams, wicker chairs and round glass-topped tables, some marble floors, some carpeted. Every room has a kitchenette, air-conditioning, direct-dial phones, and 8-channel satellite TV. The beach is tiny and too rough for swimming, but makes a pretty setting for the Steak Hut restaurant and bar, and a small pool. For swimmers, there's a second pool, with swim-up bar; it's narrow but *very* long, next to a perfect, little, shady, weathered-brick courtyard. There's also a free shuttle to the beach at Pigeon Point. If that's not enough for you, there's a small, well-equipped gym (no air-conditioning), a conference room, and a new cellar disco club, The Deep, all free to guests. *Crown Point, Tobago, tel. 809/639–8391 or 800/223–6510, fax 809/639–8495. 45 rooms, 9 studios. Facilities: restaurant, 2 bars, 2 pools, beach shuttle, on-site Jeep rentals, dive shop, boutique, conference room, gym. DC, MC, V. EP, MAP. Inexpensive–Moderate.*

The Arts and Nightlife

Trinidad Trinidadian culture doesn't end with music, but it definitely begins with it. While both calypso and steel bands are best displayed during Carnival, the steel bands play at clubs, dances, and fetes throughout the year. There's no lack of nightlife in Port-of-Spain. Music that's popular right now is "sweet Parang," a mixture of Spanish patois and calypso sung to tunes played on a string instrument much like a mandolin.

Mas Camp Pub (corner of Ariapata and French Sts., Woodbrook, tel. 809/627–8449) is Port-of-Spain's most comfortable and dependable night spot. There are tables, a bar, an ample stage in one room, and an open-air patio with more tables and a bar with a TV. There's a kitchen if you're hungry, and **Hush,** which makes delicious fruit-flavored ice cream, is right next door. **Cricket Wicket** (149 Tragarete Rd., tel. 809/622–1808), a popular watering hole with a cupola-shape bar in the center, is a fine place to hear top bands, dance, or just sit and enjoy the nocturnal scenery. **Wazo Deyzeel** (23 Sydenham Ave., St. Ann's, tel. 809/623–0115) is the current fave with a mixed age group, for its music, dancing, drinking, views, and great food cooked by three Jamaican ladies; while the **Pelican** (2–4 Coblentz Ave., St. Ann's, tel. 809/627–6271), an English-style pub, gets increasingly frenetic as the week closes, with a singles bar atmosphere. Collect gossip over a beer at **Smokey & Bunty** (Western Main Rd. and Dengue St., St James, no tel.), which calls itself a sports bar, but is really just the essential liming corner. Finally, **Moon Over Bourbon Street** (Southern Landing, Westmall, Westmoorings, tel. 809/637–3448) has comedy or music most nights, plus long, long happy hours.

There are several excellent theaters in Port-of-Spain. Consult local newspapers for listings.

Tobago People will tell you there's no nightlife on Tobago. Don't believe them. Some kind of organized cabaret-style event happens every night at the **Grafton Beach Resort** (tel. 809/639–0191). Even if you hate that touristy stuff, check out Les Couteaux Cultural Group, who does a high-octane dance version of Tobagonian history, and also appears at **Turtle Beach,** where similar shows are staged Wednesday and Sunday. Hip hotel entertainment, frequented as much by locals as tourists, is found at the **Kariwak Village** Friday and Saturday nights—almost always one of the better local jazz/calypso bands. But the most authentic nightlife of all is anywhere in downtown Scarborough, any weekend. The entire town throbs with competing sound systems and impromptu or prearranged parties, any of which will welcome extra guests.

Between the two extremes, the **Starting Gate** (Shirvan Rd., tel. 809/639–0225), an indoor-outdoor pub, is the venue for frequent party-discos, while Sunday nights at Buccoo, there is an informal hop, affectionately dubbed **Sunday School,** at Henderson's disco. It's great fun. "Blockos" (spontaneous block parties) spring up all over the island; look for the hand-painted signs. Tobago also has Harvest parties on Sundays, when a particular village opens its doors to visitors for hospitality. These occur throughout the year and are a great way to meet the locals.

26 Turks and Caicos Islands

Updated by Laurie S. Senz

The Turks and Caicos islands are relatively unknown except to aficionados of beautiful beaches and scuba divers, who religiously return to these waters year after year. The people of these islands have officially adopted the designation "Beautiful by Nature" to reflect the islands' tranquility and natural wonders.

It is claimed that Columbus's first landfall was on Grand Turk. First settled by the English more than 200 years ago, the British Crown Colony of Turks and Caicos is renowned in two respects: Its booming banking and insurance institutions lure investors from the United States and elsewhere; and its offshore reef formation entices divers to a world of colorful marine life surrounding its 40 islands, only eight of which are inhabited.

The Turks and Caicos are two groups of islands in an archipelago lying 575 miles southeast of Miami and about 90 miles north of Haiti. Some 12,350 people live on the eight large islands and more than 40 small cays that have a total landmass of 193 square miles. The Turks Islands include Grand Turk, which is the capital and seat of government, and Salt Cay, with a population of about 200. According to local legend, these islands were named by early settlers who thought the scarlet blossoms on the local cactus resembled the Turkish fez.

Some 22 miles west of Grand Turk, across the 7,000-foot-deep Christopher Columbus Passage, is the Caicos group, which includes South, East, West, Middle, and North Caicos and Providenciales. South Caicos, Middle Caicos, North Caicos, and Providenciales (nicknamed Provo) are the only inhabited islands in this group; Pine Cay, Parrot Cay, and Salt Cay are the only inhabited cays. "Caicos" is derived from *cayos*, the Spanish word for cay, and is believed to mean "string of islands."

In the years following Ponce de León's landing in 1515, a band of pirates also established communities in the archipelago. Around 1678, Bermudians, lured by the wealth of salt in these islands, began raking salt from the flats and returning to Bermuda to sell their crop. Despite French and Spanish attacks and pirate raids, the Bermudians persisted and established a trade that became the bedrock of the Bermudian economy. In 1766, Andrew Symmers settled here to hold the islands for England. Later, Loyalists from Georgia obtained land grants in the Caicos Islands, imported slaves, and continued the lifestyle of the pre–Civil War American South.

With an eye toward tourism dollars to create jobs and increase the standard of living, the government has devised a long-term development plan to improve the visibility of the Turks and the Caicos in the Caribbean tourism market. Providenciales, in particular, is slated not only for tourism development, but also for the development of banking, registration of business companies, and offshore insurance.

Before You Go

Tourist Information

Contact the **Turks and Caicos Islands Tourist Board** (tel. 800/241–0824). The **Caribbean Tourist Organization** (20 E. 46th St., New York, NY 10017, tel. 212/682–0435) is another reliable source of information. In the United Kingdom, contact **Morris-Kevan International Ltd.** (International House, 47 Chase Side, Enfield Middlesex EN2 6NB, tel. 081/367–5175).

Arriving and Departing
By Plane

American Airlines (tel. 800/433–7300) flies daily between Miami and Provo. **Turks & Caicos Islands Airlines** (tel. 800/845–2161 or 809/94–64255) flies nonstop several days a week from Miami to both Provo and Grand Turk. It also serves Provo from Nassau three days a week. **Carnival Airlines** (tel. 800/824–7386) flies nonstop from Miami to Grand Turk twice a week. Both **Turks & Caicos Islands Airlines** and **InterIsland Airways** (tel. 809/94–15481) provide regularly scheduled service between Provo and Grand Turk.

From the Airport Taxis are available at the airports; expect to share a ride. Rates are fixed. A trip between Provo's airport and most major hotels runs about $15. On Grand Turk, a trip from the airport to town is about $5; from the airport to hotels outside town, $6–$11.

By Boat Because of the superb diving, three live-aboard dive boats call regularly. Contact the *Aquanaut* (c/o See & Sea, tel. 800/DIV–XPRT), the *Sea Dancer* (c/o Peter Hughes Diving, tel. 800/DANCER), or the *Turks and Caicos Aggressor* (c/o Aggressor Fleet, tel. 504/385–2628 or 800/348–2628, fax 504/384–0817).

Passports and Visas U.S. citizens need some proof of citizenship, such as a birth certificate plus a photo I.D. or a current passport. British subjects require a current passport. All visitors must have an ongoing or return ticket.

Language The official language of the Turks and Caicos is English.

Precautions Petty crime does occur here, and you're advised to leave your valuables in the hotel safe-deposit box. During the rainy season bring along a can of insect repellent because the mosquitoes can be vicious.

If you plan to explore the uninhabited island of West Caicos, be advised that the interior is overgrown with dense shrubs that include manchineel, which has a milky, poisonous sap that can cause painful, scarring blisters.

In some hotels on Grand Turk, Salt Cay, and South Caicos, there are signs that read, "Please help us conserve our precious water." These islands have no freshwater supply other than rainwater collected in cisterns, and rainfall is scant. Drink only from the decanter of fresh water your hotel provides, but tap water is safe for brushing your teeth or other hygiene uses.

Staying in the Turks and Caicos Islands

Important Addresses **Tourist Information:** The **Government Tourist Office** (Front St., Cockburn Town, Grand Turk, tel. 809/94–62321; and Turtle Cove Landing, Provo, tel. 809/94–64970) is open Monday–Thursday 8–4:30 and Friday 8–5.

Emergencies **Police:** Grand Turk, tel. 809/94–62299; Providenciales, tel. 809/94–64259; South Caicos, tel. 809/94–63299. **Hospitals:** There is a 24-hour emergency room at **Grand Turk Hospital** (Hospital Rd., tel. 809/94–62333) and at **Providenciales Health-Medical Center** (Leeward Hwy. and Airport Rd., tel. 809/94–64201). **Pharmacies:** Prescriptions can be filled at the **Government Clinic** (Grand Turk Hospital, tel. 809/94–62040) and at the **Providenciales Health-Medical Center** in Provo (Leeward Hwy. and Airport Rd., tel. 809/94–64910).

Currency The unit of currency is U.S. dollars.

Taxes and Service Charges Most hotels collect a 7% government tax; however, some are now charging 8%. The departure tax is $15. Hotels add a 10%–15% service charge to your bill. In restaurants, a tip of 10%–15% is appropriate and sometimes already added to your bill. Taxi drivers expect a token tip.

Guided Tours A **taxi** tour of the islands costs between $25 and $30 for the first hour and $25 for each additional hour. On Provo, contact **Nell's Taxi** (tel. 809/94–65585, 809/94–64595, or 809/94–64393). The drivers are friendly and know everything and everybody. **Executive Tours** (tel. 809/94–64524 or 809/94–67310 from North Caicos) offers a guided tour in an air-conditioned bus for $10 per person, for a minimum of eight people and a maximum of 22. **Turtle Tours** (tel. 809/94–65585) offers a variety of bus and small-plane tours. A bus tour takes in all of Provo, including the conch farm, and stops for drinks at Hey Jose. You can also fly to Middle Caicos, the largest of the islands, for a visit to its mysterious caves or to North Caicos to see the ruins of a former slave plantation. If you want to island-hop on your own schedule, air charters are available through **Blue Hills Aviation** (tel. 809/94–64388), and **Flamingo Air Services** (tel. 809/94–62109).

Getting Around
Bus On Provo, shuttle buses operated by **Executive Tours** (tel. 809/94–64524) run from the hotels into town every hour, Mon.–Sat. 7 AM–9 PM. Depending on where you board, fares run from $2–$4 each way. A new public bus system on Grand Turk charges 50¢ one-way to any scheduled stop.

Taxis Taxis are unmetered, and rates, posted in the taxis, are regulated by the government.

Ferries **Caicos Express** (tel. 809/94–67111 or 809/94–67258) offers two scheduled interisland ferries between Provo, Pine Cay, Middle Caicos, Parrot Cay, and North Caicos daily except Sunday. Tickets cost $15 each way.

Rental Cars Local rental agencies on Provo are **Budget** (tel. 809/94–64079), **Provo Rent-A-Car** (tel. 809/94–64404), **Rent A Buggy** (tel. 809/94–64158), and **Turquoise Jeep Rentals** (tel. 809/94–64910); on Grand Turk, **Dutchie's Car Rental** (tel. 809/94–62244). Rates average $40 to $65 per day, plus a $10-per-rental-agreement Government Stamp duty. To rent cars on South Caicos, check with your hotel manager for rates and information.

Scooters You can scoot around Provo by contacting **Holiday Scooter Rentals** (tel. 809/94–64422) or the **Honda Shop** (tel. 809/94–64397). On Grand Turk, contact **Kittina Scooter Rental** (tel. 809/94–62232). Rates generally start at $25 per day for a one-seater, and $40 a day for a two-seater, plus a one-time $5 government tax, plus gas.

Telephones and Mail You can call the islands direct from the United States by dialing 809 and the number. Calling home from Turks and Caicos, dial direct from most hotels, from some pay phones, and from **Cable and Wireless,** which has offices in Provo (tel. 809/94–64499) and Grand Turk (tel. 809/94–62200), open Monday–Thursday 8–4:30 and Friday 8–4. You must dial 0, followed by the country code (1 for U.S. and Canada; 44 for U.K.), area code, and local number.

Postal rates for letters to the United States, Bahamas, and Caribbean are 50¢ per half ounce; postcards, 35¢. Letters to the United Kingdom and Europe, 65¢ per half ounce; postcards, 45¢. Letters to Canada, Puerto Rico, and South America, 65¢; postcards, 45¢.

Opening and Closing Times Most offices are open weekdays from 8 or 8:30 till 4 or 4:30. Banks are open Monday–Thursday 8:30–2:30, Friday 8:30–12:30 and 2:30–4:30.

Exploring the Turks and Caicos Islands

Numbers in the margin correspond to points of interest on the Turks and Caicos Islands map.

Grand Turk Horses and cattle wander around as if they owned the place, and the occasional donkey cart clatters by, carrying a load of water or freight. Front Street, the main drag, lazes along the western side of ❶ the island and eases through **Cockburn Town,** the colony's capital and seat of government. Buildings in the capital reflect the 19th-century Bermudian style of architecture, and the narrow streets are lined with low stone walls and old street lamps, now powered by electricity.

The **Turks & Caicos National Museum** opened in 1993 in the restored Guinep House. One of the oldest native stone buildings in the islands, the museum now houses the Molasses Reef wreck of 1513, the earliest shipwreck discovered in the Americas, and natural history exhibits that include artifacts left by African, North American, Bermudian, French, Hispanic, and Taino settlers. *Tel. 809/94– 62160. Admission: $5. Open weekdays 10–4, Sat. 10–1.*

Time Out The **Pepper Pot** (tel. 809/94–62389) is a little blue shack at the end of Front Street where Peanuts Butterfield is famous for his conch fritters.

Fewer than 4,000 people live on this 7½-square-mile island. Diving is definitely the big deal here. Grand Turk's Wall, with a sheer drop to 7,000 feet, is well known to divers.

Salt Cay This tiny 2½-square-mile dot in the water is home to about 200 people. The island boasts the Windmills Plantation hotel, a few stores in ❷ **Balfour Town,** and splendid beaches on the north coast. Old windmills, salt sheds, and salt ponds are silent reminders of the days when the island was a leading producer of salt.

South Caicos **Cockburn Harbour,** the best natural harbor in the Caicos chain, is ❸ home to the South Caicos Regatta, held each year in May. This 8½-square-mile island was once an important salt producer; today it's the heart of the fishing industry. Spiny lobster and queen conch may be found in the shallow Caicos bank to the west and are harvested for export by local processing plants. Bonefishing here is some of the best in the West Indies.

At the northern end of the island there are fine, white-sand beaches; the south coast is great for scuba diving along the drop-off; and the windward (east) side is excellent for snorkeling, where large stands of elkhorn and staghorn coral shelter a variety of small tropical fish.

East Caicos Uninhabited and accessible only by boat, **East Caicos** has on its ❹ north coast a magnificent 17-mile beach. It was once a cattle range and the site of a major sisal-growing industry.

Middle Caicos The largest (48 square miles) and least-developed of the inhabited ❺ Turks and Caicos islands, Middle Caicos is home to limestone **Conch Bar Caves,** with their eerie underground lakes and milky-white stalactites and stalagmites. Archaeologists have discovered Arawak and Lucayan Indian artifacts in the caves and the surrounding area. Since telephones are a rare commodity here, the boats that dock here and the planes that land on the little airstrip provide the island's 270 residents with their main connection to the outside world. **Executive Tours** can fly you over and take you through the mysterious caves (*see* Guided Tours, *above*).

North Caicos The **Prospect of Whitby Hotel** is on the north end of this 41-square-❻ mile island. To the south of Whitby is **Flamingo Pond,** a nesting place for the beautiful pink birds. If you take a taxi tour of the island, you'll see the ruins of the old plantations and, in the little settle-

⑦ ⑧ ments of **Kew** and **Sandy Point,** a profusion of tropical trees bearing limes, papayas, and custard apples. The beaches here are superb for shelling and lolling, and the waters offshore offer excellent snorkeling, scuba diving, and fishing.

Pine Cay One of a chain of small cays connecting North Caicos and Provo, 800-
⑨ acre **Pine Cay** is privately owned and under development as a planned community. It's home to the exclusive **Meridian Club** resort, playground of jet-setters, and its 2½-mile beach is the most beautiful in the archipelago. The island has a 3,800-foot airstrip and electric carts for getting around.

Providenciales In the mid-18th century, so the story goes, a French ship was wrecked near here and the survivors were washed ashore on an island they gratefully christened La Providentielle. Under the Span-
⑩ ish, the name was changed to **Providenciales.**

Provo's 44 square miles are by far the most developed in the Turks and Caicos. With its rolling ridges and 12-mile beach, the island is a prime target for developers. More than 17 years ago a group of U.S. investors, including the DuPonts, Ludingtons, and Roosevelts, opened up this island for visitors and those seeking homesites in the Caribbean. In 1990 the island's first luxury resort, the **Ramada Turquoise Reef Resort & Casino,** opened, and with it, the island's first gourmet Italian restaurant. The luxurious **Ocean Club,** a condominium resort at Grace Bay, was also completed in 1990, and was followed by the upscale **Grace Bay Club** resort in 1992. The competition of these new resorts spurred many of the older hotels to undergo much-needed renovations.

Downtown Provo, near Providenciales International Airport, is a cluster of stone and stucco buildings that house car-rental agencies, law offices, boutiques, banks, and other businesses.

Time Out Stop in at **Fast Eddie's** (Airport Rd., tel. 809/94–64075), a casual eatery, for a relaxing drink and a platter of seafood.

Provo is home to the **Island Sea Center** (on the northeast coast, tel. 809/94–65330), where tourists can learn about the sea and its inhabitants. Here you'll find the **Caicos Conch Farm** (tel. 809/94–65849), a major mariculture operation where the mollusks are farmed commercially. The farm's tourist facilities, including a geodesic dome, a video show, and a "hands-on" tank, were damaged by a fire in 1993, but at press time restoration was underway for a reopening in late 1994. Established by the PRIDE Foundation (Protection of Reefs and Islands from Degradation and Exploitation) and now funded by Into the Blue, the **JoJo Dolphin Project,** named after a 7-foot male bottle-nosed dolphin who cruises these waters and enjoys playing with local divers, is also here. You can watch a video on JoJo and learn how to interact with him safely if you see him on one of your dives.

About 6,000 people live on Provo, a considerable number of whom are expatriate U.S. and Canadian businesspeople and retirees.

West Caicos Over the past few centuries numerous wrecks have occurred in the area between West Caicos and Provo, and author Peter Benchley is among the treasure-seekers who have been lured to this island.
⑪ **Molasses Reef** is rumored to be the last resting site of the *Pinta,* which is thought to have been wrecked here in the early 1500s.

Accessible only by boat, this island is uninhabited and untamed, and there are no facilities whatsoever. A glorious white beach stretches

Turks and Caicos Islands

Caicos Passage

Mary Cays

Parrot Cay

Fort George Cay
Pine Cay **9**
Water Cay **26**

Providenciales
10

South Bluff

Jubber Point

13 — **25**

8

27

6
7

North
Caicos

Spanish
Point

Highas
Cay

Juniper
Hole

Middle C

12

Northwest
Point

West
Caicos

Southwest Point

C A I C O S   I S L A

Ocean
Hole

Vine Point

11

C A I C O S   B A N K

N

0		14 miles
0		21 km

White Cay

Exploring
Balfour Town, **2**
Cockburn Harbour, **3**
Cockburn Town, **1**
Conch Bar Caves, **5**
East Caicos, **4**

Flamingo Pond, **6**
Kew, **7**
Molasses Reef, **11**
Northwest Reef, **12**
Pine Cay, **9**
Providenciales, **10**
Sandy Point, **8**

Dining
Alfred's Place, **13**
Dora's, **14**
Fast Eddie's, **15**
Hey, José, **16**
Hong Kong
Restaurant, **17**
Regal Begal, **32**

Salt Raker Inn, **30**
Sandpiper, **31**
Top O' The Cove
Gourmet
Delicatessen, **18**
Yum Yum's, **19**

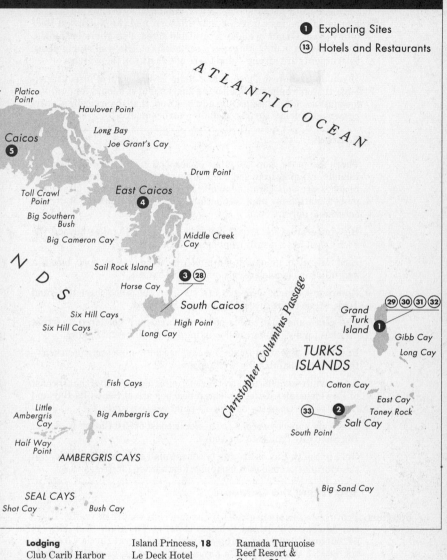

● Exploring Sites

⑬ Hotels and Restaurants

ATLANTIC OCEAN

Platico
Point

Haulover Point

Long Bay

Joe Grant's Cay

Caicos
❺

Drum Point

Toll Crawl
Point

East Caicos
❹

Big Southern
Bush

Middle Creek
Cay

Big Cameron Cay

N
D
S

Sail Rock Island

Horse Cay

❸ ㉘

South Caicos

Six Hill Cays

High Point

Six Hill Cays

Long Cay

Christopher Columbus Passage

Grand
Turk
Island ●

㉙ ㉚ ㉛ ㉜

Gibb Cay

Long Cay

TURKS
ISLANDS

Fish Cays

Cotton Cay

Little
Ambergris
Cay

Big Ambergris Cay

㉝ ❷

East Cay

Toney Rock

Salt Cay

Half Way
Point

South Point

AMBERGRIS CAYS

SEAL CAYS

Big Sand Cay

Shot Cay

Bush Cay

Lodging

Club Carib Harbor
Hotel, **28**

Club Med Turkoise, **22**

Coral Reef Resort, **29**

Erebus Inn, **15**

Grace Bay Club, **23**

Hotel Kittina, **31**

Island Princess, **18**

Le Deck Hotel
& Beach Club, **20**

The Meridian Club, **26**

Prospect of Whitby
Hotel, **27**

Ramada Turquoise
Reef Resort &
Casino, **21**

Salt Raker Inn, **30**

Treasure Beach
Villas, **24**

Turtle Cove Inn, **25**

Windmill's
Plantation, **33**

for a mile along the northwest point, and offshore diving is among the most exotic in the islands. A wall inhabited by every kind of large marine life begins a quarter-mile offshore, and the **Northwest Reef** offers great stands of elkhorn coral and acres of staghorn brambles. But this area is only for experienced divers. The wall starts deep, the currents are strong—and there are sharks in the waters.

If you do tour West Caicos, take along several vats of insect repellent. It won't help much with the sharks, but it should fend off the mosquitoes and sand flies. Be advised, too, that the interior is overgrown with dense shrubs, including manchineel.

Beaches

There are more than 230 miles of beaches in the Turks and Caicos Islands, ranging from secluded coves to miles-long stretches. Most beaches are soft coralline sand. Tiny uninhabited cays offer complete isolation for nude sunbathing and skinny-dipping. Many are accessible only by boat.

Big Ambergris Cay, an uninhabited cay about 14 miles beyond the Fish Cays, has a magnificent beach at **Long Bay.**

East Caicos, an uninhabited island accessible only by boat, boasts a magnificent 17-mile beach along its north coast.

Governor's Beach, a long white strip on the west coast of **Grand Turk,** is one of the nicest beaches on this island.

The north and east coasts of **North Caicos** are bordered by great beaches for swimming, scuba diving, snorkeling, and fishing.

Pine Cay, a private upscale retreat, has a 2½-mile strip of beach—the most beautiful in the archipelago.

A fine white-sand beach stretches 12 miles along the northeast coast of **Providenciales.** Other splendid beaches are at **Sapodilla Bay** and rounding the tip of the northwest point of the island.

There are superb beaches on the north coast of **Salt Cay,** as well as at **Big Sand Cay** 7 miles to the south.

Only in South Caicos are the beaches small and unremarkable, but the vibrant reef makes it a popular destination for divers.

Sports and the Outdoors

Bicycling   Provo has a few steep grades to conquer, but very little traffic. Bikes can be rented at **Island Princess Hotel** at The Bight (tel. 809/94–64260) for $10 per day, through **Turtle Inn Divers** (Turtle Cove Inn, tel. 809/94–64203) for $12 a day and $60 a week, or at the **Ramada Turquoise Reef Resort & Casino** (tel. 809/94–65555), in Grace Bay, for $14 a day. In Grand Turk on Duke Street, both the **Salt Raker Inn** (tel. 809/94–62260) and the **Hotel Kittina** (tel. 809/94–62232) rent bikes to their guests and the public for $10 per day, $40 per week.

Boat Rentals   You can rent a boat with private pilot for a half or full day of sportfishing through **Black Diamond Tours** (Provo, tel. 809/94–64451) or **Porpoise** (Salt Cay tel. 809/94–66927) for about $300 a day. **Dive Provo** (Ramada Turquoise Reef Resort, Provo, tel. 809/94–65040) rents small sailboats for $20 per hour and provides beginning instruction for $40 for up to two hours. Sailing not your bent? Try open-cockpit ocean kayaking, available at Dive Provo for $10 per hour for one and $15 per hour for two.

Fishing **Black Diamond Tours** (Provo, tel. 809/94–64451) will take a maximum of three people out for half- or full-day bonefish or bottom fishing expeditions, bait and tackle included, for $150 per half day. The same outfit will arrange half- or full-day deep-sea fishing trips in search of shark, marlin, kingfish, sawfish, wahoo, and tuna, with all equipment furnished. Deep-sea, bonefishing, and bottom fishing are also available aboard the *Sakitumi* (tel. 809/94–64203 or 809/94–64393).

Golf This arid archipelago introduced a 6,529-yard golf course on Providenciales in late 1991. **Provo Golf Club** (tel. 809/94–65991) is an 18-hole par-72 championship course designed by Karl Litten, sustained by a desalination plant producing 250,000 gallons of water a day. The turf is sprinkled in green islands over 12 acres of natural limestone outcroppings, creating a desert-style design of narrow "target areas" and sandy waste areas—a formidable challenge to anyone playing from the championship tees. Fees are $65 plus $15 for a mandatory electric cart. A pro shop, driving ranges, and a restaurant and bar round out the club's facilities.

Horseback Riding Horses roam lazily around the main roads on Grand Turk. While there is no organized riding program, most hotels will make arrangements for their guests, and rates can be negotiated with individual owners.

Parasailing A 15-minute flight is available for $45 at either **Dive Provo** (Ramada Turquoise Reef Resort, Provo, tel. 809/94–65040) or **Turtle Inn Divers** (Turtle Cove Inn, tel. 809/94-64203).

Scuba Diving Diving is the top attraction here. (All divers must carry and present a valid certificate card before they'll be allowed to dive.) These islands are surrounded by a reef system of more than 200 square miles—much of it unexplored. Grand Turk's famed wall drops more than 7,000 feet and is one side of a 22-mile-wide channel called the Christopher Columbus Passage. From January through March, an estimated 6,000 eastern Atlantic humpback whales swim through this passage en route to their winter breeding grounds. There are undersea cathedrals, coral gardens, and countless tunnels. Among the operations that provide instruction, equipment rentals, underwater video equipment, and trips are **Omega Divers** (Hotel Kittina, Grand Turk, tel. 809/94–62232), **Blue Water Divers** (Salt Raker Inn, Grand Turk, tel. 809/94–62432), **Off the Wall Divers** (Grand Turk, tel. 809/94–62159 or 809/94–62135), **Dive Provo** (Ramada Turquoise Reef Resort, Provo, tel. 809/94–65040 or 800/234–7768), **Flamingo Divers** (Provo, tel. 809/94–64193), **Provo Turtle Divers** (Provo, tel. 809/94–64232), **Porpoise Divers** (Salt Cay, tel. 809/94–66927), and **Tradewinds Divers** (Prospect of Whitby Hotel, North Caicos, tel. 809/94–67377).

Note: A modern hyperbaric/recompression chamber is located on Provo (tel. 809/94–64242) in the **Menzies Medical Centre** on Leeward Highway. Divers in need on Grand Turk are airlifted to Provo—a 30-minute flight.

Sea Excursions The *Ocean Outback* (tel. 809/94–64080), a 70-foot motor cruiser, does barbecue-and-snorkel cruises to uninhabited islands. Both the 37-foot catamaran *Beluga* (tel. 809/94–65040, $39 per half day) and the 56-foot trimaran *Tao* (tel. 809/94–65040) run sunset cruises, as well as sailing and snorkeling outings. A full-day outing on the Tao is $59 per person, including snorkel rental and lunch. The Provo Turtle Divers' 20-foot glass-bottom *Grouper Snooper* (Provo, tel. 809/94–64232) offers sightseeing and snorkeling excursions. For $20 per person, **Dive Provo** (Ramada Turquoise Reef Resort, tel. 809/94–

65040) gives two-hour glass-bottom boat tours of the spectacular reefs. **Turtle Inn Divers** (tel. 809/94–64203) offers full-day Sunday excursions for divers for $64.50 per person and $25 per person for nondivers and snorkelers. The *Turks and Caicos Aggressor* (tel. 504/385–2628 or 800/348–2628, fax 504/384–0817) offers luxury six-day dive cruises with full accommodations.

Snorkeling **Dive Provo** (Provo, tel. 809/94–65040), **Blue Water Divers** (Salt Raker Inn, Grand Turk, tel. 809/94–62432), and **Provo Turtle Divers** (Provo, tel. 809/94–64232) all provide rentals for about $10 and trips for $20. **Omega Diving International** (Grand Turk, tel. 809/94–62978) offers equipment and trips, as well as diving packages and instruction.

Tennis On Provo, there are two lighted courts at **Turtle Cove Inn** (tel. 809/94–64203), eight courts (four lighted) at **Club Med Turkoise** (tel. 809/94–64491), two courts at the **Ramada Turquoise Reef Resort** (tel. 809/94–65555), two lighted courts at the **Erebus Inn** (tel. 809/94–64240), two courts at **Treasure Beach Villas** (tel. 809/94–64211), and two lighted courts at **Grace Bay Club** (tel. 809/94–65050). On Grand Turk, the **Coral Reef Resort** (tel. 809/94–62055 has one court. There is also one court at the **Meridian Club** (Pine Cay, tel. 800/225–4255), and one court at the **Prospect of Whitby Hotel** (North Caicos, tel. 809/94–67119).

Waterskiing Waterskiers will find the calm turquoise water ideal for long-distance runs. **Dive Provo** (Ramada Turquoise Reef Resort, Provo, tel. 809/94–65040) will take you at $35 for a 15-minute run.

Windsurfing Rental and instruction are available at **Prospect of Whitby Hotel** (North Caicos, tel. 800/346–67119) and **Dive Provo** (Ramada Turquoise Reef Resort, Provo, tel. 809/94–65040).

Spectator Sports Cricket is the most popular game in town. The season runs from July through August. Tennis, basketball, softball, and darts are also well cheered by locals. You're welcome to join in. Inquire at the tourist board (tel. 800/241–0824) for a list of events.

Shopping

Delicate baskets woven from the local top grasses are the only craft native to the Turks and Caicos, and they are sold at the airport. Crafts from other islands are available at Turtle Cove's shopping district.

Bamboo Gallery (Leeward Hwy., Provo, tel. 809/94–64748) sells all types of Caribbean art, from vivid Haitian paintings to wood carvings.

Greensleeves (MarketPlace, Provo, tel. 809/94–64147) is the place to go for paintings by local artists, island-made rag rugs, baskets, jewelry, and sisal mats and bags.

Local Color (MarketPlace, and at Le Deck Hotel, Provo, tel. 809/94–65547) sells art and sculpture made by local artists as well as native basketry, hand-painted tropical clothing, tie-dyed pareos, and silk-screened T-shirts.

Tropical Fashions (Turtle Cove, Provo, tel. 809/94–64343) is where you'll find resortwear, sandals, Provo T-shirts, perfumes, and gold jewelry.

Dining

Like everything else on these islands, dining out is a very laid-back affair, which is not to say that it is cheap. Because of the high cost of importing all edibles, the cost of a meal is usually higher than that of a comparable meal in the United States, and all the menus are à la carte. A 7% government tax and a 10%–15% service charge are added to your check. Reservations are not required, and dress is casual.

Highly recommended restaurants are indicated by a star ★.

Category	Cost*
Expensive	over $25
Moderate	$15–$25
Inexpensive	under $15

per person, excluding drinks, service, and 7% sales tax

Grand Turk **Salt Raker Inn.** In this rustic, informal patio restaurant you may start with tomato and mozzarella salad or melon and ginger. Popular entrées include lobster in cream and sherry sauce, barbecued steak, and seafood curry. For dessert, try apple pie. The Sunday dinner and sing-along is a fun way to end the week. *Salt Raker Inn, tel. 809/94–62260. AE, D, MC, V. Moderate.*

Sandpiper. Candles flicker on the Sandpiper's terrace beside a flower-filled courtyard. A peaceful, leisurely atmosphere pervades this restaurant, whose blackboard specialties may include pork chops with applesauce, lobster, filet Mignon, or seafood platter. *Hotel Kittina, tel. 809/94–62232. AE, D, MC, V. Moderate.*

Regal Begal. This popular local eatery is the place to get native specialties, such as cracked conch, minced lobster, and fish-and-chips. The atmosphere is casual and the decor unmemorable, but the portions are large and the prices easy on your wallet. *Hospital Rd., tel. 809/94–62274. No credit cards. Inexpensive.*

Providenciales **Alfred's Place.** Austrian owner Alfred Holzfeind caters to an American palate on his extensive menu with everything from prime rib to ★ chicken salad. The alfresco lounge is a popular watering hole for locals and tourists alike. *Turtle Cove, tel. 809/94–64679. AE, D, MC, V. Closed Mon. July–Oct. Moderate–Expensive.*

Dora's. Open seven days a week from 7 AM until the last person leaves the bar, this popular eatery specializes in island fare—turtle, shredded lobster, and spicy conch chowder. Plastic print and lace tablecloths, hanging plants, and Haitian art add to the island ambience. Dora's is a favorite haunt of locals and expatriates alike. Soups ($4) come with homemade bread, and entrées such as fish-and-chips, conch Creole, and grilled pork chops come with a choice of vegetable. Be sure to come early for the packed Monday- and Thursday-night all-you-can-eat $20 seafood buffet. The price includes free round-trip transportation to your hotel. *Leeward Hwy., tel. 809/94–64558. No credit cards. Inexpensive–Moderate.*

Fast Eddie's. Located across from the airport, this cheerful, plant-festooned restaurant serves island specialties such as broiled turtle steak and fried grouper fingers alongside old American standbys such as cheeseburgers and cherry pie. Wednesday evening is their $20 ($10 for children) all-you-can-eat seafood buffet. Friday is prime rib and live music night. Diners are provided with free transportation to and from their hotels. *Airport Rd., tel. 809/94–64075. MC, V. Inexpensive–Moderate.*

Hong Kong Restaurant. A no-frills place with plain wood tables and chairs, the Hong Kong offers dine-in, delivery, or takeout, and a menu that includes lobster with ginger and green onions, chicken with black-bean sauce, sliced duck with salted mustard greens, and sweet-and-sour chicken. The Peking duck is a house specialty. *Leeward Hwy., tel. 809/94–65678. AE, MC, V. Open for dinner only on Sundays. Inexpensive–Moderate.*

★ **Hey, José.** This restaurant with an atrium boasts that it serves the island's best margaritas. People also keep coming back for the tasty Tex-Mex treats: tacos, tostados, nachos, burritos, fajitas, and José's special-recipe hot chicken wings. Creative types can build their own pizzas; dieters need not despair, as the limited menu also offers a lean beef patty. *Leeward Hwy., tel. 809/94–64812. AE, MC, V. Closed Sun. Inexpensive.*

Top O' the Cove Gourmet Delicatessen. On Leeward Highway, this tiny café is a convenient walk from the Turtle Cove and Erebus Inns and offers a rare cup of potable coffee, as well as genuine espresso and frothy cappuccino. Open every day but Christmas and New Year's from 7 AM to 3:30 PM, the café, owned by Angela Belvin, serves breakfast, deli subs, sandwiches, and salads. You can get your food to go or you can eat at bistro tables topped with colorful tropical cloths that belie the restaurant's location in the Napa Auto Parts plaza. *Leeward Hwy., tel. 809/94–64694. No credit cards. Inexpensive.*

Yum Yum's. One of the newer eateries in town, this restaurant is a good place to come when you want an affordable, reasonably quick, good meal with no frills. The menu features native dishes, deli sandwiches, ice cream, yogurt, and fresh pastries—served in a modern, air-conditioned setting. *Town Centre Mall, Butterfield Sq., tel. 809/94–64480. No credit cards. Inexpensive.*

Lodging

Hotel accommodations are available on Grand Turk, North Caicos, South Caicos, Pine Cay, and Provo. There are also some small, non-air-conditioned guest houses on Salt Cay and Middle Caicos. Accommodations range from small island inns to the splashy Club Med Turkoise to the new luxury Grace Bay Club in Providenciales. Because of the popularity of scuba diving here, virtually all the hotels have dive shops and offer attractive dive packages. Dive packagers offering air/hotel/dive packages include **Dive Provo** (tel. 800/234–7768) and **Undersea Adventures** (tel. 800/234–7768). Most of the medium and large hotels offer a choice of EP and MAP. People who don't rent a car or scooter tend to eat at their hotels, so MAP may be the better option. Please note that the government hotel tax does not apply to guest houses with fewer than four rooms.

Highly recommended lodgings are indicated by a star ★.

Category	Cost*
Very Expensive	over $250
Expensive	$170–$250

Moderate	$110–$170
Inexpensive	under $110

All prices are for a standard double room for two in winter season, excluding 7% tax and 10% service charge. Please note that some hotels are now charging 8% tax.

Grand Turk ★ **Hotel Kittina.** This family-owned hostelry is the largest hotel on Grand Turk. Choose between the sleek, balconied, air-conditioned suites with kitchens, which sit on a gleaming white-sand beach, or the older main house across the street, which oozes island atmosphere. Rooms in the latter are simple; strong winds blow through the rooms and keep things so cool you don't need the ceiling fans. Be sure to catch the hotel's occasional Friday-night poolside barbecue. *Duke St., Box 42, tel. 809/94–62232 or 800/548–8462, fax 809/94–62877. 43 rooms and 2 suites. Facilities: 2 restaurants, 2 bars, pool, boutique, Omega Dive Shop, T&C Travel Agency, scooter and bicycle rentals, windsurfing, baby-sitting, room service, boat rentals. AE, MC, V. EP, MAP. Moderate.*

Coral Reef Resort. These modern, air-conditioned efficiency one- and two-bedroom units sit on a ridge on the eastern coast, where you can stroll out of your room and onto the beach. It's a combination of apartment and hotel, with each unit boasting contemporary furnishings and a complete electric kitchen. Located a short drive from town. *Box 10, tel. 809/94–62055, fax 809/94–62911. 21 rooms. Facilities: restaurant, bar, tennis, pool, boutique, mini–fitness center, water sports arranged with dive operations. AE, MC, V. EP, MAP. Inexpensive.*

Salt Raker Inn. Across the street from the beach, this galleried house was the home of a Bermudian shipwright 180 years ago. The rooms and suites are not elegant, but are individually decorated and have a homelike atmosphere. Accommodations include a garden house with screened porches and three one- bedroom suites, all with air-conditioning, TV, telephone, and minifridge. *Duke St., Box 1, tel. 809/94–62260, fax 809/94–62432. In U.K., 44 Birchington Rd., London NW6 4LJ, tel. 071/328–6474. 10 rooms and 2 suites. Facilities: restaurant, bar, dive packages with Blue Water Diving, bicycle rentals. AE, D, MC, V. EP. Inexpensive.*

North Caicos ★ **Prospect of Whitby Hotel.** This secluded retreat is a quiet getaway located on a 7-mile-long beach. If you want them, diversions can include windsurfing, snorkeling, and bonefishing. The spacious rooms are tasteful island basic with air-conditioning. In true getaway fashion, they lack both TVs and radios. Both the service and the food are superb. *Kew Post Office, North Caicos, tel. 809/94–67119, fax 809/94–67114. 28 rooms and 4 suites. Facilities: restaurant, bar, pool, bicycles, 1 tennis court, windsurfing, dive shop, baby-sitting, tour desk. Some years closed from Sept. 1–Nov. 15. AE, MC, V. EP, MAP. Moderate.*

Pine Cay ★ **The Meridian Club.** High rollers get away from it all in high style on this privately owned 800-acre island. Club guests enjoy an unspoiled cay with 2½ miles of soft white sand and a 500-acre nature reserve, with tropical landscaping, freshwater ponds, and nature trails that lure bird-watchers and botanists. A stay here is truly getting away from it all, as there are no air conditioners, telephones, or TVs. The ceiling-fan-and-breeze-cooled accommodations range from spacious rooms with king-size beds (or twin beds on request) and patios to one- to four-bedroom cottage-homes that range in decor and amenities from rustic to well-appointed. There's also a newly renovated "round room" cottage and two new ocean-view atrium units that are separated by a lovely interior garden. Rooms in the main complex run over $550 a night for two in winter and include all meals. Cottage homes start at $2,300 a week EP. *Pine Cay, tel. 800/331–9154, fax 809/94–65128. RMI Marketing, 201½ E. 29th St., New York, NY 10016. 12 rooms and 13 cottage-homes. Facilities: restaurant, bar, pool, tennis court, bicycles, windsurfing, sailing. No credit cards. EP, FAP. Very Expensive.*

Providenciales **Club Med Turkoise.** This lavish $23 million resort is one of the most sumptuous of all Club Med's villages. One-, two-, and three-story bungalows line a mile-long beach, and all the usual sybaritic pleasures are here. This club is especially geared toward couples, singles aged 28 and over, and divers. The one-price-covers-all-except-drinks package includes all the diving, water sports, and daytime activities you can handle. *Providenciales, tel. 809/94–65500 or 800–CLUBMED; in NY, 212/750–1684 or 212/750–1685, fax 809/94–65501. 298 rooms. Facilities: 3 restaurants, snack bar, bar, disco, boutique, 8 tennis courts (4 lighted), bicycles, TV/video room, library, beach, pool, dive center, deep-sea-fishing excursions, watersports center, fitness center, nightly entertainment. AE, MC, V. All-inclusive (except for drinks). Expensive.*

Grace Bay Club. Managed by the Ricketts Group, Grace Bay, which opened in 1992, is the epitome of comfort and elegance. At the touch of your fingers you can order in a chef, who supplies the ingredients, whips up a gourmet meal, and then serves it to you in your own dining room. You can also request a nanny or a massage therapist. The rooms are furnished with rattan and pickled wood, and the Mexican-tile floors are elegantly appointed with throw rugs from Turkey and India. Accommodations range from standard rooms to studio apartments to one-and two-bedroom suites and feature air-conditioning, ceiling fans, cable TVs and VCRs, clock radios, and safety vaults. Studio apartments and suites also have terraces, full kitchens, and a washing machine and dryer. Complimentary amenities include windsurfing, Sunfish day sailers, and snorkeling gear. Rooms fall into our moderate category, while one-bedroom suites fall into our expensive category. *Box 128, Provo, tel. 809/94–65050 or 800/677–9192, fax 809/94–65758. 37 rooms and suites. Facilities: restaurant, bar pool, beach, Jacuzzi, water sports, 2 lighted tennis courts, and video/book library. AE, MC, V. EP, MAP. Expensive.*

★ **Le Deck Hotel & Beach Club.** This 27-room pink hostelry was built in classic Bermudian style around a tropical courtyard that opens onto a tiki hut- and palm tree–dotted beach on Grace Bay. Popular with divers, it offers clean rooms with a tile floor, color TV, service-bar, phone, and air-conditioning. The atmosphere is informal and lively with a mostly thirty-something-and-over crowd. *Box 144, Grace Bay, Provo, tel. 809/94–65547 or 800/282–4753, fax 809/94–65770. 27 rooms, including 2 honeymoon suites. Facilities: restaurant, bar, pool, boutique, water sports, beach. AE, D, MC, V. EP, BP, MAP, FAP. Expensive.*

★ **Ramada Turquoise Reef Resort & Casino.** This beachfront hotel is still the island's leading full-service luxury resort. Oversize ocean-front rooms have rattan furniture and an aqua, deepgreen, gold, and mauve color scheme. Furnished with a king or two double beds, all rooms are air-conditioned and have a color TV and ceiling fan, and either a terrace or a patio. The island's first gourmet Italian restaurant is located here, as is the island's only casino. Guests enjoy a free daily-activities program that includes pool volleyball and children's treasure hunts. *Box 205, Provo, tel. 809/94–65555, 800/228–9898, or 800/854–7854;fax 809/94–65522. 228 rooms. Facilities: 3 restaurants, 3 bars, beach, free-form pool, Jacuzzi, water-sports facility,*

2 tennis courts, dive shop, boutiques, duty-free shop, exercise/fitness room, room service, live nightly entertainment/disco, casino, tour desk, baby-sitting, daily activities program. AE, MC, V. EP, MAP. Expensive.

Island Princess. Wood walkways at the hotel lead up to and around the rooms, which are situated in two wings. All rooms have cable TV and a private balcony. This is a great little hotel for families. It's on the beach, the restaurant serves excellent Italian and Caribbean food, and there's nightly entertainment. *The Bight, tel. 809/94-64260, fax 809/946-4666. 80 rooms. Facilities: restaurant, bar, 2 pools, game room, children's playground, boat rentals, watersports center. AE, D, MC, V. MAP. Moderate.*

Treasure Beach Villas. These one- and two-bedroom modern self-catering apartments have fully equipped kitchens, fans, and Provo's 12 miles of white sandy beach for beachcombing and snorkeling. Laundry service and bicycle and car rentals are available, and arrangements can be made for fishing, snorkeling, or scuba diving. It's best to have a car or scooter here, although guests can also take the bus to a nearby grocery store or to several restaurants. *The Bight, tel. 809/94-64211 or 800/282-4753; fax 809/94-64108. Box 8409, Hialeah, FL 33012. 8 single,10 double rooms. Facilities: pool, tennis court. AE, D, MC, V. EP. Moderate.*

Turtle Cove Inn. Occupying 1½ acres, this two-story recreational facility has rooms facing either the marina or the free-form pool and sundeck. This quiet inn, geared toward tennis players, divers, and boaters, offers free boat shuttles to a nearby beach and snorkeling reef. All rooms have a TV, phone, and air-conditioning, and eight also have minifridges. A new dive facility is on-premises, and a handful of good restaurants are within walking distance. *Providenciales, tel. 809/94-64203 or 800/633-7411, fax 809/94-64040. 30 rooms, 1 suite. Facilities: 2 restaurants, 2 bars, lounge, game room, 2 lighted tennis courts, pool, marina, dive shop, bicycle rentals. AE, D, MC, V. EP. Moderate.*

★ **Erebus Inn Resort.** All units in this modest resort have two double beds and modern wicker furnishings. Rooms in the older chalet cost under $110 a night double occupancy in the winter. For those preferring creature comforts, we recommend the units in the newer section (even though rates here are in our moderate-priced category); each features air-conditioning,13-channel cable TV, and phone. Face-lifted and expanded in 1992, the hotel sits on a cliff overlooking Turtle Cove, which affords a wonderful view of the marina and the Caribbean beyond. A frequent shuttle service ferries guests by bus to a nearby beach. The restaurant and bar, always one of Provo's liveliest spots, has a menu of French and Caribbean cuisine. Five affordable restaurants are within walking distance, as is a shopping center and several dive operations. *Turtle Cove, Box 238, Providenciales, tel. 809/94-64240, fax 809/94-64704. 30 rooms. Facilities: restaurant, bar, 2 pools (1 saltwater), fitness center, aqua-aerobics, 2 lighted tennis courts, baby-sitting. AE, MC, V. EP, MAP. Inexpensive-Moderate.*

Salt Cay
★ **Windmills Plantation.** The attraction here is the lack of distraction: no nightlife, no cruise ships, no crowds, and no shopping. Owner-manager-architect Guy Lovelace and his interior designer wife, Patricia, built the hotel as their version of a colonial-era plantation. The great house has four suites, each with a sitting area, four-poster bed, ceiling fans, and a veranda or balcony with a view of the sea. All are furnished in a mix of antique English and wicker furniture. Four other rooms are housed in two adjacent buildings. Room rates, which during the height of winter run from $415 a night and up for

two people, include snorkeling equipment, three meals, and unlimited bar drinks, wine, and beer. *Salt Cay, tel. 800/822–7715 or 809/ 94–66962, fax 809/94–66930. 4 rooms, 4 suites. Facilities: restaurant, bar. pool, library, 2.5-mile nature trail, nearby diving, fishing, horseback riding, snorkeling, beach. AE, MC, V. FAP. Very Expensive.*

South Caicos **Club Carib Beach & Harbour Hotel.** Within walking distance of the township, this small resort overlooking Cockburn Harbour and the fishing district was, at press time, in the midst of an overall face-lift. Room refurnishing and renovation was under way at the time of this inspection, with air-conditioners, color TVs, new paint, and new furniture in store for the resort's 24 harbor rooms. The 16 beachfront rooms (which can also be rented as one- or two-bedroom villas) are larger, with tiled floors, minirefrigerators, and microwaves, but they lack air-conditioning. Management also plans to add a pool. There's a small dive operation, and guests can rent Windsurfers and bicycles. *Box 1, South Caicos, tel. 809/94–63444 or 800/722–2582, fax 809/94–63446. 40 rooms. Facilities: restaurant, bar, bicycle rentals, Windsurfers, dive shop. AE, D, MC, V. EP, MAP. Inexpensive–Moderate.*

Nightlife

On Provo, a full band plays native, reggae, and contemporary music on Thursday nights at the **Erebus Inn** (tel. 809/94–64240). **Le Deck** (tel. 809/94–65547) offers one-armed bandits every night. A lively lounge can be found at the **Ramada Turquoise Reef Resort** (tel. 809/ 94–65555) disco, where a musician plays to the mostly tourist crowd. The Ramada is also the location of **Port Royale** (tel. 809/94–65508), the island's only gambling casino. **Bacchus** (opposite the Ramada Turquoise Reef Resort, tel. 809/94–65214) is Provo's newest nightclub and is open Thursday, Friday and Saturday night. **Disco Elite** (Airport Rd., tel. 809/94–64592) sports strobe lights and an elevated dance floor. On Grand Turk, Xavier Tonneau leads singalongs in his bar almost every night (**Turks Head Inn,** tel. 809/94–62466), and there's music at the **Salt Raker Inn** on Wednesday and Sunday nights. Night owls can head over to the **Lady** for dancing (near the airport, no tel.).

27 The U.S. Virgin Islands

St. Thomas, St. Croix,
St. John

*Updated by
Pamela
Acheson and
Jordan
Simon*

It is the combination of the familiar and the exotic found in the United States Virgin Islands that defines this "American Paradise" and explains much of its appeal. The effort to be all things to all people—while remaining true to the best of itself—has created a sometimes paradoxical blend of island serenity and American practicality in this U.S. territory 1,000 miles from the southern tip of the U.S. mainland.

The postcard images you'd expect from a tropical paradise are here: Stretches of beach arc into the distance, and white sails skim across water so blue and clear it stuns the senses; red-roof houses add their spot of color to the green hillsides' mosaic, along with the orange of the flamboyant tree, the red of the hibiscus, the magenta of the bougainvillea, and the blue stone ruins of old sugar mills; and towns of pastel-tone European-style villas, decorated by filigree wrought-iron terraces, line narrow streets climbing up from a harbor.

The other part of the equation are all those things that make it so easy and appealing to visit this cluster of islands. The official language is English, the money is the dollar, and the U.S. government runs things. There's cable TV, Pizza Hut, and McDonald's. There's unfettered immigration to and from the mainland, and investments are protected by the U.S. flag. Visitors to the U.S.V.I. have the opportunity to delve into a "foreign" culture, while anchored by familiar language and landmarks.

Your destination here will be St. Thomas (13 miles long); its neighbor St. John (9 miles long); or, 40 miles to the south, St. Croix (23 miles long). A pro/con thumbnail sketch of these three might have it that St. Thomas is bustling (hustling) and the place for shopping and discos (commercial glitz and overdevelopment); St. Croix is more Danish, picturesque, and rural (more provincial and duller, particularly after dark); and St. John is matchless in the beauty of its National Park Service–protected land and beaches (a one-village island mostly for the rich or for campers). Surely not everything will suit your fancy, but chances are that between the three islands you'll find your own idea of paradise.

Before You Go

**Tourist
Information**

Information about the United States Virgin Islands is available through the following organizations. **U.S.V.I. government tourist offices:** 225 Peachtree St., Suite 760, Atlanta, GA 30303, tel. 404/688–0906, fax 404/525–1102; 122 S. Michigan Ave., Suite 1270, Chicago, IL 60603, tel. 312/461–0180, fax 312/461–0765; 3460 Wilshire Blvd., Suite 412, Los Angeles, CA 90010, tel. 213/739–0138, fax 213/739–2005; 2655 Le Jeune Rd., Suite 907, Coral Gables, FL 33134, tel. 305/442–7200, fax 305/445–9044; 1270 6th Ave., New York, NY 10020, tel. 212/582–4520, fax 212/581–3405; 900 17th Ave. NW, Suite 500, Washington, DC 20006, tel. 202/293–3707, fax 202/785–2542; 1300 Ashford St., Condado, Santurce, Puerto Rico 00907, tel. 809/724–3816, fax 809/724–7223; and 2 Cinnamon Row, Plantation Wharf, York Place, London, England SW11 3TW, tel. 071/978–5262, telex 27231, fax 071/924–3171.

You can also call the Division of Tourism's toll-free number (tel. 800/USVI–INFO).

**Arriving and
Departing**
By Plane

One advantage of visiting the U.S.V.I. is the abundance of nonstop flights that can have you at the beach in a relatively short time (three to four hours from most East Coast departures). You may fly into the U.S.V.I. direct via **Continental** (tel. 800/231–0856), **Delta** (tel.

800/221–1212), **USAir** (tel. 800/428–4322), or **American** (tel. 800/ 433–7300), or you may fly via San Juan on all the above plus **Sunaire Express** (tel. 809/495–2480).

By Boat   Some 20 cruise lines stop at St. Thomas or St. Croix, offering everything from budget floating hotels to small luxury yachts taking only 100 passengers.

Among the cruise-ship lines that offer stopovers at St. Thomas are **Holland American Line** (300 Elliott Ave. W, Seattle, WA 98119, tel. 206/281–3535), **Princess Cruises** (2029 Century Park E, Suite 3000, Los Angeles, CA 90067, tel. 213/553–1770 or 800/421–0522), **Royal Caribbean Cruises** (903 South America Way, Miami, FL 33132, tel. 800/327–6700; in Canada, 800/245–7225), **Royal Viking Line** (1 Embarcadero Center, San Francisco, CA 94111, tel. 800/422–8000), **Cunard Line** (555 5th Ave., New York, NY 10017, tel. 800/528–6273 or 800/458–9000), and **Home Lines** (1 World Trade Center, Suite 3939, New York, NY 10048, tel. 212/432–1414; in Canada, 514/842–1441). Port calls to St. Croix will be irregular until work on the new cruise-ship pier is completed in December 1994.

For a smaller luxury cruise on which caviar-and-champagne service is the norm 24 hours a day, contact **Seabourne Cruise Line** (55 San Francisco St., San Francisco, CA 94133, tel. 415/391–7444).

Increasingly popular are cruises aboard over-size sailboats. Although the sails on these rather odd-looking ships are more often cosmetic than functional, the ships usually offer a more relaxed itinerary and stop at less traveled anchorages. **Club Med** (tel. 800/-258–2633) expanded its all-inclusive vacations to the sea with the launching in February 1990 of *Club Med I,* a 614-foot ship with seven computerized sails that Club Med bills as the largest sailing ship in the world. The ship sails out of Guadeloupe on seven-day winter cruises (it's in St. Thomas for one day) and spends summers in the Mediterranean. **Windjammer Cruises** (Box 120, Miami Beach, FL 33119–0120, tel. 800/327–2601) sails out of the U.S.V.I. on cruises to neighboring islands for two- to seven-day durations. **Star Clippers** (Clipper Ship Cruises, 2833 Bird Ave., Dept. ETLF, Miami, FL 33133–4604, tel. 800/442–0551) offers seven-day cruises.

Passports and Visas   Upon entering the U.S.V.I., U.S. and Canadian citizens are required to present some proof of citizenship—if not a passport, then a birth certificate or voter-registration card with a driver's license or photo ID. If you are arriving from the U.S. mainland or Puerto Rico, you need no inoculation or health certificate.

Britons need a valid 10-year passport to enter the U.S.V.I. (cost: £15 for a standard 32-page passport, £30 for a 94-page passport). You do not need a visa for the U.S.V.I. if you are visiting either on business or pleasure, are staying fewer than 90 days, have a return ticket or ongoing ticket, are traveling with a major airline (in effect, any airline that flies from the United Kingdom to the United States), and complete visa waiver I-94W, which is supplied either at the airport of departure or on the plane.

Language   English, often with a Creole or West Indian lilt, is the medium of communication in these islands.

Precautions   Crime exists here, but not to the same degree that it does in larger cities on the U.S. mainland. Still, it's best to stick to well-lit streets at night and use the same kind of street sense (don't wander the back alleys of Charlotte Amalie after five rum punches, for example) that you would in any unfamiliar territory. If you plan on carrying things around, rent a car, not a Jeep, and lock possessions in the trunk.

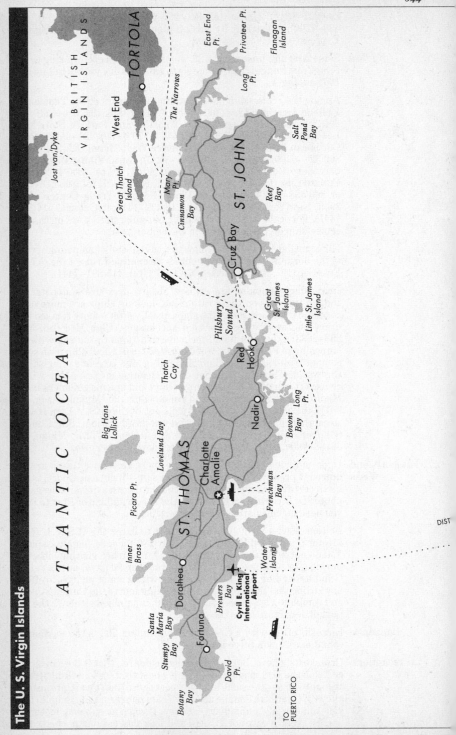

The U. S. Virgin Islands

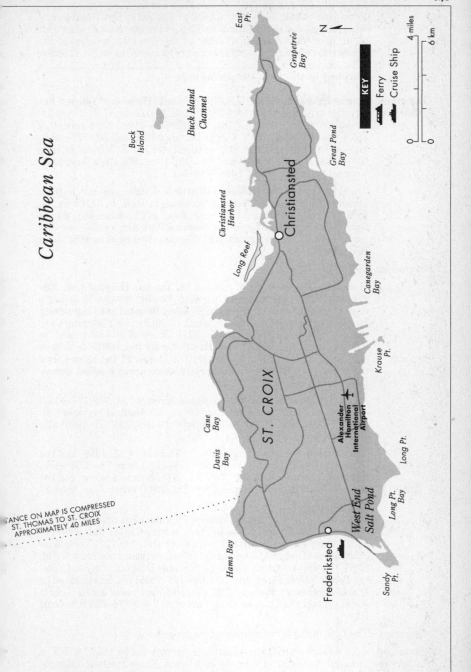

Caribbean Sea

East Pt.

Grapetree Bay

Buck Island

Buck Island Channel

Great Pond Bay

Long Reef

Christiansted Harbor

Christiansted

Canegarden Bay

Cane Bay

Davis Bay

ST. CROIX

Krause Pt.

Alexander Hamilton International Airport

Long Pt.

Long Pt. Bay

Hams Bay

West End Salt Pond

Frederiksted

Sandy Pt.

DISTANCE ON MAP IS COMPRESSED
ST. THOMAS TO ST. CROIX
APPROXIMATELY 40 MILES

N

KEY

Ferry

Cruise Ship

4 miles

6 km

Keep your rental car locked wherever you park. Don't leave cameras, purses, and other valuables lying on the beach while you're off on an hour-long snorkel, whether at the deserted beaches of St. John or the more crowded Magens and Coki beaches on St. Thomas.

Staying in the U.S. Virgin Islands

Important Addresses

Tourist Information: The U.S. Virgin Islands Division of Tourism has an office in St. Thomas (Box 6400, Charlotte Amalie, U.S. Virgin Islands 00804, tel. 809/774–8784, fax 809/774–4390), St. Croix (Box 4538, Christiansted, U.S. Virgin Islands 00822, tel. 809/773–0495, and on the pier, Strand St., Frederiksted, U.S. Virgin Islands 00840, tel. 809/772–0357), and St. John (Box 200, Cruz Bay, U.S. Virgin Islands 00830, tel. 809/776–6450).

There are two **visitor centers** in Charlotte Amalie: one across from Emancipation Square and one at Havensight Mall. In St. Croix, go to the Old Scale House at the waterfront in Christiansted, across from Fort Christiansvaern. The **National Park Service** also has visitor centers at the ferry areas on St. Thomas (Red Hook) and St. John (Cruz Bay).

Emergencies

Police: Dial 915.

Hospitals: The emergency room of **St. Thomas Hospital** (tel. 809/776–8311) in Sugar Estate, Charlotte Amalie, is open 24 hours a day. In Christiansted there is the **St. Croix Hospital and Community Health Center** (6 Diamond Bay, north of Sunny Isle Shopping Center, on Route 79, tel. 809/778–6311 or 809/778–5895), and in Frederiksted, the **Frederiksted Health Center** (tel. 809/772–1992 or 809/772–0750). On St. John contact the **Morris F. DeCastro Clinic** (Cruz Bay, tel. 809/776–6400) or call an **emergency medical technician** directly (tel. 809/776–6222).

Air Ambulances: Bohlke International Airways (tel. 809/778–9177) operates out of the airport in St. Croix. **Air Medical Services** (tel. 800/443–0013) and **Air Ambulance Network** (tel. 800/327–1966) also service the area from Florida.

Coast Guard: For emergencies on St. Thomas or St. John, call the **Marine Safety Detachment** (tel. 809/776–3497) from 7 to 3:30 weekdays; on St. Croix, call 809/773–7614. If there is no answer, call the **Rescue Coordination Center** (tel. 809/722–2943) in San Juan, open 24 hours a day.

Pharmacies: On St. Thomas, **Sunrise Pharmacy** has branches in Red Hook (tel. 809/775–6600) and in the Wheatley Center (tel. 809/774–5333); **Drug Farm Pharmacy's** main store (tel. 809/776–7098) is located across from the General Post Office, with another branch (tel. 809/776–1880) situated next to St. Thomas Hospital. On St. Croix, try **People's Drug Store, Inc.** (tel. 809/778–7355) in Christiansted or **D & D Apothecary Hall** (tel. 809/772–1890) in Frederiksted. On St. John, contact the **St. John Drug Center** (tel. 809/776–6353) in Cruz Bay.

Currency

The U.S. dollar is the medium of exchange here.

Taxes and Service Charges

A 7.5% tax is added to hotel rates. Departure tax for the U.S.V.I. is included in the cost of your airplane ticket. Some hotels and restaurants add a 10% or 15% service charge to your bill, generally only if you are part of a group of 15 or more. There is no sales tax in the U.S.V.I.

Guided Tours On St. Thomas, the **V.I. Taxi Association City-Island Tour** (tel. 809/ 774–4550) gives a two-hour tour aimed at cruise-ship passengers that includes stops at Drake's Seat and Mountain Top. **Tropic Tours** (tel. 809/774–1855) offers half-day shopping and sightseeing tours of St. Thomas by bus on Mondays, Wednesdays, Fridays, and Saturdays for $18 per person and full-day snorkeling tours to St. John every day for $40 per person (including lunch). It picks up at all the major hotels. Bird-watching, whale-watching, and a chance to wait hidden on a beach while the magnificent hawksbill turtles come ashore to lay their eggs are all open to visitors. Write the **Virgin Islands Conservation Society** (Box 3839, St. Croix 00822, tel. 809/773–1989) for more information on hikes and special programs, or check the community calendar in the *Daily News* for up-to-date information.

Van tours of St. Croix are offered by **St. Croix Safari Tours** (tel. 809/ 773–6700) and **St. Croix Transit** (tel. 809/772–3333). The tours, which depart from Christiansted and last about three hours, cost from $20 per person. One of the best ways to see the rain forest and hills of the west end may be a tour by horseback with **Paul and Jill's Equestrian Stable** (tel. 809/772–2880 or tel. 809/772–2627).

On St. John, the park service gives a variety of guided tours on- and off-shore. For more information, or to arrange a tour, contact the **St. John National Park Visitor Center** (Cruz Bay, tel. 809/776–6201).

Getting Around **Car** Any U.S. driver's license is good for 90 days here; the minimum age for drivers is 18, although many agencies won't rent to anyone under the age of 25. Driving is on the left side of the road (although your steering wheel will be on the left side of the car). Many of the roads are narrow and the islands are dotted with hills, so there is ample reason to drive carefully. Jeeps are particularly recommended on St. John, where dirt roads prevail.

On St. Thomas, you can rent a car from **ABC Rentals** (tel. 809/776– 1222 or 800/524–2080), **Anchorage E-Z Car** (tel. 809/775–6255), **Avis** (tel. 809/774–1468), **Budget** (tel. 809/776–7575), **Cowpet Car Rental** (tel. 809/775–7376 or 800/524–2072), **Dependable** (tel. 809/774–2253 or 800/522–3076), **Discount** (tel. 809/776–4858), **Hertz** (tel. 809/774– 1879), **Sea Breeze** (tel. 809/774–7200), **Sun Island** (tel. 809/774– 3333), or **Thrifty** (tel. 809/776–8600).

On St. Croix, call **Atlas** (tel. 809/773–2886), **Avis** (tel. 809/778–9355), **Budget** (tel. 809/778–9636), **Caribbean Jeep & Car** (tel. 809/773– 4399), **Hertz** (tel. 809/778–1402), **Olympic** (tel. 809/773–2208), and **Thrifty** (tel. 809/773–7200).

On St. John, call **Avis** (tel. 809/776–6374), **Budget** (tel. 809/776– 7575), **Cool Breeze** (tel. 809/776–6588), **Hertz** (tel. 809/776–6695), **O'Connor Jeep** (tel. 809/776–6343), **St. John Car Rental** (tel. 809/776– 6103), or **Spencer's Jeep** (tel. 809/776–7784).

Taxis Taxis of all shapes and sizes are available at various ferry, shopping, resort, and airport areas on St. Thomas and St. Croix and respond quickly to a call.

In Charlotte Amalie, taxi stands are located across from **Emancipation Gardens** (in front of Little Switzerland behind the post office) and along the waterfront. Away from Charlotte Amalie, you'll find taxis available at all major hotels and at such public beaches as Magens Bay and Coki Point. Calling taxis will work, too, but allow plenty of time.

Taxis on St. Croix, generally station wagons or minivans, are a phone call away from most hotels and are available in downtown Christiansted, at the Alexander Hamilton Airport, and at the Frederiksted pier during cruise-ship arrivals. Rates, set by law, are prominently displayed at the airport. Try the **St. Croix Taxi Association** (tel. 809/778–1088) at the airport and **Antilles Taxi Service** (tel. 809/773–5020) or **Cruzan Taxi Association** (tel. 809/773–6388) in Christiansted.

On St. John buses and taxis are the same thing: open-air safari buses. Technically the safari buses are private taxis, but everyone uses them as an informal bus system. You'll find them congregated at the Cruz Bay Dock, ready to take you to any of the beaches or other island destinations, but you can also pick them up anywhere on the road by signaling.

Buses Public buses are not the quickest way to get around on the islands because service is minimal, but the deluxe mainland-size buses on St. Thomas make public transportation a very reasonable and comfortable way to get from east and west to town and back (there is no service north, however). Fares are $1 between outlying areas and town and 75¢ in town. St. Croix and St. John have no public bus system, and residents rely on the kindness of taxi vans and safari buses for mass transportation.

Ferries Ferries ply two routes between St. Thomas and St. John—either between the Charlotte Amalie waterfront and Cruz Bay or between Red Hook and Cruz Bay. The schedules for daily service between Red Hook, St. Thomas, and Cruz Bay, St. John: Ferries leave Red Hook weekdays 6:30 and 7:30 AM, and all week long hourly 8 AM to midnight. They leave Cruz Bay for Red Hook hourly 6 AM to 10 PM and at 11:15 PM. The 15–20 minute ferry ride is $3 one way for adults, $1.50 for children under 12.

Telephones The area code for all the U.S.V.I. is 809, and there is direct dial to **and Mail** the mainland. Local calls from a public phone cost 25¢ for each five minutes. On St. John the place to go for any telephone or message needs is **Connections** (tel. 809/776–6922). On St. Thomas, it's **Islander Services** (tel. 809/774–8128), behind the Greenhouse Restaurant in Charlotte Amalie, or **East End Secretarial Services** (tel. 809/775–5262, fax 809/775–3590), upstairs at the Red Hook Plaza. On St. Croix, visit the **Business Bureau** (42–43 Strand St., Christiansted, tel. 809/773–7601) or **St. Croix Communications Centre** (61 King St., Frederiksted, tel. 809/772–5800).

By late 1994 the telephone exchange throughout St. John will be switched to **693**. However, at press time the change had not been fully implemented. When you dial the current listing, a recording will redirect you if necessary.

The main **U.S. post office** on St. Thomas is near the hospital, with branches in Charlotte Amalie and Frenchtown; there's a post office at Christiansted and Fredriksted on St. Croix and at Cruz Bay on St. John. Postal rates are the same as elsewhere in the United States: 29¢ for a letter, 19¢ for a postcard to anywhere in the United States, 45¢ for a ½-oz. letter mailed to a foreign country.

Opening and On **St. Thomas,** Charlotte Amalie's Main Street–area shops are open **Closing Times** weekdays and Saturday 9–5. Havensight Mall shops (next to the cruise-ships dock) hours are the same, though some shops sometimes stay open until 9 on Friday, depending on how many cruise ships are staying late at the dock. You may also find some shops open on Sunday if a lot of cruise ships are in port. **St. Croix** store hours are usually weekdays 9 to 5, but you will definitely find some shops in Christiansted open in the evening. On **St. John,** store hours are reliably similar to those on the other two islands, and Wharfside Village shops in Cruz Bay are often open into the evening.

Exploring St. Thomas

Numbers in the margin correspond to points of interest on the St. Thomas map.

Charlotte Amalie ❶   This tour of historic (and sometimes hilly) **Charlotte Amalie** and environs is on foot, so wear comfortable shoes, start early, and stop often to refresh. A note about the street names: In deference to the island's heritage, the streets downtown are labeled by their Danish names. Locals will use both the Danish name and the English name (such as Dronnigen's Gade and Main Street).

Begin at the waterfront. Waterfront and Main streets are connected by cobblestone-paved alleys kept cool by overhanging green plants and the thick stone walls of the warehouses on either side. The alleys (particularly Royal Dane Mall and Palm Passage, Main Street between the post office and Market Square, and Bakery Square on Back Street) are where you'll find the unique and glamorous—and duty-free—shops for which Charlotte Amalie is famous (*see* Shopping, *below*).

At the end of Kronprindsens Alley north of the waterfront is the pale-pink Roman Catholic **Cathedral of St. Peter and St. Paul,** consecrated as a parish church in 1848. The ceiling and walls of the church are covered in the soft tones of murals painted in 1899 by two Belgian artists, Father Leo Servais and Brother Ildephonsus. The San Juan–marble altar and side walls were added in the 1960s. *Tel. 809/774–0201. Open Mon.–Sat. 8–5.*

At **Market Square,** east of the church on Main Street, try to block out the signs advertising cameras and electronics and imagine this place as it was in the early 1800s, when plantation owners stood on the delicately draped wrought-iron balconies and chose from the human merchandise below, where the slaves for sale were displayed. Today in the square, a cadre of old-timers sell papaya, tania roots, and herbs, and sidewalk vendors offer a variety of African fabrics and artifacts, tie-dyed cotton clothes at good prices, and fresh-squeezed fruit juices. Go east on Back Street, then turn left on Store Tvaer Gade; walk a short block to the right, and take a left on Bjerge Gade.

As you walk up Bjerge Gade you'll end up facing a weather-beaten but imposing two-story red house known as the **Crystal Palace,** so named because it was the first building on the island to have glass windows. The Crystal Palace anchors the corner of Bjerge and Crystal Gade. Here the street becomes stairs, which you can climb to Denmark Hill and the old Greek Revival **Danish Consulate building** (1830)—look for the red-and-white flag.

Descend to Crystal Gade and go east. At Number 15 you'll come to the **Synagogue of Beracha Veshalom Vegmiluth Hasidim.** Its Hebrew name translates as the Congregation of Blessing, Peace, and Loving Deeds. Since the synagogue first opened its doors in 1833, it has held a weekly Sabbath service, making it the oldest synagogue building in continuous use under the American flag and the second-oldest (after the one on Curaçao) in the Western Hemisphere. *15 Crystal Gade, tel. 809/774–4312. Open Mon.–Fri. 9–4.*

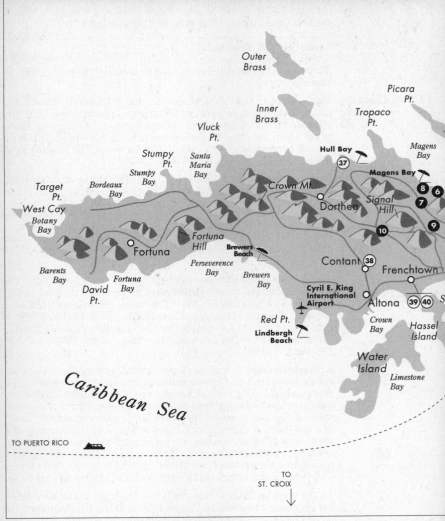

TO PUERTO RICO

TO
ST. CROIX

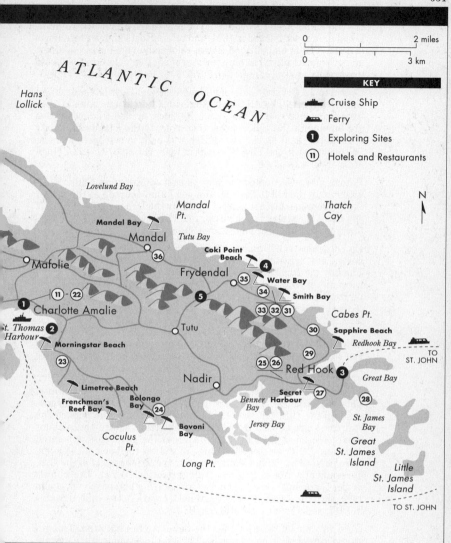

ATLANTIC OCEAN

Hans
Lollick

Lovelund Bay

Mandal Bay

Mandal

Mandal
Pt.

Tutu Bay

Thatch
Cay

Mafolie

(36)

**Coki Point
Beach**

Frydendal

(4)

(35)   **Water Bay**

(11) - (22)

(5)

(34)   **Smith Bay**

(33)(32)(31)

Charlotte Amalie

Cabes Pt.

(1)

Sapphire Beach

St. Thomas
Harbour

(2)

Tutu

(30)

Redhook Bay

TO
ST. JOHN

Morningstar Beach

(29)

(23)

(25)(26)   Red Hook   (3)

Great Bay

Nadir

Limetree Beach

**Secret
Harbour**

(27)

(28)

**Frenchman's
Reef Bay**

**Bolongo
Bay**

(24)

Benner
Bay

Jersey Bay

St. James
Bay

Great
St. James
Island

**Bovoni
Bay**

Little
St. James
Island

Coculus
Pt.

Long Pt.

TO ST. JOHN

KEY

- Cruise Ship
- Ferry
- ① Exploring Sites
- ⑪ Hotels and Restaurants

| 0 | | 2 miles |
| 0 | | 3 km |

N

Lodging

Blackbeard's
Castle, **16**

Bolongo Elysian Beach
Resort, **26**

Bolongo Inclusive
Beach Resort, **24**

Bunker Hill Hotel, **19**

Grand Palazzo, **28**

Heritage Manor, **18**

Hotel 1829, **12**

Island View
Guesthouse, **38**

Marriott's
Frenchman's Reef
and Morning Star
Beach Resorts, **23**

Pavilions & Pools, **29**

Point Pleasant
Resort, **32**

Sapphire Beach Resort
and Marina, **30**

Sign of the Griffin, **36**

Stouffer Grand Beach
Resort, **33**

Sugar Bay
Plantation, **31**

Villa Blanca Hotel, **20**

One block east, down the hill, you'll come to the corner of Nye Gade. On the right corner is the St. Thomas **Dutch Reformed Church,** founded in 1744, burned in 1804, and rebuilt to its austere loveliness in 1844. The unembellished cream-color hall exudes peace—albeit monochromatically. The only touches of another color are the forest green shutters and carpet. *Tel. 809/776-8255. Open Mon.-Fri. 9-5.*

Continue on Crystal Gade one block east and turn left (north) on Garden Street. The **All Saints Anglican Church** was built in 1848 from stone quarried on the island. Its thick, arched window frames are lined with the yellow brick that came to the islands as ballast aboard merchant ships. The church was built in celebration of the end of slavery in the Virgin Islands in 1848. *Tel. 809/774-0214. Open Mon.-Sat. 6 AM-3 PM.*

Return down Garden Street and go east on Kongen's Gade. Keep walking up the hill to the east and you'll find yourself at the foot of the **99 Steps,** a staircase "street" built by the Danes in the 1700s. (If you count the stairs as you go up, you'll discover, like thousands before you, that there are more than 99.)

Up the steps you'll find the neighborhood of **Queen's Street.** The homes are privately owned except for two inns—The Mark St. Thomas and Blackbeard's Castle. The tower of **Blackbeard's Castle** was built in 1679 and is believed to have been used by the notorious pirate Edward Teach. The castle is now a charming inn whose restaurant serves up some of the island's best food and jazz.

Time Out You might want to stop at Blackbeard's Castle for a bite to eat and a swim, since the swimming pool is open to daytime customers. As you lunch on the terrace, you can take in the view of Charlotte Amalie and the harbor.

Go back down the steps and continue east to **Government House.** This elegant home, built in 1867, is the official residence of the governor of the U.S.V.I., and the first floor is open to the public. The staircases are carved from native mahogany, as are the plaques hand-lettered in gold with the names of the governors appointed and, since 1970, elected. The three murals at the back of the lobby were painted by Pepino Mangravatti in the 1930s as part of the U.S. government's Works Projects Administration (WPA). The murals depict Columbus's landing on St. Croix during his second voyage in 1493, the transfer of the islands from Denmark to the United States in 1917, and a sugar plantation on St. John.

Head to your left and look for the **Seven Arches Museum.** This restored West Indian home was built around 1800 and is still a private residence. Ring the bell, and you'll be invited inside to see historic furnishings, cannonballs, gas lamps, and a quaint West Indian cottage that sits behind the house. *Tel. 809/774-9295. Open Mon.-Fri. 9-3.*

Return west on Norre Gade (Main Street) toward town. In the block before the post office you'll pass the **Frederick Lutheran Church,** the second-oldest Lutheran church in the Western Hemisphere. The inside is highlighted by a massive mahogany altar. The pews, each with its own door, were once rented to families of the congregation. *Tel. 809/776-1315. Open Mon.-Sat. 9-4.*

Directly across from the Lutheran Church, through a small side street, you'll see **Fort Christian,** St. Thomas's oldest standing structure, built 1672-87, and a U.S. national landmark. The clock tower was added in the 19th century. This remarkable redoubt has, over time, been used as a jail, governor's residence, town hall, court-house, and church. The building is currently being restored, but some rooms are open to the public. *Tel. 809/776-4566. Open Mon.–Fri. 8:30–4:30, Sat. 9:30–4, Sun. noon–4.*

Across from the fort is **Emancipation Garden,** which honors the freeing of slaves in 1848. On the other side of the garden is the **legislature building,** its pastoral-looking lime green exterior concealing the vociferous political wrangling going on inside. Built originally by the Danish as a police barracks, the building was later used to billet U.S. Marines, and much later it housed a public school.

Stop in the **post office** to contemplate the murals of waterfront scenes by *Saturday Evening Post* artist Stephen Dohanos. His art was commissioned as part of the WPA in the 1930s. Behind the post office, on the waterfront side of Little Switzerland, are the hospitality lounge and **V.I. Visitor's Information Center.**

As you head back toward Market Square along Main Street, you'll pass the Tropicana Perfume Shop, between Store Tvaer Gade and Trompeter Gade. The building the shop is in is also known as the **Pissarro Building,** the birthplace of French Impressionist painter Camille Pissarro.

The South Shore and East End

❷ Leaving Charlotte Amalie, take Veterans Drive (Route 30) east along the waterfront. Once you bear to the right at **Nelson Mandela Circle** (Yacht Haven is on your right), you'll make quicker progress. You may want to stop at **Havensight Mall,** across from the dock. This shopping center is a less crowded (and less charming) version of the duty-free shopping district along Main Street in town. Or turn left across the street from Havensight Mall and head straight up the hill to Paradise Point, a scenic overlook with breathtaking views of Charlotte Amalie and the harbor; it also has a bar, restaurant, and several shops.

Route 30 is narrow and winds up and down. It also changes names several times along the way; it is called Frenchman's Bay Road just outside town (take a sharp left turn just before the entrance to Marriott's Frenchman's Reef Hotel and its luxurious companion, Morning Star Beach Resort). It then becomes Bovoni Road around Bolongo Bay. Whatever it is called, you will be treated to some southerly vistas of the Caribbean Sea (and, on clear days, St. Croix, 40 miles away).

❸ Eventually, Route 30 forks into Route 322 on the right, which heads out to several hotels and the **Virgin Island National Park Headquarters,** and Route 32 on the left, which heads into **Red Hook,** where you can catch the ferry to St. John (parking available for $5 a day). Red Hook has grown from a sleepy little town connected to the rest of the island only by dirt roads (or by boat) to an increasingly self-sustaining village. There's a new waterfront arcade with branches of many Charlotte Amalie shops. You can walk along the docks and visit with sailors and fishermen and stop for a beer at Piccola Marina Cafe or the Warehouse bar.

❹ Above Red Hook the main road swings toward the north shore and becomes Route 38, or Smith Bay Road, taking you past Sapphire Beach, a resort and restaurant with water-sports rentals and a popular snorkeling and windsurfing spot, Sugar Bay Resort, Pavilions & Pools, Point Pleasant Resort, and Stouffer Grand Beach Resort. Look for the turnoff to the right for Coki Point Beach and **Coral World,** with its three-level underwater observatory, the world's largest reef tank, and an aquarium with more than 20 TV-size tanks providing capsulized views of sea life. A new semisubmarine (a craft that has glass sides below deck for underwater viewing) offers 20-minute undersea tours for $12 per person. Coral World's staff will answer your questions about the turtles, iguanas, parrots, and flamingos that inhabit the park, and there's a restaurant, souvenir shop, and the world's only underwater mailbox, from which you can send postcards home. *Tel. 809/775–1555. Admission: $14 adults, $9 children. Open daily 9–6.*

5 Continue west on Route 38 and you'll come to **Tillet's Gardens,** where local artisans craft stained glass, pottery, and ceramics, and where well-known artist Jim Tillet's paintings and silk-screened fabrics are on display and for sale.

North Shore, Center Islands, and West The north shore is home to many inviting attractions, not to mention much lusher vegetation than is found on the rest of the island. The most direct route from Charlotte Amalie is Mafolie Road (Route 35), which can be picked up east of Government Hill.

6 In the heights above Charlotte Amalie is **Drake's Seat,** the mountain lookout from which Sir Francis Drake was supposed to have kept watch over his fleet, looking for enemy ships of the Spanish fleet. Magens Bay and Mahogany Run are to the north, with the British Virgin Islands and Drake's Passage to the east. Off to the left, or west, are Fairchild Park, Mountain Top, Hull Bay, and such smaller islands as the Inner and Outer Brass islands. The panoramic vista is especially striking (and romantic) at dusk, and if you arrive late in the day you'll miss the hordes of day-trippers on taxi tours who stop at Drake's Seat to take a picture and buy a T-shirt from one of the vendors there. The vendors are gone by the afternoon.

7 West of Drake's is the island's newest attraction, the **Estate St. Peter Greathouse Botanical Gardens.** Set on a mountainside 1,000 feet above sea level, with views of more than 20 other islands and islets, the estate has a gallery displaying local art and a nature trail that winds through nearly 200 varieties of tropical trees and plants, including an orchid jungle.

8 West from Drake's Seat is **Mountain Top,** which offers an interesting collection of shops, a bar that claims to have invented the banana daiquiri, and, from its setting 1,500 feet above sea level, some spectacular views.

9 Below Mountain Top is **Fairchild Park,** a gift to the people of the U.S.V.I. from the philanthropist Arthur Fairchild.

10 If you head west from Mountain Top, on Crown Mountain Road (Route 33) you'll come to **Four Corners.** Take the extreme right turn and drive along the northwestern ridge of the mountain through **Caret Bay, Sorgenfri,** and **Pearl.** There's not much here except peace and quiet, junglelike foliage, and spectacular vistas.

Turn onto Route 301 to Route 30 and head south to Brewer's Bay, then follow Route 30 east back to Frenchtown and Charlotte Amalie.

Time Out Pull into Frenchtown and reward yourself for a long day's travels with a stop at **Epernay,** a Frenchtown wine bar tucked behind Alexander's Cafe. You'll find wines and champagnes by the glass and hors d'oeuvres and light snacks to linger over while you contemplate life on the islands. *Open Mon.–Sat. 4:30 PM–1 AM (often until later Fri. and Sat.). Food served 5 PM–midnight. AE, MC, V.*

Exploring St. Croix

Numbers in the margin correspond to points of interest on the St. Croix map.

❶ This tour starts in the historic, Danish-style town of **Christiansted,** St. Croix's commercial center. Many of the structures, which are built from the harbor up into the gentle hillsides, date from the 18th century. An easy-to-follow walking tour begins at the **visitors' bureau,** set at the harbor. The building was constructed in 1856, and once served as a scale house, where goods passing through the port were weighed and inspected. Directly across the parking lot, at the edge of D. Hamilton Jackson Park (the park is named for a famed labor leader, journalist, and judge), is the **Old Customs House.** Completed in 1829, this building now houses the island's national park offices. To the east stands yellow **Fort Christiansvaern.** Built by the Danish from 1738 to 1749 to protect the harbor against attacks on commercial shipping, the fort was repeatedly damaged by hurricane-force winds and was partially rebuilt in 1772. It is now part of the National Historic Site and the best-preserved of the remaining Danish-built forts in the Virgin Islands. Five rooms, including military barracks and a dungeon, have been restored to demonstrate how the fort looked in the 1840s, when it was at its height as a military establishment. There is also an exhibit that documents the Danish military's 150-year presence in Christiansted. *Box 160, Christiansted 00822, tel. 809/773-1460. Admission: $2 (includes admission to Steeple Building); free to children under 16 and senior citizens. Open weekdays 8-5, weekends and holidays 9-5. Closed Christmas.*

Cross Hospital Street from the customs house to reach the **post office building.** Built in 1749, it once housed the Danish West India & Guinea Company warehouse. To the south of the post office, across Company Street, stands the maroon-and-white **Steeple Building.** Built by the Danes in 1754, the building once housed the first Danish Lutheran church on St. Croix. It is now a national-park museum and contains exhibits documenting the island's habitation by native Americans through an extensive array of archaeological artifacts. There are also displays on the architectural development of Christiansted and the African American experience in the town during the Danish colonial rule. *Box 160, Christiansted 00822, tel. 809/773-1460. Admission: $2 (includes admission to fort). Open Wed. and weekends 9-4.*

One of the town's most elegant buildings is **Government House,** on King Street. Built as a home for a Danish merchant in 1747, the building today houses U.S.V.I. government offices and the U.S. District Court. Slip into the peaceful inner courtyard to admire the still pools and gardens. A sweeping staircase leads visitors to a second-story ballroom, still the site of official government functions.

To leave Christiansted, drive up Hospital Street from the tourist office and turn right onto Company Street. Follow Company Street for several blocks and turn right with the flow of traffic past the police station. Make a quick left onto King Street, and follow it out of town. At the second traffic light, make a right onto Route 75, Northside Road. A few miles up the road, you can make a side trip by turning right, just past the St. Croix Avis building, onto Route 751, which
❷ leads you past the St. Croix by the Sea hotel to **Judith's Fancy,** where you can see the ruins of an old great house and the tower left from a 17th-century château that was once home to the governor of the Knights of Malta. The "Judith" comes from the first name of a

St. Croix

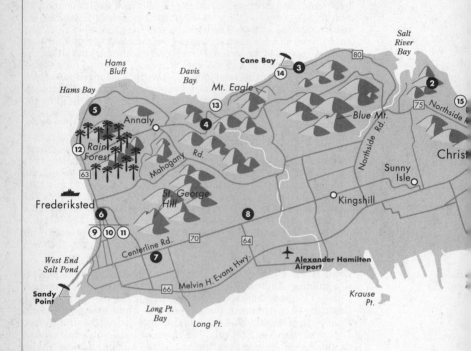

Exploring
Cane Bay, **3**
Christiansted, **1**
Estate Mount
Washington
Plantation, **5**

Estate Whim
Plantation Museum, **7**
Frederiksted, **6**
Judith's Fancy, **2**
Mahogany Road, **4**
St. George Village
Botanical Gardens, **8**

Dining
Blue Moon, **9**
Cafe Madeleine, **27**
Camille's, **20**
Dino's, **19**
Harvey's, **24**
Kendricks, **23**

Le St. Tropez, **11**
Pangaea, **25**
Top Hat, **21**

Buck Island

Buck Island Beach

Long Reef

Christiansted Harbor

5
16
Rd.
17 18 25

Tamarind Reef Beach 26

Green Cay

Pull Pt.

Coakley Bay

Teague Bay

Cramer Park

Cottongarden Pt.

Reef Beach

Sugarloaf Hill

Pt. Udall (East Pt.)

1

Gallow's Bay

East End Rd. 82

27

Isaac Bay

Grapetree Bay

stiansted

60

Recovery Hill

Prospect Hill

South Side Rd.

Grass Pt.

Robin Bay

62

Great Pond Bay

Milord Pt.

South Side Rd.

Manchenil Bay

Canegarden Bay

N

0   2 miles

0   3 km

Lodging

The Buccaneer, **26**

Carambola Beach Resort, **13**

Club St. Croix, **17**

Cormorant Beach Club, **16**

The Frederiksted, **10**

Hibiscus Beach Hotel, **15**

Hotel Caravelle, **18**

The Pink Fancy, **22**

Sprat Hall, **12**

Villa Madeleine, **27**

Waves at Cane Bay, **14**

woman buried on the property. From the guardhouse at the entrance to the neighborhood, follow Hamilton Drive to its end for a view of Salt River Bay, where Christopher Columbus anchored in 1493. The area surrounding Salt River Landing was made a National Historic Park and Ecological Preserve in 1993. It holds sites of cultural significance, such as a prehistoric ceremonial ball court and burial site; and it includes a biologically diverse coastal estuary that's home to several endangered species and boasts the largest remaining mangrove forest in the U.S.V.I. Plans are being developed for a museum, interpretive walking trails, and a replica of a Carib village.

After driving back to Route 75, continue west for 2 miles and turn right at Tradewinds Road onto Route 80, which quickly returns to **③** the grassy coastline and **Cane Bay.** This is one of St. Croix's best beaches for scuba diving, and near the small stone jetty you may see a few wet-suited, tank-backed figures making their way out to the drop-off (a bit farther out there is a steeper drop-off to 12,000 feet). Rising behind you is Mt. Eagle, St. Croix's highest peak, at 1,165 feet. Leaving Cane Bay and passing North Star beach, follow the beautiful coastal road as it dips briefly into the forest, then turn left. There is no street sign, but you'll know the turn: The pavement is marked with the words "The Beast" and a set of giant paw prints—the hill you are about to climb is the infamous Beast of the America's Paradise Triathlon, an annual St. Croix event in which participants must bike up this intimidating slope.

Follow this road, Route 69, as it twists and climbs up the hill and south across the island. The golf course you pass on the right is a Robert Trent Jones course, part of the Carambola resort complex. **④** You will eventually bear right to join Route 76, **Mahogany Road.** Follow Mahogany Road through the heart of the rain forest until you reach the end of the road at Ham's Bluff Road (Route 63), running along the west coast of the island. Turn right and, after a few miles, **⑤** look to the right side of the road for the **Estate Mount Washington Plantation** (tel. 809/772–1026). Several years ago, while surveying the property, the owners discovered the ruins of a historic sugar plantation buried beneath the rain-forest brush. The grounds have since been cleared and opened to the public. A free, self-guided walking tour of the animal-powered mill, rum factory, and other ruins is available daily, and the antiques shop located in the old stables is open on Saturdays.

⑥ Double back along Ham's Bluff Road to reach **Frederiksted,** founded in 1751. A single long cruise-ship pier juts into the sparkling sea from this historic coastal town, noted less for its Danish than for its Victorian architecture (dating from after the uprising of former slaves and the great fire of 1878). A stroll around will take you no more than an hour.

Begin your tour at the **visitor center** (tel. 809/772–0357) on the pier. From here, it's a short walk across Emancipation Park to **Fort Frederik** where, in 1848, the slaves of the Danish West Indies were freed by Governor-general Peter van Scholten. The fort, completed in 1760, houses a number of interesting historical exhibits as well as an art gallery. *Tel. 809/772–2021. Admission free. Open Mon.–Fri. 8:30–4:30.*

Time Out   Set back in a hidden courtyard on the corner of Market and King streets is **Tradewinds Bar and Deli** (tel. 809/772–0718). Serving well-built sandwiches and well-priced daily specials, Tradewinds is an ideal spot for casual lunches on the west end.

Stroll along King Street to Market Street and turn left. At the corner of Queen Street is the **Market Place,** where fresh fruits and vegetables are sold in the early morning, just as they have been for over 200 years. One block farther on the left is the coral-stone **St. Patrick's Church,** a Roman Catholic church built in 1842.

Head back to King Street and follow it to King Cross Street. A left turn here will bring you to **Apothecary Hall,** built in 1839, and on the next block, **St. Paul's Episcopal Church,** a mixture of classical and Gothic Revival architecture, built in 1812. Double back along King Cross Street to Strand Street and the waterfront. Turn right and walk along the water to the pier, where the tour began.

❼ Take Strand Street south to its end, turn left, then bear right before the post office to leave Frederiksted. Make a left at the first stop light to get on Centerline Road (Queen Mary Highway). A few miles along this road, on the right, is the **Estate Whim Plantation Museum.** The lovingly restored estate, with a windmill, cook house, and other buildings, will give you a true sense of what life was like on St. Croix's sugar plantations in the 1800s. The oval-shaped, high-ceilinged great house has antique furniture, decor, and utensils well worth seeing. Notice that it has a fresh and airy atmosphere. (The waterless moat around the great house was used not for defense but for gathering cooling air.) It is built of stone, coral, and lime. Its apothecary exhibit is the largest in all the West Indies. You will also find a museum gift shop. *Box 2855, Frederiksted 00841, tel. 809/772–0598. Admission: $5 adults, $1 children. Open Tues.–Sat. 10–4.*

❽ Continue along Centerline Road to the St. George Estate. Turn left here to reach the **St. George Village Botanical Gardens,** 17 acres of lush and fragrant flora amid the ruins of a 19th-century sugarcane plantation village. The gardens include miniature versions of each ecosystem on St. Croix, from a semi-arid cactus grove to a verdant rain forest. *Box 3011, Kingshill 00851–3011, tel. 809/772–3874. Admission: $3 adults, $1 children. Open Tues.–Sat. 10–3. Closed federal holidays.*

Continue east along Centerline Road all the way back to Christiansted.

Exploring St. John

Numbers in the margin correspond to points of interest on the St. John map.

St. John may be small, but the roads are narrow and wind up and down steep hills, so don't expect to get anywhere in a hurry. Bring along your swimsuit for stops at some of the most beautiful beaches in the world.

❶ **Cruz Bay** town dock is the starting point for just about everything on St. John. Take a leisurely stroll through the streets of this colorful, compact town: There are plenty of shops through which to browse, along with a number of watering holes where you can stop to take a breather.

Follow the waterfront out of town (about 100 yards) to another dock at the edge of a parking lot. At the far side of the lagoon here you'll find the **St. John National Park Service Visitors Center** (tel. 809/776–

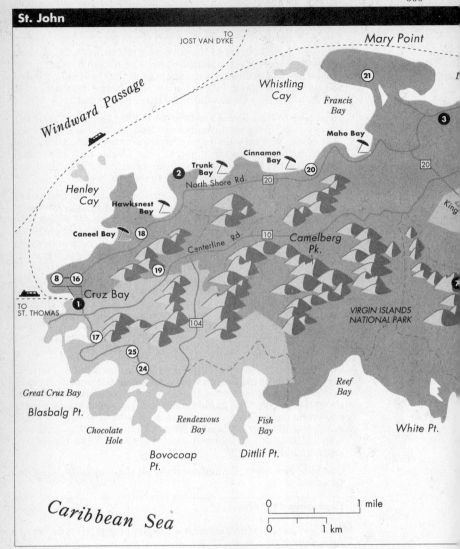

St. John

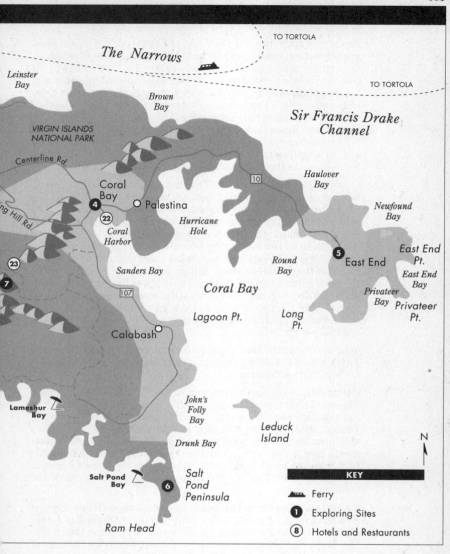

6201), where you can pick up a handy guide to St. John's hiking trails or see various large maps of the island.

Begin your tour traveling north out of Cruz Bay. You'll pass **Mongoose Junction,** recently expanded to include Mongoose Junction II, one of the prettiest shopping areas to be found in the Caribbean. At the ½-mile mark you'll come to the well-groomed gardens and beaches of **Caneel Bay,** purchased from the Danish West India Company and developed by Laurance Rockefeller in the 1950s, who then turned over much of the island to the U.S. government as parkland. Caneel Bay Beach (home of two friendly stingrays that have been fed by snorkelers) is reached by parking in the Caneel parking lot and walking through the grounds (ask for directions). Visitors are welcome at the three restaurants and other designated areas.

Continue east on North Shore Road and you'll see, one after another, four of the most beautiful beaches in all of the Caribbean. The road is narrow and hilly (it was actually just expanded, believe it or not) with switchbacks and steep curves that make driving a challenge. **Hawksnest,** the first beach you will come to, is where Alan Alda shot scenes for his film the *Four Seasons.* Just past Hawksnest Hill swing left to Peace Hill, sometimes called Sugarloaf Hill, to the **2** *Christ of the Caribbean* statue and an old sugar-mill tower. Park in the small unmarked parking lot and walk about 100 yards up a rocky path. The area is grassy, and views of the ocean do not get much better than this. *Christ of the Caribbean* was erected in 1953 by Colonel Julius Wadsworth and donated, along with nine acres of land, to the national park in 1975.

Your next stop, and that of quite a few tourist-filled safari buses, is **Trunk Bay,** a beautiful beach with an underwater trail that's good for beginner snorkelers.

Continuing on the beach hunt, you'll come to wide **Cinnamon Bay.** The snorkeling around the point to the right is good—look for the big angelfish and the swarms of purple triggerfish that live here. The national-park campground is at Cinnamon Bay and includes a snack bar, bathhouse, boutique, restaurant, general store, watersports equipment rental, and a self-guided museum. Across the road from the beach parking lot is the beginning of the Cinnamon Bay hiking trail: look for the ruins of a sugar mill to mark the trailhead.

As you leave Cinnamon, the road flattens out and you'll find yourself on a shaded lane running under flowering trees. **Maho Bay** comes almost to the road here, and you may want to stop and take a dip. The Maho Bay Campground is here, too—a wonderful mélange of open-air cottages nestled in the hillside above.

3 The partially restored **Annaberg Plantation** at Leinster Bay, built in the 1780s and once an important sugar mill, is just ahead on North Shore Road. As you stroll around, look up at the steep hillsides and imagine cutting sugarcane against that grade in the hot sun. Slaves, Danes, and Dutchmen toiled here to harvest the sugarcane that produced sugar, molasses, and rum for export. There are no official visiting hours, no charge for entry, and no official tours, although some well-informed taxi drivers will show you around. Each day from 9 to noon, artisans provide free demonstrations of various island crafts, while local ladies bake luscious johnnycakes (the Caribbean Egg McMuffin). *For more information on talks and cultural demonstrations, contact the St. John National Park Service Visitors Center, tel. 809/776–6201.*

From Annaberg keep to the left and go south, then head uphill and
➍ bear left at the junction to Route 10, to **Coral Bay,** named for its
shape rather than for its underwater life. (The word *coral* comes
from *krawl,* Danish for *corral.*) The community at the dry, eastern
end of the island is the ultimate in laid-back style. It's quiet,
neighborhoody, local, and independent. The small wood-and-stucco
West Indian homes here house everyone from families born here to
newer residents who offer palm readings and massage. This is a
place to get away from it all.

The road forms a loop around Coral Bay. Head northeast along
➎ Route 10 to Hurricane Hole at the remote and pristine **East End,**
only a 15- to 20-minute ride from Coral Bay, where Arawak Indians
are believed to have first settled on the island 2,000 years ago. At
Haulover Bay, only a couple hundred yards separate the Atlantic
Ocean from the Caribbean.

➏ Route 107 takes you south to the peninsula of **Salt Pond,** which is
only about 1 foot above sea level. If you're weary of driving, you can
hike the trail south to the spectacular cliffs of **Ram Head.** In any case
you or your rented car can't proceed much farther on 107 without
venturing onto a truly rocky road that heads west. Be sure at least
to get a view of **Lameshur Bay,** one of the best snorkeling places on
St. John and an area used for underwater training by the U.S.
Navy.

Once you've run out of road on Route 107, retrace your steps to Coral
Bay and go west (left) on Route 10 again, which takes you over the
heights of the island toward Cruz Bay. On your left is the turnoff for
➐ **Bordeaux Mountain,** at 1,277 feet St. John's highest peak. Stop for a
moment hereabouts and you'll find bay trees. Crackle a leaf from
one, and you'll get a whiff of the spicy aroma that you may recognize
from the bay rum for which St. John is famous. To appreciate the
Bordeaux Mountain region fully, save some time during your stay to
hike the **Reef Bay Trail.** Join a hike led by a National Park Service
ranger, who can identify the trees and plants on the hike down, fill
you in on the history of the Reef Bay Plantation, and tell you about
the carvings you'll find in the rocks at the bottom of the trail. The
National Park Service provides a boat ($10) to take you back to Cruz
Bay, saving you the uphill return climb (*see* Guided Tours, *above*).

Beaches

All beaches on these islands are open to the public, but often you will
have to walk through a resort to reach them. Once there, you'll find
that resort guests will often have access to lounge chairs and beach
bars that are off limits to you; for this reason, you may feel more
comfortable at one of the beaches not associated with a resort.
Whichever one you choose, remember to remove your valuables
from the car.

St. Thomas **Coki Point Beach,** next to Coral World, is a popular snorkeling spot
for cruise-ship passengers; it's common to find a group of them
among the reefs on the east and west ends of the beach. If you are
visiting Coral World, you can use its lockers and changing rooms.
Magens Bay is usually lively because of its spectacular arc of white
sand, more than a half-mile long, and its calm waters—two peninsu-
las protect it. The bottom is flat and sandy, so this is a place for sunning and swimming rather than snorkeling. The condo resort at
Secret Harbour doesn't at all detract from the attractiveness of this
covelike East End beach. Not only is it pretty, it is also superb for
snorkeling—go out to the left, near the rocks. At **Morningstar**

Beach, close to Charlotte Amalie, many young residents show up for body surfing or volleyball. This pretty curve of beach fronts the Morning Star section of the Marriott's Frenchman's Reef Hotel. Snorkeling is good here near the rocks. From **Sapphire Beach** there is a fine view of St. John and other islands. Snorkeling is excellent at the reef to the right or east, near Pettyklip Point. All kinds of watersports gear are for rent. **Hull Bay,** on the north shore, faces Inner and Outer Brass cays and attracts fishermen and beachcombers. It is open to rough Atlantic waves and is the only place to surf on the island.

St. Croix **Buck Island** and its reef, which is under environmental protection, can be reached only by boat; nonetheless, a visit here is a must on any trip to St. Croix. Its beach is beautiful, but its finest treasures are those you can see when you plop off the boat and adjust your face mask, snorkel, and flippers. The waters are not always gentle at **Cane Bay,** a breezy north-shore beach, but the scuba diving and snorkeling are wondrous, and there are never many people around. Just swim straight out to see elkhorn and brain corals. Less than 200 yards out is the drop-off or so-called Cane Bay Wall. **Tamarind Reef Beach** is a small but attractive beach east of Christiansted. Both Green Cay and Buck Island seem smack in front of you and make the view arresting. Snorkeling is good. There are several popular West End beaches along the coast north of Frederiksted. The beach at the **West End Beach Club** features a bar, water sports, and volleyball. South of Frederiksted, try the beach at the **King Frederik Hotel,** where palm trees can provide plenty of shade for those who need it, and there is a fine beachside restaurant for a casual lunch on weekends.

St. John **Caneel Bay.** This is actually seven white-sand beaches on the north shore, six of which can be reached only by water if you are not a hotel guest. The main beach (ask for directions) provides easy access to the public. **Hawksnest Beach** is becoming more popular every day; it's narrow and lined with sea grape trees. There are rest rooms, cooking grills, and a covered shed for picnicking. It's popular for group outings, but most of the time it's quiet. **Trunk Bay** is probably St. John's most-photographed beach and the most popular spot for beginning snorkelers because of its underwater trail. It's the St. John stop for cruise-ship passengers who choose a snorkeling tour for the day, so if you're looking for seclusion, check cruise-ship listings in *St. Thomas This Week* to find out what days the highest number are in port. There are changing rooms, a snack bar, picnic tables, and snorkeling equipment for rent. **Cinnamon Bay,** a long, sandy beach facing beautiful cays, serves the adjoining national-park campground. Facilities (showers, toilets, commissary, restaurant, beach shop) are open to all. There's good snorkeling off the point to the right, and rental equipment is available. **Salt Pond Bay,** on the southeastern coast of St. John, is a scenic area to explore, next to Coral Bay and rugged Drunk Bay. This beach is for the adventurous. It's a short hike down a hill from the parking lot, and the only facility is an outhouse. The beach is a little rockier here, but there are interesting tide pools and the snorkeling is good. Take special care to leave nothing valuable in the car, because reports of thefts are numerous here.

Sports and the Outdoors

Fishing In the past quarter-century, some 20 world records, many for blue marlin, have been set in the waters surrounding the Virgin Islands, most notably at St. Thomas's famed North Drop. To book a boat from St. Thomas or St. John, call **St. Thomas Sportfishing Center** (tel. 809/775–7990) or **American Yacht Harbor** (tel. 809/775–0685). On St. Croix, contact **Cruzan Divers** (tel. 809/772–3701), **Mile Mark** (tel. 809/773–2628), or **Ruffian Enterprises** (St. Croix Marina, tel. 809/773–6011 day, 809/773–0917 night).

Golf On St. Thomas, scenic *Mahogany Run* (tel. 809/775–5000), with a par-70, 18-hole course and a view of the B.V.I., lies to the north of Charlotte Amalie and has the especially tricky "Devil's Triangle" trio of holes. On St. Croix, the **Buccaneer's** (tel. 809/773–2100) 18-hole course is conveniently close to (east of) Christiansted. Yet more spectacular is **Carambola** (tel. 809/778–5638), in the valleyed northwestern part of the island, designed by Robert Trent Jones. The **Reef Club** (tel. 809/773–8844), at the northeastern part of the island, has nine holes.

Horseback At Sprat Hall on St. Croix, near Frederiksted, Jill Hurd runs **Paul**
Riding **and Jill's Equestrian Stables** (tel. 809/772–2880 or 809/772–2627) and will take you clip-clopping through the rain forest, along the coast, or on moonlit rides. Costs range from $50 to $75 for the three-hour rides. On St. John, join a trail ride with **Pony Express** (tel. 809/776–6494). A one-hour ride costs $40; the two- and three-hour tours ($75 and $100) can take you both along the beach and through the rain forest. There is also a Moonlight Ride, offered the three days before and after a full moon. All rides are by appointment only.

Sailing/ The U.S.V.I. constitutes the biggest charter-boat fleet base in the
Boating Western Hemisphere. You can go through a broker to book a private sailing vessel with crew or contact a charter-boat company directly. Among brokers for the U.S.V.I., **Blue Water Cruises** (Box 292, Islisboro, MA 04848, tel. 800/524–2020) has an excellent worldwide reputation. Charter-boat companies on St. Thomas include **Avery's Marine, Inc.** (Box 5248, St. Thomas 00803, tel. 809/776–0113), at Charlotte Amalie, or **Island Yachts** (6100 Red Hook, Suite 4, Red Hook 00802, tel. 809/775–6666 or 800/524–2019), in Red Hook. On St. Croix, the **Annapolis Sailing School** (Box 3334, 601 6th St., Annapolis, MD 21403, tel. 410/267–7205 or 800/638–9192) offers one-week live-aboard cruises leaving from Christiansted. On St. John, **Hinckley Charters Caribbean** (Box 70, Cruz Bay 00830, tel. 809/776–6256) is a small operation based out of Caneel Bay.

Small This is an interesting—and surprisingly affordable—way to see the
Powerboat islands. **Club Nautico** (American Yacht Harbor, 00802, tel. 809/779–
Rentals 2555) and **Nauti Nymph** (American Yacht Harbor, 00802, tel. 809/779–5066) both have a variety of 21- to 27-foot boats.

Day Sail The following businesses can effortlessly book you on a submarine
Charter ride, a parasail boat, a kayak trip, a jet ski ride, a Hobie Cat sail, or a
Companies half-day inshore light-tackle fishing excursion. They get customer feedback on a daily basis and know exactly what type of boats and crew they are booking. They will be happy to answer any questions.

On St. Thomas, call the **Red Hook Charter office** (Box 57, 00802, tel. 809/775–9333). **Coconut Charters** (Suite 202, Red Hook Plaza, 00802, tel. 809/775–5959) usually has a number of multihull vessels doing day sails.

On St. Croix, try **Mile-Mark Charters** (Box 3045, 59 King's Wharf, Christiansted 00822, tel. 809/773–2628 or 800/524–2012, fax 809/773–9411). **Big Beard's Adventure Tours** (Box 4534, Pan Am Pavilion, Christiansted 00822, tel. 809/773–4482) runs trips to Buck Island and beach barbecues using two catamarans, one with a glass bottom. **Buck Island Charters,** with Captain Heinz's trimaran, the *Teroro II*

(Box 2881, Christiansted, tel. 809/773–3161) departs for full- or half-day Buck Island trips from Green Cay Marina.

On St. John, **Connections** (Box 37, 00831, tel. 809/776–6922) represents a dozen of the finest local boats; many of its employees have actually worked on the boats they book.

Scuba Diving/ Snorkeling There are numerous dive operators on the three islands, and some of the hotels offer dive packages. Many of the operators listed below also offer snorkeling trips; call individual operators for details.

St. Thomas **Aqua Action Watersports** (Box 15, Red Hook 00802, tel. 809/775–6285) is a full-service, PADI five-star shop with all levels of instruction. They also rent sea kayaks and Windsurfers.

Joe Vogel Diving Co. (Box 7322, 00801, tel. 809/775–7610 for the shop), the oldest certified diving operation in the U.S.V.I., leaves from the West Indies Inn for day or night, reef or wreck dives. It has both PADI and NAUI instructors and will dive even if only one person shows up.

Seahorse Dive Boats (Crown Bay Marina, Suite 505, St. Thomas, U.S.V.I. 00802, tel. 809/774–2001) now has two locations and an expanding teaching facility at Emerald Beach. It is a PADI five-star operation and does both day and night dives on local wrecks and reefs.

Underwater Safaris (Box 8469, St. Thomas, U.S.V.I. 00801, tel. 809/774–1350) is conveniently located in Long Bay at the Ramada Yacht Haven Marina—which is also home to the U.S.V.I. charter-boat fleet. It is a PADI five-star dive operation that specializes in Buck Island dives to the wreck of the World War I cargo ship *Cartenser Sr.*

St. Croix **Anchor Dive** (Box 5588, Salt River Marina, Sunny Isle 00823, tel. 809/778–1522).

Dive Experience, Inc. (Box 4254, Strand St., Christiansted 00822–4254, tel. 809/773–3307 or 800/235–9047) is a PADI five-star training facility providing the range from certification to introductory dives.

Dive St. Croix (59 King's Wharf, Box 3045, Christiansted 00820, tel. 809/773–3434 or 800/523–3483, fax 809/773–9411), takes divers to walls and wrecks—over 50 sites—and offers introductory, certification, and PADI, NAUI, and SSI C-card completion courses. It has custom packages with five hotels. Dive St. Croix is the only dive operation on the island allowed to run dives to Buck Island.

V.I. Divers, Ltd. (Pan Am Pavilion, Christiansted 00820, tel. 809/773–6045 or 800/544–5911) is a PADI five-star training facility with a 35-foot dive boat and hotel packages.

St. John **Cruz Bay Watersports Co., Inc.** (Box 252, 00830, tel. 809/776–6234 or 800/835–7730, fax 809/776–8303) is a PADI five-star diving center with two locations in Cruz Bay. Owner-operators Patty and Marcus Johnson offer regular reef, wreck, and night dives aboard three custom dive vessels.

Low Key Water Sports (Box 431, 00831, tel. 809/776–7048), located at the Wharfside Village, offers PADI certification and resort courses, one- and two-tank dives, wreck dives, and specialty courses.

St. John Watersports (Box 70, 00830, tel. 809/776–6256) is a five-star PADI center located in the Mongoose Junction shopping mall.

Tennis *St. Thomas* Most hotels rent time to nonguests. For reservations call **Bluebeard's Castle Hotel** (tel. 809/774–1600, ext. 195 or 196), **Bolongo Bay** (tel. 809/775–1800, ext. 486), **Limetree Tennis Center** (tel. 809/774–8990), **Mahogany Run Tennis Club** (tel. 809/775–5000), **Sapphire Beach Resort** (tel. 809/775–6100), **Stouffer Grand Beach Resort** (tel. 809/775–1510), and **Sugar Bay Plantation Resort** (tel. 809/

771–7100). All the above courts have lights and are open into the evening. **Frenchman's Reef Tennis Courts** (tel. 809/776–8500) and **Grand Palazzo** (tel. 809/775–3333) have courts for the use of guests only. There are two public courts at **Sub Base** (next to the Water and Power Authority), open on a first-come, first-served basis.

St. Croix There are courts at the **Buccaneer, Carambola Beach Resort, Chenay Bay Beach Resort, St. Croix by the Sea, Cormorant Beach Club, The Reef, Villa Madeleine,** and **Club St. Croix** hotels. Public courts can be found at Conegata Park (two) and Fort Frederik (two), though they may not be in the best condition.

St. John **Caneel Bay** (tel. 809/776–6111) has 11 courts (none lighted) and a pro shop. The **Hyatt Regency** (tel. 809/776–7171) has six lighted courts and a pro shop. The public courts near the fire station are lighted until 10 PM, and are available on a first-come, first-served basis.

Shopping

St. Thomas Most people would agree that St. Thomas lives up to its self-described billing as a shopper's paradise. Even if shopping isn't your idea of paradise, you still may want to slip in on a quiet day (check the cruise-ship listings—Monday and Saturday are usually the least crowded) to check out the prices. Among the best buys are liquor, linens, imported china, crystal (most stores ship), and jewelry. The sheer volume of jewelry available makes this one of the few items for which comparison shopping is worth the effort.

Most stores take major credit cards. There is no sales tax in the U.S.V.I., and shoppers can take advantage of the $1,200 duty-free allowance per family member and the additional 10% discount on the next $1,000 worth of goods, but remember to save your receipts.

Shopping The prime shopping area in **Charlotte Amalie** is between Post Office
Districts and Market squares and consists of three parallel streets running east to west (Waterfront, Main Street, and Back Street) and the alleyways connecting them. **Vendors Plaza,** located on the waterfront at Emancipation Gardens, is a centralized location for all the vendors who used to clog the sidewalks with their merchandise.

Havensight Mall, next to the cruise-ship dock, though not as charming as Charlotte Amalie, has parking and many of the same stores. West of town, the pink-stucco **Nisky Center** is more of a hometown shopping center than a tourist area, but there's a bookstore (next to a bakery and yogurt shop), as well as a bank, gift shops, and clothing stores.

Out east, at Red Hook, there is a waterfront shopping arcade with small branches of the same stores found in Charlotte Amalie.

Art Galleries **A.H. Riise Caribbean Print Gallery** (Riise's Alley off Main St., tel. 809/776–2303). Haitian and Virgin Islands art are displayed and sold here, along with art books and the exquisite botanical prints and note cards from Mapes de Monde.

The Gallery (Veteran's Dr., tel. 809/776–4641). The Gallery carries Haitian art, along with works by a number of Virgin Islands artists.

Books and **Dockside Bookshop** (Havensight Mall, Bldg. IV, tel. 809/774–4937).
Magazines There's a wide selection of books, including those written in and about the Caribbean and the Virgin Islands, from literature to chartering guides to books on seashells and tropical flowers.

Cameras and Electronics

Boolchand's (31 Main St., tel. 809/776–0794, and Havensight Mall, tel. 809/776–0302). A variety of brand-name cameras as well as audio and video equipment are featured here.

Royal Caribbean (two locations on Main St., tel. 809/776–4110, and Havensight Mall, tel. 809/776–8890). This store has attractive prices on some cameras and accessories; portable cassette players are usually good buys here.

China and Crystal

A.H. Riise Gift Shops (Main St. and Riise's Alley and Havensight Mall, tel. 809/776–2303). A.H. Riise carries Waterford, Wedgwood, Royal Crown, and Royal Doulton at good prices.

The English Shop (Waterfront, tel. 809/776–5399, and Havensight Mall, tel. 809/776–3776). This store offers china and crystal from major European and Japanese manufacturers.

Little Switzerland (two locations on Main St. and one at Havensight Mall, tel. 809/776–2010). All of this establishment's shops carry crystal from Lalique, Baccarat, Waterford, Riedel, and Orrefors and china from Villeroy & Boch and Wedgwood, among others.

Clothing

G'Day (waterfront at Royal Dane Mall, tel. 809/774–8855). Everything in this tiny shop—from umbrellas to silk scarves to reasonably priced sportswear—is drenched in the bright colors of Australian artist Ken Done.

Janine's Boutique (8A-2 Palm Passage, tel. 809/774–8243). Here you'll find women's and men's dressy and casual apparel from European designers and manufacturers, including the Louis Feraud collection, and select finds from Valentino, Christian Dior, YSL, and Pierre Cardin.

Java Wraps (24 Palm Passage, tel. 809/774–3700). Indonesian batik creations are the specialty here. This store offers a complete line of beach cover-ups, swimwear, and leisure wear for women, men, and children.

Lion in the Sun (Riise's Alley, tel. 809/776–4203). This is one of the best locations for upscale sportswear, suits, and dresses. Go Linen, Go Silk, Donna Karan, Sonya Rykiel, Giorgio Armani, and Hugo Boss are a few of the brands sold here.

Local Color (Garden St., tel. 809/774–3727). St. Thomas artist Kerry Topper exhibits her island designs on cool cotton T-shirts and other casual clothing. Brightly printed sundresses, shorts, and shirts by Jams; big-brim straw hats dipped in fuchsia, turquoise, and other tropical colors; and unique jewelry are also for sale.

Polo/Ralph Lauren Factory Store (Garden Street, tel. 809/774–3806). The selection here changes frequently, and it's worthwhile to check often for amazing markdowns on a range of men's and women's clothing.

Thriving Tots Boutique (Garden St., tel. 809/776–0009). You'll find Caribbean clothing for children (infants to size 16), including locally made shorts sets and sundresses.

Crafts and Gifts

The Caribbean Marketplace (Havensight Mall, Bldg. III, tel. 809/776–5400). This is the place to look for Caribbean handicrafts, including Caribelle batiks from St. Lucia; bikinis from the Cayman Islands; and Sunny Caribee spices, soaps, teas, and coffees from Tortola.

The Cloth Horse (Fort Mylner Shopping Center, tel. 809/774–4761). Here you'll find signed pottery from the Dominican Republic; wicker and rattan furniture and household goods from the island of Hispaniola; and pottery, rugs, and bedspreads from all over the world.

Down Island Traders (Bakery Sq., Veteran's Dr., and Frenchman's Reef, tel. 809/774–3419). These traders deal in hand-painted calabash bowls ($10); finely printed Caribbean note cards; jams, jellies, spices, and herbs; herbal teas made of rum, passion fruit, and mango; high-mountain coffee from Jamaica; and a variety of handicrafts from throughout the Caribbean.

Food **Gourmet Gallery,** at Yacht Haven and the Sub Base, has an excellent and reasonably priced wine selection, as well as condiments, cheeses, and specialty ingredients for everything from tacos to curries to chow mein. For fruits and vegetables, go to the **Fruit Bowl,** at Wheatley Center.

Jewelry **A.H. Riise Gift Shops** (Main St. and Riise's Alley and Havensight Mall, tel. 809/776–2303). St. Thomas's oldest and largest shop for luxury items, with jewelry, pearls, ceramics, china, crystal, flatware, perfumes, and watches.

Amsterdam Sauer (14 Main St., tel. 809/774–2222). Many fine one-of-a-kind designs are displayed here.

Aperiton (3A Main St., tel. 809/776–0780). A good spot for lovely jewelry made by Greek and Italian designers.

Cardow's (three stores on Main St., tel. 809/776–1140; two on the waterfront, one at Frenchman's Reef Hotel, three at Havensight, tel. 809/776–1140). Cardow's offers an enormous "chain bar" more than 100 feet long, where you're guaranteed 30%–50% savings off U.S. retail prices or your money will be refunded (within 30 days of purchase).

Cartier (30 Trompeter Gade, tel. 809/774–1590). In addition to the fantastically beautiful and fantastically priced items, there are a surprising number of affordable ones as well.

Colombian Emeralds (one on Main St., two on the waterfront, and one at Havensight Mall, tel. 809/774–0581). Well known in the Caribbean, this store offers set and unset gems of every description, including high-quality emeralds.

H. Stern (two on Main St., Havensight Mall, Frenchman's Reef, Stouffer Grand Beach Resort, and Bluebeards, tel. 809/776–1939). One of the most respected names in gems.

Irmela's Jewel Studio (Tolbod Gade, tel. 809/774–5875). For 22 years Irmela has been offering some of the Caribbean's most exquisite jewelry designs inside the historic stone walls of the Grand Hotel.

Little Switzerland (two locations on Main St., one at Havensight Mall, tel. 809/776–2010). The sole U.S.V.I. distributor for Rolex watches, the store also does a booming mail-order business.

Leather Goods **Gucci** (Riise's Alley off Main St., tel. 809/774–7841 and at Havensight Mall, tel. 809/774–4090). Traditional Gucci insignia designs for men and women are offered here.

The Leather Shop (Main St., tel. 809/776–3995 and Havensight Mall, Bldg. II, tel. 809/776–0040). You'll find big names at big prices here: Fendi and Bottega Veneta are prevalent. However, there are also reasonably priced purses, wallets, and briefcases.

Louis Vuitton (24 Main St. at Palm Passage, tel. 809/774–3633). Here is an example of St. Thomas shopping at its most elegant.

Traveler's Haven (Havensight Mall, tel. 809/775–1798). This store features leather bags, backpacks, vests, and money belts.

Zora's (Norre Gade across from Roosevelt Park, tel. 809/774–2559). Fine leather sandals made to order are the specialty here.

Linens **Shanghai Silk and Handicrafts** (Royal Dane Mall, tel. 809/776–8118) and **Shanghai Linen** (Waterfront, tel. 809/776–2828). These two stores do a brisk trade in linens and silks.

Mr. Tablecloth (Main St., tel. 809/774–4343). The friendly staff here will help you choose from their floor-to-ceiling array of linens.

Liquor and **A.H. Riise Liquors** (Main St. and Riise's Alley and Havensight Mall,
Wine tel. 809/774–6900). This Riise venture offers a large selection of liquors, cordials, wines, and tobacco, including rare vintage cognacs, Armagnacs, ports, and Madeiras. They also stock imported cigars, fruits in brandy, and barware from England.

Al Cohen's Discount Liquor (across from Havensight Mall, Long Bay Rd., tel. 809/774–3690). A warehouse-style store with a large wine department.

Music **Parrot Fish Records and Tapes** (Back St., tel. 809/776–4514). Standard Stateside tapes and compact discs are stocked here, plus a good selection of Caribbean artists, including local groups. For a catalogue of calypso, soca, steel band, and reggae music, write to Parrot Fish, Box 9206, St. Thomas 00801.

Modern Music (across from Havensight Mall, tel 809/774–3100). This place has the latest Stateside and Caribbean CD and cassette releases plus oldies, classical, and new age music.

Perfumes **Sparky's** (Main St., tel. 809/776–7510). The impeccably turned-out salesclerks can give you a facial and makeup lesson.

Tropicana Perfume Shoppes (2 Main St., tel. 809/774–0010 and 14 Main St., tel. 809/774–1834). Tropicana has the largest selection of fragrances for men and women in all of the Virgin Islands; both shops give small free samples to customers.

Sunglasses **Fashion Eyewear** (Garden Street, tel. 809/776–9075). Tucked into a tiny building is this even tinier shop that sells sunglasses priced from $40 to $450. They'll also copy your prescription from your current glasses and make new clear or sunglasses in a few hours.

Toys **Animal Crackers Fun Factory** (Inside Sparky's, off Royal Dane Mall, tel. 809/774–4939). This place is a must-visit, whether the children are with you or back home anticipating their gifts. It's a playland jungle aswarm with parrots and pirates, teddy bears and penguins.

Land of Oz (Royal Dane Mall, tel. 809/776–7888). This Oz has a huge selection of toys fashioned by European craftsmen that include Royal Doulton collector dolls, Brio wood trains, German nutcrackers, and English wood sailboats.

St. Croix Although St. Croix doesn't offer as many shopping opportunities as St. Thomas, the island does provide an array of smaller stores with unique merchandise. In Christiansted, the best shopping areas are the Pan Am Pavilion and Caravelle Arcade off Strand Street and along King and Company streets.

Books **The Writer's Block** (36C Strand St., Christiansted, tel. 809/773–5101) carries a full line of fiction and nonfiction, as well as travel guides and other books about St. Croix.

China and   **The Royal English Shop** (5 Strand St., Frederiksted, tel. 809/772–
Crystal   2040). Saint-Louis and Beyer crystal and Wedgwood china are carried here at prices significantly lower than those on the mainland.
Store hours vary, depending on the cruise-ship schedule, so check
ahead.

Little Switzerland (Hamilton House, 56 King St., Christiansted, tel.
809/773–1976). The St. Croix branch of this Virgin Islands institution features a variety of Rosenthal flatware, Lladro figurines, Waterford and Baccarat crystal, Lalique figurines, and Wedgwood and
Royal Doulton china.

Clothing   **Caribbean Clothing Company** (55 Company St., Christiansted, tel.
809/773–5012). This fashionable store features contemporary
sportswear by top American designers.

From the Gecko (1233 Queen Cross St., tel. 809/778–9433) offers the
hippest buys on St. Croix, from superb batik sarongs to hammocks.

Java Wraps (Pan Am Pavilion, 42–43 Strand St., Christiansted, tel.
809/773–3770). Indonesian batik cover-ups and resort wear for men,
women, and children are featured here.

Polo/Ralph Lauren Factory Store (52 C Company St., Christiansted,
tel. 809/773–4388). The factory outlet for this popular, upscale clothing line presents men's and women's clothes at huge discounts.

Wayne James Boutique (42 Queen Cross St., tel. 809/773–8585). This
engaging Crucian has designed vestments for the pope and evening
wear for the queen of Denmark. His bright, savvy clothes are in-
spired by island traditions and colors.

Crafts and   **American West India Company** (1 Strand St., Christiansted, tel. 809/
Gifts   773–7325). In the market for some Jamaican allspice or perhaps a
piece of Haitian metalwork? Goods from around the Caribbean, including St. Croix, are available here.

Designworks (3 Queen Cross St., Christiansted, tel. 809/773–5355).
This store features "everything for the home," from Danish candles
and hand-woven palm baskets to heavy Mexican glassware and
Marimekko fabrics imported from Finland.

Folk Art Traders (1B Queen Cross St. at Strand St., Christiansted,
tel. 809/773–1900). The owners travel to Haiti, Jamaica, Guayama,
and elsewhere in the Caribbean to find the treasures sold in this
shop, including baskets, masks, pottery, and ceramics.

Jewelry   **Colombian Emeralds** (43 Queen Cross St., Christiansted, tel. 809/
773–1928 or 809/773–9189). Specializing—of course—in emeralds,
including some that are under $100, this store also carries dia-
monds, rubies, sapphires, and gold.

Crucian Gold (57A Company St., Christiansted, tel. 809/773–5241).
Located in a small courtyard in a West Indian–style cottage, this
store carries the unique gold creations of St. Croix native Brian
Bishop.

Sonya's (1 Company St., Christiansted, tel. 809/778–8605). This is
the home of the island's signature hook bracelet, which was designed by owner Sonya Hough.

Liquor   **Grog and Spirits** (59 Kings Wharf, Christiansted, tel. 809/778–8400
and Chandlers Wharf, Gallows Bay, tel. 809/773–8485). A good selection of liquor is available at these conveniently located shops.

Woolworth's (Sunny Isle Shopping Center, Centerline Rd., tel. 809/ 778–5466). This department store carries a huge line of discount, duty-free liquor.

Perfumes **St. Croix Shoppes** (53AB Company St., Christiansted tel. 809/773– 2727). One of these side-by-side shops specializes solely in Estee Lauder and Clinique products, while the other carries a full line of fragrances.

St. Croix Perfume Center (1114 King St., Christiansted, tel. 809/ 773–7604). An extensive array of fragrances, including all the major brands, is available here.

St. John With so much natural beauty to offer, the pleasures of shopping on St. John are all but overlooked in travel literature, but the blend of luxury items and handicrafts found in the shops on St. John offers excellent opportunities. Two new shopping areas have widened the choices. Two levels of cool, stone-wall shops, set off by colorfully planted terraces and courtyards, make **Mongoose Junction** one of the prettiest shopping malls in the Caribbean. **Wharfside Village,** on the other side of Cruz Bay, is a painted-clapboard village with shops and restaurants.

Dining

Just about every kind of cuisine you can imagine is available in the U.S.V.I. The beauty and freedom of the islands has attracted a cadre of professionally trained chefs who know their way around fresh fish and local fruits. If you are staying in a large hotel, you will pay prices similar to those in New York City or Paris—in other words, dining out is usually expensive.

St. Thomas is the most cosmopolitan of the islands and has the most visitors, so it is not surprising that the island also has the largest number and greatest variety of restaurants. St. Croix restaurants are both more relaxed and, in some ways, more elegant. Dining on St. John is, in general, more casual; the emphasis is on simple food prepared to order in an informal setting at reasonable prices.

Highly recommended restaurants are indicated by a star ★.

Category*	Cost*
Very Expensive	over $35
Expensive	$25–$35
Moderate	$15–$25
Inexpensive	under $15

average cost of a three-course dinner, per person, excluding drinks and service

St. Thomas **Blackbeard's Castle.** This romantic hillside spot is home to one of the
★ best restaurants on St. Thomas. Diners here have a spectacular view of Charlotte Amalie and the harbor as they dine alfresco on such gourmet delights as veal chop stuffed with fresh vegetables, Black Forest ham, and mozzarella; grilled swordfish with tropical salsa; or fettuccine with grilled chicken, sun-dried tomatoes, and feta cheese. Lunch offerings include excellent soups, sandwiches, and several pasta dishes. The à la carte Sunday brunch is immensely popular. *Blackbeard's Castle, Charlotte Amalie, tel. 809/776–1234. Reservations required. AE, MC, V. Very Expensive.*

Entre Nous. The view here, from the terrace of Bluebeard's Castle high over Charlotte Amalie's harbor, is as exhilarating as the dining is elegant. In the evening, you can watch the light-bedecked cruise ships pull slowly out of the harbor, while deciding between such main courses as rack of lamb, Caribbean lobster, veal, and chateaubriand. *Bluebeard's Castle, Charlotte Amalie, tel. 809/774–4050. Reservations required. AE, MC, V. No lunch. Very Expensive.*

Fiddle Leaf. This longtime favorite is on Government Hill, and tables are on a covered terrace that's open to the breezes and offers views of the sparkling nighttime lights of St. Thomas. Specialties include sautéed shrimp West Indian style, grilled yellowfin tuna on a garlicky bed of spinach and roasted sweet peppers, and rack of lamb roasted with a pecan crust. The Caesar salad prepared tableside is excellent. *Government Hill, near Main St., Charlotte Amalie, tel. 809/775–2810. Reservations advised. Closed Sun. No lunch. AE, MC, V. Very Expensive.*

Hotel 1829. You'll dine by candlelight flickering over stone walls and pink table linens at this restaurant on the terrace of the hotel. The menu and wine list are extensive, from Caribbean rock lobster to rack of lamb. Many items, including a warm spinach salad, are prepared tableside, and the restaurant is justly famous for its dessert soufflés, made of chocolate, Grand Marnier, raspberry, or coconut, to name a few. *Government Hill, near Main St., Charlotte Amalie, tel. 809/776–1829. Reservations required. No lunch. AE, MC, V. Very Expensive.*

★ **Romanos.** Inside this huge old stucco house in Smith Bay is a delightful surprise: a spare, elegant setting and superb northern Italian cuisine. Owner Tony hasn't advertised since the restaurant opened five years ago, and it is always packed. Try the pastas, either with a classic sauce or one of the unique combinations created by Tony, such as a cream sauce with mushrooms, prosciutto, pine nuts, and Parmesan. *97 Smith Bay, tel. 809/775–0045. Reservations advised. Closed Sun. Very Expensive.*

★ **Virgilio's.** This intimate, elegant hideaway serves the best northern Italian cuisine on the island. Eclectic groupings of paintings and prints cover the two-story-high brick walls. Come here for superb minestrone, perfectly cooked capellini with fresh tomatoes and garlic, Spaghetti Peasant Style (a rich tomato sauce with mushrooms and prosciutto), exquisite fresh fish, veal, and chicken dishes, and a host of daily specials. Maître d' Alfredo is on hand day and night, welcoming customers and helping the very gracious staff. Don't leave without having a Virgilio's cappuccino, a chocolate-and-coffee drink so rich it's dessert. *Back St., Charlotte Amalie, tel. 809/776–4920. Reservations advised. AE, MC, V. Closed Sun. Very Expensive.*

Piccola Marina Cafe. Dockside dining at its friendliest is the trademark of this open-air restaurant close to the St. John ferry dock at Red Hook. The clientele is a mix of sailors and fishermen who work on the docks that your table overlooks. The food is so-so, but the atmosphere is delightful. New this year is a wood-burning pizza oven. *Red Hook, tel. 809/775–6350. Reservations advised. AE, MC, V. Expensive.*

★ **Alexander's Cafe.** This charming restaurant is a favorite with the people in the restaurant business on St. Thomas—always a sign of quality. Local media types and wine aficionados (the always-changing wine list offers the best value on the island) are often among the crowd that packs this place seven nights a week. Alexander is Austrian, and the schnitzels are delicious and reasonably priced; the baked-brie-and-fruit plate and pasta specials are fresh and tasty.

Save room for strudel. *24A Honduras, Frenchtown, tel. 809/776–4211. Reservations advised. AE, MC, V. Moderate–Expensive.*

The Chart House. Located in an old great house on the tip of the Frenchtown peninsula, this restaurant features kebab and teriyaki dishes, lobster, Hawaiian chicken, and a large salad bar. *Villa Olga, Frenchtown, tel. 809/774–4262. Reservations accepted for 10 or more. AE, DC, MC, V. Moderate–Expensive.*

For the Birds. The beer is served in mason jars, and margaritas are available in 46-ounce servings at this beach restaurant with a disco floor (Sunday is ladies' night). You can have sizzling fajitas, barbecued baby-back ribs, seafood, or steak. For children there are coloring place mats and crayons. *Scott Beach, near Compass Point, East End, tel. 809/775–6431. Reservations required for 6 or more. AE, MC, V. Moderate–Expensive.*

★ **Little Bopeep.** Inside this unpretentious restaurant tucked behind the shops of Main Street is some of the best West Indian food on the island. Try the curried chicken, conch in Creole sauce, sweet potato stuffing, and fried plantains. *Back St., Charlotte Amalie, tel. 809/776–9292. AE, MC, V. Moderate.*

Zorba's Cafe. Tired of shopping? Summon up one last ounce of energy and head up Government Hill to Zorba's. Sit and have a cold beer or bracing iced tea in the 19th-century stone-paved courtyard surrounded by banana trees. Greek salads and appetizers, moussaka, and an excellent vegetarian plate top the menu. *Government Hill, Charlotte Amalie, tel. 809/776–0444. AE, MC, V. Moderate.*

Bryan's Bar and Restaurant. Located high on the cool north side of the island, overlooking Hull Bay, this surfer's bar offers gargantuan portions of grilled fish, steaks, and a great teriyaki-chicken sandwich. A local hangout complete with pool table, it's casual and cheap. *Hull Bay, tel. 809/774–3522. No credit cards. No lunch. Inexpensive–Moderate.*

Eunice's Terrace. Eunice is deservedly famous for her excellent West Indian cooking. Her roomy two-story restaurant has a spacious bar and a menu of native dishes, including callaloo (a West Indian soup), conch fritters, fried fish, local sweet potato, fungi, and green banana. *Rte. 38, near Stouffer Grand Beach Resort and Coral World, Smith Bay, tel. 809/775–3975. AE, MC, V. Inexpensive–Moderate.*

Hard Rock Cafe. A hot spot from the day it opened, this waterfront restaurant is pretty much like its namesakes around the world. Rock-and-roll memorabilia dominate the decor, and the menu offers hamburgers, sandwiches, salads, and great desserts. Doors open at 11 AM and stay open until 2 AM, and there's always a wait during prime meal times. *International Plaza on the Waterfront, tel. 809/775–5555. AE, MC, V. Inexpensive–Moderate.*

I Cappuccini. In the lower courtyard of A Taste of Italy shopping area is this quiet indoor-outdoor café that serves a variety of sandwiches (including an excellent Italian ham sandwich) and pasta dishes. *A Taste of Italy. 4-5 Back Street, tel. 809/775–1090. AE, MC, V. No dinner. Inexpensive–Moderate.*

St. Croix   **Cafe Madeleine.** This elegant restaurant, part of the Villa Madeleine resort nestled in the hills on St. Croix's East End, features such diverse cuisine as lamb and polenta soup, swordfish medallions sautéed with green tomato and asparagus, and a number of fine beef dishes. The wine list is extensive. *Teague Bay (take Rte. 82 out of Christiansted and turn right at the Reef Condominiums), tel. 809/778–7377. Reservations advised. AE, DC, MC, V. Closed Mon. and Tues. Very Expensive.*

★ **Kendricks.** This restaurant is a tranquil oasis of civility in the heart of Christiansted. Waiters dote on diners seated at tables laid with crisp linens and fine china, serving such dishes as coconut shrimp with jalapeño and chive aioli or roasted pecan–crusted pork loin with ginger mayonnaise. Stop by their informal eatery across the street, Simply Lobster, which serves daily lunches of reasonably priced lobster dishes, including their signature lobster spring rolls. *Queen Cross St., Christiansted, tel. 809/773–9199. Reservations advised. AE. No lunch. Closed Sun. and Mon. Very Expensive.*

★ **Dino's.** Homemade Italian food, often with a West Indian twist, is served at this cozy restaurant, one of the island's best. Creative, boldly flavored pastas (try the eggplant or sweet potato ravioli) are made fresh daily by chefs/owners Dwight DeLude and Dino Natale. The hot antipasto appetizer features bacon-wrapped and grilled shrimp; broiled tomato with a veil of fresh pesto; fried eggplant in a tomato-butter sauce; and grilled, succulent scallops. *4-C Hospital St., Christiansted, tel. 809/778–8005. Reservations advised. No credit cards. Closed Sun., Thurs., and Sept. Expensive.*

★ **Pangaea.** The restaurant's name—meaning all-earth—is certainly reflected in the ambitious, eclectic menu, which synthesizes African, Caribbean, and Middle Eastern influences and ingredients with aplomb. Specials might include mahimahi in two salsas (mango and tomato cilantro) and slow-roasted duck breast in honey-raspberry glaze. The owner has created an ambience best described as Peace Corps–bohemian with incense, wind chimes, and travel souvenirs such as Hawaiian coconut masks and Japanese watercolors. The waitstaff is hip and very friendly; the house's cat, Shadow, even more so. *2203 Queen Cross St., tel. 809/773–7743. No credit cards. No lunch. Closed Tues. and Wed. Expensive.*

Top Hat. This restaurant, owned by a delightful Danish couple, has been in business for 20 years, serving international cuisine with an emphasis on Danish specialties—roast duck stuffed with apples and prunes, fried Camembert with lingonberries, and smoked eel. The old West Indian structure, complete with gingerbread trim, is nicely accented in gray, white, and pink. The photographs on the walls are the work of owner and European-trained chef Hans Rasmussen. *52 Company St., Christiansted, tel. 809/773–2346. Reservations advised. AE, MC, V. Closed Sun., lunch, and May–Oct. Expensive.*

Blue Moon. This terrific little bistro, popular for its live jazz on Friday nights, has an eclectic, often-changing menu that draws heavily on Asian, Cajun, and French influences. Try the seafood chowder as an appetizer and leave room for the bittersweet chocolate torte for dessert. *17 Strand St., Frederiksted, tel. 809/772–2222. AE. No lunch. Closed Mon. and July–Sept. Moderate.*

Le St. Tropez. A dark-wood bar and soft lighting add to the Mediterranean atmosphere at this pleasant bistro, tucked into a courtyard off Frederiksted's main thoroughfare. Diners, seated either inside or on the adjoining patio, enjoy light French fare, such as quiches, salads, brochettes, and crepes. Daily specials often take advantage of fresh local seafood. *67 King St., Frederiksted, tel. 809/772–3000. Reservations accepted. AE, MC, V. Closed Sun. Moderate.*

Camille's. This tiny, lively spot is perfect for lunch or a light supper. Sandwiches and burgers are the big draw here, though the daily seafood special, often wahoo or mahimahi, is also popular. *Queen Cross St., Christiansted, tel. 809/773–2985. No credit cards. Closed Sun. Inexpensive.*

Harvey's. The plain, even dowdy room contains just 12 tables, whose plastic flowered tablecloths qualify as the sole attempt at decor; but the delicious local food ranks among the island's best. Daily specials such as mouth-watering goat stew and melting whelks in butter, sided with heaping helpings of rice, fungi, and vegetables, are listed on the blackboard. Genial owner Sarah Harvey takes great pride in her kitchen, bustling out from behind the stove to chat and urge you to eat up. *11 Company St., tel. 809/773–3343. No credit cards. No lunch. Closed Sun. Call for hours during high season. Inexpensive.*

St. John **Chow Bella.** The maître d' describes the menu at this strikingly contemporary restaurant in the Hyatt as "transcultural"—Chinese and Italian, as you might have surmised from the name. Order from one side of the menu and you'll have pot stickers; from the other side you'll have pasta. *Hyatt Regency Beach Hotel, tel. 809/776–7171. Reservations advised. No shorts or collarless shirts. AE, MC, V. No lunch. Closed Mon. Expensive–Very Expensive.*

★ **Ellington's.** Extending onto the second-story veranda of the Gallows Point Suite Resort's central building, Ellington's is a pleasant surprise, informal yet a cut above Cruz Bay's typical ultracasual fishfry joint. The menu leans heavily toward fish nevertheless: Start with the jumbo shrimp cooked in sweet coconut and served with a mango sauce or the seafood chowder. Entrées include flawlessly presented sea scallops and pesto, swordfish scampi, or filet Mignon. Save room for dessert, perhaps the banana chocolate chip cake or the white chocolate brownie. *Gallows Point Suite Resort, tel. 809/ 776–7166. Reservations accepted. AE, MC, V. Expensive.*

★ **Le Chateau de Bordeaux.** The best view you're going to find to dine by is on the terrace here or in the air-conditioned dining room (go at sunset). The rustic cabin is magically transformed into an elegant, ultraromantic aerie by wrought-iron chandeliers, lace tablecloths, and antiques. The innovative preparations appeal equally to the eye and the palate. You might start with velvety carrot soup, perfectly contrasted with roasted chiles, then segue into the rack of lamb perfumed with rosemary with a honey-dijon-nut crust in a shallot-and-port-wine sauce, or macadamia-coated salmon with creme fraîche dill glaze. *Rte. 10, just east of Centerline Rd., tel. 809/776–6611. AE, MC, V. Expensive.*

The Fish Trap. Resting on a series of open-air wooden balconies among banana trees and coconut palms, this local favorite serves up six kinds of fresh fish nightly, along with tasty appetizers, such as conch fritters and Fish Trap chowder. The menu also includes steak, pasta, and chicken. *Downtown, Cruz Bay, tel. 809/776–9817. AE, D, MC, V. No lunch. Closed Mon. Moderate.*

★ **Etta's.** This simple courtyard eatery in the Inn at Tamarind Court has long been a popular locals' hangout. They come for the scrumptious island food: sublime callaloo soup with okra and fungi, mouthwatering chicken, conch and grouper fritters served with *very* hot sauces, and true curries. The festive happy hours and tremendous live music weekends also draw crowds. *Downtown, bear right at the Texaco, tel. 809/776–6378. AE, D, MC, V. Inexpensive.*

Shipwreck Landing. Start with a house drink, perhaps a freshsqueezed concoction of lime, coconut, and rum, then move on to hearty taco salads, fried shrimp, teriyaki chicken, and conch fritters. The birds keep up a lively chatter in the bougainvillea that surround the open-air restaurant, and there's live music on Sunday nights in season. *Coral Bay, tel. 809/776–8640. MC, V. Inexpensive.*

Lodging

The U.S.V.I. has a myriad of lodging options to suit any style, from luxury five-star resorts to casual condominiums and national campgrounds.

On St. Thomas, guest houses and smaller hotels are not typically on the beach, but they offer pools and shuttle service to nearby beaches (St. Thomas is not a walking island), and the several historic inns above town offer a pleasing island ambience. In keeping with its small-town atmosphere and more relaxed pace, St. Croix offers a good variety of more moderately priced small hotels and guest houses, which are either on the beach or in a rural setting where a walk to the beach is easy. Accommodations on St. John defy easy categorization. The national-park campground offerings start with bare campsites and progress through standing tents, tent cabins, and small cottages. At the other end of the spectrum are luxury retreats of understated elegance that offer rest and relaxation of a high—and pricey—order.

The prices below reflect rates during high season, which generally runs from December 15 to April 15. Rates are from 25% to 50% lower the rest of the year.

Category	Cost*
Very Expensive	over $200
Expensive	$150–$200
Moderate	$100–$150
Inexpensive	under $100

All prices are for a standard double room, excluding 7.5% accommodations tax.

The most highly recommended lodgings are indicated by a star ★.

St. Thomas   **Bolongo Elysian Beach Resort.** At this East End property, coral-color villas are stepped down the hillside to the edge of Cowpet Bay. Rooms are decorated in muted tropical floral prints. Activity is centered on a kidney-shape pool complete with waterfall and thatched-roof pool bar. The Palm Court restaurant has gained a strong local following, a sure sign of success. All rooms have air-conditioning, terraces, ceiling fans, cable TV, telephone, and honor bar, and some have kitchenettes. There is shuttle service to Bolongo Club Everything. *Box 51, Red Hook, 00802, tel. 809/775–1000 or 800/343–4079, fax 809/776–0910. 175 rooms. Facilities: 3 restaurants, 2 bars, freshwater pool, lighted tennis court. AE, MC, V. CP. Very Expensive.*

★ **Grand Palazzo.** You step into another world as you walk through the entrance of this premier luxury resort. Reception is at the far end of a marble-floored Venetian-style villa that wraps around a two-story courtyard. Here, you look through French doors to exquisite landscaping, a small white beach, and islands in the distance. Guest rooms, in six buildings that fan out from the entrance villa, are spacious and luxuriously decorated with European fabrics. When you venture out, you'll find elegance everywhere, from the stunning free-form pool to the gourmet restaurant and casual alfresco lunch area. A multilingual staff, classical music, and 24-hour room service complete the sophisticated package. Reserve and elegance abide in this resort, but the service can be inconsistent. *Great Bay, 00802, tel. 809/775–3333 or 800/223–7637. 150 rooms. Facilities: 2 restaurants, 3 bars, health club, pool, beach, 4 tennis courts, water sports. AE, D, DC, MC, V. Very Expensive.*

★ **Marriott's Frenchman's Reef Hotel and Morning Star Beach Resorts.** Sprawling, luxurious, and situated on a prime harbor promontory east of Charlotte Amalie like a permanently anchored cruise ship, this resort is still St. Thomas's full-service American superhotel. All rooms are spacious and decorated with contemporary furniture and soft pastels. Many Frenchman's Reef rooms have glorious ocean and harbor views (but a few look out over the parking lot). Morning Star rooms are more luxurious and are in buildings tucked among the foliage that stretches along the fine white sand of Morningstar Beach. Here you can be lulled to sleep by the sound of the surf. This is a property you don't have to leave. In addition to various snack and sandwich stops and a raw bar, there are alfresco American and Italian restaurants, a Japanese steak house, and extravagant buffets at the Windows on the Harbour restaurant overlooking the sparkling lights of Charlotte Amalie and the harbor. There are also a dinner theater, live entertainment and disco, scheduled activities for all ages, branches of several duty-free shops, and a shuttle boat to town. *Box 7100, 00801, tel. 809/776–8500 or 800/524–7100, fax 809/777–8820. 518 rooms. Facilities: 7 restaurants, several snack bars, 6 bars, 2 pools, 4 tennis courts, beach, water sports, helicopter tours. AE, DC, MC, V. EP, MAP. Very Expensive.*

★ **Pavilions & Pools.** Simple, tropical-cool decor and privacy set the mood here, where each island-style room has its own very private 20-by-14-foot or 18-by-16-foot pool and a small sun deck. The unpretentious accommodations include air-conditioning, telephones, full kitchens, and VCRs. Water sports are available at Sapphire Beach on the adjacent property. The management is particularly attentive and does everything to preserve the general quiet. *Rte. 6, East End, 00802, tel. 809/775–6110 or 800/524–2001, fax 809/775–6110. 25 rooms. Facilities: restaurant, bar, private pools. AE, MC, V. CP. Very Expensive.*

★ **Point Pleasant Resort.** The beautiful setting of this resort's natural vegetation has been lovingly preserved, and a wonderful nature trail winds through the 15 acres of grounds. Stretching up a steep and tree-filled hill from Smith Bay are 15 buildings containing a range of air-conditioned accommodations, from simple bedrooms to multiroom suites, all with balconies and full kitchens. Every guest gets four hours' free use of a car daily. There are three beautiful pools built into the hillside, and a full watersports program is offered. The beach is rocky and small, so guests are granted beach privileges next door on the Stouffer Grand's long stretch of sand, just a minute's walk away. *Estate Smith Bay, 00802, tel. 809/775–7200, 800/524–2300, or 800/645–5306, fax 809/776–5694. 135 rooms. Facilities: 2 restaurants, bar, tiny beach, 3 pools, lighted tennis court, exercise room, water sports. AE, MC, V. EP, MAP. Very Expensive.*

★ **Sapphire Beach Resort and Marina.** This resort sits right on Sapphire Beach, one of St. Thomas's prettiest, where on a clear day the lush green mountains of the neighboring B.V.I. seem close enough to touch. There's excellent snorkeling on the reefs to each side of the beach. This is a quiet retreat where you can nap while swinging in one of the hammocks strung between the palm trees in your front yard, but on Sunday the place rocks with a beach party. All units have fully equipped kitchens, air-conditioning, telephones, and cable TV. Children are welcome and may join the Little Gems Kids Klub. Children under age 12 eat free at the resort's restaurant. *Box 8088, Red Hook, 00801, tel. 809/775–6100 or 800/524–2090, fax 809/775–4024. 141 rooms. Facilities: restaurant, bar, beach, marina, 4 tennis courts, water sports. AE, MC, V. EP, MAP. Very Expensive.*

Stouffer Grand Beach Resort. This resort's zigzag architectural angles spell luxury, from the marble atrium lobby to the one-bedroom suites with private whirlpool baths. The beach is excellent, and there's a fitness center with Nautilus machines. The lobby is often populated by those lucky business types whose companies favor the resort as a convention-and-conference center. Daily organized activities for children include iguana hunts, T-shirt painting, and sand-castle building. *Smith Bay Rd., Box 8267, 00801, tel. 809/775–1510 or 800/468–3571, fax 809/775–2185. 297 rooms. Facilities: 2 restaurants, beach, 6 lighted tennis courts, 2 pools, water sports. AE, DC, MC, V. EP. Very Expensive.*

Sugar Bay Plantation Resort. From afar, this large property is a rather overwhelming landmark of bulky white buildings clustered together. It was built as a Holiday Inn Crowne Plaza, but is now owned by Carnival Cruise Lines. All units have balconies and are spacious with comfortable and contemporary furnishings and such Stateside amenities as hair dryers and coffeemakers. Most rooms have water views and some have great views of the British Virgin Islands. The beach is small for the size of the property, but there is a giant free-form pool with waterfalls, a plethora of water sports, tennis courts and a tennis stadium, and plenty of other activities for all ages. Children under 19 stay free when sharing a room with their parents. *Estate Smith Bay, 00802, tel. 809/777–7100, fax 809/777–7200. 300 rooms. Facilities: 2 restaurants, 4 bars, 3 pools, health club, beach, 7 tennis courts, snorkeling equipment. AE, D, DC, MC, V. BP, MAP. Very Expensive.*

Bolongo Inclusive Beach Resort. Neighboring resorts Bolongo Bay Beach and Tennis Club and Limetree Beach Resort have combined into one mega-resort. Oceanfront and garden-view rooms and villas all have air-conditioning, cable TV, VCR, phone, and an electronic safe. All villas have full kitchens, and many rooms have kitchenettes. All guests are part of Club Everything; the room rates include full breakfast, airport transfers, shuttle to town, use of tennis courts, snorkel gear, canoes, Sunfish sailboats, windsurfing and paddleboats, a scuba lesson, and vouchers for an all-day sail, a cocktail cruise, and a half-day snorkel tour on one of the resort's yachts. Guests can also choose the All-Inclusive Club Everything rate (three-night minimum), which includes lunch, dinner, and some drinks. The complimentary Kids Corner entertains the young ones all day. *50 Estate Bolongo, 00802, tel. 809/779–2844 or 800/524–4746; fax 809/775–3208. 225 units, from hotel rooms to 1–3-bedroom villas. Facilities: 5 restaurants, 3 pools, 2 beaches, 6 tennis courts, extensive health club, water sports, 2 nightclubs, volleyball, shuffleboard. AE, DC, MC, V. BP, All-inclusive. Expensive–Very Expensive.*

Hotel 1829. This historic Spanish-style inn is popular with visiting government officials and people with business at Government House down the street. It's located on Government Hill, at the edge of Charlotte Amalie's shopping area. Rooms are on several levels and range from elegant and roomy to quite small; they are priced accordingly, so there is one for every budget. It is said that author Graham Greene stayed here, and it is easy to imagine him musing over a drink in the small, dark bar. The restaurant is one of the best on the island. The rooms have a wet bar, TV, and air-conditioning. There's a tiny pool for cooling off. *Box 1567, Charlotte Amalie, 00801, tel. 809/776–1828 or 800/524–2002. 15 rooms. Facilities: restaurant, pool. AE, DC, MC, V. EP. Inexpensive–Very Expensive.*

★ **Blackbeard's Castle.** This small and very popular hillside inn is laid out around a tower from which, it's said, Blackbeard kept watch on the horizon for invaders. It's an elegantly informal kind of place, where guests while away Sunday mornings with the *New York Times.* There are stunning views of the harbor and Charlotte Amalie from the gourmet restaurant (*see* Dining, *above*), the large freshwater pool, and the outdoor terrace, where locals come for sunset cocktails. Charlotte Amalie is a short walk down the hill and beaches are close by. Rates include a complimentary breakfast. *Box 6041, Charlotte Amalie, 00801, tel. 809/776–1234, fax 809/776–4321. 20 rooms. Facilities: restaurant, bar, freshwater pool. AE, DC, MC, V. CP. Expensive.*

Heritage Manor. The four rooms in the vintage 1830 main structure of this European-style guest house have gleaming tile floors, brass beds, and 12-foot ceilings with equally expansive windows. These rooms, along with the other four that cluster around a tiny gem of a pool and a courtyard, are all decorated with city theme prints (the "Tokyo Room" is coziness incarnate). Suites have refrigerators, and two rooms have kitchens. Guests should be cautious about wandering around after dark because the hotel is somewhat secluded. This is a place for those as interested in history as in the beach. Continental breakfast is complimentary during the winter season. *1A Snegle Gade, Charlotte Amalie, Box 90, 00804, tel. 809/774–3003 or 800/ 828–0757, fax 809/776–9585. 8 air-conditioned rooms, 4 with bath (another 4 rooms share 2 baths). Facilities: pool. AE, MC, V. CP. Moderate.*

Sign of the Griffin. If it's a house party you have in mind, you might want to consider these privately owned, furnished, one- and two-bedroom homes with great views on a hillside 500 feet above Tutu Bay. Each house has a fully equipped kitchen, telephone, private garden, and covered terrace. You'll need a car to get around from here. Maid service is provided on weekdays, and for stays of three weeks or more you'll receive a 10% discount. *Box 11668, 00801, tel. 809/775–1715. MC, V. EP. Moderate.*

Villa Blanca Hotel. Located above Charlotte Amalie on Raphune Hill, the hotel is surrounded by an attractive garden and has modern, balconied rooms with rattan furniture, kitchenettes, cable TVs, and ceiling fans. The eastern rooms face the Charlotte Amalie harbor; the western ones look out on rolling hills and a partial view of Drake's Channel and the B.V.I. *Box 7505, Charlotte Amalie, 00801, tel. 809/776–0749 or 800/237–0034, fax 809/779–2661. 12 rooms. Facilities: pool. AE, MC, V. EP. Moderate.*

Bunker Hill Hotel. The clean, air-conditioned rooms at this very modestly furnished hotel are at different levels above the rooftops of the historic district and centered around a pool and terrace. All rooms have baths, and some have small balconies. The two suites have kitchens and broad porches. Because it is tucked in the quaint back streets of town (often deserted at night), be sure to take a taxi when returning after dark. Rates include complimentary breakfast. *9 Commandant Gade, Charlotte Amalie, 00802, tel. 809/774–8056, fax 809/774–3172. 15 rooms. Facilities: restaurant, pool, kitchenettes, TV. MC, V. BP. Inexpensive.*

Island View Guest House. This clean, simply furnished guest house rests amid tropical foliage on the southern face of 1500-foot Crown Mountain, the highest point on St. Thomas. As a result, its pool and shaded terrace, where complimentary breakfast is served, have one of the most sweeping views of Charlotte Amalie harbor around. All rooms have some view of the harbor, but on the balconies of the six newer rooms (all of which have air-conditioning and ceiling fans) that are perched on the very edge of the hill, you feel suspended in mid-air. *Box 1903, 00801, tel. 809/774–4270 or 800/524–2023, fax 809/ 774–6167. 12 rooms with bath (the other two share a bath) and 3 rooms with kitchenettes. Facilities: pool. AE, MC, V. CP. Inexpensive.*

St. Croix **The Buccaneer.** If you want a self-contained tropical beach resort of-
★ fering golf, all water sports, tennis, a nature/jogging trail, shopping
arcade, health spa, and several restaurants, this 300-acre property
on the East End of the island is the place for you. A palm tree–lined
main drive leads to the large pink hotel at the top of a hill, and a number of smaller guest cottages, shops, and restaurants are scattered
throughout the property's rolling, manicured lawns. Stroll through
the elegant lobby, with its green and white marble checkerboard
floor, into the open-air terrace, where guests can relax and take in
the view. Most of the guest rooms in this former sugar plantation
have been renovated to incorporate eye-catching marble or colorful
tile floors; they also feature four-poster beds and massive wardrobes
of pale wood, pastel fabrics, and locally produced artwork, along
with such modern conveniences as refrigerators and cable TVs. Spacious bathrooms are noteworthy for their marble bench showers and
double sinks. *Box 218, Christiansted 00821–0218, tel. 809/773–2100
or 800/223–1108, fax 809/778–8215. 150 rooms. Facilities: 4 restaurants, beach, golf, health spa, 2 pools, 8 tennis courts (2 lighted),
jogging trail, water sports, shopping arcade, in-room safes, holiday
activities for children. AE, DC, MC, V. EP. Very Expensive.*

★ **Carambola Beach Resort.** This superb resort has finally reopened its
doors after Hugo's devastation and is better than ever. The 25
quaint two-story red-roofed villas connected by lovely arcades appear to have grown from the luxuriant foliage around them. The
rooms are identical; the only difference is the view—ocean or garden. Decor recalls an English country house, with rocking chairs
and sofas upholstered in soothing floral patterns, terra-cotta floors,
rough-textured ceramic lamps, and mahogany ceilings and furnishings. All rooms have a private patio and huge bath (shower only).
There are two fine restaurants, and the Sunday brunch is already
legendary for its table laden with everything from sushi and blackened shark to pork stew and pasta puttanesca. There's an exquisite
ecru beach and lots of quiet, secluded nooks perfect for a relaxing
drink. *Box 3031, Kingshill, tel. 809/778–3800, fax 809/778–1682.
151 rooms. Facilities: 2 restaurants, deli, lounge, pool, water-
sports center, 4 tennis courts (2 lighted), library, gift shop. AE, D,
DC, MC, V. Very Expensive.*

★ **Cormorant Beach Club.** Breeze-bent palm trees, hammocks, the
thrum of North Shore waves, and a blissful sense of respected privacy rule here. The open-air public spaces are filled with tropical
plants and comfy wicker furniture in cool peach and mint green
shades. Ceiling fans and tile floors add to the atmosphere at this top-
shelf resort, which resembles a series of connected Moorish villas.
The beachfront rooms are lovely, with dark wicker furniture, pale
peach walls, white-tile floors, and floral-print spreads and curtains.
All rooms have a patio or balcony and telephone, and cable TV and
safes were being installed at press time. Bathrooms stand out for
their coral-rock-wall showers, marble-top double sinks, and brass
fixtures. Morning coffee and afternoon tea are set out daily in the
building breezeways, and you'll receive a "CBC" terry robe to wear
when you walk to the beautifully ledged polygonal pool. The airy,
high-ceilinged restaurant is one of St. Croix's best. *4126 La Grande
Princesse, Christiansted 00820, tel. 809/778–8920 or 800/548–4460,
fax 809/778–9218. 34 rooms, 4 suites. Facilities: restaurant, bar,
beach, pool, snorkeling, 2 tennis courts, library with TV and VCR,
croquet lawns. AE, DC, MC, V. EP, FAP. Very Expensive.*

★ **Villa Madeleine.** This exquisite hotel on the East End opened in 1990
and has quickly earned a reputation as one of St. Croix's best. The
main building was patterned after a turn-of-the-century West Indian plantation great house. The richly upholstered furniture, Orien-

tal rugs, teal walls, and whimsically painted driftwood that set the mood in the billiards room, the austere library-and-sitting room, and at Cafe Madeleine, the resort's highly praised Continental restaurant, seem straight from the pages of *Architectural Digest*. The great house sits atop a hill, on which private guest villas are scattered in both directions, affording views of the north and south shores. The villas' decor is modern tropical, with rattan and plush cushions, and many bedrooms have bamboo four-poster beds. Each villa has a full kitchen and a private swimming pool. Special touches in the rooms include 5-foot-square pink-marble showers and, in many cottages, hand-painted floral borders along the walls, done in splashy tropical colors. *Box 3109, Christiansted 00822, tel. 809/778–7377 or 800/548–4461, fax 809/773–7518. 43 villas. Facilities: restaurant, bar, private pools, billiards room, library, tennis court, concierge, nearby golf course. EP. Very Expensive.*

Sprat Hall. This 20-acre seaside Frederiksted property is a restored 1670 plantation estate, the oldest in the U.S.V.I. The homey, antiques-filled great house (no smoking, please) has guest rooms that harken back to more genteel days, with high-standing four-poster beds, antique furniture, bowls of fresh-cut bougainvillea and ginger thomas, and no air-conditioning. There are also family cottages on the grounds, but these are rather dingy and not in the same class as the great house rooms. The Hurd family also operates extensive horseback riding facilities here. Guests receive complimentary Continental breakfasts, and may also arrange for one of the Hurds' fine dinners. *Box 695, Frederiksted 00841, tel. 809/772–0305 or 800/843–3584. 9 rooms, 8 suites. Facilities: restaurant, beach, horseback riding, water sports. AE. EP. Moderate–Expensive.*

★ **Waves at Cane Bay.** Owners Kevin and Suzanne Ryan have done wonders with this 25-year-old property since purchasing it in 1989. The two peach-and-mint-green buildings house enormous, balconied guest rooms done in cream and light pastel prints, all with kitchens or kitchenettes. The small inn caters to divers, who take advantage of the fine reef located just offshore, as well as to couples. The hotel is rather isolated and its beachfront rocky, but Cane Bay is right next door, and there is a small patch of sand at poolside for sunbathing. The pool itself is unusual, having been carved from the coral along the shore: The floor and one wall are concrete, but the seaside wall is made of natural coral, and the pool water is circulated as the waves crash over the side, creating a foamy Jacuzzi on rough days. *Box 1749, Kings Hill, 00851, tel. 809/778–1805 or 800/545–0603. 12 rooms, 1 suite. Facilities: bar, pool, complimentary snorkeling gear, Tues. night all-you-can-eat barbecue, in-room safes. AE, MC, V. EP. Moderate–Expensive.*

★ **Club St. Croix.** Popular with honeymooners, this condominium resort north of Christiansted made a strong comeback from Hurricane Hugo: Newly refurbished inside and out, the studio, one-, and two-bedroom apartments are spacious and bright. Indian-print throw rugs and cushions complement the bamboo furniture and rough, white-tile floors; the modern decor is further highlighted by glass-top tables and mirrored closet doors. Penthouses have loft bedrooms reached by spiral staircases, and studios have Murphy beds in the sitting rooms. Every room has a full kitchen and a sun deck, with waterfront views of Christiansted and Buck Island. On the beach you'll find a poolside restaurant and bar and a dock. Guests can take a sunset sail or go snorkeling with the hotel's 42-foot catamaran, the *Cruzan Cat. Estate Golden Rock, Christiansted 00820, tel. 809/773–4800 or 800/635–1533, fax 809/773–4805. 54 suites. Facilities: restaurant, bar, 3 tennis courts, conference room, dock, pool, whirlpool, laundry room, water sports. AE, MC, V. EP. Moderate.*

Hibiscus Beach Hotel. This appealing, affordable property is found on the same stretch of palm tree–lined beach as its sister hotel, the Cormorant. Guest rooms are divided among five two-story pink buildings, each named for a tropical flower. All have views of the oceanfront, thanks to the staggered placement of the buildings, and every room has a spacious balcony facing the sea. Request a room in the Hibiscus building—it's closest to the water. Rooms offer cable TV, safe, and minibar and are tastefully furnished: white-tile floors and white walls are brightened with pink-striped curtains; bright, flowered bedspreads; and fresh-cut hibiscus blossoms. The bathrooms are nondescript (both the shower stalls and the vanity mirrors are on the small side) but clean. The staff is friendly and helpful, and the Tuesday night manager's party in the open-air bar-and-restaurant is a pleasant gathering. *Box 4131, La Grande Princesse 00820–4441, tel. 809/773–4042, fax 809/773–7668. 38 rooms with bath. Facilities: bar, restaurant, 2 wheelchair-accessible rooms, 1 kitchenette-equipped room, pool, complimentary snorkel equipment, minibar, room safes. AE, DC, MC, V. EP. Moderate.*

Hotel Caravelle. The charming three-story Caravelle is an excellent choice for moderately priced lodging in Christiansted. All rooms have refrigerators and are done in tasteful dusky blues and whites, with floral-print bedspreads and curtains and vaulted ceilings. Baths are clean and new, though the unique tile in the showers is a holdover from when the hotel was built 22 years ago. Superior rooms overlook the harbor, but most rooms do have some sort of ocean view. Owners Sid and Amy Kalmans are friendly and helpful. The Banana Bay Club, a casual terrace eatery serving seafood and Continental cuisine, is also on the premises. *44A Queen Cross St., Christiansted, 00820, tel. 809/773–0687 or 800/524–0410, fax 809/778–7004. 43 rooms. Facilities: restaurant, bar, pool, water sports, conference room, gift shops, guest parking. AE, D, DC, MC, V. EP. Moderate.*

The Frederiksted. Don't be put off by the neat but unprepossessing exterior: This modern four-story inn is your best bet for lodging in Fredriksted. An inviting tiled courtyard holds a small freshwater swimming pool surrounded by the glass-topped tables and yellow chairs of the hotel's bar and restaurant; live music completes the scene on Friday and Saturday nights. Yellow-stripe awnings and tropical greenery create a sunny, welcoming atmosphere. Steps at one side of the courtyard lead to the second floor's main desk and sun deck. The bright, pleasant guest rooms are outfitted with bar, refrigerator, and microwave, and are decorated with light-color rattan furniture and print bedspreads. Bathrooms are on the small side but are bright and clean. The choice rooms are those with an ocean view; these are also the only rooms that have a bathtub in addition to a shower. *20 Strand St., Frederiksted, 00840, tel. 809/773–9150 or 800/524–2025, fax 809/778–4009. 40 rooms. Facilities: restaurant, bar, outdoor pool, sun deck, live entertainment. AE, DC, MC, V. EP. Inexpensive.*

The Pink Fancy. This homey, restful place is located a few blocks west of the center of town in a much less touristy neighborhood. The oldest of the four buildings here is a 1780 Danish town house, and old stone walls and foundations enhance the setting. The inn's efficiency rooms are basic but clean, with hardwood floors, tropical print fabrics, wicker furniture, and air-conditioning. The hotel is laid out around the pool, where pink-and-white awnings throw shade over the patio and small bar. Complimentary breakfast and cocktails are included in room rates. *27 Prince St., Christiansted, 00820, tel. 809/773–8460 or 800/524–2045, fax 809/773–6448. 13 rooms. Facilities: bar, pool. MC, V. CP. Inexpensive.*

St. John
Hotels and Inns
★

Caneel Bay Resort. This 170-acre peninsula resort was originally part of the Durloo plantation owned by the Danish West India Company, and at one time extended as far as Cinnamon Bay (*caneel* is Danish for cinnamon). It was opened as a resort in 1936 and was bought by Laurance Rockefeller in the 1950s. Attention is paid to every detail, and the grounds are immaculately maintained. The flamboyant trees here even seem to shed their blossoms neatly. There are seven beaches, three restaurants, and a restored 18th-century sugar mill. The spacious rooms have simple interiors and no telephone or TV. Jackets are requested for men (during winter season) in restaurants after 6 PM. Formerly an all-inclusive resort, Caneel Bay now offers a choice of rooms with all meals or none. *Box 720, Cruz Bay, 00830, tel. 809/776–6111 or 800/223–7637, fax 809/776–2030. 171 rooms. Facilities: 3 restaurants, 7 beaches, 11 tennis courts, water sports. AE, MC, V. EP, MAP. Very Expensive.*

Hyatt Regency St. John. This 34-acre property at Great Cruz Bay shuns the weathered, old-money elegance of Caneel and lays on the gloss and glitz to the point that even the landscaping looks freshly polished. It's a beautiful place: The grounds are positively iridescent, and the pool area is a sybarite's delight, with waterfalls and islands and a poolside bar. Spacious, well-appointed guest rooms line the beach and encircle the pool, while some suites and luxurious town houses are set back slightly from the water. Try the on-site Chow Bella restaurant's "transcultural" menu of Italian and Chinese specialties. There are morning, afternoon, and evening children's programs that include beach olympics, stargazing, island tours, and arts and crafts. *Box 8310, Great Cruz Bay, 00830, tel. 809/776–7171 or 800/323–7249, fax 809/779–4985. 285 rooms. Facilities: 3 restaurants, beach, marina, pool, water sports, fitness room, tennis. AE, DC, MC, V. EP, MAP. Very Expensive.*

★ **Gallows Point Suite Resort.** These soft-gray buildings with peaked roofs and shuttered windows grace the peninsula south of the Cruz Bay ferry dock. The garden apartments have sky-lit, plant-filled showers big enough to frolic in. The upper-level apartments have loft bedrooms. There's no air-conditioning; harborside villas get better trade winds but are noisier. Daily maid service is included in the rates. The entranceway is bridged by Ellington's restaurant. *Box 58, Cruz Bay, 00831, tel. 809/776–6434 or 800/323–7229, fax 809/776–6520. 60 rooms. Facilities: beach, pool, snorkeling. AE, DC, MC, V. EP. Expensive.*

Raintree Inn. If you want to be right in the center of the action in town and bunk at an affordable island-style place, go no farther. The dark-wood rooms, some with air-conditioning, have a nicely simple, tropical-cabin decor. Three efficiencies have kitchens and—if you don't mind climbing an indoor ladder—a comfortable sleeping loft. The Fish Trap restaurant is next door. *Box 566, Cruz Bay, 00831, tel. and fax 809/776–7449 or 800/666–7449. 11 rooms. AE, D, MC, V. EP. Inexpensive–Moderate.*

The Inn at Tamarind Court. If you can just barely afford a vacation on St. John, try this inexpensive hostelry located on the east side of town. It's especially suited to singles. Its mismatched furnishing and somewhat shabby decor reflect the prices, but the helpful staff and youthful fun-loving clientele compensate somewhat. Choose among traditional hotel rooms (some with shared bath), suites, or a one-bedroom apartment. The front-courtyard bar is a friendly hangout, as well as home to one of Cruz Bay's best West Indian restaurants. Continental breakfast is included. *Box 350, Cruz Bay, 00831, tel. 809/776–6378. 20 rooms, some with shared bath. Facilities: restaurant and bar. AE, D, MC, V. CP. Inexpensive.*

Homes and Villas   **Caribbean Villas and Resorts** (Box 458, Cruz Bay 00830, tel. 809/776–6152 or 800/338–0987, fax 809/779–4044) is the island's largest short-term villa rental agent, with some 60 homes available on St. John. Its luxury properties are usually within a mile or two of Cruz Bay and are often right on the beach. **Vacation Vistas** (Box 476, Cruz Bay 00831, tel. 809/776–6462) has a smaller roster of select waterview properties, ranging from the extravagant (an indoor swimming pool and retractable living room walls that draw back to bring the indoors outside) to the merely lovely. **Villa Portfolio** (tel. 809/693–5050) represents several charming properties just outside Cruz Bay, including Battery Hill, Villas Caribe and Coconut Coast Villas. **Destination St. John** (Box 37, Cruz Bay 00831, tel. 809/774–3843 or 800/562–1901) represents a number of properties, all perched high on hills overlooking fine views. **Catered To, Inc.** (Box 704, Cruz Bay 00831, tel. 809/776–6641, fax 809/779–6191) represents a number of luxury homes, many of which have pools and beach access. Other home-rental agents on the island include **Private Homes for Private Vacations** (Mamey Peak 00830, tel. 809/776–6876), **Paradise Hideaways** (Box 149, Cruz Bay 00831, tel. 809/776–6518), and **Vacation Homes** (Box 272, Cruz Bay 00831, tel. 809/776–6094).

Condominiums   Among the condominiums controlled by Caribbean Villas and Resorts (*see above*) are **Cruz Views, Pastory Estates,** and **Cruz Bay Villas,** all of which have dynamite ocean views from their one- and two-bedroom units. The 12 units at **Lavender Hill Estates** (Box 3606, Cruz Bay 00831, tel. 809/776–6969) are just a few minutes' walk into the center of town. Affordable **Serendip** (Box 273, Cruz Bay 00831, tel. 809/776–6646), just a short drive outside town, has been remodeled and makes a good budget option. The luxurious **Virgin Grand Villas** (Great Cruz Bay 00830, tel. 809/775–3856, fax 809/779–4760) are somewhat removed from the Virgin Grand Resort, though guests at these one-, two-, and three-bedroom town houses and villas have full use of the facilities at the Hyatt.

Campgrounds   **Maho Bay Camp.** Eight miles from Cruz Bay, this private campground is a lush hillside community of tent cottages (canvas and screens) linked by boardwalks, stairs, and ramps that also lead down to the beach. The 16-by-16-foot shelters have beds, dining table and chairs, electric lamps (and outlets), propane stove, ice cooler, kitchenware, and cutlery. The camp has the chummy feel of a retreat and is very popular, so book well in advance. *Cruz Bay, 00830, tel. 212/472–9453 or 800/392–9004. 113 tent cottages. Facilities: restaurant, commissary, barbecue areas, beach, bathhouses (showers, sinks, and toilets), water sports. No credit cards. Moderate.*

Cinnamon Bay Campground. Tents, cottages with four one-room units in each cottage, and bare sites are available at this National Park Service location surrounded by jungle and set at the edge of big, beautiful Cinnamon Bay Beach. The tents are 10-by-14 feet, with flooring, and come with living, eating, and sleeping furnishings and necessities; the 15-by-15-foot cottages have twin beds. Bare sites, which come with a picnic table and a charcoal grill, can be reserved up to eight months in advance. You can reserve by phone with a credit card. The bare sites are cheap—at press time they were $14 a site—but, if you're thinking of this option for budgetary reasons alone, be warned: the tent sites and cottages range from around $65 to $87 in season for two people per night. *Cruz Bay, 00830–0720, tel. 809/776–6330 or 800/223–7637. 44 tents, 40 cottages, 26 bare sites. Facilities: cafeteria, beach, commissary, bath-*

houses (showers and toilets), water sports. AE, MC, V. Inexpensive–Moderate.

Nightlife

Nightlife in the U.S.V.I. is a spontaneous affair. Although there are many tourist-oriented cultural shows that can make for a fun night out—including Calypso Carnival at the Reef and some broken-bottle dancing at various hotels—socializing is what nightlife is about. Most of the music scene takes place in small clubs with dance floors.

St. Thomas Nightspots At **Barnacle Bill's** (tel. 809/774–7444), Bill Grogan has turned this Crown Bay landmark with the bright red lobster on its roof into a musicians' home away from home.

Castaways (tel. 809/776–8410) is the watering hole and dance floor for the crews, owners, and those chartering the fleet of boats anchored at Yacht Haven.

Club Z (tel. 809/776–4655), still one of the hottest spots on the island, is a disco-style club located on Contant Hill, with a spectacular view of glittering harbor lights to enjoy on the terrace between dances.

Sugar Bay Disco (tel. 809/777–7100) is now one of the island's most popular night spots, and the dance floor is crowded until the early morning hours six nights a week.

Top of the Reef at Marriott's Frenchman's Reef Resort (tel. 809/776–8500) has two "Calypso Carnival" shows nightly (except Sunday). Have dinner or just drinks and take in the music and rhythms of the Caribbean.

Jazz and Piano Bars **Blackbeard's Castle** (tel. 809/776–1234) has live jazz every night except Monday from 8 PM to midnight. Come here and listen to Stateside artists (generally a singer and a piano player) who head here for three- to four-week gigs.

You'll find piano bars at **Fiddle Leaf** (tel. 809/775–2810), on Government Hill, and at the East End at the **Grand Palazzo** (tel. 809/775–3333) and **Raffles** (tel. 809/775–6004). The player at Raffles has been entertaining with his show "Gray, Gray, Gray" for many years and shouldn't be missed.

St. Croix Christiansted has a lively and eminently casual club scene near the waterfront. At **Mango Grove** (53 King St., tel. 809/778–8103) you'll hear live guitar and vocals in an open-air courtyard with a bar and Cinzano umbrella-covered tables. The upstairs **Moonraker Lounge** (43A Queen Cross St., tel. 809/773–1535) presents a constant calendar of live music, usually a singer with an acoustic guitar playing all your favorites, from Jimmy Buffet to Bob Dylan. More mellow piano music can be heard on the broad veranda of **Club Comanche** (1 Strand St., tel. 809/773–0210). To party under the stars, head to the **Wreck Bar** (tel. 809/773–6092), on Christiansted's Hospital Street, for crab races as well as rock and roll. At **Calabash** (Strand St., tel. 809/778–0001) you'll find steel band music from Wednesday through Saturday, and on Friday there's a broken-bottle dancer. **Hotel on the Cay** (Protestant Cay, tel. 809/773–2035) has a West Indian Buffet on Tuesday nights that features a broken-bottle dancer and Mocko Jumbie. On Thursday nights, the **Cormorant** (La Grande Princess, tel. 809/778–8920) throws a similar event. The **2 Plus 2 Disco** (17 La Grande Princesse, tel. 809/773–3710) spins a great mix of calypso, soul, disco and reggae, with live acts on weekends.

Although less hopping than Christiansted, Frederiksted restaurants and clubs have a variety of weekend entertainment. **Blue Moon** (17 Strand St., tel. 809/772–2222), a waterfront restaurant, is the place to be for live jazz on Friday 9 PM–1 AM. The island's premiere calypso band, Blinky and the Roadmasters, performs every Sunday night at **Stars of the West** (14 Strand St., tel. 809/772–9039). The **Lost Dog Pub** (King St., tel. 809/772–3526) is a favorite spot for a casual drink, a game of darts, and occasional live rock and roll on Sunday nights. Head north of town to the **Sand Bar** (Estate La Grange, no tel.) on Sunday night to hear Green Flash play rock and roll. For another outdoor lime, head up to Mahogany Road to the **Mt. Pellier Hut Domino Club** (50 Mt. Pellier, tel. 809/772–9914). Piro, the one-man band, plays on Sunday.

St. John Some friendly hubbub can be found at the rough-and-ready **Backyard** (tel. 809/776–8553), *the* place for sports watching as well as grooving to Bonnie Raitt et al. There's calypso and reggae on Wednesday and Friday at **Fred's** (tel. 809/776–6363). The **Etta's** at the Inn at Tamarind Court (tel. 809/776–6378) serves up a blend of jazz and rock on Friday and reggae on Saturday.

Notices on the bulletin board across from the **U.S. post office** and at **Connections** (and on telephone poles) will keep you posted on special events: comedy nights, movies, and the like.

Index

Personal Itinerary

Departure *Date*

Time

Transportation

Arrival *Date* *Time*

Departure *Date* *Time*

Transportation

Accommodations

Arrival *Date* *Time*

Departure *Date* *Time*

Transportation

Accommodations

Arrival *Date* *Time*

Departure *Date* *Time*

Transportation

Accommodations

Personal Itinerary

Arrival *Date*   *Time*

Departure *Date*   *Time*

Transportation

Accommodations

Arrival *Date*   *Time*

Departure *Date*   *Time*

Transportation

Accommodations

Arrival *Date*   *Time*

Departure *Date*   *Time*

Transportation

Accommodations

Arrival *Date*   *Time*

Departure *Date*   *Time*

Transportation

Accommodations

Personal Itinerary

Arrival   *Date*   *Time*

Departure   *Date*   *Time*

Transportation

Accommodations

Arrival   *Date*   *Time*

Departure   *Date*   *Time*

Transportation

Accommodations

Arrival   *Date*   *Time*

Departure   *Date*   *Time*

Transportation

Accommodations

Arrival   *Date*   *Time*

Departure   *Date*   *Time*

Transportation

Accommodations

Personal Itinerary

Arrival	*Date*	*Time*
Departure	*Date*	*Time*
Transportation		
Accommodations		

Arrival	*Date*	*Time*
Departure	*Date*	*Time*
Transportation		
Accommodations		

Arrival	*Date*	*Time*
Departure	*Date*	*Time*
Transportation		
Accommodations		

Arrival	*Date*	*Time*
Departure	*Date*	*Time*
Transportation		
Accommodations		

Personal Itinerary

Arrival *Date*   *Time*

Departure *Date*   *Time*

Transportation

Accommodations

Arrival *Date*   *Time*

Departure *Date*   *Time*

Transportation

Accommodations

Arrival *Date*   *Time*

Departure *Date*   *Time*

Transportation

Accommodations

Arrival *Date*   *Time*

Departure *Date*   *Time*

Transportation

Accommodations

Personal Itinerary

Arrival	*Date*	*Time*
Departure	*Date*	*Time*
Transportation		
Accommodations		

Arrival	*Date*	*Time*
Departure	*Date*	*Time*
Transportation		
Accommodations		

Arrival	*Date*	*Time*
Departure	*Date*	*Time*
Transportation		
Accommodations		

Arrival	*Date*	*Time*
Departure	*Date*	*Time*
Transportation		
Accommodations		

Personal Itinerary

Arrival *Date*   *Time*

Departure *Date*   *Time*

Transportation

Accommodations

Arrival *Date*   *Time*

Departure *Date*   *Time*

Transportation

Accommodations

Arrival *Date*   *Time*

Departure *Date*   *Time*

Transportation

Accommodations

Arrival *Date*   *Time*

Departure *Date*   *Time*

Transportation

Accommodations

Addresses

Name	*Name*
Address	*Address*
Telephone	*Telephone*
Name	*Name*
Address	*Address*
Telephone	*Telephone*
Name	*Name*
Address	*Address*
Telephone	*Telephone*
Name	*Name*
Address	*Address*
Telephone	*Telephone*
Name	*Name*
Address	*Address*
Telephone	*Telephone*
Name	*Name*
Address	*Address*
Telephone	*Telephone*
Name	*Name*
Address	*Address*
Telephone	*Telephone*
Name	*Name*
Address	*Address*
Telephone	*Telephone*

Addresses

Name	*Name*
Address	*Address*
Telephone	*Telephone*
Name	*Name*
Address	*Address*
Telephone	*Telephone*
Name	*Name*
Address	*Address*
Telephone	*Telephone*
Name	*Name*
Address	*Address*
Telephone	*Telephone*
Name	*Name*
Address	*Address*
Telephone	*Telephone*
Name	*Name*
Address	*Address*
Telephone	*Telephone*
Name	*Name*
Address	*Address*
Telephone	*Telephone*
Name	*Name*
Address	*Address*
Telephone	*Telephone*

Addresses

Name	*Name*
Address	*Address*
Telephone	*Telephone*
Name	*Name*
Address	*Address*
Telephone	*Telephone*
Name	*Name*
Address	*Address*
Telephone	*Telephone*
Name	*Name*
Address	*Address*
Telephone	*Telephone*
Name	*Name*
Address	*Address*
Telephone	*Telephone*
Name	*Name*
Address	*Address*
Telephone	*Telephone*
Name	*Name*
Address	*Address*
Telephone	*Telephone*
Name	*Name*
Address	*Address*
Telephone	*Telephone*

The only guide to explore a *Disney World you've never seen before:*

The one for grown-ups.

This is the only guide written specifically for the millions of adults who visit Walt Disney World each year <u>without</u> kids. Upscale, sophisticated, packed full of facts and maps, *Walt Disney World for Adults* provides up-to-date information on hotels, restaurants, sports facilities, and health clubs, as well as unique itineraries for adults. With *Walt Disney World for Adults* in hand, you'll get the most out of one of the world's most fascinating, most complex playgrounds.

At bookstores everywhere, or call **1-800-533-6478.**

At last — a guide for Americans with disabilities that makes traveling a delight

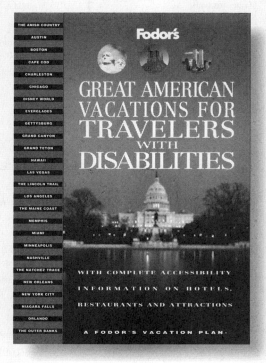

THE AMISH COUNTRY
AUSTIN
BOSTON
CAPE COD
CHARLESTON
CHICAGO
DISNEY WORLD
EVERGLADES
GETTYSBURG
GRAND CANYON
GRAND TETON
HAWAII
LAS VEGAS
THE LINCOLN TRAIL
LOS ANGELES
THE MAINE COAST
MEMPHIS
MIAMI
MINNEAPOLIS
NASHVILLE
THE NATCHEZ TRACE
NEW ORLEANS
NEW YORK CITY
NIAGARA FALLS
ORLANDO
THE OUTER BANKS

Fodor's
GREAT AMERICAN VACATIONS FOR TRAVELERS WITH DISABILITIES
WITH COMPLETE ACCESSIBILITY INFORMATION ON HOTELS, RESTAURANTS AND ATTRACTIONS
A FODOR'S VACATION PLAN

This is the first and only complete guide to great American vacations for the 35 million North Americans with disabilities, as well as for those who care for them or for aging parents and relatives. Provides:

- Essential trip-planning information for travelers with mobility, vision, and hearing impairments
- Specific details on a huge array of facilities, along with solid descriptions of attractions, hotels, restaurants, and other destinations
- Up-to-date information on ISA-designated parking, level entranceways, accessibility to pools, lounges, bathrooms

At bookstores everywhere, or call **1-800-533-6478**

Fodor's Travel Guides

Available at bookstores everywhere, or call 1–800–533–6478, 24 hours a day.

U.S. Guides

Alaska

Arizona

Boston

California

Cape Cod, Martha's Vineyard, Nantucket

The Carolinas & the Georgia Coast

Chicago

Colorado

Florida

Hawaii

Las Vegas, Reno, Tahoe

Los Angeles

Maine, Vermont, New Hampshire

Maui

Miami & the Keys

New England

New Orleans

New York City

Pacific North Coast

Philadelphia & the Pennsylvania Dutch Country

The Rockies

San Diego

San Francisco

Santa Fe, Taos, Albuquerque

Seattle & Vancouver

The South

The U.S. & British Virgin Islands

USA

The Upper Great Lakes Region

Virginia & Maryland

Waikiki

Walt Disney World and the Orlando Area

Washington, D.C.

Foreign Guides

Acapulco, Ixtapa, Zihuatanejo

Australia & New Zealand

Austria

The Bahamas

Baja & Mexico's Pacific Coast Resorts

Barbados

Berlin

Bermuda

Brittany & Normandy

Budapest

Canada

Cancún, Cozumel, Yucatán Peninsula

Caribbean

China

Costa Rica, Belize, Guatemala

The Czech Republic & Slovakia

Eastern Europe

Egypt

Euro Disney

Europe

Florence, Tuscany & Umbria

France

Germany

Great Britain

Greece

Hong Kong

India

Ireland

Israel

Italy

Japan

Kenya & Tanzania

Korea

London

Madrid & Barcelona

Mexico

Montréal & Québec City

Morocco

Moscow & St. Petersburg

The Netherlands, Belgium & Luxembourg

New Zealand

Norway

Nova Scotia, Prince Edward Island & New Brunswick

Paris

Portugal

Provence & the Riviera

Rome

Russia & the Baltic Countries

Scandinavia

Scotland

Singapore

South America

Southeast Asia

Spain

Sweden

Switzerland

Thailand

Tokyo

Toronto

Turkey

Vienna & the Danube Valley

Special Series

Fodor's Affordables

Caribbean

Europe

Florida

France

Germany

Great Britain

Italy

London

Paris

Fodor's Bed & Breakfast and Country Inns Guides

America's Best B&Bs

California

Canada's Great Country Inns

Cottages, B&Bs and Country Inns of England and Wales

Mid-Atlantic Region

New England

The Pacific Northwest

The South

The Southwest

The Upper Great Lakes Region

The Berkeley Guides

California

Central America

Eastern Europe

Europe

France

Germany & Austria

Great Britain & Ireland

Italy

London

Mexico

Pacific Northwest & Alaska

Paris

San Francisco

Fodor's Exploring Guides

Australia

Boston & New England

Britain

California

The Caribbean

Florence & Tuscany

Florida

France

Germany

Ireland

Italy

London

Mexico

New York City

Paris

Prague

Rome

Scotland

Singapore & Malaysia

Spain

Thailand

Turkey

Fodor's Flashmaps

Boston

New York

Washington, D.C.

Fodor's Pocket Guides

Acapulco

Bahamas

Barbados

Jamaica

London

New York City

Paris

Puerto Rico

San Francisco

Washington, D.C.

Fodor's Sports

Cycling

Golf Digest's Best Places to Play

Hiking

The Insider's Guide to the Best Canadian Skiing

Running

Sailing

Skiing in the USA & Canada

USA Today's Complete Four Sports Stadium Guide

Fodor's Three-In-Ones (guidebook, language cassette, and phrase book)

France

Germany

Italy

Mexico

Spain

Fodor's Special-Interest Guides

Complete Guide to America's National Parks

Condé Nast Traveler Caribbean Resort and Cruise Ship Finder

Cruises and Ports of Call

Euro Disney

France by Train

Halliday's New England Food Explorer

Healthy Escapes

Italy by Train

London Companion

Shadow Traffic's New York Shortcuts and Traffic Tips

Sunday in New York

Sunday in San Francisco

Touring Europe

Touring USA: Eastern Edition

Walt Disney World and the Orlando Area

Walt Disney World for Adults

Fodor's Vacation Planners

Great American Learning Vacations

Great American Sports & Adventure Vacations

Great American Vacations

Great American Vacations for Travelers with Disabilities

National Parks and Seashores of the East

National Parks of the West

The Wall Street Journal Guides to Business Travel

What's hot, where it's hot!

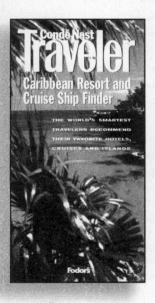

Condé Nast Traveler Caribbean Resort and Cruise Ship Finder
The World's Smartest Travelers Recommend Their Favorite Hotels, Cruises and Islands

Incorporating the results of the enormously influential *Condé Nast Traveler* survey with comprehensive Fodor's travel information — this brand new guide features 150 hotels and resorts, 30 cruise lines, 28 islands, and 60 pages of maps.

Cruises and Ports of Call 1995
Choosing the Perfect Ship and Enjoying Your Time Ashore

The most comprehensive cruise guide available offers all the essentials for planning a cruise: selecting the right ship, getting the best deals, and making the most of your time in port.
"A gold mine of information."
—*New York Post*

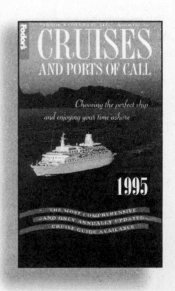

At bookstores everywhere, or call **1-800-533-6478**

AT LAST

YOUR OWN PERSONALIZED LIST
OF WHAT'S GOING ON IN THE
CITIES YOU'RE VISITING.

KEYED TO THE DAYS WHEN
YOU'LL BE THERE, CUSTOMIZED
FOR YOUR INTERESTS,
AND SENT TO YOU BEFORE YOU
LEAVE HOME.

Fodor's WORLDVIEW TRAVEL UPDATE

GET THE INSIDER'S PERSPECTIVE. . .

UP-TO-THE-MINUTE
ACCURATE
EASY TO ORDER
DELIVERED WHEN YOU NEED IT

Fodor's WORLDVIEW
TRAVEL UPDATE

Now there is a revolutionary way to get customized, time-sensitive travel information just before your trip.

Now you can obtain detailed information about what's going on in each city you'll be visiting <u>before</u> you leave home—up-to-the-minute, objective information about the events and activities that interest you most.

Your Itinerary:
Customized reports available for 160 destinations

Travel Updates contain the kind of time-sensitive insider information you can get only from local contacts – or from city magazines and newspapers once you arrive. But now you can have the same information before you leave for your trip.

The choice is yours: current art exhibits, theater, music festivals and special concerts, sporting events, antiques and flower shows, shopping, fitness, and more.

The information comes from hundreds of correspondents and thousands of sources worldwide. Updated continuously, it's like having your own personal concierge or friend in the city.

You specify the cities and when you'll be there. We'll do the rest — personalizing the information for you the way no guidebook can.

It's the perfect extension to your Fodor's guide and the best way to make the most of your valuable travel time.

**Use Order Form on back
or call 1-800-799-9609**

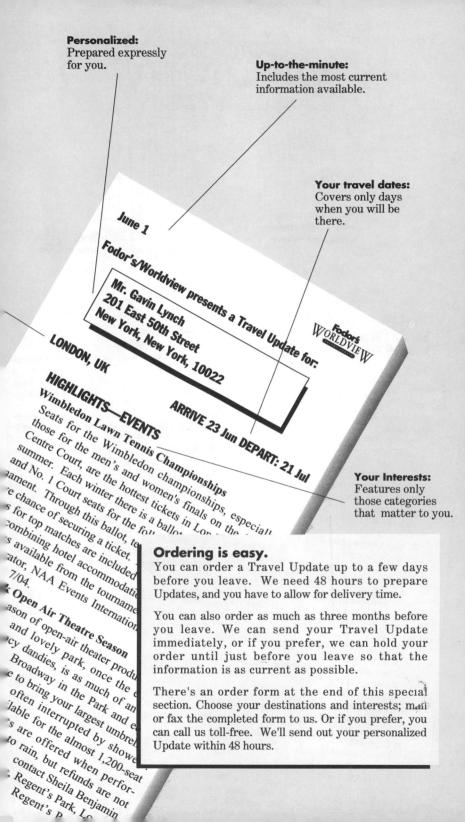

Personalized:
Prepared expressly for you.

Up-to-the-minute:
Includes the most current information available.

Your travel dates:
Covers only days when you will be there.

June 1

Fodor's/Worldview presents a Travel Update for:

Mr. Gavin Lynch
201 East 50th Street
New York, New York, 10022

Fodor's
WORLDVIEW

LONDON, UK

ARRIVE 23 Jun DEPART: 21 Jul

Your Interests:
Features only those categories that matter to you.

HIGHLIGHTS—EVENTS

Wimbledon Lawn Tennis Championships

Seats for the Wimbledon championships, especiall
those for the men's and women's finals on the
Centre Court, are the hottest tickets in Lon
summer. Each winter there is a ballo
and No. 1 Court seats for the foll
nament. Through this ballot, te
e chance of securing a ticket.
s for top matches are included
combining hotel accommodati
s available from the tournam
ator, NAA Events Internation
7/04.

k Open Air Theatre Season

ason of open-air theater produ
and lovely park, once the e
cy dandies, is as much of an
Broadway in the Park and e
e to bring your largest umbrel
often interrupted by showe
lable for the almost 1,200-seat
s are offered when perfor-
to rain, but refunds are not
contact Sheila Benjamin
Regent's Park, Lo
Regent's P

Ordering is easy.

You can order a Travel Update up to a few days before you leave. We need 48 hours to prepare Updates, and you have to allow for delivery time.

You can also order as much as three months before you leave. We can send your Travel Update immediately, or if you prefer, we can hold your order until just before you leave so that the information is as current as possible.

There's an order form at the end of this special section. Choose your destinations and interests; mail or fax the completed form to us. Or if you prefer, you can call us toll-free. We'll send out your personalized Update within 48 hours.

Fodor's WORLDVIEW TRAVEL UPDATE

Special concerts—
who's performing
what and where

One-of-a-kind,
one-time-only events

Special interest,
in-depth listings

Children — Events
Angel Canal Festival
The festivities include a children's funfair, entertainers, a boat rally and displays on the water. Regent's Canal. Islington. N1. Tube: Angel. Tel: 267 9100. 11:30am-5:30pm. 7/04.

Blackheath Summer Kite Festival
Stunt kite displays with parachuting teddy bears and trade stands. Free admission. SE3. BR: Blackheath. 10am. 6/27.

Megabugs
Children will delight in this infestation of giant robotic insects, including a praying mantis 60 times life size. Mon-Sat 10am-6pm; Sun 11am-6pm. Admission 4.50 pounds. Natural History Museum, Cromwell Road. SW7. Tube: South Kensington. Tel: 938 9123. Ends 10/01.

Childminders
This establishment employs only women, providing nurses and qualified nannies to

Music — Jazz & Blues
Tito Puente's Golden Men of Latin Jazz
The father of mambo and Cuban rumba king comes to town. Royal Festival Hall. South Bank. SE1. Tube: Waterloo. Tel: 928 8800. 8pm. 7/15.

Georgie Fame and The New York Band
Riding a popular tide with his latest album, the smoky-voiced Fame and his keyboard are on a tour yet again. The Grand. Clapham Junction. SW11. BR: Clapham Junction. Tel: 738 9000. 7:30pm. 7/07.

Jacques Loussier Play Bach Trio
The French jazz classicist and colleagues. Kenwood Lakeside. Hampstead Lane. Kenwood. NW3. Tube: Golders Green, then bus 210. Tel: 413 1443. 7pm. 7/10.

Tony Bennett and Ronnie Scott
Royal Festival Hall. South Bank. SE1. Tube: Waterloo. Tel: 928 8800. 8pm. 7/11.

Santana
Royal Festival Hall. South Bank. SE1. Tube: Waterloo. Tel: 928 8800. 8pm. 7/12.

Count Basie Orchestra and Nancy Wilson Trio
Royal Festival Hall. South Bank. SE1. Tube: Waterloo. Tel: 928 8800. 8pm. 7/14.

King Pleasure and the Biscuit Boys
Royal Festival Hall. South Bank. SE1. Tube: Waterloo. Tel: 928 8800. 6:30 and 9pm. 7/16.

Al Green and the London Community Gospel Choir
Royal Festival Hall. South Bank. SE1. Tube: Waterloo. Tel: 928 8800. 8pm. 7/13.

BB King and Linda Hopkins
Mother of the blues and successor to Bessie Smith, Hopkins meets up with "Blues Boy" King. Royal Festival Hall. South Bank. SE1. Tel: 928 8800. 6:30 and 9pm.

Music — Classical
Marylebone Sinfonia
Kenneth Gowen conducts music by Puccini and Rossini. Queen Elizabeth Hall. South Bank. SE1. Tube: Waterloo. Tel: 928 8800. 7:45pm. 7/16.

London Philharmonic
Franz Welser-Moest and George Benjamin conduct selections by Alexander Goehr, Messiaen, and some of Benjamin's own compositions. Queen Elizabeth Hall. South Bank. SE1. Tube: Waterloo. Tel: 928 8800. 8pm.

London Pro Arte Orchestra and Forest Choir
Murray Stewart conducts selections by Rossini, Haydn and Jonathan Willcocks. Queen Elizabeth Hall. South Bank. Tube: Waterloo. Tel: 928 8800. 7:45pm.

Kensington Symphony Orchestra
Russell Keable conducts Dvorak's D Queen Elizabeth Hall. South Bank.

Here's what you get . . .

Detailed information about what's going on — precisely when you'll be there.

Reviews by local critics

Show openings during your visit

Handy pocket-size booklet

Exhibitions & Shows—Antique & Flower
Westminster Antiques Fair
Over 50 stands with pre-1830 furniture and other Victorian and earlier items. Thu-Fri 11am-8pm; Sat-Sun 11am-6pm. Admission 4 pounds, children free. Old Royal Horticultural Hall. Vincent Square. SW1. Tel: 0444/48 25 14. 6-24 thru 6/27.

Royal Horticultural Society Flower Show
The show includes displays of carnations, summer fruit and vegetables. Tue 11am-7pm; Wed 10am-5pm. Admission Tue 4 pounds, Wed 2 pounds. Royal Horticultural Halls. Greycoat Street and Vincent Square. SW1. Tube: Victoria. 7/20 thru 7/21.

Hampton Court Palace International Flower Show
Major international garden and flower show taking place in conjunction with

Theater — Musical
Sunset Boulevard
In June, the four Andrew Lloyd Webber musicals which dominated London's stages in the 1980s (Cats, Starlight Express, Phantom of the Opera and Aspects of Love) are joined by the composer's latest work, a show rumored to have his best music to date. The 1950 Billy Wilder film about a helpless young writer who is drawn into the world of a possessive, aging silent screen star offers rich opportunities for Webber's evolving style. Soaring, aching melodies, lush technical effects and psychological thrills are all expected. Patti Lupone stars. Mon-Sat at 8pm; matinee Thu-Sat at 3pm. In-person sales only at the box office; credit card bookings, Tel: 344 0055. Admission 15-32.50 pounds. Adelphi Theatre. The Strand. WC2. Tube: Charing Cross. Tel: 836 7611. Starts: 6/21.

Leonardo A Portrait of Love
A new musical about the great Renaissance artist and inventor comes in for a London pre-... tested by a brief run at Oxford's Old ... The work explores ...

Spectator Sports — Other Sports
Greyhound Racing: Wembley Stadium
This dog track offers good views of greyhound racing held on Mon, Wed and Fri. No credit cards. Stadium Way. Wembley. HA9. Tube: Wembley Park. Tel: 902 8833.

Benson & Hedges Cricket Cup Final
Lord's Cricket Ground. St. John's Wood Road. NW8. Tube: St. John's Wood. Tel: 289 1611. 11am. 7/10.

Business-Fax & Overnight Mail
Post Office, Trafalgar Square Branch
Offers a network of fax services, the Intelpost system, throughout the country and abroad. Mon-Sat 8am-8pm, Sun 9am-5pm. William IV Street. WC2. Tube: Charing Cross. Tel: 930 9580.

Fodor's WORLDVIEW
TRAVEL UPDATE

London, England
Arriving: June 23
Departing: July 21

Interest Categories

For <u>your</u> personalized Travel Update, choose the categories you're most interested in from this list. Every Travel Update automatically provides you with *Event Highlights* - the best of what's happening during the dates of your trip.

1.	**Business Services**	Fax & Overnight Mail, Computer Rentals, Photocopying, Protocol, Secretarial, Messenger, Translation Services

Dining

2.	**All Day Dining**	Breakfast & Brunch, Cafes & Tea Rooms, Late-Night Dining
3.	**Local Cuisine**	In Every Price Range—from Budget Restaurants to the Special Splurge
4.	**European Cuisine**	Continental, French, Italian
5.	**Asian Cuisine**	Chinese, Far Eastern, Japanese, Other
6.	**Americas Cuisine**	American, Mexican & Latin
7.	**Nightlife**	Bars, Dance Clubs, Casinos, Comedy Clubs, Ethnic, Pubs & Beer Halls
8.	**Entertainment**	Theater—Comedy, Drama, English Language, Musicals, Dance, Ticket Agencies
9.	**Music**	Country/Western/Folk, Classical, Traditional & Ethnic, Opera, Jazz & Blues, Pop, Rock
10.	**Children's Activities**	Events, Attractions
11.	**Tours**	Local Tours, Day Trips, Overnight Excursions, Cruises
12.	**Exhibitions, Festivals & Shows**	Antiques & Flower, History & Cultural, Art Exhibitions, Fairs & Craft Shows, Music & Art Festivals
13.	**Shopping**	Districts & Malls, Markets, Regional Specialities
14.	**Fitness**	Bicycling, Health Clubs, Hiking, Jogging
15.	**Recreational Sports**	Boating/Sailing, Fishing, Golf, Ice Skating, Skiing, Snorkeling/Scuba, Swimming, Tennis & Racquet
16.	**Spectator Sports**	Auto Racing, Baseball, Basketball, Boating & Sailing, Football, Golf, Horse Racing, Ice Hockey, Rugby, Soccer, Tennis, Track & Field, Other Sports

Please note that interest category content will vary by season, destination, and length of stay.

Destinations

The Fodor's/Worldview Travel Update covers more than 160 destinations worldwide. Choose the destinations that match your itinerary from this list. (Choose bulleted destinations only.)

Europe
- Amsterdam
- Athens
- Barcelona
- Berlin
- Brussels
- Budapest
- Copenhagen
- Dublin
- Edinburgh
- Florence
- Frankfurt
- French Riviera
- Geneva
- Glasgow
- Istanbul
- Lausanne
- Lisbon
- London
- Madrid
- Milan
- Moscow
- Munich
- Oslo
- Paris
- Prague
- Provence
- Rome
- Salzburg
* Seville
- St. Petersburg
- Stockholm
- Venice
- Vienna
- Zurich

United States (Mainland)
- Albuquerque
- Atlanta
- Atlantic City
- Baltimore
- Boston
* Branson, MO
* Charleston, SC
- Chicago
- Cincinnati
- Cleveland
- Dallas/Ft. Worth
- Denver
- Detroit
- Houston
* Indianapolis
- Kansas City
- Las Vegas
- Los Angeles
- Memphis

- Miami
- Milwaukee
- Minneapolis/ St. Paul
* Nashville
- New Orleans
- New York City
- Orlando
- Palm Springs
- Philadelphia
- Phoenix
- Pittsburgh
- Portland
* Reno/ Lake Tahoe
- St. Louis
- Salt Lake City
- San Antonio
- San Diego
- San Francisco
* Santa Fe
- Seattle
- Tampa
- Washington, DC

Alaska
- Alaskan Destinations

Hawaii
- Honolulu
- Island of Hawaii
- Kauai
- Maui

Canada
- Quebec City
- Montreal
- Ottawa
- Toronto
- Vancouver

Bahamas
- Abaco
- Eleuthera/ Harbour Island
- Exuma
- Freeport
- Nassau & Paradise Island

Bermuda
- Bermuda Countryside
- Hamilton

British Leeward Islands
- Anguilla

- Antigua & Barbuda
- St. Kitts & Nevis

British Virgin Islands
- Tortola & Virgin Gorda

British Windward Islands
- Barbados
- Dominica
- Grenada
- St. Lucia
- St. Vincent
- Trinidad & Tobago

Cayman Islands
- The Caymans

Dominican Republic
- Santo Domingo

Dutch Leeward Islands
- Aruba
- Bonaire
- Curacao

Dutch Windward Island
- St. Maarten/ St. Martin

French West Indies
- Guadeloupe
- Martinique
- St. Barthelemy

Jamaica
- Kingston
- Montego Bay
- Negril
- Ocho Rios

Puerto Rico
- Ponce
- San Juan

Turks & Caicos
- Grand Turk/ Providenciales

U.S. Virgin Islands
- St. Croix
- St. John
- St. Thomas

Mexico
- Acapulco
- Cancun & Isla Mujeres
- Cozumel
- Guadalajara
- Ixtapa & Zihuatanejo
- Los Cabos
- Mazatlan
- Mexico City
- Monterrey
- Oaxaca
- Puerto Vallarta

South/Central America
* Buenos Aires
* Caracas
* Rio de Janeiro
* San Jose, Costa Rica
* Sao Paulo

Middle East
* Jerusalem

Australia & New Zealand
- Auckland
- Melbourne
* South Island
- Sydney

China
- Beijing
- Guangzhou
- Shanghai

Japan
- Kyoto
- Nagoya
- Osaka
- Tokyo
- Yokohama

Pacific Rim/Other
* Bali
- Bangkok
- Hong Kong & Macau
- Manila
- Seoul
- Singapore
- Taipei

* Destinations available by 1/1/95

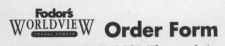

Order Form

THIS TRAVEL UPDATE IS FOR (Please print):

Name

Address

City   State   Country   ZIP

Tel #   (   )   -   Fax #   (   )   -

Title of this Fodor's guide:

Store and location where guide was purchased:

INDICATE YOUR DESTINATIONS/DATES: You can order up to three (3) destinations from the previous page. Fill in your arrival and departure dates for each destination. **Your Travel Update itinerary (all destinations selected) cannot exceed 30 days from beginning to end.**

		Month	Day		Month	Day
(Sample) LONDON	From:	6 /	21	To:	6 /	30
1	From:	/		To:	/	
2	From:	/		To:	/	
3	From:	/		To:	/	

CHOOSE YOUR INTERESTS: Select up to eight (8) categories from the list of interest categories shown on the previous page and circle the numbers below:

1   2   3   4   5   6   7   8   9   10   11   12   13   14   15   16

CHOOSE WHEN YOU WANT YOUR TRAVEL UPDATE DELIVERED (Check one):
❑ Please send my Travel Update immediately.
❑ Please hold my order until a few weeks before my trip to include the most up-to-date information.
    Completed orders will be sent within 48 hours. Allow 7-10 days for U.S. mail delivery.

ADD UP YOUR ORDER HERE. *SPECIAL OFFER FOR FODOR'S PURCHASERS ONLY!*

	Suggested Retail Price	Your Price	This Order
First destination ordered	$ 9.95	$ 7.95	$ 7.95
Second destination (if applicable)	$ 6.95	$ 4.95	+
Third destination (if applicable)	$ 6.95	$ 4.95	+

DELIVERY CHARGE (Check one and enter amount below)

	Within U.S. & Canada	Outside U.S. & Canada
First Class Mail	❑ $2.50	❑ $5.00
FAX	❑ $5.00	❑ $10.00
Priority Delivery	❑ $15.00	❑ $27.00

ENTER DELIVERY CHARGE FROM ABOVE: +

TOTAL: $

METHOD OF PAYMENT IN U.S. FUNDS ONLY (Check one):
❑ AmEx   ❑ MC   ❑ Visa   ❑ Discover   ❑ Personal Check (U. S. & Canada only)
❑ Money Order/ International Money Order
    Make check or money order payable to: Fodor's Worldview Travel Update

Credit Card —/—/—/—/—/—/—/—/—/—/—/—/—/—/—/ Expiration Date:___/___

Authorized Signature

SEND THIS COMPLETED FORM WITH PAYMENT TO:
Fodor's Worldview Travel Update, 114 Sansome Street, Suite 700, San Francisco, CA 94104

OR CALL OR FAX US 24-HOURS A DAY
Telephone **1-800-799-9609** • Fax **1-800-799-9619** (From within the U.S. & Canada)
(Outside the U.S. & Canada: Telephone 415-616-9988 • Fax 415-616-9989)

(Please have this guide in front of you when you call so we can verify purchase.)
Code: FTG   Offer valid until 12/31/95.